W9-BRA-906

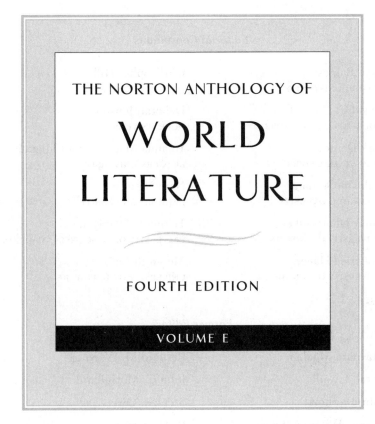

THE NORTON ANTHOLOGY OF

WORLD LITERATURE

FOURTH EDITION

VOLUME E

THE NORTON ANTHOLOGY OF WORLD LITERATURE

FOURTH EDITION

MARTIN PUCHNER, *General Editor*
HARVARD UNIVERSITY

SUZANNE AKBARI
UNIVERSITY OF TORONTO

WIEBKE DENECKE
BOSTON UNIVERSITY

BARBARA FUCHS
UNIVERSITY OF CALIFORNIA, LOS ANGELES

CAROLINE LEVINE
CORNELL UNIVERSITY

PERICLES LEWIS
YALE UNIVERSITY

EMILY WILSON
UNIVERSITY OF PENNSYLVANIA

VOLUME E

W. W. NORTON & COMPANY | New York · London

W. W. Norton & Company has been independent since its founding in 1923, when William Warder Norton and Mary D. Herter Norton first published lectures delivered at the People's Institute, the adult education division of New York City's Cooper Union. The firm soon expanded its program beyond the Institute, publishing books by celebrated academics from America and abroad. By midcentury, the two major pillars of Norton's publishing program—trade books and college texts—were firmly established. In the 1950s, the Norton family transferred control of the company to its employees, and today—with a staff of four hundred and a comparable number of trade, college, and professional titles published each year—W. W. Norton & Company stands as the largest and oldest publishing house owned wholly by its employees.

Printed in the United States of America

Editor: Peter Simon
Associate Editor: Gerra Goff
Project Editor: Christine D'Antonio
Manuscript Editor: Mike Fleming
Managing Editor, College: Marian Johnson
Managing Editor, College Digital Media: Kim Yi
Production Manager: Sean Mintus
Media Editor: Carly Fraser-Doria
Media Project Editor: Cooper Wilhelm
Assistant Media Editor: Ava Bramson
Editorial Assistant, Media: Joshua Bianchi
Marketing Manager, Literature: Kimberly Bowers
Art Direction: Rubina Yeh
Book Design: Jo Anne Metsch
Permissions Manager: Megan Schindel
Permissions Clearer: Margaret Gorenstein
Photo Editor: Catherine Abelman
Composition: Westchester Book Services
Cartographer: Adrian Kitzinger
Manufacturing: LSC Communications—Crawfordsville

ISBN 978-0-393-60285-2 (pbk.)

W. W. Norton & Company, Inc., 500 Fifth Avenue, New York, NY 10110-0017
wwnorton.com
W. W. Norton & Company Ltd., 15 Carlisle Street, London W1D 3BS

1 2 3 4 5 6 7 8 9 0

Contents

II. AT THE CROSSROADS OF EMPIRE 433

Preface

They arrive in boats, men exhausted from years of warfare and travel. As they approach the shore, their leader spots signs of habitation: flocks of goats and sheep, smoke rising from dwellings. A natural harbor permits them to anchor their boats so that they will be safe from storms. The leader takes an advance team with him to explore the island. It is rich in soil and vegetation, and natural springs flow with cool, clear water. With luck, they will be able to replenish their provisions and be on their way.

In the world of these men, welcoming travelers is a sacred custom, sanctioned by the gods themselves. It is also good policy among seafaring people. Someday, the roles may very well be reversed: today's host may be tomorrow's guest. Yet the travelers can never be certain whether a particular people will honor this custom. Wondering what to expect, the thirteen men enter one of the caves dotting the coastline.

The owner isn't home, but the men enter anyway, without any compunction. There are pens for sheep and goats, and there is plenty of cheese and milk, so the men begin eating. When the owner returns, they are terrified, but their leader, boldly, asks for gifts. The owner is not pleased. Instead of giving the intruders what they demand, he kills two of them and eats them for dinner. And then two more the next day. All the while, he keeps the men trapped in his cave.

A wily man, the leader devises a scheme to escape. He offers the owner wine, enough to make him drunk and sleepy. Once he dozes off, the men take a staff that they have secretly sharpened and they plunge it into the owner's eye, blinding him. Without sight, he cannot see the men clinging to the undersides of his prized sheep as they stroll, one by one, out of the cave to graze, and cleverly the men cling only to the male sheep, not the females, which get milked.

* * *

This story of hospitality gone wrong comes from *The Odyssey*, one of the best-known works in all of world literature. We learn of this strange encounter of Greek soldiers with the one-eyed Cyclops named Polyphemus from Odysseus, the protagonist of the epic, when he recounts his exploits at the court of another host, the king of the Phaeacians. Unsurprisingly, Polyphemus isn't presented in the best light. Odysseus describes the Cyclopes as a people without a "proper" community, without agriculture, without hospitality. Is Odysseus, who has been wined and dined by his current host, trying to curry favor with the king of the Phaeacians by telling him how terribly he was treated by these non-Greek others? Reading the passage closely, we can see that Polyphemus and the other Cyclopes are adroit makers of cheese, so they can't be all that lazy. When the blinded Polyphemus cries out for help, his associates come to help him as a matter of course, so they don't live quite as isolated from one another as Odysseus claims. Even though Odysseus asserts that Polyphemus is godless, the land is blessed by the gods with fertility, and Polyphemus's divine father comes to his aid when he prays. Odysseus says that the Cyclopes lack laws and custom, yet we are also shown the careful, regular, customary way that Polyphemus takes care of his household. In a touching scene toward the end of his encounter with Odysseus, after he is blinded, Polyphemus speaks gently and respectfully to his favorite ram, so he can't be all that monstrous. The one-eyed giants assist one another, they are shepherds and artisans, and they are capable of kindness. The passage's ambiguities suggest that perhaps it was partly Odysseus's fault that this encounter between cultures went so badly. Were he and his companions simply travelers badly in need of food, or were they looters hoping to enrich themselves? The passage suggests that it's a matter of narrative perspective, from whose point of view the story is told.

Scenes of hospitality (or the lack thereof) are everywhere in world literature, and questions about hospitality, about the courtesies that we owe to strangers and that strangers owe to us (whether we are guests or hosts), are as important today as they were in the ancient world. Although many writers and thinkers today are fond of saying that our era is the first "truly global" one, stories such as this episode from Homer's *Odyssey* remind us that travel, trade, exile, migration, and cultural encounters of all kinds have been features of human experience for thousands of years.

The experience of reading world literature, too, is a form of travel—a mode of cultural encounter that presents us with languages, cultural norms, customs, and ideas that may be unfamiliar to us, even strange. As readers, each time we begin to read a new work, we put ourselves in the role of a traveler in a foreign land, trying to understand its practices and values and hoping to feel, to some degree and in some way, connected to and welcome among the people we meet there. *The Epic of Gilgamesh*, for example, takes its readers on a tour of Uruk, the first large city in human history, in today's Iraq, boasting of its city walls, its buildings and temples with their stairways and foundations, all made of clay bricks. Like a tour guide, the text even lets its readers inspect the city's clay pits, over one square mile large, that provided the material for this miraculous city made from clay. The greatest marvel of them all is of course *The Epic of Gilgamesh* itself, which was inscribed on clay tablets—the first monument of literature.

Foundational Texts

From its beginnings, *The Norton Anthology of World Literature* has been committed to offering students and teachers as many complete or substantially represented texts as possible. This Fourth Edition emphasizes the importance of *foundational* texts as never before by offering new translations of some of the best-known and most-loved works in the history of world literature. *The Epic of Gilgamesh* stands first in line of these foundational texts, which capture the story of an entire people, telling them where they came from and who they are. Some foundational texts become an object of worship and are deemed sacred, while others are revered as the most consequential story of an entire civilization. Because foundational texts inspire countless retellings—as Homer did for the Greek tragedians—these texts are reference points for the entire subsequent history of literature.

Perhaps no text is more foundational than the one with which we opened this preface: Homer's *Odyssey*. In this Fourth Edition, we feature *The Odyssey* in a new translation by our classics editor, Emily Wilson. This version captures the fast pace and rhythmic regularity of the original and offers a fresh perspective on cultural encounters such as the one between Odysseus and Polyphemus that is described above. Astonishingly, Wilson's translation is the first translation of *The Odyssey* into English by a woman. For centuries, commentators have remarked that *The Odyssey* is unusually attuned to the lives of women, especially in its portrait of Odysseus's wife, Penelope, a compelling and powerful character who cunningly holds a rowdy group of suitors at bay. Wilson's translation pays special attention to the poem's characterization of this remarkable woman, who is every bit as intriguing as the "complicated man" who is the eponymous hero of the tale. Other female characters, too, are given a new voice in this translation. For example, Helen, wife of the Greek king Menelaus and (according to legend) possessor of "the face that launched a thousand ships," is revealed through Wilson's translation to speak of herself not as a "whore" for whose sake so many young Greek men fought, suffered, and died (as she does in most other translations) but instead as a perceptive, clever person, onto whom the Greeks, already eager to fight the Trojans, projected their own aggressive impulses: "They made my face the cause that hounded them," she says. The central conflicts of the epic, the very origin of the Trojan War, appear here in a startling new light.

We are also delighted to feature a new translation of the great Indian epic *The Mahabharata* by Carole Satyamurti, whose modern retelling captures the careful, patterned language of the original by rendering it in a fluent blank verse, a form familiar in English literature from Shakespeare to Wordsworth and also used in Wilson's *Odyssey*, a form particularly suitable to narrative. Readers used to older prose versions will find that the quest for honor and fame at the heart of this epic comes across as never before.

These two examples highlight an exciting dimension of our emphasis on new translations. The first several volumes of this anthology have always been dominated by male voices because men enjoyed privileged access to literacy and cultural influence in the centuries prior to modernity. Our focus on new translations has allowed us to introduce into these volumes many female voices—the voices of translators. So, for example, we present Homer's *Iliad* in a new translation by Caroline Alexander, Sophocles' *Antigone* in a recent translation by Ruby Blondell, and Euripides' *Medea* in a new, specially commissioned translation by Sheila H. Murnaghan, and we continue to offer work in the first volumes translated by female translators such as Laura Gibbs (Aesop's *Fables*), Dorothy Gilbert (Marie de France's *Lais*), Sholeh Wolpé (*The Conference of the Birds*), Wendy Belcher (*Kebra Nagast*), Sheila Fisher (Chaucer's *Canterbury Tales*), Rosalind Brown-Grant (Christine de Pizan's *Book of the City of Ladies*), and Pauline Yu (Wang Wei's poetry), among others. This commitment to featuring the work of female translators extends beyond these early centuries as well, for example in the brilliant new translation by Susan Bernofsky of a foundational text of literary modernity—Kafka's *Metamorphosis*. The result throughout the anthology is that these works now speak to today's readers in new and sometimes surprising ways.

Our emphasis in this edition on new translations is based on and amplifies the conviction expressed by the original editors of this anthology over fifty years ago: that world literature gains its power when it travels from its place of origin and speaks to people in different places. While purists sometimes insist on studying literature only in the original language, a dogma that radically shrinks what one can read, world literature not only relies on translation but actually thrives on it. Translation is a necessity; it is what enables a worldwide circulation of literature. It also is an art. One need only think of the way in which translations of the Bible shaped the history of Latin or English or German. Translations are re-creations of works for new readers. This edition pays keen attention to translation, featuring dozens of new translations that make classic texts newly readable and capture the originals in compelling ways. With each choice of translation, we have sought a version that would spark a sense of wonder while still being accessible to a contemporary reader.

Among other foundational texts presented in new translations and selections is the Qur'an, in a verse translation that is the product of a collaboration between M. A. Rafey Habib, a poet, literary scholar, and Muslim, and Bruce Lawrence, a renowned scholar of Islam. Their team effort captures some of the beauty of this extraordinary, and extraordinarily influential, sacred text. Augustine's *Confessions* are newly presented in a version by Peter Constantine, and Dante's *Inferno* is featured in the long-respected and highly readable translation by the American poet John Ciardi.

We have also maintained our commitment to exciting epics that deserve wider recognition such as the Maya *Popol Vuh*, the East African *Kebra Nagast*, and the *Sunjata*, which commemorates the founding of a West African empire in the late Middle Ages. Like *The Odyssey* and *The Mahabharata*, *Sunjata* was transmitted for centuries in purely oral form. But while *The Odyssey* was written down around 800 B.C.E. and *The Mahabharata* several hundred years later, the *Sunjata* was written down only in the twentieth century. We feature it here in a new prose translation by David C. Conrad, who personally recorded this version from a Mande storyteller, Djanka Tassey Condé, in 1994. In this way, *Sunjata* speaks to the continuing importance of oral storytelling, the origin of all foundational epics, from South Asia via Greece and Africa to Central America. Throughout the anthology, we remind readers that writing has coexisted with oral storytelling since the invention of literature and that it will continue to do so in the future.

A Network of Stories

In addition to foundational texts, we include in this edition a great number of story collections. The origins of this form of literature reach deep into the ancient world, as scribes collected oral stories and assembled them in larger works. We've substantially increased our offerings from what is undoubtedly the most famous of these collections, *The Thousand and One Nights*, to give readers a better sense of the intricate structure of this work, with its stories within stories within stories, all neatly framed by the overarching narrative of Shahrazad, who is telling them to her sister and the king to avoid being put to death. What is most notable about these story collections is how interconnected they are. Stories travel with striking ease from one collection to the next, appearing in *The Jataka*, one of the oldest Indian story collections framed by the

Buddha, and the *Pañcatantra*, an Indian collection put together for the education of princes, to *The Thousand and One Nights*, and, in Greece, Aesop's *Fables*. There existed a continent-spanning network of stories that allowed storytellers and scribes to recycle and reframe what they learned in ever new ways; it proved so compelling that later writers, from Marie de France to Chaucer, borrowed from it frequently. To give readers a sense of these connections, we have rethought our selection of stories by including those that appear in different collections, allowing readers to track the changes that occur when a story is told by the Buddha, by Shahrazad, or on a pilgrimage to Canterbury Cathedral.

Expanded Selections

Along with our focus on making foundational texts and story collections fresh and accessible, we have pruned the overall number of authors and were therefore able to increase our offerings from major texts that feature in many world literature courses. *Don Quixote* now includes the compelling "Captive's Tale," in which Cervantes draws on his own experiences as a slave in Algiers, where he spent five years after having been captured by pirates. Sor Juana Inés de la Cruz, whose significance is steadily increasing, is now represented by an additional selection from her mystery play, *The Divine Narcissus*, in Edith Grossman's elegant translation. Other major texts with increased selections include Machiavelli's *Prince* and, in the twentieth century, Lu Xun, who now can be introduced to students as the author not only of *Diary of a Madman* but also of *Ah Q—The Real Story*.

Despite this focus on foundational texts, story collections, and other major works, there are plenty of entirely new texts in this Fourth Edition. The Spanish Renaissance tale *The Abencerraje* tells of a Moorish knight who is taken prisoner by a Christian on his wedding day. Ultimately his captor relents and allows the knight to marry his beloved. This enormously popular tale speaks of the complex relations between Christianity and Islam in the early modern era and is featured here in a new translation by our Renaissance editor, Barbara Fuchs. Equally exciting is our representation of Korean literature. The *Tale of Hong Kiltong*, a story of a Korean Robin Hood endowed with magical powers, is a classic that we paired with excerpts from Lady Hyegyŏng's memoirs, which chronicle with deep psychological insight the horror and violence at the Korean royal court. These older Korean texts are complemented by a modern writer, Park Wansuh, whose work reflects the upheavals of the twentieth century on the Korean peninsula, from Japanese occupation and the Korean War to economic development. One of the first women to achieve critical success in modern Korea, Park offers readers keen insight into Korea's modern struggles.

We are particularly excited to now close the anthology with a story by the Nigerian writer Chimamanda Ngozi Adichie called "The Headstrong Historian," which, since its publication in 2008, has already become a favorite in world literature classrooms. This compact work introduces us to three generations of Nigerians as they navigate a complicated series of personal and cultural displacements. A thought-provoking exploration of the complex results of cultural contact and influence, this probing, searching journey seemed to us the most fitting conclusion to the anthology's survey of 4,000 years of literature.

Cultural Contact

Odysseus's encounter with the Cyclopes speaks not only to hospitality but also to the theme of cultural contact more generally. The earliest civilizations—those that invented writing and hence literature—sprang up where they did because they were located along strategic trading and migration routes. Contact was not just something that happened between fully formed cultures but something that made these cultures possible in the first place.

Committed to presenting the anthology's riches in a way that conveys this central fact of world literature, we have created sections that encompass broad contact zones—areas of intense trade in peoples, goods, art, and ideas where the earliest literatures emerged and intermingled. One of these is the Mediterranean Sea, whose central importance we visualize with four new maps. It was not just a hostile environment that could derail a journey home, as it did for Odysseus, or where nontravelers, like Polyphemus, might encounter violent invaders willing to attack and steal; it was also a connecting tissue, allowing for intense contact around its harbors. Medieval maps of the Mediterranean pay tribute to this fact: so-called portolan charts show a veritable mesh of lines connecting hundreds of ports. For this edition, we have further emphasized these contact zones, the location of intense conflict (including Cervantes's experience as a slave in North Africa) as well as friendly exchange. In a similar manner, the two major traditions of East Asia—China and Japan—are presented in the context of the larger region, including our new emphasis on Korea.

The importance of cultural contact and encounter is expressed not just in the overall organization of the anthology and the selection of material; it is also made visible in clusters of texts on the theme of travel and conquest, giving students access to documents related to travel, contact, trade, and conflict. For not all travel was voluntary. People traveled to escape wars and famine, plagues and environmental disasters. They were abducted, enslaved, and trafficked. Beginning with the early modern era, European empires dominated global politics and economics and accelerated the pace of globalization by laying down worldwide trade routes and communication networks, but old empires, such as China, continued to be influential as well. We added more material to our cluster "At the Crossroads of Empire," including a letter by Machemba, a chief in East Africa under German colonial control, and Mark Twain's trenchant soliloquy of Belgian King Leopold defending his brutal rule in Congo.

To these expanded clusters, we added a new one, "Poetry and Politics," which includes the Polish national poet Adam Mickiewicz and Latin American poet Rubén Darío's *To Roosevelt*, a powerful reminder of the crucial role poetry played in the gaining of national independence across the world. Poets captured the aspirations of nations and often enshrined those aspirations in national anthems, which also led us to include the Puerto Rican national anthem (one poet included in our anthology, Rabindranath Tagore, wrote not one but two national anthems, of both India and Bangladesh).

In the same volume, we also enhanced our cluster "Realism across the Globe," which traces one of the most successful global literary movements, one that found expression in France, Britain, Russia, Brazil, Mexico, and Japan. In keeping with our commitment to frequently taught authors, we increased our selection of Chekhov and present Tolstoy's *Death of Ivan Ilyich* in a new, acclaimed translation by Peter Carson.

The Birth of World Literature

In 1827, a provincial German writer, living in small-town Weimar, recognized that he was in the privileged position of having access not only to European literature but also to literature from much further afield, including Persian poetry, Chinese novels, and Sanskrit drama. The writer was Johann Wolfgang von Goethe, and in 1827, he coined a term to capture this new force of globalization in literature: "world literature." (We now include the "prologue" to Goethe's play *Faust*, which he wrote after encountering a similar prologue in the classical Sanskrit play *Śhakuntalā*, also included in the anthology.)

Since 1827, for less than 200 years, we have been living in an era of world literature. This era has brought many lost masterpieces back to life, including *The Epic of Gilgamesh*, which was rediscovered in the nineteenth century, and the *Popol Vuh*, which languished in a library until well into the twentieth century. Other works of world literature weren't translated and therefore didn't begin to circulate outside their sphere of origin until the last 200 years, including *The Tale of Genji*. With more literature becoming more widely available than ever before, Goethe's vision of world literature has become a reality today.

In presenting world literature from the dawn of writing to the early twenty-first century, and from oral storytelling to literary experiments of the avant-garde, this anthology raises the question not only of what world literature is but also of the nature of literature itself. We call attention to the changing nature of literature with thematic clusters on literature in the early volumes, to give students and teachers access to how early writers from different cultures thought about literature. But the changing role and nature of literature are visible in the anthology as a whole. Greek tragedy and comedy are experienced by modern students as literary genres, encountered in written texts; but for the ancient Athenians, they were primarily dramas, experienced live in an outdoor theater in the context of a religious and civic ritual. Other texts, such as the Qur'an or the Bible, are sacred pieces of writing, central to many people's religious faith, while others appreciate them primarily or exclusively as literature. Some texts, such as those by Laozi or Plato or Kant, belong in philosophy, while others, such as the Declaration of Independence, are primarily political documents. Our modern conception of literature as imaginative literature, as fiction, is very recent, about 200 years old. We have therefore opted for a much-expanded conception of literature that includes creation myths, wisdom literature, religious texts, philosophy, political writing, and fairy tales in addition to poems, plays, and narrative fiction. This answers to an older definition of literature as writing of high quality or of great cultural significance. There are many texts of philosophy or religion or politics that are not remarkable or influential for their literary qualities and that would therefore have no place in an anthology of world literature. But the works presented here do: in addition to or as part of their other functions, they have acquired the status of literature.

This brings us to the last and perhaps most important question: When we study the world, why study it through its literature? Hasn't literature lost some of its luster for us, we who are faced with so many competing media and art forms? Like no other art form or medium, literature offers us a deep history of human thinking. As our illustration program shows, writing was invented not for the composition of literature but for much more mundane purposes, such as the recording of ownership, contracts, or astronomical observations. But literature is writing's most glorious by-product. Literature can be reactivated with each reading. Many of the great architectural monuments of the past are now in ruins. Literature, too, often has to be excavated, as with many classical texts. But once a text has been found or reconstructed it can be experienced as if for the first time by new readers. Even though many of the literary texts collected in this anthology are at first strange, because they originated so very long ago, they still speak to today's readers with great eloquence and freshness. No other art form can capture the human past with the precision and scope of literature because language expresses human consciousness. Language shapes our thinking, and literature, the highest expression of language, plays an important role in that process, pushing the boundaries of what we can think and how we think it. This is especially true with great, complex, and contradictory works that allow us to explore different narrative perspectives, different points of view.

Works of world literature continue to elicit strong emotions and investments. The epic *Rāmāyana*, for example, plays an important role in the politics of India, where it has been used to bolster Hindu nationalism, just as the *Bhagavad-Gītā* continues to be a moral touchstone in the ethical deliberation about war. The so-called religions of the book, Judaism, Christianity, and Islam, make our selections from their scriptures a more than historical exercise as well. China has recently elevated the sayings of Confucius, whose influence on Chinese attitudes about the state had waned in the twentieth century, creating Confucius Institutes all over the world to promote Chinese culture in what is now called New Confucianism. World literature is never neutral. We know its relevance precisely by the controversies it inspires.

There are many ways of studying other cultures and of understanding the place of our own culture in the world. Archaeologists can show us objects and buildings from the past and speculate, through material remains, how people in the past ate, fought, lived, died, and were buried; scientists can date layers of soil. Literature is capable of something much more extraordinary: it allows us a glimpse into the imaginative lives, the thoughts and feelings of humans from thousands of years ago or living halfway around the world. This is the true magic of world literature as captured in this anthology, our shared human inheritance.

About the Fourth Edition

New Selections and Translations

Following is a list of the new translations, selections, and works in the Fourth Edition, in order:

VOLUME A

A new translation of Homer's *The Iliad* by Caroline Alexander • A new translation of Homer's *The Odyssey* by Emily Wilson, complete • Six new Aesop's *Fables*: "The Onager, the Donkey and the Driver," "The Eagle and the Farmer," "The Dung Beetle and the Eagle," "The Fox, the Donkey, and the Lion Skin," "Aesop and His Lamp," and "The Lion, the Fox, and the Deer" • New translations of Sappho's poetry by Philip Freeman, including ten new poems • New translations of *Oedipus the King* by David Grene, *Antigone* by Ruby Blondell, *Medea* by Sheila H. Murnaghan, and *Lysistrata* by Jeffrey Henderson • Benjamin Jowett's translation of *Symposium*, new to this edition • New translations of Catullus's poetry by Charles Martin • A new selection from *The Aeneid* from "The Kingdom of the Dead" • A new translation of *The Mahabharata* by Carole Satyamurti, including new selections from "The Book of Drona" and "Books 17 and 18: The Books of the Final Journey and the Ascent to Heaven" • New selections from *Zhuangzi* from "The Way of Heaven," "Outer Things," and "Of Swords"

VOLUME B

A new translation of Augustine's *Confessions* by Peter Constantine with a new selection from "Book XI [Time]" • A new translation of the Qur'an by M. A. Rafey Habib and Bruce Lawrence with new selections from "Light," "Ya Sin," and "The Sun" • A new translation of Marie de France's *Lais* by Dorothy Gilbert, including the new selection "Bisclavret" • A selection from *Vis and Ramin* translated by Dick Davis • A new translation of *The Conference of the Birds* by Sholeh Wolpé • A new translation and selection of Rumi's poetry, including six new poems: "[The nights I spend with you]," "[Like blood beneath my skin]," "[Profession, profit, trade]," "[A rose is still a rose]," "[How marvelous, that moment]," and "[On death's day]," as well as selections from *The Masnavi* translated by Dick Davis: "[On the Prohibition of Wine]," "[This World as a Dream]," "[On Men's Behavior with Women]," "[Man's Life Compared to That of an Embryo in the Womb]," and "[Moses and the Shepherd]" • John Ciardi's translation of *The Divine Comedy*, newly included, supplemented by two additional translations from Canto 3 of *Inferno* by Clive James and Mark Musa • A new translation of *Kebra Nagast* by Wendy Belcher and Michael Kleiner, including a new chapter, "About How King Solomon Swore an Oath to the Queen" • Seven new tales from *The Thousand and One Nights*: "[The Story of the Porter and the Three Ladies]," "[The First Dervish's Tale]," "[The Second Dervish's Tale]," "[The Tale of the Envious and the Envied]," "[The Third Dervish's Tale]," "[The Tale of the First Lady]," and "[The Tale of the Second Lady]" • "The Nun's Priest's Tale" from *The Canterbury Tales* • Three new tales from the *Pañcatantra*: "The Bird with Golden Dung" and "The Ass in the Tiger Skin" translated by Arthur W. Ryder and "The Ass without Ears or a Heart" translated by Patrick Olivelle • New selections from *The Tale of Genji*: "Sakaki: A Branch of Sacred Evergreens," "Maboroshi: Spirit Summoner," "Hashihime: The Divine Princess at Uji Bridge," "Agemaki: A Bowknot Tied in Maiden's Loops," "Yadoriki: Trees Encoiled in Vines of Ivy," and "Tenarai: Practicing Calligraphy"

VOLUME C

A new prose translation of *Sunjata: A West African Epic of the Mande* by David C. Conrad • New selections from *The Prince*: "[Liberality and Parsimony]," "[Love and Fear]," "[Dissimulation]," "[Contempt and Hatred]," "[Princely Devices; Fortresses]," "[The Excellent Prince]," "[Flatterers]," and "[The Princes of Italy]" • "The Abencerraje" translated by Barbara Fuchs, Larissa Brewer-García, and Aaron J. Ilika • A new selection from *Don Quixote*, "[A Story of Captivity in North Africa, Told to Don Quixote at the Inn]" • A revised *Fuenteovejuna* translated by G. J. Racz

VOLUME D

A new translation of "What Is Enlightenment?" by Mary C. Smith • A new translation of Sor Juana Inés de la Cruz's work translated by Edith Grossman, including three new sonnets, "[O World, why do you wish to persecute me?]," "[I adore Lisi but do not pretend]," and "[Because you have died, Laura, let affections]," as well as *Loa* to the Mystery Play *The Divine Narcissus: An Allegory* translated by Edith Grossman • Hŏ Kyun's "The Tale of Hong Kiltong" translated by Marshall R. Pihl • A selection from Lady Hyegyŏng's *The Memoirs of Lady Hyegyŏng* translated by JaHyun Kim Haboush

VOLUME E

A new selection from *Faust*, "Prelude in the Theatre" • Machemba's "Letter to Major von Wissmann" translated by Robert Sullivan and Sarah Lawall • A selection from Mark Twain's "King Leopold's Soliloquy" • A new cluster, "Poetry and Politics," including four new works, Adam Mickiewicz's "The Prisoner's Return" translated by Jerzy Peterkiewicz and Burns Singer, Speranza's (Lady Jane Wilde's) "A Lament for the Potato" and "The Exodus," and Lola Rodríguez de Tió's "The Song of the Borinquen" translated by José Nieto, as well as the new translation of "Guantanamera" by Elinor Randall • A new translation of *The Death of Ivan Ilyich* by Peter Carson • A new translation of "The Cane" by Margaret Jull Costa • José López Portillo y Rojas's "Unclaimed Watch" translated by Roberta H. Kimble • Anton Chekhov's "The Lady with the Dog" translated by Ivy Litvinov

VOLUME F

A new translation of *The Metamorphosis* by Susan Bernofsky • Lu Xun's "Ah Q—The Real Story" translated by William A. Lyell • Eric Bentley's translation, new to this edition, of Pirandello's *Six Characters in Search of an Author* • A new translation of "The Dancing Girl of Izu" by J. Martin Homan • Jorge Luis Borges's "The Library of Babel" translated by James E. Irby • M. D. Herder Norton's translations of Rainer Maria Rilke's poems, newly included • A new translation of "Lament for Ignacio Sánchez Mejías" by Pablo Medina • A new translation of "Matryona's Home" by Michael Glenny • Derek Walcott's "Sea Grapes" • Park Wansuh's "Mother's Hitching Post, Part 2" • Yu Hua's "On the Road at Eighteen" • Chimamanda Ngozi Adichie's "The Headstrong Historian"

Resources for Students and Instructors

Norton is pleased to provide students and instructors with abundant resources to make the teaching and study of world literature an even more interesting and rewarding experience.

We are pleased to launch the new *Norton Anthology of World Literature* website, found at digital.wwnorton.com/worldlit4pre1650 (for volumes A, B, C) and digital.wwnorton.com/worldlit4post1650 (for volumes D, E, F). This searchable and sortable site contains thousands of resources for students and instructors in one centralized place at no additional cost. Following are some highlights:

- A series of eight brand-new video modules are designed to enhance classroom presentation and spark student interest in the anthology's works. These videos, conceived of and narrated by the anthology editors, ask students to consider why it is important for them to read and engage with this literature.
- Hundreds of images—maps, author portraits, literary places, and manuscripts—are available for student browsing or instructor download for in-class presentation.
- Several hours of audio recordings are available, including a 10,000-term audio glossary that helps students pronounce the character and place names in the anthologized works.

The site also provides a wealth of teaching resources that are unlocked with an instructor's log-in:

- "Quick read" summaries, teaching notes, discussion questions, and suggested resources for every work in the anthology, from the much-praised *Teaching with* The Norton Anthology of World Literature: *A Guide for Instructors*
- Downloadable Lecture PowerPoints featuring images, quotations from the texts, and lecture notes in the notes view for in-class presentation

In addition to the wealth of resources in *The Norton Anthology of World Literature* website, Norton offers a downloadable Coursepack that allows instructors to easily add high-quality Norton digital media to online, hybrid, or lecture courses—all at no cost. Norton Coursepacks work within existing learning management systems; there's no new system to learn, and access is free and easy. Content is customizable and includes over seventy reading-comprehension quizzes, short-answer questions, links to the videos, and more.

Acknowledgments

The editors would like to thank the following people, who have provided invaluable assistance by giving us sage advice, important encouragement, and help with the preparation of the manuscript: Sara Akbari, Alannah de Barra, Wendy Belcher, Jodi Bilinkoff, Daniel Boucher, Freya Brackett, Psyche Brackett, Michaela Bronstein, Rachel Carroll, Sookja Cho, Kyeong-Hee Choi, Amanda Claybaugh, Lewis Cook, David Damrosch, Dick Davis, Burghild Denecke, Amanda Detry, Anthony Domestico, Megan Eckerle, Marion Eggert, Merve Emre, Maria Fackler, Guillermina de Ferrari, Alyssa Findley, Karina Galperín, Stanton B. Garner, Kimberly Dara Gordon, Elyse Graham, Stephen Greenblatt, Sara Guyer, Langdon Hammer, Emily Hayman, Iain Higgins, Paulo Lemos Horta, Mohja Kahf, Peter Kornicki, Paul W. Kroll, Peter H. Lee, Sung-il Lee, Lydia Liu, Bala Venkat Mani, Ann Matter, Barry McCrea, Alexandra McCullough-Garcia, Rachel McGuiness, Jon McKenzie, Mary Mullen, Djibril Tamsir Niane, Johann Noh, Felicity Nussbaum, Andy Orchard, John Peters, Michael Pettid, Daniel Taro Poch, Daniel Potts, Megan Quigley, Payton Phillips Quintanilla, Catherine de Rose, Imogen Roth, Katherine Rupp, Ellen Sapega, Jesse Schotter, Stephen Scully, Kyung-ho Sim, Sarah Star, Brian Stock, Tomi Suzuki, Joshua Taft, Sara Torres, J. Keith Vincent, Lisa Voigt, Kristen Wanner, Emily Weissbourd, Karoline Xu, Yoon Sun Yang, and Catherine Vance Yeh.

All the editors would like to thank the wonderful people at Norton, principally our editor Pete Simon, the driving force behind this whole undertaking, as well as Marian Johnson (Managing Editor, College), Christine D'Antonio and Kurt Wildermuth (Project Editors), Michael Fleming (Copyeditor), Gerra Goff (Associate Editor), Megan Jackson (College Permissions Manager), Margaret Gorenstein (Permissions), Catherine Abelman (Photo Editor), Debra Morton Hoyt (Art Director; cover design), Rubina Yeh (Design Director), Jo Anne Metsch (Designer; interior text design), Adrian Kitzinger (cartography), Agnieszka Gasparska (timeline design), Carly Fraser-Doria (Media Editor), Ava Bramson (Assistant Editor, Media), Sean Mintus (Production Manager), and Kim Bowers (Marketing Manager, Literature). We'd also like to thank our Instructor's Guide authors: Colleen Clemens (Kutztown University), Elizabeth Watkins (Loyola University New Orleans), and Janet Zong (Harvard University).

This anthology represents a collaboration not only among the editors and their close advisers but also among the thousands of instructors who teach from the anthology and provide valuable and constructive guidance to the publisher and editors. *The Norton Anthology of World Literature* is as much their book as it is ours, and we are grateful to everyone who has cared enough about this anthology to help make it better. We're especially grateful to the professors of world literature who responded to an online survey in 2014, whom we have listed below. Thank you all.

Michelle Abbott (Georgia Highlands College), Elizabeth Ashworth (Castleton State College), Clinton Atchley (Henderson State University), Amber Barnes (Trinity Valley Community College), Rosemary Baxter (Clarendon College), Khani Begum (Bowling Green State University), Joyce Boss (Wartburg College), Floyd

Brigdon (Trinity Valley Community College), James Bryant-Trerise (Clackamas Community College), Barbara Cade (Texas College), Kellie Cannon (Coastal Carolina Community College), Amee Carmines (Hampton University), Farrah Cato (University of Central Florida), Brandon Chitwood (Marquette University), Paul Cohen (Texas State University), Judith Cortelloni (Lincoln College), Randall Crump (Kennesaw State University), Sunni Davis (Cossatot Community College), Michael Demson (Sam Houston State University), Richard Diguette (Georgia Perimeter College, Dunwoody), Daniel Dooghan (University of Tampa), Jeff Doty (West Texas A&M University), Myrto Drizou (Valdosta State University), Ashley Dugas (Copiah-Lincoln Community College), Richmond Eustis (Nicholls State University), David Fell (Carroll Community College), Allison Fetters (Chattanooga State Community College), Francis Fletcher (Folsom Lake College), Kathleen D. Fowler (Surry Community College), Louisa Franklin (Young Harris College), James Gamble (University of Arkansas), Antoinette Gazda (Averett University), Adam Golaski (Central Connecticut State University), Anissa Graham (University of North Alabama), Eric Gray (St. Gregory's University), Jared Griffin (Kodiak College), Marne Griffin (Hilbert College), Frank Gruber (Bergen Community College), Laura Hammons (Hinds Community College), Nancy G. Hancock (Austin Peay State University), C. E. Harding (Western Oregon University), Leslie Harrelson (Dalton State College), Eleanor J. Harrington-Austin (North Carolina Central University), Matthew Hokom (Fairmont State University), Scott Hollifield (University of Nevada, Las Vegas), Catherine Howard (University of Houston, Downtown), Jack Kelnhofer (Ocean County College), Katherine King (University of California, Los Angeles), Pam Kingsbury (University of North Alabama), Sophia Kowalski (Hillsborough Community College), Roger Ladd (University of North Carolina at Pembroke), Jameela Lares (University of Southern Mississippi), Susan Lewis (Delaware Technical Community College), Christina Lovin (Eastern Kentucky University), Richard Mace (Pace University), Nicholas R. Marino (Borough of Manhattan Community College, CUNY), Brandi Martinez (Mountain Empire Community College), Kathy Martinez (Sandhills Community College), Matthew Masucci (State College of Florida), Kelli McBride (Seminole State College), Melissa McCoy (Clarendon College), Geoffrey McNeil (Notre Dame de Namur University), Renee Moore (Mississippi Delta Community College), Anna C. Oldfield (Coastal Carolina University), Keri Overall (Texas Woman's University), Maggie Piccolo (Rutgers University), Oana Popescu-Sandu (University of Southern Indiana), Jonathan Purkiss (Pulaski Technical College), Rocio Quispe-Agnoli (Michigan State University), Evan Radcliffe (Villanova University), Ken Raines (Eastern Arizona College), Jonathan Randle (Mississippi College), Kirk G. Rasmussen (Utah Valley University), Helaine Razovsky (Northwestern State University of Louisiana), Karin Rhodes (Salem State University), Stephanie Roberts (Georgia Military College), Allen Salerno (Auburn University), Shannin Schroeder (Southern Arkansas University), Heather Seratt (University of Houston, Downtown), Conrad Shumaker (University of Central Arkansas), Edward Soloff (St. John's University), Eric Sterling (Auburn University Montgomery), Ron Stormer (Culver-Stockton College), Marianne Szlyk (Montgomery College), Tim Tarkington (Georgia Perimeter College), Allison Tharp (University of Southern Mississippi), Diane Thompson (Northern Virginia Community College), Sevinc Turkkan (College at Brockport, State University of New York), Verne Underwood (Rogue Community College), Patricia Vazquez (College of Southern Nevada), William Wallis (Los Angeles Valley College), Eric Weil (Elizabeth City State University), Denise C. White (Kennesaw State University), Tamora Whitney (Creighton University), Todd Williams (Kutztown University of Pennsylvania), Bertha Wise (Oklahoma City Community College), and Lindsey Zanchettin (Auburn University).

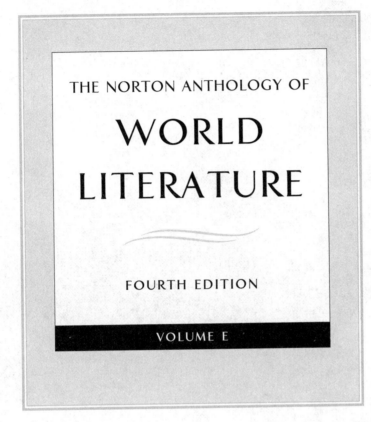

THE NORTON ANTHOLOGY OF

WORLD LITERATURE

FOURTH EDITION

VOLUME E

I

An Age of Revolutions in Europe and the Americas

If you were born in 1765, and you happened to live to a ripe old age, you would witness two dramatic revolutions. Together these revolutions would create a period of staggering upheaval unparalleled in prior human history. Whether you happened to find yourself in Texas or London or Buenos Aires, you would see daily life change for almost everyone—rich and poor, rural and urban—and the workings of governments and markets forever transformed. You would have to learn a whole new vocabulary to describe your social world: the terms "factory," "middle class," "capitalism," "industry," "journalism," "liberal," and "conservative" would come into use during your lifetime. You would learn of workers moving to cities in vast numbers. They would live in dismal conditions of filth, disease, and hunger, and at times would erupt in violent protest. You would listen to orators denouncing tyranny and demanding new rights and freedoms. You would hear about an ordinary soldier who rose to conquer most of Europe, and his name, Napoleon, would provoke either a chill of fear or a shiver of exhilaration. You would watch new constitutions take effect and new nations assert themselves. You would see the very map of the world redrawn.

Liberty Leading the People, 1830, Eugène Delacroix.

THE INDUSTRIAL REVOLUTION

The first of the two great upheavals was the industrial revolution, which began in England and then radiated outward, as other nations copied English innovations and as England's increasing commercial and military power conquered large portions of the globe. Before the 1780s economies everywhere changed only at a glacially slow pace. Most of Europe's inhabitants were peasants who worked the land which their forefathers had worked for generations before them, typically growing their own food and making their own clothes, and paying rent to their landowners in exchange for military protection. Many, including Russian serfs, were under the legal control of their landowners and thus forbidden to move from the places where they were born. But agriculture in England was different. There, large landowners rented tracts of land to tenant farmers, who then hired laborers to work for them. The farmers could get rich by finding new markets for their products, and the workers could move if they saw opportunities elsewhere. Here were the seeds of an entirely new, fast-growing capitalist economy. In the eighteenth century, English farmers started to turn into entrepreneurs, looking for faster and better ways to make profits from their lands. In order to attract investors, the nation needed to keep the economy growing, and in order to keep the economy growing, it needed to increase production and find new markets. Colonial expansion seemed like a perfect solution: England fought to acquire and control vast territories abroad, especially in North America, which would provide new land to till and new natural resources to use. Entrepreneurs also found new markets in the colonies to buy the goods which England produced.

An engraving depicting the interior of the Swainson & Birley Mill in Lancashire, England, ca. 1830.

The great spur for this new global economy was cotton. Grown and harvested by slaves in the colonies, the raw material was shipped to English entrepreneurs, whose textile factories spun and wove the slave-picked cotton into finished cloth. They eagerly developed new technologies to keep production growing, and that meant that iron and steel industries grew too, allowing for the ever faster production of machines for manufacture and transportation. Railways expanded swiftly. Historians often date the great acceleration of the economy to the 1780s, which was the moment when English exports surpassed imports for the first time. The growth was breathtaking and unprecedented. In 1785 England imported 11 million pounds of raw cotton; by 1850 the English were importing 588 million pounds. They established trade monopolies with India and Latin America, compelling overseas consumers to buy English goods, which meant that exports grew at an astonishing rate: English mill owners had sold more than two billion yards of cotton cloth by the middle of the nineteenth century. England had become the hub of a new world economy, and other nations rushed to imitate English techniques of production. Factories sprang up everywhere.

Not everyone benefited from this extraordinary growth. The workers who moved off ancestral lands to crowd into new industrial centers labored in unregulated factories, often inhaling dust or having their limbs broken in machines. Employers looked for the cheapest labor, typically hiring women and children, and forced them to work 14- and even 16-hour days. Barely paid a subsistence wage, the new urban working class made do with living conditions that were even more appalling than conditions in the factories where they worked. Cities grew at such a fast rate that urban populations quickly outpaced the availability of necessities such as adequate housing and the supply of clean water. The result was a sequence of major epidemics, including cholera and typhoid fever, which overwhelmed congested slums but hardly touched the middle and upper classes. To add to the general hardships for the poor, the economy had already begun the international cycles of boom and bust that would characterize the next two centuries. In periods of poor growth, unemployed workers literally starved. Feelings of angry discontent grew rapidly alongside the new economy.

Overseas, too, large populations began to suffer from industrialization. The huge acceleration in the English economy had absolutely depended on slavery. Six million slaves had been captured and sent from Africa to the Americas in the eighteenth century alone, many to serve the booming cotton trade. Meanwhile, India's economy plunged. Until the eighteenth century, India had had a thriving manufacturing sector that produced gorgeous textiles for export, but the new factory-made cloth from England came in at low prices and depressed the market. Many workers in India were forced back into agriculture, which deindustrialized India's economy, setting it on a slower track. Latin America, too, increasingly organized its economies of mining and agriculture around exports to England—including sugar, coffee, and silver—which made the new Latin American nations worryingly dependent on agriculture and on economic decisions made in England.

DEMOCRATIC REVOLUTIONS

As the industrial revolution was producing vast wealth, changing labor practices, molding a class of angry urban workers, rapidly expanding cities, and creating new and uneven global trade relations, a second revolution was also taking place. This revolution was political. Intent on throwing off old hierarchies that gave power to kings and compelled everyone else to act as obedient subjects, revolutionaries in North America and France argued that ordinary people should take political decision making into their own hands. This was a democratic revolution that, like the industrial revolution, had global effects, transforming expectations about basic rights and freedoms worldwide.

In North America, colonial subjects became increasingly resentful of the power of the English king, who made both political and economic decisions that favored England. In 1776 they declared independence not only from English rule but from the whole structure of the old regime, rejecting its hereditary monarchy in favor of a new elected president. They vested power in "the people," insisting that governments should derive their power only from the consent of the governed. This was a radical new foundation for politics, and it inspired many later constitutions.

In Europe, another, even more dramatic political revolution was brewing. The French monarchy had become ever more absolutist, and peasants were growing resentful of the traditional taxes and tithes they had to pay. Bad harvests in 1788 and 1789 doubled the cost of bread, but the king seemed entirely indifferent to the fate of a starving people. (When told that the peasants were calling for bread, Queen Marie Antoinette is famous for responding, "Let them eat cake.") On July 14, 1789, a loosely organized armed mob stormed the Bastille prison—a symbol of royal power—and called for the liberation of the French people. The news spread quickly. Within a month, uprisings all across France had wrecked the traditional feudal social hierarchy and ushered in a new era. **The Declaration of the Rights of Man and of the Citizen**, issued by the French National Assembly in August, asserted the equality and freedom of all men and abolished all privileges based on birth. The revolutionary government insisted on ruling by reason, not by tradition. They adopted the innovative new metric system, separated church and state, abolished slavery in the French colonies, and granted equal rights to everyone, including, for the first time, Jews. The French Revolution also helped to unleash a new force in world affairs: nationalism. France was no longer a land possessed by a powerful ruling family, but stood for a self-governing and autonomous "people." In a powerful symbolic gesture, the revolutionaries renamed 1789 as "Year Zero," suggesting that nothing that had happened before the revolution mattered. They then stunned Europe by sending the king to his death in 1793, executing him with a sleek new machine intended to make killing more humane: the guillotine.

The French Revolution sent shock waves around the world. Throughout Europe and the Americas, suddenly it seemed possible that people might rise up against their oppressors, violently opposing traditional authority in the name of individual human rights. Huge divisions emerged between those who saw the revolutionaries as vicious and reckless, and those who heralded them as the opening of a whole new chapter in human history.

Other European powers, fearful that revolution might spread into their territories, went to war with France in 1792, and the whole country threatened to collapse in disarray. A small group of radicals, called the Jacobins, seized control and united the nation under a strong centralized dictatorship, mobilizing the nation for war and sending all traitors—and potential

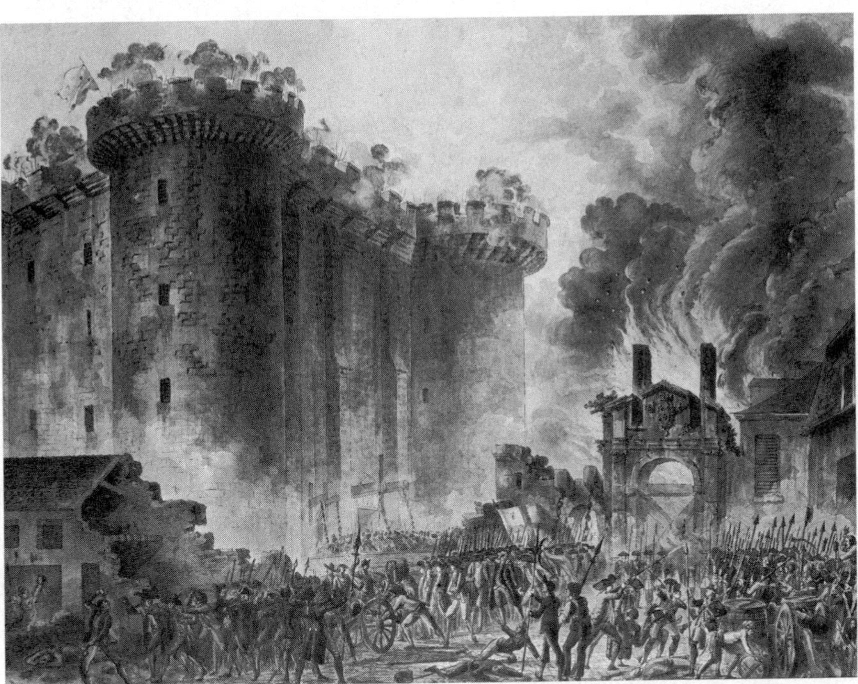

The siege of the Bastille, July 1789.

traitors—to the guillotine. Their short period of leadership in 1793–94 has come to be known as the "Reign of Terror." The blood they shed sickened many observers who had once sympathized with the aims of the revolution, and the "Reign of Terror" has, ever since, been seen as a symbol of revolutionary violence taken too far.

As the new French government faltered and changed leadership, a talented young soldier who had helped the French to defeat the British at Toulon in 1793 was rising up through the ranks. Born on the remote island of Corsica, Napoleon Bonaparte had few advantages of birth or connections, but his genius for military strategy, his extraordinary ambition, and his own huge popularity allowed him to take advantage of government weakness during a wave of foreign invasions and to position himself as the new leader of France. In 1799 he installed a new dictatorship and through a vast military campaign redrew the map of Europe, bringing large parts of Spain, Germany, Austria, Italy, and Poland under French control. He crowned himself emperor in 1804. Ravenous for power, he tried and failed to conquer the vast territories of Russia, and he did not succeed in controlling Egypt for long, but his meteoric career was unlike any the world had ever seen. When he was finally defeated by the British at the Battle of Waterloo in 1815, he left a powerful myth behind: the brilliant individual who, by sheer talent, could conquer whole nations.

Napoleon left a number of crucial political legacies too. Though he ruled by dictatorship and reinstated slavery in the French colonies, he also consolidated many of the principles of the French Revolution. Known as the Napoleonic Code, his new legal system was modeled after the civil code of ancient Rome: it

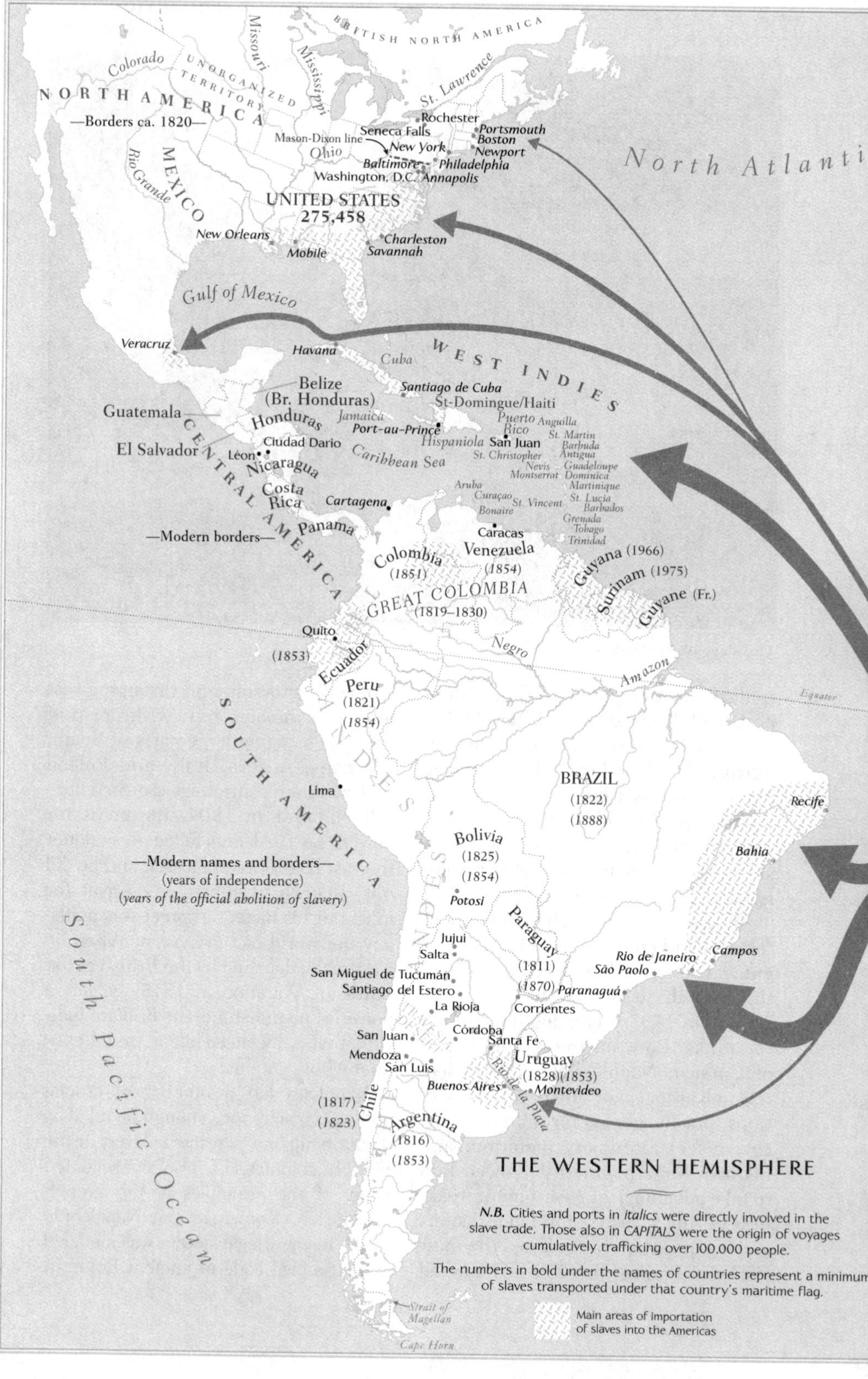
BRITISH NORTH AMERICA
Missouri
Mississippi
Colorado
UNORGANIZED TERRITORY
NORTH AMERICA
—Borders ca. 1820—
St. Lawrence
Rochester
Seneca Falls
Portsmouth
Boston
Newport
Mason-Dixon line
New York
Ohio
Baltimore
Philadelphia
Washington, D.C.
Annapolis
North Atlantic
Rio Grande
MEXICO
UNITED STATES
275,458
New Orleans
Mobile
Charleston
Savannah
Gulf of Mexico
Veracruz
Havana
Cuba
WEST INDIES
Belize
(Br. Honduras)
Santiago de Cuba
St-Domingue/Haiti
Guatemala
Honduras
Jamaica
Port-au-Prince
Puerto Rico
Anguilla
St. Martin
Barbuda
Antigua
Guadeloupe
Dominica
Martinique
St. Lucia
Barbados
Grenada
Tobago
Trinidad
Hispaniola
San Juan
St. Christopher
Nevis
Montserrat
Ciudad Dario
El Salvador
Léon
Nicaragua
Caribbean Sea
CENTRAL AMERICA
Costa Rica
Cartagena
Aruba
Curaçao
Bonaire
St. Vincent
Panama
Caracas
—Modern borders—
Venezuela
(1854)
Colombia
(1851)
Guyana (1966)
Surinam (1975)
Guyane (Fr.)
GREAT COLOMBIA
(1819–1830)
Quito
(1853)
Ecuador
Negro
Amazon
Equator
Peru
(1821)
(1854)
ANDES
SOUTH AMERICA
Lima
BRAZIL
(1822)
(1888)
Recife
Bolivia
(1825)
(1854)
Bahia
—Modern names and borders—
(years of independence)
(years of the official abolition of slavery)
Potosi
Paraguay
(1811)
(1870)
South Pacific Ocean
Jujui
Salta
San Miguel de Tucumán
Santiago del Estero
La Rioja
Rio de Janeiro
São Paolo
Campos
Paranaguá
Corrientes
San Juan
Córdoba
Santa Fe
Mendoza
San Luis
Uruguay
(1828)(1853)
Buenos Aires
Montevideo
Rio de la Plata
Chile
(1817)
(1823)
Argentina
(1816)
(1853)
Strait of Magellan
Cape Horn
THE WESTERN HEMISPHERE
N.B. Cities and ports in italics were directly involved in the slave trade. Those also in CAPITALS were the origin of voyages cumulatively trafficking over 100,000 people.
The numbers in bold under the names of countries represent a minimum of slaves transported under that country's maritime flag.
Main areas of importation of slaves into the Americas

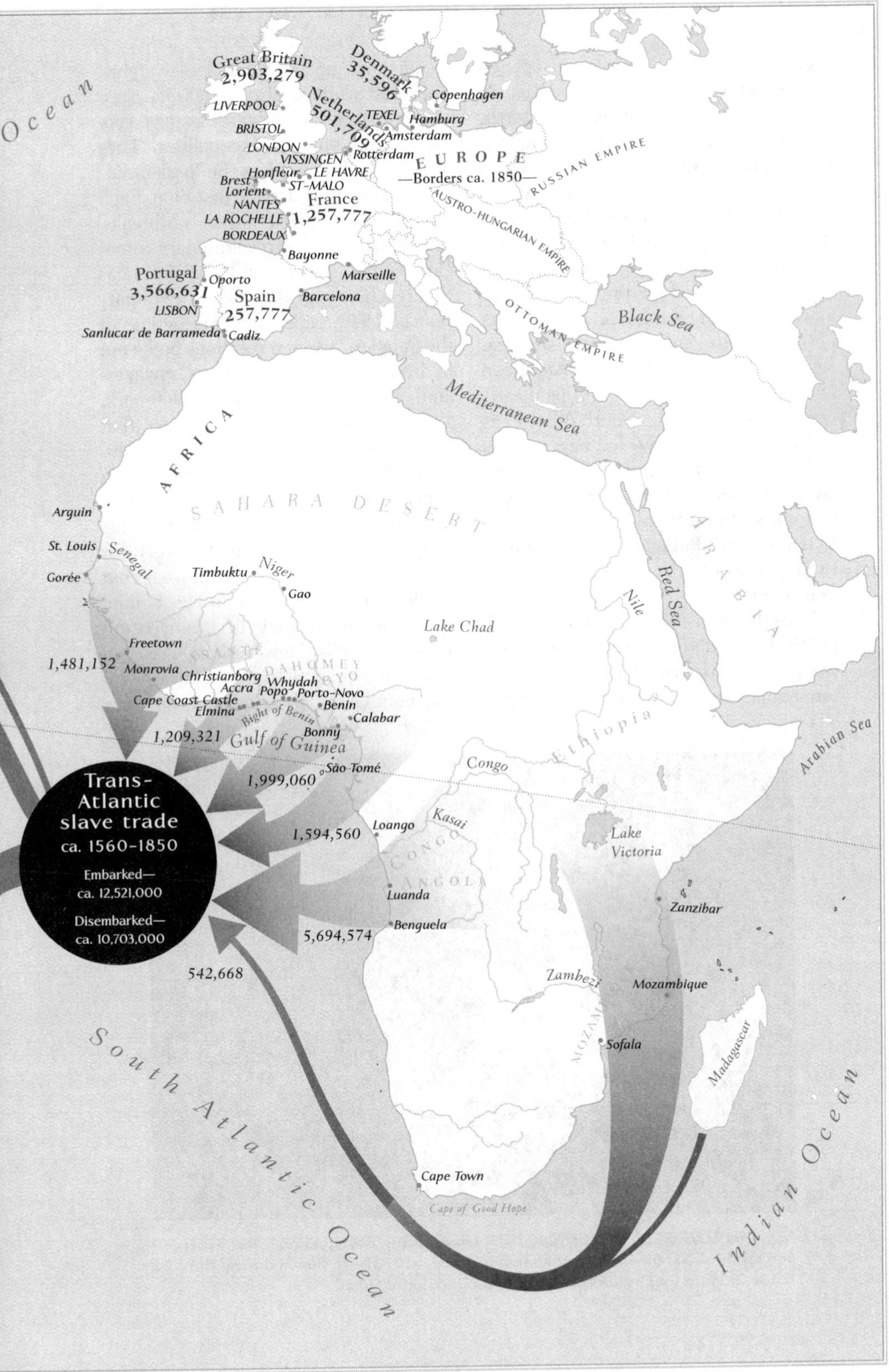
Ocean
Great Britain
2,903,279
LIVERPOOL
BRISTOL
LONDON
Denmark
35,596
Copenhagen
Netherlands
501,709
TEXEL
Hamburg
Amsterdam
VISSINGEN
Rotterdam
Honfleur
LE HAVRE
Brest
Lorient
ST-MALO
NANTES
LA ROCHELLE
BORDEAUX
France
1,257,777
EUROPE
—Borders ca. 1850—
RUSSIAN EMPIRE
AUSTRO-HUNGARIAN EMPIRE
Bayonne
Marseille
Portugal
3,566,631
Oporto
LISBON
Spain
257,777
Barcelona
Sanlucar de Barrameda
Cadiz
OTTOMAN EMPIRE
Black Sea
Mediterranean Sea
AFRICA
SAHARA DESERT
ARABIA
Arguin
St. Louis
Senegal
Gorée
Timbuktu
Niger
Gao
Lake Chad
Nile
Red Sea
Freetown
1,481,152
Monrovia
Christianborg
Accra
Whydah
Popo
Porto-Novo
Cape Coast Castle
Elmina
Bight of Benin
Benin
Calabar
Bonny
1,209,321
Gulf of Guinea
São Tomé
1,999,060
Ethiopia
Arabian Sea
Congo
Trans-Atlantic slave trade
ca. 1560–1850
Embarked—
ca. 12,521,000
Disembarked—
ca. 10,703,000
Kasai
Loango
1,594,560
Lake Victoria
Luanda
Zanzibar
Benguela
5,694,574
542,668
Zambezi
Mozambique
Sofala
Madagascar
South Atlantic Ocean
Indian Ocean
Cape Town
Cape of Good Hope

abolished hereditary privileges, opened government careers to individuals on the basis of ability rather than birth, and established freedom of religion. In conquering much of Europe, Napoleon managed to wipe away many vestiges of old feudal institutions across the continent. And when he occupied Spain in 1808, he destabilized its power over its colonies, opening the way for a wave of independence movements across South and Central America. Inspired by the ideals of the American and French Revolutions, groups mostly composed of *criollos*—South Americans of European ancestry—led new nations to freedom from Spanish imperial rule. By 1825 Mexico, Peru, Brazil, Bolivia, Colombia, Venezuela, Chile, Uruguay, Ecuador, and Paraguay had all taken their places on the map as independent states.

Both the industrial revolution and the political revolution continued to haunt the generations that followed. Absolute monarchies kept crumbling, as outraged people rose up to demand new rights. Exploited workers also mobilized, organizing strikes and protests against economic and political inequalities. They began to call themselves the "proletariat" or "working class" for the first time. Each insurgency inspired other outbreaks, producing a kind of revolutionary contagion across Europe and the Americas that reached its peak in the extraordinary year of 1848, called the "Springtime of the Peoples," when revolutions broke out in France, Austria, Hungary, Switzerland, Spain, Germany, Italy, Denmark, and Romania. This was the year that Karl Marx and Friedrich Engels published the *Communist Manifesto*, which ended with the battle cry: "Workers of the world, unite!" It was in this year that the French abolished slavery for good. And it was in the same year that women's rights activists in the United States organized their first convention at Seneca Falls, New York, where, in a deliberate echo of the Declaration of Independence, they made the case

Napoleon at the Battle of Waterloo, 1815, Charles Auguste Steuben. Most artists' portrayals of Napoleon, even in defeat (as here, where he is shown during the Battle of Waterloo), reinforced a romanticized, heroic ideal.

"that all men and women are created equal."

LITERATURE IN THE AGE OF REVOLUTIONS

Utopian dreams have always driven political revolutionaries. In fact, there can be no revolution without acts of imagination. If the old world must be banished and a new world put in its place, what should that new world look like? The first wave of American and French revolutionaries were inspired by the work of eighteenth-century Enlightenment thinkers who envisioned a society governed by reason rather than by custom or superstition. In particular, the philosopher and novelist **Jean-Jacques Rousseau** powerfully stirred the French revolutionaries by imagining a universal emancipation from tyranny: "Man is born free," he wrote, "but everywhere is in chains." The industrial revolution, too, depended on the workings of the imagination: it was spurred by new schemes for increasing the speed of production, for the invention of huge new machines and the creation of fast modes of communication and transportation. It was fueled, too, by dreams of unprecedented wealth.

Since imagination seemed so crucial to the making of these modern revolutions, writers and artists began to see themselves as playing an important role in the tumult of the times. Art, it seemed, could have the power to transform the world. Many writers eagerly threw themselves into the fray. In the 1790s, for example, the English poet **William Blake** boldly wore the red cap symbolizing the liberty and equality of the French Revolution, and he used his poetry to decry the corruption of church and government, as well as the poverty and enslavement of the people. Still strongly inspired by the French Revolution, in the 1840s the German poet **Heinrich Heine** supported a workers' uprising in a poem called "**The Silesian Weavers**," which cursed unbearable economic and political inequalities. Similarly, English poet **Elizabeth Barrett Browning** helped to persuade her contemporaries to put limits on child labor in factories with her poem, "**The Cry of the Children**." Later the Cuban **José Martí** combined the roles of revolutionary fighter, political prisoner, and heroic national poet. All of these writers are included in this volume.

For a hundred years, the French Revolution continued to haunt literary writers. Had it ushered in a great new world based on equality and freedom, or had its violence and bloodshed produced meaningless destruction? The Anglo-Irish writer **Edmund Burke** called the French revolutionaries a "swinish multitude"; British poets **William Wordsworth** and **Samuel Taylor Coleridge** were at first caught up in the enthusiasm for the democratic ideals of the French Revolution, but the Reign of Terror horrified them and turned them into conservative voices. Charles Dickens, in his *Tale of Two Cities* (1859), exposed the terrible impoverishment of both the London poor and the French peasantry, and yet did not support the French Revolution: the sinister revolutionary Madame Defarge represents vengeful bloodshed. On the other hand, the revolutionaries continued to inspire passionate adherents. "Whatever else may be said of it," asserts a character in Victor Hugo's novel *Les Misérables* (1862), "the French Revolution was the greatest step forward by mankind since the coming of Christ." And whichever side one took, according to the English poet **Percy Shelley**, the French Revolution was simply "the master theme of the epoch in which we live."

Napoleon provided inspiration for novelists, who used his remarkable

Atlantic Ocean
North Sea
NORWAY
Oslo
SWEDEN
DENMARK
Copenhagen
GREAT BRITAIN
Scotland
Glasgow
Belfast
Ireland
Dublin
Leeds
Manchester
England
Wales
Thames
LONDON
Amsterdam
Rotterdam
NETHERLANDS
Brussels
BELGIUM
Elbe
Hamburg
Mecklenburg
Oldenburg
PRUSSIA
Hanover
BERLIN
Oder
Brunswick
Anhalt
GERMAN CONFEDERATION
Cologne
Leipzig
Dresden
Weimar
Thuringia
Hesse
Saxony
Bohemia
Frankfurt
Prague
AUSTRO-
Palatinate
Bavaria
Stuttgart
Alsace
Baden
Württemberg
Danube
Munich
VIENNA
Rhine
Rouen
Seine
PARIS
FRANCE
Nantes
Loire
SWITZERLAND
ALPS
Sava
Geneva
Lyon
Bordeaux
SAVOY
Rhône
Milan
Brescia
Turin
Piedmont
Venice
Po
Genoa
Bologna
Adriatic Sea
La Coruña
Oviedo
Marseille
Pamplona
PYRENEES
Florence
TUSCANY
PAPAL STATES
Macerata
Ebro
Oporto
Douro
Zaragoza
KINGDOM OF SARDINIA
Tiber
Madrid
Barcelona
Rome
Corsica
KINGDOM OF THE TWO SICILIES
PORTUGAL
Tagus
Naples
Salerno
Lisbon
SPAIN
Valencia
Sardinia
Tyrrhenian Sea
Mediterranean Sea
Sicily
Palermo
Reggio
Cádiz
AFRICA
Malta
0 200 400 600 800 kilometers
0 100 200 300 400 500 miles

REVOLUTIONARY EUROPE
1848
Centers of major revolutionary uprisings, 1819–1848
ST. PETERSBURG
Stockholm
Baltic Sea
Riga
MOSCOW
RUSSIAN EMPIRE
Vistula
Warsaw
Łodz
Dneiper
Volga
Kiev
Silesia
Kraków
Dneister
HUNGARIAN EMPIRE
Prut
Pest
Buda
CARPATHIAN MOUNTAINS
Danube
Belgrade
Bucharest
Danube
Black Sea
OTTOMAN EMPIRE
ISTANBUL
Bari
Asia Minor
GREECE
Aegean Sea
Euphrates
Rhodes
Cyprus
Crete

The artist Francisco Goya, whose life spanned the years covered in this section of the anthology, spent most of his career as a portraitist for the wealthy. But late in his career, he also privately devoted his art to chronicling the horrors of war during and after Napoleon's siege of Spain in the early 1800s. The series of prints that resulted—called *The Disasters of War* (*Los Desastres de la Guerra*)—hinted at the stylistic upheavals that would follow later in the century. In this image, called simply *Why?* (*Por qué?*), French soldiers garrotte a Spanish prisoner.

rise to shape both sensational adventures and political reflections. Alexandre Dumas, the grandson of a slave whose father had been dismissed from the French army by Napoleon because of the color of his skin, wrote an enormously popular novel called *The Count of Monte Cristo* (1844), where the protagonist is imprisoned for helping Napoleon. Russian writer **Leo Tolstoy** later set his magisterial *War and Peace* (1869) in Russia at the time of Napoleon's invasion, and **Herman Melville**, an American, looked back to the Napoleonic wars in *Billy Budd* (1891) to tell the story of a sailor on a British ship fighting against the French army.

The upheavals of this revolutionary moment did not only provide compelling subject matter for writers. This was a period that dramatically altered the very forms of art. Until the nineteenth century, artists in Europe had mostly worked for the old wealthy elites: powerful aristocrats or the Catholic Church. Now they began to create works of art for "the people." In this context, traditional modes of writing often seemed ill-suited to new democratic ideals. What was needed was a revolution in style and form. Thus when Wordsworth and Coleridge collaborated on a volume of poetry in 1798, they outright rejected "the gaudiness and inane phraseology" of earlier poetry in favor of "language really used by men." For generations to follow, writers would struggle to capture the revolutionary tumult of the times in startling and sometimes uncomfortable new forms, insisting on experimenting, on innovating, on seeing the world afresh—and never getting buried in old routines. This impulse to revolutionize the way people saw the world was to become part of the definition of art itself. The late nineteenth-century painter Paul Gauguin maintained that every artist was "either a plagiarist or a revolutionary." And if those were the only choices, then what self-respecting artist wouldn't choose revolution?

REVOLUTIONARY CONTEXTS

The word *revolution* comes from the Latin *revolvere*, "to turn." Once associated with astronomy to refer to the rotation of celestial bodies, in the eighteenth century the word came more and more frequently to signify a total overthrow of the existing political and social order. The American Revolution of 1776, the French Revolution of 1789, the Latin American independence movements, the outbreak of revolutions across Europe and the Americas in 1848, and the ongoing industrial revolution that spread worldwide throughout the nineteenth century all promised that kind of comprehensive transformation. Not every revolution delivered on that promise, however. While it might seem relatively straightforward to topple tyrants and resist established hierarchies, it turned out to be intensely difficult to put something radically different—and better—in their place. Thus revolutionary leaders often labored to create powerful declarations, proclamations, and constitutions that would lay down convincing foundations for a wholly new society. Many turned to traditions of philosophical thought, and in particular to the European philosophers of the Enlightenment, to answer the most difficult questions. What values and principles should guide relationships between governments and those they govern? Should ordinary life be transformed as well as political institutions? What laws does a just society require? In this context, writing mattered. For the first time, societies around the world claimed to be governed by principles laid down in founding documents. The words that articulated the very grounds of new societies had to be forceful, widely persuasive, and durable.

Collected here are some of the most influential of those documents—the **US Declaration of Independence**, the **Declaration of the Rights of Man and of the Citizen** issued by the revolutionary French government, two assertions of the rights of women (one from France and one from the United States), a proclamation from the Haitian Revolution, and **Simón Bolívar**'s letter, in which an anticolonial leader announces the principles for revolution in Latin America. Each seeks to establish not only new laws and governments but also what it means to be human, what responsibilities we have to one another, and what justice and freedom entail. Included here with these documents are also the comments of two influential observers: **Edmund Burke**, a British politician who bitterly opposed the French Revolution and became one of the most influential voices for those ever since who favor conserving, rather than overthrowing, existing social arrangements; and **William Wordsworth**, a poet who had been inspired by the French Revolution, horrified by the Reign of Terror that followed it, and then sympathetic to the Haitian Revolution, though not hopeful. He captures in poetic form some of the ambivalence of living through the promise and the violence of revolutionary upheaval.

The execution of French King Louis XVI, an engraving by Georg Heinrich Sieveking (1793).

US DECLARATION OF INDEPENDENCE

Written by Thomas Jefferson (1743–1826), the Declaration of Independence draws on principles propounded by Enlightenment philosophers. Among these are the notion that human beings are given natural or "inalienable" rights by God, and that governments are not entitled to impose their will arbitrarily but instead derive their power from the people. Although these ideas were not new at the time of the American Revolution, no society before this moment had ever tried to found a state upon them. The Declaration passed the Continental Congress in Philadelphia on July 4, 1776.

The Declaration is celebrated not only for its affirmation of radical principles for government but also for its compelling style. Rather than beginning with defenses or accusations, it "declares" a series of truths—foundational ideas about human nature and government—which it simply asserts as "self-evident." After affirming these general truths, it builds a dramatic picture of King George III's tyranny, presented as a sequence of incontrovertible facts which any impartial observer would decry. It builds to the rousing conclusion that the colonists are willing to stake their lives and their honor on the necessity of independence. Jefferson's brilliant writing—compact and logical, but also stirring and musical—has made this one of the most famous of all political documents.

The Declaration of Independence:

IN CONGRESS, JULY 4, 1776.

The unanimous Declaration of the thirteen united States of America,

When in the Course of human events, it becomes necessary for one people to dissolve the political bands which have connected them with another, and to assume among the powers of the earth, the separate and equal station to which the Laws of Nature and of Nature's God entitle them, a decent respect to the opinions of mankind requires that they should declare the causes which impel them to the separation.

We hold these truths to be self-evident, that all men are created equal, that they are endowed by their Creator with certain unalienable Rights, that among these are Life, Liberty and the pursuit of Happiness.—That to secure these rights, Governments are instituted among Men, deriving their just powers from the consent of the governed,—That whenever any Form of Government becomes destructive of these ends, it is the Right of the People to alter or to abolish it, and to institute new Government, laying its foundation on such principles and organizing its powers in such form, as to them shall seem most likely to effect their Safety and Happiness. Prudence, indeed, will dictate that

Governments long established should not be changed for light and transient causes; and accordingly all experience hath shewn, that mankind are more disposed to suffer, while evils are sufferable, than to right themselves by abolishing the forms to which they are accustomed. But when a long train of abuses and usurpations, pursuing invariably the same Object evinces a design to reduce them under absolute Despotism, it is their right, it is their duty, to throw off such Government, and to provide new Guards for their future security.—Such has been the patient sufferance of these Colonies; and such is now the necessity which constrains them to alter their former Systems of Government. The history of the present King of Great Britain[1] is a history of repeated injuries and usurpations, all having in direct object the establishment of an absolute Tyranny over these States. To prove this, let Facts be submitted to a candid world.

He has refused his Assent to Laws, the most wholesome and necessary for the public good.

He has forbidden his Governors to pass Laws of immediate and pressing importance, unless suspended in their operation till his Assent should be obtained; and when so suspended, he has utterly neglected to attend to them.

He has refused to pass other Laws for the accommodation of large districts of people, unless those people would relinquish the right of Representation in the Legislature, a right inestimable to them and formidable to tyrants only.

He has called together legislative bodies at places unusual, uncomfortable, and distant from the depository of their public Records, for the sole purpose of fatiguing them into compliance with his measures.

He has dissolved Representative Houses repeatedly, for opposing with manly firmness his invasions on the rights of the people.

He has refused for a long time, after such dissolutions, to cause others to be elected; whereby the Legislative powers, incapable of Annihilation, have returned to the People at large for their exercise; the State remaining in the mean time exposed to all the dangers of invasion from without, and convulsions within.

He has endeavoured to prevent the population of these States; for that purpose obstructing the Laws for Naturalization of Foreigners; refusing to pass others to encourage their migrations hither, and raising the conditions of new Appropriations of Lands.

He has obstructed the Administration of Justice, by refusing his Assent to Laws for establishing Judiciary powers.

He has made Judges dependent on his Will alone, for the tenure of their offices, and the amount and payment of their salaries.

He has erected a multitude of New Offices, and sent hither swarms of Officers to harrass our people, and eat out their substance.

He has kept among us, in times of peace, Standing Armies without the Consent of our legislatures.

He has affected to render the Military independent of and superior to the Civil power.

He has combined with others to subject us to a jurisdiction foreign to our constitution, and unacknowledged by our laws; giving his Assent to their Acts of pretended Legislation:

1. George III (1738–1820).

For Quartering large bodies of armed troops among us:
For protecting them, by a mock Trial, from punishment for any Murders which they should commit on the Inhabitants of these States:
For cutting off our Trade with all parts of the world:
For imposing Taxes on us without our Consent:
For depriving us in many cases, of the benefits of Trial by Jury:
For transporting us beyond Seas to be tried for pretended offences:
For abolishing the free System of English Laws in a neighbouring Province, establishing therein an Arbitrary government, and enlarging its Boundaries so as to render it at once an example and fit instrument for introducing the same absolute rule into these Colonies:
For taking away our Charters, abolishing our most valuable Laws, and altering fundamentally the Forms of our Governments:
For suspending our own Legislatures, and declaring themselves invested with power to legislate for us in all cases whatsoever.
He has abdicated Government here, by declaring us out of his Protection and waging War against us.
He has plundered our seas, ravaged our Coasts, burnt our towns, and destroyed the lives of our people.
He is at this time transporting large Armies of foreign Mercenaries to compleat the works of death, desolation and tyranny, already begun with circumstances of Cruelty & perfidy scarcely paralleled in the most barbarous ages, and totally unworthy the Head of a civilized nation.
He has constrained our fellow Citizens taken Captive on the high Seas to bear Arms against their Country, to become the executioners of their friends and Brethren, or to fall themselves by their Hands.
He has excited domestic insurrections amongst us, and has endeavoured to bring on the inhabitants of our frontiers, the merciless Indian Savages, whose known rule of warfare, is an undistinguished destruction of all ages, sexes and conditions.

In every stage of these Oppressions We have Petitioned for Redress in the most humble terms: Our repeated Petitions have been answered only by repeated injury. A Prince whose character is thus marked by every act which may define a Tyrant, is unfit to be the ruler of a free people.

Nor have We been wanting in attentions to our Brittish brethren. We have warned them from time to time of attempts by their legislature to extend an unwarrantable jurisdiction over us. We have reminded them of the circumstances of our emigration and settlement here. We have appealed to their native justice and magnanimity, and we have conjured them by the ties of our common kindred to disavow these usurpations, which, would inevitably interrupt our connections and correspondence. They too have been deaf to the voice of justice and of consanguinity. We must, therefore, acquiesce in the necessity, which denounces our Separation, and hold them, as we hold the rest of mankind, Enemies in War, in Peace Friends.

We, therefore, the Representatives of the united States of America, in General Congress, Assembled, appealing to the Supreme Judge of the world for the rectitude of our intentions, do, in the Name, and by Authority of the good

People of these Colonies, solemnly publish and declare, That these United Colonies are, and of Right ought to be Free and Independent States; that they are Absolved from all Allegiance to the British Crown, and that all political connection between them and the State of Great Britain, is and ought to be totally dissolved; and that as Free and Independent States, they have full Power to levy War, conclude Peace, contract Alliances, establish Commerce, and to do all other Acts and Things which Independent States may of right do. And for the support of this Declaration, with a firm reliance on the protection of divine Providence, we mutually pledge to each other our Lives, our Fortunes and our sacred Honor.

DECLARATION OF THE RIGHTS OF MAN AND OF THE CITIZEN

After the storming of the Bastille Prison in Paris on July 14, 1789, leaders of the French Revolution agreed on the need to draw up a declaration of rights. They debated whether to craft a short document that focused entirely on general rights, or to produce a detailed explanation of each principle. And should they include duties and obligations as well as rights? In the end, they opted for something easy to read and disseminate. Brief enough to take up one side of a sheet of paper, the Declaration of the Rights of Man and of the Citizen appeared all over France immediately after its passage on August 26, 1789. It was soon translated into every major European language and so conveyed the universalizing ideals of the French Revolution well beyond France.

Like the Continental Congress in the United States, the French National Assembly rested their founding document on the assertion of natural human rights. In fact, Thomas Jefferson, who was the US envoy to France at the time, lent his help in drafting the language, though the rights asserted in France are interestingly different from those found in the **US Declaration of Independence.**

Declaration of the Rights of Man and of the Citizen[1]

The representatives of the French people, organized in National Assembly,[2] considering that ignorance, forgetfulness or contempt of the rights of man are the sole causes of the public miseries and of the corruption of governments,

1. Translated by Frank Maloy Anderson.
2. The new French people's government, convened in 1789, responsible for the radical transformations that mark the beginning of the French Revolution.

have resolved to set forth in a solemn declaration the natural, inalienable, and sacred rights of man, in order that this declaration, being ever present to all the members of the social body, may unceasingly remind them of their rights and their duties; in order that the acts of the legislative power and those of the executive power may be each moment compared with the aim of every political institution and thereby may be more respected; and in order that the demands of the citizens, grounded henceforth upon simple and incontestable principles, may always take the direction of maintaining the constitution and the welfare of all.

In consequence, the National Assembly recognizes and declares, in the presence and under the auspices of the Supreme Being,[3] the following rights of man and citizen.

1. Men are born and remain free and equal in rights. Social distinctions can be based only upon public utility.

2. The aim of every political association is the preservation of the natural and imprescriptible rights of man. These rights are liberty, property, security, and resistance to oppression.

3. The source of all sovereignty is essentially in the nation; no body, no individual can exercise authority that does not proceed from it in plain terms.

4. Liberty consists in the power to do anything that does not injure others; accordingly, the exercise of the natural rights of each man has for its only limits those that secure to the other members of society the enjoyment of these same rights. These limits can be determined only by law.

5. The law has the right to forbid only such actions as are injurious to society. Nothing can be forbidden that is not interdicted by the law and no one can be constrained to do that which it does not order.

6. Law is the expression of the general will. All citizens have the right to take part personally or by their representatives in its formation. It must be the same for all, whether it protects or punishes. All citizens being equal in its eyes, are equally eligible to all public dignities, places, and employments, according to their capacities, and without other distinction than that of their virtues and their talents.

7. No man can be accused, arrested, or detained except in the cases determined by the law and according to the forms that it has prescribed. Those who procure, expedite, execute, or cause to be executed arbitrary orders ought to be punished; but every citizen summoned or seized in virtue of the law ought to render instant obedience; he makes himself guilty by resistance.

8. The law ought to establish only penalties that are strictly and obviously necessary and no one can be punished except in virtue of a law established and promulgated prior to the offence and legally applied.

9. Every man being presumed innocent until he has been pronounced guilty, if it is thought indispensable to arrest him, all severity that may not be necessary to secure his person ought to be strictly suppressed by law.

10. No one ought to be disturbed on account of his opinions, even religious, provided their manifestation does not derange the public order established by law.

3. Common term for divine power as understood by deists, who did not believe in a god who intervened in human affairs.

11. The free communication of ideas and opinions is one of the most precious of the rights of man; every citizen then can freely speak, write, and print, subject to responsibility for the abuse of this freedom in the cases determined by law.

12. The guarantee of the rights of man and citizen requires a public force; this force then is instituted for the advantage of all and not for the personal benefit of those to whom it is entrusted.

13. For the maintenance of the public force and for the expenses of administration a general tax is indispensable; it ought to be equally apportioned among all the citizens according to their means.

14. All the citizens have the right to ascertain, by themselves or by their representatives, the necessity of the public tax, to consent to it freely, to follow the employment of it, and to determine the quota, the assessment, the collection, and the duration of it.

15. Society has the right to call for an account from every public agent of its administration.

16. Any society in which the guarantee of the rights is not secured or the separation of powers not determined has no constitution at all.

17. Property being a sacred and inviolable right, no one can be deprived of it unless a legally established public necessity evidently demands it, under the condition of a just and prior indemnity.

OLYMPE DE GOUGES

One of the most radical voices for women's rights in the period was Olympe de Gouges (1748–1793). Born Marie Gouzes, the daughter of a rural butcher and a serving woman, Olympe de Gouges reinvented herself as a playwright and Parisian intellectual. She advanced highly progressive ideas, including the abolition of slavery and the rights of orphans and unwed mothers. Her political writings were so unsettling that they alienated many of her fashionable social and intellectual allies. The Rights of Woman (1791), which explicitly revises **the Declaration of the Rights of Man and of the Citizen**, insists that the logic of the French Revolution—its demands for freedom and equality and the overthrow of an old system of oppression—must be extended to women. Among her most famous assertions was article X: "Woman has the right to mount the scaffold; she must also have the right to take to the rostrum." That is, if women can be executed, then surely they should be permitted to make public speeches. She herself provided an ironic and tragic coda to this argument. Olympe de Gouges was guillotined during the Reign of Terror as a consequence of her inflammatory words. Too radical even for the revolutionaries, she died a "public enemy" in 1793.

The Rights of Woman[1]

Man, are you capable of being just? It is a WOMAN who asks you this question; you will not deprive her at least of this right. Tell me what gave you the supreme authority to oppress my sex? Your strength? Your talents? Observe the creator in his wisdom; Go through nature in all its grandeur, to which you seem to wish to be close. And if you dare, give me one example of this tyrannical empire. Go back to the animals, consult the elements, study plant life, and finally cast a glance, on all modifications in organized matter; and bow down before the evidence when I offer you the means to do so. Search, dig deeper and try to distinguish, if you can, sex in nature's administration. Everywhere you will find them indistinct; everywhere they cooperate in a harmonious whole in this immortal masterpiece.

Man alone is in principle tied down to this exception. Bizarre, blind, bloated with science and degenerated, in this century of enlightenment and wisdom, in the crassest of ignorance. He wishes to rule as a despot over a sex that is endowed with all intellectual faculties; he claims to enjoy the revolution and reclaim his rights to equality, in order to say nothing more.

The Rights of Woman

Declaration of the Rights of Woman and of the Woman-Citizen

To be decreed by the National Assembly in its last sessions or in those of the next legislature.

PREAMBLE

Mothers, daughters, sisters, representatives of the nation, demand to be constituted into a national assembly, considering that ignorance, forgetfulness or contempt of the rights of the WOMAN, are the sole causes of public miseries, and of the corruption of governments, have resolved to set forth in a solemn declaration, the natural inalienable and sacred rights of the WOMAN, in order that this declaration, being ever present to all members of the social body, may unceasingly remind them of their rights and duties, in order that the acts of the power of women, and those of the power of men may at each moment be compared with the aim of all political institutions and thereby be more respected, in order that the demands of women-citizens henceforth founded on simple and incontestable principles, may always turn to maintaining the constitution, good mores, and the happiness of all. In consequence, the sex superior in beauty as in courage, in maternal sufferings, recognizes and declares, in the presence and under the auspices of the Supreme Being, the following Rights of the Woman and of the Woman-Citizen.

1. Translated under the direction of Nirupama Rastogi.

I

Woman is born free and remains equal to man in rights. Social distinctions can be based only upon common utility.

II

The aim of every political association is the preservation of the natural and unwritten rights of woman and of man: these rights are liberty, prosperity, security and especially resistance to oppression.

III

The principle of all sovereignty resides essentially in the Nation, which is nothing but the coming together of woman and man: no body, no individual can exercise any authority that does not expressly emanate from it.

IV

Liberty and justice consist in restoring all that which belongs to others: accordingly the exercise of the natural rights of the woman has for its only limits the perpetual tyranny that man imposes on her; these limits must be reformed according to the laws of nature and of reason.

V

The laws of nature and of reason prohibit all actions injurious to society: all that is not forbidden by these wise and divine laws, cannot be prohibited, and no one can be constrained to do what they do not order.

VI

Law must be the expression of the general will; all women and male citizens must take part, personally, or through their representatives in its formation; it must be the same for all: all women and male citizens, being equal in its eyes, must be equally eligible to all dignities, places and public offices, according to their capacities, and without other distinctions than those of their virtues and talents.

VII

No woman is an exception; she is accused, arrested and detained according to cases determined by law. Women obey, just as men, this rigorous law.

VIII

The law must establish only penalties that are strictly and obviously necessary, and no one can be punished except by virtue of a law established and promulgated prior to the offence and legally applicable to women.

IX

Any woman being declared guilty, all severity is exercised by the law.

X

No one ought to be harmed on account of his opinions, even the fundamental ones. Woman has the right to mount the scaffold; she must also have the right to take to the rostrum;[2] provided her manifestations do not disturb the public order established by law.

XI

The free communication of thought and of opinion is one of the most precious rights of women, as this liberty assures the legitimacy of fathers in relation to children. Every woman-citizen can therefore say freely, I am the mother of the child that belongs to you without having to conceal the truth due to a barbarous prejudice only to respond to the abuse of this liberty in cases determined by law.

XII

The guarantee of the rights of women and the woman-citizen requires a major service, this guarantee must be instituted for the advantage of all, and not for the specific utility of the women to whom it is entrusted.

XIII

For the maintenance of the public force, and for administrative expenditure, the contribution of women and men is equal; she has a share in all chores, in all painful tasks; she should therefore have the same share in the distribution of posts, employment, responsibilities, dignities and industry.

XIV

Women and men-citizens have the right to ascertain, for themselves, or through their representatives, the necessity for a public fund. Women-citizens can become members only if they are eligible for an equal share, not only in fortune, but even in public administration, and to establish the quota, the taxable property, the collection and the duration of the tax.

XV

The mass of women along with men contributing to the public fund, have the right to ask for an account, from every public agent and its administration.

XVI

Every society, where guarantee of rights is not assured, nor the separation of powers determined, has no constitution: the constitution is nothing if the majority of the individuals who constitute the nation, has not cooperated in its drafting.

2. Women can be executed; they should also be allowed to make speeches.

XVII

Properties belong to all sexes united or separated; they are for everyone an inviolable and sacred right; no one can be deprived of it as a true heritage of nature, unless a public necessity, legally established, evidently demands it, and under the condition of a just and prior indemnity.

POSTAMBULE

Women, rouse yourself, the tolling of the bell of reason can be heard throughout the universe; recognize your rights. Nature's mighty empire is no longer encircled by prejudices, fanaticism, superstition and lies. Truth's flaming torch has dispelled all clouds of foolishness and usurpation. Man-slave has multiplied his strengths and he needs to resort to yours to break his shackles. Once free, he has become unjust towards his companion. O women! Women, when will you cease to be blind? What are the benefits that you have reaped from the revolution? A contempt all the more marked, a disdain all the more evident. During centuries of corruption you have only reigned over the weakness of men. Your empire is destroyed, what then are you left with? The conviction of man's injustices, the demand for your heritage, founded on wise decrees of nature; what would you have to fear for in such a beautiful enterprise? The wit of the legislator in the marriage of Cana?[3] Are you afraid that our French legislators, correctors of these morals, hanging for long to the branches of politics, but which are no longer in season, will repeat to you: WOMEN, what is common between you and us? Everything, you would have to answer. If they persisted stubbornly in their weaknesses, in putting this thoughtlessness in contradiction with their principles; oppose courageously with the force of reason the vain pretensions of superiority; assemble under the banner of philosophy; unfurl all the energy of your character, and you will soon see these arrogant ones become your servile worshippers, cringing at your feet, but proud to share with you the treasures of the Supreme Being. Whatever be the barriers against you, it is within your power to cross them; you only have to wish it. Let us move on now to the appalling picture of what you have been in society, and since there is talk, at this moment, of a national education, let us see if our wise legislators will think soundly about women's education.

Women have done more harm than good. Constraint and dissimulation have been their lot. What force took from them, has been returned to them by guile; they have resorted to all the resources of their charms, and the most irreproachable man could not resist them. Poison, chains, everything was subjugated to them; they controlled crime as well as virtue. The French government specially, for centuries, depended on the nocturnal administration of women,[4] the cabinet had no secrets to be indiscreet about. Be it the embassy, the armed forces, the ministry, the presidency, the pontificate or the cardinalship; in short all that characterizes the stupidity of men, secular or religious, all was submitted to the cupidity and to the ambition of this sex earlier disdainful and respected, and since the revolution, respectable and disdained.

3. At which Jesus performed his first miracle, turning water into wine.

4. The manipulations of women at night, presumably through "pillow talk."

In this sort of antithesis, how many remarks do I not have to offer! I only have a moment to make them, but this moment will arrest the attention of the most remote posterity. Under the Ancien Régime,[5] all was perverted, all guilty; but could we not notice an improvement of things in the very substance of vices? A woman only needed to be beautiful or pleasant; when she possessed these two qualities, she saw a hundred fortunes at her feet. If she did not take advantage of them, she had a bizarre personality, or a less common philosophy, which led her to scorn riches, thus she was only considered headstrong. The most indecent woman made herself respected with gold. Trade in women was a kind of industry accepted in the highest classes and which, henceforth, will have no credit. If it yet had any, the REVOLUTION would be lost, and under new relationships, we would still be corrupt. However, can reason conceal the fact that any other path to fortune is closed to the woman bought by man, like a slave on the African coast? The difference is considerable, we know it. The slave has command over the master, but if the master gives her freedom without reward, and at an age when the slave has lost all her charms, what becomes of this unfortunate woman? The toy of contempt; the very doors of charity are shut for her; she is poor and old, one says; why did she not know how to become rich? Other examples, even more touching, come to the mind. A young woman without any experience, seduced by the man she loves, will abandon her parents to follow him; the ungrateful man will leave her after a few years, and the more she has aged with him, the more inhuman his fickleness will be; if she has children he will abandon her all the same. If he is rich, he will think himself exempted from sharing his fortune with his noble victims. If some commitment binds him to his duties, he will violate its power, but hope for everything from the law. If he is married, all other commitments lose their force. What laws remain then to be formed in order to extirpate vice from its very roots? That of sharing wealth between men and women, and that of public administration. One can easily imagine that a woman born in a rich family earns a lot with equal sharing. But she who is born in a poor family, with merits and virtues, what is her lot? Poverty and opprobrium. If she does not excel precisely in music or in painting, she cannot be admitted to any public function even if she is fully capable. I will speak at length about them in the new edition of all my political writings, which I propose to give to the public in a few days' time, with notes.

I take up my text concerning mores.[6] Marriage is the tomb of confidence and love. The married woman can with impunity give bastards to her husband, and fortune which does not belong to them. The unmarried one, has but one weak right; the old and inhuman laws refused her and her children this right in the name and property of the father, and no new laws have been made on this subject. If an attempt to give an honorable and just place to my sex is, at this moment, considered as a paradox on my part and as attempting the impossible, I leave to future men the glory of treating this subject; but in the meanwhile, it can be prepared through national education by restoring customs and conjugal conventions.

5. The old monarchical, hierarchical system. 6. Morally binding customs.

EDMUND BURKE

Not everyone found the revolutionary tumult of the times inspiring or hopeful. The Anglo-Irish politician and writer Edmund Burke (1729–1797) was horrified when he read pamphlets enthusiastically supporting the French Revolution in England, and the response he wrote made him one of history's most famous champions of conservatism. His *Reflections on the Revolution in France* supports tradition for the sake of stability and freedom. It upholds monarchy, the inheritance of wealth and political power, and the value of conventional wisdom. To Burke, abstract rights and new constitutions seem monstrous and unnatural, and the angry mob violence of the French Revolution disrupts longstanding institutions and generates nothing better than terrifying chaos. The book was an immediate best seller when it appeared in 1790: thirteen thousand copies sold in the first month after publication, and it was reprinted eleven times in the next year. Part of its popularity had to do with Burke's sensational and gripping style. He is especially famous for his description of the march on Versailles in October of 1789, when a hungry mob composed mostly of women stormed the royal palace and captured the French king and queen.

From Reflections on the Revolution in France

* * * All circumstances taken together, the French revolution is the most astonishing that has hitherto happened in the world. The most wonderful things are brought about in many instances by means the most absurd and ridiculous; in the most ridiculous modes; and apparently, by the most contemptible instruments. Every thing seems out of nature in this strange chaos of levity and ferocity, and of all sorts of crimes jumbled together with all sorts of follies. In viewing this monstrous tragi-comic scene, the most opposite passions necessarily succeed, and sometimes mix with each other in the mind; alternate contempt and indignation; alternate laughter and tears; alternate scorn and horror.

* * *

A spirit of innovation is generally the result of a selfish temper and confined views. People will not look forward to posterity, who never look backward to their ancestors. Besides, the people of England well know, that the idea of inheritance furnishes a sure principle of conservation, and a sure principle of transmission; without at all excluding a principle of improvement. It leaves acquisition free; but it secures what it acquires. Whatever advantages are obtained by a state proceeding on these maxims, are locked fast as in a sort of family settlement; grasped as in a kind of mortmain[1] for ever. By a constitutional policy, working

1. Land held in perpetuity by an institution, such as a church.

after the pattern of nature, we receive, we hold, we transmit our government and our privileges, in the same manner in which we enjoy and transmit our property and our lives. The institutions of policy, the goods of fortune, the gifts of Providence, are handed down, to us and from us, in the same course and order. Our political system is placed in a just correspondence and symmetry with the order of the world, and with the mode of existence decreed to a permanent body composed of transitory parts; wherein, by the disposition of a stupendous wisdom, moulding together the great mysterious incorporation of the human race, the whole, at one time, is never old, or middle-aged, or young, but in a condition of unchangeable constancy, moves on through the varied tenour of perpetual decay, fall, renovation, and progression. Thus, by preserving the method of nature in the conduct of the state, in what we improve we are never wholly new; in what we retain we are never wholly obsolete. By adhering in this manner and on those principles to our forefathers, we are guided not by the superstition of antiquarians, but by the spirit of philosophic analogy. In this choice of inheritance we have given to our frame of polity the image of a relation in blood; binding up the constitution of our country with our dearest domestic ties; adopting our fundamental laws into the bosom of our family affections; keeping inseparable, and cherishing with the warmth of all their combined and mutually reflected charities, our state, our hearths, our sepulchres, and our altars.

Through the same plan of a conformity to nature in our artificial institutions, and by calling in the aid of her unerring and powerful instincts, to fortify the fallible and feeble contrivances of our reason, we have derived several other, and those no small benefits, from considering our liberties in the light of an inheritance. Always acting as if in the presence of canonized forefathers, the spirit of freedom, leading in itself to misrule and excess, is tempered with an awful gravity. This idea of a liberal descent inspires us with a sense of habitual native dignity, which prevents that upstart insolence almost inevitably adhering to and disgracing those who are the first acquirers of any distinction. By this means our liberty becomes a noble freedom. It carries an imposing and majestic aspect. It has a pedigree and illustrating ancestors. It has its bearings and its ensigns armorial. It has its gallery of portraits; its monumental inscriptions; its records, evidences, and titles. We procure reverence to our civil institutions on the principle upon which nature teaches us to revere individual men; on account of their age; and on account of those from whom they are descended. All your sophisters[2] cannot produce any thing better adapted to preserve a rational and manly freedom than the course that we have pursued, who have chosen our nature rather than our speculations, our breasts rather than our inventions, for the great conservatories and magazines of our rights and privileges.

* * *

History will record, that on the morning of the 6th of October 1789, the king and queen of France, after a day of confusion, alarm, dismay, and slaughter, lay down, under the pledged security of public faith, to indulge nature in a few hours of respite, and troubled melancholy repose. From this sleep the queen was

2. People who make devious or deceptive arguments.

first startled by the voice of the centinel at her door, who cried out to her, to save herself by flight—that this was the last proof of fidelity he could give—that they were upon him, and he was dead. Instantly he was cut down. A band of cruel ruffians and assassins, reeking with his blood, rushed into the chamber of the queen, and pierced with an hundred strokes of bayonets and poniards the bed, from whence this persecuted woman had but just time to fly almost naked, and through ways unknown to the murderers had escaped to seek refuge at the feet of a king and husband, not secure of his own life for a moment.

This king, to say no more of him, and this queen, and their infant children (who once would have been the pride and hope of a great and generous people) were then forced to abandon the sanctuary of the most splendid palace in the world, which they left swimming in blood, polluted by massacre, and strewed with scattered limbs and mutilated carcases. Thence they were conducted into the capital of their kingdom. Two had been selected from the unprovoked, unresisted, promiscuous slaughter, which was made of the gentlemen of birth and family who composed the king's body guard. These two gentlemen, with all the parade of an execution of justice, were cruelly and publickly dragged to the block, and beheaded in the great court of the palace. Their heads were stuck upon spears, and led the procession; whilst the royal captives who followed in the train were slowly moved along, amidst the horrid yells, and shrilling screams, and frantic dances, and infamous contumelies, and all the unutterable abominations of the furies of hell, in the abused shape of the vilest of women. After they had been made to taste, drop by drop, more than the bitterness of death, in the slow torture of a journey of twelve miles, protracted to six hours, they were, under a guard, composed of those very soldiers who had thus conducted them through this famous triumph, lodged in one of the old palaces of Paris, now converted into a Bastile[3] for kings.

* * *

As a man, it became [the king] to feel for his wife and his children, and the faithful guards of his person, that were massacred in cold blood about him; as a prince, it became him to feel for the strange and frightful transformation of his civilized subjects, and to be more grieved for them, than solicitous for himself. It derogates little from his fortitude, while it adds infinitely to the honor of his humanity. I am very sorry to say it, very sorry indeed, that such personages are in a situation in which it is not unbecoming in us to praise the virtues of the great.

I hear, and I rejoice to hear, that the great lady, the other object of the triumph, has borne that day (one is interested that beings made for suffering should suffer well) and that she bears all the succeeding days, that she bears the imprisonment of her husband, and her own captivity, and the exile of her friends, and the insulting adulation of addresses, and the whole weight of her accumulated wrongs, with a serene patience, in a manner suited to her rank and race, and becoming the offspring of a sovereign distinguished for her piety and her courage;[4] that like her she has lofty sentiments; that she feels with the

3. Political prison in Paris that was attacked at the start of the French Revolution.

4. Marie Antoinette, the queen of France, was the daughter of the empress of Austria, Maria Theresa.

dignity of a Roman matron; that in the last extremity she will save herself from the last disgrace,[5] and that if she must fall, she will fall by no ignoble hand.

It is now sixteen or seventeen years since I saw the queen of France, then the dauphiness,[6] at Versailles; and surely never lighted on this orb, which she hardly seemed to touch, a more delightful vision. I saw her just above the horizon, decorating and cheering the elevated sphere she just began to move in,—glittering like the morning-star, full of life, and splendor, and joy. Oh! what a revolution! and what an heart must I have, to contemplate without emotion that elevation and that fall! Little did I dream when she added titles of veneration to those of enthusiastic, distant, respectful love, that she should ever be obliged to carry the sharp antidote against disgrace concealed in that bosom; little did I dream that I should have lived to see such disasters fallen upon her in a nation of gallant men, in a nation of men of honor and of cavaliers. I thought ten thousand swords must have leaped from their scabbards to avenge even a look that threatened her with insult.—But the age of chivalry is gone.—That of sophisters, oeconomists, and calculators, has succeeded; and the glory of Europe is extinguished for ever. Never, never more, shall we behold that generous loyalty to rank and sex, that proud submission, that dignified obedience, that subordination of the heart, which kept alive, even in servitude itself, the spirit of an exalted freedom. The unbought grace of life, the cheap defence of nations, the nurse of manly sentiment and heroic enterprize is gone! It is gone, that sensibility of principle, that chastity of honor, which felt a stain like a wound, which inspired courage whilst it mitigated ferocity, which ennobled whatever it touched, and under which vice itself lost half its evil, by losing all its grossness.

This mixed system of opinion and sentiment had its origin in the antient chivalry; and the principle, though varied in its appearance by the varying state of human affairs, subsisted and influenced through a long succession of generations, even to the time we live in. If it should ever be totally extinguished, the loss I fear will be great. It is this which has given its character to modern Europe. It is this which has distinguished it under all its forms of government, and distinguished it to its advantage, from the states of Asia, and possibly from those states which flourished in the most brilliant periods of the antique world. It was this, which, without confounding ranks, had produced a noble equality, and handed it down through all the gradations of social life. It was this opinion which mitigated kings into companions, and raised private men to be fellows with kings. Without force, or opposition, it subdued the fierceness of pride and power; it obliged sovereigns to submit to the soft collar of social esteem, compelled stern authority to submit to elegance, and gave a domination vanquisher of laws, to be subdued by manners.

But now all is to be changed. All the pleasing illusions, which made power gentle, and obedience liberal, which harmonized the different shades of life, and which, by a bland assimilation, incorporated into politics the sentiments which beautify and soften private society, are to be dissolved by this new conquering empire of light and reason. All the decent drapery of life is to be rudely torn off. All the superadded ideas, furnished from the wardrobe of a

5. She is willing to commit suicide rather than submit to rape.

6. Wife of the heir to the French throne.

moral imagination, which the heart owns, and the understanding ratifies, as necessary to cover the defects of our naked shivering nature, and to raise it to dignity in our own estimation, are to be exploded as a ridiculous, absurd, and antiquated fashion.

On this scheme of things, a king is but a man; a queen is but a woman; a woman is but an animal; and an animal not of the highest order. All homage paid to the sex[7] in general as such, and without distinct views, is to be regarded as romance and folly. Regicide, and parricide, and sacrilege, are but fictions of superstition, corrupting jurisprudence by destroying its simplicity. The murder of a king, or a queen, or a bishop, or a father, are only common homicide; and if the people are by any chance, or in any way gainers by it, a sort of homicide much the most pardonable, and into which we ought not to make too severe a scrutiny.

On the scheme of this barbarous philosophy, which is the offspring of cold hearts and muddy understandings, and which is as void of solid wisdom, as it is destitute of all taste and elegance, laws are to be supported only by their own terrors, and by the concern, which each individual may find in them, from his own private speculations, or can spare to them from his own private interests. In the groves of *their* academy, at the end of every visto, you see nothing but the gallows. Nothing is left which engages the affections on the part of the commonwealth. On the principles of this mechanic philosophy, our institutions can never be embodied, if I may use the expression, in persons; so as to create in us love, veneration, admiration, or attachment. But that sort of reason which banishes the affections is incapable of filling their place. These public affections, combined with manners, are required sometimes as supplements, sometimes as correctives, always as aids to law. The precept given by a wise man, as well as a great critic, for the construction of poems, is equally true as to states. *Non satis est pulchra esse poemata, dulcia sunto.*[8] There ought to be a system of manners in every nation which a well-formed mind would be disposed to relish. To make us love our country, our country ought to be lovely.

But power, of some kind or other, will survive the shock in which manners and opinions perish; and it will find other and worse means for its support. The usurpation which, in order to subvert antient institutions, has destroyed antient principles, will hold power by arts similar to those by which it has acquired it. When the old feudal and chivalrous spirit of *Fealty*,[9] which, by freeing kings from fear, freed both kings and subjects from the precautions of tyranny, shall be extinct in the minds of men, plots and assassinations will be anticipated by preventive murder and preventive confiscation, and that long roll of grim and bloody maxims, which form the political code of all power, not standing on its own honor, and the honor of those who are to obey it. Kings will be tyrants from policy when subjects are rebels from principle.

When antient opinions and rules of life are taken away, the loss cannot possibly be estimated. From that moment we have no compass to govern us; nor

7. The female sex.
8. "It is not enough for poems to be beautiful; they must also be sweet" (Latin, from the Roman writer Horace [65–8 B.C.E.]).
9. A pledge of fidelity to a person of higher rank.

can we know distinctly to what port we steer. Europe undoubtedly, taken in a mass, was in a flourishing condition the day on which your Revolution was compleated. How much of that prosperous state was owing to the spirit of our old manners and opinions is not easy to say; but as such causes cannot be indifferent in their operation, we must presume, that, on the whole, their operation was beneficial.

We are but too apt to consider things in the state in which we find them, without sufficiently adverting to the causes by which they have been produced, and possibly may be upheld. Nothing is more certain, than that our manners, our civilization, and all the good things which are connected with manners, and with civilization, have, in this European world of ours, depended for ages upon two principles; and were indeed the result of both combined; I mean the spirit of a gentleman, and the spirit of religion. The nobility and the clergy, the one by profession, the other by patronage, kept learning in existence, even in the midst of arms and confusions, and whilst governments were rather in their causes than formed. Learning paid back what it received to nobility and to priesthood; and paid it with usury,[1] by enlarging their ideas, and by furnishing their minds. Happy if they had all continued to know their indissoluble union, and their proper place! Happy if learning, not debauched by ambition, had been satisfied to continue the instructor, and not aspired to be the master! Along with its natural protectors and guardians, learning will be cast into the mire, and trodden down under the hoofs of a swinish multitude.

If, as I suspect, modern letters owe more than they are always willing to own to antient manners, so do other interests which we value full as much as they are worth. Even commerce, and trade, and manufacture, the gods of our oeconomical politicians, are themselves perhaps but creatures; are themselves but effects, which, as first causes, we choose to worship. They certainly grew under the same shade in which learning flourished. They too may decay with their natural protecting principles. With you, for the present at least, they all threaten to disappear together. Where trade and manufactures are wanting to a people, and the spirit of nobility and religion remains, sentiment supplies, and not always ill supplies their place; but if commerce and the arts should be lost in an experiment to try how well a state may stand without these old fundamental principles, what sort of a thing must be a nation of gross, stupid, ferocious, and at the same time, poor and sordid barbarians, destitute of religion, honor, or manly pride, possessing nothing at present, and hoping for nothing hereafter?

I wish you may not be going fast, and by the shortest cut, to that horrible and disgustful situation. Already there appears a poverty of conception, a coarseness and vulgarity in all the proceedings of the assembly and of all their instructors. Their liberty is not liberal. Their science is presumptuous ignorance. Their humanity is savage and brutal.

* * *

1. Interest.

JEAN-JACQUES DESSALINES

The French colony of Saint-Domingue—the western portion of the Caribbean island of Hispaniola—was the jewel of the French empire in the eighteenth century. A fertile source of sugar, coffee, tobacco and cotton, its 500,000 slaves produced extraordinary wealth for France. The slaves also chafed against their oppression, erupting frequently in rebellion. As the French Revolution abolished old hierarchies, the people of Saint-Domingue hotly debated new questions about natural rights, especially freedom and equality. The colony's free blacks, white plantation owners, and the poorer white population began to fight among themselves over property and privileges under the new French Declaration of the Rights of Man. In this unstable context in 1791, the slaves who made up the vast majority of the island rose up under the leadership of the brilliant strategist Toussaint L'Ouverture and launched a war that would last more than a decade. During this period, Britain and Spain struggled to take control of Saint-Domingue, and fearful of losing its richest colony, France officially liberated the slaves in the hope of retaining power there. The plan worked for a period: Toussaint L'Ouverture joined the French Republic and defeated the British and the Spanish. By 1801 he had succeeded in abolishing slavery on the island and had declared himself governor for life. Napoleon, however, nervous about this independent black leader, captured Toussaint and in 1802 forced him into exile in Europe, where he died less than a year later.

Toussaint's astute but ruthless second-in-command, Jean-Jacques Dessalines (1758–1806), then took charge of the revolution. He successfully defeated the increasingly brutal French troops in 1803. Dessalines proclaimed a new nation, which he called Haiti, and had himself crowned emperor. His proclamation, "Liberty or Death," was published in June 1804, shortly after he had ordered the massacre of thousands of white Haitians and declared Haiti an all-black nation.

Rhetorically, the document is creative and skillful, especially for a former slave who had received no schooling: Dessalines recasts the French Revolutionary motif of the "Tree of Liberty" as "the ancient tree of slavery and prejudices," and portrays the slave trade as a cannibalistic consumption of fellow human beings. The proclamation is also explicitly critical of Toussaint, arguing for the need for absolutely ruthless determination. Dessalines was canny about targeting international audiences. His secretary sent letters accompanying this proclamation to American newspaper publishers, urging them to publish them. It appeared in about fifty different US newspapers. Dessalines's violence was in fact long remembered and discussed throughout the American South in the decades that followed, and served as an important source of white Southern fears about what might await them if slavery were abolished in the United States.

Assassinated in 1806, Dessalines left a complex legacy: on the one hand, horror at his autocratic rule and willingness to be brutal in battle, and on the other hand, admiration at his power to fight back against strong oppressors with both words and weapons. The Haitian national anthem is called the *Dessalinienne*.

LIBERTY or DEATH[1]

PROCLAMATION

Jean Jacques Dessalines, governor-general, to the inhabitants of Hayti.

CRIMES, the most atrocious, such as were until then unheard of, and would cause nature to shudder, have been perpetrated. The measure was over-heaped. At length the hour of vengeance has arrived, and the implacable enemies of the rights of man have suffered the punishment due to their crimes.

My arm, raised over their heads, has too long delayed to strike. At that signal which the justice of God has urged, your hands righteously armed, have brought the axe upon the ancient tree of slavery and prejudices. In vain had time, and more especially the infernal politics of Europeans, surrounded it with triple brass; you have stripped it of its armor: you have placed it upon your heart that you may become (like your natural enemies) cruel and merciless. Like an overflowing mighty torrent that tears down all opposition, your vengeful fury has carried away everything in its impetuous course. Thus perish all tyrants over innocence—all oppressors of mankind!

What then? bent for many ages under an iron yoke; the sport of the passions of men, of their injustice, and of the caprices of fortune; mutilated victims of the cupidity of white French men: after having fattened with our toils these insatiate bloodsuckers, with a patience and resignation unexampled, we should again have seen that sacrilegious horde make an attempt upon our destruction, without any distinction of sex or age; and we, men without energy, of no virtue, of no delicate sensibility, should not we have plunged in their breasts the dagger of desperation? Where is that vile Haytian, so unworthy of his regeneration, who thinks he has not accomplished the decrees of the eternal, by exterminating these blood-thirsty tigers? If there is one let him fly: indignant nature discards him our bosom; let him hide his shame far from hence; the air we breathe is not suited to his gross organs, it is the pure air of liberty, august and triumphant.

Yes, we have rendered to these true cannibals war for war, crime for crime, outrage for outrage; Yes, I have saved my country, I have avenged America. The avowal I make of it in the face of earth and heaven, constitutes my pride and my glory. Of what consequence to me is the opinion which contemporary and future generations will pronounce upon my conduct? I have performed my duty; I enjoy my own approbation; for me, that is sufficient. But what do I say? The preservation of my unfortunate brothers, the testimony of my own conscience, are not my only recompence: I have seen two classes of men,[2] born to

1. Published in the *New York Commercial Advertiser*, June 4, 1804.
2. Black slaves and *gens de couleur* (free people of color); they united under Dessalines's leadership.

cherish, assist and succour one another—mixed, in a word, and blended together—crying vengeance, and disputing the honor of the first blow.

Blacks and yellows,[3] whom the refined duplicity of Europeans has for a long time endeavoured to divide: you who are now consolidated and make but one family; without doubt it was necessary that our perfect reconciliation should be sealed with the blood of our butchers. Similar calamities have hung over your proscribed heads: a similar ardour to strike your enemies has signalized you; the like fate is reserved for you: and the like interests must therefore render you forever one, indivisible and inseparable. Maintain that precious concord, that happy harmony amongst yourselves: it is the pledge of your happiness, your salvation, and your success: it is the secret of being invincible.

It is necessary, in order to strengthen these ties, to recall to your remembrance the catalogue of atrocities committed against our species; the massacre of the entire population of this island, meditated in the silence and sang froid of the cabinet:[4] the execution of that abominable project to me unblushingly proposed, and already begun by the French with the calmness and serenity of a countenance accustomed to similar crimes. Guadeloupe, pillaged and destroyed: its victims still reeking with the blood of the children, women and old men put to the sword. . . . Unfortunate people of Martinique,[5] could I but fly to your assistance, and break your fetters! Alas! an insurmountable barrier separates us. Perhaps a spark from the same fire which inflames us, will alight into your bosoms: perhaps at the sound of this commotion, suddenly awakening from your lethargy, with arms in your hands, you will reclaim your sacred and imprescriptable rights.

After the terrible example which I have just given, that sooner or later divine Justice will unchain on earth some mighty minds, above the weakness of the vulgar, for the destruction and terror of the wicked; tremble, tyrants, usurpers, scourges of the new world! our daggers are sharpened; your punishment is ready! sixty thousand men, equipped, inured to war, obedient to my orders, burn to offer a new sacrifice to the manes of their assassinated brothers. Let that nation come who may be mad and daring enough to attack me. Already at its approach, the irritated genius of Hayti, rising out of the bosom of the ocean, appears; his menacing aspect throws the waves into commotion, excites tempests, and with his mighty hand disperses ships, or dashes them in pieces; to his formidable voice the laws of nature pay obeisence: diseases, plague,[6] famine, conflagration, poison, are his constant attendants. But why calculate on the assistance of the climate and of the elements? Have I forgot that I command a people of no common cast, brought up in adversity, whose audacious daring frowns at obstacles, and increases by dangers? Let them come, then, these homicidal cohorts! I wait for them with

3. People of mixed-race ancestry.
4. The French military leader Donatien-Marie-Joseph de Vimeur, Viscount of Rochambeau, had written to Napoleon to tell him that ruthless violence against slaves was the only way for France to reassert control over Saint-Domingue.
5. French islands in the Caribbean that, unlike Saint-Domingue, did not achieve independence from France.
6. Yellow fever helped to propel Dessalines to victory when it killed Napoleon's brother-in-law Le Clerc, the leader of French troops in Saint-Domingue, and thousands of his troops.

firmness and with a steady eye. I abandon to them freely the sea shore, and the places where cities have existed; but woe to those who may approach us too near the mountains! It were better for them that the sea received them into its profound abyss, than to be devoured by the anger of the children of Hayti.

"War to death to tyrants!" this is my motto; "Liberty! Independence!" this is our rallying cry.

Generals, officers, soldiers, a little unlike him who has preceded me, the ex-general TOUSSAINT LOUVERTURE, I have been faithful to the promise which I made to you when I took up arms against tyranny, and whilst the last spark of life remains in me I shall keep my oath. *Never again shall a colonist or a European set his foot upon this territory with the title of master or proprietor*. This resolution shall henceforward form the fundamental basis of our constitution.

Should other chiefs, after me, by pursuing a conduct diametrically opposite to mine, dig their own grave and those of their species, you will have to accuse only the law of destiny which shall have taken me away from the happiness and welfare of my fellow citizens. May my successors follow the path I shall have traced out for them! It is the system best adapted for consolidating their power; it is the highest homage they can render to my memory.

As it is derogatory to my character and my dignity to punish the innocent for the crimes of the guilty, a handful of whites, commendable by the religion they have always professed, and who have besides taken the oath to live with us in the woods, have experienced my clemency. I order that the sword respect them, and that they be unmolested.

I recommend anew and order to all the generals of department, etc. to grant succours encouragement and protection, to all neutral and friendly nations who may wish to establish commercial relations in this island.

WILLIAM WORDSWORTH

The English poet William Wordsworth (1770–1850) went through contradictory emotions as he watched the political revolutions of the period unfold. Living in France between 1790 and 1792, he caught the joyful spirit of freedom and possibility. He visited sites made famous by the revolutionaries and picked up rubble from the attack on the Bastille prison. At one point he saw a starving girl trudging through the streets. "'Tis against *that* / That we are fighting," a French friend explained, and Wordsworth committed himself to the cause of toppling monarchy and eradicating poverty and inequality.

Wordsworth's autobiographical poem, *The Prelude*, composed in 1799 and 1805 but not published (in a greatly revised version) until 1850, registers both the elation felt by the poet and his growing horror at the increasingly bloody revolution. The first passage selected here conveys his misery as he hears about the Terror; the second shows how the French Revolution raised exciting and profound political questions: what kind of new society was now possible? Had the Revolution unleashed the promise of a world based on freedom and reason?

In 1802 Wordsworth also published a poem to the Haitian revolutionary Toussaint l'Ouverture, who was at the time locked in a French prison, though the world did not know where he was or what his fate would be. Here the poet opts for the compact fourteen-line sonnet, a strict and traditional form usually associated with love. In this particular sonnet the poet offers a troubling and ambivalent conclusion: Toussaint may die, but he should take comfort in the fact that nature—and human experience—will survive him.

The Prelude

From *Book X*

Domestic carnage now filled the whole year
With feast-days; old men from the chimney-nook,
The maiden from the bosom of her love,
The mother from the cradle of her babe,
The warrior from the field—all perished, all—
Friends, enemies, of all parties, ages, ranks,
Head after head, and never heads enough
For those that bade them fall. They found their joy,
They made it proudly, eager as a child,
(If like desires of innocent little ones
May with such heinous appetites be compared),
Pleased in some open field to exercise
A toy that mimics with revolving wings

The motion of a wind-mill; though the air
Do of itself blow fresh, and make the vanes
Spin in his eyesight, *that* contents him not,
But, with the plaything at arm's length, he sets
His front against the blast, and runs amain,
That it may whirl the faster.
Amid the depth
Of those enormities, even thinking minds
Forgot, at seasons, whence they had their being;
Forgot that such a sound was ever heard,
As Liberty upon earth: yet all beneath
Her innocent authority was wrought,
Nor could have been, without her blessed name.
The illustrious wife of Roland,[1] in the hour
Of her composure, felt that agony,
And gave it vent in her last words. O Friend![2]
It was a lamentable time for man,
Whether a hope had e'er been his or not;
A woful time for them whose hopes survived
The shock; most woful for those few who still
Were flattered, and had trust in human kind:
They had the deepest feeling of the grief.
Meanwhile the Invaders[3] fared as they deserved:
The Herculean Commonwealth had put forth her arms,
And throttled with an infant godhead's might
The snakes about her cradle;[4] that was well,
And as it should be; yet no cure for them
Whose souls were sick with pain of what would be
Hereafter brought in charge against mankind.
Most melancholy at that time, O Friend!
Were my day-thoughts,—my nights were miserable;
Through months, through years, long after the last beat
Of those atrocities, the hour of sleep
To me came rarely charged with natural gifts,
Such ghastly visions had I of despair
And tyranny, and implements of death;
And innocent victims sinking under fear,
And momentary hope, and worn-out prayer,
Each in his separate cell, or penned in crowds
For sacrifice, and struggling with fond mirth
And levity in dungeons, where the dust
Was laid with tears. Then suddenly the scene

1. Madame Roland (1754–1793), a prominent supporter of the moderate Girondist faction during the French Revolution, executed by the Jacobins during the Reign of Terror. Her last words were reportedly, "Oh Liberty, how you have been played with!"

2. Samuel Taylor Coleridge (1772–1834), Wordsworth's friend and collaborator.

3. Counterrevolutionary and foreign armies attacking the new French Republic.

4. In Greek mythology, the infant Heracles (Hercules to the Romans) strangled two snakes sent by Hera to kill him.

Changed, and the unbroken dream entangled me
In long orations, which I strove to plead
Before unjust tribunals,—with a voice
Laboring, a brain confounded, and a sense,
Death-like, of treacherous desertion, felt
In the last place of refuge—my own soul.

* * *

From *Book XI*

O pleasant exercise of hope and joy!
For mighty were the auxiliars which then stood
Upon our side, us who were strong in love!
Bliss was it in that dawn to be alive,
But to be young was very Heaven! O times,
In which the meagre, stale, forbidding ways
Of custom, law, and statute, took at once
The attraction of a country in romance!
When Reason seemed the most to assert her rights
When most intent on making of herself
A prime enchantress—to assist the work,
Which then was going forward in her name!
Not favored spots alone, but the whole Earth,
The beauty wore of promise—that which sets
(As at some moments might not be unfelt
Among the bowers of Paradise itself)
The budding rose above the rose full blown.
What temper at the prospect did not wake
To happiness unthought of? The inert
Were roused, and lively natures rapt away!
They who had fed their childhood upon dreams,
The play-fellows of fancy, who had made
All powers of swiftness, subtilty, and strength
Their ministers,—who in lordly wise had stirred
Among the grandest objects of the sense,
And dealt with whatsoever they found there
As if they had within some lurking right
To wield it;—they, too, who of gentle mood
Had watched all gentle motions, and to these
Had fitted their own thoughts, schemers more mild,
And in the region of their peaceful selves;—
Nor was it that *both* found, the meek and lofty
Did both find helpers to their heart's desire,
And stuff at hand, plastic as they could wish,—
Were called upon to exercise their skill,
Not in Utopia,—subterranean fields,—
Or some secreted island, Heaven knows where!
But in the very world, which is the world
Of all of us,—the place where, in the end,
We find our happiness, or not at all!

Why should I not confess that Earth was then
To me, what an inheritance, new-fallen,
Seems, when the first time visited, to one
Who thither comes to find in it his home?
He walks about and looks upon the spot
With cordial transport, moulds it and remoulds,
And is half pleased with things that are amiss,
'Twill be such joy to see them disappear.

* * *

To Toussaint L'Ouverture[1]

Toussaint, the most unhappy Man of Men!
Whether the rural Milk-maid by her Cow
Sing in thy hearing, or thou liest now
Alone in some deep dungeon's earless den,
O miserable chieftain! where and when
Wilt thou find patience? Yet die not; do thou
Wear rather in thy bonds a chearful brow:
Though fallen Thyself, never to rise again,
Live, and take comfort. Thou hast left behind
Powers that will work for thee; air, earth, and skies;
There's not a breathing of the common wind
That will forget thee; thou hast great allies;
Thy friends are exultations, agonies,
And love, and Man's unconquerable mind.

1. L'Ouverture (1743–1803) was the slave-born leader of the Haitian Revolution, captured and imprisoned in France in 1802.

SIMÓN BOLÍVAR

Known as "El Libertador"—the Liberator—Simón Bolívar (1783–1830) led the movement for Latin American independence from Spain. Born in Venezuela, he took part in a battle that achieved a fragile independence there in 1811 before turning his attention to the rest of New Granada, a huge Spanish colony that comprised what are now Venezuela, Colombia, Ecuador, Guyana, Panama, Costa Rica, and Nicaragua, as well as the colony of Perú, comprising modern-day Peru, Chile, and Bolivia. In 1819 Bolívar's army beat back Spanish forces, liberating the Republic of Colombia, and he was elected president. Six years later he achieved victory in what was then known as Upper Perú, now named Bolivia in his honor.

Bolívar was a thinker as well as a fighter. He wrote Bolivia's constitution and a series of influential political manifestos. He had read works of French Enlightenment philosophers in his youth, including **Rousseau** and **Voltaire**, and was inspired by the French Revolution. After a defeat in 1815, Bolívar went into exile in Jamaica to reflect on the ideal course of action. His famous "Letter from Jamaica," ostensibly written to a single Englishman in Jamaica, was published with the intention of winning Britain over to the side of South American independence. Bolívar lists the crimes of Spain and its tenuous hold on the vast territories of Latin America, and he offers a theory of colonial power that is different, he argues, from other kinds of tyranny. Bolívar makes the case that Latin American independence will serve the interests of all of Europe. And he ends with a call to unity among all Latin American nations, foreseeing a great future for the continent.

Reply of a South American to a Gentleman of This Island[1] [Jamaica]

* * * With what a feeling of gratitude I read that passage in your letter in which you say to me: "I hope that the success which then followed Spanish arms may now turn in favor of their adversaries, the badly oppressed people of South America." I take this hope as a prediction, if it is justice that determines man's contests. Success will crown our efforts, because the destiny of America has been irrevocably decided; the tie that bound her to Spain has been severed. Only a concept maintained that tie and kept the parts of that immense monarchy together. That which formerly bound them now divides them. The hatred that the Peninsula has inspired in us is greater than the ocean between us. It would be easier to have the two continents meet than to reconcile the spirits of the two countries. The habit of obedience; a community of interest, of understanding, of religion; mutual goodwill; a tender regard for the birthplace and good name of our forefathers; in short, all that gave rise to our hopes, came to us from Spain. As a result there was born a principle of affinity

1. Translated by Lewis Bertrand.

that seemed eternal, notwithstanding the misbehavior of our rulers which weakened that sympathy, or, rather, that bond enforced by the domination of their rule. At present the contrary attitude persists: we are threatened with the fear of death, dishonor, and every harm; there is nothing we have not suffered at the hands of that unnatural step-mother—Spain. The veil has been torn asunder. We have already seen the light, and it is not our desire to be thrust back into darkness. The chains have been broken; we have been freed, and now our enemies seek to enslave us anew. For this reason America fights desperately, and seldom has desperation failed to achieve victory.

Because successes have been partial and spasmodic, we must not lose faith. In some regions the Independents triumph, while in others the tyrants have the advantage. What is the end result? Is not the entire New World in motion, armed for defense? We have but to look around us on this hemisphere to witness a simultaneous struggle at every point.

The war-like state of the La Plata River provinces has purged that territory and led their victorious armies to Upper Perú, arousing Arequipa and worrying the royalists in Lima.[2] Nearly one million inhabitants there now enjoy liberty.

The territory of Chile, populated by 800,000 souls, is fighting the enemy who is seeking her subjugation; but to no avail, because those who long ago put an end to the conquests of this enemy, the free and indomitable Araucanians,[3] are their neighbors and compatriots. Their sublime example is proof to those fighting in Chile that a people who love independence will eventually achieve it.

The viceroyalty of Perú, whose population approaches a million and a half inhabitants, without doubt suffers the greatest subjection and is obliged to make the most sacrifices for the royal cause; and, although the thought of coöperating with that part of America may be vain, the fact remains that it is not tranquil, nor is it capable of restraining the torrent that threatens most of its provinces.

New Granada,[4] which is, so to speak, the heart of America, obeys a general government, save for the territory of Quito which is held only with the greatest difficulty by its enemies, as it is strongly devoted to the country's cause; and the provinces of Panamá and Santa Marta endure, not without suffering, the tyranny of their masters. Two and a half million people inhabit New Granada and are actually defending that territory against the Spanish army under General Morillo,[5] who will probably suffer defeat at the impregnable fortress of Cartagena. But should he take that city, it will be at the price of heavy casualties, and he will then lack sufficient forces to subdue the unrestrained and brave inhabitants of the interior.

With respect to heroic and hapless Venezuela, events there have moved so rapidly and the devastation has been such that it is reduced to frightful desolation and almost absolute indigence, although it was once among the fairest

2. The Viceroyalty of Perú had been the center of Spanish power in Latin America for centuries; the city of Lima remained loyal to Spain, but the southern region of Arequipa housed many Peruvian nationalists.

3. Spanish name given to the Mapuche people, an indigenous group who live in Chile and Argentina.

4. Spanish colony fighting for independence in 1815; its territory has since been divided to become the nations of Panama, Colombia, Ecuador, and Venezuela.

5. Pablo Morillo y Morillo (1775–1837), commander of Spanish troops sent to quell revolts in the Latin American colonies.

regions that are the pride of America. Its tyrants govern a desert, and they oppress only those unfortunate survivors who, having escaped death, lead a precarious existence. A few women, children, and old men are all that remain. Most of the men have perished rather than be slaves; those who survive continue to fight furiously on the fields and in the inland towns, until they expire or hurl into the sea those who, insatiable in their thirst for blood and crimes, rival those first monsters who wiped out America's primitive race. Nearly a million persons formerly dwelt in Venezuela, and it is no exaggeration to say that one out of four has succumbed either to the land, sword, hunger, plague, flight, or privation, all consequences of the war, save the earthquake.

According to Baron von Humboldt, New Spain,[6] including Guatemala, had 7,800,000 inhabitants in 1808. Since that time, the insurrection, which has shaken virtually all of her provinces, has appreciably reduced that apparently correct figure, for over a million men have perished, as you can see in the report of Mr. Walton,[7] who describes faithfully the bloody crimes committed in that abundant kingdom. There the struggle continues by dint of human and every other type of sacrifice, for the Spaniards spare nothing that might enable them to subdue those who have had the misfortune of being born on this soil, which appears to be destined to flow with the blood of its offspring. In spite of everything, the Mexicans will be free. They have embraced the country's cause, resolved to avenge their forefathers or follow them to the grave. Already they say with Raynal:[8] The time has come at last to repay the Spaniards torture for torture and to drown that race of annihilators in its own blood or in the sea.

The islands of Puerto Rico and Cuba, with a combined population of perhaps 700,000 to 800,000 souls, are the most tranquil possessions of the Spaniards, because they are not within range of contact with the Independents. But are not the people of those islands Americans? Are they not maltreated? Do they not desire a better life?

This picture represents, on a military map, an area of 2,000 longitudinal and 900 latitudinal leagues at its greatest point, wherein 16,000,000 Americans either defend their rights or suffer repression at the hands of Spain, which, although once the world's greatest empire, is now too weak, with what little is left her, to rule the new hemisphere or even to maintain herself in the old. And shall Europe, the civilized, the merchant, the lover of liberty allow an aged serpent, bent only on satisfying its venomous rage, devour the fairest part of our globe? What! Is Europe deaf to the clamor of her own interests? Has she no eyes to see justice? Has she grown so hardened as to become insensible? The more I ponder these questions, the more I am confused. I am led to think that America's disappearance is desired; but this is impossible because all Europe is not Spain. What madness for our enemy to hope to reconquer America when she has no navy, no funds, and almost no soldiers! Those troops

6. Alexander von Humboldt (1769–1859), German explorer who published scientific accounts of Latin American geography. "New Spain": vast Spanish colony covering territory that today includes California, New Mexico, Texas, most of Central America, the Caribbean, and the Philippines.

7. William Walton (1784–1857), British resident of Santo Domingo, now capital of the Dominican Republic, who wrote *The Present State of the Spanish Colonies* (1810) and *An Exposé of the Dissensions of Spanish America* (1814).

8. Guillaume Thomas Raynal (1713–1796), French historian and philosopher who condemned European colonialism.

which she has are scarcely adequate to keep her own people in a state of forced obedience and to defend herself from her neighbors. On the other hand, can that nation carry on the exclusive commerce of one-half the world when it lacks manufactures, agricultural products, crafts and sciences, and even a policy? Assume that this mad venture were successful, and further assume that pacification ensued, would not the sons of the Americans of today, together with the sons of the European *reconquistadores*[9] twenty years hence, conceive the same patriotic designs that are now being fought for?

Europe could do Spain a service by dissuading her from her rash obstinacy, thereby at least sparing her the costs she is incurring and the blood she is expending. And if she will fix her attention on her own precincts she can build her prosperity and power upon more solid foundations than doubtful conquests, precarious commerce, and forceful exactions from remote and powerful peoples. Europe herself, as a matter of common sense policy, should have prepared and executed the project of American independence, not alone because the world balance of power so necessitated, but also because this is the legitimate and certain means through which Europe can acquire overseas commercial establishments. A Europe which is not moved by the violent passions of vengeance, ambition, and greed, as is Spain, would seem to be entitled, by all the rules of equity, to make clear to Spain where her best interests lie.

All of the writers who have treated this matter agree on this point. Consequently, we have had reason to hope that the civilized nations would hasten to our aid in order that we might achieve that which must prove to be advantageous to both hemispheres. How vain has been this hope! Not only the Europeans but even our brothers of the North have been apathetic bystanders in this struggle which, by its very essence, is the most just, and in its consequences the most noble and vital of any which have been raised in ancient or in modern times. Indeed, can the far-reaching effects of freedom for the hemisphere which Columbus discovered ever be calculated?

* * *

It is even more difficult to foresee the future fate of the New World, to set down its political principles, or to prophesy what manner of government it will adopt. Every conjecture relative to America's future is, I feel, pure speculation. When mankind was in its infancy, steeped in uncertainty, ignorance, and error, was it possible to foresee what system it would adopt for its preservation? Who could venture to say that a certain nation would be a republic or a monarchy; this nation great, that nation small? To my way of thinking, such is our own situation. We are a young people. We inhabit a world apart, separated by broad seas. We are young in the ways of almost all the arts and sciences, although, in a certain manner, we are old in the ways of civilized society. I look upon the present state of America as similar to that of Rome after its fall. Each part of Rome adopted a political system conforming to its interest and situation or was led by the individual ambitions of certain chiefs, dynasties, or associations. But this important difference exists: those dispersed parts later re-established their ancient nations, subject to the changes imposed by cir-

9. Reconquerors (Spanish).

cumstances or events. But we scarcely retain a vestige of what once was; we are, moreover, neither Indian nor European, but a species midway between the legitimate proprietors of this country and the Spanish usurpers. In short, though Americans by birth we derive our rights from Europe, and we have to assert these rights against the rights of the natives, and at the same time we must defend ourselves against the invaders. This places us in a most extraordinary and involved situation. Notwithstanding that it is a type of divination to predict the result of the political course which America is pursuing, I shall venture some conjectures which, of course, are colored by my enthusiasm and dictated by rational desires rather than by reasoned calculations.

The rôle of the inhabitants of the American hemisphere has for centuries been purely passive. Politically they were non-existent. We are still in a position lower than slavery, and therefore it is more difficult for us to rise to the enjoyment of freedom. Permit me these transgressions in order to establish the issue. States are slaves because of either the nature or the misuse of their constitutions; a people is therefore enslaved when the government, by its nature or its vices, infringes on and usurps the rights of the citizen or subject. Applying these principles, we find that America was denied not only its freedom but even an active and effective tyranny. Let me explain. Under absolutism there are no recognized limits to the exercise of governmental powers. The will of the great sultan, khan, bey, and other despotic rulers is the supreme law, carried out more or less arbitrarily by the lesser pashas, khans, and satraps of Turkey and Persia, who have an organized system of oppression in which inferiors participate according to the authority vested in them. To them is entrusted the administration of civil, military, political, religious, and tax matters. But, after all is said and done, the rulers of Ispahan are Persians; the viziers of the Grand Turk are Turks; and the sultans of Tartary are Tartars. China does not bring its military leaders and scholars from the land of Genghis Khan,[1] her conqueror, notwithstanding that the Chinese of today are the lineal descendants of those who were reduced to subjection by the ancestors of the present-day Tartars.

How different is our situation! We have been harassed by a conduct which has not only deprived us of our rights but has kept us in a sort of permanent infancy with regard to public affairs. If we could at least have managed our domestic affairs and our internal administration, we could have acquainted ourselves with the processes and mechanics of public affairs. We should also have enjoyed a personal consideration, thereby commanding a certain unconscious respect from the people, which is so necessary to preserve amidst revolutions. That is why I say we have even been deprived of an active tyranny, since we have not been permitted to exercise its functions.

Americans today, and perhaps to a greater extent than ever before, who live within the Spanish system occupy a position in society no better than that of serfs destined for labor, or at best they have no more status than that of mere consumers. Yet even this status is surrounded with galling restrictions, such as being forbidden to grow European crops, or to store products which are

1. Mongol chieftain (1165–1227), founder of the Mongol Empire in central Asia, who conquered huge swaths of territory, including present-day China, Korea, Russia, and Afghanistan.

royal monopolies, or to establish factories of a type the Peninsula[2] itself does not possess. To this add the exclusive trading privileges, even in articles of prime necessity, and the barriers between American provinces, designed to prevent all exchange of trade, traffic, and understanding. In short, do you wish to know what our future held?—simply the cultivation of the fields of indigo, grain, coffee, sugar cane, cacao, and cotton; cattle raising on the broad plains; hunting wild game in the jungles: digging in the earth to mine its gold—but even these limitations could never satisfy the greed of Spain.

So negative was our existence that I can find nothing comparable in any other civilized society, examine as I may the entire history of time and the politics of all nations. Is it not an outrage and a violation of human rights to expect a land so splendidly endowed, so vast, rich, and populous, to remain merely passive?

* * *

Surely unity is what we need to complete our work of regeneration. The division among us, nevertheless, is nothing extraordinary, for it is characteristic of civil wars to form two parties, *conservatives* and *reformers*. The former are commonly the more numerous, because the weight of habit induces obedience to established powers; the latter are always fewer in number although more vocal and learned. Thus, the physical mass of the one is counterbalanced by the moral force of the other; the contest is prolonged, and the results are uncertain. Fortunately, in our case, the mass has followed the learned.

I shall tell you with what we must provide ourselves in order to expel the Spaniards and to found a free government. It is *union*, obviously; but such union will come about through sensible planning and well-directed actions rather than by divine magic. America stands together because it is abandoned by all other nations. It is isolated in the center of the world. It has no diplomatic relations, nor does it receive any military assistance; instead, America is attacked by Spain, which has more military supplies than any we can possibly acquire through furtive means.

When success is not assured, when the state is weak, and when results are distantly seen, all men hesitate; opinion is divided, passions rage, and the enemy fans these passions in order to win an easy victory because of them. As soon as we are strong and under the guidance of a liberal nation which will lend us her protection, we will achieve accord in cultivating the virtues and talents that lead to glory. Then will we march majestically toward that great prosperity for which South America is destined. Then will those sciences and arts which, born in the East, have enlightened Europe, wing their way to a free Colombia, which will cordially bid them welcome.

Such, Sir, are the thoughts and observations that I have the honor to submit to you, so that you may accept or reject them according to their merit. I beg you to understand that I have expounded them because I do not wish to appear discourteous and not because I consider myself competent to enlighten you concerning these matters.

2. The Iberian Peninsula, comprising Spain and Portugal.

DECLARATION OF SENTIMENTS

At the World Anti-Slavery Convention in London in 1840, two American delegates were denied the right to speak because they were women. Disturbed not least by the hypocrisy of the antislavery movement, supposedly dedicated to freedom and human rights, these two delegates—Lucretia Mott (1793–1880) and Elizabeth Cady Stanton (1815–1902)—convened a Women's Rights Convention in Seneca Falls, New York, in 1848. There more than 300 delegates hotly debated whether or not it was practical for the new women's movement to demand the right to vote. The great abolitionist leader **Frederick Douglass**, himself a former slave, spoke out powerfully in support of women's suffrage.

Stanton wrote the Declaration of Sentiments that was presented at Seneca Falls. Modeled explicitly on the **US Declaration of Independence**, this document uses the language of the American Revolution to argue for freedom and equal rights for the half of the nation that had been excluded by the original Declaration. Ironically, the American men who had enumerated the wrongs perpetrated by a foreign tyrant were now the ones accused of tyranny. Many voices in the press, including religious leaders, treated the plea for women's rights with contempt or outright horror. It would be another seventy years before US women won the right to vote.

Declaration of Sentiments

Put forth at Seneca Falls, N.Y., July 19th and 20th, 1848

When, in the course of human events, it becomes necessary for one portion of the family of man to assume among the people of the earth a position different from that which they have hitherto occupied, but one to which the laws of nature, and of nature's God entitle them, a decent respect to the opinions of mankind requires that they should declare the causes that impel them to such a course.

We hold these truths to be self-evident; that all men and women are created equal; that they are endowed by their Creator with certain inalienable rights; that among these are life, liberty, and the pursuit of happiness; that to secure these rights governments are instituted, deriving their just powers from the consent of the governed. Whenever any form of Government becomes destructive of those ends, it is the right of those who suffer from it, to refuse allegiance to it, and to insist upon the institution of a new government, laying its foundation on such principles, and organizing its powers in such form as to them shall seem most likely to effect their safety and happiness. Prudence, indeed, will dictate that governments long established should not be changed for light and transient causes; and accordingly, all experience hath shown that mankind are more disposed to suffer, while evils are sufferable, than to right themselves by abolishing the forms to which they are accustomed. But when a long train of abuses and usurpations, pursuing invariably the same object, evinces a design to reduce them under absolute despotism, it is their duty to throw off such government, and provide new guards for their future security. Such has been the patient sufferance of the women under this government, and such is now the necessity which constrains them to demand the equal station, to which they are entitled.

The history of mankind is a history of repeated injuries and usurpations on the part of man toward woman, having in direct object the establishment of an absolute tyranny over her. To prove this, let facts be submitted to a candid world.

He has never permitted her to exercise her inalienable right to the elective franchise.

He has compelled her to submit to laws, in the formation of which she had no voice.

He has withheld from her rights which are given to the most ignorant and degraded men—both natives and foreigners.

Having deprived her of this first right of a citizen, the elective franchise, thereby leaving her without representation in the halls of legislation, he has oppressed her on all sides.

He has made her, if married, in the eye of the law, civilly dead.[1]

He has taken from her all right in property, even to the wages she earns.

He has made her, morally, an irresponsible being, as she can commit many crimes with impunity, provided they be done in the presence of her husband. In the covenant of marriage, she is compelled to promise obedience to her husband, he becoming, to all intents and purposes, her master—the law giving him power to deprive her of her liberty, and to administer chastisement.

He has so framed the laws of divorce, as to what shall be the proper causes of divorce, in case of separation, to whom the guardianship of children shall be given; as to be wholly regardless of the happiness of women—the law, in all cases, going upon the false supposition of the supremacy of man, and giving all power into his hands.

After depriving her of all rights as a woman, if single and the owner of property, he has taxed her to support a government, which recognizes her only when her property can be made profitable to it.

He has monopolized nearly all the profitable employments; and from those she is permitted to follow, she receives but a scanty remuneration.

He closes against her all avenues to wealth and distinction, which he considers most honorable to himself. As a teacher of Theology, Medicine or Law, she is not known.

He has denied her the facilities for obtaining a thorough education—all colleges being closed against her.

He allows her in Church as well as State, but a subordinate position, claiming Apostolic authority for her exclusion from the ministry, and with some exceptions, from any public participation in the affairs of the Church.

1. "Civil death" is a legal term for those who have lost their civil rights, traditionally because they have committed a felony.

He has created a false public sentiment, by giving to the world a different code of morals for man and woman, by which moral delinquencies which exclude women from society, are not only tolerated but deemed of little account when committed by man.

He has usurped the prerogative of Jehovah himself, claiming it as his right to assign for her a sphere of action, when that belongs to her conscience and her God.

He has endeavored in every way that he could, to destroy her confidence in her own powers, to lessen her self-respect, and to make her willing to lead a dependent and abject life.

Now, in view of this entire disfranchisement of one half the people of this country, their social and religious degradation—in view of the unjust laws above mentioned and because women do feel themselves aggrieved, oppressed and fraudulently deprived of their most sacred rights, we insist that they have immediate admission to all the rights and privileges, which belong to them as citizens of these United States.

In entering upon the great work before us, we anticipate no small amount of misconception; misrepresentation and ridicule; but we shall use every instrumentality within our power to effect our object. We shall employ agents, circulate tracts, petition the State and National Legislatures, and endeavor to enlist the pulpit and the press in our behalf. We hope this Convention will be followed by a series of Conventions, embracing every part of the country.

Firmly relying upon the final triumph of the Right and the True, we do this day affix our signatures to this declaration.

JEAN-JACQUES ROUSSEAU

1712–1778

Jean-Jacques Rousseau played a significant role in three different revolutions: in politics, his work inspired and shaped revolutionary sentiment in the American colonies and France; in philosophy, he proposed radically unsettling ideas about human nature, justice, and progress that disrupted the dominant Enlightenment thinking of the moment and helped to spark the Romantic movement; and in literature, he invented a major new genre: the modern autobiography. The kind of life story he tells in the *Confessions* is now so familiar as to feel ordinary, recounting in detail the author's emotional life, including formative childhood experiences of desire, pain, and guilt. But in its moment this narrative broke with established conventions, erupting onto the literary scene as a shock so great that it was banned altogether. The text did not appear in full until more than a hundred years after it was written.

LIFE

As a young man, Rousseau did not seem bound for intellectual greatness. Born in the Protestant city of Geneva in 1712, the second son of a watchmaker, he spent very little time in school. Rousseau's mother died a few days after he was born, and his father, after having gotten himself involved in a violent quarrel, fled Geneva when Jean-Jacques was ten, sending his son to live with relatives. The boy did not seem adept enough to learn watchmaking, so at the age of thirteen he was apprenticed to an engraver, who turned out to be cruel and violent. Three years later, Rousseau ran away from Geneva and, craving the protection of a beautiful Catholic woman named Françoise-Louise de Warens, converted to Catholicism. Then began a period of aimless wandering, as Rousseau lived on and off with Madame de Warens, working for short periods as a domestic servant, a music teacher, a surveyor's clerk, and a tutor. Even in his thirties, he was given to idle drifting and was unable to hold down a job for long.

Despite his lack of formal schooling, the young Rousseau always read voraciously. In early childhood he developed a passionate enthusiasm for ancient Greek and Roman writers. A particular favorite was Plutarch, who wrote morally instructive biographies of ancient emperors and military leaders, including Julius Caesar and Alexander the Great. Rousseau was such an avid reader that while he was an apprentice he went so far as to sell his clothes in order to get his hands on books.

Madame de Warens helped the young man to pursue his intellectual interests and encouraged him to learn music. Their emotional relationship has become well known thanks to Rousseau's account of it in the *Confessions*. Rousseau called her "Mamma," while she called him "Little One." They became lovers in the period from 1733 to 1738, although, Rousseau writes, he felt considerable discomfort joining sexual longings with his love for this maternal figure. To make matters more complicated still, their household often included other men, with Rousseau at times the less favored figure in the *ménage à trois*. And yet, long after their relationship was over, he continued to speak of his lasting love for Madame de Warens and her pivotal importance in his life.

At the age of thirty, Rousseau went to Paris, where he became a personal assistant to a powerful and aristocratic family. In this period he met **Denis Diderot** and other important Enlightenment philosophers, and he contributed a few entries to the grand ***Encyclopédie*** they were compiling. At the same time that he was attracting patronage in the most refined Parisian circles, he started living with a barely literate chambermaid named Thérèse Levasseur, a relationship that lasted for three decades and finally resulted in marriage. He had five children with her—all of whom, shockingly, he insisted on leaving in a Paris orphanage.

Late in 1749 Rousseau was considering competing for an essay prize: the challenge was to write about whether advances in the arts and sciences had brought about a purification of human morals. As he was thinking about this question, he experienced a sudden flash of inspiration that would change his life. In one moment of "illumination," he said, he realized that intellectual advances had brought not moral purification but corruption, not improvement but decline. Human beings in a state of nature were compassionate and good; it was society itself that was to blame for creating inequality, greed, and aggression. He abruptly rejected the achievements that the Enlightenment philosophers were calling "progress." The essay won first prize, and it made

Rousseau famous. "I dared to strip man's nature naked," he wrote, "and showed that his supposed improvement was the true fount of all his miseries."

In the years that followed, Rousseau developed these innovative ideas. In 1754 he ascribed all of the evils of human experience to property and inequality: "You are undone if you once forget that the fruits of the earth belong to us all, and the earth itself to nobody." Deciding to live the simple life that he extolled in his works, he returned to Geneva, where he converted back to Protestantism. This second conversion prompted some detractors to accuse him of insincerity and opportunism. Soon after, he made a new enemy when he published a condemnation of the French philosopher **Voltaire**. Two years later he denounced the theater as a cause of moral corruption, and inserted a personal attack on his former friend Diderot. He soon found himself isolated and labeled a traitor. From this point onward, he constantly suspected that others were conspiring against him.

Julie, or the New Heloise, Rousseau's only novel, was published in 1761. The best-selling novel of the entire eighteenth century, *Julie* extolled passionate, authentic feeling, sincere faith, and rustic nature, and it struck audiences as dramatically different from most contemporary fiction, which prized artful wit and sophistication. Readers were enthralled, and Rousseau became one of the first literary celebrities. "Women were intoxicated by both the book and its author," he boasted, "and there were hardly any, even in the highest ranks, whose conquest I might not have made if I had undertaken it."

The year after *Julie* appeared, Rousseau developed his thinking in two major philosophical works. The first, *The Social Contract*, made the radical case that legitimate government rests on the will of the people. When rulers fail to protect the populace, Rousseau argued, they break the social contract, and the people are then free to choose new rulers. Thomas Jefferson would rely on this argument when he came to write the **Declaration of Independence**. The second major work, *Émile*, another major best seller, was a treatise on education which argued that children should be allowed to develop according to their senses and lived experience, and should be kept from books until the age of 12. This idea inspired numerous educational programs, including Montessori schools. In *Émile*, Rousseau also made a case for "natural religion," arguing that a knowledge of God comes not from orthodox doctrine or from revelation, but from one's own observations of nature. Parliaments in both Paris and Geneva saw the book as subversive and called for it to be banned and burned, while the French government ordered Rousseau's arrest. He escaped to a Prussian town, where he asked a priest if he could take communion. His detractors were shocked: was this the man who had just condemned all established religion? Then, in 1764, an anonymous pamphlet—which turned out to have been written by Voltaire—revealed that Rousseau had abandoned all five of his children. Since the moral purpose of *Émile* was to teach readers how to raise and educate children, this latest scandal seemed to many to expose Rousseau as a thoroughgoing hypocrite. In response, he began to write a defense of himself that would shield him from public blame—a story of his own life. This was to become the *Confessions*.

Looking for refuge from scandal and capture, Rousseau fled to England to stay with the philosopher **David Hume** in 1766. He had become so suspicious of those around him that after a few months he became convinced that Hume was part of a large conspiracy against him, and he wrote a public letter accusing his host of persecuting him. After wandering in exile, he finally settled down in Paris in 1770. A warrant was still out for his arrest, but no one seemed eager to enforce it, and he quietly took up copying music for a living. He also finished the *Confessions*. Since he knew that he would not be permitted to publish it, he confined himself to reading portions aloud to intimate aristocratic audiences. Even these readings alarmed many of his listeners, however, who feared that their own secrets would become public in Rousseau's narrative. Former friends convinced the police to ban these events. After an intense period of despair and hopelessness, Rousseau grew comparatively serene until his death in 1778.

CENSORSHIP AND SUBVERSION IN ROUSSEAU'S FRANCE

Rousseau was not the only writer of his time to endure censorship. At the beginning of the eighteenth century, France had been ruled for decades by an absolute monarch, Louis XIV, who consolidated power so effectively that he is remembered for his stark declaration, "I am the state." Under his rule, Catholic France became the most powerful nation in Europe. It was also highly repressive, silencing criticism of the state and persecuting Protestants who lived within French borders. The king's great-grandson, Louis XV, came to the throne in 1715, a less able and decisive ruler than his predecessor. After several serious military losses, sex scandals, and spending sprees, his popularity sank, and although the government controlled all publications and ordered the death penalty for any writer who attacked religious or state authority, a lively underground book and pamphlet trade flourished. The literate population of France almost doubled between 1680 and 1780, and it included an ever greater variety of readers, including women and artisans. Printed works became cheaper and more available, and audiences began to change their habits, shifting from the conventional practice of reading a small number of works many times over to a new pattern of reading numerous works quickly, thereby gaining access to an unprecedented array of genres and points of view.

From the 1720s onward, a large network of underground printers published philosophical works outside of France in Protestant cities such as Geneva or Amsterdam and had them smuggled across the borders in oxcarts, or sewn into women's petticoats. A few publishers hid inflammatory pages inside respectable books such as Bibles. The king's advisors realized that they were losing the battle and in the 1750s became more permissive, but such an outpouring of radical publications followed that the state imposed new bans. Paradoxically, outlawing a work helped it to sell more copies, which meant that Louis XV's censorship helped to set off a vigorous public debate. For the first time, a democratic public sphere was emerging. Literary success began to depend on a wide reading public, rather than on specific patrons. And as those beyond the elite enjoyed a growing access to such innovative works, their willingness to tolerate the conventions of the old regime would start to falter.

Among the most influential critics of authority in Rousseau's time were the Enlightenment philosophers, such as Voltaire, who forcefully attacked the Catholic Church, and the Baron de Montesquieu, who denounced despotism and the slave trade. These thinkers called for individual reason to take the place of traditional authority, and they argued that human history was progressing toward perfection by casting off old habits and fetters. This was no marginal academic argument: it threatened to rock the very foundations of the state. Rousseau's friend Denis Diderot remained under police surveillance for years and was for a time imprisoned in a dungeon for writing subversively about religion. Later, his great Enlightenment project, the *Encyclopédie*, worried those in power by promising to diffuse knowledge widely, allowing ordinary people access to unsettling new ideas about natural rights, science, and religious tolerance. In the late 1750s Enlightenment thinkers felt intensely vulnerable, and it was in these same years that Rousseau—subversive and inflammatory in his own right—began to attack them from a new angle. Exalting feeling over reason, rejecting scientific advances, and imagining a return to uncorrupted nature as the key to human happiness, Rousseau became the lightning rod for critiques of Enlightenment reason and the personification of a whole new movement that would come to be known as Romanticism. Indeed, it was Rousseau's writing that first introduced a wide audience to the values that Romantic writers and artists would enthusiastically take up in the generations to follow: an admiration for simplicity and naturalness, a pleasure in the imagination, an assertion of the importance of unique, sincere, individual experience, and, in place of reason, a celebration of the whole range of emotions, from passionate love and intense horror to patriotic loyalty and harrowing grief.

WORK

Before Rousseau's *Confessions*, European readers had sometimes encountered life stories written by aristocrats and military heroes, which recounted their heroic exploits, and they had read confessional religious works, where authors had told stories about faith and conversion. But they had never seen anything quite like a modern autobiography. For the first time, an author's intimate emotional life became the subject of his work. The *Confessions* therefore helped to revolutionize notions of what a life was and what it meant. This was a text that took the uniqueness of individual feeling more seriously than any text had done before, prizing honest self-knowledge as a new moral value. In the process, it also offered a new kind of hero: the isolated but extraordinary individual, unhappy in his solitude but brave in his resistance to social mores. Rousseau departed from convention, too, in his insistence on the importance of childhood memories as essential to the formation of adult personality. Since previous writers had generally considered children's experience inconsequential, the *Confessions* challenged the most basic expectations about what was relevant to an understanding of the self. And then, even more strangely, the narrative focused specifically on sexual pleasures—including the pleasure of being spanked as a child—which struck many of Rousseau's first readers as embarrassingly petty. But these episodes would turn out to have a lasting impact. More than a century later, Sigmund Freud looked back on the *Confessions* as the forerunner of psychoanalysis, and into our own time, biographers, memoir writers, novelists, therapists, and talk-show hosts continue to understand childhood sexuality as a crucial shaping factor in an adult's life.

The book opens with Rousseau's own sense of his radical originality: "I am resolved on an undertaking that has no model and will have no imitator." Given this claim to being without precedent, Rousseau's title intriguingly suggests the opposite: by calling his autobiography the *Confessions*, he suggests that he is in fact modeling his own work on a famous fourth-century Christian story of spiritual conversion, St. Augustine's *Confessions*. And so he invites us to consider whether or not Augustine's autobiography acts as a "model" for his own work.

This is just one of many paradoxes and contradictions that readers have noticed in Rousseau. On the one hand, for example, he casts himself as a solitary outcast. On the other hand, the *Confessions* repeatedly mentions that its author is an international celebrity, hounded by adoring fans across Europe. In another seeming paradox, Rousseau borrows from the conventionally masculine genre of the public figure's memoir, while he draws equally from the much more feminine, private, domestic style of the novel to describe his childhood and love affairs. Rousseau himself said, "I would rather be a man of paradoxes than a man of prejudices," and it is possible to see these paradoxes forming the very backbone of the work. After all, while the *Confessions* presents the private, emotional life of a unique person, it also uses this personal experience to explore larger ideas about the relationship between the individual and society—the very ideas that are also at the heart of Rousseau's philosophical works. The *Confessions* can therefore be seen to interrogate and break down conventional distinctions between private and public, unique and representative, masculine and feminine.

Many readers have been troubled by yet another tension in the text. Rousseau insists throughout that he is telling the unvarnished truth about himself, however shameful, including acts of theft and masturbation. And yet, he also says that he intends the text to vindicate him to a wide public—to show that he is, by nature, essentially good. The struggle for truth and the attempt at self-justification can seem starkly at odds. In his own time, however, Rousseau's innovative style strengthened his claims to truth telling. Most contemporary writers reveled in elaborate wit and wordplay, but Rousseau spoke frankly and powerfully in the first person, giving his readers a startling new sense of direct contact with the author. Inventing a style of prose that felt unusually plain and honest, Rousseau helped to provoke a new appetite for authenticity in life-writing. Meanwhile, his insistence on direct democracy, natural rights, the value of authentic emotion, and the perils of property ownership would win numerous followers, political, philosophical, and literary. Napoleon himself is reputed to have said that Rousseau caused the French Revolution, and added, "without the Revolution, you would not have had me."

Confessions[1]

This is the only portrait of a man, painted exactly according to nature and in all its truth, that exists and will probably ever exist. Whoever you may be, whom destiny or my trust has made the arbiter of the fate of these notebooks, I entreat you, in the name of my misfortunes, of your compassion, and of all human kind, not to destroy a unique and useful work, which may serve as a first point of comparison in the study of man that certainly is yet to be begun, and not to take away from the honour of my memory the only sure monument to my char-

1. Translated by Angela Scholar.

acter that has not been disfigured by my enemies. Finally, were you yourself to be one of those implacable enemies, cease to be so towards my ashes, and do not pursue your cruel injustice beyond the term both of my life and yours; so that you might do yourself the credit of having been, once at least, generous and good, when you might have been wicked and vindictive; if, that is, the evil directed at a man who has never himself done nor wanted to do any could properly bear the name of vengeance.

Part One

BOOK ONE

Intus, et in cute.[2]

I am resolved on an undertaking that has no model and will have no imitator. I want to show my fellow-men a man in all the truth of nature; and this man is to be myself.

Myself alone. I feel my heart and I know men. I am not made like any that I have seen; I venture to believe that I was not made like any that exist. If I am not more deserving, at least I am different. As to whether nature did well or ill to break the mould in which I was cast, that is something no one can judge until after they have read me.

Let the trumpet of judgement sound when it will, I will present myself with this book in my hand before the Supreme Judge. I will say boldly: 'Here is what I have done, what I have thought, what I was. I have told the good and the bad with equal frankness. I have concealed nothing that was ill, added nothing that was good, and if I have sometimes used some indifferent ornamentation, this has only ever been to fill a void occasioned by my lack of memory; I may have supposed to be true what I knew could have been so, never what I knew to be false. I have shown myself as I was, contemptible and vile when that is how I was, good, generous, sublime, when that is how I was; I have disclosed my innermost self as you alone know it to be. Assemble about me, Eternal Being, the numberless host of my fellow-men; let them hear my confessions, let them groan at my unworthiness, let them blush at my wretchedness. Let each of them, here on the steps of your throne, in turn reveal his heart with the same sincerity; and then let one of them say to you, if he dares: *I was better than that man.*'

I was born in 1712 in Geneva, the son of Isaac Rousseau and Suzanne Bernard, citizens.[3] Since an already modest family fortune to be divided between fifteen children had reduced to almost nothing my father's share of it, he was obliged to depend for his livelihood on his craft as a watchmaker, at which, indeed, he excelled. My mother, who was the daughter of M. Bernard, the minister, was wealthier; she was beautiful and she was good; and my father had not won her easily. They had loved one another almost from the day they were

2. "Inside and under the skin" (Latin), from Roman satirist Aulus Persius Flaccus (34–62 C.E.), referring to a man who looks back sadly on his loss of virtue.

3. Geneva, unlike its larger neighbors Savoy and France, was a republic with an elected legislature, though only a small number of adult men counted as citizens.

born; at the age of eight or nine years they were already taking walks together every evening along the Treille; by ten years they were inseparable. The sympathy, the harmony between their souls, reinforced the feelings that habit had formed. Tender and sensitive by nature, they were both of them waiting only for the moment when they would find another person of like disposition, or rather this moment was waiting for them, and each of them gave his heart to the first that opened to receive it. The destiny that had seemed to oppose their passion served only to kindle it. Unable to win his lady, the young man was consumed with grief; she counselled him to travel and to forget her. He travelled, to no avail, and returned more in love than ever. He found the woman he loved still tender and true. After such a test all that remained was for them to love one another till the end of their days; they swore to do so, and Heaven blessed the vow.

Gabriel Bernard, my mother's brother, fell in love with one of my father's sisters; but she consented to marry the brother only on condition that her brother marry the sister. Love prevailed, and the two weddings took place on the same day. And so my uncle was the husband of my aunt, and their children were my first cousins twice over. By the end of the first year a child had been born on each side; but there was to be a further separation.

My uncle Bernard was an engineer; he went away to serve in the Empire and in Hungary under Prince Eugène. He distinguished himself during the siege and the battle of Belgrade.[4] After the birth of my only brother, my father departed for Constantinople to take up a post as watchmaker to the seraglio. While he was away my mother's beauty, intelligence, and accomplishments[5] won her many admirers. M. de La Closure, the French resident in Geneva, was one of the most assiduous in his attentions. His passion must have been keenly felt; since thirty years later he still softened visibly when he spoke of her to me. My mother had more than her virtue with which to defend herself, she loved her husband tenderly; she pressed him to return; he abandoned everything and came. I was the sad fruit of this homecoming. Ten months later, I was born, weak and sickly; I cost my mother her life, and my birth was the first of my misfortunes.

I never knew how my father bore his loss; but I do know that he never got over it. He thought he could see my mother in me, without being able to forget that I had deprived him of her; he never caressed me without my sensing, from his sighs, from his urgent embraces, that a bitter regret was mingled with them, for which, however, they were the more tender. He had only to say to me: 'Let's talk about your mother, Jean-Jacques,' and I would reply: 'Very well,

4. François-Eugène, Prince of Savoy (1663–1736), led the Hungarian army to victory in the Battle of Belgrade, a famous and surprising triumph over the Turkish army in 1717.

5. These were too brilliant for her condition in life, for her father, the minister, adored her, and had taken great care over her education. She could draw and sing, she accompanied herself on the theorbo [a stringed instrument], she was well read and could write tolerable verse. Here is a little rhyme she wrote impromptu, while out walking with her sister-in-law and their children during the absence of her brother and her husband, in response to a remark that someone made to her about these latter:

> These two young men, though far from here,
> In many ways to us are dear;
> They are our friends, our lovers;
> Our husbands and our brothers,
> And the fathers of these children here.

[Rousseau's note]

Father, and then we'll weep together,' and these words alone were enough to move him to tears. 'Ah!' he would sigh, 'bring her back to me, comfort me for losing her; fill the emptiness she has left in my soul. Would I love you as much if you were only my son?' Forty years after losing her he died in the arms of a second wife, but with the name of the first on his lips, and her image deep in his heart.

Such were the authors of my days. Of all the gifts bestowed on them by heaven, the only one they bequeathed to me was a tender heart; but to this they owed their happiness, just as I owe it all my misfortune.

I was born almost dying; they despaired of saving me. I already carried within me the germ of an indisposition which has worsened with the years, and which now allows me some occasional respite only in order that I might endure another, more cruel, form of suffering. One of my father's sisters, an amiable and virtuous young woman, took such good care of me that she saved me. She is still alive as I write this, and at eighty years old cares for a husband who is younger than she, but ravaged by drink. I forgive you, dear Aunt, for having preserved my life, and it grieves me that I cannot, at the end of your days, repay you for the tender care you lavished on me at the beginning of mine. My nurse Jacqueline, too, is still alive and in sound health. The hands that opened my eyes at my birth may yet close them at my death.

I had feelings before I had thoughts: that is the common lot of humanity. But I was more affected by it than others are. I have no idea what I did before the age of five or six: I do not know how I learned to read; all I remember is what I first read and its effect on me; this is the moment from which I date my first uninterrupted consciousness of myself. My mother had left some romances.[6] We began to read them after supper, my father and I. Our first intention was simply that I should practise my reading with the help of some entertaining books; but we soon became so engrossed in them that we spent whole nights taking it in turns to read to one another without interruption, unable to break off until we had finished the whole volume. Sometimes my father, hearing the swallows at dawn, would say shamefacedly: 'We'd better go to bed now; I'm more of a child than you are.'

By this dangerous method I acquired in a short time not only a marked facility for reading and comprehension, but also an understanding, unique in one of my years, of the passions. I had as yet no ideas about things, but already I knew every feeling. I had conceived nothing; I had felt everything. This rapid succession of confused emotions did not damage my reason, since as yet I had none; but it provided me with one of a different temper; and left me with some bizarre and romantic notions about human life, of which experience and reflection have never quite managed to cure me.

The romances lasted us until the summer of 1719. The following winter we found something else. Since my mother's books were exhausted, we resorted to what we had inherited of her father's library. Fortunately it contained some good books; and this could scarcely have been otherwise, since this library had been collected by a man who was not only an ordained minister and even, for such was the fashion of the day, a scholar, but also a man of taste and intelligence. Le

6. Novels, often fanciful tales of adventure and heroism.

Sueur's *History of Church and Empire*, Bossuet's discourses on universal history, Plutarch's on famous men, Nani's *History of Venice*, Ovid's *Metamorphoses*, La Bruyère, Fontenelle's *Plurality of Worlds* and his *Dialogues of the Dead*, and some volumes of Molière,[7] all these were moved into my father's studio, and there, every day, I read to him while he worked. I acquired a taste for these works that was rare, perhaps unique, in one of my age. Plutarch, in particular, became my favourite author. The pleasure I took in reading and rereading him cured me in part of my passion for romances, and I soon preferred Agesilaus, Brutus, and Aristides to Orondate, Artamène, and Juba.[8] These interesting books, and the conversations they occasioned between my father and me, shaped that free, republican spirit, that proud and indomitable character, that impatience with servitude and constraint, which it has been my torment to possess all my life in circumstances not at all favourable to its development. My mind was full of Athens and Rome; I lived, as it were, in the midst of their great men; I was, besides, by birth a citizen of a republic and the son of a father whose love for his country was his greatest passion, and I was fired by his example; I thought of myself as a Greek or a Roman; I became the person whose life I was reading: when I recounted acts of constancy and fortitude that had particularly struck me, my eyes would flash and my voice grow louder. One day at table, while I was relating the story of Scaevola,[9] my family were alarmed to see me stretch out my hand and, in imitation of his great deed, place it on a hot chafing-dish.

I had a brother seven years older than I, who was learning my father's trade. The extreme affection that was lavished upon me meant that he was a little neglected, which is not something of which I can approve. His upbringing suffered in consequence. He fell into dissolute ways even before the age at which one can, properly speaking, be considered dissolute. He was placed with a new master, from whom he ran away just as he had done at home. I hardly ever saw him; I can hardly claim to have known him; but I nevertheless loved him dearly, and he loved me too, in as far as such a rascal is capable of love. I remember once when my father, in a rage, was chastising him severely, throwing myself impetuously between the two of them and flinging my arms around him. I thus protected him by taking on my own body all the blows destined for him, and I kept this up so determinedly that my father was obliged in the end to spare him, either because he was moved by my cries and my tears, or because he was afraid of hurting me more than him. My brother went from bad to worse and in the end ran off and disappeared forever. A little while later

7. The pseudonym of Jean Baptiste de Poquelin (1622–1673), French comic playwright. Jean Le Sueur (c. 1602–1681), French historian and Protestant minister. Jacques-Bénigne Bossuet (1627–1704), French bishop, writer, and orator. Plutarch (46–119), Roman historian and biographer. Giovanni Battista Nani (1616–1678), Venetian writer, historian, and ambassador. Ovid (43 B.C.E.–16 C.E.), Roman poet. Jean de la Bruyère (1645–1696), French satirist. Bernard le Bovier de Fontenelle (1657–1757), French writer, scientist, and philosopher.

8. Agesilaus, Brutus, and Aristides are historical figures; Orondate and Juba are characters from novels by Gauthier de Costes, called la Calprenède (1610–1663); Artamène is the hero of a long novel by Madeleine de Scudéry (1607–1701).

9. Gaius Mucius Scaevola, a mythical Roman hero who held his right hand in a fire without showing any signs of pain.

we heard that he was in Germany. He never once wrote. No more was ever heard of him; and so it was that I became an only son.

If this poor boy's upbringing was neglected, the same could not be said of his brother, for royal princes could not have been cared for more zealously than I was during my early years, idolized by everyone around me, and, which is rarer, treated always as a much-loved child and never as a spoiled one. Never once while I remained in my father's house was I allowed to roam the streets alone with the other children; never was it necessary either to discourage in me or to indulge any of those fanciful whims which are generally attributed to nature, and which are entirely the product of upbringing. I had my childish faults: I prattled, I was greedy, I sometimes told lies. No doubt I stole fruit, sweets, things to eat; but I never, just for the fun of it, did any harm or damage, got others into trouble, or teased dumb animals. I remember on one occasion, however, peeing into the kettle belonging to one of our neighbours, Mme Clot, while she was at church. I must confess, too, that this memory still makes me laugh, for Mme Clot, although otherwise a thoroughly good person, was the grumpiest old woman I ever knew in my life. Such is the true but brief history of my childhood misdemeanours.

How could I have learnt bad ways, when I was offered nothing but examples of mildness and surrounded by the best people in the world? It was not that the people around me—my father, my aunt, my nurse, our relatives, our friends, our neighbours—obeyed me, but rather that they loved me; and I loved them in return. My whims were so little encouraged and so little opposed that it never occurred to me to have any. I am ready to swear that, until I was myself subjected to the rule of a master, I never even knew what a caprice was. When I was not reading or writing with my father, or going for walks with my nurse, I was always with my aunt, watching her at her embroidery, hearing her sing, sitting or standing at her side; and I was happy. Her good-humour, her gentleness, her agreeable features, all these have so imprinted themselves on my memory, that I can still see in my mind's eye her manner, her glance, her whole air; I still remember the affectionate little things she used to say; I could describe how she was dressed, and how she wore her hair, even to the two black curls which, after the fashion of the day, framed her temples.

I am convinced that it is to her that I owe the taste, or rather passion, for music that developed in me fully only much later. She knew a prodigious number of songs and airs, which she sang in a small, sweet voice. This excellent young woman possessed a serenity of soul that banished far from her and from everyone around her any reverie or sadness. I was so enchanted by her singing that, not only have many of her songs lingered in my memory, but, now that I have lost her, others too, totally forgotten since childhood, return to haunt me as I grow older, with a charm I cannot convey. Who would have thought that, old driveller that I am, worn out with worry and care, I should suddenly catch myself humming these little tunes in a voice already cracked and quavering, and weeping like a child? One air in particular has come back to me in full, although the words of the second verse have repeatedly resisted all my efforts to remember them, even though I dimly recall the rhymes. Here is the beginning followed by what I have been able to remember of the rest.

Tircis,[1] I dare not stay
Beneath the sturdy oak
To hear your pipe's sweet play;
Already I'm the talk
Of all our village folk
. . . .
. . . a shepherd's vows
. . . his repose
. . . allows
For always the thorn lies under the rose.

What is it about this song, I wonder, that so beguiles and moves my heart? It has a capricious charm I do not understand at all; nevertheless, I am quite incapable of singing it through to the end without dissolving into tears. I have often been on the point of writing to Paris to enquire about the rest of the words, in case there should be anyone there who still knows them. But I suspect that some of the pleasure I take in recalling this little tune would fade if I knew for certain that others apart from my poor aunt Suzanne had sung it.

Such were the affections that marked my entry into life; thus there began to take shape or to manifest themselves within me this heart, at once so proud and so tender, and this character, effeminate and yet indomitable, which, continually fluctuating between weakness and courage, between laxity and virtue, has to the end divided me against myself and ensured that abstinence and enjoyment, pleasure and wisdom have all eluded me equally.

This upbringing was interrupted by an accident whose consequences have affected my life ever since. My father had a quarrel with a M. Gautier, a French captain, who had relatives in the council.[2] This Gautier, an insolent and cowardly fellow, suffered a nose-bleed and, out of revenge, accused my father of having drawn his sword on him inside the city limits. My father, threatened with imprisonment, insisted that, in accordance with the law, his accuser be taken into custody with him. Unable to obtain this, he chose to leave Geneva and to exile himself for the rest of his life rather than give way on a point where it seemed to him that both his honour and his liberty were compromised.

I remained behind under the guardianship of my uncle Bernard, who at the time was employed on the fortifications of Geneva. His eldest daughter had died, but he had a son the same age as myself. We were sent off together to Bossey to board with the minister, M. Lambercier, so that, along with some Latin, we might acquire that hotchpotch of knowledge which usually accompanies it under the name of education.

Two years spent in this village softened, somewhat, my Roman harshness and restored my childhood to me. At Geneva, where nothing was imposed on me, I had loved reading and study; it was almost my only amusement. At Bossey I was made to work, and thus grew to love the games that served as relaxation. The countryside was so new to me that I never tired of enjoying it. I came to love it with a passion that has never faded. The memory of the happy days I spent there has filled me with regret for rural life and its pleasures at every

1. A shepherd from pastoral poetry.

2. The legislature of Geneva.

stage of my existence until the one that took me back there. M. Lambercier was a sensible man who, while not neglecting our education, did not overburden us with schoolwork. The proof that he went about this in the right way is that, in spite of my dislike of any form of compulsion, I have never remembered my hours of study with any distaste, and that, while I did not learn much from him, what I did learn, I learned without difficulty and have never forgotten.

This simple country life bestowed on me a gift beyond price in opening up my heart to friendship. Up until then I had only known feelings that, although exalted, were imaginary. Living peaceably day after day with my cousin Bernard, I became warmly attached to him, and soon felt a more tender affection for him than I had for my brother, and one that has not been erased by time. He was a tall boy, lanky and very thin, as mild-tempered as he was feeble-bodied, and who did not take unfair advantage of the preference that, as the son of my guardian, he was shown by the whole household. We shared the same tasks, the same amusements, the same tastes; we were on our own together; we were of the same age; each of us needed a friend; so that to be separated was for both of us, so to speak, to be annihilated. Although we rarely had occasion to demonstrate our mutual attachment, it was strong, and not only could we not bear to be separated for a moment, but we could not imagine ever being able to bear it. Since we both of us responded readily to affection and were good-humoured when not crossed, we always agreed about everything. If, as the favourite of our guardians, he took precedence over me when we were with them, when we were alone the advantage was mine, and this redressed the balance between us. When he was at a loss during lessons, I whispered the answer to him; when my exercise was finished, I helped him with his, and in games, where I was the more inventive, he always followed my lead. In other words, our characters were so compatible and the friendship that united us so real, that, during the more than five years that we were virtually inseparable, whether at Bossey or in Geneva, we often, it is true, fell out, but we never needed to be separated, none of our quarrels lasted for more than a quarter of an hour, and neither of us ever once informed against the other. These remarks may seem puerile, but they nevertheless draw attention to an example that is perhaps unique among children.

The kind of life I led at Bossey suited me so well that it would have fixed my character for ever, if only it had lasted longer. It was founded on feelings that were at once tender, affectionate, and tranquil. Never, I believe, has any individual of our species possessed less natural vanity than I do. I would soar to heights of sublime feeling, but as promptly fall back into my habitual indolence. To be loved by all who came near me was my most urgent wish. I was by nature gentle, so too was my cousin; so indeed were our guardians. During two whole years I neither witnessed nor was the victim of any kind of violence. Everything fostered the tendencies that nature herself had planted in my heart. I knew no greater happiness than to see everyone content with me and with the world in general. I will never forget how, when it was my turn in chapel to recite my catechism, nothing distressed me more, if I happened to hesitate in my replies, than to see on Mlle Lambercier's face signs of anxiety and distress. I was more upset by this than by the shame of failing in public, although that, too, affected me greatly: for, not much moved by praise, I was always susceptible to shame, and I can safely say that the expectation of a reprimand from Mlle Lambercier alarmed me less than did the fear of causing her pain.

And indeed, she was not afraid, any more than was her brother, to show severity when this was necessary; but since her severity was almost always justified and never excessive, it provoked in me feelings of distress rather than of rebellion. I was more concerned about occasioning displeasure than about being chastised, for marks of disapprobation seemed more cruel to me than physical punishment. I find it embarrassing to go into greater detail, but I must. How promptly we would change our methods of dealing with the young if only the long-term effects of the one that is presently employed, always indiscriminately and often indiscreetly, could be foreseen! The lesson that may be learned from just one example of this, as common as it is pernicious, is so important that I have decided to give it.

Just as Mlle Lambercier felt for us the affection of a mother, so too she had a mother's authority, which she sometimes exerted to the point of inflicting common childhood punishments on us, when we had deserved this. For a while she restricted herself to threats of punishment which were quite new to me and which I found very frightening; but after the threat had been carried out, I discovered that it was less terrible in the event than it had been in anticipation, and, what is even more bizarre, that this punishment made me even fonder of the woman who had administered it. Indeed, it took all the sincerity of my affection for her and all my natural meekness to prevent me from seeking to merit a repetition of the same treatment; for I had found in the pain inflicted, and even in the shame that accompanied it, an element of sensuality which left me with more desire than fear at the prospect of experiencing it again from the same hand. It is true that, since without doubt some precocious sexual instinct entered into all this, the same punishment received from her brother would not have seemed to me at all pleasant. But given his temperament, this arrangement was not something that needed to be feared, so that, if I resisted the temptation to earn punishment, this was solely because I was afraid of vexing Mlle de Lambercier; for so great is the power that human kindness exercises over me, even if it has its origin in the senses, that in my heart the former will always prevail over the latter.

This second offence, which I had avoided without fearing it, duly occurred, but without involving any misdeed or at least any conscious act of will on my part, so that it was with a clear conscience that I as it were profited from it. But this second was also the last: for Mlle de Lambercier, who no doubt inferred from some sign I gave that the punishment was not achieving its aim, declared that she could not continue with it, that it exhausted her too much. Up until then we had slept in her room and sometimes, in winter, even in her bed. Two days later we were moved to another room, and I had henceforward the honour, which I would gladly have foregone, of being treated by her as a big boy.

Who would have believed that this ordinary form of childhood punishment, meted out to a boy of eight years[3] by a young woman of thirty, should have

3. Rousseau was in fact eleven years old at the time, not eight.

decided my tastes, my desires, my passions, my whole self, for the rest of my life, and in a direction that was precisely the opposite of what might naturally have been expected? My senses were inflamed, but at the same time my desires, confused and indeed limited by what I had already experienced, never thought of looking for anything else. My blood had burned within my veins almost from the moment of my birth, but I kept myself pure of any taint until an age when even the coldest and slowest of temperaments begins to develop. Long tormented, but without knowing why, I devoured with ardent gaze all the beautiful women I encountered. My imagination returned to them again and again, but only to deploy them in its own way, and to make of each of them another Mlle de Lambercier.

This bizarre taste, which persisted beyond adolescence and indeed drove me to the verge of depravity and madness, nevertheless preserved in me those very standards of upright behaviour which it might have been expected to undermine. If ever an upbringing was proper and chaste, it was certainly the one that I had received. My three aunts were not only persons of exemplary respectability, they also practised a reticence that women have long since abandoned. My father, who liked his pleasures but was gallant in the old style, never uttered, even in the presence of the women he most admired, a single word that would make a virgin blush, and the consideration that is due to children has never been more scrupulously observed than it was in my family and in front of me. M. Lambercier's household was no less strict in this regard, and indeed a very good servant was dismissed for having said something a little too free and easy in front of us. Not only had I reached adolescence before I had any clear idea about sexual union, but such confused ideas as I did have always took some odious and disgusting form. I had a horror of common prostitutes that I have never lost; I could not look at a debauchee without disdain, without dread even, so extreme was the aversion that I had felt for debauchery ever since, going to Saconnex one day along a hollow lane, I saw holes in the earth along both sides of the path and was told that this was where these people did their coupling. What I had seen dogs doing always came into my mind too when I thought of how it might be for people, and the very memory was enough to sicken me.

These prejudices, which I owed to my upbringing and which were sufficient in themselves to delay the first eruptions of a combustible temperament, were further reinforced, as I have said, by the false direction in which I had been led by the first stirrings of sensuality. I imagined only what I had experienced; in spite of a troublesome agitation in the blood, I concentrated all my desires on the kind of pleasure I already knew, without ever getting as far as that which I had been made to think of as odious, and which so closely resembled the other, although I had not the least suspicion of this. When, in the midst of my foolish fantasies, of my wild erotic flights, and of the extravagant actions to which they sometimes drove me, I resorted in imagination to the assistance of the other sex, I never dreamt that it could be put to any other use than that which I burned to make of it.

In this way, then, in spite of an ardent, lascivious, and very precocious temperament, not only did I pass beyond the age of puberty without desiring, without knowing, any sensual pleasures beyond those to which Mlle de Lambercier had quite innocently introduced me; but also, when at last the passing years had made me a man, it was again the case that what should have ruined me preserved me. The taste I had acquired as a child, instead of disappearing, became so identified with that other pleasure that I was never able to dissociate it from the desires aroused through the senses; and this vagary, in conjunction with my natural timidity, has always inhibited me in my approaches to women, because I dare not tell them everything, but nor am I able to perform everything; since my kind of pleasure, of which the other sort is only the end point, cannot be extracted by the man who desires it, nor guessed at by the woman who alone can bestow it. And so I have spent my life coveting but never declaring myself to the women I loved most. Never daring to reveal my proclivities, I have at least kept them amused with relationships that allowed my mind to dwell on them. To lie at the feet of an imperious mistress, to obey her commands, to be obliged to beg for her forgiveness, these were sweet pleasures, and the more my inflamed imagination roused my blood, the more I played the bashful lover. This way of making love does not, needless to say, result in very rapid progress, nor does it pose much threat to the virtue of the women who are its object. I have thus possessed very few, but have nevertheless achieved much pleasure in my own way, that is, through my imagination. Thus it is that my senses, conspiring with my timid nature and my romantic spirit, have kept my heart pure and my behaviour honourable, thanks to those very inclinations which, if I had been a little bolder perhaps, would have plunged me into the most brutish pleasure-seeking.

I have taken the first step, and the most painful, into the dark and miry labyrinth of my confessions. It is not what is criminal that it is the hardest to reveal, but what is laughable or shameful. But from now on I can feel certain of myself: after what I have just dared to say, nothing can stop me.

* * *

BOOK TWO

My landlady who, as I have said, had taken a liking to me, told me that she might have found a situation for me, and that a lady of quality wanted to see me. This was enough to convince me that I was at last embarked upon adventures in high places, for this was the idea I always came back to. It turned out, however, not to be as brilliant as I had imagined. I was taken to see the lady by the servant who had told her about me. She questioned me, cross-examined me, and was, apparently, satisfied, for all of a sudden I found myself in her service, not exactly as a favourite, but as a footman. I was dressed in the same colour as the other servants, except that they had a shoulder-knot which I was not given; since there was no braid on her livery, it looked very little different from any ordinary suit of clothes. Such was the unexpected fulfilment of all my high hopes!

The Comtesse de Vercellis, whose household I had entered, was a widow with no children. Her husband had been from Piedmont; as for her, I have always assumed that she came from Savoy, since I could not imagine a Piedmontese speaking French so well and with such a pure accent. She was in her middle years, distinguished in appearance, cultivated in mind, with a great love and knowledge of French literature. She wrote a great deal and always in French. Her letters had the turn of phrase and the grace, almost, of Mme de Sévigné's:[4] some of them might even have been taken for hers. My main task, not at all an unpleasant one, was to take dictation of these letters, since she was prevented by a breast cancer, which caused her much suffering, from writing them herself.

Mme de Vercellis possessed not only great intelligence but a steadfast and noble soul. I watched her during her last illness, I saw her suffer and die without betraying a moment's weakness, without making the least apparent effort to contain herself, without abandoning her woman's dignity, and without suspecting that there was any philosophy in all of this; indeed, the word 'philosophy' was not yet in vogue, and she would not have known it in the sense in which it is used today. This strength of character was so marked as to be indistinguishable, sometimes, from coldness. She always seemed to me to be as indifferent to the feelings of others as she was to her own, so that, if she performed good works among the poor and needy, she did so because this was good in itself rather than out of any true compassion. I experienced something of this indifference during the three months I was with her. It would have been natural for her to conceive a liking for a young man of some promise, who was continually in her presence, and for it to occur to her, as she felt death approach, that afterwards he would still need help and support; however, either because she did not think me worthy of any special attention, or because the people who watched over her saw to it that she thought only of them, she did nothing for me.

I well remember, however, the curiosity she showed while getting to know me. She would sometimes ask me about myself; she liked me to show her the letters I was writing to Mme de Warens, and to describe my feelings to her. But she went about discovering them in quite the wrong way, since she never revealed hers to me. My heart was eager to pour itself out, provided it felt that another was open to receive it. Cold and curt interrogation, however, with no hint either of approbation or of blame at my replies, did not inspire me with confidence. Unable to judge whether my chatter was pleasing or displeasing, I became fearful and would try, not so much to say what I felt, as to avoid saying anything that might harm me. I have since observed that this habit of coldly interrogating people whom you are trying to get to know is fairly common among women who pride themselves on their intelligence. They imagine that, by revealing nothing of their own feelings, they will the better succeed in discovering yours; what they do not realize is that they thereby deprive you of the courage to reveal them. Anyone subjected to close questioning will, for that very reason, be put on his guard, and if he suspects that, far from inspiring any real interest, he is merely being made to talk, he will either lie, say nothing, or watch his tongue even more carefully than before, preferring to be thought a fool than to be the dupe of someone's mere curiosity. It is, in short, pointless to attempt to see into the heart of another while affecting to conceal one's own.

Mme de Vercellis never said a word to me that expressed affection, pity, or benevolence. She questioned me coldly, I replied with reserve. My replies were

4. French writer Marie de Rabutin-Chantal, marquise de Sévigné (1626–1696), famous for her letters.

so timid that she must have found them beneath her notice, and become bored. Towards the end she asked me no more questions and spoke to me only if she wanted me to do something for her. She judged me on the basis not so much of what I was but of what she had made me, and because she regarded me as nothing more than a footman, she prevented me from appearing to be anything else.

I think that this was my first experience of that malign play of hidden self-interest which has so often impeded me in life and which has left me with a very natural aversion towards the apparent order that produces it. Mme de Vercellis's heir, since she had no children, was a nephew, the Comte de la Roque, who was assiduous in his attentions towards her. In addition, her principal servants, seeing that her end was near, were determined not to be forgotten, and all in all she was surrounded by so many over-zealous people that it was unlikely that she would find time to think of me. The head of her household was a certain M. Lorenzini, an artful man, whose wife, even more artfully, had so insinuated herself into the good graces of her mistress that she was treated by her as a friend rather than a paid servant. She had persuaded her to take on as chambermaid a niece of hers, called Mlle Pontal, a crafty little creature who gave herself the airs of a lady's maid; together, she and her aunt were so successful in ingratiating themselves with their mistress that she saw only through their eyes and acted only through their agency. I had not the good fortune to find favour with these three people; I obeyed them, but I did not serve them; I did not see why, as well as attending our common mistress, I should be a servant to her servants. I presented, moreover, something of a threat to them. They could see very well that I was not in my rightful place; they feared that Madame would see it too, and that what she might do to rectify this would diminish their own inheritance; for people of that sort are too greedy to be fair, and look upon any legacy made to others as depriving them of what is properly theirs. And so they made a concerted effort to keep me out of her sight. She liked writing letters. It was a welcome distraction for someone in her condition; they discouraged it and persuaded her doctor to oppose it on the grounds that it was too tiring for her. On the pretext that I did not understand my duties, they hired in my place two great oafs to carry her about in her chair; and in short, they were so successful in all this that, when she came to make her will, I had not even entered her room during the whole of the previous week. It is true that thereafter I entered as before, and was more assiduous in my attentions than anyone else; for the poor woman's sufferings distressed me greatly, while the constancy with which she bore them inspired admiration and affection in me; indeed I shed genuine tears in that room, unnoticed by her or by anyone else.

At last we lost her. I saw her die. In life she had been a woman of wit and good sense; in death she was a sage. I can safely say that she endeared the Catholic religion to me by the serenity of spirit with which she fulfilled its duties, without omission and without affectation. She was by nature serious, but towards the end of her illness she assumed an air of gaiety, which was too constant to be simulated, and which was as though lent her by reason itself to compensate for the gravity of her situation. It was only during her last two days that she stayed in bed, and even then she kept up a tranquil conversation with the people round about her. At last, unable to speak and already in the throes of death, she gave a great fart. 'Good,' she said, as she turned over: 'A woman who farts cannot be dead.' These were the last words she uttered.

She had bequeathed a year's wages to each of her menial servants; but, since my name did not appear on her household list, I received nothing; in spite of this, the Comte de la Roque gave me thirty francs and let me keep the new suit of clothes which, although I was wearing it, M. Lorenzini had wanted to take away from me. He even promised to try to find me a new position and gave me permission to go and see him. I went two or three times, but without managing to speak to him. Easily deterred, I did not go again. As we will soon see, this was a mistake.

If only this were all that I have to relate about my time with Mme de Vercellis! But although my situation appeared unchanged, I was not the same on leaving her house as I had been when I entered it. I took away with me the enduring memory of a crime and the intolerable burden of a remorse, with which even now, after forty years, my conscience is still weighed down, and whose bitter knowledge, far from fading, becomes more painful with the years. Who would have thought that a child's misdeed could have such cruel consequences? But it is because of these all too probable consequences that my heart is denied any consolation. I may have caused to perish, in shameful and miserable circumstances, a young woman who, amiable, honest, and deserving, was, without a doubt, worth a great deal more than I.

It is almost inevitable that the dispersal of a household should generate a certain confusion and that items should go astray. And yet, such was the loyalty of the servants and the vigilance of M. and Mme Lorenzini that nothing was missing from the inventory. All that was lost was a little ribbon, silver and rose-coloured and already quite old, which belonged to Mlle Pontal. Many other, better things had been within my reach; but I was tempted only by this ribbon, I stole it, and since I made little attempt to conceal it, I was soon found with it. They asked me where I had got it. I hesitated, stammered, and finally said, blushing, that Marion had given it to me. Marion was a young girl from the Maurienne,[5] whom Mme de Vercellis had engaged as a cook when, because she no longer entertained and had more need of nourishing soups than of delicate ragouts, she decided to dismiss her own. Not only was Marion pretty, with a freshness of complexion that is found only in the mountains, and, above all, an air of modesty and sweetness that won the heart of everyone who saw her, she was also a good girl, virtuous and totally loyal. There was thus great surprise when I named her. I was regarded as scarcely less trustworthy, and so an enquiry was thought to be necessary to establish which of us was the thief. She was summoned; a large crowd of people was present, among them the Comte de la Roque. She arrived, was shown the ribbon, and, shamelessly, I made my accusation; taken aback, she said nothing, then threw me a glance which would have disarmed the devil himself, but which my barbarous heart resisted. At length she denied the charge, firmly but calmly, remonstrated with me, urged me to recollect myself and not to bring disgrace upon an innocent girl who had never done me any harm; I persisted in my infernal wickedness, however, repeated my accusation, and asserted to her face that it was she who had given me the ribbon. The poor girl began to cry,

5. A province in the kingdom of Savoy.

but said no more than, 'Ah Rousseau, and I always thought you had a good character! How wretched you are making me, and yet I would not for anything be in your place.' And that was all. She continued to defend herself with steadfast simplicity but without permitting herself any attack on me. The contrast between her moderation and my decided tone worked against her. It did not seem natural to suppose that there could be such diabolical effrontery on the one hand and such angelic sweetness on the other. No formal conclusion was reached, but the presumption was in my favour. Because of the general upheaval, the matter was left there, and the Comte de la Roque, dismissing us both, contented himself with saying that the conscience of the guilty party would be certain to avenge the innocent. This was no vain prophecy, but is every day fulfilled anew.

I do not know what became of the victim of my false witness; it seems unlikely that, after this, she would easily have found another good situation. She had suffered an imputation to her honour that was cruel in every way. The theft was trifling; nevertheless, it was a theft and, what was worse, had been used to seduce a young boy; finally, the lie and the obstinacy with which she clung to it left nothing to be hoped for from someone who combined so many vices. I fear, too, that wretchedness and destitution were not the worst of the dangers I exposed her to. Who knows to what extremes despair and injured innocence might not, at her age, have driven her? Ah, if my remorse at having made her unhappy is intolerable, only judge how it feels to have perhaps reduced her to being worse off than myself!

At times I am so troubled by this cruel memory, and so distressed, that I lie sleepless in my bed, imagining the poor girl advancing towards me to reproach me for my crime as though I had committed it only yesterday. While I still enjoyed some tranquillity in life it tormented me less, but in these tempestuous times it deprives me of the sweetest consolation known to persecuted innocence; it brings home to me the truth of an observation I think I have made in another work, that remorse is lulled during times of good fortune and aggravated in adversity. And yet I have never been able to bring myself to unburden my heart of this confession by entrusting it to a friend. I have never, in moments of the greatest intimacy, divulged it to anyone, even to Mme de Warens. The most that I have been able to do has been to confess my responsibility for an atrocious deed, without ever saying of what exactly it consisted. This burden, then, has lain unalleviated on my conscience until this very day; and I can safely say that the desire to be in some measure relieved of it has greatly contributed to the decision I have taken to write my confessions.

I have been outspoken in the confession I have just made, and surely no one could think that I have in any way sought to mitigate the infamy of my crime. But I would not be fulfilling the purpose of this book if I did not at the same time reveal my own innermost feelings, and if I were afraid to excuse myself, even where the truth of the matter calls for it. I have never been less motivated by malice than at this cruel moment, and when I accused this unfortunate girl, it is bizarre, but it is true, that it was my fondness for her that was the cause of it. She was on my mind, and I had simply used as an excuse the first object that presented itself to me. I accused her of having done what I wanted to do, and of having given me the ribbon, because my intention had been to give it to her. When she appeared shortly afterwards I was stricken with remorse, but the presence of so many people was stronger than my repentance. It was not that I was afraid of being punished but that I was afraid of being put to shame; and I feared shame more than death, more than crime, more than anything in the world. I would have wanted the earth to swallow me up and bury me in its depths. It was shame alone, unconquerable shame, that prevailed over everything and was the cause of all my impudence; and the more criminal I became, the more my terror at having to admit it made me bold. All I could think of was the horror of being found out and of being denounced, publicly and to my face, as a thief, a liar, a slanderer. The confusion that seized my whole being robbed me of any other feeling. If I had been given time to collect myself, I would unquestionably have admitted everything. If M. de la Roque had taken me aside and had said to me: 'Don't ruin this poor girl. If you are guilty, own up to it now,' I would have thrown myself at his feet forthwith; of that I am perfectly certain. But, when what I needed was encouragement, all I received was intimidation. My age, too, was a consideration that it is only fair to take into account. I was scarcely more than a child, or rather I still was one. Real wickedness is even more criminal in a young person than in an adult, but what is merely weakness is much less so, and my offence, when it comes down to it, was little more. Thus its memory distresses me less because of any evil in the act itself than because of that which it must have caused. It has even had the good effect of preserving me for the rest of my life from any inclination towards crime, because of the terrible impression that has remained with me of the only one I ever committed, and I suspect that my aversion towards lying comes in large part from remorse at having been capable of one that was so wicked. If, as I venture to believe, such a crime can be expiated, it must surely have been so by the many misfortunes that burden my old age; by forty years of rectitude and honour in difficult circumstances; indeed, poor Marion has found so many avengers in this world that, however grave my offence against her, I am not too afraid that I will carry the guilt for it into the next. That is all that I had to say on this subject. May I be spared from ever having to speak of it again.

OLAUDAH EQUIANO

ca. 1745–1797

To proslavery writers in Europe and the United States who insisted that Africans were not human beings, Olaudah Equiano offered an unsettling challenge. *The Interesting Narrative of the Life of Olaudah Equiano, Or Gustavus Vassa, the African, Told by Himself* was the first autobiography to have been written by a freed slave. Barred from education, most slaves had to tell their stories to ghostwriters, but Equiano used his unusual access to literacy to present an intelligent, honest, and feeling self in his own compelling words. It was difficult to argue that Africans were not human when here was a person who evidently faced new experiences with puzzlement and curiosity; a person who encountered hardship with sensitivity; a person who felt love, pain, friendship, and deep religious faith. When the text first appeared in 1789, reviewers speculated that Equiano's story would shift the debate about slavery. "Written with much truth and simplicity," and showing "extraordinary intellectual powers," Equiano's story might be "sufficient to wipe off the stigma" attached to Africans. It was so popular that it went through 36 editions before 1857, and was translated into German, Dutch, and Russian. The debate about slavery might not have been the only source of the book's popularity: Equiano was one of the most widely traveled men of the eighteenth century, having been in Africa, the West Indies, the United States, Europe, Central America, Turkey, and even the Arctic Circle. His life made fascinating reading for European and American audiences who were showing a keen and growing appetite for stories of remote and exotic places.

LIFE

Equiano was born in about 1745 in the Niger River Delta area of present-day Nigeria. Kidnapped by local raiders around the age of eleven, he was carried to the coast and sold into slavery. There is no record of what price he commanded, but traders often exchanged several yards of fabric, a couple of barrels of rum, or a keg of gunpowder for a slave. After a harrowing journey across the Atlantic, Equiano was purchased by a Virginia slaveholder who put him to work in the fields. Soon after, a former British naval officer, Michael Henry Pascal, bought him as a present for friends in England. In a gesture of cruel irony, Pascal renamed his new slave "Gustavus Vassa," after a sixteenth-century Swedish hero who had liberated Sweden from Danish oppression.

On board Pascal's commercial ship, Equiano befriended a young American sailor named Dick Baker, who taught him the habits and values of his new environment. In England, Equiano received comparatively kind treatment; he learned to read and write, and was baptized. He also went to sea a number of times on Pascal's ship, serving under him in the Seven Years' War. In 1762 Equiano insisted to Pascal that he had a right to his freedom. Pascal promptly responded by selling him to a ship bound for the West Indies. There Equiano was lucky enough to be sold to a "charitable and humane" Quaker merchant from Philadelphia. He eventually earned the money he needed to purchase his freedom, and chose to live in London, where he worked as a hairdresser, valet, and doctor's assistant. In 1773 he joined an expedition to the

Arctic, in search of a route from Europe, over the North Pole, to Asia; and two years later he went to Nicaragua as a missionary. He had by this point become a devout Methodist.

Equiano came to know the leading British abolitionists and with them, he took part in an effort to resettle former slaves in a colony in Sierra Leone. He was given the job of outfitting the ship with adequate food and equipment. As he worked, he discovered that other administrators were pocketing the money intended for the colony, and he drew public attention to their scheme. This attempt to redress injustice backfired, and it was Equiano who was dismissed. History proved him right, however: Equiano had warned that the colony would fail without sufficient funds, and in fact it was so ill-equipped that fewer than one in five of the settlers survived the first few years.

The Interesting Narrative appeared in 1789. Equiano dedicated the book to the English Parliament; he then cannily persuaded prominent readers to pay for the book in advance, and published the list of all of his subscribers, beginning with the Prince of Wales and including eight dukes. Soon after the book's publication, he became the first modern author to go on a book tour. He lectured throughout Great Britain and Ireland, his presence helping to authenticate the claim that the text was "written by himself"—that is, that an African had been capable of writing this powerful story. A few years later, Equiano married an Englishwoman named Susannah Cullen, and had two daughters. He died in London at the age of fifty-two.

TIMES

Between the sixteenth century and the middle of the nineteenth, slave traders transported about 12 million Africans across the Atlantic Ocean to North America, South America, and the Caribbean. The journey across the Atlantic—called the Middle Passage—is infamous: chained and crowded together so closely that they could barely breathe, Africans had to be prevented from jumping overboard to their deaths to escape the sickness and pain that surrounded them. Often severed from family members and from anyone who shared their local language, faith, and customs, slaves endured a traumatic rupture from everything that had made life meaningful for them. And this was only the beginning. They then underwent the horrors of slavery itself: they were beaten, muzzled, raped, forced to work through sickness and hunger, separated from parents and children, and denied education and freedom of movement.

The slave trade reached its peak in the 1780s, when seventy thousand or more slaves traveled across the Atlantic to North and South America and the Caribbean each year. And the rewards for slave traders were considerable: if a voyage went smoothly, a trader might reap a profit of more than a hundred percent. Then, after selling the slaves that had survived the journey, traders used their profits to buy products of American slave labor, such as sugar, cotton, coffee, and tobacco, which they proceeded to sell in Europe.

As the traffic in slaves grew, so too did opposition to slavery. Quakers and Methodists were particularly active in the antislavery movement in Britain and the United States. They worked vigorously to publicize the horrors of the slave trade, organizing societies, publications, lectures, and petitions. Thanks to Olaudah Equiano's efforts, one incident in particular prompted public outcry. In 1781 the captain of the slave ship *Zong* ordered more than a hundred sick slaves to be thrown overboard. He reasoned that his insurance policy would pay for the loss of living slaves but would hold him responsible for those who had died of illness.

Appalled by such brutality, the British Parliament eventually outlawed the transport of slaves to Britain or any of its colonies; the United States soon followed suit. The traffic in bodies did not stop, however; plenty of illicit ships continued to carry Africans across the Atlantic. In 1833 Britain outlawed slavery altogether, but it remained legal in the United States, Brazil, and Cuba well past midcentury.

WORK

Equiano begins the story of his life with a detailed description of the Ibo community of his childhood. Recent anthropologists have authenticated his account, praising Equiano for his meticulous depiction of a whole way of life. His own contemporaries were often fascinated by his images of contented African people, living in a bountiful nature, who existed without the luxuries and technologies of the Europeans but seemed happy and honorable. Some took *The Interesting Narrative* as confirmation of **Jean-Jacques Rousseau**'s claims that human beings are morally best when they are closest to nature.

To be sure, Equiano's writing goes far beyond mere anthropological interest: combining elements of the travelogue, spiritual autobiography, and antislavery argument, Equiano combined genres to create a new prototype which many later slave narratives would follow. The rootless Equiano also calls to mind the picaresque wanderers of popular eighteenth-century novels, such as **Gulliver** and Robinson Crusoe, who are thrown into unfamiliar situations and forced to survive among strangers. Like these heroes, too, the young slave comments on social conventions as he travels, using episodes in his story as opportunities for both wonder and critique.

Among the most famous of these episodes is Equiano's experience of "the talking book." Having seen Captain Pascal and his friend Dick reading, the slave puts a book to his ear to see if it will talk to him likewise, and is disappointed when it seems to say nothing. Here, he narrates the story from the perspective of the bewildered child, and so allows readers to see their own cultural habits and expectations through fresh, unfamiliar eyes. This scene also draws attention to the vast distance the hero himself will travel, moving from an illiterate slave to a successful author in his own right. Equiano tells us that the name Olaudah means "having a loud voice and well spoken," which suggests that his own book will speak more loudly than the silent ones he has tried to read as a child. *The Interesting Narrative* has certainly won a wide array of admiring readers over the centuries. And if recent audiences have been impressed by Equiano's complex and sophisticated narrative self-representation, his first readers were often most taken with his appealing, sensitive, and trustworthy persona. As one of his early reviewers put it, "anyone is to be pitied who does not feel affection for Vassa, after reading his memoirs."

From The Interesting Narrative of the Life of Olaudah Equiano, or Gustavus Vassa, the African, Written by Himself

Volume I

Behold, God is my salvation; I will trust and not be afraid, for the Lord Jehovah is my strength and my song; he also is become my salvation. And in that day shall ye say, Praise the Lord, call upon his name, declare his doings among the people.

—Isaiah 12:2, 4

To the Lords Spiritual and Temporal, and the Commons of the Parliament of Great Britain.

My Lords and Gentlemen,

Permit me, with the greatest deference and respect, to lay at your feet the following genuine Narrative; the chief design of which is to excite in your august assemblies a sense of compassion for the miseries which the Slave-Trade has entailed on my unfortunate countrymen. By the horrors of that trade was I first torn away from all the tender connexions that were naturally dear to my heart; but these, through the mysterious ways of Providence, I ought to regard as infinitely more than compensated by the introduction I have thence obtained to the knowledge of the Christian religion, and of a nation which, by its liberal sentiments, its humanity, the glorious freedom of its government, and its proficiency in arts and sciences, has exalted the dignity of human nature.

I am sensible I ought to entreat your pardon for addressing to you a work so wholly devoid of literary merit; but, as the production of an unlettered African, who is actuated by the hope of becoming an instrument towards the relief of his suffering countrymen, I trust that *such a man*, pleading in *such a cause*, will be acquitted of boldness and presumption.

May the God of heaven inspire your hearts with peculiar benevolence on that important day when the question of Abolition is to be discussed, when thousands, in consequence of your Determination, are to look for Happiness or Misery!

I am,
My Lords and Gentlemen,
Your most obedient,
And devoted humble Servant,
Olaudah Equiano,
or
Gustavus Vassa.

Union-Street, Mary-le-bone,
March 24, 1789.

CHAPTER I

I believe it is difficult for those who publish their own memoirs to escape the imputation of vanity; nor is this the only disadvantage under which they labour: it is also their misfortune, that what is uncommon is rarely, if ever, believed, and what is obvious we are apt to turn from with disgust, and to charge the writer with impertinence. People generally think those memoirs only worthy to be read or remembered which abound in great or striking events, those, in short, which in a high degree excite either admiration or pity: all others they consign to contempt and oblivion. It is therefore, I confess, not a little hazardous in a private and obscure individual, and a stranger too, thus to solicit the indulgent attention of the public; especially when I own I offer here the history of neither a saint, a hero, nor a tyrant. I believe there are few events in my life, which have not happened to many: it is true the incidents of it are numerous; and, did I consider myself an European, I might say my sufferings were great: but when I compare my lot with that of most of my countrymen, I regard myself as a *particular favourite of Heaven*, and acknowledge the mercies of Providence in every occurrence of my life. If then the following narrative does not appear sufficiently interesting to engage general attention, let my motive be some excuse for its publication. I am not so foolishly vain as to expect from it either immortality or literary reputation. If it affords any satisfaction to my numerous friends, at whose request it has been written, or in the smallest degree promotes the interests of humanity, the ends for which it was undertaken will be fully attained, and every wish of my heart gratified. Let it therefore be remembered, that, in wishing to avoid censure, I do not aspire to praise.

That part of Africa, known by the name of Guinea, to which the trade for slaves is carried on, extends along the coast above 3400 miles, from the Senegal to Angola, and includes a variety of kingdoms. Of these the most considerable is the kingdom of Benen,[1] both as to extent and wealth, the richness and cultivation of the soil, the power of its king, and the number and warlike disposition of the inhabitants. It is situated nearly under the line,[2] and extends along the coast about 170 miles, but runs back into the interior part of Africa to a distance hitherto I believe unexplored by any traveller; and seems only terminated at length by the empire of Abyssinia,[3] near 1500 miles from its beginning. This kingdom is divided into many provinces or districts: in one of the most remote and fertile of which, called Eboe,[4] I was born, in the year 1745, in a charming fruitful vale, named Essaka. The distance of this province from the capital of Benin and the sea coast must be very considerable; for I had never heard of white men or Europeans, nor of the sea: and our subjection to the king of Benin was little more than nominal; for every transaction of the government, as far as my slender observation extended, was conducted by the chiefs or elders of the place. The manners and government of a people who have little commerce with other countries are generally very simple; and the history of what passes in one family or village may serve as a specimen of a nation. My father was one of those elders or chiefs I have spoken of, and was styled Embrenche; a term, as I remember, importing the highest distinction, and signifying in our language a *mark* of grandeur. This mark is conferred on the person entitled to it, by cutting the skin across at the top of the forehead, and drawing it down to the eye-brows; and while it is in this situation applying a warm hand, and rubbing it until it shrinks up into a thick *weal* across the lower part of the forehead. Most of the judges and senators were thus marked; my father had long borne it: I had seen it conferred on one of my brothers, and I was also *destined* to receive it by my parents. Those Embrenche, or chief men, decided disputes and punished crimes; for which purpose they always assembled together. The proceedings were generally short; and in most cases the law of retaliation prevailed. I remember a man was brought before my father, and the other judges, for kidnapping a boy; and, although he was the son of a chief or senator, he was condemned to make recompense by a man or woman slave. Adultery, however, was sometimes punished with slavery or death; a punishment which I believe is inflicted on it throughout most of the

1. Benin, a country in West Africa.
2. South of the equator.
3. African empire that lasted for almost three millennia; it includes present-day Ethiopia and Eritreia, as well as parts of Egypt and Sudan.
4. The Ibo people of Nigeria.

nations of Africa:[5] so sacred among them is the honour of the marriage bed, and so jealous are they of the fidelity of their wives. Of this I recollect an instance:—a woman was convicted before the judges of adultery, and delivered over, as the custom was, to her husband to be punished. Accordingly he determined to put her to death: but it being found, just before her execution, that she had an infant at her breast; and no woman being prevailed on to perform the part of a nurse, she was spared on account of the child. The men, however, do not preserve the same constancy to their wives, which they expect from them; for they indulge in a plurality, though seldom in more than two. Their mode of marriage is thus:—both parties are usually betrothed when young by their parents, (though I have known the males to betroth themselves). On this occasion a feast is prepared, and the bride and bridegroom stand up in the midst of all their friends, who are assembled for the purpose, while he declares she is thenceforth to be looked upon as his wife, and that no other person is to pay any addresses to her. This is also immediately proclaimed in the vicinity, on which the bride retires from the assembly. Some time after she is brought home to her husband, and then another feast is made, to which the relations of both parties are invited: her parents then deliver her to the bridegroom, accompanied with a number of blessings, and at the same time they tie round her waist a cotton string of the thickness of a goose-quill, which none but married women are permitted to wear: she is now considered as completely his wife; and at this time the dowry is given to the new married pair, which generally consists of portions of land, slaves, and cattle, household goods, and implements of husbandry. These are offered by the friends of both parties; besides which the parents of the bridegroom present gifts to those of the bride, whose property she is looked upon before marriage; but after it she is esteemed the sole property of her husband. The ceremony being now ended the festival begins, which is celebrated with bonfires, and loud acclamations of joy, accompanied with music and dancing.

We are almost a nation of dancers, musicians, and poets. Thus every great event, such as a triumphant return from battle, or other cause of public rejoicing is celebrated in public dances, which are accompanied with songs and music suited to the occasion. The assembly is separated into four divisions, which dance either apart or in succession, and each with a character peculiar to itself. The first division contains the married men, who in their dances frequently exhibit feats of arms, and the representation of a battle. To these succeed the married women, who dance in the second division. The young men occupy the third; and the maidens the fourth. Each represents some interesting scene of real life, such as a great achievement, domestic employment, a pathetic story, or some rural sport; and as the subject is generally founded on some recent event, it is therefore ever new. This gives our dances a spirit and variety which I have scarcely seen elsewhere.[6] We have many musical instruments, particularly drums of different kinds, a piece of music which resembles a guitar, and another much like a stickado.[7] These last are chiefly used by betrothed virgins, who play on them on all grand festivals.

5. See Benezet's 'Account of Guinea' throughout [Equiano's note]. Anthony Benezet (1713–1784) was an antislavery writer from the United States.

6. When I was in Smyrna I have frequently seen the Greeks dance after this manner [Equiano's note]. Smyrna is a city that was once in Greece, now in Turkey.

7. The sticcado pastorale is an Italian instrument like a xylophone.

As our manners are simple, our luxuries are few. The dress of both sexes is nearly the same. It generally consists of a long piece of callico, or muslin, wrapped loosely round the body, somewhat in the form of a highland plaid. This is usually dyed blue, which is our favourite colour. It is extracted from a berry, and is brighter and richer than any I have seen in Europe. Besides this, our women of distinction wear golden ornaments; which they dispose with some profusion on their arms and legs. When our women are not employed with the men in tillage, their usual occupation is spinning and weaving cotton, which they afterwards dye, and make it into garments. They also manufacture earthen vessels, of which we have many kinds. Among the rest tobacco pipes, made after the same fashion, and used in the same manner, as those in Turkey.[8]

Our manner of living is entirely plain; for as yet the natives are unacquainted with those refinements in cookery which debauch the taste: bullocks, goats, and poultry, supply the greatest part of their food. These constitute likewise the principal wealth of the country, and the chief articles of its commerce. The flesh is usually stewed in a pan, to make it savoury we sometimes use also pepper, and other spices, and we have salt made of wood ashes. Our vegetables are mostly plantains, eadas, yams, beans, and Indian corn.[9] The head of the family usually eats alone; his wives and slaves have also their separate tables. Before we taste food we always wash our hands: indeed our cleanliness on all occasions is extreme; but on this it is an indispensable ceremony. After washing, libation is made, by pouring out a small portion of the food, in a certain place, for the spirits of departed relations, which the natives suppose to preside over their conduct, and guard them from evil. They are totally unacquainted with strong or spirituous liquors; and their principal beverage is palm wine. This is gotten from a tree of that name by tapping it at the top, and fastening a large gourd to it; and sometimes one tree will yield three or four gallons in a night. When just drawn it is of a most delicious sweetness; but in a few days it acquires a tartish and more spirituous flavour: though I never saw any one intoxicated by it. The same tree also produces nuts and oil. Our principal luxury is in perfumes; one sort of these is an odoriferous wood of delicious fragrance: the other a kind of earth; a small portion of which thrown into the fire diffuses a most powerful odour.[1] We beat this wood into powder, and mix it with palm oil; with which both men and women perfume themselves.

In our buildings we study convenience rather than ornament. Each master of a family has a large square piece of ground, surrounded with a moat or fence, or enclosed with a wall made of red earth tempered; which, when dry, is as hard as brick. Within this are his houses to accommodate his family and slaves; which, if numerous, frequently present the appearance of a village. In the middle stands the principal building, appropriated to the sole use of the master, and consisting of two apartments; in one of which he sits in the day

8. The bowl is earthen, curiously figured, to which a long reed is fixed as a tube. The tube is sometimes so long as to be borne by one, and frequently out of grandeur by two boys [Equiano's note].

9. Corn that comes from the New World. "Eadas": a species of yam.

1. When I was in Smyrna, I saw the same kind of earth, and brought some of it with me to England; it resembles musk in strength but is more delicious in scent, and is not unlike the smell of a rose [Equiano's note].

with his family, the other is left apart for the reception of his friends. He has besides these a distinct apartment in which he sleeps, together with his male children. On each side are the apartments of his wives, who have also their separate day and night houses. The habitations of the slaves and their families are distributed throughout the rest of the enclosure. These houses never exceed one story in height: they are always built of wood, or stakes driven into the ground, crossed with wattles,[2] and neatly plastered within, and without. The roof is thatched with reeds. Our day-houses are left open at the sides; but those in which we sleep are always covered, and plastered in the inside, with a composition mixed with cowdung, to keep off the different insects, which annoy us during the night. The walls and floors also of these are generally covered with mats. Our beds consist of a platform, raised three or four feet from the ground, on which are laid skins, and different parts of a spungy tree called plaintain. Our covering is calico or muslin, the same as our dress. The usual seats are a few logs of wood; but we have benches, which are generally perfumed, to accommodate strangers: these compose the greater part of our household furniture. Houses so constructed and furnished require but little skill to erect them. Every man is a sufficient architect for the purpose. The whole neighbourhood afford their unanimous assistance in building them and in return receive, and expect no other recompense than a feast.

As we live in a country where nature is prodigal of her favours, our wants are few and easily supplied; of course we have few manufactures. They consist for the most part of calicoes, earthern ware, ornaments, and instruments of war and husbandry. But these make no part of our commerce, the principal articles of which, as I have observed, are provisions. In such a state money is of little use; however we have some small pieces of coin, if I may call them such. They are made something like an anchor; but I do not remember either their value or denomination. We have also markets, at which I have been frequently with my mother. These are sometimes visited by stout mahogany-coloured men from the south west of us: we call them Oye-Eboe, which term signifies red men living at a distance. They generally bring us fire-arms, gunpowder, hats, beads, and dried fish. The last we esteemed a great rarity, as our waters were only brooks and springs. These articles they barter with us for odoriferous woods and earth, and our salt of wood ashes. They always carry slaves through our land; but the strictest account is exacted of their manner of procuring them before they are suffered to pass. Sometimes indeed we sold slaves to them, but they were only prisoners of war, or such among us as had been convicted of kidnapping, or adultery, and some other crimes, which we esteemed heinous. This practice of kidnapping induces me to think, that, notwithstanding all our strictness, their principal business among us was to trepan[3] our people. I remember too they carried great sacks along with them, which not long after I had an opportunity of fatally seeing applied to that infamous purpose.

Our land is uncommonly rich and fruitful, and produces all kinds of vegetables in great abundance. We have plenty of Indian corn, and vast quantities of cotton and tobacco. Our pine apples grow without culture; they are about the size of the largest sugar-loaf,[4] and finely flavoured. We have also spices of dif-

2. Woven reeds or thin branches.
3. Deceive, betray.
4. Block of refined sugar for sale.

ferent kinds, particularly pepper; and a variety of delicious fruits which I have never seen in Europe; together with gums of various kinds, and honey in abundance. All our industry is exerted to improve those blessings of nature. Agriculture is our chief employment; and every one, even the children and women, are engaged in it. Thus we are all habituated to labour from our earliest years. Every one contributes something to the common stock; and as we are unacquainted with idleness, we have no beggars. The benefits of such a mode of living are obvious. The West India planters prefer the slaves of Benin or Eboe to those of any other part of Guinea, for their hardiness, intelligence, integrity, and zeal. Those benefits are felt by us in the general healthiness of the people, and in their vigour and activity; I might have added too in their comeliness. Deformity is indeed unknown amongst us, I mean that of shape. Numbers of the natives of Eboe now in London might be brought in support of this assertion: for, in regard to complexion, ideas of beauty are wholly relative. I remember while in Africa to have seen three negro children, who were tawny, and another quite white, who were universally regarded by myself, and the natives in general, as far as related to their complexions, as deformed. Our women too were in my eyes at least uncommonly graceful, alert, and modest to a degree of bashfulness; nor do I remember to have ever heard of an instance of incontinence amongst them before marriage. They are also remarkably cheerful. Indeed cheerfulness and affability are two of the leading characteristics of our nation.

Our tillage is exercised in a large plain or common, some hours walk from our dwellings, and all the neighbours resort thither in a body. They use no beasts of husbandry; and their only instruments are hoes, axes, shovels, and beaks, or pointed iron to dig with. Sometimes we are visited by locusts, which come in large clouds, so as to darken the air, and destroy our harvest. This however happens rarely, but when it does, a famine is produced by it. I remember an instance or two wherein this happened. This common is often the theatre of war; and therefore when our people go out to till their land, they not only go in a body, but generally take their arms with them for fear of a surprise; and when they apprehend an invasion they guard the avenues to their dwellings, by driving sticks into the ground, which are so sharp at one end as to pierce the foot, and are generally dipped in poison. From what I can recollect of these battles, they appear to have been irruptions of one little state or district on the other, to obtain prisoners or booty. Perhaps they were incited to this by those traders who brought the European goods I mentioned amongst us. Such a mode of obtaining slaves in Africa is common; and I believe more are procured this way and by kidnapping, than any other.[5] When a trader wants slaves, he applies to a chief for them, and tempts him with his wares. It is not extraordinary, if on this occasion he yields to the temptation with as little firmness, and accepts the price of his fellow creatures liberty with as little reluctance as the enlightened merchant. Accordingly he falls on his neighbours, and a desperate battle ensues. If he prevails and takes prisoners, he gratifies his avarice by selling them; but, if his party be vanquished, and he falls into the hands of the enemy, he is put to death: for, as he has been known to foment their quarrels, it is thought dangerous to let him survive, and

5. See Benezet's 'Account of Guinea' throughout [Equiano's note].

no ransom can save him, though all other prisoners may be redeemed. We have fire-arms, bows and arrows, broad two-edged swords and javelins: we have shields also which cover a man from head to foot. All are taught the use of these weapons; even our women are warriors, and march boldly out to fight along with the men. Our whole district is a kind of militia: on a certain signal given, such as the firing of a gun at night, they all rise in arms and rush upon their enemy. It is perhaps something remarkable, that when our people march to the field a red flag or banner is borne before them. I was once a witness to a battle in our common. We had been all at work in it one day as usual, when our people were suddenly attacked. I climbed a tree at some distance, from which I beheld the fight. There were many women as well as men on both sides; among others my mother was there, and armed with a broad sword. After fighting for a considerable time with great fury, and after many had been killed our people obtained the victory, and took their enemy's Chief prisoner. He was carried off in great triumph, and, though he offered a large ransom for his life, he was put to death. A virgin of note among our enemies had been slain in the battle, and her arm was exposed in our market-place, where our trophies were always exhibited. The spoils were divided according to the merit of the warriors. Those prisoners which were not sold or redeemed we kept as slaves: but how different was their condition from that of the slaves in the West Indies! With us they do no more work than other members of the community, even their masters; their food, clothing and lodging were nearly the same as theirs, (except that they were not permitted to eat with those who were free-born); and there was scarce any other difference between them, than a superior degree of importance which the head of a family possesses in our state, and that authority which, as such, he exercises over every part of his household. Some of these slaves have even slaves under them as their own property, and for their own use.

As to religion, the natives believe that there is one Creator of all things, and that he lives in the sun, and is girted round with a belt that he may never eat or drink; but, according to some, he smokes a pipe, which is our own favourite luxury. They believe he governs events, especially our deaths or captivity; but, as for the doctrine of eternity, I do not remember to have ever heard of it: some however believe in the transmigration of souls[6] in a certain degree. Those spirits, which are not transmigrated, such as our dear friends or relations, they believe always attend them, and guard them from the bad spirits or their foes. For this reason they always before eating, as I have observed, put some small portion of the meat, and pour some of their drink, on the ground for them; and they often make oblations of the blood of beasts or fowls at their graves. I was very fond of my mother, and almost constantly with her. When she went to make these oblations at her mother's tomb, which was a kind of small solitary thatched house, I sometimes attended her. There she made her libations, and spent most of the night in cries and lamentations. I have been often extremely terrified on these occasions. The loneliness of the place, the darkness of the night, and the ceremony of libation, naturally awful and gloomy, were heightened by my mother's lamentations; and these, concuring with the cries of doleful birds, by which these places were frequented, gave an inexpressible terror to the scene.

6. Reincarnation.

We compute the year from the day on which the sun crosses the line, and on its setting that evening there is a general shout throughout the land; at least I can speak from my own knowledge throughout our vicinity. The people at the same time make a great noise with rattles, not unlike the basket rattles used by children here, though much larger, and hold up their hands to heaven for a blessing. It is then the greatest offerings are made; and those children whom our wise men foretell will be fortunate are then presented to different people. I remember many used to come to see me, and I was carried about to others for that purpose. They have many offerings, particularly at full moons; generally two at harvest before the fruits are taken out of the ground: and when any young animals are killed, sometimes they offer up part of them as a sacrifice. These offerings, when made by one of the heads of a family, serve for the whole. I remember we often had them at my father's and my uncle's, and their families have been present. Some of our offerings are eaten with bitter herbs. We had a saying among us to any one of a cross temper, "That if they were to be eaten, they should be eaten with bitter herbs."

We practised circumcision like the Jews, and made offerings and feasts on that occasion in the same manner as they did. Like them also, our children were named from some event, some circumstance, or fancied foreboding at the time of their birth. I was named *Olaudah*, which, in our language, signifies vicissitude or fortune also, one favoured, and having a loud voice and well spoken. I remember we never polluted the name of the object of our adoration; on the contrary, it was always mentioned with the greatest reverence; and we were totally unacquainted with swearing, and all those terms of abuse and reproach which find their way so readily and copiously into the languages of more civilized people. The only expressions of that kind I remember were "May you rot, or may you swell, or may a beast take you."

I have before remarked that the natives of this part of Africa are extremely cleanly. This necessary habit of decency was with us a part of religion, and therefore we had many purifications and washings; indeed almost as many, and used on the same occasions, if my recollection does not fail me, as the Jews. Those that touched the dead at any time were obliged to wash and purify themselves before they could enter a dwelling house. Every woman too, at certain times, was forbidden to come into a dwelling house, or touch any person, or any thing we ate. I was so fond of my mother I could not keep from her, or avoid touching her at some of those periods, in consequence of which I was obliged to be kept out with her, in a little house made for that purpose, till offering was made, and then we were purified.

Though we had no places of public worship, we had priests and magicians, or wise men. I do not remember whether they had different offices, or whether they were united in the same persons, but they were held in great reverence by the people. They calculated our time, and foretold events, as their name imported, for we called them Ah-affoe-way-cah, which signifies calculators or yearly men, our year being called Ah-affoe. They wore their beards, and when they died they were succeeded by their sons. Most of their implements and things of value were interred along with them. Pipes and tobacco were also put into the grave with the corpse, which was always perfumed and ornamented, and animals were offered in sacrifice to them. None accompanied their funerals but those of the same profession or tribe. These buried them after sunset, and always returned from the grave by a different way from that which they went.

These magicians were also our doctors or physicians. They practised bleeding by cupping;[7] and were very successful in healing wounds and expelling poisons. They had likewise some extraordinary method of discovering jealousy, theft, and poisoning; the success of which no doubt they derived from their unbounded influence over the credulity and superstition of the people. I do not remember what those methods were, except that as to poisoning: I recollect an instance or two, which I hope it will not be deemed impertinent here to insert, as it may serve as a kind of specimen of the rest, and is still used by the negroes in the West Indies. A virgin had been poisoned, but it was not known by whom: the doctors ordered the corpse to be taken up by some persons, and carried to the grave. As soon as the bearers had raised it on their shoulders, they seemed seized with some[8] sudden impulse, and ran to and fro unable to stop themselves. At last, after having passed through a number of thorns and prickly bushes unhurt, the corpse fell from them close to a house, and defaced it in the fall; and, the owner being taken up, he immediately confessed the poisoning.[9]

The natives are extremely cautious about poison. When they buy any eatable the seller kisses it all round before the buyer, to shew him it is not poisoned; and the same is done when any meat or drink is presented, particularly to a stranger. We have serpents of different kinds, some of which are esteemed ominous when they appear in our houses, and these we never molest. I remember two of those ominous snakes, each of which was as thick as the calf of a man's leg, and in colour resembling a dolphin in the water, crept at different times into my mother's night-house, where I always lay with her, and coiled themselves into folds, and each time they crowed like a cock. I was desired by some of our wise men to touch these, that I might be interested in the good omens, which I did, for they were quite harmless, and would tamely suffer themselves to be handled; and then they were put into a large open earthen pan, and set on one side of the highway. Some of our snakes, however, were poisonous: one of them crossed the road one day when I was standing on it, and passed between my feet without offering to touch me, to the great surprise of many who saw it; and these incidents were accounted by the wise men, and therefore by my mother and the rest of the people, as remarkable omens in my favour.

7. The use of glass cups to create a heated air vacuum for drawing blood from the body.

8. See also Leut. Matthew's Voyage, p. 123 [Equiano's note]. He is referring to John Matthews, *A Voyage to the River Sierra Leone* (1788).

9. An instance of this kind happened at Montserrat in the West Indies in the year 1763. I then belonged to the Charming Sally, Capt. Doran.—The chief mate, Mr. Mansfield, and some of the crew being one day on shore, were present at the burying of a poisoned negro girl. Though they had often heard of the circumstance of the running in such cases, and had even seen it, they imagined it to be a trick of the corpse-bearers. The mate therefore desired two of the sailors to take up the coffin, and carry it to the grave. The sailors, who were all of the same opinion, readily obeyed; but they had scarcely raised it to their shoulders, before they began to run furiously about, quite unable to direct themselves, till, at last, without intention, they came to the hut of him who had poisoned the girl. The coffin then immediately fell from their shoulders against the hut, and damaged part of the wall. The owner of the hut was taken into custody on this, and confessed the poisoning.—I give this story as it was related by the mate and crew on their return to the ship. The credit which is due to it I leave with the reader [Equiano's note].

Such is the imperfect sketch my memory has furnished me with of the manners and customs of a people among whom I first drew my breath. And here I cannot forbear suggesting what has long struck me very forcibly, namely, the strong analogy which even by this sketch, imperfect as it is, appears to prevail in the manners and customs of my countrymen and those of the Jews, before they reached the Land of Promise, and particularly the patriarchs[1] while they were yet in that pastoral state which is described in Genesis—an analogy, which alone would induce me to think that the one people had sprung from the other.

* * *

Like the Israelites in their primitive state, our government was conducted by our chiefs or judges, our wise men and elders; and the head of a family with us enjoyed a similar authority over his household with that which is ascribed to Abraham and the other patriarchs. The law of retaliation obtained almost universally with us as with them: and even their religion appeared to have shed upon us a ray of its glory, though broken and spent in its passage, or eclipsed by the cloud with which time, tradition, and ignorance might have enveloped it; for we had our circumcision (a rule I believe peculiar to that people:) we had also our sacrifices and burnt-offerings, our washings and purifications, on the same occasions as they had.

As to the difference of colour between the Eboan Africans and the modern Jews, I shall not presume to account for it. It is a subject which has engaged the pens of men of both genius and learning, and is far above my strength. The most able and Reverend Mr. T. Clarkson, however, in his much admired Essay on the Slavery and Commerce of the Human Species,[2] has ascertained the cause, in a manner that at once solves every objection on that account, and, on my mind at least, has produced the fullest conviction. I shall therefore refer to that performance for the theory,[3] contenting myself with extracting a fact as related by Dr. Mitchel.[4] "The Spaniards, who have inhabited America, under the torrid zone, for any time, are become as dark coloured as our native Indians of Virginia; of which *I myself have been a witness.*" There is also another instance[5] of a Portuguese settlement at Mitomba, a river in Sierra Leona;[6] where the inhabitants are bred from a mixture of the first Portuguese discoverers with the natives, and are now become in their complexion, and in the woolly quality of their hair, *perfect negroes*, retaining however a smattering of the Portuguese language.

These instances, and a great many more which might be adduced, while they shew how the complexions of the same persons vary in different climates, it is hoped may tend also to remove the prejudice that some conceive against the natives of Africa on account of their colour. Surely the minds of the Span-

1. In the Bible, the patriarchs are the ancestors of the Israelites. "Land of Promise": land promised to the Israelites by God.
2. This was written in 1785 by antislavery writer Thomas Clarkson (1760–1846).
3. Page 178 to 216 [Equiano's note].
4. Philos. Trans. No. 476, Set. 4, cited by Mr. Clarkson, p. 205 [Equiano's note]. John Mitchell was the author of an "Essay on the Causes of the Different Colours of People in Different Climates," *Philosophical Transactions* (1744).
5. Same page [Equiano's note].
6. Portuguese port in West Africa for commerce in slaves and ivory; later used by the British government to resettle freed slaves.

iards did not change with their complexions! Are there not causes enough to which the apparent inferiority of an African may be ascribed, without limiting the goodness of God, and supposing he forbore to stamp understanding on certainly his own image, because "carved in ebony." Might it not naturally be ascribed to their situation? When they come among Europeans, they are ignorant of their language, religion, manners, and customs. Are any pains taken to teach them these? Are they treated as men? Does not slavery itself depress the mind, and extinguish all its fire and every noble sentiment? But, above all, what advantages do not a refined people possess over those who are rude and uncultivated! Let the polished and haughty European recollect that his ancestors were once, like the Africans, uncivilized, and even barbarous. Did Nature make *them* inferior to their sons? and should *they too* have been made slaves? Every rational mind answers, No. Let such reflections as these melt the pride of their superiority into sympathy for the wants and miseries of their sable brethren, and compel them to acknowledge, that understanding is not confined to feature or colour. If, when they look round the world, they feel exultation, let it be tempered with benevolence to others, and gratitude to God, "who hath made of one blood all nations of men for to dwell on all the face of the earth;[7] and whose wisdom is not our wisdom, neither are our ways his ways."[8]

CHAPTER II

I hope the reader will not think I have trespassed on his patience in introducing myself to him with some account of the manners and customs of my country. They had been implanted in me with great care, and made an impression on my mind, which time could not erase, and which all the adversity and variety of fortune I have since experienced served only to rivet and record; for, whether the love of one's country be real or imaginary, or a lesson of reason, or an instinct of nature, I still look back with pleasure on the first scenes of my life, though that pleasure has been for the most part mingled with sorrow.

I have already acquainted the reader with the time and place of my birth. My father, besides many slaves, had a numerous family, of which seven lived to grow up, including myself and a sister, who was the only daughter. As I was the youngest of the sons, I became, of course, the greatest favourite with my mother, and was always with her; and she used to take particular pains to form my mind. I was trained up from my earliest years in the art of war; my daily exercise was shooting and throwing javelins; and my mother adorned me with emblems, after the manner of our greatest warriors. In this way I grew up till I was turned the age of eleven, when an end was put to my happiness in the following manner:—Generally when the grown people in the neighbourhood were gone far in the fields to labour, the children assembled together in some of the neighbours' premises to play; and commonly some of us used to get up a tree to look out for any assailant, or kidnapper, that might come upon us; for they sometimes took those opportunities of our parents' absence to attack and carry off as many as they could seize. One day, as I was watching at the top of a tree in our yard, I saw one of those people come into the yard of our next neighbour but one, to kidnap, there being many stout young people in it. Immediately on

7. Acts 17.26.

8. A paraphrase of Isaiah 5.58.

this I gave the alarm of the rogue, and he was surrounded by the stoutest of them, who entangled him with cords, so that he could not escape till some of the grown people came and secured him. But alas! ere long it was my fate to be thus attacked, and to be carried off, when none of the grown people were nigh. One day, when all our people were gone out to their works as usual, and only I and my dear sister were left to mind the house, two men and a woman got over our walls, and in a moment seized us both, and, without giving us time to cry out, or make resistance, they stopped our mouths, and ran off with us into the nearest wood. Here they tied our hands, and continued to carry us as far as they could, till night came on, when we reached a small house, where the robbers halted for refreshment, and spent the night. We were then unbound, but were unable to take any food; and, being quite overpowered by fatigue and grief, our only relief was some sleep, which allayed our misfortune for a short time. The next morning we left the house, and continued travelling all the day. For a long time we had kept the woods, but at last we came into a road which I believed I knew. I had now some hopes of being delivered; for we had advanced but a little way before I discovered some people at a distance, on which I began to cry out for their assistance: but my cries had no other effect than to make them tie me faster and stop my mouth, and then they put me into a large sack. They also stopped my sister's mouth, and tied her hands; and in this manner we proceeded till we were out of the sight of these people. When we went to rest the following night they offered us some victuals; but we refused it; and the only comfort we had was in being in one another's arms all that night, and bathing each other with our tears. But alas! we were soon deprived of even the small comfort of weeping together. The next day proved a day of greater sorrow than I had yet experienced; for my sister and I were then separated, while we lay clasped in each other's arms. It was in vain that we besought them not to part us; she was torn from me, and immediately carried away, while I was left in a state of distraction not to be described. I cried and grieved continually; and for several days I did not eat any thing but what they forced into my mouth. At length, after many days travelling, during which I had often changed masters, I got into the hands of a chieftain, in a very pleasant country. This man had two wives and some children, and they all used me extremely well, and did all they could to comfort me; particularly the first wife, who was something like my mother. Although I was a great many days journey from my father's house, yet these people spoke exactly the same language with us. This first master of mine, as I may call him, was a smith, and my principal employment was working his bellows, which were the same kind as I had seen in my vicinity. They were in some respects not unlike the stoves here in gentlemen's kitchens; and were covered over with leather, and in the middle of that leather a stick was fixed, and a person stood up, and worked it, in the same manner as is done to pump water out of a cask with a hand pump. I believe it was gold he worked, for it was of a lovely bright yellow colour, and was worn by the women on their wrists and ankles. I was there I suppose about a month, and they at last used to trust me some little distance from the house. This liberty I used in embracing every opportunity to inquire the way to my own home: and I also sometimes, for the same purpose, went with the maidens, in the cool of the evenings, to bring pitchers of water from the springs for the use of the house. I had also remarked where the sun rose in the morning, and set in the evening, as I had travelled along; and I had observed that my father's house was towards the rising of the sun. I therefore determined to seize the first opportunity of making my escape, and to shape my course for that quarter; for I was quite oppressed and weighed down by grief after my mother and friends; and my love of liberty, ever great, was strengthened by the mortifying circumstance of not daring to eat with the free-born children, although I was mostly their companion. While I was projecting my escape, one day an unlucky event happened, which quite disconcerted my plan, and put an end to my hopes. I used to be sometimes employed in assisting an elderly woman slave to cook and take care of the poultry; and one morning, while I was feeding some chickens, I happened to toss a small pebble at one of them, which hit it on the middle and directly killed it. The old slave, having soon after missed the chicken, inquired after it; and on my relating the accident (for I told her the truth, because my mother would never suffer me to tell a lie) she flew into a violent passion, threatened that I should suffer for it; and, my master being out, she immediately went and told her mistress what I had done. This alarmed me very much, and I expected an instant flogging, which to me was uncommonly dreadful; for I had seldom been beaten at home. I therefore resolved to fly; and accordingly I ran into a thicket that was hard by, and hid myself in the bushes. Soon afterwards my mistress and the slave returned, and, not seeing me, they searched all the house, but not finding me, and I not making answer when they called to me, they thought I had run away, and the whole neighbourhood was raised in the pursuit of me. In that part of the country (as in ours) the houses and villages were skirted with woods, or shrubberies, and the bushes were so thick that a man could readily conceal himself in them, so as to elude the strictest search. The neighbours continued the whole day looking for me, and several times many of them came within a few yards of the place where I lay hid. I then gave myself up for lost entirely, and expected every moment, when I heard a rustling among the trees, to be found out, and punished by my master: but they never discovered me, though they were often so near that I even heard their conjectures as they were looking about for me; and I now learned from them, that any attempt to return home would be hopeless. Most of them supposed I had fled towards home; but the distance was so great, and the way so intricate, that they thought I could never reach it, and that I should be lost in the woods. When I heard this I was seized with a violent panic, and abandoned myself to despair. Night too began to approach, and aggravated all my fears. I had before entertained hopes of getting home, and I had determined when it should be dark to make the attempt; but I was now convinced it was fruitless, and I began to consider that, if possibly I could escape all other animals, I could not those of the human kind; and that, not knowing the way, I must perish in the woods. Thus was I like the hunted deer:

—Ev'ry leaf and ev'ry whisp'ring breath
Convey'd a foe, and ev'ry foe a death.[9]

I heard frequent rustlings among the leaves; and being pretty sure they were snakes I expected every instant to be stung by them. This increased my anguish, and the horror of my situation became now quite insupportable. I at length

9. Lines from "Cooper's Hill," a 1642 work by British poet John Denham (1615–1669).

quitted the thicket, very faint and hungry, for I had not eaten or drank any thing all the day; and crept to my master's kitchen, from whence I set out at first, and which was an open shed, and laid myself down in the ashes with an anxious wish for death to relieve me from all my pains. I was scarcely awake in the morning when the old woman slave, who was the first up, came to light the fire, and saw me in the fire place. She was very much surprised to see me, and could scarcely believe her own eyes. She now promised to intercede for me, and went for her master, who soon after came, and, having slightly reprimanded me, ordered me to be taken care of, and not to be ill-treated.

Soon after this my master's only daughter, and child by his first wife, sickened and died, which affected him so much that for some time he was almost frantic, and really would have killed himself, had he not been watched and prevented. However, in a small time afterwards he recovered, and I was again sold. I was now carried to the left of the sun's rising, through many different countries, and a number of large woods. The people I was sold to used to carry me very often, when I was tired, either on their shoulders or on their backs. I saw many convenient well-built sheds along the roads, at proper distances, to accommodate the merchants and travellers, who lay in those buildings along with their wives, who often accompany them; and they always go well armed.

From the time I left my own nation I always found somebody that understood me till I came to the sea coast. The languages of different nations did not totally differ, nor were they so copious as those of the Europeans, particularly the English. They were therefore easily learned; and, while I was journeying thus through Africa, I acquired two or three different tongues. In this manner I had been travelling for a considerable time, when one evening, to my great surprise, whom should I see brought to the house where I was but my dear sister! As soon as she saw me she gave a loud shriek, and ran into my arms—I was quite overpowered: neither of us could speak; but, for a considerable time, clung to each other in mutual embraces, unable to do any thing but weep. Our meeting affected all who saw us; and indeed I must acknowledge, in honour of those sable destroyers of human rights, that I never met with any ill treatment, or saw any offered to their slaves, except tying them, when necessary, to keep them from running away. When these people knew we were brother and sister they indulged us [to be] together; and the man, to whom I supposed we belonged, lay with us, he in the middle, while she and I held one another by the hands across his breast all night; and thus for a while we forgot our misfortunes in the joy of being together: but even this small comfort was soon to have an end; for scarcely had the fatal morning appeared, when she was again torn from me for ever! I was now more miserable, if possible, than before. The small relief which her presence gave me from pain was gone, and the wretchedness of my situation was redoubled by my anxiety after her fate, and my apprehensions lest her sufferings should be greater than mine, when I could not be with her to alleviate them.

Yes, thou dear partner of all my childish spats, thou sharer of my joys and sorrows; happy should I have ever esteemed myself to encounter every misery for you, and to procure your freedom by the sacrifice of my own! Though you were early forced from my arms, your image has been always rivetted in my heart, from which neither *time nor fortune* have been able to remove it; so that, while the thoughts of your sufferings have damped my prosperity, they have mingled with adversity and increased its bitterness. To that Heaven which protects the weak from the strong, I commit the care of your innocence and virtues, if they have not already received their full reward, and if your youth and delicacy have not long since fallen victims to the violence of the African trader, the pestilential stench of a Guinea ship, the seasoning[1] in the European colonies, or the lash and lust of a brutal and unrelenting overseer.

I did not long remain after my sister. I was again sold, and carried through a number of places, till, after travelling a considerable time, I came to a town called Tinmah, in the most beautiful country I had yet seen in Africa. It was extremely rich, and there were many rivulets which flowed through it, and supplied a large pond in the centre of the town, where the people washed. Here I first saw and tasted cocoa-nuts, which I thought superior to any nuts I had ever tasted before; and the trees, which were loaded, were also interspersed amongst the houses, which had commodious shades adjoining, and were in the same manner as ours, the insides being neatly plastered and white-washed. Here I also saw and tasted for the first time sugar-cane. Their money consisted of little white shells, the size of the finger nail. I was sold here for one hundred and seventy-two of them by a merchant who lived and brought me there. I had been about two or three days at his house, when a wealthy widow, a neighbour of his, came there one evening, and brought with her an only son, a young gentleman about my own age and size. Here they saw me; and, having taken a fancy to me, I was bought of the merchant, and went home with them. Her house and premises were situated close to one of those rivulets I have mentioned, and were the finest I ever saw in Africa: they were very extensive, and she had a number of slaves to attend her. The next day I was washed and perfumed, and when meal-time came I was led into the presence of my mistress, and ate and drank before her with her son. This filled me with astonishment; and I could scarce help expressing my surprise that the young gentleman should suffer me, who was bound, to eat with him who was free; and not only so, but that he would not at any time either eat or drink till I had taken first, because I was the eldest, which was agreeable to our custom. Indeed every thing here, and all their treatment of me, made me forget that I was a slave. The language of these people resembled ours so nearly, that we understood each other perfectly. They had also the very same customs as we. There were likewise slaves daily to attend us, while my young master and I with other boys sported with our darts and bows and arrows, as I had been used to do at home. In this resemblance to my former happy state I passed about two months; and I now began to think I was to be adopted into the family, and was beginning to be reconciled to my situation, and to forget by degrees my misfortunes, when all at once the delusion vanished; for, without the least previous knowledge, one morning early, while my dear master and companion was still asleep, I was wakened out of my reverie to fresh sorrow, and hurried away even amongst the uncircumcised.

Thus, at the very moment I dreamed of the greatest happiness, I found myself most miserable; and it seemed as if fortune wished to give me this taste of joy, only to render the reverie more poignant. The change I now experienced was as painful as it was sudden and unexpected. It was a change indeed from

1. One of the stages of the slave trade—first came capture; then the voyage across the ocean; then "seasoning," which was the preparation of slaves for hard labor; then enslavement.

a state of bliss to a scene which is inexpressible by me, as it discovered to me an element I had never before beheld, and till then had no idea of, and wherein such instances of hardship and cruelty continually occurred as I can never reflect on but with horror.

All the nations and people I had hitherto passed through resembled our own in their manners, customs, and language: but I came at length to a country, the inhabitants of which differed from us in all those particulars. I was very much struck with this difference, especially when I came among a people who did not circumcise, and are without washing their hands. They cooked also in iron pots, and had European cutlasses and cross bows, which were unknown to us, and fought with their fists amongst themselves. Their women were not so modest as ours, for they ate, and drank, and slept, with their men. But, above all, I was amazed to see no sacrifices or offerings among them. In some of those places the people ornamented themselves with scars, and likewise filed their teeth very sharp. They wanted sometimes to ornament me in the same manner, but I would not suffer them; hoping that I might some time be among a people who did not thus disfigure themselves, as I thought they did. At last I came to the banks of a large river, which was covered with canoes, in which the people appeared to live with their household utensils and provisions of all kinds. I was beyond measure astonished at this, as I had never before seen any water larger than a pond or a rivulet: and my surprise was mingled with no small fear when I was put into one of these canoes, and we began to paddle and move along the river. We continued going on thus till night; and when we came to land, and made fires on the banks, each family by themselves, some dragged their canoes on shore, others stayed and cooked in theirs, and laid in them all night. Those on the land had mats, of which they made tents, some in the shape of little houses: in these we slept; and after the morning meal we embarked again and proceeded as before. I was often very much astonished to see some of the women, as well as the men, jump into the water, dive to the bottom, come up again, and swim about. Thus I continued to travel, sometimes by land, sometimes by water, through different countries and various nations, till, at the end of six or seven months after I had been kidnapped, I arrived at the sea coast. It would be tedious and uninteresting to relate all the incidents which befell me during this journey, and which I have not yet forgotten; of the various hands I passed through, and the manners and customs of all the different people among whom I lived. I shall therefore only observe, that in all the places where I was the soil was exceedingly rich; the pomkins, eadas, plantains, yams, etc., etc. were in great abundance, and of incredible size. There were also vast quantities of different gums, though not used for any purpose; and every where a great deal of tobacco. The cotton even grew quite wild; and there was plenty of red-wood. I saw no mechanics whatever in all the way, except such as I have mentioned. The chief employment in all these countries was agriculture, and both the males and females, as with us, were brought up to it, and trained in the arts of war.

The first object which saluted my eyes when I arrived on the coast was the sea, and a slave ship, which was then riding at anchor, and waiting for its cargo. These filled me with astonishment, which was soon converted into terror when I was carried on board. I was immediately handled and tossed up to see if I were found by some of the crew; and I was now persuaded that I had gotten into a world of bad spirits, and that they were going to kill me. Their complexions too differing so much from ours, their long hair, and the language they spoke, (which was very different from any I had ever heard) united to confirm me in this belief. Indeed such were the horrors of my views and fears at the moment, that, if ten thousand worlds had been my own, I would have freely parted with them all to have exchanged my condition with that of the meanest slave in my own country. When I looked round the ship too and saw a large furnace or copper boiling, and a multitude of black people of every description chained together, every one of their countenances expressing dejection and sorrow, I no longer doubted of my fate; and, quite overpowered with horror and anguish, I fell motionless on the deck and fainted. When I recovered a little I found some black people about me, who I believed were some of those who brought me on board, and had been receiving their pay; they talked to me in order to cheer me, but all in vain. I asked them if we were not to be eaten by those white men with horrible looks, red faces, and loose hair. They told me I was not; and one of the crew brought me a small portion of spirituous liquor in a wine glass; but, being afraid of him, I would not take it out of his hand. One of the blacks therefore took it from him and gave it to me, and I took a little down my palate, which, instead of reviving me, as they thought it would, threw me into the greatest consternation at the strange feeling it produced, having never tasted any such liquor before. Soon after this the blacks who brought me on board went off, and left me abandoned to despair. I now saw myself deprived of all chance of returning to my native country, or even the least glimpse of hope of gaining the shore, which I now considered as friendly; and I even wished for my former slavery in preference to my present situation, which was filled with horrors of every kind, still heightened by my ignorance of what I was to undergo. I was not long suffered to indulge my grief; I was soon put down under the decks, and there I received such a salutation in my nostrils as I had never experienced in my life: so that, with the loathsomeness of the stench, and crying together, I became so sick and low that I was not able to eat, nor had I the least desire to taste any thing. I now wished for the last friend, death, to relieve me; but soon, to my grief, two of the white men offered me eatables; and, on my refusing to eat, one of them held me fast by the hands, and laid me across I think the windlass, and tied my feet, while the other flogged me severely. I had never experienced any thing of this kind before; and although, not being used to the water, I naturally feared that element the first time I saw it, yet nevertheless, could I have got over the nettings, I would have jumped over the side, but I could not; and, besides, the crew used to watch us very closely who were not chained down to the decks, lest we should leap into the water: and I have seen some of these poor African prisoners most severely cut for attempting to do so, and hourly whipped for not eating. This indeed was often the case with myself. In a little time after, amongst the poor chained men, I found some of my own nation, which in a small degree gave ease to my mind. I inquired to these what was to be done with us; they gave me to understand we were to be carried to these white people's country to work for them. I then was a little revived, and thought, if it were no worse than working, my situation was not so desperate: but still I feared I should be put to death, the white people looked and acted, as I thought, in so savage a manner; for I had never seen among any people such instances of brutal cruelty; and this not only shewn towards us blacks, but also to some of the whites themselves. One white man in particular I saw, when we were permitted to be on deck, flogged so unmercifully with a large rope near the foremast, that he died in consequence of it; and they tossed him over the side as they would have done a brute. This made me fear these people the more; and I expected nothing less than to be treated in the same manner. I could not help expressing my fears and apprehensions to some of my countrymen: I asked them if these people had no country, but lived in this hollow place (the ship): they told me they did not, but came from a distant one. "Then," said I, "how comes it in all our country we never heard of them?" They told me because they lived so very far off. I then asked where were their women? had they any like themselves? I was told they had: "and why," said I, "do we not see them?" They answered, because they were left behind. I asked how the vessel could go? they told me they could not tell; but that there were cloths put upon the masts by the help of the ropes I saw, and then the vessel went on; and the white men had some spell or magic they put in the water when they liked in order to stop the vessel. I was exceedingly amazed at this account, and really thought they were spirits. I therefore wished much to be from amongst them, for I expected they would sacrifice me: but my wishes were vain; for we were so quartered that it was impossible for any of us to make our escape. While we stayed on the coast I was mostly on deck; and one day, to my great astonishment, I saw one of these vessels coming in with the sails up. As soon as the whites saw it, they gave a great shout, at which we were amazed; and the more so as the vessel appeared larger by approaching nearer. At last she came to an anchor in my sight, and when the anchor was let go I and my countrymen who saw it were lost in astonishment to observe the vessel stop; and were now convinced it was done by magic. Soon after this the other ship got her boats out, and they came on board of us, and the people of both ships seemed very glad to see each other. Several of the strangers also shook hands with us black people, and made motions with their hands, signifying I suppose we were to go to their country; but we did not understand them. At last, when the ship we were in had got in all her cargo they made ready with many fearful noises and we were all put under deck, so that we could not see how they managed the vessel.

But this disappointment was the least of my sorrow. The stench of the hold while we were on the coast was so intolerably loathsome, that it was dangerous to remain there for any time, and some of us had been permitted to stay on the deck for the fresh air; but now that the whole ship's cargo were confined together, it became absolutely pestilential. The closeness of the place, and the heat of the climate, added to the number in the ship, which was so crowded that each had scarcely room to turn himself, almost suffocated us. This produced copious perspirations, so that the air soon became unfit for respiration, from a variety of loathsome smells, and brought on a sickness among the slaves, of which many died, thus falling victims to the improvident avarice, as I may call it, of their purchasers. This wretched situation was again aggravated by the galling of the chains, now become insupportable; and the filth of the necessary tubs, into which the children often fell, and were almost suffocated. The shrieks of the women, and the groans of the dying, rendered the whole a scene of horror almost inconceivable. Happily perhaps for myself I was soon reduced so low here that it was thought necessary to keep me almost always on deck; and from my extreme youth I was not put in fetters. In this situation I expected every hour to share the fate of my companions, some of whom were almost daily brought upon deck at the point of death, which I began to hope would soon put an end to my miseries. Often did I think many of the inhabitants of the deep much more happy than myself. I envied them the freedom they enjoyed, and as often wished I could change my condition for theirs. Every circumstance I met with served only to render my state more painful, and heighten my apprehensions, and my opinion of the cruelty of the whites. One day they had taken a number of fishes; and when they had killed and satisfied themselves with as many as they thought fit, to our astonishment who were on the deck, rather than give any of them to us to eat as we expected, they tossed the remaining fish into the sea again, although we begged and prayed for some as well as we could, but in vain; and some of my countrymen, being pressed by hunger, took an opportunity, when they thought no one saw them, of trying to get a little privately; but they were discovered, and the attempt procured them some very severe floggings. One day, when we had a smooth sea and moderate wind, two of my wearied countrymen who were chained together (I was near them at the time), preferring death to such a life of misery, somehow made through the nettings and jumped into the sea: immediately another quite dejected fellow, who, on account of his illness, was suffered to be out of irons, also followed their example; and I believe many more would very soon have done the same if they had not been prevented by the ship's crew, who were instantly alarmed. Those of us that were the most active were in a moment put down under the deck, and there was such a noise and confusion amongst the people of the ship as I never heard before, to stop her, and get the boat out to go after the slaves. However two of the wretches were drowned, but they got the other, and afterwards flogged him unmercifully for thus attempting to prefer death to slavery. In this manner we continued to undergo more hardships than I can now relate, hardships which are inseparable from this accursed trade. Many a time we were near suffocation from the want of fresh air, which we were often without for whole days together. This, and the stench of the necessary tubs, carried off many. During our passage I first saw flying fishes, which surprised me very much: they used frequently to fly across the ship, and many of them fell on the deck. I also now first saw the use of the quadrant;[2] I had often with astonishment seen the mariners make observations with it, and I could not think what it meant. They at last took notice of my surprise; and one of them, willing to increase it, as well as to gratify my curiosity, made me one day look through it. The clouds appeared to me to be land, which disappeared as they passed along. This heightened my wonder; and I was now more persuaded than ever that I was in another world, and that every thing about me was magic. At last we came in sight of the island of Barbadoes, at which the whites on board gave a great shout, and made many signs of joy to us. We did not know what to think of this; but as the vessel drew nearer we plainly saw the harbour, and other ships of different kinds and sizes; and we soon anchored amongst them off Bridge Town.[3] Many merchants and planters now came on board, though it was in the evening. They put us in separate parcels, and examined us attentively. They also made us jump, and pointed to the land, signifying we were to go there. We thought by this we should be eaten by these ugly men, as they appeared to us; and, when

2. Measurement device used for the navigation of ships.

3. Capital of Barbados.

soon after we were all put down under the deck again, there was much dread and trembling among us, and nothing but bitter cries to be heard all the night from these apprehensions, insomuch that at last the white people got some old slaves from the land to pacify us. They told us we were not to be eaten, but to work, and were soon to go on land, where we should see many of our country people. This report eased us much; and sure enough, soon after we were landed, there came to us Africans of all languages. We were conducted immediately to the merchant's yard, where we were all pent up together like so many sheep in a fold, without regard to sex or age. As every object was new to me every thing I saw filled me with surprise. What struck me first was that the houses were built with stories, and in every other respect different from those in Africa: but I was still more astonished on seeing people on horseback. I did not know what this could mean; and indeed I thought these people were full of nothing but magical arts. While I was in this astonishment one of my fellow prisoners spoke to a countryman of his about the horses, who said they were the same kind they had in their country. I understood them, though they were from a distant part of Africa, and I thought it odd I had not seen any horses there; but afterwards, when I came to converse with different Africans, I found they had many horses amongst them, and much larger than those I then saw. We were not many days in the merchant's custody before we were sold after their usual manner, which is this:—On a signal given, (as the beat of a drum) the buyers rush at once into the yard where the slaves are confined, and make choice of that parcel they like best. The noise and clamour with which this is attended, and the eagerness visible in the countenances of the buyers, serve not a little to increase the apprehensions of the terrified Africans, who may well be supposed to consider them as the ministers of that destruction to which they think themselves devoted. In this manner, without scruple, are relations and friends separated, most of them never to see each other again. I remember in the vessel in which I was brought over, in the men's apartment, there were several brothers, who, in the sale, were sold in different lots; and it was very moving on this occasion to see and hear their cries at parting. O, ye nominal Christians! might not an African ask you, learned you this from your God, who says unto you, Do unto all men as you would men should do unto you? Is it not enough that we are torn from our country and friends to toil for your luxury and lust of gain? Must every tender feeling be likewise sacrificed to your avarice? Are the dearest friends and relations, now rendered more dear by their separation from their kindred, still to be parted from each other, and thus prevented from cheering the gloom of slavery with the small comfort of being together and mingling their sufferings and sorrows? Why are parents to lose their children, brothers their sisters, or husbands their wives? Surely this is a new refinement in cruelty, which, while it has no advantage to atone for it, thus aggravates distress, and adds fresh horrors even to the wretchedness of slavery.

FROM CHAPTER III

I now totally lost the small remains of comfort I had enjoyed in conversing with my countrymen; the women too, who used to wash and take care of me, were all gone different ways, and I never saw one of them afterwards.

I stayed in this island for a few days; I believe it could not be above a fortnight; when I, and some few more slaves, that were not saleable amongst the rest, from very much fretting, were shipped off in a sloop for North America. On the passage we were better treated than when we were coming from Africa, and we had plenty of rice and fat pork. We were landed up a river a good way from the sea, about Virginia county, where we saw few or none of our native Africans, and not one soul who could talk to me. I was a few weeks weeding grass, and gathering stones in a plantation; and at last all my companions were distributed different ways, and only myself was left. I was now exceedingly miserable, and thought myself worse off than any of the rest of my companions, for they could talk to each other, but I had no person to speak to that I could understand. In this state, I was constantly grieving and pining, and wishing for death rather than anything else. While I was in this plantation the gentleman, to whom I suppose the estate belonged, being unwell, I was one day sent for to his dwelling-house to fan him; when I came into the room where he was I was very much affrighted at some things I saw, and the more so as I had seen a black woman slave as I came through the house, who was cooking the dinner, and the poor creature was cruelly loaded with various kinds of iron machines; she had one particularly on her head, which locked her mouth so fast that she could scarcely speak; and could not eat nor drink. I was much astonished and shocked at this contrivance, which I afterwards learned was called the iron muzzle. Soon after I had a fan put in my hand, to fan the gentleman while he slept; and so I did indeed with great fear. While he was fast asleep I indulged myself a great deal in looking about the room, which to me appeared very fine and curious. The first object that engaged my attention was a watch which hung on the chimney, and was going. I was quite surprised at the noise it made, and was afraid it would tell the gentleman anything I might do amiss; and when I immediately after observed a picture hanging in the room, which appeared constantly to look at me, I was still more affrighted, having never seen such things as these before. At one time I thought it was something relative to magic; and not seeing it move I thought it might be some way the whites had to keep their great men when they died, and offer them libations as we used to do to our friendly spirits. In this state of anxiety I remained till my master awoke, when I was dismissed out of the room, to my no small satisfaction and relief; for I thought that these people were all made up of wonders. In this place I was called Jacob; but on board the *African Snow*, I was called Michael. I had been some time in this miserable, forlorn, and much dejected state, without having anyone to talk to, which made my life a burden, when the kind and unknown hand of the Creator (who in very deed leads the blind in a way they know not) now began to appear, to my comfort; for one day the captain of a merchant ship, called the *Industrious Bee*, came on some business to my master's house. This gentleman, whose name was Michael Henry Pascal, was a lieutenant in the royal navy, but now commanded this trading ship, which was somewhere in the confines of the county many miles off. While he was at my master's house it happened that he saw me, and liked me so well that he made a purchase of me. I think I have often heard him say he gave thirty or forty pounds sterling for me; but I do not now remember which. However, he meant me for a present to some of his friends in England: and as I was sent accordingly from the house of my then master (one Mr. Campbell) to the place where the ship lay; I was conducted on horseback by an elderly black man (a mode of travelling which appeared very odd to me). When I arrived I was carried on board a fine large ship, loaded with tobacco, etc., and just ready to sail for England. I now thought my condition much mended; I had sails to lie on, and plenty of good victuals to eat; and everybody on board used me very kindly, quite contrary to what I had seen of any white people before; I therefore began to think that they were not all of the same disposition. A few days after I was on board we sailed for England. I was still at a loss to conjecture my destiny. By this time, however, I could smatter a little imperfect English; and I wanted to know as well as I could where we were going. Some of the people of the ship used to tell me they were going to carry me back to my own country, and this made me very happy. I was quite rejoiced at the sound of going back; and thought if I should get home what wonders I should have to tell. But I was reserved for another fate, and was soon undeceived when we came within sight of the English coast. While I was on board this ship, my captain and master named me *Gustavas Vassa*.[4] I at that time began to understand him a little, and refused to be called so, and told him as well as I could that I would be called Jacob; but he said I should not, and still called me Gustavus: and when I refused to answer to my new name, which at first I did, it gained me many a cuff; so at length I submitted, and was obliged to bear the present name, by which I have been known ever since.

* * *

It was about the beginning of the spring 1757, when I arrived in England and I was near twelve years of age at that time. I was very much struck with the buildings and the pavement of the streets in Falmouth; and, indeed, every object I saw, filled me with new surprise. One morning, when I got upon deck, I saw it covered all over with the snow that fell over-night. As I had never seen anything of the kind before, I thought it was salt; so I immediately ran down to the mate and desired him, as well as I could, to come and see how somebody in the night had thrown salt all over the deck. He, knowing what it was, desired me to bring some of it down to him. Accordingly I took up a handful of it, which I found very cold indeed; and when I brought it to him he desired me to taste it. I did so, and I was surprised beyond measure. I then asked him what it was; he told me it was snow, but I could not in anywise understand him. He asked me if we had no such thing in my country; I told him, No. I then asked him the use of it, and who made it; he told me a great man in the heavens, called God. But here again I was to all intents and purposes at a loss to understand him; and the more so, when a little after I saw the air filled with it, in a heavy shower, which fell down on the same day. After this I went to church; and having never been at such a place before, I was again amazed at seeing and hearing the service. I asked all I could about it; and they gave me to understand it was worshipping God, who made us and all things. I was still at a great loss, and soon got into an endless field of inquiries, as well as I was able to speak and ask about things. However, my little friend Dick[5] used to be my

4. King Gustav of Sweden, called Gustav Vasa (1496–1560), who liberated the Swedes from the Danes but then ruled the nation as a brutal tyrant.

5. Richard Baxter, an American boy who befriends Equiano on his first voyage to England.

best interpreter; for I could make free with him, and he always instructed me with pleasure. And from what I could understand by him of this God, and in seeing these white people did not sell one another as we did, I was much pleased; and in this I thought they were much happier than we Africans. I was astonished at the wisdom of the white people in all things I saw; but was amazed at their not sacrificing, or making any offerings, and eating with unwashed hands, and touching the dead. I likewise could not help remarking the particular slenderness of their women, which I did not at first like; and I thought they were not so modest and shame faced as the African women.

I had often seen my master and Dick employed in reading; and I had a great curiosity to talk to the books, as I thought they did; and so to learn how all things had a beginning: for that purpose I have often taken up a book, and have talked to it, and then put my ears to it, when alone, in hopes it would answer me; and I have been very much concerned when I found it remained silent.

* * *

JOHANN WOLFGANG VON GOETHE

1749–1832

Few writers have ever surpassed Goethe in global fame and influence. He was perhaps the last European to live up to the ideal of the Renaissance man: skilled in the arts, in science, and in politics. He made groundbreaking contributions not only in all the major literary genres, but also in art criticism and the study of classical culture. He did extensive work in the fields of botany, mineralogy, comparative anatomy, and optics. And he occupied many administrative and political positions at the court of Weimar, where he was responsible for finance, the military, and mining, as well as for the Weimar Court Theatre, which he turned from an amateur theater to a professional troupe that premiered many of his own plays. Distrusting both the French Revolution, whose effects he witnessed at close hand, and growing nationalist movements in Germany and elsewhere, Goethe did not consider himself a German, but a European, and he coined the visionary notion of "world literature," eager to open Europe to the intellectual and artistic production of the non-European world.

Goethe was born into a middle-class family in Frankfurt. Despite an early interest in the arts and the theater, he followed his father's wishes and studied law. But Goethe's artistic ambitions could not be held back for long and he soon started to publish literary works. His first significant play, *Götz of Berlechingen* (1773), was shaped by his discovery of Shakespeare, whom he especially admired for being willing to violate the strict rules of drama that prevailed at the time. Yet the most important work of Goethe's early period was a novel, *The Sorrows of Young Werther*

(1774), which turned Goethe into the representative of a literary movement called *Sturm und Drang* ("storm and stress") that emphasized the expression of feelings over the strictures of literary form. Centered on subjective impressions, extreme emotions, and literary outbursts, the novel leads its tragic protagonist, who is caught in a love triangle, to his eventual suicide. *The Sorrows of Young Werther* prompted mass hysteria, also called "Werther fever," allegedly leading to several copycat suicides as well as to the marketing of Werther paraphernalia. Goethe became a European celebrity virtually overnight.

A year later, Duke Karl August of Weimar called the young writer to his elegant but provincial court, where Goethe first served as educator, but soon fulfilled more important functions and was ultimately elevated to the aristocracy. It was here, amid his extensive duties, that Goethe began his mature, more classical works: his influential novel, *Wilhelm Meister's Apprenticeship*, as well as the plays *Egmont, Iphigenia on Tauris, Torquato Tasso*, and *Faust*. He began all of these works shortly after he had arrived at Weimar, but they went through innumerable revisions, during which he slowly forged a new, less unruly and more measured style, leaving the earlier "storm and stress" behind.

Goethe was inspired by an extended voyage to Italy (1786–88), and he became the chief representative of a revival of classical forms and ideas in Germany and Europe more generally. This journey led him to revise *Faust* and other works in accordance with the classical ideal. He collected classical sculpture (he contented himself with replicas) and adapted classical stories, poetry, and drama. But the theater stood at the center of the classical revival. He worried about the training of actors, developing guidelines later published as *Rules for Actors* (1803, 1832), and intervened in all other aspects of theater production. He also insisted on introducing international playwrights, including Shakespeare, Calderón, and Goldoni, to his provincial audience. Thus, although Goethe had started the Weimar Court Theatre as a vehicle for his revival of classical drama, he opened it to a variety of dramatic styles.

In the first decades of the nineteenth century, Goethe finally completed the long-awaited first part of *Faust* (1806). While he left his mark on numerous fields and genres, *Faust* stands out as his masterpiece. He began writing it in his early twenties and continued to work on it until his death. Even more than many of his other texts, it underwent significant changes, from the first drafts in the 1770s, through the publication of the first part in 1808, to the final version of the second part, completed just before his last birthday in 1832.

For *Faust* Goethe relied on an old folk legend, a quintessentially medieval morality tale, in which an arrogant scholar gives in to the temptations of the devil, makes a famous pact to trade his soul for the use of black magic, and finally suffers in hell for his sins. In the course of his many revisions, Goethe transformed this simple material into a text that captured the spirit and desires of modernity. Although he preserved important set pieces such as the pact with the devil, what mattered to Goethe was the relation between abstract learning and sensuous experience, as well as the nature of human striving. He used the character of Faust to explore the transformative energies unleashed by modern science, philosophy, and industry.

In revising the old legend, Goethe changed its moral structure. While earlier Fausts were always lost to the devil, Goethe has Faust escape Mephistopheles' clutches at the end of *Faust II*. This decision thoroughly alters the morality play, which had punished a blaspheming protagonist as a warning to Christian audiences. Goethe still depicts Faust as a sinner, as the earlier versions had done. But now Faust's sinning has to be balanced against his irreverent and limitless thirst for knowledge, which for Goethe has great esteem. Paradoxically, the very quality that drives Faust to his pact with the devil is the one that will lead him to salvation.

Several scenes frame the play before its proper action begins. First Goethe presents a kind of curtain riser, a "Prelude in the Theater," in which a Manager, a Poet, and a Clown debate their respective visions of a theater, poised between popular entertainment and high art, a debate undoubtedly grounded in Goethe's experience as a dramatist and theater director. He then moves on to the "Prologue in Heaven," which is borrowed from the biblical book of of Job. It depicts a debate between God and Mephistopheles that ends in a wager. Mephistopheles has permission to lead Faust into temptation because God is certain that Faust's restless striving, his search for true knowledge, will eventually lead him back on the right path. Goethe then introduces the text with a "Dedication," in which he evokes the youthful world in which began this work some thirty years ago.

The main drama of *Faust I* can be divided into two parts. The first part introduces us to the medieval Doctor, who has mastered all the higher disciplines of the university—philosophy, law, medicine, and theology—but who still has not learned the inner essence of the world. Dissatisfied with this insufficient knowledge, he turns to the dangerous domains of magic and alchemy, and it is this daring that is, for Goethe, Faust's most modern attribute. Shunning inherited pieties and religious prejudices, Faust is ready to sacrifice everything to knowledge. He also longs to experience life to the fullest, and this makes him especially susceptible to the enticements of Mephistopheles, who offers him wide experience and the satisfaction of his sensual desires.

In the second part of *Faust I*, Mephistopheles tries to satisfy Faust's demands and yearnings. Although he often dismisses Mephistopheles' efforts at satisfaction as "mere spectacle," Faust nevertheless tries them all, culminating in the famous, orgiastic "Walpurgisnight" scene, a delirious meeting of all creatures of the night. None of these sensuous pleasures, however, can give Faust the kind of satisfaction he derives from the culminating event of the play: the seduction of Gretchen. It is with Gretchen that *Faust* earns its title to tragedy. Gretchen represents different pleasures from the other experiences provided by Mephistopheles. Faust genuinely falls in love with her, praising her innocence and simple religious faith. And yet he alternately neglects her and showers her with presents as he pursues, and finally achieves, his physical satisfaction, leading to a tragic end. Here the first part of *Faust* ends. These tragic events will be blissfully forgotten in the second part, which takes Faust and Mephistopheles on a wild tour through politics, science, and learning.

Not only did Goethe revise the Faust legend to rescue Faust from damnation at the end of part two, but in the first part, he shaped another, and possibly more radical, revision of the historical tale. For the real protagonist of this part is not Faust, who is alternatively pompous, idealistic, and fatuous, who does not know himself, and who manages to bring everything, including poor Gretchen, to ruin. Instead, the real protagonist is the witty, realistic, and caustic Mephistopheles. It is Mephistopheles who criticizes the medieval world of Faust, and who deflates his grandiose speeches, including his self-serving declarations of love for Gretchen. Mephistopheles is the spirit of negation, as he says of himself, but it is a negation that serves to criticize authority. Mephistopheles thus embodies the principle of critique, of questioning all kinds of inherited religious belief and orthodoxies. Since this critical spirit is central to modernity, Mephistopheles becomes the truly modern character in the play. And Goethe clandestinely turns Mephistopheles into the main protagonist. He has all the best and wittiest lines. In the theater, he simply steals the show.

Outdoing a modernized Faust with an even more modern Mephistopheles, Goethe was also daring in his use of structure and form. The play rejects the narrow rules of Aristotelian drama, constraining time and space, and instead presents a play of epic length that is composed of loosely connected scenes. *Faust* contains passages in different meters and rhyme schemes as well as in prose. It includes interludes, an allegorical dream, a satire of the university, erotic songs, and scenes of outright bacchanalia. It seeks to encompass the entirety of the modern world, aspiring to a rare totality in its hybrid form. Thus *Faust* has been considered a total work of art, a modern epic, and a strikingly new type of drama.

Faust is so startling in its dramatic innovations that Goethe himself never sought to mount even the more manageable first part in his own Weimar Court Theatre, and in fact he did not even consider it fit for the stage. When it was performed at another theater a few years before his death, he did not show much interest in the production. The much more difficult, allegorical second part has been performed even less often. Given the length of both parts taken together, few theaters have ever tried to produce the entirety of Goethe's *Faust*. In the course of the twentieth century, however, the first part attracted the most renowned theater directors, composers, and actors. French composers Hector Berlioz and Charles Gounod based operas on it, and in the twentieth century, Gertrude Stein's *Doctor Faustus Lights the Lights* is among the most modernist responses to Goethe's text. Filmmakers have turned to it again and again for inspiration, including F. W. Murnau in 1926 and Czech director Jan Švankmajer in 1994. Goethe's *Faust* has thus remained an important touchstone for two centuries of art, a testament to Goethe's ability to turn a simple medieval morality tale into a complex investigation of modernity.

Faust[1]

Prelude in the Theater

MANAGER, POET, CLOWN

MANAGER You two who've always stood by me
When times were hard and the playhouse empty,
What do you think we may hope for
From this tour of ours through German country?
I'd like to please the crowd here, for
They're really so easy-going, so patient,
The posts are up, the floorboards laid,
And in they came in search of entertainment.
Taking their seats they look around, at ease,
Wishing to be surprised, each one,
Well, I know with this audience how to please,

1. Translated by Martin Greenberg.

But I've never been in a fix like this one.
It's not to the best these good people are used,
But Lord, all the books all of them have perused.
So we need to comes up with something lively and new,
A piece with some meaning that amuses them too.
I don't deny what pleases me most
Are droves of people, a great host,
Trying with all their might to squeeze
Through the strait gate to our paradise,
When it's daylight still, not even four,
Using elbow and fist to get to the ticket seller,
Like starving men rushing the baker's door—
For the sake of a seat prepared to commit murder.
Who works on such a mixed lot such a wonder?
Do I need to tell you? Why, of course it's the poet,
So fall to, dear colleague, and let's see you do it!

POET Don't talk to me about that crazy crowd,
One look at them and all my wits desert me!
Oh shield me from that shoving, shouting horde
That swallows you up against your will completely!
No, lead me to some quiet, remote place
Where poets know their only happiness,
Where love and dearest friends inspire and nurse
The blessed gift that is the power of verse.
Oh dear, what struggles up from deep inside us,
Syllables our lips shape hesitantly
Into scenes ineffective now, and now effective,
Is drowned out in the present's hurlyburly;
Years must pass till, seen in time's perspective,
Its shape and soul shine forth as they are truly.
What's all flash and glitter lives a day,
The real thing's treasured by posterity.

CLOWN Posterity! Oh that word—but let's not start a row!
If all *I* ever thought of was the hereafter,
Who'd set the audience laughing in the here and now?
To be amused, that's their hearts' desire.
Having a clown on the stage who knows what his business is
Is not to be sneezed at—it matters to know how to please.
When yours is the stuff to delight and content a whole theaterful,
You don't sourly mutter the public's a mob, always changeable.
What you want's a full house, the sign out saying Standing Room Only,
For the bigger the house, the better the response you can count on,
So be a good fellow and show us what drama is really.
Your imagination, let it pour out like a fountain,
Its marvels matched by wisdom, good sense, feeling,
By passion too—but mind you, show us some fooling!

MANAGER But what's the first requirement? Plenty of action!
They're spectators so what they want to see is things happen.
If you've got business going on every minute

That catches people's attention, their roving eyes rivet,
Then you don't have to worry, they're yours, they're won over,
When the curtain comes down they'll shout "Author! Author!"
With a public so large you need an abundance to please them all
Something for everyone, that's how to seize them all,
The last thing you want is to be classically economical.
In the theater today only scenes and set pieces do,
The way to succeed is to serve up a stew,
You can cook it up fast, dish it out easy too.
Now tell me, what good is your artistic unity,
The public will only make hash of it anyway.

POET You don't understand—all that's just hackwork,
A true artist never stoops to such stuff!
Those cheap purveyors of tawdry patchwork
For you are the measure of dramatic truth.

MANAGER Go ahead, scold me, I don't mind your censure.
To do a job right you use the tools that are called for,
Remember, it's soft wood you've got to split,
Consider the people for whom you write:
One's here because he's bored, another
Comes stuffed from eating a seven-course dinner,
But worst are the ones who come to fill up our seats
Straight from reading the very latest news sheets.
The crowd arrives here distracted, distrait,
Thinking of this and that, not of a play,
The reason they come is mere curiosity,
The ladies exhibit their shoulders and finery,
Put on a great show, don't require a salary.
Oh, the dreams poets dream in their ivory tower!
Flattered, are you, to see the house full?
Well, take a good look at our clientele,
The half vulgar and loud, half unmoved and sour,
One's mind's on his card game after the play,
Another's on tumbling a girl in the hay.
It's for people like that you fools torture the Muses?
Listen to me: You'll never go wrong
If you pile it on, pile it on, and still pile it on.
Bewilder, confound them with all your variety,
The public's the public, they're a hard lot to satisfy.
But goodness, how worked up you seem to be!
What's wrong? Is it anguish or is it ecstasy?

POET Go out and find yourself some other lackey!
You expect the poet, do you, frivolously,
For the sake of your blue eyes to debase
Nature's finest gift to the human race?
How does he teach humanity feeling,
Master the elements, every one?
I'll tell you, by the music pealing
Forth from his breast orphically,

Which then by reflux back on him returning
Reverberates as Nature's deep-voiced harmony.
When Nature winds life's endless thread
Indifferently on the bobbin, when
The noisy cries of her countless creatures
No music make, uproar instead,
Who melodizes the monotonous din
And makes all move in living measures?
Who calls each mute particular
To sing its part in the general chorus
In a glorious concord of myriad voices?
Who links our passions to wild tempests,
Our solemn moods to fading sunsets?
Unrolls before the feet of lovers
A lovely carpet of spring flowers?
Twines leaves which in themselves mean nothing at all
To crown those who have proven most worthy of all?
Assures us of Olympus, upon it assembled the gods?—
That revelation of man's powers, the poet, does!

CLOWN Then go on and use them, your marvelous powers!
Go at your business of making verses
The way you go at a love adventure:
A chance encounter, you're attracted, linger,
And little by little you find yourself caught.
You're so happy, later you're not;
First you're enraptured, then it's nothing but trouble,
And before you know it it's a whole novel,
Write the play we want that way, you know how to do it!
Jump right into life's richness and riot,
All of us live life, few have an idea about it,
And my, how it interests wherever you scratch it!
Color, confusion, a wild hurlyburly,
With a glimmer of truth amid errors' obscurity,
And there you have it, exactly the right brew
To refresh everyone, make them think a bit too.
Then the best of our youth will flock here to listen,
Gripping their seats in anticipation.
The sensitive soul will find in your play
Food to feed his melancholy;
One thing touches one man, another another,
The end result is, all discover
What's in their hearts. The young are still ready
To laugh at a good thrust, let their tears flow in pity,
Warmly respond to lofty ambitions,
Cherishing still their bright dreams and illusions.
You'll never please those whose race is run,
For them there are no more surprises,
But the youth for whom all's just begun,
They will shower you with praises.

POET Then give me back those times again
When I, too, was a leaf uncurled,
When mists still filled the morning world,
And song after song poured out of me
Like a fountain flowing uninterruptedly,
When a bud was a promised miracle,
And I plucked the thousand flowers that filled
The vales with their rich spectacle.
The nothing I owned was more than enough,
By fictions delighted, impelled toward truth—
Oh give me back that unquelled ardor,
The happiness whose depth is pain,
The strength of hate, love's superpower,
Oh give me back my youth again!
CLOWN Youth, my dear colleague, you need in the following cases:
When the enemy's crowding you hard in the fight,
When pretty girls in summer dresses
Kiss and squeeze you with all their might,
When running hard, you glimpse in the distance
The wreath that rewards the fleetest foot,
When after the madly whirling dances
With drinking you wear the night out.
But to sweep the old familiar harp strings
Boldly yet with fine grace too,
To make by pleasing indirections
For the end your drama has in view—
That's a job for you old fellows,
And we respect you for your skill;
Age doesn't make us childish, God knows,
Just finds us the same old children still.
MANAGER We've talked enough, now let me see
Your tardy quill produce results,
Our business is to stage a play,
Not waste the time in compliments.
And please—don't say you're not in the mood,
It never arrives if you hesitate timidly.
You say you're a poet, good, very good,
Let's hear it, then, your poetry.
You know what's wanted, good strong stuff—
To work now, work, go right at it,
What's put off today, tomorrow's put off;
How precious to us is every minute.
A resolute spirit, acting timely,
Seizes occasion by the short hairs,
It won't let go but hangs on grimly,
Once committed, it perseveres.

You know how on our German stage
We're free to try whatever we please,

So don't imagine I want you to save
Me money on paint and properties.
Hang out heaven's big and little lamps,
Scatter stars over the canvas sky,
Let's have fire and flood and dizzying steeps,
All sorts of birds and beasts—do the thing liberally.
And thus on a narrow platform you're able
To go all the way round Creation's great circle
At a brisk enough pace, yet deliberately as well,
From Heaven, through this our world, down to Hell.

Prologue in Heaven[1]

THE LORD. THE HEAVENLY HOST. *Then* MEPHISTOPHELES.[2] *The three* ARCHANGELS *advance to front.*

RAPHAEL The sun as always sounds his music
In contest with each brother sphere,
Marching round and around, with steps terrific,
His appointed circle, year after year.
To see him lends us angels strength,
But what he *is*, oh who can say?
The inconceivably great works are great
As on the first creating day.
GABRIEL And swift, past all conception swift,
The jeweled globe spins on its axletree,
Celestial brightness alternating
With shuddering night's obscurity.
Against the rock-bound littoral[3]
The sea is backwards seething hurled,
And rock and sea together hurtle
With the eternally turning world.
MICHAEL And tempests vying, howling, riot
From sea to land, from land to sea,
Linking in tremendous circuit
A chain of blazing energy.
The thunderbolt makes ready for
The thunderclap a ruinous way—
Yet Lord, your servants most prefer
The stiller motions of your day.
ALL THREE From seeing this we draw our strength,
But what You *are*, oh who can say?
And all your great works are as great
As on the first creating day.

1. The scene is patterned on Job 1.6–12 and 2.1–6.
2. The origin of the name remains debatable. It may come from Hebrew, Persian, or Greek, with such meanings as "destroyer-liar," "no friend of Faust," and "no friend of light."
3. Near the seaside.

MEPHISTOPHELES Lord, since you've stopped by here again, liking to know
How all of us are doing, for which we're grateful,
And since you've never made me feel *de trop*,[4]
Well, here I am too with your other people.
Excuse, I hope, my lack of eloquence,
Though this whole host, I'm sure, will think I'm stupid.
Coming from me, high-sounding sentiments
Would only make you laugh—that is, provided
Laughing is a thing Your Worship still did
About suns and worlds I don't know beans, I only see
How mortals find their lives pure misery.
Earth's little god's shaped out of the same old clay,
He's the same queer fish he was on the first day.
He'd be much better off, in my opinion, without
The bit of heavenly light you dealt him out.
He calls it Reason, and the use he puts it to?
To act more beastly than beasts ever do.
To me he seems, if you'll pardon my saying so,
Like a long-legged grasshopper all of whose leaping
Only lands him back in the grass again chirping
The tune he's always chirped. And if only he'd
Stay put in the grass! But no! It's an absolute need
With him to creep and crawl and strain and sweat
And stick his nose in every pile of dirt.

THE LORD Is that all you have got to say to me?
Is that all you can do, accuse eternally?
Is nothing ever right for you down there, sir?

MEPHISTOPHELES No, nothing, Lord—all's just as bad as ever.
I really pity humanity's myriad miseries,
I swear I hate tormenting the poor ninnies.

THE LORD Do you know Faust?

MEPHISTOPHELES The Doctor?[5]

THE LORD My good servant!

MEPHISTOPHELES You[6] don't say! He serves you, I think, very queerly,
Finds meat and drink, the fool, in nothing earthly,
Drives madly on, there's in him such a torment,
He himself is half aware he's crazy;
Heaven's brightest stars he imperiously requires
And from the earth its most exciting pleasures;
All, all, the near at hand and far and wide,
Leave your good servant quite unsatisfied.

THE LORD If today his service shows confused, disordered,
With my help he will see the way clear forward;
When the sapling greens, the gardener can feel certain

4. Over the top, too much.
5. Of philosophy.
6. In the German text, Mephistopheles shifts back and forth between the informal word for "you" (*du*) and the more formal, respectful mode of address (*ihr*).

Flower and fruit will follow in due season.
MEPHISTOPHELES Would you care to bet on that? You'll lose, I tell you,
If you'll give me leave to lead the fellow
Gently down my broad, my primrose path.
THE LORD As long as Faustus walks the earth
I shan't, I promise, interfere.
While still man strives, still he must err.
MEPHISTOPHELES Well thank you, Lord—it's not the dead and gone
I like dealing with. By far what I prefer
Are round and rosy cheeks. When corpses come
A-knocking, sorry, Master's left the house;
My way of working's the cat's way with a mouse.
THE LORD So it's agreed, you have my full consent.
Divert the soul of Faust from its true source
And if you're able, lead him along, Hell bent
With you, upon the downward course—
Then blush for shame to find you must admit:
For all his dark impulses, imperfect sight,
A good man always knows the way that's right.
MEPHISTOPHELES Of course, of course! Yet I'll seduce him from it
Soon enough. I'm not afraid I'll lose my bet.
And after I have won it,
You won't, I trust, begrudge me
My whoops of triumph, shouts of victory.
Dust he'll eat
And find that he enjoys it, exactly like
That old aunt of mine, the famous snake.
THE LORD There too feel free, you have carte blanche.
I've never hated your likes much;
I find of all the spirits of denial,
You jeerers not my severest trial.
Man's very quick to slacken in his effort,
What he likes best is Sunday peace and quiet;
So I'm glad to give him a devil—for his own good,
To prod and poke and incite him as a devil should.
[*To the Angels*] But you who are God's true and faithful progeny—
Delight in the world's wealth of living beauty!
May the force that makes all life-forms to evolve,
Enfold you in the dear confines of love,
And the fitfulness, the flux of all appearance,
By enduring thoughts give enduring forms to its transience.
[*The Heavens close, the Archangels withdraw.*]
MEPHISTOPHELES I like to see the Old Man now and then,
And take good care I don't fall out with him.
How very decent of a Lord Celestial
To talk man to man with the Devil of all people.

Part I

Night

In a narrow, high-vaulted Gothic room, FAUST, *seated restlessly in an armchair at his desk.*

FAUST I've studied, alas, philosophy,
Law and medicine, recto and verso,[1]
And how I regret it, theology also,
Oh God, how hard I've slaved away,
With what result? Poor foolish old man,
I'm no whit wiser than when I began!
I've got a Master of Arts degree,
On top of that a Ph.D.,
For ten long years, around and about,
Upstairs, downstairs, in and out,
I've led my students by the nose
With what result? that nobody knows,
Or ever shall know, the tiniest crumb!
Which is why I feel completely undone.
Of course I'm cleverer than these stuffed shirts,
These Doctors, M.A.s, scribes and priests,
I'm not bothered by a doubt or a scruple,
I'm not afraid of Hell or the Devil—
But the consequence is, my mirth's all gone.
No longer can I fool myself
I'm able to teach anyone
How to be better, love true worth;
I've got no money or property,
Worldly honors or celebrity—
A dog wouldn't put up with this life!
Which is why I've turned to magic,
Seeking to know, by ways occult,
From ghostly mouths spells difficult,
So I no longer need to sweat
Painfully explaining what
I don't know anything about;
So I may penetrate the power
That holds the universe together,
Behold the source whence all proceeds
And deal no more in words, words, words.

O full moon, melancholy-bright,
Friend I've watched for, many a night,
Till your quiet-shining circle
Appeared above my book-heaped table,

1. "Recto and verso": Latin terms for the front and back of a sheet of paper.

If only you might never again
Look down from above on my pain,
If only I might stray at will
In your mild light, high on the hill,
Haunt with spirits upland hollows,
Fade with you in dim-lit meadows,
And soul no longer gasping in
The stink of learning's midnight oil,
Bathe in your dews till well again!

Oh misery! Oh am I still
Stuck here in this dismal prison?
A musty goddamned hole in the wall
Where even the golden light of heaven
Can only weakly make its way through
The painted panes of the gothic window;
Where all about me shelves of books
Rise up to the vault in stacks,
Books gray with dust, worm-eaten, rotten,
With soot-stained paper for a curtain;
Where instruments, retorts and glasses
Are crammed in everywhere a space is;
And squeezed in somehow with these things
My family's ancient furnishings
Make complete the sad confusion—
Call this a world, this world you live in?

Can you still wonder why your heart
Should clench in your breast so anxiously?
Why your every impulse is stopped short
By an inexplicable misery?
Instead of the living house of Nature
God created man to dwell in,
About you all is dust, mold, ordure,
Bones of beasts and long dead men.

Up! Fly to the open countryside!
And do you have a better guide
Than this mysterious book inscribed
By Nostradamus's[2] own hand?
What better help to master the secrets
Of how the stars turn in their orbits,
From Nature learn to understand
The spirits' power to speak to spirits.
Sitting here and racking your brains
To puzzle out the sacred signs—

2. The Latin name of the French astrologer and physician Michel de Notredame (1503–1566). His collection of rhymed prophecies, *The Centuries*, appeared in 1555.

What a sterile, futile business!
You hover, spirits, all around me—
Announce yourselves if you can hear me!
[*He opens the book and his eye encounters the sign of the Macrocosm.*[3]]
The pure bliss flooding all my senses,
Seeing this! Through every nerve and vein
I feel youth's fiery, fresh spirit race again.
Was it a god marked out this sign
By which my agitated bosom's stilled,
By which my bleak heart's filled with joy,
By whose mysterious agency
The forces of Nature about me stand revealed?
Am *I* a god? All's bright as day!
By these pure tracings I can see,
At my soul's feet, great Nature unconcealed.
And the sage's words I understand them finally:
"The spirit world is not barred shut,
It's your closed mind, your dead heart!
Stand up unappalled, my scholar,
And bathe your breast in the rose of aurora!"
[*He contemplates the sign.*]
How all is woven one, uniting
Each in the other, living, working!
Heavenly powers rise, descend,
Passing gold vessels from hand to hand!
On wings that scatter sweet-smelling blessings
Everywhere they post in earth,
And make a universal harmony sound forth!
Oh, what a show! But a show, nothing more.
How, infinite Nature, lay hold of you, where?
Where find your all-life-giving fountains?—breasts that sustain
The earth and the heavens which my shrunken breast
Yearns for with a feverish thirst—
You flow, overflow, must I keep on thirsting in vain?
[*Morosely, he turns the pages of the book and comes on the sign of the Spirit of Earth*][4]
How different an effect this sign has on me!
O Spirit of Earth, how near, how much nearer to me!
Already fresh life-blood pours through every vein,
Already I'm aglow as if with new wine—
Now, now I possess the courage to dare
To adventure into the wide world, bear
Earth's ill, earth's well, and bravely battle
The howling storms, when the ship splits, not to tremble.

3. The great world (literal trans.); the universe as a whole. It represents the ordered, harmonious universe in its totality.

4. This figure seems to be a symbol for the energy of terrestrial nature—neither good nor bad, merely powerful.

The air grows dark overhead—
The moon's put out her light.
The oil lamp's nearly dead.
Vapors rise, red flashes dart
Around my head—fright,
Shuddering down from the vault,
Seizes me by the throat!
Spirit I have invoked, hovering near:
Reveal yourself!
Ha! How my heart beats! All of my being's
Fumbling and groping amid never felt feelings!
Appear! Oh, you must! Though it costs me my life!

[*He seizes the book and pronounces the Spirit's mystic spell. A red flame flashes, in the midst of which the* SPIRIT *appears.*]

SPIRIT Who's calling?
FAUST (*Averting his face*) Overpowering! Dreadful!
SPIRIT Potently you've drawn me here,
A parched mouth sucking at my sphere.
And now—?
FAUST But you're unbearable!
SPIRIT You're breathless from your implorations
To see my face, to hear me speak.
I've yielded to your supplications
And here I am.—Well, shrinking, weak,
I find the superman! You call, I come,
And you're struck dumb. Is yours the breast
Inside of which an entire world was nursed
Into existence, a creation
On which you doted with mad elation,
Puffed up to think yourself the equal
Of us spirits, on our level?
Wherever is that fellow Faust
Who urged himself just now with all
His strength on me, made such a fuss?
You're Faust? The one who at my breath's
Least touch, shudders to his depths,
A thing that wriggles off, scared, a worm!
FAUST *I* shrink back from you, an airy flame?
I'm him, yes Faust, your equal, the same.
SPIRIT In flood tides of life, in tempests of doing,
Up and down running,
The here with there joining,
Birth with the grave,
An eternal ocean,
A weaving, reweaving,
A life aglow, burning—
So seated before time's humming loom,
I weave the Godhead's living costume.
FAUST We're equals, I know! I feel so close to you, near,

You busy spirit ranging everywhere!
SPIRIT You equal the spirit you think I am,
Not me! [*Vanishes.*]
FAUST [*Deflated*] Not you?
Then who?
Me, made in God's own image,
Not even equal to you?
[*A knocking*]
Death! My famulus[5]—I know that knock.
Finis my supremest moment—worse luck!
That visions richer than I could have guessed
Should be scattered by a shuffling dryasdust!
[WAGNER *in dressing gown and nightcap, carrying a lamp.* FAUST *turns around impatiently.*]
WAGNER Excuse me, sir, but that was your voice, wasn't it,
I heard declaiming? A Greek tragedy,
I'm sure. Well, that's an art that comes in handy
Nowadays, I'd love to master it.
People say, how often I have heard it,
Actors could really give lessons to the clergy.
FAUST Yes, so parsons can make a stage out of the pulpit—
Something I have seen in more than one case.
WAGNER Oh dear, to be so cooped up in one's study all day,
Seeing the world only now and then, on holiday,
Seeing people from far off, as if through a spyglass—
How persuade them to any effect in that way?
FAUST Unless you really feel it, no, you cannot—
Unless the words your lips declare are heartfelt
And by their soul-born spontaneous power,
Seize with delight the soul of your hearer.
But no! Stick in your seats, you scholars!
Paste bits and pieces together, cook up
A beggar's stew from others' leftovers
Over a flame you've sweated to coax up
From your own little heap of smoldering ashes,
Filling with wonder all the jackasses,
If that's the kind of stuff your taste favors.
But you'll never get heart to cleave to heart
Unless you speak from your own heart.
WAGNER Still and all, a good delivery is what
Makes the orator. I'm far behind in that art.
FAUST Advance yourself in an honest way,
Don't play the fool in cap and bells!
Good sense, good understanding, they
Are art enough, speak for themselves.
When you have something serious to say,
What need is there for hunting up

5. Assistant to a medieval scholar.

Fancy words, high-sounding phrases?
Your brilliant speeches, smartened up
With bits and pieces collected out
Of a miscellany of commonplaces
From all the languages spoken by all the races,
Are about as bracing as the foggy autumnal breeze
Swaying the last leaves on the trees.
WAGNER Dear God, but art is long,
And our life—much shorter.
Often in the middle of my labor
My confidence and courage falter.
How hard it is to master all the stuff
For dealing with each and every source,
And before you've traveled half the course,
Poor devil, you have gone and left this life.
FAUST Parchment, tell me—that's the sacred fount
You drink out of, to slake your eternal thirst?
The only true refreshment that exists
You get from where? Yourself—where all things start.
WAGNER But sir, it's such a pleasure, isn't it,
To enter into another age's spirit,
To see what the sages before us thought
And measure how far since we've got.
FAUST As far as to the stars, no doubt!
Your history, why, it's a joke;
Bygone times are a seven-sealed book.[6]
What you call an age's spirit,
What is it? Nothing but your own poor spirit
With the age reflected as you see it.
And it's pathetic, what's to be seen in your mirror.
One look and I head straight for the exit.
A trash can, strewn attic, junk-filled cellar,
At best a blood-and-thunder thriller
Improved with the most high-minded sentiments
Exactly suited for mouthing by marionettes.
WAGNER But this great world, the human mind and heart,
They are things all want to know about.
FAUST Yes, know as the world knows knowing!
Who wants to know the real truth, tell me?
Those few with vision, feeling, understanding
Who failed to stand guard, most unwisely,
Over their tongues, speaking their minds and hearts
For the mob to hear—you know what's been their fate:
They were crucified, burnt, torn to bits.
But we must break off, friend, it's getting late.
WAGNER I love such serious conversation, I do!
I'd stay up all night gladly talking to you.

6. Revelation 5.1.

But sir, it's Easter Sunday in the morning
And perhaps I may ask you a question or two then, if you're willing?
I've studied hard, with unrelaxing zeal,
I know a lot, but I want, sir, to know all. [*Exit.*]

FAUST [*Alone*] Such fellows keep their hopes up by forever
Busying themselves with trivialities,
Dig greedily in the ground for treasure
And when they turn a worm up—what ecstacies!
That banal, commonplace human accents
Should fill air just now filled with spirit voices!
Still, this one time you've earned my thanks,
Oh sorriest, oh shallowest of wretches!
You snatched me from the grip of a dejection
So profound, I was nearly driven off
My head. So gigantic was the apparition,
It made me feel no bigger than a dwarf—

Me, the image of God, certain in my belief
Soon, soon I'd behold the mirror of eternal truth,
Whose near presence I felt, already savoring
The celestial glory, stripped of my mortal clothing;
Me, higher placed than the angels, dreaming brashly
With the strength I possess I could flow freely,
Godlike creative, through Nature's live body—
Well, it had to be paid for: a single word
Thundered out knocked me flat, all my vain conceit curbed.
No, I can't claim we are equals, presumptuously!
Though I was strong enough to draw you down to me,
Holding on to you was another matter entirely.
In that exalted-humbling moment of pure delight
I felt myself at once both small and great.
And then you thrust me remorselessly back
Into uncertainty, which is all of humanity's fate.
Who'll tell me what to do? Not to do?
Still seek out the spirits to learn what they know?
Alas, what we do as much as what's done to us,
Obstructs the way stretching clearly before us.
The noblest conceptions to which our minds ever attained
Are more and more violated, oh how profaned!
When we've gained a bit of the good of this world for our prize,
Then the better's dismissed as delusion and lies;
Those radiant sentiments, once our breath of life,
Grow dim and expire in the madding crowd's strife.

Time was that hope and brave imagination
Boldly reached as far as to infinity,
But now misfortune piling on misfortune,
A little, confined space will satisfy.
It's then, heart deep, Care builds her nest,

Dithering nervously, killing joy, ruining rest,
Masking herself as this, as that concern
For house and home, for wife and children,
Fearing fire and flood, daggers and poison;
You shrink back in terror from imagined blows
And cry over losing what you never in fact lose.

Oh no, I'm no god, only too well do I know it!
A worm's what I am, wriggling through the dirt
And finding its nourishment in it,
Whom the passerby treads underfoot.

These high walls, every shelf crammed, every niche,
Dust is what shrinks them to a stifling cell,
This moth-eaten world with its all kinds of trash,
They are the reasons I feel shut up in jail.
And here I'll discover what it is that I lack?
Devour thousands of books so as to learn, shall I,
Mankind has always been stretched on the rack
With now and then somebody, somewhere's been happy?
You, empty skull there, smirking so, I know why—
What does it tell me, if not that your brain,
Whirling like mine, sought the bright sun of truth,
Only to wander, night-bewildered, in vain.
And all this apparatus, you mock me, you laugh
With your every wheel, cylinder, cog and ratchet,
I stood at the door, sure that you were the key,
Yet for all the bit's cunning design I couldn't unlatch it.
Mysterious even in broad daylight,
Nature lets no one part her veil,
And what she keeps hidden, out of sight,
All your levers and wrenches can't make her reveal.
You, ancient stuff I've left lying about,
You're here, and why?—my father[7] found you useful,
And you, old scrolls, have gathered soot
For as long as the lamp's smoked on this table.
Much better to have squandered the little I got
Than find myself sweating under the lot.
It's from our fathers, what we inherit,
To possess it really, we've got to earn it.
What you don't use is a dead weight,
What's worthwhile is what you spontaneously create.

But why do I find I must stare in that corner,
Is that bottle a magnet enchanting my sight?
Why is everything all at once brighter, clearer,
Like woods when the moon's up and floods them with light?

7. Later we learn that Faust's father was a doctor of medicine.

Vial, I salute you, exceptional, rare thing,
And reverently bring you down from the shelf,
Honoring in you man's craft and cunning—
Quintessence of easeful sleeping potions,
Pure distillation of subtle poisons,
Do your master the kindness that lies in your power!
One look at you and my agony lessens,
One touch and my feverish straining grows calmer
And my tight-stretched spirit bit by bit slackens.
The spirit's flood tide runs more and more out,
My way is clear, into death's immense sea,
The bright waters glitter before my feet,
A new day is dawning, new shores calling to me.

A fiery chariot, bird-winged, swoops down on me,
I am ready to follow new paths and higher,
Aloft into new spheres of purest activity—
An existence so exalted, so godlike a rapture,
Does the worm of a minute ago deserve it?
No matter. Never falter! Turn your back bravely
On the sunlight, sweet sunlight, of our earth forever,
Tear wide open those dark gates boldly
Which the whole world skulks past with averted heads.
The time has come to disprove by deeds,
Because the gods are great, man's a derision,
To cringe back no more from that black pit
Whose unspeakable tortures are your own invention,
To struggle toward that narrow gate
Around which all Hell flames in constant eruption,
To do it calmly, without regret;
Even at the risk of utter extinction.
And now let me lift this long forgotten
Crystal wine cup out of its chest.
You used to shine bright at the family feast,
Making the solemn guests' faces lighten
When you went round with each lively toast.
The figures artfully cut in the crystal
Which it was the duty of all at the table,
In turn, to make up rhymes about,
Then drain the cup at a single draught—
How they recall many nights of my youth!
But now there's no passing you on to my neighbor
Or thinking up rhymes to parade my quick wit;[8]
Here is a juice that is quick too—to intoxicate,
A brownish liquid, see, filling the beaker,

8. Faust here alludes to the drinking of toasts. The maker of a toast often produced impromptu rhymes.

Chosen by me, by me mixed together,
My last drink! Which now I lift up in festive greeting
To the bright new day I see dawning!
[He raises the cup to his lips. Bells peal, a choir bursts into song.]

CHORUS OF ANGELS
Christ is arisen!
Joy to poor mortals
By their own baleful,
Inherited, subtle
Failings imprisoned.

FAUST What deep-sounding burden, what tremelo strain
Arrest the glass before I can drink?
Does that solemn ringing already proclaim
The glorious advent of Holy Week?
Already, choirs, are you intoning
What angels' lips sang once, a comforting chant,
Above the sepulcher's darkness sounding,
Certain assurance of a new covenant?

CHORUS OF WOMEN
With spices and balm, we
Prepared the body,
Faithful ones, we
Laid him out in the tomb,
Clean in linen we wound him
And bound up his hair,
Oh, what do we find now?
Christ is not here.

CHORUS OF ANGELS
Christ is arisen!
Blest is the man of love,
He who the anguishing,
Bitter, exacting test,
Salvation bringing, passed.

FAUST But why do you seek me out in the dust,
You music of Heaven, mild and magnificent?
Sound out where men and women are simple,
Your message is clear but it leaves me indifferent,
And where belief's lacking no miracle's possible.
The spheres whence those glad tidings ring
Are not for me to try and enter,
Yet all's familiar from when I was young
And back to life I feel myself sent for.
Years ago loving Heaven's embrace
Flew down to me in the Sabbath stillness,
Oh, how the bells rang with such promise,
And fervently praying to Jesus, what bliss!
A yearning so sweet, not to be comprehended,
Drove me out into green wood and field,
In me an inner world expanded

As my cheeks ran wet from eyes tear-filled.
Your song gave the signal for the games we all joined in
When the springtime arrived with its gay festival,
Innocent childhood's remembered emotion
Holds me back from the last step of all—
O sound away, sound away, sweet songs of Heaven,
Earth claims me again, my tears well up, fall!

CHORUS OF DISCIPLES

Only just buried,
Ascended already.
Who lived sublimely,
On high rose in glory!
Joy of becoming, his,
Near to creating's bliss.
He on the earth's hard crust
Left us, his own, his best,
To languish and wait—
Oh, how we pity,
Master, your fate!

CHORUS OF ANGELS

Christ is arisen
From the bowels of decay,
Strike off your fetters
And shout for joy,
By good works praising him,
By loving, upraising him.
Feeding the least of all,
Preaching him east and west to all,
Promising bliss to all.
You have the Master near,
You have him here.

Outside the Town Gate

All sorts of people out walking.

SOME APPRENTICES Where are you fellows off to?
OTHERS To the hunters' lodge over that way.
FIRST BUNCH Well, we're on our way to the old mill.
ONE APPRENTICE The river inn—that's what I say.
SECOND APPRENTICE But the way I don't care for at all.
SECOND APPRENTICE And what about you?
THIRD APPRENTICE I'll stick with the rest of us here.
FOURTH APPRENTICE Let's go up to the village. There, I can promise you
The best-looking girls, the best tasting beer,
And some very good roughhousing too.
FIFTH APPRENTICE My, but aren't you greedy!
A third bloody nose—don't you care?
I'll never go there, it's too scary.

SERVANT GIRL No, no, I'm turning back, no, I won't stay.
ANOTHER We're sure to find him at those poplar trees.
FIRST GIRL Is that supposed to make me jump for joy?
It's you he wants to walk with, wants to please,
And you're the one he'll dance with. Fine
For you. And for me what? The spring sunshine!
THE OTHER He's not alone, I know, today. He said
He'd bring his friend—you know, that curlyhead.
A STUDENT Those fast-stepping girls there, look at the heft of them!
Into action, old fellow, we're taking out after them.
Beer with body, tobacco with a good rich taste,
And red-cheeked housemaids in their Sunday best
Are just the things to make your Hermann happiest.
A BURGHER'S DAUGHTER Oh look over there, such fine looking boys!
Really, I think they are simply wretches,
They have their pick of the nicest girls,
Instead they run after overweight wenches.
SECOND STUDENT [*To the first*] Hold up, go slow! I see two more,
And the pair of them dressed so pretty, so proper.
But I know that one! She lives next door,
And her, I can tell you, I think I could go for.
They loiter along, eyes lowered decorously.
After saying no twice, they'll jump at our company.
FIRST STUDENT No, no—all that bowing and scraping, it makes me feel ill at ease,
If we don't get a move on we'll lose our two birds in the bushes;
The work-reddened hand that swings the broom Saturday
On Sunday knows how to give the softest caresses.
A BURGHER No, you can have him; our new Mayor,
Since he took office he's been a dictator,
All he's done is make the town poorer,
Every day I get madder and madder,
When he says a thing's so, not a peep, not a murmur
Dare we express—and the taxes climb higher.
A BEGGAR [*Singing*]
Good sirs and all you lovely ladies,
Healthy in body and handsome in dress,
Turn, oh turn your eyes on me, please,
And pity the beggarman's distress!
Must I grind the organ fruitlessly?
Only the charitable know true joy.
This day when the whole world dances merrily,
Make it for me a harvest day.
ANOTHER BURGHER On a Sunday or holiday nothing in all my experience
Beats talking about war and rumors of war,
When leagues away, in Turkey, for instance,
Armies are wading knee deep in gore.
You stand at the window, take long pulls at your schooner,
And watch the gaily colored boats glide past,

And then at sunset go home in the best of humor
And praise God for the peace by which we're blest.

THIRD BURGHER Yes, neighbor, yes, exactly my opinion.
Let them go and beat each other's brains in,
Let them turn the whole world upside down,
As long as things are just as always in our town.

OLD CRONE [*To the* BURGHERS' DAUGHTERS]
How smart we all are! And so pretty and young,
I'd like to see the man who could resist you.
But not so proud, my dears. Just come along,
Oh I know how to get what you want for you.

BURGHER'S DAUGHTER Agatha, come! The awful fright!
I'm afraid of being seen with that witchwoman.
It's true that last St. Andrew's Night[1]
She showed me in a glass my very own one.

HER FRIEND And mine she showed me in a crystal sphere
Looking a soldier, with swaggering friends around him,
And though I watch out everywhere,
I have no luck, I never seem to find him.

SOLDIERS

Castles have ramparts,
Great walls and towers,
Girls turn their noses up
At soldier-boy lovers—
We'll make both ours!
Boldly adventure
And rake in the pay!

Hear the shrill bugle
Summon to battle,
Forward to rapture
Or forward to ruin!
Oh what a struggle!
Our life—oh how stirring!
Haughty girls, high-walled castles,
We'll make them surrender!
Boldly adventure
And rake in the pay!
—And after, the soldiers
Go marching away.

FAUST *and* WAGNER.

FAUST The streams put off their icy mantle
Under the springtime's quickening smile,
Hope's green banner flies in the valley;
White-bearded winter, old and frail,

1. November 29, the traditional time for young girls to consult fortune tellers about their future lovers or husbands.

Retreats back up into the mountains,
And still retreating, down he sends
Feeble volleys of sleet showers,
Whitening in patches new-green plains.
But the sun can bear with white no longer,
When life stirs, shaping all anew,
He wants a scene that has some color,
And since there's nowhere yet one flower,
Holiday crowds have got to do.
Now face about and looking down
From the hilltop back to town,
See the brightly colored crowd
Pouring like a spring flood
Through the gaping, gloomy arch
To bask in the sun all love so much.
They celebrate the Savior's rising,
For they themselves today are risen:
From airless rooms in huddled houses,
From drudgery at counters and benches,
From under cumbrous roofs and gables,
From crowded, suffocating alleys,
From the mouldering dimness of the churches,
They hurry to where all is brightness.
And look there, how the eager crowd
Scatters through the fields and gardens,
How over the river's length and breadth
Skiffs and sculls are busily darting,
And that last boat, packed near to sinking,
Already's pulled a good ways off.
Even from distant mountain slopes
Bright colored clothes wink back at us.
Now I can hear it, the village commotion,
Out here, you can tell, is the people's true heaven,
Young and old crying exultingly—
Here I am human, here I can be free!

WAGNER To go for a walk with you, dear Doctor,
Is a treat for my mind as well as honoring me,
But by myself I'd never come near here,
For I can't abide the least vulgarity.
The fiddling, shrieking, clashing bowls,
For me are all an unbearable uproar,
All scream and shout like possessed souls
And call it music, call it pleasure.

PEASANTS [*Singing and dancing under the linden tree*]
The shepherd dressed up in his best,
Pantaloons and flowered vest,
Oh my, how brave and handsome!
Within the broad-leaved linden's shade
Madly spun both man and maid,

Tra-la! Tra-la!
Tra-la-la-la! Tra-lay!
The fiddle bow flew and then some.
He flung himself into their midst
And seized a young thing round the waist,
While saying, "Care to dance, ma'am?"
The snippy miss she tossed her head,
"You boorish shepherd boy!" she said,
Tra-la! Tra-la!
Tra-la-la-la! Tra-lay!
"Observe, do, some decorum!"
But round the circle swiftly wheeled,
To right and left the dancers whirled,
Till all the breath flew from them.
They got so red, they got so warm,
They rested, panting, arm in arm,
Tra-la! Tra-la!
Tra-la-la-la! Tra-lay!
And breast to breast—a twosome.

"I'll thank you not to make so free!
We girls know well how men betray,
What snakes lurk in your bosom!"
But still he wheedled her away—
Far off they heard the fiddle play,
Tra-la! Tra-la!
Tra-la-la-la! Tra-lay!
The screaming, uproar, bedlam!

OLD PEASANT Professor, welcome! Oh how kind
To join us common folk today,
Though such a fine man, learned mind,
Not to scorn our holiday.
So please accept our best cup, sir,
Brimful with the freshest beer.
We hope that it will quench your thirst,
But more than that, we pray and hope
Your sum of days may be increased
By as many drops are in the cup.

FAUST Friends, thanks for this refreshment, I
In turn wish you all health and joy.
[*The people make a circle around him.*]

OLD PEASANT Indeed it's only right that you
Should be with us this happy day,
Who when our times were hard, a true
Friend he proved in every way.
Many a one stands in his boots here
Whom your good father, the last minute,
Snatched from the hot grip of the fever,

That time he quelled the epidemic.[2]
And you yourself, a youngster then,
Never shrank back; every house
The pest went in, you did too.
Out they carried many a corpse,
But never yours. Much you went through;
Us you saved, and God saved you.

ALL Health to our tried and trusty friend,
And may his kindness have no end.

FAUST Bow down to him who dwells above
Whose love shows us how we should love.
[*He continues on with* WAGNER.]

WAGNER What gratification must be yours
To win such popular applause.
Lucky the man, thanks to his gifts,
Can count on receiving handsome emoluments!
Fathers point you out to their boys,
The fiddle stops, the dancers pause,
And as you pass between the rows
Of people, caps fly in the air. Why,
Next you know they'll all be on their knees
As if the host itself[3] were passing by.

FAUST A few steps more to that rock where we'll rest
A bit, shall we, from our walk. How often
I would sit alone here, musing, thinking, sighing,
And torture myself with praying, fasting, crying.
So much hope I had then, such great trust—
I'd wring my hands, I'd weep, fall on my knees,
Believing God, in this way forced
To look below, must call a halt to the disease.
But now these people's generous praise of me
I find a mockery. If only you could see
Into my heart, you would realize
How little worthy father and son were really.
My father was an upright man, a lonely,
Brooding soul who searched great Nature's processes
With a head crammed full of the most bizarre hypotheses.
Shutting himself with fellow masters up in
The vaulted confines of their vaporous Black Kitchen,[4]
He mixed together opposites according
To innumerable recipes. A bold Red Lion,[5]
Handsome suitor he, took for wedding

2. Pestilence or plague.
3. The Eucharist, the consecrated bread of the Sacrament.
4. Laboratory where Faust experiments with black magic and alchemy.
5. Name for the red-colored mercuric oxide which Faust here "marries" to hydrochloric acid (which he calls "White Lily") to produce "the young Queen," a medicine to be used to cure the plague.

Partner a pure White Lily, the two uniting
In a tepid bath; then being tested by fire,
The pair precipitately fled
From one bridal chamber to another,
Till there appeared, within the glass,
The young Queen, dazzlingly dressed
In every color of the spectrum:
The Sovereign Remedy—a futile nostrum.
The patients died; none stopped to inquire
How many there were who got better.[6]
So with our infernal electuary
We killed our way across the country.
I poisoned, myself, by prescription, thousands,
They sickened and faded; yet I must live to see
On every side the murderers' fame emblazoned.

WAGNER But why be so distressed, there is no reason.
If you conscientiously, with full devotion,
Practise all the arts your father practised,
You've done enough, done all can be expected.
A youth who is respectful of his father
Listens and learns all that he has to teach.
If he's able himself to lengthen science's reach,
His son in turn can reach goals even farther.

FAUST Oh, he's a happy man who hopes
To keep from drowning in these seas of error!
What we know least we need the most,
And what we do know is no use whatever.
But such cheerlessness blasphemes
The quiet sweetness of this shining hour,
Look, how the sunset's level beams
Gild those cottages in their green bower,
The brightness fades, the sun makes his adieu,
Hurrying off to kindle new life elsewhere—
If only I had wings to rise into
The air and follow ever after!
Then I would see the whole world at my feet,
Quietly shining in the eternal sunset,
The peaks ablaze, the valleys gone to sleep,
And babbling into golden stream the silver runlet.
The savage mountain with its plunging cliffs
Should never balk my godlike soaring,
And there's the ocean, see, already swelling
Before my wondering gaze, with its sun-warmed gulfs.
But finally the bright god looks like sinking,
Whereupon a renewed urgency
Drives me on to drink his eternal light,
The day always before, behind the night,

6. This confusing sequence evokes a kind of medicine closely allied to magic.

The heavens overhead, below the heaving sea . . .
A lovely dream!—and meanwhile it grows dark.
Oh dear, oh dear, that our frames should lack
Wings with which to match our soaring spirit,
Yet every soul there is, no matter whose it,
Knows feelings that strive upwards, onwards, straining,
When high above, lost in the azure evening,
The skylark pours out his shrill rhapsody,
When over fir-clad mountain peaks
The eagle on his broad wings gyres silently,
And passing over prairies, over lakes,
The homeward-bound crane labors steadily.

WAGNER Well, I've had more than one odd moment, I have,
But I have never felt those impulses you have.
Soon enough you get your fill of woods and things,
I don't really envy birds their wings.
How different are the pleasures of the intellect,
Sustaining one from page to page, from book to book,
And warming winter nights with dear employment
And with the consciousness your life's so lucky.
And goodness, when you spread out an old parchment,
Heaven's fetched straight down into your study.

FAUST You know the one great driving force,
May you never know the other!
Two souls live in me, alas,
Irreconcilable with one another.
One, lusting for the world with all its might,
Grapples it close, greedy of all its pleasures,
The other rises up, up from the dirt,
Up to the blest fields where dwell our great forbears.

O beings of the air if you exist,
Holding sway between the heaven and earth,
Come down to me out of the golden mist
And translate me to a new, a vivid life!
Oh, if I only had a magic mantle
To bear me off to foreign lands, strange people,
I'd never trade it for the costliest gown
Or for a cloak however rich and royal.

WAGNER Never call them down, the dreadful swarm
That swoop and hover through the atmosphere,
Bringing mankind every kind of harm
From every corner of the terrestrial sphere.
From the North they bare their razor teeth
And prick you with their arrow-pointed tongues,
From the East, sighing with parched breath,
They eat away your dessicated lungs.
And when from southern wastes they gust and sough.
Fire on fire on your sunk head heaping,

From the West they send for your relief
Cooling winds—then drown fields just prepared for reaping.
Their ears are cocked, on trickery intent,
Seem dutiful while scheming to defeat us,
Their pretense is that they are heaven sent
And lisp like angels even as they cheat us.
However, come, let's go, the world's turned gray
And chilly, evening mists are rising,
At nightfall it's indoors you want to be.
But why should you stand still, astonished, staring?
What can you see in the dusk to find upsetting?

FAUST Don't you see that black dog in the stubble
Coursing back and forth?

WAGNER I do. I saw that one
A while back. What about him?

FAUST Look again.
What kind of creature is it?

WAGNER Kind? A poodle—
Worried where his master is and always
Sniffing about to find his scent.

FAUST Look, he's
Circling around us, coming near and nearer.
Unless I'm much mistaken, a wake of fire
'S streaming after him.

WAGNER I see nothing
But a black-haired poodle. Your eyes are playing
Tricks on you, perhaps.

FAUST I think I see
Him winding a magic snare, quietly,
Around our feet, a noose which he'll pull tight
In the future when the time is right.

WAGNER He's circling us because he's timid and uncertain,
He's missed his master, come on men unknown to him.

FAUST The circle's getting tighter, he's much closer!

WAGNER You see!—a dog, and no ghost, sir.
He growls suspiciously, he hesitates,
He wags his tail, lies down and waits.
Never fear, it's all just dog behavior.

FAUST Come here, doggie, come here, do!

WAGNER A silly poodle, a poor creature,
When you stop, he stops too,
Speak to him, he'll leap and bark,
Throw something and he'll fetch it back,
Go after your stick right into the river.

FAUST I guess you're right, it's just what he's been taught,
I see no sign of anything occult.

WAGNER A dog whose conduct is so good, so clever,
Why, even a philosopher would stoop to pet him.

Some student trained him, he proved an apt scholar—
Sir, he deserves you should adopt him.
[*They enter at the Town Gate*]

Faust's Study [I]

FAUST [*Entering with the poodle*]
Behind me lie the fields and meadows
Shrouded in the lowering dark,
In dread of what waits in the shadows
Our better soul now starts awake.
Our worser one, unruly, reckless,
Quietens and starts to nod;
In me the love of my own fellows
Begins to stir, and the love of God.

Quiet, poodle! Stop! A dozen
Dogs you seem, all sniffing at the doorsill!
Here's my own cushion for you to doze on
Behind the stove—if you are gentle.
Just now when we came down the hillside
You gambolled like the friendliest beast.
I'm glad to take you in, provide
Your keep—provided you're a silent guest.

When once again the lamp light brightens
With its soft glow your narrow cell,
Oh in your breast how then it lightens,
And deeper in your heart as well.
Again you hear the voice of reason
And hope revives, it breathes afresh,
You long to drink the living waters,
Mount upwards to our being's source.

You're growling, poodle! Animal squealings
Hardly suit the exalted feelings
Filling my soul to overflowing.
We're used to people ridiculing
What they hardly understand,
Grumbling at the good and the beautiful—
It makes them so uncomfortable!
Do dogs now emulate mankind?
Yet even with the best of will
I feel my new contentment fail.
Why must the waters cease so soon
And leave us thirsting once again?
Oh, this has happened much too often!
But there's an answer to it all:

I mean the supernatural,
I mean our hope of revelation,
Which nowhere shines so radiant
As here in the New Testament.
I'll look right now at the original[1]
And see if it is possible
For me to make a true translation
Into my beloved German.
[*He opens the volume and begins.*]
"In the beginning was the Word"[2]—so goes
The text. And right off I am given pause,
A little help, please, someone, I'm unable
To see the *word* as first, most fundamental.
If I am filled with the true spirit
I'll find a better way to say it.
So: "In the beginning *mind* was—right?
Give plenty of thought to what you write,
Lest your pen prove too impetuous.
Is it mind that makes and moves the universe?
Shouldn't it be: "In the beginning
Power was," before it nothing?
Yet even as I write this down on paper
Something tells me don't stop there, go farther.
The Spirit's prompt in aid; now, now indeed,
I know for sure: "In the beginning was the *Deed*!"

If this cell's one we'll share, each helping.
Poodle, stop that barking, yelping!
You're giving me a splitting headache,
I can't put up with such a roommate.
One of us
Has got to quit the premises.
It goes against the grain with me
To renege on hospitality,
But there's the door, dog, leave, goodbye.

But what's that I'm seeing,
A shadow or real thing?
It beggars belief—
My poodle's swelled up huger than life!
He heaves up his hulk—
No dog has such bulk!
What a spook I have brought
In my house without thought.
He looks, with his fierce eyes and jaws,
Just like a hippopotamus—
But I've got you, you're caught!

1. That is, the Greek.
2. John 1.1.

For a half-hellhound like you are,
Solomon's Key[3] is what is called for.

SPIRITS [*Outside the door*]
Someone is locked in there!
No one's allowed in there!
Like a fox hunters snared,
Old Scratch, he shivers, scared.
Be careful, watch out!
Hover this way, now that,
About and again about,
And you'll soon see he's out.
If you can help him,
Don't let him sit there,
All of us owe him
For many a favor.

FAUST Against such a creature my first defense,
The Spell of the Four Elements:

Let the salamander turn red,
The undine winding flow,
Let the sylph disappear,
The kobold[4] go to work.

Ignorance
Of the elements,
Their power and properties,
Denies you all mastery
Over the demonry.

Up in flames fly,
Salamander!
In soft murmurings,
Undine, die!
Meteor bright glitter,
Sylph!
Help, help bring us,
Incubus!
Come out, come out, enough's enough.

None of the four
Is in the cur,
Calmly he lies there grinning at me;
My spells glance off him harmlessly.
—Now hear me conjure
With something stronger.

3. The *Clavicula Salomonis*, a standard work used by magicians for conjuring. In many medieval legends, Solomon was noted as a great magician.

4. A spirit of the earth. "Salamander": spirit of fire. "Undine": spirit of water. "Sylph": spirit of air.

Are you, grim fellow,
Escaped here from Hell below?
Then look at this symbol
Before which the legions
Of devils and demons
Fearfully bow.

How his hair bristles, how he swells up now!

Creature cast into darkness,
Can you make out its meaning?
—The never-begotten One,
Wholly ineffable One,
Carelessly-pierced-in-the-side One,
Whose blood in the heavens
Is everywhere streaming,

Behind the stove by me sent,
Bulging big as an elephant,
The entire cell filling,
Into mist himself willing—
No, no! Not through the ceiling!
At my feet fall, Master's bidding,
My threats, as you see, are hardly idle,
With holy fire, out I'll rout you, I will!
Wait if you wish
For my triune[5] light's hot flash,
Wait till you force me
To use my potentest sorcery.

[*The mist clears, and* MEPHISTOPHELES, *dressed as a traveling student, emerges from behind the stove.*]

MEPHISTO Why all the racket? What's your wish, sir?

FAUST So it's you who was the poodle!
I have to laugh—a wandering scholar.

MEPHISTO My greetings to you, learned doctor,
You really had me sweating hard there.

FAUST And what's your name?

MEPHISTO Your question's trivial
From one who finds words superficial,
Who strives to pass beyond mere seeming
And penetrate the heart of being.[6]

FAUST With gentry like yourself, it's common
To find the name declares who you are
Very plainly. I'll just mention

5. Perhaps the Trinity or a triangle with divergent rays.

6. Mephistopheles refers to Faust's substitution of "*Deed*" or "*Word*" in the passage from John (see line 904).

Lord of the Flies,[7] Destroyer, Liar.
So say who you are, if you would.
MEPHISTO A humble part of that great power
Which always means evil, always does good.
FAUST Those riddling words mean what, I'd like to know.
MEPHISTO I am the spirit that says no, no,
Always! And how right I am! For surely
It's right that everything that comes to be
Should cease to be. And so they do. Still better
Would be nothing ever was. Hence sin
And havoc and ruin—all you call evil, in sum—
For me's the element in which I swim.
FAUST A part, you say? You look like the whole works to me.
MEPHISTO I say what's so, it isn't modesty—
Man in his world of self's a fool,
He likes to think he's all in all.
I'm part of the part which was all at first,
A part of the dark out of which light burst,
Arrogant light which now usurps the air
And seeks to thrust Night from her ancient chair,
To no avail. Since light is one with all
Things bodily, making them beautiful,
Streams from them, from them is reflected,
Since light by matter's manifested—
When by degrees all matter's burnt up and no more,
Why, then light shall not matter any more.
FAUST Oh, now I understand your office:
Since you can't wreck Creation wholesale,
You're going at it bit by bit, retail.
MEPHISTO And making, I fear, little progress.
The opposite of nothing-at-all,
The *something*, this great shambling world,
In spite of how I exert myself against it,
Phlegmatically endures my every onset
By earthquake, fire, tidal wave and storm:
Next day the land and sea again are calm.
And all that *stuff*, those animal and human species—
I can hardly make a dent in them.
The numbers I've already buried, armies!
Yet fresh troops keep on marching up again.
That's how it is, it's enough to drive you crazy!
From air, from water, from the earth
Seeds innumerable sprout forth
In dry and wet and cold and warm!
If I hadn't kept back fire for myself,
What the devil could I call my own?
FAUST So against the goodly, never-resting,

7. An almost literal translation of the name of the Philistine deity Beelzebub.

Beneficent creative force,
In impotent spite you ball your fist and
Try to arrest life's onward course?
Look around for work that's more rewarding,
You singular son of old Chaos!
MEPHISTO Well, it's a subject for discussion—
At our next meeting. Now I wish
To go. That is, with your permission.
FAUST But why should *you* ask *me* for leave?
We've struck up an acquaintance, we two,
Drop in on me whenever you please.
There's the door and there's the window,
And ever reliable, there's the chimney.
MEPHISTO Well . . . you see . . . an obstacle
Keeps me from dropping *out*—so sorry!
That witch's foot chalked on your doorsill.
FAUST The pentagram's[8] the difficulty?
But if it's that that has you stopped,
How did you ever manage an entry?
And how should a devil like you get trapped?
MEPHISTO Well, look close and you'll see that
A corner's open: the outward pointing
Angle's lines don't quite meet.
FAUST What a stroke of luck! I'm thinking
Now you are my prisoner.
Pure chance has put you in my power!
MEPHISTO The poodle dashed right in, saw nothing,
But now the case is the reverse;
The Devil can't get out of the house!
FAUST There's the window, why don't you use it?
MEPHISTO It's an iron law we devils can't flout,
The way we come in we've got to go out,
We're free as to entrée but not as to exit.
FAUST So even in Hell there's law and order!
I'm glad, for then a man might sign
A contract with you gentlemen.
MEPHISTO Whatever we promise, you get, full measure,
There's no cutting corners, no skulduggery—
But it's not a thing to be done in a hurry;
Let's save the subject for our next get-together.
And as for now, I beg you earnestly:
Release me from the spell that binds me!
FAUST Why rush off, stay a while, do.
I'd love to hear some more from you.
MEPHISTO Let me go now, I swear I'll come back,

8. A magic five-pointed star designed to keep away evil spirits.

Then you can ask me whatever you like.
FAUST Trapping you was never my thought,
You trapped yourself, it's your own fault.
Who's nabbed the Devil must keep a tight grip,
You don't grab him again once he gives you the slip.
MEPHISTO Oh, all right! To please you, I
Will stay and keep you company,
Provided with my arts you let me
Entertain you in my own way.
FAUST Delighted, go ahead. But please
Make sure those arts of yours amuse!
MEPHISTO You'll find, my friend, your senses in one hour
More teased and roused than all the long dull year,
The songs the fluttering spirits murmur in your ear,
The visions they unfold of sweet desire,
Oh they are more than just tricks meant to fool.
By Arabian scents you'll be delighted,
Your palate tickled, never sated,
The ravishing sensations you will feel!
No preparation's needed, none,
Here we are. Let the show begin!
SPIRITS Open, you gloomy
Vaulted ceiling above him,
Let the blue ether
Look benignly in on him,
And dark cloudbanks scatter
So that all is fair for him!
Starlets are glittering,
Milder suns glowing,
Angelic troops shining
In celestial beauty
Hover past smiling,
Bending and bowing.
Ardent desire
Follows them yearning,
And their robes
Veil the fields, veil the meadows,
Veil the arbors where lovers
In pensive surrender
Give themselves to each other
For ever and ever.
Arbor on arbor!
Vines clambering and twining!
Their heavy clusters,
Poured into presses,
Pour out purple wines
Which descend in dark streams
Over beds of bright stones

Down the vineyards' steep slopes
To broaden to lakes
At the foot of green hills.
Birds blissfully drink there,
With beating wings sunwards soar,
Soar towards the golden isles
Shimmering hazily
On the horizon,
Where we hear voices
Chorusing jubilantly,
Where we see dancers
Whirling exuberantly
Over the meadows,
Here, there and everywhere.
Some climb the heights,
Some swim in the lakes,
Others float in the air—
Joying in life, all,
Beneath the paradisal
Stars glowing with love
Afar in the distance.

MEPHISTO Asleep! Well done, my every airy youngling!
Into a drowse you've sung him, never stumbling,
I am in your debt for this performance.
—As for you, sir, you were never born
To keep the Prince of Darkness down!
Let sweet dream-shapes crowd round him in confusion,
Drown him in a deep sea of delusion.
But from this doorsill-magic to be freed
A rat's tooth is the thing I need.
No point to conjuring long-windedly,
There's one rustling nearby, he'll soon hear me.

The lord of flies and rats and mice,
Of frogs and bedbugs, worms and lice,
Commands you forth from your dark hole
To gnaw, beast, for me that doorsill
Whereon I dab this drop of oil!
—And there you are! Begin, begin!
The corner that is pointing in,
That's the one that shuts me in;
One last crunch to clear my way.
Now Faustus, till we meet next—dream away!

FAUST [*Awakening*] Deceived again, am I, by tricks,
Those vanished spirits just a hoax,
A dream the Devil, nothing more,
The dog I took home just a cur?

Faust's Study [II]

FAUST, MEPHISTOPHELES.

FAUST A knock, was that? Come in! Who is it this time?
MEPHISTO Me.
FAUST Come in!
MEPHISTO You have to say it still a third time.
FAUST
All right, all right—come in!
MEPHISTO Good, very good!
We two shall get along, I see, just as we should.
I've come here dressed up as a Junker[1] Why?
To help you drive your blues away!
In a scarlet suit, all over gold braid,
Across my shoulders a stiff silk cape,
A gay cock's feather in my cap,
At my side a gallant's bold blade—
And bringing you advice that's short and sweet:
Put fine clothes on like me, cut loose a bit,
Be free and easy, man, throw off your yoke
And find out what real life is like.
FAUST In any clothes, I'd feel the misery
Of this cramped, suffocating life on earth.
I'm too old to live for amusement only,
Too young to wish for nothing, wait for death.
The world—what has it got to say to me?
Renounce all that you long for, all—renounce!
That's the truth that all pronounce
So sagely, so interminably,
The non-stop croak, the universal chant:
You can't have what you want, you can't!
I awake each morning, how? Horrified,
On the verge of tears, to confront a day
Which at its close will not have satisfied
One smallest wish of mine, not one. Why,
Even the hope of a bit of pleasure, some pleasantness,
Withers in the atmosphere of mean-spirited fault-finding,
My lively nature's quick inventiveness
Is thwarted by cares that seem to have no ending,
And when the night draws on and all is hushed,
I go to bed not soothed at last, but apprehensively,
Well knowing what awaits me is not rest,
But wild and whirling dreams that terrify me.
The god who dwells inside my breast,
Able to stir me to my depths, so powerfully,

1. A noble. In the popular plays based on the Faust legend, the Devil often appeared as a monk when the play catered to a Protestant audience and as a noble squire when the audience was mainly Catholic.

The master strength of all my strengths,
Is impotent to effect a single thing outside me.
And so I find existence burdensome, wretched,
Death eagerly desired, my life hated.
MEPHISTO Yet the welcome men give death is never wholehearted.
FAUST Happy the man, even as he conquers gloriously,
Death sets the blood-stained laurel on his brows,
Happy the man, after dancing the night through furiously,
Death finds him in a girl's arms in a drowse.
If only, overwhelmed by the Spirit's power,
In raptures I had died right then and there!
MEPHISTO And yet that very night, I seem to remember,
A fellow didn't down a drink I saw him prepare.
FAUST Spying around, I see, is what you like to do.
MEPHISTO I don't know everything, but I know a thing or two.
FAUST If a sweet, familiar harmony
When I was staggering, arrested me,
Beguiled what's left of childhood feeling
From a time when all was gay and smiling—
Well, never again, I pronounce a curse on
All false and flattering persuasion,
All tales that cheat the soul, constrain
It to endure this house of pain.
First I curse man's mind for thinking
Much too well of itself; I curse
The show of things, bedazzling, blinding,
That assails us through our every sense;
Our dreams of fame, of our name's enduring,
Oh what a sham, I curse them too;
I curse as hollow all our having,
Curse wife and child, peasant and plow;
I curse Mammon[2] when he incites us
With dreams of treasure to reckless deeds,
Or plumps the cushions for our pleasure
As we lie lazily at ease;
Curse comfort sucked out of the grape,
Curse love on its pinnacle of bliss,
Curse faith, so false, curse all vain hope,
And patience most of all I curse!
SPIRIT CHORUS [*Invisible*]
Pity, oh pity!
Now you have done it—
Spoiled
The lovely world!
One mighty blow
And down it falls

2. The Aramaic word for "riches," used in the New Testament of the Bible. Medieval writers interpreted the word as a proper noun, the name of the Devil, as representing greed.

Smashed
By a demigod's fist.
We sweep the rubble
Away into nothing,
And mourn
All the beauty gone.
Omnificent
Son of the earth,
Rebuild it,
Magnificent,
Inside your heart,
With a clear head and strong,
Singing a new song.
Come,
Make a fresh start!

MEPHISTO Lesser ones, these are
Of my order,
Active be, cheerful,
Is their sage counsel.
Out of your loneliness,
Weak-blooded languidness,
Their voices draw you
Into the wide world before you.

Stop making love to your misery,
It eats away at you like a vulture!
Even in the meanest company
You'd feel a man like any other.
Not that I'm proposing to
Put you down among the rabble.
I'm not your grandest devil, no.
But still, throw in with me—that way, united,
Together life's long road we'll travel,
And my, how I would be delighted!
I'll do your will as if my will,
Every wish of yours fulfill,
By your leave
Be your bond servant, be your slave.

FAUST And in return what must I do?

MEPHISTO There's plenty of time for that, forget it.

FAUST No, no, the Devil must have his due,
He doesn't do things for the hell of it,
Just to see another fellow through.
So let's hear the terms, what the fine print is,
Having you for a servant's a tricky business.

MEPHISTO I promise I will serve your wishes—here,
A slave who does your bidding faithfully;
But if we meet each other—there,
Why, you must do the same for me.

FAUST That "there" of yours—it doesn't scare me off;
If you pull this world down about my ears,
Let the other one come on, who cares?
My joys are part and parcel of this earth.
It's under this sun that I suffer,
And once it's goodbye, last leave taken,
Then let whatever happens happen,
And that is that. About the hereafter
We have had enough palaver,
More than I want to hear, by far:
If still we love and hate each other,
If some stand high and some stand lower,
Et cetera, et cetera.

MEPHISTO In that case, an agreement's easy.
Come, dare it! Come, your signature!
Oh, how my tricks will tickle your fancy!
I'll show you things no man has seen before.

FAUST You poor devil, really, what have you got to offer?
The mind of man in its sublime endeavor,
Tell me, have you ever understood it?
Oh yes indeed, you've bread, and when I eat it
I'm hungry still; you've yellow gold—it's flighty,
Quicksilver-like it's gone and my purse empty;
Games of chance no man can win at, ever;
Girls who wind me in their arms, their lover,
While eyeing up a fresh one over my shoulder;
There's fame, last failing of a noble nature,
It shoots across the sky a second, then it's over.
Oh yes, do show me fruit that rots as you try
To pick it, trees whose leaves bud daily, daily die!

MEPHISTO Marvels like that? For a devil, not so daunting,
I'm good for whatever you have in mind.
—But friend, the day comes when you find
A share of your own in life's good things,
And peace and quiet, are what you're wanting.

FAUST If ever you see me loll at ease,
Then it's all yours, you can have it, my life!
If ever you fool me with flatteries
Into feeling satisfied with myself,
Or tempt me with visions of luxuries,
That's it, the last day that I breathe this air,
I'll bet you!

MEPHISTO Done! A bet!

FAUST A bet! I swear!
If ever I plead with the passing moment,
"Linger a while, you are so fair!"
Then chain me up in close confinement,
Then serving me no more's your care,
Then let the death bell toll my finish,

Then unreluctantly I'll perish,
The clock may stop, the hands fall off,
And time for me be over with!

MEPHISTO Think twice. Forgetting's not a thing we do.

FAUST Of course, quite right—a bet's a bet,
This isn't anything I'm rushing into.
But if I stagnate, fall into a rut,
I'm a slave, no matter who to,
To this one, that one, or to you.

MEPHISTO My service starts now—no procrastinating!—
At the dinner tonight for the just-made Ph.D.s.
But there's one thing: you know, for emergencies,
I'd like to have our arrangement down in writing.

FAUST In black and white you want it—oh the pedantry!
You've never learnt a *man's* word's your best guarantee?
It's not enough for you that I'm committed
By what I promise till the end of days?
—Yet the world's a flood sweeps all along before it,
And why should I feel my word holds always?
A strange idea, but that's the way we are,
And who would want it otherwise?
That man's blessed who keeps his conscience clear,
He'll regret no sacrifice,
Yet parchment signed and stamped and sealed,
Is a bogey all recoil from, scared.
The pen does in the living word,
Only sealing wax and vellum[3] count, honor must yield.
Base spirit, say what you require!
Brass or marble, parchment or paper?
Shall I use a quill, a stylus, chisel?
I leave it up to you, you devil!

MEPHISTO Why get so hot, make extravagant speeches?
Ranting away does no good.
A scrap of paper takes care of the business.
And sign it with a drop of blood.

FAUST Oh, all right. If that's what makes you happy,
I'll go along with the tomfoolery.

MEPHISTO Blood's a very special ink, you know.

FAUST Are you afraid that I won't keep our bargain?
With every inch of me I'll strive, I'll never slacken!
So I've promised, that's what I will do.
I had ideas too big for me,
Your level's mine, that's all I'm good for.
The Spirit laughed derisively,
Nature won't allow me near her.
Thinking's done with for me, I'm through,

3. Sealing wax is melted to close documents, and vellum is a kind of parchment used for writing.

Learning I've loathed since long ago.
—Then fling ourselves into the dance
Of sensual extravagance!
Bring on your miracles, each one,
Inscrutably veiled in your sorcery!
We'll plunge into time's pell-mell run.
The vortex of activity,
Where pleasure and distress,
Setbacks and success,
May come as they come, by turn-about, however;
To be always up and doing is man's nature.

MEPHISTO No limits restrain you, do just as you like,
A little taste here, a nibble, a lick,
You see something there, snatch it up on the run,
Let all that you do with gusto be done,
Only don't be bashful, wade right in.

FAUST I told you, I'm not out to enjoy myself, have fun,
I want frenzied excitements, gratifications that are painful,
Love and hatred violently mixed,
Anguish that enlivens, inspiriting trouble;
Cured of my thirst to know at last,
I'll never again shun anything distressful.
From now on my wish is to undergo
All that men everywhere undergo, their whole portion,
Make mine their heights and depths, their weal and woe,
Everything human encompass in my one person,
And so enlarge myself to embrace theirs, all,
And shipwreck with them when at last we shipwreck, all.

MEPHISTO Believe me, I have chewed and chewed
At that tough meat, mankind, since long ago,
From birth to death work at it, still that food
Is indigestible as sourdough.
Only a God can take in all of them,
The whole lot, for He dwells in eternal light,
While we poor devils are stuck down below
In darkness and gloom, lacking even candlelight,
And all *you* qualify for is, half day, half night.

FAUST Nevertheless I will!

MEPHISTO All right, all right.
Still, one thing worries me.
The time allotted you is very short,
But art has always been around and shall be,
So listen, hear what is my thought:
Hire a poet, learn by his instruction.
Let the good gentleman search his mind
By careful, persevering reflection,
And every noble trait he can find,
Heap on your head, his honored creation:

The lion's fierceness,
Mild hart's swiftness,
Italian fieriness,
Northern steadiness.
Let him master for you the difficult feat
Of combining magnanimity with deceit,
How, driven by youthful impulsiveness, unrestrained,
To fall in love as beforehand you have planned.
Such a creature—my, I'd love to know him!—
I'd call him Mr. Microcosm.

FAUST What am I, then, if it can never be:
The realization of all human possibility,
That crown my soul so avidly reaches for?

MEPHISTO In the end you are—just what you are.
Wear wigs high-piled with curls, oh millions,
Stick your legs in yard-high hessians,
You're still you, the one you always were.

FAUST I feel it now, how pointless my long grind
To make mine all the treasures of man's mind;
When I sit back and interrogate my soul,
No new powers answer to my call;
I'm not a hair's breadth more in height,
A step nearer to the infinite.

MEPHISTO The way you see things, my dear Faust,
Is superficial—I speak frankly.
If you go on repining weakly,
We'll lose our seat at life's rich feast.
Hell, man, you have hands and feet,
A headpiece and a pair of balls,
And savors from fruit fresh and sweet,
That pleasure's yours, entirely yours.
If I've six studs, a sturdy span,
That horsepower's mine, my property,
My coach bowls on, ain't I the man.
Two dozen legs I've got for me!
Sir, come on, quit all that thinking,
Into the world, the pair of us!
The man who lives in his head only's
Like a donkey in the rough,
Led round and round by the bad fairies,
While green grass grows a stone's throw off.

FAUST And how do we begin?

MEPHISTO By clearing out—just leaving.
A torture chamber this place is, and that's the truth.
You call it living, to be boring
Yourself and your young men to death?
Leave that to Dr. Bacon Fat next door!
Why toil and moil at threshing heaps of straw?

Anyhow, the deepest knowledge you possess
You daren't let on to before your class.
—Oh now I hear one in the passageway!
FAUST I can't see him—tell him to go away.
MEPHISTO The poor boy's been so patient, don't be cross;
We mustn't let him leave here *désolé*.[4]
Let's have your cap and gown, Herr Doctor.
Won't I look the fine professor!
[*Changes clothes.*]
Count on me to know just what to say!
Fifteen minutes's all I need for it—
Meanwhile get ready for our little junket!
Exit FAUST
MEPHISTO [*Wearing* FAUST*'s gown*] Despise learning, heap contempt on reason,
The human race's best possession,
Only let the lying spirit draw you
Over into mumbo-jumbo,
Make-believe and pure illusion—
And then you're mine for sure, I have you,
No matter what we just agreed to.
Fate's given him a spirit knows no measure,
On and on it strives, relentlessly,
It soars away disdaining every pleasure,
Yet I will drag him deep into debauchery
Where all proves shallow, meaningless,
I'll have him writhing, ravening, berserk;
Before his lips' insatiable greediness
I'll dangle food and drink; he'll shriek
In vain for relief from his torturing dryness!
And even if he weren't the Devil's already,
He'd still be sure to perish miserably.
[*Enter a student.*]
STUDENT Allow me, sir, but I am a beginner
And come in quest of an adviser,
One whom all the people here
Greatly esteem, indeed revere.
MEPHISTO I thank you for your courtesy.
But I'm a man, as you can see,
Like any other. I wonder, shouldn't you look further?
STUDENT It's you, sir, you, I want for adviser!
I came here full of youthful zeal,
Eager to learn everything worthwhile.
Mother cried to see me go;
I've got an allowance, it's small, but will do.
MEPHISTO You've come to the right place, my son.
STUDENT But I'm ready to turn right around and run!

4. Sorry (French).

It seems so sad inside these walls,
My heart misgives me. I find all's
Confined, shut in, there's nothing green,
Not even a single tree, to be seen.
I can't, on the bench in the lecture hall,
Hear or see or think at all!

MEPHISTO It's a matter of getting used to things first.
An infant starts out fighting the breast,
But soon it's feeding lustily.
Just so your appetite'll sharpen by the day
The more you nurse at Wisdom's bosom.

STUDENT I'll cling tight to her bosom, happily,
But where do I find her, by what way?

MEPHISTO First of all, then—have you chosen
A faculty?

STUDENT Oh well, you see,
I'd like to be a learned man.
The earth below, the heavens on high—
All those things I long to understand,
All the sciences, all nature.

MEPHISTO You've got the right idea; however,
It demands close application.

STUDENT Oh never fear, I'm in this heart and soul;
But still, a fellow gets so dull
Without time off for recreation,
In the long and lovely days of summer.

MEPHISTO Time slips away so fast you need to use it
Rationally, and not abuse it.
And for that reason I advise you:
The Principles of Logic *primo*![5]
We will drill your mind by rote,
Strap it in the Spanish boot[6]
So it never shall forget
The road that's been marked out for it
And stray about incautiously,
A will-o'-the-wisp, this way, that way.
Day after day you'll be taught
All you once did just like that,
Like eating and drinking, thoughtlessly,
Now needs a methodology—
Order and system: *A, B, C!*
Our thinking instrument behaves
Like a loom: every thread,
At a step on the treadle's set in motion,
Back and forth the shuttle's sped,
The strands flow too fast for the eye,

5. First (Spanish).
6. The Spanish boot is an instrument of torture.

A blow of the batten and there's cloth, woven!
Now enter your philosopher, he
Proves all is just as it should be:
A being thus and *B* also,
Then *C* and *D* inevitably follow;
And if there were no *A* and *B*,
There'd never be a *C* and *D*.
They're struck all of a heap, his admiring hearers,
But still, it doesn't make them weavers.
How do you study something living?
Drive out the spirit, deny it being,
So there're just parts with which to deal,
Gone is what binds it all, the soul.
With lifeless pieces as the only things real,
The wonder's where's the life of the whole—
Encheiresis naturae,[7] the chemists then call it,
Make fools of themselves and never know it.

STUDENT I have trouble following what you say.

MEPHISTO You'll get the hang of it by and by
When you learn to distinguish and classify.

STUDENT How stupid all this makes me feel;
It spins around in my head like a wheel.

MEPHISTO Next metaphysics, a vital part
Of scholarship, its very heart.
Exert your faculties to venture
Beyond the boundaries of our nature,
Gain intelligence the brain
Has difficulty taking in,
And whether it goes in or not,
There's always a big word for it.
Be very sure, your first semester,
To do things right, attend each lecture;
Five of them you'll have daily,
Be in your seat when the bell peals shrilly;
Come to class with your homework done,
The sections memorized, each one,
So you are sure nothing's mistook
And nothing's said not in the book.
Still, note down all, not one word lost,
As if it came from the Holy Ghost.

STUDENT No need to say that to me twice,
They help a lot, notes do, all right.
What you've got down in black and white
Goes home with you, to a safe place.

MEPHISTO But your faculty—you've still not told me.

STUDENT Well, I don't believe the law would hold me.

7. The natural process by which substances are united into a living organism—a name for an action no one understands.

MEPHISTO I can't blame you, law is no delight.
What's jurisprudence?—a stupid rite
That's handed down, a kind of contagion,
From generation to generation,
From people to people, region to region.
Good sense is treated as nonsensical,
Benefactions as a botheration.
O future grandsons, how I wince for you all!
As for the rights with which we're born—
Not a word!—as if they were unknown.
STUDENT I hate the stuff now more than ever!
How lucky I am to have you for adviser.
Perhaps I'll take theology.
MEPHISTO I shouldn't want to lead you astray,
But it's a science, if you'll allow me to say it,
Where it's easy to lose your way.
There's so much poison hidden in it
It's very nearly impossible
To tell what's toxic from what's medicinal.
Here again it's safer to choose
One single master and echo his words dutifully—
As a general rule, put your trust in *words*,
They'll guide you safely past doubt and dubiety
Into the Temple of Absolute Certainty.
STUDENT But shouldn't words convey ideas, a meaning?
MEPHISTO Of course they should! But why overdo it?
It's exactly when ideas are wanting,
Words come in so handy as a substitute.
With words we argue pro and con,
With words invent a whole system.
Believe in words! Have faith in them!
No jot or tittle shall pass from them.
STUDENT Forgive me, I've another query,
My last one and then I'll go.
Medicine, sir—what might you care to tell me
About that study I should know?
Three years, my God, are terribly short
For so vast a field for the mind to survey.
A pointer or two would provide a start
And advance one quicker on one's way.
MEPHISTO [*Aside*] Enough of all this academic chatter,
Back again to devilry!
[*Aloud*] Medicine's an easy art to master.
Up and down you study the whole world
Only so as to discover
In the end it's all up to the Lord.
Plough your way through all the sciences you please,
Each learns only what he can,
But the man who understands his opportunities,

Him I call a man.
You seem a pretty strapping fellow,
Not one to hang back bashfully,
If you don't doubt yourself, I know,
Nobody else will doubt you, nobody.
Above all learn your way with women
If you mean to practise medicine.
The aches and pains that torture them
From one place only, one, all stem—
Cure there, cure all. Act halfway decent
And you'll find the whole sex acquiescent.
With an M.D. you enjoy great credit,
Your art, they're sure, beats others' arts;
The doctor, when he pays a visit,
For greeting reaches for those parts
It takes a layman years to come at;
You feel her pulse with extra emphasis
And your arm slipping with an ardent glance
Around her slender waist,
See if it's because she's so tight-laced.

STUDENT Oh, that's much better—practical, down to earth!

MEPHISTO All theory, my dear boy, is gray,
And green the golden tree of life.

STUDENT I swear it seems a dream to me!
Would you permit me, sir, to impose on
Your generous kindness another day
And drink still more draughts of your wisdom?

MEPHISTO I'm glad to help you in any way.

STUDENT I mustn't leave without presenting
You my album. Do write something
In it for me, would you?

MEPHISTO Happily.
[*Writes and hands back the album.*]

STUDENT [*Reading*] *Eritis sicut Deus, scientes bonum et malum.*[8]
[*Closes the book reverently and exits.*]

MEPHISTO Faithfully follow that good old verse,
That favorite line of my aunt's, the snake,
And for all your precious godlikeness
You'll end up how? A nervous wreck.

Enter FAUST.

FAUST And now where to?

MEPHISTO Wherever you like.
First we'll mix with little people, then with great,
The pleasure and the profit you will get
From our course—and never pay tuition for it.

FAUST But me and my long beard—we're hardly suited

8. A slight alteration of the serpent's words to Eve in Genesis: "Ye shall be as God, knowing good and evil" (Latin).

For the fast life. I feel myself defeated
Even before we start. I've never been
A fellow to fit in. Among other men
I feel so small, so mortified—I freeze.
Oh, in the world I'm always ill at ease!

MEPHISTO My friend, that's all soon changed, it doesn't matter;
With confidence comes *savoir-vivre.*[9]

FAUST But how do we get out of here?
Where are your horses, groom and carriage?

MEPHISTO By air's how we make our departure,
On my cloak—you'll enjoy the voyage.
But take care, on so bold a venture,
You're sparing in the matter of luggage.
I'll heat some gas, that way we'll rise up
Quickly off the face of earth;
If we're light enough we'll lift right up—
I offer my congratulations, sir, on your new life!

Auerbach's Cellar in Leipzig

Drinkers carousing.

FROSCH Faces glum and glasses empty?
I don't call this much of a party.
You fellows seem wet straw tonight
Who always used to blaze so bright.

BRANDER It's your fault—he just sits there, hardly speaks!
Where's the horseplay, where're the dirty jokes?

FROSCH [*Emptying a glass of wine on his head*]
There! Both at once!

BRANDER O horse and swine!

FROSCH You asked for it, so don't complain.

SIEBEL Out in the street if you want to punch noses!
—Now take a deep breath and roar out a chorus
In praise of the grape and the jolly god Bacchus.[1]
Come, all together with a rollicking round-o!

ALTMAYER Stop, stop, man, I'm wounded, cotten, quick, someone fetch some,
The terrible fellow has burst me an eardrum!

SIEBEL Hear the sound rumble above in the vault?
That tells you you're hearing the true bass note.

FROSCH That's right! Out the door, whoever don't like it!
With a do-re-mi,

ALTMAYER And a la-ti-do,

FROSCH We will have us a concert!
[*Sings.*]

9. French for knowing how to live in polite society.

1. Roman god of wine.

Our dear Holy Roman Empire,[2]
How does the damn thing hold together?

BRANDER Oh, but that's dreadful, and dreadfully sung,
A dreary, disgusting *political* song!
Thank the Lord when you wake each morning
You're not the one must keep the Empire running.
It's a blessing I'm grateful for
To be neither Kaiser nor Chancellor.[3]
But we, too, need a chief for our group
So let's elect ourselves a pope.
To all of us here I'm sure it's well known
What a man must do to sit on that throne.

FROSCH [*Singing*]
Nightingale, fly away, o'er lawn, o'er bower,
Tell her I love her ten thousand times over.

SIEBEL Enough of that love stuff, it turns my stomach.

FROSCH Ten thousand times, though it drives you frantic!
[*Sings.*]
Unbar the door, the night is dark!
Unbar the door, my love, awake!
Bar up the door now it's daybreak.

SIEBEL Go on, then, boast about her charms, her favor,
But I will have the latest laugh of all.
She played me false—just wait, she'll play you falser.
A horned imp's what I wish her, straight from Hell,
To dawdle with her in the dust of crossroads;
And may an old goat stinking from the Brocken[4]
Bleat "Goodnight, dearie," to her, galloping homewards.
A fellow made of honest flesh and blood
For a slut like that is much too good.
What kind of love note would I send that scarecrow?—
A beribboned rock tossed through her kitchen window.

BRANDER [*Banging on the table*]
Good fellows, your attention! None here will deny
I know what should be done and shouldn't at all.
Now we have lovers in our company
Whom we must treat in manner suitable
To their condition, our jollity,
With a song just lately written. So mind the air
And come in on the chorus loud and clear!
[*He sings.*]
A rat lived downstairs in the cellar,
Dined every day on lard and butter,
His paunch grew round as any burgher's,

2. Group of Central European lands ruled by Frankish and German kings from the ninth to the nineteenth centuries.

3. Head of the government. Kaiser: German for emperor.

4. The highest mountain in northern Germany.

As round as Dr. Martin Luther's.[5]
The cook put poison down for it.
Oh, how it groaned, the pangs it felt,
As if by Cupid smitten.

CHORUS [*Loud and clear*]
As if by Cupid smitten!

BRANDER
It rushed upstairs, it raced outdoors
And drank from every gutter,
It gnawed the woodwork, scratched the floors,
Its fever burned still hotter.
In agony it hopped and squealed,
Oh, piteously the beast appealed,
As if by Cupid smitten.

CHORUS
As if by Cupid smitten!

BRANDER
Its torment drove it, in broad day,
Out into the kitchen,
Collapsing on the hearth, it lay
Panting hard and twitching.
But that cruel Borgia[6] smiled with pleasure,
That's it, that's that rat's final seizure,
As if by Cupid smitten.

CHORUS
As if by Cupid smitten!

SIEBEL You find it funny, you coarse louts,
Oh, quite a stunt, so very cunning,
To put down poison for poor rats!

BRANDER You like rats, do you, find them charming?

ALTMAYER O big of gut and bald of pate!
Losing out's subdued the oaf;
What he sees in the bloated rat
'S the spitting image of himself.

[FAUST *and* MEPHISTOPHELES *enter.*]

MEPHISTO What your case calls for, Doctor, first,
Is some diverting company,
To teach you life affords some gaiety.
For these men every night's a feast
And every day a holiday;
With little wit but lots of zest
All spin inside their little orbit
Like young cats chasing their own tails.
As long as the landlord grants them credit
And they are spared a splitting headache,

5. Martin Luther (1483–1546), German leader of the Protestant Reformation, hence an object of distaste for Catholics.

6. Spanish and Italian family that grew powerful during the Renaissance; famous for poisoning their enemies.

They find life good, unburdened by travails.
BRANDER They're travelers is what your Brander says,
You can tell it by their foreign ways,
They've not been here, I'll bet, an hour.
FROSCH Right, right! My Leipzig's an attraction, how I love her,
A little Paris spreading light and culture!
SIEBEL Who might they be? What's your guess?
FROSCH Leave it to me. I'll fill their glass,
Gently extract, as you do a baby's tooth,
All there's to know about them, the whole truth.
I'd say we're dealing with nobility,
They look so proud, so dissatisfied, to me.
BRANDER They're pitchmen at the Fair, is what I think.
ALTMAYER Maybe so.
FROSCH Now watch me go to work.
MEPHISTO [*To* FAUST]
These dolts can't ever recognize Old Nick[7]
Even when he's got them by the neck.
FAUST Gentlemen, good day.
SIEBEL Thank you, the same.
[*Aside, obliquely studying* MEPHISTOPHELES]
What the hell, the fellow limps, he's lame![8]
MEPHISTO We'd like to join you, sirs, if you'll allow it.
But our landlord's wine looks so-so, I am thinking,
So the company shall make up for it.
ALTMAYER Particular, you are, about your drinking?
FROSCH Fresh from Dogpatch, right? From supper
On cabbage soup with Goodman Clodhopper?
MEPHISTO We couldn't stop on this trip, more's the pity!
But last time he went on so tenderly
About his Leipzig kith and kin,
And sent his very best to you, each one.

Bowing to FROSCH.

ALTMAYER [*Aside to* FROSCH]
Score one for him. He's got some wit.
SIEBEL A sly one, he is.
FROSCH Wait, I'll fix him yet!
MEPHISTO Unless I err, weren't we just now hearing
Some well-schooled voices joined in choral singing?
Voices, I am sure, must resonate
Inside this vault to very fine effect.
FROSCH You know music professionally, I think.
MEPHISTO Oh no—the spirit's eager, but the voice is weak.
ALTMAYER Give us a song!
MEPHISTO Whatever you'd like to hear.

7. Nickname for the devil.
8. By tradition, the Devil had cloven feet, split like sheep's hooves.

SIEBEL A new one, nothing we've heard before.
MEPHISTO Easily done. We've just come back from Spain,
Land where the air breathes song, the rivers run wine.
[*Sings.*]
Once upon a time a King
Had a flea, a big one—
FROSCH Did you hear that? A flea, goddamn!
I'm all for fleas, myself, I am.
MEPHISTO [*Sings*]
Once upon a time a King
Had a flea, a big one,
Doted fondly on the thing
With fatherly affection.
Calling his tailor in, he said,
Fetch needles, thread and scissors,
Measure the Baron up for shirts,
Measure him, too, for trousers.
BRANDER And make it perfectly clear to the tailor
He must measure exactly, sew perfect stitches,
If he's fond of his head, not the least little error,
Not a wrinkle, you hear, not one, in those breeches!
MEPHISTO
Glowing satins, gleaming silks
Now were the flea's attire,
Upon his chest red ribbons crossed
And a great star shone like fire,
In sign of his exalted post
As the King's First Minister.
His sisters, cousins, uncles, aunts
Enjoyed great influence too—
The bitter torments that that Court's
Nobility went through!
And the Queen as well, and her lady's-maid,
Though bitten till delirious,
Forbore to squash the fleas, afraid
To incur the royal animus.
But we free souls, we squash all fleas
The instant they light on us!
CHORUS [*Loud and clear*]
But we free souls, we squash all fleas
The instant they light on us!
FROSCH Bravo, bravo! That was fine!
SIEBEL May every flea's fate be the same!
BRANDER Between finger and nail, then crack! and they're done for.
ALTMAYER Long live freedom, long live wine!
MEPHISTO I'd gladly drink a glass in freedom's honor,
If only your wine looked a little better.[9]

9. That is, not cursed.

SIEBEL Again! You try, sir, our good humor.
MEPHISTO I'm sure our landlord wouldn't take it kindly.
For otherwise I'd treat this company
To wine that's wine—straight out of our own cellar.
SIEBEL Go on, go on, let the landlord be my worry.
FROSCH You're princes, you are, if you're able
To put good wine upon the table;
But a drop or two, hell, that's no trial at all,
To judge right what I need's a real mouthful.
ALTMAYER [*In an undertone*] They're from the Rhineland,
I would swear.
MEPHISTO Let's have an auger,[1] please.
BRANDER What for?
Don't tell me you've barrels piled outside the door!
ALTMAYER There's a basket of tools—look, over there.
MEPHISTO [*Picking out an auger, to* FROSCH]
Now gentlemen, name what you'd have, please.
FROSCH What do you mean? We have a choice?
MEPHISTO Whatever you wish. I will produce.
ALTMAYER [*To* FROSCH] Licking his lips already, he is!
FROSCH Fine, fine! For me—a Rhine wine any day,
The best stuff's from the fatherland, I say.
MEPHISTO [*Boring a hole in the table edge at Frosch's place*]
Some wax to stop the holes with, quick!
ALTMAYER Hell, it's just a sideshow trick.
MEPHISTO [*To* BRANDER]
And you?
BRANDER The best champagne you have, friend, please,
With lots of sparkle, lots of fizz.

[MEPHISTOPHELES *goes round the table boring holes at all the places, which one of the drinkers stops with bungs made of wax.*]

You can't always avoid what's foreign,
About pleasure I'm nonpartisan.
A man who's a true German can't stand Frenchmen,
But he can stand their wine, oh yes he can!
SIEBEL [*As* MEPHISTOPHELES *reaches his place*]
I confess your dry wines don't
Please me, sweet is what I want.
MEPHISTO Tokay[2] for you! Coming up shortly!
ALTMAYER No, fellows, slow down, just look at it calmly—
The whole thing's meant to make fools of us.
MEPHISTO Ei me! With noble guests such as you are,
That would be going a bit far.
Do you imagine I'd be so obtuse?
So what's your pleasure, I'm waiting—speak.
ALTMAYER Whatever you like, just don't take all week.

1. Tool used to bore holes.
2. A sweet Hungarian wine.

MEPHISTO [*All the holes are now bored and stopped; gesturing grotesquely*]
Grapes grow on the vine,
Horns on the head of the goat,
O vinestock of hard wood,
O juice of the tender grape!
And a wooden table shall,
When summoned, yield wine as well!
O depths of Nature, mysterious, secret,
Here is a miracle—if you believe it!
Now pull the plugs, all, drink and be merry!

ALL [*Drawing the bungs and the wine each drinker asked for gushing into his glass*]
Sweet fountain, flowing for us only!

MEPHISTO But take good care you don't spill any.
[*They drink glass after glass.*]

ALL [*Singing*]
Lovely, oh lovely, I must be dreaming!
A party so cannabalistically cozy—
Five hundred pigs swilling slops!

MEPHISTO The people are free! What a time they're having!

FAUST I'd like to go now. Nincompoops!

MEPHISTO Before we do, you must admire
Their swinishness in all its splendor.

SIEBEL [*Spilling wine on the floor, where it bursts into flame*]
All Hell's afire, I burn, I burn!

MEPHISTO [*Conjuring the flame*]
Peace, my own element, down, down!
[*To the drinkers*]
Only a pinch, for the present, of the purgatorial fire.

SIEBEL What's going on here? For this you'll pay dear!
You don't seem to know the kind of men you have here.

FROSCH Once is enough for that kind of business!

ALTMAYER Throw him out on his ear, but quietly, no fuss!

SIEBEL You've got your nerve, trying out upon us
Stuff like that—damned hocus-pocus!

MEPHISTO Quiet, you tub of guts!

SIEBEL Bean pole, you!
Now he insults us. I know what to do.

BRANDER A taste of our fists is what: one-two, one-two.

ALTMAYER [*Drawing a bung and flames shooting out at him*]
I'm on fire, I'm on fire!

SIEBEL It's witchcraft, no mistaking!
Stick him, the rogue, he's free for the taking!
[*They draw their knives and fall on* MEPHISTOPHELES.]

MEPHISTO [*Gesturing solemnly*]
False words, false shapes
Addle wits, muddle senses!
Let here and otherwheres
Exchange places!

[*All stand astonished and gape at each other.*]

ALTMAYER Where am I? What a lovely country!
FROSCH Such vineyards! Do my eyes deceive me?
SIEBEL And grapes you only need to reach for!
BRANDER Just look inside this green arbor!
What vines, what grapes! Cluster on cluster!

[*He seizes* SIEBEL *by the nose. The others do the same to each other, and raise their knives.*]

MEPHISTO Unspell, illusion, eyes and ears!
—Take note the Devil's a jester, my dears!

[*He vanishes with* FAUST; *the drinkers recoil from each other.*]

SIEBEL What's happened?
ALTMAYER What?
FROSCH Was that your nose?
BRANDER [*To* SIEBEL] And I'm still holding on to yours!
ALTMAYER The shock I felt—in every limb!
Get me a chair, I'm caving in.
FROSCH What happened? That man, and his wine—so strange!
SIEBEL If only I could lay hands on that scoundrel,
I'd give him something in exchange!
ALTMAYER I saw him, horsed upon a barrel,
Vault straight out through the cellar door—
My feet feel leaden, so unnatural.

[*Turning toward the table.*]

Well—maybe some wine's still trickling here.
SIEBEL Lies, all lies! Deluded! Dupes!
FROSCH I was drinking wine, I'd swear.
BRANDER But what was it with all those grapes?
ALTMAYER Now try and tell me, you know-it-alls,
There's no such thing as miracles!

Witch's Kitchen

A low hearth, and on the fire a large cauldron. In the steam rising up from it, various figures can be glimpsed. A she-ape is seated by the cauldron, skimming it to keep it from boiling over. The male with their young crouches close by, warming himself. Hanging on the walls and from the ceiling are all sorts of strange objects, the household gear of a witch.

FAUST, MEPHISTOPHELES.

FAUST Why, it's revolting, all this crazy witchery!
Are you telling me that I'll be born a new man
Here amid this lunatic confusion?
Is an ancient hag the doctor who will cure me?
And the mess that that beast's boiling, that's the remedy
To cancel thirty years, unbow my back?
If you can do no better, the outlook's black
For me, the hopes I nursed are dead already.

Hasn't man's venturesome mind, instructed by Nature,
Discovered some sort of potent elixer?

MEPHISTO Now you're speaking sensibly!
There is a natural way to recover your youth;
But that's another business entirely
And not your sort of thing, is my belief.

FAUST No, no, come on, I want to hear it.

MEPHISTO All right. It's simple: you don't need to worry
About money, or doctors, or necromancy.
Go out into the fields right now, this minute,
Start digging and hoeing, with never a stop or respite,
Confine yourself and your thoughts to the narrowest sphere,
Eat nothing but the plainest kind of fare,
Live with the cattle as cattle, don't think it too low
To spread your own dung on the fields that you sow.
So there you have it, the sane way, the healthy,
To keep yourself young till the age of eighty!

FAUST Yes, not my sort of thing, I'm afraid,
Humbling myself to work with a spade;
So straitened a life would never suit me.

MEPHISTO So it's back to the witch, my friend, are we?

FAUST That horrible hag—no one else will do?
Why can't *you* concoct the brew?

MEPHISTO A nice thing that, to waste the time of the Devil
When his every moment is claimed by the business of evil!
Please understand. Not only skill and science
Are called for here, but also patience:
A mind must keep at it for years, very quietly,
Only time can supply the mixture its potency.
Such a deal of stuff goes into the process,
All very strange, all so secret.
The Devil, it's true, taught her how to do it.
But it's no business of his to brew it.

[*Seeing the* APES]

See here, those creatures, aren't they pretty!
That one's the housemaid, that one's the flunkey.

[*To the* APES]

Madam is not at home, it seems?

APES
Flew up the chimney
To dine out with friends.

MEPHISTO And her feasting, how long does it usually take her?

APES As long as we warm our paws by the fire.

MEPHISTO [*To* FAUST] What do you think of these elegant folk?

FAUST Noisome enough to make me choke.

MEPHISTO Well, just this sort of causerie
Is what I find most pleases me.

[*To the* APES]

Tell me, you ugly things, oh do.

What's that you're stirring there, that brew?
APES Beggars' soup, it's thin stuff, goes down easy.
MEPHISTO Your public's assured—they like what's wishy-washy.
HE-APE [*Sidling up to* MEPHISTOPHELES *fawningly*]
Roll, roll the dice quick,
And this monkey make rich,
Have himself at last luck,
The rich have too much.
With a few dollars and cents
The credit I'd have for sense!
MEPHISTO How very happy that monkey would be
If he could buy chances in the lottery.
[*Meanwhile the young* APES *have been rolling around a big ball to which they now give a push forward.*]
HE-APE
The world, sirs, behold it!
Down goes the up side,
Up goes the down side,
And never a respite.
Touch it, it'll ring,
It's like glass, fractures easily.
When all's said and done,
A hollow, void thing.
See, it shines bright here,
Here even brighter.
—Oops, ain't I nimble!
But you, son, be careful
And keep a safe distance,
Or it's your last day.
The thing's made of clay,
A knock, and it's fragments.
MEPHISTO What is that sieve for?
HE-APE [*Taking it down*]
If you came here to thieve,
It would be my informer.
[*He scampers across to the* SHE-APE *and has her look through it.*]
Look through the sieve!
Now say, do you know him?
Or you daren't name him?
MEPHISTO [*Approaching the fire*] And this pot over here?
APES
Oh, you're a dolt, sir,
Don't know what a pot's for!
Nor a kettle neither.
MEPHISTO What a rude creature!
HE-APE
Here, take this duster,
Sit down in the armchair.
[*Presses* MEPHISTOPHELES *down in the chair.*]

FAUST [*Who meanwhile has been standing in front of a mirror, going forward to peer into it from close up and then stepping back*]
What do I see? What a marvellous vision
Shows itself in this magic glass!
Love, land me your wings, your swiftest to pass
Through the air to the heaven she must dwell in!
Unless I stay firmly fixed to this spot,
If I dare to move nearer the least bit,
Mist blurs the vision and obscures her quite.
Woman unrivaled, beauty absolute!
Can such things be, a creature made perfectly?
The body so indolently stretched out there
Surely epitomizes all that is heavenly.
Can such a marvel inhabit down here?

MEPHISTO Of course when a god's sweated six whole days
And himself cries bravo in his works praise,
You can be certain the results are first class.
Look all you want now in the glass,
But I can find you just such a prize,
And lucky the man, his bliss assured,
Brings home such a beauty to his bed and board.

[FAUST *continues to stare into the mirror, while* MEPHISTOPHELES, *leaning back comfortably in the armchair and toying with the feather duster, talks on.*]

Here I sit like a king on a throne,
Scepter in hand, all I'm lacking's my crown.

APES [*Who have been performing all sorts of queer, involved movements, with loud cries bring* MEPHISTOPHELES *a crown*]
Here, your majesty,
If you would,
Glue up the crown
With sweat and blood!

[*Their clumsy handling of the crown causes it to break apart and they cavort around with the pieces.*]

Oh no, now it's broken!
We look and we listen.
We chatter, scream curses,
And make up our verses—

FAUST [*Still gazing raptly into the mirror*]
Good God, how my mind reels, it's going to snap!

MEPHISTO [*Nodding toward the* APES]
My own head's starting to spin like a top.

APES
And if by some fluke
The words happen to suit
Then the rhyme makes a thought!

FAUST [*As above*] My insides burn as if on fire!
Come on, we must get out of here.

MEPHISTO [*Keeping his seat*] They tell the truth, these poets do.

You've got to give the creatures their due.
[*The cauldron, neglected by the* SHE-APE, *starts to boil over, causing a great tongue of flame to shoot up the chimney.* THE WITCH *comes riding down the flame, shrieking hideously.*]

THE WITCH It hurts, it hurts!
Monkeys, apes, incompetent brutes!
Forgetting the pot and singeing your mistress—
The servants I have! Utterly useless!
[*Catching sight of* FAUST *and* MEPHISTOPHELES]
What's going on here?
Who are this pair?
What's all this about?
Sneaking in when I'm out!
Hellfire burn
Them to a turn!
[*She plunges the spoon into the cauldron and scatters fire over* FAUST, MEPHISTOPHELES *and the* APES. *The* APES *whine.*]

MEPHISTOPHELES [*Turning the duster upside down and hitting out violently among the glasses and jars with the butt end*]
In pieces, in pieces,
Spilt soup and smashed dishes!
It's all in fun, really—
Beating time, you old carcass,
To your melody.
[THE WITCH *starts back in rage and fear.*]
Can't recognize me, rattlebones, old donkey, you?
Can't recognize your lord and master?
Why I don't chop up you and your monkey crew
Into the littlest bits and pieces is a wonder!
No respect at all for my red doublet?
And my cock's feather means nothing to you, beldam?
Is my face masked or can you plainly see it?
Must I tell *you* of all people who I am?

THE WITCH Oh sir, forgive my discourteous salute!
But I look in vain for your cloven foot,
And your two ravens, where are they?

MEPHISTO All right, this time you're let off—I remember
It's been so long since we've seen each other.
Also, the world's grown so cultured today,
Even the Devil's been caught up in it;
The Northern bogey has made his departure,
No horns now, no tail, to make people shiver,
And as for my hoof, though I can't do without it,
Socially it would raise too many eyebrows—
So like a lot of other young fellows
I've padded my calves to try and conceal it.

THE WITCH [*Dancing with glee*]
I'm out of my mind with delight, I swear!
My lord Satan's dropped out of the air.

MEPHISTO Woman, that name—I forbid you to use it.
THE WITCH Why not? Whyever now refuse it?
MEPHISTO Since God knows when it belongs to mythology,
But that's hardly improved the temper of humanity.
The Evil One's no more, evil ones more than ever.
Address me as Baron, that will do,
A gentleman of rank like any other,
And if you doubt my blood is blue,
See, here's my house's arms, the noblest ever!
[*He makes an indecent gesture.*]
THE WITCH [*Laughing excessively*]
Ha, ha! It's you, I see now, it's clear—
The same old rascal you always were!
MEPHISTO [*To* FAUST] Observe, friend, my diplomacy
And learn the art of witch-mastery.
THE WITCH Gentlemen, now, what is your pleasure?
MEPHISTO A generous glass of your famous liquor,
But please, let it be from your oldest supply;
It doubles in strength as the years multiply.
THE WITCH At once! Here I've got, as it happens, a bottle
From which I myself every now and then tipple,
And what is more, it's lost all its stink.
I'll gladly pour you out a cup.
[*Under her breath*]
But if the fellow's unprepared, the drink
Might kill him, you know, before an hour's up.
MEPHISTO I know the man well, he'll thrive upon it.
I wish him the best your kitchen affords.
Now draw your circle, say the right words,
And pour him out a brimming goblet.
[*Making bizarre gestures,* THE WITCH *draws a circle and sets down an assortment of strange objects inside it. All the glasses start to ring and the pots to resound, providing a kind of musical accompaniment. Last of all, she brings out a great tome and stands the apes in the circle to serve as a lectern and to hold up the torches. Then she signals* FAUST *to approach.*]
FAUST [*To* MEPHISTOPHELES]
What can I hope for here, would you tell me?
That junk of hers, her arms waving crazily,
All the vulgar tricks she's performing,
Well do I know them, I don't find them amusing.
MEPHISTO Jokes, just jokes! It's not all that serious,
Really, you're being much too difficult.
Of course hocus-pocus! She's a sorceress—
How else can her potion produce a result?
[*He presses* FAUST *inside the circle.*]
THE WITCH [*Declaiming from the book, with great emphasis*]
Listen and learn!
From one make ten,
And let two go,

And add three in,
And you are rich.
Now cancel four!
From five and six,
So says the witch,
Make seven and eight—
Thus all's complete.
And nine is one
And ten is none
And that's the witch's one-times-one.

FAUST I think the old woman's throwing a fit.

MEPHISTO We're nowhere near the end of it.
I know the book, it's all like that,
The time I've wasted over it!
For a thoroughgoing paradox is what
Bemuses fools and wise men equally.
The trick's old as the hills yet it's still going strong;
With Three-in-One and One-in-Three[1]
Lies are sown broadcast, truth may go hang;
Who questions professors about the claptrap they teach—
Who wants to debate and dispute with a fool?
People dutifully think, hearing floods of fine speech,
It can't be such big words mean nothing at all.

THE WITCH [*Continuing*].
The power of science
From the whole world kept hidden!
Who don't have a thought,
To them it is given
Unbidden, unsought,
It's theirs without sweat.

FAUST Did you hear that, my God, what nonsense,
It's giving me a headache, phew!
It makes me think I'm listening to
A hundred thousand fools in chorus.

MEPHISTO Enough, enough, O excellent Sibyl![2]
Bring on the potion, fill the stoup,
Your drink won't give my friend here trouble,
He's earned his Ph.D. in many a bout.

[THE WITCH *very ceremoniously pours the potion into a bowl; when* FAUST *raises it to his lips, a low flame plays over it.*]

Drink, now drink, no need to diddle,
It'll put you into a fine glow,
When you've got a sidekick in the Devil,
Why should some fire frighten you so?

[THE WITCH *breaks the circle and* FAUST *steps out.*]

Now let's be off, you mustn't dally.

THE WITCH I hope that little nip, sir, hits the spot!

1. The Christian doctrine of the Trinity.
2. Prophetess.

MEPHISTO [*To* THE WITCH] Madam, thanks. If I can help *you* out,
Don't fail, upon Walpurgis Night,[3] to ask me.
THE WITCH [*To* FAUST] Here is a song, sir, carol it now and then,
You'll find it assists the medicine.
MEPHISTO Come away quick! You must do as I say.
To soak up the potion body and soul,
A man's got to sweat a bucketful.
And after, I'll teach you the gentleman's way
Of wasting your time expensively.
Soon yours the delight outdelights all things—
Boy Cupid astir in you, stretching his wings.
FAUST One more look in the mirror, let me—
That woman was inexpressibly lovely!
MEPHISTO No, no, soon enough, before you, vis-à-vis,
Yours the fairest of fair women, I guarantee.
[*Aside*] With that stuff in him, old Jack will
Soon see a Helen in every Jill.

A Street

FAUST. MARGARETE *passing by.*

FAUST Pretty lady, here's my arm,
Would you allow me to see you home?
MARGARETE I'm neither pretty nor a lady,
Can find my way home quite unaided.
[*She escapes his arm and passes by.*]
FAUST By God, what a lovely girl,
I've never seen her like, a pearl!
A good girl, too, with a quick wit,
Her manner modest and yet pert.
Those red, ripe lips and cheeks abloom
Will haunt me till the crack of doom.
The way she looked down, so demure,
Had for me such allure!
The way she cut short my come-on
Charmed me—charmed by a turn-down!
Enter MEPHISTOPHELES.
FAUST Get me that girl, do you hear, you must!
MEPHISTO What girl?
FAUST The one who just went past.
MEPHISTO Oh, her. She's just been to confession
To be absolved of all her sins.
I sidled near the box to listen:
She could have spared herself her pains,
She is the soul of innocence

3. May Day Eve (April 30), when witches are supposed to assemble on the Brocken, the highest peak in the Harz Mountains, which are in central Germany.

And has no reason, none at all,
To visit the confessional.
Her kind is too much for me.

FAUST She's over fourteen, isn't she?

MEPHISTO Well, listen to him, an instant Don Juan,[1]
Demands every favor, his shyness all gone,
Conceitedly thinks it offends his honor
To leave unplucked every pretty flower.
But it doesn't go so easy always.

FAUST My dear Doctor of What's Proper,
Spare me your lectures, I beg you, please.
Let me tell it to you straight:
If I don't hold that darling creature
Tight in my arms this very night,
We're through, we two, come twelve midnight.

MEPHISTO Impossible! That's out of the question!
I require two weeks at the least
To spy out a propitious occasion.

FAUST With several hours or so, at the most,
I could seduce her handily—
Don't need the Devil to pimp for me,

MEPHISTO You're talking like a Frenchman now.
Calm down, there's no cause for vexation.
You'll find that instant gratification
Disappoints. If you allow
For compliments and billets doux,
Whisperings and rendezvous,
The pleasure's felt so much more keenly.
Italian novels teach you exactly.

FAUST I've no use for your slow-paced courting,
My appetite needs no supporting.

MEPHISTO Please, I'm being serious.
With such a pretty little miss
You mustn't be impetuous
And assault the fortress frontally.
What's called for here is strategy.

FAUST Something of hers, do you hear, I require!
Come, show me the way to the room she sleeps in,
Get me a scarf, a glove, a ribbon,
A garter with which to feed my desire!

MEPHISTO To prove to you my earnest intention
By every means to further your passion,
Not losing a minute, without delay,
I'll take you to her room today.

FAUST I'll see her, yes? And have her?

MEPHISTO No!

1. The German reads *Hans Liederlich*, meaning a profligate because *liederlich* means "careless" or "dissolute."

She'll be at a neighbor's—you *must* go slow!
Meanwhile alone there, in her room,
You'll steep yourself in her perfume
And dream of the delights to come.

FAUST Can we start now?

MEPHISTO Too soon! Be patient!

FAUST Then find me a pretty thing for a present.

Exit.

MEPHISTO Presents already? The man's proving a lover!—
Now for his gift, I know there's treasure
Buried in many an out-of-the way corner.
Off I go to reconnoiter!

Evening

A small room, very neat and clean.

MARGARETE [*As she braids her hair and puts it up*]
I'd give a lot to know, I would,
Who the gentleman was today.
He seemed a fine man, decent, good,
And from a noble house, I'm sure;
It shows on him as plain as day—
To be so bold! Who else would dare?

Exit.

MEPHISTOPHELES, FAUST.

MEPHISTO Come in now, in!—but quietly, take care.

FAUST [*After a silent interval*] Leave, please, leave me on my own.

MEPHISTO [*Sniffing around*] Not every girl keeps things so spic and span.

Exit.

FAUST Welcome, evening's twilight gloom,
Stealing through this holy room,
Possess my heart, oh love's sweet anguish,
That lives in hope, in hope must languish.
How still it's here, how happily
It breathes good order and contentment,
What riches in this poverty,
What bliss there is in this confinement!
[*He flings himself into a leather armchair by the bed.*]
Receive me as in generations past
You received the happy and distressed.
How often, I know, children crowded round
This chair where their grandfather sat enthroned.
Perhaps my darling too, a round-cheeked child,
Grateful for her Christmas present, held
Reverentially his shrunken hand.

I feel, dear girl, where you are all is comfort,
Where you are, order, goodness all abound.
Maternally instructed by your spirit,
Daily you spread the clean cloth on the table,
Sprinkle the sand on the floor so carefully—[1]
O lovely hand! Hand of a lovely angel
That's made of this home something heavenly.
And here—!
[*He lifts a bed curtain.*]
I tremble, frightened, with delight!
Here I could linger hour after hour.
Here the dear creature, gently dreaming, slept,
Her angel substance slowly shaped by Nature.
Here warm life in her tender bosom swelled,
Here by a pure and holy weaving
Of the strands, was revealed
The angelic being.

But me? What is it brought me here?
See how shaken I am, how nervous!
What do I want? Why am I so anxious?
Poor Faust, I hardly know you any more.

Has this room put a spell on me?
I came here burning up with lust,
And melt with love now, helplessly.
Are we blown about by every gust?

And if she came in now, this minute,
How I'd pay dear, I would, for it.
The big talker, Herr Professor,
Would dwindle to nothing, grovel before her.

MEPHISTO [*Entering*] Hurry! I saw her, she's coming up.

FAUST Hurry indeed, I'll never come here again!

MEPHISTO Here's a jewel box I snatched up
When I—but who cares how or when.
Put it in the closet there,
She'll jump for joy when she comes on it.
It's got a number of choice things in it,
Meant for another—but I declare,
Girls are girls, they're all the same,
The only thing that matters is the game.

FAUST Should I, I wonder?

MEPHISTO *Should* you, you say!
Do you mean to keep it for yourself?
If what you're after's treasure, pelf,
Then I have wasted my whole day,

1. Floors were sprinkled with sand after cleaning.

Been put to a lot of needless bother,
I hope you aren't some awful miser—
After all my head-scratching, scheming, labor!
[*He puts the box in the closet and shuts it.*]
Come on, let's go!
Our aim? Your darling's favor,
So you may do with her as you'd like to do.
And you do what? Only gape,
As if going into your lecture hall,
Looming before you in human shape
Stood physics and metaphysics, ancient, stale.
Come on!

Exit

MARGARETE [*With a lamp*] How close, oppressive it's in here.
[*She opens the window.*]
And yet outside it isn't warm.
I feel, I don't know why, so queer—
I wish Mother would come home,
I'm shivering so in every limb.
What a foolish, frightened girl I am!
[*She sings as she undresses.*]
There was a king in Thule,[2]
No truer man drank up,
To whom his mistress, dying,
Gave a golden cup.

Nothing he held dearer,
And mid the feasters' cries,
Each time he drained the beaker
Tears started in his eyes.

And when death knocked, he tallied
His towns and treasure up,
Yielded his heirs all gladly,
All except the cup.

In the great hall of his fathers,
In the castle by the sea,
He and his knights sat down to
Their last revelry.

Up stood the old carouser,
A last time knew wine's warmth,
Then pitched his beloved beaker
Down into the gulf.

2. The fabled *Ultima Thule* of Latin literature—those distant lands just beyond the reach of every explorer. Goethe wrote the ballad in 1774; it was published in 1782 and set to music by several composers.

He saw it fall and founder,
Deep, deep down it sank,
His eyes grew dim and never
Another drop he drank.
[*She opens the closet to put her clothes away and sees the jewel box.*]
How did this pretty box get here?
I locked the closet, I'm quite sure.
Whatever's in the box? Maybe
Mother took it in pledge today.
And there's the little key on a ribbon.
I think I'd like to open it!
—Look at all this, God in Heaven!
I've never seen the like of it!
Jewels! And *such* jewels, that a fine lady
Might wear on a great holiday.
How would the necklace look on me?
Who is it owns these wonderful things?
[*She puts the jewelry on and stands in front of the mirror.*]
I wish they were mine, these fine earrings!
When you put them on, you're changed completely.
What good's your pretty face, your youth,
Nice to have but little worth.
Men praise you, do it half in pity,
What's on their minds is money, money,
Gold is their god, all—
Oh us poor people!

Out Walking

FAUST *strolling up and down, thinking. To him* MEPHISTOPHELES.

MEPHISTO By true love cruelly scorned! By Hellfire fierce and fiery!
If only I could think of worse to swear by!
FAUST What's eating you, now what's the trouble?
Such a face I've not seen till today.
MEPHISTO The Devil take me, that's what I would say,
If it didn't so happen I'm the Devil.
FAUST Are you in your right mind—behaving
Like a madman, wildly raving?
MEPHISTO The jewels I got for Gretchen,[1] just imagine—
Every piece a damned priest's stolen!
The minute her mother saw them, she
Began to tremble fearfully.
The woman has a nose! It's stuck
Forever in her prayerbook,
She knows right off, by the smell alone,
If something's sacred or profane;

1. Diminutive of the German *Margarete.* She is called Gretchen for much of the play.

One whiff of the jewelry was enough
To tell her something's wrong with the stuff.
My child—she cried—and listen well to me,
All property obtained unlawfully
Does body and soul a mortal injury.
These jewels we'll consecrate to the Blessed Virgin,
And for reward have showers of manna from Heaven.
Our little Margaret pouted, loath—
Why look a gift horse[2] in the mouth?
And surely the one who gave her it
So generously, was hardly wicked.
Her mother sent for the priest, and he,
Seeing how the land lay,
Was mightily pleased. You've done, he said,
Just as you should, mother and maid;
Who overcometh is repaid.
The Church's maw's remarkably capacious,
Gobbles up whole realms, everything precious,
Nor once suffers qualms, not even belches;
The Church alone is able to digest
Goods illegitimately possessed.

FAUST That's the way the whole world over,
From a King to a Jew, so all do ever.

MEPHISTO So then he pockets brooches, chains and rings
As if they were the cheapest household things,
And gives the women as much of a thank-you
As a body gets for a mouldy potato.
In Heaven, he says, you will receive your reward:
The women, uplifted, are reassured.

FAUST And Gretchen?

MEPHISTO Sits there restlessly,
Her mind confused, her will uncertain,
Thinks about jewels night and day,
Even more about her unknown patron.

FAUST I can't bear that she should suffer;
Find her new ones immediately!
Poor stuff, those others, hardly suit her.

MEPHISTO Oh yes indeed! With a snap of the fingers!

FAUST Do what I say, march, man—how he lingers!
Insinuate yourself with her neighbor.
Damn it, devil, you move so sluggishly!
Fetch Gretchen new and better jewelry!

MEPHISTO Yes, yes, just as you wish, Your Majesty.

Exit FAUST.

2. Like the wooden horse in which Greek soldiers entered Troy to capture it; an emblem of potential treachery.

A lovesick fool! To amuse his girl he'd blow up
Sun, moon, stars, the whole damned shop.

The Neighbor's House

MARTHE [*Alone*] May God that man of mine condone!
He's done me wrong—like a bird
Flew right off without a word
And left me here to sleep alone.
I never gave him cause for grief
But loved him as a faithful wife.
[*She weeps.*]
Suppose he's dead—oh I feel hopeless!
If only I had an official notice.
Enter MARGARETE.
MARGARETE Frau Marthe!
MARTHE Gretel, what's wrong, tell me!
MARGARETE My knees are shaking, near collapse!
Just now I found another box
Inside my closet. Ebony,
And such things in it, much more splendid
Than the first ones, I'm dumbfounded!
MARTHE Never a word to your mother about it,
Or the priest will have all the next minute.
MARGARETE Just look at this, and this, and this here!
MARTHE [*Decking her out in the jewels*]
Oh, what a lucky girl you are!
MARGARETE But I mustn't be seen in the street with such jewelry,
And never in church. Oh, it's too cruel!
MARTHE Come over to me whenever you're able,
Here you can wear them without any trouble,
March back and forth in front of the mirror—
Won't we enjoy ourselves together!
And when it's a holiday, some such occasion,
You can start wearing them, with discretion.
First a necklace, then a pearl earring,
Your mother, she'll never notice anything,
And if she does, why, we'll think of something.
MARGARETE Who put the jewelry in my closet?
There's something that's not right about it.
[*A knock.*]
Dear God above, can that be Mother?
MARTHE [*Peeping through the curtain*]
Please come in!—No, it's a stranger.
Enter MEPHISTOPHELES.
MEPHISTO Good women, pardon, with your permission!
I beg you to excuse the intrusion.
[*Steps back deferentially from* MARGARETE.]
I'm looking for Frau Marthe Schwerdtlein.

MARTHE I'm her. And what have you to say, sir?
MEPHISTO [*Under his breath to her*]
Now I know who you are, that's enough.
You have a lady under your roof,
I'll go away and come back later.
MARTHE [*Aloud*] Goodness, child, you won't believe me,
What the gentleman thinks is, you're a lady!
MARGARETE A poor girl's what I am, no more.
The gentleman's kind—I thank you, sir.
These jewels don't belong to me.
MEPHISTO Oh, it's not just the jewelry,
It's the Fräulein herself, so clear-eyed, serene.
—So delighted I'm allowed to remain.
MARTHE Why are you here, if you'll pardon the question.
MEPHISTO I wish my news were pleasanter.
Don't blame me, the messenger:
Your husband's dead, he sent his affection.
MARTHE The good man's dead and gone, departed?
Then I'll die too. Oh, I'm broken-hearted!
MARGARETE Marthe dear, it's too violent, your sorrow!
MEPHISTO Hear the sad story I've come to tell you.
MARGARETE As long as I live I'll love nobody, no!
It would kill me with grief to lose my man so.
MEPHISTO Joy's latter end is sorrow—and sorrow's joy.
MARTHE Tell me how the dear man died.
MEPHISTO He's buried in Padua, beside
The blessed saint, sweet Anthony,[1]
In hallowed ground where he can lie
In rest eternal, quietly.
MARTHE And nothing else, sir, that is all?
MEPHISTO A last request. He enjoins you solemnly:
Let three hundred masses be sung for his soul!
As for anything else, my pocket's empty.
MARTHE What! No jewel, nice souvenir,
Such as every journeyman keeps in his wallet,
And would sooner go hungry and beg than sell it?
MEPHISTO Nothing, I'm sorry to say, Madam dear.
However—he never squandered his money,
And he sincerely regretted his sins,
Regretted even more he was so unlucky.
MARGARETE Why must so many be so unhappy!
I'll pray for him often, sing requiems.
MEPHISTO What a lovable creature, there's none dearer!
What you should have now, right away,
Is a good husband. It's true what I say.

1. Known for his care for the poor and the sick, St. Anthony of Padua is the patron saint of lost things.

MARGARETE Oh no, it's not time yet, that must come later.
MEPHISTO If not now a husband, meanwhile a lover.
What blessing from Heaven, which one of life's charms
Rivals holding a dear thing like you in one's arms.
MARGARETE With us people here it isn't the custom.
MEPHISTO Custom or not, it's what's done and by more than some.
MARTHE Go on with your story, more's surely to come.
MEPHISTO He lay on a bed of half-rotten straw,
Better at least than a dunghill, and there
He died as a Christian, knowing well
Much remained outstanding on his bill.
"Oh how," he cried, "I hate myself!
To abandon my trade, desert my wife!
It kills me even to think of it,
If only she would forgive and forget!"
MARTHE [*Weeping*] I did, long ago! He's forgiven, the dear man.
MEPHISTO "But she's more to blame, God knows, than I am."
MARTHE Liar! How shameless! At death's very door!
MEPHISTO His mind wandered as the end drew near,
If I'm anything of a connoisseur here.
"No pleasure," he said, "no good times, nor anything nice;
First getting children, then getting them fed,
By fed meaning lots more things than bread,
With never a moment for having my bite in peace."
MARTHE How could he forget my love and loyalty,
My hard work day and night, the drudgery!
MEPHISTO He didn't forget, he remembered all tenderly.
"When we set sail from Malta's port," he said,
"For wife and children fervently I prayed.
And Heaven, hearing, smiled down kindly,
For we captured a Turkish vessel, stuffed
With the Sultan's treasure. How we rejoiced!
Our courage being recompensed,
I left the ship with a fatter purse
Than ever I'd owned before in my life."
MARTHE Treasure! Do you think he buried it?
MEPHISTO Who knows what's become of it?
In Naples, where he wandered about,
A pretty miss with a kind heart
Showed the stranger such good will,
Till the day he died he felt it still.
MARTHE The villain! Robbing his children, his wife!
And for all our misery, dire need,
He would never give up his scandalous life.
MEPHISTO Well, he's been paid, the man is dead.
If I were in your shoes, my dear,
I'd mourn him decently a year
And meanwhile keep an eye out for another.
MARTHE Dear God, I'm sure it won't be easy
To find, on this earth, his successor;

So full of jokes he was, so merry!
But he was restless, always straying,
Loved foreign women, foreign wine,
And how he loved, drat him, dice-playing.
MEPHISTO Oh well, I'm sure things worked out fine
If he was equally forgiving.
With such an arrangement, why, I swear,
I'd marry you myself, my dear!
MARTHE Oh sir, you would? You're joking, I'm sure!
MEPHISTO [*Aside*] Time to leave! This one's an ogress,
She'd sue the Devil for breach of promise!
[*To* GRETCHEN]
And what's your love life like, my charmer?
MARGARETE What do you mean?
MEPHISTO [*Aside*] Oh you good girl,
All innocence! [*Aloud*] And now farewell.
MARGARETE Farewell.
MARTHE Quick, one last matter.
If you would. I want to know
If I might have some proof to show
How and when my husband died
And where the poor man now is laid?
I like to have things right and proper,
With a notice published in the paper.
MEPHISTO Madam, yes. To attest the truth,
Two witnesses must swear an oath.
I know someone, a good man, we
Will go before the notary.
I'll introduce you to him.
MARTHE Do.
MEPHISTO And she'll be here, your young friend, too?—
A very fine fellow who's been all over,
So polite to ladies, so urbane his behavior.
MARGARETE I'd blush for shame before the gentleman.
MEPHISTO No, not before a king or any man!
MARTHE We'll wait for you tonight, the two of us,
Inside my garden, just behind the house.

A Street

FAUST, MEPHISTOPHELES

FAUST Well, speak! It's on? When will I have her?
MEPHISTO Bravo, bravo, aren't you on fire!
Very shortly Gretchen will be all yours;
This evening you will meet her at her neighbor's.
The worthy Mistress Marthe, I confess,
Needs no instruction as a procuress.
FAUST
Well done.

MEPHISTO But something we must do for her.
FAUST One good turn deserves another.
MEPHISTO All it is is swear an oath
Her husband's laid out in the earth
At Padua in consecrated ground.
FAUST So we must make a trip there—very smart!
MEPHISTO Sancta simplicitas![1] Whoever said that?
Just swear an oath, is all. You frowned?
FAUST If that's the best you're able, count me out.
MEPHISTO The saintly fellow! Turned devout.
Declaring falsely—Heaven forbid!—
Is something Faustus never did.
Haven't you pontificated
About God and the world, undisconcerted,
About man, man's mind and heart and being,
As bold as brass, without blushing?
Look at it closely and what's the truth?
You know as much about those things
As you know about Herr Schwerdtlein's death.
FAUST You always were a sophist[2] and a liar.
MEPHISTO Indeed, indeed. If we look ahead a little further,
To tomorrow, what do we see?
You swearing, oh so honorably,
Your soul is Gretchen's, for ever and ever.
FAUST My soul, and all my heart as well.
MEPHISTO Oh noble, great!
You'll swear undying faith and love eternal,
Go on about desire unique and irresistable,
About longing, boundless, infinite.
That, too, with all your loving heart.
FAUST With all my heart! And now enough.
What I feel, an emotion of such depth,
Such turbulence—when I try to find
A name for it and nothing comes to mind,
And cast about, search heaven and earth
For words to express its transcendent worth,
And call the fire in which I burn
Eternal, yes, eternal, yes, undying,
Do you really mean to tell me
That's just devil's doing, deception, lying?
MEPHISTO
Say what you please, I'm right.
FAUST One word more, one only,
And then I'll save my breath. A man who is unyielding,
Sure, absolutely, he's right, and has a tongue in his mouth—
Is right. So come, I'm sick of arguing.

1. Holy simplicity (Latin).
2. Philosopher.

You're right, and the reason's simple enough:
I must do what I must, can't help myself.

A Garden

MARGARETE *with* FAUST, *her arm linked with his:* MARTHE *with* MEPHISTOPHELES. *The two couples stroll up and down.*

MARGARETE You are too kind, sir, I am sure it's meant
To spare a simple girl embarrassment.
A traveler finds whatever amusement he can,
You've been all over, you're a gentleman—
How can anything I say
Interest you in any way?
FAUST One word of yours, a single look's
Worth all the science in our books.
[*He kisses her hand.*]
MARGARETE No, no, sir, please, you mustn't! How could you kiss
A hand so ugly—red and coarse?
You can't imagine all the work I do:
My mother must have things just so.
[*They walk on.*]
MARTHE And you, sir, I believe you constantly travel?
MEPHISTO Business, business! It is so demanding!
Leaving a place you like, oh, it is dismal,
But on you've got to go, it's just unending.
MARTHE How fine when young and full of ginger
To roam the world, go everywhere,
But grim days come, come even grimmer,
When no one likes what lies in store—
Likes crawling to his grave a lonely bachelor.
MEPHISTO When I look at what's ahead, I tremble.
MARTHE Then think about it while you're able.
[*They walk on.*]
MARGARETE Yes, out of sight is out of mind.
It's second nature with you, gallantry;
But you have friends of every kind,
Cleverer by far, oh much, than me.
FAUST Dear girl, believe me, what's called cleverness
Is mostly shallowness and vanity.
MARGARETE What do you mean?
FAUST God, isn't it a pity
That unspoiled innocence and simpleness
Should never know itself and its own worth,
That meekness, lowliness, those highest gifts
Kindly Nature endows us with—
MARGARETE You'll think of me for a moment or two,
I'll have hours enough to think of you.
FAUST You're alone a good deal, are you?

MARGARETE Our family's very small, it's true,
But still it has to be looked to.
We have no maid, I sweep the floors, I cook and knit
And sew, do all the errands, morning and night.
Mother's very careful about money,
All's accounted for to the last penny.
Not that she really needs to pinch and save,
We can afford much more than others have.
My father left us a good bit,
With a small dwelling part of it,
And a garden just outside the city.
But lately I've lived quietly.
My brother is a soldier. My little sister died.
The trouble that she cost me, the poor child!
But I loved her very much, I'd gladly do
It all again.

FAUST An angel, if at all like you.

MARGARETE All the care of her was mine,
And she was very fond of her sister.
My father died before she was born,
And Mother, well, we nearly lost her;
It took so long, oh many months, till she got better.
It was out of the question she should nurse
The poor little crying thing herself.
So I nursed her, on milk and water.
I felt she was my own daughter,
In my arms, upon my lap,
She smiled and kicked, grew round and plump.

FAUST The happiness it must have given you!

MARGARETE But it was hard on me so often, too.
Her crib stood at my bedside, near my head,
A slightest movement, cradle's creak,
And instantly I was awake;
I'd give her a bottle or take her into my bed.
If still she fretted, up I'd raise,
Walk up and down with her swaying and crooning,
And be at the washtub early the next morning.
To market after that and getting the hearth to blaze,
And so it went day after day, always.
Home's not always cheerful, be it said,
But still—how good your supper, good your bed.

[*They walk on.*]

MARTHE It's very hard on us poor women.
You bachelors don't listen, you're so stubborn.

MEPHISTO What's needed are more charmers like yourself
To bring us bachelors down from off the shelf.

MARTHE There's never, sir, been anyone? Confess!
You've never lost your heart to one of us?

MEPHISTO How does the proverb go? A loving wife,

And one's own hearthside, are more worth
Than all the gold that's hidden in the earth.
MARTHE I mean, you've had no wish, yourself?
MEPHISTO Oh, everywhere I've been received politely.
MARTHE No, what I mean is, hasn't there been somebody
Who ever made your heart beat? Seriously?
MEPHISTO It's never a joking matter with women, believe me.
MARTHE Oh, you don't understand!
MEPHISTO So sorry. Still,
I can see that you are—amiable.
[*They walk on.*]
FAUST You recognized me, angel, instantly
When I came through the gate into the garden?
MARGARETE I dropped my eyes. Didn't you see?
FAUST And you'll forgive the liberty, you'll pardon
My swaggering up in that insulting fashion
When you came out of the church door?
MARGARETE I was shocked. Never before
Had I been spoken to like that.
I'm a good girl. Who would dare
To be so free with me, so smart?
It seemed to me at once you thought
There's a girl who can be bought
On the spot. Did I look a flirt?
Is that so, tell! Well, I'll admit
A voice spoke "Isn't he nice?" in my breast,
And oh how vexed with myself I felt
When I wasn't vexed with you in the least.
FAUST Dear girl!
MARGARETE Just wait.
[*Picking a daisy and plucking the petals one by one*]
FAUST What is it for, a bouquet?
MARGARETE Only a little game of ours.
FAUST A game, is it?
MARGARETE Never mind. I'm afraid you'll laugh at me.
[*Murmuring to herself as she plucks the petals*]
FAUST What are you saying!
MARGARETE [*Under her breath*]
Loves me—loves me not—
FAUST Oh, what a creature, heavenly!
MARGARETE [*Continuing*] He loves me—not—he loves me—not—
[*Plucking the last petal and crying out delightedly*]
He loves me!
FAUST Dearest, yes! Yes, let the flower be
The oracle by which the truth is said.
He loves you! Do you understand?
He loves you! Let me take your hand.
[*He takes her hands in his.*]
MARGARETE I'm afraid!

FAUST Read the look on my face,
Feel my hands gripping yours,
They say what is the case,
Can't ever be put in words:
Utter surrender, and such rapture
As must never end, must last forever!
Yes, forever! An end—it would betoken
Utter despair! a heart forever broken!
No—no end! No end!

[MARGARETE *squeezes his hands, frees herself and runs away. He doesn't move for a moment, thinking, then follows her.*]

MARTHE It's getting dark.
MEPHISTO That's right. We have to go.
MARTHE Please forgive me if I don't invite
You in. But ours is such a nasty-minded street,
You'd think people had no more to do
Than watch their neighbors' every coming and going.
The gossip that goes on here, about nothing!
But where are they, our little couple?
MEPHISTO Flew
Up that path like butterflies.
MARTHE He seems to like her.
MEPHISTO And she him. Which is the way the world wags ever.

A Summerhouse

GRETCHEN *runs in and hides behind the door, putting her fingertips to her lips and peeping through a crack.*

MARGARETE Here he comes!
FAUST You're teasing me, yes, are you?
I've got you now! [*Kisses her.*]
MARGARETE [*Holding him around and returning the kiss*]
My heart! Oh, how I love you!

MEPHISTOPHELES *knocks.*

FAUST [*Stamping his foot*]
Who's there?
MEPHISTO A friend.
FAUST A fiend!
MEPHISTO We must be on our way.
MARTHE [*Coming up*] Yes, sir, it's late.
FAUST I'd like to walk you home.
MARGARETE My mother, I'm afraid . . . Goodbye!
FAUST So we must say
Goodbye? Goodbye!
MARGARETE I hope I'll see you soon.

Exit FAUST *and* MEPHISTOPHELES.

Good God, the thoughts that fill the head
Of such a man, oh it's astounding!
I stand there dumbly, my face red,
And stammer yes to everything.
I don't understand. What in the world
Does he see in me, an ignorant child?

Forest and Cavern

FAUST [*Alone*] Sublime Spirit, all that I asked for, all,
You gave me. Not for nothing was it,
The face you showed me all ablaze with fire.
You gave me glorious Nature for my kingdom,
With the power to feel, to delight in her—nor as
A spectator only, coolly admiring her wonders,
But letting me see deep into her bosom
As a man sees deep into a dear friend's heart.
Before me you make pass all living things,
From high to low, and teach me how to know
My brother creatures in the woods, the streams, the air.
And when the shrieking storm winds make the forest
Groan, toppling the giant fir whose fall
Bears nearby branches down with it and crushes
Neighboring trees so that the hill returns
A hollow thunder—oh, then you lead me to
The shelter of this cave, lay bare my being to myself,
And all the mysteries hidden in my depths
Unfold themselves and open to the day.
And when I see the moon ascend the sky,
Shedding a pure, assuaging light, out
Of the walls of rock, the dripping bushes, float
The silver figures of antiquity
And temper meditation's austere joy.

That nothing perfect's ever ours, oh but
I know it now. Together with the rapture
That I owe you, by which I am exalted
Nearer and still nearer to the gods, you gave me
A familiar, a creature whom already
I can't do without, though he's a cold
And shameless devil who drags me down
In my own eyes and with a whisper turns
All the gifts you gave me into nothing.
The longing that I feel for that enchanting
Figure of a girl he busily blows up
Into a leaping flame. And so desire
Whips me stumbling on to seize enjoyment,
And once enjoyed, I languish for desire.

Enter MEPHISTOPHELES.

MEPHISTO Aren't you fed up with it by now,
This mooning about? How can it still
Amuse you? You do it for a while,
All right, but enough's enough, on to the new!

FAUST I wish you'd more to do than criticize
The peace I feel on one of my good days.

MEPHISTO A breather you want? Very well, I grant it;
But don't speak so, as if you really meant it.
I wouldn't shed tears losing a companion
Who is so mad, so rude, so sullen;
I have my hands full every minute—
Impossible to tell what pleases you or doesn't.

FAUST Why, that's just perfect, isn't it?
He bores me stiff and wants praise for it.

MEPHISTO You poor earthly creature, would
You ever have managed at all without me?
Whom do you have to thank for being cured
Of your mad ideas, your feverish frenzy?
If not for me you would have disappeared
From off the face of earth already.
A life, you call it, to be brooding
Owl-like in caves or toad-like feeding
On oozing moss and dripping stones?
That's a way to spend your time?
The old Doctor still lives in your bones.

FAUST Try to understand, my life's renewed
When I wander in communion with wild Nature;
But even if you could I know you would
Begrudge me, Devil that you are, my rapture.

MEPHISTO Oh my! Your rapture—superterrestrial!
Sprawled on a hillside in the nocturnal dewfall,
Penetrating intuitively the bowels of the earth,
All the six days of Creation unfolding inside yourself,
In your arrogance enjoying I don't know what satisfaction,
Amorously immerging with the all in its perfection,
Nary a trace left of the child born of this earth,
And then as finis to your deep, deep insight—
[*Making a gesture*]
I forbid myself to say, it's not polite.

FAUST Ugh! Oh ugly!

MEPHISTO That's not what you care for?
You're right, "ugh"'s right, the moral comment called for.
Never a word, when chaste ears are about,
Of what chaste souls can't do without.
Oh well, go on amuse yourself
By duping now and then yourself.
Yet you can't keep on like this any longer,
You look done in again, almost a goner.

If you persist so, in this fashion,
You'll go mad with baffled passion.
Enough, I say! Your sweetheart sits down there
And all's a dismal prison for her.
You haunt her mind continually,
She's mad about you, oh completely.
At first your passion, like a freshet[1]
Swollen with melted snow, overflowing
Its peaceful banks, engulfed a soul unknowing,
But now the flood's thinned to a streamlet.
Instead of playing monarch of the wood,
My opinion is the Herr Professor
Should make the silly little creature
Some return in gratitude.
For her the hours creep along,
She stands at the window watching the clouds
Pass slowly over the old town walls,
"Lend me, sweet bird, your wings," is the song
She sings all day and half the night.
Sometimes she's cheerful, mostly she's downhearted,
Sometimes she cries as if brokenhearted,
Then she's calm again and seems all right,
And heart-sick always.

FAUST Serpent! Snake!

MEPHISTO [*Aside*] I'll have you yet!

FAUST Away, you monster from some stinking fen!
Don't mention her, the soul itself of beauty,
Don't make my half-crazed senses crave again
The sweetness of that lovely body!

MEPHISTO Then what? She thinks you've taken flight,
And I must say, the girl's half right.

FAUST Far off as I may go, still she is near me,
She fills my thoughts both day and night,
I even envy the Lord's flesh the kiss
Her lips bestow upon it at the mass.[2]

MEPHISTO I understand. I've often envied *you*
Her pair of roes that feed among the lilies.[3]

FAUST Pimp! I won't hear your blasphemies.

MEPHISTO Fine! Insult me! And I laugh at you.
The God that made you girls and boys
Himself was first to recognize,
And practice, what's the noblest calling,
The furnishing of opportunities.
Away! A crying shame this, never linger!

1. Stream.
2. That is, when Margarete takes Communion, in which bread is miraculously turned to the body of Christ.
3. Compare the Song of Solomon 4.5: "Thy two breasts are like two young roes that are twins, which feed among the lilies."

You act as if hard fate were dragging
You to death, not to your truelove's chamber.
FAUST Heaven's out-heavened when she holds me tight,
And though I'm warmed to life upon her breast,
Do I ever once forget her plight?
Am I not a fugitive, a beast,
That's houseless, restless, purposeless,
A furious, impatient cataract
That plunges down from rock to rock to the abyss?
And she, her senses unawakened, a child still,
Dwelt in her cottage on the Alpine meadow,
Her life the same domestic ritual
Within a little world where fell no shadow.
And I, abhorred by God,
Was not content to batter
Rocks to bits, I had
To undermine her peace and overwhelm her!
This sacrifice you claimed, Hell, as your due!
Help me, Devil, please, to shorten
The anxious time I must go through!
Let happen quick what has to happen!
Let her fate fall on me, too, crushingly,
And both together perish, her and me!
MEPHISTO All worked up again, all in a sweat!
On your way, you fool, and comfort her.
When dolts like you are baffled, don't know what,
They think it's hopeless, the end near.
Long live the man who keeps on undeterred!
I'd rate your progress as a devil pretty fair;
But tell me, what is there that's more absurd
Than a moping devil, mewling in despair?

Gretchen's Room

GRETCHEN [*Alone at her spinning wheel*]
My heart is heavy,
My peace gone,
I'll never know any
Peace again.

For me it's death
Where he is not,
The whole earth
Waste, desert, rot.

My poor poor head
Is in a whirl,
For sure I'm mad,
A poor mad girl.

My heart is heavy,
My peace gone,
I'll never know any
Peace again.

I look out the window,
Walk out the door,
Him, only him,
I look for.

His bold walk,
His princely person,
His smiling look,
His eyes' persuasion,

And his sweet speech—
Magicalness!
His fingers' touch
And oh his kiss!

My heart is heavy,
My peace gone,
I'll never know any
Peace again.

With aching breast
I strain so toward him,
Oh if I just
Could catch and hold him,

And kiss him and kiss him,
Never ceasing,
Though I should die in
His arms kissing.

Marthe's Garden

MARGARETE, FAUST.

MARGARETE Heinrich,[1] the truth—I have to insist!
FAUST As far as I'm able.
MARGARETE Well, tell me, you must,
About your religion—how do you feel?
You're such a good man, kind and intelligent,
Yet I suspect you are indifferent.
FAUST Enough of that, my child. You know quite well

1. That is, Faust. In the legend, Faust's name was generally Johann (John). Goethe changed it to Heinrich (Henry).

I cherish you so very dearly,
For those I love I'd give my life up gladly,
And I never interfere with people's faith.
MARGARETE That isn't right, you've got to have belief!
FAUST You do?
MARGARETE I know you think I am a dunce!
You don't respect the sacraments.
FAUST I do respect them.
MARGARETE Not enough to go to mass.
And tell me when you last went to confess?
Do you believe in God?
FAUST Who, my dear,
Can say, I believe in God?
Ask any priest or learned scholar
And what you get by way of answer
Sounds like mockery of a fool.
MARGARETE So you don't believe in God.
FAUST Don't misunderstand me, lovely girl.
Who dares name him,
Dares affirm him,
Dares say he believes?
Who, feeling doubt,
Ventures to say right out,
I don't believe?
The All-embracing,
All-sustaining,
Sustains and embraces
Himself and you and me.
Overhead the great sky arches,
Firm lies the earth beneath our feet,
And the friendly shining stars, don't they
Mount aloft eternally?
Don't my eyes, seeking your eyes, meet?
And all that is, doesn't it weigh
On your mind and heart,
In eternal secrecy working,
Visibly, invisibly, about you?—
Fill heart with it to overflowing
In an ecstasy of blissful feeling
Which then call what you would:
Happiness! Heart! Love! Call it God!—
I know no name for it, nor look
For one. Feeling is all,
Names noise and smoke
Dimming the heavenly fire.
MARGARETE I guess what you say is all right,
The priest speaks so, or pretty near,
Except his language isn't yours, not quite.
FAUST I speak as all speak here below,

All souls beneath bright heaven's day,
They use the language that they know,
And I use mine. Why shouldn't I?
MARGARETE It sounds fine when it's put your way,
But something's wrong, there's still a question;
The truth is, you are not a Christian.
FAUST Now darling!
MARGARETE I have suffered so much, I can't sleep
To see the company you keep.
FAUST Company?
MARGARETE That man you always have with you,
I loathe him, oh how much I do
In all my life I can't remember
Anything that's made me shiver
More than his face has, so horrid, hateful!
FAUST Silly thing, don't be so fearful.
MARGARETE His presence puts my blood into a turmoil.
I like people, most of them indeed;
But even as I long for you,
I think of him with secret dread—
And he's a scoundrel, he is too!
If I'm unjust, forgive me, Lord.
FAUST It takes all kinds to make a world.
MARGARETE I wouldn't want to have his kind around me!
His lips curl so sarcastically,
Half angrily,
When he pokes his head inside the door.
You can see there's nothing he cares for;
It's written on his face as plain as day
He loves no one, we're all his enemy.
I'm so happy with your arms around me,
I'm yours, and feel so warm, so free, so easy,
But when he's here it knots up so inside me.
FAUST You angel, you, atremble with foreboding!
MARGARETE What I feel's so strong, so overwhelming,
That let him join us anywhere
And right away I almost fear
I don't love you anymore.
And when he's near, my lips refuse to pray,
Which causes me such agony.
Don't you feel the same way too?
FAUST It's just that you dislike him so.
MARGARETE I must go now.
FAUST Shall we never
Pass a quiet time alone together,
Breast pressed to breast, our two beings one?
MARGARETE Oh, if I only slept alone!
I'd draw the bolt for you tonight, yes, gladly;
But my mother sleeps so lightly,

And if we were surprised by her
I know I'd die right then and there.
FAUST Angel, there's no need to worry.
Here's a vial—three drops only
In her cup will subdue nature
And lull her into pleasant slumber.
MARGARETE What would I say no
To when you ask?
It won't harm her, though
There is no risk?
FAUST If there were,
Would I suggest you give it her?
MARGARETE Let me only look at you
And I don't know, I have to do
Your least wish.
I have gone so far already,
How much farther's left for me to go?

Exit.

Enter MEPHISTOPHELES.

MEPHISTO The girl's a goose! I hope she's gone.
FAUST Spying around are you, again?
MEPHISTO I heard it all, yes, every bit of it,
How she put the Doctor through his catechism,
From which he'll have, I trust, much benefit.
Does a fellow stick to the old, the true religion?—
That's what all the girls are keen to know.
If he minds there, they think, he'll mind us too.
FAUST Monster, lacking the least comprehension
How such a soul, so loving, pure,
Whose faith is all in all to her,
The sole means to obtain salvation,
Should be tormented by the fear
The one she loves is damned forever!
MEPHISTO You transcendental, hot and sensual Romeo,
See how a little skirt's got you in tow.
FAUST You misbegotten thing of filth and fire!
MEPHISTO And she's an expert, too, in physiognomy.
When I come in, she feels—what, she's not sure;
This face I wear hides a dark mystery;
I'm a genius of some kind, a bad one,
About that she is absolutely certain,
Even the Devil, very possibly.
Now about tonight—?
FAUST What's that to you?
MEPHISTO I get my fun out of it too.

At the well

GRETCHEN *and* LIESCHEN *carrying pitchers.*

LIESCHEN You've heard about our Barbara, have you?
GRETCHEN No, not a word. I hardly see a soul.
LIESCHEN Sybil told me; yes, the whole thing's true.
She's gone and done it now, the little fool.
You see what comes of being so stuck up!
GRETCHEN What comes?
LIESCHEN Oh, it smells bad, it stinks.
She's feeding two now when she eats and drinks.
GRETCHEN Oh dear!
LIESCHEN Serves her right, if you ask me.
How she kept after him, without a let-up,
Gadding about, the pair, and gallivanting
Off to the village for the music, dancing;
She had to be first always, everywhere,
While he with wine and sweet cakes courted her.
She thought her beauty echoed famously,
Accepted his gifts shamelessly,
They kissed and fondled by the hour,
Till it was goodbye to her little flower.
GRETCHEN The poor thing!
LIESCHEN Poor thing, you say!
While we two sat home spinning the whole day
And our mothers wouldn't let us out at night,
She was where? Out—hugging her sweetheart
On a bench or up a dark alley,
And never found an hour passed too slowly.
Well, now she's got to pay for it—
Shiver in church in her sinner's shift.
GRETCHEN He'll marry her. How can he not?
LIESCHEN He won't—he can.
That one's too smart,
He'll find a girlfriend elsewhere in a trice.
In fact he's gone.
GRETCHEN But that's not nice!
LIESCHEN And if he does, she'll rue the day,
The boys will snatch her bridal wreath away
And we'll throw dirty straw down in her doorway.[1]

Exit.

GRETCHEN [*Turning to go home*]
How full of blame I used to be, how scornful
Of any girl who got herself in trouble!

1. In Germany, this treatment was reserved for young women who had sexual relations before marriage.

I couldn't find words enough to express
My disgust for others' sinfulness.
Black as all their misdeeds seemed to be,
I blackened them still more, so cruelly,
And still they weren't black enough for me.
I blessed myself, was smug and proud
To think I was so very good,
And who's the sinner now? Me, me, oh God!
Yet everything that brought me to it,
God, was so good, oh, was so sweet!

The City Wall

In a niche in the wall, an image of the Mater Dolorosa[1] *at the foot of the cross, with pots of flowers before it.*

GRETCHEN [*Putting fresh flowers in the pots*]
Look down, O
Thou sorrow-rich Lady,
On my need, in thy mercifulness aid me!

With the sword in your heart,
With your infinite hurt,
Upwards you look to your son's death.

To the Father you gaze up.
Send sighs upon sighs up,
For his grief and your own sore grief.

Who's there knows
How it gnaws
Deep inside me, the pain?
The heart-anguish I suffer,
Fright, tremblings, desire?
You only know, you alone!

Wherever I go, no matter,
The woe, the woe I suffer
Inside my bosom, aching!

No sooner I'm alone
I moan, I moan, I moan,
Mary, my heart is breaking!

From the box outside my window,
Dropping tears like dew,
Leaning into the dawning,
I picked these flowers for you.

1. Sorrowful mother (Latin; literal trans.); that is, the Virgin Mary in mourning.

Into my bedroom early
The bright sun put his head,
Found me bolt upright sitting
Miserably on my bed.

Help! Save me from shame and death!
Look down, O
Thou sorrow-rich Lady,
On my need, in thy mercifulness aid me!

Night

The street outside GRETCHEN*'s door.*

VALENTINE [*A soldier, Gretchen's brother*]
Whenever at a bout the boys
Would fill the tavern with the noise
Of their loud bragging, swearing Mattie,
Handsome Kate or blushing Mary
The finest girl in all the country,
Confirming what they said by drinking
Many a bumper,[1] I'd say nothing,
My elbows on the table propped,
Till all their boasting at last stopped.
And then I'd stroke my beard, and smiling,
Say there was no point in quarrelling
About taste; but tell me where
There was one who could compare,
A virgin who could hold a candle
To my beloved sister, Gretel?
Clink, clank, you heard the tankards rattle
All around, and voices shout
He's right, he is, she gets our vote,
Among all her sex she has no equal!
Which stopped those others cold. But now—
I could tear my hair out, all,
Run right up the side of the wall!
All the drunks are free to crow
Over me, to needle, sneer,
And I'm condemned to sitting there
Like a man with debts unpaid
Who sweats in fear lest something's said.
I itch to smash them all, those beggars,
But still that wouldn't make them liars.

Who's sneaking up here? Who is that?
There's two! And one I bet's that rat.
When I lay my hands on him

1. A drinking vessel filled to the top.

He won't be going home again!

FAUST, MEPHISTOPHELES.

FAUST How through the window of the vestry, look,
The flickering altar lamp that's always lit
Upward throws its light, while dim and weak,
By darkness choked, a gleam dies at our feet.
Just so all's night and gloom within my soul.

MEPHISTO But me, I'm itching like a tomcat on the prowl
That slinks past fire ladders, hugs the wall.
An honest devil I am, after all;
It's nothing serious, the little thievery
I have in mind, the little lechery—
It merely shows Walpurgis Night's already
Spooking up and down inside me.
Still another night of waiting, then
The glorious season's here again
When a fellow finds out waking beats
Sleeping life away between the sheets.

FAUST That flickering light I see, is that
Buried treasure rising, what?

MEPHISTO Very soon you'll have the pleasure
Of lifting out a pot of treasure.
The other day I stole a look—
Such lovely coins, oh you're in luck!

FAUST No necklace, bracelet, some such thing
My darling can put on, a ring?

MEPHISTO I think I glimpsed a string of pearls—
Just the thing to please the girls.

FAUST Good, good. It makes me feel unhappy
When I turn up with my hands empty.

MEPHISTO Why should you mind it if you can
Enjoy a free visit now and then?
Look up, how the heavens sparkle, star-full,
Time for a song, a cunning one, artful:
I'll sing her a ballad that's moral, proper,
So as to delude the baggage the better.

[*Sings to the guitar.*]

What brings you out before[2]
Your sweet William's door,
O Katherine, my dear,
  In morning's chill?
You pretty child, beware,
The maid that enters there,
Out she'll not come here
  A maiden still.

Girls, listen, trust no one,
Or when all's said and done,

2. Lines 3407–22 are adapted by Goethe from Shakespeare's *Hamlet* 4.5.

You'll find yourselves undone
 And poor things, damned.
Of your good souls take care,
Yield nothing though he swear,
Until your finger wear
 A silver band.

VALENTINE [*Advancing*]
Luring who here with that braying,
Abominable rat catcher?
The devil take that thing you're playing,
And then take you, you guitar scratcher!

MEPHISTO Smashed my guitar! Now it's no good at all.

VALENTINE And now I think I'll split your no good skull.

MEPHISTO [*To* FAUST] Hold your ground, Professor! At the ready!
Stick close to me, I'll show you how.
Out with your pigsticker now!
You do the thrusting, I will parry.

VALENTINE Parry that!

MEPHISTO Why not?

VALENTINE And this one too!

MEPHISTO Delighted, I am, oh much, to oblige you.

VALENTINE It's the Devil I think I'm fighting!—Who's grinning.
What's this? My hand is feeling feeble.

MEPHISTO [*To* FAUST] Stick him!

VALENTINE [*Falling*] Oh!

MEPHISTO See how the lout's turned civil.
What's called for now is legwork. Off and running!
In no time they will raise a hue and cry;
I can manage sheriffs without trouble,
But not the High Judiciary.

Exeunt.

MARTHE [*Leaning out of the window*]
Neighbors, help!

GRETCHEN [*Leaning out of her window*]
 A light, a light!

MARTHE They curse and brawl, they scream and fight.

CROWD Here's one on the ground. He's dead.

MARTHE [*Coming out*] Where are the murderers? All fled?

GRETCHEN [*Coming out*]
Who's lying here?

CROWD Your mother's son.

GRETCHEN My God, the misery, on and on.

VALENTINE I'm dying! Well, it's soon said, that,
And sooner done. You women, don't
Stand there blubbering away.
Come here, I've something I must say.
 [*All gather around him.*]
Gretchen, look here, you're young yet,
A green girl, not so smart about

Managing her business.
We know it, don't we, you and me,
You're a whore, privately—
Go public, don't be shy, miss.

GRETCHEN My brother! God! What wretchedness!

VALENTINE You can leave God out of this.
What's done can't ever be undone,
And as things went, so they'll go on.
You let in one at the back door,
Soon there'll be others, more and more—
A whole dozen, hot for pleasure,
And then the whole town for good measure.

Shame is born in hugger-mugger,[3]
The lying-in veiled in black night,
And she is swaddled up so tight
In hopes the ugly thing will smother.
But as she thrives, grows bigger, bolder,
The hussy's eager to step out,
Though she has grown no prettier.
The more she's hateful to the sight,
The more the creature seeks the light.

I look ahead and I see what?
The honest people of this place
Standing back from you, you slut,
As from a plague-infected corpse.
When they look you in the face
You'll cringe with shame, pierced to the heart.
In church they'll drive you from the altar,
No wearing gold chains any more,
No putting on a fine lace collar
For skipping round on the dance floor.
You'll hide in dark and dirty corners
With limping cripples, lousy beggars.
God may pardon you at last,
But here on earth you stand accurst.

MARTHE Look up to God and ask his mercy!
Don't add to all your other sins
Sacrilege and blasphemy.

VALENTINE If I could only lay my hands
On your scrawny, dried up body,
Vile panderer, repulsive bawd,
Then I might hope to find forgiveness
Ten times over from the Lord!

GRETCHEN My brother! Hell's own wretchedness!

VALENTINE Stop your bawling, all your to-do.

3. Mess, disorder.

When you said goodbye to honor,
That is what gave me the worst blow.
And now I go down in the earth,
Passing through the sleep of death,
To God—who in his life was a brave soldier.

Dies.

The Cathedral

Requiem mass, organ music, singing. GRETCHEN *among a crowd of worshippers. Behind her an* EVIL SPIRIT.

EVIL SPIRIT How different then, Gretchen,
It was when, all innocent,
Here at the altar
You babbled your prayers
From the worn little prayer book,
Half a game playing,
Half God adoring
In your childish heart,
Gretchen!
And how is it now?
In your heart how now is it,
What wickedness there?
Do you pray for the soul of your mother
Who through you slept on and still on,
Into pain and more pain?
There at your door whose blood is it?
—And already under your heart
A stirring, a quickening, is it,
Affrighting you both
With its foreboding presence?

GRETCHEN Misery! Misery!
To be rid of these thoughts
That go round and around in me.
Accusing, accusing!

CHOIR *Dies irae, dies illa*
Solvet saeclum in favilla.[1]
[*Organ music.*]

EVIL SPIRIT The wrath of God grips you!
The trumpet sounds,
The grave mounds are heaving,
And your heart,
From its ashen rest waking
Into billowing flames,
Agonizingly burns!

1. Day of wrath, that day that dissolves the world into ashes (Latin). The choir sings a famous mid-13th-century hymn by Thomas Celano (ca. 1200–ca. 1255).

GRETCHEN How hateful it's here!
I feel as if stifling
In the organ tones!
The chanting is shrivelling
My heart into dust.
CHOIR *Judex ergo cum sedebit,*
Quidquid latet adparebit,
Nil inultum remanebit.[2]
GRETCHEN How shut in I feel,
The pillars imprison me!
The vaulting presses
Down on me!—Air!
EVIL SPIRIT Hide yourself, do! Sin and shame
Never stay hidden.
Air? Light?
Poor thing that you are!
CHOIR *Quid sum miser tunc dicturus?*
Quem patronum rogaturus,
Cum vix justus sit securus?[3]
EVIL SPIRIT The blessed avert
Their faces from you.
Pure souls with a shudder
Snatch their hands back from you.
Poor thing!
CHOIR *Quid sum miser tunc dicturus?*
GRETCHEN Your smelling salts, neighbor!
[*She swoons.*]

Walpurgis Night

The Harz Mountains, near Schierke and Elend. FAUST, MEPHISTOPHELES.

MEPHISTO What you would like now is a broomstick, right?
Myself, give me a tough old billy goat.
We've got a ways to go still, on this route.
FAUST While legs hold up and breath comes freely,
This knotty blackthorn's all I want.
Hastening our journey, what's the point?
To loiter through each winding valley,
Then clamber up this rocky slope
Down which that stream there tumbles ceaselessly—
That's what gives the pleasure to our tramp.
The spring has laid her finger on the birch,
Even the fir tree feels her touch,

2. When the judge shall be seated, what is hidden shall appear, nothing shall remain unavenged (Latin).

3. What shall I say in my wretchedness? To whom shall I appeal when scarcely the righteous man is safe? (Latin.)

Then mustn't our limbs feel new energy?
MEPHISTO Must they? I don't feel that way, not me.
My season's strictly wintertime,
I'd much prefer we went through ice and snow.
The waning moon, making its tardy climb
Up the sky, gives off a reddish glow
So sad and dim, at every step you run
Into a tree or stumble on a stone.
You won't mind my begging assistance
Of a will-o'-the wisp[1]—and there's one no great distance,
Shining for all he's worth, so merrily.
—Hello there, friend, we'd like your company!
Why blaze away so uselessly, for nothing?
Do us a favor, light up this path we're climbing.
WILL-O'-THE-WISP I hope the deep respect I hold you in, sir,
Will keep in check my all-too-skittish temper;
The way we go is zigzag, that's our nature.
MEPHISTO Trying to ape mankind, poor silly flame.
Now listen to me: fly straight, in the Devil's name,
Or out I'll blow your feeble light immediately.
WILL-O'-THE-WISP Yes, yes, you give the orders here, quite right;
I'll do what you require, happily,
But don't forget, the mountain on this night
Is mad with magic, witchcraft, sorcery,
And if Jack-o'-Lantern is your guide,
Don't expect more than he can provide.
FAUST, MEPHISTOPHELES, WILL-O'-THE-WISP [*Singing in turn*]
We have entered, as it seems,
Realm of magic, realm of dreams,
Lead us well and win such honor
His to have, bright-shining creature,
By whose flicker we may hasten
Forward through this wide, waste region!

See the trees, one then another,
Spinning past us fast and faster,
And the cliffs impending over,
And the jutting crags, like noses
Winds blow through with snoring noises!

Over stones and through the heather
Rills and runnels downwards hasten.
Is that water splashing, listen,
Is it singing, that soft murmur,
Is it love's sweet voice, lamenting,

1. A wavering light formed by marsh gas. In German folklore, it was thought to lead travelers to their destruction.

For the days when all was heaven?
How our hearts hoped, loving, yearning!
And like a tale, an old, familiar,
Echo once more tells it over.

Whoo-oo! Owl's hoot's heard nearer,
Cry of cuckoo and of plover—
Still not nested, still awake?
Are those lizards in the brake,
Straggle-legged, big of belly?
And roots winding every which way
In the rock and sand send far out
Shoots to snare and make us cry out.
Tree warts, swollen, gross excrescents,
Send their tentacles like serpents
Out to catch us. And mice scamper
In great packs of every color
Through the moss and through the heather,
And the glowworms swarm around us
In dense clouds and only lead us
Hither, thither, to confuse us.

Tell me, are we standing still, or
Still advancing, climbing higher?
Everything spins round us wildly,
Rocks and trees grin at us madly,
And the errant lights, more of them ever,
Puff themselves up, big and bigger.

MEPHISTO Seize hold of my coattails, quick,
We're coming to a middling peak
Where you'll marvel at the sight
Of Mammon's Mountain burning bright.[2]

FAUST How strange that glow is, there, far down,
Sad and pinkish, like the dawn.
Its faint luminescence reaches
Deep into the yawning gorges,
Mist rises here and streams away there,
Penetrated by pale fire.
Here, like a thin thread, the glitter
Winds along, then like a fountain
Overflowing, spills down the mountain,
And vein-like, branching all about,
Holds in gleaming embrace the valley,
And here, squeezed through a narrow gully,

2. Mammon is imagined as leading a group of fallen angels in digging out gold and gems from the ground of hell, presumably for Satan's palace, as described in Milton's *Paradise Lost* 1.678 ff.

Collects into a pool apart,
Sparks fly about as if a hand
Were scattering golden grains of sand,
And look there, how from base to top,
The whole cliffside is lit up.

MEPHISTO Holiday time Lord Mammon's castle
Puts on a show that has no equal.
Don't you agree? You saw it, very luckily.
I hear our guests arriving—not so quietly!

FAUST What a gale of wind is blowing,
Buffeting my back and shoulders!

MEPHISTO Clutch with your fingers that outcropping
Or you'll fall to your death among the boulders.
The mist is making it darker than ever.
Hear how the trees are pitching and tossing!
Frightened, the owls fly up in a flutter,
The evergreen palace's pillars are creaking
And cracking, boughs snapping and breaking,
As down the trunks thunder
With a shriek of roots tearing,
Piling up on each other
In a fearful disorder!
And through the wreckage-strewn ravines
The hurtling storm blast howls and screams.
And hear those voices in the air,
Some far-off and others near?
That's the witches' wizard singing,
Along the mountain shrilly ringing.

CHORUS OF WITCHES

The witches ride up to the Brocken,
Stubble's yellow, new grain green,
The great host meets upon the peak and
There Urian[3] mounts his throne.
So over stock and stone go stumping,
Witches farting, billy goats stinking!

VOICE Here comes Mother Baubo[4] now,
Riding on an old brood sow.

CHORUS

Honor to whom honor is due!
Old Baubo to the head of the queue!
A fat pig and a fat frau on her,
And all the witches following after!

VOICE How did you come?

VOICE Ilsenstein way.
I peeked in an owl's nest, passing by.

3. A name for the devil.
4. In Greek mythology, the nurse of Demeter, noted for her obscenity and bestiality.

VOICE Oh, I wish you'd go to hell, all,
Why such a rush, such an insane scramble?
VOICE Too fast, too fast, my bottom's skinned sore!
Oh, my wounds! Look here and here!
CHORUS OF WITCHES
Broad the way and long the road,
What a bumbling, stumbling crowd!
Broomstraw scratches, pitchfork's pushed,
Mother's ripped and baby's crushed.
HALF-CHORUS OF WARLOCKS
We crawl like snails lugging their whorled shell,
The women have got a good mile's lead.
When where you're going's to the Devil,
It's woman knows how to get up speed.
OTHER HALF-CHORUS
A mile or so, why should we care?
Women may get the start of us,
But for all of their forehandedness,
One jump carries a man right there.
VOICE [*Above*] Come along with us, you down at the lake.
VOICE [*From below*] Is there anything better we would like?
We scrub ourselves clean as a whistle,
But it's no use, still we're infertile.
BOTH CHORUSES
The wind is still, the stars are fled,
The veiled moon's glad to hide her head,
Rushing, roaring, the mad chorus
Scatters sparks by the thousands about us.
VOICE [*From below*] Wait, please, wait, only a minute!
VOICE [*Above*] A voice from that crevice, did you hear it?
VOICE [*From below*] Take me along, don't forget me!
For three hundred years I've tried to climb
Up to the summit—all in vain.
I long for creatures who are like me.
BOTH CHORUSES
Straddle a broomstick, a pitchfork's fine too,
Get up on a goat, a plain stick will do.
Who can't make it up tonight,
Forever is done for, and so good night.
HALF-WITCH [*From below*] I trot breathlessly, and yet
How far ahead the rest have got.
No peace at all at home, and here
It's no better. Dear, oh dear!
CHORUS OF WITCHES
The unction[5] gives us hags a lift,
A bit of rag will do for a sail,
Any tub's a fine sky boat—
Don't fly now and you never will.

BOTH CHORUSES
And when we've gained the very top,
Light down, swooping, to a stop,
We'll darken the heath entirely
With all our swarming witchery.
[*They alight.*]

MEPHISTO What a crowding and shoving, rushing and clattering,
Hissing and shrieking, pushing and chattering,
Burning and sparking, stinking and shaking,
We're among witches, no mistaking!
Stick close to me or we'll lose one another.
But where are you?

FAUST Here, over here!

MEPHISTO Already swept away so far!
I must show this mob who is master—
Out of the way of Voland the Devil,
Out of the way, you charming rabble!
Doctor, hang on, we'll make a quick dash
And get ourselves out of this terrible crush—
Even for me it's too much to endure.
Yonder's a light has a strange lure,
Those bushes, I don't know why, attract me.
Quick now, dive in that shrubbery!

FAUST Spirit of Contradiction! However,
Lead the way!—He's clever, my devil:
Walpurgis Night up the Brocken we scramble
So as to do what? Hide ourselves in a corner!

MEPHISTO Look at that fire there, burning brightly,
Clubmen meeting, all seeming so sprightly;
You don't feel alone when the company's fewer.

FAUST But I would like it better higher,
On the summit, where I make out
A red glow and black smoke swirling,
Satanwards a great crowd's toiling,
And there, I haven't the least doubt,
Many a riddle at last is resolved.

MEPHISTO And many another one revealed.
Let the world rush on crazily,
We'll pass the time here cozily,
And doing what customarily's the thing done,
Inside the great world contrive us a little one.
Look there, young witches, all stark naked,
And old ones wisely petticoated.
Don't sulk, be nice, if only to please me;
Plenty of fun—as for trouble, hardly.
I hear music, a damned racket!

5. Magical ointment made from the fat of unborn babies that witches smear on their broomsticks.

You must learn not to mind it.
No backing out now, follow me in
And find you are my debtor again.
—Now what do you think of this place, my friend?
Our eyes can hardly see to its end.
A hundred fires, in a row blinking,
The people shouting, dancing, drinking,
Eating, loving, oh what a party!
Where is there anything better, show me.

FAUST To get us admitted to the revel,
You'll appear how, as magician or devil?

MEPHISTO I travel incognito normally,
But when it comes to celebrations
A man must show his decorations.
The Garter's never been awarded me,[6]
But in these parts the split hoof's much respected.
That snail there, do you see it, creeping forwards,
Its face pushing this way, that way, towards us?
Already I've been smelt out, I'm detected.
Even if deception was my aim,
Here there's no denying who I am.
Come on, we'll go along from fire to fire,
The go-between me, you the cavalier.
[*Addressing figures huddled around a fire*]
Old sirs, you keep apart, not very merry,
You'd please me better if you joined the party.
You ought to be carousing with the youngsters,
At home we're all alone enough, we oldsters.

GENERAL Put no trust in nations, for the people,
In spite of all you've done, are never grateful.
It's with them always as it is with women,
The young come first, and we—ignored, forgotten.

MINISTER OF STATE The world has got completely off the track.
Oh, they were men, the older generation!
When we held every high position,
That was the golden age, and no mistake.

PARVENU We were no simpletons ourselves, we weren't,
And often did so many things we shouldn't.
But everything's turned topsy-turvy now,
Just when we're foursquare with the status quo.

AUTHOR Who wants, today, to read a book
With a modicum of sense or wit?
And as for our younger folk,
I've never seen such rude conceit.

MEPHISTO [*Suddenly transformed into an old man*]
For Judgment Day all now are ripe and ready,

6. That is, he has no decoration of nobility, such as the Order of the Garter, the highest order of chivalry, bestowed by the king or queen of England.

Since I shan't ever again climb Brocken's top;
And considering too my wine of life is running cloudy,
The world also is coming to a stop.

JUNK-DEALER WITCH Good sirs, don't pass me unawares,
Don't miss this opportunity!
Look here, will you, at my wares,
What richness, what variety!
Yet there is not a single item
Hasn't served to claim a victim,
Nowhere on earth will you find such a stall!
No dagger here but it has drunk hot blood,
No cup but from it deadly poison's flowed
To waste a body once robust and hale,
No gem but has seduced a loving girl,
No sword but has betrayed an ally or a friend,
Or struck an adversary from behind.

MEPHISTO Auntie, think about the times you live in—
What's past is done. Done and gone!
The new, the latest, that's what you should deal in,
The nouveau only, turns us on.

FAUST Oh let me not forget I'm me, me, solely!
A fair to beat all fairs this is, believe me.

MEPHISTO The scrambling mob climbs upwards, jostling, crushed,
You think you're pushing and you're being pushed.

FAUST Who's that there?

MEPHISTO Look at her close.
Lilith.[7]

FAUST Lilith? What's she to us?

MEPHISTO Adam's wife, his first. Beware of her.
Her beauty's one boast is her dangerous hair.
When Lilith winds it tight around young men
She doesn't soon let go of them again.

FAUST Look, one old witch, one young one, there they sit—
They've waltzed around a lot already, I will bet!

MEPHISTO Tonight's no night for resting but for fun,
Let's join the dance, a new one's just begun.

FAUST [*Dancing with the young witch*]
A lovely dream I dreamt one day:
I saw a green-leaved apple tree,
Two apples swayed upon a stem,
So tempting! I climbed up for them.

THE PRETTY WITCH Ever since the days of Eden
Apples have been man's desire,
How overjoyed I am to know, sir,
Apples grow, too, in my garden.

7. According to rabbinical legend, Adam's first wife; the *female* mentioned in Genesis 1.27: "So God created man in his own image, in the image of God created he him; male and female created he them." After Eve was created, Lilith became a ghost who seduced men and inflicted evil on children.

MEPHISTO [*Dancing with the old witch*]
A naughty dream I dreamt one day:
I saw a tree split up the middle—
A huge cleft, phenomenal!
And yet it pleased me every way.
THE OLD WITCH Welcome, welcome, to you, sire,
Cloven-footed cavalier!
Stand to with a proper stopper,
Unless you fear to come a cropper.
PROCTOPHANTASMIST[8] Accursed tribe, so bold, presumptuous!
Hasn't it been proven past disputing
Spirits all are footless, they lack standing?
And here you're footing like the rest of us!
THE PRETTY WITCH [*Dancing*]
What's he doing here, at our party?
FAUST [*Dancing*]
Him? You find him everywhere, that killjoy,
We others dance, he does the criticizing,
Every step one takes requires analyzing,
Until it's jawed about, it hasn't yet occurred.
He can't stand how we go forwards undeterred;
If you keep going around in the same old circle,
As he plods year in, year out on his treadmill,
You might be favored with his good opinion,
Provided you most humbly beg it of him.
PROCTOPHANTASMIST Still here, are you? It's an outrage!
Vanish, ours is the Enlightened Age—
You devils, no respect for law and regulation,
We've grown so wise, yet ghosts still walk in Tegel.[9]
How long I've toiled to banish superstition,
Yet it lives on. The whole thing is a scandal!
THE PRETTY WITCH Stop, stop, how boring you are with your gabble!
PROCTOPHANTASMIST I tell you to your face, you ghostly freaks,
I'll not endure this tyranny of spooks
My spirit finds you spirits much too spiritual!
[*They go on dancing.*]
I see I'm getting nowhere with these devils,
Still, it will add a chapter to my travels,
And I hope, before my sands of life run out,
To put foul fiends and poets all to rout.
MEPHISTO He'll go and plump himself down in a puddle—
It solaces him for all his ghostly trouble—

8. A German coinage meaning "one who exorcises evil spirits by sitting in a pond and applying leeches to his behind" (see lines 3908–11). The figure caricatures Friedrich Nicolai (1733–1811), who opposed modern movements in German thought and literature and had parodied Goethe's *The Sorrows of Young Werther* (1774).

9. A town near Berlin where ghosts had been reported.

And purge away his ghost and all the other spirits
By having leeches feed on where the M'sieur sits.[1]
[*To* FAUST, *who has broken off dancing and withdrawn*]
What's this? You've left your partner in the lurch
As she was sweetly singing, pretty witch.

FAUST Ugh! From her mouth a red mouse sprung
In the middle of her song.

MEPHISTO Is that anything to fuss about?
And anyway it wasn't gray, was it?
To take on so, to me, seems simply rudeness
When you are sporting with your Amaryllis.

FAUST And then I saw—

MEPHISTO Saw what?

FAUST Look over there,
At that lovely child, pale-faced with fear,
Standing by herself. How laboriously
She pushes herself forwards, wracked by pains,
As if her feet were shackled tight in chains.
I must confess, it looks like Gretchen.

MEPHISTO Let it be!
It's bad, that thing, a lifeless shape, a wraith
No man ever wants to meet up with.
Your blood freezes under her dead stare,
Almost turned to stone, you are.
Medusa,[2] did you ever hear of her?

FAUST Yes, yes, those are a corpse's eyes
No loving hand was by to close.
That's Gretchen's breast, which she so often
Gave to me to rest my head on,
That shape her dear, her lovely body,
She gave to me to enjoy freely.

MEPHISTO It's all magic, hocus-pocus, idiot!
Her power is, each thinks she's his own sweetheart.

FAUST What rapture! And what suffering!
I stand here spellbound by her look.
How strange, that bit of scarlet string
That ornaments her lovely neck,
No thicker than a knife blade's back.

MEPHISTO Right you are. I see it, too.
She's also perfectly able to
Tuck her head beneath her arm
And stroll about. Perseus—remember him?—
He is the one that hacked it off her.
—Man, I'd think you'd have enough of

1. Nicolai claimed that he had been bothered by ghosts but had repelled them by applying leeches to his rump.

2. The Gorgon with hair of serpents whose glance turned people to stone.

The mad ideas your head is stuffed with!
Come, we'll climb this hill, discover
All's as lively as inside the Prater.[3]
And unless somebody has bewitched me,
The thing I see there is a theater.
What's happening?

SERVIBILIS A play, a new one, starting shortly,
Last of seven. With us here it's customary
To offer a full repertory.
The playwright's a rank amateur,
Amateurs, too, the whole company.
Well, I must hurry off now, please excuse me,
I need to raise the curtain—amateurishly!

MEPHISTO How right it is that I should find you here, sirs;
The Blocksberg's just the place for amateurs.

Walpurgis Night's Dream
or
OBERON AND TITANIA'S GOLDEN WEDDING

INTERMEZZO[1]

STAGE MANAGER [*To crew*] Today we'll put by paint and canvas,
Mieding's[2] brave sons, all.
Nature paints the scene for us:
Gray steep and mist-filled vale.

HERALD For the wedding to be golden,
Years must pass, full fifty;
But if the quarrel is made up, then
It is golden truly.

OBERON Spirits, if you hover round,
Appear, it's right, the hour;
King and Queen are once more bound
Lovingly together.

PUCK[3] Here's Puck, my lord, who spins and whirls
And cuts a merry caper,
A hundred follow at his heels,
Skipping to the measure.

ARIEL[4] Ariel strikes up his song,
The notes as pure as silver;
Philistines[5] all around him throng,
Those, too, with true culture.

OBERON Wives and husbands, learn from us
How two hearts unite:

3. A famous park in Vienna.
1. Brief interlude. Oberon and Titania are king and queen of the fairies.
2. Johann Martin Mieding (d. 1782), a master carpenter and scene builder in the Weimar theater.
3. A mischievous spirit.
4. A helpful sprite.
5. Those who disregard intellectual or artistic values.

To find connubial happiness,
Only separate.

TITANIA If Master sulks and Mistress pouts,
Here's the remedy:
Send her on a trip down south,
Him the other way.

FULL ORCHESTRA [*Fortissimo*][6] Buzzing fly and humming gnat,
And all their consanguinity,
Frog's hoarse croak, cicada's chat
Compose our symphony.

SOLO Here I come, the bagpipes, who's
Really a soap bubble;
Hear me through my stumpy nose
Go tootle-doodle-doodle.

A BUDDING IMAGINATION A spider's foot, a green toad's gut,
Two winglets—though they hardly
Compose a living creature, yet
Make do as nonsense poetry.

A COUPLE Short steps, smart leaps, all done neatly
In the honeyed air.
I grant you foot it very featly,
We stay planted here.

AN INQUIRING TRAVELER Can it be a fairground fraud,
The shape at which I'm looking?
Oberon the handsome god
Still alive and kicking?

A PIOUS BELIEVER I don't see claws, nor any tail,
And yet it's indisputable:
Like Greece's gods, his dishabille[7]
Betrays the pagan devil.

AN ARTIST OF THE NORTH Here everything I undertake
Is weak, is thin, is sketchy;
But I'm preparing soon to make
My Italian journey.

A STICKLER FOR DECORUM I'm here, and most unhappily,
Where all's impure, improper;
Among this riotous witchery
Only two wear powder.

A YOUNG WITCH Powder, like a petticoat,
Is right for wives with gray hair;
But I'll sit naked on my goat,
Show off my strapping figure.

A MATRON We are too well bred by far
To bandy words about,
But may you, young thing that you are,
Drop dead, and soon, cheap tart!

6. Italian, used as a direction in music to play very loudly.

7. Carelessly dressed or partly undressed.

THE CONDUCTOR Mosquito's nose, gnat's proboscis,
Mind you keep the tempo.
Let be, you bugs, the naked miss—
On with the concerto!

A WEATHERCOCK [*Pointing one way*]
No better company than maids
Like these, so kind, complaisant;
And bachelors to match, old boys,
Agog all, all impatient!

WEATHERCOCK [*Pointing the other way*]
And if the earth don't open up
And swallow this lewd rabble,
Off I'll race at a great clip,
Myself go to the Devil.

SATIRICAL EPIGRAMS [XENIEN][8] Gadflies, we, who plant our sting
In hides highborn and bourgeois,
In so doing honoring
Great Satan, our dear Papa.

HENNINGS[9] Look there at the pack of them,
Like schoolboys jeering meanly.
Next, I'm sure, they all will claim
It's all in fun, friends, really.

MUSAGET[1] ["LEADER OF THE MUSES"]
If I joined these witches here
I'm sure I'd not repine;
I know I'd find it easier
To lead them than the Nine.[2]

THE QUONDAM "SPIRIT OF THE AGE."[3]
What counts is knowing the right people,
Catch hold and we'll go places;
Blocksberg's top holds lots, so ample,
Like Germany's Parnassus.[4]

THE INQUIRING TRAVELER Who's that fellow who's so stiff
And marches so majestical?
He sniffs away for all he's worth,
"Pursuing things Jesuitical."[5]

A CRANE An earnest fisherman I am,
In clear and troubled waters.
And thus you see a pious man
Hobnobbing with devils.

A CHILD OF THIS WORLD All occasions serve the godly

8. Literally, polemical verses written by Goethe and Friedrich von Schiller (1759–1805). The characters here are versions of Goethe himself.

9. August Adolf von Hennings (1746–1826), publisher of *Genius of the Age*, a journal that had attacked Schiller.

1. The title of a collection of Hennings's poetry.

2. The nine muses, or Greek goddesses of art and science.

3. That is, former "Genius of the Age"; probably alludes to the journal's change of title in 1800 to *Genius of the Nineteenth Century*.

4. A mountain sacred to Apollo and the Muses; hence, figuratively, the locale of poetic excellence.

5. The Jesuits were a Catholic religious order, famous for their cunning, case-by-case arguments.

In their work. Atop
The Blocksberg, even there, they
Set up religious shop.

A DANCER What's that booming, a new team
Of musicians coming?
No, no, they're bitterns in the stream
All together drumming.

THE DANCING MASTER How cautiously they lift their feet—
Draw back in fear of tripping!
The knock-kneed hop, they jump the stout,
Heedless how they're looking.

THE FIDDLER This riffraff's so hate-filled, each lusts
To slit the other's throat;
Orpheus with his lute tamed beasts:[6]
These march to the bagpipes' note.

A DOGMATIST I can't be rattled, no, by your
Doubts, suspicions, quibbles;
The Devil's real, he is, that's sure,
Else how would there be devils?

AN IDEALIST The mind's creative faculty
This time has gone too far;
If everything I see is me,
Daft I am for sure.

A REALIST It's pandemonium, it's mad,
I'm floored, I am, dumbfounded!
This is the first time I have stood
On ground on nothing founded.

A SUPERNATURALIST The presence of these devils here
For me is reassuring evidence:
From the demonical I infer
The angelical's existence.

A SKEPTIC They see a flickering light and gloat,
There's treasure there, oh surely;
Devil's a word that pairs with doubt,
This is a place made for me.

CONDUCTOR Frogs in leaves, grasshoppers grass—
What damned amateurs!
Cicadas chirr, mosquitos buzz—
Call yourselves performers!

THE SMART ONES Sans all souci[7] we are, shift
About with lightning speed;
When walking on the feet is out,
We walk on the head.

THE NOT-SO SMART ONES At court we sat down to free dinners,
And now all doors are shut;
We've worn out our dancing slippers
And must limp barefoot.

6. In Greek mythology, Orpheus's music was said to have the power to quiet wild animals.

7. Without any care or unhappiness (French).

WILL-O-THE-WISPS We're from the muddy flats, marais,[8]
Such is our lowly origin;
But now we shine as chevaliers
And dance in the cotillion.

A SHOOTING STAR I shot across the sky's expanse,
A meteor, blazing bright.
Now fallen, I sprawl in the grass—
Who'll help me to my feet?

THE BRUISERS Make way, make way, we're coming through,
Trampling your lawn,
We're spirits too, but spirits who
Have lots of beef and brawn.

PUCK How you tramp, so heavily,
Like infant elephants!
Elfin Puck's stamp be today
The heaviest of tramps.

ARIEL Or gave you wings, our loving Nature,
Or gave you them the Spirit,
Come, my light trace fly after,
Up to the rose hill's summit.

ORCHESTRA [*Pianissimo*][9]
Shrouding mists and trailing clouds
Lighten in the dawning,
Breeze stirs leaves, wind rattles reeds,
And all, all, gone in the morning.

An Overcast Day. A Field

FAUST *and* MEPHISTOPHELES.

FAUST In misery! In despair! Stumbling about pitifully over the earth for so long, and now a prisoner! A condemned criminal, shut up in a dungeon and suffering horrible torments, the poor unfortunate child! It's come to this, to this! And not a word about it breathed to me, you treacherous, odious spirit! Stand there rolling your Devil's eyes around in rage, oh do! Brazen it out with your intolerable presence! A prisoner! In misery, irremediable misery! Delivered up to evil spirits and the stony-hearted justice of mankind! And meanwhile you distract me with your insipid entertainments, keep her situation, more desperate every day, from me, and leave her to perish helplessly!

MEPHISTO She's not the first.

FAUST You dog, you monster! Change him, O you infinite Spirit, change the worm back into a dog, give it back the shape it wore those evenings when it liked to trot ahead of me and roll at the feet of some innocent wayfarer, tripping him up and leaping on him as he fell. Give it back its favorite shape so it can crawl on its belly in the sand before me, and I can kick it as it deserves, the abomination!—Not the first!—Such mis-

8. French for marsh or swamp.
9. Italian, direction in music to play very softly.

ery, such misery! It's inconceivable, humanly inconceivable, that more than one creature should ever have plumbed such depths of misery, that the first who did, writhing in her last agony under the eyes of the Eternal Forgiveness, shouldn't have expiated the guilt of all the others who came after! I am cut to the quick, pierced to the marrow, by the suffering of this one being—you grin indifferently at the fate of thousands!

MEPHISTO So once again we're at our wits' end, are we—reached the point where you fellows start feeling your brain is about to explode? Why did you ever throw in with us if you can't see the thing through? You'd like to fly, but can't stand heights. Did we force ourselves on you or you on us?

FAUST Don't snarl at me that way with those wolfish fangs of yours, it sickens me!—Great and glorious Spirit, Spirit who vouchsafed to appear to me, who knows me in my heart and soul, why did you fasten me to this scoundrel who diets on destruction, delights to hurt?

MEPHISTO Finished yet?

FAUST Save her or you'll pay for it! With a curse on you, the dreadfullest there is, for thousands of years to come!

MEPHISTO I'm powerless to strike off the Great Avenger's chains or draw his bolts.—Save her indeed!—Who's the one who ruined her, I would like to know—you or me?

[FAUST *looks around wildly.*]

Looking for a thunderbolt, are you? A good thing you wretched mortals weren't given them. That's the tyrant's way of getting out of difficulties—strike down any innocent person who makes an objection, gets in his way.

FAUST Take me to where she is, you hear? She's got to be set free.

MEPHISTO In spite of the risk you would run? There's blood guilt on the town because of what you did. Where murder was, there the avenging spirits hover, waiting for the murderer to return.

FAUST That, from you, that too? Death and destruction, a world's worth, on your head, you monster! Take me there, I say, and set her free!

MEPHISTO All right, all right, I'll take you there. But hear what I can do—do you think all the powers of heaven and earth are mine? I'll muddle the turnkey's senses, then you seize his keys and lead her out. Only a human hand can do it. I'll keep watch. The spirit horses are ready. Off I'll carry both of you. That's what I can do.

FAUST Away then!

Night. Open Country

FAUST *and* MEPHISTOPHELES *going by on black horses at a furious gallop.*

FAUST What's that going on at the ravenstone?[1]
MEPHISTO Brewing something, doing something, don't know.
FAUST Soaring up, swooping down, bowing, genuflecting.
MEPHISTO A pack of witches.
FAUST Strewing stuff, consecrating.
MEPHISTO Keep going, keep going!

1. The block on which Gretchen will be beheaded.

A PRISON

FAUST [*With a bunch of keys and carrying a lamp, at a narrow iron door*]
I shudder as I haven't for so long—
Oh, how it suffers, our humanity!
She's shut up inside these dank walls, poor thing,
And all her crime was love, the brave, the illusory.
You're hanging back from going in!
You're afraid of meeting her eyes again!
In, in, your hesitation's her death, hurry!
[*He puts the key in the lock.*]

SINGING [*From within*]
My mother, the whore,
She's the one slew me,
My father, the knave,
He's the one ate me,
My sister, wee thing,
Heaped up my bones
Under cold stones,
Turned into a wood bird, I sing
Fly away, fly away!

FAUST [*Unlocking the door*] She doesn't dream her lover's listening,
Hears her chains rattle, the straw rustling.
[*He enters.*]

MARGARETE [*Cowering on her paillasse*][2]
They're coming, they're coming! How bitter, death, bitter!

FAUST [*Whispering*] Hush, dear girl, hush! You'll soon be free.

MARGARETE [*Groveling before him*]
If your heart's human, think how I suffer.

FAUST You'll wake the guards. Speak quietly.
[*Taking hold of the chains to unlock them*]

MARGARETE [*On her knees*] Headsman, so early, it isn't right.
Have mercy on me! Too soon, too soon!
You come for me in the dead of night—
Isn't it time enough at dawn?
[*Stands up.*]
I'm still so young, too young surely—
Still I must die.
How pretty I was, that's what undid me,
He held me so close, now he's far away,
My wreath pulled apart, the flowers scattered,
Don't grip me so hard! Please, won't you spare me?
What did I ever do to you?
Don't let me beg in vain for mercy.
I never before laid eyes on you.

FAUST It's unendurable, her misery!

MARGARETE What can I do, I'm in your power,

2. Thin straw mattress (French).

Only let me nurse my baby first,
All night long I hugged the dear creature;
How mean they were, snatched it from my breast,
And now they say I murdered it.
I'll never be happy, no, never again.
They sing songs about me in the street,
It's wicked of them.
There's an old fairy tale ends that way,
What has it got to do with me?

FAUST [*Falling at her feet*] It's me here who loves you, me at your feet
To rescue you from this miserable fate.

MARGARETE [*Kneeling beside him*]
We'll kneel down, that's right, and pray to the saints.
Look, under those steps,
Below the doorsill,
All Hell's a-boil.
The Evil One
In his horrible rage
Makes such a noise.

FAUST [*Crying out*] Gretchen! Gretchen!

MARGARETE [*Listening*] That was my darling's own dear voice!
[*She jumps up, the chains fall away.*]
I heard him call. Where can he be?
No one may stop me now, I'm free!
Into his arms I'll fly so fast,
Lie on his breast at last, at last.
Gretchen, he called, from there on the sill,
Through all the howlings and gnashings of Hell,
Through the furious, devilish sneering and scorn,
I heard a dear voice, its sound so well known.

FAUST It's me!

MARGARETE It's you! Oh, say it again.
[*Catching hold of him.*]
It's him! Where's the torture now, it's him!
Where's my fear of the prison, the chains they hung on me?
It's you, it's you! You've come here to save me!
I'm saved!
—I see it before me, so very plain,
The street I saw you the first time on,
I see Marthe and me where we waited for you
In the sunlit garden.

FAUST [*Pulling her toward the door*]
Come along, come!

MARGARETE Don't go, stay here!
I love it so being wherever you are.
[*Caressing him.*]

FAUST Hurry!
If you don't hurry
The price we will pay!

MARGARETE What? Don't know how to kiss anymore?
Parted from me a short time only
And quite forgotten what lips are for?
Why am I frightened with your arms around me?
Time was, at a word or a look from you,
Heaven herself threw her arms around me
And you kissed me as if you'd devour me.
Kiss me, kiss me,
Or I'll kiss you!
[*She embraces him.*]
Oh the cold lips you have,
Cold and dumb.
What's become of your love,
All gone?
Who stole it from me?
[*She turns away from him.*]

FAUST Come, follow me! Darling, be brave!
Oh, the kisses I'll give you, my love—
Only come now, we'll slip through the door.

MARGARETE [*Turning back to him*]
It's you, is it really? For sure?

FAUST Yes, it's me—you must come!

MARGARETE You strike off my chains,
Take me into your arms.
How is it you don't shrink away from me?
Have you any idea who you're setting free?

FAUST Hurry, hurry! The night's almost over.

MARGARETE I murdered my mother,
Drowned my infant,
Weren't both of us given it—you too its parent—
Equally? It's you, I can hardly believe it.
Give me your hand. No, I haven't dreamt it.
Your dear hand!—But your hand is wet!
Wipe it off, there's blood on it!
My God, my God, what did you do?
Put away your sword,
I beg you to!

FAUST What's past is done, forget it all.
You're killing me.

MARGARETE No, live on still.
I'll tell you how the graves should be;
Tomorrow you must see to it.
Give my mother the best spot,
My brother put alongside her,
Me, put me some distance off,
Yet not too far,
And at my right breast put my baby,
Nobody else shall lie beside me.
When I used to press up close to you,

How sweet it was, pure happiness,
But now I can't, it's over, all such bliss—
I feel it as an effort I must make,
That I must force myself on you,
And you, I feel, resist me, push me back.
And yet it's you, with your good, kind look.
FAUST If it's me, then come, we can't delay.
MARGARETE Out there?
FAUST Out there, away!
MARGARETE If the grave's out there, death ready,
Yes, come, the two of us together,
But only to the eternal place, no other.
—You're going now?
I'd go too if I could, Heinrich, believe me!
FAUST You can! All you need is the will. Oh come!
The way is clear.
MARGARETE No, I mayn't. For me all hope is gone.
It's useless, flight. They'd keep, I'm sure,
A sharp watch out. I'd find it dreadful
To have to beg my bread of people,
Beg with a bad conscience, too;
Dreadful to have to wander about
Where all is strange and new,
Only to end up getting caught.
FAUST But I'll stick with you!
MARGARETE Hurry! Be quick!
Save your poor child—
Run! Keep to the track
That follows the brook,
Over the bridge.
Into the wood
Left to the plank,
There in the pool—
Reach down, quick, catch it!
It's fighting for breath!
It's struggling still!
Save it, oh, save it!
FAUST Get hold of yourself.
One step and you're free, dear girl.
MARGARETE If only we were well past the hill.
There on a rock Mother sits, all a-tremble—
Not a sign does she make, doesn't speak.
There on a rock Mother sits, head a-wobble—
To look at her gives me a chill.
She slept so long she will never wake,
She slept so we might have our pleasure—
The happy hours we spent together!
FAUST If all my persuading is no use,
I'll have to carry you off by force.

MARGARETE Let go, let go, how dare you compel me!
You're gripping my arm so brutally!
I always did what you wanted, once.
FAUST Soon day will be breaking! Darling, darling!
MARGARETE Day? Yes, day, my last one, dawning,
My wedding day it should have been.
Not a word to a soul you've already been with your Gretchen.
My poor wreathe!
All's over and done.
We'll see one another again,
But not to go dancing.
The crowd presses in—not a sound, nothing,
Not the cry of a child.
There are too many
For square and alley
To hold.
The bell calls, staff's shattered,
I'm seized and I'm fettered
And borne away, bound, to the block.
Every neck shivers with shock
As the sharp blade's brought down on my own.
Dumb lies the world as the grave.
FAUST I wish I had never been born.
MEPHISTOPHELES [*Appearing outside*]
Come, come, or all's up with you, friend—
Debating, delaying, useless jabbering!
My horses are trembling.
A minute or two and it's day.
MARGARETE Who's that rising up out of the ground?
It's him, him, oh drive him away!
It's holy here, what is he after?
It's me he is after, me!
FAUST Live, hear me, live!
MARGARETE It's the judgment of God! I surrender!
MEPHISTO Die both of you, I have to leave.
MARGARETE In your hands, our Father, oh save me!
You angelical hosts, stand about me!
Draw up in your ranks to protect me!
I'm afraid of you, Heinrich, afraid!
MEPHISTO She's condemned.
VOICE [*From above*]
She is saved!
MEPHISTO [*To* FAUST, *peremptorily*]
Come with me!
[*He disappears with* FAUST.]
VOICE [*From within, dying away*]
Heinrich! Heinrich!

FREDERICK DOUGLASS

1818?–1895

There was no more important African American public figure in the nineteenth century than Frederick Douglass. Born into slavery, he could easily have remained illiterate his whole life. But with extraordinary ingenuity and perseverance, he taught himself to read, and soon turned himself into such an electrifying antislavery speaker and writer that some audiences simply could not believe that he had grown up a slave. Even skeptics found themselves won over by his charismatic personality, acerbic wit, and skillful arguments. Douglass's eloquence became a powerful weapon in the war against slavery, as he edited an influential abolitionist newspaper, stirred crowded lecture halls in the United States, Great Britain, and Ireland, and published his bestselling *Narrative of the Life of Frederick Douglass, an American Slave, Written by Himself* (1845).

LIFE

Frederick Augustus Washington Bailey was born in Talbot County in the slave state of Maryland sometime around 1818. He barely knew his mother, a slave, and never knew the identity of his father, probably a white man and perhaps his owner. At first he lived in his grandmother's cabin, and then at the age of six he went to live in the house of his owner, the chief overseer of a vast plantation belonging to one of the wealthiest men in Maryland. It was during this period, as Douglass recounts in horrifying detail in his autobiography, that he first witnessed the daily cruelty suffered by plantation slaves.

An important turning point came in 1826 when Frederick was sent to live with Hugh and Sophia Auld, relatives of his owner in Baltimore. One of the most famous episodes in the autobiography tells of the moment when Hugh Auld discovered that his wife was teaching the slave to read. He burst out angrily that literacy would make Frederick "discontented" and "unmanageable" and so "would forever unfit him to be a slave." This reprimand transformed the slave's life: "From that moment," Douglass writes, "I understood the pathway from slavery to freedom." In the seven years that he remained with the Aulds, Douglass used his best resources to learn how to read and write, discovering two texts that would significantly shape his later career: Caleb Bingham's *The Columbian Orator* (1807), and the speeches of Thomas Sheridan, an eighteenth-century Irish actor and educator. Both were guides to public speaking.

In 1833 Hugh Auld's brother, Thomas, who had become Frederick Bailey's official owner, called him back to work on his plantation. Thomas Auld was a cruel master, but he found the slave so unruly that he sent him to a harsh "slave breaker" for a year to tame him. Douglass was not tamed, however; he defied and bested this notoriously brutal master in a long physical struggle, which, he says, resolved him to break free from slavery altogether: "however long I might remain a slave in form, the day passed forever when I could be a slave in fact."

After a first abortive attempt at escape, Douglass returned to Hugh Auld in Baltimore, where he learned caulking skills in the shipyard and began to turn his weekly wages over to his master. During this period of relative independence he met and fell in love with a free black woman named Anna Murray. Then, in 1838, he managed a successful escape. In the *Narrative* he was reluctant to divulge his strategies in case publicizing them would endanger other slaves trying to escape, but much later, after slavery had ended, he told the full story. First he disguised himself as a sailor and borrowed the identification papers of a free black seaman; then he traveled by train and ferry to New York, and with the help of abolitionists, moved to New Bedford, Massachusetts. There he married Murray, changed his name, and worked odd jobs to make a living. He also began to read an abolitionist newspaper, *The Liberator.* In 1841 he met its celebrated and controversial editor, William Lloyd Garrison, who invited Douglass to work for him as a traveling lecturer, telling the story of his life and selling subscriptions to the newspaper.

This marked the beginning of Douglass's extraordinarily successful public career. From the outset, his lectures moved his audiences to laughter, tears, and rapt attention. "As a speaker, he has few equals," claimed a contemporary editor. "I would give twenty thousand dollars if I could deliver an address in that manner," said another. In a context where apologists for slavery argued that Southern slaves were contented—living comfortable lives with kindly owners—Douglass's story offered a compelling counternarrative. And yet, from the beginning, he was also accused of fabricating the facts. His oratorical elegance and skill were so striking that a few abolitionists pleaded with him to put a little more "plantation" into his speech, so that he would seem more authentic. Douglass refused.

The public lectures paved the way for the *Narrative of the Life of Frederick Douglass* in two ways. First, although Douglass's speeches regularly told of the cruelties of slaveholding, mocked hypocritical proslavery ministers, and asked Northern audiences to confront inequality and prejudice in the free states, the centerpiece of his lectures was his own life story. He had tested it out on audience after audience; he knew it had power, and he was eager to disseminate it widely. Second, given the many accusations of fraud against Douglass, he wanted to publish details about the people and places he had known as a slave, so that others could confirm the truthfulness of his account. But publishing the details also put Douglass in danger. There was always the threat that a fugitive slave would be recaptured and sent back to the South, and now his owners could recognize him from his narrative and come to claim him. Douglass left the United States for England in 1845, just a few months after the autobiography appeared.

For two years Douglass traveled through Great Britain and Ireland, lecturing to enthusiastic crowds. By 1848 the *Narrative* had gone through nine editions in England alone, and it was translated into French and German. Douglass was surprised at the relative lack of racial prejudice he encountered in Britain. Among the warmest receptions he had was from Daniel O'Connell, the leader of the struggle against British colonial rule in Ireland. In England two Quakers gave Douglass the money to buy his own freedom, and in December of 1846 he became officially a free man.

Back in the United States, Douglass broke from Garrison's organization. Garrison was a powerful voice in the antislavery cause, but he paid Douglass less than the white lecturers on his circuit and patronized him, urging him to focus only on telling the story of his own life because, Garrison suggested, a black man was not capable of analyzing slavery as a large-scale social problem. Garrison also refused to fight for the vote for African Americans. Setting up on his own, Douglass launched an antislavery newspaper called the *North Star* in Rochester, New York. This city was an important stop on the underground railroad—the secret route organized around safe houses which fugitive slaves followed to Canada. The Douglass household harbored so many runaway slaves that there were sometimes as many as eleven fugitives staying in the house at a time. But the city was less committed to full racial equality than the Douglasses had hoped: their oldest daughter, Rosetta, was not allowed to attend public school, and the private school she attended forbade her to learn with the white students. Douglass began a campaign to end segregation in the schools. In 1848 he attended the women's rights convention in Seneca Falls, and he emerged as a stalwart champion of women's suffrage. The motto of the *North Star* marked his commitment to gender as well as racial equality: "Right is of no sex," it read. "Truth is of no color."

When the Civil War broke out in 1861, Douglass led efforts to persuade Congress and President Lincoln to allow African American men to enlist in the Union Army. This struggle succeeded, and in 1863, Douglass actively recruited soldiers to fight, including his own two sons, Lewis and Charles. After the war was over, he led the campaign for black suffrage, and prevailed in 1870 with the passage of the Fifteenth Amendment to the US Constitution, which states that citizens cannot be denied the vote "on account of race, color, or previous condition of servitude."

The following years saw Douglass working tirelessly to expose and denounce discrimination and violence. He moved to Washington, DC, where he held several government offices. In 1889 he accepted the position of consul-general to Haiti and moved there, but later resigned when he was told that he was too sympathetic to Haitian interests. His wife died in 1882, and Douglass later married Helen Pitts, a white woman. After speaking at the National Council of Women, he died of a heart attack in 1895. On hearing the news of Douglass's death, the women's rights activist Elizabeth Cady Stanton remembered hearing him speak for the first time: "He stood there like an African prince, majestic in his wrath, as with wit, satire, and indignation he graphically described the bitterness of slavery. . . . Thus it was that I first saw Frederick Douglass, and wondered that any mortal man should have ever tried to subjugate a being with such talents, intensified with the love of liberty."

SLAVERY AND ABOLITION

In the southern United States in the nineteenth century, slaves worked in fields, in homes, and in mines; they built railroads and canals; they processed sugar and iron. But by far the most significant use of slave labor involved cotton production. Eli Whitney's 1793 invention of the cotton gin had accelerated the cleaning of cotton, and worldwide demand for cotton textiles—a source of cheap and lightweight clothing—had skyrocketed. But this was a crop that still needed to be handpicked in the fields. The booming cotton trade therefore demanded lots of arable land and a huge supply of labor—conditions met easily by the slave economy of the United States South. Nearly three quarters of all US slaves labored on cotton plantations, and by 1840 the southern United States produced more than half of the world's cotton. Cotton helped to drive the whole nation's economy, contributing substantially to the growth of Northern industry, shipping, and banking. It powered the global economy too. African traders used the term *americani* to refer to inexpensive cottons from the United States. And even after Britain had officially abolished slavery in its own territories, British traders imported vast quantities of cotton picked by US slaves, and British mills turned this raw material into textiles for sale around the world. About 10 percent of Britain's wealth came from the cotton trade. In 1858 US Senator James Hammond of South Carolina declared, "You dare not make war upon cotton. No power on earth dare make war upon it. Cotton is king!"

Intent on reaping as much profit as possible from their crops, plantation holders increasingly turned to the "gang system" to organize slave labor. Groups of slaves, under the command of an overseer, were forced—typically with whips, clubs, and threats—to perform a single repetitive task from the break of dawn until night. To increase efficiency, slaveholders would often rotate corn and cotton—ready at different times of the year—and use the corn to feed both slaves and animals on the plantation.

The state of Maryland, where Douglass was a slave, differed from most of the South. Maryland farms mostly grew tobacco rather than cotton, and the demand for tobacco was on the decline. Also, by the time that Frederick Douglass was born, Maryland had the highest number of free black men and women in the United States, more than half of its African American population. (By contrast, more than 99 percent of black people in Alabama, Texas, and Mississipi were slaves.) Working in the bustling city of Baltimore, surrounded by free blacks, Douglass had significantly more opportunities for escape than the plantation would have afforded.

Maryland was reputed to have a less harsh and dehumanizing slaveholder population than the "deep" South. In this respect as in many others, Douglass's *Narrative* challenged his readers' assumptions. In general the abolitionists felt that the best weapon against slavery was a campaign to reveal its horrors as fully and as accurately as possible. They went to significant trouble to demonstrate the evils of slavery and to confirm the truth of their claims. Some former slaves on the lecture circuit corroborated their accounts of violence by baring scars on their backs to horrified audiences.

Apart from organizing lecture tours and publishing books, abolitionists also sent volleys of pamphlets by mail to Southern states. But Southerners were not the only targets. As the abolitionist movement grew in the 1830s, activists increasingly focused their attention on the indifference of white Northerners, who mostly kept quiet on the subject of slavery. Neither major political party would mention it. And even in the North, angry mobs would descend on antislavery meetings and smash their printing presses. Douglass himself had his hand broken in Indiana. Dedicating themselves to exposing slavery to a wide public, abolitionists showed just how risky—and how powerful—words could be.

WORK

While the truthfulness of Douglass's story was a central question for his contemporaries, recent readers have been more inclined to admire the literary artfulness of the *Narrative*, its metaphorical richness, rhetorical complexity, and careful construction. Douglass casts his life as a long process of self-transformation—from an object, or an animal, to a free human being with a name. The contrast between the openings of the *Narrative* and of **Rousseau**'s ***Confessions*** is instructive. Rousseau begins by proclaiming that he differs from everyone else in his unique personality and character. Douglass, on the other hand, starts by reporting what he does *not* know of himself. He must guess his own age, he doesn't know his birthday, he has only rumor to tell him of his father's identity. Although he knows his mother, he spends virtually no time with her; she comes to him and leaves him in the dark. Most children develop their sense of who they are by precisely the clues missing in Douglass's experience: age, parentage, and such ritual occasions as birthdays. Douglass has only a generic identity: slave. Everything in Douglass's early experience denies his individuality and declares his lack of particularized identity. By the end, however, he claims a right to affirm himself: "I subscribe myself, FREDERICK DOUGLASS." The name itself is a triumph, not his father's or his mother's but the freshly bestowed name of his freedom. Each step of the way to this point—learning to read, learning to write, acquiring a name—has involved a painful self-testing, but the *word* proves for Douglass quite literally a means to salvation.

If Douglass wins himself a name and an identity by the end of the *Narrative*, the triumphant individual is not the sole focus of the story. Along the way, Douglass uses his own experience to throw light on slavery in general. The first pages in fact tell us little about the uniqueness of the author, and Douglass is careful to explain how his own circumstances are common to many slaves. He also repeatedly argues that individuals emerge out of their circumstances. He goes to some trouble to show how masters systematically *create* the slaves' mindset, deliberately starving them of intellectual or spiritual nourishment. But he makes it clear that the masters, too, are created by their conditions. Sophia Auld begins as a compassionate and generous person, but the experience of owning another human being makes her suspicious and mean-spirited. Many readers have seen the *Narrative* as fundamentally a story of self-transformation in which the illiterate and unthinking slave is prompted to recognize the injustice of his experience and to insist on his full personhood, but Douglass reminds us many times along the way that self-transformation always involves a set of opportunities, and that under slightly different conditions, this slave might never have sought out his freedom.

There is one way that Douglass's story has disappointed recent readers. He affirms his own manhood—rejecting the bestial and objectified status of the slave—but does so at the expense of women's experience. He entirely omits descriptions of important women in his life, such as his grandmother, who raised him, and his wife-to-be. He does give graphic depictions of women slaves enduring physical violence, and he refers to the rape of slaves by masters more than once. But since his central image for slavery is a physical struggle for dominance between men, and since he depicts women mostly as lacerated bodies, Douglass's *Narrative* cannot be said to speak for all slaves.

In recounting the internal and external shifts that take him from slave to free man, Douglass's story draws on a number of other genres. As in spiritual autobiographies, the *Narrative* calls attention to moments of revelation, when the central figure undergoes a kind of conversion experience, and sees himself and his world in a fresh light. As in rags-to-riches stories, Douglass tells us how he makes a dramatic rise in social status and wealth through virtues such as perseverance, bravery, self-reliance, and determination. He draws on the sentimental novel, too, in offering us images of innocent victims whose abuses tug at our heartstrings. And the *Narrative* draws on the language of politics, economics, and religious sermons, woven together throughout the text. But perhaps most important, this autobiography belongs in the tradition of the slave narrative, which, by Douglass's time, had become a well-established genre. There had been thousands of first-person accounts of slavery published since the late eighteenth century, and slave narratives had become a major American genre. They were so popular that most American readers might never have encountered an autobiography written by anyone other than a slave. Among these many narratives, Douglass's has been widely recognized as the richest, most subtle, and most beautifully conceived, remaining worthwhile reading not only for its searing indictment of slavery, but also for its complex literary artistry.

Narrative of the Life of Frederick Douglass, An American Slave[1]

CHAPTER I

I was born in Tuckahoe, near Hillsborough, and about twelve miles from Easton, in Talbot county, Maryland. I have no accurate knowledge of my age, never having seen any authentic record containing it. By far the larger part of the slaves know as little of their ages as horses know of theirs, and it is the wish of most masters within my knowledge to keep their slaves thus ignorant. I do not remember to have ever met a slave who could tell of his birthday. They seldom come nearer to it than planting-time, harvest-time, cherry-time, spring-time, or fall-time. A want of information concerning my own was a source of unhappiness to me even during childhood. The white children could tell their ages. I could not tell why I ought to be deprived of the same privilege. I was not allowed to make any inquiries of my master concerning it. He deemed all such inquiries on the part of a slave improper and impertinent, and evidence of a restless spirit. The nearest estimate I can give makes me now between twenty-seven and twenty-eight years of age. I come to this, from hearing my master say, some time during 1835, I was about seventeen years old.

My mother was named Harriet Bailey. She was the daughter of Isaac and Betsey Bailey, both colored, and quite dark. My mother was of a darker complexion than either my grandmother or grandfather.

My father was a white man. He was admitted to be such by all I ever heard speak of my parentage. The opinion was also whispered that my master was my father; but of the correctness of this opinion, I know nothing; the means of knowing was withheld from me. My mother and I were separated when I was but an infant—before I knew her as my mother. It is a common custom, in the part of Maryland from which I ran away, to part children from their mothers at a very early age. Frequently, before the child has reached its twelfth month, its mother is taken from it, and hired out on some farm a considerable distance

1. The text, printed in its entirety, is that of the first American edition, published by the Massachusetts Anti-Slavery Society in Boston in 1845.

off, and the child is placed under the care of an old woman, too old for field labor. For what this separation is done, I do not know, unless it be to hinder the development of the child's affection toward its mother, and to blunt and destroy the natural affection of the mother for the child. This is the inevitable result.

I never saw my mother, to know her as such, more than four or five times in my life; and each of those times was very short in duration, and at night. She was hired by a Mr. Stewart, who lived about twelve miles from my home. She made her journeys to see me in the night, travelling the whole distance on foot, after the performance of her day's work. She was a field hand, and a whipping is the penalty of not being in the field at sunrise, unless a slave has special permission from his or her master to the contrary—a permission which they seldom get, and one that gives to him that gives it the proud name of being a kind master. I do not recollect of ever seeing my mother by the light of day. She was with me in the night. She would lie down with me, and get me to sleep, but long before I waked she was gone. Very little communication ever took place between us. Death soon ended what little we could have while she lived, and with it her hardships and suffering. She died when I was about seven years old, on one of my master's farms, near Lee's Mill. I was not allowed to be present during her illness, at her death, or burial. She was gone long before I knew anything about it. Never having enjoyed, to any considerable extent, her soothing presence, her tender and watchful care, I received the tidings of her death with much the same emotions I should have probably felt at the death of a stranger.

Called thus suddenly away, she left me without the slightest intimation of who my father was. The whisper that my master was my father, may or may not be true; and, true or false, it is of but little consequence to my purpose whilst the fact remains, in all its glaring odiousness, that slaveholders have ordained, and by law established, that the children of slave women shall in all cases follow the condition of their mothers; and this is done too obviously to administer to their own lusts, and make a gratification of their wicked desires profitable as well as pleasurable; for by this cunning arrangement, the slaveholder, in cases not a few, sustains to his slaves the double relation of master and father.

I know of such cases; and it is worthy of remark that such slaves invariably suffer greater hardships, and have more to contend with, than others. They are, in the first place, a constant offence to their mistress. She is ever disposed to find fault with them; they can seldom do any thing to please her; she is never better pleased than when she sees them under the lash, especially when she suspects her husband of showing to his mulatto children favors which he withholds from his black slaves. The master is frequently compelled to sell this class of his slaves, out of deference to the feelings of his white wife; and, cruel as the deed may strike any one to be, for a man to sell his own children to human flesh-mongers, it is often the dictate of humanity for him to do so; for, unless he does this, he must not only whip them himself, but must stand by and see one white son tie up his brother, of but few shades darker complexion than himself, and ply the gory lash to his naked back; and if he lisp one word of disapproval, it is set down to his parental partiality, and only makes a bad matter worse, both for himself and the slave whom he would protect and defend.

Every year brings with it multitudes of this class of slaves. It was doubtless in consequence of a knowledge of this fact, that one great statesman of the south predicted the downfall of slavery by the inevitable laws of population. Whether this prophecy is ever fulfilled or not, it is nevertheless plain that a very different-looking class of people are springing up at the south, and are now held in slavery, from those originally brought to this country from Africa; and if their increase will do no other good, it will do away the force of the argument, that God cursed Ham,[2] and therefore American slavery is right. If the lineal descendants of Ham are alone to be scripturally enslaved, it is certain that slavery at the south must soon become unscriptural; for thousands are ushered into the world, annually, who, like myself, owe their existence to white fathers, and those fathers most frequently their own masters.

I have had two masters. My first master's name was Anthony. I do not remember his first name. He was generally called Captain Anthony—a title which, I presume, he acquired by sailing a craft on the Chesapeake Bay. He was not considered a rich slaveholder. He owned two or three farms, and about thirty slaves. His farms and slaves were under the care of an overseer. The overseer's name was Plummer. Mr. Plummer was a miserable drunkard, a profane swearer, and a savage monster. He always went armed with a cowskin and a heavy cudgel. I have known him to cut and slash the women's heads so horribly, that even master would be enraged at his cruelty, and would threaten to whip him if he did not mind himself. Master, however, was not a humane slaveholder. It required extraordinary barbarity on the part of an overseer to affect him. He was a cruel man, hardened by a long life of slaveholding. He would at times seem to take great pleasure in whipping a slave. I have often been awakened at the dawn of day by the most heartrending shrieks of an own aunt of mine, whom he used to tie up to a joist, and whip upon her naked back till she was literally covered with blood. No words, no tears, no prayers, from his gory victim, seemed to move his iron heart from its bloody purpose. The louder she screamed, the harder he whipped; and where the blood ran fastest, there he whipped longest. He would whip her to make her scream, and whip her to make her hush; and not until overcome by fatigue, would he cease to swing the blood-clotted cowskin. I remember the first time I ever witnessed this horrible exhibition. I was quite a child, but I well remember it. I never shall forget it whilst I remember any thing. It was the first of a long series of such outrages, of which I was doomed to be a witness and a participant. It struck me with awful force. It was the blood-stained gate, the entrance to the hell of slavery, through which I was about to pass. It was a most terrible spectacle. I wish I could commit to paper the feelings with which I beheld it.

This occurrence took place very soon after I went to live with my old master, and under the following circumstances. Aunt Hester went out one night,—where or for what I do not know,—and happened to be absent when my master desired her presence. He had ordered her not to go out evenings, and warned

2. It was widely thought that Noah cursed his second son, Ham, for mocking him; that black skin resulted from the curse; and that all black people descended from Ham. In fact, according to Genesis 9.20–27 and 10.6–14, Noah cursed not Ham but Ham's son Canaan, while Ham's son Cush was black.

her that she must never let him catch her in company with a young man, who was paying attention to her, belonging to Colonel Lloyd. The young man's name was Ned Roberts, generally called Lloyd's Ned. Why master was so careful of her, may be safely left to conjecture. She was a woman of noble form, and of graceful proportions, having very few equals, and fewer superiors, in personal appearance, among the colored or white women of our neighborhood.

Aunt Hester had not only disobeyed his orders in going out, but had been found in company with Lloyd's Ned; which circumstance, I found, from what he said while whipping her, was the chief offence. Had he been a man of pure morals himself, he might have been thought interested in protecting the innocence of my aunt; but those who knew him will not suspect him of any such virtue. Before he commenced whipping Aunt Hester, he took her into the kitchen, and stripped her from neck to waist, leaving her neck, shoulders, and back, entirely naked. He then told her to cross her hands, calling her at the same time a d—d b—h. After crossing her hands, he tied them with a strong rope, and led her to a stool under a large hook in the joist, put in for the purpose. He made her get upon the stool, and tied her hands to the hook. She now stood fair for his infernal purpose. Her arms were stretched up at their full length, so that she stood upon the ends of her toes. He then said to her, "Now, you d—d b—h, I'll learn you how to disobey my orders!" and after rolling up his sleeves, he commenced to lay on the heavy cowskin, and soon the warm, red blood (amid heart-rending shrieks from her, and horrid oaths from him) came dripping to the floor. I was so terrified and horror-stricken at the sight, that I hid myself in a closet, and dared not venture out till long after the bloody transaction was over. I expected it would be my turn next. It was all new to me. I had never seen any thing like it before. I had always lived with my grandmother on the outskirts of the plantation, where she was put to raise the children of the younger women. I had therefore been, until now, out of the way of the bloody scenes that often occurred on the plantation.

CHAPTER II

My master's family consisted of two sons, Andrew and Richard; one daughter, Lucretia, and her husband, Captain Thomas Auld. They lived in one house, upon the home plantation of Colonel Edward Lloyd. My master was Colonel Lloyd's clerk and superintendent. He was what might be called the overseer of the overseers. I spent two years of childhood on this plantation in my old master's family. It was here that I witnessed the bloody transaction recorded in the first chapter; and as I received my first impressions of slavery on this plantation, I will give some description of it, and of slavery as it there existed. The plantation is about twelve miles north of Easton, in Talbot county, and is situated on the border of Miles River. The principal products raised upon it were tobacco, corn, and wheat. These were raised in great abundance; so that, with the products of this and the other farms belonging to him, he was able to keep in almost constant employment a large sloop, in carrying them to market at Baltimore. This sloop was named *Sally Lloyd*, in honor of one of the colonel's daughters. My master's son-in-law, Captain Auld, was master of the vessel; she was otherwise manned by the colonel's own slaves. Their names were Peter,

Isaac, Rich, and Jake. These were esteemed very highly by the other slaves, and looked upon as the privileged ones of the plantation; for it was no small affair, in the eyes of the slaves, to be allowed to see Baltimore.

Colonel Lloyd kept from three to four hundred slaves on his home plantation, and owned a large number more on the neighboring farms belonging to him. The names of the farms nearest to the home plantation were Wye Town and New Design. "Wye Town" was under the overseership of a man named Noah Willis. New Design was under the overseership of a Mr. Townsend. The overseers of these, and all the rest of the farms, numbering over twenty, received advice and direction from the managers of the home plantation. This was the great business place. It was the seat of government for the whole twenty farms. All disputes among the overseers were settled here. If a slave was convicted of any high misdemeanor, became unmanageable, or evinced a determination to run away, he was brought immediately here, severely whipped, put on board the sloop, carried to Baltimore, and sold to Austin Woolfolk, or some other slave-trader, as a warning to the slaves remaining.

Here, too, the slaves of all the other farms received their monthly allowance of food, and their yearly clothing. The men and women slaves received, as their monthly allowance of food, eight pounds of pork, or its equivalent in fish, and one bushel of corn meal. Their yearly clothing consisted of two coarse linen shirts, one pair of linen trousers, like the shirts, one jacket, one pair of trousers for winter, made of coarse negro cloth, one pair of stockings, and one pair of shoes; the whole of which could not have cost more than seven dollars. The allowance of the slave children was given to their mothers, or the old women having the care of them. The children unable to work in the field had neither shoes, stockings, jackets, nor trousers, given to them; their clothing consisted of two coarse linen shirts per year. When these failed them, they went naked until the next allowance-day. Children from seven to ten years old, of both sexes, almost naked, might be seen at all seasons of the year.

There were no beds given the slaves, unless one coarse blanket be considered such, and none but the men and women had these. This, however, is not considered a very great privation. They find less difficulty from the want of beds, than from the want of time to sleep; for when their day's work in the field is done, the most of them having their washing, mending, and cooking to do, and having few or none of the ordinary facilities for doing either of these, very many of their sleeping hours are consumed in preparing for the field the coming day; and when this is done, old and young, male and female, married and single, drop down side by side, on one common bed,—the cold, damp floor,—each covering himself or herself with their miserable blankets; and here they sleep till they are summoned to the field by the driver's horn. At the sound of this, all must rise, and be off to the field. There must be no halting; every one must be at his or her post; and woe betides them who hear not this morning summons to the field; for if they are not awakened by the sense of hearing, they are by the sense of feeling: no age nor sex finds any favor. Mr. Severe, the overseer, used to stand by the door of the quarter, armed with a large hickory stick and heavy cowskin, ready to whip any one who was so unfortunate as not to hear, or, from any other cause, was prevented from being ready to start for the field at the sound of the horn.

Mr. Severe was rightly named: he was a cruel man. I have seen him whip a woman, causing the blood to run half an hour at the time; and this, too, in the midst of her crying children, pleading for their mother's release. He seemed to take pleasure in manifesting his fiendish barbarity. Added to his cruelty, he was a profane swearer. It was enough to chill the blood and stiffen the hair of an ordinary man to hear him talk. Scarce a sentence escaped him but that was commenced or concluded by some horrid oath. The field was the place to witness his cruelty and profanity. His presence made it both the field of blood and of blasphemy. From the rising till the going down of the sun, he was cursing, raving, cutting, and slashing among the slaves of the field, in the most frightful manner. His career was short. He died very soon after I went to Colonel Lloyd's; and he died as he lived, uttering, with his dying groans, bitter curses and horrid oaths. His death was regarded by the slaves as the result of a merciful providence.

Mr. Severe's place was filled by a Mr. Hopkins. He was a very different man. He was less cruel, less profane, and made less noise, than Mr. Severe. His course was characterized by no extraordinary demonstrations of cruelty. He whipped, but seemed to take no pleasure in it. He was called by the slaves a good overseer.

The home plantation of Colonel Lloyd wore the appearance of a country village. All the mechanical operations for all the farms were performed here. The shoemaking and mending, the blacksmithing, cartwrighting, coopering, weaving, and grain-grinding, were all performed by the slaves on the home plantation. The whole place wore a business-like aspect very unlike the neighboring farms. The number of houses, too, conspired to give it advantage over the neighboring farms. It was called by the slaves the *Great House Farm.* Few privileges were esteemed higher, by the slaves of the out-farms, than that of being selected to do errands at the Great House Farm. It was associated in their minds with greatness. A representative could not be prouder of his election to a seat in the American Congress, than a slave on one of the out-farms would be of his election to do errands at the Great House Farm. They regarded it as evidence of great confidence reposed in them by their overseers; and it was on this account, as well as a constant desire to be out of the field from under the driver's lash, that they esteemed it a high privilege, one worth careful living for. He was called the smartest and most trusty fellow, who had this honor conferred upon him the most frequently. The competitors for this office sought as diligently to please their overseers, as the office-seekers in the political parties seek to please and deceive the people. The same traits of character might be seen in Colonel Lloyd's slaves, as are seen in the slaves of the political parties.

The slaves selected to go to the Great House Farm, for the monthly allowance for themselves and their fellow-slaves, were peculiarly enthusiastic. While on their way, they would make the dense old woods, for miles around, reverberate with their wild songs, revealing at once the highest joy and the deepest sadness. They would compose and sing as they went along, consulting neither time nor tune. The thought that came up, came out—if not in the word, in the sound;—and as frequently in the one as in the other. They would sometimes sing the most pathetic sentiment in the most rapturous tone, and the most rapturous sentiment in the most pathetic tone. Into all of their songs they would manage to weave something of the Great House Farm. Especially would they do this, when leaving home. They would then sing most exultingly the following words:—

"I am going away to the Great House Farm!
O, yea! O, yea! O!"

This they would sing, as a chorus, to words which to many would seem unmeaning jargon, but which, nevertheless, were full of meaning to themselves. I have sometimes thought that the mere hearing of those songs would do more to impress some minds with the horrible character of slavery, than the reading of whole volumes of philosophy on the subject could do.

I did not, when a slave, understand the deep meaning of those rude and apparently incoherent songs. I was myself within the circle; so that I neither saw nor heard as those without might see and hear. They told a tale of woe which was then altogether beyond my feeble comprehension; they were tones loud, long, and deep; they breathed the prayer and complaint of souls boiling over with the bitterest anguish. Every tone was a testimony against slavery, and a prayer to god for deliverance from chains. The hearing of those wild notes always depressed my spirit, and filled me with ineffable sadness. I have frequently found myself in tears while hearing them. The mere recurrence to those songs, even now, afflicts me; and while I am writing these lines, an expression of feeling has already found its way down my cheek. To those songs I trace my first glimmering conception of the dehumanizing character of slavery. I can never get rid of that conception. Those songs still follow me, to deepen my hatred of slavery, and quicken my sympathies for my brethren in bonds. If any one wishes to be impressed with the soul-killing effects of slavery, let him go to Colonel Lloyd's plantation, and, on allowance-day, place himself in the deep pine woods, and there let him, in silence, analyze the sounds that shall pass through the chambers of his soul,—and if he is not thus impressed, it will only be because "there is no flesh in his obdurate heart."

I have often been utterly astonished, since I came to the north, to find persons who could speak of the singing, among slaves, as evidence of their contentment and happiness. It is impossible to conceive of a greater mistake. Slaves sing most when they are most unhappy. The songs of the slave represent the sorrows of his heart; and he is relieved by them, only as an aching heart is relieved by its tears. At least, such is my experience. I have often sung to drown my sorrow, but seldom to express my happiness. Crying for joy, and singing for joy, were alike uncommon to me while in the jaws of slavery. The singing of a man cast away upon a desolate island might be as appropriately considered as evidence of contentment and happiness, as the singing of a slave; the songs of the one and of the other are prompted by the same emotion.

CHAPTER III

Colonel Lloyd kept a large and finely cultivated garden, which afforded almost constant employment for four men, besides the chief gardener (Mr. M'Durmond). This garden was probably the greatest attraction of the place. During the summer months, people came from far and near—from Baltimore, Easton, and

Annapolis—to see it. It abounded in fruits of almost every description, from the hardy apple of the north to the delicate orange of the south. This garden was not the least source of trouble on the plantation. Its excellent fruit was quite a temptation to the hungry swarms of boys, as well as the older slaves, belonging to the colonel, few of whom had the virtue or the vice to resist it. Scarcely a day passed, during the summer, but that some slave had to take the lash for stealing fruit. The colonel had to resort to all kinds of stratagems to keep his slaves out of the garden. The last and most successful one was that of tarring his fence all around; after which, if a slave was caught with tar upon his person, it was deemed sufficient proof that he had either been into the garden, or had tried to get in. In either case, he was severely whipped by the chief gardener. This plan worked well; the slaves became as fearful of tar as of the lash. They seemed to realize the impossibility of touching *tar* without being defiled.[3]

The colonel also kept a splendid riding equipage. His stable and carriage-house presented the appearance of some of our large city livery establishments. His horses were of the finest form and noblest blood. His carriage-house contained three splendid coaches, three or four gigs, besides dearborns and barouches[4] of the most fashionable style.

This establishment was under the care of two slaves—old Barney and young Barney—father and son. To attend to this establishment was their sole work. But it was by no means an easy employment; for in nothing was Colonel Lloyd more particular than in the management of his horses. The slightest inattention to these was unpardonable, and was visited upon those, under whose care they were placed, with the severest punishment; no excuse could shield them, if the colonel only suspected any want of attention to his horses—a supposition which he frequently indulged, and one which, of course, made the office of old and young Barney a very trying one. They never knew when they were safe from punishment. They were frequently whipped when least deserving, and escaped whipping when most deserving it. Every thing depended upon the looks of the horses, and the state of Colonel Lloyd's own mind when his horses were brought to him for use. If a horse did not move fast enough, or hold his head high enough, it was owing to some fault of his keepers. It was painful to stand near the stable-door, and hear the various complaints against the keepers when a horse was taken out for use. "This horse has not had proper attention. He has not been sufficiently rubbed and curried, or he has not been properly fed; his food was too wet or too dry; he got it too soon or too late; he was too hot or too cold; he had too much hay, and not enough of grain; or he had too much grain, and not enough of hay; instead of old Barney's attending to the horse, he had very improperly left it to his son." To all these complaints, no matter how unjust, the slave must answer never a word. Colonel Lloyd could not brook any contradiction from a slave. When he spoke, a slave must stand, listen, and tremble; and such was literally the case. I have seen Colonel Lloyd make old Barney, a man between fifty and sixty years of age, uncover his bald head, kneel down upon the cold, damp ground, and receive upon his

3. Cf. the proverb "He who touches pitch shall be defiled."

4. Light four-wheeled carriages (*dearborns*) and carriages with a front seat for the driver and two facing back seats for couples (*barouches*).

naked and toil-worn shoulders more than thirty lashes at the time. Colonel Lloyd had three sons—Edward, Murray, and Daniel,—and three sons-in-law, Mr. Winder, Mr. Nicholson, and Mr. Lowndes. All of these lived at the Great House Farm, and enjoyed the luxury of whipping the servants when they pleased, from old Barney down to William Wilkes, the coach-driver. I have seen Winder make one of the house-servants stand off from him a suitable distance to be touched with the end of his whip, and at every stroke raise great ridges upon his back.

To describe the wealth of Colonel Lloyd would be almost equal to describing the riches of Job.[5] He kept from ten to fifteen house-servants. He was said to own a thousand slaves, and I think this estimate quite within the truth. Colonel Lloyd owned so many that he did not know them when he saw them; nor did all the slaves of the out-farms know him. It is reported of him, that, while riding along the road one day, he met a colored man, and addressed him in the usual manner of speaking to colored people on the public highways of the south: "Well, boy, whom do you belong to?" "To Colonel Lloyd," replied the slave. "Well, does the colonel treat you well?" "No, sir," was the ready reply. "What, does he work you too hard?" "Yes, sir." "Well, don't he give you enough to eat?" "Yes, sir, he gives me enough, such as it is."

The colonel, after ascertaining where the slave belonged, rode on; the man also went on about his business, not dreaming that he had been conversing with his master. He thought, said, and heard nothing more of the matter, until two or three weeks afterwards. The poor man was then informed by his overseer that, for having found fault with his master, he was now to be sold to a Georgia trader. He was immediately chained and handcuffed; and thus, without a moment's warning, he was snatched away, and forever sundered, from his family and friends, by a hand more unrelenting than death. This is the penalty of telling the truth, of telling the simple truth, in answer to a series of plain questions.

It is partly in consequence of such facts, that slaves, when inquired of as to their condition and the character of their masters, almost universally say they are contented, and that their masters are kind. The slaveholders have been known to send in spies among their slaves, to ascertain their views and feelings in regard to their condition. The frequency of this has had the effect to establish among the slaves the maxim, that a still tongue makes a wise head. They suppress the truth rather than take the consequences of telling it, and in so doing prove themselves a part of the human family. If they have any thing to say of their masters, it is generally in their masters' favor, especially when speaking to an untried man. I have been frequently asked, when a slave, if I had a kind master, and do not remember ever to have given a negative answer; nor did I, in pursuing this course, consider myself as uttering what was absolutely false; for I always measured the kindness of my master by the standard of kindness set up among slaveholders around us. Moreover, slaves are like other people, and imbibe prejudices quite common to others. They think their own better than that of others. Many, under the influence of this prejudice,

5. Job 1.3: "His substance also was seven thousand sheep, and three thousand camels, and five hundred yoke of oxen, and five hundred she asses, and a very great household; so that this man was the greatest of all the men of the East."

think their own masters are better than the masters of other slaves; and this, too, in some cases, when the very reverse is true. Indeed, it is not uncommon for slaves even to fall out and quarrel among themselves about the relative goodness of their masters, each contending for the superior goodness of his own over that of the others. At the very same time, they mutually execrate their masters when viewed separately. It was so on our plantation. When Colonel Lloyd's slaves met the slaves of Jacob Jepson, they seldom parted without a quarrel about their masters; Colonel Lloyd's slaves contending that he was the richest, and Mr. Jepson's slaves that he was the smartest, and most of a man. Colonel Lloyd's slaves would boast his ability to buy and sell Jacob Jepson. Mr. Jepson's slaves would boast his ability to whip Colonel Lloyd. These quarrels would almost always end in a fight between the parties, and those that whipped were supposed to have gained the point at issue. They seemed to think that the greatness of their masters was transferable to themselves. It was considered as being bad enough to be a slave; but to be a poor man's slave was deemed a disgrace indeed!

CHAPTER IV

Mr. Hopkins remained but a short time in the office of overseer. Why his career was so short, I do not know, but suppose he lacked the necessary severity to suit Colonel Lloyd. Mr. Hopkins was succeeded by Mr. Austin Gore, a man possessing, in an eminent degree, all those traits of character indispensable to what is called a first-rate overseer. Mr. Gore had served Colonel Lloyd, in the capacity of overseer, upon one of the out-farms, and had shown himself worthy of the high station of overseer upon the home or Great House Farm.

Mr. Gore was proud, ambitious, and persevering. He was artful, cruel, and obdurate. He was just the man for such a place, and it was just the place for such a man. It afforded scope for the full exercise of all his powers, and he seemed to be perfectly at home in it. He was one of those who could torture the slightest look, word, or gesture, on the part of the slave, into impudence, and would treat it accordingly. There must be no answering back to him; no explanation was allowed a slave, showing himself to have been wrongfully accused. Mr. Gore acted fully up to the maxim laid down by slaveholders,—"It is better that a dozen slaves suffer under the lash, than that the overseer should be convicted, in the presence of the slaves, of having been at fault." No matter how innocent a slave might be—it availed him nothing, when accused by Mr. Gore of any misdemeanor. To be accused was to be convicted, and to be convicted was to be punished; the one always following the other with immutable certainty. To escape punishment was to escape accusation; and few slaves had the fortune to do either, under the overseership of Mr. Gore. He was just proud enough to demand the most debasing homage of the slave, and quite servile enough to crouch, himself, at the feet of the master. He was ambitious enough to be contented with nothing short of the highest rank of overseers, and persevering enough to reach the height of his ambition. He was cruel enough to inflict the severest punishment, artful enough to descend to the lowest trickery, and obdurate enough to be insensible to the voice of a reproving conscience. He was, of all the overseers, the most dreaded by the slaves. His presence was painful; his eye flashed confusion; and seldom was his sharp, shrill voice heard, without producing horror and trembling in their ranks.

Mr. Gore was a grave man, and, though a young man, he indulged in no jokes, said no funny words, seldom smiled. His words were in perfect keeping with his looks, and his looks were in perfect keeping with his words. Overseers will sometimes indulge in a witty word, even with the slaves; not so with Mr. Gore. He spoke but to command, and commanded but to be obeyed; he dealt sparingly with his words, and bountifully with his whip, never using the former where the latter would answer as well. When he whipped, he seemed to do so from a sense of duty, and feared no consequences. He did nothing reluctantly, no matter how disagreeable; always at his post, never inconsistent. He never promised but to fulfil. He was, in a word, a man of the most inflexible firmness and stone-like coolness.

His savage barbarity was equalled only by the consummate coolness with which he committed the grossest and most savage deeds upon the slaves under his charge. Mr. Gore once undertook to whip one of Colonel Lloyd's slaves, by the name of Demby. He had given Demby but few stripes, when, to get rid of the scourging, he ran and plunged himself into a creek, and stood there at the depth of his shoulders, refusing to come out. Mr. Gore told him that he would give him three calls, and that, if he did not come out at the third call, he would shoot him. The first call was given. Demby made no response, but stood his ground. The second and third calls were given with the same result. Mr. Gore then, without consultation or deliberation with any one, not even giving Demby an additional call, raised his musket to his face, taking deadly aim at his standing victim, and in an instant poor Demby was no more. His mangled body sank out of sight, and blood and brains marked the water where he had stood.

A thrill of horror flashed through every soul upon the plantation, excepting Mr. Gore. He alone seemed cool and collected. He was asked by Colonel Lloyd and my old master, why he resorted to this extraordinary expedient. His reply was, (as well as I can remember,) that Demby had become unmanageable. He was setting a dangerous example to the other slaves,—one which, if suffered to pass without some such demonstration on his part, would finally lead to the total subversion of all rule and order upon the plantation. He argued that if one slave refused to be corrected, and escaped with his life, the other slaves would soon copy the example; the result of which would be, the freedom of the slaves, and the enslavement of the whites. Mr. Gore's defence was satisfactory. He was continued in his station as overseer upon the home plantation. His fame as an overseer went abroad. His horrid crime was not even submitted to judicial investigation. It was committed in the presence of slaves, and they of course could neither institute a suit, nor testify against him; and thus the guilty perpetrator of one of the bloodiest and most foul murders goes unwhipped of justice, and uncensured by the community in which he lives. Mr. Gore lived in St. Michael's, Talbot county, Maryland, when I left there; and if he is still alive, he very probably lives there now; and if so, he is now, as he was then, as highly esteemed and as much respected as though his guilty soul had not been stained with his brother's blood.

I speak advisedly when I say this,—that killing a slave, or any colored person, in Talbot county, Maryland, is not treated as a crime, either by the courts or the community. Mr. Thomas Lanman, of St. Michael's, killed two slaves, one of whom he killed with a hatchet, by knocking his brains out. He used to boast of the commission of the awful and bloody deed. I have heard him do so laughingly, saying, among other things, that he was the only benefactor of his country in the company, and that when others would do as much as he had done, we should be relieved of "the d——d niggers."

The wife of Mr. Giles Hicks, living but a short distance from where I used to live, murdered my wife's cousin, a young girl between fifteen and sixteen years of age, mangling her person in the most horrible manner, breaking her nose and breastbone with a stick, so that the poor girl expired in a few hours afterward. She was immediately buried, but had not been in her untimely grave but a few hours before she was taken up and examined by the coroner, who decided that she had come to her death by severe beating. The offence for which this girl was thus murdered was this:—She had been set that night to mind Mrs. Hicks's baby, and during the night she fell asleep, and the baby cried. She, having lost her rest for several nights previous, did not hear the crying. They were both in the room with Mrs. Hicks. Mrs. Hicks, finding the girl slow to move, jumped from her bed, seized an oak stick of wood by the fireplace, and with it broke the girl's nose and breastbone, and thus ended her life. I will not say that this most horrid murder produced no sensation in the community. It did produce sensation, but not enough to bring the murderess to punishment. There was a warrant issued for her arrest, but it was never served. Thus she escaped not only punishment, but even the pain of being arraigned before a court for her horrid crime.

Whilst I am detailing bloody deeds which took place during my stay on Colonel Lloyd's plantation, I will briefly narrate another, which occurred about the same time as the murder of Demby by Mr. Gore.

Colonel Lloyd's slaves were in the habit of spending a part of their nights and Sundays in fishing for oysters, and in this way made up the deficiency of their scanty allowance. An old man belonging to Colonel Lloyd, while thus engaged, happened to get beyond the limits of Colonel Lloyd's, and on the premises of Mr. Beal Bondly. At this trespass, Mr. Bondly took offence, and with his musket came down to the shore, and blew its deadly contents into the poor old man.

Mr. Bondly came over to see Colonel Lloyd the next day, whether to pay him for his property, or to justify himself in what he had done, I know not. At any rate, this whole fiendish transaction was soon hushed up. There was very little said about it at all, and nothing done. It was a common saying, even among little white boys, that it was worth a half-cent to kill a "nigger," and a half-cent to bury one.

CHAPTER V

As to my own treatment while I lived on Colonel Lloyd's plantation, it was very similar to that of the other slave children. I was not old enough to work in the field, and there being little else than field work to do, I had a great deal of leisure time. The most I had to do was to drive up the cows at evening, keep the fowls out of the garden, keep the front yard clean, and run off errands for my old master's daughter, Mrs. Lucretia Auld. The most of my leisure time I spent in helping Master Daniel Lloyd in finding his birds, after he had shot them. My connection with Master Daniel was of some advantage to me. He became quite attached to me, and was a sort of protector of me. He would not allow the older boys to impose upon me, and would divide his cakes with me.

I was seldom whipped by my old master, and suffered little from any thing else than hunger and cold. I suffered much from hunger, but much more from cold. In hottest summer and coldest winter, I was kept almost naked—no shoes, no stockings, no jacket, no trousers, nothing on but a coarse tow linen shirt, reaching only to my knees. I had no bed. I must have perished with cold, but that, the coldest nights, I used to steal a bag which was used for carrying corn to the mill. I would crawl into this bag, and there sleep on the cold, damp, clay floor, with my head in and feet out. My feet had been so cracked with the frost, that the pen with which I am writing might be laid in the gashes.

We were not regularly allowanced. Our food was coarse corn meal boiled. This was called *mush*. It was put into a large wooden tray or trough, and set down upon the ground. The children were then called, like so many pigs, and like so many pigs they would come and devour the mush; some with oyster-shells, others with pieces of shingle, some with naked hands, and none with spoons. He that ate fastest got most; he that was strongest secured the best place; and few left the trough satisfied.

I was probably between seven and eight years old when I left Colonel Lloyd's plantation. I left it with joy. I shall never forget the ecstasy with which I received the intelligence that my old master (Anthony) had determined to let me go to Baltimore, to live with Mr. Hugh Auld, brother to my old master's son-in-law, Captain Thomas Auld. I received this information about three days before my departure. They were three of the happiest days I ever enjoyed. I spent the most part of all these three days in the creek, washing off the plantation scurf, and preparing myself for my departure.

The pride of appearance which this would indicate was not my own. I spent the time in washing, not so much because I wished to, but because Mrs. Lucretia had told me I must get all the dead skin off my feet and knees before I could go to Baltimore; for the people in Baltimore were very cleanly, and would laugh at me if I looked dirty. Besides, she was going to give me a pair of trousers, which I should not put on unless I got all the dirt off me. The thought of owning a pair of trousers was great indeed! It was almost a sufficient motive, not only to make me take off what would be called by pig-drovers the mange, but the skin itself. I went at it in good earnest, working for the first time with the hope of reward.

The ties that ordinarily bind children to their homes were all suspended in my case. I found no severe trial in my departure. My home was charmless; it was not home to me; on parting from it, I could not feel that I was leaving any thing which I could have enjoyed by staying. My mother was dead, my grandmother lived far off, so that I seldom saw her. I had two sisters and one brother, that lived in the same house with me; but the early separation of us from our mother had well nigh blotted the fact of our relationship from our memories. I looked for home elsewhere, and was confident of finding none which I should relish less than the one which I was leaving. If, however, I found in my new home hardship, hunger, whipping, and nakedness, I had the consolation that I should not have escaped any one of them by staying. Having already had more than a taste of them in the house of my old master, and having endured them there, I very naturally inferred my ability to endure them elsewhere, and especially at Baltimore; for I had something of the feeling about Baltimore that is expressed in the proverb, that "being hanged in England is preferable to dying a natural death in Ireland." I had the strongest desire to see Baltimore.

Cousin Tom, though not fluent in speech, had inspired me with that desire by his eloquent description of the place. I could never point out any thing at the Great House, no matter how beautiful or powerful, but that he had seen something at Baltimore far exceeding, both in beauty and strength, the object which I pointed out to him. Even the Great House itself, with all its pictures, was far inferior to many buildings in Baltimore. So strong was my desire, that I thought a gratification of it would fully compensate for whatever loss of comforts I should sustain by the exchange. I left without a regret, and with the highest hopes of future happiness.

We sailed out of Miles River for Baltimore on a Saturday morning. I remember only the day of the week, for at that time I had no knowledge of the days of the month, nor the months of the year. On setting sail, I walked aft, and gave to Colonel Lloyd's plantation what I hoped would be the last look. I then placed myself in the bows of the sloop, and there spent the remainder of the day in looking ahead, interesting myself in what was in the distance rather than in things near by or behind.

In the afternoon of that day, we reached Annapolis, the capital of the State. We stopped but a few moments, so that I had no time to go on shore. It was the first large town that I had ever seen, and though it would look small compared with some of our New England factory villages, I thought it a wonderful place for its size—more imposing even than the Great House Farm!

We arrived at Baltimore early on Sunday morning, landing at Smith's Wharf, not far from Bowley's Wharf. We had on board the sloop a large flock of sheep; and after aiding in driving them to the slaughterhouse of Mr. Curtis on Louden Slater's Hill, I was conducted by Rich, one of the hands belonging on board of the sloop, to my new home in Alliciana Street, near Mr. Gardner's ship-yard, on Fells Point.

Mr. and Mrs. Auld were both at home, and met me at the door with their little son Thomas, to take care of whom I had been given. And here I saw what I had never seen before; it was a white face beaming with the most kindly emotions; it was the face of my new mistress, Sophia Auld. I wish I could describe the rapture that flashed through my soul as I beheld it. It was a new and strange sight to me, brightening up my pathway with the light of happiness. Little Thomas was told, there was his Freddy,—and I was told to take care of little Thomas; and thus I entered upon the duties of my new home with the most cheering prospect ahead.

I look upon my departure from Colonel Lloyd's plantation as one of the most interesting events of my life. It is possible, and even quite probable, that but for the mere circumstance of being removed from that plantation to Baltimore, I should have to-day, instead of being here seated by my own table, in the enjoyment of freedom and the happiness of home, writing this Narrative, been confined in the galling chains of slavery. Going to live at Baltimore laid the foundation, and opened the gateway, to all my subsequent prosperity. I have ever regarded it as the first plain manifestation of that kind providence which has ever since attended me, and marked my life with so many favors. I regarded the selection of myself as being somewhat remarkable. There were a number of slave children that might have been sent from the plantation to Baltimore. There were those younger, those older, and those of the same age. I was chosen from among them all, and was the first, last, and only choice.

I may be deemed superstitious, and even egotistical, in regarding this event as a special interposition of divine Providence in my favor. But I should be false to the earliest sentiments of my soul, if I suppressed the opinion. I prefer to be true to myself, even at the hazard of incurring the ridicule of others, rather than to be false, and incur my own abhorrence. From my earliest recollection, I date the entertainment of a deep conviction that slavery would not always be able to hold me within its foul embrace; and in the darkest hours of my career in slavery, this living word of faith and spirit of hope departed not from me, but remained like ministering angels to cheer me through the gloom. This good spirit was from God, and to him I offer thanksgiving and praise.

CHAPTER VI

My new mistress proved to be all she appeared when I first met her at the door,—a woman of the kindest heart and finest feelings. She had never had a slave under her control previously to myself, and prior to her marriage she had been dependent upon her own industry for a living. She was by trade a weaver; and by constant application to her business, she had been in a good degree preserved from the blighting and dehumanizing effects of slavery. I was utterly astonished at her goodness. I scarcely knew how to behave towards her. She was entirely unlike any other white woman I had ever seen. I could not approach her as I was accustomed to approach other white ladies. My early instruction was all out of place. The crouching servility, usually so acceptable a quality in a slave, did not answer when manifested toward her. Her favor was not gained by it; she seemed to be disturbed by it. She did not deem it impudent or unmannerly for a slave to look her in the face. The meanest slave was put fully at ease in her presence, and none left without feeling better for having seen her. Her face was made of heavenly smiles, and her voice of tranquil music.

But, alas! this kind heart had but a short time to remain such. The fatal poison of irresponsible power was already in her hands, and soon commenced its infernal work. That cheerful eye, under the influence of slavery, soon became red with rage; that voice, made all of sweet accord, changed to one of harsh and horrid discord; and that angelic face gave place to that of a demon.

Very soon after I went to live with Mr. and Mrs. Auld, she very kindly commenced to teach me the A, B, C. After I had learned this, she assisted me in learning to spell words of three or four letters. Just at this point of my progress, Mr. Auld found out what was going on, and at once forbade Mrs. Auld to instruct me further, telling her, among other things, that it was unlawful, as well as unsafe, to teach a slave to read. To use his own words, further, he said, "If you give a nigger an inch, he will take an ell. A nigger should know nothing but to obey his master—to do as he is told to do. Learning would *spoil* the best nigger in the world. Now," said he, "if you teach that nigger (speaking of myself) how to read, there would be no keeping him. It would forever unfit him to be a slave. He would at once become unmanageable, and of no value to his master. As to himself, it could do him no good, but a great deal of harm. It would make him discontented and unhappy." These words sank deep into my heart, stirred up sentiments within that lay slumbering, and called into existence an entirely new train of thought. It was a new and special revelation, explaining dark and mysterious things, with which my youthful understanding had struggled, but struggled in vain. I now understood what had been to me a most perplexing difficulty—to wit, the white man's power to enslave the black man. It was a grand achievement, and I prized it highly. From that moment, I understood the pathway from slavery to freedom. It was just what I wanted, and I got it at a time when I the least expected it. Whilst I was saddened by the thought of losing the aid of my kind mistress, I was gladdened by the invaluable instruction which, by the merest accident, I had gained from my master. Though conscious of the difficulty of learning without a teacher, I set out with high hope, and a fixed purpose, at whatever cost of trouble, to learn how to read. The very decided manner with which he spoke, and strove to impress his wife with the evil consequences of giving me instruction, served to convince me that he was deeply sensible of the truths he was uttering. It gave me the best assurance that I might rely with the utmost confidence on the results which, he said, would flow from teaching me to read. What he most dreaded, that I most desired. What he most loved, that I most hated. That which to him was a great evil, to be carefully shunned, was to me a great good, to be diligently sought; and the argument which he so warmly urged, against my learning to read, only served to inspire me with a desire and determination to learn. In learning to read, I owe almost as much to the bitter opposition of my master, as to the kindly aid of my mistress. I acknowledge the benefit of both.

I had resided but a short time in Baltimore before I observed a marked difference, in the treatment of slaves, from that which I had witnessed in the country. A city slave is almost a freeman, compared with a slave on the plantation. He is much better fed and clothed, and enjoys privileges altogether unknown to the slave on the plantation. There is a vestige of decency, a sense of shame, that does much to curb and check those outbreaks of atrocious cruelty so commonly enacted upon the plantation. He is a desperate slaveholder, who will shock the humanity of his nonslaveholding neighbors with the cries of his lacerated slave. Few are willing to incur the odium attaching to the reputation of being a cruel master; and above all things, they would not be known as not giving a slave enough to eat. Every city slaveholder is anxious to have it known of him, that he feeds his slaves well; and it is due to them to say, that most of them do give their slaves enough to eat. There are, however, some painful exceptions to this rule. Directly opposite to us, on Philpot Street, lived Mr. Thomas Hamilton. He owned two slaves. Their names were Henrietta and Mary. Henrietta was about twenty-two years of age, Mary was about fourteen; and of all the mangled and emaciated creatures I ever looked upon, these two were the most so. His heart must be harder than stone, that could look upon these unmoved. The head, neck, and shoulders of Mary were literally cut to pieces. I have frequently felt her head, and found it nearly covered with festering sores, caused by the lash of her cruel mistress. I do not know that her master ever whipped her, but I have been an eye-witness to the cruelty of Mrs. Hamilton. I used to be in Mr. Hamilton's house nearly every day. Mrs. Hamilton used to sit in a large chair in the middle of the room, with a heavy cowskin always by her side, and scarce an hour passed during the day but was marked by the blood of one of these slaves. The girls seldom passed her without her saying, "Move faster, you *black gip*!"[6] at the same time giving

6. Cheat, swindler.

them a blow with the cowskin over the head or shoulders, often drawing the blood. She would then say, "Take that, you *black gip*!"—continuing, "If you don't move faster, I'll move you!" Added to the cruel lashings to which these slaves were subjected, they were kept nearly half-starved. They seldom knew what it was to eat a full meal. I have seen Mary contending with the pigs for the offal thrown into the street. So much was Mary kicked and cut to pieces, that she was oftener called "*pecked*" than by her name.

CHAPTER VII

I lived in Master Hugh's family about seven years. During this time, I succeeded in learning to read and write. In accomplishing this, I was compelled to resort to various stratagems. I had no regular teacher. My mistress, who had kindly commenced to instruct me, had, in compliance with the advice and direction of her husband, not only ceased to instruct, but had set her face against my being instructed by any one else. It is due, however, to my mistress to say of her, that she did not adopt this course of treatment immediately. She at first lacked the depravity indispensable to shutting me up in mental darkness. It was at least necessary for her to have some training in the exercise of irresponsible power, to make her equal to the task of treating me as though I were a brute.

My mistress was, as I have said, a kind and tender-hearted woman; and in the simplicity of her soul she commenced, when I first went to live with her, to treat me as she supposed one human being ought to treat another. In entering upon the duties of a slaveholder, she did not seem to perceive that I sustained to her the relation of a mere chattel, and that for her to treat me as a human being was not only wrong, but dangerously so. Slavery proved as injurious to her as it did to me. When I went there, she was a pious, warm, and tender-hearted woman. There was no sorrow or suffering for which she had not a tear. She had bread for the hungry, clothes for the naked, and comfort for every mourner that came within her reach. Slavery soon proved its ability to divest her of these heavenly qualities. Under its influence, the tender heart became stone, and the lamblike disposition gave way to one of tiger-like fierceness. The first step in her downward course was in her ceasing to instruct me. She now commenced to practise her husband's precepts. She finally became even more violent in her opposition than her husband himself. She was not satisfied with simply doing as well as he had commanded; she seemed anxious to do better. Nothing seemed to make her more angry than to see me with a newspaper. She seemed to think that here lay the danger. I have had her rush at me with a face made all up of fury, and snatch from me a newspaper, in a manner that fully revealed her apprehension. She was an apt woman; and a little experience soon demonstrated, to her satisfaction, that education and slavery were incompatible with each other.

From this time I was most narrowly watched. If I was in a separate room any considerable length of time, I was sure to be suspected of having a book, and was at once called to give an account of myself. All this, however, was too late. The first step had been taken. Mistress, in teaching me the alphabet, had given me the *inch*, and no precaution could prevent me from taking the *ell*.

The plan which I adopted, and the one by which I was most successful, was that of making friends of all the little white boys whom I met in the street. As many of these as I could, I converted into teachers. With their kindly aid, obtained at different times and in different places, I finally succeeded in learning to read. When I was sent of errands, I always took my book with me, and by going one part of my errand quickly, I found time to get a lesson before my return. I used also to carry bread with me, enough of which was always in the house, and to which I was always welcome; for I was much better off in this regard than many of the poor white children in our neighborhood. This bread I used to bestow upon the hungry little urchins, who, in return, would give me that more valuable bread of knowledge. I am strongly tempted to give the names of two or three of those little boys, as a testimonial of the gratitude and affection I bear them; but prudence forbids;—not that it would injure me, but it might embarrass them; for it is almost an unpardonable offence to teach slaves to read in this Christian country. It is enough to say of the dear little fellows, that they lived on Philpot Street, very near Durgin and Bailey's shipyard. I used to talk this matter of slavery over with them. I would sometimes say to them, I wished I could be as free as they would be when they got to be men. "You will be free as soon as you are twenty-one, *but I am a slave for life!* Have not I as good a right to be free as you have?" These words used to trouble them; they would express for me the liveliest sympathy, and console me with the hope that something would occur by which I might be free.

I was now about twelve years old, and the thought of being *a slave for life* began to bear heavily upon my heart. Just about this time, I got hold of a book entitled "The Columbian Orator."[7] Every opportunity I got, I used to read this book. Among much of other interesting matter, I found in it a dialogue between a master and his slave. The slave was represented as having run away from his master three times. The dialogue represented the conversation which took place between them, when the slave was retaken the third time. In this dialogue, the whole argument in behalf of slavery was brought forward by the master, all of which was disposed of by the slave. The slave was made to say some very smart as well as impressive things in reply to his master—things which had the desired though unexpected effect; for the conversation resulted in the voluntary emancipation of the slave on the part of the master.

In the same book, I met with one of Sheridan's[8] mighty speeches on and in behalf of Catholic emancipation. These were choice documents to me. I read them over and over again with unabated interest. They gave tongue to interesting thoughts of my own soul, which had frequently flashed through my mind, and died away for want of utterance. The moral which I gained from the dialogue was the power of truth over the conscience of even a slaveholder. What I got from Sheridan was a bold denunciation of slavery, and a powerful vindication of human rights. The reading of these documents enabled me to utter my thoughts, and to meet the arguments brought forward to sustain slavery; but while they relieved me of one difficulty, they brought on another even more painful than the one of which I was relieved. The more I read, the more I was led to abhor and detest my enslavers. I could regard them in no other

7. Caleb Bingham, *The Columbian Orator: Containing a Variety of Original and Selected Pieces: Together with Rules, Calculated to Improve Youth and Others in the Ornamental and Useful Art of Eloquence* (1807).

8. Thomas Sheridan (1719–1788), Irish actor, lecturer, and writer on elocution.

light than a band of successful robbers, who had left their homes, and gone to Africa, and stolen us from our homes, and in a strange land reduced us to slavery. I loathed them as being the meanest as well as the most wicked of men. As I read and contemplated the subject, behold! that very discontentment which Master Hugh had predicted would follow my learning to read had already come, to torment and sting my soul to unutterable anguish. As I writhed under it, I would at times feel that learning to read had been a curse rather than a blessing. It had given me a view of my wretched condition, without the remedy. It opened my eyes to the horrible pit, but to no ladder upon which to get out. In moments of agony, I envied my fellow-slaves for their stupidity. I have often wished myself a beast. I preferred the condition of the meanest reptile to my own. Any thing, no matter what, to get rid of thinking! It was this everlasting thinking of my condition that tormented me. There was no getting rid of it. It was pressed upon me by every object within sight or hearing, animate or inanimate. The silver trump of freedom had roused my soul to eternal wakefulness. Freedom now appeared, to disappear no more forever. It was heard in every sound, and seen in every thing. It was ever present to torment me with a sense of my wretched condition. I saw nothing without seeing it, I heard nothing without hearing it, and felt nothing without feeling it. It looked from every star, it smiled in every calm, breathed in every wind, and moved in every storm.

I often found myself regretting my own existence, and wishing myself dead; and but for the hope of being free, I have no doubt but that I should have killed myself, or done something for which I should have been killed. While in this state of mind, I was eager to hear any one speak of slavery. I was a ready listener. Every little while, I could hear something about the abolitionists. It was some time before I found what the word meant. It was always used in such connections as to make it an interesting word to me. If a slave ran away and succeeded in getting clear, or if a slave killed his master, set fire to a barn, or did any thing very wrong in the mind of a slaveholder, it was spoken of as the fruit of *abolition*. Hearing the word in this connection very often, I set about learning what it meant. The dictionary afforded me little or no help. I found it was "the act of abolishing"; but then I did not know what was to be abolished. Here I was perplexed. I did not dare to ask any one about its meaning, for I was satisfied that it was something they wanted me to know very little about. After a patient waiting, I got one of our city papers, containing an account of the number of petitions from the north, praying for the abolition of slavery in the District of Columbia, and of the slave trade between the States. From this time I understood the words *abolition* and *abolitionist*, and always drew near when that word was spoken, expecting to hear something of importance to myself and fellow-slaves. The light broke in upon me by degrees. I went one day down on the wharf of Mr. Waters; and seeing two Irishmen unloading a scow of stone, I went, unasked, and helped them. When we had finished, one of them came to me and asked me if I were a slave. I told him I was. He asked, "Are ye a slave for life?" I told him that I was. The good Irishman seemed to be deeply affected by the statement. He said to the other that it was a pity so fine a little fellow as myself should be a slave for life. He said it was a shame to hold me. They both advised me to run away to the north; that I should find friends there, and that I should be free. I pretended not to be interested in what they said, and treated them as if I did not understand them; for I feared they might be treacherous. White men have been known to encourage slaves to escape, and then, to get the reward, catch them and return them to their masters. I was afraid that these seemingly good men might use me so; but I nevertheless remembered their advice, and from that time I resolved to run away. I looked forward to a time at which it would be safe for me to escape. I was too young to think of doing so immediately; besides, I wished to learn how to write, as I might have occasion to write my own pass. I consoled myself with the hope that I should one day find a good chance. Meanwhile, I would learn to write.

The idea as to how I might learn to write was suggested to me by being in Durgin and Bailey's ship-yard, and frequently seeing the ship carpenters, after hewing, and getting a piece of timber ready for use, write on the timber the name of that part of the ship for which it was intended. When a piece of timber was intended for the larboard side, it would be marked thus—"L." When a piece was for the starboard side, it would be marked thus—"S." A piece for the larboard forward, would be marked thus—"L.F." When a piece was for starboard side forward, it would be marked thus—"S.F." For larboard aft, it would be marked thus—"L.A." For starboard aft, it would be marked thus—"S.A." I soon learned the names of these letters, and for what they were intended when placed upon a piece of timber in the ship-yard. I immediately commenced copying them, and in a short time was able to make the four letters named. After that, when I met with any boy who I knew could write, I would tell him I could write as well as he. The next word would be, "I don't believe you. Let me see you try it." I would then make the letters which I had been so fortunate as to learn, and ask him to beat that. In this way I got a good many lessons in writing, which it is quite possible I should never have gotten in any other way. During this time, my copy-book was the board fence, brick wall, and pavement; my pen and ink was a lump of chalk. With these, I learned mainly how to write. I then commenced and continued copying the Italics in Webster's Spelling Book, until I could make them all without looking on the book. By this time, my little Master Thomas had gone to school, and learned how to write, and had written over a number of copy-books. These had been brought home, and shown to some of our near neighbors, and then laid aside. My mistress used to go to class meeting at the Wilk Street meetinghouse every Monday afternoon, and leave me to take care of the house. When left thus, I used to spend the time in writing in the spaces left in Master Thomas's copy-book, copying what he had written. I continued to do this until I could write a hand very similar to that of Master Thomas. Thus, after a long, tedious effort for years, I finally succeeded in learning how to write.

CHAPTER VIII

In a very short time after I went to live at Baltimore, my old master's youngest son Richard died; and in about three years and six months after his death, my old master, Captain Anthony, died, leaving only his son, Andrew, and daughter, Lucretia, to share his estate. He died while on a visit to see his daughter at Hillsborough. Cut off thus unexpectedly, he left no will as to the disposal of his property. It was therefore necessary to have a valuation of the property, that it might be equally divided between Mrs. Lucretia and Master Andrew. I was immediately sent for, to be valued with the other property. Here again my feelings rose up in detestation of slavery. I had now a new conception of my degraded condition. Prior to this, I had become, if not insensible to my lot, at least partly so. I left Baltimore with a young heart overborne with sadness, and a soul full of apprehension. I took passage with Captain Rowe, in the schooner *Wild Cat*, and, after a sail of about twenty-four hours, I found myself near the place of my birth. I had now been absent from it almost, if not quite, five years. I, however, remembered the place very well. I was only about five years old when I left it, to go and live with my old master on Colonel Lloyd's plantation; so that I was now between ten and eleven years old.

We were all ranked together at the valuation. Men and women, old and young, married and single, were ranked with horses, sheep, and swine. There were horses and men, cattle and women, pigs and children, all holding the same rank in the scale of being, and all were subjected to the same narrow examination. Silvery-headed age and sprightly youth, maids and matrons, had to undergo the same indelicate inspection. At this moment, I saw more clearly than ever the brutalizing effects of slavery upon both slave and slaveholder.

After the valuation, then came the division. I have no language to express the high excitement and deep anxiety which were felt among us poor slaves during this time. Our fate for life was now to be decided. We had no more voice in that decision than the brutes among whom we were ranked. A single word from the white men was enough—against all our wishes, prayers, and entreaties—to sunder forever the dearest friends, dearest kindred, and strongest ties known to human beings. In addition to the pain of separation, there was the horrid dread of falling into the hands of Master Andrew. He was known to us all as being a most cruel wretch,—a common drunkard, who had, by his reckless mismanagement and profligate dissipation, already wasted a large portion of his father's property. We all felt that we might as well be sold at once to the Georgia traders, as to pass into his hands; for we knew that that would be our inevitable condition,—a condition held by us all in the utmost horror and dread.

I suffered more anxiety than most of my fellow-slaves. I had known what it was to be kindly treated; they had known nothing of the kind. They had seen little or nothing of the world. They were in very deed men and women of sorrow, and acquainted with grief.[9] Their backs had been made familiar with the bloody lash, so that they had become callous; mine was yet tender; for while at Baltimore I got few whippings, and few slaves could boast of a kinder master and mistress than myself; and the thought of passing out of their hands into those of Master Andrew—a man who, but a few days before, to give me a sample of his bloody disposition, took my little brother by the throat, threw him on the ground, and with the heel of his boot stamped upon his head till the blood gushed from his nose and ears—was well calculated to make me anxious as to my fate. After he had committed this savage outrage upon my brother, he turned to me, and said that was the way he meant to serve me one of these days,—meaning, I suppose, when I came into his possession.

Thanks to a kind Providence, I fell to the portion of Mrs. Lucretia, and was sent immediately back to Baltimore, to live again in the family of Master Hugh. Their joy at my return equalled their sorrow at my departure. It was a

9. In Isaiah 53.3, the Lord's servant is described as "a man of sorrows, and acquainted with grief."

glad day to me. I had escaped a [fate] worse than lion's jaws. I was absent from Baltimore, for the purpose of valuation and division, just about one month, and it seemed to have been six.

Very soon after my return to Baltimore, my mistress, Lucretia, died, leaving her husband and one child, Amanda; and in a very short time after her death, Master Andrew died. Now all the property of my old master, slaves included, was in the hands of strangers,—strangers who had had nothing to do with accumulating it. Not a slave was left free. All remained slaves, from the youngest to the oldest. If any one thing in my experience, more than another, served to deepen my conviction of the infernal character of slavery, and to fill me with unutterable loathing of slaveholders, it was their base ingratitude to my poor old grandmother. She had served my old master faithfully from youth to old age. She had been the source of all his wealth; she had peopled his plantation with slaves; she had become a great grandmother in his service. She had rocked him in infancy, attended him in childhood, served him through life, and at his death wiped from his icy brow the cold death-sweat, and closed his eyes forever. She was nevertheless left a slave—a slave for life—a slave in the hands of strangers; and in their hands she saw her children, her grandchildren, and her great-grandchildren, divided, like so many sheep, without being gratified with the small privilege of a single word, as to their or her own destiny. And, to cap the climax of their base ingratitude and fiendish barbarity, my grandmother, who was now very old, having outlived my old master and all his children, having seen the beginning and end of all of them, and her present owners finding she was of but little value, her frame already racked with the pains of old age, and complete helplessness fast stealing over her once active limbs, they took her to the woods, built her a little hut, put up a little mud-chimney, and then made her welcome to the privilege of supporting herself there in perfect loneliness; thus virtually turning her out to die! If my poor old grandmother now lives, she lives to suffer in utter loneliness; she lives to remember and mourn over the loss of children, the loss of grandchildren, and the loss of great-grandchildren. They are, in the language of the slave's poet, Whittier,—

"Gone, gone, sold and gone
To the rice swamp dank and lone,
Where the slave-whip ceaseless swings,
Where the noisome insect stings,
Where the fever-demon strews
Poison with the falling dews,
Where the sickly sunbeams glare
Through the hot and misty air:—
　Gone, gone, sold and gone
　To the rice swamp dank and lone,
　From Virginia hills and waters—
　Woe is me, my stolen daughters!"[1]

1. John Greenleaf Whittier, American poet (1807–1892), wrote a large group of antislavery poems. This one is *The Farewell of a Virginia Slave Mother to her Daughters Sold into Southern Bondage.*

The hearth is desolate. The children, the unconscious children, who once sang and danced in her presence, are gone. She gropes her way, in the darkness of age, for a drink of water. Instead of the voices of her children, she hears by day the moans of the dove, and by night the screams of the hideous owl. All is gloom. The grave is at the door. And now, when weighed down by the pains and aches of old age, when the head inclines to the feet, when the beginning and ending of human existence meet, and helpless infancy and painful old age combine together—at this time, this most needful time, the time for the exercise of that tenderness and affection which children only can exercise towards a declining parent—my poor old grandmother, the devoted mother of twelve children, is left all alone, in yonder little hut, before a few dim embers. She stands—she sits—she staggers—she falls—she groans—she dies—and there are none of her children or grandchildren present, to wipe from her wrinkled brow the cold sweat of death, or to place beneath the sod her fallen remains. Will not a righteous God visit[2] for these things?

In about two years after the death of Mrs. Lucretia, Master Thomas married his second wife. Her name was Rowena Hamilton. She was the eldest daughter of Mr. William Hamilton. Master now lived in St. Michael's. Not long after his marriage, a misunderstanding took place between himself and Master Hugh; and as a means of punishing his brother, he took me from him to live with himself at St. Michael's. Here I underwent another most painful separation. It, however, was not so severe as the one I dreaded at the division of property; for, during this interval, a great change had taken place in Master Hugh and his once kind and affectionate wife. The influence of brandy upon him, and of slavery upon her, had effected a disastrous change in the characters of both; so that, as far as they were concerned, I thought I had little to lose by the change. But it was not to them that I was attached. It was to those little Baltimore boys that I felt the strongest attachment. I had received many good lessons from them, and was still receiving them, and the thought of leaving them was painful indeed. I was leaving, too, without the hope of ever being allowed to return. Master Thomas had said he would never let me return again. The barrier betwixt himself and brother he considered impassable.

I then had to regret that I did not at least make the attempt to carry out my resolution to run away; for the chances of success are tenfold greater from the city than from the country.

I sailed from Baltimore for St. Michael's in the sloop *Amanda*, Captain Edward Dodson. On my passage, I paid particular attention to the direction which the steamboats took to go to Philadelphia. I found, instead of going down, on reaching North Point they went up the bay, in a north-easterly direction. I deemed this knowledge of the utmost importance. My determination to run away was again revived. I resolved to wait only so long as the offering of a favorable opportunity. When that came, I was determined to be off.

CHAPTER IX

I have now reached a period of my life when I can give dates. I left Baltimore, and went to live with Master Thomas Auld, at St. Michael's, in March, 1832.

2. I.e., visit vengeance. Cf. Exodus 32.34: "Nevertheless, in the day when I visit I will visit their sin upon them."

It was now more than seven years since I lived with him in the family of my old master, on Colonel Lloyd's plantation. We of course were now almost entire strangers to each other. He was to me a new master, and I to him a new slave. I was ignorant of his temper and disposition; he was equally so of mine. A very short time, however, brought us into full acquaintance with each other. I was made acquainted with his wife not less than with himself. They were well matched, being equally mean and cruel. I was now, for the first time during a space of more than seven years, made to feel the painful gnawings of hunger—a something which I had not experienced before since I left Colonel Lloyd's plantation. It went hard enough with me then, when I could look back to no period at which I had enjoyed a sufficiency. It was tenfold harder after living in Master Hugh's family, where I had always had enough to eat, and of that which was good. I have said Master Thomas was a mean man. He was so. Not to give a slave enough to eat, is regarded as the most aggravated development of meanness even among slaveholders. The rule is, no matter how coarse the food, only let there be enough of it. This is the theory; and in the part of Maryland from which I came, it is the general practice,—though there are many exceptions. Master Thomas gave us enough of neither coarse nor fine food. There were four of us slaves in the kitchen—my sister Eliza, my aunt Priscilla, Henny, and myself; and we were allowed less than a half of a bushel of corn-meal per week, and very little else, either in the shape of meat or vegetables. It was not enough for us to subsist upon. We were therefore reduced to the wretched necessity of living at the expense of our neighbors. This we did by begging and stealing, whichever came handy in the time of need, the one being considered as legitimate as the other. A great many times have we poor creatures been nearly perishing with hunger, when food in abundance lay mouldering in the safe and smoke-house, and our pious mistress was aware of the fact; and yet that mistress and her husband would kneel every morning, and pray that God would bless them in basket and store!

Bad as all slaveholders are, we seldom meet one destitute of every element of character commanding respect. My master was one of this rare sort. I do not know of one single noble act ever performed by him. The leading trait in his character was meanness; and if there were any other element in his nature, it was made subject to this. He was mean; and, like most other mean men, he lacked the ability to conceal his meanness. Captain Auld was not born a slaveholder. He had been a poor man, master only of a Bay craft. He came into possession of all his slaves by marriage; and of all men, adopted slaveholders are the worst. He was cruel, but cowardly. He commanded without firmness. In the enforcement of his rules, he was at times rigid, and at times lax. At times, he spoke to his slaves with the firmness of Napoleon and the fury of a demon; at other times, he might well be mistaken for an inquirer who had lost his way. He did nothing of himself. He might have passed for a lion, but for his ears.[3] In all things noble which he attempted, his own meanness shone most conspicuous. His airs, words, and actions, were the airs, words, and actions of born slaveholders, and, being assumed, were awkward enough. He was not even a good imitator. He possessed all the disposition to deceive, but wanted

3. A variation on Aesop's fable of the ass in a lion's skin who frightened all of the animals. The fox says: "I would have been frightened too if I had not heard you bray."

the power. Having no resources within himself, he was compelled to be the copyist of many, and being such, he was forever the victim of inconsistency; and of consequence he was an object of contempt, and was held as such even by his slaves. The luxury of having slaves of his own to wait upon him was something new and unprepared for. He was a slaveholder without the ability to hold slaves. He found himself incapable of managing his slaves either by force, fear, or fraud. We seldom called him "master"; we generally called him "Captain Auld," and were hardly disposed to title him at all. I doubt not that our conduct had much to do with making him appear awkward, and of consequence fretful. Our want of reverence for him must have perplexed him greatly. He wished to have us call him master, but lacked the firmness necessary to command us to do so. His wife used to insist upon our calling him so, but to no purpose. In August, 1832, my master attended a Methodist camp-meeting held in the Bay-side, Talbot county, and there experienced religion. I indulged a faint hope that his conversion would lead him to emancipate his slaves, and that, if he did not do this, it would, at any rate, make him more kind and humane. I was disappointed in both these respects. It neither made him to be humane to his slaves, nor to emancipate them. If it had any effect on his character, it made him more cruel and hateful in all his ways; for I believe him to have been a much worse man after his conversion than before. Prior to his conversion, he relied upon his own depravity to shield and sustain him in his savage barbarity; but after his conversion, he found religious sanction and support for his slaveholding cruelty. He made the greatest pretensions to piety. His house was the house of prayer. He prayed morning, noon, and night. He very soon distinguished himself among his brethren, and was soon made a class-leader and exhorter. His activity in revivals was great, and he proved himself an instrument in the hands of the church in converting many souls. His house was the preachers' home. They used to take great pleasure in coming there to put up; for while he starved us, he stuffed them. We have had three or four preachers there at a time. The names of those who used to come most frequently while I lived there, were Mr. Storks, Mr. Ewery, Mr. Humphry, and Mr. Hickey. I have also seen Mr. George Cookman at our house. We slaves loved Mr. Cookman. We believed him to be a good man. We thought him instrumental in getting Mr. Samuel Harrison, a very rich slaveholder, to emancipate his slaves; and by some means got the impression that he was laboring to effect the emancipation of all the slaves. When he was at our house, we were sure to be called in to prayers. When the others were there, we were sometimes called in and sometimes not. Mr. Cookman took more notice of us than either of the other ministers. He could not come among us without betraying his sympathy for us, and, stupid as we were, we had the sagacity to see it.

While I lived with my master in St. Michael's, there was a white young man, a Mr. Wilson, who proposed to keep a Sabbath school for the instruction of such slaves as might be disposed to learn to read the New Testament. We met but three times, when Mr. West and Mr. Fairbanks, both class-leaders, with many others, came upon us with sticks and other missiles, drove us off, and forbade us to meet again. Thus ended our little Sabbath school in the pious town of St. Michael's.

I have said my master found religious sanction for his cruelty. As an example, I will state one of many facts going to prove the charge. I have seen him tie up a lame young woman, and whip her with a heavy cowskin upon her naked shoulders, causing the warm red blood to drip; and, in justification of the bloody deed, he would quote this passage of Scripture—"He that knoweth his master's will, and doeth it not, shall be beaten with many stripes."[4]

Master would keep this lacerated young woman tied up in this horrid situation four or five hours at a time. I have known him to tie her up early in the morning, and whip her before breakfast; leave her, go to his store, return to dinner, and whip her again, cutting her in the places already made raw with his cruel lash. The secret of master's cruelty toward "Henny" is found in the fact of her being almost helpless. When quite a child, she fell into the fire, and burned herself horribly. Her hands were so burnt that she never got the use of them. She could do very little but bear heavy burdens. She was to master a bill of expense; and as he was a mean man, she was a constant offence to him. He seemed desirous of getting the poor girl out of existence. He gave her away once to his sister; but, being a poor gift, she was not disposed to keep her. Finally, my benevolent master, to use his own words, "set her adrift to take care of herself." Here was a recently-converted man, holding on upon the mother, and at the same time turning out her helpless child, to starve and die! Master Thomas was one of the many pious slaveholders who hold slaves for the very charitable purpose of taking care of them.

My master and myself had quite a number of differences. He found me unsuitable to his purpose. My city life, he said, had had a very pernicious effect upon me. It had almost ruined me for every good purpose, and fitted me for every thing which was bad. One of my greatest faults was that of letting his horse run away, and go down to his father-in-law's farm, which was about five miles from St. Michael's. I would then have to go after it. My reason for this kind of carelessness, or carefulness, was, that I could always get something to eat when I went there. Master William Hamilton, my master's father-in-law, always gave his slaves enough to eat. I never left there hungry, no matter how great the need of my speedy return. Master Thomas at length said he would stand it no longer. I had lived with him nine months, during which time he had given me a number of severe whippings, all to no good purpose. He resolved to put me out, as he said, to be broken; and, for this purpose, he let me for one year to a man named Edward Covey. Mr. Covey was a poor man, a farm-renter. He rented the place upon which he lived, as also the hands with which he tilled it. Mr. Covey had acquired a very high reputation for breaking young slaves, and this reputation was of immense value to him. It enabled him to get his farm tilled with much less expense to himself than he could have had it done without such a reputation. Some slaveholders thought it not much loss to allow Mr. Covey to have their slaves one year, for the sake of the training to which they were subjected, without any other compensation. He could hire young help with great ease, in consequence of this reputation. Added to the natural good qualities of Mr. Covey, he was a professor of religion—a pious soul—a member and a class-leader in the Methodist church. All of this added weight to his reputation as a "nigger-breaker." I was aware of all the facts, having been made acquainted with them by a young man who had lived

4. Luke 12.47.

there. I nevertheless made the change gladly; for I was sure of getting enough to eat, which is not the smallest consideration to a hungry man.

CHAPTER X

I left Master Thomas's house, and went to live with Mr. Covey, on the 1st of January, 1833. I was now, for the first time in my life, a field hand. In my new employment, I found myself even more awkward than a country boy appeared to be in a large city. I had been at my new home but one week before Mr. Covey gave me a very severe whipping, cutting my back, causing the blood to run, and raising ridges on my flesh as large as my little finger. The details of this affair are as follows: Mr. Covey sent me, very early in the morning of one of our coldest days in the month of January, to the woods, to get a load of wood. He gave me a team of unbroken oxen. He told me which was the in-hand ox, and which the off-hand ox. He then tied the end of a large rope around the horns of the in-hand ox, and gave me the other end of it, and told me, if the oxen started to run, that I must hold on upon the rope. I had never driven oxen before, and of course I was very awkward. I, however, succeeded in getting to the edge of the woods with little difficulty; but I had got a very few rods into the woods, when the oxen took fright, and started full tilt, carrying the cart against trees, and over stumps, in the most frightful manner. I expected every moment that my brains would be dashed out against the trees. After running thus for a considerable distance, they finally upset the cart, dashing it with great force against a tree, and threw themselves into a dense thicket. How I escaped death, I do not know. There I was, entirely alone, in a thick wood, in a place new to me. My cart was upset and shattered, my oxen were entangled among the young trees, and there was none to help me. After a long spell of effort, I succeeded in getting my cart righted, my oxen disentangled, and again yoked to the cart. I now proceeded with my team to the place where I had, the day before, been chopping wood, and loaded my cart pretty heavily, thinking in this way to tame my oxen. I then proceeded on my way home. I had now consumed one half of the day. I got out of the woods safely, and now felt out of danger. I stopped my oxen to open the woods gate; and just as I did so, before I could get hold of my ox-rope, the oxen again started, rushed through the gate, catching it between the wheel and the body of the cart, tearing it to pieces, and coming within a few inches of crushing me against the gate-post. Thus twice, in one short day, I escaped death by the merest chance. On my return, I told Mr. Covey what had happened, and how it happened. He ordered me to return to the woods again immediately. I did so, and he followed on after me. Just as I got into the woods, he came up and told me to stop my cart, and that he would teach me how to trifle away my time, and break gates. He then went to a large gum-tree, and with his axe cut three large switches, and, after trimming them up neatly with his pocket-knife, he ordered me to take off my clothes. I made him no answer, but stood with my clothes on. He repeated his order. I still made him no answer, nor did I move to strip myself. Upon this he rushed at me with the fierceness of a tiger, tore off my clothes, and lashed me till he had worn out his switches, cutting me so savagely as to leave the marks visible for a long time after. This whipping was the first of a number just like it, and for similar offences.

I lived with Mr. Covey one year. During the first six months, of that year, scarce a week passed without his whipping me. I was seldom free from a sore back. My awkwardness was almost always his excuse for whipping me. We were worked fully up to the point of endurance. Long before day we were up, our horses fed, and by the first approach of day we were off to the field with our hoes and ploughing teams. Mr. Covey gave us enough to eat, but scarce time to eat it. We were often less than five minutes taking our meals. We were often in the field from the first approach of day till its last lingering ray had left us; and at saving-fodder time, midnight often caught us in the field binding blades.[5]

Covey would be out with us. The way he used to stand it was this. He would spend the most of his afternoons in bed. He would then come out fresh in the evening, ready to urge us on with his words, example, and frequently with the whip. Mr. Covey was one of the few slaveholders who could and did work with his hands. He was a hard-working man. He knew by himself just what a man or a boy could do. There was no deceiving him. His work went on in his absence almost as well as in his presence; and he had the faculty of making us feel that he was ever present with us. This he did by surprising us. He seldom approached the spot where we were at work openly, if he could do it secretly. He always aimed at taking us by surprise. Such was his cunning, that we used to call him, among ourselves, "the snake." When we were at work in the cornfield, he would sometimes crawl on his hands and knees to avoid detection, and all at once he would rise nearly in our midst, and scream out, "Ha, ha! Come, come! Dash on, dash on!" This being his mode of attack, it was never safe to stop a single minute. His comings were like a thief in the night. He appeared to us as being ever at hand. He was under every tree, behind every stump, in every bush, and at every window, on the plantation. He would sometimes mount his horse, as if bound to St. Michael's, a distance of seven miles, and in half an hour afterwards you would see him coiled up in the corner of the wood-fence, watching every motion of the slaves. He would, for this purpose, leave his horse tied up in the woods. Again, he would sometimes walk up to us, and give us orders as though he was upon the point of starting on a long journey, turn his back upon us, and make as though he was going to the house to get ready; and, before he would get half way thither, he would turn short and crawl into a fence-corner, or behind some tree, and there watch us till the going down of the sun.

Mr. Covey's *forte* consisted in his power to deceive. His life was devoted to planning and perpetrating the grossest deceptions. Every thing he possessed in the shape of learning or religion, he made conform to his disposition to deceive. He seemed to think himself equal to deceiving the Almighty. He would make a short prayer in the morning, and a long prayer at night; and, strange as it may seem, few men would at times appear more devotional than he. The exercises of his family devotions were always commenced with singing; and, as he was a very poor singer himself, the duty of raising the hymn generally came upon me. He would read his hymn, and nod at me to commence. I would at times do so; at others, I would not. My noncompliance would almost always produce much

5. Gathering cut grain into bundles or sheaves.

confusion. To show himself independent of me, he would start and stagger through with his hymn in the most discordant manner. In this state of mind, he prayed with more than ordinary spirit. Poor man! such was his disposition, and success at deceiving, I do verily believe that he sometimes deceived himself into the solemn belief, that he was a sincere worshipper of the most high God; and this, too, at a time when he may be said to have been guilty of compelling his woman slave to commit the sin of adultery. The facts in the case are these: Mr. Covey was a poor man; he was just commencing in life; he was only able to buy one slave; and, shocking as is the fact, he bought her, as he said, for a *breeder*. This woman was named Caroline. Mr. Covey bought her from Mr. Thomas Lowe, about six miles from St. Michael's. She was a large, able-bodied woman, about twenty years old. She had already given birth to one child, which proved her to be just what he wanted. After buying her, he hired a married man of Mr. Samuel Harrison, to live with him one year; and him he used to fasten up with her every night! The result was, that, at the end of the year, the miserable woman gave birth to twins. At this result Mr. Covey seemed to be highly pleased, both with the man and the wretched woman. Such was his joy, and that of his wife, that nothing they could do for Caroline during her confinement was too good, or too hard, to be done. The children were regarded as being quite an addition to his wealth.

If at any one time of my life more than another, I was made to drink the bitterest dregs of slavery, that time was during the first six months of my stay with Mr. Covey. We were worked in all weathers. It was never too hot or too cold; it could never rain, blow, hail, or snow, too hard for us to work in the field. Work, work, work, was scarcely more the order of the day than of the night. The longest days were too short for him, and the shortest nights too long for him. I was somewhat unmanageable when I first went there, but a few months of this discipline tamed me. Mr. Covey succeeded in breaking me. I was broken in body, soul, and spirit. My natural elasticity was crushed, my intellect languished, the disposition to read departed, the cheerful spark that lingered about my eye died; the dark night of slavery closed in upon me; and behold a man transformed into a brute!

Sunday was my only leisure time. I spent this in a sort of beast-like stupor, between sleep and wake, under some large tree. At times I would rise up, a flash of energetic freedom would dart through my soul, accompanied with a faint beam of hope, that flickered for a moment, and then vanished. I sank down again, mourning over my wretched condition. I was sometimes prompted to take my life, and that of Covey, but was prevented by a combination of hope and fear. My sufferings on this plantation seem now like a dream rather than a stern reality.

Our house stood within a few rods of the Chesapeake Bay, whose broad bosom was ever white with sails from every quarter of the habitable globe. Those beautiful vessels, robed in purest white, so delightful to the eye of freemen, were to me so many shrouded ghosts, to terrify and torment me with thoughts of my wretched condition. I have often, in the deep stillness of a summer's Sabbath, stood all alone upon the lofty banks of that noble bay, and traced, with saddened heart and tearful eye, the countless number of sails moving off to the mighty ocean. The sight of these always affected me powerfully. My thoughts would compel utterance; and there, with no audience but the Almighty, I would pour out my soul's complaint, in my rude way, with an apostrophe[6] to the moving multitude of ships:—

"You are loosed from your moorings, and are free; I am fast in my chains, and am a slave! You move merrily before the gentle gale, and I sadly before the bloody whip! You are freedom's swift-winged angels, that fly round the world; I am confined in bands of iron! O that I were free! O, that I were on one of your gallant decks, and under your protecting wing! Alas! betwixt me and you, the turbid waters roll. Go on, go on. O that I could also go! Could I but swim! If I could fly! O, why was I born a man, of whom to make a brute! The glad ship is gone; she hides in the dim distance. I am left in the hottest hell of unending slavery. O God, save me! God, deliver me! Let me be free! Is there any God? Why am I a slave? I will run away. I will not stand it. Get caught, or get clear, I'll try it. I had as well die with ague as the fever. I have only one life to lose. I had as well be killed running as die standing. Only think of it; one hundred miles straight north, and I am free! Try it? Yes! God helping me, I will. It cannot be that I shall live and die a slave. I will take to the water. This very bay shall bear me into freedom. The steam boats steered in a north-east course from North Point. I will do the same; and when I get to the head of the bay, I will turn my canoe adrift, and walk straight through Delaware into Pennsylvania. When I get there, I shall not be required to have a pass; I can travel without being disturbed. Let but the first opportunity offer, and, come what will, I am off. Meanwhile, I will try to bear up under the yoke. I am not the only slave in the world. Why should I fret? I can bear as much as any of them. Besides, I am but a boy, and all boys are bound to some one. It may be that my misery in slavery will only increase my happiness when I get free. There is a better day coming."

Thus I used to think, and thus I used to speak to myself; goaded almost to madness at one moment, and at the next reconciling myself to my wretched lot.

I have already intimated that my condition was much worse, during the first six months of my stay at Mr. Covey's, than in the last six. The circumstances leading to the change in Mr. Covey's course toward me form an epoch in my humble history. You have seen how a man was made a slave; you shall see how a slave was made a man. On one of the hottest days of the month of August, 1833, Bill Smith, William Hughes, a slave named Eli, and myself, were engaged in fanning wheat.[7] Hughes was clearing the fanned wheat from before the fan, Eli was turning, Smith was feeding, and I was carrying wheat to the fan. The work was simple, requiring strength rather than intellect; yet, to one entirely unused to such work, it came very hard. About three o'clock of that day, I broke down; my strength failed me; I was seized with a violent aching of the head, attended with extreme dizziness; I trembled in every limb. Finding what was coming, I nerved myself up, feeling it would never do to stop work. I stood as long as I could stagger to the hopper with grain. When I could stand no longer, I fell, and felt as if held down by an immense weight. The fan of course stopped; every one had his own work to do; and no one could do the work of the other, and have his own go on at the same time.

6. An exclamatory form of address.

7. Separating the grain from the chaff.

Mr. Covey was at the house, about one hundred yards from the treading-yard where we were fanning. On hearing the fan stop, he left immediately, and came to the spot where we were. He hastily inquired what the matter was. Bill answered that I was sick, and there was no one to bring wheat to the fan. I had by this time crawled away under the side of the post and rail-fence by which the yard was enclosed, hoping to find relief by getting out of the sun. He then asked where I was. He was told by one of the hands. He came to the spot, and, after looking at me awhile, asked me what was the matter. I told him as well as I could, for I scarce had strength to speak. He then gave me a savage kick in the side, and told me to get up. I tried to do so, but fell back in the attempt. He gave me another kick, and again told me to rise. I again tried, and succeeded in gaining my feet; but, stooping to get the tub with which I was feeding the fan, I again staggered and fell. While down in this situation, Mr. Covey took up the hickory slat with which Hughes had been striking off the half-bushel measure, and with it gave me a heavy blow upon the head, making a large wound, and the blood ran freely; and with this again told me to get up. I made no effort to comply, having now made up my mind to let him do his worst. In a short time after receiving this blow, my head grew better. Mr. Covey had now left me to my fate. At this moment I resolved, for the first time, to go to my master, enter a complaint, and ask his protection. In order to [do] this, I must that afternoon walk seven miles; and this, under the circumstances, was truly a severe undertaking. I was exceedingly feeble; made so as much by the kicks and blows which I received, as by the severe fit of sickness to which I had been subjected. I, however, watched my chance, while Covey was looking in an opposite direction, and started for St. Michael's. I succeeded in getting a considerable distance on my way to the woods, when Covey discovered me, and called after me to come back, threatening what he would do if I did not come. I disregarded both his calls and his threats, and made my way to the woods as fast as my feeble state would allow; and thinking I might be overhauled by him if I kept the road, I walked through the woods, keeping far enough from the road to avoid detection, and near enough to prevent losing my way. I had not gone far before my little strength again failed me. I could go no farther. I fell down, and lay for a considerable time. The blood was yet oozing from the wound on my head. For a time I thought I should bleed to death; and think now that I should have done so, but that the blood so matted my hair as to stop the wound. After lying there about three quarters of an hour, I nerved myself up again, and started on my way, through bogs and briers, barefooted and bareheaded, tearing my feet sometimes at nearly every step; and after a journey of about seven miles, occupying some five hours to perform it, I arrived at master's store. I then presented an appearance enough to affect any but a heart of iron. From the crown of my head to my feet, I was covered with blood. My hair was all clotted with dust and blood; my shirt was stiff with blood. My legs and feet were torn in sundry places with briers and thorns, and were also covered with blood. I suppose I looked like a man who had escaped a den of wild beasts, and barely escaped them. In this state I appeared before my master, humbly entreating him to interpose his authority for my protection. I told him all the circumstances as well as I could, and it seemed, as I spoke, at times to affect him. He would then walk the floor, and seek to justify Covey by saying he expected I deserved it. He asked me what I wanted. I told him, to let me get a new home; that as sure as I lived with Mr. Covey again, I should live with but to die with him; that Covey would surely kill me; he was in a fair way for it. Master Thomas ridiculed the idea that there was any danger of Mr. Covey's killing me, and said that he knew Mr. Covey; that he was a good man, and that he could not think of taking me from him; that, should he do so, he would lose the whole year's wages; that I belonged to Mr. Covey for one year, and that I must go back to him, come what might; and that I must not trouble him with any more stories, or that he would himself *get hold of me*. After threatening me thus, he gave me a very large dose of salts, telling me that I might remain in St. Michael's that night, (it being quite late) but that I must be off back to Mr. Covey's early in the morning; and that if I did not, he would *get hold of me*, which meant that he would whip me. I remained all night, and, according to his orders, I started off to Covey's in the morning, (Saturday morning), wearied in body and broken in spirit. I got no supper that night, or breakfast that morning. I reached Covey's about nine o'clock; and just as I was getting over the fence that divided Mrs. Kemp's fields from ours, out ran Covey with his cowskin, to give me another whipping. Before he could reach me, I succeeded in getting to the cornfield; and as the corn was very high, it afforded me the means of hiding. He seemed very angry, and searched for me a long time. My behavior was altogether unaccountable. He finally gave up the chase, thinking, I suppose, that I must come home for something to eat; he would give himself no further trouble in looking for me. I spent that day mostly in the woods, having the alternative before me,—to go home and be whipped to death, or stay in the woods and be starved to death. That night, I fell in with Sandy Jenkins, a slave with whom I was somewhat acquainted. Sandy had a free wife who lived about four miles from Mr. Covey's; and it being Saturday, he was on his way to see her. I told him my circumstances, and he very kindly invited me to go home with him. I went home with him, and talked this whole matter over, and got his advice as to what course it was best for me to pursue. I found Sandy an old adviser. He told me, with great solemnity, I must go back to Covey; but that before I went, I must go with him into another part of the woods, where there was a certain *root*, which, if I would take some of it with me, carrying it *always on my right side*, would render it impossible for Mr. Covey, or any other white man, to whip me. He said he had carried it for years; and since he had done so, he had never received a blow, and never expected to while he carried it. I at first rejected the idea, that the simple carrying of a root in my pocket would have any such effect as he had said, and was not disposed to take it; but Sandy impressed the necessity with much earnestness, telling me it could do no harm, if it did no good. To please him, I at length took the root, and, according to his direction, carried it upon my right side. This was Sunday morning. I immediately started for home; and upon entering the yard gate, out came Mr. Covey on his way to meeting. He spoke to me very kindly, bade me drive the pigs from a lot near by, and passed on towards the church. Now, this singular conduct of Mr. Covey really made me begin to think that there was something in the *root* which Sandy had given me; and had it been on any other day than Sunday, I could have attributed the conduct to no other cause than the influence of that root; and as it was, I was half inclined to think the *root* to be something more than I at first had taken it to be. All went well till Monday morning. On this morning, the virtue of the *root* was fully tested. Long before daylight, I was called to go and rub, curry, and feed, the horses. I obeyed, and was glad to obey. But whilst thus engaged, whilst in the act of throwing down some blades from the loft, Mr. Covey entered the stable with a long rope; and just as I was half out of the loft, he caught hold of my legs, and was about tying me. As soon as I found what he was up to, I gave a sudden spring, and as I did so, he holding to my legs, I was brought sprawling on the stable floor. Mr. Covey seemed now to think he had me, and could do what he pleased; but at this moment—from whence came the spirit I don't know—I resolved to fight; and, suiting my action to the resolution, I seized Covey hard by the throat; and as I did so, I rose. He held on to me, and I to him. My resistance was so entirely unexpected, that Covey seemed taken all aback. He trembled like a leaf. This gave me assurance, and I held him uneasy, causing the blood to run where I touched him with the ends of my fingers. Mr. Covey soon called out to Hughes for help. Hughes came, and, while Covey held me, attempted to tie my right hand. While he was in the act of doing so, I watched my chance, and gave him a heavy kick close under the ribs. This kick fairly sickened Hughes, so that he left me in the hands of Mr. Covey. This kick had the effect of not only weakening Hughes, but Covey also. When he saw Hughes bending over with pain, his courage quailed. He asked me if I meant to persist in my resistance. I told him I did, come what might; that he had used me like a brute for six months, and that I was determined to be used so no longer. With that, he strove to drag me to a stick that was lying just out of the stable door. He meant to knock me down. But just as he was leaning over to get the stick, I seized him with both hands by his collar, and brought him by a sudden snatch to the ground. By this time, Bill came. Covey called upon him for assistance. Bill wanted to know what he could do. Covey said, "Take hold of him, take hold of him!" Bill said his master hired him out to work, and not to help to whip me; so he left Covey and myself to fight our own battle out. We were at it for nearly two hours. Covey at length let me go, puffing and blowing at a great rate, saying that if I had not resisted, he would not have whipped me half so much. The truth was, that he had not whipped me at all. I considered him as getting entirely the worst end of the bargain; for he had drawn no blood from me, but I had from him. The whole six months afterwards, that I spent with Mr. Covey, he never laid the weight of his finger upon me in anger. He would occasionally say, he didn't want to get hold of me again. "No," thought I, "you need not; for you will come off worse than you did before."

This battle with Mr. Covey was the turning-point in my career as a slave. It rekindled the few expiring embers of freedom, and revived within me a sense of my own manhood. It recalled the departed self-confidence, and inspired me again with a determination to be free. The gratification afforded by the triumph was a full compensation for whatever else might follow, even death itself. He only can understand the deep satisfaction which I experienced, who has himself repelled by force the bloody arm of slavery. I felt as I never felt before. It was a glorious resurrection, from the tomb of slavery, to the heaven of freedom. My long-crushed spirit rose, cowardice departed, bold defiance took its place; and I now resolved that, however long I might remain a slave in form, the day had passed forever when I could be a slave in fact. I did not hesitate to let it be known of me, that the white man who expected to succeed in whipping, must also succeed in killing me.

From this time I was never again what might be called fairly whipped, though I remained a slave four years afterwards. I had several fights, but was never whipped.

It was for a long time a matter of surprise to me why Mr. Covey did not immediately have me taken by the constable to the whipping-post, and there regularly whipped for the crime of raising my hand against a white man in defence of myself. And the only explanation I can now think of does not entirely satisfy me; but such as it is, I will give it. Mr. Covey enjoyed the most unbounded reputation for being a first-rate overseer and negro-breaker. It was of considerable importance to him. That reputation was at stake; and had he sent me—a boy about sixteen years old—to the public whipping-post, his reputation would have been lost; so, to save his reputation, he suffered me to go unpunished.

My term of actual service to Mr. Edward Covey ended on Christmas day, 1833. The days between Christmas and New Year's day are allowed as holidays; and, accordingly, we were not required to perform any labor, more than to feed and take care of the stock. This time we regarded as our own, by the grace of our masters; and we therefore used or abused it nearly as we pleased. Those of us who had families at a distance, were generally allowed to spend the whole six days in their society. This time, however, was spent in various ways. The staid, sober, thinking and industrious ones of our number would employ themselves in making corn-brooms, mats, horse-collars, and baskets; and another class of us would spend the time in hunting opossums, hares, and coons. But by far the larger part engaged in such sports and merriments as playing ball, wrestling, running foot-races, fiddling, dancing, and drinking whisky; and this latter mode of spending the time was by far the most agreeable to the feelings of our masters. A slave who would work during the holidays was considered by our masters as scarcely deserving them. He was regarded as one who rejected the favor of his master. It was deemed a disgrace not to get drunk at Christmas; and he was regarded as lazy indeed, who had not provided himself with the necessary means, during the year, to get whisky enough to last him through Christmas.

From what I know of the effect of these holidays upon the slave, I believe them to be among the most effective means in the hands of the slaveholder in keeping down the spirit of insurrection. Were the slaveholders at once to abandon this practice, I have not the slightest doubt it would lead to an immediate insurrection among the slaves. These holidays serve as conductors, or safety-valves, to carry off the rebellious spirit of enslaved humanity. But for these, the slave would be forced up to the wildest desperation; and woe betide the slaveholder, the day he ventures to remove or hinder the operation of those conductors! I warn him that, in such an event, a spirit will go forth in their midst, more to be dreaded than the most appalling earthquake.

The holidays are part and parcel of the gross fraud, wrong, and inhumanity of slavery. They are professedly a custom established by the benevolence of the slaveholders; but I undertake to say, it is the result of selfishness, and one of the grossest frauds committed upon the down-trodden slave. They do not give the slaves this time because they would not like to have their work during its continuance, but because they know it would be unsafe to deprive them of it. This will be seen by the fact, that the slaveholders like to have their slaves spend those days just in such a manner as to make them as glad of their ending as of their beginning. Their object seems to be, to disgust their slaves with freedom, by plunging them into the lowest depths of dissipation. For instance, the slaveholders not only like to see the slave drink of his own accord, but will adopt various plans to make him drunk. One plan is, to make bets on their slaves, as to who can drink the most whisky without getting drunk; and in this way they succeed in getting whole multitudes to drink to excess. Thus, when the slave asks for virtuous freedom, the cunning slaveholder, knowing his ignorance, cheats him with a dose of vicious dissipation, artfully labelled with the name of liberty. The most of us used to drink it down, and the result was just what might be supposed: many of us were led to think that there was little to choose between liberty and slavery. We felt, and very properly too, that we had almost as well be slaves to man as to rum. So, when the holidays ended, we staggered up from the filth of our wallowing, took a long breath, and marched to the field,—feeling, upon the whole, rather glad to go, from what our master had deceived us into a belief was freedom, back to the arms of slavery.

I have said that this mode of treatment is a part of the whole system of fraud and inhumanity of slavery. It is so. The mode here adopted to disgust the slave with freedom, by allowing him to see only the abuse of it, is carried out in other things. For instance, a slave loves molasses; he steals some. His master, in many cases, goes off to town, and buys a large quantity; he returns, takes his whip, and commands the slave to eat the molasses, until the poor fellow is made sick at the very mention of it. The same mode is sometimes adopted to make the slaves refrain from asking for more food than their regular allowance. A slave runs through his allowance, and applies for more. His master is enraged at him; but, not willing to send him off without food, gives him more than is necessary, and compels him to eat it within a given time. Then, if he complains that he cannot eat it, he is said to be satisfied neither full nor fasting, and is whipped for being hard to please! I have an abundance of such illustrations of the same principle, drawn from my own observation, but think the cases I have cited sufficient. The practice is a very common one.

On the first of January, 1834, I left Mr. Covey, and went to live with Mr. William Freeland, who lived about three miles from St. Michael's. I soon found Mr. Freeland a very different man from Mr. Covey. Though not rich, he was what would be called an educated southern gentleman. Mr. Covey, as I have shown, was a well-trained negro-breaker and slave-driver. The former (slaveholder though he was) seemed to possess some regard for honor, some reverence for justice, and some respect for humanity. The latter seemed totally insensible to all such sentiments. Mr. Freeland had many of the faults peculiar to slaveholders, such as being very passionate and fretful; but I must do him the justice to say, that he was exceedingly free from those degrading vices to which Mr. Covey was constantly addicted. The one was open and frank, and we always knew where to find him. The other was a most artful deceiver, and could be understood only by such as were skilful enough to detect his cunningly-devised frauds. Another advantage I gained in my new master was, he made no pretensions to, or profession of, religion; and this, in my opinion, was truly a great advantage. I assert most unhesitatingly, that the religion of the south is a mere covering for the most horrid crimes,—a justifier of the most appalling barbarity,—a sanctifier of the most hateful frauds,—and a dark shelter under which the darkest, foulest, grossest, and most infernal deeds of slaveholders find the strongest protection. Were I to be again reduced to the chains of slavery, next to that enslavement, I should regard being the slave of a religious master the greatest calamity that could befall me. For of all slaveholders with whom I have ever met, religious slaveholders are the worst. I have ever found them the meanest and basest, the most cruel and cowardly, of all others. It was my unhappy lot not only to belong to a religious slaveholder, but to live in a community of such religionists. Very near Mr. Freeland lived the Rev. Daniel Weeden, and in the same neighborhood lived the Rev. Rigby Hopkins. These were members and ministers in the Reformed Methodist Church. Mr. Weeden owned, among others, a woman slave, whose name I have forgotten. This woman's back, for weeks, was kept literally raw, made so by the lash of this merciless, *religious* wretch. He used to hire hands. His maxim was, Behave well or behave ill, it is the duty of a master occasionally to whip a slave, to remind him of his master's authority. Such was his theory, and such his practice.

Mr. Hopkins was even worse than Mr. Weeden. His chief boast was his ability to manage slaves. The peculiar feature of his government was that of whipping slaves in advance of deserving it. He always managed to have one or more of his slaves to whip every Monday morning. He did this to alarm their fears, and strike terror into those who escaped. His plan was to whip for the smallest offences, to prevent the commission of large ones. Mr. Hopkins could always find some excuse for whipping a slave. It would astonish one, unaccustomed to a slaveholding life, to see with what wonderful ease a slaveholder can find things, of which to make occasion to whip a slave. A mere look, word, or motion,—a mistake, accident, or want of power,—are all matters for which a slave may be whipped at any time. Does a slave look dissatisfied? It is said, he has the devil in him, and it must be whipped out. Does he speak loudly when spoken to by his master? Then he is getting high-minded, and should be taken down a button-hole lower. Does he forget to pull off his hat at the approach of a white person? Then he is wanting in reverence, and should be whipped for it. Does he ever venture to vindicate his conduct, when censured for it? Then he is guilty of impudence,—one of the greatest crimes of which a slave can be guilty. Does he ever venture to suggest a different mode of doing things from that pointed out by his master? He is indeed presumptuous, and getting above himself; and nothing less than a flogging will do for him. Does he, while ploughing, break a plough,—or, while hoeing, break a hoe? It is owing to his carelessness, and for it a slave must always be whipped. Mr. Hopkins could always find something of this sort to justify the use of the lash, and he seldom failed to embrace such opportunities. There was not a man in the whole county, with whom the slaves who had the getting their own home, would not prefer to live, rather than with this Rev. Mr. Hopkins. And yet there was not a man any where round, who made higher professions of religion, or was more active in revivals,—more attentive to the class, love-feast, prayer and preaching meetings, or more devotional in his family,—that prayed earlier, later, louder, and longer,—than this same reverend slave-driver, Rigby Hopkins.

But to return to Mr. Freeland, and to my experience while in his employment. He, like Mr. Covey, gave us enough to eat; but, unlike Mr. Covey, he also gave us sufficient time to take our meals. He worked us hard, but always between sunrise and sunset. He required a good deal of work to be done, but gave us good tools with which to work. His farm was large, but he employed hands enough to work it, and with ease, compared with many of his neighbors. My treatment, while in his employment, was heavenly, compared with what I experienced at the hands of Mr. Edward Covey.

Mr. Freeland was himself the owner of but two slaves. Their names were Henry Harris and John Harris. The rest of his hands he hired. These consisted of myself, Sandy Jenkins,[8] and Handy Caldwell. Henry and John were quite intelligent, and in a very little while after I went there, I succeeded in creating in them a strong desire to learn how to read. This desire soon sprang up in the others also. They very soon mustered up some old spelling-books, and nothing would do but that I must keep a Sabbath school. I agreed to do so, and accordingly devoted my Sundays to teaching these my loved fellow-slaves how to read. Neither of them knew his letters when I went there. Some of the slaves of the neighboring farms found what was going on, and also availed themselves of this little opportunity to learn to read. It was understood, among all who came, that there must be as little display about it as possible. It was necessary to keep our religious masters at St. Michael's unacquainted with the fact, that, instead of spending the Sabbath in wrestling, boxing, and drinking whisky, we were trying to learn how to read the will of God; for they had much rather see us engaged in those degrading sports, than to see us behaving like intellectual, moral, and accountable beings. My blood boils as I think of the bloody manner in which Messrs. Wright Fairbanks and Garrison West, both class-leaders, in connection with many others, rushed in upon us with sticks and stones, and broke up our virtuous little Sabbath school, at St. Michael's—all calling themselves Christians! humble followers of the Lord Jesus Christ! But I am again digressing.

I held my Sabbath school at the house of a free colored man, whose name I deem it imprudent to mention; for should it be known, it might embarrass him greatly, though the crime of holding the school was committed ten years ago. I had at one time over forty scholars, and those of the right sort, ardently desiring to learn. They were of all ages, though mostly men and women. I look back to those Sundays with an amount of pleasure not to be expressed. They were great days to my soul. The work of instructing my dear fellow-slaves was the sweetest engagement with which I was ever blessed. We loved each other, and to leave them at the close of the Sabbath was a severe cross indeed. When I think that those precious souls are to-day shut up in the prison-house of slavery, my feelings overcome me, and I am almost ready to ask, "Does a righteous God govern the universe? and for what does he hold the thunders in his right hand, if not to smite the oppressor, and deliver the spoiled out of the hand of the spoiler?" These dear souls came not to Sabbath school because it was popular to do so, nor did I teach them because it was reputable to be thus engaged. Every moment they spent in that school, they were liable to be taken up, and given thirty-nine lashes. They came because they wished to learn. Their minds had been starved by their cruel masters. They had been shut up

8. This is the same man who gave me the roots to prevent my being whipped by Mr. Covey. He was "a clever soul." We used frequently to talk about the fight with Covey, and as often as we did so, he would claim my success as the result of the roots which he gave me. This superstition is very common among the more ignorant slaves. A slave seldom dies but that his death is attributed to trickery [Douglass's note].

in mental darkness. I taught them, because it was the delight of my soul to be doing something that looked like bettering the condition of my race. I kept up my school nearly the whole year I lived with Mr. Freeland; and, beside my Sabbath school, I devoted three evenings in the week, during the winter, to teaching the slaves at home. And I have the happiness to know, that several of those who came to Sabbath school learned how to read; and that one, at least, is now free through my agency.

The year passed off smoothly. It seemed only about half as long as the year which preceded it. I went through it without receiving a single blow. I will give Mr. Freeland the credit of being the best master I ever had, *till I became my own master*. For the ease with which I passed the year, I was, however, somewhat indebted to the society of my fellow-slaves. They were noble souls; they not only possessed loving hearts, but brave ones. We were linked and interlinked with each other. I loved them with a love stronger than any thing I have experienced since. It is sometimes said that we slaves do not love and confide in each other. In answer to this assertion, I can say, I never loved any or confided in any people more than my fellow-slaves, and especially those with whom I lived at Mr. Freeland's. I believe we would have died for each other. We never undertook to do any thing, of any importance, without a mutual consultation. We never moved separately. We were one; and as much so by our tempers and dispositions, as by the mutual hardships to which we were necessarily subjected by our condition as slaves.

At the close of the year 1834, Mr. Freeland again hired me of my master, for the year 1835. But, by this time, I began to want to live *upon free land* as well as *with Freeland*; and I was no longer content, therefore, to live with him or any other slaveholder. I began, with the commencement of the year, to prepare myself for a final struggle, which should decide my fate one way or the other. My tendency was upward. I was fast approaching manhood, and year after year had passed, and I was still a slave. These thoughts roused me—I must do something. I therefore resolved that 1835 should not pass without witnessing an attempt, on my part, to secure my liberty. But I was not willing to cherish this determination alone. My fellow-slaves were dear to me. I was anxious to have them participate with me in this, my life-giving determination. I therefore, though with great prudence, commenced early to ascertain their views and feelings in regard to their condition, and to imbue their minds with thoughts of freedom. I bent myself to devising ways and means for our escape, and meanwhile strove, on all fitting occasions, to impress them with the gross fraud and inhumanity of slavery. I went first to Henry, next to John, then to the others. I found, in them all, warm hearts and noble spirits. They were ready to hear, and ready to act when a feasible plan should be proposed. This was what I wanted. I talked to them of our want of manhood, if we submitted to our enslavement without at least one noble effort to be free. We met often, and consulted frequently, and told our hopes and fears, recounted the difficulties, real and imagined, which we should be called on to meet. At times we were almost disposed to give up, and try to content ourselves with our wretched lot; at others, we were firm and unbending in our determination to go. Whenever we suggested any plan, there was shrinking—the odds were fearful. Our path was beset with the greatest obstacles; and if we succeeded in gaining the end of it, our right to be free was yet questionable—we were yet liable to be returned to bondage. We could see no spot, this side of the ocean, where we could be free. We knew nothing about Canada. Our knowledge of the north did not extend farther than New York; and to go there, and be forever harassed with the frightful liability of being returned to slavery—with the certainty of being treated tenfold worse than before—the thought was truly a horrible one, and one which it was not easy to overcome. The case sometimes stood thus: At every gate through which we were to pass, we saw a watchman—at every ferry a guard—on every bridge a sentinel—and in every wood a patrol. We were hemmed in upon every side. Here were the difficulties, real or imagined—the good to be sought, and the evil to be shunned. On the one hand, there stood slavery, a stern reality, glaring frightfully upon us,—its robes already crimsoned with the blood of millions, and even now feasting itself greedily upon our own flesh. On the other hand, away back in the dim distance, under the flickering light of the north star, behind some craggy hill or snow-covered mountain, stood a doubtful freedom—half frozen—beckoning us to come and share its hospitality. This in itself was sometimes enough to stagger us; but when we permitted ourselves to survey the road, we were frequently appalled. Upon either side we saw grim death, assuming the most horrid shapes. Now it was starvation, causing us to eat our own flesh;—now we were contending with the waves, and were drowned;—now we were overtaken, and torn to pieces by the fangs of the terrible blood-hound. We were stung by scorpions, chased by wild beasts, bitten by snakes, and finally, after having nearly reached the desired spot,—after swimming rivers, encountering wild beasts, sleeping in the woods, suffering hunger and nakedness,—we were overtaken by our pursuers, and, in our resistance, we were shot dead upon the spot! I say, this picture sometimes appalled us, and made us

> "rather bear those ills we had,
> Than fly to others, that we knew not of."[9]

In coming to a fixed determination to run away, we did more than Patrick Henry,[1] when he resolved upon liberty or death. With us it was a doubtful liberty at most, and almost certain death if we failed. For my part, I should prefer death to hopeless bondage.

Sandy, one of our number, gave up the notion, but still encouraged us. Our company then consisted of Henry Harris, John Harris, Henry Bailey, Charles Roberts, and myself. Henry Bailey was my uncle, and belonged to my master. Charles married my aunt: he belonged to my master's father-in-law, Mr. William Hamilton.

The plan we finally concluded upon was, to get a large canoe belonging to Mr. Hamilton, and upon the Saturday night previous to Easter holidays, paddle directly up the Chesapeake Bay. On our arrival at the head of the bay, a distance of seventy or eighty miles from where we lived, it was our purpose to turn our canoe adrift, and follow the guidance of the north star till we got beyond the limits of Maryland. Our reason for taking the water route was, that

9. Shakespeare's *Hamlet* 3.1.81–82: "rather bear those ills we have, / Than fly to others, that we know not of."

1. American statesman and orator (1736–1799) whose most famous utterance was "Give me liberty or give me death."

we were less liable to be suspected as runaways; we hoped to be regarded as fishermen; whereas, if we should take the land route, we should be subjected to interruptions of almost every kind. Any one having a white face, and being so disposed, could stop us, and subject us to examination.

The week before our intended start, I wrote several protections, one for each of us. As well as I can remember, they were in the following words, to wit:—

> "This is to certify that I, the undersigned, have given the bearer, my servant, full liberty to go to Baltimore, and spend the Easter holidays. Written with mine own hand, &c., 1835.
>
> "William Hamilton,
> "Near St. Michael's, in Talbot county, Maryland."

We were not going to Baltimore; but, in going up the bay, we went toward Baltimore, and these protections were only intended to protect us while on the bay.

As the time drew near for our departure, our anxiety became more and more intense. It was truly a matter of life and death with us. The strength of our determination was about to be fully tested. At this time, I was very active in explaining every difficulty, removing every doubt, dispelling every fear, and inspiring all with the firmness indispensable to success in our undertaking; assuring them that half was gained the instant we made the move; we had talked long enough; we were now ready to move; if not now, we never should be; and if we did not intend to move now, we had as well fold our arms, sit down, and acknowledge ourselves fit only to be slaves. This, none of us were prepared to acknowledge. Every man stood firm; and at our last meeting, we pledged ourselves afresh, in the most solemn manner, that, at the time appointed, we would certainly start in pursuit of freedom. This was in the middle of the week, at the end of which we were to be off. We went, as usual, to our several fields of labor, but with bosoms highly agitated with thoughts of our truly hazardous undertaking. We tried to conceal our feelings as much as possible; and I think we succeeded very well.

After a painful waiting, the Saturday morning, whose night was to witness our departure, came. I hailed it with joy, bring what of sadness it might. Friday night was a sleepless one for me. I was, by common consent, at the head of the whole affair. The responsibility of success or failure lay heavily upon me. The glory of the one, and the confusion of the other, were alike mine. The first two hours of that morning were such as I never experienced before, and hope never to again. Early in the morning, we went, as usual, to the field. We were spreading manure; and all at once, while thus engaged, I was overwhelmed with an indescribable feeling, in the fulness of which I turned to Sandy, who was near by, and said, "We are betrayed!" "Well," said he, "that thought has this moment struck me." We said no more. I was never more certain of any thing.

The horn was blown as usual, and we went up from the field to the house for breakfast. I went for the form, more than for want of any thing to eat that morning. Just as I got to the house, in looking out at the lane gate, I saw four white men, with two colored men. The white men were on horseback, and the colored ones were walking behind, as if tied. I watched them a few moments till they got up to our lane gate. Here they halted, and tied the colored men to the gate-post. I was not yet certain as to what the matter was. In a few moments, in rode Mr. Hamilton, with a speed betokening great excitement. He came to the door, and inquired if Master William was in. He was told he was at the barn. Mr. Hamilton, without dismounting, rode up to the barn with extraordinary speed. In a few moments, he and Mr. Freeland returned to the house. By this time, the three constables rode up, and in great haste dismounted, tied their horses, and met Master William and Mr. Hamilton returning from the barn; and after talking awhile, they all walked up to the kitchen door. There was no one in the kitchen but myself and John. Henry and Sandy were up at the barn. Mr. Freeland put his head in at the door, and called me by name, saying, there were some gentlemen at the door who wished to see me. I stepped to the door, and inquired what they wanted. They at once seized me, and, without giving me any satisfaction, tied me—lashing my hands closely together. I insisted upon knowing what the matter was. They at length said, that they had learned I had been in a "scrape," and that I was to be examined before my master; and if their information proved false, I should not be hurt.

In a few moments, they succeeded in tying John. They then turned to Henry, who had by this time returned, and commanded him to cross his hands. "I won't!" said Henry, in a firm tone, indicating his readiness to meet the consequences of his refusal. "Won't you?" said Tom Graham, the constable. "No, I won't!" said Henry, in a still stronger tone. With this, two of the constables pulled out their shining pistols, and swore, by their Creator, that they would make him cross his hands or kill him. Each cocked his pistol, and, with fingers on the trigger, walked up to Henry, saying, at the same time, if he did not cross his hands, they would blow his damned heart out. "Shoot me, shoot me!" said Henry; "you can't kill me but once. Shoot, shoot,—and be damned! *I won't be tied!*" This he said in a tone of loud defiance; and at the same time, with a motion as quick as lightning, he with one single stroke dashed the pistols from the hand of each constable. As he did this, all hands fell upon him, and, after beating him some time, they finally overpowered him, and got him tied.

During the scuffle, I managed, I know not how, to get my pass out, and, without being discovered, put it into the fire. We were all now tied; and just as we were to leave for Easton jail, Betsy Freeland, mother of William Freeland, came to the door with her hands full of biscuits, and divided them between Henry and John. She then delivered herself of a speech, to the following effect:—addressing herself to me, she said, "*You devil! You yellow devil!* it was you that put it into the heads of Henry and John to run away. But for you, you long-legged mulatto devil! Henry nor John would never have thought of such a thing." I made no reply, and was immediately hurried off towards St. Michael's. Just a moment previous to the scuffle with Henry, Mr. Hamilton suggested the propriety of making a search for the protections which he had understood Frederick had written for himself and the rest. But, just at the moment he was about carrying his proposal into effect, his aid was needed in helping to tie Henry; and the excitement attending the scuffle caused them either to forget, or to deem it unsafe, under the circumstances, to search. So we were not yet convicted of the intention to run away.

When we got about half way to St. Michael's, while the constables having us in charge were looking ahead, Henry inquired of me what he should do with his pass. I told him to eat it with his biscuit, and own nothing; and we passed the word around, "*Own nothing*"; and "*Own nothing!*" said we all. Our confidence in each other was unshaken. We were resolved to succeed or fail together, after the calamity had befallen us as much as before. We were now prepared for any thing. We were to be dragged that morning fifteen miles behind horses, and then to be placed in the Easton jail. When we reached St. Michael's, we underwent a sort of examination. We all denied that we ever intended to run away. We did this more to bring out the evidence against us, than from any hope of getting clear of being sold; for, as I have said, we were ready for that. The fact was, we cared but little where we went, so we went together. Our greatest concern was about separation. We dreaded that more than any thing this side of death. We found the evidence against us to be the testimony of one person; our master would not tell who it was; but we came to a unanimous decision among ourselves as to who their informant was. We were sent off to the jail at Easton. When we got there, we were delivered up to the sheriff, Mr. Joseph Graham, and by him placed in jail. Henry, John, and myself, were placed in one room together—Charles, and Henry Bailey, in another. Their object in separating us was to hinder concert.

We had been in jail scarcely twenty minutes, when a swarm of slave traders, and agents for slave traders, flocked into jail to look at us, and to aseertain if we were for sale. Such a set of beings I never saw before! I felt myself surrounded by so many fiends from perdition. A band of pirates never looked more like their father, the devil. They laughed and grinned over us, saying, "Ah, my boys! we have got you, haven't we?" And after taunting us in various ways, they one by one went into an examination of us, with intent to ascertain our value. They would impudently ask us if we would not like to have them for our masters. We would make them no answer, and leave them to find out as best they could. Then they would curse and swear at us, telling us that they could take the devil out of us in a very little while, if we were only in their hands.

While in jail, we found ourselves in much more comfortable quarters than we expected when we went there. We did not get much to eat, nor that which was very good; but we had a good clean room, from the windows of which we could see what was going on in the street, which was very much better than though we had been placed in one of the dark, damp cells. Upon the whole, we got along very well, so far as the jail and its keeper were concerned. Immediately after the holidays were over, contrary to all our expectations, Mr. Hamilton and Mr. Freeland came up to Easton, and took Charles, the two Henrys, and John, out of jail, and carried them home, leaving me alone. I regarded this separation as a final one. It caused me more pain than any thing else in the whole transaction. I was ready for any thing rather than separation. I supposed that they had consulted together, and had decided that, as I was the whole cause of the intention of the others to run away, it was hard to make the innocent suffer with the guilty; and that they had, therefore, concluded to take the others home, and sell me, as a warning to the others that remained. It is due to the noble Henry to say, he seemed almost as reluctant at leaving the prison as at leaving home to come to the prison. But we knew we should, in all probability, be separated, if we were sold; and since he was in their hands, he concluded to go peaceably home.

I was now left to my fate. I was all alone, and within the walls of a stone prison. But a few days before, and I was full of hope. I expected to have been safe in a land of freedom; but now I was covered with gloom, sunk down to the utmost despair. I thought the possibility of freedom was gone. I was kept in this way about one week, at the end of which, Captain Auld, my master, to my surprise and utter astonishment, came up, and took me out, with the intention of sending me, with a gentleman of his acquaintance, into Alabama. But, from some cause or other, he did not send me to Alabama, but concluded to send me back to Baltimore, to live again with his brother Hugh, and to learn a trade.

Thus, after an absence of three years and one month, I was once more permitted to return to my old home at Baltimore. My master sent me away, because there existed against me a very great prejudice in the community, and he feared I might be killed.

In a few weeks after I went to Baltimore, Master Hugh hired me to Mr. William Gardner, an extensive ship-builder, on Fell's Point. I was put there to learn how to calk. It, however, proved a very unfavorable place for the accomplishment of this object. Mr. Gardner was engaged that spring in building two large man-of-war brigs, professedly for the Mexican government. The vessels were to be launched in the July of that year, and in failure thereof, Mr. Gardner was to lose a considerable sum; so that when I entered, all was hurry. There was no time to learn any thing. Every man had to do that which he knew how to do. In entering the shipyard, my orders from Mr. Gardner were, to do whatever the carpenters commanded me to do. This was placing me at the beck and call of about seventy-five men. I was to regard all these as masters. Their word was to be my law. My situation was a most trying one. At times I needed a dozen pair of hands. I was called a dozen ways in the space of a single minute. Three or four voices would strike my ear at the same moment. It was—"Fred., come help me to cant this timber here."—"Fred., come carry this timber yonder."—"Fred., bring that roller here."—"Fred., go get a fresh can of water."—"Fred., come help saw off the end of this timber."—"Fred., go quick, and get the crowbar."—"Fred., hold on the end of this fall."—"Fred., go to the blacksmith's shop, and get a new punch."—"Hurra,[2] Fred.! run and bring me a cold chisel."—"I say, Fred., bear a hand, and get up a fire as quick as lightning under that steam-box."—"Halloo, nigger! come, turn this grindstone."—"Come, come! move, move! and *bowse*[3] this timber forward."—"I say, darky, blast your eyes, why don't you heat up some pitch?"—"Halloo! halloo! halloo!" (Three voices at the same time.) "Come here!—Go there!—Hold on where you are! Damn you, if you move, I'll knock your brains out!"

This was my school for eight months, and I might have remained there longer, but for a most horrid fight I had with four of the white apprentices, in which my left eye was nearly knocked out, and I was horribly mangled in other respects. The facts in the case were these: Until a very little while after I went there, white and black ship-carpenters worked side by side, and no one seemed to see any impropriety in it. All hands seemed to be very well satisfied. Many of the black carpenters were freemen. Things seemed to be going on very well. All at once, the white carpenters knocked off, and said they would not work

2. Hurry.

3. Lift or haul (usually with the help of block and tackle).

with free colored workmen. Their reason for this, as alleged, was, that if free colored carpenters were encouraged, they would soon take the trade into their own hands, and poor white men would be thrown out of employment. They therefore felt called upon at once to put a stop to it. And, taking advantage of Mr. Gardner's necessities, they broke off, swearing they would work no longer, unless he would discharge his black carpenters. Now, though this did not extend to me in form, it did reach me in fact. My fellow-apprentices very soon began to feel it degrading to them to work with me. They began to put on airs, and talk about the "niggers" taking the country, saying we all ought to be killed; and, being encouraged by the journeymen, they commenced making my condition as hard as they could, by hectoring me around, and sometimes striking me. I, of course, kept the vow I made after the fight with Mr. Covey, and struck back again, regardless of consequences; and while I kept them from combining, I succeeded very well; for I could whip the whole of them, taking them separately. They, however, at length combined, and came upon me, armed with sticks, stones, and heavy handspikes. One came in front with a half brick. There was one at each side of me, and one behind me. While I was attending to those in front, and on either side, the one behind ran up with the handspike, and struck me a heavy blow upon the head. It stunned me. I fell, and with this they all ran upon me, and fell to beating me with their fists. I let them lay on for a while, gathering strength. In an instant, I gave a sudden surge, and rose to my hands and knees. Just as I did that, one of their number gave me, with his heavy boot, a powerful kick in the left eye. My eyeball seemed to have burst. When they saw my eye closed, and badly swollen, they left me. With this I seized the handspike, and for a time pursued them. But here the carpenters interfered, and I thought I might as well give it up. It was impossible to stand my hand against so many. All this took place in sight of not less than fifty white ship-carpenters, and not one interposed a friendly word; but some cried, "Kill the damned nigger! Kill him! kill him! He struck a white person." I found my only chance for life was in flight. I succeeded in getting away without an additional blow, and barely so; for to strike a white man is death by Lynch law,—and that was the law in Mr. Gardner's ship-yard; nor is there much of any other out of Mr. Gardner's ship-yard.

I went directly home, and told the story of my wrongs to Master Hugh; and I am happy to say of him, irreligious as he was, his conduct was heavenly, compared with that of his brother Thomas under similar circumstances. He listened attentively to my narration of the circumstances leading to the savage outrage, and gave many proofs of his strong indignation of it. The heart of my once overkind mistress was again melted into pity. My puffed-out eye and blood-covered face moved her to tears. She took a chair by me, washed the blood from my face, and, with a mother's tenderness, bound up my head, covering the wounded eye with a lean piece of fresh beef. It was almost compensation for my suffering to witness, once more, a manifestation of kindness from this, my once affectionate old mistress. Master Hugh was very much enraged. He gave expression to his feelings by pouring out curses upon the heads of those who did the deed. As soon as I got a little the better of my bruises, he took me with him to Esquire Watson's, on Bond Street, to see what could be done about the matter. Mr. Watson inquired who saw the assault committed. Master Hugh told him it was done in Mr. Gardner's ship-yard, at midday, where there were a large company of men at work. "As to that," he said, "the deed was done, and there was no question as to who did it." His answer was, he could do nothing in the case, unless some white man would come forward and testify. He could issue no warrant on my word. If I had been killed in the presence of a thousand colored people, their testimony combined would have been insufficient to have arrested one of the murderers. Master Hugh, for once, was compelled to say this state of things was too bad. Of course, it was impossible to get any white man to volunteer his testimony in my behalf, and against the white young men. Even those who may have sympathized with me were not prepared to do this. It required a degree of courage unknown to them to do so; for just at that time, the slightest manifestation of humanity toward a colored person was denounced as abolitionism, and that name subjected its bearer to frightful liabilities. The watchwords of the bloody-minded in that region, and in those days, were, "Damn the abolitionists!" and "Damn the niggers!" There was nothing done, and probably nothing would have been done if I had been killed. Such was, and such remains, the state of things in the Christian city of Baltimore.

Master Hugh, finding he could get no redress, refused to let me go back again to Mr. Gardner. He kept me himself, and his wife dressed my wound till I was again restored to health. He then took me into the ship-yard of which he was foreman, in the employment of Mr. Walter Price. There I was immediately set to calking, and very soon learned the art of using my mallet and irons. In the course of one year from the time I left Mr. Gardner's, I was able to command the highest wages given to the most experienced calkers. I was now of some importance to my master. I was bringing him from six to seven dollars per week. I sometimes brought him nine dollars per week: my wages were a dollar and a half a day. After learning how to calk, I sought my own employment, made my own contracts, and collected the money which I earned. My pathway became much more smooth than before; my condition was now much more comfortable. When I could get no calking to do, I did nothing. During these leisure times, those old notions about freedom would steal over me again. When in Mr. Gardner's employment, I was kept in such a perpetual whirl of excitement, I could think of nothing, scarcely, but my life; and in thinking of my life, I almost forgot my liberty. I have observed this in my experience of slavery,—that whenever my condition was improved, instead of its increasing my contentment, it only increased my desire to be free, and set me to thinking of plans to gain my freedom. I have found that, to make a contented slave, it is necessary to make a thoughtless one. It is necessary to darken his moral and mental vision, and, as far as possible, to annihilate the power of reason. He must be made to feel that slavery is right; and he can be brought to that only when he ceases to be a man.

I was now getting, as I have said, one dollar and fifty cents per day. I contracted for it; I earned it; it was paid to me; it was rightfully my own; yet, upon each returning Saturday night, I was compelled to deliver every cent of that money to Master Hugh. And why? Not because he earned it,—not because he had any hand in earning it,—not because I owed it to him,—nor because he possessed the slightest shadow of a right to it; but solely because he had the power to compel me to give it up. The right of the grim-visaged pirate upon the high seas is exactly the same.

CHAPTER XI

I now come to that part of my life during which I planned, and finally succeeded in making, my escape from slavery. But before narrating any of the peculiar circumstances, I deem it proper to make known my intention not to state all the facts connected with the transaction. My reasons for pursuing this course may be understood from the following: First, were I to give a minute statement of all the facts, it is not only possible, but quite probable, that others would thereby be involved in the most embarrassing difficulties. Secondly, such a statement would most undoubtedly induce greater vigilance on the part of slaveholders than has existed heretofore among them; which would, of course, be the means of guarding a door whereby some dear brother bondman might escape his galling chains. I deeply regret the necessity that impels me to suppress any thing of importance connected with my experience in slavery. It would afford me great pleasure indeed, as well as materially add to the interest of my narrative, were I at liberty to gratify a curiosity, which I know exists in the minds of many, by an accurate statement of all the facts pertaining to my most fortunate escape. But I must deprive myself of this pleasure, and the curious of the gratification which such a statement would afford. I would allow myself to suffer under the greatest imputations which evil-minded men might suggest, rather than exculpate myself, and thereby run the hazard of closing the slightest avenue by which a brother slave might clear himself of the chains and fetters of slavery.

I have never approved of the very public manner in which some of our western friends have conducted what they call the *underground railroad*,[4] but which, I think, by their open declarations, has been made most emphatically the *upperground railroad*. I honor those good men and women for their noble daring, and applaud them for willingly subjecting themselves to bloody persecution, by openly avowing their participation in the escape of slaves. I, however, can see very little good resulting from such a course, either to themselves or the slaves escaping; while, upon the other hand, I see and feel assured that those open declarations are a positive evil to the slaves remaining, who are seeking to escape. They do nothing towards enlightening the slave, whilst they do much towards enlightening the master. They stimulate him to greater watchfulness, and enhance his power to capture his slave. We owe something to the slaves south of the line[5] as well as to those north of it; and in aiding the latter on their way to freedom, we should be careful to do nothing which would be likely to hinder the former from escaping from slavery. I would keep the merciless slaveholder profoundly ignorant of the means of flight adopted by the slave. I would leave him to imagine himself surrounded by myriads of invisible tormentors, ever ready to snatch from his infernal grasp his trembling prey. Let him be left to feel his way in the dark; let darkness commensurate with his crime hover over him; and let him feel that at every step he takes, in pursuit of the flying bondman, he is running the frightful risk of having his hot brains dashed out by an invisible agency. Let us render the tyrant no aid;

4. A system set up by opponents of slavery to help fugitive slaves from the South escape to free states and to Canada.

5. The Mason-Dixon line, the boundary between Pennsylvania and Maryland and between slave and free states.

let us not hold the light by which he can trace the footprints of our flying brother. But enough of this. I will now proceed to the statement of those facts, connected with my escape, for which I am alone responsible, and for which no one can be made to suffer but myself.

In the early part of the year 1838, I became quite restless. I could see no reason why I should, at the end of each week, pour the reward of my toil into the purse of my master. When I carried to him my weekly wages, he would, after counting the money, look me in the face with a robber-like fierceness, and ask, "Is this all?" He was satisfied with nothing less than the last cent. He would, however, when I made him six dollars, sometimes give me six cents, to encourage me. It had the opposite effect. I regarded it as a sort of admission of my right to the whole. The fact that he gave me any part of my wages was proof, to my mind, that he believed me entitled to the whole of them. I always felt worse for having received any thing; for I feared that the giving me a few cents would ease his conscience, and make him feel himself to be a pretty honorable sort of robber. My discontent grew upon me. I was ever on the look-out for means of escape; and, finding no direct means, I determined to try to hire my time, with a view of getting money with which to make my escape. In the spring of 1838, when Master Thomas came to Baltimore to purchase his spring goods, I got an opportunity, and applied to him to allow me to hire my time. He unhesitatingly refused my request, and told me this was another stratagem by which to escape. He told me I could go nowhere but that he could get me; and that, in the event of my running away, he should spare no pains in his efforts to catch me. He exhorted me to content myself, and be obedient. He told me, if I would be happy, I must lay out no plans for the future. He said, if I behaved myself properly, he would take care of me. Indeed, he advised me to complete thoughtlessness of the future, and taught me to depend solely upon him for happiness. He seemed to see fully the pressing necessity of setting aside my intellectual nature, in order to [insure] contentment in slavery. But in spite of him, and even in spite of myself, I continued to think, and to think about the injustice of my enslavement, and the means of escape.

About two months after this, I applied to Master Hugh for the privilege of hiring my time. He was not acquainted with the fact that I had applied to Master Thomas, and had been refused. He too, at first, seemed disposed to refuse; but, after some reflection, he granted me the privilege, and proposed the following terms: I was to be allowed all my time, make all contracts with those for whom I worked, and find my own employment; and, in return for this liberty, I was to pay him three dollars at the end of each week; find myself in calking tools, and in board and clothing. My board was two dollars and a half per week. This, with the wear and tear of clothing and calking tools, made my regular expenses about six dollars per week. This amount I was compelled to make up, or relinquish the privilege of hiring my time. Rain or shine, work or no work, at the end of each week the money must be forthcoming, or I must give up my privilege. This arrangement, it will be perceived, was decidedly in my master's favor. It relieved him of all need of looking after me. His money was sure. He received all the benefits of slave-holding without its evils; while I endured all the evils of a slave, and suffered all the care and anxiety of a freeman. I found it a hard bargain. But, hard as it was, I thought it better than the old mode of getting along. It was a step towards freedom to be allowed to bear the responsibilities of a freeman, and I was determined to hold on upon it. I bent myself to the work of making money. I was ready to work at night as well as day, and by the most untiring perseverance and industry, I made enough to meet my expenses, and lay up a little money every week. I went on thus from May till August. Master Hugh then refused to allow me to hire my time longer. The ground for his refusal was a failure on my part, one Saturday night, to pay him for my week's time. This failure was occasioned by my attending a camp meeting about ten miles from Baltimore. During the week, I had entered into an engagement with a number of young friends to start from Baltimore to the camp ground early Saturday evening; and being detained by my employer, I was unable to get down to Master Hugh's without disappointing the company. I knew that Master Hugh was in no special need of the money that night. I therefore decided to go to camp meeting, and upon my return pay him the three dollars. I staid at the camp meeting one day longer than I intended when I left. But as soon as I returned, I called upon him to pay him what he considered his due. I found him very angry; he could scarce restrain his wrath. He said he had a great mind to give me a severe whipping. He wished to know how I dared go out of the city without asking his permission. I told him I hired my time, and while I paid him the price which he asked for it, I did not know that I was bound to ask him when and where I should go. This reply troubled him, and, after reflecting a few moments, he turned to me, and said I should hire my time no longer; that the next thing he should know of, I would be running away. Upon the same plea, he told me to bring my tools and clothing home forthwith. I did so; but instead of seeking work, as I had been accustomed to do previously to hiring my time, I spent the whole week without the performance of a single stroke of work. I did this in retaliation. Saturday night, he called upon me as usual for my week's wages. I told him I had no wages; I had done no work that week. Here we were upon the point of coming to blows. He raved, and swore his determination to get hold of me. I did not allow myself a single word; but was resolved, if he laid the weight of his hand upon me, it should be blow for blow. He did not strike me, but told me that he would find me in constant employment in future. I thought the matter over during the next day, Sunday, and finally resolved upon the third day of September, as the day upon which I would make a second attempt to secure my freedom. I now had three weeks during which to prepare for my journey. Early on Monday morning, before Master Hugh had time to make any engagement for me, I went out and got employment of Mr. Butler, at his shipyard near the draw-bridge, upon what is called the City Block, thus making it unnecessary for him to seek employment for me. At the end of the week, I brought him between eight and nine dollars. He seemed very well pleased, and asked me why I did not do the same the week before. He little knew what my plans were. My object in working steadily was to remove any suspicion he might entertain of my intent to run away; and in this I succeeded admirably. I suppose he thought I was never better satisfied with my condition than at the very time during which I was planning my escape. The second week passed, and again I carried him my full wages; and so well pleased was he, that he gave me twenty-five cents, (quite a large sum for a slaveholder to give a slave,) and bade me to make a good use of it. I told him I would.

Things went on without very smoothly indeed, but within there was trouble. It is impossible for me to describe my feelings as the time of my contemplated start drew near. I had a number of warm-hearted friends in Baltimore,—friends that I loved almost as I did my life,—and the thought of being separated from them forever was painful beyond expression. It is my opinion that thousands would escape from slavery, who now remain, but for the strong cords of affection that bind them to their friends. The thought of leaving my friends was decidedly the most painful thought with which I had to contend. The love of them was my tender point, and shook my decision more than all things else. Besides the pain of separation, the dread and apprehension of a failure exceeded what I had experienced at my first attempt. The appalling defeat I then sustained returned to torment me. I felt assured that, if I failed in this attempt, my case would be a hopeless one—it would seal my fate as a slave forever. I could not hope to get off with any thing less than the severest punishment, and being placed beyond the means of escape. It required no very vivid imagination to depict the most frightful scenes through which I should have to pass, in case I failed. The wretchedness of slavery, and the blessedness of freedom, were perpetually before me. It was life and death with me. But I remained firm, and, according to my resolution, on the third day of September, 1838, I left my chains, and succeeded in reaching New York without the slightest interruption of any kind. How I did so,— what means I adopted,—what direction I travelled, and by what mode of conveyance,—I must leave unexplained, for the reasons before mentioned.

I have been frequently asked how I felt when I found myself in a free State. I have never been able to answer the question with any satisfaction to myself. It was a moment of the highest excitement I ever experienced. I suppose I felt as one may imagine the unarmed mariner to feel when he is rescued by a friendly man-of-war from the pursuit of a pirate. In writing to a dear friend, immediately after my arrival at New York, I said I felt like one who had escaped a den of hungry lions. This state of mind, however, very soon subsided; and I was again seized with a feeling of great insecurity and loneliness. I was yet liable to be taken back, and subjected to all the tortures of slavery. This in itself was enough to damp the ardor of my enthusiasm. But the loneliness overcame me. There I was in the midst of thousands, and yet a perfect stranger; without home and without friends, in the midst of thousands of my own brethren—children of a common Father, and yet I dared not to unfold to any one of them my sad condition. I was afraid to speak to any one for fear of speaking to the wrong one, and thereby falling into the hands of money-loving kidnappers, whose business it was to lie in wait for the panting fugitive, as the ferocious beasts of the forest lie in wait for their prey. The motto which I adopted when I started from slavery was this—"Trust no man!" I saw in every white man an enemy, and in almost every colored man cause for distrust. It was a most painful situation; and, to understand it, one must needs experience it, or imagine himself in similar circumstances. Let him be a fugitive slave in a strange land—a land given up to be the hunting-ground for slaveholders—whose inhabitants are legalized kidnappers—where he is every moment subjected to the terrible liability of being seized upon by his fellow-men, as the hideous crocodile seizes upon his prey!—I say, let him place himself in my situation—without home or friends—without money or credit—wanting shelter, and no one to give it—wanting bread, and no money to buy it,—and at the same time let him feel that he is pursued by merciless men-hunters, and in total darkness as to what to do, where to go, or where to stay,—perfectly helpless both as to the means of defence and means of escape,—in the midst of plenty, yet suffering the terrible gnawings of hunger,—in the midst of houses, yet having no home,—among fellow-men, yet feeling as if in the midst of wild beasts, whose greediness to swallow up the trembling and half-famished fugitive is only equalled by that with which the monsters of the deep swallow up the helpless fish upon which they subsist,—I say, let him be placed in this most trying situation,—the situation in which I was placed,—then, and not till then, will he fully appreciate the hardships of, and know how to sympathize with, the toil-worn and whip-scarred fugitive slave.

Thank Heaven, I remained but a short time in this distressed situation. I was relieved from it by the humane hand of Mr. David Ruggles,[6] whose vigilance, kindness, and perseverance, I shall never forget. I am glad of an opportunity to express, as far as words can, the love and gratitude I bear him. Mr. Ruggles is now afflicted with blindness, and is himself in need of the same kind offices which he was once so forward in the performance of toward others. I had been in New York but a few days, when Mr. Ruggles sought me out, and very kindly took me to his boarding-house at the corner of Church and Lespenard Streets. Mr. Ruggles was then very deeply engaged in the memorable *Darg* case, as well as attending to a number of other fugitive slaves, devising ways and means for their successful escape; and, though watched and hemmed in on almost every side, he seemed to be more than a match for his enemies. Very soon after I went to Mr. Ruggles, he wished to know of me where I wanted to go; as he deemed it unsafe for me to remain in New York. I told him I was a calker, and should like to go where I could get work. I thought of going to Canada; but he decided against it, and in favor of my going to New Bedford, thinking I should be able to get work there at my trade. At this time, Anna,[7] my intended wife, came on; for I wrote to her immediately after my arrival at New York, (notwithstanding my homeless, houseless, and helpless condition,) informing her of my successful flight, and wishing her to come on forthwith. In a few days after her arrival, Mr. Ruggles called in the Rev. J. W. C. Pennington, who, in the presence of Mr. Ruggles, Mrs. Michaels, and two or three others, performed the marriage ceremony, and gave us a certificate, of which the following is an exact copy:—

> "This may certify, that I joined together in holy matrimony Frederick Johnson[8] and Anna Murray, as man and wife, in the presence of Mr. David Ruggles and Mrs. Michaels.
>
> "James W. C. Pennington.
> "*New York, Sept.* 15, 1838."

Upon receiving this certificate, and a five-dollar bill from Mr. Ruggles, I shouldered one part of our baggage, and Anna took up the other, and we set out forthwith to take passage on board of the steamboat *John W. Richmond* for Newport, on our way to New Bedford. Mr. Ruggles gave me a letter to a Mr. Shaw in Newport, and told me, in case my money did not serve me to New

6. A black abolitionist (1810–1849), at this time living in New York, who helped many slaves to escape.

7. She was free [Douglass's note].

8. I had changed my name from Frederick *Bailey* to that of *Johnson* [Douglass's note].

Bedford, to stop in Newport and obtain further assistance; but upon our arrival at Newport, we were so anxious to get to a place of safety, that, notwithstanding we lacked the necessary money to pay our fare, we decided to take seats in the stage, and promise to pay when we got to New Bedford. We were encouraged to do this by two excellent gentlemen, residents of New Bedford, whose names I afterward ascertained to be Joseph Ricketson and William C. Taber. They seemed at once to understand our circumstances, and gave us such assurance of their friendliness as put us fully at ease in their presence. It was good indeed to meet with such friends, at such a time. Upon reaching New Bedford, we were directed to the house of Mr. Nathan Johnson, by whom we were kindly received, and hospitably provided for. Both Mr. and Mrs. Johnson took a deep and lively interest in our welfare. They proved themselves quite worthy of the name of abolitionists. When the stage-driver found us unable to pay our fare, he held on upon our baggage as security for the debt. I had but to mention the fact to Mr. Johnson, and he forthwith advanced the money.

We now began to feel a degree of safety, and to prepare ourselves for the duties and responsibilities of a life of freedom. On the morning after our arrival at New Bedford, while at the breakfast-table, the question arose as to what name I should be called by. The name given me by my mother was, "Frederick Augustus Washington Bailey." I, however, had dispensed with the two middle names long before I left Maryland so that I was generally known by the name of "Frederick Bailey." I started from Baltimore bearing the name of "Stanley." When I got to New York, I again changed my name to "Frederick Johnson," and thought that would be the last change. But when I got to New Bedford, I found it necessary again to change my name. The reason of this necessity was, that there were so many Johnsons in New Bedford, it was already quite difficult to distinguish between them. I gave Mr. Johnson the privilege of choosing me a name, but told him he must not take from me the name of "Frederick." I must hold on to that, to preserve a sense of my identity. Mr. Johnson had just been reading the "Lady of the Lake,"[9] and at once suggested that my name be "Douglass." From that time until now I have been called "Frederick Douglass"; and as I am more widely known by that name than by either of the others, I shall continue to use it as my own.

I was quite disappointed at the general appearance of things in New Bedford. The impression which I had received respecting the character and condition of the people of the north, I found to be singularly erroneous. I had very strangely supposed, while in slavery, that few of the comforts, and scarcely any of the luxuries, of life were enjoyed at the north, compared with what were enjoyed by the slaveholders of the south. I probably came to this conclusion from the fact that northern people owned no slaves. I supposed that they were about upon a level with the non-slaveholding population of the south. I knew *they* were exceedingly poor, and I had been accustomed to regard their poverty as the necessary consequence of their being non-slaveholders. I had somehow imbibed the opinion that, in the absence of slaves, there could be no wealth, and very little refinement. And upon coming to the north, I expected to meet with a rough, hard-handed, and uncultivated population, living in the most Spartan-like simplicity, knowing

9. A narrative poem by Sir Walter Scott (1810) about the fortunes of the Douglas clan in Scotland.

nothing of the ease, luxury, pomp, and grandeur of southern slaveholders. Such being my conjectures, any one acquainted with the appearance of New Bedford may very readily infer how palpably I must have seen my mistake.

In the afternoon of the day when I reached New Bedford, I visited the wharves, to take a view of the shipping. Here I found myself surrounded with the strongest proofs of wealth. Lying at the wharves, and riding in the stream, I saw many ships of the finest model, in the best order, and of the largest size. Upon the right and left, I was walled in by granite warehouses of the widest dimensions, stowed to their utmost capacity with the necessaries and comforts of life. Added to this, almost every body seemed to be at work, but noiselessly so, compared with what I had been accustomed to in Baltimore. There were no loud songs heard from those engaged in loading and unloading ships. I heard no deep oaths or horrid curses on the laborer. I saw no whipping of men; but all seemed to go smoothly on. Every man appeared to understand his work, and went at it with a sober, yet cheerful earnestness, which betokened the deep interest which he felt in what he was doing, as well as a sense of his own dignity as a man. To me this looked exceedingly strange. From the wharves I strolled around and over the town, gazing with wonder and admiration at the splendid churches, beautiful dwellings, and finely-cultivated gardens; evincing an amount of wealth, comfort, taste, and refinement, such as I had never seen in any part of slaveholding Maryland.

Every thing looked clean, new, and beautiful. I saw few or no dilapidated houses, with poverty-stricken inmates; no half-naked children and barefooted women, such as I had been accustomed to see in Hillsborough, Easton, St. Michael's, and Baltimore. The people looked more able, stronger, healthier, and happier, than those of Maryland. I was for once made glad by a view of extreme wealth, without being saddened by seeing extreme poverty. But the most astonishing as well as the most interesting thing to me was the condition of the colored people, a great many of whom, like myself, had escaped thither as a refuge from the hunters of men. I found many, who had not been seven years out of their chains, living in finer houses, and evidently enjoying more of the comforts of life, than the average of slave-holders in Maryland. I will venture to assert that my friend Mr. Nathan Johnson (of whom I can say with a grateful heart, "I was hungry, and he gave me meat; I was thirsty, and he gave me drink; I was a stranger, and he took me in")[1] lived in a neater house; dined at a better table; took, paid for, and read, more newspapers; better understood the moral, religious, and political character of the nation,—than nine tenths of the slave-holders in Talbot county Maryland. Yet Mr. Johnson was a working man. His hands were hardened by toil, and not his alone, but those also of Mrs. Johnson. I found the colored people much more spirited than I had supposed they would be. I found among them a determination to protect each other from the blood-thirsty kidnapper, at all hazards. Soon after my arrival, I was told of a circumstance which illustrated their spirit. A colored man and a fugitive slave were on unfriendly terms. The former was heard to threaten the latter with informing his master of his whereabouts. Straightway a meeting was called among the colored people, under the stereotyped notice, "Business of importance!" The

1. Matthew 25.35: "For I was an hungered, and ye gave me meat: I was thirsty, and ye gave me drink: I was a stranger, and ye took me in."

betrayer was invited to attend. The people came at the appointed hour, and organized the meeting by appointing a very religious old gentleman as president, who, I believe, made a prayer, after which he addressed the meeting as follows: "*Friends, we have got him here, and I would recommend that you young men just take him outside the door, and kill him!*" With this, a number of them bolted at him; but they were intercepted by some more timid than themselves, and the betrayer escaped their vengeance, and has not been seen in New Bedford since. I believe there have been no more such threats, and should there be hereafter, I doubt not that death would be the consequence.

I found employment, the third day after my arrival, in stowing a sloop with a load of oil. It was new, dirty, and hard work for me; but I went at it with a glad heart and a willing hand. I was now my own master. It was a happy moment, the rapture of which can be understood only by those who have been slaves. It was the first work, the reward of which was to be entirely my own. There was no Master Hugh standing ready, the moment I earned the money, to rob me of it. I worked that day with a pleasure I had never before experienced. I was at work for myself and newly-married wife. It was to me the starting-point of a new existence. When I got through with that job, I went in pursuit of a job of calking; but such was the strength of prejudice against color, among the white calkers, that they refused to work with me, and of course I could get no employment.[2] Finding my trade of no immediate benefit, I threw off my calking habiliments, and prepared myself to do any kind of work I could get to do. Mr. Johnson kindly let me have his woodhorse and saw, and I very soon found myself a plenty of work. There was no work too hard—none too dirty. I was ready to saw wood, shovel coal, carry the hod, sweep the chimney, or roll oil casks,—all of which I did for nearly three years in New Bedford, before I became known to the anti-slavery world.

In about four months after I went to New Bedford there came a young man to me, and inquired if I did not wish to take the "Liberator."[3] I told him I did; but, just having made my escape from slavery, I remarked that I was unable to pay for it then. I, however, finally became a subscriber to it. The paper came, and I read it from week to week with such feelings as it would be quite idle for me to attempt to describe. The paper became my meat and my drink. My soul was set all on fire. Its sympathy for my brethren in bonds—its scathing denunciations of slaveholders—its faithful exposures of slavery—and its powerful attacks upon the upholders of the institution—sent a thrill of joy through my soul, such as I had never felt before!

I had not long been a reader of the "Liberator," before I got a pretty correct idea of the principles, measures and spirit of the anti-slavery reform. I took right hold of the cause. I could do but little; but what I could, I did with a joyful heart, and never felt happier than when in an anti-slavery meeting. I seldom had much to say at the meetings, because what I wanted to say was said so much better by others. But, while attending an anti-slavery convention at Nantucket, on the 11th of August, 1841, I felt strongly moved to speak, and was at the same time much urged to do so by Mr. William C. Coffin, a gentle-

2. I am told that colored persons can now get employment at calking in New Bedford—a result of antislavery effort [Douglass's note].

3. William Lloyd Garrison's antislavery newspaper, which began publication in 1831.

man who had heard me speak in the colored people's meeting at New Bedford. It was a severe cross, and I took it up reluctantly. The truth was, I felt myself a slave, and the idea of speaking to white people weighed me down. I spoke but a few moments, when I felt a degree of freedom, and said what I desired with considerable ease. From that time until now, I have been engaged in pleading the cause of my brethren—with what success, and with what devotion, I leave those acquainted with my labors to decide.

APPENDIX

I find, since reading over the foregoing Narrative, that I have, in several instances, spoken in such a tone and manner, respecting religion, as may possibly lead those unacquainted with my religious views to suppose me an opponent of all religion. To remove the liability of such misapprehension, I deem it proper to append the following brief explanation. What I have said respecting and against religion, I mean strictly to apply to the *slaveholding religion* of this land, and with no possible reference to Christianity proper; for, between the Christianity of this land, and the Christianity of Christ, I recognize the widest possible difference—so wide, that to receive the one as good, pure, and holy, is of necessity to reject the other as bad, corrupt, and wicked. To be the friend of the one, is of necessity to be the enemy of the other. I love the pure, peaceable, and impartial Christianity of Christ: I therefore hate the corrupt, slaveholding, women-whipping, cradle-plundering, partial and hypocritical Christianity of this land. Indeed, I can see no reason, but the most deceitful one, for calling the religion of this land Christianity. I look upon it as the climax of all misnomers, the boldest of all frauds, and the grossest of all libels. Never was there a clearer case of "stealing the livery of the court of heaven to serve the devil in." I am filled with unutterable loathing when I contemplate the religious pomp and show, together with the horrible inconsistencies, which every where surround me. We have men-stealers for ministers, women-whippers for missionaries, and cradle-plunderers for church members. The man who wields the blood-clotted cowskin during the week fills the pulpit on Sunday, and claims to be a minister of the meek and lowly Jesus. The man who robs me of my earnings at the end of each week meets me as a class-leader on Sunday morning, to show me the way of life, and the path of salvation. He who sells my sister, for purposes of prostitution, stands forth as the pious advocate of purity. He who proclaims it a religious duty to read the Bible denies me the right of learning to read the name of the God who made me. He who is the religious advocate of marriage robs whole millions of its sacred influence, and leaves them to the ravages of wholesale pollution. The warm defender of the sacredness of the family relation is the same that scatters whole families,—sundering husbands and wives, parents and children, sisters and brothers,—leaving the hut vacant, and the hearth desolate. We see the thief preaching against theft, and the adulterer against adultery. We have men sold to build churches, women sold to support the gospel, and babes sold to purchase Bibles for the *poor heathen! all for the glory of God and the good of souls*! The slave auctioneer's bell and the church-going bell chime in with each other, and the bitter cries of the heart-broken slave are drowned in the religious shouts of his pious master. Revivals of religion and revivals in the slave-trade go hand in hand together. The slave prison and the church stand near each other. The clanking of fetters and the rattling of chains in the prison, and the pious psalm and solemn prayer in the church, may be heard at the same time. The dealers in the bodies and souls of men erect their stand in the presence of the pulpit, and they mutually help each other. The dealer gives his blood-stained gold to support the pulpit, and the pulpit, in return, covers his infernal business with the garb of Christianity. Here we have religion and robbery the allies of each other—devils dressed in angels' robes, and hell presenting the semblance of paradise.

"Just God! and these are they,
Who minister at thine altar, God of right!
Men who their hands, with prayer and blessing, lay
On Israel's ark of light.

"What! preach, and kidnap men?
Give thanks, and rob thy own afflicted poor?
Talk of thy glorious liberty, and then
Bolt hard the captive's door?

"What! servants of thy own
Merciful Son, who came to seek and save
The homeless and the outcast, fettering down
The tasked and plundered slave!

"Pilate and Herod friends!
Chief priests and rulers, as of old, combine!
Just God and holy! is that church which lends
Strength to the spoiler thine?"

The Christianity of America is a Christianity, of whose votaries it may be as truly said, as it was of the ancient scribes and Pharisees, "They bind heavy burdens, and grievous to be borne, and lay them on men's shoulders, but they themselves will not move them with one of their fingers. All their works they do for to be seen of men.—— They love the uppermost rooms at feasts, and the chief seats in the synagogues, ... and to be called of men, Rabbi, Rabbi.—— But woe unto you, scribes and Pharisees, hypocrites! for ye neither go in yourselves, neither suffer ye them that are entering to go in. Ye devour widows' houses, and for a pretence make long prayers; therefore ye shall receive the greater damnation. Ye compass sea and land to make one proselyte, and when he is made, ye make him twofold more the child of hell than yourselves.—— Woe unto you, scribes and Pharisees, hypocrites! for ye pay tithe of mint, and anise, and cumin, and have omitted the weightier matters of the law, judgment, mercy, and faith; these ought ye to have done, and not to leave the other undone. Ye blind guides! which strain at a gnat, and swallow a camel. Woe unto you, scribes and Pharisees, hypocrites! for ye make clean the outside of the cup and of the platter; but within, they are full of extortion and excess.——Woe unto you, scribes and Pharisees, hypocrites! for ye are like unto whited sepulchres, which indeed appear beautiful outward, but are within full of dead men's bones, and of all uncleanness. Even so ye also outwardly appear righteous unto men, but within ye are full of hypocrisy and iniquity."[4]

4. Matthew 23.

Dark and terrible as is this picture, I hold it to be strictly true of the overwhelming mass of professed Christians in America. They strain at a gnat, and swallow a camel. Could anything be more true of our churches? They would be shocked at the proposition of fellowshipping a *sheep*-stealer; and at the same time they hug to their communion a *man*-stealer, and brand me with being an infidel, if I find fault with them for it. They attend with Pharisaical strictness to the outward forms of religion, and at the same time neglect the weightier matters of the law, judgment, mercy, and faith. They are always ready to sacrifice, but seldom to show mercy. They are they who are represented as professing to love God whom they have not seen, whilst they hate their brother whom they have seen. They love the heathen on the other side of the globe. They can pray for him, pay money to have the Bible put into his hand, and missionaries to instruct him; while they despise and totally neglect the heathen at their own doors.

Such is, very briefly, my view of the religion of this land; and to avoid any misunderstanding, growing out of the use of general terms, I mean, by the religion of this land, that which is revealed in the words, deeds, and actions, of those bodies, north and south, calling themselves Christian churches, and yet in union with slaveholders. It is against religion, as presented by these bodies, that I have felt it my duty to testify.

I conclude these remarks by copying the following portrait of the religion of the south, (which is, by communion and fellowship, the religion of the north) which I soberly affirm is "true to the life," and without caricature or the slightest exaggeration. It is said to have been drawn, several years before the present anti-slavery agitation began, by a northern Methodist preacher, who, while residing at the south, had an opportunity to see slaveholding morals, manners, and piety, with his own eyes. "Shall I not visit for these things? saith the Lord. Shall not my soul be avenged on such a nation as this?"[5]

"A *Parody*.

"Come, saints and sinners, hear me tell
How pious priests whip Jack and Nell,
And women buy and children sell,
And preach all sinners down to hell,
  And sing of heavenly union.

"They'll bleat and baa, dona[6] like goats,
Gorge down black sheep, and strain at motes,
Array their backs in fine black coats,
Then seize their negroes by their throats,
  And choke, for heavenly union.

"They'll church you if you sip a dram,
And damn you if you steal a lamb;
Yet rob old Tony, Doll, and Sam,
Of human rights, and bread and ham;
  Kidnapper's heavenly union.

5. Jeremiah 5.9.

6. Believed to be a printer's error in the original edition for "go on" or "go n-a-a-ah."

"They'll loudly talk of Christ's reward,
And bind his image with a cord,
And scold, and swing the lash abhorred,
And sell their brother in the Lord
To handcuffed heavenly union.

"They'll read and sing a sacred song,
And make a prayer both loud and long,
And teach the right and do the wrong,
Hailing the brother, sister throng,
With words of heavenly union.

"We wonder how such saints can sing,
Or praise the Lord upon the wing,
Who roar, and scold, and whip, and sting,
And to their slaves and mammon cling,
In guilty conscience union.

"They'll raise tobacco, corn, and rye,
And drive, and thieve, and cheat, and lie,
And lay up treasures in the sky,
By making switch and cowskin fly,
In hope of heavenly union.

"They'll crack old Tony on the skull,
And preach and roar like Bashan bull,
Or braying ass, of mischief full,
Then seize old Jacob by the wool,
And pull for heavenly union.

"A roaring, ranting, sleek man-thief,
Who lived on mutton, veal, and beef,
Yet never would afford relief
To needy, sable sons of grief,
Was big with heavenly union.

"'Love not the world,' the preacher said,
And winked his eye, and shook his head;
He seized on Tom, and Dick, and Ned,
Cut short their meat, and clothes, and bread,
Yet still loved heavenly union.

"Another preacher whining spoke
Of One whose heart for sinners broke:
He tied old Nanny to an oak,
And drew the blood at every stroke,
And prayed for heavenly union.

"Two others oped their iron jaws,
And waved their children-stealing paws;
There sat their children in gewgaws;
By stinting negroes' backs and maws,
They kept up heavenly union.

"All good from Jack another takes,
And entertains their flirts and rakes,

Who dress as sleek as glossy snakes,
And cram their mouths with sweetened cakes;
And this goes down for union."

Sincerely and earnestly hoping that this little book may do something toward throwing light on the American slave system, and hastening the glad day of deliverance to the millions of my brethren in bonds—faithfully relying upon the power of truth, love, and justice, for success in my humble efforts—and solemnly pledging my self anew to the sacred cause,—I subscribe myself,

FREDERICK DOUGLASS.

Lynn, Mass., April 28, 1845.

HERMAN MELVILLE
1819–1891

"Bartleby, the Scrivener" takes place within a dark office on Wall Street, and its main character refuses to budge. This confined setting might seem unusual for a writer whose most famous works, including his most celebrated novel, *Moby-Dick*, are tales of adventure at sea. But "Bartleby" is typical of Melville's major work in that it revolves around questions of authority and rebellion, asking how and whether we may choose our own fates. Melville's memorable character Bartleby simply refuses to go along with the demands and expectations of others. "I would prefer not to," he repeats, politely but without compromise. And in his immovable way, he raises vexing social and philosophical questions: is it possible to opt out of the routines of modern life? Why should people continue to participate in the daily grind if it brings them neither satisfaction nor social mobility? And to what extent are we genuinely free to make our own choices?

LIFE

Two of the great literary giants of the United States in the nineteenth century—**Walt Whitman** and Herman Melville—were born in New York in 1819. Both believed in democracy and both opposed slavery. But Melville boasted an unusually patriotic pedigree: his paternal grandfather had participated in the Boston Tea Party, so attached to that revolutionary moment that he refused to change the style of his clothing even decades later, long after fashions had changed. His maternal grandfather, too, had been a hero in the American Revolutionary War. While Melville could claim a proud ancestry, however, his immediate family suffered shame and poverty after a series of poor business decisions. He and his father fled New York under cover of night when Herman was eleven years old to escape creditors, and they barely managed on loans from relatives until his father died in 1832. His own adulthood was hardly better financially: losing money even on his best-selling works, Melville would remain impoverished for most of his life.

In his teens, Melville worked unhappily as a copyist and errand boy in a bank, and then became a sailor, setting out for the South Pacific at the age of twenty. His first captain was harsh, and Melville jumped ship on an island reputed to be inhabited by cannibals. The local people treated Melville kindly, however, and he would remember them in his autobiographical novel *Typee* (1846) as sexually frank but also innocent, and morally good compared to the European missionaries then contributing to the disappearance of Polynesian cultural and spiritual traditions.

Back in the United States, Melville married Elizabeth Shaw, the daughter of a family friend, and they would go on to have four children. The marriage was not a happy one, and in the 1860s Elizabeth considered a legal separation, claiming that she was afraid of her husband. Their younger son Malcolm died in 1867 of a self-inflicted gunshot wound—almost certainly suicide—at the age of eighteen.

Melville's career as a writer went no more smoothly than his family life. *Typee* and its successor, *Omoo* (1847), both novels about the South Seas, proved popular with readers throughout the British Empire as well as the United States, but critics disliked the writer's defense of the "savages," his scenes of sexual pleasure, and his scathing portraits of Christian missionaries. Melville followed these early popular successes with a fantasy called *Mardi* (1849), which neither publishers nor readers liked much. And when he published *Moby-Dick* (1851)—which would later be seen by many readers as the best of all American novels—Melville lost the admiration of his contemporaries. A vast and bulky novel that folds into its story philosophy, science, and detailed myths and facts about whales and whaling, it seemed to reviewers to be muddled, eccentric, and rambling. Most critics then agreed that Melville's next novel, *Pierre* (1852), was nothing more than the ravings of a "lunatic." This book lost him substantial money, and set him on the path to near total obscurity. He was dispirited. "What I feel most moved to write, that is banned,—it will not pay. Yet, altogether, write the *other* way I cannot. So the product is a final hash, and all my books are botches." It was in 1853, while still smarting from the hostile reviews of *Moby-Dick* and badly in need of money, that Melville published an anonymous short story in *Putnam's Magazine* called "Bartleby the Scrivener." It garnered little notice until a century later.

Though he continued to write for the rest of his life, Melville was forced to take up work as a customs inspector to pay his bills. He faded from the public eye almost entirely. One day in 1885 the English writer Robert Buchanan went to look for him: "I sought everywhere for this Triton, who is still living somewhere in New York. No one seemed to know anything of the one great writer fit to stand shoulder to shoulder with Whitman on that continent." At the very end of his life, Melville wrote *Billy Budd*, considered another of his greatest works, but it was not published until thirty-three years later. When the writer died in his sleep in 1891, some obituary writers declared themselves surprised to discover that he had been so recently alive.

It was not until the 1920s that Melville's star would begin to rise. Writers in the United States and Europe who were experimenting with new and unsettling techniques for writing fiction understood Melville's peculiarities as signs of brilliant originality and exciting innovation. Seen today as one of the greatest of all American writers, Herman Melville has ultimately earned a profound respect denied to him in his own time.

TIMES

The full title of Melville's story is "Bartleby, the Scrivener: A Story of Wall-Street." Already in the mid-nineteenth century, New York's Wall Street had become the major financial center of the United States. It was associated with the accumulation of tremendous wealth, often symbolized by one of the richest men in the nation, John Jacob Astor. But New York's financial district was also associated with large-scale economic meltdowns—such as the "Panic of 1837," which prompted a major economic depression and helped to put Melville's own father deep into debt. Mysterious and powerful, Wall Street already seemed like the hub of a vast web of economic transactions. Fluctuations in the stock market could put coal miners out of work in Pennsylvania, depress interest rates in Europe, bankrupt Southern slaveholders, and create a need for Chinese immigrants to help build railroads in California.

While some made fortunes on Wall Street and others lost all they had, many ordinary laborers were dissatisfied with their working conditions. Wages dropped in the northeastern United States in the 1830s and '40s, in part because large numbers of immigrants fleeing famine-wracked Ireland and political unrest in Germany brought new competition for scarce jobs. The quality of work was changing, too. Disappearing was the life of the self-sufficient artisan who grew materials and sold handmade products to buyers at local markets; now, more and more often, workers made only parts of objects in factories, to be assembled elsewhere and sold to far-flung consumers. Labor activists objected fiercely to the replacement of workers by machines, and to the transformation of workers *into* machines, performing repetitive, mind-numbing tasks. Some warned that a whole class of people was becoming violent as workers grew increasingly alienated from their labor. Meanwhile, entrepreneurs in New York and Philadelphia set out to defeat the growing trade unions, and more generally they preached the value of the free market as a cornerstone of American freedom. In the 1840s numerous labor struggles broke out in New York, including strikes by bookbinders, upholsterers, shoemakers, tailors, and railroad workers. Walt Whitman wrote admiringly of their resistance: "in all of them burns, almost with a fierceness, the divine fire which more or less, during all ages, has only waited a chance to leap forth and confound the calculations of tyrants, hunkers, and all their tribe. At this moment, New York is the most radical city in America."

A different version of resistance was emerging in the same moment. The writer Henry David Thoreau, outraged that the US government was fighting to extend slavery into Mexico in the late 1840s, refused to pay his taxes and willingly went to prison to demonstrate his dissent. "I simply wish to refuse allegiance to the State, to withdraw and stand aloof from it effectually," wrote Thoreau in his essay "Civil Disobedience." The idea here was to resist unjust laws without violence, simply to refuse to cooperate and voluntarily to take the consequences as a form of peaceful protest. Thoreau would later have world-famous followers in Mohandas Gandhi and Martin Luther King Jr., but one of his first imitators may have been Melville's fictional Bartleby, who, by declining to make copies, ironically himself becomes a copy of Thoreau.

WORK

It could be said that Melville himself, like Bartleby, refused to make copies. That is, he would not write a predictable kind of literature that would sell but insisted on writing his own eccentric, highly original kind of work. Many readers have interpreted Bartleby, accordingly, as a figure for Melville the principled artist, punished for his unwillingness to go along with the crowd. But Bartleby can also be seen as an alienated member of the working class, a white-collar clerk only slightly higher on the social ladder than the angry factory workers agitating at the time, whose job of mechanically copying documents holds no possibility of fulfillment and whose comfortable employer lives off the proceeds of his labor. Or he can be read as the failure of freedom in modern society—the doomed struggle to assert a self in the face of economic and social pressures. Or even, as the narrator concludes, Bartleby cannot be interpreted at all: he is an unknowable cipher, one of the enigmas of a plural and puzzling "humanity."

And in fact, the narrator's response to Bartleby is as worthy of critical attention as Bartleby himself. In a story about a worker's refusal to obey, what can we make of the character who is both the boss and the storyteller? The prosperous lawyer who spins the narrative has a series of reactions to his employee's eccentric behavior, including first accommodating him, offering him friendship, then losing his temper, pleading, threatening, sympathizing, bribing, and eventually even fleeing altogether, as he feels compelled to abandon his own office to the unmoving Bartleby. Along the way, we hear far more about the narrator's thoughts than we do about Bartleby's: his unambitious life of ease, his anxiety about what other people think, his feelings about employees, and the prickings of his conscience. Most of all, we hear about his struggle to make some sense of Bartleby's resistance.

In his efforts to interpret the mysterious Bartleby, the narrator repeatedly runs into a wall, figuratively speaking, but the story is also filled with literal walls: the Wall Street of the title, the blank wall that can be seen from the office window, Bartleby's inclination to fall into "dead-wall reveries," and the high wall of the Tombs, New York's infamous prison. Filled with blockages and barriers, the story ends with the news that Bartleby has once worked for the Dead Letter Office—the resting place for undeliverable letters. Melville may have worried that his own writing was a kind of dead letter—doomed never to reach its destination, and thus to remain forever unread. Luckily for us, his work did not share the fate of its unfortunate character. And perhaps the story, in being read today, has finally reached the right address.

Bartleby, the Scrivener

A Story of Wall-Street

I am a rather elderly man. The nature of my avocations for the last thirty years has brought me into more than ordinary contact with what would seem an interesting and somewhat singular set of men, of whom as yet nothing that I know of has ever been written:—I mean the law-copyists or scriveners. I have known very many of them, professionally and privately, and if I pleased, could relate divers histories, at which good-natured gentlemen might smile, and sentimental souls might weep. But I waive the biographies of all other scriveners for a few passages in the life of Bartleby, who was a scrivener the strangest I ever saw or heard of. While of other law-copyists I might write the complete life, of Bartleby nothing of that sort can be done. I believe that no materials exist for a full and satisfactory biography of this man. It is an irreparable loss to literature. Bartleby was one of those beings of whom nothing is ascertainable, except from the original sources, and in his case those are very small. What my own astonished eyes saw of Bartleby, *that* is all I know of him, except, indeed, one vague report which will appear in the sequel.

Ere introducing the scrivener, as he first appeared to me, it is fit I make some mention of myself, my *employés*, my business, my chambers, and general surroundings; because some such description is indispensable to an adequate understanding of the chief character about to be presented.

Imprimis:[1] I am a man who, from his youth upwards, has been filled with a profound conviction that the easiest way of life is the best. Hence, though I belong to a profession proverbially energetic and nervous, even to turbulence, at times, yet nothing of that sort have I ever suffered to invade my peace. I am one of those unambitious lawyers who never addresses a jury, or in any way draws down public applause; but in the cool tranquillity of a snug retreat, do a snug business among rich men's bonds and mortgages and title-deeds. All who know me, consider me an eminently *safe* man. The late John Jacob Astor,[2] a personage little given to poetic enthusiasm, had no hesitation in pronouncing my first grand point to be prudence; my next, method. I do not speak it in vanity, but simply record the fact, that I was not unemployed in my profession by the late John Jacob Astor; a name which, I admit, I love to repeat, for it hath a rounded and orbicular sound to it, and rings like unto bullion. I will freely add, that I was not insensible to the late John Jacob Astor's good opinion.

Some time prior to the period at which this little history begins, my avocations had been largely increased. The good old office, now extinct in the State of New-York, of a Master in Chancery,[3] had been conferred upon me. It was not a very arduous office, but very pleasantly remunerative. I seldom lose my temper; much more seldom indulge in dangerous indignation at wrongs and outrages; but I must be permitted to be rash here and declare, that I consider the sudden and violent abrogation of the office of Master in Chancery, by the new Constitution, as a—premature act; inasmuch as I had counted upon a life-lease of the profits, whereas I only received those of a few short years. But this is by the way.

My chambers were up stairs at No. — Wall-street. At one end they looked upon the white wall of the interior of a spacious sky-light shaft, penetrating the building from top to bottom. This view might have been considered rather tame than otherwise, deficient in what landscape painters call "life." But if so, the view from the other end of my chambers offered, at least, a contrast, if nothing more. In that direction my windows commanded an unobstructed view of a lofty brick wall, black by age and everlasting shade; which wall required no spy-glass to bring out its lurking beauties, but for the benefit of all near-sighted spectators, was pushed up to within ten feet of my window panes. Owing to the great height of the surrounding buildings, and my chambers being on the

1. In the first place (Latin).
2. John Jacob Astor (1763–1848), successful businessman in the American fur trade and the country's first multimillionaire.
3. An anachronistic court position, associated with the British royalty, abolished in New York in 1848.

second floor, the interval between this wall and mine not a little resembled a huge square cistern.

At the period just preceding the advent of Bartleby, I had two persons as copyists in my employment, and a promising lad as an office-boy. First, Turkey; second, Nippers; third, Ginger Nut. These may seem names, the like of which are not usually found in the Directory.[4] In truth they were nicknames, mutually conferred upon each other by my three clerks, and were deemed expressive of their respective persons or characters. Turkey was a short, pursy Englishman of about my own age, that is, somewhere not far from sixty. In the morning, one might say, his face was of a fine florid hue, but after twelve o'clock, meridian—his dinner hour—it blazed like a grate full of Christmas coals; and continued blazing—but, as it were, with a gradual wane—till 6 o'clock, P.M. or thereabouts, after which I saw no more of the proprietor of the face, which gaining its meridian with the sun, seemed to set with it, to rise, culminate, and decline the following day, with the like regularity and undiminished glory. There are many singular coincidences I have known in the course of my life, not the least among which was the fact, that exactly when Turkey displayed his fullest beams from his red and radiant countenance, just then, too, at that critical moment, began the daily period when I considered his business capacities as seriously disturbed for the remainder of the twenty-four hours. Not that he was absolutely idle, or averse to business then; far from it. The difficulty was, he was apt to be altogether too energetic. There was a strange, inflamed, flurried, flighty recklessness of activity about him. He would be incautious in dipping his pen into his inkstand. All his blots upon my documents, were dropped there after twelve o'clock, meridian. Indeed, not only would he be reckless and sadly given to making blots in the afternoon, but some days he went further, and was rather noisy. At such times, too, his face flamed with augmented blazonry, as if cannel coal had been heaped on anthracite.[5] He made an unpleasant racket with his chair; spilled his sand-box;[6] in mending his pens, impatiently split them all to pieces, and threw them on the floor in a sudden passion; stood up and leaned over his table, boxing his papers about in a most indecorous manner, very sad to behold in an elderly man like him. Nevertheless, as he was in many ways a most valuable person to me, and all the time before twelve o'clock, meridian, was the quickest, steadiest creature too, accomplishing a great deal of work in a style not easy to be matched—for these reasons, I was willing to overlook his eccentricities, though indeed, occasionally, I remonstrated with him. I did this very gently, however, because, though the civilest, nay, the blandest and most reverential of men in the morning, yet in the afternoon he was disposed, upon provocation, to be slightly rash with his tongue, in fact, insolent. Now, valuing his morning services as I did, and resolved not to lose them; yet, at the same time made uncomfortable by his inflamed ways after twelve o'clock; and being a man of peace, unwilling by my admonitions to call forth unseemly retorts from him; I took upon me, one Saturday noon (he was always worse on Saturdays), to hint to him, very kindly, that perhaps now that he was growing old, it

4. List of the most established upper-class families in New York society.

5. Cannel coal burns quickly and brightly, whereas anthracite produces a dim, smokeless flame.

6. Sand was used to blot ink.

might be well to abridge his labors; in short, he need not come to my chambers after twelve o'clock, but, dinner over, had best go home to his lodgings and rest himself till tea-time. But no; he insisted upon his afternoon devotions. His countenance became intolerably fervid, as he oratorically assured me—gesticulating with a long ruler at the other end of the room—that if his services in the morning were useful, how indispensable, then, in the afternoon?

"With submission, sir," said Turkey on this occasion, "I consider myself your right-hand man. In the morning I but marshal and deploy my columns; but in the afternoon I put myself at their head, and gallantly charge the foe, thus!"—and he made a violent thrust with the ruler.

"But the blots, Turkey," intimated I.

"True,—but, with submission, sir, behold these hairs! I am getting old. Surely, sir, a blot or two of a warm afternoon is not to be severely urged against gray hairs. Old age—even if it blot the page—is honorable. With submission, sir, we *both* are getting old."

This appeal to my fellow-feeling was hardly to be resisted. At all events, I saw that go he would not. So I made up my mind to let him stay, resolving, nevertheless, to see to it, that during the afternoon he had to do with my less important papers.

Nippers, the second on my list, was a whiskered, sallow, and, upon the whole, rather piratical-looking young man of about five and twenty. I always deemed him the victim of two evil powers—ambition and indigestion. The ambition was evinced by a certain impatience of the duties of a mere copyist, an unwarrantable usurpation of strictly professional affairs, such as the original drawing up of legal documents. The indigestion seemed betokened in an occasional nervous testiness and grinning irritability, causing the teeth to audibly grind together over mistakes committed in copying; unnecessary maledictions, hissed, rather than spoken, in the heat of business; and especially by a continual discontent with the height of the table where he worked. Though of a very ingenious mechanical turn, Nippers could never get this table to suit him. He put chips under it, blocks of various sorts, bits of pasteboard, and at last went so far as to attempt an exquisite adjustment by final pieces of folded blotting-paper. But no invention would answer. If, for the sake of easing his back, he brought the table lid at a sharp angle well up towards his chin, and wrote there like a man using the steep roof of a Dutch house for his desk:—then he declared that it stopped the circulation in his arms. If now he lowered the table to his waistbands, and stooped over it in writing, then there was a sore aching in his back. In short, the truth of the matter was, Nippers knew not what he wanted. Or, if he wanted any thing, it was to be rid of a scrivener's table altogether. Among the manifestations of his diseased ambition was a fondness he had for receiving visits from certain ambiguous-looking fellows in seedy coats, whom he called his clients. Indeed I was aware that not only was he, at times, considerable of a ward-politician, but he occasionally did a little business at the Justices' courts, and was not unknown on the steps of the Tombs.[7] I have good reason to believe, however, that one individual who called upon him at my chambers, and who, with a grand air, he insisted was his client, was no other than a dun, and the alleged title-deed, a bill. But with all his

7. A New York prison and municipal court building complex.

failings, and the annoyances he caused me, Nippers, like his compatriot Turkey, was a very useful man to me; wrote a neat, swift hand; and, when he chose, was not deficient in a gentlemanly sort of deportment. Added to this, he always dressed in a gentlemanly sort of way; and so, incidentally, reflected credit upon my chambers. Whereas with respect to Turkey, I had much ado to keep him from being a reproach to me. His clothes were apt to look oily and smell of eating-houses. He wore his pantaloons very loose and baggy in summer. His coats were execrable; his hat not to be handled. But while the hat was a thing of indifference to me, inasmuch as his natural civility and deference, as a dependent Englishman, always led him to doff it the moment he entered the room, yet his coat was another matter. Concerning his coats, I reasoned with him; but with no effect. The truth was, I suppose, that a man with so small an income, could not afford to sport such a lustrous face and a lustrous coat at one and the same time. As Nippers once observed, Turkey's money went chiefly for red ink. One winter day I presented Turkey with a highly-respectable looking coat of my own, a padded gray coat, of a most comfortable warmth, and which buttoned straight up from the knee to the neck. I thought Turkey would appreciate the favor, and abate his rashness and obstreperousness of afternoons. But no. I verily believe that buttoning himself up in so downy and blanket-like a coat had a pernicious effect upon him; upon the same principle that too much oats are bad for horses. In fact, precisely as a rash, restive horse is said to feel his oats, so Turkey felt his coat. It made him insolent. He was a man whom prosperity harmed.

Though concerning the self-indulgent habits of Turkey I had my own private surmises, yet touching Nippers I was well persuaded that whatever might be his faults in other respects, he was, at least, a temperate young man. But indeed, nature herself seemed to have been his vintner, and at his birth charged him so thoroughly with an irritable, brandy-like disposition, that all subsequent potations were needless. When I consider how, amid the stillness of my chambers, Nippers would sometimes impatiently rise from his seat, and stooping over his table, spread his arms wide apart, seize the whole desk, and move it, and jerk it, with a grim, grinding motion on the floor, as if the table were a perverse voluntary agent, intent on thwarting and vexing him; I plainly perceive that for Nippers, brandy and water were altogether superfluous.

It was fortunate for me that, owing to its peculiar cause—indigestion—the irritability and consequent nervousness of Nippers, were mainly observable in the morning, while in the afternoon he was comparatively mild. So that Turkey's paroxysms only coming on about twelve o'clock, I never had to do with their eccentricities at one time. Their fits relieved each other like guards. When Nippers' was on, Turkey's was off; and *vice versa*. This was a good natural arrangement under the circumstances.

Ginger Nut, the third on my list, was a lad some twelve years old. His father was a carman,[8] ambitious of seeing his son on the bench instead of a cart, before he died. So he sent him to my office as student at law, errand boy, and cleaner and sweeper, at the rate of one dollar a week. He had a little desk to himself, but he did not use it much. Upon inspection, the drawer exhibited a great array of the shells of various sorts of nuts. Indeed, to this quick-witted

8. Railway car mechanic.

youth the whole noble science of the law was contained in a nut-shell. Not the least among the employments of Ginger Nut, as well as one which he discharged with the most alacrity, was his duty as cake and apple purveyor for Turkey and Nippers. Copying law papers being proverbially a dry, husky sort of business, my two scriveners were fain to moisten their mouths very often with Spitzenbergs[9] to be had at the numerous stalls nigh the Custom House and Post Office. Also, they sent Ginger Nut very frequently for that peculiar cake—small, flat, round, and very spicy—after which he had been named by them. Of a cold morning when business was but dull, Turkey would gobble up scores of these cakes, as if they were mere wafers—indeed they sell them at the rate of six or eight for a penny—the scrape of his pen blending with the crunching of the crisp particles in his mouth. Of all the fiery afternoon blunders and flurried rashnesses of Turkey, was his once moistening a ginger-cake between his lips, and clapping it on to a mortgage for a seal. I came within an ace of dismissing him then. But he mollified me by making an oriental bow, and saying—"With submission, sir, it was generous of me to find you in stationery on my own account."

Now my original business—that of a conveyancer and title hunter, and drawer-up of recondite documents of all sorts—was considerably increased by receiving the master's office. There was now great work for scriveners. Not only must I push the clerks already with me, but I must have additional help. In answer to my advertisement, a motionless young man one morning, stood upon my office threshold, the door being open, for it was summer. I can see that figure now—pallidly neat, pitiably respectable, incurably forlorn! It was Bartleby.

After a few words touching his qualifications, I engaged him, glad to have among my corps of copyists a man of so singularly sedate an aspect, which I thought might operate beneficially upon the flighty temper of Turkey, and the fiery one of Nippers.

I should have stated before that ground glass folding-doors divided my premises into two parts, one of which was occupied by my scriveners, the other by myself. According to my humor I threw open these doors, or closed them. I resolved to assign Bartleby a corner by the folding-doors, but on my side of them, so as to have this quiet man within easy call, in case any trifling thing was to be done. I placed his desk close up to a small side-window in that part of the room, a window which originally had afforded a lateral view of certain grimy back-yards and bricks, but which, owing to subsequent erections, commanded at present no view at all, though it gave some light. Within three feet of the panes was a wall, and the light came down from far above, between two lofty buildings, as from a very small opening in a dome. Still further to a satisfactory arrangement, I procured a high green folding screen, which might entirely isolate Bartleby from my sight, though not remove him from my voice. And thus, in a manner, privacy and society were conjoined.

At first Bartleby did an extraordinary quantity of writing. As if long famishing for something to copy, he seemed to gorge himself on my documents. There was no pause for digestion. He ran a day and night line, copying by sun-light and by candle-light. I should have been quite delighted with his application, had he been cheerfully industrious. But he wrote on silently, palely, mechanically.

9. Variety of apple.

It is, of course, an indispensable part of a scrivener's business to verify the accuracy of his copy, word by word. Where there are two or more scriveners in an office, they assist each other in this examination, one reading from the copy, the other holding the original. It is a very dull, wearisome, and lethargic affair. I can readily imagine that to some sanguine temperaments it would be altogether intolerable. For example, I cannot credit that the mettlesome poet Byron[1] would have contentedly sat down with Bartleby to examine a law document of, say five hundred pages, closely written in a crimpy hand.

Now and then, in the haste of business, it had been my habit to assist in comparing some brief document myself, calling Turkey or Nippers for this purpose. One object I had in placing Bartleby so handy to me behind the screen, was to avail myself of his services on such trivial occasions. It was on the third day, I think, of his being with me, and before any necessity had arisen for having his own writing examined, that, being much hurried to complete a small affair I had in hand, I abruptly called to Bartleby. In my haste and natural expectancy of instant compliance, I sat with my head bent over the original on my desk, and my right hand sideways, and somewhat nervously extended with the copy, so that immediately upon emerging from his retreat, Bartleby might snatch it and proceed to business without the least delay.

In this very attitude did I sit when I called to him, rapidly stating what it was I wanted him to do—namely, to examine a small paper with me. Imagine my surprise, nay, my consternation, when without moving from his privacy, Bartleby in a singularly mild, firm voice, replied, "I would prefer not to."

I sat awhile in perfect silence, rallying my stunned faculties. Immediately it occurred to me that my ears had deceived me, or Bartleby had entirely misunderstood my meaning. I repeated my request in the clearest tone I could assume. But in quite as clear a one came the previous reply, "I would prefer not to."

"Prefer not to," echoed I, rising in high excitement, and crossing the room with a stride. "What do you mean? Are you moon-struck? I want you to help me compare this sheet here—take it," and I thrust it towards him.

"I would prefer not to," said he.

I looked at him steadfastly. His face was leanly composed; his gray eye dimly calm. Not a wrinkle of agitation rippled him. Had there been the least uneasiness, anger, impatience or impertinence in his manner; in other words, had there been any thing ordinarily human about him, doubtless I should have violently dismissed him from the premises. But as it was, I should have as soon thought of turning my pale plaster-of-paris bust of Cicero[2] out of doors. I stood gazing at him awhile, as he went on with his own writing, and then reseated myself at my desk. This is very strange, thought I. What had one best do? But my business hurried me. I concluded to forget the matter for the present, reserving it for my future leisure. So calling Nippers from the other room, the paper was speedily examined.

A few days after this, Bartleby concluded four lengthy documents, being quadruplicates of a week's testimony taken before me in my High Court of

1. George Gordon, Lord Byron (1788–1824), aristocratic British poet noted for his rejection of social restrictions.

2. Marcus Tullius Cicero (106–43 B.C.E.), Roman philosopher, politician, and lawyer.

Chancery. It became necessary to examine them. It was an important suit, and great accuracy was imperative. Having all things arranged I called Turkey, Nippers and Ginger Nut from the next room, meaning to place the four copies in the hands of my four clerks, while I should read from the original. Accordingly Turkey, Nippers and Ginger Nut had taken their seats in a row, each with his document in hand, when I called to Bartleby to join this interesting group.

"Bartleby! quick, I am waiting."

I heard a slow scrape of his chair legs on the uncarpeted floor, and soon he appeared standing at the entrance of his hermitage.

"What is wanted?" said he mildly.

"The copies, the copies," said I hurriedly. "We are going to examine them. There"—and I held towards him the fourth quadruplicate.

"I would prefer not to," he said, and gently disappeared behind the screen.

For a few moments I was turned into a pillar of salt,[3] standing at the head of my seated column of clerks. Recovering myself, I advanced towards the screen, and demanded the reason for such extraordinary conduct.

"*Why* do you refuse?"

"I would prefer not to."

With any other man I should have flown outright into a dreadful passion, scorned all further words, and thrust him ignominiously from my presence. But there was something about Bartleby that not only strangely disarmed me, but in a wonderful manner touched and disconcerted me. I began to reason with him.

"These are your own copies we are about to examine. It is labor saving to you, because one examination will answer for your four papers. It is common usage. Every copyist is bound to help examine his copy. Is it not so? Will you not speak? Answer!"

"I prefer not to," he replied in a flute-like tone. It seemed to me that while I had been addressing him, he carefully revolved every statement that I made; fully comprehended the meaning; could not gainsay the irresistible conclusion; but, at the same time, some paramount consideration prevailed with him to reply as he did.

"You are decided, then, not to comply with my request—a request made according to common usage and common sense?"

He briefly gave me to understand that on that point my judgment was sound. Yes: his decision was irreversible.

It is not seldom the case that when a man is browbeaten in some unprecedented and violently unreasonable way, he begins to stagger in his own plainest faith. He begins, as it were, vaguely to surmise that, wonderful as it may be, all the justice and all the reason is on the other side. Accordingly, if any disinterested persons are present, he turns to them for some reinforcement for his own faltering mind.

"Turkey," said I, "what do you think of this? Am I not right?"

"With submission, sir," said Turkey, with his blandest tone, "I think that you are."

"Nippers," said I, "what do *you* think of it?"

3. In the Book of Genesis, Lot's wife disregards the angel's command not to look back while fleeing Sodom; as a punishment she is turned into a pillar of salt.

"I think I should kick him out of the office."

(The reader of nice perceptions will here perceive that, it being morning, Turkey's answer is couched in polite and tranquil terms, but Nippers replies in ill-tempered ones. Or, to repeat a previous sentence, Nippers's ugly mood was on duty, and Turkey's off.)

"Ginger Nut," said I, willing to enlist the smallest suffrage in my behalf, "what do *you* think of it?"

"I think, sir, he's a little *luny*," replied Ginger Nut, with a grin.

"You hear what they say," said I, turning towards the screen, "come forth and do your duty."

But he vouchsafed no reply. I pondered a moment in sore perplexity. But once more business hurried me. I determined again to postpone the consideration of this dilemma to my future leisure. With a little trouble we made out to examine the papers without Bartleby, though at every page or two, Turkey deferentially dropped his opinion that this proceeding was quite out of the common; while Nippers, twitching in his chair with a dyspeptic nervousness, ground out between his set teeth occasional hissing maledictions against the stubborn oaf behind the screen. And for his (Nippers's) part, this was the first and the last time he would do another man's business without pay.

Meanwhile Bartleby sat in his hermitage, oblivious to every thing but his own peculiar business there.

Some days passed, the scrivener being employed upon another lengthy work. His late remarkable conduct led me to regard his ways narrowly. I observed that he never went to dinner; indeed that he never went any where. As yet I had never of my personal knowledge known him to be outside of my office. He was a perpetual sentry in the corner. At about eleven o'clock though, in the morning, I noticed that Ginger Nut would advance toward the opening in Bartleby's screen, as if silently beckoned thither by a gesture invisible to me where I sat. The boy would then leave the office jingling a few pence, and reappear with a handful of ginger-nuts which he delivered in the hermitage, receiving two of the cakes for his trouble.

He lives, then, on ginger-nuts, thought I; never eats a dinner, properly speaking; he must be a vegetarian then; but no; he never eats even vegetables, he eats nothing but ginger-nuts. My mind then ran on in reveries concerning the probable effects upon the human constitution of living entirely on ginger-nuts. Ginger-nuts are so called because they contain ginger as one of their peculiar constituents, and the final flavoring one. Now what was ginger? A hot, spicy thing. Was Bartleby hot and spicy? Not at all. Ginger, then, had no effect upon Bartleby. Probably he preferred it should have none.

Nothing so aggravates an earnest person as a passive resistance. If the individual so resisted be of a not inhumane temper, and the resisting one perfectly harmless in his passivity; then, in the better moods of the former, he will endeavor charitably to construe to his imagination what proves impossible to be solved by his judgment. Even so, for the most part, I regarded Bartleby and his ways. Poor fellow! thought I, he means no mischief; it is plain he intends no insolence; his aspect sufficiently evinces that his eccentricities are involuntary. He is useful to me. I can get along with him. If I turn him away, the chances are he will fall in with some less indulgent employer, and then he will be rudely treated, and perhaps driven forth miserably to starve. Yes. Here I can cheaply purchase a delicious self-approval. To befriend Bartleby; to humor him in his strange wilfulness, will cost me little or nothing, while I lay up in my soul what will eventually prove a sweet morsel for my conscience. But this mood was not invariable with me. The passiveness of Bartleby sometimes irritated me. I felt strangely goaded on to encounter him in new opposition, to elicit some angry spark from him answerable to my own. But indeed I might as well have essayed to strike fire with my knuckles against a bit of Windsor soap. But one afternoon the evil impulse in me mastered me, and the following little scene ensued:

"Bartleby," said I, "when those papers are all copied, I will compare them with you."

"I would prefer not to."

"How? Surely you do not mean to persist in that mulish vagary?"

No answer.

I threw open the folding-doors near by, and turning upon Turkey and Nippers, exclaimed:

"Bartleby a second time says, he won't examine his papers. What do you think of it, Turkey?"

It was afternoon, be it remembered. Turkey sat glowing like a brass boiler, his bald head steaming, his hands reeling among his blotted papers.

"Think of it?" roared Turkey; "I think I'll just step behind his screen, and black his eyes for him!"

So saying, Turkey rose to his feet and threw his arms into a pugilistic position. He was hurrying away to make good his promise, when I detained him, alarmed at the effect of incautiously rousing Turkey's combativeness after dinner.

"Sit down, Turkey," said I, "and hear what Nippers has to say. What do you think of it, Nippers? Would I not be justified in immediately dismissing Bartleby?"

"Excuse me, that is for you to decide, sir. I think his conduct quite unusual, and indeed unjust, as regards Turkey and myself. But it may only be a passing whim."

"Ah," exclaimed I, "you have strangely changed your mind then—you speak very gently of him now."

"All beer," cried Turkey; "gentleness is effects of beer—Nippers and I dined together to-day. You see how gentle *I* am, sir. Shall I go and black his eyes?"

"You refer to Bartleby, I suppose. No, not to-day, Turkey," I replied; "pray, put up your fists."

I closed the doors, and again advanced towards Bartleby. I felt additional incentives tempting me to my fate. I burned to be rebelled against again. I remembered that Bartleby never left the office.

"Bartleby," said I, "Ginger Nut is away; just step round to the Post Office, won't you? (it was but a three minutes walk,) and see if there is any thing for me."

"I would prefer not to."

"You *will* not?"

"I *prefer* not."

I staggered to my desk, and sat there in a deep study. My blind inveteracy returned. Was there any other thing in which I could procure myself to be ignominiously repulsed by this lean, penniless wight?—my hired clerk? What added thing is there, perfectly reasonable, that he will be sure to refuse to do?

"Bartleby!"

No answer.

"Bartleby," in a louder tone.

No answer.

"Bartleby," I roared.

Like a very ghost, agreeably to the laws of magical invocation, at the third summons, he appeared at the entrance of his hermitage.

"Go to the next room, and tell Nippers to come to me."

"I prefer not to," he respectfully and slowly said, and mildly disappeared.

"Very good, Bartleby," said I, in a quiet sort of serenely severe self-possessed tone, intimating the unalterable purpose of some terrible retribution very close at hand. At the moment I half intended something of the kind. But upon the whole, as it was drawing towards my dinner-hour, I thought it best to put on my hat and walk home for the day, suffering much from perplexity and distress of mind.

Shall I acknowledge it? The conclusion of this whole business was, that it soon became a fixed fact of my chambers, that a pale young scrivener, by the name of Bartleby, had a desk there; that he copied for me at the usual rate of four cents a folio (one hundred words); but he was permanently exempt from examining the work done by him, that duty being transferred to Turkey and Nippers, out of compliment doubtless to their superior acuteness; moreover, said Bartleby was never on any account to be dispatched on the most trivial errand of any sort; and that even if entreated to take upon him such a matter, it was generally understood that he would prefer not to—in other words, that he would refuse point-blank.

As days passed on, I became considerably reconciled to Bartleby. His steadiness, his freedom from all dissipation, his incessant industry (except when he chose to throw himself into a standing revery behind his screen), his great stillness, his unalterableness of demeanor under all circumstances, made him a valuable acquisition. One prime thing was this,—*he was always there*;—first in the morning, continually through the day, and the last at night. I had a singular confidence in his honesty. I felt my most precious papers perfectly safe in his hands. Sometimes to be sure I could not, for the very soul of me, avoid falling into sudden spasmodic passions with him. For it was exceeding difficult to bear in mind all the time those strange peculiarities, privileges, and unheard of exemptions, forming the tacit stipulations on Bartleby's part under which he remained in my office. Now and then, in the eagerness of dispatching pressing business, I would inadvertently summon Bartleby, in a short, rapid tone, to put his finger, say, on the incipient tie of a bit of red tape with which I was about compressing some papers. Of course, from behind the screen the usual answer, "I prefer not to," was sure to come; and then, how could a human creature with the common infirmities of our nature, refrain from bitterly exclaiming upon such perverseness—such unreasonableness. However, every added repulse of this sort which I received only tended to lessen the probability of my repeating the inadvertence.

Here it must be said, that according to the custom of most legal gentlemen occupying chambers in densely-populated law buildings, there were several keys to my door. One was kept by a woman residing in the attic, which person weekly scrubbed and daily swept and dusted my apartments. Another was kept by Turkey for convenience sake. The third I sometimes carried in my own pocket. The fourth I knew not who had.

Now, one Sunday morning I happened to go to Trinity Church, to hear a celebrated preacher, and finding myself rather early on the ground, I thought I would walk round to my chambers for a while. Luckily I had my key with me; but upon applying it to the lock, I found it resisted by something inserted from the inside. Quite surprised, I called out; when to my consternation a key was turned from within; and thrusting his lean visage at me, and holding the door ajar, the apparition of Bartleby appeared, in his shirt sleeves, and otherwise in a strangely tattered dishabille, saying quietly that he was sorry, but he was deeply engaged just then, and—preferred not admitting me at present. In a brief word or two, he moreover added, that perhaps I had better walk round the block two or three times, and by that time he would probably have concluded his affairs.

Now, the utterly unsurmised appearance of Bartleby, tenanting my law-chambers of a Sunday morning, with his cadaverously gentlemanly *nonchalance*, yet withal firm and self-possessed, had such a strange effect upon me, that incontinently I slunk away from my own door, and did as desired. But not without sundry twinges of impotent rebellion against the mild effrontery of this unaccountable scrivener. Indeed, it was his wonderful mildness chiefly, which not only disarmed me, but unmanned me, as it were. For I consider that one, for the time, is a sort of unmanned when he tranquilly permits his hired clerk to dictate to him, and order him away from his own premises. Furthermore, I was full of uneasiness as to what Bartleby could possibly be doing in my office in his shirt sleeves, and in an otherwise dismantled condition of a Sunday morning. Was any thing amiss going on? Nay, that was out of the question. It was not to be thought of for a moment that Bartleby was an immoral person. But what could he be doing there?—copying? Nay again, whatever might be his eccentricities, Bartleby was an eminently decorous person. He would be the last man to sit down to his desk in any state approaching to nudity. Besides, it was Sunday; and there was something about Bartleby that forbade the supposition that he would by any secular occupation violate the proprieties of the day.

Nevertheless, my mind was not pacified; and full of a restless curiosity, at last I returned to the door. Without hindrance I inserted my key, opened it, and entered. Bartleby was not to be seen. I looked round anxiously, peeped behind his screen; but it was very plain that he was gone. Upon more closely examining the place, I surmised that for an indefinite period Bartleby must have ate, dressed, and slept in my office, and that too without plate, mirror, or bed. The cushioned seat of a ricketty old sofa in one corner bore the faint impress of a lean, reclining form. Rolled away under his desk, I found a blanket; under the empty grate, a blacking box and brush; on a chair, a tin basin, with soap and a ragged towel; in a newspaper a few crumbs of ginger-nuts and a morsel of cheese. Yes, thought I, it is evident enough that Bartleby has been making his home here, keeping bachelor's hall all by himself. Immediately then the thought came sweeping across me, What miserable friendlessness and loneliness are here revealed! His poverty is great; but his solitude, how horrible! Think of it.

Of a Sunday, Wall-street is deserted as Petra;[4] and every night of every day it is an emptiness. This building too, which of week-days hums with industry and life, at nightfall echoes with sheer vacancy, and all through Sunday is forlorn. And here Bartleby makes his home, sole spectator of a solitude which he has seen all populous—a sort of innocent and transformed Marius brooding among the ruins of Carthage![5]

For the first time in my life a feeling of overpowering stinging melancholy seized me. Before, I had never experienced aught but a not-unpleasing sadness. The bond of a common humanity now drew me irresistibly to gloom. A fraternal melancholy! For both I and Bartleby were sons of Adam. I remembered the bright silks and sparkling faces I had seen that day, in gala trim, swan-like sailing down the Mississippi of Broadway; and I contrasted them with the pallid copyist, and thought to myself, Ah, happiness courts the light, so we deem the world is gay; but misery hides aloof, so we deem that misery there is none. These sad fancyings—chimeras, doubtless, of a sick and silly brain—led on to other and more special thoughts, concerning the eccentricities of Bartleby. Presentiments of strange discoveries hovered round me. The scrivener's pale form appeared to me laid out, among uncaring strangers, in its shivering winding sheet.

Suddenly I was attracted by Bartleby's closed desk, the key in open sight left in the lock.

I mean no mischief, seek the gratification of no heartless curiosity, thought I; besides, the desk is mine, and its contents too, so I will make bold to look within. Every thing was methodically arranged, the papers smoothly placed. The pigeon holes were deep, and removing the files of documents, I groped into their recesses. Presently I felt something there, and dragged it out. It was an old bandanna handkerchief, heavy and knotted. I opened it, and saw it was a savings' bank.

I now recalled all the quiet mysteries which I had noted in the man. I remembered that he never spoke but to answer; that though at intervals he had considerable time to himself, yet I had never seen him reading—no, not even a newspaper; that for long periods he would stand looking out, at his pale window behind the screen, upon the dead brick wall; I was quite sure he never visited any refectory or eating house; while his pale face clearly indicated that he never drank beer like Turkey, or tea and coffee even, like other men; that he never went any where in particular that I could learn; never went out for a walk, unless indeed that was the case at present; that he had declined telling who he was, or whence he came, or whether he had any relatives in the world; that though so thin and pale, he never complained of ill health. And more than all, I remembered a certain unconscious air of pallid—how shall I call it?—of pallid haughtiness, say, or rather an austere reserve about him, which had positively awed me into my tame compliance with his eccentricities, when I had feared to ask him to do the slightest incidental thing for me, even though I might know, from his long-continued motionlessness, that behind his screen he must be standing in one of those dead-wall reveries of his.

4. Ancient city in what is now Jordan, rediscovered in 1812 after centuries of neglect.

5. Gaius Marius (155–86 B.C.E.), a Roman general who was exiled from Rome and denied sanctuary in the African city of Carthage.

Revolving all these things, and coupling them with the recently discovered fact that he made my office his constant abiding place and home, and not forgetful of his morbid moodiness; revolving all these things, a prudential feeling began to steal over me. My first emotions had been those of pure melancholy and sincerest pity; but just in proportion as the forlornness of Bartleby grew and grew to my imagination, did that same melancholy merge into fear, that pity into repulsion. So true it is, and so terrible too, that up to a certain point the thought or sight of misery enlists our best affections; but, in certain special cases, beyond that point it does not. They err who would assert that invariably this is owing to the inherent selfishness of the human heart. It rather proceeds from a certain hopelessness of remedying excessive and organic ill. To a sensitive being, pity is not seldom pain. And when at last it is perceived that such pity cannot lead to effectual succor, common sense bids the soul be rid of it. What I saw that morning persuaded me that the scrivener was the victim of innate and incurable disorder. I might give alms to his body; but his body did not pain him; it was his soul that suffered, and his soul I could not reach.

I did not accomplish the purpose of going to Trinity Church that morning. Somehow, the things I had seen disqualified me for the time from church-going. I walked homeward, thinking what I would do with Bartleby. Finally, I resolved upon this;—I would put certain calm questions to him the next morning, touching his history, &c., and if he declined to answer them openly and unreservedly (and I supposed he would prefer not), then to give him a twenty dollar bill over and above whatever I might owe him, and tell him his services were no longer required; but that if in any other way I could assist him, I would be happy to do so, especially if he desired to return to his native place, wherever that might be; I would willingly help to defray the expenses. Moreover, if, after reaching home, he found himself at any time in want of aid, a letter from him would be sure of a reply.

The next morning came.

"Bartleby," said I, gently calling to him behind his screen.

No reply.

"Bartleby," said I, in a still gentler tone, "come here; I am not going to ask you to do any thing you would prefer not to do—I simply wish to speak to you."

Upon this he noiselessly slid into view.

"Will you tell me, Bartleby, where you were born?"

"I would prefer not to."

"Will you tell me *any thing* about yourself?"

"I would prefer not to."

"But what reasonable objection can you have to speak to me? I feel friendly towards you."

He did not look at me while I spoke, but kept his glance fixed upon my bust of Cicero, which as I then sat, was directly behind me, some six inches above my head.

"What is your answer, Bartleby?" said I, after waiting a considerable time for a reply, during which his countenance remained immovable, only there was the faintest conceivable tremor of the white attenuated mouth.

"At present I prefer to give no answer," he said, and retired into his hermitage.

It was rather weak in me I confess, but his manner on this occasion nettled me. Not only did there seem to lurk in it a certain calm disdain, but his perverseness seemed ungrateful, considering the undeniable good usage and indulgence he had received from me.

Again I sat ruminating what I should do. Mortified as I was at his behavior, and resolved as I had been to dismiss him when I entered my office, nevertheless I strangely felt something superstitious knocking at my heart, and forbidding me to carry out my purpose, and denouncing me for a villain if I dared to breathe one bitter word against this forlornest of mankind. At last, familiarly drawing my chair behind his screen, I sat down and said: "Bartleby, never mind then about revealing your history; but let me entreat you, as a friend, to comply as far as may be with the usages of this office. Say now you will help to examine papers to-morrow or next day: in short, say now that in a day or two you will begin to be a little reasonable:—say so, Bartleby."

"At present I would prefer not to be a little reasonable," was his mildly cadaverous reply.

Just then the folding-doors opened, and Nippers approached. He seemed suffering from an unusually bad night's rest, induced by severer indigestion than common. He overheard those final words of Bartleby.

"*Prefer not*, eh?" gritted Nippers—"I'd *prefer* him, if I were you, sir," addressing me—"I'd *prefer* him; I'd give him preferences, the stubborn mule! What is it, sir, pray, that he *prefers* not to do now?"

Bartleby moved not a limb.

"Mr. Nippers," said I, "I'd prefer that you would withdraw for the present."

Somehow, of late I had got into the way of involuntarily using this word "prefer" upon all sorts of not exactly suitable occasions. And I trembled to think that my contact with the scrivener had already and seriously affected me in a mental way. And what further and deeper aberration might it not yet produce? This apprehension had not been without efficacy in determining me to summary measures.

As Nippers, looking very sour and sulky, was departing, Turkey blandly and deferentially approached.

"With submission, sir," said he, "yesterday I was thinking about Bartleby here, and I think that if he would but prefer to take a quart of good ale every day, it would do much towards mending him, and enabling him to assist in examining his papers."

"So you have got the word too," said I, slightly excited.

"With submission, what word, sir," asked Turkey, respectfully crowding himself into the contracted space behind the screen, and by so doing, making me jostle the scrivener. "What word, sir?"

"I would prefer to be left alone here," said Bartleby, as if offended at being mobbed in his privacy.

"*That's* the word, Turkey," said I—"*that's* it."

"Oh, *prefer*? oh yes—queer word. I never use it myself. But, sir, as I was saying, if he would but prefer—"

"Turkey," interrupted I, "you will please withdraw."

"Oh certainly, sir, if you prefer that I should."

As he opened the folding-doors to retire, Nippers at his desk caught a glimpse of me, and asked whether I would prefer to have a certain paper copied on blue paper or white. He did not in the least roguishly accent the word prefer. It was plain that it involuntarily rolled from his tongue. I thought to myself, surely I must get rid of a demented man, who already has in some degree turned the tongues, if not the heads of myself and clerks. But I thought it prudent not to break the dismission at once.

The next day I noticed that Bartleby did nothing but stand at his window in his dead-wall revery. Upon asking him why he did not write, he said that he had decided upon doing no more writing.

"Why, how now? what next?" exclaimed I, "do no more writing?"

"No more."

"And what is the reason?"

"Do you not see the reason for yourself," he indifferently replied.

I looked steadfastly at him, and perceived that his eyes looked dull and glazed. Instantly it occurred to me, that his unexampled diligence in copying by his dim window for the first few weeks of his stay with me might have temporarily impaired his vision.

I was touched. I said something in condolence with him. I hinted that of course he did wisely in abstaining from writing for a while; and urged him to embrace that opportunity of taking wholesome exercise in the open air. This, however, he did not do. A few days after this, my other clerks being absent, and being in a great hurry to dispatch certain letters by the mail, I thought that, having nothing else earthly to do, Bartleby would surely be less inflexible than usual, and carry these letters to the post-office. But he blankly declined. So, much to my inconvenience, I went myself.

Still added days went by. Whether Bartleby's eyes improved or not, I could not say. To all appearance, I thought they did. But when I asked him if they did, he vouchsafed no answer. At all events, he would do no copying. At last, in reply to my urgings, he informed me that he had permanently given up copying.

"What!" exclaimed I; "suppose your eyes should get entirely well—better than ever before—would you not copy then?"

"I have given up copying," he answered, and slid aside.

He remained as ever, a fixture in my chamber. Nay—if that were possible—he became still more of a fixture than before. What was to be done? He would do nothing in the office: why should he stay there? In plain fact, he had now become a millstone to me, not only useless as a necklace, but afflictive to bear. Yet I was sorry for him. I speak less than truth when I say that, on his own account, he occasioned me uneasiness. If he would but have named a single relative or friend, I would instantly have written, and urged their taking the poor fellow away to some convenient retreat. But he seemed alone, absolutely alone in the universe. A bit of wreck in the mid Atlantic. At length, necessities connected with my business tyrannized over all other considerations. Decently as I could, I told Bartleby that in six days' time he must unconditionally leave the office. I warned him to take measures, in the interval, for procuring some other abode. I offered to assist him in this endeavor, if he himself would but take the first step towards a removal. "And when you finally quit me, Bartleby," added I, "I shall see that you go not away entirely unprovided. Six days from this hour, remember."

At the expiration of that period, I peeped behind the screen, and lo! Bartleby was there.

I buttoned up my coat, balanced myself; advanced slowly towards him, touched his shoulder, and said, "The time has come; you must quit this place; I am sorry for you; here is money; but you must go."

"I would prefer not," he replied, with his back still towards me.

"You *must.*"

He remained silent.

Now I had an unbounded confidence in this man's common honesty. He had frequently restored to me sixpences and shillings carelessly dropped upon the floor, for I am apt to be very reckless in such shirt-button affairs. The proceeding then which followed will not be deemed extraordinary.

"Bartleby," said I, "I owe you twelve dollars on account; here are thirty-two; the odd twenty are yours.—Will you take it?" and I handed the bills towards him.

But he made no motion.

"I will leave them here then," putting them under a weight on the table. Then taking my hat and cane and going to the door I tranquilly turned and added—"After you have removed your things from these offices, Bartleby, you will of course lock the door—since every one is now gone for the day but you—and if you please, slip your key underneath the mat, so that I may have it in the morning. I shall not see you again; so good-bye to you. If hereafter in your new place of abode I can be of any service to you, do not fail to advise me by letter. Good-bye, Bartleby, and fare you well."

But he answered not a word; like the last column of some ruined temple, he remained standing mute and solitary in the middle of the otherwise deserted room.

As I walked home in a pensive mood, my vanity got the better of my pity. I could not but highly plume myself on my masterly management in getting rid of Bartleby. Masterly I call it, and such it must appear to any dispassionate thinker. The beauty of my procedure seemed to consist in its perfect quietness. There was no vulgar bullying, no bravado of any sort, no choleric hectoring, and striding to and fro across the apartment, jerking out vehement commands for Bartleby to bundle himself off with his beggarly traps. Nothing of the kind. Without loudly bidding Bartleby depart—as an inferior genius might have done—I *assumed* the ground that depart he must; and upon that assumption built all I had to say. The more I thought over my procedure, the more I was charmed with it. Nevertheless, next morning, upon awakening, I had my doubts,—I had somehow slept off the fumes of vanity. One of the coolest and wisest hours a man has, is just after he awakes in the morning. My procedure seemed as sagacious as ever,—but only in theory. How it would prove in practice—there was the rub. It was truly a beautiful thought to have assumed Bartleby's departure; but, after all, that assumption was simply my own, and none of Bartleby's. The great point was, not whether I had assumed that he would quit me, but whether he would prefer so to do. He was more a man of preferences than assumptions.

After breakfast, I walked down town, arguing the probabilities *pro* and *con.* One moment I thought it would prove a miserable failure, and Bartleby would be found all alive at my office as usual; the next moment it seemed certain that I should find his chair empty. And so I kept veering about. At the corner of Broadway and Canal-street, I saw quite an excited group of people standing in earnest conversation.

"I'll take odds he doesn't," said a voice as I passed.

"Doesn't go?—done!" said I, "put up your money."

I was instinctively putting my hand in my pocket to produce my own, when I remembered that this was an election day. The words I had overheard bore no reference to Bartleby, but to the success or non-success of some candidate for the mayoralty. In my intent frame of mind, I had, as it were, imagined that all Broadway shared in my excitement, and were debating the same question with me. I passed on, very thankful that the uproar of the street screened my momentary absent-mindedness.

As I had intended, I was earlier than usual at my office door. I stood listening for a moment. All was still. He must be gone. I tried the knob. The door was locked. Yes, my procedure had worked to a charm; he indeed must be vanished. Yet a certain melancholy mixed with this: I was almost sorry for my brilliant success. I was fumbling under the door mat for the key, which Bartleby was to have left there for me, when accidentally my knee knocked against a panel, producing a summoning sound, and in response a voice came to me from within—"Not yet; I am occupied."

It was Bartleby.

I was thunderstruck. For an instant I stood like the man who, pipe in mouth, was killed one cloudless afternoon long ago in Virginia, by summer lightning; at his own warm open window he was killed, and remained leaning out there upon the dreamy afternoon, till some one touched him, when he fell.

"Not gone!" I murmured at last. But again obeying that wondrous ascendancy which the inscrutable scrivener had over me, and from which ascendancy, for all my chafing, I could not completely escape, I slowly went down stairs and out into the street, and while walking round the block, considered what I should next do in this unheard-of perplexity. Turn the man out by an actual thrusting I could not; to drive him away by calling him hard names would not do; calling in the police was an unpleasant idea; and yet, permit him to enjoy his cadaverous triumph over me,—this too I could not think of. What was to be done? or, if nothing could be done, was there any thing further that I could *assume* in the matter? Yes, as before I had prospectively assumed that Bartleby would depart, so now I might retrospectively assume that departed he was. In the legitimate carrying out of this assumption, I might enter my office in a great hurry, and pretending not to see Bartleby at all, walk straight against him as if he were air. Such a proceeding would in a singular degree have the appearance of a home-thrust. It was hardly possible that Bartleby could withstand such an application of the doctrine of assumptions. But upon second thoughts the success of the plan seemed rather dubious. I resolved to argue the matter over with him again.

"Bartleby," said I, entering the office, with a quietly severe expression, "I am seriously displeased. I am pained, Bartleby. I had thought better of you. I had imagined you of such a gentlemanly organization, that in any delicate dilemma a slight hint would suffice—in short, an assumption. But it appears I am deceived. Why," I added, unaffectedly starting, "you have not even touched that money yet," pointing to it, just where I had left it the evening previous.

He answered nothing.

"Will you, or will you not, quit me?" I now demanded in a sudden passion, advancing close to him.

"I would prefer *not* to quit you," he replied, gently emphasizing the *not*.

"What earthly right have you to stay here? Do you pay any rent? Do you pay my taxes? Or is this property yours?"

He answered nothing.

"Are you ready to go on and write now? Are your eyes recovered? Could you copy a small paper for me this morning? or help examine a few lines? or step round to the post-office? In a word, will you do any thing at all, to give a coloring to your refusal to depart the premises?"

He silently retired into his hermitage.

I was now in such a state of nervous resentment that I thought it but prudent to check myself at present from further demonstrations. Bartleby and I were alone. I remembered the tragedy of the unfortunate Adams and the still more unfortunate Colt in the solitary office of the latter;[6] and how poor Colt, being dreadfully incensed by Adams, and imprudently permitting himself to get wildly excited, was at unawares hurried into his fatal act—an act which certainly no man could possibly deplore more than the actor himself. Often it had occurred to me in my ponderings upon the subject, that had that altercation taken place in the public street, or at a private residence, it would not have terminated as it did. It was the circumstance of being alone in a solitary office, up stairs, of a building entirely unhallowed by humanizing domestic associations—an uncarpeted office, doubtless, of a dusty, haggard sort of appearance;—this it must have been, which greatly helped to enhance the irritable desperation of the hapless Colt.

But when this old Adam of resentment rose in me and tempted me concerning Bartleby, I grappled him and threw him. How? Why, simply by recalling the divine injunction: "A new commandment give I unto you, that ye love one another."[7] Yes, this it was that saved me. Aside from higher considerations, charity often operates as a vastly wise and prudent principle—a great safeguard to its possessor. Men have committed murder for jealousy's sake, and anger's sake, and hatred's sake, and selfishness' sake, and spiritual pride's sake; but no man that ever I heard of, ever committed a diabolical murder for sweet charity's sake. Mere self-interest, then, if no better motive can be enlisted, should, especially with high-tempered men, prompt all beings to charity and philanthropy. At any rate, upon the occasion in question, I strove to drown my exasperated feelings towards the scrivener by benevolently construing his conduct. Poor fellow, poor fellow! thought I, he don't mean any thing; and besides, he has seen hard times, and ought to be indulged.

I endeavored also immediately to occupy myself, and at the same time to comfort my despondency. I tried to fancy that in the course of the morning, at such time as might prove agreeable to him, Bartleby, of his own free accord, would emerge from his hermitage, and take up some decided line of march in the direction of the door. But no. Half-past twelve o'clock came; Turkey began to glow in the face, overturn his inkstand, and become generally obstreperous;

6. In 1841 Samuel Adams, a New York printer, was murdered by John C. Colt, an accountant, after badgering Colt in his office about an outstanding loan; the distraught Colt committed suicide before he could be executed.

7. Jesus's command to his disciples before he is crucified (John 13.34).

Nippers abated down into quietude and courtesy; Ginger Nut munched his noon apple; and Bartleby remained standing at his window in one of his profoundest dead-wall reveries. Will it be credited? Ought I to acknowledge it? That afternoon I left the office without saying one further word to him.

Some days now passed, during which, at leisure intervals I looked a little into "Edwards on the Will," and "Priestley on Necessity."[8] Under the circumstances, those books induced a salutary feeling. Gradually I slid into the persuasion that these troubles of mine touching the scrivener, had been all predestinated from eternity, and Bartleby was billeted upon me for some mysterious purpose of an all-wise Providence, which it was not for a mere mortal like me to fathom. Yes, Bartleby, stay there behind your screen, thought I; I shall persecute you no more; you are harmless and noiseless as any of these old chairs; in short, I never feel so private as when I know you are here. At last I see it, I feel it; I penetrate to the predestinated purpose of my life. I am content. Others may have loftier parts to enact; but my mission in this world, Bartleby, is to furnish you with office-room for such period as you may see fit to remain.

I believe that this wise and blessed frame of mind would have continued with me, had it not been for the unsolicited and uncharitable remarks obtruded upon me by my professional friends who visited the rooms. But thus it often is, that the constant friction of illiberal minds wears out at last the best resolves of the more generous. Though to be sure, when I reflected upon it, it was not strange that people entering my office should be struck by the peculiar aspect of the unaccountable Bartleby, and so be tempted to throw out some sinister observations concerning him. Sometimes an attorney having business with me, and calling at my office, and finding no one but the scrivener there, would undertake to obtain some sort of precise information from him touching my whereabouts; but without heeding his idle talk, Bartleby would remain standing immovable in the middle of the room. So after contemplating him in that position for a time, the attorney would depart, no wiser than he came.

Also, when a Reference[9] was going on, and the room full of lawyers and witnesses and business was driving fast; some deeply occupied legal gentleman present, seeing Bartleby wholly unemployed, would request him to run round to his (the legal gentleman's) office and fetch some papers for him. Thereupon, Bartleby would tranquilly decline, and yet remain idle as before. Then the lawyer would give a great stare, and turn to me. And what could I say? At last I was made aware that all through the circle of my professional acquaintance, a whisper of wonder was running round, having reference to the strange creature I kept at my office. This worried me very much. And as the idea came upon me of his possibly turning out a long-lived man, and keep occupying my chambers, and denying my authority; and perplexing my visitors; and scandalizing my professional reputation; and casting a general gloom over the premises, keeping soul and body together to the last upon his savings (for doubtless he spent but half a dime a day), and in the end perhaps outlive me, and claim

8. Jonathan Edwards's *Freedom of the Will* (1754) claimed that God determines the kinds of choices that human beings will make; Joseph Priestley's *Doctrine of Philosophical Necessity Illustrated* (1777) argued that people cannot be blamed for wrongdoing because all human action ultimately fulfills the divine will.

9. Legal case referred to the Court of Chancery to be resolved.

possession of my office by right of his perpetual occupancy: as all these dark anticipations crowded upon me more and more, and my friends continually intruded their relentless remarks upon the apparition in my room; a great change was wrought in me. I resolved to gather all my faculties together, and for ever rid me of this intolerable incubus.

Ere revolving any complicated project, however, adapted to this end, I first simply suggested to Bartleby the propriety of his permanent departure. In a calm and serious tone, I commended the idea to his careful and mature consideration. But having taken three days to meditate upon it, he apprised me that his original determination remained the same; in short, that he still preferred to abide with me.

What shall I do? I now said to myself, buttoning up my coat to the last button. What shall I do? what ought I to do? what does conscience say I *should* do with this man, or rather ghost? Rid myself of him, I must; go, he shall. But how? You will not thrust him, the poor, pale, passive mortal,—you will not thrust such a helpless creature out of your door? you will not dishonor yourself by such cruelty? No, I will not, I cannot do that. Rather would I let him live and die here, and then mason up his remains in the wall. What then will you do? For all your coaxing, he will not budge. Bribes he leaves under your own paper-weight on your table; in short, it is quite plain that he prefers to cling to you.

Then something severe, something unusual must be done. What! surely you will not have him collared by a constable, and commit his innocent pallor to the common jail? And upon what ground could you procure such a thing to be done?—a vagrant, is he? What! he a vagrant, a wanderer, who refuses to budge? It is because he will *not* be a vagrant, then, that you seek to count him *as* a vagrant. That is too absurd. No visible means of support: there I have him. Wrong again: for indubitably he *does* support himself, and that is the only unanswerable proof that any man can show of his possessing the means so to do. No more then. Since he will not quit me, I must quit him. I will change my offices; I will move elsewhere; and give him fair notice, that if I find him on my new premises I will then proceed against him as a common trespasser.

Acting accordingly, next day I thus addressed him: "I find these chambers too far from the City Hall; the air is unwholesome. In a word, I propose to remove my offices next week, and shall no longer require your services. I tell you this now, in order that you may seek another place."

He made no reply, and nothing more was said.

On the appointed day I engaged carts and men, proceeded to my chambers, and having but little furniture, every thing was removed in a few hours. Throughout, the scrivener remained standing behind the screen, which I directed to be removed the last thing. It was withdrawn; and being folded up like a huge folio, left him the motionless occupant of a naked room. I stood in the entry watching him a moment, while something from within me upbraided me.

I re-entered, with my hand in my pocket—and—and my heart in my mouth.

"Good-bye, Bartleby; I am going—good-bye, and God some way bless you; and take that," slipping something in his hand. But it dropped upon the floor, and then,—strange to say—I tore myself from him whom I had so longed to be rid of.

Established in my new quarters, for a day or two I kept the door locked, and started at every footfall in the passage. When I returned to my rooms after any little absence, I would pause at the threshold for an instant, and attentively listen, ere applying my key. But these fears were needless. Bartleby never came nigh me.

I thought all was going well, when a perturbed looking stranger visited me, inquiring whether I was the person who had recently occupied rooms at No. — Wall-street.

Full of forebodings, I replied that I was.

"Then sir," said the stranger, who proved a lawyer, "you are responsible for the man you left there. He refuses to do any copying; he refuses to do any thing; he says he prefers not to; and he refuses to quit the premises."

"I am very sorry, sir," said I, with assumed tranquillity, but an inward tremor, "but, really, the man you allude to is nothing to me—he is no relation or apprentice of mine, that you should hold me responsible for him."

"In mercy's name, who is he?"

"I certainly cannot inform you. I know nothing about him. Formerly I employed him as a copyist; but he has done nothing for me now for some time past."

"I shall settle him then,—good morning, sir."

Several days passed, and I heard nothing more; and though I often felt a charitable prompting to call at the place and see poor Bartleby, yet a certain squeamishness of I know not what withheld me.

All is over with him, by this time, thought I at last, when through another week no further intelligence reached me. But coming to my room the day after, I found several persons waiting at my door in a high state of nervous excitement.

"That's the man—here he comes," cried the foremost one, whom I recognized as the lawyer who had previously called upon me alone.

"You must take him away, sir, at once," cried a portly person among them, advancing upon me, and whom I knew to be the landlord of No. — Wall-street. "These gentlemen, my tenants, cannot stand it any longer; Mr. B——" pointing to the lawyer, "has turned him out of his room, and he now persists in haunting the building generally, sitting upon the banisters of the stairs by day, and sleeping in the entry by night. Every body is concerned; clients are leaving the offices; some fears are entertained of a mob; something you must do, and that without delay."

Aghast at this torrent, I fell back before it, and would fain have locked myself in my new quarters. In vain I persisted that Bartleby was nothing to me—no more than to any one else. In vain:—I was the last person known to have any thing to do with him, and they held me to the terrible account. Fearful then of being exposed in the papers (as one person present obscurely threatened) I considered the matter, and at length said, that if the lawyer would give me a confidential interview with the scrivener, in his (the lawyer's) own room, I would that afternoon strive my best to rid them of the nuisance they complained of.

Going up stairs to my old haunt, there was Bartleby silently sitting upon the banister at the landing.

"What are you doing here, Bartleby?" said I.

"Sitting upon the banister," he mildly replied.

I motioned him into the lawyer's room, who then left us.

"Bartleby," said I, "are you aware that you are the cause of great tribulation to me, by persisting in occupying the entry after being dismissed from the office?"

No answer.

"Now one of two things must take place. Either you must do something, or something must be done to you. Now what sort of business would you like to engage in? Would you like to re-engage in copying for some one?"

"No; I would prefer not to make any change."

"Would you like a clerkship in a dry-goods store?"

"There is too much confinement about that. No, I would not like a clerkship; but I am not particular."

"Too much confinement," I cried, "why you keep yourself confined all the time!"

"I would prefer not to take a clerkship," he rejoined, as if to settle that little item at once.

"How would a bar-tender's business suit you? There is no trying of the eyesight in that."

"I would not like it at all; though, as I said before, I am not particular."

His unwonted wordiness inspirited me. I returned to the charge.

"Well then, would you like to travel through the country collecting bills for the merchants? That would improve your health."

"No, I would prefer to be doing something else."

"How then would going as a companion to Europe, to entertain some young gentleman with your conversation,—how would that suit you?"

"Not at all. It does not strike me that there is any thing definite about that. I like to be stationary. But I am not particular."

"Stationary you shall be then," I cried, now losing all patience, and for the first time in all my exasperating connection with him fairly flying into a passion. "If you do not go away from these premises before night, I shall feel bound—indeed I *am* bound—to—to—to quit the premises myself!" I rather absurdly concluded, knowing not with what possible threat to try to frighten his immobility into compliance. Despairing of all further efforts, I was precipitately leaving him, when a final thought occurred to me—one which had not been wholly unindulged before.

"Bartleby," said I, in the kindest tone I could assume under such exciting circumstances, "will you go home with me now—not to my office, but my dwelling—and remain there till we can conclude upon some convenient arrangement for you at our leisure? Come, let us start now, right away."

"No: at present I would prefer not to make any change at all."

I answered nothing; but effectually dodging every one by the suddenness and rapidity of my flight, rushed from the building, ran up Wall-street towards Broadway, and jumping into the first omnibus was soon removed from pursuit. As soon as tranquillity returned I distinctly perceived that I had now done all that I possibly could, both in respect to the demands of the landlord and his tenants, and with regard to my own desire and sense of duty, to benefit Bartleby, and shield him from rude persecution. I now strove to be entirely carefree and quiescent; and my conscience justified me in the attempt; though indeed it was not so successful as I could have wished. So fearful was I of being again hunted out by the incensed landlord and his exasperated tenants, that, surrendering my business to Nippers, for a few days I drove about the upper part of the town and through the suburbs, in my rockaway;[1] crossed over to Jersey City and Hoboken, and paid fugitive visits to Manhattanville and Astoria. In fact I almost lived in my rockaway for the time.

When again I entered my office, lo, a note from the landlord lay upon the desk. I opened it with trembling hands. It informed me that the writer had sent to the police, and had Bartleby removed to the Tombs as a vagrant. Moreover, since I knew more about him than any one else, he wished me to appear at that place, and make a suitable statement of the facts. These tidings had a conflicting effect upon me. At first I was indignant; but at last almost approved. The landlord's energetic, summary disposition, had led him to adopt a procedure which I do not think I would have decided upon myself; and yet as a last resort, under such peculiar circumstances, it seemed the only plan.

As I afterwards learned, the poor scrivener, when told that he must be conducted to the Tombs, offered not the slightest obstacle, but in his pale unmoving way, silently acquiesced.

Some of the compassionate and curious bystanders joined the party; and headed by one of the constables arm in arm with Bartleby, the silent procession filed its way through all the noise, and heat, and joy of the roaring thoroughfares at noon.

The same day I received the note I went to the Tombs, or to speak more properly, the Halls of Justice. Seeking the right officer, I stated the purpose of my call, and was informed that the individual I described was indeed within. I then assured the functionary that Bartleby was a perfectly honest man, and greatly to be compassionated, however unaccountably eccentric. I narrated all I knew, and closed by suggesting the idea of letting him remain in as indulgent confinement as possible till something less harsh might be done—though indeed I hardly knew what. At all events, if nothing else could be decided upon, the alms-house must receive him. I then begged to have an interview.

Being under no disgraceful charge, and quite serene and harmless in all his ways, they had permitted him freely to wander about the prison, and especially in the inclosed grass-platted yards thereof. And so I found him there, standing all alone in the quietest of the yards, his face towards a high wall, while all around, from the narrow slits of the jail windows, I thought I saw peering out upon him the eyes of murderers and thieves.

"Bartleby!"

"I know you," he said, without looking round,—"and I want nothing to say to you."

"It was not I that brought you here, Bartleby," said I, keenly pained at his implied suspicion. "And to you, this should not be so vile a place. Nothing reproachful attaches to you by being here. And see, it is not so sad a place as one might think. Look, there is the sky, and here is the grass."

"I know where I am," he replied, but would say nothing more, and so I left him.

As I entered the corridor again, a broad meat-like man, in an apron, accosted me, and jerking his thumb over his shoulder said—"Is that your friend?"

"Yes."

1. A type of four-wheeled carriage.

"Does he want to starve? If he does, let him live on the prison fare, that's all."

"Who are you?" asked I, not knowing what to make of such an unofficially speaking person in such a place.

"I am the grub-man. Such gentlemen as have friends here, hire me to provide them with something good to eat."

"Is this so?" said I, turning to the turnkey.

He said it was.

"Well then," said I, slipping some silver into the grub-man's hands (for so they called him). "I want you to give particular attention to my friend there; let him have the best dinner you can get. And you must be as polite to him as possible."

"Introduce me, will you?" said the grub-man, looking at me with an expression which seemed to say he was all impatience for an opportunity to give a specimen of his breeding.

Thinking it would prove of benefit to the scrivener, I acquiesced; and asking the grub-man his name, went up with him to Bartleby.

"Bartleby, this is Mr. Cutlets; you will find him very useful to you."

"Your sarvant, sir, your sarvant," said the grub-man, making a low salutation behind his apron. "Hope you find it pleasant here, sir; nice grounds—cool apartments, sir—hope you'll stay with us some time—try to make it agreeable. May Mrs. Cutlets and I have the pleasure of your company to dinner, sir, in Mrs. Cutlets' private room?"

"I prefer not to dine to-day," said Bartleby, turning away. "It would disagree with me; I am unused to dinners." So saying he slowly moved to the other side of the inclosure, and took up a position fronting the dead-wall.

"How's this?" said the grub-man, addressing me with a stare of astonishment. "He's odd, aint he?"

"I think he is a little deranged," said I, sadly.

"Deranged? deranged is it? Well now, upon my word, I thought that friend of yourn was a gentleman forger; they are always pale and genteel-like, them forgers. I can't help pity 'em—can't help it, sir. Did you know Monroe Edwards?"[2] he added touchingly, and paused. Then, laying his hand pityingly on my shoulder, sighed, "he died of consumption at Sing-Sing.[3] So you weren't acquainted with Monroe?"

"No, I was never socially acquainted with any forgers. But I cannot stop longer. Look to my friend yonder. You will not lose by it. I will see you again."

Some few days after this, I again obtained admission to the Tombs, and went through the corridors in quest of Bartleby; but without finding him.

"I saw him coming from his cell not long ago," said a turnkey, "may be he's gone to loiter in the yards."

So I went in that direction.

"Are you looking for the silent man?" said another turnkey passing me. "Yonder he lies—sleeping in the yard there. 'Tis not twenty minutes since I saw him lie down."

2. Monroe Edwards (ca. 1808–1847), the "Great Forger" who posed as a wealthy southern plantation owner.

3. Prison on the Hudson River in New York State.

The yard was entirely quiet. It was not accessible to the common prisoners. The surrounding walls, of amazing thickness, kept off all sounds behind them. The Egyptian character of the masonry weighed upon me with its gloom. But a soft imprisoned turf grew under foot. The heart of the eternal pyramids, it seemed, wherein, by some strange magic, through the clefts, grass-seed, dropped by birds, had sprung.

Strangely huddled at the base of the wall, his knees drawn up, and lying on his side, his head touching the cold stones, I saw the wasted Bartleby. But nothing stirred. I paused; then went close up to him; stooped over, and saw that his dim eyes were open; otherwise he seemed profoundly sleeping. Something prompted me to touch him. I felt his hand, when a tingling shiver ran up my arm and down my spine to my feet.

The round face of the grub-man peered upon me now. "His dinner is ready. Won't he dine to-day, either? Or does he live without dining?"

"Lives without dining," said I, and closed the eyes.

"Eh!—He's asleep, aint he?"

"With kings and counsellors,"[4] murmured I.

• • • • • • •

There would seem little need for proceeding further in this history. Imagination will readily supply the meagre recital of poor Bartleby's interment. But ere parting with the reader, let me say, that if this little narrative has sufficiently interested him, to awaken curiosity as to who Bartleby was, and what manner of life he led prior to the present narrator's making his acquaintance, I can only reply, that in such curiosity I fully share, but am wholly unable to gratify it. Yet here I hardly know whether I should divulge one little item of rumor, which came to my ear a few months after the scrivener's decease. Upon what basis it rested, I could never ascertain; and hence, how true it is I cannot now tell. But inasmuch as this vague report has not been without a certain strange suggestive interest to me, however sad, it may prove the same with some others; and so I will briefly mention it. The report was this: that Bartleby had been a subordinate clerk in the Dead Letter Office[5] at Washington, from which he had been suddenly removed by a change in the administration. When I think over this rumor, hardly can I express the emotions which seize me. Dead letters! does it not sound like dead men? Conceive a man by nature and misfortune prone to a pallid hopelessness, can any business seem more fitted to heighten it than that of continually handling these dead letters, and assorting them for the flames? For by the cart-load they are annually burned. Sometimes from out the folded paper the pale clerk takes a ring:—the finger it was meant for, perhaps, moulders in the grave; a bank-note sent in swiftest charity:—he whom it would relieve, nor eats nor hungers any more; pardon for those who died despairing; hope for those who died unhoping; good tidings for those who died stifled by unrelieved calamities. On errands of life, these letters speed to death.

Ah Bartleby! Ah humanity!

4. After many misfortunes, the biblical Job longs for eternal rest "with kings and counselors" (Job 3.14).

5. The US Postal Service's depository for undeliverable mail.

CHRISTINA RO
del. SEPT

ROMANTIC POETS AND THEIR SUCCESSORS

The twentieth century is often considered the era of radical experimentation in poetry, but in fact throughout the nineteenth century poets in Europe and the Americas were inventing startling new poetic forms and resisting traditional expectations. It all began with the period we now know as Romanticism, a movement across the arts—literature, visual art, and music—that lasted roughly from the 1780s to the 1830s in Europe and the Americas. *Romanticism* often feels like a frustratingly loose term, encompassing so many styles and practices that it ceases to mean anything at all. It is associated with nature, and especially wild and untamed natural settings. It is often defined as a rejection of neoclassical styles—the revival of Greek and Roman traditions that had grown dominant in the eighteenth century—as well as a rejection of reason as the organizing principle for art and society. Romanticism tended to valorize the ordinary individual, the solitary soul, the visionary, even the outcast. The term evokes imagination, excess, spontaneity, freedom, and revolution. Romantic art often dwells in wild, ghostly, and exotic settings, and embraces a turn inward to the emotions, dreams, and fantasies. Romanticism is also associated with nationalism and folk traditions. Its dominant literary form is the lyric poem, though there were Romantic novels, dramas, plays, and autobiographies.

Portrait of Christina Rossetti by her brother Dante Gabriel Rossetti (1866).

One way to grasp Romanticism as a concept is to investigate the crucial role that nature plays in the period. Before the 1780s in Europe, there was very little art that depicted natural scenes apart from the highly artful tradition of pastoral—which tended to portray flute-playing, classical-style shepherds in distinctly sheepless environments. Romantic artists were really the first group in the West to take nature as an important subject matter in and of itself: turning away from the manners and artifices of social life, writers and artists celebrated the beauties of vast skies and towering mountains, a world free from court intrigues and urban poverty. But why did this new focus on nature emerge at this particular moment? Two different historical explanations help to make sense of the shift. First, as the industrial revolution forced huge masses of people out of agricultural life and into crowded cities, nature became exotic—and therefore interesting and valuable—in a whole new way. That is, when the majority of people lived in the countryside, it had seemed ordinary, mundane. But as more and more people began to lead urban lives, while railways cut ugly gashes through the fields and black smoke billowed into the sky, nature's beauty began to seem rare and precious—and increasingly under threat. From this perspective, the sudden upsurge in artistic treatments of nature makes sense as a way to capture and honor an increasingly vulnerable natural environment.

There is also a second explanation for the new embrace of nature. In the eighteenth century, both absolute monarchies and new kinds of human knowledge—including science and statistics—valued control over nature. The gardens built by King Louis XIV of France at his grand palace of Versailles followed a rigid geometrical design, marking the power to subdue and order the natural world in accordance with the demands of human reason. Resisting old regimes of power, some radical late-eighteenth-century thinkers rejected this entwining of order and authority, and saw a return to the wildness of nature as a new model of expressive freedom, liberated from the constraints of reason and authority. Nature could be not only a source of beauty and inspiration, but a very foundation for a new kind of society that would replace the rule of absolute monarchs and rigid regulations. This new society would be based on the fulfillment of what was natural within human beings. Thus thinkers started to explore and celebrate nature as a kind of foundation for human experience, putting forward "natural laws" as the basis for social organizations, and crafting new state constitutions based on them. Here we see the emergence of new ideas about human rights—the notion that certain freedoms are given by nature alone and cannot justly be taken away by any government. Also emergent was a notion of a human community based not on kings or laws but on natural ties that united a group—an organic set of folk traditions that bound a people together indissolubly. Called "romantic nationalists," these thinkers celebrated local folklore, language, and customs—and often ethnic and racial differences—as the basis for national identity.

This revolutionary set of political ideals went hand in hand with a thoroughgoing revolution in poetry. Throwing off classical models, poets now looked to children and to "primitive" peoples who seemed closer to nature as models for social experience. They sought out new poetic forms that would capture natural rhythms and patterns of human speech. They turned to traditional folk and fairy tales for inspiration, and wrote in local dialects that had seemed low and coarse in the era of neoclassicism. And they valued not rigid conventions but what seemed most natural in the self: impulsiveness, excess, imaginative freedom. **William Wordsworth** cast the best new poetry as "the spontaneous overflow of powerful feelings," and **John Keats** wrote that "if poetry comes not as naturally as the leaves to a tree it had better not come at all." Instead of insisting on reason, art, and order as their sources of inspiration, poets looked to the unconscious mind, to spiritual awakening, and to dreams. They also valued ruins and relics of past times and exotic settings—anything that would jolt readers out of their entrenched sense of order and habit. Some of these Romantic themes contradicted each other—exotic settings and local traditions, individualism and racial foundations for communities—but they coexisted as a constellation of reactions against the dominant eighteenth-century values of order, reason, and authority.

For many writers—especially in England—the ideal poetic form for these new principles seemed to be the lyric. A lyric poem expresses a process of perception, thought, or emotion, often in the first person. Traditionally a marginal European form compared to epic, elegy, pastoral, and the satires popular in the eighteenth century, lyric grew so powerfully central to the definition of poetry in the nineteenth century that today it seems to have little in the way of competition. And it is thanks to the Romantics, with their insistence on turning away from the imitation of classical forms and toward the truth of inner experience—toward the individual's sincere, spontaneous feeling—that lyric came to prominence. Lyric has few set rules—one can choose any meter, stanza length, or structuring arc—and so it embodies the freedom from set conventions that Romantic poets valued. And its focus on processes of thought and feeling allowed poets to celebrate the great range of human emotion that seemed to have been suddenly released from rigid authority—imagination and desire, memory and mourning, speculation and idealism, and above all, a passionate interest in the truth of nature as a guide to beauty, freedom, community, and humanity itself.

EMERGENT MODERNISM

Just after the midpoint of the nineteenth century, a handful of French poets transformed Romantic poetry in ways that would have a profound influence on world literature. **Charles Baudelaire** is sometimes called "the first modern poet." His successors—**Stéphane Mallarmé** and **Arthur Rimbaud**—built on his resistance to poetic convention and together came to be known as the Symbolists. Preserving the Romantic notion of the poet as a seer or visionary, they brought together intensely evocative images that were not necessarily related by any external logic. In fact, they rejected the notion that poetic language should communicate or resolve itself into clear meanings. The goal was not to make sense; rather, they developed a deliberately allusive, sometimes brutally coarse poetry that played with multiple and shifting perspectives and frequently led to a blurring of boundaries between real and imaginary. They even abandoned the notion of the lyric speaker as a stable self, assuming that language precedes and makes up the self, rather than the other way around. For the Symbolists, poetry should be purified of everything but language itself.

The Symbolists were the first of a series of movements that would soon come to be known as *avant-garde*. Originally a military term, it means "advance guard" and evokes the image of artists doing battle. In this case, the war was being waged in the name of the future. Artists of the avant-garde saw themselves not as representing the world as it was but as bringing in a new world through startling breaks in perception. They shattered old views in favor of disconcerting new modes of seeing, which they hoped would then usher in radically new ways of living. Impressionism in painting, a famous avant-garde movement like Symbolism in poetry, literally broke color apart to lay bare its components of light and human perception.

In their struggle to make a radical break from the past, the Symbolists marked the beginnings of Modernism, an international movement that would flourish in the first half of the twentieth century. Already in the 1890s, the influence of the Symbolists could be felt far from Paris. Nicaraguan-born poet **Rubén Darío** was in fact the first person to use the term *modernismo* to describe what was happening in the arts. He drew on the inspiration of the French Symbolists but also brought indigenous American traditions into his work to create a new poetic movement in Latin America.

But perhaps the spirit of these avant-garde movements was not so new as it sometimes claimed to be. It was the Romantics of a century before, after all, who had insisted on freeing art from the past and experimenting with new forms and styles. The Modernists therefore drew upon a tradition of innovation launched by their Romantic precursors. And thus, while they inaugurated revolutionary new art forms for the new century, the Modernists remained in many ways Romanticism's rightful heirs.

ANNA LAETITIA BARBAULD

A fierce opponent of war and slavery and an early defender of animal rights, Anna Laetitia Barbauld (1743–1825) was a sophisticated woman poet whose work was widely known and respected in England and the United States. Called "one of the great minds which belong to all time," she entered bravely into public debates that were traditionally the province of male writers, urging her readers to live up to the highest principles of morality and citizenship. But Barbauld was not only a fearless and tough-minded public poet: she also wrote playful and reflective poems on family life, exploring childhood, married love, and grief.

Born Anna Laetitia Aikin in rural England, she was the daughter of two Presbyterians. As a child, she persuaded her father to teach her Latin and Greek—typically forbidden to women in the period. Her first book of poems in 1772 met with excitement on the part of the literary world, and she soon came to prominence as a major poet in a culture that esteemed poetry as the highest of the arts. **Samuel Taylor Coleridge** walked forty miles just to meet her, and **William Wordsworth** regretted that he had not himself written some of her great lines. In 1774 she married Rochemont Barbauld, a convert to Presbyterianism, and together they administered a school for boys. "Mrs. Barbauld," as she became known, wrote poetry and popular textbooks for children in this period, including *Lessons for Children of Two to Three Years Old*. In 1808 her husband succumbed to mental illness, and they separated after he violently assaulted her. He soon committed suicide.

Taking women's domestic experience as seriously as she took national politics, Barbauld's poetry crossed back and forth between traditionally masculine and feminine domains. Her poem "To a little invisible Being, who is expected soon to become visible," written about 1795, considers the mysterious existence of the unborn child, a being, the poem speculates, that has senses but no objects to sense and a mind but no thoughts to fill it. Barbauld reflects on the baffling problem of individuality in pregnancy—still unresolved in our own time. Is the child the same as the mother, or different? In the poem, the mother eagerly awaits the arrival of a complex being—a "stranger guest," "Part of herself, yet to herself unknown."

To a Little Invisible Being Who Is Expected Soon to Become Visible

Germ of new life, whose powers expanding slow
For many a moon their full perfection wait,—
Haste, precious pledge of happy love, to go
Auspicious borne through life's mysterious gate.

What powers lie folded in thy curious frame,—
Senses from objects locked, and mind from thought!

How little canst thou guess thy lofty claim
To grasp at all the worlds the Almighty wrought!

And see, the genial season's warmth to share,
Fresh younglings shoot, and opening roses glow.
Swarms of new life exulting fill the air,—
Haste, infant bud of being, haste to blow!

For thee the nurse prepares her lulling songs,
The eager matrons count the lingering day;
But far the most thy anxious parent longs
On thy soft cheek a mother's kiss to lay.

She only asks to lay her burden down,
That her glad arms that burden may resume;
And nature's sharpest pangs her wishes crown,
That free thee living from thy living tomb.

She longs to fold to her maternal breast
Part of herself, yet to herself unknown;
To see and to salute the stranger guest,
Fed with her life through many a tedious moon.

Come, reap thy rich inheritance of love!
Bask in the fondness of a Mother's eye!
Nor wit nor eloquence her heart shall move
Like the first accents of thy feeble cry.

Haste, little captive, burst thy prison doors!
Launch on the living world, and spring to light!
Nature for thee displays her various stores,
Opens her thousand inlets of delight.

If charmed verse or muttered prayers had power,
With favouring spells to speed thee on thy way,
Anxious I'd bid my beads each passing hour,
Till thy wished smile thy mother's pangs o'erpay.

WILLIAM BLAKE

William Blake condemned authority of all kinds. He cast priests and kings as responsible for exploiting the poor, repressing sexuality, and stifling art, and he admired the devil himself for his disobedience. "I must Create a System or be enslaved by another Man's," claims one of his characters.

But the rebellious Blake also harbored profound religious beliefs, developing his own unorthodox visions of divine love, justice, and creativity. When asked if he believed in the divinity of Jesus Christ, he is reported to have said, *"He is the only God,"* and then added: "And so am I and so are you." Some of his contemporaries hailed him as a saint: one legend has it that on his deathbed he burst out in songs of joy. To many others, he seemed a pitiable madman. Only a few admirers in his own time acclaimed him as the creative visionary he would appear to later generations.

LIFE

Born in 1757 in London, Blake was the third of six children. His father kept a hosiery shop, and both parents were lower-middle-class Londoners, radical in their politics and unorthodox in their religion. He grew up among small tradesmen and artisans, who typically took pride in their skilled labor and had a tradition of political radicalism that pitted them against the aristocratic elite. At the age of ten, Blake started drawing school, and at fourteen he was apprenticed to an engraver who taught him complex techniques of engraving and printmaking. He had no formal education beyond drawing school, but he read widely, including history, philosophy, classical literature, the Bible, Shakespeare, Milton, and other English poets, and he began writing poetry himself at around the age of thirteen. From childhood onward he repeatedly saw visions. "I write when commanded by the spirits," he once said, "and the moment I have written I see the words fly about the room in all directions." After exhibiting engravings and watercolors at the prestigious Royal Academy of Arts in 1779, Blake went to work as an engraver for Joseph Johnson, a bookseller and publisher who associated with the most influential radical thinkers of the Enlightenment period.

At the age of 25 Blake married Catherine Boucher, an illiterate daughter of a small farmer, whom he taught to read and write. By all accounts, their married life was a happy one, if occasionally tempestuous, and Catherine actively helped William in his work. The couple had no children.

In the late 1780s Blake developed a revolutionary new technique which he called "illuminated printing." Conventional print shops at the time separated the printing of images and words, integrating them only in the final stage of book production. Blake's method, by contrast, involved combining visual and written materials. He drew and wrote directly on the same copper plate, which then formed the basis for print reproductions. This process allowed Blake to adopt a much more spontaneous multimedia artistic practice than was usual, and ensured that the end product was entirely his own: he was at once the writer, the illustrator, and the printer. In characteristically visionary fashion, Blake explained that the spirit of his dead brother Robert had come to teach him this new technique.

Excited by the radical energies unleashed by the French Revolution in 1789, Blake threw himself into his creative endeavors and produced many of his greatest works in the following few years. *Songs of Innocence* in 1789 marked the beginnings of Blake's innovations. Frustrated with the poetry of his contemporaries, he looked backward to ancient ballads and sixteenth- and seventeenth-century English poetry for models. But he also took his work into some startlingly new poetic directions, including experimental rhythms, prophecies, themes of madness and jealousy, and the beginnings of a grand cosmological history. He wrote directly about politics while also pursuing his growing interest in myths and symbols.

One day in 1803 a soldier came into the Blakes' garden uttering threats and curses; Blake physically pushed him out. Because he had supposedly assaulted a soldier, the artist went on trial for sedition, or inciting rebellion, then punishable by hanging. In the end, he was acquitted, but the experience drove him further into isolation than ever. He spent the rest of his life poor and obscure. In his final years, a group of young painters recognized Blake's innovations in visual art, hailing him as a genius and an inspiration. He began to feel less angry and isolated, and his last few years were probably his happiest. But although he had finally won admiration as a visual artist, it was only long after his death in 1827 that Blake's extraordinary inventiveness as a poet would be understood and acclaimed.

TIMES

Blake was not alone in wanting to see tyrannical and corrupt authorities toppled, but he was often seen as eccentric even among revolutionaries. He rejected the Enlightenment insistence on cold rationality, mechanical science, and individual rights, envisioning a more spiritual, imaginative, and collective future. He wrote, "God is not a mathematical diagram." His famous poem "Mock On, Mock On, **Voltaire**, **Rousseau**" expresses his sense of the dangers of Enlightenment philosophy.

Blake put a much greater emphasis on economic inequality than most English supporters of the French Revolution. While many of his Enlightenment contemporaries argued for legal rights and political representation, Blake fiercely condemned the vast economic gulf between rich and poor. This was a moment when working conditions were changing dramatically: factories were springing up in urban centers, drawing vast numbers of laborers from the rural countryside, and machines were beginning to replace traditional craftsmanship. Blake angrily denounced a society willing to thrust workers into "dark Satanic Mills." Chimney sweeps, notorious as emblems of child labor, endured particularly severe hardships. Typically, these boys started working around the age of five, and by the time they had grown too large to climb chimneys, at twelve or thirteen, their bodies had been deformed and broken, rendered incapable of further work. In "The Chimney Sweeper," Blake expressed horror at the life of the laboring child who worked in darkness, inhaled soot and smoke, and had to endure burns, bruises, and debilitating illnesses.

It was not an easy time to speak out against injustice. The 1790s saw a wave of repressive laws that clamped down on dissenting expression in Britain. Public speakers, inflamed by the French Revolution, were trying to whip up antimonarchical sentiment and crowds were actively protesting—even at one point attacking the king's carriage. The British government responded harshly, suspending habeas corpus (the right not to be detained indefinitely without trial), banning most meetings larger than fifty people, and prosecuting "wicked and seditious writing." In 1793 France declared war on England, and the two nations were at war almost continuously until 1815. The wars intensified popular unrest, and revolutionary sympathizers were forced underground. Blake's former employer, Joseph Johnson, landed in jail for nine months for publishing an antiwar pamphlet. During this time, Blake's explicit engagements with poverty, slavery, and revolution gave way to more cryptic, biblical, and mythological themes.

But it would also be a mistake to imagine too strict a separation between Blake's politics and his religion. British law had long denied civil liberties to those who did not belong to the Church of England, and many Protestants, such as Methodists, Baptists, and Presbyterians—called Dissenters—had a robust tradition of resistance to official power. They wove together their religious beliefs with their political opposition. Blake was no exception. He was drawn to the mystical, charitable Swedenborg Church of the New Jerusalem, though he later criticized and rejected its doctrines. The 1780s and '90s saw a rise in evangelical and millenarian enthusiasm, and many Dissenters took the French Revolution to be the sign of a coming apocalypse. Blake repeatedly treated politics in terms of biblical models, and he, like many of his dissenting contemporaries, understood political revolutions as a violent purifying process that would bring about prophecies foretold in the Bible. In Blake's *Jerusalem*, one character asks, "Are not Religion & Politics the same thing? Brotherhood is Religion." Although Blake can seem eccentric among his rationalist Enlightenment contemporaries, then, his fusion of radical political beliefs and unorthodox, mystical spirituality was not entirely unusual among Dissenters in London.

WORK

Blake called for an open, accessible, democratic poetry and claimed that children were often the best readers of his work. His poems typically reject regular rhythms and conventional images in favor of unorthodox forms and unusually plain, forceful language. But he also opted for complicated systems of allegorical images and symbols, and in his stories characters often meld into others, change names, and appear and disappear in new guises. Not surprisingly, then, Blake's meanings remain a subject of fierce debate after two centuries. Many readers protest that much of his work is impenetrable and obscure—precisely the opposite of what Blake himself seems to have intended. And yet this debate might not have surprised or bothered Blake, since deliberate oppositions are often at the very heart of his work. He moves back and forth between innocence and experience, mystical vision and wry irony, joyful optimism and bleak prophecy, visual art and poetry.

In *Songs of Innocence*, Blake explores in simple language what it would be like to perceive the world through the eyes of a child. This means rendering familiar ideas radically unfamiliar. For instance, if we are accustomed to living in a culture that associates darkness with evil, then what does it feel like to be a dark-skinned child? His later *Songs of Experience* (1794) offers a set of companion pieces that return to the same subject matter from a more knowing perspective. Blake juxtaposes the two sets of poems, inviting us to think about the different ways that an innocent child and an experienced adult might understand God, love, and justice. There are echoes and recurrences within as well as across these two groups of poems, and perhaps this is not surprising: after all, Blake's major occupation throughout his life involved making copies—as an engraver, printmaker, and printer—and he seems to have been at least as interested in ideas of doubling and repetition as he was in uniqueness and originality. But he also complicates many of these echoes. In the famous "Tyger," for example, he rhymes "symmetry" and "eye"—a sight rhyme or pairing that might look like a rhyme but does not sound like one. He also unsettles conventional distinctions: the usual lines dividing human and divine states dissolve, for example, and the child leads the poet, rather than the other way around. These apparently simple but highly complex poems have remained Blake's most famous and beloved works.

Songs of Innocence and of Experience

SHEWING THE TWO CONTRARY STATES OF THE HUMAN SOUL

From Songs of Innocence[1]

Introduction

Piping down the valleys wild
Piping songs of pleasant glee
On a cloud I saw a child,
And he laughing said to me,

"Pipe a song about a Lamb";
So I piped with merry chear;
"Piper pipe that song again"—
So I piped, he wept to hear.

"Drop thy pipe thy happy pipe
Sing thy songs of happy chear";
So I sung the same again
While he wept with joy to hear.

"Piper sit thee down and write
In a book that all may read"—
So he vanished from my sight.
And I plucked a hollow reed,

And I made a rural pen,
And I stained the water clear,
And I wrote my happy songs
Every child may joy to hear.

The Lamb

  Little Lamb, who made thee?
  Dost thou know who made thee?
Gave thee life & bid thee feed,
By the stream & o'er the mead;
Gave thee clothing of delight,
Softest clothing wooly bright;
Gave thee such a tender voice,
Making all the vales rejoice!

1. The text for all of Blake's works is edited by David V. Erdman and Harold Bloom. *Songs of Innocence* (1789) was later combined with *Songs of Experience* (1794), and the poems were etched and accompanied by Blake's illustrations, the process accomplished by copper engravings stamped on paper, then colored by hand.

Little Lamb who made thee?
Dost thou know who made thee?

Little Lamb I'll tell thee,
Little Lamb I'll tell thee!
He is callèd by thy name,
For he calls himself a Lamb:
He is meek & he is mild,
He became a little child:
I a child & thou a lamb,
We are callèd by his name.[1]
Little Lamb God bless thee.
Little Lamb God bless thee.

The Little Black Boy

My mother bore me in the southern wild,
And I am black, but O! my soul is white;
White as an angel is the English child:
But I am black as if bereaved of light.

My mother taught me underneath a tree,
And sitting down before the heat of day,
She took me on her lap and kissèd me,
And pointing to the east, began to say:

"Look on the rising sun: there God does live,
And gives his light, and gives his heat away;
And flowers and trees and beasts and men receive
Comfort in morning, joy in the noon day.

"And we are put on earth a little space,
That we may learn to bear the beams of love,
And these black bodies and this sun-burnt face
Is but a cloud, and like a shady grove.

"For when our souls have learned the heat to bear,
The cloud will vanish; we shall hear his voice,
Saying: 'Come out from the grove, my love & care,
And round my golden tent like lambs rejoice.'"

Thus did my mother say, and kissèd me;
And thus I say to little English boy:
When I from black and he from white cloud free,
And round the tent of God like lambs we joy,

I'll shade him from the heat till he can bear
To lean in joy upon our father's knee;

1. I.e., Christians use the name of Christ to designate themselves.

And then I'll stand and stroke his silver hair,
And be like him, and he will then love me.

Holy Thursday[1]

'Twas on a Holy Thursday, their innocent faces clean,
The children walking two & two, in red & blue & green,[2]
Grey headed beadles[3] walked before with wands as white as snow,
Till into the high dome of Paul's they like Thames' waters flow.

O what a multitude they seemed, these flowers of London town!
Seated in companies they sit with radiance all their own.
The hum of multitudes was there, but multitudes of lambs,
Thousands of little boys & girls raising their innocent hands.

Now like a mighty wind they raise to heaven the voice of song,
Or like harmonious thunderings the seats of heaven among.
Beneath them sit the agèd men, wise guardians[4] of the poor;
Then cherish pity, lest you drive an angel from your door.[5]

The Chimney Sweeper

When my mother died I was very young,
And my father sold me[1] while yet my tongue
Could scarcely cry " 'weep![2] 'weep! 'weep! 'weep!"
So your chimneys I sweep & in soot I sleep.

There's little Tom Dacre, who cried when his head
That curled like a lamb's back, was shaved, so I said,
"Hush, Tom! never mind it, for when your head's bare,
You know that the soot cannot spoil your white hair."

And so he was quiet, & that very night,
As Tom was a-sleeping he had such a sight!
That thousands of sweepers, Dick, Joe, Ned, & Jack,
Were all of them locked up in coffins of black;

And by came an Angel who had a bright key,
And he opened the coffins & set them all free;

1. Ascension Day, forty days after Easter, when children from charity schools were marched to St. Paul's Cathedral.
2. Each school had its own distinctive uniform.
3. Ushers and minor functionaries, whose job was to maintain order.
4. The governors of the charity schools.
5. See Hebrews 13.2: "Be not forgetful to entertain strangers: for thereby some have entertained angels unawares."

1. It was common practice in Blake's day for fathers to sell, or indenture, their children to become chimney sweeps. The average age at which such children began working was six or seven; they were generally employed for seven years, until they were too big to ascend the chimneys.
2. The child's lisping effort to say "sweep," as he walks the streets looking for work.

Then down a green plain, leaping, laughing they run,
And wash in a river and shine in the Sun;

Then naked[3] & white, all their bags left behind,
They rise upon clouds, and sport in the wind.
And the Angel told Tom, if he'd be a good boy,
He'd have God for his father & never want joy.

And so Tom awoke; and we rose in the dark
And got with our bags & our brushes to work.
Tho' the morning was cold, Tom was happy & warm;
So if all do their duty, they need not fear harm.

From Songs of Experience

Introduction

Hear the voice of the Bard!
Who Present, Past, & Future sees;
  Whose ears have heard
  The Holy Word
  That walked among the ancient trees;[1]

  Calling the lapsèd Soul
  And weeping in the evening dew;[2]
  That might control
  The starry pole,
  And fallen, fallen light renew!

  "O Earth, O Earth, return!
  Arise from out the dewy grass;
  Night is worn,
  And the morn
  Rises from the slumberous mass.

  "Turn away no more;
  Why wilt thou turn away?
  The starry floor
  The watery shore
  Is given thee till the break of day."

3. They climbed up the chimneys naked.
1. Genesis 3.8: "And [Adam and Eve] heard the voice of the Lord God walking in the garden in the cool of the day."
2. Blake's ambiguous use of pronouns makes for interpretative difficulties. It would seem that *The Holy Word* (Jehovah, a name for God in the Old Testament of the Bible) calls *the lapsèd Soul*, and weeps—not the Bard.

Earth's Answer

Earth raised up her head,
From the darkness dread & drear.
Her light fled:
Stony dread!
And her locks covered with grey despair.

"Prisoned on watery shore
Starry Jealousy does keep my den,
Cold and hoar
Weeping o'er
I hear the Father[1] of the ancient men.

"Selfish father of men,
Cruel, jealous, selfish fear!
Can delight
Chained in night
The virgins of youth and morning bear?

"Does spring hide its joy
When buds and blossoms grow?
Does the sower
Sow by night,
Or the plowman in darkness plow?

"Break this heavy chain
That does freeze my bones around;
Selfish! vain!
Eternal bane!
That free Love with bondage bound."

The Tyger

Tyger! Tyger! burning bright
In the forests of the night,
What immortal hand or eye
Could frame thy fearful symmetry?

In what distant deeps or skies
Burnt the fire of thine eyes?
On what wings dare he aspire?
What the hand dare seize the fire?

1. In Blake's later prophetic works, one of the four Zoas, representing the four chief faculties of humankind, is Urizen. In general, he stands for the orthodox conception of the Divine Creator, sometimes Jehovah in the Old Testament, often the God conceived by Newton and Locke—in all instances a tyrant associated with excessive rationalism and sexual repression, and the opponent of the imagination and creativity. This may be "the Holy Word" in line 4 of "Introduction" (p. 316).

And what shoulder, & what art,
Could twist the sinews of thy heart?
And when thy heart began to beat,
What dread hand? & what dread feet?

What the hammer? what the chain?
In what furnace was thy brain?
What the anvil? what dread grasp
Dare its deadly terrors clasp?

When the stars threw down their spears,
And watered heaven with their tears,
Did he smile his work to see?
Did he who made the Lamb make thee?

Tyger! Tyger! burning bright
In the forests of the night,
What immortal hand or eye
Dare frame thy fearful symmetry?

The Sick Rose

O Rose, thou art sick.
The invisible worm
That flies in the night
In the howling storm

Has found out thy bed
Of crimson joy,
And his dark secret love
Does thy life destroy.

London

I wander thro' each chartered[1] street,
Near where the chartered Thames does flow,
And mark in every face I meet
Marks of weakness, marks of woe.

In every cry of every Man,
In every Infant's cry of fear,
In every voice, in every ban,
The mind-forged manacles I hear:

1. Hired (literally). Blake implies that the streets and the river are controlled by commercial interests.

How the Chimney-sweeper's cry
Every blackening Church appalls;[2]
And the hapless Soldier's sigh
Runs in blood down Palace walls.

But most thro' midnight streets I hear
How the youthful Harlot's curse
Blasts the new-born Infant's tear,[3]
And blights with plagues the Marriage hearse.

The Chimney Sweeper

A little black thing among the snow
Crying "'weep, 'weep," in notes of woe!
"Where are thy father & mother? say?"
"They are both gone up to the church to pray.

"Because I was happy upon the heath,
And smiled among the winter's snow;
They clothèd me in the clothes of death,
And taught me to sing the notes of woe.

"And because I am happy, & dance & sing,
They think they have done me no injury,
And are gone to praise God & his Priest & King,
Who make up a heaven of our misery."

Mock On, Mock On, Voltaire, Rousseau

Mock on, Mock on, Voltaire, Rousseau;
Mock on, Mock on, 'tis all in vain.
You throw the sand against the wind,
And the wind blows it back again.

And every sand becomes a Gem
Reflected in the beams divine;
Blown back, they blind the mocking Eye,
But still in Israel's paths they shine.

The Atoms of Democritus[1]
And Newton's Particles of light[2]
Are sands upon the Red sea shore,
Where Israel's tents do shine so bright.

2. Makes white (literally), punning also on *appall* (to dismay) and *pall* (the cloth covering a corpse or bier).

3. The harlot infects the parents with venereal disease, and thus the infant is inflicted with neonatal blindness.

1. Greek philosopher (460?–362? B.C.E.), who advanced a theory that all things are merely patterns of atoms.

2. Sir Isaac Newton's (1642–1727) corpuscular theory of light. For Blake, both men were condemned as materialists.

And Did Those Feet

And did those feet[1] in ancient time
Walk upon England's mountains green?
And was the holy Lamb of God
On England's pleasant pastures seen?

And did the Countenance Divine
Shine forth upon our clouded hills?
And was Jerusalem builded here,
Among those dark Satanic Mills?[2]

Bring me my Bow of burning gold:
Bring me my Arrows of desire:
Bring me my Spear: O clouds unfold!
Bring me my Chariot of fire!

I will not cease from Mental Fight,
Nor shall my Sword sleep in my hand,
Till we have built Jerusalem
In England's green & pleasant Land.

1. A reference to an ancient legend that Jesus came to England with Joseph of Arimathea.
2. Possibly industrial England, but for Blake *mills* also meant 18th-century arid, mechanistic philosophy.

WILLIAM WORDSWORTH

After William Wordsworth, English poetry would never be the same again. The sense that poets should convey intensely personal, individual expression, which now feels like the ordinary stuff of poetry, can be traced to Wordsworth's deliberate rejection of his eighteenth-century precursors. He turned readers' attention away from classical models and Gothic supernatural stories to everyday emotion and imagination, championing the spontaneity of authentic feeling. Like **Jean-Jacques Rousseau**, Wordsworth approached children's experience as crucial and determinative, in defiance of many of his contemporaries, who considered childhood trivial. And he chose to focus on common people—often poor and marginal figures such as elderly farmers and vagrant beggars. Just as important, Wordsworth also launched a new set of stylistic values for poetry, jettisoning "the gaudiness and inane phraseology" of contemporary poets in favor of a language that would feel direct, authentic, and plain. And finally, Wordsworth committed himself in surprising new ways to honoring the natural world as a benevolent nurturer and guide, and many have credited him with launching an ecological consciousness that continues to inspire environmentalists today.

LIFE

William Wordsworth was born in the small town of Cockermouth, in England's wild and rugged Lake District, in 1770. As a boy he was sent to a grammar school in the countryside, where he learned Greek and Latin and committed large portions of Shakespeare and Milton to memory. After his father's death in 1783, he began to feel restless and unsettled. While at Cambridge University, he failed to apply himself to his studies. "I am doomed to be an idler thro' my whole life," he wrote.

Wordsworth's perspective on the world took a turn in the summer of 1790, when he and a friend set off for a walking tour of France and the Alps. It was a critical moment in French history: the country was "mad with joy in consequence of the revolution," as Wordsworth put it. He also had a love affair with a Frenchwoman named Annette Vallon and had a child with her. He returned to England in 1793, meaning to make some money so that he could marry Vallon, but Britain went to war with France, and Wordsworth was not permitted to cross back for a decade.

The following few years were the most difficult of Wordsworth's life. He had no source of income, and his revolutionary sympathies made him an outsider in England. He moved to London and for a time became a disciple of the anarchist William Godwin, who favored the abolition of marriage and all forms of government. In 1795 Wordsworth began a formative friendship with another young radical poet, **Samuel Taylor Coleridge**. So close did Wordsworth and Coleridge become that they deliberately moved to within walking distance of one another in rural Somerset. There they entertained revolutionary thinkers and were suspected of being spies: "a mischievous gang of disaffected Englishmen," reported a government agent, "a Sett of violent Democrats." In fact, however, both Wordsworth and Coleridge were horrified by the bloody turn the revolution in France had taken, and they soon began to lose faith in radical politics. Loving the beauty of the countryside and each other's company, the two poets started to work together on a different kind of revolutionary ideal: the production of a new kind of poetry. Together, in 1798, they published a collection of poems called *Lyrical Ballads*. It contained works that would count among their best loved, including Wordsworth's "Tintern Abbey" and "We Are Seven," and Coleridge's "Rime of the Ancient Mariner." They published the first edition anonymously. ("Wordsworth's name is nothing," Coleridge explained, and "to a large number of persons mine *stinks*.")

This book succeeded in accomplishing a revolution in English poetry. Radically democratic, it focused on subject matter conventionally ignored by poets—the lives of lowly people, such as the very poor, the insane, children, shepherds, and tinkers. This new subject matter, Wordsworth wrote, demanded a simple and unaffected language, like the prose spoken by ordinary people. Thus *Lyrical Ballads* prized not only humble and simple subjects but also the poet's own internal state of mind, a focus that would become ever more important to Wordsworth's work. In 1801 he included a new preface, which has become as well known as his poetry. Here he put forward his revolutionary new ideas: "I have proposed to myself to imitate, and, as far as is possible, to adopt the very language of men," he wrote. Famously, he defined poetry as "the spontaneous overflow of powerful feelings," explaining that it comes from "emotion recollected in tranquility."

Critics were not prepared for this innovative volume, and Wordsworth's poetry garnered almost entirely hostile reviews. One critic wrote, "Than the volumes now before us we never saw any thing better calculated to excite disgust and anger in a lover of poetry. The drivelling nonsense of some of Mr. Wordsworth's poems is insufferable, and it is equally insufferable that such nonsense should have been written by a man capable, as he is, of writing well."

Wordsworth was appalled by Napoleon's rise to power across Europe, and his political views turned increasingly conservative. In the following years, Wordsworth became very much part of the conservative establishment. He was appointed distributor of stamps, collecting taxes on government documents, a civil service job that seemed to many contemporary radicals to represent a betrayal of his earlier commitment to the artist's independence. In 1818 he campaigned for the Tories—the conservative party—in local elections.

Wordsworth died on April 23, traditionally thought to be Shakespeare's birth- and death-day, in 1850.

WORK

Since Wordsworth's style is often purposefully simple, his poetry can seem deceptively uncomplicated. For many readers, its pleasures lie in the philosophical questions it poses. "Tintern Abbey" asks what makes a self a self: how do we become what we are? "We Are Seven" interrogates the abstraction of death and asks whether the dead may be considered part of the human community. And the "Ode on Intimations of Immortality" considers the immortality of the soul, using Plato's ideas as a touchstone.

But the poems also reward close attention to their language. Even the most seemingly straightforward Wordsworthian lines often yield more questions than answers. Consider, for example, the title of the poem "Lines Composed a Few Miles above Tintern Abbey, on Revisiting the Banks of the Wye during a Tour, July 13, 1798." Why such a curiously long and descriptive title, going to such trouble to mark the place and date of composition? The poem itself, surprisingly, says nothing at all about the ruined abbey. Some readers have noted that Wordsworth is careful to use the title to note his position "above" the landscape; others have remarked on the date, which commemorates the anniversary of the day *before* the French Revolution started, hinting that Wordsworth's explorations of memory and selfhood in this poem are bound up with his ambivalence about the revolution. In another example, the central tension of "We Are Seven" turns on the definition of one of the simplest and most common words in the English language—"we." The poem explores the idea that two different uses of an ordinary pronoun reveal radically dissimilar ways of seeing the world. How is it, Wordsworth's poetry insistently asks, that complex conceptions of faith, nature, selfhood, community, and knowledge are revealed in the most commonplace language that we use?

Wordsworth is famous for his plain style and his philosophical explorations, but he is also notable for his ease in moving among poetic forms and genres. While "Tintern Abbey" is composed in the regular and highly traditional English form of iambic pentameter, "Ode on Intimations of Immortality" is strikingly irregular, with both lines and stanzas varying widely in length. Wordsworth borrows here from an English tradition of deliberately irregular odes in which the poet meditates on a problem or object in changing rhythms. Since both "Tintern Abbey" and the "Ode" are about time and memory, it is intriguing that Wordsworth should choose such different forms for the two poems.

The other genre represented here is the sonnet, a form that had languished for a couple of centuries but became popular again in the late eighteenth century. Wordsworth was among many Romantic poets—among them, numerous women—who brought the sonnet back to prominence. He wrote a poem called "Scorn not the Sonnet," which reminds the reader of the sonnet's illustrious history, begun by the Italian poet Petrarch and later taken up by Shakespeare and Milton. Wordsworth was clearly self-conscious about his place in this poetic tradition. The two examples included here, "Composed upon Westminster Bridge" and "The World Is Too Much with Us," steer clear of the sonnet's traditional focus on romantic love, meditating instead on the specific conditions of modern, industrial, and urban society, thus pointedly bringing this traditional poetic form into the present. In re-imagining the sonnet, then, as in his innovative ideas about democracy, poetic style, nature, childhood, and the importance of individual experience, Wordsworth is a quintessentially modern poet.

We Are Seven

——A simple Child,
That lightly draws its breath,
And feels its life in every limb,
What should it know of death?

I met a little cottage Girl:
She was eight years old, she said;
Her hair was thick with many a curl
That clustered round her head.

She had a rustic, woodland air,
And she was wildly clad:
Her eyes were fair, and very fair;
—Her beauty made me glad.

"Sisters and brothers, little Maid,
How many may you be?"
"How many? Seven in all," she said,
And wondering looked at me.

"And where are they? I pray you tell."
She answered, "Seven are we;
And two of us at Conway[1] dwell,
And two are gone to sea.

"Two of us in the church-yard lie,
My sister and my brother;
And, in the church-yard cottage, I
Dwell near them with my mother."

"You say that two at Conway dwell,
And two are gone to sea,
Yet ye are seven! I pray you tell,
Sweet Maid, how this may be."

1. Port town in Wales.

Then did the little Maid reply,
"Seven boys and girls are we;
Two of us in the church-yard lie,
Beneath the church-yard tree."

"You run about, my little Maid,
Your limbs they are alive;
If two are in the church-yard laid,
Then ye are only five."

"Their graves are green, they may be seen,"
The little Maid replied,
"Twelve steps or more from my mother's door,
And they are side by side.

"My stockings there I often knit,
My kerchief there I hem;
And there upon the ground I sit,
And sing a song to them.

"And often after sun-set, Sir,
When it is light and fair,
I take my little porringer,[2]
And eat my supper there.

"The first that died was sister Jane;
In bed she moaning lay,
Till God released her of her pain;
And then she went away.

"So in the church-yard she was laid;
And, when the grass was dry,
Together round her grave we played,
My brother John and I.

"And when the ground was white with snow,
And I could run and slide,
My brother John was forced to go,
And he lies by her side."

"How many are you, then," said I,
"If they two are in heaven?"
Quick was the little Maid's reply,
"O Master! we are seven."

"But they are dead; those two are dead!
Their spirits are in heaven!"
'Twas throwing words away; for still
The little Maid would have her will,
And said, "Nay, we are seven!"

2. A bowl or dish.

Lines Composed a Few Miles above Tintern Abbey

On Revisiting the Banks of the Wye During a Tour, July 13, 1798

Five years have past; five summers, with the length
Of five long winters! and again I hear
These waters, rolling from their mountain-springs
With a soft inland murmur.—Once again
Do I behold these steep and lofty cliffs,
That on a wild secluded scene impress
Thoughts of more deep seclusion; and connect
The landscape with the quiet of the sky.
The day is come when I again repose
Here, under this dark sycamore, and view
These plots of cottage-ground, these orchard-tufts,
Which at this season, with their unripe fruits,
Are clad in one green hue, and lose themselves
'Mid groves and copses. Once again I see
These hedge-rows, hardly hedge-rows, little lines
Of sportive wood run wild: these pastoral farms,
Green to the very door; and wreaths of smoke
Sent up, in silence, from among the trees!
With some uncertain notice, as might seem
Of vagrant dwellers in the houseless woods,
Or of some Hermit's cave, where by his fire
The Hermit sits alone.

These beauteous forms,
Through a long absence, have not been to me
As is a landscape to a blind man's eye:
But oft, in lonely rooms, and 'mid the din
Of towns and cities, I have owed to them,
In hours of weariness, sensations sweet,
Felt in the blood, and felt along the heart;
And passing even into my purer mind,
With tranquil restoration:—feelings too
Of unremembered pleasure: such, perhaps,
As have no slight or trivial influence
On that best portion of a good man's life,
His little, nameless, unremembered, acts
Of kindness and of love. Nor less, I trust,
To them I may have owed another gift,
Of aspect more sublime; that blessèd mood,
In which the burthen of the mystery,
In which the heavy and the weary weight
Of all this unintelligible world,
Is lightened:—that serene and blessèd mood,
In which the affections gently lead us on,—
Until, the breath of this corporeal frame
And even the motion of our human blood
Almost suspended, we are laid asleep

In body, and become a living soul:
While with an eye made quiet by the power
Of harmony, and the deep power of joy,
We see into the life of things.

If this
Be but a vain belief, yet, oh! how oft—
In darkness and amid the many shapes
Of joyless daylight; when the fretful stir
Unprofitable, and the fever of the world,
Have hung upon the beatings of my heart—
How oft, in spirit, have I turned to thee,
O sylvan Wye! thou wanderer thro' the woods,
How often has my spirit turned to thee!

And now, with gleams of half-extinguished thought,
With many recognitions dim and faint,
And somewhat of a sad perplexity,
The picture of the mind revives again:
While here I stand, not only with the sense
Of present pleasure, but with pleasing thoughts
That in this moment there is life and food
For future years. And so I dare to hope,
Though changed, no doubt, from what I was when first
I came among these hills; when like a roe
I bounded o'er the mountains, by the sides
Of the deep rivers, and the lonely streams,
Wherever nature led: more like a man
Flying from something that he dreads, than one
Who sought the thing he loved. For nature then
(The coarser pleasures of my boyish days,
And their glad animal movements all gone by)
To me was all in all.—I cannot paint
What then I was. The sounding cataract
Haunted me like a passion: the tall rock,
The mountain, and the deep and gloomy wood,
Their colours and their forms, were then to me
An appetite; a feeling and a love,
That had no need of a remoter charm,
By thought supplied, nor any interest
Unborrowed from the eye.—That time is past,
And all its aching joys are now no more,
And all its dizzy raptures. Not for this
Faint I, nor mourn nor murmur; other gifts
Have followed; for such loss, I would believe,
Abundant recompense. For I have learned
To look on nature, not as in the hour
Of thoughtless youth; but hearing oftentimes
The still, sad music of humanity,
Nor harsh nor grating, though of ample power
To chasten and subdue. And I have felt
A presence that disturbs me with the joy

Of elevated thoughts; a sense sublime
Of something far more deeply interfused,
Whose dwelling is the light of setting suns,
And the round ocean and the living air,
And the blue sky, and in the mind of man:
A motion and a spirit, that impels
All thinking things, all objects of all thought,
And rolls through all things. Therefore am I still
A lover of the meadows and the woods,
And mountains; and of all that we behold
From this green earth; of all the mighty world
Of eye, and ear,—both what they half create,
And what perceive; well pleased to recognise
In nature and the language of the sense,
The anchor of my purest thoughts, the nurse,
The guide, the guardian of my heart, and soul
Of all my moral being.

Nor perchance,
If I were not thus taught, should I the more
Suffer my genial[1] spirits to decay:
For thou art with me here upon the banks
Of this fair river; thou my dearest Friend,
My dear, dear Friend; and in thy voice I catch
The language of my former heart, and read
My former pleasures in the shooting lights
Of thy wild eyes. Oh! yet a little while
May I behold in thee what I was once,
My dear, dear Sister! and this prayer I make,
Knowing that Nature never did betray
The heart that loved her; 'tis her privilege,
Through all the years of this our life, to lead
From joy to joy: for she can so inform
The mind that is within us, so impress
With quietness and beauty, and so feed
With lofty thoughts, that neither evil tongues,
Rash judgments, nor the sneers of selfish men,
Nor greetings where no kindness is, nor all
The dreary intercourse of daily life,
Shall e'er prevail against us, or disturb
Our cheerful faith, that all which we behold
Is full of blessings. Therefore let the moon
Shine on thee in thy solitary walk;
And let the misty mountain-winds be free
To blow against thee: and, in after years,
When these wild ecstasies shall be matured
Into a sober pleasure; when thy mind
Shall be a mansion for all lovely forms,
Thy memory be as a dwelling-place
For all sweet sounds and harmonies; oh! then,

1. Generative, creative.

If solitude, or fear, or pain, or grief
Should be thy portion, with what healing thoughts
Of tender joy wilt thou remember me,
And these my exhortations! Nor, perchance—
If I should be where I no more can hear
Thy voice, nor catch from thy wild eyes these gleams
Of past existence—wilt thou then forget
That on the banks of this delightful stream
We stood together; and that I, so long
A worshipper of Nature, hither came
Unwearied in that service; rather say
With warmer love—oh! with far deeper zeal
Of holier love. Nor wilt thou then forget
That after many wanderings, many years
Of absence, these steep woods and lofty cliffs,
And this green pastoral landscape, were to me
More dear, both for themselves and for thy sake!

Ode on Intimations of Immortality

From Recollections of Early Childhood

The Child is father of the Man:
And I could wish my days to be
Bound each to each by natural piety.

I

There was a time when meadow, grove, and stream,
The earth, and every common sight,
To me did seem
Apparelled in celestial light,
The glory and the freshness of a dream.
It is not now as it hath been of yore;—
Turn wheresoe'er I may,
By night or day,
The things which I have seen I now can see no more.

II

The Rainbow comes and goes,
And lovely is the Rose;
The Moon doth with delight
Look round her when the heavens are bare,
Waters on a starry night
Are beautiful and fair;
The sunshine is a glorious birth;
But yet I know, where'er I go,
That there hath passed away a glory from the earth.

III

Now, while the birds thus sing a joyous song,
And while the young lambs bound
As to the tabor's sound,
To me alone there came a thought of grief:
A timely utterance gave that thought relief,
And I again am strong:
The cataracts blow their trumpets from the steep;
No more shall grief of mine the season wrong;
I hear the Echoes through the mountains throng,
The Winds come to me from the fields of sleep,
And all the earth is gay;
Land and sea
Give themselves up to jollity,
And with the heart of May
Doth every Beast keep holiday;—
Thou Child of Joy,
Shout round me, let me hear thy shouts, thou happy
Shepherd-boy!

IV

Ye blessèd Creatures, I have heard the call
Ye to each other make; I see
The heavens laugh with you in your jubilee;
My heart is at your festival,
My head hath its coronal,
The fulness of your bliss, I feel—I feel it all.
Oh evil day! if I were sullen
While Earth herself is adorning,
This sweet May-morning,
And the Children are culling
On every side,
In a thousand valleys far and wide,
Fresh flowers; while the sun shines warm,
And the Babe leaps up on his Mother's arm:—
I hear, I hear, with joy I hear!
—But there's a Tree, of many, one,
A single Field which I have looked upon,
Both of them speak of something that is gone:
The Pansy at my feet
Doth the same tale repeat:
Whither is fled the visionary gleam?
Where is it now, the glory and the dream?

V

Our birth is but a sleep and a forgetting:
The Soul that rises with us, our life's Star,
Hath had elsewhere its setting,

And cometh from afar:
Not in entire forgetfulness,
And not in utter nakedness,
But trailing clouds of glory do we come
From God, who is our home:
Heaven lies about us in our infancy!
Shades of the prison-house begin to close
Upon the growing Boy,
But He beholds the light, and whence it flows,
He sees it in his joy;
The Youth, who daily farther from the east
Must travel, still is Nature's Priest,
And by the vision splendid
Is on his way attended;
At length the Man perceives it die away,
And fade into the light of common day.

VI

Earth fills her lap with pleasures of her own;
Yearnings she hath in her own natural kind,
And, even with something of a Mother's mind,
And no unworthy aim,
The homely Nurse doth all she can
To make her Foster-child, her Inmate, Man,
Forget the glories he hath known,
And that imperial palace whence he came.

VII

Behold the Child among his new-born blisses,
A six years' Darling of a pigmy size!
See, where 'mid work of his own hand he lies,
Fretted by sallies of his mother's kisses,
With light upon him from his father's eyes!
See, at his feet, some little plan or chart,
Some fragment from his dream of human life,
Shaped by himself with newly-learnèd art;
A wedding or a festival,
A mourning or a funeral;
And this hath now his heart,
And unto this he frames his song:
Then will he fit his tongue
To dialogues of business, love, or strife;
But it will not be long
Ere this be thrown aside,
And with new joy and pride
The little Actor cons another part;
Filling from time to time his "humorous stage"
With all the Persons, down to palsied Age,
That Life brings with her in her equipage;
As if his whole vocation
Were endless imitation.

VIII

Thou, whose exterior semblance doth belie
Thy Soul's immensity;
Thou best Philosopher, who yet dost keep
Thy heritage, thou Eye among the blind,
That, deaf and silent, read'st the eternal deep,
Haunted for ever by the eternal mind,—
Mighty Prophet! Seer blest!
On whom those truths do rest,
Which we are toiling all our lives to find,
In darkness lost, the darkness of the grave;
Thou, over whom thy Immortality
Broods like the Day, a Master o'er a Slave,
A Presence which is not to be put by;
[To whom the grave
Is but a lonely bed without the sense or sight
Of day or the warm light,
A place of thought where we in waiting lie;][1]
Thou little Child, yet glorious in the might
Of heaven-born freedom on thy being's height,
Why with such earnest pains dost thou provoke
The years to bring the inevitable yoke,
Thus blindly with thy blessedness at strife?
Full soon thy Soul shall have her earthly freight,
And custom lie upon thee with a weight,
Heavy as frost, and deep almost as life!

IX

O joy! that in our embers
Is something that doth live,
That nature yet remembers
What was so fugitive!
The thought of our past years in me doth breed
Perpetual benediction: not indeed
For that which is most worthy to be blest;
Delight and liberty, the simple creed
Of Childhood, whether busy or at rest,
With new-fledged hope still fluttering in his breast—
Not for these I raise
The song of thanks and praise;
But for those obstinate questionings
Of sense and outward things,
Fallings from us, vanishings;
Blank misgivings of a Creature
Moving about in worlds not realized,
High instincts before which our mortal Nature
Did tremble like a guilty Thing surprised:

1. The lines within brackets were included in the 1807 and 1815 editions of Wordsworth's poems but omitted in the 1820 and subsequent editions, as a result of Coleridge's severe censure of them.

But for those first affections,
Those shadowy recollections,
Which, be they what they may,
Are yet the fountain-light of all our day,
Are yet a master-light of all our seeing;
Uphold us, cherish, and have power to make
Our noisy years seem moments in the being
Of the eternal Silence: truths that wake,
To perish never;
Which neither listlessness, nor mad endeavour,
Nor Man nor Boy,
Nor all that is at enmity with joy,
Can utterly abolish or destroy!
Hence in a season of calm weather
Though inland far we be,
Our Souls have sight of that immortal sea
Which brought us hither,
Can in a moment travel thither,
And see the Children sport upon the shore,
And hear the mighty waters rolling evermore.

X

Then sing, ye Birds, sing, sing a joyous song!
And let the young Lambs bound
As to the tabor's sound!
We in thought will join your throng,
Ye that pipe and ye that play,
Ye that through your hearts to-day
Feel the gladness of the May!
What though the radiance which was once so bright
Be now for ever taken from my sight,
Though nothing can bring back the hour
Of splendour in the grass, of glory in the flower;
We will grieve not, rather find
Strength in what remains behind;
In the primal sympathy
Which having been must ever be;
In the soothing thoughts that spring
Out of human suffering;
In the faith that looks through death,
In years that bring the philosophic mind.

XI

And O, ye Fountains, Meadows, Hills, and Groves,
Forebode not any severing of our loves!
Yet in my heart of hearts I feel your might;
I only have relinquished one delight
To live beneath your more habitual sway.
I love the Brooks which down their channels fret,
Even more than when I tripped lightly as they;

The innocent brightness of a new-born Day
Is lovely yet;
The Clouds that gather round the setting sun
Do take a sober colouring from an eye
That hath kept watch o'er man's mortality;
Another race hath been, and other palms are won.
Thanks to the human heart by which we live,
Thanks to its tenderness, its joys, and fears,
To me the meanest flower that blows can give
Thoughts that do often lie too deep for tears.

Composed upon Westminster Bridge, September 3, 1802

Earth has not anything to show more fair:
Dull would he be of soul who could pass by
A sight so touching in its majesty;
This City now doth, like a garment, wear
The beauty of the morning; silent, bare,
Ships, towers, domes, theatres, and temples lie
Open unto the fields, and to the sky;
All bright and glittering in the smokeless air.
Never did sun more beautifully steep
In his first splendour, valley, rock, or hill;
Ne'er saw I, never felt, a calm so deep!
The river glideth at his own sweet will:
Dear God! the very houses seem asleep;
And all that mighty heart is lying still!

The World Is Too Much with Us

The world is too much with us; late and soon,
Getting and spending, we lay waste our powers:
Little we see in Nature that is ours;
We have given our hearts away, a sordid boon![1]
This Sea that bares her bosom to the moon,
The winds that will be howling at all hours,
And are up-gathered now like sleeping flowers;
For this, for everything, we are out of tune;
It moves us not.—Great God! I'd rather be
A Pagan suckled in a creed outworn;
So might I, standing on this pleasant lea,
Have glimpses that would make me less forlorn;
Have sight of Proteus[2] rising from the sea;
Or hear old Triton[3] blow his wreathèd horn.

1. Gift. "Sordid": refers to the act of giving the heart away.
2. An old man of the sea who, in the *Odyssey*, could assume a variety of shapes.
3. A sea deity, usually represented as blowing on a conch shell.

SAMUEL TAYLOR COLERIDGE

Intellectually brilliant and highly learned, Samuel Taylor Coleridge (1772–1834) led a chaotic life, addicted to opium, hopelessly in love with one woman while married to another, and typically unable to complete his literary and philosophical projects. But his groundbreaking poetic innovations, his wide and deep knowledge of religion, politics, and philosophy, and his compelling, improvised public lectures marked him as one of the most exceptional minds of his time. For many of his contemporaries, he was first and foremost a sparkling and impassioned conversationalist, so notable that admirers recorded and published his dinner table talk after his death. But long after his spirited conversation had gone, generations of readers would remember Coleridge for his most famous poem, "The Rime of the Ancient Mariner"—much quoted, imitated, and parodied—and for his dense philosophical meditations on literature and the mind.

LIFE

The youngest of ten children, Coleridge was a child prodigy who had read the Bible by the age of three. At school he was taught to read literature with exacting precision: "I learnt . . . that Poetry, even that of the loftiest, and, seemingly, that of the wildest odes, had a logic of its own, as severe as that of science." Always a voracious reader, Coleridge chose to immerse himself in philosophy and theology even as an adolescent. While studying at Cambridge University he won a medal for a poem he wrote on the slave trade, and found himself caught up in the enthusiasm for the French Revolution. But his commitment to "liberty" subjected him to intense anxieties. When the British declared war on France in 1793, antirevolutionary forces gathered strength, and Coleridge became vulnerable to accusations of treason. Plagued by uncertainty, he enlisted in the army under the unlikely alias of "Silas Tomkyn Comberbache." He was thoroughly unsuited to military life, and his brother, a military captain, obtained a release for him under the army's insanity clause.

Outside of the military context, Coleridge gained fame as a learned figure who spoke passionately in support of liberty. He published a radical journal and gave compelling lectures critical of the government and the slave trade. But he had no source of income, and when his wife gave birth to his first son, Hartley, in 1796, it was clear that he needed some stability. He set up house near his new friend, the poet **William Wordsworth**, and the two began a close relationship that would propel Coleridge into a period of intense poetic productivity that saw the composition of his most famous works. It was during 1797–98 that Coleridge wrote all three of the poems collected here.

Around this time, Coleridge began to shift his political sympathies. He rejected the ideals of the French Revolution and adopted a patriotic, anti-Napoleonic position, which brought him under attack by radicals. Disillusioned with French thought, Coleridge grew increasingly fascinated by German philosophers, including G. W. F. Hegel, **Immanuel Kant**, and Friedrich Schelling, and he is often credited with having introduced these thinkers to British readers.

In the first years of the nineteenth century, Coleridge's life seemed bleak indeed. He found himself unable to write poetry, estranged from his wife, and in love with Sara Hutchinson, Wordsworth's future sister-in-law. She was highly intelligent, but thanks to Coleridge's marriage she remained permanently out of reach, and in his anguish the poet became increasingly dependent on both opium and alcohol. He left his family and worked as a journalist and lecturer. Addiction and both physical and mental illness brought Coleridge close to suicide in 1810, and he broke off his friendship with Wordsworth. He had a thoroughgoing breakdown a few years later, tormented by a sense of failure.

In 1814, however, Coleridge's fortunes began to change. A new generation of poets, including **Percy Shelley**, **John Keats**, and most enthusiastically George Gordon Byron, professed themselves admirers of Coleridge's poetry, and he embarked on a new work, an exploration of poetic principles and practices, which grew into a complex intellectual autobiography—a combination of philosophy, theories of mind and language, literary history and criticism, and personal development—called the *Biographia Literaria*. In this work, Coleridge elaborates theories of the imagination that would have great influence a century later. He also describes a rigorous discipline of reading poetry, a practice that would inspire literary critics in the twentieth century who wanted to foster skills of "close reading"—still a staple of literature classrooms today. Coleridge died a famous poet and thinker in 1834.

COLERIDGE'S WORKS IN A GLOBAL CONTEXT

The poems collected here give a sense of Coleridge's breadth as a poet. His conversation poem "Frost at Midnight," written soon after Hartley's birth, is sometimes considered the inspiration for Wordsworth's "Tintern Abbey," both of them meditations on childhood, memory, and nature written in a soothing blank verse. Intriguingly, Coleridge first published this in a pamphlet along with two highly political poems, "France: An Ode" and "Fears in Solitude," and some readers have interpreted this quiet work as a response to the atmosphere of censorship and oppressive government that prevailed during the wars with France.

Coleridge's supernatural poems, by contrast, are startling in their strangeness. "Kubla Khan" is haunting and fragmentary, and Coleridge prefaced it with a story about how the poem had come to him in an opium-induced dream that was unfortunately interrupted by a "person from Porlock." This account has become as famous as the poem itself. "The Ancient Mariner" also accumulated interpretive materials beyond the poem itself: it is written with archaic words and spellings, and over the years Coleridge made the language feel even more foreign by adding an explanatory gloss in the margins, also in an antiquated idiom, and a Latin epigraph. When it first appeared in the collection of poems by Wordsworth and Coleridge called *Lyrical Ballads,* critics were largely derisive, and the "Ancient Mariner" was called the worst in the volume. Wordsworth said later that "the old words and the strangeness of it have deterred readers from going on." (In the first version of *Lyrical Ballads,* Wordsworth had given it pride of place as the very first poem; just two years later he buried it second to last in the volume.)

Generations of readers have puzzled over Coleridge's theories of the human mind, and they have read "The Ancient Mariner" and "Kubla Khan" as meditations on the power and limits of the poetic imagination. But in recent years, readers have noticed that both poems depend on evocations of distant places. The Ancient Mariner travels as far as the South Pole, and "Kubla Khan" is quite specific in beginning with a Mongol emperor and ending with a girl from Abysinnia (now known as Ethiopia). Scholars have uncovered evidence of Coleridge's fascination with travel narratives, one of the most popular genres of his moment. And they have recommended reading these two poems in the context of Britain's global empire and the explosion of travel writing that accompanied it.

In Coleridge's time, books and newspapers brought constant news of imperial affairs: the loss of the American colonies, tensions with Spain and France over colonial territory, the first contact with Australia, the exploration of African territories unknown to Europeans, and the continuing administration of Ireland, India, Canada, and much of the Caribbean. Among the most popular books in late-eighteenth-century Britain were accounts of Captain James Cook's voyages around the globe. His crew brought back new maps of the world, accounts of cultures profoundly different from those of the Europeans, and also botanical and zoological specimens that surprised and fascinated English audiences. And yet the global explorations described in British travel writing of the time were not simply undertaken for the pursuit of knowledge: they formed an integral part of the British desire for the discovery and control of new raw materials, new trade goods, and new markets. Travel writing thus formed one popular part of a wider colonizing culture preoccupied with economic gain and global conquest.

"The Rime of the Ancient Mariner" was partly inspired by Cook's second voyage, which attempted to discover the South Pole. "Kubla Khan" too might have evoked the British Empire for Coleridge's first readers, since the Khan was a legendary emperor: the grandson of Genghis Khan, he ruled over the Mongols of Northern China in the thirteenth century and controlled the largest empire that had existed up to that time, stretching as far as modern Korea, Iraq, Western Russia, and Hungary. It was the Mongols who first allowed trade between Europe and China, but they were also famous for their brutal violence—massacring and plundering wherever they encountered opposition.

As his poetry imaginatively ranges over the globe, Coleridge also explores the inner frontier, probing the powers and limits of the mind. And in all of his work, he offers a dense and thoughtful contemplation of human capacities: our knowledge, our inner vision, and our powers of creation and destruction.

The Rime of the Ancient Mariner

IN SEVEN PARTS

Facile credo, plures esse Naturas invisibiles quam visibiles in rerum universitate. Sed horum [sic] omnium familiam quis nobis enarrabit, et gradus et cognationes et discrimina et singulorum munera? Quid agunt? quae loca habitant? Harum rerum notitiam semper ambivit ingenium humanum, nunquam attigit. Juvat, interea, non diffiteor, quandoque in animo, tanquam in tabulâ, majoris et melioris mundi imaginem contemplari: ne mens assuefacta hodiernae vitae minutiis se contrahat nimis, et tota subsidat in pusillas cogitationes. Sed veritati interea invigilandum est, modusque servandus, ut certa ab incertis, diem a nocte, distinguamus.

T. BURNET, Archaeol. Phil. p. 68.[1]

Part 1

An ancient Mariner meeteth three gallants bidden to a wedding-feast, and detaineth one.

It is an ancient Mariner
And he stoppeth one of three.
"By thy long grey beard and glittering eye,
Now wherefore stopp'st thou me?

The Bridegroom's doors are opened wide,
And I am next of kin;
The guests are met, the feast is set:
May'st hear the merry din."

He holds him with his skinny hand,
"There was a ship," quoth he.
"Hold off! unhand me, grey-beard loon!"
Eftsoons[2] his hand dropt he.

The wedding guest is spellbound by the eye of the old sea-faring man, and constrained to hear his tale.

He holds him with his glittering eye—
The wedding-guest stood still,
And listens like a three years' child:
The Mariner hath his will.[3]

The wedding-guest sat on a stone:
He cannot choose but hear;

1. "I readily believe that there are more invisible Natures in the universe than visible ones. But who will explain the ways that these beings are related, their ranks and connections and features and functions? What do they do? Where do they dwell? The human mind has always searched for this knowledge but has never attained it. Meanwhile, I do not deny that from time to time it is useful to picture in the mind, as on a tablet, the image of a greater and better world, so that our minds, preoccupied with everyday trivial matters, do not narrow themselves too much and sink entirely into petty ideas. And yet we must watch for the truth and keep a sense of proportion, so that we may distinguish between the certain and uncertain, day and night" (Latin). Adapted by Coleridge from Thomas Burnet, *Archaeologiae philosophicae* (1692).

2. Immediately.

3. I.e., the mariner has mesmerized the wedding guest.

And thus spake on that ancient man,
The bright-eyed Mariner.

"The ship was cheered, the harbor cleared,
Merrily did we drop
Below the kirk,[4] below the hill,
Below the light house top.

The Mariner tells how the ship sailed southward with a good wind and fair weather, till it reached the line.

The sun came up upon the left,
Out of the sea came he!
And he shone bright, and on the right
Went down into the sea.

Higher and higher every day,
Till over the mast at noon—"
The wedding-guest here beat his breast,
For he heard the loud bassoon.

The Wedding Guest heareth the bridal music; but the mariner continueth his tale.

The bride hath paced into the hall,
Red as a rose is she;
Nodding their heads before her goes
The merry minstrelsy.

The wedding-guest he beat his breast,
Yet he cannot choose but hear;
And thus spake on that ancient man,
The bright-eyed Mariner.

The ship driven by a storm toward the south pole.

"And now the storm-blast came, and he
Was tyrannous and strong:
He struck with his o'ertaking wings,
And chased us south along.

With sloping masts and dipping prow,
As who pursued with yell and blow
Still treads the shadow of his foe,
And forward bends his head,
The ship drove fast, loud roared the blast,
And southward aye we fled.

And now there came both mist and snow,
And it grew wondrous cold:
And ice, mast-high, came floating by,
As green as emerald.

The land of ice, and of fearful sounds where no living thing was to be seen.

And through the drifts the snowy clifts
Did send a dismal sheen:
Nor shapes of men nor beasts we ken—
The ice was all between.

4. Church.

The ice was here, the ice was there,
The ice was all around:
It cracked and growled, and roared and howled,
Like noises in a swound![5]

Till a great sea-bird, called the Albatross, came through the snow-fog, and was received with great joy and hospitality.

At length did cross an Albatross,
Thorough the fog it came;
As if it had been a Christian soul,
We hailed it in God's name.

It ate the food it ne'er had eat,
And round and round it flew.
The ice did split with a thunder-fit;
The helmsman steered us through!

And lo! the Albatross proveth a bird of good omen, and followeth the ship as it returned northward through fog and floating ice.

And a good south wind sprung up behind;
The Albatross did follow,
And every day, for food or play,
Came to the mariners' hollo!

In mist or cloud, on mast or shroud,
It perched for vespers nine;
Whiles all the night, through fog-smoke white,
Glimmered the white moon-shine."

The ancient Mariner inhospitably killeth the pious bird of good omen.

"God save thee, ancient Mariner!
From the fiends, that plague thee thus!—
Why look'st thou so?"—With my cross-bow
I shot the Albatross.

Part 2

The Sun now rose upon the right:
Out of the sea came he,
Still hid in mist, and on the left
Went down into the sea.

And the good south wind still blew behind,
But no sweet bird did follow,
Nor any day for food or play
Came to the mariners' hollo!

His shipmates cry out against the ancient Mariner, for killing the bird of good luck.

And I had done a hellish thing,
And it would work 'em woe:
For all averred, I had killed the bird
That made the breeze to blow.
Ah wretch! said they, the bird to slay,
That made the breeze to blow!

5. Swoon.

But when the fog cleared off, they justify the same, and thus make themselves accomplices in the crime.

Nor dim nor red, like God's own head,
The glorious Sun uprist:
Then all averred, I had killed the bird
That brought the fog and mist.
'Twas right, said they, such birds to slay,
That bring the fog and mist.

The fair breeze continues; the ship enters the Pacific Ocean, and sails northward, even till it reaches the Line.

The fair breeze blew, the white foam flew,
The furrow followed free;
We were the first that ever burst
Into that silent sea.

The ship hath been suddenly becalmed.

Down dropt the breeze, the sails dropt down,
'Twas sad as sad could be;
And we did speak only to break
The silence of the sea!

All in a hot and copper sky,
The bloody Sun, at noon,
Right up above the mast did stand,
No bigger than the Moon.

Day after day, day after day,
We stuck, nor breath nor motion;
As idle as a painted ship
Upon a painted ocean.

And the Albatross begins to be avenged.

Water, water, every where,
And all the boards did shrink;
Water, water, every where,
Nor any drop to drink.

The very deep did rot: O Christ!
That ever this should be!
Yea, slimy things did crawl with legs
Upon the slimy sea.

About, about, in reel and rout
The death-fires danced at night;
The water, like a witch's oils,
Burnt green, and blue and white.

A spirit had followed them; one of the invisible inhabitants of this planet, neither departed souls nor angels; concerning whom the learned Jew, Josephus, and the Platonic Constantinopolitan, Michael Psellus, may be consulted. They are very numerous, and there is no climate or element without one or more.

And some in dreams assured were
Of the spirit that plagued us so;
Nine fathom deep he had followed us
From the land of mist and snow.

And every tongue, through utter drought,
Was withered at the root;
We could not speak, no more than if
We had been choked with soot.

The shipmates, in their sore distress, would fain throw the whole guilt on the ancient Mariner: in sign whereof they hang the dead sea bird round his neck.

Ah! well-a-day! what evil looks
Had I from old and young!
Instead of the cross, the Albatross
About my neck was hung.

Part 3

There passed a weary time. Each throat
Was parched, and glazed each eye.
A weary time! a weary time!
How glazed each weary eye,
When looking westward, I beheld
A something in the sky.

The ancient Mariner beholdeth a sign in the element afar off.

At first it seemed a little speck,
And then it seemed a mist;
It moved and moved, and took at last
A certain shape, I wist.[6]

A speck, a mist, a shape, I wist!
And still it neared and neared:
As if it dodged a water-sprite,
It plunged and tacked and veered.

At its nearer approach, it seemeth him to be a ship; and at a dear ransom he freeth his speech from the bonds of thirst.

With throats unslaked, with black lips baked,
We could nor laugh nor wail;
Through utter drought all dumb we stood!
I bit my arm, I sucked the blood,
And cried, A sail! a sail!

A flash of joy;

With throats unslaked, with black lips baked,
Agape they heard me call:
Gramercy![7] they for joy did grin,
And all at once their breath drew in,
As they were drinking all.

And horror follows. For can it be a ship that comes onward without wind or tide?

See! see! (I cried) she tacks no more!
Hither to work us weal;[8]
Without a breeze, without a tide,
She steadies with upright keel!

6. Knew.
7. Great thanks!
8. Benefit.

The western wave was all a-flame.
The day was well nigh done!
Almost upon the western wave
Rested the broad bright Sun;
When that strange shape drove suddenly
Betwixt us and the Sun.

It seemeth him but the skeleton of a ship.

And straight the Sun was flecked with bars,
(Heaven's Mother send us grace!)
As if through a dungeon-grate he peered
With broad and burning face.

Alas! (thought I, and my heart beat loud)
How fast she nears and nears!
Are those her sails that glance in the Sun,
Like restless gossameres?

And its ribs are seen as bars on the face of the setting Sun. The specter-woman and her death-mate, and no other on board the skeleton-ship.

Are those her ribs through which the Sun
Did peer, as through a grate?
And is that Woman all her crew?
Is that a Death? and are there two?
Is Death that woman's mate?

Like vessel, like crew!

Her lips were red, her looks were free,
Her locks were yellow as gold:
Her skin was as white as leprosy,
The Night-mare Life-in-Death was she,
Who thicks man's blood with cold.

Death and Life-in-death have diced for the ship's crew, and she (the latter) winneth the ancient Mariner.

The naked hulk alongside came,
And the twain were casting dice;
"The game is done! I've won! I've won!"
Quoth she, and whistles thrice.

No twilight within the courts of the sun.

The Sun's rim dips; the stars rush out:
At one stride comes the dark;
With far-heard whisper, o'er the sea,
Off shot the spectre-bark.

At the rising of the Moon,

We listened and looked sideways up!
Fear at my heart, as at a cup,
My life-blood seemed to sip!
The stars were dim, and thick the night,
The steersman's face by his lamp gleamed white;

From the sails the dew did drip—
Till clomb above the eastern bar
The horned Moon, with one bright star
Within the nether tip.

One after another,

One after one, by the star-dogged Moon,
Too quick for groan or sigh,
Each turned his face with a ghastly pang,
And cursed me with his eye.

His shipmates drop down dead.

Four times fifty living men,
(And I heard nor sigh nor groan)
With heavy thump, a lifeless lump,
They dropped down one by one.

But Life-in-Death begins her work on the ancient Mariner.

The souls did from their bodies fly,—
They fled to bliss or woe!
And every soul, it passed me by,
Like the whizz of my cross-bow!

Part 4

The wedding guest feareth that a spirit is talking to him.

"I fear thee, ancient Mariner!
I fear thy skinny hand!
And thou art long, and lank, and brown,
As is the ribbed sea-sand.

But the ancient Mariner assureth him of his bodily life, and proceedeth to relate his horrible penance.

I fear thee and thy glittering eye,
And thy skinny hand, so brown."—
Fear not, fear not, thou wedding-guest!
This body dropt not down.

Alone, alone, all, all alone,
Alone on a wide wide sea!
And never a saint took pity on
My soul in agony.

He despiseth the creatures of the calm,

The many men, so beautiful!
And they all dead did lie:
And a thousand thousand slimy things
Lived on; and so did I.

And envieth that they should live, and so many lie dead.

I looked upon the rotting sea,
And drew my eyes away;
I looked upon the rotting deck,
And there the dead men lay.

I looked to heaven, and tried to pray;
But or ever a prayer had gusht,
A wicked whisper came, and made
My heart as dry as dust.

I closed my lids, and kept them close,
And the balls like pulses beat;
For the sky and the sea, and the sea and the sky

Lay like a load on my weary eye,
And the dead were at my feet.

But the curse liveth for him in the eye of the dead men.

The cold sweat melted from their limbs,
Nor rot nor reek did they:
The look with which they looked on me
Had never passed away.

An orphan's curse would drag to hell
A spirit from on high;
But oh! more horrible than that
Is the curse in a dead man's eye!
Seven days, seven nights, I saw that curse,
And yet I could not die.

In his loneliness and fixedness he yearneth towards the journeying Moon, and the stars that still sojourn, yet still move onward; and everywhere the blue sky belongs to them, and is their appointed rest, and their native country and their own natural homes, which they enter unannounced, as lords that are certainly expected and yet there is a silent joy at their arrival.

The moving Moon went up the sky,
And no where did abide:
Softly she was going up,
And a star or two beside—

Her beams bemocked the sultry main,
Like April hoar-frost spread;
But where the ship's huge shadow lay,
The charmed water burnt alway
A still and awful red.

By the light of the Moon he beholdeth God's creatures of the great calm.

Beyond the shadow of the ship,
I watched the water-snakes:
They moved in tracks of shining white,
And when they reared, the elfish light
Fell off in hoary flakes.

Within the shadow of the ship
I watched their rich attire:
Blue, glossy green, and velvet black,
They coiled and swam; and every track
Was a flash of golden fire.

Their beauty and their happiness.

O happy living things! no tongue
Their beauty might declare:
A spring of love gushed from my heart,

He blesseth them in his heart.

And I blessed them unaware:
Sure my kind saint took pity on me,
And I blessed them unaware.

The spell begins to break.

The selfsame moment I could pray;
And from my neck so free
The Albatross fell off, and sank
Like lead into the sea.

Part 5

Oh sleep! it is a gentle thing,
Beloved from pole to pole!
To Mary Queen the praise be given!
She sent the gentle sleep from Heaven,
That slid into my soul.

By grace of the holy Mother, the ancient Mariner is refreshed with rain.

The silly[9] buckets on the deck,
That had so long remained,
I dreamt that they were filled with dew;
And when I awoke, it rained.

My lips were wet, my throat was cold,
My garments all were dank;
Sure I had drunken in my dreams,
And still my body drank.

I moved, and could not feel my limbs:
I was so light—almost
I thought that I had died in sleep,
And was a blessed ghost.

He heareth sounds and seeth strange sights and commotions in the sky and the element.

And soon I heard a roaring wind:
It did not come anear;
But with its sound it shook the sails,
That were so thin and sere.

The upper air burst into life!
And a hundred fire-flags sheen,[1]
To and fro they were hurried about!
And to and fro, and in and out,
The wan stars danced between.

And the coming wind did roar more loud,
And the sails did sigh like sedge;[2]
And the rain poured down from one black cloud;
The Moon was at its edge.

The thick black cloud was cleft, and still
The Moon was at its side:
Like waters shot from some high crag,
The lightning fell with never a jag,
A river steep and wide.

The bodies of the ship's crew are inspired, and the ship moves on;

The loud wind never reached the ship,
Yet now the ship moved on!
Beneath the lightning and the moon
The dead men gave a groan.

9. Simple.
1. Shone.
2. Flowering plant like a grass or rush.

They groaned, they stirred, they all uprose,
Nor spake, nor moved their eyes;
It had been strange, even in a dream,
To have seen those dead men rise.

The helmsman steered, the ship moved on;
Yet never a breeze up blew;
The mariners all 'gan work the ropes,
Where they were wont to do;
They raised their limbs like lifeless tools—
We were a ghastly crew.

The body of my brother's son
Stood by me, knee to knee:
The body and I pulled at one rope,
But he said nought to me.

But not by the souls of the men, nor by dæmons of earth or middle air, but by a blessed troop of angelic spirits, sent down by the invocation of the guardian saint.

"I fear thee, ancient Mariner!"
Be calm, thou Wedding-Guest!
'Twas not those souls that fled in pain,
Which to their corses[3] came again,
But a troop of spirits blest:

For when it dawned—they dropped their arms,
And clustered round the mast;
Sweet sounds rose slowly through their mouths,
And from their bodies passed.

Around, around, flew each sweet sound,
Then darted to the Sun;
Slowly the sounds came back again,
Now mixed, now one by one.

Sometimes a-dropping from the sky
I heard the sky-lark sing;
Sometimes all little birds that are,
How they seemed to fill the sea and air
With their sweet jargoning![4]

And now 'twas like all instruments,
Now like a lonely flute;
And now it is an angel's song,
That makes the heavens be mute.

It ceased; yet still the sails made on
A pleasant noise till noon,

3. Corpses.

4. Twittering.

A noise like of a hidden brook
In the leafy month of June,
That to the sleeping woods all night
Singeth a quiet tune.

Till noon we quietly sailed on,
Yet never a breeze did breathe:
Slowly and smoothly went the ship,
Moved onward from beneath.

The lonesome spirit from the south-pole carries on the ship as far as the line, in obedience to the angelic troop, but still requireth vengeance.

Under the keel nine fathom deep,
From the land of mist and snow,
The spirit slid: and it was he
That made the ship to go.
The sails at noon left off their tune,
And the ship stood still also.

The Sun, right up above the mast,
Had fixed her to the ocean:
But in a minute she 'gan stir,
With a short uneasy motion—
Backwards and forwards half her length
With a short uneasy motion.

Then like a pawing horse let go,
She made a sudden bound:
It flung the blood into my head,
And I fell down in a swound.

The Polar Spirit's fellow dæmons, the invisible inhabitants of the element, take part in his wrong; and two of them relate, one to the other, that penance long and heavy for the ancient Mariner hath been accorded to the Polar Spirit, who returneth southward.

How long in that same fit I lay,
I have not to declare;
But ere my living life returned,
I heard and in my soul discerned
Two voices in the air.

"Is it he?" quoth one, "Is this the man?
By him who died on cross,
With his cruel bow he laid full low
The harmless Albatross.

The spirit who bideth by himself
In the land of mist and snow,
He loved the bird that loved the man
Who shot him with his bow."

The other was a softer voice,
As soft as honey-dew:
Quoth he, "The man hath penance done,
And penance more will do."

Part 6

FIRST VOICE

"But tell me, tell me! speak again,
Thy soft response renewing—
What makes that ship drive on so fast?
What is the ocean doing?"

SECOND VOICE

"Still as a slave before his lord,
The ocean hath no blast;
His great bright eye most silently
Up to the Moon is cast—

If he may know which way to go;
For she guides him smooth or grim.
See, brother, see! how graciously
She looketh down on him."

The Mariner hath been cast into a trance; for the angelic power causeth the vessel to drive northward faster than human life could endure.

FIRST VOICE

"But why drives on that ship so fast,
Without or wave or wind?"

SECOND VOICE

"The air is cut away before,
And closes from behind.

Fly, brother, fly! more high, more high!
Or we shall be belated:
For slow and slow that ship will go,
When the Mariner's trance is abated."

The supernatural motion is retarded; the Mariner awakes, and his penance begins anew.

I woke, and we were sailing on
As in a gentle weather:
'Twas night, calm night, the moon was high;
The dead men stood together.

All stood together on the deck,
For a charnel-dungeon fitter:
All fixed on me their stony eyes,
That in the Moon did glitter.

The pang, the curse, with which they died,
Had never passed away:
I could not draw my eyes from theirs,
Nor turn them up to pray.

The curse is finally expiated.

And now this spell was snapt: once more
I viewed the ocean green,
And looked far forth, yet little saw
Of what had else been seen—

Like one, that on a lonesome road
Doth walk in fear and dread,
And having once turned round walks on,
And turns no more his head;
Because he knows, a frightful fiend
Doth close behind him tread.

But soon there breathed a wind on me,
Nor sound nor motion made:
Its path was not upon the sea,
In ripple or in shade.

It raised my hair, it fanned my cheek
Like a meadow-gale of spring—
It mingled strangely with my fears,
Yet it felt like a welcoming.

Swiftly, swiftly flew the ship,
Yet she sailed softly too:
Sweetly, sweetly blew the breeze—
On me alone it blew.

And the ancient Mariner beholdeth his native country.

Oh! dream of joy! is this indeed
The light-house top I see?
Is this the hill? is this the kirk?
Is this mine own countree?

We drifted o'er the harbour-bar,
And I with sobs did pray—
O let me be awake, my God!
Or let me sleep alway.

The harbour-bay was clear as glass,
So smoothly it was strewn!
And on the bay the moonlight lay,
And the shadow of the moon.

The rock shone bright, the kirk no less,
That stands above the rock:
The moonlight steeped in silentness
The steady weathercock.

And the bay was white with silent light,
Till rising from the same,

The angelic spirits leave the dead bodies,

Full many shapes, that shadows were,
In crimson colours came.

And appear in their own forms of light.

A little distance from the prow
Those crimson shadows were:
I turned my eyes upon the deck—
Oh, Christ! what saw I there!

Each corse lay flat, lifeless and flat,
And, by the holy rood![5]
A man all light, a seraph-man,
On every corse there stood.

This seraph-band, each waved his hand:
It was a heavenly sight!
They stood as signals to the land,
Each one a lovely light;

This seraph-band, each waved his hand,
No voice did they impart—
No voice; but oh! the silence sank
Like music on my heart.

But soon I heard the dash of oars,
I heard the Pilot's cheer;
My head was turned perforce away,
And I saw a boat appear.

The Pilot and the Pilot's boy,
I heard them coming fast:
Dear Lord in Heaven! it was a joy
The dead men could not blast.

I saw a third—I heard his voice:
It is the Hermit good!
He singeth loud his godly hymns
That he makes in the wood.
He'll shrieve my soul, he'll wash away
The Albatross's blood.

Part 7

The Hermit of the wood,

This Hermit good lives in that wood
Which slopes down to the sea.
How loudly his sweet voice he rears!
He loves to talk with marineres
That come from a far countree.

5. Cross.

He kneels at morn, and noon, and eve—
He hath a cushion plump:
It is the moss that wholly hides
The rotted old oak-stump.

The skiff-boat neared: I heard them talk,
"Why, this is strange, I trow!
Where are those lights so many and fair,
That signal made but now?"

Approacheth the ship with wonder.

"Strange, by my faith!" the Hermit said—
"And they answered not our cheer!
The planks looked warped! and see those sails,
How thin they are and sere!
I never saw aught like to them,
Unless perchance it were

Brown skeletons of leaves that lag
My forest-brook along;
When the ivy-tod[6] is heavy with snow,
And the owlet whoops to the wolf below,
That eats the she-wolf's young."

"Dear Lord! it hath a fiendish look"—
(The Pilot made reply)
"I am a-feared"—"Push on, push on!"
Said the Hermit cheerily.

The boat came closer to the ship,
But I nor spake nor stirred;
The boat came close beneath the ship,
And straight a sound was heard.

The ship suddenly sinketh.

Under the water it rumbled on,
Still louder and more dread:
It reached the ship, it split the bay;
The ship went down like lead.

The ancient Mariner is saved in the Pilot's boat.

Stunned by that loud and dreadful sound,
Which sky and ocean smote,
Like one that hath been seven days drowned
My body lay afloat;
But swift as dreams, myself I found
Within the Pilot's boat.

Upon the whirl, where sank the ship,
The boat spun round and round;
And all was still, save that the hill
Was telling of the sound.

6. Ivy bush.

I moved my lips—the Pilot shrieked
And fell down in a fit;
The holy Hermit raised his eyes,
And prayed where he did sit.

I took the oars: the Pilot's boy,
Who now doth crazy go,
Laughed loud and long, and all the while
His eyes went to and fro.
"Ha! ha!" quoth he, "full plain I see,
The Devil knows how to row."

And now, all in my own countree,
I stood on the firm land!
The Hermit stepped forth from the boat,
And scarcely he could stand.

The ancient Mariner earnestly entreateth the Hermit to shrieve him; and the penance of life falls on him.

"O shrieve me, shrieve me, holy man!"
The Hermit crossed his brow.
"Say quick," quoth he, "I bid thee say—
What manner of man art thou?"

Forthwith this frame of mine was wrenched
With a woful agony,
Which forced me to begin my tale;
And then it left me free.

And ever and anon throughout his future life an agony constraineth him to travel from land to land.

Since then, at an uncertain hour,
That agony returns:
And till my ghastly tale is told,
This heart within me burns.

I pass, like night, from land to land;
I have strange power of speech;
That moment that his face I see,
I know the man that must hear me:
To him my tale I teach.

What loud uproar bursts from that door!
The wedding-guests are there:
But in the garden-bower the bride
And bride-maids singing are:
And hark the little vesper bell,
Which biddeth me to prayer!

O Wedding-Guest! this soul hath been
Alone on a wide wide sea:
So lonely 'twas, that God himself
Scarce seemed there to be.

O sweeter than the marriage-feast,
'Tis sweeter far to me,
To walk together to the kirk
With a goodly company!—

To walk together to the kirk,
And all together pray,
While each to his great Father bends,
Old men, and babes, and loving friends,
And youths and maidens gay!

And to teach, by his own example, love and reverence to all things that God made and loveth.

Farewell, farewell! but this I tell
To thee, thou Wedding-Guest!
He prayeth well, who loveth well
Both man and bird and beast.

He prayeth best, who loveth best
All things both great and small;
For the dear God who loveth us,
He made and loveth all.

The Mariner, whose eye is bright,
Whose beard with age is hoar,
Is gone: and now the Wedding-Guest
Turned from the bridegroom's door.

He went like one that hath been stunned,
And is of sense forlorn:
A sadder and a wiser man,
He rose the morrow morn.

Kubla Khan

Or, a Vision in a Dream. A Fragment

The following fragment is here published at the request of a poet of great and deserved celebrity [Lord Byron], and, as far as the Author's own opinions are concerned, rather as a psychological curiosity, than on the ground of any supposed *poetic* merits.

In the summer of the year 1797, the Author, then in ill health, had retired to a lonely farm-house between Porlock and Linton, on the Exmoor confines of Somerset and Devonshire.[1] In consequence of a slight indisposition, an anodyne had been prescribed, from the effects of which he fell asleep in his chair at the moment that he was reading the following sentence, or words of the

1. A high moorland shared by the two southwestern counties in England.

same substance, in "Purchas's Pilgrimage":[2] "Here the Khan Kubla commanded a palace to be built, and a stately garden thereunto. And thus ten miles of fertile ground were inclosed with a wall." The Author continued for about three hours in a profound sleep, at least of the external senses, during which time he has the most vivid confidence, that he could not have composed less than from two to three hundred lines; if that indeed can be called composition in which all the images rose up before him as *things*, with a parallel production of the correspondent expressions, without any sensation or consciousness of effort.[3] On awaking he appeared to himself to have a distinct recollection of the whole, and taking his pen, ink, and paper, instantly and eagerly wrote down the lines that are here preserved. At this moment he was unfortunately called out by a person on business from Porlock, and detained by him above an hour, and on his return to his room, found, to his no small surprise and mortification, that though he still retained some vague and dim recollection of the general purport of the vision, yet, with the exception of some eight or ten scattered lines and images, all the rest had passed away like the images on the surface of a stream into which a stone has been cast, but, alas! without the after restoration of the latter!

Then all the charm
Is broken—all that phantom-world so fair
Vanishes, and a thousand circlets spread,
And each mis-shape[s] the other. Stay awhile,
Poor youth! who scarcely dar'st lift up thine eyes—
The stream will soon renew its smoothness, soon
The visions will return! And lo, he stays,
And soon the fragments dim of lovely forms
Come trembling back, unite, and now once more
The pool becomes a mirror.[4]

Yet from the still surviving recollections in his mind, the Author has frequently purposed to finish for himself what had been originally, as it were, given to him. Σαμερον αδιον ασω:[5] but the to-morrow is yet to come. . . .

In Xanadu did Kubla Khan[6]
A stately pleasure-dome decree:
Where Alph,[7] the sacred river, ran

2. Samuel Purchas (1575?–1626) published *Purchas, his Pilgrimage; or, Relations of the World and the Religions observed in all Ages* in 1613. The passage in Purchas is slightly different: "In Xamdu did Cublai Can build a stately Palace, encompassing sixteene miles of plaine ground with a wall, wherein are fertile meddowes, pleasant Springs, delightfull Streames, and all sorts of beasts of chase and game, and in the middest thereof a sumptuous house of pleasure, which may be removed from place to place" (IV.13).

3. Coleridge's statement that he dreamed the poem and wrote down what he could later remember verbatim has been queried, most recently by medical opinion. The belief that opium produces special dreams or even any dreams at all lacks confirmation.

4. From Coleridge's poem *The Picture; or, The Lover's Resolution*, lines 91–100.

5. From Theocritus's *Idylls* 1.145: "I'll sing a sweeter song tomorrow" (Greek).

6. Mongol emperor (1215?–1294), visited by Marco Polo.

7. J. L. Lowes, in *The Road to Xanadu* (1927), thinks that Coleridge may have had in mind the river Alpheus—linked with the Nile—mentioned by Virgil.

Through caverns measureless to man
  Down to a sunless sea.
So twice five miles of fertile ground
With walls and towers were girdled round:
And there were gardens bright with sinuous rills,
Where blossomed many an incense-bearing tree;
And here were forests ancient as the hills,
Enfolding sunny spots of greenery.

But oh! that deep romantic chasm which slanted
Down the green hill athwart a cedarn cover!
A savage place! as holy and enchanted
As e'er beneath a waning moon was haunted
By woman wailing for her demon-lover!
And from this chasm, with ceaseless turmoil seething,
As if this earth in fast thick pants were breathing,
A mighty fountain momently was forced:
Amid whose swift half-intermitted burst
Huge fragments vaulted like rebounding hail,
Or chaffy grain beneath the thresher's flail:
And 'mid these dancing rocks at once and ever
It flung up momently the sacred river.
Five miles meandering with a mazy motion
Through wood and dale the sacred river ran,
Then reached the caverns measureless to man,
And sank in tumult to a lifeless ocean:
And 'mid this tumult Kubla heard from far
Ancestral voices prophesying war!

  The shadow of the dome of pleasure
  Floated midway on the waves;
  Where was heard the mingled measure
  From the fountain and the caves.
It was a miracle of rare device,
A sunny pleasure-dome with caves of ice!
  A damsel with a dulcimer
  In a vision once I saw:
  It was an Abyssinian maid,
  And on her dulcimer she played,
  Singing of Mount Abora.[8]
  Could I revive within me
  Her symphony and song,
  To such a deep delight 'twould win me,
That with music loud and long,
I would build that dome in air,
That sunny dome! those caves of ice!
And all who heard should see them there,
And all should cry, Beware! Beware!

8. Lowes argues that this may have been "Mt. Amara," mentioned by Milton in *Paradise Lost* (4.28), or Amhara in Samuel Johnson's *Rasselas*.

His flashing eyes, his floating hair!
Weave a circle round him thrice,
And close your eyes with holy dread,
For he on honey-dew hath fed,
And drunk the milk of Paradise.

Frost at Midnight

The frost performs its secret ministry,
Unhelped by any wind. The owlet's cry
Came loud—and hark, again! loud as before.
The inmates of my cottage, all at rest,
Have left me to that solitude, which suits
Abstruser musings: save that at my side
My cradled infant slumbers peacefully.
'Tis calm indeed! so calm, that it disturbs
And vexes meditation with its strange
And extreme silentness. Sea, hill, and wood,
This populous village! Sea, and hill, and wood,
With all the numberless goings on of life,
Inaudible as dreams! the thin blue flame
Lies on my low burnt fire, and quivers not;
Only that film,[1] which fluttered on the grate,
Still flutters there, the sole unquiet thing.
Methinks, its motion in this hush of nature
Gives it dim sympathies with me who live,
Making it a companionable form,
Whose puny flaps and freaks the idling Spirit
By its own moods interprets, every where
Echo or mirror seeking of itself,
And makes a toy of Thought.

But O! how oft,
How oft, at school, with most believing mind,
Presageful, have I gazed upon the bars,
To watch that fluttering stranger! and as oft
With unclosed lids, already had I dreamt
Of my sweet birth-place, and the old church-tower,
Whose bells, the poor man's only music, rang
From morn to evening, all the hot Fair-day,
So sweetly, that they stirred and haunted me
With a wild pleasure, falling on mine ear

1. In all parts of the kingdom these films are called *strangers* and supposed to portend the arrival of some absent friend [Coleridge's note]. The term "film" here refers to a piece of soot fluttering on the fire grate.

Most like articulate sounds of things to come!
So gazed I, till the soothing things I dreamt
Lulled me to sleep, and sleep prolonged my dreams!
And so I brooded all the following morn,
Awed by the stern preceptor's[2] face, mine eye
Fixed with mock study on my swimming book:
Save if the door half opened, and I snatched
A hasty glance, and still my heart leaped up,
For still I hoped to see the stranger's face,
Townsman, or aunt, or sister more beloved,
My play-mate when we both were clothed alike![3]

Dear Babe, that sleepest cradled by my side,
Whose gentle breathings, heard in this deep calm,
Fill up the interspersed vacancies
And momentary pauses of the thought!
My babe so beautiful! it thrills my heart
With tender gladness, thus to look at thee,
And think that thou shalt learn far other lore
And in far other scenes! For I was reared
In the great city, pent 'mid cloisters dim,
And saw nought lovely but the sky and stars.
But thou, my babe! shalt wander like a breeze
By lakes and sandy shores, beneath the crags
Of ancient mountain, and beneath the clouds,
Which image in their bulk both lakes and shores
And mountain crags: so shalt thou see and hear
The lovely shapes and sounds intelligible
Of that eternal language, which thy God
Utters, who from eternity doth teach
Himself in all, and all things in himself.
Great universal Teacher! he shall mould
Thy spirit, and by giving make it ask.

Therefore all seasons shall be sweet to thee,
Whether the summer clothe the general earth
With greenness, or the redbreast sit and sing
Betwixt the tufts of snow on the bare branch
Of mossy apple-tree, while the nigh thatch
Smokes in the sun-thaw; whether the eave-drops fall
Heard only in the trances of the blast,
Or if the secret ministry of frost
Shall hang them up in silent icicles,
Quietly shining to the quiet Moon.

2. Teacher's.
3. Boys and girls were dressed in the same clothes when very young.

JOHN KEATS

John Keats (1795–1821) established himself as one of the greatest of all English poets in a career that lasted less than five years. His first published work appeared in 1816, and his life ended—"blighted in the bud," as the poet **Percy Shelley** put it—in 1821, just as he had reached the height of his powers. Readers have long speculated about what would have happened to his writing, and to the history of English poetry, if he had lived just a few years longer. Keats himself knew well that his life could be cut short; he had watched his mother and brother die of tuberculosis, and he diagnosed his own mortal illness. Written in the full awareness of a terrifying mortality, Keats's poetry exults in the intensity of bodily, sensual experience. And even in this briefest of writing careers, Keats produced a varied, original, and formally dazzling body of work. His linguistic richness, taut craftsmanship, and skill in harmonizing sounds and rhythms have influenced many poets to follow, while he grapples with themes that have moved generations of readers: aching desire, the dreadful coming of death, and the seductive power of beauty.

LIFE

John Keats began his life in comparatively lowly surroundings. He was the eldest son of an ostler, a laborer who looked after horses at a London inn, and the inn-owner's daughter. His father died when he was eight years old, and Keats's mother remarried within a few months. At the time Keats was a student at the progressive Enfield Academy, where the schoolmasters embraced political reform, skepticism, and religious dissent. The young Keats often started fights with other boys, earning a reputation for a hot temper. Called "little Keats" into adulthood, he never grew taller than five feet in height. After his father's death he began to work extraordinarily hard at his studies, hungrily reading poetry in particular, including the work of Edmund Spenser—his favorite poet—as well as Virgil, Chaucer, Dante, Shakespeare, Milton, **Wordsworth**, and Byron.

Miserable in her second marriage, Keats's mother disappeared altogether for some time. Eventually she returned to her children, but only after she had begun to suffer from a deadly case of tuberculosis. John nursed her in her final illness, caring for her passionately and possessively. She died when he was fourteen years old. Soon afterward, Keats's guardian decided to apprentice him to a surgeon. These were the days before anesthesia, which meant patients writhed in pain under the surgeon's knife. Keats found this horrifying, and he stayed with his medical training only long enough to become an apothecary—the lowest rung on the medical ladder—before dedicating himself to writing poetry. His first volume garnered many harshly critical reviews, including one that called him "an uneducated and flimsy stripling."

At the end of 1818 Keats's younger brother Tom died of tuberculosis, and the poet threw himself into writing, producing all of his greatest work in just one remarkable year: "The Eve of Saint Agnes," "La Belle Dame sans Merci," "Lamia," the completion of his long poem *Hyperion*, all of his great odes, and a group of dazzling sonnets, including "Bright Star." This was the same year as the Peterloo Massacre, the government's violent killing of peaceful civilians. (Shelley's poem in this volume, "England in 1819," describes the corruption and severity of government censorship at this moment.) It was also the year that Keats fell in love with a London neighbor named Fanny Brawne. He was possessive, she flirtatious, and his letters reveal him as an impassioned and jealous lover.

Their love was doomed, however, by Keats's poverty and growing ill-health. A history of debts, unwise loans, and ongoing struggles to earn money prevented Keats from proposing marriage. Then, early in 1820, he suffered a lung hemorrhage. His medical training led him to recognize this as his "death warrant." He was told that he would not survive another British winter, and so he set out for Italy. It was in this final stretch of his life that his work finally earned favorable reviews, and Keats felt hopeful that he would eventually be ranked with the great English poets. He died in Rome at the age of twenty-five.

KEATS AND THE "COCKNEY SCHOOL" OF POETRY

In 1817 the radical poet and editor Leigh Hunt published Keats's first poem and hailed him as one of the most exciting of a new generation of poets who were casting off the orderly, decorous, neoclassical poetic styles associated with the eighteenth century—in particular the work of **Alexander Pope**. Detractors lumped Keats and Hunt together as the "Cockney School" of poets. Cockneys are working-class Londoners from the heart of the city, and this name conveyed contempt for what critics saw as the poets' low social class, lack of education, and vulgarity.

There was no question that the Cockney poets were up to something quite new. They flagrantly broke with poetic convention in a number of obvious ways: their work sparkled with clever, innovative turns of phrase—often making adverbs out of participles, such as "crushingly," or turning verbs into adjectives, as in "scattery light." They also refused Pope's favorite form of "closed couplets," which contained a completed sentence in two rhyming lines, in favor of "open couplets," where the thought spilled out beyond the end of the rhyme. Even more shockingly, they delighted in erotic imagery and sensuous language, which invited readers to linger on bodily pleasures: "delicious" was a particular favorite.

The Cockney poets also led a return to the roughness and sensuous vitality of the pagan ancient Greeks, which they saw as fundamentally different from the eighteenth-century English version of the Greeks as delicate "toys." Keats's poem "On First Looking into Chapman's Homer" would have seemed polemical at the time: the poet is pointedly celebrating Chapman's "loud and bold" seventeenth-century translation of the ancient Greek poet over the neatly rhymed, standard translation of his own time—that of Alexander Pope. (When one of Keats's readers expressed surprise that he evoked the Greeks so well, despite his meager education, Percy Shelley answered curtly, "He *was* a Greek.")

Contemporaries contrasted the Cockney School with the poets they called the "Lake School"—most prominently **William Wordsworth** and **Samuel Taylor Coleridge**. Keats mulled a great deal on Wordsworth, who provided both inspiration and irritation for the younger poet. In place of the "egotistical sublime"—Keats's term for Wordsworth's focus on the self—he embraced the model of the "chameleon poet" who has "no identity" but takes delight in things other than himself. Keats also criticized Coleridge, who lacked what he famously called "negative capability": "when a man is capable of being in uncertainties, Mysteries, doubts, without any irritable reaching after fact & reason."

WORKS

Keats's work richly rewards the reader in a broad range of ways. His luxurious language and sumptuous imagery invite us to take pleasure in the sensuous beauty of poetry; his meticulous crafting of poetic forms—the architecture of lines, stanzas, and figures—is flawless; his numerous allusions to other writers are thoughtful and suggestive; and his uses of poetic forms to dwell on death, love, pain, art, and nature are philosophically penetrating. For many readers, Keats is among the very few poets in English who have combined these elements with such skill.

Keats's poetry insistently dwells on antitheses and contradictions. "Bright Star" invokes the paradox of "sweet unrest," for example, while the "Ode to a Nightingale" opens with the oxymoronic claim that "numbness" can give "pain." These two poems also foreground a fundamental Keatsian opposition: the distance between the fully sensuous experience of human bodies, which are doomed to die, and that which lasts beyond the human lifespan but has no experience of its pleasures—the star or the transcendent song of the nightingale. But far from offering a simple contrast between these two states, Keats often pushes one of these so far that it turns into its opposite: in "Ode to a Nightingale," the poet longs for a lived experience of wine and sunshine so intense that he will "fade away" and become like the immortal nightingale, remote from lived experience. Leigh Hunt spoke of Keats's "poetical *concentrations*," and it is typical of his poetry to find conflicting experiences fused together. In "Ode to a Nightingale," for example, the poet speaks of "tasting . . . the country green," an example of synaesthesia—the mixing up of the senses—that violates conventional distinctions. His poems are thick with linguistic activity—meticulously wrought metaphors, puns, allusions, echoes within and across poems, and multiple kinds of poetic diction—all working together in a single text.

Keats's odes, perhaps his greatest works of all, participate in a tradition of English odes that are addressed to a serious and dignified object—such as an artwork, a mood, or a mythological figure. Keats, like other writers of odes, uses these objects to reflect on the nature and power of poetry. Each of his odes responds to and builds on the one before, and they echo and oppose one another in provocative ways. For example, "Ode to a Nightingale" and "Ode on a Grecian Urn" are like mirror images: the first compares poetry to music, suppressing visual experience in favor of aural; the second contrasts poetry to visual art while suppressing sound. Keats also builds his odes around repeated rhetorical forms: his insistent questions in "Ode on a Grecian Urn," for example, or the recurring form of the list in "To Autumn."

Collected here are four of Keats's greatest odes, as well as some shorter poems that give a sense of his variety as a writer: three sonnets and a ballad, "La Belle Dame sans Merci," a spare and haunting half-told story that draws on medieval style and subject matter. Two sonnets—"When I Have Fears That I May Cease to Be" and "Bright Star"—follow the Shakespearian sonnet form: three quatrains (groups of four alternately rhyming lines: abab) followed by one rhyming couplet. Keats complained that the closing rhyme of Shakespearian sonnets was "seldom pleasing." He also disliked the "pouncing rhymes" of the traditional Petrarchan sonnet, though he used the form sometimes (as in "On First Looking into Chapman's Homer"). The ten-line stanza form of his odes can be seen as a joining of the two traditions: each starts with a Shakespearian quatrain and ends with a Petrarchan sestet (six lines that rhyme every third: cdecde). His discomfort with traditional forms and the desire for a more balanced and varied rhyme scheme attests to Keats's seriousness and originality as an architect of poetic structure: he cares deeply about the ways that stanzas, rhymes, rhythms, and line lengths punctuate, organize, and work together in complex composite wholes. But he is more than a mere craftsman: Keats's intricate structures are there to serve his exquisite meditations on poetry, love, and the looming fact of death.

On First Looking into Chapman's Homer[1]

Much have I traveled in the realms of gold,
And many goodly states and kingdoms seen;
Round many western islands have I been
Which bards in fealty to Apollo[2] hold.
Oft of one wide expanse had I been told
That deep-browed Homer ruled as his demesne;[3]
Yet did I never breathe its pure serene
Till I heard Chapman speak out loud and bold:
Then felt I like some watcher of the skies
When a new planet swims into his ken;
Or like stout Cortez[4] when with eagle eyes
He stared at the Pacific—and all his men
Looked at each other with a wild surmise—
Silent, upon a peak in Darien.

When I Have Fears That I May Cease to Be

When I have fears that I may cease to be
Before my pen has glean'd my teeming brain,
Before high piled books, in charactry,[1]
Hold like rich garners the full ripen'd grain;
When I behold, upon the night's starr'd face,

1. Keats's friend and former teacher Charles Cowden Clarke had introduced Keats to George Chapman's (1559?–1634) translations of the *Iliad* (1611) and the *Odyssey* (1616) the night before this poem was written.
2. The Greek god of poetic inspiration.
3. Realm, kingdom.
4. In fact, Vasco Núñez de Balboa (ca. 1475–1519), Spanish conquistador, not Hernán Cortés (1485–1547), another Spaniard, was the European explorer who first saw the Pacific from Darién, Panama.

1. Printed letters.

Huge cloudy symbols of a high romance,
And think that I may never live to trace
Their shadows, with the magic hand of chance;
And when I feel, fair creature of an hour,
That I shall never look upon thee more,
Never have relish in the fairy power
Of unreflecting love;—then on the shore
Of the wide world I stand alone, and think
Till love and fame to nothingness do sink.

Bright Star

Bright star, would I were steadfast as thou art—
Not in lone splendor hung aloft the night,
And watching, with eternal lids apart,
Like nature's patient, sleepless Eremite,[1]
The moving waters at their priestlike task
Of pure ablution round earth's human shores,
Or gazing on the new soft fallen mask
Of snow upon the mountains and the moors—
No—yet still steadfast, still unchangeable,
Pillowed upon my fair love's ripening breast,
To feel forever its soft fall and swell,
Awake forever in a sweet unrest,
Still, still to hear her tender-taken breath,
And so live ever—or else swoon to death.

La Belle Dame sans Merci[1]

I

O what can ail thee, knight at arms,
Alone and palely loitering?
The sedge has withered from the lake
And no birds sing!

II

O what can ail thee, knight at arms,
So haggard, and so woebegone?
The squirrel's granary is full
And the harvest's done.

1. Hermit.
1. "The beautiful lady without pity" (French); from a medieval poem by Alain Chartier.

III

I see a lily on thy brow
  With anguish moist and fever dew,
And on thy cheeks a fading rose
  Fast withereth too.

IV

I met a lady in the meads,[2]
  Full beautiful, a faery's child,
Her hair was long, her foot was light
  And her eyes were wild.

V

I made a garland for her head,
  And bracelets too, and fragrant zone;[3]
She looked at me as she did love
  And made sweet moan.

VI

I set her on my pacing steed
  And nothing else saw all day long,
For sidelong would she bend and sing
  A faery's song.

VII

She found me roots of relish sweet,
  And honey wild, and manna[4] dew,
And sure in language strange she said
  "I love thee true."

VIII

She took me to her elfin grot[5]
  And there she wept and sighed full sore,[6]
And there I shut her wild wild eyes
  With kisses four.

IX

And there she lullèd me asleep,
  And there I dreamed, ah woe betide!

2. Meadows. Here the knight answers the question asked in lines 5–6.
3. Girdle.
4. The supernatural substance with which God fed the children of Israel in the wilderness (Exodus 16 and Joshua 5.12).
5. Cavern.
6. With great grief.

The latest[7] dream I ever dreamt
   On the cold hill's side.

X

I saw pale kings, and princes too,
   Pale warriors, death-pale were they all;
They cried, "La belle dame sans merci
   Thee hath in thrall!"[8]

XI

I saw their starved lips in the gloam[9]
   With horrid warning gapèd wide,
And I awoke, and found me here
   On the cold hill's side.

XII

And this is why I sojourn here,
   Alone and palely loitering;
Though the sedge withered from the lake
   And no birds sing.

Ode on a Grecian Urn

I

Thou still unravished bride of quietness,
   Thou foster-child of silence and slow time,
Sylvan historian, who canst thus express
   A flowery tale more sweetly than our rhyme:
What leaf-fringed legend haunts about thy shape
   Of deities or mortals, or of both,
      In Tempe or the dales of Arcady?[1]
   What men or gods are these? What maidens loth?
What mad pursuit? What struggle to escape?
      What pipes and timbrels? What wild ecstasy?

II

Heard melodies are sweet, but those unheard
   Are sweeter; therefore, ye soft pipes, play on;
Not to the sensual ear, but, more endeared,

7. Last.
8. Bondage.
9. Twilight.
1. A mountainous region in the Peloponnese, traditionally regarded as the place of ideal rustic, bucolic contentment. "Tempe": a valley in Thessaly between Mount Olympus and Mount Ossa.

Pipe to the spirit ditties of no tone:
Fair youth, beneath the trees, thou canst not leave
Thy song, nor ever can those trees be bare;
Bold lover, never, never canst thou kiss,
Though winning near the goal—yet, do not grieve;
She cannot fade, though thou hast not thy bliss,
For ever wilt thou love, and she be fair!

III

Ah, happy, happy boughs! that cannot shed
Your leaves, nor ever bid the Spring adieu;
And, happy melodist, unwearièd,
For ever piping songs for ever new;
More happy love! more happy, happy love!
For ever warm and still to be enjoyed,
For ever panting, and for ever young;
All breathing human passion far above,
That leaves a heart high-sorrowful and cloyed,
A burning forehead, and a parching tongue.

IV

Who are these coming to the sacrifice?
To what green altar, O mysterious priest,
Lead'st thou that heifer lowing at the skies,
And all her silken flanks with garlands drest?
What little town by river or sea shore,
Or mountain-built with peaceful citadel,
Is emptied of this folk, this pious morn?
And, little town, thy streets for evermore
Will silent be; and not a soul to tell
Why thou art desolate, can e'er return.

V

O Attic shape! Fair attitude! with brede[2]
Of marble men and maidens overwrought,
With forest branches and the trodden weed;
Thou, silent form, dost tease us out of thought
As doth eternity: Cold Pastoral!
When old age shall this generation waste,
Thou shalt remain, in midst of other woe
Than ours, a friend to man, to whom thou say'st,
"Beauty is truth, truth beauty,"—that is all
Ye know on earth, and all ye need to know.

2. Pattern. "Attic": classical (literally, Athenian).

Ode to a Nightingale

I

My heart aches, and a drowsy numbness pains
My sense, as though of hemlock I had drunk,
Or emptied some dull opiate to the drains
One minute past, and Lethe-wards[1] had sunk:
'Tis not through envy of thy happy lot,
But being too happy in thy happiness,
That thou, light-wingèd Dryad[2] of the trees,
In some melodious plot
Of beechen green, and shadows numberless,
Singest of summer in full-throated ease.

II

O for a draught of vintage! that hath been
Cooled a long age in the deep-delvèd earth,
Tasting of Flora[3] and the country green,
Dance, and Provençal[4] song, and sunburnt mirth!
O for a beaker full of the warm South!
Full of the true, the blushful Hippocrene,[5]
With beaded bubbles winking at the brim,
And purple-stainèd mouth;
That I might drink, and leave the world unseen,
And with thee fade away into the forest dim:

III

Fade far away, dissolve, and quite forget
What thou among the leaves hast never known,
The weariness, the fever, and the fret
Here, where men sit and hear each other groan;
Where palsy shakes a few, sad, last gray hairs,
Where youth grows pale, and spectre-thin, and dies;
Where but to think is to be full of sorrow
And leaden-eyed despairs;
Where beauty cannot keep her lustrous eyes,
Or new love pine at them beyond tomorrow.

IV

Away! away! for I will fly to thee,
Not charioted by Bacchus and his pards,[6]

1. I.e., toward Lethe, the river of forgetfulness in Greek mythology.
2. Wood nymph.
3. The goddess of flowers and spring; here, flowers.
4. From Provence, the region in France associated with the troubadours.
5. The fountain on Mount Helicon, in Greece, sacred to the muse of poetry.
6. Leopards. Bacchus (Dionysus) was traditionally supposed to be accompanied by leopards, lions, goats, and so on.

But on the viewless wings of Poesy,
Though the dull brain perplexes and retards:
Already with thee! tender is the night,
And haply[7] the Queen-Moon is on her throne,
Clustered around by all her starry Fays;[8]
But here there is no light,
Save what from heaven is with the breezes blown
Through verdurous glooms and winding mossy ways.

V

I cannot see what flowers are at my feet,
Nor what soft incense hangs upon the boughs,
But, in embalmèd darkness, guess each sweet
Wherewith the seasonable month endows
The grass, the thicket, and the fruit-tree wild;
White hawthorn, and the pastoral eglantine;
Fast-fading violets covered up in leaves;
And mid-May's eldest child,
The coming musk-rose, full of dewy wine,
The murmurous haunt of flies on summer eves.

VI

Darkling[9] I listen; and for many a time
I have been half in love with easeful Death,
Called him soft names in many a musèd rhyme,
To take into the air my quiet breath;
Now more than ever seems it rich to die,
To cease upon the midnight with no pain,
While thou art pouring forth thy soul abroad
In such an ecstasy!
Still wouldst thou sing, and I have ears in vain—
To thy high requiem become a sod.[1]

VII

Thou wast not born for death, immortal Bird!
No hungry generations tread thee down;
The voice I hear this passing night was heard
In ancient days by emperor and clown:
Perhaps the self-same song that found a path
Through the sad heart of Ruth, when, sick for home,
She stood in tears amid the alien corn;[2]
The same that ofttimes hath
Charmed magic casements, opening on the foam
Of perilous seas, in faery lands forlorn.

7. By chance.
8. Fairies.
9. In the dark.
1. I.e., like dirt, unable to hear.
2. See the Book of Ruth. After her Ephrathite husband died, she returned to his native land with her mother-in-law.

VIII

Forlorn! the very word is like a bell
  To toll me back from thee to my sole self!
Adieu! the fancy cannot cheat so well
  As she is famed to do, deceiving elf.
Adieu! adieu! thy plaintive anthem fades
  Past the near meadows, over the still stream,
    Up the hill-side; and now 'tis buried deep
        In the next valley-glades:
  Was it a vision, or a waking dream?
    Fled is that music:—do I wake or sleep?

Ode on Melancholy

I

No, no, go not to Lethe,[1] neither twist
  Wolfsbane, tight-rooted, for its poisonous wine;
Nor suffer thy pale forehead to be kissed
  By nightshade, ruby grape of Proserpine;[2]
Make not your rosary of yew-berries,[3]
  Nor let the beetle, nor the death-moth[4] be
    Your mournful Psyche,[5] nor the downy owl
A partner in your sorrow's mysteries;
  For shade to shade will come too drowsily,
    And drown the wakeful anguish of the soul.

II

But when the melancholy fit shall fall
  Sudden from heaven like a weeping cloud,
That fosters the droop-headed flowers all,
  And hides the green hill in an April shroud;
Then glut thy sorrow on a morning rose,
  Or on the rainbow of the salt sand-wave,
    Or on the wealth of globèd peonies;
Or if thy mistress some rich anger shows,
  Imprison her soft hand, and let her rave,
    And feed deep, deep upon her peerless eyes.

1. The river of forgetfulness in Hades.
2. Wife of Pluto, queen of the underworld.
3. Wolfsbane, nightshade, and yew berries are all poisonous.
4. The death's-head moth has markings that resemble a skull. The scarab beetle, often depicted in Egyptian tombs, was an emblem of death.
5. The soul, portrayed by the Greeks as a butterfly.

III

She[6] dwells with Beauty—Beauty that must die;
And Joy, whose hand is ever at his lips
Bidding adieu; and aching Pleasure nigh,
Turning to Poison while the bee-mouth sips:
Aye, in the very temple of Delight
Veiled Melancholy has her sovereign shrine,
Though seen of none save him whose strenuous tongue
Can burst Joy's grape against his palate fine;
His soul shall taste the sadness of her might,
And be among her cloudy trophies hung.[7]

To Autumn

I

Season of mists and mellow fruitfulness,
Close bosom-friend of the maturing sun;
Conspiring with him how to load and bless
With fruit the vines that round the thatch-eaves run;
To bend with apples the mossed cottage-trees,
And fill all fruit with ripeness to the core;
To swell the gourd, and plump the hazel shells
With a sweet kernel; to set budding more,
And still more, later flowers for the bees,
Until they think warm days will never cease,
For Summer has o'er-brimmed their clammy cells.

II

Who hath not seen thee oft amid thy store?
Sometimes whoever seeks abroad may find
Thee sitting careless on a granary floor,
Thy hair soft-lifted by the winnowing wind;
Or on a half-reaped furrow sound asleep,
Drowsed with the fume of poppies, while thy hook
Spares the next swath and all its twinèd flowers:
And sometimes like a gleaner thou dost keep
Steady thy laden head across a brook;
Or by a cyder-press, with patient look,
Thou watchest the last oozings hours by hours.

6. Melancholy.
7. The Greeks placed war trophies in their temples to commemorate victories.

III

Where are the songs of Spring? Ay, where are they?
  Think not of them, thou hast thy music too,—
While barrèd clouds bloom the soft-dying day,
  And touch the stubble-plains with rosy hue;
Then in a wailful choir the small gnats mourn
  Among the river sallows,[8] borne aloft
    Or sinking as the light wind lives or dies;
And full-grown lambs loud bleat from hilly bourn;
  Hedge-crickets sing; and now with treble soft
  The red-breast whistles from a garden-croft;
    And gathering swallows twitter in the skies.

8. Willows.

GIACOMO LEOPARDI

Giacomo Leopardi (1798–1837) is one of Italy's greatest lyric poets. Born into an aristocratic family in a dreary provincial town, he was extraordinarily precocious, learning faster than any tutor could teach him. As an adolescent, he read several hundred pages a day, translated and commented on ancient texts, and wrote volumes of his own plays, essays, and poems. Yet it was far from a happy childhood. In his well-known diary, Leopardi explained that his mother purposefully reproached her children in order to "make them well aware of their defects . . . and to convince them with a fierce, pitiless veracity of their inevitable misery." In late adolescence, Leopardi's health began to break down—he became almost blind, his spine curved over—and his family encouraged him to become a priest. But he had begun to lose faith in God, and what followed was thoroughgoing, even paralyzing skepticism, as he began to see human life as little more than agonizing suffering. Even as he grew to be a famous poet, he remained almost completely trapped in his parents' house, with no income of his own. He had three painful experiences of unrequited love, and died at the age of thirty-nine.

It is not surprising, then, that Leopardi is, above all, a poet of despair, one who casts life as doomed, sorrowful, and purposeless. And yet both natural and artistic beauty seem to provide a brief respite from this anguish. His own art has often felt to readers strangely uplifting, filled with pleasure and solace, despite the sadness of his themes. In his most famous lyric, "The Infinite" (1819), the poet has the sublime feeling—both pleasurable and frightening—of imagining infinity, which extends beyond his own restricted vision, and he willingly celebrates the feeling of drowning in this endlessness. Readers have long appreciated the musical beauty of "To Silvia" (1828). The despairing late poem "To Himself" (1833) was written after Leopardi had been rejected by a woman he loved. While most other Italian Romantic writers looked outward—toward national political struggles—Leopardi resolutely turned inward, to explore the painful intensity of an individual human life.

The Infinite[1]

This lonely hill has always been so dear
To me, and dear the hedge which hides away
The reaches of the sky. But sitting here
And wondering, I fashion in my mind
The endless spaces far beyond, the more
Than human silences, and deepest peace;
So that the heart is on the edge of fear.
And when I hear the wind come blowing through
The trees, I pit its voice against that boundless
Silence and summon up eternity,
And the dead seasons, and the present one,
Alive with all its sound. And thus it is
In this immensity my thought is drowned:
And sweet to me the foundering in this sea.

To Himself

Now you may rest forever,
My tired heart. The last illusion is dead
That I believed eternal. Dead. I can
So clearly see—not only hope is gone
But the desire to be deceived as well.
Rest, rest forever.
You have beaten long enough. Nothing is worth
Your smallest motion, nor the earth your sighs.
This life is bitterness
And vacuum, nothing else. The world is mud.
From now on calm yourself.
Despair for the last time. The only gift
Fate gave our kind was death. Henceforth, heap scorn
Upon yourself, Nature, the ugly force
That, hidden, orders universal ruin,
And the boundless emptiness of everything.

1. All three poems are translated by Ottavio M. Casale.

To Sylvia

Sylvia. Do you remember still
The moments of your mortal lifetime here,
When such a loveliness
Shone in the elusive laughter of your eyes,
And you, contemplative and gay, climbed toward
The summit of your youth?

The tranquil chambers held,
The paths re-echoed, your perpetual song,
When at your woman's tasks
You sat, content to concentrate upon
The future beckoning within your mind.
It was the fragrant May,
And thus you passed your time.

I often used to leave
The dear, belabored pages which consumed
So much of me and of my youth, and from
Ancestral balconies
Would lean to hear the music of your voice,
Your fingers humming through
The intricacies of the weaving work.
And I would gaze upon
The blue surrounding sky,
The paths and gardens golden in the sun,
And there the far-off sea, and here the mountain.
No human tongue can tell
What I felt then within my brimming heart.

What tendernesses then,
What hopes, what hearts were ours, O Sylvia mine!
How large a thing seemed life, and destiny!
When I recall those bright anticipations,
Bitterness invades,
And I turn once again to mourn my lot.
O Nature, Nature, why
Do you not keep the promises you gave?
Why trick the children so?

Before the winter struck the summer grass,
You died, my gentle girl,
Besieged by hidden illness and possessed.
You never saw the flowering of your years.
Your heart was never melted by the praise
Of your dark hair, your shy,
Enamoured eyes. Nor did you with your friends
Conspire on holidays to talk of love.

The expectation failed
As soon for me, and fate denied my youth.
Ah how gone by, gone by,
You dear companion of my dawning time,
The hope that I lament!
Is this the world we knew? And these the joys
The love, the labors, happenings we shared?
And this the destiny
Of human beings? My poor one, when
The truth rose up, you fell,
And from afar you pointed me the way
To coldest death and the stark sepulchre.

CHARLES BAUDELAIRE

Crowds and prostitutes, boredom and hypocrisy, garbage and cheap perfume: from these ugly materials, Charles Baudelaire crafted such shocking, painful, and exquisite poetry that he became the most widely read French poet around the globe. Haunted by a vision of human nature as fallen and corrupt, he was drawn to explore his own weaknesses and transgressions, as well as the sins of society. Lust, hatred, laziness, a disabling self-awareness, a horror of death and decay, and above all an all-encompassing *ennui*—a kind of disgusted, existential boredom—consumed the poet. But it is not only this anguished worldview that makes Baudelaire so significant: for many thinkers who followed, he opened the way to understanding what it means to be modern, to live in the exciting, disorienting, technologically changing, often hideous world of the industrialized city. And for writers, what is so extraordinary about Baudelaire is that he examined the unsettling shocks of modernity through perfectly controlled and beautiful art forms.

LIFE

Born in Paris in 1821, Baudelaire quickly became a rebellious youth. His elderly father died when he was six, and his mother married a stern military man whom the young Baudelaire came to detest. In his late teens, he was expelled from boarding school and sent away on a boat to India to remove him from bad influences. He jumped ship on the African island of Mauritius, then slowly wended his way home without ever reaching India. Back in Paris, he began to consort with artists, bohemians, and prostitutes in the famous Latin Quarter. By his early twenties, he had contracted syphilis and had started to spend his father's inheritance with alarming speed, buying up gorgeous furniture, dandyish clothing, and costly paintings. In 1842 he fell passionately in love with a woman named Jeanne Duval, an actress of African descent, who lived with him on and off for most of his adult life. To his family, he seemed to be going nowhere. His mother was disturbed at his spending habits and obtained a court order to control his finances. Humiliated, Baudelaire remained for the rest of his life dependent on an allowance dispensed by the family lawyer.

In 1845 he published a work of art criticism that established his reputation as a writer, and he would go on to write important reviews of painting and photography, championing the most daring contemporary art. In the 1850s he reviewed and translated the works of American writer Edgar Allan Poe, who shared his dedication to beauty, his fascination with death, and his passion for perfectly crafted writing. Only in 1857, at the age of thirty-six, did his first slim volume of poetry appear. With its horrifyingly evocative images of lust, duplicity, and decay, *The Flowers of Evil* was fully intended to scandalize its readers. It succeeded. French authorities seized the book and fined the writer, making Baudelaire famous—but more reviled than admired. Ever more ill and in debt, Baudelaire spent his last years in distress. He added new poems to *The Flowers of Evil* and began to write some experimental works that would come to be known as *Paris Spleen*. He died in 1867, leaving behind few admirers. At the graveside, in the pouring rain, accompanied by a few stragglers, only one close friend predicted that Baudelaire would someday be recognized as a "poet of genius."

BAUDELAIRE'S PARIS

Most French poets of the first half of the nineteenth century were drawn to the beauties of the natural world: to mountains, lakes, and flowers. Baudelaire was different. "I find myself incapable of feeling moved by vegetation," he wrote. Instead, he observed the social life of the city.

At the time, Paris was an exciting and disorienting place. It grew rapidly over the first few decades of the nineteenth century, as new industries drew peasants from the impoverished countryside in search of work. Competing for badly paid jobs, the urban poor were visible everywhere, many of them sick from factory smoke, or reduced to beggary and prostitution. Also visible in the city, however, were the glossy carriages and flamboyant dresses of the rich. Commentators often remarked that on a single stroll through the city one might find ragpickers searching through street refuse for scraps to sell, as well as glittering new shopping arcades offering seductive, mass-produced commodities for wealthy consumers. Everything in this modern world, it seemed, could be bought and sold.

During the 1850s the streets of Paris underwent a huge transformation, as the government razed winding old alleyways and installed clean, wide boulevards in their place. These smooth streets radiated outward to allow easy access to the city center from many directions. The poor were evicted and moved in large numbers to the suburbs, while gleaming new apartment houses, street cafes, shops, and theaters rose up quickly. In this new urban milieu, one encountered vast numbers of strangers. Dramatically unlike village life, the city typically felt both crowded and lonely, both stimulating and alienating. Baudelaire used the term *flâneur*—meaning "saunterer"—to refer to those who wandered alone and detached through urban streets to experience the city's fleeting spectacles. Many of the first *flâneurs* were writers who found a new kind of inspiration in this fragmented experience. And so the bustling commercial city became an important literary theme, supplanting rural beauty for self-consciously "modern" writers in the decades to follow.

WORK

It is difficult to grasp just how shocking Baudelaire's work must have seemed to his contemporaries. French poets before him typically worked in what was called the "noble style," which was formal and elevated, deliberately remote from everyday speech. Poets were not supposed to refer to ordinary objects (even the word "nose" was forbidden as prosaic). We can only imagine, then, how outrageous Baudelaire's deliberately brutal wording—"pissing hogwash" or "lecherous whore"—must have seemed. And not only did he offer up explicit, often coarse, images of the body, but his contemporaries were horrified to find him willing to connect sexual desire to the horrors of sadism and putrefaction, as we see in his poem "A Carcass."

And yet it would be misleading to see Baudelaire as rejecting beauty: he luxuriated in gorgeous, lavish, and exotic images, and crafted passages of lyrical magnificence. Unlike some of his other rebellious-poet contemporaries—such as **Walt Whitman**, born just two years before him—Baudelaire loved strictly traditional metrical forms and rhyme schemes. And so it is worth exploring the ways that the poet associates the shockingly foul with the traditionally lovely. Even the very title of his volume, *The Flowers of Evil*, signals the juxtaposition of beauty with corruption.

Always attracted by dissonance and contrast, Baudelaire is famous for his irony—his willingness to undermine one perspective with another more-knowing, cynical point of view. Many of his works explore both lived experience and the desire to stand skeptically apart from that experience. In the process, Baudelaire's poetic speakers often emerge as self-divided, torn between beautiful ideals and what he called "spleen," a thoroughgoing disgust with life. (The ancient Greeks had believed that sadness originated with fluids of the spleen.)

Late in his life, Baudelaire experimented with "prose poems"—then highly innovative and, according to many of his contemporaries, confusingly paradoxical. Dissolving the distinction between poetry and prose, these brief pieces lack the line breaks associated with poetry, but they feel like lyric, capturing brief moments of experience in compressed and meditative passages. For Baudelaire, this kind of writing was momentous: he claimed to dream of "the miracle of a poetic prose, musical, without rhythm and without rhyme, supple enough and rugged enough to adapt itself to the lyrical impulses of the soul."

The Flowers of Evil

To the Reader[1]

Infatuation, sadism, lust, avarice
possess our souls and drain the body's force;
we spoonfeed our adorable remorse,
like whores or beggars nourishing their lice.

Our sins are mulish, our confessions lies;
we play to the grandstand with our promises,

1. Translated by Robert Lowell. The translation pays primary attention to the insistent rhythm of the original poetic language and keeps the *abba* rhyme scheme.

we pray for tears to wash our filthiness,
importantly pissing hogwash through our styes.

The devil, watching by our sickbeds, hissed
old smut and folk-songs to our soul, until
the soft and precious metal of our will
boiled off in vapor for this scientist.

Each day his flattery[2] makes us eat a toad,
and each step forward is a step to hell,
unmoved, though previous corpses and their smell
asphyxiate our progress on this road.

Like the poor lush who cannot satisfy,
we try to force our sex with counterfeits,
die drooling on the deliquescent tits,
mouthing the rotten orange we suck dry.

Gangs of demons are boozing in our brain—
ranked, swarming, like a million warrior-ants,[3]
they drown and choke the cistern of our wants;
each time we breathe, we tear our lungs with pain.

If poison, arson, sex, narcotics, knives
have not yet ruined us and stitched their quick,
loud patterns on the canvas of our lives,
it is because our souls are still too sick.[4]

Among the vermin, jackals, panthers, lice,
gorillas and tarantulas that suck
and snatch and scratch and defecate and fuck
in the disorderly circus of our vice,

there's one more ugly and abortive birth.
It makes no gestures, never beats its breast,
yet it would murder for a moment's rest,[5]
and willingly annihilate the earth.

It's BOREDOM. Tears have glued its eyes together.
You know it well, my Reader. This obscene
beast chain-smokes yawning for the guillotine—
you—hypocrite Reader—my double—my brother!

2. The devil is literally described as a puppet master controlling our strings.
3. Literally, intestinal worms.
4. Literally, not bold enough.
5. Literally, swallow the world in a yawn.

Correspondences[1]

Nature is a temple whose living colonnades
Breathe forth a mystic speech in fitful sighs;
Man wanders among symbols in those glades
Where all things watch him with familiar eyes.

Like dwindling echoes gathered far away
Into a deep and thronging unison
Huge as the night or as the light of day,
All scents and sounds and colors meet as one.

Perfumes there are as sweet as the oboe's sound,
Green as the prairies, fresh as a child's caress,[2]
—And there are others, rich, corrupt, profound[3]

And of an infinite pervasiveness,
Like myrrh, or musk, or amber,[4] that excite
The ecstasies of sense, the soul's delight.

Her Hair[1]

O fleece, that down the neck waves to the nape!
O curls! O perfume nonchalant and rare!
O ecstacy! To fill this alcove[2] shape
With memories that in these tresses sleep,
I would shake them like pennons in the air!

Languorous Asia, burning Africa,
And a far world, defunct almost, absent,
Within your aromatic forest stay!
As other souls on music drift away,
Mine, o my love! still floats upon your scent.

I shall go there where, full of sap, both tree
And man swoon in the heat of southern climes;
Strong tresses, be the swell that carries me!
I dream upon your sea of ebony
Of dazzling sails, of oarsmen, masts and flames:

A sun-drenched and reverberating port,
Where I imbibe color and sound and scent;

1. Translated by Richard Wilbur. The translation keeps the intricate melody of the sonnet's original rhyme scheme.
2. Literally, flesh.
3. Literally, triumphant.
4. Or ambergris, a substance secreted by whales. Ambergris and musk (a secretion of the male musk deer) are used in making perfume.

1. Translated by Doreen Bell. The translation emulates the French original's challenging *abaab* rhyme pattern.
2. Bedroom.

Where vessels, gliding through the gold and moire,
Open their vast arms as they leave the shore
To clasp the pure and shimmering firmament.

I'll plunge my head, enamored of its pleasure,
In this black ocean where the other hides;
My subtle spirit then will know a measure
Of fertile idleness and fragrant leisure,
Lulled by the infinite rhythm of its tides!

Pavilion, of blue-shadowed tresses spun,
You give me back the azure from afar;
And where the twisted locks are fringed with down
Lurk mingled odors I grow drunk upon
Of oil of coconut, of musk and tar.

A long time! always! my hand in your hair
Will sow the stars of sapphire, pearl, ruby,
That you be never deaf to my desire,
My oasis and gourd whence I aspire
To drink deep of the wine of memory![3]

A Carcass[1]

Remember, my love, the item you saw
  That beautiful morning in June:
By a bend in the path a carcass reclined
  On a bed sown with pebbles and stones;

Her legs were spread out like a lecherous whore,
  Sweating out poisonous fumes,
Who opened in slick invitational style
  Her stinking and festering womb.

The sun on this rottenness focused its rays
  To cook the cadaver till done,
And render to Nature a hundredfold gift
  Of all she'd united in one.

And the sky cast an eye on this marvelous meat
  As over the flowers in bloom.

3. The last two lines are a question: "Are you not . . . ?"

1. Translated by James McGowan with special attention to imagery. The alternation of long and short lines in English emulates the French meter's rhythmic swing between twelve- and eight-syllable lines in an *abab* rhyme scheme.

The stench was so wretched that there on the grass
You nearly collapsed in a swoon.

The flies buzzed and droned on these bowels of filth
Where an army of maggots arose,
Which flowed like a liquid and thickening stream
On the animate rags of her clothes.

And it rose and it fell, and pulsed like a wave,
Rushing and bubbling with health.
One could say that this carcass, blown with vague breath,
Lived in increasing itself.

And this whole teeming world made a musical sound
Like babbling brooks and the breeze,
Or the grain that a man with a winnowing-fan
Turns with a rhythmical ease.

The shapes wore away as if only a dream
Like a sketch that is left on the page
Which the artist forgot and can only complete
On the canvas, with memory's aid.

From back in the rocks, a pitiful bitch
Eyed us with angry distaste,
Awaiting the moment to snatch from the bones
The morsel she'd dropped in her haste.

—And you, in your turn, will be rotten as this:
Horrible, filthy, undone,
Oh sun of my nature and star of my eyes,
My passion, my angel[2] in one!

Yes, such will you be, oh regent of grace,
After the rites have been read,
Under the weeds, under blossoming grass
As you molder with bones of the dead.

Ah then, oh my beauty, explain to the worms
Who cherish your body so fine,
That I am the keeper for corpses of love
Of the form, and the essence divine![3]

2. Series of conventional Petrarchan images that idealize the beloved.

3. "Any form created by man is immortal. For form is independent of matter . . ." (from Baudelaire's journal *My Heart Laid Bare* 80).

Invitation to the Voyage[1]

My child, my sister, dream
How sweet all things would seem
Were we in that kind land to live together,
And there love slow and long,
There love and die among
Those scenes that image you, that sumptuous weather.
Drowned suns that glimmer there
Through cloud-disheveled air
Move me with such a mystery as appears
Within those other skies
Of your treacherous eyes
When I behold them shining through their tears.

There, there is nothing else but grace and measure,
Richness, quietness, and pleasure.

Furniture that wears
The lustre of the years
Softly would glow within our glowing chamber,
Flowers of rarest bloom
Proffering their perfume
Mixed with the vague fragrances of amber;
Gold ceilings would there be,
Mirrors deep as the sea,
The walls all in an Eastern splendor hung—
Nothing but should address
The soul's loneliness,
Speaking her sweet and secret native tongue.

There, there is nothing else but grace and measure,
Richness, quietness, and pleasure.

See, sheltered from the swells
There in the still canals
Those drowsy ships that dream of sailing forth;
It is to satisfy
Your least desire, they ply
Hither through all the waters of the earth.
The sun at close of day
Clothes the fields of hay,
Then the canals, at last the town entire
In hyacinth and gold:
Slowly the land is rolled
Sleepward under a sea of gentle fire.

1. Translated by Richard Wilbur. The translation maintains both the rhyme scheme and the rocking motion of the original meter, which follows an unusual pattern of two five-syllable lines followed by one seven-syllable line, and a seven-syllable couplet as refrain.

There, there is nothing else but grace and measure,
Richness, quietness, and pleasure.

Song of Autumn I[1]

Soon we shall plunge into the chilly fogs;
Farewell, swift light! our summers are too short!
I hear already the mournful fall of logs
Re-echoing from the pavement of the court.

All of winter will gather in my soul:
Hate, anger, horror, chills, the hard forced work;
And, like the sun in his hell by the north pole,
My heart will be only a red and frozen block.

I shudder, hearing every log that falls;
No scaffold could be built with hollower sounds.
My spirit is like a tower whose crumbling walls
The tireless battering-ram brings to the ground.

It seems to me, lulled by monotonous shocks,
As if they were hastily nailing a coffin today.
For whom?—Yesterday was summer. Now autumn knocks.
That mysterious sound is like someone's going away.

Spleen LXXVIII[1]

Old Pluvius,[2] month of rains, in peevish mood
Pours from his urn chill winter's sodden gloom
On corpses fading in the near graveyard,
On foggy suburbs pours life's tedium.

My cat seeks out a litter on the stones,
Her mangy body turning without rest.
An ancient poet's soul in monotones
Whines in the rain-spouts like a chilblained ghost.

A great bell mourns, a wet log wrapped in smoke
Sings in falsetto to the wheezing clock,
While from a rankly perfumed deck of cards
(A dropsical old crone's fatal bequest)

1. Translated by C. F. MacIntyre to follow the original rhyme pattern.

1. Translated by Kenneth O. Hanson, with emphasis on the imagery. The French original uses identical *abab* rhymes in the two quatrains and shifts to *ccd, eed* in the tercets.

2. "The rainy time" (Latin, literal trans.); a period extending from January 20 to February 18 as the fifth month of the French Revolutionary calendar.

The Queen of Spades, the dapper Jack of Hearts
Speak darkly of dead loves, how they were lost.

Spleen LXXIX[1]

I have more memories than if I had lived a thousand years.

Even a bureau crammed with souvenirs,
Old bills, love letters, photographs, receipts,
Court depositions, locks of hair in plaits,
Hides fewer secrets than my brain could yield.
It's like a tomb, a corpse-filled Potter's Field,[2]
A pyramid where the dead lie down by scores.
I am a graveyard that the moon abhors:
Like guilty qualms, the worms burrow and nest
Thickly in bodies that I loved the best.
I'm a stale boudoir where old-fashioned clothes
Lie scattered among wilted fern and rose,
Where only the Boucher girls[3] in pale pastels
Can breathe the uncorked scents and faded smells.

Nothing can equal those days for endlessness
When in the winter's blizzardy caress
Indifference expanding to Ennui[4]
Takes on the feel of Immortality.
O living matter, henceforth you're no more
Than a cold stone encompassed by vague fear
And by the desert, and the mist and sun;
An ancient Sphinx ignored by everyone,
Left off the map, whose bitter irony
Is to sing as the sun sets in that dry sea.[5]

Spleen LXXXI[1]

When the low heavy sky weighs like a lid
Upon the spirit aching for the light
And all the wide horizon's line is hid
By a black day sadder than any night;

1. Translated by Anthony Hecht. The translation follows the original rhymed couplets, except for one technical impossibility: Baudelaire's repetition (in a poem about monotony) of an identical rhyme for eight lines (lines 11–18, the sound of long *a*).
2. A general term describing the common cemetery for those buried at public expense.
3. François Boucher (1703–1770), court painter for Louis XV of France, drew many pictures of young women clothed and nude.
4. Melancholy, paralyzing boredom.
5. Baudelaire combines two references to ancient Egypt, the Sphinx and the legendary statue of Memnon at Thebes, which was supposed to sing at sunset.
1. Translated by Sir John Squire in accord with the original rhyme scheme.

When the changed earth is but a dungeon dank
Where batlike Hope goes blindly fluttering
And, striking wall and roof and mouldered plank,
Bruises his tender head and timid wing;

When like grim prison bars stretch down the thin,
Straight, rigid pillars of the endless rain,
And the dumb throngs of infamous spiders spin
Their meshes in the caverns of the brain,

Suddenly, bells leap forth into the air,
Hurling a hideous uproar to the sky
As 'twere a band of homeless spirits who fare
Through the strange heavens, wailing stubbornly.

And hearses, without drum or instrument,
File slowly through my soul; crushed, sorrowful,
Weeps Hope, and Grief, fierce and omnipotent,
Plants his black banner on my drooping skull.

The Voyage[1]

To Maxime du Camp[2]

I

The child, in love with prints and maps,
Holds the whole world in his vast appetite.
How large the earth is under the lamplight!
But in the eyes of memory, how the world is cramped!

We set out one morning, brain afire,
Hearts fat with rancor and bitter desires,
Moving along to the rhythm of wind and waves,
Lull the inner infinite on the finite of seas:

Some are glad, glad to leave a degraded home;
Others, happy to shake off the horror of their hearts,
Still others, astrologers drowned in the eyes of woman—
Oh the perfumes of Circe,[3] the power and the pig!—

To escape conversion to the Beast, get drunk
On space and light and the flames of skies;

1. Translated by Charles Henri Ford. The French poem is written in the traditional twelve-syllable (alexandrine) line with an *abab* rhyme scheme.
2. A wry dedication to the progress-oriented author of *Modern Songs* (1855), which began "I was born a traveler."
3. In Homer's *Odyssey*, an island sorceress who changed visitors into beasts. Odysseus's men were transformed into pigs.

The tongue of the sun and the ice that bites
Slowly erase the mark of the Kiss.

But the true voyagers are those who leave
Only to be going; hearts nimble as balloons,
They never diverge from luck's black sun,
And with or without reason, cry, Let's be gone!

Desire to them is nothing but clouds,
They dream, as a draftee dreams of the cannon,
Of vast sensualities, changing, unknown,
Whose name the spirit has never pronounced!

II

We imitate—horrible!—the top and ball
In their waltz and bounce; even in sleep
We're turned and tormented by Curiosity,
Who, like a mad Angel, lashes the stars.

Peculiar fortune that changes its goal,
And being nowhere, is anywhere at all!
And Man, who is never untwisted from hope,
Scrambling like a madman to get some rest!

The soul's a three-master seeking Icaria;[4]
A voice on deck calls: "Wake up there!"
A voice from the mast-head, vehement, wild:
"Love . . . fame . . . happiness!" We're on the rocks!

Every island that the lookout hails
Becomes the Eldorado[5] foretold by Fortune;
Then Imagination embarks on its orgy
But runs aground in the brightness of morning.

Poor little lover of visionary fields!
Should he be put in irons, dumped in the sea,
This drunken sailor, discoverer of Americas,
Mirage that makes the gulf more bitter?

So the old vagabond, shuffling in mud,
Dreams, nose hoisted, of a shining paradise,
His charmed eye lighting on Capua's[6] coast
At every candle aglow in a hovel.

4. Greek island in the Aegean Sea named after the mythological Icarus, who, escaping from prison using wings made by his father, Daedalus, plunged into nearby waters and drowned when the wings gave way. His name was associated with utopian flights, as in Étienne Cabet's novel about a utopian community, *Voyage to Icaria* (1840). "Three-master": a ship.

5. Fabled country of gold and abundance.

6. City on the Volturno River in southern Italy, famous for its luxury and sensuality.

III

Astounding voyagers! what noble stories
We read in your eyes, deeper than seas;
Show us those caskets, filled with rich memories,
Marvelous jewels, hewn from stars and aether.

Yes, we would travel, without sail or steam!
Gladden a little our jail's desolation,
Sail over our minds, stretched like a canvas,
All your memories, framed with gold horizons.

Tell us, what have you seen?

IV

"We have seen stars
And tides; we have seen sands, too,
And, despite shocks and unforeseen disasters,
We were often bored, just as we are here.

The glory of sun on a violet sea,
The glory of cities in the setting sun,
Kindled our hearts with torment and longing
To plunge into the sky's magnetic reflections.

Neither the rich cities nor sublime landscapes,
Ever possessed that mysterious attraction
Of Change and Chance having fun with the clouds.
And always Desire kept us anxious!

—Enjoyment adds force to Appetite!
Desire, old tree nurtured by pleasure,
Although your dear bark thicken and harden,
Your branches throb to hold the sun closer!

Great tree, will you outgrow the cypress?
Still we have gathered carefully
Some sketches for your hungry album,
Brothers, for whom all things from far away

Are precious! We've bowed down to idols;
To thrones encrusted with luminous rocks;
To figured palaces whose magic pomp
Would ruin your bankers with a ruinous dream;

To costumes that intoxicate the eye,
To women whose teeth and nails are dyed,
To clever jugglers, fondled by the snake."[7]

7. Snake charmers. The images in this stanza evoke India.

V

And then, and what more?

VI

"O childish minds!

Not to forget the principal thing,
We saw everywhere, without looking for it,
From top to toe of the deadly scale,
The tedious drama of undying sin:

Woman, low slave, vain and stupid,
Without laughter self-loving, and without disgust,
Man, greedy despot, lewd, hard and covetous,
Slave of the slave, rivulet in the sewer;

The hangman exulting, the martyr sobbing;
Festivals that season and perfume the blood;[8]
The poison of power unnerving the tyrant,
The masses in love with the brutalizing whip;

Many religions, very like our own,
All climbing to heaven; and Holiness,
Like a delicate wallower in a feather bed,
Seeking sensation from hair shirts and nails.

Jabbering humanity, drunk with its genius,
As crazy now as it was in the past,
Crying to God in its raging agony:
'O master, fellow creature, I curse thee forever!'

And then the least stupid, brave lovers of Lunacy,
Fleeing the gross herd that Destiny pens in,
Finding release in the vast dreams of opium!
—Such is the story, the whole world over."

VII

Bitter knowledge that traveling brings!
The globe, monotonous and small, today,
Yesterday, tomorrow, always, throws us our image:
An oasis of horror in a desert of boredom!

Should we go? Or stay? If you can stay, stay;
But go if you must. Some run, some hide

8. Literally, "Festivals seasoned and perfumed by blood."

To outwit Time, the enemy so vigilant and
Baleful. And many, alas, must run forever

Like the wandering Jew[9] and the twelve apostles,
Who could not escape his relentless net[1]
By ship or by wheel; while others knew how
To destroy him without leaving home.

When finally he places his foot on our spine,
May we be able to hope and cry, Forward!
As in days gone by when we left for China,
Eyes fixed on the distance, hair in the wind,

With heart as light as a young libertine's
We'll embark on the sea of deepening shadows.
Do you hear those mournful, enchanting voices[2]
That sing: "Come this way, if you would taste

The perfumed Lotus. Here you may pick
Miraculous fruits for which the heart hungers.
Come and drink deep of this strange,
Soft afternoon that never ends?"

Knowing his voice, we visualize the phantom—
It is our Pylades there, his arms outstretched.
While she whose knees we used to kiss cries out,
"For strength of heart, swim back to your Electra!"[3]

VIII

O Death, old captain, it is time! weigh anchor!
This country confounds us; hoist sail and away!
If the sky and sea are black as ink,
Our hearts, as you know them, burst with blinding rays.

Pour us your poison, that last consoling draft!
For we long, so the fire burns in the brain,
To sound the abyss, Hell or Heaven, what matter?
In the depths of the Unknown, we'll discover the New!

9. According to medieval legend, a Jew who mocked Christ on his way to the cross and was condemned to wander unceasingly until Judgment Day.
1. These three stanzas describe Time (ultimately Death) as a Roman gladiator, the *retiarius*, who used a net to trap his opponent.
2. The voices of the dead, luring the sailor to the Lotus-land of ease and forgetfulness.
3. In Greek mythology, Orestes and Pylades were close friends ready to sacrifice their lives for each other. Electra was Orestes' faithful sister, who saved him from the Furies.

EMILY DICKINSON

In the 1880s, visitors to Amherst, Massachusetts, gossiped about the strange woman, dressed only in white gowns, who never left her father's house—except once, it was rumored, "to see a new church, when she crept out by night, and viewed it by moonlight." Neighbors and friends knew that this woman wrote, but she published only ten poems during her lifetime, and even those appeared anonymously. She begged those closest to her to burn her papers after her death. They refused, instead startling audiences by publishing Emily Dickinson's (1830–1886) unusual lyrics, with their passionate intensity, broken meter, slant rhymes, and unconventional dashes and capitalizations. From the moment that they first appeared, these poems have been beloved by both readers and critics. Dickinson's works can seem, on the one hand, like childlike and accessible meditations on such universal themes as death, faith, and nature, and on the other hand, like highly artful, philosophically demanding, and radically innovative experiments in lyric form. It is with this unlikely combination of innocence and sophistication that the mysterious Dickinson has become one of the best-known of American poets.

LIFE

Born to a prominent Amherst family—her father was elected to Congress—Dickinson attended Amherst Academy and later, for a year, the Mount Holyoke Female Seminary. Conflicted and ambivalent about Christian orthodoxy even as a child, she resisted the Puritan attitudes that surrounded her, especially at school. "Christ is calling everyone here," she wrote, "and I am standing alone in rebellion." This sense of isolation would only deepen. From early in her twenties, she confined herself almost entirely to her family home, leading the life of a recluse with her tyrannical father and absent-minded mother. She did have close attachments to her brother and sister, and she developed a few close friendships, though she pursued these mainly through correspondence. Some of her works reflect on the pain of unrequited love and erotic desire, and biographers have speculated about Dickinson's passions, but no scholar has been able to determine indisputably the name of the one—or ones—she loved.

Dickinson began writing verse seriously in the 1850s, putting groups of her poems together in fascicles (booklets of pages bound together by hand). In these works she seldom remarked on the burning issues of the day, from slavery and women's rights to the violence of the Civil War. Concerned with domestic matters and the torments of the soul, she can seem excruciatingly inward-looking. But her literary life was expansive. She wrote more than a thousand letters, linking herself to the outside world more readily by mail than by face-to-face contact. Dickinson also read widely. Shakespeare was a major touchstone (she once asked: "why is any other book needed?"), and she named **John Keats**, **Elizabeth Barrett Browning**, Robert Browning, and Charlotte Brontë as among her foremost inspirations.

In 1862, after seeing an article with advice for aspiring writers by Thomas Wentworth Higginson, Dickinson wrote to solicit his opinion of her poems. He was both enthusiastic and shocked, warning her away from publishing such unconventional work. Their friendship continued to the end of Dickinson's life. After her death, Dickinson's sister Lavinia was surprised to discover almost two thousand poems stashed away in a box, and she began the difficult task of trying to figure out how to edit and organize these works for publication, a process that has puzzled and divided editors ever since. Higginson was one of the first to publish volumes of Dickinson's poetry, editing the work to make it seem as conventional as he could.

WORK

With singular conviction and independence, Dickinson produced poetry unlike anyone else of her time. Her works are noteworthy, first of all, for their brevity and compression, throwing readers immediately into the thick of the poem, eschewing any preparation. And while she draws on familiar poetic themes—nature, death, love, and faith—she pushes her explorations of feeling to their most extreme intensity, and her images persistently unsettle expectation. Nature can turn out to be revolting, as when a bird devours a worm; the grandest subjects can turn ordinary, as when death appears as an everyday conveyance; and the human body can be estranged from itself, turned into a corpse, a gun, or a tomb.

Dickinson's use of meter is as striking as her imagery. She relies most heavily on popular metrical patterns associated with Protestant hymns, such as common meter (quatrains that begin with one line of eight syllables followed by a line of six syllables, repeated to form an 8/6/8/6 pattern). But while she depends on the hymnal, she also breaks with it. Sometimes she speeds up or slows down its familiar rhythms; and sometimes she even interrupts them altogether. For example, she introduces dashes that cluster syllables together in a way that interrupts the feeling of a smooth rhythm (as in the first line of one of her most famous poems, "I heard a Fly buzz—when I died"); or she changes meter suddenly (as in "I like to see it lap the Miles," a poem that opens and closes with common-meter quatrains but swerves into a different pattern altogether in the third stanza). Dickinson's rhymes also play with traditional patterns. In "A Bird came down the Walk," for example, she offers us a couple of perfect rhymes (saw/raw, Grass/pass). But in the same poem she gives us two slant rhymes (Crumb/home, seam/swim), and in the middle, where one expects a rhyme, she presents sounds that share a rough resemblance but do not rhyme at all (around/Head).

Perhaps most strikingly experimental of all is Dickinson's use of punctuation. Her dramatic dashes are famous, and the manuscripts suggest that they are even more innovative than they look on the printed page. In her own handwriting, Dickinson's dashes are of varying lengths, and sometimes turn up or down (a few are completely vertical). These marks do not always work the same way: sometimes her dashes draw thoughts together; at other times they separate them. And finally, while Dickinson capitalizes many important proper nouns, such as Soul and Beauty, she also opts to capitalize some unexpected words: Onset, for example, or Buckets.

That Dickinson never published these outrageously unconventional and demanding poems might not surprise us. Higginson had led her to believe that the world would not appreciate them, and the few of her poems that did appear in print in her lifetime were heavily edited to conform to unadventurous tastes. "Publication—is the Auction / Of the Mind of Man," she wrote, disgusted by the idea of selling what she cared for most. And so she withdrew to what she called the "freedom" of her narrow room to create great poetry for herself alone.

216

Safe in their Alabaster Chambers—
Untouched by Morning
And untouched by Noon—
Sleep the meek members of the Resurrection—
Rafter of satin,
And Roof of stone.

Light laughs the breeze
In her Castle above them—
Babbles the Bee in a stolid Ear,
Pipe the Sweet Birds in ignorant cadence—
Ah, what sagacity perished here!

258

There's a certain Slant of light,
Winter Afternoons—
That oppresses, like the Heft
Of Cathedral Tunes—

Heavenly Hurt, it gives us—
We can find no scar,
But internal difference,
Where the Meanings, are—

None may teach it—Any—
'Tis the Seal Despair—
An imperial affliction
Sent us of the Air—

When it comes, the Landscape listens—
Shadows—hold their breath—
When it goes, 'tis like the Distance
On the look of Death—

303

The Soul selects her own Society—
Then—shuts the Door—
To her divine Majority—
Present no more—

Unmoved—she notes the Chariots—pausing
At her low Gate—
Unmoved—an Emperor be kneeling
Upon her Mat—

I've known her—from an ample nation—
Choose One—
Then—close the Valves of her attention—
Like Stone—

328

A Bird came down the Walk—
He did not know I saw—
He bit an Angleworm in halves
And ate the fellow, raw,

And then he drank a Dew
From a convenient Grass—
And then hopped sidewise to the Wall
To let a Beetle pass—

He glanced with rapid eyes
That hurried all around—
They looked like frightened Beads, I thought—
He stirred his Velvet Head

Like one in danger, Cautious,
I offered him a Crumb
And he unrolled his feathers
And rowed him softer home—

Than Oars divide the Ocean,
Too silver for a seam—
Or Butterflies, off Banks of Noon
Leap, plashless as they swim.

341

After great pain, a formal feeling comes—
The Nerves sit ceremonious, like Tombs—

The stiff Heart questions was it He, that bore,
And Yesterday, or Centuries before?

The Feet, mechanical, go round—
Of Ground, or Air, or Ought[1]—
A Wooden way
Regardless grown,
A Quartz contentment, like a stone—

This is the Hour of Lead—
Remembered, if outlived,
As Freezing persons, recollect the Snow—
First—Chill—then Stupor—then the letting go—

435

Much Madness is divinest Sense—
To a discerning Eye—
Much Sense—the starkest Madness—
'Tis the Majority
In this, as All, prevail—
Assent—and you are sane—
Demur—you're straightway dangerous—
And handled with a Chain—

449

I died for Beauty—but was scarce
Adjusted in the Tomb
When One who died for Truth, was lain
In an adjoining Room—

He questioned softly "Why I failed"?
"For Beauty", I replied—
"And I—for Truth—Themself are One—
We Brethren, are", He said—

And so, as Kinsmen, met a Night—
We talked between the Rooms—
Until the Moss had reached our lips—
And covered up—our names—

465

I heard a Fly buzz—when I died—
The Stillness in the Room

1. Zero.

Was like the Stillness in the Air—
Between the Heaves of Storm—

The Eyes around—had wrung them dry—
And Breaths were gathering firm
For that last Onset—when the King
Be witnessed—in the Room—

I willed my Keepsakes—Signed away
What portion of me be
Assignable—and then it was
There interposed a Fly—

With Blue—uncertain stumbling Buzz—
Between the light—and me—
And then the Windows failed—and then
I could not see to see—

519

'Twas warm—at first—like Us—
Until there crept upon
A Chill—like frost upon a Glass—
Till all the scene—be gone.

The Forehead copied Stone—
The Fingers grew too cold
To ache—and like a Skater's Brook—
The busy eyes—congealed—

It straightened—that was all—
It crowded Cold to Cold
It multiplied indifference—
As[1] Pride were all it could—

And even when with Cords—
'Twas lowered, like a Weight—
It made no Signal, nor demurred,
But dropped like Adamant.

585

I like to see it lap the Miles—
And lick the Valleys up—
And stop to feed itself at Tanks—
And then—prodigious step

Around a Pile of Mountains—
And supercilious peer

1. As if.

In Shanties—by the sides of Roads—
And then a Quarry pare

To fit its Ribs
And crawl between
Complaining all the while
In horrid—hooting stanza—
Then chase itself down Hill—

And neigh like Boanerges[1]—
Then—punctual as a Star
Stop—docile and omnipotent
At its own stable door—

632

The Brain—is wider than the Sky—
For—put them side by side—
The one the other will contain
With ease—and You—beside—

The Brain is deeper than the sea—
For—hold them—Blue to Blue—
The one the other will absorb—
As Sponges—Buckets—do—

The Brain is just the weight of God—
For—Heft them—Pound for Pound—
And they will differ—if they do—
As Syllable from Sound—

657

I dwell in Possibility—
A fairer House than Prose—
More numerous of Windows—
Superior—for Doors—

Of Chambers as the Cedars—
Impregnable of Eye—
And for an Everlasting Roof
The Gambrels[1] of the Sky—

Of Visitors—the fairest—
For Occupation—This—

1. "Sons of thunder," name given by Jesus to the brothers and disciples James and John, presumably because they were thunderous preachers.

1. Slopes, as in the large, arched roofs often seen on barns.

The spreading wide my narrow Hands
To gather Paradise—

712

Because I could not stop for Death—
He kindly stopped for me—
The Carriage held but just Ourselves—
And Immortality.

We slowly drove—He knew no haste
And I had put away
My labor and my leisure too,
For His Civility—

We passed the School, where Children strove
At Recess—in the Ring—
We passed the Fields of Gazing Grain—
We passed the Setting Sun—

Or rather—He passed Us—
The Dews drew quivering and chill—
For only Gossamer, my Gown—
My Tippet—only Tulle[1]—

We paused before a House that seemed
A Swelling of the Ground—
The Roof was scarcely visible—
The Cornice—in the Ground—

Since then—'tis Centuries—and yet
Feels shorter than the Day
I first surmised the Horses' Heads
Were toward Eternity—

754

My Life had stood—a Loaded Gun—
In Corners—till a Day
The Owner passed—identified—
And carried Me away—

And now We roam in Sovereign Woods—
And now We hunt the Doe—
And every time I speak for Him—
The Mountains straight reply—

1. Fine, silken netting. "Tippet": a scarf.

And do I smile, such cordial light
Upon the Valley glow—
It is as a Vesuvian face[1]
Had let its pleasure through—

And when at Night—Our good Day done—
I guard My Master's Head—
'Tis better than the Eider-Duck's
Deep Pillow—to have shared—

To foe of His—I'm deadly foe—
None stir the second time—
On whom I lay a Yellow Eye—
Or an emphatic Thumb—

Though I than He—may longer live
He longer must—than I—
For I have but the power to kill,
Without—the power to die—

1084

At Half past Three, a single Bird
Unto a silent Sky
Propounded but a single term
Of cautious melody.

At Half past Four, Experiment
Had subjugated test
And lo, Her silver Principle
Supplanted all the rest.

At Half past Seven, Element
Nor Implement, be seen—
And Place was where the Presence was
Circumference between.

1129

Tell all the Truth but tell it slant—
Success in Circuit lies
Too bright for our infirm Delight
The Truth's superb surprise

As Lightning to the Children eased
With explanation kind

1. A face glowing with light like that from an erupting volcano.

The Truth must dazzle gradually
Or every man be blind—

1207

He preached upon "Breadth" till it argued him narrow—
The Broad are too broad to define
And of "Truth" until it proclaimed him a Liar—
The Truth never flaunted a Sign—

Simplicity fled from his counterfeit presence
As Gold the Pyrites[1] would shun—
What confusion would cover the innocent Jesus
To meet so enabled[2] a Man!

1564

Pass to thy Rendezvous of Light,
Pangless except for us—
Who slowly ford the Mystery
Which thou hast leaped across!

1593

There came a Wind like a Bugle—
It quivered through the Grass
And a Green Chill upon the Heat
So ominous did pass
We barred the Windows and the Doors
As from an Emerald Ghost—
The Doom's electric Moccasin[1]
That very instant passed—
On a strange Mob of panting Trees
And Fences fled away
And Rivers where the Houses ran
Those looked that lived—that Day—
The Bell within the steeple wild
The flying tidings told—
How much can come
And much can go,
And yet abide the World!

1. Iron bisulfide, sometimes called fool's gold.
2. Competent.

1. I.e., water moccasin, a poisonous snake.

CHRISTINA ROSSETTI

Poems of thwarted desire and painful self-renunciation fill Christina Rossetti's (1830–1894) body of work. But even as she explores the intensity of grief, longing, and death, her poems often express a whimsical playfulness and a wry humor. Like **Emily Dickinson**, born in the same year across the Atlantic, Rossetti refused a conventional life with marriage and children, and she broke poetic rules in ways that startled her first readers. Like Dickinson, too, she was secretive and largely withdrawn from social contact. "Beautiful, delightful, noble, memorable, as is the world," she wrote to her brother, "I yet am well content in my shady crevice."

Rossetti was born in London in 1830, the youngest of four talented children of an exiled Italian intellectual. Rossetti's two older brothers would go on to become famous artists, members of a group that called themselves the Pre-Raphaelite Brotherhood. Working in poetry and paint, they aimed to revitalize the arts in England by representing the details of the natural world and by returning to medieval themes and images. William Michael Rossetti was also a great admirer of the American poet **Walt Whitman** and introduced his work to English readers. Christina Rossetti's gender prevented her from being a central member of the Pre-Raphaelite Brotherhood, but her first volume, *Goblin Market and Other Poems* (1862) was the first popular success associated with their movement, and it established her as a leading English poet.

Intensely religious and drawn to Christian models of austerity and self-renunciation, Rossetti rejected two suitors on the grounds that their faith was not firm enough for her, and gave up going to the theater and playing chess because these gave her too much pleasure. She wrote 450 devotional poems, and many of her other works also deal with questions of spirituality. Her mother led her to become an Anglo-Catholic, a member of the Protestant Church of England who wanted to revive traditional elements of the Catholic liturgy dating back centuries. This movement favored the doctrine of "reserve," which meant keeping sacred truths hidden from the profane and the uninitiated. Rossetti's secretiveness and her fascination with mysteries are sometimes associated with this doctrine. The Anglo-Catholic movement also encouraged women to work together, and Rossetti spent many years doing charitable service at a home for prostitutes. Her most famous poem, *Goblin Market*, ends with a moral about sisterhood which many readers have linked to Rossetti's membership in the Anglo-Catholic movement and her work with "fallen women."

But *Goblin Market* has also puzzled and captivated readers since it first appeared. "Is it a fable—or a mere fairy story—or an allegory against the pleasures of sinful love—or what is it?" asked the poet Caroline Norton. On the one hand, it is lavishly sensuous and wracked by aching temptation, a daring poem that refuses conventional patterns of rhyme and meter. On the other hand, it is moralizing and childlike, a didactic tale of temptation and redemption. On closer inspection, even its Christian warning against temptation starts to break down: the sinner is restored to her earlier happiness, and her savior is not

Christ but her sister. Indeterminate, the poem has continued to tantalize readers with multiple meanings, and audiences have reached no consensus even about its central theme: the poem has been taken as a reflection on sin, on women's sexual desire, on addiction, and on imperial consumption (the fruit described in the poem comes from all over the world, like commodities to Britain from its colonies). The poem has also been celebrated as a feminist work that sets the violence of the male goblins against the solidarity of the sisters. In the end, like so much of Rossetti's life and work, it continues to entice us with its perpetually fascinating secrets.

After Death

The curtains were half drawn, the floor was swept
   And strewn with rushes, rosemary and may[1]
   Lay thick upon the bed on which I lay,
Where thro' the lattice ivy-shadows crept.
He leaned above me, thinking that I slept
   And could not hear him; but I heard him say:
   "Poor child, poor child": and as he turned away
Came a deep silence, and I knew he wept.
He did not touch the shroud, or raise the fold
   That hid my face, or take my hand in his,
      Or ruffle the smooth pillows for my head:
      He did not love me living; but once dead
   He pitied me; and very sweet it is
To know he still is warm tho' I am cold.

Winter: My Secret

I tell my secret? No indeed, not I:
Perhaps some day, who knows?
But not today; it froze, and blows, and snows,
And you're too curious: fie!
You want to hear it? well:
Only, my secret's mine, and I won't tell.

Or, after all, perhaps there's none:
Suppose there is no secret after all,
But only just my fun.
Today's a nipping day, a biting day;
In which one wants a shawl,
A veil, a cloak, and other wraps:
I cannot ope to every one who taps,
And let the draughts come whistling thro' my hall;

1. Plants that symbolize death.

Come bounding and surrounding me,
Come buffeting, astounding me,
Nipping and clipping thro' my wraps and all.
I wear my mask for warmth: who ever shows
His nose to Russian snows
To be pecked at by every wind that blows?
You would not peck? I thank you for good will,
Believe, but leave that truth untested still.

Spring's an expansive time: yet I don't trust
March with its peck of dust,
Nor April with its rainbow-crowned brief showers,
Nor even May, whose flowers
One frost may wither thro' the sunless hours.

Perhaps some languid summer day,
When drowsy birds sing less and less,
And golden fruit is ripening to excess,
If there's not too much sun nor too much cloud,
And the warm wind is neither still nor loud,
Perhaps my secret I may say,
Or you may guess.

Goblin Market

Morning and evening
Maids heard the goblins cry:
"Come buy our orchard fruits,
Come buy, come buy:
Apples and quinces,
Lemons and oranges,
Plump unpecked cherries,
Melons and raspberries,
Bloom-down-cheeked peaches,
Swart-headed mulberries,
Wild free-born cranberries,
Crab-apples, dewberries,
Pine-apples, blackberries,
Apricots, strawberries;—
All ripe together
In summer weather,—
Morns that pass by,
Fair eves that fly;
Come buy, come buy:
Our grapes fresh from the vine,
Pomegranates full and fine,
Dates and sharp bullaces,
Rare pears and greengages,

Damsons[1] and bilberries,
Taste them and try:
Currants and gooseberries,
Bright-fire-like barberries,
Figs to fill your mouth,
Citrons from the South,
Sweet to tongue and sound to eye;
Come buy, come buy."

Evening by evening
Among the brookside rushes,
Laura bowed her head to hear,
Lizzie veiled her blushes:
Crouching close together
In the cooling weather,
With clasping arms and cautioning lips,
With tingling cheeks and finger tips.
"Lie close," Laura said,
Pricking up her golden head:
"We must not look at goblin men,
We must not buy their fruits:
Who knows upon what soil they fed
Their hungry thirsty roots?"
"Come buy," call the goblins
Hobbling down the glen.
"Oh," cried Lizzie, "Laura, Laura,
You should not peep at goblin men."
Lizzie covered up her eyes,
Covered close lest they should look;
Laura reared her glossy head,
And whispered like the restless brook:
"Look, Lizzie, look, Lizzie,
Down the glen tramp little men.
One hauls a basket,
One bears a plate,
One lugs a golden dish
Of many pounds weight.
How fair the vine must grow
Whose grapes are so luscious;
How warm the wind must blow
Thro' those fruit bushes."
"No," said Lizzie: "No, no, no;
Their offers should not charm us,
Their evil gifts would harm us."
She thrust a dimpled finger
In each ear, shut eyes and ran:
Curious Laura chose to linger

1. Types of plum.

Wondering at each merchant man.
One had a cat's face,
One whisked a tail,
One tramped at a rat's pace,
One crawled like a snail,
One like a wombat prowled obtuse and furry,
One like a ratel[2] tumbled hurry scurry.
She heard a voice like voice of doves
Cooing all together:
They sounded kind and full of loves
In the pleasant weather.

Laura stretched her gleaming neck
Like a rush-imbedded swan,
Like a lily from the beck,
Like a moonlit poplar branch,
Like a vessel at the launch
When its last restraint is gone.

Backwards up the mossy glen
Turned and trooped the goblin men,
With their shrill repeated cry,
"Come buy, come buy."
When they reached where Laura was
They stood stock still upon the moss,
Leering at each other,
Brother with queer brother;
Signalling each other,
Brother with sly brother.
One set his basket down,
One reared his plate;
One began to weave a crown
Of tendrils, leaves and rough nuts brown
(Men sell not such in any town);
One heaved the golden weight
Of dish and fruit to offer her:
"Come buy, come buy," was still their cry.
Laura stared but did not stir,
Longed but had no money:
The whisk-tailed merchant bade her taste
In tones as smooth as honey,
The cat-faced purr'd,
The rat-paced spoke a word
Of welcome, and the snail-paced even was heard;
One parrot-voiced and jolly
Cried "Pretty Goblin" still for "Pretty Polly;"—
One whistled like a bird.

2. The honey badger, a mammal from Africa and south Asia.

But sweet-tooth Laura spoke in haste:
"Good folk, I have no coin;
To take were to purloin:
I have no copper in my purse,
I have no silver either,
And all my gold is on the furze
That shakes in windy weather
Above the rusty heather."
"You have much gold upon your head,"
They answered all together:
"Buy from us with a golden curl."
She clipped a precious golden lock,
She dropped a tear more rare than pearl,
Then sucked their fruit globes fair or red:
Sweeter than honey from the rock.
Stronger than man-rejoicing wine,
Clearer than water flowed that juice;
She never tasted such before,
How should it cloy with length of use?
She sucked and sucked and sucked the more
Fruits which that unknown orchard bore;
She sucked until her lips were sore;
Then flung the emptied rinds away
But gathered up one kernel-stone,
And knew not was it night or day
As she turned home alone.

Lizzie met her at the gate
Full of wise upbraidings:
"Dear, you should not stay so late,
Twilight is not good for maidens;
Should not loiter in the glen
In the haunts of goblin men.
Do you not remember Jeanie,
How she met them in the moonlight,
Took their gifts both choice and many,
Ate their fruits and wore their flowers
Plucked from bowers
Where summer ripens at all hours?
But ever in the noonlight
She pined and pined away;
Sought them by night and day,
Found them no more but dwindled and grew grey;
Then fell with the first snow,
While to this day no grass will grow
Where she lies low:
I planted daisies there a year ago
That never blow.
You should not loiter so."
"Nay, hush," said Laura:
"Nay, hush, my sister:

I ate and ate my fill,
Yet my mouth waters still;
Tomorrow night I will
Buy more:" and kissed her:
"Have done with sorrow;
I'll bring you plums tomorrow
Fresh on their mother twigs,
Cherries worth getting;
You cannot think what figs
My teeth have met in,
What melons icy-cold
Piled on a dish of gold
Too huge for me to hold,
What peaches with a velvet nap,
Pellucid grapes without one seed:
Odorous indeed must be the mead
Whereon they grow, and pure the wave they drink
With lilies at the brink,
And sugar-sweet their sap."

Golden head by golden head,
Like two pigeons in one nest
Folded in each other's wings,
They lay down in their curtained bed:
Like two blossoms on one stem,
Like two flakes of new-fall'n snow,
Like two wands of ivory
Tipped with gold for awful[3] kings.
Moon and stars gazed in at them,
Wind sang to them lullaby,
Lumbering owls forbore to fly,
Not a bat flapped to and fro
Round their rest:
Cheek to cheek and breast to breast
Locked together in one nest.

Early in the morning
When the first cock crowed his warning,
Neat like bees, as sweet and busy,
Laura rose with Lizzie:
Fetched in honey, milked the cows,
Aired and set to rights the house,
Kneaded cakes of whitest wheat,
Cakes for dainty mouths to eat,
Next churned butter, whipped up cream,
Fed their poultry, sat and sewed;
Talked as modest maidens should:
Lizzie with an open heart,
Laura in an absent dream,

3. Awe-inspiring.

One content, one sick in part;
One warbling for the mere bright day's delight,
One longing for the night.

At length slow evening came:
They went with pitchers to the reedy brook;
Lizzie most placid in her look,
Laura most like a leaping flame.
They drew the gurgling water from its deep;
Lizzie plucked purple and rich golden flags,
Then turning homewards said: "The sunset flushes
Those furthest loftiest crags;
Come, Laura, not another maiden lags
No wilful squirrel wags,
The beasts and birds are fast asleep."
But Laura loitered still among the rushes
And said the bank was steep.

And said the hour was early still,
The dew not fall'n, the wind not chill:
Listening ever, but not catching
The customary cry,
"Come buy, come buy,"
With its iterated jingle
Of sugar-baited words:
Not for all her watching
Once discerning even one goblin
Racing, whisking, tumbling, hobbling;
Let alone the herds
That used to tramp along the glen,
In groups or single,
Of brisk fruit-merchant men.
Till Lizzie urged, "O Laura, come:
I hear the fruit-call but I dare not look:
You should not loiter longer at this brook:
Come with me home.
The stars rise, the moon bends her arc,
Each glowworm winks her spark,
Let us get home before the night grows dark:
For clouds may gather
Tho' this is summer weather,
Put out the lights and drench us thro';
Then if we lost our way what should we do?"

Laura turned cold as stone
To find her sister heard that cry alone,
That goblin cry,
"Come buy our fruits, come buy."
Must she then buy no more such dainty fruit?
Must she no more such succous pasture find,
Gone deaf and blind?

Her tree of life drooped from the root:
She said not one word in her heart's sore ache;
But peering thro' the dimness, nought discerning,
Trudged home, her pitcher dripping all the way;
So crept to bed, and lay
Silent till Lizzie slept;
Then sat up in a passionate yearning,
And gnashed her teeth for baulked desire, and wept
As if her heart would break.

Day after day, night after night,
Laura kept watch in vain
In sullen silence of exceeding pain.
She never caught again the goblin cry:
"Come buy, come buy;"—
She never spied the goblin men
Hawking their fruits along the glen:
But when the noon waxed bright
Her hair grew thin and gray;
She dwindled, as the fair full moon doth turn
To swift decay and burn
Her fire away.

One day remembering her kernel-stone
She set it by a wall that faced the south;
Dewed it with tears, hoped for a root,
Watched for a waxing shoot,
But there came none;
It never saw the sun,
It never felt the trickling moisture run:
While with sunk eyes and faded mouth
She dreamed of melons, as a traveller sees
False waves in desert drouth
With shade of leaf-crowned trees,
And burns the thirstier in the sandful breeze.
She no more swept the house,
Tended the fowls or cows,
Fetched honey, kneaded cakes of wheat,
Brought water from the brook:
But sat down listless in the chimney-nook
And would not eat.

Tender Lizzie could not bear
To watch her sister's cankerous care
Yet not to share.
She night and morning
Caught the goblins' cry:
"Come buy our orchard fruits,
Come buy, come buy:"—
Beside the brook, along the glen,

She heard the tramp of goblin men,
The voice and stir
Poor Laura could not hear;
Longed to buy fruit to comfort her,
But feared to pay too dear.
She thought of Jeanie in her grave,
Who should have been a bride;
But who for joys brides hope to have
Fell sick and died
In her gay prime,
In earliest Winter time,
With the first glazing rime,
With the first snow-fall of crisp Winter time.

Till Laura dwindling
Seemed knocking at Death's door:
Then Lizzie weighed no more
Better and worse;
But put a silver penny in her purse,
Kissed Laura, crossed the heath with clumps of furze
At twilight, halted by the brook:
And for the first time in her life
Began to listen and look.

Laughed every goblin
When they spied her peeping:
Came towards her hobbling,
Flying, running, leaping,
Puffing and blowing,
Chuckling, clapping, crowing,
Clucking and gobbling,
Mopping and mowing,
Full of airs and graces,
Pulling wry faces,
Demure grimaces,
Cat-like and rat-like,
Ratel-and wombat-like,
Snail-paced in a hurry,
Parrot-voiced and whistler,
Helter skelter, hurry skurry,
Chattering like magpies,
Fluttering like pigeons,
Gliding like fishes,—
Hugged her and kissed her,
Squeezed and caressed her:
Stretched up their dishes,
Panniers, and plates:
"Look at our apples
Russet and dun,
Bob at our cherries,

Bite at our peaches,
Citrons and dates,
Grapes for the asking,
Pears red with basking
Out in the sun,
Plums on their twigs;
Pluck them and suck them,
Pomegranates, figs."—

"Good folk," said Lizzie,
Mindful of Jeanie:
"Give me much and many:"—
Held out her apron,
Tossed them her penny.
"Nay, take a seat with us,
Honour and eat with us,"
They answered grinning:
"Our feast is but beginning.
Night yet is early,
Warm and dew-pearly,
Wakeful and starry:
Such fruits as these
No man can carry;
Half their bloom would fly,
Half their dew would dry,
Half their flavour would pass by.
Sit down and feast with us,
Be welcome guest with us,
Cheer you and rest with us."—
"Thank you," said Lizzie: "But one waits
At home alone for me:
So without further parleying,
If you will not sell me any
Of your fruits tho' much and many,
Give me back my silver penny
I tossed you for a fee."—
They began to scratch their pates,
No longer wagging, purring,
But visibly demurring,
Grunting and snarling.
One called her proud,
Cross-grained, uncivil;
Their tones waxed loud,
Their looks were evil.
Lashing their tails
They trod and hustled her,
Elbowed and jostled her,
Clawed with their nails.
Barking, mewing, hissing, mocking,
Tore her gown and soiled her stocking,

Twitched her hair out by the roots,
Stamped upon her tender feet,
Held her hands and squeezed their fruits
Against her mouth to make her eat.

White and golden Lizzie stood,
Like a lily in a flood,—
Like a rock of blue-veined stone
Lashed by tides obstreperously,—
Like a beacon left alone
In a hoary roaring sea,
Sending up a golden fire,—
Like a fruit-crowned orange-tree
White with blossoms honey-sweet
Sore beset by wasp and bee,—
Like a royal virgin town
Topped with gilded dome and spire
Close beleaguerred by a fleet
Mad to tug her standard down.

One may lead a horse to water,
Twenty cannot make him drink.
Tho' the goblins cuffed and caught her,
Coaxed and fought her,
Bullied and besought her,
Scratched her, pinched her black as ink,
Kicked and knocked her,
Mauled and mocked her,
Lizzie uttered not a word;
Would not open lip from lip
Lest they should cram a mouthful in:
But laughed in heart to feel the drip
Of juice that syruped all her face,
And lodged in dimples of her chin,
And streaked her neck which quaked like curd.
At last the evil people
Worn out by her resistance
Flung back her penny, kicked their fruit
Along whichever road they took,
Not leaving root or stone or shoot;
Some writhed into the ground,
Some dived into the brook
With ring and ripple,
Some scudded on the gale without a sound,
Some vanished in the distance.

In a smart, ache, tingle,
Lizzie went her way;
Knew not was it night or day;
Sprang up the bank, tore thro' the furze,

Threaded copse and dingle,
And heard her penny jingle
Bouncing in her purse,
Its bounce was music to her ear.
She ran and ran
As if she feared some goblin man
Dogged her with gibe or curse
Or something worse:
But not one goblin skurried after,
Nor was she pricked by fear;
The kind heart made her windy-paced
That urged her home quite out of breath with haste
And inward laughter.

She cried "Laura," up the garden,
"Did you miss me?
Come and kiss me.
Never mind my bruises,
Hug me, kiss me, suck my juices
Squeezed from goblin fruits for you,
Goblin pulp and goblin dew.
Eat me, drink me, love me;
Laura, make much of me:
For your sake I have braved the glen
And had to do with goblin merchant men."

Laura started from her chair,
Flung her arms up in the air,
Clutched her hair:
"Lizzie, Lizzie, have you tasted
For my sake the fruit forbidden?
Must your light like mine be hidden,
Your young life like mine be wasted,
Undone in mine undoing
And ruined in my ruin,
Thirsty, cankered, goblin-ridden?"—
She clung about her sister,
Kissed and kissed and kissed her:
Tears once again
Refreshed her shrunken eyes,
Dripping like rain
After long sultry drouth;
Shaking with aguish fear, and pain,
She kissed and kissed her with a hungry mouth.

Her lips began to scorch,
That juice was wormwood to her tongue,
She loathed the feast:
Writhing as one possessed she leaped and sung,
Rent all her robe, and wrung

Her hands in lamentable haste,
And beat her breast.
Her locks streamed like the torch
Borne by a racer at full speed,
Or like the mane of horses in their flight,
Or like an eagle when she stems the light
Straight toward the sun,
Or like a caged thing freed,
Or like a flying flag when armies run.

Swift fire spread thro' her veins, knocked at her heart,
Met the fire smouldering there
And overbore its lesser flame;
She gorged on bitterness without a name:
Ah! fool, to choose such part
Of soul-consuming care!
Sense failed in the mortal strife:
Like the watch-tower of a town
Which an earthquake shatters down,
Like a lightning-stricken mast,
Like a wind-uprooted tree
Spun about,
Like a foam-topped waterspout
Cast down headlong in the sea,
She fell at last;
Pleasure past and anguish past,
Is it death or is it life?

Life out of death.
That night long Lizzie watched by her,
Counted her pulse's flagging stir,
Felt for her breath,
Held water to her lips, and cooled her face
With tears and fanning leaves:
But when the first birds chirped about their eaves,
And early reapers plodded to the place
Of golden sheaves,
And dew-wet grass
Bowed in the morning winds so brisk to pass,
And new buds with new day
Opened of cup-like lilies on the stream,
Laura awoke as from a dream,
Laughed in the innocent old way,
Hugged Lizzie but not twice or thrice;
Her gleaming locks showed not one thread of grey,
Her breath was sweet as May
And light danced in her eyes.

Days, weeks, months, years
Afterwards, when both were wives

With children of their own;
Their mother-hearts beset with fears,
Their lives bound up in tender lives;
Laura would call the little ones
And tell them of her early prime,
Those pleasant days long gone
Of not-returning time:
Would talk about the haunted glen,
The wicked, quaint fruit-merchant men,
Their fruits like honey to the throat
But poison in the blood;
(Men sell not such in any town:)
Would tell them how her sister stood
In deadly peril to do her good,
And win the fiery antidote:
Then joining hands to little hands
Would bid them cling together,
"For there is no friend like a sister
In calm or stormy weather;
To cheer one on the tedious way,
To fetch one if one goes astray,
To lift one if one totters down,
To strengthen whilst one stands."

ROSALÍA DE CASTRO

In northwestern Spain, just north of Portugal, lies the province called Galicia, where for centuries people have spoken a language, Galician, that is closer to Portuguese than to Castilian Spanish. Most writers considered this a low and vulgar dialect until the middle of the nineteenth century, when a poet and novelist named Rosalía de Castro (1837–1885) began to celebrate this region, its customs, its folkways, and the language of its ordinary people. Her works helped to usher in what is called the "Galician Renaissance," and even now, every May 17, the anniversary of Rosalía de Castro's first Galician poetry collection, is celebrated as "Galician Literature Day."

Born in Santiago de Compostela, Rosalía de Castro was the child of an aristocratic mother and a Catholic priest who refused any contact with her. Doubly shamed as not only illegitimate but also "sacrilegious," she was raised by an aunt. Her first volume of poems, written in Castilian Spanish, brought her to the attention of an editor named Manuel Martinez Murguía, a champion of Galician culture. He published her work and encouraged her to write in Galician. Soon the two married and would go on to have seven children.

Over the course of her career, Rosalía de Castro wrote five novels and five volumes of poetry. Her fiction explores the subordinate position of women in Spanish society, and her poems turn again and again to quintessentially Romantic themes: the natural world, folk traditions, feelings of agonized, turbulent passion, and forebodings of death. Her intention, she said, was "to evoke all the splendor, and the sudden flashes of beauty, that emanate from every custom and thought of a people who have often been called stupid and sometimes judged insensitive or unfamiliar with refined poetry." She deliberately chose simple and accessible poetic forms, which would inspire such later Spanish writers as **Rubén Darío** and **Federico García Lorca**.

[As I composed this little book][1]

As I composed this little book, I thought:
Although my songs may never bring me fame,
Simple they are and brief,
And may achieve, perhaps, my longed-for aim.
For they can be sure-fixed in memory
As are the prayers and rituals of belief,
Fervent though short, we learned in infancy.
Those we do not forget, in spite of grief
And time and distance and the destroying flame
Of passion. That is why my songs are brief
And simple,—though they may not bring me fame.

[A glowworm scatters flashes through the moss]

A glowworm scatters flashes through the moss;
A star gleams in its high remote domain.
Abyss above, and in the depths abyss:
What things come to an end and what remain?
Man's thought—we call it science!—peers and pries
Into the soundless dark. But it is vain:
When all is done, we still are ignorant
Of what things reach an end, and what remain.

Kneeling before an image rudely carved,
I sink my spirit in the Infinite,
And—is it impious?—I vacillate
And tremble, questioning Heaven and Hell of it.

My Deity, shattered in a thousand bits,
Has fallen to chasms where I cannot see.
I rush to seek Him, and my groping meets
A solitary vast vacuity.

1. This and the following two poems were translated by S. Griswold Morley.

When lo! from their lofty marble niches,
Angels gazed down in sorrow; and in my ears
Murmured a gentle voice: "Unhappy soul,
Take hope; pour out thy tears
Before the feet of the Most High;
But well remember this: No insolent cry
To Heaven makes its way
From one whose heart adores material things,
Who makes an idol out of Adam's clay."

[The ailing woman felt her forces ebb]

The ailing woman felt her forces ebb
With summer, and knew her time was imminent.
"In autumn I shall die,"
She thought, half-melancholy, half-content,
"And I shall feel the leaves, that will be dead
Like me, drop on the grave in which I lie."

Not even Death would do her so much pleasure.
Cruel to her he too,
In winter spared her life, and when anew
The earth was being born in blossoming,
Slew her by inches to the joyous hymns
Of fair and merry spring!

[I well know there is nothing][1]

I well know there is nothing
new under the sky,
that what I think of now
others have thought before.

Well, why do I write?
Well, because we are so,
clocks that repeat
forever the same.

[As the clouds]

As the clouds
borne by the wind,
now darken, now brighten
the immense spaces of the sky,
just so the mad
ideas I have,

1. This and the following three poems are translated by Michael Smith.

the images of multiple forms,
of strange features, of vague colour,
now darken,
now brighten,
the abysmal depths of my mind.

[You will say about these verses, and it's true]

You will say about these verses, and it's true,
that they have a strange, unusual harmony,
that in them ideas wanly glow
as straying sparks
that explode at intervals
soon vanished;
that they resemble the unsteady leaf-fall
churning in the backyards,
and the pines monotonous sough
by the wild seashore.

And I will tell you, my songs
issue from my soul in confusion
as out of the deep oakwoods,
at the day's start,
an indefinable hum,
maybe the chafing of the breeze,
or the kissing of flowers,
or the rustic, mysterious harmonies
that in this sad world
are at a loss to find their way to Heaven.

[Some say plants don't speak]

Some say plants don't speak, nor fountains, nor birds,
nor the wave with its swish, nor stars with their sparkle:
so say some, but it isn't true, since always as I pass by,
things whisper about me and exclaim:
—There goes the madwoman, dreaming
of the eternal spring of life and the fields,
though soon enough, all too soon, she will comb grey hair,
and shivering, numb, see the hoarfrost shroud the meadow.

—There's white hair on my head, hoarfrost in the meadows;
but I, poor soul, incurable sleepwalker, dream on and on
of expiring life's eternal spring
and the perennial freshness of fields and souls
even though these burn up and those wither.

Stars and fountains and flowers, don't murmur against my dreams;
could I delight in you without them, without them, could I live?

[The feet of Spring are on the stair][1]

The feet of Spring are on the stair;
Her breath is sweet and warm and rare;
Beneath the soil in amorous heat
Seeds are astir with restless beat,
And atoms drifting in the air,
Afloat and silent, pair by pair,
Kiss as they meet.

Youth's blood is eager, youth's heart is hot,
Its courage leaps, its bold mad thought
Believes that man—oh, dreams of youth!—
Is, like the gods, immortal. What
If dreams are lies? This much is truth:
Unblest are they who dreamless draw their breath,
And fortunate who in a dream find death.

How swift the passage of each thing
In our sad world!
By a wild giant, quivering
Our lives are whirled!
Yesterday bud, today a rose,
And then the sun-scorched blossom goes
As Summer masters Spring.

1. Translated by S. Griswold Morley.

STÉPHANE MALLARMÉ

What would it be like to try to free poetry from the world of ordinary things? For Stéphane Mallarmé, it meant trying to figure out what makes poetry *poetry*—and not just another way of speaking about experience. It meant liberating poetic language from conventional everyday uses, such as the communication of facts and the reporting of events in newspapers. It meant refusing standard syntax, embracing incompleteness, moving fluidly among strange and disconnected images, and focusing on the sounds as much as the sense of words. The result was a kind of writing so deliberately strange and difficult that it has bewildered readers from its own time to ours. The writer **Marcel Proust** lamented, "How unfortunate that so gifted a man should become insane every time he takes up the pen." And the painter Edgar Degas ran out of a lecture by Mallarmé, shouting, "I do not understand!" But Mallarmé's poetry also sparked the intense enthusiasm of fellow writers, visual artists, and musicians—later called the "Symbolists"—who devoted themselves to creating an art of evocative moods and mysterious images and sensations.

LIFE

Mallarmé was born into a well-to-do middle-class family in Paris in 1842. His mother died when he was five, and his sister (his only sibling, whom Mallarmé adored) died when he was fifteen. Many critics have ascribed his existential anxiety and fascination with death to these painful early losses. As a young man, he married a German woman named Maria Gerhard, and together they had two children. Their son died at the age of eight.

Mallarmé had a long career as an English teacher, and even wrote an English textbook for French students. He was not a particularly good language teacher, had little aptitude for drills and discipline, and was often a figure of fun for his students. Frustrated that the French government repeatedly assigned him to teaching positions in the provinces, in 1871 he was relieved, finally, that he was able to move to Paris, capital of the arts. There he wrote reviews for newspapers and magazines, and he labored for months—sometimes even years—to perfect each of his innovative poems.

It was in Paris in 1880 that Mallarmé began holding exciting gatherings for artists, musicians, and writers, who flocked to hear him talk about the nature of art. These Tuesday-evening meetings became famous, and a whole generation of young artists found Mallarmé charismatic and inspiring. His influence spread widely: the painter Edouard Manet illustrated his verse, and the composer Claude Debussy famously set Mallarmé's "Afternoon of a Faun" to music. After he retired from teaching, he lectured on poetry and continued his radical experimentation with poetic form. He was elected "Prince of Poets" by his colleagues two years before his death in 1898.

WORK

"To tell, to teach, and even to describe have their place," wrote Mallarmé—but not in literature. Instead of "reporting," he insisted, literary writers should offer mysterious symbols and allusions. Thus readers should not expect to enter a coherent and recognizable world, with descriptions and relationships explained. The poet urges us to take delight, instead, in images that remain elusive: "*To name* an object is to suppress three-quarters of the enjoyment of the poem, which derives from the pleasure of step-by-step discovery; to *suggest*, that is the dream . . . to evoke an object little by little, so as to bring to light a state of the soul or, inversely, to choose an object and bring out of it a state of the soul through a series of unravelings."

Mallarmé's best known and most influential work is the dramatic poem "The Afternoon of a Faun." The speaker is a woodland spirit from Roman mythology, part man and part goat, who is known both for his lustful appetites and for his skill in playing the flute. Mallarmé's faun tells us of his erotic pursuit of two beautiful water nymphs. Or was it a dream? The poem contemplates desire for beautiful objects that remain forever out of reach, and it interweaves erotic desire with questions about imagination and creativity. It has been especially celebrated for the extraordinary musicality of its verse, and the flute-playing faun may be a figure for the poet. In fact, Mallarmé often thought of music as a model for poetry, and in many of his works he focused intently on rhythm and sound. Sometimes he even began with a particular rhyme and worked backward to the text's images.

Mallarmé's poetry grew increasingly experimental with time. His last published work, "A Throw of the Dice Will Never Abolish Chance," took the form of a carefully designed visual object, printed in multiple typefaces with words arranged in unconventional ways, with huge gaps, across the page. This text is an important precursor to the concrete poetry of the twentieth century. Although Mallarmé's poems are immediately accessible on the level of visual imagery, they also offer the pleasure of a chess game for those who like to pursue intricate structures of thought. He works with sounds and letters, plays on words, and punning rhymes to produce rich patterns and echoes across each poem. Many of his early works also compel us to dwell on absences: hallmarks of his writing include hesitation and discontinuity, interruption and incompleteness. But his early poems, such as those included here, stay close to traditional verse forms. In French, "The Afternoon of a Faun" follows the alexandrine, or twelve-syllable line, in keeping with the most traditional French poetry, and "The Tomb of Edgar Poe," written for a memorial service for the American writer, is a sonnet.

So thought-provoking are his experiments in language that Mallarmé has been appreciated not only by poets and other artists but also by philosophers. This might not have surprised him. "Poetry," he insisted, is "the only possible human creation."

The Afternoon of a Faun[1]

Eclogue[2]

THE FAUN

These nymphs that I would perpetuate:
so clear
And light, their carnation,[3] that it floats in the air
Heavy with leafy slumbers.
My doubt, night's ancient hoard, pursues its theme
In branching labyrinths, which, being still
The veritable woods themselves, alas, reveal
My triumph as the ideal fault of roses.
Consider . . .

if the women of your glosses
Are phantoms of your fabulous[4] desires!
Faun, the illusion flees from the cold, blue eyes
Of the chaster nymph like a fountain gushing tears;
But the other, all in sighs, you say, compares

1. All poems translated by Henry Michael Weinfield. In Greek mythology, a faun was a woodland satyr with goatlike hooves and horns.
2. A pastoral poem, usually in dialogue form, originating in Greek poetry. Here, italics indicate the divisions of the faun's internal dialogue.
3. A rosy flesh pink.
4. Fabled; i.e., both marvelous and narrated.

To a hot wind through the fleece that blows at noon?
No! through the motionless and weary swoon
Of stifling heat that suffocates the morning,
Save from my flute, no waters murmuring
In harmony flow out into the groves;
And the only wind on the horizon no ripple moves,
Exhaled from my twin pipes and swift to drain
The melody in arid drifts of rain,
Is the visible, serene and fictive air
Of inspiration rising as if in prayer.

RELATE, Sicilian shores,[5] whose tranquil fens
My vanity disturbs as do the suns,
Silent beneath the brilliant flowers of flame:
"That cutting hollow reeds my art would tame,
I saw far off, against the glaucous gold
Of foliage twined to where the springs run cold,
An animal whiteness languorously swaying;
To the slow prelude that the pipes were playing,
This flight of swans—no! naiads[6]—rose in a shower
Of spray . . ."
Day burns inert in the tawny hour
And excess of hymen is escaped away—
Without a sign, from one who pined for the primal A:[7]
And so, beneath a flood of antique light,
As innocent as are the lilies white,
To my first ardors I awake alone.

Besides sweet nothings by their lips made known,
Kisses that only mark their perfidy,
My chest reveals an unsolved mystery . . .
The toothmarks of some strange, majestic creature:
Enough! Arcana such as these disclose their nature
Only through vast twin reeds played to the skies,
That, turning to music all that clouds the eyes,
Dream, in a long solo, that we amused
The beauty all around us by confused
Equations[8] with our credulous melody;
And dream that the song can make love soar so high
That, purged of all ordinary fantasies
Of back or breast—incessant shapes that rise
In blindness—it distills sonorities
From every empty and monotonous line.[9]

5. An invocation to the surrounding countryside, which recalls the openings of classical poems like the *Iliad* and the *Aeneid*.
6. Water nymphs.
7. The musical note A. In the French text it is *la* (from the *do-re-mi* scale), which is also the feminine article "the."
8. Playing his reed pipes, the faun creates a musical line that is equated with the nymphs' silhouette as he remembers it behind closed eyes.
9. Lines 51 and 52 are one line in the French text.

Then, instrument of flights; Syrinx[1] malign,
At lakes where you attend me, bloom once more!
Long shall my discourse from the echoing shore
Depict those goddesses: by masquerades,[2]
I'll strip the veils that sanctify their shades;
And when I've sucked the brightness out of grapes,
To quell the flood of sorrow that escapes,
I'll lift the empty cluster to the sky,
Avidly drunk till evening has drawn nigh,
And blow in laughter through the luminous skins.

Let us inflate our MEMORIES, O nymphs.
"Piercing the reeds, my darting eyes transfix,
Plunged in the cooling waves, immortal necks,
And cries of fury echo through the air;
Splendid cascades of tresses disappear
In shimmering jewels. Pursuing them, I find
There, at my feet, two sleepers intertwined,
Bruised in the languor of duality,
Their arms about each other heedlessly.
I bear them, still entangled, to a height
Where frivolous shadow never mocks the light
And dying roses yield the sun their scent,
That with the day our passions might be spent."
I adore you, wrath of virgins—fierce delight
Of the sacred burden's writhing naked flight
From the fiery lightning of my lips that flash
With the secret terror of the thirsting flesh:
From the cruel one's feet to the heart of the shy,
Whom innocence abandons suddenly,
Watered in frenzied or less woeful tears.
"Gay with the conquest of those traitorous fears,
I sinned when I divided the dishevelled
Tuft of kisses that the gods had ravelled.
For hardly had I hidden an ardent moan
Deep in the joyous recesses of one
(Holding by a finger, that her swanlike pallor
From her sister's passion might be tinged with color,
The little one, unblushingly demure,
When from my arms, loosened[3] by death obscure,
This prey, ungrateful to the end, breaks free,
Spurning the sobs that still transported me."

Others will lead me on to happiness,
Their tresses knotted round my horns, I guess.
You know, my passion, that, crimson with ripe seeds,
Pomegranates burst in a murmur of bees,

1. In Greek mythology, a nymph who fled from the god Pan and was changed into a reed, from which flutes, or panpipes, are made.

2. Literally, idolatrous pictures (of the nymphs).

3. I.e., his arms were momentarily weakened.

And that our blood, seized by each passing form,
Flows toward desire's everlasting swarm.
In the time when the forest turns ashen and gold
And the summer's demise in the leaves is extolled,
Etna![4] when Venus visits her retreat,
Treading your lava with innocent feet,
Though a sad sleep thunders and the flame burns cold,
I hold the queen!
Sure punishment[5] . . .

No, but the soul,
Weighed down by the body, wordless, struck dumb,
To noon's proud silence must at last succumb:
And so, let me sleep, oblivious of sin,
Stretched out on the thirsty sand, drinking in
The bountiful rays of the wine-growing star!

Couple, farewell; I'll see the shade that now you are.

The Tomb[1] of Edgar Poe

As to Himself at last eternity changes him
The Poet reawakens with a naked sword
His century appalled at never having heard
That in this voice triumphant death had sung its hymn.

They, like a writhing hydra, hearing seraphim[2]
Bestow a purer sense on the language of the horde,
Loudly proclaimed that the magic potion[3] had been poured
From the dregs of some dishonored mixture of foul slime.

From the war between earth and heaven, what grief!
If understanding cannot sculpt a bas-relief
To ornament the dazzling tomb of Poe:
Calm block here fallen from obscure disaster,[4]
Let this granite at least mark the boundaries evermore
To the dark flights of Blasphemy[5] hurled to the future.

4. A volcano in Sicily.
5. The faun imagines swift punishment when in his heightened desire he fantasizes seizing Venus, the goddess of love.
1. A *tomb* is also a funeral poem. The poem was written for a memorial ceremony honoring Edgar Allan Poe (1809–1849) in Baltimore, Maryland, and was first published in the 1877 memorial volume.
2. The Angel: the above said Poet [Mallarmé's note]. Mallarmé explained this in English to the memorial organizers. "Hydra": a mythical many-headed serpent; here compared with those who slandered Poe when he was alive.
3. In plain prose: Charged him with always being drunk [Mallarmé's note]. Critics accused Poe of finding inspiration in drunken fantasies.
4. The memorial marker ("Calm block") is seen as a meteorite fallen from a dark or negative star ("disaster"); a play on words: "aster" is Greek for "star."
5. Blasphemy: against poets, such as the charge of Poe being drunk [Mallarmé's note]. "Boundaries": literally, the milestone along French roads, intended here to limit the batlike flights of slander.

Saint[1]

At the window frame concealing
The viol old and destitute
Whose gilded sandalwood, now peeling,
Once shone with mandolin or flute,

Is the Saint, pale, unfolding
The old, worn missal,[2] a divine
Magnificat[3] in rivers flowing
Once at vespers and compline:[4]

At the glass of this monstrance,[5] vessel
Touched by a harp that took its shape
From the evening flight of an Angel
For the delicate fingertip
Which, without the old, worn missal
Or sandalwood, she balances
On the plumage instrumental,
Musician of silences.

[The virginal, vibrant, and beautiful dawn]

II

The virginal, vibrant, and beautiful dawn,
Will a beat of its drunken wing[1] not suffice
To rend this hard lake haunted beneath the ice
By the transparent glacier of flights never flown?

A swan of former times remembers it's the one
Magnificent but hopelessly struggling to resist
For never having sung of a land in which to exist
When the boredom of the sterile winter has shone.

Though its quivering neck will shake free of the agonies
Inflicted on the bird by the space it denies,
The horror of the earth will remain where it lies.
Phantom whose pure brightness assigns it this domain,
It stiffens in the cold dream of disdain
That clothes the useless exile of the Swan.[2]

1. The original title was "Saint Cecilia Playing on the Wing of an Angel."
2. Literally, an old book, probably containing the music for the old instruments. Cecilia is the patron saint of music.
3. A hymn of praise to God.
4. Evening church services. "Once": formerly.
5. An altar receptacle to hold the Host, with a small glass window in front.

1. A wild, impulsive gesture; also, an astonishing pun with "delivers" in French: *d'aile ivre/délivre.*
2. The word *swan* rhymes with *sign* in French (*cygne / signe*), and the capitalized Swan may be read as a symbol of the writer's futile quest for the absolute Sign.

ARTHUR RIMBAUD

In a brief, dazzling literary career, which lasted from the age of fifteen to the age of twenty, Arthur Rimbaud expanded the visionary and experimental possibilities of modern poetry. Taking literally the ancient notion of the poet as a prophet, he determined to push poetic vision beyond all familiar bounds, violently and dramatically, "by the systematic derangement *of all the senses.*" Rimbaud dedicated himself to a transformation of existence that exceeded even the written word: in ordinary life, he actively rebelled against rules of etiquette and conventional morality to produce a revolutionary reimagining of experience intended to explode entrenched patterns of thought and usher in a radically different future. Idealistic, defiant, deliberately rude, bitter, profoundly anti-conventional and astonishingly talented, Rimbaud, as one admirer explained, passed like a lightning bolt through French literature.

Jean-Nicholas-Arthur Rimbaud was born on October 20, 1854, in Charleville, a town in northeastern France. His military father abandoned the family when Arthur was seven, and his embittered mother raised her four children in a repressive, disciplinary atmosphere. Rimbaud was a highly gifted student who read widely, but he was also unruly, running away from home more than once to live as a vagrant. In 1871 the seventeen-year-old writer sent some of his work to an established Parisian poet, Paul Verlaine, who was so impressed that he invited Rimbaud to stay with him in Paris. Expecting to meet a man in his twenties, Verlaine was shocked to behold the "real head of a child, chubby and fresh, on a big, bony rather clumsy body of a still-growing adolescent." Far from innocent, however, Rimbaud sneered and swore, stole books and broke objects, and deliberately used literary magazines as toilet paper. He also wrote staggeringly innovative works of poetry. Verlaine was drawn to this gifted and uncompromising outsider, and the two began a tumultuous love affair, which ended two years later when Verlaine went to prison for shooting his young lover in a fight. At the age of nineteen Rimbaud decided to renounce poetry, and he traveled as a commercial trader to Cyprus, Java, and Aden, eventually becoming a gunrunner in Abyssinia (now Ethiopia). Falling ill with a cancerous tumor in one knee, he returned to France to die in 1891, one month after his thirty-seventh birthday.

Rimbaud's work resists Romantic traditions of lyric poetry that cherish the self as the site and source of meaningful experience. He suggests instead that multiple, disjointed, and borrowed experiences precede the self, making it what it is. One should not say "I think," he wrote, but rather "I am being thought," as if our thoughts come before us, rather than the other way around. In one of his most famous lines, he claimed "je est un autre" ("I is an other"), his deliberate grammatical error signaling a whole new way of regarding the self as if it were an external object.

We can see one radical revision of the lyric "I" in Rimbaud's most famous poem, "The Drunken Boat," which speaks from the perspective of the boat itself, one that leaves the rivers of Europe for the sea, where it experiences a thoroughgoing freedom and encounters a kind of total reality, both beautiful and terrifying, both creative and destructive, and ends in failure and the desire for self-annihilation, longing to be only a poor child's paper boat sailing in a black puddle. Rimbaud had at this point in his life never seen the sea, but the images he has borrowed from adventure novels, newspapers, and epic poetry allow him to bring together bits and pieces of imaginative intensity to see the world from the strange and unknowable vantage point of a boat.

The Drunken Boat[1]

As I descended black, impassive Rivers,
I sensed that haulers[2] were no longer guiding me:
Screaming Redskins took them for their targets,
Nailed nude to colored stakes: barbaric trees.

I was indifferent to all my crews;
I carried English cottons, Flemish wheat.
When the disturbing din of haulers ceased,
The Rivers let me ramble where I willed.

Through the furious ripping of the sea's mad tides,
Last winter, deafer than an infant's mind,
I ran! And drifting, green Peninsulas
Did not know roar more gleefully unkind.

A tempest blessed my vigils on the sea.
Lighter than a cork I danced on the waves,
Those endless rollers, as they say, of graves:
Ten nights beyond a lantern's[3] silly eye!

Sweeter than sourest apple-flesh to children,
Green water seeped into my pine-wood hull
And washed away blue wine[4] stains, vomitings,
Scattering rudder, anchor, man's lost rule.

And then I, trembling, plunged into the Poem
Of the Sea,[5] infused with stars, milk-white,
Devouring azure greens; where remnants, pale
And gnawed, of pensive corpses fell from light;

Where, staining suddenly the blueness, delirium.
The slow rhythms of the pulsing glow of day,
Stronger than alcohol and vaster than our lyres,
The bitter reds of love ferment the way!

1. Translated by Stephen Stepanchev.
2. The image is of a commercial barge being towed along a canal.
3. Port beacons.
4. A cheap, ordinary, bitter wine.
5. A play on words, "Poem" suggests "creation" (Greek *poiein*, "making"); "Sea," the source or "mother" of life, sounds the same as "mother" in French (*mer / mère*).

I know skies splitting into light, whirled spouts
Of water, surfs, and currents: I know the night,
The dawn exalted like a flock of doves, pure wing,
And I have seen what men imagine they have seen.

I saw the low sun stained with mystic horrors,
Lighting long, curdled clouds of violet,
Like actors in a very ancient play,
Waves rolling distant thrills like lattice[6] light!

I dreamed of green night, stirred by dazzling snows,
Of kisses rising to the sea's eyes, slowly,
The sap-like coursing of surprising currents,
And singing phosphors,[7] flaring blue and gold!

I followed, for whole months, a surge like herds
Of insane cattle in assault on the reefs,
Unhopeful that three Marys,[8] come on luminous feet,
Could force a muzzle on the panting seas!

Yes, I struck incredible Floridas[9]
That mingled flowers and the eyes of panthers
In skins of men! And rainbows bridled green
Herds beneath the horizon of the seas.

I saw the ferment of enormous marshes, weirs
Where a whole Leviathan[1] lies rotting in the weeds!
Collapse of waters within calms at sea,
And distances in cataract toward chasms!

Glaciers, silver suns, pearl waves, and skies like coals,
Hideous wrecks at the bottom of brown gulfs
Where giant serpents eaten by red bugs
Drop from twisted trees and shed a black perfume!

I should have liked to show the young those dolphins
In blue waves, those golden fish, those fish that sing.
—Foam like flowers rocked my sleepy drifting,
And, now and then, fine winds supplied me wings.

When, feeling like a martyr, I tired of poles and zones,
The sea, whose sobbing made my tossing sweet,
Raised me its dark flowers, deep and yellow whirled,
And, like a woman, I fell on my knees . . .[2]

6. Like the ripple of venetian blinds.
7. *Noctiluca*, tiny marine animals.
8. A legend that the three biblical Marys crossed the sea during a storm to land in Camargue, a region in southern France famous for its horses and bulls.
9. A name (plural) given to any exotic country.
1. Vast biblical sea monster (Job 41.1–10).
2. The poet's ellipses; nothing has been omitted.

Peninsula, I tossed upon my shores
The quarrels and droppings of clamorous, blond-eyed birds.
I sailed until, across my rotting cords,
Drowned men, spinning backwards, fell asleep! . . .

Now I, a lost boat in the hair of coves,[3]
Hurled by tempest into a birdless air,
I, whose drunken carcass neither Monitors
Nor Hansa ships[4] would fish back for men's care;

Free, smoking, rigged with violet fogs,
I, who pierced the red sky like a wall
That carries exquisite mixtures for good poets,
Lichens of sun and azure mucus veils;

Who, spotted with electric crescents, ran
Like a mad plank, escorted by seashores,
When cudgel blows of hot Julys struck down
The sea-blue skies upon wild water spouts;

I, who trembled, feeling the moan at fifty leagues
Of rutting Behemoths[5] and thick Maelstroms, I,
Eternal weaver of blue immobilities,
I long for Europe with its ancient quays!

I saw sidereal archipelagoes! and isles
Whose delirious skies are open to the voyager:
—Is it in depthless nights you sleep your exile,
A million golden birds, O future Vigor?—

But, truly, I have wept too much! The dawns disturb.
All moons are painful, and all suns break bitterly:
Love has swollen me with drunken torpors.
Oh, that my keel might break and spend me in the sea!

Of European waters I desire
Only the black, cold puddle in a scented twilight
Where a child of sorrows squats and sets the sails
Of a boat as frail as a butterfly in May.

I can no longer, bathed in languors, O waves,
Cross the wake of cotton-bearers on long trips,
Nor ramble in a pride of flags and flares,
Nor swim beneath the horrible eyes of prison ships.[6]

3. Seaweed.

4. Vessels belonging to the German Hanseatic League of commercial maritime cities. "Monitors": armored coast guard ships, after the iron-clad Union warship *Monitor* of the American Civil War.

5. Biblical animal resembling a hippopotamus (Job 40.15–24).

6. Portholes of ships tied at anchor and used as prisons.

RUBÉN DARÍO

Rubén Darío (1867–1916) was the first poet of *Modernismo*—a movement that revolutionized Spanish American poetry. He was inspired by the French Symbolists, and he fused their poetic innovations with a range of traditions, including his own indigenous ancestry, occult science, and ancient Greek mythology, to create a startling new sensibility. Darío's life, like his poetry, spanned continents and historical moments. He was born in Nicaragua, lived in Chile and Argentina, worked for the Colombian government, and spent many years in Europe as a reporter and diplomat, managing to serve as a bridge between countries and generations. When two later writers, **Pablo Neruda** and **García Lorca**, paid homage to Darío in 1933, they called him "that great Nicaraguan, Argentinian, Chilean, and Spanish poet" whose poetry, "crisscrossed with sounds and dreams . . . stands solidly outside of norms, forms, and schools."

LIFE

Rubén Darío was born Félix Rubén García y Sarmiento in a small village in Nicaragua now called Ciudad Darío (Darío City). His parents separated when he was only eight months old, and he was sent to live with an aunt and uncle in the old city of Léon. His autobiography describes the impression made on him by the antiquated house and the ghostly horror stories told after dinner, which gave him nightmares. Before he was eight, he had made a name for himself as a child-poet and soon became well known in the region. At fourteen he began submitting articles to newspapers, and in 1886 he moved to Chile, where he worked as a journalist and wrote poetry. It was here, two years later, that he published *Azul* (*Blue*), a collection of his writing that would come to be recognized as a turning point in Spanish American literary history.

In 1891 Nicaragua arranged to send a delegation to Spain for the fourth centennial of the European discovery of America, and Darío went as secretary to the delegation. Exhilarated by the warm reception he experienced as a representative of Spanish American letters, he moved to Argentina with new confidence in his role as a spokesperson for Latin American literature and culture.

Darío married twice and had two children who survived to adulthood. In the early years of the twentieth century, he lived in Madrid and then in Paris. Eventually, suffering from cirrhosis of the liver and barely making a living in Europe, he returned to Nicaragua, where he died in 1916. After his death, the government ordered national mourning and granted him the burial honors of a high-level minister, while the Church performed funeral services usually reserved for royalty.

WORK

Although Darío is known for modernizing Latin American poetry, he was not one to discard traditional literary forms and conventions. His works deliberately recall forms with a long history—such as the *blasón* (blazon), a love poem that lists the beauties of the beloved. He also drew on age-old images: the swan was Darío's favorite symbol of artistic inspiration—ideally beautiful, and yet haunted by doubt, with its neck swerving into the shape of a question mark. All of this suggests a deep debt to tradition. But what felt strikingly new to his contemporaries was Darío's style. The poems, short stories, and sketches in the early collection *Blue* seemed far more similar to the evocative, jewel-like recent work of French Symbolist writers—such as Paul Verlaine, one of Darío's great heroes—than to contemporary Spanish-language writers, who tended to favor long rhetorical passages. His sentences were surprisingly short, with rhythmic and stylistic variations; he preferred foreign, even exotic subjects, and rare and musical words. "Words should paint the color of a sound, the aroma of a star; they should capture the very soul of things," he wrote. Like many of the French Symbolists, then, he evoked ideal beauties in rich images rather than describing gritty realities, and he concentrated his attention on the musical qualities of his verse. He also purified his language of anything coarse or vulgar and produced a rigorously flawless technical brilliance that was entirely different from any poetry that had been written in Spanish before. At the same time, there was always a sense of melancholy, of longing and doubt, as if the pursuit of the ideal was always doomed to failure.

Darío's final collection, *Songs of Life and Hope*, continued the emphasis on musicality and technical perfection but also displayed a new poetic awakening to contemporary political and cultural concerns, as well as a somber interrogation of the poet's own mortality, as we see in the poem "Fatality." His final poems invite a new sense of violence that breaks from the perfectly crafted, ideal gems that are the early work.

Darío's influence was already so overpowering by 1910 that a young Mexican poet named Enrique González Martínez urged his fellow poets to "wring the swan's neck." And yet poets have continued to return to Darío for inspiration. Indeed, his work has had such a profound impact that some literary historians have broken the story of Spanish-language poetry into two periods—before and after Darío.

Blazon[1]

For the Countess of Peralta

The snow-white Olympic[2] swan,
with beak of rose-red agate,
preens his eucharistic[3] wing,
which he opens to the sun like a fan.

1. This and the following poems are translated by Lysander Kemp. "Blazon": both a heraldic coat of arms and a poem that enumerates various qualities of the beloved.

2. Associated with Mount Olympus, home of the gods in Greek mythology.

3. Like the white wafer used in the Eucharist, the Christian ritual of communion.

His shining neck is curved
like the arm of a lyre,
like the handle of a Greek amphora,[4]
like the prow of a ship.

He is the swan of divine origin
whose kiss mounted through fields
of silk to the rosy peaks
of Leda's[5] sweet hills.

White king of Castalia's fount,
his triumph illumines the Danube;[6]
Da Vinci was his baron in Italy;
Lohengrin[7] is his blond prince.

His whiteness is akin to linen,
to the buds of white roses,
to the diamantine white
of the fleece of an Easter lamb.

He is the poet of perfect verses,
and his lyric cloak is of ermine;
he is the magic, the regal bird
who, dying, rhymes the soul in his song.

This wingèd aristocrat displays
white lilies on a blue field;
and Pompadour,[8] gracious and lovely,
has stroked his feathers.

He rows and rows on the lake
where dreams wait for the unhappy,
where a golden gondola waits
for the sweetheart of Louis of Bavaria.[9]

Countess, give the swans your love,
for they are gods of an alluring land
and are made of perfume and ermine,
of white light, of silk, and of dreams.

4. Large two-handled jar used in ancient Greece for storing wine or oil.
5. In Greek mythology, a nymph raped by Zeus, who had taken the form of a swan; she gave birth to Helen of Troy.
6. A major river in central Europe. "Castalia's fount": the spring of Castalia on Mount Parnassus, home of the Greek Muses.
7. The "Swan Knight" of Wagner's opera *Lohengrin* (1850). "Da Vinci": Leonardo da Vinci (1452–1519), the Renaissance artist and inventor.
8. The Marquise de Pompadour (1721–1764) was the mistress of King Louis XV of France. "White lilies on a blue field": the fleur-de-lis. The coat of arms of the French kings displayed white lilies on a blue background.
9. The mad king of Bavaria (1864–86) who built a fairytale castle and retired from the world; he was Wagner's patron for many years.

I Seek a Form . . .

I seek a form that my style cannot discover,
a bud of thought that wants to be a rose;
it is heralded by a kiss that is placed on my lips
in the impossible embrace of the Venus de Milo.[1]

The white peristyle[2] is decorated with green palms;
the stars have predicted that I will see the goddess;
and the light reposes within my soul like the bird
of the moon reposing on a tranquil lake.

And I only find the word that runs away,
the melodious introduction that flows from the flute,[3]
the ship of dreams that rows through all space,

and, under the window of my sleeping beauty,[4]
the endless sigh from the waters of the fountain,
and the neck of the great white swan, that questions me.

Leda

The swan in shadow seems to be of snow;
his beak is translucent amber in the daybreak;
gently that first and fleeting glow of crimson
tinges his gleaming wings with rosy light.

And then, on the azure waters of the lake,
when dawn has lost its colors, then the swan,
his wings outspread, his neck a noble arc,
is turned to burnished silver by the sun.

The bird from Olympus, wounded by love, swells out
his silken plumage, and clasping her in his wings
he ravages Leda there in the singing water,
his beak seeking the flower of her lips.

She struggles, naked and lovely, and is vanquished,
and while her cries turn sighs and die away,
the screen of teeming foliage parts and the wild
green eyes of Pan[1] stare out, wide with surprise.

1. Ancient Greek statue of Venus, goddess of love and beauty, found on the island of Melos; the statue's arms are missing.
2. A courtyard surrounded by columns.
3. Compare Mallarmé's *The Afternoon of a Faun*, lines 16–20.
4. Sleeping Beauty (capitalized in the original).
1. The horned shepherd god of woods and field.

Fatality

The tree is happy because it is scarcely sentient;
the hard rock is happier still, it feels nothing:
there is no pain as great as being alive,
no burden heavier than that of conscious life.

To be, and to know nothing, and to lack a way,
and the dread of having been, and future terrors . . .
And the sure terror of being dead tomorrow,
and to suffer all through life and through the darkness,

and through what we do not know and hardly suspect . . .
And the flesh that tempts us with bunches of cool grapes,
and the tomb that awaits us with its funeral sprays,
and not to know where we go,
nor whence we came! . . .

ourne 1218

II

At the Crossroads of Empire

Many a ruler has dreamed of acquiring a great empire. The first challenge is to subjugate neighboring peoples and then, as one grows rich and powerful from those conquests, to vanquish ever-more-distant peoples and lands. And yet maintaining an empire turns out to be a grueling task. Crossing vast distances is difficult enough, but keeping control of far-off places requires canny and forceful administration. The subjugated peoples may well rise up, and they have some advantages: they know the local terrain, and they may be able to rally substantial popular support for resistance to foreign domination. Meanwhile, imperial troops and administrators can easily grow weary of spending their lives far from home, in places where local people resent them. Their families back home may not benefit much, if at all, from the new imperial possessions, and popular enthusiasm for conquest at home may dwindle, as people begrudge the cost in lives and taxes that it takes to maintain an empire. Emperors need to persuade their own subjects to value the mission of empire, which means that they must invoke a sense of urgent or high purpose. For this, rulers depend in part on the use of words, on rousing rhetoric to muster broad support for their dreams of conquest. Thus,

The Amar Singh Gate of the Agra Fort, India; picture taken by British photographer Samuel Bourne in 1865.

writers can play a crucial role in the making and keeping of empires.

Of course, many a subjugated people has also dreamed of throwing out foreign invaders. The humiliation of being conquered is often the primary source of their discontent. But foreign empires not only inflict armies from far away, they also typically impose their language, their laws, and their religion. New imperial administrators disrupt long-standing ways of life with imported rules; they exploit local resources, including the people themselves; and they assert the superiority of the conquering state, insisting on wiping away values and traditions they see as backward or primitive in favor of their own ways of life. The occupied people may well feel outraged to the point of violence and begin to rally support for rebellion against the foreign invaders. This support is often easy enough to rouse at the beginning, but it can get difficult if the conquered people begin to believe that the conquering power is too strong or too advanced to unseat. Perhaps, after a few generations of intermarriage between the conquerors and the conquered, it becomes difficult to wrench the two peoples apart. Hence those who wish to fight off the bonds of empire feel the need for writers just as the mighty emperors do: they crave stirring words to capture the value of native customs and beliefs under threat and to build up the people's determination to struggle against the empire—knowing full well that any resistance may entail horrific sacrifices.

A great deal of our experience of the world today is a consequence of the dominance of European empires in the nineteenth century. Our feelings of global interconnectedness as well as our sense of the deep economic inequalities that divide the developed world from developing nations are effects of Europe's imperial reach. Britain and France became the world's major superpowers then, centers of vast empires that stretched across the globe. These empires had emerged out of fierce economic competition among European nations going back several centuries. Hoping to profit from new natural resources and new markets, England, France, Spain, Holland, and Portugal had sent ships both eastward and westward, trying to establish monopolies on trade relations with Turkey, Russia, India, and China, and establishing colonies in North and South America. European consumers developed a growing appetite for products from these distant places, goods such as tea, coffee, sugar, furs, cotton, silver, tobacco, rubber, silk, spices, and opium. The profits reaped by European companies soared. The slave trade played a crucial role in this new economy: traders would buy slaves in Africa and sell them to plantation owners in the United States, Brazil, and the Caribbean. Slave traders would then use the profits to buy products of slave labor, such as tobacco and sugar, which they would transport to Europe to sell to eager customers there.

Since all of Europe coveted the same valuable markets, tensions rose among European nations, frequently erupting into outright war. In the eighteenth century, France lost a series of wars with Britain, which frustrated its dreams of controlling North America, the Caribbean, and India. France then looked elsewhere. Long interested in opening up trade with Vietnam, the French army invaded in the 1850s and took control. They industrialized the Vietnamese economy, investing in railroads and factories, and made huge profits from Vietnamese rubber, coal, and sugar. But few Vietnamese people benefited: under French rule, poverty, disease, and starvation became commonplace.

Conflicts among European empires redrew the maps of whole continents. When Napoleon invaded Spain and put his brother on the throne there, he destabilized monarchical authority so profoundly that emboldened Latin Americans were able to win wars of independence from Spanish rule. Many of

A colonial French family in Vietnam with a machine gun, ca. 1900.

these struggles were aided by Britain, which was eager to limit Spanish economic and political power. In the 1880s, European powers that had held various territories on the African coast began to compete for power inland, dividing up Africa into spheres of control. The diverse territories of South Africa prompted the Boer Wars, battles between the British army and Dutch settlers. In west central Africa, Great Britain, Germany, France, and Portugal vied for territory. By the turn of the century, 90 percent of the African continent was under European control. Around this time, the United States and Japan also began to build empires, entering into the competition with European states. In 1898, the United States intervened in Cuba and the Philippines, sparking the Spanish–American War and beginning its new role as another powerful imperial player on the world stage.

Until the nineteenth century, European nations had been unashamed to admit that their imperial missions were above all about profits. But if the Europeans traveled to distant lands for economic reasons, they often stayed for political ones. Over the course of the nineteenth century, the rhetoric of racial difference deepened, as Europeans saw themselves less and less as economic actors and more and more as liberators and civilizers of less "advanced" races. Advocates of colonialism often argued that empires existed not for the benefit of the conquerors but for the sake of the conquered "primitive" peoples, who were believed incapable of self-government but who could, with European guidance, eventually become civilized. Global empires had filled European coffers, but this the Europeans often conveniently forgot, speaking of themselves instead as responsible world leaders, reluctantly taking up what Rudyard Kipling famously called "the white man's burden."

But while Europeans often claimed to be motivated by a high-minded responsibility to spread reason and progress, reports of atrocities made it clear that the zeal to civilize was often a mask for brutal exploitation. King Leopold II of Belgium

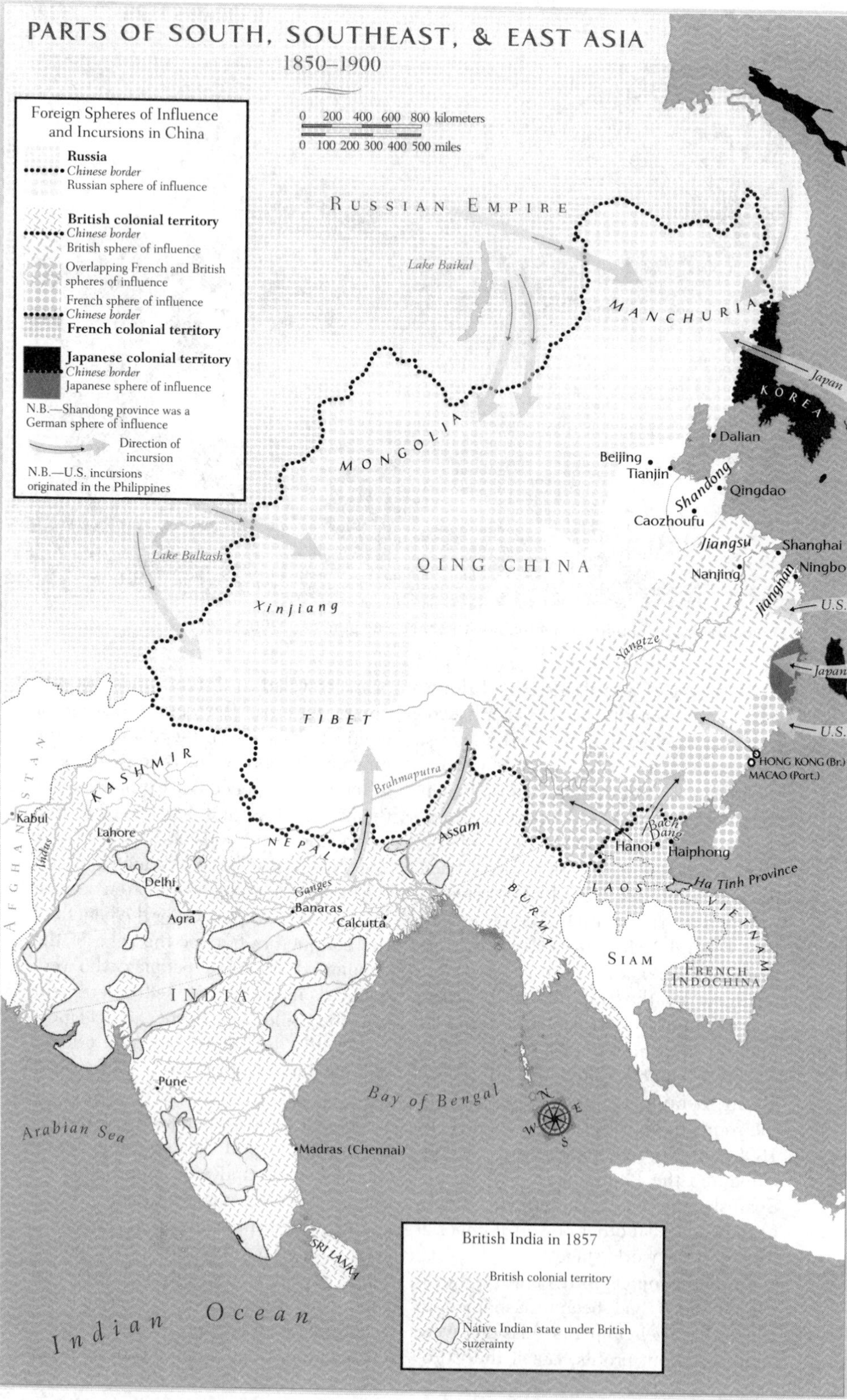

PARTS OF SOUTH, SOUTHEAST, & EAST ASIA
1850–1900
0 200 400 600 800 kilometers
0 100 200 300 400 500 miles
Foreign Spheres of Influence and Incursions in China
Russia
Chinese border
Russian sphere of influence
British colonial territory
Chinese border
British sphere of influence
Overlapping French and British spheres of influence
French sphere of influence
Chinese border
French colonial territory
Japanese colonial territory
Chinese border
Japanese sphere of influence
N.B.—Shandong province was a German sphere of influence
Direction of incursion
N.B.—U.S. incursions originated in the Philippines
RUSSIAN EMPIRE
Lake Baikal
MANCHURIA
Japan
KOREA
Dalian
Beijing
Tianjin
Shandong
Qingdao
Caozhoufu
MONGOLIA
Lake Balkash
QING CHINA
Jiangsu
Shanghai
Nanjing
Ningbo
Jiangnan
U.S.
Xinjiang
Yangtze
Japan
U.S.
TIBET
HONG KONG (Br.)
MACAO (Port.)
KASHMIR
AFGHANISTAN
Brahmaputra
Kabul
Lahore
Indus
NEPAL
Assam
Bach Dang
Hanoi
Haiphong
Delhi
Agra
Ganges
Banaras
Calcutta
BURMA
LAOS
Ha Tinh Province
VIETNAM
SIAM
FRENCH INDOCHINA
INDIA
Pune
Bay of Bengal
Arabian Sea
Madras (Chennai)
SRI LANKA
Indian Ocean
British India in 1857
British colonial territory
Native Indian state under British suzerainty

sent explorers to the Congo Free State, for example, under the guise of a scientific and charitable association, but in fact intending to subdue the Congolese through economic and military force. Eager to profit from the rubber trade, Leopold's agents enslaved Congolese workers and brutally tortured and mutilated them, often leaving them to starve. As much as half the population—ten million people—died under Leopold's regime. Around the globe, the violence and exploitation of European empires fostered resentment and out-and-out insurrection. A major blow to British imperialism, for example, came in 1857 when Indian soldiers rebelled against the British army. The British violently suppressed the rebellion, resorting to brutality that left lasting scars. Indian subjects began to feel a profound mistrust of the British that would fuel increasingly insistent movements for independence.

Writers in South and East Asia in the nineteenth century faced particularly daunting challenges. Struggling to define their own linguistic and literary roles in relation to long-standing local and imperial traditions, they also got caught up in new collisions between vast empires. For many centuries China had been the great unchallenged superpower in East Asia, and the Islamic Mughal Empire successfully ruled India, but in the eighteenth and nineteenth centuries the expanding European empires headed eastward and began to establish significant power in Asia. Britain, which managed to conquer a full quarter of the world's population, building the largest empire in human history, had taken over from the Mughals in India and by the middle of the nineteenth century had made inroads into China. Meanwhile, France, Russia, Portugal, the Netherlands, and Japan claimed land and trading rights in different places across Asia, leading to hostility with one another and with Britain and China.

What was it like to write at the crossroads of contending empires? The writers collected in this section reveal a complex variety of attitudes, all of them profoundly ambivalent. Vietnam's **Nguyễn Du** cherished a deep love and respect for the intellectual traditions of imperial China, which had ruled Vietnam for many centuries and remained a menacing neighbor. But Nguyễn Du resisted the easy assumption of Chinese superiority: he deliberately chose to write in vernacular Vietnamese, crafting a new heroic epic for his nation in the language of the people. A generation later in India, the poet **Ghalib** belonged to the Muslim ruling elite and wrote in two different imperial languages—Persian, the official court language imported from afar, and Urdu, an Indian idiom that reflected his particular hybrid Indo-Muslim culture. When Indian princes and soldiers rose up in an unsuccessful revolt against the British in 1857, Ghalib's court patronage ended and the poet struggled to make a living as he refused to show the mandatory deference to the British Empire. Born a half century after Ghalib, **Pandita Ramabai** followed yet another kind of path; an Indian writer who came from an orthodox Hindu family, she converted to Christianity—the religion of the British—and became a missionary, traveling to the United States and Britain and devoting herself to reforming the lives of Indian women, who, she argued, were essential to the well-being of her beloved homeland. Like Ghalib, Ramabai wrote in two languages: her native Marathi and English. A final example comes from China. The writer **Liu E** came of age at a moment when European ideas, products, and technologies had begun to transform traditional Chinese ways of life and were triggering a violent backlash. Liu E supported industrialization and was willing to borrow ideas from the West, but he opposed foreign power over China. He was eventually forced into exile, accused of betraying the nation to foreign invaders.

All of these writers remained torn between loyalty to local traditions and

A photograph of men in a Chinese opium den, ca. 1900.

respect or even admiration for a conquering imperial power. All of them had to negotiate between two or more languages and power structures. But their responses were strikingly varied. And so together they give a rich sense of the multiple ways that bitterness, inspiration, and responsibility combine to create the complex experience of writing at the crossroads of powerful empires.

NGUYỄN DU

1765–1820

Memorized by illiterate farmers, consulted by lovers, esteemed by learned scholars, and popular with readers of all classes, *The Tale of Kiều* has no rival in Vietnamese literature. Many Vietnamese people can recite the whole narrative by heart—more than 3,000 lines of poetry—and some use the text to divine the future. This story of a young woman buffeted by fate—forced into prostitution and slavery—has come to stand for a nation that has been repeatedly attacked by foreign invaders and oppressed by tyrants. But it is also a gripping love story whose talented and heroic protagonist lives on in the memory long after we have finished reading. And it is a work of literary genius that displays the richness of Vietnamese linguistic and cultural traditions while addressing themes—lust, loyalty, sacrifice, corruption, faith, and justice—that extend beyond any single nation.

LIFE AND TIMES

China ruled Vietnam for over a thousand years (111 B.C.E.–939 C.E.). Periodically, Vietnamese rebels tried to unseat Chinese rule until the tenth century, when Vietnamese leaders defeated the Chinese in the famous Battle of Bạch Dàng River, thus ending a millennium of Chinese domination and asserting independence. Buddhism and Confucianism remained the dominant religious traditions, along with Taoism, and these merged to become a distinctively Vietnamese religion. Classical Chinese remained the nation's official language for many hundreds of years, a period in which Vietnam was wracked by civil war and continued to repel threats of invasion by Chinese armies, often successfully adopting tactics of guerilla warfare.

Nguyễn Du was born in 1766 to a learned and powerful family in the Nghệ Tĩnh province in northern Vietnam. He was well educated. His father had been prime minister under the Lê dynasty, but his father's high rank was hardly an advantage in late-eighteenth-century Vietnam, as the Lê rulers came under attack by the Tây Sơn, a unified peasant uprising that brought the nation together and drove out Chinese and Siamese invaders. Since Nguyễn Du's family had been loyal to the old Lê dynasty, the poet spent the first thirty years of his life struggling to survive the tumult of the Tây Sơn revolution, remaining poor and obscure. In 1802, however, he reluctantly pledged his loyalty to a new ruler, Gia Long, who had suppressed the Tây Sơn revolution and established a national capital in central Vietnam. So began an era of relative peace and national unity.

The writer felt suspicious of Gia Long, who seemed to him an illegitimate ruler, and *The Tale of Kiều* suggests that he may even have felt some admiration for the peasant revolution, since his own glorious war hero, Tu-Hai, is possibly modeled on the rebel Tây Sơn leader. It is well known, too, that Nguyễn Du wrote his great poem while oppressed with a sense of great loss and disenchantment, his family's long-standing loyalty to the Lê dynasty having given way to pretensions of loyalty to an upstart regime. Nguyễn Du's heroine, Kiều, battered by fate and forced to prostitute herself, has long been a folk symbol of what it means to suffer injustice and struggle to survive, but she may also stand for Nguyễn Du's own discontent, resentment, and shame at having betrayed his own convictions to play the part of a faithful official in order to protect himself and his family.

Under the new regime, Nguyễn Du was highly regarded as a poet, but was granted only official positions that had no real power. He became ambassador to China in 1813, for example, but this post was by custom reserved for scholars who had a wide knowledge of Chinese poetry and were not expected to exert any political control. It was on one of his diplomatic visits to China that Nguyễn Du may have come across his inspiration for *The Tale of Kiều*—a prose narrative called *The Tale of Jin, Yun, and Qiao*, written in Chinese, probably in the seventeenth century. Nguyễn Du also wrote other poems, some of them in Chinese style, though none reached the stature of his great verse novel. He died in 1820.

The Tale of Kiều continued to resonate as a symbol of Vietnam's troubled history well after its first publication. When France invaded Vietnam in 1862, some Vietnamese leaders who collaborated with the foreign invaders saw themselves, like Kiều, as victims of circumstance who must bow to fate. They were cast as traitors by others, who claimed they resembled Scholar Mã—a greedy pimp in the story—rather than his innocent prey.

French missionaries had been in Vietnam since the sixteenth century, and the French, eager especially for new markets for their own products, had long been interested in opening up trade with Vietnam. For the first half of the nineteenth century, Vietnamese leaders remained divided: should they ban foreign trade and the Christian religion, or should they welcome wealth and influence from overseas? Emperors leaned one way and then the other until the late 1850s when the French army invaded, intent on establishing an empire that could compete with the British in Asia. By the end of the nineteenth century, the French colony of Indochina had grown to include all of Vietnam as well as Laos and Cambodia. French companies made huge profits from Vietnamese rubber, coal, and sugar, while poverty, disease, and starvation became commonplace for the indigenous people. As late as 1939, 80 percent of the population was still illiterate. Numerous anti-French resistance movements took shape, none of them successful until the Second World War, when Imperial Japan occupied Vietnam and temporarily expelled the French.

Vietnam would remain a battleground for competing world powers through most of the rest of the twentieth century. The struggle for control of Vietnam by China, the Soviet Union, and the United States reinforced the idea that the nation was, like Kiều, cursed by fate to suffer at the hands of others, and those who were forced to flee Vietnam have often turned to the story as solace meant for sufferers and survivors.

WORK

The Tale of Kiều is widely considered one of the greatest achievements of Vietnamese literature. For the first time, the Vietnamese language was on display in all of the diversity of its rhythms, moods, and expressions. And for its contemporaries, the text triumphantly broke the tradition of dominance by classical Chinese in favor of a gorgeous and distinguished vernacular.

Some of the poem's power lies in Nguyễn Du's rich blending of folk traditions and scholarly knowledge. On the one hand, the text owes a great deal to popular oral songs and poetry. Its metrical regularity of alternating lines of six and eight syllables is derived from folk ballads, and one reason for the lasting popularity of the poem is that its quintessentially oral rhyming patterns make it easy to memorize. This meter also differs markedly from the patterns of classical Chinese poetry, which favor odd numbers of syllables (often five and seven). The poem thus transforms traditional oral patterns into highly crafted written form, but retains enough of the feeling of a popular ballad that it is easily reincorporated back into a predominantly oral culture, learned and loved by people who do not have access to literacy.

On the other hand, *Kiều* is a remarkable storehouse of classical Chinese learning, including over a hundred quotations from the *Classics of Poetry* and other Confucian texts, over a hundred references to Chinese poetry and fiction, and two dozen mentions of Buddhist or Daoist texts. Analogous in some ways to the role of ancient Greece in nineteenth-century Western Europe, classical Chinese tradition was a rich philosophical and literary resource for Vietnamese thinkers. Both Buddhism and Confucianism were dominant religious traditions in Vietnam, with Chinese religious texts exerting a powerful influence. And even nine centuries after Vietnamese independence, classical Chinese remained both the language of official business and the prevailing language of literature. It was in this context that we can recognize what a remarkable achievement it was for Nguyễn Du to take the vernacular language of folktales and ordinary people and transform it into the consummately literary language of *The Tale of Kiều*.

Admirers of the poem have often noted that Nguyễn Du weaves Chinese allusions gracefully into the text without their seeming dreary or pedantic. And for those who recognize the references to Chinese tradition, such allusions lend a depth to the poem. For example, the poet represents his war hero Từ Hải as both a powerful soldier and a lover of music: "Plying his oar, he roved the streams and lakes / with sword and lute upon his shoulders slung" (lines 2173–74). The combination of martial bravery and aesthetic sensitivity communicates itself to any reader, but those who grasp the reference will know that Nguyễn Du is also alluding to Huang Chao, the ninth-century Chinese warlord who rebelled against the Tang court and established himself as emperor for two short years, helping to bring about the demise of the Tang dynasty.

It is intriguing that Nguyễn Du chose a female protagonist for his great poem. In doing so, he drew on his Chinese model, but he also followed in the footsteps of other male Vietnamese writers, who often chose heroines to explore life's struggles. Some have speculated that the focus on central female characters might be a ploy, in a context of strict political censorship, to distract political leaders from potentially subversive political messages: that is, by putting rebellious ideas in the mouth of a relatively powerless character who is clearly distant from the author's own life and experience, the writer could gain a measure of freedom. It was also true that Vietnam adopted a far more liberal set of norms for women than did neighboring China. For many centuries, women had nearly equal rights in matters of marriage and inheritance, and two sisters, the legendary "Trưng queens," had even successfully rebelled against the Chinese Han Empire for a few years during the first century C.E. (a poem in their honor is included in Volume B). At the same time, Confucianism was influential throughout Vietnam and dictated a subordinate role for women. It is possible that oppressed women seemed like ideal vehicles for male Vietnamese writers feeling frustrated at their subjection to unjust political leaders who insisted on strict obedience, in keeping with Confucian principles.

And indeed, some scholars suggest that *The Tale of Kiều* offers a rebellious response to both Confucian and Buddhist ideas. The text certainly draws on Buddhist thinking, including the notion that past, present, and future existences are interwoven, but it seems to reject the idea that living for passion will necessarily result in sorrow and punishment. Instead, the story rewards individual acts in the name of love, and it imagines a woman who remains pure and good despite many lovers—a terrible breach of Confucian principles. Kiều's decision to meet her young lover privately in his room would have seemed unthinkable to Confucian believers, and the story celebrates the worst of Confucian transgressions—rebellion—when it lavishes adoring attention on Từ Hải, a hero so noble and brave, in Nguyễn Du's narrative, that even his enemies are in awe of him. Từ Hải actively redresses injustices rather than passively bowing to fate, and seems much more like a stirring folk hero than a proper follower of the Buddha or of Confucius.

The complexity of moral decision making in *The Tale of Kiều* is clearly part of the story's lasting power. For example, Nguyễn Du does not offer Kiều's agonizing choice between loyalty to her family, who have raised and nurtured her, and loyalty to the young man she loves passionately, as a matter of clear or straightforward judgment. Kiều must reason her way through it, with compelling arguments made on both sides. Similarly, when a victorious Từ Hải compels all of those who have wronged Kiều to come before her and receive justice, Kiều surprises onlookers by forgiving Miss Hoạn, who has tormented and enslaved her. This wrongdoer has acted out of jealousy, Kiều concludes, responding to passionate feeling and expressing a genuine remorse. Given the text's thought-provoking engagement with ethical questions, it is perhaps not surprising that readers have turned to *The Tale of Kiều* not only for the richness of its language, for the fascinating possiblities of its political messages, or for its exciting plot and vivid characters, but also for guidance in the struggle to figure out how to live in the face of suffering and cruelty, divided loyalties and intoxicating love.

From The Tale of Kiều[1]

I

A hundred years—in this life span on earth
talent and destiny are apt to feud.
You must go through a play of ebb and flow
and watch such things as make you sick at heart.
Is it so strange that losses balance gains?
Blue Heaven's wont to strike a rose[2] from spite.

By lamplight turn these scented leaves and read
a tale of love recorded in old books.
Under the Jiajing reign when Ming held sway,
all lived at peace—both capitals stood strong.[3]
There was a burgher in the clan of Vương,
a man of modest wealth and middle rank.
He had a last-born son, Vương Quan—his hope
to carry on a line of learned folk.
Two daughters, beauties both, had come before:
Thúy Kiều was oldest, younger was Thúy Vân.
Bodies like slim plum branches, snow-pure souls:
each her own self, each perfect in her way.
In quiet grace Vân was beyond compare:
her face a moon, her eyebrows two full curves;
her smile a flower, her voice the song of jade;
her hair the sheen of clouds, her skin white snow.
Yet Kiều possessed a keener, deeper charm,
surpassing Vân in talents and in looks.
Her eyes were autumn streams, her brows spring hills.
Flowers grudged her glamour, willows her fresh hue.
A glance or two from her, and kingdoms rocked!
Supreme in looks, she had few peers in gifts.
By Heaven blessed with wit, she knew all skills:
she could write verse and paint, could sing and chant.
Of music she had mastered all five tones,

1. Translated by Huynh Sanh Thông.
2. From the Vietnamese "má hồng," an expression referring to beautiful women.
3. There were two capitals of China during the Ming dynasty (1368–1644)—Beijing in the north and Nanjing in the south. "Jiaqing": name given to the reign of Chinese emperor Shizong (r. 1522–66).

and played the lute far better than Ai Zhang.[4]
She had composed a song called *Cruel Fate*
to mourn all women in soul-rending strains.
A paragon of grace for womanhood,
she neared that time when maidens pinned their hair.[5]
She calmly lived behind drawn shades and drapes,
as wooers swarmed, unheeded, by the wall.

Swift swallows and spring days were shuttling by—
of ninety radiant ones three score had fled.
Young grass spread all its green to heaven's rim;
some blossoms marked pear branches with white dots.
Now came the Feast of Light[6] in the third month
with graveyard rites and junkets on the green.
As merry pilgrims flocked from near and far,
the sisters and their brother went for a stroll.
Fine men and beauteous women on parade:
a crush of clothes, a rush of wheels and steeds.
Folks clambered burial knolls to strew and burn
sham gold or paper coins, and ashes swirled.
Now, as the sun was dipping toward the west,
the youngsters started homeward, hand in hand.
With leisured steps they walked along a brook,
admiring here and there a pretty view.
The rivulet, babbling, curled and wound its course
under a bridge that spanned it farther down.
Beside the road a mound of earth loomed up
where withered weeds, half yellow and half green.
Kiều asked: "Now that the Feast of Light is on,
why is no incense burning for this grave?"
Vương Quan told her this tale from first to last:
"She was a famous singer once, Đam Tiên.
Renowned for looks and talents in her day,
she lacked not lovers jostling at her door.
But fate makes roses fragile—in mid-spring
off broke the flower that breathed forth heaven's scents.
From overseas a stranger came to woo
and win a girl whose name spread far and wide.
But when the lover's boat sailed into port,
he found the pin had snapped, the vase had crashed.[7]
A death-still silence filled the void, her room;
all tracks of horse or wheels had blurred to moss.
He wept, full of a grief no words could tell:
'Harsh is the fate that has kept us apart!
Since in this life we are not meant to meet,

4. The most famous lute player in China during the Han dynasty (206 B.C.E.–265 C.E.). "Five tones": traditional Chinese music follows a five-tone (pentatonic) system.

5. An old Chinese custom held that when girls were fifteen and ready for marriage, they would pin up their hair.

6. Chinese spring festival when people tend the graves of the dead and make offerings to them.

7. Chinese metaphors for the death of a wife or lover.

let me pledge you my troth for our next life.'
He purchased both a coffin and a hearse
and rested her in dust beneath this mound,
among the grass and flowers. For many moons,
who's come to tend a grave that no one claims?"
  A well of pity lay within Kiều's heart:
as soon as she had heard her tears burst forth.
"How sorrowful is women's lot!" she cried.
"We all partake of woe, our common fate.
Creator, why are you so mean and cruel,
blighting green days and fading rose-fresh cheeks?
Alive, she played the wife to all the world,
alas, to end down there without a man!
Where are they now who shared in her embrace?
Where are they now who lusted for her charms?
Since no one else gives her a glance, a thought,
I'll light some incense candles while I'm here.
I'll mark our chance encounter on the road—
perhaps, down by the Yellow Springs,[8] she'll know."
  She prayed in mumbled tones, then she knelt down
to make a few low bows before the tomb.
Dusk gathered on a patch of wilted weeds—
reed tassels swayed as gently blew the breeze.
She pulled a pin out of her hair and graved
four lines of stop-short verse[9] on a tree's bark.
Deeper and deeper sank her soul in trance—
all hushed, she tarried there and would not leave.
The cloud on her fair face grew darker yet,
as sorrow ebbed or flowed, tears dropped or streamed.
  Vân said: "My sister, you should be laughed at,
lavishing tears on one long dead and gone!"
"Since ages out of mind," retorted Kiều,
"harsh fate has cursed all women, sparing none.
As I see her lie there, it hurts to think
what will become of me in later days."
  "A fine speech you just made!" protested Quan.
"It jars the ears to hear you speak of her
and mean yourself. Dank air hangs heavy here—
day's failing, and there's still a long way home."
  Kiều said: "When one who shines in talent dies,
the body passes on, the soul remains.
In her, perhaps, I've found a kindred heart:
let's wait and soon enough she may appear."
  Before they could respond to what Kiều said,
a whirlwind rose from nowhere, raged and raved.
It blustered, strewing buds and shaking trees
and scattering whiffs of perfume in the air.
They strode along the path the whirlwind took

8. The underworld.
9. Compact poetic form of four lines developed by poets in Tang-dynasty China (618–907).

and plainly saw fresh footprints on the moss.
They stared at one another, terror-struck.
"You've heard the prayer of my pure faith!" Kiều cried.
"As kindred hearts, we've joined each other here—
transcending life and death, soul sisters meet."
  Đam Tiên had cared to manifest herself;
to what she'd written Kiều now added thanks.
A poet's feelings, rife with anguish, flowed:
she carved an old-style poem[1] on the tree.

  To leave or stay—they all were wavering still
when nearby rang the sound of harness bells.
They saw a youthful scholar come their way
astride a colt he rode with slackened rein.
He carried poems packing half his bag,
and tagging at his heels were some page boys.
His frisky horse's coat was dyed with snow.
His gown blent tints of grass and pale blue sky.
He spied them from afar, at once alit
and walked toward them to pay them his respects.
His figured slippers trod the green—the field
now sparkled like some jade-and-ruby grove.
Young Vương stepped forth and greeted him he knew
while two shy maidens hid behind the flowers.
  He came from somewhere not so far away,
Kim Trong, a scion of the noblest stock.
Born into wealth and talent, he'd received
his wit from heaven, a scholar's trade from men.
Manner and mien set him above the crowd:
he studied books indoors, lived high abroad.
Since birth he'd always called this region home—
he and young Vương were classmates at their school.
  His neighbors' fame had spread and reached his ear:
two beauties locked in their Bronze Sparrow Tower![2]
But, as if hills and streams had barred the way,
he had long sighed and dreamt of them, in vain.
How lucky, in this season of new leaves,
to roam about and find his yearned-for flowers!
He caught a fleeting glimpse of both afar:
spring orchid, autumn mum—a gorgeous pair!
  Beautiful girl and talented young man—
what stirred their hearts their eyes still dared not say.
They hovered, rapture-bound, 'tween wake and dream;
they could not stay, nor would they soon depart.
The dusk of sunset prompted thoughts of gloom—
he left, and longingly she watched him go.
Below a stream flowed clear, and by the bridge
a twilit willow rustled threads of silk.

1. Ancient poetic form with a five-word meter.
2. In the Three Kingdoms period of Chinese history (220–280), the heroic leader Cao Cao tried to capture two beautiful sisters from his enemies and lock them in his palace, the Bronze Sparrow Tower, but was defeated by a young commander named Zhou Yu.

When Kiều got back behind her flowered drapes,
the sun had set, the curfew gong had rung.
Outside the window, squinting, peeped the moon—
gold spilled on waves, trees shadowed all the yard.
East drooped a red camellia, toward the next house:
as dewdrops fell, the spring branch bent and bowed.
Alone, in silence, she beheld the moon,
her heart a raveled coil of hopes and fears.
"Lower than that no person could be brought!
It's just a bauble then, the glittering life.
And who is he? Why did we chance to meet?
Does fate intend some tie between us two?"
Her bosom heaved in turmoil—she poured forth
a wondrous lyric fraught with all she felt.
The moonlight through the blinds was falling slant.
Leaning against the window, she drowsed off.
Now out of nowhere there appeared a girl
of worldly glamour joined to virgin grace:
face washed with dewdrops, body clad in snow,
and hovering feet, two golden lotus blooms.[3]
With joy Kiều hailed the stranger, asking her:
"Did you stray here from that Peach Blossom Spring?"[4]
"We two are sister souls," the other said.
"Have you forgotten? We just met today!
My cold abode lies west of here, out there,
above a running brook, below a bridge.
By pity moved, you stooped to notice me
and strew on me poetic pearls and gems.
I showed them to our League Chief[5] and was told
your name is marked in the Book of the Damned.
We both reap what we sowed in our past lives:
of the same League, we ride the selfsame boat.
Well, ten new subjects our League Chief just set;
again please work your magic with a brush."
Kiều did as asked and wrote—with nymphic grace
her hand dashed off ten lyrics at one stroke.
Đam Tiên read them and marveled to herself:
"Rich-wrought embroidery from a heart of gold!
Included in the Book of Sorrow Songs,[6]
they'll yield the palm to none but win first prize."
The caller crossed the doorsill, turned to leave,
but Kiều would hold her back and talk some more.
A sudden gust of wind disturbed the blinds,
and Kiều awakened, knowing she had dreamed.
She looked, but nowhere could she see the girl,
though hints of perfume lingered here and there.

3. Bound feet, traditionally considered beautiful for women in China, but not a custom adopted in Vietnam.
4. Legendary paradise, once found by a fisherman and then lost again forever, described by the Chinese poet Tao Qian (365–427).
5. Chief of the League of Sorrow, a group of beautiful and talented women who are doomed.
6. Collection of poetry and songs written by members of the League of Sorrow.

Alone with her dilemma in deep night,
she viewed the road ahead and dread seized her.
A rose afloat, a water fern adrift:
such was the lot her future held in store.
Her inmost feelings surged, wave after wave—
again and yet again she broke and cried.
Kiều's sobs sent echoes through the phoenix drapes.
Aroused, her mother asked: "What troubles you
that you still stir and fret at dead of night,
your cheeks like some pear blossoms drenched with rain?"
Kiều said: "You once bore me, you've brought me up,
a double debt I've not repaid one whit.
Today, while strolling, I found Đam Tiên's grave,
then in a dream she just revealed herself.
She told me how by fate I'm doomed to grief,
delivered themes on which I wrote some songs.
As I interpret what the dream portends,
my life in days ahead won't come to much!"
Her mother said: "Are dreams and vapors grounds
whereon to build a tale of woe? Just think!"
Kiều tried to heed such words of sound advice,
but soon her tears welled up and flowed again.
Outside the window chirped an oriole—
over the wall a catkin flew next door.
The tilting moonlight lay aslant the porch—
she stayed alone, alone with her own grief.

How strange, the race of lovers! Try as you will,
you can't unsnarl their hearts' entangled threads.
Since Kim was back inside his book-lined walls,
he could not drive her from his haunted mind.
He drained the cup of gloom: it filled anew—
one day without her seemed three autumns long.
Silk curtains veiled her windows like dense clouds,
and toward the rose within he'd dream his way.
The moon kept waning, oil kept burning low,
his face yearned for her face, his heart her heart.
The study-room turned icy, metal-cold—
brushes lay dry, lute strings hung loose on frets.
Xiang bamboo blinds[7] stirred rustling in the wind—
incense roused longing, tea lacked love's sweet taste.
If fate did not mean them to join as mates,
why had the temptress come and teased his eyes?
Forlorn, he missed the scene, he missed the girl:
he rushed back where by chance the two had met.
A tract of land with grasses lush and green,
with waters crystal-clear: he saw naught else.
The breeze at twilight stirred a mood of grief—
the reeds waved back and forth as if to taunt.

7. According to legend, when the Emperor Shun died, his wives Ehuang and Nüying wept so heavily that their tears stained this species of bamboo.

A lover's mind is full of her he loves:
he walked straight on and made toward her Blue Bridge.[8]
  Fast gate, high wall: no stream for his red leaf,
no passage for his bluebird bearing word.[9]
A willow dropped its curtain of silk threads—
perched on a branch, an oriole chirped jeers.
All doors were shut, all bolts were locked in place.
A threshold strewn with flowers—where was she?
  He lingered, standing there as time passed by,
then to the rear he strolled—he saw a house.
Its owner, traveling heathen climes for trade,
was still away—left vacant were the rooms.
  Young Kim, as student, came to rent the house—
he brought his lute, his books, and settled in.
He lacked for nothing—trees and rocks, a porch
inscribed in vivid gold: "Kingfisher View."[1]
The porch's name made him exult inside:
"It must be Heaven's will that we should meet!"
He left his window open just a crack
and daily glanced his eyes toward that east wall.
Nearby both spring and grotto stayed tight shut:
he failed to see the nymph flit in and out.
  Since he left home to dwell at this strange lodge,
twice on its rounds the moon had come and gone.
Now, on a balmy day, across the wall,
he glimpsed a lissome form beneath peach trees.
He dropped the lute, smoothed down his gown, rushed out:
her scent was wafting still—of her no trace.
  As he paced round the wall, his eye espied
a golden hairpin caught on a peach branch.
He reached for it and took it home. He thought:
"It left a woman's chamber and came here.
This jewel must be hers. Why, fate binds us—
if not, could it have fallen in my hands?"
Now sleepless, he admired and stroked the pin
still faintly redolent of sandalwood.
  At dawn when mists had cleared, he found the girl
peering along the wall with puzzled eyes.
The student had been lurking there in wait—
across the wall he spoke to test her heart:
"From nowhere I have found this hairpin here:
I would send back the pearl, but where's Hepu?"[2]
  Now from the other side Kiều's voice was heard:
"I thank him who won't keep a jewel found.

8. The place where a man will meet the woman he will marry, an expression that comes from a Chinese legend about a man who encounters an immortal nymph near a blue bridge and marries her, becoming immortal himself.

9. In Chinese Daoist literature, the bluebird brings messages of love; the red leaf is a symbol of love determined by fate.

1. Kiều's other name, Thuy, means kingfisher.

2. The Chinese city of Hepu was famous for its pearls, but when too many people fished for pearls, the supply threatened to disappear; thus a prudent ruler regulated the fisheries. A "pearl going back to Hepu" is an expression that means that something is being returned to its proper place.

A pin's worth little, but it means so much
that in your scale what's right weighs more than gold."
He said: "We come and go in these same parts—
we're neighbors, not two strangers, not at all!
I owe this moment to some scent you dropped,
but countless torments I've endured till now.
So long I've waited for just this one day!
Stay on and let me ask your private thoughts."
He hurried off and fetched some things from home:
gold bracelets in a pair, a scarf of silk.
By ladder he could climb across the wall:
she was the one he'd met that day, no doubt!
Ashamed, the girl maintained a shy reserve:
while he gazed at her face, she hung her head.
He said: "We chanced to meet—and ever since
I have in secret yearned and pined for you.
My slender frame has wasted—who'd have thought
that I could linger on to see this day?
For months I dreamt my goddess in the clouds:
lovelorn, I hugged my post, prepared to drown.[3]
But you are here—I beg to ask one thing:
will on a leaf of grass the mirror shine?"[4]
She faltered—after some demur she said:
"Our ways are snow-pure, plain as turnip greens.
When comes the time for love, the marriage bond,
my parents' wish will tie it or will not.
You deign to care for me, but I'm too young
to know what's right and dare not give my word."
He said: "It blows one day and rains the next—
how often does chance favor us in spring?
If you ignore and scorn my desperate love,
you'll hurt me—yet what will it profit you?
Let's pledge our troth with something—once that's done,
I'll plan our wedding through a go-between.
Should Heaven disappoint my fondest hopes,
I'll throw away a life in vernal bloom.
If to a lover's plea you shut your heart,
I'll have pursued you all in vain, for naught!"
All hushed, she drank in words whose music lulled—
love stirred the autumn calm of her fair eyes.
She said: "Although our friendship's still quite new,
how can my heart resist your heart's behest?
To your kind bosom you have taken me—
I'll etch your word, our troth, in stone and bronze."
Her words untied a knot within his breast—
to her he passed gold bracelets and red scarf.
"Henceforth I'm bound to you for life," he said.

3. Having arranged a meeting with his beloved under a bridge, a young man named Wei Sheng waited for her so long that he eventually drowned, as he held onto a pillar.

4. The leaf of grass here is an image of someone worthless; elsewhere in the poem water plants are metaphors for women destined to wander.

"Call these small gifts a token of my love."
In hand she had a sunflower-figured fan:[5]
she traded it that instant for her pin.
  They had just sworn an oath to seal their pact
when from the backyard voices came, abuzz.
Both fled—in flurries leaves and flowers fell,
and he regained his study, she her room.

  The stone and gold had touched—and from that time,
their love grew deeper, more distraught their minds.
The Xiang, the stream of longing tears, ran low:
he waited at the spring, she at the mouth.[6]
The wall rose like a snow-capped mountain range,
and words of love could not go back and forth.
  As windswept days and moonlit nights wheeled round,
red dimmed, green deepened—spring was past and gone.
A birthday feast fell due in Mother's clan:
with their two younger children, both old folks
in gay attire left home to journey forth
presenting their best wishes and a gift.
  A hushed, deserted house—she stayed alone:
a chance to see him on this day, she thought.
She set out fare in season, treats galore,
then toward the wall she bent her nimble steps.
She sent a soft-voiced call across the flowers:
he was already there awaiting her.
  He said: "Your heart cares not for what I feel—
so long you've let love's fire burn to cold ash.
Sorrow and yearning I have felt by turns,
and half my head of hair frost's tinged with gray."
She said: "Wind's held me up, rain's kept me back—
I've hurt your feelings much against my wish.
I'm home alone today—I've come out here
to make amends repaying love for love."
  She slid around the rock garden and reached
a fresh-barred passage at the wall's far end.
She rolled up sleeves, unlocked the fairy cave[7]
and cleared through clouds the path to Paradise!
  Face gazed at face to glow with purest joy.
Fond greetings they exchanged. Then, side by side,
they walked together toward his study-room
while mingling words of love and vows of troth.
  Brush rack and tube for poems on his desk—
above, there hung a sketch of pale green pines.
Frost-bitten and wind-battered, they looked real;

5. In the Confucian tradition, the sunflower stands for feminine submission and fidelity; the fan is a symbol of femininity across East Asia.

6. According to an old Chinese song, "He stays at the source of the Xiang. / She stays at the mouth of the Xiang. / Unseeing, both yearn for each other. / Both drink the water of the Xiang."

7. Legendary cave that leads to paradise.

the more she gazed, the more they sprang to life.
"It's something I dashed off just now," he said.
"Please write your comments, lending it some worth."
Her nymphic hand moved like a lashing storm
and penned some quatrains right atop the pines.
"Your magic conjures gems and pearls!" he cried.
"Could Ban and Xie[8] have measured up to this?
If I did not earn merit in past lives,
could I be blessed with you, my treasure, now?"
She said: "I've dared to peek and read your face:
you shall wear jade or cross the Golden Gate.[9]
But I deem my own lot a mayfly's wing:
will Heaven square things out and round things off?
Back in my childish years, I still recall,
a seer observed my features—he foretold,
'All charms and splendors from within burst forth:
she'll live an artist's life, a life of woe.'
I look at you, then on myself look back:
how could good luck, ill luck conjoin and thrive?"
He said: "That we have met means fate binds us.
Man's will has often vanquished Heaven's whim.
But should the knot which ties us fall apart,
I'll keep my troth and sacrifice my life."
They bared and shared all secrets of their souls—
spring feelings quivered hearts, spring wine turned heads.
A happy day is shorter than a span:
the western hills had swallowed up the sun.
With none at home, she could no longer stay:
she left him, rushing back to her own room.

News of her folks she learned when she reached home:
her feasting parents would not soon be back.
She dropped silk curtains at the entrance door,
then crossed the garden in dark night, alone.
The moon through branches cast shapes bright or dark—
through curtains glimmered flickers of a lamp.
The student at his desk had nodded off,
reclining half awake and half asleep.
The girl's soft footsteps woke him from his drowse:
the moon was setting as she hovered near.
He wondered—was this Wuxia the fairy hill,[1]
where he was dreaming now a spring night's dream?
"Along a lonesome, darkened path," she said,
"for love of you I found my way to you.
Now we stand face to face—but who can tell
we shan't wake up and learn it was a dream?"

8. Famous Chinese women scholars: Ban Zhao (ca. 45–116) and Xie Daoyun (4th century).
9. Only highly ranked court ministers could pass through the Golden Portal. Officials who were also scholars typically wore jade emblems to indicate their high position.
1. Where the goddess of love lives.

He bowed and welcomed her, then he replaced
the candle and refilled the incense urn.
Both wrote a pledge of troth, and with a knife
they cut in two a lock of her long hair.
The stark bright moon was gazing from the skies
as with one voice both mouths pronounced the oath.
Their hearts' recesses they explored and probed,
etching their vow of union in their bones.
Both sipped a nectar wine from cups of jade—
silks breathed their scents, the mirror glassed their selves.
"The breeze blows cool, the moon shines clear," he said,
"but in my heart still burns a thirst unquenched.
The pestle's yet to pound on the Blue Bridge—
I fear my bold request might give offense."
She said: "By the red leaf, the crimson thread,[2]
we're bound for life—our oath proves mutual faith.
Of love make not a sport, a dalliance,
and what would I begrudge you otherwise?"
He said: "You've won wide fame as lutanist:
like Zhong Ziqi I've longed to hear you play."[3]
"It's no great art, my luting," answered she,
"but if you so command, I must submit."
In the back porch there hung his moon-shaped lute:
he hastened to present it in both hands,
at eyebrow's height. "My petty skill," she cried,
"is causing you more bother than it's worth!"
By turns she touched the strings, both high and low,
to tune all four to five tones, then she played.
An air, *The Battlefield of Han and Chu*,[4]
made one hear bronze and iron clash and clang.
The Sima tune, *A Phoenix Seeks His Mate*,[5]
sounded so sad, the moan of grief itself.
Here was Ji Kang's famed masterpiece, *Guangling*[6]—
was it a stream that flowed, a cloud that roamed?
Crossing the Border-gate—here was Zhaojun,
half lonesome for her lord, half sick for home.[7]
Clear notes like cries of egrets flying past:
dark tones like torrents tumbling in mid-course.
Andantes languid as a wafting breeze:
allegros rushing like a pouring rain.

2. The Wedlock God ties two people together in marriage with a red thread.
3. According to Confucian tradition, Zhong Ziqi always appreciated and understood the lute playing of his friend Bo Ya. When he died Bo Ya smashed his lute.
4. Liu Bang (256–195 B.C.E.) defeated Xiang Yu of the state of Chu and went on to found the Han dynasty.
5. Song played on a lute by the writer Sima Xiangru (179–117 B.C.E.) to win the heart of a young woman, who married him against her family's wishes.
6. Ji Kang (223–262) was a famous Chinese musician and music theorist who was best known for a song called *Guangling*.
7. The emperor Han Yuandi sent his concubine Zhaojun as a gift to the leader of the Xiongnu tribes, who wanted a Chinese wife.

The lamp now flared, now dimmed—and there he sat
hovering between sheer rapture and deep gloom.
He'd hug his knees or he'd hang down his head—
he'd feel his entrails wrenching, knit his brows.
"Indeed, a master's touch," he said at last,
"but it betrays such bitterness within!
Why do you choose to play those plaintive strains
which grieve your heart and sorrow other souls?"
"I'm settled in my nature," she replied.
"Who knows why Heaven makes one sad or gay?
But I shall mark your golden words, their truth,
and by degrees my temper may yet mend."
A fragrant rose, she sparkled in full bloom,
bemused his eyes, and kindled his desire.
When waves of lust had seemed to sweep him off,
his wooing turned to wanton liberties.
She said: "Treat not our love as just a game—
please stay away from me and let me speak.
What is a mere peach blossom that one should
fence off the garden, thwart the bluebird's quest?
But you've named me your bride—to serve her man,
she must place chastity above all else.
They play in mulberry groves along the Pu,[8]
but who would care for wenches of that ilk?
Are we to snatch the moment, pluck the fruit,
and in one sole day wreck a lifelong trust?
Let's ponder those love stories old and new—
what well-matched pair could equal Cui and Zhang?[9]
Yet passion's storms did topple stone and bronze:
she cloyed her lover humoring all his whims.
As wing to wing and limb to limb they lay,
contempt already lurked beside their hearts.
Under the western roof the two burned out
the incense of their vow, and love turned shame.
If I don't cast the shuttle in defense,[1]
we'll later blush for it—who'll bear the guilt?
Why force your wish on your shy flower so soon?
While I'm alive, you'll sometime get your due."
The voice of sober reason gained his ear,
and tenfold his regard for her increased.
As silver paled along the caves, they heard
an urgent call from outside his front gate.
She ran back toward her chamber while young Kim
rushed out and crossed the yard where peaches bloomed.

8. The mulberry groves along the Pu River were traditional places for lovers' secret meetings.

9. Famous lovers in Chinese literature; they appear in "The Story of Yingying" by the Tang writer Yuan Zhen (779–831).

1. According to legend, a girl working at a loom threw the shuttle at an unwelcome suitor and broke his teeth.

II

The brush wood gate unbolted, there came in
a houseboy with a missive fresh from home.
It said Kim's uncle while abroad had died,
whose poor remains were now to be brought back.
To far Liaoyang, beyond the hills and streams,[2]
he'd go and lead the cortege, Father bade.
What he'd just learned astounded Kim—at once
he hurried to her house and broke the news.
In full detail he told her how a death,
striking his clan, would send him far away:
"We've scarcely seen each other—now we part.
We've had no chance to tie the marriage tie.
But it's still there, the moon that we swore by:
not face to face, we shall stay heart to heart.
A day will last three winters far from you:
my tangled knot of grief won't soon unknit.
Care for yourself, my gold, my jade, that I,
at the world's ends, may know some peace of mind."
She heard him speak, her feelings in a snarl.
With broken words, she uttered what she thought:
"Why does he hate us so who spins silk threads?[3]
Before we've joined in joy we part in grief.
Together we did swear a sacred oath:
my hair shall gray and wither, not my love.
What matter if I must wait months and years?
I'll think of my wayfaring man and grieve.
We've pledged to wed our hearts—I'll never leave
and play my lute aboard another's boat.[4]
As long as hills and streams endure, come back,
remembering her who is with you today."
They lingered hand in hand and could not part,
but now the sun stood plumb above the roof.
Step by slow step he tore himself away—
at each farewell their tears would fall in streams.
Horse saddled and bags tied in haste, he left:
they split their grief in half and parted ways.
Strange landscapes met his mournful eyes—on trees
cuckoos galore, at heaven's edge some geese.
Grieve for him who must bear through wind and rain
a heart more loaded down with love each day.

There she remained, her back against the porch,
her feelings snarled like raveled skeins of silk.
Through window bars she gazed at mists beyond—
a washed-out rose, a willow gaunt and pale.
Distraught, she tarried walking back and forth

2. Province in Manchuria, now in northeast China.
3. The Wedlock God.
4. To play a lute aboard another man's boat is an expression meaning that a woman betrays her lover, leaving him for someone else.

LIBERTÉ DE LA PRESSE

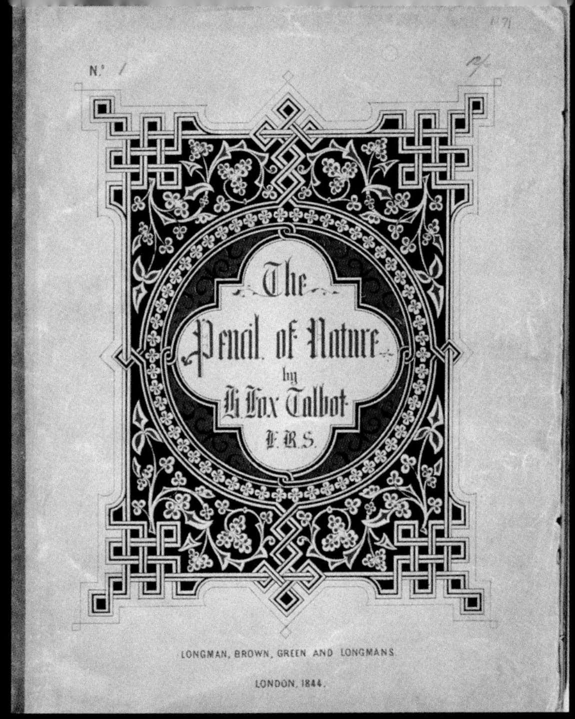

The Pencil of Nature, assembled and published in 1844 by William Henry Fox Talbot (1800–1877), was the first commercially available book illustrated with photographs. Shown here are the cover of the first issue (it was published in six installments) and one of the "plates" inside that issue: Fox's 1841 photograph "Bust of Patroclus."

During the nineteenth century, inventors raced to improve the speed and output of printing technologies. Richard Hoe, an American inventor, pushed the technology significantly forward with his design in 1847 of the lithographic rotary press. The version of Hoe's printing machine pictured here was used to produce *The Daily Telegraph* newspaper in London during the 1860s.

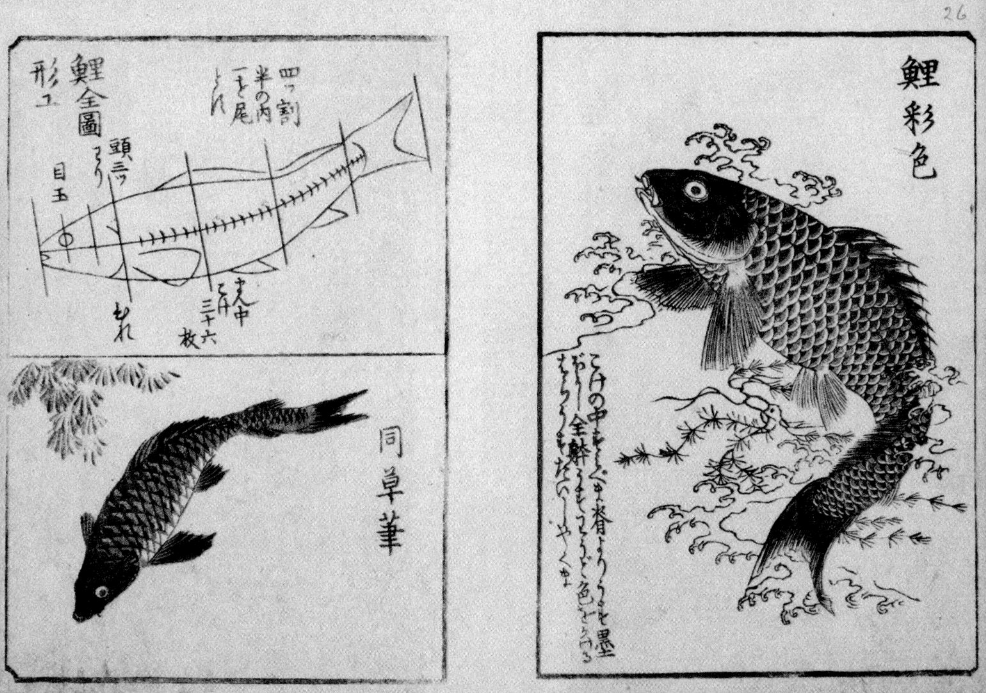

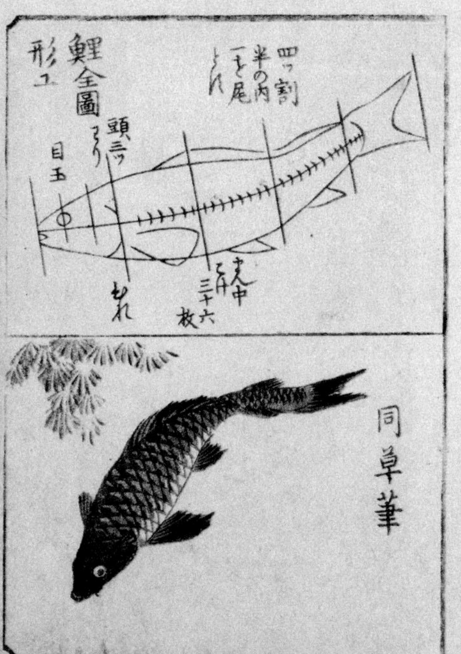

Sketches of swimming carp from *A Picture Book Miscellany* (1849), a book by the Japanese ukiyo-e artist Utagawa Hiroshige (1797–1858) that displays his commitment to realistic renderings of subjects from nature.

SKETCHES IN JAPAN BY OUR SPECIAL ARTIST: THE STORYTELLER (A DAILY SCENE) IN YOKUHAMA.

A street scene from 1861 in Yokohoma, Japan, shows a storyteller (center, seated on small stage) accompanying himself with a stringed instrument.

The world's first commercially produced typewriter: the Hansen Writing Ball designed by Rasmus Malling-Hansen (1835–1890), minister and principal at the Danish Royal Institute for the Deaf. First designed in 1865 and improved over the next fifteen years, Hansen's machine would eventually be overshadowed by late nineteenth-century typewriters that allowed one to see the result on paper as one typed (rather than operating 'blind,' as with the writing ball).

when from the birthday feast her folks returned.
Before they could trade news of health and such,
in burst a mob of bailiffs on all sides.
With cudgels under arm and swords in hand,
those fiends and monsters rushed around, berserk.
They cangued[5] them both, the old man, his young son—
one cruel rope trussed two dear beings up.
Then, like bluebottles buzzing through the house,
they smashed workbaskets, shattered looms to bits.
They grabbed all jewels, fineries, personal things,
scooping the household clean to fill greed's bag.
From nowhere woe had struck—who'd caused it all?
Who'd somehow set the snare and sprung the trap?
Upon inquiry it was later learned
some knave who sold raw silk had brought a charge.
Fear gripped the household—cries of innocence
shook up the earth, injustice dimmed the clouds.
All day they groveled, begged, and prayed—deaf ears
would hear no plea, harsh hands would spare no blow.
A rope hung each from girders, by his heels—
rocks would have broken, let alone mere men.
Their faces spoke sheer pain and fright—this wrong
could they appeal to Heaven far away?
Lawmen behaved that day as is their wont,
wreaking dire havoc just for money's sake.

By what means could she save her flesh and blood?
When evil strikes, you bow to circumstance.
As you must weigh and choose between your love
and filial duty, which will turn the scale?
She put aside all vows of love and troth—
a child first pays the debts of birth and care.
Resolved on what to do, she said: "Hands off—
I'll sell myself and Father I'll redeem."
There was an elderly scrivener surnamed Chung,
a bureaucrat who somehow had a heart.
He witnessed how a daughter proved her love
and felt some secret pity for her plight.
Planning to pave this way and clear that path,
he reckoned they would need three hundred liang.
He'd have her kinsmen freed for now, bade her
provide the sum within two days or three.
Pity the child, so young and so naive—
misfortune, like a storm, swooped down on her.
To part from Kim meant sorrow, death in life—
would she still care for life, much less for love?
A raindrop does not brood on its poor fate:
a leaf of grass repays three months of spring.
Matchmakers were advised of her intent—
brisk rumor spread the tidings near and far.

5. Forced them to wear a cangue, a heavy wooden collar worn by criminals as punishment.

There lived a woman in that neighborhood,
who brought a suitor, one from out of town.
When asked, he gave his name as Scholar Mâ
and claimed his home to be "Lin-ching, near here."
Past forty, far beyond the bloom of youth,
he wore a smooth-shaved face and smart attire.
Master and men behind came bustling in—
the marriage broker ushered him upstairs.
He grabbed the best of seats and sat in state
while went the broker bidding Kiều come out.
  Crushed by her kinsfolk's woe and her own grief,
she crossed the sill, tears flowing at each step.
She felt the chill of winds and dews, ashamed
to look at flowers or see her mirrored face.
The broker smoothed her hair and stroked her hand,
coaxing a wilted mum, a gaunt plum branch.
  He pondered looks, gauged skills—he made her play
the moon-shaped lute, write verses on a fan.
Of her lush charms he relished each and all:
well pleased, he set to bargaining a deal.
  He said: "For jade I've come to this Blue Bridge:
tell me how much the bridal gift will cost."
The broker said: "She's worth her weight in gold!
But in distress they'll look to your big heart."
They haggled hard and long, then struck a deal:
the price for her, four hundred and some liang.
All was smooth paddling once they gave their word—
as pledges they swapped horoscopic cards
and set the day when, full paid for, she'd wed.
When cash is ready, what cannot be fixed?
Old Chung was asked to help—at his request,
old Vương could on probation go back home.
  Pity the father facing his young child.
Looking at her, he bled and died within:
"You raise a daughter wishing she might find
a fitting match, might wed a worthy mate.
O Heaven, why inflict such woes on us?
Who slandered us to tear our home apart?
I would not mind the ax for these old bones,
but how can I endure my child's ordeal?
Death now or later happens only once—
I'd rather pass away than suffer so."
  After he'd said those words he shed more tears
and made to knock his head against a wall.
They rushed to stop him, then she softly spoke
and with some words of comfort calmed him down:
"What is she worth, a stripling of a girl
who's not repaid one whit a daughter's debts?
Ying once shamed me, petitioning the throne—

could I fall short of Li who sold herself?[6]
As it grows old, the cedar is a tree
that singly shoulders up so many boughs.
If moved by love you won't let go of me.
I fear a storm will blow and blast our home.
You'd better sacrifice just me—one flower
will turn to shreds, but green will stay the leaves.
Whatever lot befalls me I accept—
think me a blossom nipped when budding green.
Let no wild notions run around your head
or you shall wreck our home and hurt yourself."
Words of good sense sank smoothly in his ear—
they stared at one another, pouring tears.
Outside, that Scholar Mâ appeared again—
they signed the contract, silver then changed hands.
A wanton god, the Old Man of the Moon,[7]
at random tying couples with his threads!
When money's held in hand it's no great trick
swaying men's hearts and turning black to white.
Old Chung did all he could and gave all help:
gifts once presented, charges were dismissed.

* * *

How to express her grief while on the tower
a watchman tolled and tolled the hours of night?
A carriage, flower-decked, arrived outside
with flutes and lutes to bid dear kin part ways.
She grieved to go, they grieved to stay behind:
tears soaked stone steps as parting tugged their hearts.
Across a twilit sky dragged sullen clouds—
grasses and branches drooped, all drenched with dew.
He led her to an inn and left her there
within four walls, a maiden in her spring.
The girl felt torn between dire dread and shame—
she'd sadly brood, her heart would ache and ache.
A rose divine lay fallen in vile hands,
once kept from sun or rain for someone's sake.
"If only I had known I'd sink so low,
I should have let my true love pluck my bud.
Because I fenced it well from the east wind,[8]
I failed him then and make him suffer now.
When we're to meet again, what will be left
of my poor body here to give much hope?
If I indeed was born to float and drift,

6. Li Ji, the heroine of a Tang story, sold herself as a sacrifice to a snake demon to save her parents.

7. A name for the god of marriage.

8. The east wind blows in the springtime and is supposed to bring love.

how can a woman live with such a fate?"
Upon the table lay a knife at hand—
she grabbed it, hid it wrapped inside her scarf:
"Yes, if and when the flood should reach my feet,
this knife may later help decide my life."
The autumn night wore on, hour after hour—
alone, she mused, half wakeful, half asleep.
She did not know that Scholar Mã, the rogue,
had always patronized the haunts of lust.
The rake had hit a run of blackest luck:
in whoredom our whoremaster sought his bread.
Now, in a brothel, languished one Dame Tú
whose wealth of charms was taxed by creeping age.
Mere hazard, undesigned, can bring things off:
sawdust and bitter melon[9] met and merged.
They pooled resources, opening a shop
to sell their painted dolls all through the year.
Country and town they scoured for "concubines"
whom they would teach the trade of play and love.
With Heaven lies your fortune, good or ill,
and woe will pick you if you're marked for woe.
Pity a small, frail bit of womankind,
a flower sold to board a peddler's boat.
She now was caught in all his bag of tricks:
a paltry bridal gift, some slapdash rites.
He crowed within: "The flag has come to hand![1]
I view rare jade—it stirs my heart of gold!
The kingdom's queen of beauty! Heaven's scent!
One smile of hers is worth pure gold—it's true.
When she gets there, to pluck the maiden bud,
princes and gentlefolk will push and shove.
She'll bring at least three hundred liang, about
what I have paid—net profit after that.
A morsel dangles at my mouth—what God
serves up I crave, yet money hate to lose.
A heavenly peach within a mortal's grasp:
I'll bend the branch, pick it, and quench my thirst.
How many flower-fanciers on earth
can really tell one flower from the next?
Juice from pomegranate skin and cockscomb blood
will heal it up and lend the virgin look.
In dim half-light some yokel will be fooled:
she'll fetch that much, and not one penny less.
If my old broad finds out and makes a scene,
I'll take it like a man, down on my knees!
Besides, it's still a long, long way from home:
if I don't touch her, later she'll suspect."

9. Vietnamese expression meaning two con artists who are well-matched.
1. Reference to the Vietnamese proverb "Whoever holds the flag waves it," meaning that those who hold power are free to use it as they please.

Oh, shame! A pure camellia had to let
the bee explore and probe all ins and outs.
A storm of lust broke forth—it would not spare
the flawless jade, respect the pristine scent.
All this spring night was one bad dream—she woke
to lie alone beneath the nuptial torch.
Her tears of silent grief poured down like rain—
she hated him, she loathed herself as much:
"What breed is he, a creature foul and vile?
My body's now a blot on womanhood.
What hope is left to cherish after this?
A life that's come to this is life no more."
By turns she cursed her fate, she moaned her lot.
She grabbed the knife and thought to kill herself.
She mulled it over: "If I were alone,
it wouldn't matter—I've two loved ones, though.
If trouble should develop afterwards,
an inquest might ensue and work their doom.
Perhaps my plight will ease with passing time.
Sooner or later, I'm to die just once."
While she kept tossing reasons back and forth,
a rooster shrilly crowed outside the wall.
The watchtower horn soon blared through morning mists,
so Mâ gave orders, making haste to leave.
Oh, how it rends the heart, the parting hour,
when horse begins to trot and wheels to jolt!
Ten miles beyond the city, at a post,
the father gave a feast to bid farewell.
While host and guests were making cheer outside,
mother and Kiều were huddling now indoors.
As they gazed at each other through hot tears,
Kiều whispered all her doubts in mother's ear:
"I'm just a girl, so helpless, to my shame—
when could I ever pay a daughter's debts?
Lost here where water's mud and dust's soil-free,[2]
I'll leave with you my heart from now, for life.
To judge by what I've noticed these past days,
I fear a scoundrel's hands are holding me.
When we got there, he left me all alone.
He tarried coming in, but out he dashed.
He halts and stammers often when he talks.
His men make light of him, treat him with scorn.
He lacks the ease and grace of gentlefolk,
seeming just like some merchant on close watch.
What else to say? Your daughter's doomed to live
on foreign land and sleep in alien soil."
At all those words, Dame Vương let out a shriek
that would pierce heaven, crying for redress.
Before they had drunk dry the parting cup,

2. Chinese expression implying that society corrupts the innocent.

Mâ rushed outside and urged the coach to leave.
Mourning his daughter in his heavy heart,
old Vương stood by the saddle begging Mâ:
"Because fate struck her family, this frail girl
is now reduced to serving you as slave.
Henceforth, beyond the sea, at heaven's edge,
she'll live lone days with strangers, rain or shine.
On you, her lofty oak, she will depend,
a vine you'll shelter from cold frosts and snows."
Whereat the bridegroom said: "Our feet are bound
by that mysterious thread of crimson silk.
The sun's my witness—if I should break faith,
may all the demons strike me with their swords!"
  By stormwinds hurtled under rolling clouds,
the coach roared off in swirls of ocher dust.
Wiping their tears, they followed with their eyes:
on that horizon, day and night, they'd gaze.

III

  She traveled far, far into the unknown.
Bridges stark white with frost, woods dark with clouds.
Reeds huddling close while blew the cold north wind:
an autumn sky for her and her alone.
A road that stretched far off in hushed, still night:
she saw the moon, felt shame at her love vows.
Fall woods—green tiers all interlaid with red:
bird cries reminded her of her old folks.
She crossed unheard-of streams, climbed nameless hills—
the moon waxed full again: Linzi[3] was reached.
  The carriage stopped before an entrance gate—
a woman, parting curtains, stalked right out.
One noticed at first glance her pallid skin—
what did she feed upon to gain such bulk?
With wanton cheer she met them by the coach—
Kiều, at her bidding, meekly stepped indoors.
  On one side, there sat girls with penciled brows,
and on the other four or five gay blades.
Between, an altar all rigged out: above,
the image of that god with hoary brows.
In bawdyhouses old tradition bids
them worship him as patron of their trade,
offer him flowers, burn incense day and night.
When some jinxed gal drew too few customers,
in front of him she'd doff her shirt and skirt,
then light some incense candles mumbling prayer.
She'd take all faded flowers to line her mat,
and bees would swarm a-buzzing all around!
  Bewildered, unaware of what it was,
Kiều just knelt down as told—the bawd then prayed:

3. City in China's Shandong province.

"May fortune bless this house and business thrive
on nights of mirth, on days of revelry!
May all men fall in love with her and come
flocking like orioles and swallow-birds!
Let billets-doux and messages pour in!
Let clients throng both doorways, front and back!"
Strange sounds that made no sense to Kiều's stunned ears,
and that whole scene struck her as all amiss.
Once she'd paid homage to her household god,
Dame Tú installed herself upon a couch.
She ordered: "Kneel and bow before your aunt,
then go and kowtow to your uncle there."
"By fortune banished from my home," said Kiều,
"I hugged my humble lot as concubine.
A swallow's somehow turned an oriole:[4]
what's my real status I'm too young to know.
With bridal presents, wedding rites, and all,
we did share bed and board, as man and wife.
But now it seems the roles and ranks have changed:
may I beg you to make it clear for me?"
The woman heard the tale and learned the truth—
her devils, fiends, and demons all broke loose:
"What happened is as plain as day to see!
She caught my man alive for her own use!
I sent him for some lass to bring back here
and put to work as hostess, earn our bread.
But that false-hearted knave, that beastly rogue
had his damn itch—he played and messed with her.
Now that the cloth has lost all starch and glaze,
there goes to hell the money I put up!
You little strumpet, they sold you to me,
and in my house you go by my house rules.
When that old lecher tried his dirty trick,
why did you listen? Slap his face, instead!
Why did you just lie there and take it all?
The merest chit, do you already rut?
I must teach you how I lay down the law."
She grabbed a whip, about to pounce and lash.
"Heaven and earth bear witness!" Kiều cried out.
"My life I threw away when I left home.
What now remains of it to have and hold?"
At once she pulled the knife out of her sleeve—
O horror, she found heart to kill herself!
The bawd stood watching, helpless, as Kiều stabbed.
Alas, were all such perfect gifts and charms
to leave this earth, dissevered by a knife?
The girl's misfortune soon got noised abroad—
a crowd came pouring in and packed the house.
While she was lying there in slumber's lap,

4. Scholars often interpret this line as a veiled reference to the new Vietnamese dynasty, which Nguyễn Du felt had usurped the old Lê dynasty's rule.

the bawd just stared and shook, her wits scared off.
Then Kiều was carried out to the west porch—
someone nursed her, a doctor was called in.
Her ties to earth were not yet sundered, though—
asleep, Kiều sensed a girl was standing by.
And whispered she: "Your karma's still undone:
how could you shirk your debt of grief to life?
You're still to bear the fortune of a rose:
you wish to quit, but Heaven won't allow.
Live and fulfill your destiny, frail reed:
on the Qiantang[5] we two shall meet again."
With balms and salves applied all through the day,
Kiều slowly wakened from her deathlike swoon.
Dame Tú was waiting by the patient's bed
to coax her into line with chosen words:
"How many lives can anybody claim?
You are a rosebud—spring has scarcely sprung.
Something has gone awry—how could I force
your sterling virtue into games of love?
But since you've strayed and ended here, lock up
your chamber waiting for your nuptial day.
While you still have your body you have all—
you'll make a perfect match with some young heir.
Why visit havoc on a blameless head?
Why lose your life and hurt me? What's the good?"
The earnest plea she murmured in Kiều's ear
sounded like logic, sorting right from wrong.
Besides, there was the message of her dream:
in human fortune Heaven takes a hand.
If she died now and left her debt unpaid,
she'd pay with interest in some future life.

* * *

Summary Imprisoned and sorrowful, Kiều is urged to escape by a man who declares his love and wants her to escape with him. Kiều starts off, only to find that the man has tricked her and disappeared. She is recaptured and forced to work as a prostitute in the brothel. A scholar's son, Thúc, falls in love with her. They live together for a year. But he is already married, and his first wife, Miss Hoan, has heard of his infidelity. She arranges to drug and kidnap Kiều, forcing her to work in her house as a slave. Kiều begs Miss Hoan to allow her to renounce the world and devote her life to Buddhist piety. She takes refuge with a nun named Giác Duyên, who puts her in the care of a neighbor. The neighbor turns out to be another villain: she forces Kiều to marry a man who again sells her into prostitution.

5. River in China's Zhejiang province.

From V

Cool breeze, clear moon—her nights were going round
when from the far frontier a guest turned up.
A tiger's beard, a swallow's jaw, and brows
as thick as silkworms—he stood broad and tall.
A towering hero, he outfought all foes
with club or fist and knew all arts of war.
Between the earth and heaven he lived free:
he was Từ Hải, a native of Yuedong.[6]
Plying his oar, he roved the streams and lakes
with sword and lute upon his shoulders slung.
In town for fun, he heard loud praise of Kiều—
love for a woman bent a hero's will.
He brought his calling card to her boudoir—
thus eyes met eyes and heart encountered heart.
"Two kindred souls have joined," Từ said to Kiều.
"We're not those giddy fools who play at love.
For long I've heard them rave about your charms,
but none's won favor yet in your clear eyes.
How often have you lucked upon a *man*?
Why bother with caged birds or fish in pots?"
She said: "My lord, you're overpraising me.
For who am I to slight this man or that?
Within I crave the touchstone for the gold—
but whom can I turn to and give my heart?
As for all those who come and go through here,
am I allowed to sift real gold from brass?"
"What lovely words you utter!" Từ exclaimed.
"They call to mind the tale of Prince Pingyuan.[7]
Come here and take a good, close look at me
to see if I deserve a bit of trust."
"It's large, your heart," she said. "One of these days,
Jinyang[8] shall see a dragon in the clouds.
If you care for this weed, this lowly flower,
tomorrow may I count on your good grace?"
Well pleased, he nodded saying with a laugh:
"Through life how many know what moves one's soul?
Those eyes be praised that, keen and worldly-wise,
can see the hero hid in common dust!
Your words prove you discern me from the rest—
we'll sit together when I sit on high."
Two minds at one, two hearts in unison—
unbidden, love will seek those meant for love.
Now he approached a go-between—through her
he paid some hundred liang for Kiều's release.
They picked a quiet spot, built their love nest:

6. Now Guangdong, a province in southern China.

7. Tang poem about Prince Pingyuan, famous for his hospitality and generous protection.

8. The place where the rebel leader Li Yuan, founder of the Tang dynasty, took over the throne in the year 618.

a sumptuous bed and curtains decked with gods.
The hero chose a phoenix as his mate:
the beauty found a dragon for her mount.[9]
  A year half gone—their love was burning bright,
but now he heard the call of all four winds.
He gazed afar on sea and heaven, then
he leapt into the saddle with his sword.
  "A woman's place is near her man," she said.
"If go you must, I beg to go with you."
"We read each other's hearts, don't we?" Từ said.
"Yet you act like some vulgar woman—why?
When I can lead a hundred thousand men,
when drumbeats shake the earth and banners throw
thick shadows on the road, when all the world
admires this hero, then I'll take you home.
There's nowhere I belong. If you're to come,
you'll hinder me—I know not where I'll go.
Have patience—just wait here for me a while:
I shall be back no later than a year."
This said, he tore himself away and left—
wind-winged, the eagle soared to hunt the skies.
  Alone beside the window where grew plums,
she passed long nights within fast-bolted doors.
The courtyard moss bore no more marks of shoes—
the weeds ran wild, but gaunt the willow grew.
She peered through space to glimpse the elms back home
and, riding clouds, her fancy would fly there.
For her old parents how it ached, her heart!
Had time allayed their sorrow at their loss?
With more than ten years gone, if still alive,
they must have skin with scales and hair like frost.
Oh, how she pined and mourned for her old love—
cut from her mind, it clung on to her heart.
If her young sister had retied the knot,
she must be cuddling children in both arms.
An exile's yearning thoughts of her far land
entwined and interwove with other cares.
  After the eagle vanished into space,
she kept her eyes fast set on heaven's edge.
In silence she was waiting, night and day,
when through the region roared the flames of war.
Gray phantoms, fumes of slaughter leapt the skies
as sharks roved streams and armored men prowled roads.
Her friends and neighbors all exhorted her
to flee and somewhere stay out of harm's reach.
But she replied: "I once gave him my word—
though danger threatens, I shall not break faith."
  Perplexed, she was still wavering when, outside,
she now saw flags and heard the clang of gongs.

9. Expression referring to marrying a worthy husband.

Armor-clad troops had come and ringed the house—
in chorus they all asked, "Where is our queen?"
Ten officers, in two rows, laid down their arms,
took off their coats, and kowtowed on the ground.
Ladies-in-waiting followed, telling her:
"By order we'll escort you to our lord."
The phoenix-coach held ready for a queen
her glittering diadem, her sparkling robe.
They hoisted flags, beat drums, and off they marched—
musicians led the way, maids closed the rear.
A herald rushed ahead—the Southern Court
called all to its headquarters with the drum.
On ramparts banners waved and cannons boomed—
Lord Từ rode out to meet her at the gate.
Turbaned and sashed, he looked unlike himself,
but he still had the hero's face of old.
He laughed and said: "When fish and water meet,
it's love! Remember what you told me once?
To spot a hero took a heroine—
well, now, have I fulfilled your fondest hopes?"
She said: "I'm just a humble clinging vine
that by good luck may flourish in your shade.
It's only now we see it all come true,
yet from the first I felt it in my bones."
Eyes locked and laughing, hand in hand they walked
to their own niche where they could pour their hearts.
They gave a feast rewarding all their troops—
the wardrums thumped, the battle marches throbbed.
Triumph proved fair amends for hardships past,
and day by day their love bloomed forth afresh.

At camp, together in an idle hour,
they talked about those squalid days gone by.
In turn Kiều spoke of Wuxi and Linzi,[1]
where they'd betrayed her, where they'd cherished her:
"My life's now eased of burdens it once bore.
But wrongs or favors I've not yet repaid."
Lord Từ gave ear to her complete account,
then like a thunderblast his anger burst.
He mustered men, named captains—he bade them
rush off with flags unfurled and race the stars.
Red banners would show all his troops the way:
one wing bound for Wuxi, one for Linzi.
Those traitors who of old had wrought Kiều's woes
would be tracked down, dragged back to stand due trial.
A herald was dispatched to take such steps
as would protect the clan of Thúc from harm.
The woman chamberlain, the nun Giác Duyên
would both be asked to come as honored guests.

1. Places where Kiều has been ill-treated.

Kiều briefed all soldiers, swearing them to act:
all, outraged, vowed to execute her will.
Awesome is Heaven's law of recompense—
one haul and all were caught, brought back to camp.
Wielding big swords or brandishing long spears,
the guardsmen stood arrayed in rank and file.
All pomp and pageantry on ready view—
the grounds lay thick with weapons, dark with flags.
Under a tent erected in the midst,
Lord Từ and his fair lady took their seats.
No sooner had the drumroll died away
than guards checked names, led captives to the gate.
"Whether they used you well or ill," he said,
"pronounce yourself upon their just deserts."
She said: "I'll borrow your almighty power
to pay such dues as gratitude deems fit.
I'll render good, then make return for ill."
Lord Từ replied, "Consider your own wish."
A swordsman fetched young Thúc—face soaked with sweat
like indigo, frame shaking like a leaf.
Kiều said: "What I owe you weighs like the hills.
Remember me, your erstwhile Linzi mate?
A morning star weds not an evening star,[2]
but how could I deny my debt to you?
Brocade, a hundred bolts, a thousand pounds
of silver—with my heartfelt thanks take this.
Your wife, though, is a fiend in woman's guise—
this time, the thief has met the shrewd old gal!
Inside the cup the ant shan't crawl for long:
her deep-laid scheme shall reap its fit reward."
Meanwhile Thúc's face was quite a sight to see,
for sweat was dripping fast from it like rain.
His breast was bursting with both joy and fear:
fear for himself and joy for Kiều's own sake.
Next came the chamberlain, the elder nun:
to seats of honor they were promptly led.
Kiều clasped their hands, then off she took her veil:
"Flower the slave, Pure Spring, and I are one!
I yet recall how I once tripped and fell—
a hill of gold could not repay your love.
A thousand liang is meager wages, for
no gold can match the washerwoman's heart!"[3]
Both women stared at Kiều in stunned surprise,
all torn between awed dread and sheer delight.
She said: "Don't leave your seats as yet—stay on
and watch how I will take my sweet revenge."

2. Two stars that never see one another, like lovers or brothers who are separated or at odds.

3. In the 3rd century B.C.E., an old washerwoman gave a bowl of rice to a poor fisherman named Xin; later he became one of the emperor's highest generals and repaid the washerwoman with gold.

Captains were bid to turn their prisoners in,
submitting proofs of crimes to be perused.
Under the flags swords were unsheathed and raised—
the major culprit's name was called: Miss Hoan.
Kiều greeted her as soon as she appeared:
"Your ladyship has deigned to come today!
Before or now, a woman of your stamp
is seldom found, one with your heart of steel.
A woman, though, should wield a gentle hand—
more cruelties she sows, more woes she reaps."
The lady's wits and spirits all took flight—
under the tent she bowed her head and cried:
"I have a woman's mind, a petty soul,
and jealousy's a trait all humans share.
But please recall I let you tend the shrine,
and when you fled I stopped pursuing you.
I felt esteem for you in my own heart—
what woman, though, would gladly share her man?
I'm sorry I strewed thorns along your path—
may I beseech your mercy on my fate?"
In praise Kiều cried: "To tell the truth, you boast
a matchless wit, you know just what to say.
You have your luck to thank that I'll spare you,
for if I strike I'll look a small, mean soul.
You show a contrite spirit, as you should."
She gave an order setting free Miss Hoan,
who gratefully fell prostrate on the ground.
Now a long string of captives crossed the gate.
Kiều said: "High Heaven towers over all!
It's not my law that ill be paid with ill."
Before their judge, Bạc Hạnh, Dame Bạc came first,
then Hawk and Hound, these followed by Sở Khanh,
and last, not least, Dame Từ and Scholar Mã[4]—
guilty as charged, how could they go scot-free?
The executioner now received the word:
mete out such pains as fit each broken oath.
Blood flowed in streams while flesh was hacked to bits—
the scene struck terror into every soul.
With Heaven rest all matters here below:
harm people and they'll harm you in their turn.
Perfidious humans who do fiendish deeds
shall suffer, crying quarter all in vain.
All soldiers, crowded on the grounds, could watch
the scourage divine deal justice in broad day.
When Kiều had paid due wages to them all,
Giác Duyên soon begged to take her leave—Kiều said:
"Once in a thousand years! Is that the most
the best of friends may ever hope to meet?

4. All of the characters who have mistreated Kiều in the story, including those who have betrayed her and sold her into prostitution.

Two wanderers will part ways—where shall I find
the crane, the cloud that roams the wilds and heights?"
"But it will not be long," the nun replied.
"Our paths will cross again within five years.
As I remember, on my pilgrim's way,
I chanced upon a prophetess, Tam Hop.
She forecast you and I would meet this year,
then yet another time five twelvemonths hence.
Indeed, her prophecy's not missed the mark,
once proven true, it shall prove true again.
Our friendship still has many days ahead.
Why worry? Karma still binds us two fast."
Kiều said: "Yes, destiny can be foreseen:
what she predicts shall doubtless come to pass.
Should you encounter her along your road,
please bid her tell my fortune yet ahead."
Gladly the nun agreed to that request,
then said goodbye and left for other parts.
Since she'd paid good for good or ill for ill,
her soul's deep sea of wrongs soon ebbed away.
She knelt before Lord Từ to say her thanks:
"Could this frail reed once hope to live this day?
For me your lightning brought the wicked low
and cast a load of sorrows off my soul.
I've etched your favors in my heart, my bones—
my life itself could not discharge such debts."
Từ answered: "Down the ages have great men
so often found that mate, that sister soul?
And does a man live up to his proud name
If he confronts a wrong and winks at it?
Besides, it was a family matter, too!
Need you bow low and offer me your thanks?
But you still have your parents—I regret
that you should dwell in Yue and they in Qin.
May you rejoin them both beneath one roof
and see their faces—then, I'll rest at ease."
At his command, all gathered, spread the boards
to celebrate the just redress of wrongs.
Bamboos split fast; tiles slip, soon fall apart:
his martial might now thundered far and wide.
In his own corner he installed his court
for peace or war and cut the realm in two.
Time after time he stormed across the land
and trampled down five strongholds in the South.
He fought and honed his sword on wind and dust,
scorning those racks for coats, those sacks for rice.[5]
He stalked and swaggered through his border fief,
with no less stature than a prince, a king.

5. Expression referring to men whose only concerns are their desires and appetites.

Who dared oppose his flag, dispute his sway?
For five years, by the sea, he reigned sole lord.

There was an eminent province governor,
Lord Hồ Tôn Hiến, who plied a statesman's craft.
The emperor sent him off with special powers
to quell revolt and rule the borderland.
He knew Từ Hải would prove a gallant foe—
but then, in all his plans, Kiều had a voice.
He camped his troops and feigned to seek a truce,
sending an envoy with rich gifts for Từ.
For Kiều some presents, too: two waiting maids,
a thousand pounds of finest jade and gold.
When his headquarters got the plea for peace,
Lord Từ himself felt gnawing doubts and thought:
"My own two hands have built this realm—at will,
I've roamed the sea of Chu, the streams of Wu.
If I turn up at court, bound hand and foot,
what will become of me, surrendered man?
Why let them swaddle me in robes and skirts?
Why play a duke so as to cringe and crawl?
Had I not better rule my march domain?
For what can they all do against my might?
At pleasure I stir heaven and shake earth—
I come and go, I bow my head to none."
But trust in people moved Kiều's guileless heart:
sweet words and lavish gifts could make her yield.
"A fern that floats on water," she now thought,
"I've wandered long enough, endured enough.
Let's swear allegiance to the emperor's throne—
we'll travel far up fortune's royal road.
Public and private ends will both be met,
and soon I may arrange to go back home.
A lord's own consort, head erect, I'll walk
and make my parents glow with pride and joy.
Then, both the state above, my home below,
I'll have well served as liege and daughter both.
Is that not better than to float and drift,
a skiff the waves and waters hurl about?"
When they discussed the wisest course to take,
she sought to win him over to her views.
"The emperor's munificence," she would say,
"has showered on the world like drenching rain.
His virtues and good works have kept the peace,
placing each subject deeply in his debt.
Since you rose up in arms, dead men's white bones
have piled head-high along the Wayward Stream.[6]
Why should you leave an ill repute behind?

6. The Wuding River, which twists and turns.

For ages who has ever praised Huang Chao?[7]
Why not accept high post and princely purse?
Is there some surer avenue to success?"
  Her words struck home: he listened giving ground.
He dropped all schemes for war and sued for peace.
The envoy he received with pomp and rites—
he pledged to lay down arms, disband his troops.
  Trusting the truce they'd sworn below the walls,
Lord Từ let flags hang loose, watch-drums go dead.
He slackened all defense—imperial spies
observed his camp and learned of its true state.
Lord Hồ conceived a ruse to snatch this chance:
behind a screen of gifts he'd poise his troops.
The flying flag of friendship led the van,
with gifts in front and weapons hid behind.
  Lord Từ suspected nothing, caught off guard—
in cap and gown, he waited at the gate.
Afield, Lord Hồ now gave the secret cue:
flags on all sides unfurled and guns fired off.
  The fiercest tiger, taken unawares,
will lick the dust and meet an abject end.
Now doomed, Từ fought his one last fight on earth
to show them all a soldier's dauntless heart.
When his brave soul left him to join the gods,
he still stood on his feet amidst his foes.
His body, firm as rock and hard as bronze,
who in the whole wide world could shake or move?
  Imperial troops rushed forward giving chase—
death vapors choked the skies: who could resist?
All battlements tumbled down, inside and out—
some fleeing men found Kiều and led her there.
As stones and arrows flew and whizzed around,
Từ stood there still, transfixed, beneath the skies.
  "You had stout heart and clever mind," she cried,
"but you took my advice and came to this!
How can I bear to look you in the face?
I'd rather die with you on this same day."
Her pent-up grief gushed forth in floods of tears—
she flung herself head first upon the ground.
Oh, strange affinity of two wronged souls!
As she collapsed, he too fell down with her.
  Some government soldiers now were walking past—
sorry, they picked her up, helped her revive.
To their headquarters they delivered her—
Lord Hồ caught sight of her and kindly spoke:
"Defenseless, fragile woman that you are,
you've been war-tossed and suffered grievous blows.
Our plans, laid down at Court, won this campaign,

7. Rebel who proclaimed himself emperor in 881 but was defeated a few years later, disastrously weakening the Tang dynasty.

but you did help—you talked the traitor round.
Now all is well that has come off so well—
I'll leave you free to choose your own reward."
Her bitter tears poured forth, a flow of pearls—
she heaved with sobs, unburdening her breast:
"A hero was my Từ—he went his way
beneath the skies, he roamed the open seas.
I talked, he listened overtrusting me—
the victor laid down arms to serve at court!
He hoped to gain the world for man and wife—
alas, he came to nothing in a trice.
Five years he roved between the sky and sea,
then dropped his body on the field like trash.
Now you suggest I ask for my reward—
the more you praise my act, the more I grieve.
I judge myself a culprit, nothing less—
that's why I tried to end my futile life.
Please give me just a paltry patch of earth
to cover him I love in life and death."
Her plea moved him—the lord had Từ's remains
wrapped up in grass and buried by the stream.

* * *

Summary Lord Hồ decrees that Kiều must be married to a tribal chief. During the wedding procession, she throws herself into a river, and her body drifts along until it is found by Giác Duyên, the nun who saved her earlier. Meanwhile, Kiều's first love, Kim, has found Kiều's father, mother, and siblings.

From *VI*

Kim sent his card and bade Thúc visit him.
He asked his guest to settle dubious points:
"Where is Kiều's husband now? And what's his name?"
Thúc answered: "Caught in those wild times of strife,
I probed and asked some questions while at camp.
The chieftain's name was Hải, his surname Từ—
he won all battles, overwhelmed all foes.
He chanced to meet her while he was in Tai—
genius and beauty wed, a natural course.
For many years he stormed about the world:
his thunder made earth quake and heaven quail!
He garrisoned his army in the East—
since then, all signs and clues of him are lost."
Kim heard and knew the story root and branch—
anguish and dread played havoc with his heart:
"Alas for my poor leaf, a toy of winds!
When could she ever shake the world's foul dust?
As flows the stream, the flower's swept along—
I grieve her wave-tossed life, detached from mine.
From all our broken pledges I still keep
a bit of incense there, and here this lute.

Its soul has fled the strings—will incense there
give us its fire and fragrance in this life?
While she's now wandering, rootless, far from home,
how can I wallow in soft ease and wealth?"
His seal of office he'd as soon resign—
then he would cross all streams and scale all heights,
then he would venture onto fields of war
and risk his life to look for his lost love.
But heaven showed no track, the sea no trail—
where could he seek the bird or find the fish?
While he was pausing, waiting for some news,
who knows how often cycled sun and rain?
Now from the throne, on rainbow-tinted sheets,
arrived decrees that clearly ordered thus:
Kim should assume new office in Nanbing,
Vương was transferred to functions at Fuyang.[8]
In haste they purchased horse and carriage, then
both families left together for their posts.
The news broke out: The rebels had been crushed—
waves stilled, fires quenched in Fujian and Zhejiang.[9]
Informed, Kim thereupon requested Vương
to help him look for Kiều along the way.
When they both reached Hangzhou,[1] they could obtain
precise and proven facts about her fate.
This they were told: "One day, the fight was joined.
Từ, ambushed, fell a martyr on the field.
Kiều's signal service earned her no reward:
by force they made her wed a tribal chief.
She drowned that body fine as jade, as pearl:
the Qiantang river has become her grave."
Ah, torn asunder not to meet again!
They all were thriving—she had died foul death.

To rest her soul, they set her tablet up,
installed an altar on the riverbank.
The tide cast wave on silver-crested wave:
gazing, all pictured how the bird had dropped.
Deep love, a sea of griefs—so strange a fate!
Where had it strayed, the bird's disconsolate soul?[2]
How queerly fortune's wheel will turn and spin!
Giác Duyên now somehow happened by the spot.
She saw the tablet, read the written name.
She cried, astonished: "Who are you, my friends?
Are you perchance some kith or kin of hers?
But she's alive! Why all these mourning rites?"

8. City in Zhejiang province.
9. Provinces on the coast of southeast China.
1. A major city in Zhejiang province.
2. According to a Chinese legend, when the daughter of an emperor drowned, her soul turned into a bird that dropped stones into the sea in a struggle to fill it all up.

They heard the news and nearly fell with shock.
All mobbed her, talked away, asked this and that:
"Her husband here, her parents over there,
and there her sister, brother, and his wife.
From truthful sources we heard of her death,
but now you tell us this amazing news!"
"Karma drew us together," said the nun,
"first at Linzi, and next by the Qiantang.
When she would drown her beauteous body there,
I stood at hand and brought her safe to shore.
She's made her home within the Bodhi gate—
our grass-roofed cloister's not too far from here.
At Buddha's feet calm days go round and round,
but her mind's eye still fastens on her home."
At what was heard all faces glowed and beamed:
could any bliss on earth exceed this joy?
The leaf had left its grove—since that dark day,
they'd vainly searched all streams and scanned all clouds.
The rose had fallen, its sweet scent had failed:
they might see her in afterworlds, not here.
She'd gone the way of night, they dwelt with day—
now, back from those Nine Springs,[3] she walked on earth!
All knelt and bowed their thanks to old Giác Duyên,
then in a group they followed on her heels.
They cut and cleared their way through reed and rush,
their loving hearts half doubting yet her word.
By twists and turns they edged along the shore,
pushed past that jungle, reached the Buddha's shrine.
In a loud voice, the nun Giác Duyên called Kiều,
and from an inner room she hurried out.
She glanced and saw her folks—they all were here:
Father looked still quite strong, and Mother spry:
both sister Vân and brother Quan grown up:
and over there was Kim, her love of yore.
Could she believe this moment, what it seemed?
Was she now dreaming open-eyed, awake?
Tear-pearls dropped one by one and damped her smock—
she felt such joy and grief, such grief and joy.
She cast herself upon her mother's knees
and, weeping, told of all she had endured:
"Since I set out to wander through strange lands,
a wave-tossed fern, some fifteen years have passed.
I sought to end it in the river's mud—
who could have hoped to see you all on earth?"
The parents held her hands, admired her face:
that face had not much changed since she left home.
The moon, the flower, lashed by wind and rain
for all that time, had lost some of its glow.
What scale could ever weigh their happiness?

3. The underworld.

Present and past, so much they talked about!
The two young ones kept asking this or that
while Kim looked on, his sorrow turned to joy.
Before the Buddha's altar all knelt down
and for Kiều's resurrection offered thanks.
  At once they ordered sedans decked with flowers—
old Vương bade Kiều be carried home with them.
"I'm nothing but a fallen flower," she said.
"I drank of gall and wormwood half my life.
I thought to die on waves beneath the clouds—
how could my heart nurse hopes to see this day?
Yet I've survived and met you all again,
and slaked the thirst that long has parched my soul.
This cloister's now my refuge in the wilds—
to live with grass and trees befits my age.
I'm used to salt and greens in Dhyana[4] fare:
I've grown to love the drab of Dhyana garb.
Within my heart the fire of lust is quenched—
why should I roll again in worldly dust?
What good is that, a purpose half achieved?
To nunhood vowed, I'll stay here till the end.
I owe to her who saved me sea-deep debts—
how can I cut my bonds with her and leave?"
  Old Vương exclaimed: "Other times, other tides!
Even a saint must bow to circumstance.
You worship gods and Buddhas—who'll discharge
a daughter's duties, keep a lover's vows?
High Heaven saved your life—we'll build a shrine
and have our Reverend come, live there near us."
Heeding her father's word, Kiều had to yield:
she took her leave of cloister and old nun.
  The group returned to Kim's own yamen where,
for their reunion, they all held a feast.
After mum wine instilled a mellow mood,
Vân rose and begged to air a thought or two:
"It's Heaven's own design that lovers meet,
so Kim and Kiều did meet and swear their troth.
Then, over peaceful earth wild billows swept,
and in my sister's place I wedded him.
Amber and mustard seed, lodestone and pin![5]
Besides, 'when blood is split, the gut turns soft.'[6]
Day after day, we hoped and prayed for Kiều
with so much love and grief these fifteen years.
But now the mirror cracked is whole again:
wise Heaven's put her back where she belongs.
She still loves him and, luckily, still has him—

4. The Buddhist practice of meditation.
5. Expression referring to objects that are irresistibly drawn to one another, as people are in marriage.
6. Vietnamese expression meaning that when one member of a family is in pain, all the rest suffer, too.

still shines the same old moon both once swore by.
The tree still bears some three or seven plums,
the peach stays fresh—it's time to tie the knot!"[7]
  Kiều brushed her sister's speech aside and said:
"Why now retell a tale of long ago?
We once did pledge our troth, but since those days,
my life has been exposed to wind and rain.
I'd die of shame discussing what's now past—
let those things flow downstream and out to sea!"
  "A curious way to put it!" Kim cut in.
"Whatever you may feel, your oath remains.
A vow of troth is witnessed by the world,
by earth below and heaven far above.
Though things may change and stars may shift their course,
sworn pledges must be kept in life or death.
Does fate, which brought you back, oppose our love?
We two are one—why split us in two halves?"
  "A home where love and concord reign," Kiều said,
"whose heart won't yearn for it? But I believe
that to her man a bride should bring the scent
of a close bud, the shape of a full moon.
It's priceless, chastity—by nuptial torch,
am I to blush for what I'll offer you?
Misfortune struck me—since that day the flower
fell prey to bees and butterflies, ate shame.
For so long lashed by rain and swept by wind,
a flower's bound to fade, a moon to wane.
My cheeks were once two roses—what's now left?
My life is done—how can it be remade?
How dare I, boldfaced, soil with worldly filth
the homespun costume of a virtuous wife?
You bear a constant love for me, I know—
but where to hide my shame by bridal light?
From this day on I'll shut my chamber door:
though I will take no vows, I'll live a nun.
If you still care for what we both once felt,
let's turn it into friendship—let's be friends.
Why speak of marriage with its red silk thread?
It pains my heart and further stains my life."
  "How skilled you are in spinning words!" Kim said.
"You have your reasons—others have their own.
Among those duties falling to her lot,
a woman's chastity means many things.
For there are times of ease and times of stress:
in crisis, must one rigid rule apply?
True daughter, you upheld a woman's role:
what dust or dirt could ever sully you?
Heaven grants us this hour: now from our gate
all mists have cleared; on high, clouds roll away.

7. Allusion to ancient Chinese poetry, suggesting that Kiều is not too old to marry.

The faded flower's blooming forth afresh,
the waning moon shines more than at its full.
What is there left to doubt? Why treat me like
another Xiao, a passerby ignored?"[8]
He argued, pleaded, begged—she heard him through.
Her parents also settled on his plans.
Outtalked, she could no longer disagree:
she hung her head and yielded, stifling sighs.
They held a wedding-feast—bright candles lit
all flowers, set aglow the red silk rug.
Before their elders groom and bride bowed low—
all rites observed, they now were man and wife.
In their own room they traded toasts, still shy
of their new bond, yet moved by their old love.
Since he, a lotus sprout,[9] first met with her,
a fresh peach bud, fifteen full years had fled.
To fall in love, to part, to reunite—
both felt mixed grief and joy as rose the moon.
The hour was late—the curtain dropped its fringe:
under the light gleamed her peach-blossom cheeks.
Two lovers met again—out of the past,
a bee, a flower constant in their love.
"I've made my peace with my own fate," she said.
"What can this cast-off body be good for?
I thought of your devotion to our past—
to please you, I went through those wedding rites.
But how ashamed I felt in my own heart,
lending a brazen front to all that show!
Don't go beyond the outward marks of love—
perhaps, I might then look you in the face.
But if you want to get what they all want,
glean scent from dirt, or pluck a wilting flower,
then we'll flaunt filth, put on a foul display,
and only hate, not love, will then remain.
When you make love and I feel only shame,
then rank betrayal's better than such love.
If you must give your clan a rightful heir,
you have my sister—there's no need for me.
What little chastity I may have saved,
am I to fling it under trampling feet?
More tender feelings pour from both our hearts—
why toy and crumple up a faded flower?"
"An oath bound us together," he replied.
"We split, like fish to sea and bird to sky.
Through your long exile how I grieved for you!
Breaking your troth, you must have suffered so.

8. Xiao, a man who lived during the Tang dynasty, was married to a woman named Luzhu; when a high-ranking official took Luzhu as his concubine, she refused to acknowledge her husband when she passed him in the street.
9. In Chinese poetry the lotus often symbolizes love.

We loved each other, risked our lives, braved death—
now we two meet again, still deep in love.
The willow in mid-spring still has green leaves—
I thought you still attached to human love.
But no more dust stains your clear mirror now:
your vow can't but increase my high regard.
If I long searched the sea for my lost pin,[1]
it was true love, not lust, that urged me on.
We're back together now, beneath one roof:
to live in concord, need two share one bed?"
  Kiều pinned her hair and straightened up her gown,
then knelt to touch her head in gratitude:
"If ever my soiled body's cleansed of stains,
I'll thank a gentleman, a noble soul.
The words you spoke came from a kindred heart:
no truer empathy between two souls.
A home, a refuge—what won't you give me?
My honor lives again as of tonight."
  Their hands unclasped, then clasped and clasped again—
now he esteemed her, loved her all the more.
They lit another candle up, refilled
the incense urn, then drank to their new joy.
His old desire for her came flooding back—
he softly asked about her luting skill.
"Those strings of silk entangled me," she said,
"in sundry woes which haven't ceased till now.
Alas, what's done regrets cannot undo—
but I'll obey your wish just one more time."
  Her elfin fingers danced and swept the strings—
sweet strains made waves with curls of scentwood smoke.
Who sang this hymn to life and peace on earth?
Was it a butterfly or Master Zhuang?[2]
And who poured forth this rhapsody of love?
The king of Shu or just a cuckoo-bird?[3]
Clear notes like pearls dropped in a moon-lit bay.
Warm notes like crystals of new Lantian jade.[4]
  His ears drank in all five tones of the scale—
all sounds which stirred his heart and thrilled his soul.
"Whose hand is playing that old tune?" he asked.
"What sounded once so sad now sounds so gay!
It's from within that joy or sorrow comes—
have bitter days now set and sweet ones dawned?"
"This pleasant little pastime," answered she,
"once earned me grief and woe for many years.

1. Vietnamese equivalent of searching for a needle in a haystack.
2. The Daoist master Zhuang Zhou, who does not know whether he is really a man dreaming of being a butterfly or a butterfly dreaming of being a man.
3. Wangdi, the king of Shu, turned into a cuckoo when he was found to be having an affair with his minister's wife.
4. In Shaanxi, Mount Lantian (meaning "blue field") is famous for its jade.

For you my lute just sang its one last song—
henceforth, I'll roll its strings and play no more."
The secrets of their hearts were flowing still
when cocks crowed up the morning in the east.
Kim spoke, told all about their private pact.
All marveled at her wish and lauded her—
a woman of high mind, not some coquette
who'd with her favors skip from man to man.
Of love and friendship they fulfilled both claims—
they shared no bed but joys of lute and verse.
Now they sipped wine, now played a game of chess,
admiring flowers, waiting for the moon.
Their wishes all came true since fate so willed,
and of two lovers marriage made two friends.
As pledged, they built a temple on a hill,
then sent a trusted man to fetch the nun.
When he got there, he found doors shut and barred—
he saw a weed-grown rooftop, moss-filled cracks.
She'd gone to gather simples, he was told:
the cloud had flown, the crane had fled—but where?
For old times' sake, Kiều kept the temple lit,
its incense candles burning night and day.
The twice-blessed home enjoyed both weal and wealth.
Kim climbed the office ladder year by year.
Vân gave him many heirs: a stooping tree,
a yardful of sophoras and cassia shrubs.[5]
In rank or riches who could rival them?
Their garden throve, won glory for all times.

This we have learned: with Heaven rest all things.
Heaven appoints each human to a place.
If doomed to roll in dust, we'll roll in dust;
we'll sit on high when destined for high seats.
Does Heaven ever favor anyone,
bestowing both rare talent and good luck?
In talent take no overweening pride,
for talent and disaster form a pair.[6]
Our karma we must carry as our lot—
let's stop decrying Heaven's whims and quirks.
Inside ourselves there lies the root of good:
the heart outweighs all talents on this earth.

May these crude words, culled one by one and strung,
beguile an hour or two of your long night.

5. Plants symbolizing sons who will become officials and scholars.

6. The words for "talent" and "disaster" rhyme in both Chinese and Vietnamese.

GHALIB

1797–1869

Ghalib is probably the most frequently quoted poet of the nineteenth and twentieth centuries in India and Pakistan, where tens of millions of people know some of his Urdu poems by heart. His popularity, which has only grown since his death nearly a century and a half ago, is especially remarkable given the complexity of his work. Despite the fact that he is a difficult poet, his phrases, images, and ideas have become part of the common speech of Urdu and Hindi, which are closely interrelated languages. He wrote haunting love poems in a style that still seems contemporary, and his words and emotions are on the lips of lovers young and old everywhere on the subcontinent.

LIFE AND TIMES

India in the nineteenth century passed from one vast imperial power to another. The Mughal Empire, which at its height commanded 100 million people, had once boasted great wealth and military might. Babur (1483–1530), the first Mughal emperor, had brought with him rich traditions of Persian art and literature as well as his Islamic faith to create a new dynasty that would rule over the Hindu majority in India for three centuries. His grandson, the great emperor Akbar, established a well-organized bureaucracy and permitted multiple religions to flourish, allowing Hindus to serve as generals and administrators.

The British arrived in India during Akbar's reign. As Indian tea, cotton, silk, spices, and opium flowed into Britain, consumers there developed a growing appetite for Indian products. The profits of British companies soared. The French and the Dutch competed for the same goods, and tensions rose between European contenders for the Indian market. These hostilities would last until 1757, when the British defeated the French in battle and seized control of European trade with the entire subcontinent.

While the Europeans struggled for Indian markets, Akbar and his successors expanded the territory under Mughal control, bringing almost the entire Indian peninsula into the hands of the Mughals by the late seventeenth century. Their grand capital was Delhi, where they gathered the works of skilled artists in luxurious palaces. The majestic Taj Mahal, built in 1648 as the mausoleum for the favorite wife of Mughal emperor Shah Jahan, captures the sumptuousness and grandeur of this period in Indian history. To European visitors, the enviably powerful Mughal Empire seemed home to untold riches.

In the seventeenth century, Emperor Aurangzeb, a devout Muslim who dismounted from his horse in the thick of battle to recite his evening prayers, pushed to expand the empire and succeeded—but only by stretching his resources to the point of collapse. Some Hindu kingdoms continued to resist Mughal control, and by the middle of the eighteenth century they had helped to weaken the empire. Attacks on Delhi by the Hindu Marathas, as well as foreign invaders from Persia and Afghanistan, further exhausted the regime.

As the Mughal Empire weakened, the British East India Company gradually assumed more and more military and administrative power. In 1804, the East India Company officially took control of

India. At first, the British tended to leave local leaders in place rather than getting involved in direct administration; they did not try to convert Indians to Christianity. Over the course of the nineteenth century, however, the nature of British control over India underwent a major shift. A new generation of British career men, feeling superior to the Indians, began a campaign to impose their own moral, linguistic, and cultural traditions on India. Christian missionaries arrived in ever larger numbers, and increasingly the British back home were whipped into an enthusiasm for advancing the "backward" peoples of India. Ironically, it was partly thanks to British imperialism that the Indians could be seen as backward in the first place. India had once had a thriving economy based on beautiful textiles—in 1700 it had been the leading exporter of woven cloth—but Britain's cheap factory-made textiles and its demand for raw materials from India had forced many workers back into a peasant-based rural economy.

Born in Agra in December 1797, Asadullah Khan—later known by his literary pseudonym, Ghalib ("Conqueror" in Persian and Urdu)—was a descendant of Turkish military settlers in north India. His grandfather as well as his father and an uncle, who ranked as minor nobles in the Muslim ruling class of the nineteenth century, served in the Mughal emperor's army. After his father died, when he was five, and his uncle, who then supported the extended family, died only three years later, Ghalib was raised mostly among his mother's relatives. When he was thirteen, his family (then in financial decline) arranged his marriage to an eleven-year-old girl from a wealthier segment of the nobility. In 1810 he moved to Delhi, where the young couple lived in comfortable circumstances with support from her family, a dependence that was to continue for the rest of his life. The young poet, who had begun to write Urdu verse and prose at seven and in Persian by the age of nine, matured rapidly in the next few years, completing a significant portion of his oeuvre of Urdu poetry by 1816, when he was nineteen.

However, in 1822, partly in response to widespread incomprehension and criticism of his early poetry, Ghalib stopped writing verse in Urdu and switched to Persian as his only poetic medium—a practice he adhered to until 1850. Persian had been the premier literary language of Muslim society across Asia for much of the preceding seven or eight hundred years; and, since the end of the sixteenth century, it had also been the official imperial language of the subcontinent under the Mughals. By the 1840s Ghalib had produced a large body of poetry and prose in Persian, and he had become a prominent Indian authority on the language and its literature.

Despite his renown, much of Ghalib's adult life was marked by bitter disappointments. He spent most of the 1820s unsuccessfully seeking an aristocratic patron near Delhi; in 1827–30, he tried in vain to secure a British pension in Calcutta; and in 1842 he failed to get a position as Persian instructor at Delhi College, a new British-Indian institution. Ghalib's public humiliations reached a peak in 1847, when he was arrested for gambling in his home and imprisoned for three months. His personal and family life also proved to be deeply unhappy during this period. He and his wife had seven children, but none survived beyond the age of fifteen months, a cycle of tragedies that contributed to the couple's emotional alienation from each other. In the 1840s Ghalib adopted his wife's adult nephew 'Arif as his son, but the untimely deaths of both 'Arif and his wife from tuberculosis in 1852 only added to the poet's sorrows. Ghalib's elegy for 'Arif—included here as "It Was Essential"—remains one of his most famous poems today, a memorable mourning of human mortality and a celebration of family life and familial love. And yet his deepest emotional relationship—one that haunted him for more than forty years after its tragic end—may have been with a low-caste Hindu courtesan who died very young and whose loss he mourned publicly at her funeral and in his letters and poetry.

The year 1850 brought significant changes to the poet's literary and professional life, and alleviated his financial circumstances to some extent. Emperor Bahadur Shah Zafar—who proved to be the last in the long line of Mughal rulers on Delhi's throne—commissioned Ghalib to write a history of the dynasty in Persian; and, four years later, the emperor finally appointed him as royal tutor and court poet. At Zafar's urging, Ghalib also resumed writing poetry and prose in Urdu, the "mixed" language (combining Hindi syntax and Persian vocabulary) that was the first language of north-Indian Muslims. In the 1850s and 1860s Ghalib became the most sought-after master of Urdu and Persian poetry among Muslim as well as Hindu writers, developing a rich and voluminous correspondence in Urdu with more than four hundred friends and admirers of various faiths across the subcontinent.

The events of 1857, however, transformed Ghalib's life and his beloved city of Delhi irreversibly. The "Mutiny" (now often called the First Indian War of Independence from British rule) started that summer and quickly overtook the Mughal capital, where large-scale violence ravaged all segments of Muslim and Hindu society over several months, first with the arrival of large contingents of Indian soldiers rebelling against the British colonial army, and subsequently with British retaliation. After crushing the uprising and arresting and deporting the emperor, the British administration and British militias summarily executed some 3,000 citizens of Delhi and razed the most densely populated part of the city (now known as Old Delhi), exiling its inhabitants to the surrounding countryside. Several hundreds of Ghalib's fellow-courtiers, friends, acquaintances, and neighbors—Hindu, Muslim, and Sikh—lost their lives, families, homes, or property; and for many months he lived in fear for his own life and the safety of his family. In 1858 he published *Dastanbuy*, his personal account of these events, which asserted his political innocence in the Mughal court's complicity with the rebels.

Ghalib survived the catastrophe of 1857 by a dozen years, but as a broken and lonely man. He wrote some of his best late poems in Urdu in the 1850s and early 1860s, but old age, deteriorating eyesight and hearing, and long illness increasingly confined him to his dilapidated home in Delhi; much of this is foreshadowed in his first poem in our selection, "Now Go and Live in a Place." Despite his personal difficulties, however, he kept up a vivid and generous correspondence with younger poets and admirers, including the close Hindu friends who preserved his works. These letters became a celebrated part of his oeuvre in his own lifetime, when, in 1868, they were collected and published as *Urdu-i-mu'alla*.

Looking back from our own times, Ghalib's life and poetry seem to represent the Indian subcontinent's transition from tradition to modernity in all its many-sided complexity. He was the last major poet to be trained in the traditional disciplines (language, poetics, philosophy, and theology), and to work only in inherited forms, even as Indian society engaged fully with Western-style modernity. He was the first—and last—traditional writer to publish his work in the print medium in his own lifetime (which he did around its mid-point), and to experience at first hand the extraordinary transformation that print culture brings to long-standing cultures of manuscript circulation, by fundamentally changing the nature of authorship, the author-audience connection, and literary reputation itself. He also underwent this experience by positioning himself quite uniquely in the shadowy space between tradition and modernity. While most of his contemporaries confronted the British presence in India from the perspective of a traditional "Hindu" or "Muslim" identity, Ghalib explicitly located himself in a prior synthesis of Muslim and Hindu cultures (or a hybrid Indo-Islamic civilization) that was open to a productive interaction with European culture. His life and career thus give us a glimpse into the unusual "triangle" of Muslim, Hindu, and European cultures intersecting in unprecedented proximity in the turmoil of nineteenth-century India.

WORK

Ghalib composed his poetry entirely in the inherited verse forms and genres of Persian and Urdu, both influenced heavily by Arabic traditions and the literary conventions of Islam. His favorite form in both Persian and Urdu was the *ghazal*, but he also wrote the equivalents of odes, panegyrics, satires, epigrams, epithalamiums, verse-epistles, prayers, and chronograms. The *ghazal*, invented in classical Arabic but widely practiced throughout the past millennium in Persian and Urdu, among other languages, is technically one of the most demanding metrical forms in world poetry. A *ghazal* consists of a sequence of couplets—most often between five and twelve in number—in a single meter; and each couplet is end-stopped, hence representing one complete poetic thought. All the couplets in a *ghazal* have to be connected to each other by end-rhyme; the rhyme, however, has to occur at the end of each couplet, not in an isolated word but in an entire phrase. This "rhyming phrase" has two required parts: a final word or set of words that is repeated in each couplet, and hence serves as a refrain; and a word preceding the refrain that rhymes with the corresponding word in each of the other couplets. The rhyming phrase in a *ghazal* thus consists of a "monorhyme" followed by a refrain. The following metrical translation of two separate couplets from an Urdu *ghazal* by Ghalib captures this pattern in English, with the repeated word "good" at the end of each couplet defining the refrain, and "more" and "restore" representing the monorhyme that precedes it.

> The beauty of the moon, its sheer
>   beauty when it's full, is good—
> And yet, compared to it, her beauty
>   dazzles like the sun, is more than
>   good.
>
> When my face lights up merely
>   because she has looked at me,
> She thinks, mistakenly, the patient's
>   on the mend, restored for good.

The stringent rules of the *ghazal* also require that the opening couplet contain this rhyme-and-repetition pattern in both its lines (rather than only in the second one), thus defining the paradigm strongly; and that the closing couplet contain the poet's literary pseudonym, thus embedding the author's signature in the *ghazal* itself. This complicated structure leaves the poet free to make each couplet an entire miniature poem that is thematically and rhetorically independent of the other couplets. At the same time, it challenges him to create a thematic continuity against impossible prosodic odds. In the history of the *ghazal* across Arabic, Persian, and Urdu, Ghalib stands out as an astonishing craftsman who could construct continuous poetic arguments within the strictest constraints of meter, repetition, and rhyme, without sacrificing wit, emotional integrity, intellectual rigor, and range of experience. Among the examples included in our selection, his versatility with the *ghazal* is especially evident in "I've Made My Home Next Door to You," "It Was Essential," and "My Tongue Begs for the Power of Speech."

The poems below display Ghalib's imaginative range and depth in several genres in Urdu. The three poems just mentioned, together with "Now Go and Live in a Place," are translations of complete *ghazal*s, and they capture the recursive structure of the form as closely as possible in metrical English, while retaining the semantic richness of the originals. Of these, "I've Made My Home Next Door to You" is represented in two parallel translations, one rendering the *ghazal* as a "secular" piece (a lover's plea and complaint), and the other highlighting the same text as a "sacred" poem (about love between God and human beings); the original conveys both meanings simultaneously, which is impossible to achieve in a single English version. In contrast, "Where's the Foothold" is a translation of a complete poem that is composed as a single unrhymed couplet, but is nevertheless classified among Ghalib's *ghazal*s in Urdu. The separate "Selection of Couplets" offers self-contained verses taken from a dozen different *ghazal*s, each presenting a complete and independent poetic thought with epigrammatic force. The final piece, "My Salary," is an excerpt from one of Ghalib's miscellaneous poems, addressed to Emperor Bahadur Shah Zafar, who was formally his literary student as well as his royal employer; in this unusual verse epistle, he sought to improve his working conditions and salary as court poet. Most of the poems here contain "Ghalib" as the poet's signature, and hence they may belong to the latter half of his career; the exception is the prayer, "My Tongue Begs for the Power of Speech," which refers to him as "Asad," the pseudonym he used often as a young man.

Ghalib's value as a poet also rests on his larger cultural position. In the predominantly Sunni Muslim community of nineteenth-century Delhi, he professed to be a Shi'a; in the midst of organized Sunni Islam, with its mosques, public prayers and rituals, and powerful clerics, he adopted a radical and subversive Sufism in private, as evident from "I've Made My Home Next Door to You." He did not practice the five daily prayers or the weekly Friday prayer, did not fast during the month of Ramadan, and did not undertake the pilgrimage to Mecca; at the same time, he conspicuously violated the taboo against alcohol—among the "sins committed" that he mentions in the third piece in our "Selection of Couplets." Moreover, as the fifth couplet in that selection shows, he openly advocated a complete reconciliation between Islam and Hinduism, arguing for a secular merger in shared ways of everyday life. Ghalib was also a universal humanist before his time, as the sixth couplet indicates: in his view, being fully human was more essential than, and prior to, being either Muslim or Hindu, believer or infidel. He actively sympathized with, acted for, and spoke out on behalf of the poor and the dispossessed, and he was doggedly committed to freedom of thought and speech, always speaking his mind tactfully yet forcefully, regardless of his interlocutor's status or power. At the same time, his contemporaries valued him immensely for his personal kindness and generosity: he had a remarkable gift for friendship, and he conducted himself with wit, humor, and dignity even with his enemies. We see all these qualities vividly at work in his extraordinary prayer, "My Tongue Begs for the Power of Speech," which remained unpublished in his lifetime, perhaps because of its subversively modern message.

Ghalib was one of the last figures in a seven-century tradition of Persian writing in India; while his Persian prose was a model for a few later writers, his Persian poetry (about 11,000 verses) has had little effect on later poets in India or Pakistan, and none on poets in Iran. In contrast, his Urdu prose (in his letters) and especially his Urdu poetry have deeply influenced writers and readers in every generation after him. His *ghazal*s have perpetuated this traditional form among Indian, Pakistani, and diasporic Urdu writers down to the present; and, just as importantly, they have spread the *ghazal* tradition among other contemporary Indian languages, such as Punjabi, Hindi, and Marathi. Since the international commemoration of the centenary of Ghalib's death in 1969, dozens of American, British, and Irish poets—from Adrienne Rich to Paul Muldoon—have cultivated the Ghalib-style *ghazal* in English, building on its earlier history as an international form that **Goethe** had adapted in German from his Persian favorite, Hafiz, and that **Lorca** had used in his avant-garde Spanish *gacelas*. Since the mid-twentieth century, in India as well as Pakistan, Ghalib's *ghazal*s have been set to music and performed, live and in recordings, by many popular singers, and his life and work have been the subjects of several films and a television serial. A century and a half after his death, Ghalib remains a living presence in the two countries that have inherited his poetic legacy.

[Now go and live in a place][1]

Now go and live in a place where no one lives—
no one who fathoms your verse, no one who shares your speech.

Build yourself a house, as if without a wall or gate—
no neighbour to keep you company, no watchman to keep you safe.

If you fall ill, no one to nurse you there—
and if you die, no one to mourn you there.

[Be merciful and send for me]

Be merciful and send for me,
anytime you please—
  I'm not some moment

1. All the poems in this selection are translated by Vinay Dharwadker.

that has passed
   and can't come back again.

Why do I complain
about my rival's power[2]
   as though I were a weakling?
My cause isn't so lost
   it can't be taken up again.

I just can't lay my hands
on poison, darling,
   and even if I could,
I couldn't swallow it—
   because I've made a vow

that we two shall be one again.

[Where's the foothold]

Where's the foothold, Lord,
for desire's second step?

I found this barren world—
this wilderness of possibilities—

to be an imprint
of just the first step.

[I've made my home next door to you]

1. The secular version

I've made my home next door to you, without being asked,
   without a word being said—
you still can't find my whereabouts without my help,
   without a word being said.

She says to me: "Since you don't have
   the power of words, how can you tell
what's in someone else's heart—
   without a word being said?"

2. The woman addressed in this poem may be a courtesan, and one of her other suitors would then be the speaker's rival. Like other Muslim aristocrats in 19th-century India, Ghalib frequently visited courtesans, especially in his youth and early adulthood.

I've work to do with her—I have to make it work—
 though no one in the world
can even speak her name without the word
 "tormentor" having to be said.

There's nothing in my heart, or else,
 even if my life were on the line,
I wouldn't hold my tongue,
 I wouldn't leave a thing unsaid.

I won't stop worshipping the one I love—
 that idol of an infidel—
even though the world won't let me go
 without the phrase "You infidel!" being said.[3]

Ghalib, don't press your case on her
 again and again and again.
Your state's completely evident to her—
 without a word being said.

2. *The sacred version*

I've made my home next door to You, without being asked,
 without a word being said—
You still can't find my whereabouts without my help,
 without a word being said.

He says to me: "Since you don't have
 the power of words, how can you tell
what's in someone else's heart—
 without a word being said?"

I've work to do with Him—I have to make it work—
 though no one in the world
can even speak His Name without the word
 "Tormentor" having to be said.[4]

There's nothing in my heart, or else,
 even if my life were on the line,
I wouldn't hold my tongue,
 I wouldn't leave a thing unsaid.

3. Following Sufi mystical tradition, Ghalib often represents the beloved woman in his *ghazals* as an "infidel," someone who has not submitted to the true faith (Islam), and who is also sexually unfaithful or incapable of fidelity. The image is provocative because it suggests that she may not be a Muslim, which is why the speaker himself is accused of being disloyal to his religion. Ghalib may be referring here to the low-caste Hindu courtesan with whom he fell in love as a young man, and whose early tragic death he mourned throughout much of his adult life.

4. In Sufi poetry in Persian and Urdu, God is often portrayed as a Beloved who torments worshipers, much as a beloved woman may torment a suitor in order to deepen his emotional dependence on her.

I won't stop worshipping the One I love—
   that Idol of an Infidel—
even though the world won't let me go
   without the phrase "You infidel!" being said.[5]

Ghalib, don't press your case on Him
   again and again and again.
Your state's completely evident to Him—
   without a word being said.

Couplets

1

Ghalib, it's no use
forcing your way with love:
   it's a form of fire
that doesn't catch when lit
and doesn't die when doused.

2

I have hopes,
I have hopes of faithfulness
from her—
         she
who doesn't have a clue
what faithfulness might be.

3

Dear God:
if there are punishments
for sins committed,

there also ought to be
rewards
for sins craved

but not committed.

4

What I have
isn't a case of love
but madness—

5. From the perspective of orthodox Islam, this characterization is theologically provocative; it suggests that God himself is not "faithful" to the faith that focuses on him.

I grant you that.

But then it's true—
your reputation rests
upon the fact that it was you

who drove me mad.

5

We're monotheists,
we believe in the unity of God.[6]
For them, our message is:
Abandon your rituals![7]

But when communities
have cancelled their differences
and mingled and merged,
they've already converged

upon a common faith.[8]

6

Just this
    that it's so hard
to make each task
look easy.

So too
    it isn't simple
for humans
to be human.[9]

7

There are other poets
in the world
who're also very good:

6. The "we" in this verse refers to the fraternity of Muslims; Ghalib here repeats Islam's central claim that it believes in one God and in his absolute unity.
7. "They" and "them" refer to Hindus; Ghalib here alludes to the standard Muslim position that Hinduism valorizes many gods, the worship of idols, and numerous rituals.
8. This is Ghalib's famous argument for a "secularization" of both Islam and Hinduism, in which the two communities, after living with each other for centuries, have already created a shared way of life in practice, and hence ought not to be ideologically pitted against each other anymore.
9. The last word in this verse translates *insan* in the Urdu original, which points explicitly to Ghalib's emphasis on *insaniyat*, literally "humanism" as well as "the set of qualities that render a creature fully human." Like his much younger contemporary Rabindranath Tagore, Ghalib was a proponent of a "universal humanism."

but Ghalib's style
of saying things, they say,
is something else.

8

Tonight, somewhere,
 you're sleeping by the side
of another lover, a stranger:
 otherwise, what reason would you have
for visiting my dreams
 and smiling your half-smile?

9

I've been
set free
from the prison of love
a hundred times—

but what can I do
if the heart itself
proves to be
an enemy of freedom?

10

Pulling
that image
from my memory—

of your finger
imprinted with designs
in henna[1]—

was exactly like
pulling a fingernail
from my flesh.

11

If no one but You
 is manifest,
if nothing but You
 exists, O Lord,

1. Among Muslims as well as Hindus in India, henna is used as a cosmetic, both routinely and for brides at weddings. Dry henna leaves are crushed and mixed into a paste, which is applied in designs or patterns on the skin, especially the forearms, palms and hands, and soles and feet.

then what's this great commotion
  all about?

12

The news was hot—
that Ghalib would self-destruct,
and all his parts
would go flying!
I, too, went to see the show—
but the promised mayhem
never materialized.

[It was essential]

Elegy for his wife's nephew and adopted son, 'Arif[2]

It was essential
that you wait for me
  for a few more days.
Why did you leave alone—
now wait alone
  for a few more days.

If your gravestone hasn't
worn it down for me,
  my head will soon be dust—
for I'll be rubbing my brow
upon your threshold
  for a few more days.

You arrived yesterday—
and, now, today you say,
  "I'm leaving."
I agree that staying forever
isn't good—but stay with us
  for a few more days.

As you depart you say,
"We'll meet once more
  on Doomsday."[3]
How great—
that doom will have its day
  on one more day.

2. 'Arif was a young adult when Ghalib and his wife formally adopted him, but both the young man and Ghalib's wife died prematurely due to ill health. This *ghazal*, Ghalib's famous elegy for 'Arif, also celebrates family life and domesticity.

3. The day specified in the Qur'an on which the world will end, and on which Allah will call the living and the dead to Judgment.

Yes, oh yes,
O wise and ancient sky,
'Arif was young—
what would have gone so wrong
if he hadn't died
for a few more days?

You were the moon
of the fourteenth night,
the full moon of my home[4]—
why didn't that remain
the picture of my household
for a few more days?

You weren't so uptight
about the give-and-take of life—
couldn't Death have been
bribed and dissuaded
from pressing His case
for a few more days?

Fine, you hated me,
and fought with Nayyir[5]—
but you didn't even stay
to watch, with pleasure,
your children's boisterous games
for a few more days.

Our time together didn't pass
through every sort of circumstance,
to seal enduring bonds—
dead before your time,
you should have passed the time with us
for a few more days.

Those of you around me
are fools to ask,
"Ghalib, why are you still living?"
It's my destiny
to continue to wish for death
for a few more days.

4. Each month on the Muslim lunar calendar in India begins with the new moon; the full moon thus appears on the fourteenth night of the month. In Urdu *ghazals*, the full moon is a multifaceted image of beauty, happiness, and blessedness.

5. A relative of Ghalib's who lived in his neighborhood in Ballimaran, Old Delhi; for 'Arif, Nayyir was one of the "elders" in the extended family to be treated with respect and affection.

[My tongue begs for the power of speech][6]

My tongue begs
for the power of speech
   that is Your gift to us;
for silence gets
its style of representation
   from Your gift to us.

The melancholic weeping
of those who live with disappointment
   is Your gift to us;
daybreak's smothered lamp
and autumn's wilted bloom
   are Your gifts to us.

The blossoming of wonder
at the sights we see
   is tough Love's gift:
the henna on the feet of death,[7]
the blood of slaughter's victims
   are Your gifts to us.

The predawn hour's concupiscence,
the contrivance of effects
   that follow later—
the flood of tears,
the colours of grief—
   are all Your gifts to us.

Garden after garden
multiplies the mirrors
   that fill desire's lap;
the hope that flowers there,
immersed in spring's displays,
   is Your gift to us.

Devotion is the veil[8]
that keeps our hubris hidden,
   held in check;

6. One of Ghalib's most technically skilled, thematically complex, and powerful *ghazal*s, which he did not publish in his lifetime and which was discovered in the 1970s among his papers. Written with an almost entirely Persian vocabulary and syntax, linguistically and poetically it lies on the thin line separating Ghalib's Urdu and Persian verse. An intensely personal prayer, it is the poet's most direct and sustained conversation with, and tribute to, God.

7. Henna is a traditional cosmetic in India; this image suggests the death of a young woman, perhaps a bride, in the prime of her life.

8. Islam enjoins women always to remain behind a veil outside the *zenana*, the "women's quarters" in a home; theologically, God is "veiled" from human eyes, as is any form of true piety or "devotion" to God.

the brow that scrapes the ground,
the square prayer mat,[9]
  are Your gifts to us.

Our farce-like search for mercy,
our secretive retreat
  behind a festival's facade—
the firmness of our courage,
our sorrow at the tests we fail—
  are all Your gifts to us.

Asad, in the season of roses,
in an arbour that enchants us
  with its overarching latticework,
the winding walk, the bracing easterly,
the flowerbed in bloom
  are all Your gifts to us.

Petition: My Salary

The conclusion of a petition in verse,
addressed to Bahadur Shah Zafar, the last Mughal emperor,
with its famous final lines[1]

My master and my pupil! . . .
My salary, agreed upon,
is paid to me
in the strangest way.
The custom is
to consecrate the dead
once in six months—
that's the basis
on which the world runs.
But if you look at me,
you'll see that I am
a prisoner of life, not death—
and six-monthly paydays[2]
fall only twice a year.

9. One of the "pillars" of Islam is the set of five prayers that a Muslim must offer at prescribed times every day, facing in the direction of the Ka'aba in Mecca; since the prayers must be performed, in part, while kneeling on the ground, most Muslims use a personal mat for the purpose.

1. Emperor Bahadur Shah, who wrote verse under the pen name "Zafar," appointed Ghalib as his court poet and poetry teacher in 1854. This poem is a formal petition in verse addressed to the emperor.

2. Ghalib was paid his salary twice a year, rather than once a month; he compares this biannual schedule to the customary practice, among Muslims in India, of remembering the dead twice a year.

All I do each month
is take out a debt,
with wrangles over interest
repeated endlessly—
my money-lender has become
a partner
in one-third of my earnings.
Today, the world
has no one like me—
a poet of worth
who speaks beautifully.
If you wish to hear
an epic of war,
my tongue's a sharp sword;
if you convene an assembly,
my pen's a cloud
that rains down pearls.
It's a violation of etiquette
not to praise poetry,
it's an act of violence
not to love me.
I'm your slave
and I wander naked,
I'm your servant
and all I eat is debt.
Let my salary be paid
month by month,
let my life
cease to be a burden.
And now I conclude
my discourse
of prayer and supplication—
my business isn't poetry.
May you live
safe and sound
for a thousand years,
may the days
in every year
be fifty thousand.[3]

3. The final sentence of this poem, its concluding verse, has become the most widespread benediction or blessing in Urdu and Hindi in northern Indian society and is used especially on birthdays, at partings or departures, and at life-cycle ceremonies.

LIU E

1857–1909

The Travels of Lao Can has long been a favorite among Chinese readers. Although sometimes considered one of the last traditional Chinese novels, it represented a compelling new kind of fiction when it first appeared in installments between 1904 and 1907. It was the first Chinese novel to take readers inside the psychological life of its hero, borrowing as much from lyric poetry as from the fictional tradition to give us Lao Can's unfolding consciousness in expressive detail. Dedicated to unmasking government corruption and cruelty at the expense of the people, it brings together a sensitive individual and a vast social drama, revealing a nation in crisis through the eyes of a solitary and sympathetic character, one who is openly, warmly interested in the many people he encounters but also bitterly disillusioned with the world as he finds it.

LIFE

Liu E (also known as Liu Tieyun) was born in a midsized city in Jiangsu province on the east coast of China in 1857. His father was a government official. Nicknamed "that mad fellow" by people who knew him in his youth, Liu E was wild, rebellious, and energetic. He was also highly intelligent and precocious, interested in music, poetry, philosophy, economics, astronomy, and medicine. He developed a specialized knowledge of flood control, which would later propel him to a position of influence, and he saw himself as part of a group of young men who were preparing to help the cause of their nation.

In his early twenties, Liu E joined a small religious sect that combined elements of Confucianism, Daoism, and Buddhism. Here he subdued some of his unruliness, becoming more disciplined and responsible. He remained outspoken, however, and still refused to settle down. A number of failed careers and business ventures troubled his twenties: he tried to work in traditional Chinese medicine but got no customers; he gave up studying for the examinations that would allow him to enter the civil service; and he struggled to set up one of the first lithographic printing presses in China but got ensnared in a lawsuit and went bankrupt.

In 1888 Liu E's professional luck changed. The Yellow River flooded, and he went to work for the Director General of the Yellow River Conservancy. With his extensive knowledge of floods, he was able to present an innovative plan of action. It succeeded, in part because Liu E rejected the conventional role of an official and worked alongside the laborers himself, giving them instructions in person. His eccentric methods succeeded so well that he rose to become a high-ranking adviser on flood control.

As his contemporaries became ever more torn between embracing traditional Chinese business practices and following European influences, Liu E argued against both extremes. He insisted that China needed to modernize its industrial and commercial methods, but not by relying on foreign powers. He particularly favored building a system of railways, but other officials did not take up his plans. Disgusted by their apathy, he resigned from government and again pursued a number of unsuccessful business ventures that were dedicated to modernization: a coal mine that never opened, a bankrupted department store, a steam cotton mill, a mechanized silk-weaving plant, a steel refinery, a waterworks, and a streetcar line.

It was in 1904 that Liu E started work on his most successful venture: *The Travels of Lao Can*. The novel became enormously popular, the best known of a group of socially critical novels of the period that attacked both corrupt government and stultifying tradition. It appeared piecemeal, as individual chapters were published in two different magazines over the course of three years.

The book's success did not bring its author a prosperous and settled life. With his tactless criticisms and relentless condemnation of traditions, Liu E had by this time accumulated powerful enemies. In 1907 he was falsely accused of treason and corruption, and was sent 3,500 miles away to the far northwestern area of Xinjiang, which is populated by a significant number of non-Chinese minorities. He died there thirteen months later at the age of fifty-two.

THE BOXER UPRISING

For many hundreds of years, imperial China had seemed strong and self-sufficient, impervious to foreign influence. Europeans keenly desired China's products, especially their beautiful porcelain, but offered little of value to Chinese buyers in return. Thus European silver poured into China, and Chinese emperors had no incentive to create special trade relationships with any particular European power.

But the nineteenth century brought an end to this proud isolation. By 1800, population growth had begun to put a strain on food sources, and peasant rebellions—sparked by mass hunger—erupted with some frequency. The British soon began smuggling opium from India into China against the wishes of the Qing emperor. A massive consumer demand for opium followed as millions of Chinese people fell prey to the highly addictive drug. The Chinese government struggled to stem the flow. By the 1820s, tens of thousands of chests of opium crossed the border each year. Lin Zexu, a Cantonese official, wrote to Britain's Queen Victoria to ask her to stop this poisonous trade: "the wicked barbarians beguile the Chinese people into a death trap," he wrote. When British traders continued to arrive, he obstructed their way and cut off their access to supplies and then dumped huge shipments of opium into the sea. British warships responded by attacking coastal cities and taking over southern Chinese ports. The powerful British navy prevailed in what are now known as the Opium Wars (1839–42, 1856–60), gaining control of Hong Kong for over a hundred years and establishing treaty agreements that favored their own interests.

A massive civil war further weakened the Qing dynasty. Hong Xiuquan, a farmer's son who had been inspired by the teachings of an American Baptist missionary, declared that he was the younger brother of Jesus Christ, sent by God to expel foreigners from China. Promising a "Heavenly Kingdom of Great Peace," Hong Xiuquan led a huge army of poor peasants, known as the Taiping, to take control of much of southern and central China in 1851. British and French forces, who preferred a weak emperor to a strong peasant regime, supported the Qing and quelled the Taiping rebellion for good in 1864. But the costs had been colossal. Between 20 and 30 million people died, and government coffers were empty.

In the ensuing decades, Western European power and influence in China grew steadily, and so too did resentment against the West. The British insisted on continuing to sell opium to Chinese buyers, and required a change in the law to allow Christian missionaries to travel throughout the country. What resulted was a vast conversion effort, with European and American missionaries challenging Confucian tradition and pressing for modernization, building large numbers of Christian schools, clinics, and hospitals all over China. Meanwhile, French, British, German, and American merchants set up trading zones where they refused to abide by Chinese laws.

In response, groups of patriotic Chinese people formed anti-European societies, and one became both popular and powerful. Called "Boxers" by Western journalists because they made martial arts and calisthenics part of their training, they also practiced mass spirit possession. Most of them were poor peasants whose farming efforts had suffered from natural disasters and so had little to lose. In 1899 they launched a campaign of violence against Europeans and Christians—including Chinese Christians—killing missionaries and diplomats, raping European and Chinese Christian women, and destroying railway lines and the property of foreigners. They blamed the ruling Qing dynasty for China's powerlessness in the face of European influence and called for new leadership. With little love for Westerners themselves, the Qing court decided to encourage the Boxer movement and won them over to the imperial side.

This was followed by 1900, one of the most significant years in Chinese history, when the Boxers suffered a quick and humiliating reaction. An expedition of troops from overseas, including Britain, Japan, Russia, the United States, and Australia, promptly defeated the Boxers and occupied Beijing, imposing huge monetary penalties and demanding public apologies from China. Weakened and impoverished, the Qing court tried for the next few years to impose a series of sweeping reforms, but these largely failed.

During the Boxer Uprising, Liu E learned that Russian troops in Beijing were burning huge stores of rice while many Chinese people were literally dying of hunger in the streets. He had made many friends among foreigners, and he persuaded the Russians to sell the rice at a low price instead of destroying it. This earned him great respect as a humanitarian, but it also prompted his enemies to accuse him of betraying the nation and supporting the foreign invaders.

The Boxer Uprising turned out to be a major watershed in the history of China. Part of a general breakdown of the old political and economic order, it paved the way for the Revolution of 1911, which toppled the Qing dynasty and brought more than two thousand years of Chinese imperial rule to an end.

WORK

In *The Travels of Lao Can,* Liu E was shrewd to convey the nation through the eyes of a wandering doctor. Dedicated to healing, the doctor stands for justice and the alleviation of suffering. Comparatively free, he has no government role, and he remains isolated, traveling alone. Members of the official class welcome him into their circles, and he shares their sophistication about poetry and art, but as a doctor Lao Can also walks among poor and suffering people, refusing to wear silks and furs in favor of simple cotton clothing and showing as much interest in ordinary life as he does in the experience of the official elite.

There is no question that the novel in part reflects Liu E's own life, and it has often been read as autobiographical. The hero's family name, Tieyun, means "Iron Cloud," and he shares the name "iron" (*tie*) with the author, whose courtesy name was Liu Tieyun. (His nickname, Lao Can, means "old and decrepit.") Some of the most corrupt officials in the novel are thinly disguised versions of historical people in the Qing government, and Youxian, the cruel prefect described in our selection below, is modeled on a real official who was a fanatical Boxer supporter. In Youxian, Liu E departs from a long Chinese tradition of holding corruption to be the worst evil of government. In some cases, he suggests, honest officials can be so harsh and intolerant that they wreak more destruction than dishonest ones.

The novel is written in literary Chinese, invoking chivalric ideals of justice and heroism through its central character, who is like an old knight-errant. Other popular novels of the time explicitly hearkened back to chivalric themes and styles. But while Liu E's protagonist is well-meaning and brave, seeking out remedies for injustice wherever he finds them, he also turns out to be, ultimately, quite helpless. At one point he persuades a powerful governor that an unjust official should be punished, but the governor refuses to take action for fear of offending the emperor. Lao Can does manage to rescue a few isolated people, but in the process he draws attention to the plight of many thousands of others whom he is powerless to save. Thus, although *The Travels of Lao Can* draws on long traditions of Chinese storytelling and novel-writing, this is a very modern novel in its ironic treatment of old chivalric ideals. It is also groundbreaking in its exploration of an individual psychology, mixing novelistic conventions for the first time with passages of private meditation traditionally rendered through the voice of lyric poetry. And most of all, it is modern in its searching attention to contemporary political injustice, a topic that had grown urgent in the face of China's national crisis and would preoccupy Chinese writers for the whole of the twentieth century. Poignantly, it begins and ends in sadness, conveying a historical moment of frightening upheaval in China.

From The Travels of Lao Can[1]

Author's Preface

When a baby is born, he weeps, *wa-wa*; and when a man is old and dying, his family form a circle around him and wail, *haotao*. Thus weeping is most certainly that with which a man starts and finishes his life. In the interval, the quality of a man is measured by his much or little weeping, for weeping is the expression of a spiritual nature. Spiritual nature is in proportion to weeping: the weeping is not dependent on the external conditions of life being favorable or unfavorable.

Horse and ox toil and moil the year round. They eat only hay and corn and are acquainted with the whip from start to finish. They can be said to suffer, but they do not know how to weep; this is because spiritual nature is lacking to them. Apes and monkeys are creatures that jump about in the depths of the forest and fill themselves with pears and chestnuts. They live a life of ease and pleasure, yet they are given to screaming. This screaming is the monkey's way of weeping. The naturalists say that among all living things

1. Translated by Harold Shadick.

monkeys and apes are nearest to man, because they have a spiritual nature. The old poem says:

> Of the three gorges of Eastern Ba, the Sorcerer's Gorge is the longest;
> Three sounds of monkeys screaming there cut through a man's bowels.[2]

Just think what feelings they must have!

Spiritual nature gives birth to feeling; feeling gives birth to weeping. There are two kinds of weeping. One kind is strong; one kind is weak. When an addlepated boy loses a piece of fruit, he cries; when a silly girl loses a hairpin, she weeps. This is the weak kind of weeping. The sobbing of Qi's wife[3] that caused the city wall to collapse, the tears of the Imperial Concubines Xiang[4] that stained the bamboo—these were the strong kind of weeping. Moreover the strong kind of weeping divides into two varieties. If weeping takes the form of tears, its strength is small. If weeping does not take the form of tears, its strength is great: it reaches farther.

* * *

We of this age have our feelings stirred about ourselves and the world, about family and nation, about society, about the various races and religions. The deeper the emotions, the more bitter the weeping. This is why the Scholar of a Hundred Temperings from Hongdu has made this book, *The Travels of Lao Can*.[5]

The game of chess is finished. We are getting old. How can we not weep? I know that "a thousand lovely ones" and "ten thousand beauties" among mankind will weep with me and be sad with me.

* * *

From *Chapter Five*

When they had all eaten, Lao Dong[6] was still bustling about, reckoning up the bills at each table and looking after his business. Lao Can had nothing to do, so he went for a stroll down the street. Leaving the inn he walked twenty or thirty steps east to where there was a small shop selling oil, salt, and other provisions.

Lao Can went in to buy two packets of Chao tobacco[7] flavored with orchid seeds and took the chance to sit down. Looking at the man behind the counter, he judged that he was something over fifty years of age. He asked him, "Your honorable name?" "My name is Wang," said the man; "I'm a native of this place. Your honorable name, Sir?" Lao Can said, "My name is Tie[8]—I'm a Jiangnan man." "Jiangnan is certainly a fine place," said the man; " 'Above are the halls of heaven; below Su and Hang.'[9] Not like this hell of ours here!"

2. Poem by Li Daoyuan (d. 527), about the Three Gorges of the Yangtze River.
3. The legendary wife of Qi Liang of Qi; when her husband died in battle in the year 549 B.C.E., she is said to have wept so long that her tears brought down the walls of the city.
4. Daughters of the legendary emperor Yao, who gave them as concubines to his successor, Shun; when Shun died, they cried bitterly, staining the bamboo forever.
5. Reference to Lao Can, whose family name means "iron"; here, he suggests that the iron has been tempered a hundred times to make it pure.
6. Owner of the inn where Lao Can is staying.
7. Tobacco from Chaozhou in Guangdong Province in southern China.
8. Lao Can's real name (which means "iron" in Chinese).
9. Suzhou and Hangzhou are Chinese cities known for their beauty.

Lao Can said: "You have hills, you have water, you grow rice and you grow wheat. How is it different from Jiangnan?" The man sighed and answered, "It is difficult to tell in a word!" and said no more.

Lao Can asked, "Your Prefect Yu here, is he all right?" The man answered, "He's an honest official! A good official! At the gate of his yamen[1] are twelve cages which are usually full; it's a rare day when one or two are vacant!"

While they were talking, a middle-aged woman with a rough bowl in her hand came out from the back of the shop to look for something among the shelves. Noticing a man on the other side of the counter, she gave one glance at him and continued her search.

Lao Can said, "How can there be so many bandits?" The man replied, "Who knows?" Lao Can said, "Surely most of them must be unjustly condemned." The man answered, "Injustice! No, there's no injustice!" Lao Can said, "I hear that if he happens to see a man who doesn't please his eye, he simply puts him in a cage and chokes him to death; or if somebody talks unwisely and falls into his hands, he's a dead man too. Is this true?" The man said, "No! Never!"

But Lao Can noticed that as the man answered, his face began to turn gray, and his eyes reddened. When he heard the words, "if somebody talks unwisely," tears filled his eyes, though they did not fall. The woman who had come in to get things looked round and could no longer restrain the tears which rolled down her face. She stopped in her search, and carrying her bowl in one hand, and covering her eyes with her sleeve with the other, ran out through the back door. When she had reached the courtyard, she began to sob, *ru ru*.

Lao Can wanted to question the man further, but by his grief-stricken face he knew that he must be weighed down by some wrong or injustice of which he dared not speak, so he merely made a few meaningless remarks and went away.

He returned to his inn and went to sit for a while in his own room, where he read a few pages of a book. When Lao Dong was no longer busy, he wandered out to find him and have another chat. He told Lao Dong what he had seen in the little general store and asked him what it was all about.

Lao Dong said: "This man's name is Wang. There are only the two of them, man and wife, and they were not married until he was thirty. His wife is ten years younger than he. After marriage they had one son, who was twenty-one years old this year. They buy the rougher articles they sell in their shop at our village fair, but for the better-grade articles, this son of theirs always went to the city. This spring, when their son was in the *fu*[2] city he must have had one or two cups of wine too many and let his tongue run away with him, for outside somebody's shop, he started to carry on about Prefect Yu, what a fool he was, how he took pleasure in treating people unjustly. This was overheard by some of Prefect Yu's spies, and he was dragged off to the yamen. The Prefect took his seat and railed at him, 'You thing, you! So you start rumors to disturb the people! What next?' He was then stood in a cage, and in less than two days choked to death. The middle-aged woman Your Honor saw just now is the wife of this man Wang. She is now more than forty. They had only this one son, not

1. Headquarters of a government official.
2. Site of the prefecture.

another soul in the world. Your mention of Prefect Yu couldn't help hurting her!"

Lao Can said, "This Yu Xian! Death wouldn't expiate all his crimes! How is it that his reputation in the provincial capital is so great? It truly is an astonishing thing! If I had power, this man would certainly be put to death!" Lao Dong said, "Your Honor had better watch what he says! While Your Honor is here, it doesn't matter if you talk freely. But in the city don't talk like this. It will cost you your life!"

Lao Can said, "Thank you for your kind warning; I will be careful." That night, after supper, he had a good sleep. The next day he took his leave of Lao Dong, got on his cart, and set out. That night he stayed at Macunji.

* * *

From *Chapter Six*

The next day when Lao Can got up the sky was heavily overcast. Although the northwest wind was not blowing very hard, his padded gown floated about him like the garments of an immortal. Having washed his face he bought several *youtiao*[3] for his breakfast, and then feeling rather dispirited strolled aimlessly up and down the street for some time. He was just thinking of going up on the city wall to enjoy the distant view when snowflakes began to flutter down one after another. Before long the snow was coming down in wild flurries, whirling and crisscossing, ever thicker and thicker. He returned in haste to his inn and told the servant to bring in a brazier. A sheet of the window paper, bigger than the rest, hung loose, and the wind, drumming on the paper wet from the snow, made a noise, *huoduo, huoduo*. The smaller strips of paper at the sides, though they made no noise, flapped to and fro without end. The chilling wind seemed to reach every corner of the room, making it desolate and eerie. Lao Can sat with nothing to do. Even his books were in the trunk and not easy to get at. So he just sat, becoming more and more melancholy. He couldn't hold back his feelings, and finally, taking a brush and an ink slab from the box that formed his pillow, he wrote a poem on the wall, devoted to Yu Xian's actions. The poem said:

Ambition pervades his flesh and marrow,
He zealously strives to make a name.
Injustice smothers the city in gloom,
Blood stains his hat-button[4] red.
Everywhere a rain of ill-omen,
In all the hills a tigerish wind;
He kills good people as though killing bandits:
This prefect who acts like a captain of troops.

Below he put the words: "Written by Tie Ying[5] of Xuzhou in Jiangnan." When he had finished writing, he had his noon meal. By this time the snow was coming down still more heavily. He stood in the doorway and looked out. The branches of the trees, big and little, appeared to be wrapped in fresh cotton

3. Deep-fried dough served for breakfast.
4. Red button worn by the highest rank of officials, governors, and viceroys.
5. Lao Can's name.

wool. The rooks in the trees kept drawing in their necks to escape the cold and were flapping their wings for fear the snow would pile up on their backs; he saw, too, many sparrows hiding under the eaves of the house who also drew in their necks for fear of the cold. Their frozen and hungry appearance seemed to him most pitiful. He therefore thought to himself, "These poor birds! They have to depend on seeds collected from trees and plants and on little insects to satisfy their hunger and keep them alive. Now of course all the insects have gone into their winter sleep and are not to be found, and even the seeds of trees and plants are scarcely to be found under this covering of snow. Even if the sun shines tomorrow and the snow melts a little, as soon as the northwest wind blows the snow will become ice and again the birds will not be able to find them. Won't they go on starving until next spring?" When his thoughts reached this point, he felt so sorry for the suffering of the birds that he could hardly bear it. And then again he thought, "These birds may be cold and hungry, but even so they do not have men to shoot at them and hurt them; no snares are put out to catch them. They are only cold and hungry for the time being, but when it comes around to next year's springtime they will be as happy as can be. And now think of these people of Caozhoufu who have suffered calamities for several years—they are the unfortunate ones. For they have this tyrannical, 'paternal' official who, on every possible occasion, captures them and treats them as bandits, killing them in his cages. They are so frightened that not a word can they say. To cold and hunger is added fear. Are they not worse off than these birds?" At this point his tears began to fall. Again he heard a strident outburst of cawing from the rooks, as if they were not crying out from cold and hunger but rather showing off to the people of Caozhoufu because they enjoyed freedom of speech. And now he became so angry that "his angry hair pushed up his hat,"[6] angry that he could not immediately kill Yu Xian and so give vent to his anger.

He was just thinking these wild thoughts when a blue-felt sedan chair came to the gate followed by some attendants. He knew it was Shen Dongzao[7] returning to the inn after paying some calls. He thought, "Why shouldn't I write a letter telling the Governor all these things I have seen and heard?" So he took out some letter paper and envelopes from his pillow box, lifted his brush, and began to write. The ink on the slab which he had used for writing on the wall was already frozen into solid ice. He had to breathe on it and write a few characters, and then breathe on it again. When he had written not more than two sheets, it was already quite late, for while he was breathing on the ink slab, his brush would freeze; and when he was breathing on his brush, the ink slab would freeze. After each attempt to melt the ink he could not write more than four or five characters, so he wasted a lot of time.

While he was kept busy in this way, it became so dark that he could not see. Being a dull day, it got dark even earlier than usual, so he called to the servant to bring him a lamp. After he had called for a long time, the man came in carrying a lamp, his hands and feet shaking with the cold, and as he put the lamp down he exclaimed, "It's cold all right!" He had a paper spill

6. Words taken from the work of Sima Qian (ca. 145–ca. 85 B.C.E.), a historian of China.

7. A local magistrate.

stuck between his fingers, and had to blow on it many times before it flared up. The lamp had been freshly filled with solid oil which was piled up like a big spiral snail shell so that when first lit it gave very little light. The servant said, "Wait a bit: when the oil has melted, it will be bright." He shook the lamp, then drew his hands into his sleeves again and stood and watched to see whether the lamp would go out. At first the flame was only the size of a big yellow pea. Gradually it took up oil and then became as big as a kidney bean. Suddenly the servant raised his head and looked at the characters written on the wall. Greatly alarmed he said, "Did Your Honor write this? What does it say? Don't stir up trouble! It's no laughing matter!" He then quickly turned his head and looked outside. There was no one there, so he said, "If you don't watch out, your life will be in danger; and we shall get into trouble too." Lao Can laughed and said, "My name is written at the bottom, so don't worry."

While he was speaking, a man wearing a hat with a red tassel came in and called out, "Mr. Tie!" The inn servant shuffled out, and the newcomer said, "My master invites Mr. Tie to go and eat with him." It was Shen Dongzao's servant. Lao Can said, "Ask your master to have his meal alone. I've already told them to bring me something here. It will come in a minute. Please thank him all the same." The man replied, "My master said, 'The inn food is not fit to eat!' We have a brace of pheasants someone has sent which have already been sliced, and there is also some sliced mutton. He said I am to tell Mr. Tie he simply must come and share the chafing dish. My master says that if Mr. Tie really won't come he will have the food carried over and eat it in this room. It seems to me much better for Your Honor to go over there. In that room there is a brazier four or five times as big as the one in this room, and it is very much warmer. Also it will be easier for us servants. Please oblige us."

Lao Can had no excuse, so there was nothing to do but go. When Shen Dongzao saw him, he said, "Mr. Bu,[8] what have you been doing in your room? Since it's such a snowy day, let's drink a cup or two of wine. Someone has sent me some very good pheasants. They are excellent eaten scalded in the chafing dish, so I will 'offer borrowed flowers to Buddha!'"[9]

While he was speaking, they took their seats. The servants brought on the slices of pheasant, red and white, very good to look at. Eaten scalded they had a most savory taste. Dongzao said, "Do you notice a rather unusual flavor?" Lao Can answered, "Indeed there is a sort of fresh fragrance. Why is it?" Dongzao said, "These pheasants come from the Peach Blossom Mountain in Feichengxian, where there are many pine trees. The birds have this freshness and fragrance because they are so fond of eating pine flowers and pine kernels. The popular name for them is 'Pine-Flower Pheasant.' Even here they are very difficult to get."

Lao Can murmured a few words of appreciation, and then the rice and other dishes were brought from the kitchen and placed on the table. When the two men had finished their rice, Dongzao suggested that they go into the inner room for their tea and to warm themselves at the fire. Suddenly he noticed that Lao Can was wearing a cotton padded gown and said, "How is it you are still wearing a cotton gown in such cold weather as this?"

8. Bucan is a name Lao Can has given himself.
9. Expression suggesting that one has done something conveniently without going to a lot of trouble.

Lao Can replied, "I don't feel at all cold. For us who have never worn fur-lined gowns from our childhood I think the amount of warmth given by our cotton gowns is greater than that given by your fox furs." Dongzao said, "This won't do" and then shouted, "Hello, there! In my flat leather trunk there is an extra gown lined with white fox. Take it out and put it in Mr. Tie's room."

Lao Can said, "On no account do that! I am not just being polite. Think! Has there ever been an itinerant bell ringer who wore a gown lined with fox fur?" Dongzao said, "You didn't have to shake that string of bells of yours in the first place. Why must you go to such extremes in feigning vulgarity? Since you have favored me to the extent of treating me as Somebody, I have a few outspoken words I want to say, whether you get offended at me or not, Sir! Last night I heard you say that you despised those who 'live in lofty seclusion claiming to be high-minded!' You said, 'The world produces a limited number of gifted men; it is not good to belittle oneself unreasonably!' I prostrate myself in admiration of those sentiments! But your actions rather contradict your words. The Governor really wants you to come out of seclusion and be an official, but you run off in the middle of the night, determined to get away and shake your string of bells. Consider! How are you different from the one who 'knocked a hole in the wall and escaped'; or the one who 'washed his ears and would not listen'?[1] What I say can't help being rather rash and is probably offensive to you, but please think about it. Am I right or wrong?"

Lao Can said, "I admit that shaking a string of bells contributes little to the world, but then does it contribute anything to be an official? I should like to ask, now that you are magistrate of Chengwuxian and are 'father and mother' to a hundred li and to ten thousand people, where will be the benefit to the people? But perhaps you are like the painter of bamboo who 'had the complete bamboo in his mind.'[2] Why not favor me with a little enlightenment? I know that you have already held two or three official posts in the past. Please tell me what evidence you have had of achieving anything unusual by your good government?"

Dongzao replied, "This is not the way to look at it. All that mediocre talents like me can do is to muddle through. But if a man of vast ability and resourcefulness like you doesn't come out and do something, it really is a great pity! Men without ability are dying for official positions, while men of ability would die to avoid official positions; this truly is the most regrettable thing in the world!"

Lao Can said, "On the contrary; what I say is that if those without ability get into office it does not matter at all; the really bad thing is when men of ability want to be officials. After all, isn't this Excellency Yu a man of ability? But just because he is overanxious to be an official, or rather hankers after being a great official, he acts as he does, wounding heaven and damaging all principles of justice. And with so great a reputation as an administrator I fear that within a few years he will become provincial governor. The greater the official position such a man holds, the greater the harm he will do. If he controls a prefecture, then a prefecture suffers; if he governs a province, then a

1. References to scholars who refused the invitations of rulers.
2. From a poem by Chao Buzhi (1053–1110): "When Youke painted bamboo, / In his breast he had the completed bamboo."

province is maimed; if he rules the Empire, then the Empire dies! Looked at in this way, please tell me, is greater harm done when a man of ability is an official, or is the harm greater when a man without ability is the official? If he were to go about like me, shaking a string of bells and curing disease, people would not want him to treat serious disorders; and in treating minor troubles he couldn't kill anybody. And if in the course of a year he happened to cause the death of one man, in ten thousand years he would not harm as many people as he does as Prefect of Caozhoufu!"

PANDITA RAMABAI
1858–1922

A feminist well ahead of her time, Pandita Ramabai was a formidable speaker, writer, and advocate for women's emancipation in India and worldwide. Her writings in Marathi, which reached out directly to women who shared her mother tongue and also introduced them to the Anglo-American world of their time, have become modern classics in the language. Her English-language writings, in turn, fueled a fresh wave of interest throughout the Anglo-American world in the lives of Indian women. A gifted translator, both literal and figurative, of many different traditions and texts, Ramabai was also a masterful and dedicated activist who parlayed her popularity into concrete and lasting reforms for women.

LIFE AND TIMES

Ramabai's life spanned the middle decades of India's period as a British colony (1757–1947), between the end of the East India Company's rule on the subcontinent in 1858 (giving way to direct administration by Queen Victoria's imperial government) and the consolidation of the nationalist freedom movement, led by Mahatma Gandhi and others, in the 1920s. These decades witnessed the material as well as cultural transformation of India from a preindustrial and predominantly rural society to a relatively modern society with a railway system, steamships, textile factories, municipal councils, universities, modern professions, and Europeanized cities such as Bombay, Calcutta, and Madras.

Like almost everybody else in her generation on the subcontinent, Ramabai started in her childhood deep inside a traditional way of life, but found herself in a globally interconnected world in her adult years. She was born in 1858 into a *brāhmaṇa* (priestly) family from Maharashtra, in western India. Her father was a religious scholar of Sanskrit who made his living by reciting sacred texts for wealthy patrons at pilgrimage sites. Despite his traditionalism, he broke from Hindu orthodoxy by teaching Sanskrit not only to his son but also to his wife and two daughters. For over a decade, the family traveled constantly from one pilgrimage site to another to earn a meager living from recitation. The itinerant lifestyle took a heavy toll: worn out by hardship and deprivation, Ramabai's parents died during a famine in 1874, and her sister died of cholera the following year. Orphaned teenagers, Ramabai and her elder brother continued in the family occupation, traveling on foot across India. When they arrived in Calcutta in 1878, the city's Hindu priests and scholars (all male) found the twenty-year-old Ramabai's knowledge of Sanskrit and religious texts so extraordinary that, after a public examination, they awarded her the title of *paṇḍitā* ("great female scholar"), making her the first woman in modern Indian history to receive this rare honor.

Suddenly famous, Ramabai delivered lectures in Calcutta for the Brahmo Samaj, a major organization for social reform in colonial India (cofounded by **Rabindranath Tagore**'s grandfather), and she quickly established herself as a powerful public speaker for women's education and emancipation. But reversals of fortune followed just as rapidly. In 1880 her brother died of cholera; shortly afterward she married his best friend, but after two years of a very happy marriage she lost her husband also to cholera. Thus, at twenty-four, Ramabai found herself a widow, without any material resources and with an infant daughter to raise. With the help of several reformers and reformist organizations, however, she moved to Maharashtra and in 1882 established the Arya Mahila Samaj (Society of Noble Women), an organization designed to raise Hindu women's consciousness against their oppressive social conditions, and to demand social and legal reforms. Her work at the Samaj reinvigorated Ramabai's own long-standing desire to study medicine, and so the following year, accompanied by her daughter, she left for England to pursue that dream.

Ramabai's three years in England proved life-transforming. She lived with the Sisters of the Community of St. Mary in Wantage, Oxfordshire, and taught them Marathi in exchange for room and board. Early in her stay, during a period of great personal turmoil, she accepted baptism into the Church of England for herself and her infant daughter. She then enrolled at the Cheltenham Ladies' College, where she taught Sanskrit in return for an education in science, mathematics, and English. There she became friends with Dorothea Beale, the founding principal of the college and an important proponent of women's education in England at that time. Ramabai's exchanges in English with Beale and others, published in *The Letters and Correspondence of Pandita Ramabai*, are now a notable part of nineteenth-century Indian literature and history; and her short Marathi book of this period, *Pandita Ramabai Yancha Englandcha Paravas* (*Pandita Ramabai's Journey to England*), is an early instance in her mother tongue of the modern epistolary travelogue.

In 1886 Ramabai journeyed to the United States to attend the graduation ceremony at the Women's Medical College of Pennsylvania of a niece, Anandibai Joshee, India's first female doctor trained in modern medicine. There, over the next two and a half years, Ramabai was widely celebrated as the leading representative of the Indian women's emancipation movement. During her extended stay she closely studied the educational system in Philadelphia, and she traveled around the country to deliver public lectures and to raise funds for a new institution for upper-caste Hindu women back in India. The Ramabai Association of Boston was founded in 1887 in direct response to her campaign; by 1890 it had seventy-five branches around the United States, and it pledged long-term support for two secular and nonsectarian institutions for widows in India. While in America, Ramabai wrote and published her most famous book in English, *The High-Caste Hindu Woman* (1887), which became an immediate best seller. At this time she also started writing *United Stateschi Loka-sthiti ani*

Pravasa-vritta (*The Condition of the People of the United States and an Account of My Travels*, 1889)—another classic of modern Marathi literature—which she completed in Bombay after her return in early 1889. By the time she set sail from San Francisco, she had raised more than $30,000, then a very large sum, for Indian women's projects.

Over the next three decades and more, Ramabai devoted herself primarily to women's causes in India, establishing separate institutions for sexually abused women and victims of rape, for blind women, and for old women. These enterprises offered abandoned, victimized, or disabled women an alternative shelter, a chance for rehabilitation, and an opportunity for self-reliance with training in vocational crafts ranging from weaving, tailoring, and laundering, to teaching, nursing, and printing and binding. In 1898 she opened an overtly Christian institution called Mukti Sadan (Home of Salvation) that is perhaps the best-known of her activist initiatives. Nine decades after her death, it was renamed the Pandita Ramabai Mukti Mission, and it remains today a large, active, and internationally recognized organization, in many ways a model of its kind.

While Ramabai was welcomed by reformers and reformist institutions throughout India from the beginning of her public career, more conservative Hindu groups criticized her frequently and sharply for her attempts to change the status and treatment of widows. With her conversion to Christianity, and especially after her return from the United States with foreign funding for her projects, the local attacks on her integrity, style, and perceived intentions increased in intensity. In the early 1890s, allegations that she exploited the vulnerability of the Hindu women in her institutions for Christian evangelical purposes and for proselytization sparked national and international controversies—not unlike those over Mother Teresa's mission in Calcutta a hundred years later. During the next two decades, Ramabai was increasingly alienated from the mainstream Hindu society in which she had her origins, and she continued to work at an emotional distance from it, gradually moving toward the resolutely Christian position of her final years.

WORK

Ramabai had a gift for languages. In childhood she learned Sanskrit and memorized complex religious texts in it for public recitation. During her years in Calcutta and her brief marriage, she picked up Bengali; in her mid-twenties in England, she became fluent in English. In her forties and fifties, she learned Hebrew and Greek in order to translate the Bible into Marathi, a monumental project she completed shortly before her death in 1922. Like other multilingual intellectuals, Ramabai developed different styles in the languages in which she wrote—Marathi and English. The Marathi she had absorbed from her infancy was rough, because her family spent much of its time traveling outside the Marathi-speaking region. When she wrote her first book in it, she adopted an artificial prose style with a heavy Sanskrit vocabulary imported into it, rather like a Latinate diction imposed on the "natural" Anglo-Saxon base of English. For her later book in Marathi about the United States, which is represented in our selection here, she developed what her contemporary reviewers called more "elegant and heart-stirring" expression; it includes some relaxed narrative, conversational explanations, and "gripping" descriptions. Ramabai's style in English is, on the whole, more expository and argumentative, as we can see from the excerpt from *The High-Caste Hindu Woman*. Her English uses many stock phrases and the longer periodic sentences that are typical of Victorian English, but it moves briskly by pursuing its lines of reasoning without digressions.

Ramabai's work as a bilingual woman writer of nonfictional prose is represented here in two selections. "Married Life" is the third chapter of *The High-Caste Hindu Woman* (1887), written originally in English and published in the United States during her visit there. This text, addressed to an international audience, offers a lively, uncompromising picture of upper-caste Hindu marriage customs in late-nineteenth-century India. Although Ramabai was writing for common readers, her analysis is like that of a skillful anthropologist: she explains the practices of arranged marriage and early marriage (before puberty), the dowry system, the structure of the extended family, and the organization of the average household, as well as the religious, historical, socioeconomic, and regional contexts. Based primarily on personal observation and reflection, her nonfictional account of Hindu marriage corresponds very closely to the representation of marriage we find, for example, in the fictional narratives of her contemporary, Rabindranath Tagore, who shared many of her concerns.

The second selection is "Legal Rights," a short section from "The Condition of Women in the USA," which is the seventh chapter of *United Stateschi Lokasthiti ani Pravasa-vritta* (*The Condition of the People of the United States and an Account of My Travels*, 1889). Written originally in Marathi, this text offers a trenchant critique of women's lack of legal rights in the United States in the late nineteenth century. For Ramabai, this shortcoming in the law is surprising, because it appears in a "civilized" country; and it is distressing, because it treats women as "greatly inferior" to men. Despite the many advances she finds in American society, the internal contradictions in the law mean that, in some respects, the condition of women in the United States is not significantly better than, or different from, the condition of women in India. Such criticism notwithstanding, Ramabai paints a sufficiently positive picture of late-nineteenth-century American society on the whole that her women readers in India felt quite overwhelmed. When Kashibai Kanitkar, the first female novelist in Marathi, reviewed the book in 1889, she noted astutely: "It would hardly be surprising if every one of our countrywomen who reads this book mutters dejectedly that such a golden day will never dawn for us. However, we will have to swallow these words hastily before they reach anybody's ears for fear of committing 'treason against men,' just as our men are afraid of committing treason when they discuss the [British colonial] government."

Married Life[1]

It is not easy to determine when the childhood of a Hindu girl ends and the married life begins. The early marriage system, although not the oldest custom of my country, is at least five hundred years older than the Christian era. According to Manu, eight years is the minimum, and twelve years of age the maximum marriageable age for a high caste girl.[2] The earlier the act of giving

1. From *The High-Caste Hindu Woman*. Written originally in English.

2. Ramabai bases this statement on *The Laws of Manu*, a book of ancient Hindu customs, ix, 94, which she quotes in a footnote.

the daughter in marriage, the greater is the merit, for thereby the parents are entitled to rich rewards in heaven. There have always been exceptions to this rule, however. Among the eight kinds of marriages described in the law, there is one form that is only an agreement between the lovers to be loyal to each other; in this form of marriage there is no religious ceremony, nor even a third party to witness and confirm the agreement and relationship, and yet by the law this is regarded as completely lawful a marriage as any other. It is quite plain from this fact that all girls were not betrothed between the age of eight and twelve years, and also that marriage was not considered a religious institution by the Hindus in olden times. All castes and classes could marry in this form if they chose to do so. One of the most noticeable facts connected with this form is this: women as well as men were quite free to choose their own future spouses. In Europe and America women do choose their husbands, but it is considered a shame for a woman to be the first to request marriage, and both men and women will be shocked equally at such an occurrence; but in India, women had equal freedom with men, in this case at least. A woman might, without being put to shame, and without shocking the other party, come forward and select her own husband. The *svayamvara* (selecting [one's] husband) was quite common until as late as the eleventh century AD, and even now, although very rarely, this custom is practised by a few people.

I know of a woman in the Bombay Presidency who is married to a Brahman according to this form. The first wife of the man is still living; the second wife, being of another caste, he could not openly acknowledge as his religiously wedded wife, but he could do so [i.e. acknowledge her] without going through the religious ceremony had she been of his own caste, as the act is sanctioned by Hindu law. The lawless behaviour of the Mahomedan intruders from the twelfth century AD, had much to do in universalizing infant marriage in India. A great many girls are given in marriage at the present day literally while they are still in their cradles; from five to eleven years is the usual age for their marriage among the Brahmans all over India. As it is absurd to assume that girls should be allowed to choose their future husbands in their infancy, this is done for them by their parents and guardians. In the northern part of the country, the family barber is generally employed to select boys and girls to be married, it being considered too humiliating and mean an act on the part of parents and guardians to go out to seek their future daughters- and sons-in-law.

Although Manu[3] has distinctly said that twenty-four years is the minimum marriageable age for a young man, the popular custom defies the law. Boys of ten and twelve are now doomed to be married to girls of seven and eight years of age. A boy of a well-to-do family does not generally remain a bachelor after seventeen or eighteen years of age; respectable but very poor families, even if they are of high caste, cannot afford to marry their boys so soon, but even among them it is a shame for a man to remain unmarried after twenty or twenty-five. Boys as well as girls have no voice in the selection of their spouses at the first marriage but if a man loses his first wife, and marries a second time, *he* has a choice in the matter.

3. Much of what Ramabai says in this part of her discussion is a combination of summary and paraphrase from *Manu*, ix.

Although the ancient law-givers thought it desirable to marry [off] girls when quite young, and consequently ignored their right to choose their own husbands, yet they were not altogether void of humane feelings. They have positively forbidden parents and guardians to give away girls in marriage unless good suitors were offered them.

> To a distinguished, handsome suitor of equal caste should a father give his daughter in accordance with the prescribed rule, though she has not attained the proper age. (*Manu*, ix, 88.)
>
> But the maiden, though marriageable, should rather stop in the father's house until death, than that he should ever give her to a man destitute of good qualities. (*Manu*, ix, 89.)

But, alas, here too the law is defined by cruel custom! It allows some men to remain unmarried, but woe to the maiden and to her family if she is so unfortunate as to remain single after the marriageable age. Although no law has ever said so, the popular belief is that a woman can have no salvation unless she be formally married. It is not, then, a matter of wonder that parents become extremely anxious when their daughters are over eight or nine and are unsought in marriage. Very few suitors offer to marry the daughters of poor parents, though they may be of high-caste families. Wealth has its own pride and merit in India, as everywhere else in the world, but even this powerful wealth is as nothing before caste rule. A high-caste man will never condescend to marry his daughter to a low-caste man though he be a millionaire.

But wealth in one's own caste surpasses the merits of learning, beauty and honour; parents generally seek boys of well-to-do families as their sons-in-law. As the boys are too young to pass as possessing 'good qualities,' i.e. learning, common-sense, ability to support and take care of a family, and respectable character, the parents wish to see their daughter safe in a family where she will, at least, have plenty to eat and to wear; they, of course, wish her to be happy with her husband, but in their judgment that is not the one thing needful. So long as *they* have fulfilled the custom, and thereby secured a good name in this world and heavenly reward in the next, their minds are not much troubled concerning the girl's fate. If the boy be of rich or middle-class people, a handsome sum of money must be given to him and his family in order to secure the marriage; beside this, the girl's family must walk very humbly with this little god, for he is believed to be in-dwelt by the god Vishnu. Poor parents cannot have the advantage of marrying their daughters to boys of prosperous families, and as they *must* marry them to someone, it very frequently happens that girls of eight or nine are given to men of sixty and seventy, or to men utterly unworthy of the young maidens.

Parents who have the means to secure good-looking, prosperous men as their sons-in-law, take great care to consult the horoscopes of both parties in order to know the future of their daughters; in such cases, they are anxious to ascertain, over and above all things, that the girl shall not become a widow. If the daughter's horoscope reveals that her future husband is to survive her, the match is considered very satisfactory; but if it reveals the reverse, then a boy having a horoscope equally bad is sought for, because it is sincerely believed that in that case the guardian planets will wrestle with each other, and, as almost always happens, that the stronger, i.e. the husband's planet will be victorious, or else both parties will fall in the conflict, and the husband and wife [will] die together. A friend of mine informed me that three hundred horoscopes were rejected before one was found which agreed satisfactorily with her sister's guardian planet. Undoubtedly many suitors, who might make good husbands for these little girls, are for this reason rejected, and unworthy men fall to their lot; thus, the horoscope becomes a source of misery instead of blessing.

It not unfrequently [*sic*] happens that fathers give away their daughters in marriage to strangers without exercising care in making inquiry concerning the suitor's character and social position. It is enough to learn from the man's own statement, his caste and clan, and the locality of his home. I know of a most extraordinary marriage that took place in the following manner:[4] the father was on a pilgrimage with his family, which consisted of his wife and two daughters, one nine and the other, seven years of age, and they had stopped in a town to take rest for a day or two. One morning, the father was bathing in the sacred river Godavari, near the town, when he saw a fine-looking man coming to bathe there also. After the ablution and the morning prayers were over, the father inquired of the stranger who he was and whence he came; on learning his caste, and clan, and dwelling-place, also that he was a widower, the father offered him his little daughter of nine, in marriage. All things were settled in an hour or so; next day the marriage was concluded, and the little girl placed in the possession of the stranger, who took her nearly nine hundred miles away from her home. The father left the place the day after the marriage without the daughter, and pursued his pilgrimage with a light heart; fortunately, the little girl had fallen in good hands, and was well and tenderly cared for beyond all expectation, but the conduct of her father, who cared so little to ascertain his daughter's fate, is none the less censurable.

When the time to conclude the marriage ceremony draws near, the Hindu mother's affection for the girl frequently knows no bounds; she indulges her in endless ways, knowing that in a few days her darling will be torn away from her loving embrace. When she goes to pay the customary visit to her child's future mother-in-law, many are the tearful entreaties and soul-stirring solicitations that she will be as kind and forbearing towards the little stranger as though she were her own daughter. The boy's mother is moved at this time, for she has a woman's heart, and she promises to be a mother to the little bride. On the day fixed for the marriage, parents formally give their daughter away to the boy; afterwards the young people are united by priests who utter the sacred texts and pronounce them man and wife in the presence of the sacred fire and of relatives and friends. The marriage being thus concluded, it is henceforth indissoluble.

> Neither by sale nor by repudiation is a wife released from her husband; such we know the law to be which the Lord of creatures made of old. (*Manu*, ix, 46.)

Marriage is the only 'sacrament' administered to a high caste woman, accompanied with the utterance of the Vedic texts. It is to be presumed that the texts are introduced in honour of the man whom she marries, for no sacrament

4. The circumstances Ramabai narrates in this passage are those of her parents' marriage; the unnamed town is Paithan, a temple and pilgrimage center now in the state of Maharashtra.

must be administered to him without the sacred formulae. Henceforth the girl is his, not only his property, but also that of his nearest relatives.

> 'For they (the ancient sages) declare that a bride is given to the family of her husband, and not to the husband alone.' (*Apastamba, II*, 10, 27, 3.)[5]

The girl now belongs to the husband's clan; she is known by his family name, and in some parts of India the husband's relatives will not allow her to be called by the first name that was given her by her parents; henceforth she is a kind of impersonal being. She can have no merit or quality of her own.

> Whatever be the qualities of the man with whom a woman is united in lawful marriage, such qualities even she assumes, like a river united with the ocean. (*Manu*, ix, 22.)

Many of our girls, when asked in fun whether they would like soon to be married, would innocently answer in the affirmative. They often see their sisters, cousins or playmates married; the occasion is one long to be remembered with pleasure. Even the poorest families take great pains to make it pleasant to everybody; children enjoy it most of all. There are gorgeous dresses, bright coloured clothes, beautiful decorations, music, songs, fireworks, fun, plenty of fruit and sweet things to eat and to give away, lovely flowers, and the whole house is illuminated with many lamps. What can be more tempting to a child's mind than these? In addition to all this, a big elephant is sometimes brought, on which the newly-married children ride in procession amidst all sorts of fun. Is it not grand enough for a child? Oh—, . . . I shall ride on the back of the elephant, thinks the girl; and there is something more besides; all the people in the house will wait on me, will make much of me; everybody will caress and try to please me. 'Oh, what fun!'

'I like to have a cold, and be ill,' said a girl of four. 'Why, darling?' asked her mother, in surprise. 'Oh, because,' replied the little girl, 'I like to eat my breakfast in bed, and then, too, everybody waits on me!'

Who has not heard remarks such as these, and laughed heartily over them? Children like even to be ill for the sake of being waited on. What wonder, then, if Hindu girls like being married for the sake of enjoying that much-coveted privilege! But little do these poor innocents know what comes after the fun. Little do they imagine that they must bid farewell to [their] home and mother, to noisy merriment and laughter, and to the free life of pure enjoyment. Sometimes the child desires to be married when, through superstition, she is ill-treated at home by her nearest relatives, otherwise there can be no reason except the enjoyment of fun that excites the desire in the girl's heart, for when the marriage takes place she is just emerging from babyhood.

Childhood is, indeed, the heyday of a Hindu woman's life. Free to go in and out where she pleases, never bothered by caste or other social restrictions, never worried by lesson-learning, sewing, mending or knitting, loved, petted and spoiled by parents, brothers and sisters, uncles and aunts, she is little different from a young colt whose days are spent in complete liberty. Then lo, all at once the ban of marriage is pronounced and the yoke put on her neck forever!

Immediately after the marriage ceremony is concluded the boy takes his

5. A commentary on Vedic ritual, attributed to the ancient sage Apastambha.

girl-bride home and delivers her over to his own mother, who becomes from that time until the girl grows old enough to be given to her husband, her sole mistress, and who wields over the daughter-in-law undisputed authority!

It must be borne in mind that both in Northern and Southern India, the term 'marriage' does not mean anything more than an irrevocable betrothal. The ceremony gone through at that time establishes *religiously* the conjugal relationship of both parties; there is a second ceremony that confirms the relationship both religiously and socially, which does not take place until the children attain the age of puberty. In Bengal, the rule is somewhat different, and proves in many cases greatly injurious to the human system. In some very rare cases the girls are allowed to remain with their own parents for a time at least. In the North of India, the little bride's lot is a happier one to begin with, she not being forced to go to her husband's home until she is about thirteen or fourteen years of age.

The joint family system, which is one of the peculiarities of Eastern countries, is very deeply rooted in the soil of India. There may not unfrequently [*sic*] be found four generations living under one roof. The house is divided into two parts, namely, the outer and the inner court. The houses, as a rule, have but few windows, and they are usually dark; the men's court is comparatively light and good. Houses in country places are better than those in the crowded cities. Men and women have almost nothing in common.

The women's court is situated at the back of the house, where darkness reigns perpetually. There the child-bride is brought to be forever confined. She does not enter her husband's house to be the head of a new home, but rather enters the house of the father-in-law to become the lowest of its members, and to occupy the humblest position in the family. Breaking the young bride's spirit is an essential part of the discipline of this new abode. She must never talk or laugh loudly, must never speak before or to the father and elder brother-in-law, or any other distant male relative of her husband, unless commanded to do so. In Northern India, where all women wear veils,[6] the young bride or woman covers her face with it, or runs into another room to show respect to them, when these persons enter an apartment where she happens to be. In Southern India, where women, as a rule, do not wear veils, they need not cover their faces; they rise to show respect to elders and to their husbands, and remain standing as long as they are obliged to be in their presence.

The mothers-in-law employ their daughters in all kinds of household work, in order to give them a thorough knowledge of domestic duties. These children of nine or ten years of age find it irksome to work hard all day long without the hope of hearing a word of praise from the mother-in-law. As a rule, the little girl is scolded for every mistake she commits; if the work be well done, it is silently accepted, words of encouragement and praise from the elders being regarded as spoiling children and demoralizing them. The faults of the little ones are often mistaken for intentional offences, and then the artillery of abusive speech is opened upon them; thus, mortified and distressed, they seek to console themselves by shedding bitter tears in silence. In such sorrowful hours they miss the[ir own] dear mother and her loving sympathy.

6. Ramabai refers to the fact that, in northern India, after Muslims introduced the convention of Muslim women wearing veils outside the immediate family circle, Hindus and members of other religious communities also adopted the convention of their women wearing veils in public.

I must, however, do justice to the mothers-in-law. Many of them treat the young brides of their sons as their own children; many are kind and affectionate, but ignorant; they easily lose their temper and seem to be hard when they do not mean to be so. Others again, having themselves been the victims of merciless treatment in their childhood become hard-hearted; such a one will do all she can to torment the child by using abusive language, by beating her and slandering her before the neighbours. Often she is not satisfied by doing this herself, but induces and encourages the son to join her. I have several times seen young wives shamefully beaten by beastly young husbands who cherished no natural love for them.

As we have seen, the marriage is concluded without the consent of either party, and after it the bride is not allowed to speak or be acquainted with the husband until after the second ceremony, and even then the young couple must never betray any sign of their mutual attachment before a third party. Under such circumstances, they seldom meet and talk; it may therefore be easily understood that being cut off from the chief means of forming attachment, the young couple are almost strangers, and in many cases do not like their relationship; and if in the midst of all this, the mother-in-law begins to encourage the young man to torment his wife in various ways, it is not strange that a feeling akin to hatred takes root between them. A child of thirteen was cruelly beaten by her husband in my presence for telling the simple truth, that she did not like as much to be in his house as at her own home.

In spite of all these drawbacks, there is in India many a happy and loving couple that would be an honour to any nation. Where the conjugal relation is brightened by mutual love, the happy wife has nothing to complain of except the absence of freedom of thought and action; but since wives have never known from the beginning what freedom is, they are generally well content to remain in bondage; there is, however, no such thing as the family having pleasant times together.

Men spend their evenings and other leisure hours with friends of their own sex, either in the outer court or away from home. Children enjoy the company of the father and mother alternately, by going in and out when they choose, but the children of young parents are never made happy by the father's caresses or any other demonstration of his love in the presence of the elders; the notion of false modesty prevents the young father from speaking to his children freely. The women of the family usually take their meals after the men have had theirs, and the wife, as a rule, eats what her lord may please to leave on his plate.

* * *

Legal Rights[1]

It is both surprising and regrettable that for all the progress in the United States, women have been granted very few legal rights. The social restrictions prevailing in the United States stem mainly from the ancient English law, which in turn is founded on the Commandments of Moses and on Roman law. By recognizing this, one is able to solve the riddle as to why women are

1. From *United Stateschi Loka-sthiti ani Pravasa-vritta*. Written originally in Marathi in 1888; translated by Meera Kosambi.

treated as greatly inferior by American law. In the new States in the west, there are several changes in laws pertaining to women; [for example] the law stipulates that the house in which a married man lives with his wife should be treated as hers and not his. But in most of the eastern states a widow is not allowed to stay in her late husband's house without paying rent, for more than forty days after his death! The compassionate and learned men in the State of Maine have taken pity on the grieving widow and allowed her to stay in her deceased husband's house for ninety days! These days, many States have granted married women the right to dispose of their self-earned property as they wish. The law states that they do not have a right to the money earned by doing work at home, such as tailoring, sketching, etc., but only to the money earned by paid employment outside the home. In several States, women have a full right to the moveable and immoveable property gifted by their father or brother, and married women have a right to a third of their deceased husband's moveable assets. But in many States, they have no right to self-earned assets or those inherited from the father, and no share whatsoever in the husband's property.

In New York and many other States, a mother has no right over her minor children. A father may give guardianship of his children to whomsoever he wishes during his lifetime or through his last will and testament. Thus the husband has the right to give away the children his wife has borne, against her will. Only if he is of unsound mind or dies intestate, does the mother obtain custody of her minor children. The children born to legally wedded couples are the father's children by law; the mother can claim no right to them. Only the children of unmarried women or prostitutes are regarded as the mother's. A couple of years ago, there was a respectable woman whose heartless husband tried to give away her tender babes against her wishes. The poor mother could not endure the separation from her own flesh and blood. In order to get guardianship of her children, she set aside her modesty and took a false oath in the court of law that they were not her husband's children. Only then did she get her children back. See how the laws of so-called civilized countries insult women's modesty, maternal love and God-given natural rights! . . . Only in the three States of Kansas, New Jersey and Iowa can mothers obtain custody of their children.

A few years ago, in Massachusetts and some other States, women did not have the right to be buried beside their husbands' graves; now this law has changed. Immediately after getting married, a woman becomes her husband's prisoner. The priest makes her take a vow of obedience to her husband. The moveable and immoveable property gifted by her father or brother, her jewellery, and such other possessions go into her husband's hands.[2] A few

2. American society still shows vestiges of its ancient barbaric condition, and it may be said that foremost among them is the excessive dependence of married women [on their husbands]. American men are shameless, just like the men of our country. They say, 'We support our households and feed our wives by our daily toil and the sweat of our brow.' Men work for eight, ten, or at the most twelve hours a day; but women have to slog for sixteen to seventeen hours daily, to serve the menfolk, mind the children and do household chores. The wives of labourers, farmers and of men in other occupations look after their homes and children first; in addition, they share their husbands' work equally and help them. In spite of all this, a wife has no right to the family income; whenever she needs a little money for her expenses, she has to cajole her husband, supply satisfactory answers to a thousand questions

years ago a woman could not claim a right to the clothes she stood in, but now the law has forbidden husbands to sell or pawn their wives' dresses in order to fill their own pockets.

The laws governing marriage and divorce differ widely throughout the United States, which causes a great deal of confusion in the social order. The good people of this country, especially The Woman's Temperance Society and its supporters, have been striving for a long time to insist that laws regarding marriage should be just and uniform throughout the country.

There is a law that entitles citizens of the United States to obtain justice in a court of law through a jury of twelve men who are their peers. But women do not have the right to trial by a jury of their own sex, who are their real peers. Men—even though they be a hundred times more foolish than women, or full of vices—do not allow the legislature to lift a finger without consulting them while enacting Federal or State laws. But women—no matter how learned, intelligent, thoughtful and moral—have no right to vote for the Federal or State legislatures. This makes men far superior to women [and not their equals] in the eyes of the law; therefore, if they, as jurors, try a case involving a woman, it does not mean that the woman defendant is tried by a jury of her peers. Except for the Territory of Wyoming, every other part of the United States has denied women this important right of an ordinary citizen, solely on the ground that they are women. Even so, these diligent women are trying to win poltical rights, and there are hopeful signs that their efforts will be crowned with success in the course of time.

MACHEMBA

late nineteenth century

I find no reason why I should obey you. I would rather die," wrote East African chief Machemba defiantly to Major Hermann von Wissmann, the officer in command of subduing Tanganyika (most of modern-day Tanzania) for the German Empire. Von Wissmann had recently completed a bloody suppression of coastal resistance and was now turning his attention to the interior and

---

he asks, and beg him for it. If he refuses to give her any money, she cannot claim a right to her hard-earned possessions, either by law or with the support of public opinion. Nor is this all. On the contrary, her husband tells everyone how much she is obliged to him; and society—male society—says, 'Men work hard indeed to earn the money to feed and clothe their wives! Oh, how highly they oblige their wives!' In the absence of a wife in the house, at least two or three servants would need to be employed to do the work that she does singlehandedly; and they would need to be paid wages. Servants are not fed for doing nothing, nor can they be said to be obliged to their master. But a wife, even if she does the work of ten servants, is under an obligation to her husband because he feeds her! [Ramabai's note.]

requiring the submission of all local chiefs, demanding that they pay new taxes and give up their lands.

In the 1880s, European nations began vying for control over African ports and resources. At the infamous Berlin Conference in 1884–85, European powers negotiated the rules for colonizing and occupying the continent—without any representation from African people. This meeting launched the so-called Scramble for Africa, a period when Europeans rushed to seize land and power from existing African communities.

Machemba was chief of the numerous Yao tribes who lived near the southern end of Lake Malawi. He was a wealthy trader, with a vast commercial network inside and outside Tanganyika. When the Germans first tried to lure him with promises of friendship, he turned them away. But for all his wealth and power and the advantage of guerrilla warfare on his own terrain, Machemba knew he would be vulnerable in the long term to the kind of scorch-and-burn attack that had already devastated the coast. The Germans had cannons and a large military force that included hundreds of Sudanese mercenaries.

Von Wissmann wrote Machemba a letter requiring him to come to the German station at Lindi and submit. Using reason, appeals to fairness, and biblical morality, Machemba replied that he and his family presented no danger for the Germans, and he left the door open for friendship. He also emphatically refused to submit.

Friendship was not what the Germans had in mind, and they tried to subdue Machemba three times. Each time he disappeared and harassed them with guerrilla tactics until they finally returned to the coast to report failure. In 1891, after his people's villages had been destroyed, Machemba did go to Lindi to accept the Germans' conditions. The peace did not last, however; he refused to collect their taxes and in 1899 was forced to flee to neighboring Mozambique, where he conducted a similar resistance against the Portuguese.

Machemba's letter is a dramatic statement of resistance to colonial subjugation. The only copy of the document is a German translation preserved in the German Colonial Archives along with other records, which means that the lost Swahili original comes to us filtered through the conqueror's language.

Letter to Major von Wissmann[1]

[undated—ca. Fall 1890]

Addressed to my friend and brother, the Commander-in-Chief:

I am informing you that your letter has arrived, and that I have read it and know everything it contains. Moreover, I have heard what you have to say;[2] but I find no reason that I should obey you. I would rather die. I have no relationship to you, and I cannot recall that you ever gave me a paisa[3] or a quarter

1. This letter was written by Chief Machemba of the Yao people to Major Hermann von Wissmann, commander of the German forces in Tanganyika and head of the station at Lindi. Translated from the German by Robert Sullivan and Sarah Lawall.

2. The spoken message accompanying the letter.

3. Or pice, a small coin, one-sixty-fourth of the Indian rupee in the East India Company's currency system. Machemba lists a descending order of possible gifts. The colonial trading companies initially gave gifts to local rulers whom they wished to persuade. "Relationship": i.e., personal, commercial, or diplomatic ties.

paisa or a needle or a thread. I look for a reason why I should obey you, and I find not the slightest. If it is only a matter of friendship, then I am not opposed, now or in the future. But to be your subject—that I cannot do. If it is only a matter of friendship, then we are agreed.

If you want to fight, I am ready. But to be your subject—never.

What you are hearing here is said without ambush. I will not fall at your feet, for you are a creature of God,[4] and I, too, am created. I am no God to be able to help you, and if you hear anything in my message, it is that we have no relationship.

I am sultan in my land. You are sultans in your land. Behold,[5] I am by no means saying to you that you should obey me. Not at all: indeed, I know that you are a free man. Not since I was born have I ever set foot on the coast; should I set foot on it now because you summon me? I will not come, and, if you are strong enough, then come get me. I would rather lose your respect [by being captured] than submit to you.

Besides, my child is called "Weakling,"[6] and, ever since he was born, has not known what war is. God willing, if you want to get me, then come: I will not come in person. Greetings.

This letter comes from your friend Machemba, son of M'chakama of the family of Masaninga, written in his own hand.

4. In the German text, a recognizable phrase from the Lutheran Bible.
5. Echoes biblical language in German and is more than simply "look" or "see." "Sultans": kings or rulers. The sultan of Zanzibar, now displaced by the Germans, was the traditional ruler of the mainland peoples of Tanganyika.
6. Literal translation from German. The lost Swahili term may have had special cultural significance, such as describing a youth who has not yet seen combat.

MARK TWAIN (SAMUEL CLEMENS)

1835–1910

Best known around the world for *The Adventures of Tom Sawyer* (1876) and *Adventures of Huckleberry Finn* (1885), the Missouri-born humorist Mark Twain was also a fierce opponent of imperialism. When the United States went to war with Spain over the Philippines, Twain at first cheered his own nation on, believing that US power would bring freedom to Filipinos: "We can make them as free as ourselves, give them a government and country of their own, put a miniature of the American Constitution afloat in the Pacific, start a brand new republic to take its place among the free nations of the world." But Twain's views changed when he realized that the US government was subjugating Filipinos, not liberating them. He began to work for the American Anti-Imperialist League and wrote scathing critiques of other empires as well. He condemned Cecil Rhodes, the British imperialist in South

Africa, in *Following the Equator* (1898) and a few years later turned his attention to Leopold II of Belgium, whose atrocities in the Congo Free State were being reported here and there but not prompting the kind of revulsion Twain thought they should. The United States and Britain recognized Leopold's regime and looked the other way, for the most part, when they heard of his willingness to torture and mutilate Congolese workers. Twain's *King Leopold's Soliloquy* (1905), excerpted here, is an inventive kind of satire. It adopts Leopold's persona and imagines him attempting to justify himself in response to reports of his cruelties. This technique allows Twain to quote at length from horrifying eyewitness accounts of Leopold's regime while also revealing the king as a mad and ruthless monster of a ruler.

From King Leopold's Soliloquy[1]

[*Contemplating, with an unfriendly eye, a stately pile of pamphlets*] Blister the meddlesome missionaries! They write tons of these things. They seem to be always around, always spying, always eye-witnessing the happenings; and everything they see they commit to paper. They are always prowling from place to place; the natives consider them their only friends; they go to them with their sorrows; they show them their scars and their wounds, inflicted by my soldier police; they hold up the stumps of their arms and lament because their hands have been chopped off, as punishment for not bringing in enough rubber, and as proof to be laid before my officers that the required punishment was well and truly carried out. One of these missionaries saw eighty-one of these hands drying over a fire for transmission to my officials—and of course he must go and set it down and print it. They travel and travel, they spy and spy! And nothing is too trivial for them to print. [*Takes up a pamphlet. Reads a passage from Report of a "Journey made in July, August and September, 1903, by Rev. A. E. Scrivener, a British missionary"*]

> ". . . Soon we began talking, and without any encouragement on my part the natives began the tales I had become so accustomed to. They were living in peace and quietness when the white men came in from the lake with all sorts of requests to do this and that, and they thought it meant slavery. So they attempted to keep the white men out of their country but without avail. The rifles were too much for them. So they submitted and made up their minds to do the best they could under the altered circumstances. First came the command to build houses for the soldiers, and this was done without a murmur. Then they had to feed the soldiers and all the men and women—hangers on—who accompanied them. Then they were told to bring in rubber. This was quite a new thing for them to do. There was rubber in the forest several days away from their home, but that it was worth anything was news to them. A small reward was offered and a rush was made for the rubber. 'What strange white men, to give us cloth and beads for the sap of a wild vine.' They rejoiced in what they thought their good fortune. But soon the reward was reduced until at last they were told to bring in the rubber for nothing.

1. This selection is spoken in the voice of King Leopold II of Belgium (1835–1909), who was one of the most vicious of all imperial rulers, conquering the people of Congo in the 1880s and remaining their ruler until he was forced to cede control in 1908. In 1905, at the time this piece was written, reports by missionaries and other witnesses had begun to stir up international outcry over Leopold's actions.

To this they tried to demur; but to their great surprise several were shot by the soldiers, and the rest were told, with many curses and blows, to go at once or more would be killed. Terrified, they began to prepare their food for the fortnight's absence from the village which the collection of rubber entailed. The soldiers discovered them sitting about. 'What, not gone yet?' Bang! bang! bang! and down fell one and another, dead, in the midst of wives and companions. There is a terrible wail and an attempt made to prepare the dead for burial, but this is not allowed. All must go at once to the forest. Without food? Yes, without food. And off the poor wretches had to go without even their tinder boxes to make fires. Many died in the forests of hunger and exposure, and still more from the rifles of the ferocious soldiers in charge of the post. In spite of all their efforts the amount fell off and more and more were killed. I was shown around the place, and the sites of former big chiefs' settlements were pointed out. A careful estimate made the population of, say, seven years ago, to be 2,000 people in and about the post, within a radius of, say, a quarter of a mile. All told, they would not muster 200 now, and there is so much sadness and gloom about them that they are fast decreasing."

"We stayed there all day on Monday and had many talks with the people. On the Sunday some of the boys had told me of some bones which they had seen, so on the Monday I asked to be shown these bones. Lying about on the grass, within a few yards of the house I was occupying, were numbers of human skulls, bones, in some cases complete skeletons. I counted thirty-six skulls, and saw many sets of bones from which the skulls were missing. I called one of the men and asked the meaning of it. 'When the rubber palaver began,' said he, 'the soldiers shot so many we grew tired of burying, and very often we were not allowed to bury; and so just dragged the bodies out into the grass and left them. There are hundreds all around if you would like to see them.' But I had seen more than enough, and was sickened by the stories that came from men and women alike of the awful time they had passed through. The Bulgarian atrocities[2] might be considered as mildness itself when compared with what was done here. How the people submitted I don't know, and even now I wonder as I think of their patience. That some of them managed to run away is some cause for thankfulness. I stayed there two days and the one thing that impressed itself upon me was the collection of rubber. I saw long files of men come in, as at Bongo, with their little baskets under their arms; saw them paid their milk tin full of salt, and the two yards of calico flung to the headmen; saw their trembling timidity, and in fact a great deal that all went to prove the state of terrorism that exists and the virtual slavery in which the people are held."

That is their way; they spy and spy, and run into print with every foolish trifle. And that British consul, Mr. Casement, is just like them. He gets hold of a *diary which had been kept by one of my government officers*, and, although it is a private diary and intended for no eye but its owner's, Mr. Casement is so lacking in delicacy and refinement as to print passages from it. [*Reads a passage from the diary*]

"Each time the corporal goes out to get rubber, cartridges are given him. He must bring back all not used, and for every one used he must bring back a right hand. M. P. told me that sometimes they shot a cartridge at an animal in hunting; they then cut off a hand from a living man. As to the extent to which this is carried on, he informed me that in six months the State on the Mambogo River had used 6,000 cartridges, which means that 6,000 people are killed or muti-

2. In the 1870s the Ottoman Empire violently suppressed an uprising of Christians in Bulgaria who were resisting Ottoman rule.

> lated. It means more than 6,000, for the people have told me repeatedly that the soldiers kill the children with the butt of their guns."

When the subtle consul thinks silence will be more effective than words, he employs it. Here he leaves it to be recognized that a thousand killings and mutilations a month is a large output for so small a region as the Mambogo River concession, silently indicating the dimensions of it by accompanying his report with a map of the prodigious Congo State, in which there is not room for so small an object as that river. That silence is intended to say, "If it is a thousand a month in this little corner, imagine the output of the whole vast State!" A gentleman would not descend to these furtivenesses.

Now as to the mutilations. You can't head off a Congo critic and make him stay headed-off; he dodges, and straightway comes back at you from another direction. They are full of slippery arts. When the mutilations (severing hands, unsexing men, etc.) began to stir Europe, we hit upon the idea of excusing them with a retort which we judged would knock them dizzy on that subject for good and all, and leave them nothing more to say; to wit, we boldly laid the custom on the natives, and said we did not invent it, but only followed it. Did it knock them dizzy? did it shut their mouths? Not for an hour. They dodged, and came straight back at us with the remark that "if a Christian king can perceive a saving moral difference between inventing bloody barbarities, and *imitating them from savages*, for charity's sake let him get what comfort he can out of his confession!"

It is most amazing, the way that that consul acts—that spy, that busy-body. *[Takes up pamphlet "Treatment of Women and Children in the Congo State; what Mr. Casement Saw in 1903"] Hardly two years ago! Intruding* that date upon the public was a piece of cold malice. It was intended to weaken the force of my press syndicate's assurances to the public that my severities in the Congo *ceased*, and ceased utterly, *years and years ago*. This man is fond of trifles—revels in them, gloats over them, pets them, fondles them, sets them all down. One doesn't need to drowse through his monotonous report to see that; the mere subheadings of its chapters prove it. [*Reads*]

> "Two hundred and forty persons, *men, women and children*, compelled to supply government with *one ton* of carefully prepared foodstuffs *per week*, receiving in remuneration, all told, the princely sum of 15s. 10d!"[3]

Very well, it was liberal. It was not much short of a penny a week for each nigger. It suits this consul to belittle it, yet he knows very well that I could have had both the food and the labor for nothing. I can prove it by a thousand instances. [*Reads*]

> "Expedition against a village behindhand in its (compulsory) supplies; result, slaughter of sixteen persons; among them three women and a boy of five years. Ten carried off, to be prisoners till ransomed; among them a child, who died during the march."

But he is careful not to explain that we are *obliged* to resort to ransom to collect debts, where the people have nothing to pay with. Families that escape to the woods sell some of their members into slavery and thus provide the ransom. He knows that I would stop this if I could find a less objectionable way to collect

3. Fifteen shillings and ten pence in British money, worth over a hundred US dollars today.

their debts. . . . Mm—here is some more of the consul's delicacy! He reports a conversation he had with some natives:

> Q. "How do you know it was the *white* men themselves who ordered these cruel things to be done to you? These things must have been done without the white man's knowledge by the black soldiers."
>
> A. "The white men told their soldiers: 'You only kill *women*; you cannot kill men. You must prove that you kill men.' So then the soldiers when they killed us" (here he stopped and hesitated and then pointing to . . . he said:) "then they . . . and took them to the white men, who said: 'It is true, you have killed *men*.'"
>
> Q. "You say this is true? Were many of you so treated after being shot?"
>
> All [*shouting out*]: "*Nkote*! *Nkoto*!" ("Very many! Very many!")
>
> There was no doubt that these people were not inventing. Their vehemence, their flashing eyes, their excitement, were not simulated."

Of course the critic had to divulge that; he has no self-respect. All his kind reproach me, although they know quite well that I took no pleasure in punishing the men in that particular way, but only did it as a warning to other delinquents. Ordinary punishments are no good with ignorant savages; they make no impression. [*Reads more sub-heads*]

> "Devastated region; population reduced from 40,000 to 8,000."

He does not take the trouble to say how it happened. He is fertile in concealments. He hopes his readers and his Congo reformers, of the Lord-Aberdeen-Norbury-John-Morley-Sir Gilbert-Parker stripe,[4] will think they were all killed. They were not. The great majority of them escaped. They fled to the bush with their families because of the rubber raids, and it was there they died of hunger. Could we help that?

One of my sorrowing critics observes: "Other Christian rulers tax their people, but furnish schools, courts of law, roads, light, water and protection to life and limb in return; King Leopold taxes his stolen nation, but provides *nothing in return but hunger, terror, grief, shame, captivity, mutilation and massacre*." That is their style! I furnish "nothing"! I send the gospel to the survivors; these censure-mongers know it, but they would rather have their tongues cut out than mention it. I have several times required my raiders to give the dying an opportunity to kiss the sacred emblem; and if they obeyed me I have without doubt been the humble means of saving many souls. None of my traducers have had the fairness to mention this; but let it pass; there is One who has not overlooked it, and that is my solace, that is my consolation.

[*Puts down the Report, takes up a pamphlet, glances along the middle of it*]

This is where the "death-trap" comes in. Meddlesome missionary spying around—Rev. W. H. Sheppard. Talks with a black raider of mine after a raid; cozens him into giving away some particulars. The raider remarks:

> "I demanded 30 slaves from this side of the stream and 30 from the other side; 2 points of ivory, 2,500 balls of rubber, 13 goats, 10 fowls and 6 dogs, some corn chumy, etc.
>
> 'How did the fight come up?' I asked.

4. British leaders who opposed Leopold's atrocities.

'I sent for all their chiefs, sub-chiefs, men and women, to come on a certain day, saying that I was going to finish all the palaver. When they entered these small gates (the walls being made of fences brought from other villages, the high native ones) I demanded all my pay or I would kill them; so they refused to pay me, and I ordered the fence to be closed so they couldn't run away; then we killed them here inside the fence. The panels of the fence fell down and some escaped.'

'How many did you kill?' I asked.

'We killed plenty, will you see some of them?'

That was just what I wanted.

He said: 'I think we have killed between eighty and ninety, and those in the other villages I don't know, I did not go out but sent my people.'

He and I walked out on the plain just near the camp. There were three dead bodies with the flesh carved off from the waist down.

'Why are they carved so, only leaving the bones?' I asked.

'My people ate them,' he answered promptly. He then explained, 'The men who have young children do not eat people, but all the rest ate them.' On the left was a big man, shot in the back and without a head. (All these corpses were nude.)

'Where is the man's head?' I asked.

'Oh, they made a bowl of the forehead to rub up tobacco and diamba in.'

We continued to walk and examine until late in the afternoon, and counted forty-one bodies. The rest had been eaten up by the people.

On returning to the camp, we crossed a young woman, shot in the back of the head, one hand was cut away. I asked why, and Mulunba N'Cusa explained that they always cut off the right hand to give to the State on their return.

'Can you not show me some of the hands?' I asked.

So he conducted us to a framework of sticks, under which was burning a slow fire, and there they were, the right hands—I counted them, eighty-one in all.

There were not less than sixty women (Bena Pianga)[5] prisoners. I saw them.

We all say that we have as fully as possible investigated the whole outrage, and find it was a plan previously made to get all the stuff possible and to catch and kill the poor people in the 'death-trap.'"

Another detail, as we see!—cannibalism. They report cases of it with a most offensive frequency. My traducers do not forget to remark that, inasmuch as I am absolute and with a word can prevent in the Congo anything I choose to prevent, then whatsoever is done there by my permission is my act, my *personal* act; that *I* do it; that the hand of my agent is as truly *my* hand as if it were attached to my own arm; and so they picture me in my robes of state, with my crown on my head, munching human flesh, saying grace, mumbling thanks to Him from whom all good things come. Dear, dear, when the soft-hearts get hold of a thing like that missionary's contribution they quite lose their tranquility over it They speak out profanely and reproach Heaven for allowing such a fiend to live. Meaning me. They think it irregular. They go shuddering around, brooding over the reduction of that Congo population from 25,000,000 to 15,000,000 in the twenty years of my administration; then they burst out and call me "the King with Ten Million Murders on his Soul." They call me a "record." The most of them do not stop with charging merely the 10,000,000 against me. No, they reflect that but for me the population, by natural increase, would now be 30,000,000, so they charge another 5,000,000 against me and make my total death-harvest 15,000,000.

5. A Congolese group.

They remark that the man who killed the goose that laid the golden egg was responsible for the eggs she would subsequently have laid if she had been let alone. Oh, yes, they call me a "record." They remark that twice in a generation, in India, the Great Famine destroys 2,000,000 out of a population of 320,000,000, and the whole world holds up its hands in pity and horror; then they fall to wondering where the world would find room for its emotions if I had a chance to trade places with the Great Famine for twenty years! The idea fires their fancy, and they go on and imagine the Famine coming in state at the end of the twenty years and prostrating itself before me, saying: "Teach me, Lord, I perceive that I am but an apprentice." And next they imagine Death coming, with his scythe and hour-glass, and begging me to marry his daughter and reorganize his plant and run the business. For the whole world, you see! By this time their diseased minds are under full steam, and they get down their books and expand their labors, with me for text. They hunt through all biography for my match, working Attila, Torquemada, Ghengis Khan, Ivan the Terrible,[6] and the rest of that crowd for all they are worth, and evilly exulting when they cannot find it. Then they examine the historical earthquakes and cyclones and blizzards and cataclysms and volcanic eruptions: verdict, none of them "in it" with me. At last they do really hit it (as they think), and they close their labors with conceding—reluctantly—that I have *one* match in history, but only one—the *Flood*. This is intemperate.

But they are always that, when they think of me. They can no more keep quiet when my name is mentioned than can a glass of water control its feelings with a seidlitz powder[7] in its bowels. The bizarre things they can imagine, with me for an inspiration! One Englishman offers to give me the odds of three to one and bet me anything I like, up to 20,000 guineas,[8] that for 2,000,000 years I am going to be the most conspicuous foreigner in hell. The man is so beside himself with anger that he does not perceive that the idea is foolish. Foolish and unbusiness-like: you see, there could be no winner; both of us would be losers, on account of the loss of interest on the stakes; at four or five per cent. compounded, this would amount to—I do not know how much, exactly, but, by the time the term was up and the bet payable, a person could buy hell itself with the accumulation.

Another madman wants to construct a memorial for the perpetuation of my name, out of my 15,000,000 skulls and skeletons, and is full of vindictive enthusiasm over his strange project. He has it all ciphered out and drawn to scale. Out of the skulls he will build a combined monument and mausoleum to me which shall exactly duplicate the Great Pyramid of Cheops,[9] whose base covers thirteen acres, and whose apex is 451 feet above ground. He desires to stuff me and stand me up in the sky on that apex, robed and crowned, with my "pirate flag" in one hand and a butcher-knife and pendant handcuffs in the other. He will build the pyramid in the centre of a depopulated tract, a brooding solitude covered with weeds and the mouldering ruins of burned villages, where the spirits of the starved and murdered dead will voice their laments forever in the whispers of the wandering winds. Radiating from the pyramid, like the spokes of a wheel, there are to be forty grand avenues of approach, each thirty-five miles long, and each

6. All rulers infamous for their cruelty. Attila, ruler of the Huns in the fifth century (?–453). Tomás de Torquemada (1420–1498), fanatical priest who led the Spanish Inquisition. Tsar Ivan IV of Russia (1530–1584), called "the Terrible."

7. A common medication used to aid digestion.

8. A large sum, worth nearly 3 million US dollars today.

9. This ancient Egyptian pyramid is almost five hundred feet high, and considered one of the Seven Wonders of the World. It was built about 2500 B.C.E.

fenced on both sides by skulless skeletons standing a yard and a half apart and festooned together in line by short chains stretching from wrist to wrist and attached to tried and true old handcuffs stamped with my private trade-mark, a crucifix and butcher-knife crossed, with motto, "By this sign we prosper;" each osseous fence to consist of 200,000 skeletons on a side, which is 400,000 to each avenue. It is remarked with satisfaction that it aggregates three or four thousand miles (single-ranked) of skeletons,—15,000,000 all told—and would stretch across America from New York to San Francisco. It is remarked further, in the hopeful tone of a railroad company forecasting showy extensions of its mileage, that my output is 500,000 corpses a year when my plant is running full time, and that therefore if I am spared ten years longer there will be fresh skulls enough to add 175 feet to the pyramid, making it by a long way the loftiest architectural construction on the earth, and fresh skeletons enough to continue the transcontinental file (on piles) a thousand miles into the Pacific. The cost of gathering the materials from my "widely scattered and innumerable private graveyards," and transporting them, and building the monument and the radiating grand avenues, is duly ciphered out, running into an aggregate of millions of guineas, and then—why then, (—— ——!!—— ——!!) this idiot asks me to *furnish the money! [Sudden and effusive application of the crucifix]* He reminds me that my yearly income from the Congo is millions of guineas, and that *"only"* 5,000,000 would be required for his enterprise. Every day wild attempts are made upon my purse; they do not affect me, they cost me not a thought. But *this one*—this one troubles me, makes me nervous; for there is no telling what an unhinged creature like this may think of next. . . . *If he should think of Carnegie*[1]—but I must banish that thought out of my mind! it worries my days; it troubles my sleep. That way lies madness. [*After a pause*] There is no other way—I have got to buy Carnegie.

[*Harrassed and muttering, walks the floor a while, then takes to the Consul's chapter-headings again. Reads*]

> "Government starved a woman's children to death and killed her sons."
>
> "Butchery of women and children."
>
> *"The native has been converted into a being without ambition because without hope."*
>
> "Women chained by the neck by rubber sentries."
>
> "Women refuse to bear children because, with a baby to carry, they cannot well run away and hide from the soldiers."
>
> "Statement of a child. 'I, my mother, my grandmother and my sister, we ran away into the bush. A great number of our people were killed by the soldiers. . . . After that they saw a little bit of my mother's head, and the soldiers ran quickly to where we were and caught my grandmother, my mother, my sister and another little one younger than us. Each wanted my mother for a wife, and argued about it, so they finally decided to kill her. They shot her through the stomach with a gun and she fell, and when I saw that I cried very much, because they killed my grandmother and mother and I was left alone. I saw it all done!' "

It has a sort of pitiful sound, although they are only blacks. It carries me back and back into the past, to when my children were little, and would fly—to the bush, so to speak—when they saw me coming. . . . [*Resumes the reading of chapter-headings of the Consul's report*]

1. Andrew Carnegie (1835–1919) was one of the richest men in the world. Scottish born, he made his fortune in the United States in steel.

"They put a knife through a child's stomach."

"They cut off the hands and brought them to C. D. (white officer) and spread them out in a row for him to see. They left them lying there, because the white man had seen them, so they did not need to take them to P."

"Captured children left in the bush to die, by the soldiers."

"Friends came to ransom a captured girl; but sentry refused, saying the white man wanted her because she was young."

"Extract from a native girl's testimony. 'On our way the soldiers saw a little child, and when they went to kill it the child laughed, so the soldier took the butt of his gun and struck the child with it and then cut off its head. One day they killed my half-sister and cut off her head, hands and feet, because she had bangles on. Then they caught another sister, and sold her to the W. W. people, and now she is a slave there.'"

The little child laughed! [*A long pause. Musing*] That innocent creature. Somehow—I wish it had not laughed. [*Reads*]

"Mutilated children."

"Government encouragement of inter-tribal slave-traffic. The monstrous fines levied upon villages tardy in their supplies of foodstuffs compel the natives to sell their fellows—and children—to other tribes in order to meet the fine."

"A father and mother forced to sell their little boy."

"Widow forced to sell her little girl."

[*Irritated*] Hang the monotonous grumbler, what would he have me do! Let a widow off merely because she is a widow? He knows quite well that there is nothing much left, now, *but* widows. I have nothing against widows, as a class, but business is business, and I've got to live, haven't I, even if it does cause inconvenience to somebody here and there? [*Reads*]

"Men intimidated by the torture of their wives and daughters. (To make the men furnish rubber and supplies and so get their captured women released from chains and detention.) The sentry explained to me that he caught the women and brought them in (chained together neck to neck) by direction of his employer."

"An agent explained that he was forced to catch women in preference to men, as then the men brought in supplies quicker; but he did not explain how the children deprived of their parents obtained their own food supplies."

"A file of 15 (captured) women."

"Allowing women and children to die of starvation in prison."

[*Musing*] Death from *hunger*. A lingering, long misery that must be. Days and days, and still days and days, the forces of the body failing, dribbling away, little by little—yes, it must be the hardest death of all. And to see food carried by, every day, and you can have none of it! Of course the little children cry for it, and that wrings the mother's heart. . . . [*A sigh*] Ah, well, it cannot be helped; circumstances make this discipline necessary.* * *

[*Studies some photographs of mutilated negroes—throws them down. Sighs*] The kodak[2] has been a sore calamity to us. The most powerful enemy that has confronted us, indeed. In the early years we had no trouble in getting the press to "expose" the tales of the mutilations as slanders, lies, inventions of busy-body American missionaries and exasperated foreigners who had found the "open

2. The first camera that was easy to use and carry, it was extremely popular from its introduction in 1888.

door" of the Berlin-Congo charter[3] closed against them when they innocently went out there to trade; and by the press's help we got the Christian nations everywhere to turn an irritated and unbelieving ear to those tales and say hard things about the tellers of them. Yes, all things went harmoniously and pleasantly in those good days, and I was looked up to as the benefactor of a downtrodden and friendless people. Then all of a sudden came the crash! That is to say, the incorruptible *Kodak*—and all the harmony went to hell! The only witness I have encountered in my long experience that I couldn't bribe. Every Yankee missionary and every interrupted trader sent home and got one; and now—oh, well, the pictures get sneaked around everywhere, in spite of all we can do to ferret them out and suppress them. Ten thousand pulpits and ten thousand presses are saying the good word for me all the time and placidly and convincingly denying the mutilations. Then that trivial little kodak, that a child can carry in its pocket, gets up, uttering never a word, and knocks them dumb!

. . . What is this fragment? [*Reads*]

> "But enough of trying to tally off his crimes! His list is interminable, we should never get to the end of it. His awful shadow lies across his Congo Free State, and under it an unoffending nation of 15,000,000 is withering away and swiftly succumbing to their miseries. It is a land of graves; it is *The* Land of Graves; it is the Congo Free Graveyard. It is a majestic thought: that is, this ghastliest episode in all human history is the work of *one man alone*; one solitary man; just a single individual—Leopold, King of the Belgians. He is personally and solely responsible for all the myriad crimes that have blackened the history of the Congo State. He is *sole* master there; he is absolute. He could have prevented the crimes by his mere command; he could stop them today with a word. He withholds the word. For his pocket's sake.
>
> It seems strange to see a king destroying a nation and laying waste a country for mere sordid money's sake, and solely and only for that. Lust of conquest is royal; kings have always exercised that stately vice; we are used to it, by old habit we condone it, perceiving a certain dignity in it; but *lust of money—lust of shillings—lust of nickels—lust of dirty coin*, not for the nation's enrichment but for *the king's alone*—this is new. It distinctly revolts us, we cannot seem to reconcile ourselves to it, we resent it, we despise it, we say it is shabby, unkingly, out of character. Being democrats we ought to jeer and jest, we ought to rejoice to see the purple dragged in the dirt, but—well, account for it as we may, we don't. We see this awful king, this pitiless and blood-drenched king, this money-crazy king towering toward the sky in a world-solitude of sordid crime, unfellowed and apart from the human race, sole butcher for personal gain findable in all his caste, ancient or modern, pagan or Christian, proper and legitimate target for the scorn of the lowest and the highest, and the execrations of all who hold in cold esteem the oppressor and the coward; and—well, it is a mystery, but *we do not wish to look*; for he is a king, and it hurts us, it troubles us, by ancient and inherited instinct it shames us to see a king degraded to this aspect, and we shrink from hearing the particulars of how it happened. *We shudder* and *turn away* when we come upon them in print."

Why, certainly—*that* is my protection. And you will continue to do it. I know the human race.

3. In 1884–85, European powers met to decide on a policy to govern imperial activity in Africa, agreeing that any European nation could take control of African land. "Open Door": a policy allowing free trade and travel along the Congo and Niger Rivers.

POETRY AND POLITICS

Although nineteenth-century poets were often drawn to the exploration of intimate and personal experience, many also envisioned poetry as an agent of social change. Poets across the world focused attention on political corruption and social inequality. They wrote poems about war, democracy, and imperial domination.

Some of this poetry succeeded in having a real social impact. In England, Elizabeth Barrett Browning wrote a bitter poetic condemnation of child labor in factories that helped to persuade the British Parliament to pass a new law that limited the workday for children to six and a half hours. Another outspoken woman writer, Lola Rodríguez de Tió, used her poetry to call Puerto Ricans to revolution; one of her poems, in fact, became the official anthem of Puerto Rico. The Irish poet Lady Jane Wilde, who took the pen name "Speranza," worked to build the political movement for Irish independence from British rule. She wrote with particular passion about the horrors of mass starvation brought on by the potato famine of the 1840s.

New nations often celebrated poets as heroes of the people. After the death of Nicaraguan poet Rubén Darío, for example, the government ordered national mourning and granted him the burial honors of a high-level minister, while the church performed funeral services usually reserved for royalty. Adam Mickiewicz, known to this day as the national poet of Poland, is memorialized by a massive statue in Krakow's main square.

But political poetry could also spell danger to the authorities. Percy Shelley's publisher was imprisoned for distributing his blasphemous works. Mickiewicz's books were banned by the Catholic Church. The revolutionary works of Rodríguez de Tió prompted her expulsion from Puerto Rico by Spanish authorities. José Martí, who died fighting for Cuban independence, spent two of his teenage years in a Cuban prison, and Heinrich Heine's work was banned and burned in Germany multiple times, starting in 1835. Nearly all the writers included here spent years in exile from their homelands.

In order to capture and convey the sufferings of whole social groups, poets experimented with crafting new forms and styles. Barrett Browning and Heine, for example, rejected the solitary first-person "I" of lyric poetry so popular with their contemporaries to take up the collective "we" of oppressed workers, attempting an unusual poetry in which crowds would speak with one voice. Both poets also turned away from the natural landscapes that had so inspired the Romantic poets to focus poetic attention instead on the ugliness of industrial labor. US poet Walt Whitman, famous for his poems of the self, put the "I" aside in his elegies that expressed a whole nation's grief after the assassination of Abraham Lincoln. Whitman saw Lincoln's death as, like poetry, capable of unifying a nation: "a cement to the whole people, subtler, more underlying, than any thing written in constitution, or courts or armies." Martí's deliberately simple verse made it

José Martí (right) with fellow Cuban patriots Fermín Valdés Dominguez (left) and Francisco Gómez Toro (center), in Key West, Florida, ca. 1894.

especially effective politically. With its short, rhyming lines, it was easily memorized, particularly when it was set to the music of a popular folk song. Martí's words could therefore travel easily in the form of a catchy tune, reaching even those people who could not read or write. The Russian poet Anna Bunina chose a witty, bantering back-and-forth form for her investigation of the role of women writers in Russian society.

Poets often drew on folk songs, rooting their literary work in the long story of their people. Rodríguez de Tió set her call for revolutionary violence to the rhythm of a traditional dance tune. Speranza turned to the Gaelic poetry of a hundred years before her time as a source for her vivid sense of contemporary Irish hunger. The influence of political poetry could also spill across national borders. Martí and Darío drew inspiration from Whitman, who argued that a new poetry could act as the voice of independence and democracy in the Americas.

Poems might seem like strange sites for such intense political engagement, but in the nineteenth century many people understood poetry as a particularly dignified and elevated art form, to be taken especially seriously as the voice of a nation or as a call to the making of a new and better world. As Shelley's "Defence of Poetry" put it, "The most unfailing herald, companion, and follower of the awakening of a great people to work a beneficial change in opinion or institution, is Poetry." Shelley hailed poets as bringers of collective joy, as prophets. "Poets," he wrote famously, "are the unacknowledged legislators of the World."

Nineteenth-century political poets typically understood their literary work as woven together with their commitment to justice and liberty. Whitman tended wounded soldiers of the US Civil War. Darío was a diplomat. Martí, Mickiewicz, Rodríguez de Tió, and Speranza led nationalist political movements. Barrett Browning and Bunina fought for women's equality. For all of these writers, poetry and politics seemed to take part in one and the same project: the realization of human freedom.

ANNA BUNINA

It was not easy to work as a woman writer in early nineteenth-century Russia, even for those who came from the highest ranks of the aristocracy. Women were largely dependent on husbands or fathers for their keep, and they received meager educations compared to their male counterparts. The small handful of women who did publish their writing typically won disparaging and sometimes hostile comments from critics and male writers, who insisted that women could act as readers and inspirations, but could not compose anything of value. It was in this context that the remarkable Anna Petrovna Bunina (1774–1829) published a startling range of poems, in multiple styles and on themes that ranged from nationalistic military songs to conversational, intimate lyrics on love and mortality.

Born into an aristocratic family in 1774, Bunina struggled to maintain her independence. Her inheritance was so small that she soon exhausted it on attempts to improve her education, learning to read Latin and Greek and to speak a number of foreign languages. She started publishing her work in her late twenties, and soon attracted mentors and patrons. Remaining unmarried, she barely made ends meet as a poverty-stricken writer until her death in 1829 from breast cancer. And yet, although she was poor, her independence was an extraordinary accomplishment: she was the first Russian woman to earn her living as a writer. At the time it was rare for even male Russian writers to live by the pen. Only about 250 titles were published in Russia each year between 1800 and 1820, compared to 4,500 in France. As few as 6 percent of Russian men could read in 1800, and 4 percent of women. A financial turning point for Bunina came in 1808, when she published a manual for women poets called *The Rules of Poetry*. Here she explained principles of genre and meter in order to educate women who might not have taken up writing otherwise. The Administration of Schools adopted it as a textbook, and the ensuing profits allowed Bunina to become self-sufficient.

Some critics hailed Bunina as a "Russian Sappho," comparable to the great ancient Greek woman poet. Others, including the legendary writer Alexander Pushkin, scorned her as "the goddess of the lady-chatterboxes." Writers in the generation that followed hers saw her as painfully old-fashioned, and felt particular contempt for women poets who were only able to produce "a poetic knitting of stockings." Bunina's reputation never recovered, though readers have begun to show a renewed interest in recent years.

Bunina's poems frequently took gender as an explicit theme. Her "Conversation between Me and the Women" sets up a dialogue between the poet and a chorus of modern, cosmopolitan women who reject Russian poetry and want the poetess to sing them flattering verses. She refuses, claiming that male readers will be the judges of her fame. But this seems like a puzzling conclusion. Is Bunina also writing for men in *this* poem, which is so clearly focused on women readers and writers? Is she trivializing women, or taking them seriously? And is she indicating her own preference for Russian styles and subjects, or is she undermining them by claiming that she writes about tsars and heroes merely for the approbation of a masculine readership? Bunina's ironic meditation on the role of the woman poet raises more questions than it answers.

Conversation between Me and the Women[1]

THE WOMEN

Our sister dear, what joy for us!
You are a poetess! your palette's able,
Holding all shades, to paint an ode, a fable;
Your heart must brim with praise for us!

1. Translated by Sibelan Forrester.

A man's tongue, though . . . Ah, God preserve us, dear!
Sharp as a knife is sharp!
In Paris, London—as in Russia here—
  They're all the same! On just one string they harp:
Naught but abuse—and ladies always suffer!
We wait for madrigals—it's epigrams they offer.
Don't expect brothers, husbands, fathers, sons
  To praise you even once.
How long we've lacked a songstress of our own!
So, do you sing? Pray answer, yes or no?

ME

Yes, yes, dear sisters! Thanks be to Providence
I have been singing now for five years since.

THE WOMEN

And in those years, what have you sung and how?
Though few of us, in truth, have Russian educations,
And Russian verses make such complications!
Besides, you know, they aren't in fashion now.

ME

I sing all Nature's beauteous hues,
Above the flood the hornèd sickle moon;
I count the little drops of dew,
I hymn the sun's ascension in the morn.
Flocks gambolling in the fields enjoy my care:
I give reed pipes unto the shepherdesses,
Flowers I entwine in their companions' tresses,
  That are so flaxen-fair;
I order them to take each other's hands,
  To caper to a dance,
And as their fleet feet pass,
To trample not a single blade of grass.
Up to the heavens rocky crags I raise,
  I plant out branchy trees
To rest an old man in their shady breeze
  On summer's sultry days;
I search the roses for bright insects' wings,
  And, having summoned feathered birds to sing,
  I languish pale
To the sweet warble of the nightingale.
Or, all at once, freeing the horse's manes.
  I order them to race the wind;
And with their hooves dust to the clouds they fling.
I draw a corn-field crowned with ears of grain,
  Which, from the sun's bright rays

Takes on the look of seas
Of molten gold,
Sways, ripples, dazzles, shines—
Blinding the eye,
As humble ploughmen their reward behold.
In fortifying my own timid voice
Through Nature's loveliness,
I'm braver in a flash!

THE WOMEN

Fie! what balderdash!
There's not one word in this for us!
Tell us what good such singing does?
What use are all your livestock, polled and horned
To us, who weren't as herdsmen born?
So, with the beasts you feel at home?
Well! . . . if that's your topic, then,
Hide in a den,
Among the fields, pray, roam,
And never haunt the capitals in vain!

ME

O no, dear sisters, come!
People are also in my ken.

THE WOMEN

Commendable! but whom *have* you sung, then?

ME

At times I've hymned the deeds of mighty men,
Who, when the bloody fight drew near,
Declared for faith and Tsar; they knew no fear.
Shaking with my lament the field of quarrels
I bore them thence away with laurels,
Dropping a tear.
At times I've left this grievous task,
And passed to those who keep the laws,
I've filled my soul with cheer,
And rested 'neath their aegis, free from cares.
At times to poets I've inclined my ear
And bent the knee before their thunderous lyres.
At times
Moved by esteem,
I've made the chemist or astronomer my theme.

THE WOMEN

And here again we're missing from your rhymes!
You do us quite a service!
So what good *are* you? Don't you make things worse?
Why did you bother learning to sing verse?
You ought to take your themes from your own circle.
'Tis only men you honour with your lays,
As if their sex alone deserved your praise.
You traitress! Give our case some thought!
For is this what you ought?
Are their own founts of flattery too few,
Or can they boast of more than our virtue?

ME

It's true, my dears, you are no less,
But understand:
With men, not you, the courts of taste are manned
Where authors all must stand,
And all an author's fame is in their hands,
And none can help loving himself the best.[2]

2. May I be forgiven for this jest in deference to the merry Muses, who love to mix business with idleness, lies with truth, and to enliven conversation with innocent playfulness [Bunina's note].

PERCY BYSSHE SHELLEY

A forthright advocate of vegetarianism, free love, anarchism, Irish nationalism, and atheism, the English poet Percy Shelley (1792–1822) provoked so much alarm among his contemporaries that his critics accused him of spreading corruption, aligning himself with Satan, and undermining the nation. Shelley's work was inflammatory enough that only small portions of it found their way to publication in his lifetime, and he reported having escaped several attempts at assassination. Later generations would invoke an entirely different Shelley, one who looked beyond conventional pieties to a universal good, "a beautiful ineffectual angel, beating in the void his luminous wings in vain," as the poet and critic Matthew Arnold put it in 1888. Shelley remains an object of controversy into our own time: for some enthusiasts, he is the fiery radical who bravely flouted convention and inspired generations of revolutionary thinkers; for a still-sizable number of detractors he has emerged as a self-serving egoist who destroyed the lives of women he loved; and for some—

admirers and critics alike—he appears as the abstract and philosophical poet-aristocrat who crafted beautiful and dreamy poetic reconciliations of humans with their world.

LIFE

Shelley came from a wealthy and aristocratic English family. His father was a member of Parliament who held to a strict standard of respectability. In 1811, after only five months at Oxford University, the young Shelley published a pamphlet titled *The Necessity of Atheism*, which he sent to all of the professors and heads of colleges at Oxford and Cambridge and all of the bishops of the Church of England. Oxford expelled him, and his father—deeply shocked—threw him on his own resources. Alone in London, he eloped with the daughter of a coffeehouse owner, Harriet Westbrook.

In these first years of his independence, Shelley moved in radical circles. Feeling disgust at the oppressiveness of British colonial rule, in 1812 he left for Ireland, where he spoke publicly in favor of Catholic rights and Irish nationalism. He claimed to have been the victim of an assassination attempt, though some have alleged that he was just trying to avoid mounting debts. Shelley's first major poem, *Queen Mab*, was distributed privately in 1813 because it was too revolutionary to be published. Advocating sexual freedom and a new era of egalitarianism as well as the overthrow of corrupt institutions, it continued to circulate underground among radicals throughout the nineteenth century.

Within just a few years, the Shelleys' marriage had begun to falter, and in 1814 Percy fell in love with Mary Wollstonecraft Godwin, the beautiful sixteen-year-old daughter of the two most famous radicals of the time, William Godwin and **Mary Wollstonecraft**. Godwin tried to separate the couple, and in desolation, Percy attempted suicide. When he recovered, the two lovers ran away together. Percy, in keeping with his unconventional beliefs about love and marriage, tried to persuade his wife Harriet to come and live with him and Mary—as a sister. She refused.

Ostracized, the young lovers wandered restlessly around Europe. They spent the summer of 1816 at Lake Geneva with the poet George Gordon Byron. Notorious for his many love affairs, Byron had a brief liaison with Mary's stepsister Claire. It was that summer, too, that Mary Shelley first had the idea for the novel that would soon make her famous—*Frankenstein*.

Often ill and usually trying to escape creditors, Shelley continued to live a peripatetic life. He became friendly with poets and critics in London, including **John Keats**. In 1822 Shelley went boating off the coast of Italy; a sudden storm wrecked the boat, and his body later washed ashore.

WORKS

Shelley is a deeply skeptical poet, always probing the foundations of his own thought and willing to subject his own and others' beliefs to interrogation. "Our words are dead," Shelley lamented; "our thoughts are cold and borrowed." Since we can only ever reuse words that have been used thousands of times before, Shelley argues, we are unable to have new thoughts—and so unable to revolutionize our approaches to experience. Only poetic images, in all of their strangeness and novelty, can reanimate "dead" words. And since oppressive power depends on static, deadened language, the poet's renewal of words becomes a means of upending social inequalities and tyrannical authorities. Poetic language can itself turn rigid through conventional use, however, and Shelley often experiments with endings that resist resolution and heapings of mismatched metaphors in order to keep his language surprising and unsettling.

"England in 1819" stays very much within the tradition of the Shakespearian sonnet, with fourteen rhyming lines. And yet Shelley plays with the form in inventive ways. For example, he deliberately uses the sonnet, one of the smallest and most compact forms in English poetry, to convey vast wrongs that beset a whole nation. By 1819 the British government had imposed heavy taxes to pay for the nation's protracted wars with France, with the poor suffering especially from high taxes on grain. Concerned about rising unrest, Parliament imposed strict censorship, suspended the right to trial, suppressed politically subversive groups, and accused even moderate critics of treason. On August 16, 1819, a huge but orderly and unarmed crowd gathered at St. Peter's Field in the city of Manchester in support of democratic reforms. Between 60,000 and 80,000 men, women, and children arrived wearing their Sunday best. Ill-trained troops with sabers ignored the peaceful nature of the protest and charged through the crowd on horseback. Reporters counted eleven dead and estimated over 400 injured. Contemporaries gave the event the nickname "Peterloo," an ironic echo of Waterloo, the great British victory against Napoleon in 1815. Parliament refused to conduct an inquiry into the violence, and powerful government ministers, Viscounts Castlereagh and Sidmouth, used the Peterloo massacre as an excuse to pass a new round of repressive laws. Shelley purposefully squeezes large-scale historical events into his first twelve lines, and imagines their redemption in an even briefer two.

In 1820, the Shelleys settled in the Italian town of Pisa, and it was there that Percy wrote his famous *Defense of Poetry*, where he made the case that creative artists were crucial to history, poets being "the unacknowledged legislators of the world."

England in 1819

An old, mad, blind, despised, and dying King;[1]
Princes,[2] the dregs of their dull race, who flow
Through public scorn,—mud from a muddy spring;
Rulers who neither see nor feel nor know,
But leechlike to their fainting country cling
Till they drop, blind in blood, without a blow.
A people starved and stabbed in th' untilled field;[3]
An army, whom liberticide and prey
Makes as a two-edged sword to all who wield;
Golden and sanguine[4] laws which tempt and slay;
Religion Christless, Godless—a book sealed;

1. George III (1738–1820).
2. The king's sons, including the prince regent, whose dissolute behavior gave rise to public scandals.
3. A reference to the event called "Peterloo," the British military's massacre of unarmed protesters marching for political reform in St. Peter's Field, Manchester.
4. Bloody, causing bloodshed. "Golden": bought. The laws favor the rich and powerful.

A senate, Time's worst statute,[5] unrepealed—
Are graves from which a glorious Phantom may
Burst, to illumine our tempestuous day.

A Defense of Poetry

[*Conclusion*]

* * * Poetry is the record of the best and happiest moments of the happiest and best minds. We are aware of evanescent visitations of thought and feeling sometimes associated with place or person, sometimes regarding our own mind alone, and always arising unforeseen and departing unbidden, but elevating and delightful beyond all expression: so that even in the desire and the regret they leave, there cannot but be pleasure, participating as it does in the nature of its object. It is as it were the interpenetration of a diviner nature through our own; but its footsteps are like those of a wind over a sea, which the coming calm erases, and whose traces remain only as on the wrinkled sand which paves it. These and corresponding conditions of being are experienced principally by those of the most delicate sensibility and the most enlarged imagination; and the state of mind produced by them is at war with every base desire. The enthusiasm of virtue, love, patriotism, and friendship is essentially linked with these emotions, and whilst they last, self appears as what it is, an atom to a Universe. Poets are not only subject to these experiences as spirits of the most refined organization, but they can colour all that they combine with the evanescent hues of this ethereal world; a word, or a trait in the representation of a scene or a passion, will touch the enchanted chord, and reanimate, in those who have ever experienced these emotions, the sleeping, the cold, the buried image of the past. Poetry thus makes immortal all that is best and most beautiful in the world; it arrests the vanishing apparitions which haunt the interlunations of life, and veiling them or[1] in language or in form sends them forth among mankind, bearing sweet news of kindred joy to those with whom their sisters abide—abide, because there is no portal of expression from the caverns of the spirit which they inhabit into the universe of things. Poetry redeems from decay the visitations of the divinity in man.

* * *

The first part of these remarks has related to Poetry in its elements and principles; and it has been shown, as well as the narrow limits assigned them would permit, that what is called poetry, in a restricted sense, has a common source with all other forms of order and of beauty according to which the materials of human life are susceptible of being arranged, and which is poetry in an universal sense.

5. The law by which the civil liberties of Roman Catholics and dissenters from the state religion (Anglicanism) were restricted.

1. Either. "Interlunations": dark periods between the old and new moon.

The second part[2] will have for its object an application of these principles to the present state of the cultivation of Poetry, and a defense of the attempt to idealize the modern forms of manners and opinion, and compel them into a subordination to the imaginative and creative faculty. For the literature of England, an energetic development of which has ever preceded or accompanied a great and free development of the national will, has arisen as it were from a new birth. In spite of the low-thoughted envy which would undervalue contemporary merit, our own will be a memorable age in intellectual achievements, and we live among such philosophers and poets as surpass beyond comparison any who have appeared since the last national struggle for civil and religious liberty.[3] The most unfailing herald, companion, and follower of the awakening of a great people to work a beneficial change in opinion or institution, is Poetry. At such periods there is an accumulation of the power of communicating and receiving intense and impassioned conceptions respecting man and nature. The persons in whom this power resides, may often, as far as regards many portions of their nature, have little apparent correspondence with that spirit of good of which they are the ministers. But even whilst they deny and abjure, they are yet compelled to serve, the Power which is seated upon the throne of their own soul. It is impossible to read the compositions of the most celebrated writers of the present day without being startled with the electric life which burns within their words. They measure the circumference and sound the depths of human nature with a comprehensive and all-penetrating spirit, and they are themselves perhaps the most sincerely astonished at its manifestations, for it is less their spirit than the spirit of the age. Poets are the hierophants[4] of an unapprehended inspiration, the mirrors of the gigantic shadows which futurity casts upon the present, the words which express what they understand not; the trumpets which sing to battle, and feel not what they inspire: the influence which is moved not, but moves. Poets are the unacknowledged legislators of the World.

2. The second part was never written.
3. The English Civil War. The great poet of that age was Milton.
4. Interpreters, in the role of priests who interpret sacred mysteries.

HEINRICH HEINE

Born to Jewish parents in the German city of Düsseldorf, Heinrich Heine (1797–1856) became one of the most famous of all German poets. He wrote at a historical moment dominated by Romantic literature, but experienced a growing disillusionment with the ideals of his contemporaries. "The Romantic School" was "where I spent the most agreeable days of my youth," he wrote, but he "ended up by beating the schoolmaster." He turned his sardonic pen on the very themes that had first animated him: instead of dreams, he focused on harsh awakenings; in place of beautiful love, he concentrated on falling out of love; and he treated nature itself with ironic detachment. He continued to rely on traditional rhyming forms, evocative of simple folk songs, but he deliberately modernized their content, and put them to complex, ironic, and often humorous ends.

Politically, Heine was a radical. He was a friend of Karl Marx, though he remained wary of communism. Early in his life he refused to use his poetic voice as a vehicle for political opinions, arguing that poetry belonged to a higher, more transcendent realm. (He once compared political poets to dancing bears.) But in the 1840s he would write a number of rousing poems on current political events: "The Silesian Weavers" commemorates a protest by Prussian laborers whose wages had fallen below starvation levels.

Throughout his life, the poet maintained an ambivalent relationship to both his Jewishness and his Germanness. Napoleon's conquest of Germany brought with it a guarantee of full civil rights to Jews, but after his defeat, many German cities and states reverted to repressive laws. In Frankfurt, for example, only twelve Jewish couples were permitted to marry in any given year. Heine was allowed to study law but not to practice, and he converted to Christianity in order to find work. He rejected Jewish communities and beliefs until late in life, but remained fiercely critical of Christian Germany. "Wherever they burn books," he wrote, "they will also, in the end, burn human beings."

The Silesian Weavers[1]

In somber eyes no tears of grieving;
Grinding their teeth, they sit at their weaving;
"O Germany, at your shroud we sit,
We're weaving a threefold curse in it—
    We're weaving, we're weaving!

"A curse on the god we prayed to, kneeling
With cold in our bones, with hunger reeling;
We waited and hoped, in vain persevered,
He scorned us and duped us, mocked and jeered—
    We're weaving, we're weaving!

"A curse on the king[2] of the rich man's nation
Who hardens his heart at our supplication,
Who wrings the last penny out of our hides

1. Silesia was a province of the kingdom of Prussia in northeast Germany. This poem was occasioned by violent uprisings of weavers protesting intolerable working conditions during June 1844. Translated by Hal Draper.

2. Friedrich Wilhelm IV (1795–1861). Heine's poem is prophetic: in 1848 the king, though not deposed, was forced by revolution to grant a constitution to Prussia.

And lets us be shot like dogs besides—
 We're weaving, we're weaving!

"A curse on this false fatherland, teeming
With nothing but shame and dirty scheming,
Where every flower is crushed in a day,
Where worms are regaled on rot and decay—
 We're weaving, we're weaving!

"The shuttle[3] flies, the loom creaks loud,
Night and day we weave your shroud—
Old Germany, at your shroud we sit,
We're weaving a threefold curse in it,
 We're weaving, we're weaving!"

3. Device used for weaving cloth on a loom.

ADAM MICKIEWICZ

Beloved as the National Poet of Poland, Adam Mickiewicz (1798–1855) spent most of his life in exile, trying to fight for his nation from afar. He was born to an upper-class Polish-speaking family in Navahrudak, a town that is now in Belarus, then ruled by the Russian Empire. As a young man, he went to Vilnius to study to be a teacher. While there, he founded a secret Polish national independence society. Found out by the authorities, he was arrested and imprisoned, then banished to Russia.

Poland had been a major European power in the sixteenth and seventeenth centuries, but by the time Mickiewicz was born it no longer even appeared on the map, having been conquered by its neighbors, Prussia, Austria, and the Russian Empire. Poles resisted foreign rule throughout the nineteenth century, rising up against occupying empires again and again. "There remained nothing," says one Polish writer, "except a nation that refused to die." Many Polish intellectuals and revolutionaries, exiled from their birthplace, established dynamic émigré communities in Western Europe.

In 1829, Mickiewicz was granted permission to travel outside of Russia, and he spent the rest of his life on the move, taking up residence in Berlin, Prague, Rome, and Paris. As he traveled, he may have been passing messages and funds through émigré networks to Polish fighters. Along the way, he met many of the most important literary and political figures of his time, from **Johann Wolfgang von Goethe** and the American novelist of the frontier, James Fenimore Cooper, to Italian nationalist Giuseppe Mazzini and the Polish composer Frédéric Cho-pin, who set some of his verses to music. Mickiewicz died in Istanbul, where he had been supporting Polish soldiers who were fighting under the Ottoman Empire against the Russians.

Mickiewicz's first book of poems, published in 1822, famously marks the beginning of Polish Romanticism. Like other Romantic poets included in this volume, he drew on traditional folktales and ballads, and he took up mystical themes and stories of unrequited love. All of his work is intensely patriotic, and inspired generations of Polish writers and nationalists to follow. His legacy was so powerful that the Nazis destroyed a Mickiewicz monument when they occupied Cracow in 1940 in an effort to eradicate the history of Polish resistance.

The excerpt included here, "The Prisoner's Return," comes from Mickiewicz's four-part poetic drama, *Forefathers' Eve*, which was written over the course of many years. In this section, we learn about the persecution of Poles by police and spies under the Russian tsar, Alexander I. Mickiewicz draws on his own experience of being imprisoned and tried for his anti-Russian activity as a student. In this passage, the narrator begs an old friend, recently released from prison, to tell his story, but years of torture have broken him. Suffocated by fear, he refuses to talk. Here, Mickiewicz hints at a crucial role for the writer in the fight for independence. The poet is the one who must speak out against a regime intent on terrifying its opponents into silence.

The Prisoner's Return[1]

Him! So I rushed. "But there will be a spy.
Don't go today." I made another try
The morning after. Police thugs at the door.
The next week, too, I went. "His health is poor."
And then, at last, when travelling out of town
They told me that a fat but broken-down
Fellow was my friend. His hair had gone; his skin
Was a puffed sponge that wrinkles burrowed in.
Bad food had done it, that and rotten air.
I never would have known him, sitting there.
I said good day. He couldn't place my face.
I introduced myself, but not a trace
Of recognition. Then I reminded him
Of this and that. His glance grew deep, kept dim.
And all his daily tortures, all the fears
Of sleepless nights, and all the thoughts, the years,
I saw; but only for a moment: then
A monstrous veil descended once again.
His pupils, like thick glass refracting light,
Looked grey when stared at but could shine with bright
Patterns of rainbows when glimpsed from the side.
Cobwebs are like that too: their grey threads hide
Sparks and rust-reds and spots of black and green:

1. Translated by Jerzy Peterkiewicz and Burns Singer.

Yet in those pupils nothing could be seen.
Their surface, quite opaquely, showed that they
Had lain a long time in the damp dark clay.

Next month I called on him, hoping to find
A man at ease, refreshed, in his right mind.
But many questioners had had their say,
Ten thousand sleepless nights had passed away,
Too many torturers had probed, and he
Had learned that shadows make good company
And silence is the only right reply.

The city, in a month, could not defy
The laws that had been taught him year by year.
Day was a traitor, sunlight a spy: his fear
Made turnkeys of his family, hangmen of guests.
The door's click meant: "More questions. More arrests."
He'd turn his back, prop head on hand, and wait
Collecting strength enough to concentrate.
His lips pressed tight to make them one thin line.
He hid his eyes lest they should give some sign,
And any sign might tell them what he thought.
The simplest question seemed to have him caught.
He'd crouch in shadows, crying "I won't talk."
Because his mind was made of prison rock
So that his cell went with him everywhere.
His wife wept long, kneeling beside his chair.
But maybe it was mostly his child's tears
That, finally, released him from his fears.

I thought he'd tell his story in the end.
(Ex-convicts like to speak to an old friend
About their prison days.) I'd learn the truth,
The truth that tyrants hide, the Polish truth.
It flourishes in shadows. Its history
Lives in Siberia where its heroes die,
There and in dungeons. But what did my friend say?
He said he had forgotten. And, with dismay,
I listened to his silence. His memory was
Written upon, and deeply, but, because
It had long rotted in the dark, my friend
Could not read what was written: "We'd better send
For God. He will remember and tell us all."

ELIZABETH BARRETT BROWNING

Elizabeth Barrett Browning (1806–1861) was by far the most famous woman poet writing in English in the nineteenth century. She was adored to the point of hero-worship both in Britain and in the United States. In her view, poetry was capable of acting as a powerful vehicle for social protest, and in fact, when she wrote about slavery, women's rights, prostitution, and child labor, her audiences were often inspired to vocal debate and political action. Though widely acclaimed as both a poetic genius and a moral authority, after her death her fame was eclipsed by that of her husband, Robert Browning, and later writers dismissed her as a sentimental feminine soul rather than an accomplished poet in her own right. But this was a mistake. Few poets have been more technically skilled than Barrett Browning. She uses a vast range of existing poetic forms with staggering dexterity and subtlety, and when these forms are not enough, she boldly invents strange and innovative new rhythms, stanza structures, and rhyme schemes.

The eldest of twelve children, Elizabeth Barrett Moulton-Barrett was born to a prosperous English family that had made its money from slave plantations in Jamaica. Her education was highly unusual for an Englishwoman of her time: sitting in on her brother's private lessons, she learned Latin and Greek, and later taught herself Hebrew. She began writing poetry at the age of six and published her first volume at thirteen. Exceptionally learned, she translated the ancient Greek dramatist Aeschylus and experimented with writing epic poetry—something women were strongly discouraged from doing. As she came to understand the source of her family's wealth, she deliberately tried to distance herself from slavery, both renouncing money earned from plantation labor and writing antislavery poetry for abolitionist periodicals in the United States. A mysterious lung disease and a fall from a horse made her an invalid, and she spent much of her early adulthood confined to her bedroom, addicted to morphine. Her tyrannical father wanted none of his children to marry and leave his house, and he kept her secluded even as she became an increasingly prominent poet. This was to change, however, when the young poet Robert Browning launched a passionate correspondence with her. In 1846, when she was thirty-nine and he thirty-three, they eloped to Italy, where she recovered her strength and bore a son. The following years were exceptionally happy and productive. Elizabeth Barrett Browning died, in her husband's arms, unforgiven by her father, in 1861.

"The Cry of the Children" appeared in response to a government report about child laborers in mines and factories, who were expected to work as many as sixteen hours a day unprotected by any safety regulations. Rejecting the intensely personal voice of lyric poetry, Barrett Browning here makes confrontational direct addresses to her readers and adopts a collective first-person-plural "we" for the voice of the child workers. She also invents an uncomfortable, confrontational new rhythm rather than relying on existing poetic conventions. One reviewer wrote that "the cadence, lingering, broken, and full of wail, is one of the most perfect adaptations of sound to sense in literature." This poem was so powerful that Barrett Browning was credited with inspiring the British parliament to pass new laws regulating child labor.

In her own time, Barrett Browning's fierce frankness on politics, women's desire, and the power of poetry consistently drew attention to the ways that she defied conventional feminine constraints. One of her contemporaries wrote that Barrett Browning was the first woman writer to mix "masculine vigour, breadth, and culture" with "feminine subtlety of perception, feminine quickness of sensibility, and feminine tenderness."

The Cry of the Children

"Φευ, φευ, τιπροσδερκεσθέ μ' όμμασιν, τέκνα;"
—*Medea*[1]

Do ye hear the children weeping, O my brothers,
Ere the sorrow comes with years?
They are leaning their young heads against their mothers,
And *that* cannot stop their tears.
The young lambs are bleating in the meadows,
The young birds are chirping in the nest,
The young fawns are playing with the shadows,
The young flowers are blowing toward the west—
But the young, young children, O my brothers,
They are weeping bitterly!
They are weeping in the playtime of the others,
In the country of the free.

Do you question the young children in the sorrow
Why their tears are falling so?
The old man may weep for his to-morrow
Which is lost in Long Ago;
The old tree is leafless in the forest,
The old year is ending in the frost,
The old wound, if stricken, is the sorest,
The old hope is hardest to be lost:
But the young, young children, O my brothers,
Do you ask them why they stand
Weeping sore before the bosoms of their mothers,
In our happy Fatherland?

They look up with their pale and sunken faces,
And their looks are sad to see,
For the man's hoary anguish draws and presses
Down the cheeks of infancy;

1. Greek tragedy by Euripides (ca. 480–406 B.C.E.) about the mythological figure of Medea, a mother who kills her own children; Medea speaks the line in Greek: "Alas, my children, why do you look at me?"

"Your old earth," they say, "is very dreary,"
  "Our young feet," they say, "are very weak;
Few paces have we taken, yet are weary—
  Our grave-rest is very far to seek:
Ask the aged why they weep, and not the children,
      For the outside earth is cold,
And we young ones stand without, in our bewildering,
      And the graves are for the old."

"True," say the children, "it may happen
      That we die before our time:
Little Alice died last year, her grave is shapen
      Like a snowball, in the rime.
We looked into the pit prepared to take her:
  Was no room for any work in the close clay!
From the sleep wherein she lieth none will wake her,
  Crying, 'Get up, little Alice! it is day.'
If you listen by that grave, in sun and shower,
  With your ear down, little Alice never cries;
Could we see her face, be sure we should not know her,
  For the smile has time for growing in her eyes:
And merry go her moments, lulled and stilled in
      The shroud by the kirk[2] chime.
It is good when it happens," say the children,
      "That we die before our time."

Alas, alas, the children! they are seeking
      Death in life, as best to have:
They are binding up their hearts away from breaking,
      With a ceremen[3] from the grave.
Go out, children, from the mine and from the city,
  Sing out, children, as the little thrushes do;
Pluck your handfuls of the meadow-cowslips pretty,
  Laugh aloud, to feel your fingers let them through!
But they answer, "Are your cowslips of the meadows
      Like our weeds anear the mine?
Leave us quiet in the dark of the coal-shadows,
      From your pleasures fair and fine!

"For oh," say the children, "we are weary,
      And we cannot run or leap;
If we cared for any meadows, it were merely
      To drop down in them and sleep.
Our knees tremble sorely in the stooping,
  We fall upon our faces, trying to go;
And, underneath our heavy eyelids drooping,
  The reddest flower would look as pale as snow.
For, all day, we drag our burden tiring
      Through the coal-dark, underground;

2. Church.

3. Shroud.

Or, all day, we drive the wheels of iron
In the factories, round and round.

"For, all day, the wheels are droning, turning;
Their wind comes in our faces,
Till our hearts turn, our heads with pulses burning,
And the walls turn in their places:
Turns the sky in the high window blank and reeling,
Turns the long light that drops adown the wall,
Turn the black flies that crawl along the ceiling,
All are turning, all the day, and we with all.
And all day, the iron wheels are droning,
And sometimes we could pray,
'O ye wheels,' (breaking out in a mad moaning)
'Stop! be silent for to-day!'"

Ay, be silent! Let them hear each other breathing
For a moment, mouth to mouth!
Let them touch each other's hands, in a fresh wreathing
Of their tender human youth!
Let them feel that this cold metallic motion
Is not all the life God fashions or reveals:
Let them prove their living souls against the notion
That they live in you, or under you, O wheels!
Still, all day, the iron wheels go onward,
Grinding life down from its mark;
And the children's souls, which God is calling sunward,
Spin on blindly in the dark.

Now tell the poor young children; O my brothers,
To look up to Him and pray;
So the blessed One who blesseth all the others,
Will bless them another day.
They answer, "Who is God that He should hear us,
While the rushing of the iron wheels is stirred?
When we sob aloud, the human creatures near us
Pass by, hearing not, or answer not a word.
And *we* hear not (for the wheels in their resounding)
Strangers speaking at the door:
Is it likely God, with angels singing round Him,
Hears our weeping any more?

Two words, indeed, of praying we remember,
And at midnight's hour of harm,
'Our Father,' looking upward in the chamber,
We say softly for a charm.
We know no other words except 'Our Father.'
And we think that, in some pause of angels' song,
God may pluck them with the silence sweet to gather,
And hold both within His right hand which is strong.
'Our Father!' If He heard us, He would surely

(For they call Him good and mild)
Answer, smiling down the steep world very purely,
'Come and rest with me, my child.'

"But, no!" say the children, weeping faster,
"He is speechless as a stone:
And they tell us, of His image is the master
Who commands us to work on.
Go to!" say the children,—"up in Heaven,
Dark, wheel-like, turning clouds are all we find.
Do not mock us; grief has made us unbelieving:
We look up for God, but tears have made us blind."
Do you hear the children weeping and disproving,
O my brothers, what ye preach?
For God's possible is taught by His world's loving,
And the children doubt of each.

And well may the children weep before you!
They are weary ere they run;
They have never seen the sunshine, nor the glory
Which is brighter than the sun.
They know the grief of man, without its wisdom;
They sink in man's despair, without its calm;
Are slaves, without the liberty in Christdom,
Are martyrs, by the pang without the palm:
Are worn as if with age, yet unretrievingly
The harvest of its memories cannot reap,—
Are orphans of the earthly love and heavenly.
Let them weep! let them weep!

They look up with their pale and sunken faces,
And their look is dread to see,
For they mind you of their angels in high places,
With eyes turned on Deity.
"How long," they say, "how long, O cruel nation,
Will you stand, to move the world, on a child's heart,—
Stifle down with a mailed[4] heel its palpitation,
And tread onward to your throne amid the mart?
Our blood splashes upward, O gold-heaper,
And your purple shows your path!
But the child's sob in the silence curses deeper
Than the strong man in his wrath."

4. Armored, as with chainmail.

WALT WHITMAN

Walt Whitman (1819–1892) left an astonishing legacy. In rejecting conventional rhyme and meter he managed, almost single-handedly, to make free verse seem like the most appropriate form for a truly modern poetry. He insisted on a homegrown American art that would supplant European influence. He cast the poet as a fighter and a leader. He prized free and full sexual pleasure, celebrating "the body electric." And he gave voice to a vast range of ordinary people who had gone largely unnoticed by poets before him. "I am big—I contain multitudes," he wrote. Affirmative, inclusive, energetic, defiant, and radically experimental, Whitman ushered in a whole new era in American poetry.

LIFE

Born on Long Island, Whitman moved with his family to Brooklyn as a child. His father deeply admired American democracy, naming three of his sons George Washington, Thomas Jefferson, and Andrew Jackson. The young Whitman grew up among Deists and Quakers, followers of creeds that favored an internal spirituality over formal religious doctrines. He left school at the age of eleven and worked odd jobs, first as a printer, later as a schoolteacher, builder, bookstore owner, journalist, and poet. He spent a few months in New Orleans and came to love the South, though he vehemently opposed slavery and petitioned to prevent its westward expansion. During the Civil War, Whitman felt a passionate admiration for Abraham Lincoln and was devoted to the Union cause. He was also deeply moved by the soldiers at the front, so much so that he went to Washington as a volunteer nurse, helping to care for the Civil War wounded and witnessing firsthand the devastating spectacle of corpses and amputated limbs. While in Washington he worked as a clerk in several government departments, including the Bureau of Indian Affairs. In 1865 Whitman met Peter Doyle, a young horsecar conductor who became his companion and almost certainly his lover. A few years later he settled in Camden, New Jersey, where he remained for the rest of his life.

WORK

Whitman began writing in his youth, producing a good deal of bad poetry and a novel about temperance, the movement advocating abstinence from alcohol. But something altogether different emerged in 1855 with his innovative collection of poems, *Leaves of Grass*. This volume departed from convention in startling ways. First of all, it did not look like the poetry of his contemporaries: there were no rhymes; the lines varied widely in length; and the words followed no particular rhythm. Second, the collection's themes were shocking: many readers were appalled by the unusually vivid sexual imagery and the intense evocations of bodily pleasure. Whitman also overturned convention by insisting on a vehemently democratic kind of verse, appealing to the common reader and celebrating the most overlooked people, from slaves and prostitutes to immigrants and prisoners. Finally, his poetic language was eccentrically various, moving between beauty and slang, spirituality and obscenity. This was a poetry that aimed to include all of modern life. A poet fails, Whitman wrote, "if he does not flood himself with the immediate age as with vast oceanic tides . . . if he be not himself the age transfigured."

Whitman always loved the theater, and he deliberately adopted many voices and personae in his poetry. The *I* of his poems represents many selves. Perhaps most famously, the poet ventriloquizes a new urban type called the "b'hoy," a rebellious young working-class New Yorker known for his idle loafing and his willingness to fight, as well as his insolent, loud, slangy way of speaking. Whitman saw ordinary speech as the best source for poetry. "Language," he wrote, "is not an abstract construction of the learn'd, or of the dictionary-makers, but is something arising out of the work, needs, ties, joys, affections, tastes, of long generations of humanity, and has its bases broad and low, close to the ground. Its final decisions are made by the masses." Whitman's long lines also follow the patterns of ordinary language: rather than forming sentences broken up in accordance with conventions of rhyme or meter, each line is a statement complete in itself.

The innovations of *Leaves of Grass* did not sit well with the volume's first readers. "Walt Whitman," wrote one reviewer, "is as unacquainted with art as a hog is with mathematics." Another dismissed the book as "a mass of stupid filth." Even Henry David Thoreau said, "It is as if beasts spoke." Whitman was unperturbed by these attacks: he had intended to unsettle his readers, and he even publicized his most venomous reviews as a way of promoting his work.

But Whitman would soon come to be seen as one of the great poets of the United States, perhaps the greatest. In part this was because the nation was such a crucial focus for his work. He was deliberately writing a new, quintessentially American poetry, an art form that would leave European values and traditions behind to celebrate a modern, pluralistic democracy. At a moment when Europe was widely assumed to represent the standard for art and culture, Whitman wrote: "The Americans of all nations at any time upon the earth, have probably the fullest poetical nature. The United States themselves are essentially the greatest poem." And if the nation was a poem, the poet was its best leader. With the exception of Lincoln, Whitman despised politicians ("swarms of cringers, suckers, doughfaces, planners of the sly involutions for their own preferment to city offices or state legislatures or the judiciary or congress or the presidency"), and, as the United States fractured on the eve of Civil War, he imagined the poet alone as capable of healing and uniting the nation.

His way of healing, of course, involved confrontation and defiance. "I think agitation is the most important factor of all," he wrote. "To stir, to question, to suspect, to examine, to denounce!" What upset his contemporaries most was his willingness to defy conventions of silence around sex and sexuality. In 1882 he was threatened with an obscenity prosecution. Intriguingly, Whitman's contemporaries objected more to his eroticized representations of women than to the explicit expressions of male-male desire that appear often in his works. This was a cultural and historical context in which the "manly love" Whitman celebrated could be understood in idealized, nonsexual terms.

Whitman reworked *Leaves of Grass* many times, revising old poems and including new ones. Over time, he included explicitly patriotic work and toned down the most sexually offensive passages. By the end of his life he had come to seem not the rebellious purveyor of scandalous experiments, but simply "the good gray poet."

O Captain! My Captain![1]

O Captain! my Captain! our fearful trip is done,
The ship has weather'd every rack, the prize we sought is won,
The port is near, the bells I hear, the people all exulting,
While follow eyes the steady keel, the vessel grim and daring;
    But O heart! heart! heart!
        O the bleeding drops of red,
            Where on the deck my Captain lies,
                Fallen cold and dead.

O Captain! my Captain! rise up and hear the bells;
Rise up—for you the flag is flung—for you the bugle trills,
For you bouquets and ribbon'd wreaths—for you the shores a-crowding,
For you they call, the swaying mass, their eager faces turning;
    Here Captain! dear father!
        This arm beneath your head!
            It is some dream that on the deck,
                You've fallen cold and dead.

My Captain does not answer, his lips are pale and still,
My father does not feel my arm, he has no pulse nor will,
The ship is anchor'd safe and sound, its voyage closed and done,
From fearful trip the victor ship comes in with object won;
    Exult O shores, and ring O bells!
        But I with mournful tread,
            Walk the deck my Captain lies,
                Fallen cold and dead.

When Lilacs Last in the Dooryard Bloom'd[1]

I

When lilacs last in the dooryard bloom'd,
And the great star early droop'd in the western sky in the night,
I mourn'd, and yet shall mourn with ever-returning spring.

Ever-returning spring, trinity sure to me you bring,
Lilac blooming perennial and drooping star in the west,
And thought of him I love.

2

O powerful western fallen star!
O shades of night—O moody, tearful night!
O great star disappear'd—O the black murk that hides the star!

1. Elegy for Abraham Lincoln, who is imagined here as the captain of a ship.
1. Elegy written after the death of Abraham Lincoln; the poem follows Lincoln's coffin to its burial place.

O cruel hands that hold me powerless—O helpless soul of me!
O harsh surrounding cloud that will not free my soul.

3

In the dooryard fronting an old farm-house near the white-wash'd
palings,
Stands the lilac-bush tall-growing with heart-shaped leaves of
rich green,
With many a pointed blossom rising delicate, with the perfume
strong I love,
With every leaf a miracle—and from this bush in the dooryard,
With delicate-color'd blossoms and heart-shaped leaves of rich green,
A sprig with its flower I break.

4

In the swamp in secluded recesses,
A shy and hidden bird is warbling a song.
Solitary the thrush,
The hermit withdrawn to himself, avoiding the settlements,
Sings by himself a song.

Song of the bleeding throat,
Death's outlet song of life, (for well dear brother I know,
If thou wast not granted to sing thou would'st surely die.)

5

Over the breast of the spring, the land, amid cities,
Amid lanes and through old woods, where lately the violets
peep'd from the ground, spotting the gray debris,
Amid the grass in the fields each side of the lanes, passing
the endless grass,
Passing the yellow-spear'd wheat, every grain from its shroud
in the dark-brown fields uprisen,
Passing the apple-tree blows of white and pink in the orchards,
Carrying a corpse to where it shall rest in the grave,
Night and day journeys a coffin.

6

Coffin that passes through lanes and streets,
Through day and night with the great cloud darkening the land,
With the pomp of the inloop'd flags with the cities draped in
black,
With the show of the States themselves as of crape-veil'd
women standing,
With processions long and winding and the flambeaus of the night,
With the countless torches lit, with the silent sea of faces and
the unbared heads,

With the waiting depot, the arriving coffin, and the sombre faces,
With dirges through the night, with the thousand voices rising
    strong and solemn,
With all the mournful voices of the dirges pour'd around the coffin,
The dim-lit churches and the shuddering organs—where amid
    these you journey,
With the tolling tolling bells' perpetual clang,
Here, coffin that slowly passes,
I give you my sprig of lilac.

7

(Nor for you, for one alone,
Blossoms and branches green to coffins all I bring,
For fresh as the morning, thus would I chant a song for you
    O sane and sacred death.

All over bouquets of roses,
O death, I cover you over with roses and early lilies,
But mostly and now the lilac that blooms the first,
Copious I break, I break the sprigs from the bushes,
With loaded arms I come, pouring for you,
For you and the coffins all of you O death.)

8

O western orb sailing the heaven,
Now I know what you must have meant as a month since I walk'd,
As I walk'd in silence the transparent shadowy night,
As I saw you had something to tell as you bent to me night after night,
As you droop'd from the sky low down as if to my side, (while
    the other stars all look'd on,)
As we wander'd together the solemn night, (for something I know
    not what kept me from sleep,)
As the night advanced, and I saw on the rim of the west how
    full you were of woe,
As I stood on the rising ground in the breeze in the cool
    transparent night,
As I watch'd where you pass'd and was lost in the netherward
    black of the night,
As my soul in its trouble dissatisfied sank, as where you sad orb,
Concluded, dropt in the night, and was gone.

9

Sing on there in the swamp,
O singer bashful and tender, I hear your notes, I hear your call,
I hear, I come presently, I understand you,
But a moment I linger, for the lustrous star has detain'd me,
The star my departing comrade holds and detains me.

10

O how shall I warble myself for the dead one there I loved?
And how shall I deck my song for the large sweet soul that has gone?
And what shall my perfume be for the grave of him I love?

Sea-winds blown from east and west,
Blown from the Eastern sea and blown from the Western sea, till there on the prairies meeting,
These and with these and the breath of my chant,
I'll perfume the grave of him I love.

11

O what shall I hang on the chamber walls?
And what shall the pictures be that I hang on the walls,
To adorn the burial-house of him I love?

Pictures of growing spring and farms and homes,
With the Fourth-month[2] eve at sundown, and the gray smoke lucid and bright,
With floods of the yellow gold of the gorgeous, indolent, sinking sun, burning, expanding the air,
With the fresh sweet herbage under foot, and the pale green leaves of the trees prolific,
In the distance the flowing glaze, the breast of the river, with a wind-dapple here and there,
With ranging hills on the banks, with many a line against the sky, and shadows,
And the city at hand with dwellings so dense, and stacks of chimneys,
And all the scenes of life and the workshops, and the workmen homeward returning.

12

Lo, body and soul—this land,
My own Manhattan with spires, and the sparkling and hurrying tides, and the ships,
The varied and ample land, the South and the North in the light, Ohio's shores and flashing Missouri,
And ever the far-spreading prairies cover'd with grass and corn.

Lo, the most excellent sun so calm and haughty,
The violet and purple morn with just-felt breezes,
The gentle soft-born measureless light,
The miracle spreading bathing all, the fulfill'd noon,
The coming eve delicious, the welcome night and the stars,
Over my cities shining all, enveloping man and land.

2. April.

13

Sing on, sing on you gray-brown bird,
Sing from the swamps, the recesses, pour your chant from the bushes,
Limitless out of the dusk, out of the cedars and pines.

Sing on dearest brother, warble your reedy song,
Loud human song, with voice of uttermost woe.

O liquid and free and tender!
O wild and loose to my soul—O wondrous singer!
You only I hear—yet the star holds me, (but will soon depart,)
Yet the lilac with mastering odor holds me.

14

Now while I sat in the day and look'd forth,
In the close of the day with its light and the fields of spring, and the farmers preparing their crops,
In the large unconscious scenery of my land with its lakes and forests,
In the heavenly aerial beauty, (after the perturb'd winds and the storms,)
Under the arching heavens of the afternoon swift passing, and the voices of children and women,
The many-moving sea-tides, and I saw the ships how they sail'd,
And the summer approaching with richness, and the fields all busy with labor,
And the infinite separate houses, how they all went on, each with its meals and minutia of daily usages,
And the streets how their throbbings throbb'd, and the cities pent—lo, then and there,
Falling upon them all and among them all, enveloping me with the rest,
Appear'd the cloud, appear'd the long black trail,
And I knew death, its thought, and the sacred knowledge of death.

Then with the knowledge of death as walking one side of me,
And the thought of death close-walking the other side of me,
And I in the middle as with companions, and as holding the hands of companions,
I fled forth to the hiding receiving night that talks not,
Down to the shores of the water, the path by the swamp in the dimness,
To the solemn shadowy cedars and ghostly pines so still.

And the singer so shy to the rest receiv'd me,
The gray-brown bird I know receiv'd us comrades three,
And he sang the carol of death, and a verse for him I love.

From deep secluded recesses,
From the fragrant cedars and the ghostly pines so still,
Came the carol of the bird.

And the charm of the carol rapt me,
As I held as if by their hands my comrades in the night,
And the voice of my spirit tallied the song of the bird.

Come lovely and soothing death,
Undulate round the world, serenely arriving, arriving,
In the day, in the night, to all, to each,
Sooner or later delicate death.

Prais'd be the fathomless universe,
For life and joy, and for objects and knowledge curious,
And for love, sweet love—but praise! praise! praise!
For the sure-enwinding arms of cool-enfolding death.

Dark mother always gliding near with soft feet,
Have none chanted for thee a chant of fullest welcome?
Then I chant it for thee, I glorify thee above all,
I bring thee a song that when thou must indeed come, come unfalteringly.

Approach strong deliveress,
When it is so, when thou hast taken them I joyously sing the dead,
Lost in the loving floating ocean of thee,
Laved in the flood of thy bliss O death.

From me to thee glad serenades,
Dances for thee I propose saluting thee, adornments and feastings for thee,
And the sights of the open landscape and the high-spread sky are fitting,
And life and the fields, and the huge and thoughtful night.
The night in silence under many a star,
The ocean shore and the husky whispering wave whose voice I know,
And the soul turning to thee O vast and well-veil'd death,
And the body gratefully nestling close to thee.

Over the tree-tops I float thee a song,
Over the rising and sinking waves, over the myriad fields and the prairies wide,
Over the dense-pack'd cities all and the teeming wharves and ways,
I float this carol with joy, with joy to thee O death.

15

To the tally of my soul,
Loud and strong kept up the gray-brown bird,
With pure deliberate notes spreading filling the night.

Loud in the pines and cedars dim,
Clear in the freshness moist and the swamp-perfume,
And I with my comrades there in the night.

While my sight that was bound in my eyes unclosed,
As to long panoramas of visions.

And I saw askant the armies,
I saw as in noiseless dreams hundreds of battle-flags,
Borne through the smoke of the battles and pierc'd with missiles
 I saw them,
And carried hither and yon through the smoke, and torn and
 bloody,
And at last but a few shreds left on the staffs, (and all in silence,)
And the staffs all splinter'd and broken.

I saw battle-corpses, myriads of them,
And the white skeletons of young men, I saw them,
I saw the debris and debris of all the slain soldiers of the war,
But I saw they were not as was thought,
They themselves were fully at rest, they suffer'd not,
The living remain'd and suffer'd, the mother suffer'd,
And the wife and the child and the musing comrade suffer'd,
And the armies that remain'd suffer'd.

16

Passing the visions, passing the night,
Passing, unloosing the hold of my comrades' hands,
Passing the song of the hermit bird and the tallying song of
 my soul,
Victorious song, death's outlet song, yet varying ever-altering song,
As low and wailing, yet clear the notes, rising and falling,
 flooding the night,
Sadly sinking and fainting, as warning and warning, and yet
 again bursting with joy,
Covering the earth and filling the spread of the heaven,
As that powerful psalm in the night I heard from recesses,
Passing, I leave thee lilac with heart-shaped leaves,
I leave thee there in the door-yard, blooming, returning with
 spring.

I cease from my song for thee,
From my gaze on thee in the west, fronting the west,
 communing with thee,
O comrade lustrous with silver face in the night.

Yet each to keep and all, retrievements out of the night,
The song, the wondrous chant of the gray-brown bird,
And the tallying chant, the echo arous'd in my soul,
With the lustrous and drooping star with the countenance full
 of woe,
With the holders holding my hand nearing the call of the bird,
Comrades mine and I in the midst, and their memory ever to
 keep, for the dead I loved so well,
For the sweetest, wisest soul of all my days and lands—and this
 for his dear sake,
Lilac and star and bird twined with the chant of my soul,
There in the fragrant pines and the cedars dusk and dim.

SPERANZA, LADY JANE WILDE

A small minority of English and Scottish Protestants had ruled Catholic Ireland for hundreds of years by the time Jane Frances Agnes Elgee was born in 1821. Catholics were not allowed to own land or to vote. Most Irish families had no choice but to rent tiny plots of land from absentee Protestant landlords. These landowners held almost unlimited power over their tenants, hiring middlemen to raise rents and evict families whenever they chose. A third of Irish people managed to subsist on potatoes, which could grow even in the poorest soil. When potato crops suddenly failed due to blight in the 1840s, the results were catastrophic. A million Irish people died of starvation and two million more emigrated, many of them to the United States.

A child of conservative Protestant parents, Jane Elgee rebelled against her family to take up the cause of Irish nationalism. Writing under the pen name Speranza ("hope" in Italian), she wrote poems and articles for the radical Irish newspaper, *The Nation*. Her poems on the suffering of the poor during the *Gorta Mór*, or "Great Hunger," were so popular that for years to come she would be cheered by crowds when she drove through the streets of Dublin. At one point Speranza even called for an armed uprising, which prompted the government to shut down *The Nation* for a time and imprison its editor.

Speranza's "A Lament for the Potato" is a translation of a translation. It was originally an eighteenth-century song in Gaelic. An English prose version of it had reached Speranza, and she decided to translate the prose into verse. We learn from the song that famine was not new to the Irish: the Irish poor had suffered terribly before, with the devastation of potato crops in 1739.

"The Exodus" responds to the census of the United Kingdom conducted in 1851. The statistics made clear that massive numbers of people were leaving Ireland in the wake of the famine. The Irish national census commissioner was none other than William Wilde, Speranza's husband, later knighted for this achievement by Queen Victoria. In the poem Speranza expresses horror that statistics are read so "calmly and cold" by British statesmen. The poem deliberately registers the numbers of emigrants with passionate sympathy instead of cool statistical objectivity.

After her husband's early death, Lady Wilde moved to England to try to support herself with her writing. She joined her son Oscar in London, who was on his way to becoming a world-renowned playwright. Although Speranza did succeed in publishing many articles in magazines and newspapers, including rousing calls for women's equality, she struggled to make enough money to survive. She died penniless in London in 1896 and was buried in an unmarked grave.

A Lament for the Potato

(From the Irish)[1]

There is woe, there is clamour, in our desolated land,
And wailing lamentation from a famine-stricken band;
And weeping are the multitudes in sorrow and despair,
For the green fields of Munster[2] lying desolate and bare.
Woe for Lorc's[3] ancient kingdom, sunk in slavery and grief;
Plundered, ruined, are our gentry, our people, and their Chief;
For the harvest lieth scattered, more worth to us than gold,
All the kindly food that nourished both the young and the old.
Well I mind me of the cosherings,[4] where princes might dine,
And we drank until nightfall the best seven sorts of wine;
Yet was ever the Potato our old, familiar dish,
And the best of all sauces with the beeves and the fish.
But the harp now is silent, no one careth for the sound;
No flowers, no sweet honey, and no beauty can be found;
Not a bird its music thrilling through the leaves of the wood,
Nought but weeping and hands wringing in despair for our food.
And the Heavens, all in darkness, seem lamenting our doom,
No brightness in the sunlight, not a ray to pierce the gloom;
The cataract comes rushing with a fearful deepened roar,
And ocean bursts its boundaries, dashing wildly on the shore.
Yet, in misery and want, we have one protecting man,
Kindly Barry, of Fitzstephen's old hospitable clan;[5]
By mount and river working deeds of charity and grace:
Blessings ever on our champion, best hero of his race!
Save us, God! In Thy mercy bend to hear the people's cry,
From the famine-stricken fields, rising bitterly on high;
Let the mourning and the clamour cease in Lorc's ancient land,
And shield us in the death-hour by Thy strong, protecting hand!

The Exodus

I

"A million a decade!" Calmly and cold
  The units are read by our statesmen sage;
Little they think of a Nation old,
  Fading away from History's page;
    Outcast weeds by a desolate sea—
    Fallen leaves of Humanity.

1. This was a song originally written in Gaelic about a potato blight that followed a terrible frost.
2. Province in southern Ireland.
3. Legendary king of Ireland.
4. Meals and lodging provided to a feudal lord by a tenant.
5. James Barry, fourth Earl of Barrymore (1667–1748), a member of the British Parliament who claimed descent from Robert Fitz Stephen, a leader of the 12th-century Norman invasion of Ireland. Barry is said to have provided food for 4,000 starving people in Dublin during the famine.

II

"A million a decade!"—of human wrecks,
  Corpses lying in fever sheds—
Corpses huddled on foundering decks,
  And shroudless dead on their rocky beds;
    Nerve and muscle, and heart and brain,
    Lost to Ireland—lost in vain.

III

"A million a decade!" Count ten by ten,
  Column and line of the record fair;
Each unit stands for ten thousand men,
  Staring with blank, dead eye-balls there;
    Strewn like blasted trees on the sod,
    Men that were made in the image of God.

IV

"A million a decade!"—and nothing done;
  The Cæsars had less to conquer a world;
And the war for the Right not yet begun,
  The banner of Freedom not yet unfurled:
    The soil is fed by the weed that dies;
    If forest leaves fall, yet they fertilise.

V

But ye—dead, dead, not climbing the height,
  Not clearing a path for the future to tread;
Not opening the golden portals of light,
  Ere the gate was choked by your piled-up dead:
    Martyrs ye, yet never a name
    Shines on the golden roll of Fame.

VI

Had ye rent one gyve[1] of the festering chain,
  Strangling the life of the Nation's soul;
Poured your life-blood by river and plain,
  Yet touched with your dead hand Freedom's goal;
    Left of heroes one footprint more
    On our soil, tho' stamped in your gore—

VII

We could triumph while mourning the brave,
  Dead for all that was holy and just,
And write, through our tears, on the grave,

1. Shackle.

As we flung down the dust to dust—
"They died for their country, but led
Her up from the sleep of the dead."

VIII

"A million a decade!" What does it mean?
A Nation dying of inner decay—
A churchyard silence where life has been—
The base of the pyramid crumbling away:
A drift of men gone over the sea,
A drift of the dead where men should be.

IX

Was it for this ye plighted your word,
Crowned and crownless rulers of men?
Have ye kept faith with your crucified Lord,
And fed His sheep till He comes again?
Or fled like hireling shepherds away,
Leaving the fold the gaunt wolf's prey?

X

Have ye given of your purple to cover,
Have ye given of your gold to cheer,
Have ye given of your love, as a lover
Might cherish the bride he held dear,
Broken the Sacrament-bread to feed
Souls and bodies in uttermost need?

XI

Ye stand at the Judgment-bar to-day—
The Angels are counting the dead-roll, too;
Have ye trod in the pure and perfect way,
And ruled for God as the crowned should do?
Count our dead—before Angels and Men,
Ye're judged and doomed by the Statist's[2] pen.

2. A person who collects and analyzes statistics for the government.

LOLA RODRÍGUEZ DE TIÓ

On the night of September 23, 1868, a rebel army armed with machetes met to declare the independence of Puerto Rico from Spain. Puerto Ricans had been petitioning peacefully for national sovereignty for decades, and had grown increasingly frustrated with the persistence of slavery and the unrepresentative and corrupt Spanish military government that ruled them. "Puerto Rico must in the end be free," insisted a growing band of secret revolutionary societies, which used code names and underground print shops to issue plans and proclamations. When one important revolutionary leader was arrested, a thousand rebels from all classes seized the town of Lares and took local Spanish authorities prisoner. The revolt was short-lived. Spanish military forces quelled the rebel forces the next day and imprisoned or exiled its leaders.

Although the rebellion itself failed, however, the memory of the "Lares Outcry" (*Grito de Lares*) would live on. One of those deeply moved by the rebels was Lola Rodríguez de Tió (1843–1924), the first major woman poet from Puerto Rico and a passionate advocate for women's rights, the abolition of slavery, and independence from Spain. Rodríguez de Tió set new words to the tune of a popular Puerto Rican song called a *danza*. The *danza* tradition combines European classical music with an Afro-Caribbean beat. Most musicians in the nineteenth century joined *danza* sounds with themes of melancholy, pastoral beauty, and romantic love. Rodríguez de Tió's lyrics threw out all of these conventional associations, reimagining the *danza* as a call to men and women to take up machetes to fight violently for independence. Sung by Puerto Ricans of all classes, Rodríguez de Tió's 1868 lyrics soon became the unofficial national anthem. The title, "The Song of Borinquen," is drawn from *boriken*, a word used by the indigenous Taíno people to refer to the island of Puerto Rico. (Puerto Ricans sometimes identify themselves as "Boricua" as a mark of pride in the Taíno heritage of the island.)

Rodríguez de Tió's words were so inflammatory that they prompted the Spanish authorities to send her and her family into exile. She spent many years in Cuba, where she founded the Cuban Academy of Arts and Letters, and wrote poetry about both Puerto Rico and Cuba. While living in New York for a time, she gave her support to **José Martí**, the Cuban revolutionary and poet whose famous song, "La Guantanamera," is also included in this section. Rodríguez de Tió was known for her short hair, her outspoken views, and her ability to compose verses on the spot. She died in Cuba in 1924 at the age of eighty-one.

The tune of "The Song of Borinquen" grew so popular that it could not be suppressed. But the authorities adopted bland new lyrics for the song in the 1890s, recasting the same tune as an ode to the beauty of the island. The new version became the official anthem of Puerto Rico. Rodríguez de Tió's lyrics have survived, however, and are still sung in our own time.

The Song of Borinquen[1]

Awake, Borinqueños,
for they've given the signal!

Awake from your sleep
for it's time to fight!

Come! The sound of cannon
will be dear to us.

At that patriotic clamor
doesn't your heart burn?

Look! The Cuban will soon be free,
the machete will give him freedom.

The drum of war announces in its beating
that the thicket is the place, the meeting place!

Most beautiful Borinquen, we have to follow Cuba;
you have brave sons who want to fight!

Let us no more seem fearful!
Let us no more, timid, permit our enslavement!

We want to be free already
and our machete is well sharpened!

Why should we, then, remain so asleep
and deaf, asleep and deaf to that signal?

There's no need to fear, Ricans, the sound of cannon,
for saving the homeland is the duty of the heart!

We want no more despots! Let the tyrant fall!
Women, likewise wild, will know how to fight!

We want freedom and our machete will give it to us!

Let's go, Puerto Ricans, let's go already,
for LIBERTY is waiting, ever so anxious!

1. Translated by José Nieto. *Borinquen*: a name for Puerto Rico; from *Borinquén*, the island's indigenous Taíno name.

JOSÉ MARTÍ

The Cuban writer José Martí (1853–1895) always entwined his revolutionary political activities with his art. Arrested at the age of sixteen for writing subversive literature, he was killed twenty-six years later by a Spanish bullet in a war for Cuban independence. In the intervening years, he became known as an orator, a teacher, a diplomat, a widely respected journalist, a political and literary essayist, a ground-breaking poet, and a committed organizer of the struggle to free Cuba from Spanish colonial rule. His most important works, *Our America* (1891) and *Versos Sencillos* (*Simple Songs*, 1891), helped to formulate the concept of America for Latin Americans. Martí's dedication to freedom and human rights and his committed anti-racism made him a political hero (today his face appears on Cuban coins, and the Havana airport is named after him), while his deliberately simplified poetic diction and his rejection of conventional Spanish verse forms paved the way for Latin American *modernismo*, the exciting experimental poetry that emerged at the end of the nineteenth century.

Martí's best-known poem, "I Am an Honest Man," with its values of sincerity, simplicity, and intense emotion, astonished readers when it first appeared, dramatically overturning dominant traditions of Spanish poetry that had valued complex, artful structures and Romantic sentimentality. This poem has long been beloved by Cubans, but it became world famous when it was set to the tune of *Guantanamera* ("the woman from Guantánamo"), a popular Cuban melody. Julián Orbón, a musician and composer, wanted to dignify this popular song and did so by borrowing celebrated words for it from the martyred poet-hero Martí. It is now the unofficial anthem of both island and exiled Cubans, and musicians around the world have translated and recorded it. The US folk singer Pete Seeger helped to propel the song to international fame in the 1960s.

I Am an Honest Man

(Guantanamera)[1]

I am an honest man
From where the palms grow;
Before I die I want my soul
To shed its poetry.

I come from everywhere,
To everywhere I'm bound:
An art among the arts,

1. Translated by Elinor Randall.

A mountain among mountains.

I know the unfamiliar names
Of grasses and of flowers,
Of fatal deceptions
And exalted sorrows.

On darkest nights I've seen
Rays of the purest splendor
Raining upon my head
From heavenly beauty.

I've seen wings sprout
From handsome women's shoulders,
Seen butterflies fly out
Of rubbish heaps.

I've seen a man who lives
With a dagger at his side,
Never uttering the name
Of his murderess.

Twice, quick as a wink, I've seen
The soul: once when a poor
Old man succumbed, once when
She said goodby.

Once I shook with anger
At the vineyard's iron gate
When a savage bee attacked
My daughter's forehead.

Once I rejoiced as I
Had never done before,
When the warden, weeping, read
My sentence of death.

I hear a sigh across
The land and sea; it is
No sigh: it is my son
Waking from sleep.

If I am said to take
A jeweler's finest gem,
I take an honest friend,
Put love aside.

I've seen a wounded eagle
Fly to the tranquil blue,
And seen a snake die in its
Hole, of venom.

Well do I know that when
The livid world yields to repose,
The gentle brook will ripple on

In deepest silence.

I've laid a daring hand,
Rigid from joy and horror,
Upon the burnt-out star that fell
Before my door.

My manly heart conceals
The pain it suffers; sons of
A land enslaved live for it
Silently, and die.

All is permanence and beauty,
And all is melody and reason,
And all, like diamonds rather
Than light, is coal.

I know that fools are buried
Splendidly, with floods of tears,
And that no fruit on earth
Is like the graveyard's.

I understand, keep still,
Cast off the versifier's pomp,
And hang my doctoral robes upon
A withered tree.

RUBÉN DARÍO

To have grown up in Nicaragua in the late nineteenth century was to find oneself caught between two empires. Though the Spanish government had lost most of its colonies in fierce battles for independence that had been waged in the early decades of the nineteenth century, Spain continued its powerful influence over Latin America through language, institutions—including the Catholic Church—and control of Cuba and Puerto Rico. Meanwhile, the United States had become the major power in the region, and was threatening to use its military might against European states trying to assert authority in the Western Hemisphere. Hostilities between Spain and the United States over Cuba mounted until war erupted in 1898. The Spanish–American War, as it came to be called, established the United States as an imperial power far more frightening than Spain to many in Latin America.

US imperialism seemed so outrageous that even Rubén Darío (1867–1916) was moved to write a poem of protest. Darío had mostly avoided politics in his poetry, but here he responds explicitly to Theodore Roosevelt's "Big Stick" policy, which he casts as powerful but wrong—aggressive, greedy, and barbaric. He opens the poem by paying homage to the American poet **Walt Whitman**, using US culture against itself. Darío also remains fully conscious here of Spain's history of torturing and exploiting indigenous peoples. Thus like many of his contemporaries, he is wary of both empires, and presses for a Latin American cultural and political renewal that would be the result of a new kind of self-determination.

To Roosevelt[1]

The voice that would reach you, Hunter, must speak
in Biblical tones, or in the poetry of Walt Whitman.[2]
You are primitive and modern, simple and complex;
you are one part George Washington and one part Nimrod.[3]
  You are the United States
future invader of our naive America[4]
with its Indian blood, an America
that still prays to Christ and still speaks Spanish.

You are a strong, proud model of your race;
you are cultured and able; you oppose Tolstoy.[5]
You are an Alexander-Nebuchadnezzar,[6]
breaking horses and murdering tigers.
(You are a Professor of Energy,
as the current lunatics say).

You think that life is a fire,
that progress is an irruption,
that the future is wherever
your bullet strikes.

No.

The United States is grand and powerful.
Whenever it trembles, a profound shudder
runs down the enormous backbone of the Andes.[7]
If it shouts, the sound is like the roar of a lion.

1. President of the United States from 1901 to 1909, Theodore Roosevelt was well known as a hunter and as a political expansionist.
2. American poet (1819–1892) and author of *Leaves of Grass* (1855) whose poetry Darío liked and to whom he addressed a poem.
3. Mighty hunter and king of ancient Assyria (see Genesis 10.8–12).
4. I.e., Spanish-speaking Central and South America.
5. The Russian count and novelist Leo Tolstoy (1828–1910) in his later works preached piety, morality, and a simple peasant life.
6. A combination of the Macedonian conqueror Alexander the Great (356–323 B.C.E.) and Nebuchadnezzar (630–562 B.C.E.), king of Babylon, who destroyed Jerusalem and made its inhabitants slaves.
7. Mountain chain running the length of South America.

And Hugo said to Grant:[8] "The stars are yours."
(The dawning sun of the Argentine barely shines;
the star of Chile is rising . . .)[9] A wealthy country,
joining the cult of Mammon to the cult of Hercules;[1]
while Liberty, lighting the path
to easy conquest, raises her torch in New York.
But our own America, which has had poets
since the ancient times of Nezahualcóyotl;[2]
which preserved the footprints of great Bacchus,
and learned the Panic[3] alphabet once,
and consulted the stars; which also knew Atlantis[4]
(whose name comes ringing down to us in Plato)
and has lived, since the earliest moments of its life,
in light, in fire, in fragrance, and in love—
the America of Moctezuma and Atahualpa,[5]
the aromatic America of Columbus,
Catholic America, Spanish America,
the America where noble Cuauhtémoc said:
"I am not on a bed of roses"[6]—our America,
trembling with hurricanes, trembling with Love:
O men with Saxon[7] eyes and barbarous souls,
our America lives. And dreams: And loves.
And it is the daughter of the Sun. Be careful.
Long live Spanish America!
A thousand cubs of the Spanish lion are roaming free.
Roosevelt, you must become, by God's own will,
the deadly Rifleman and the dreadful Hunter
before you can clutch us in your iron claws.

And though you have everything, you are lacking one thing:
God!

8. Ulysses S. Grant (1822–1885), Union general in the Civil War and president from 1869 to 1877. "Hugo": Darío admired the 19th-century French writer Victor Hugo (1802–1885).

9. The flags of Argentina and Chile display a sun and a star, respectively.

1. The Greek demigod known for his strength. "Mammon": in the New Testament, a false god who personified riches and greed.

2. An Aztec ruler and early poet.

3. Belonging to the woodland god Pan, a follower of Bacchus. "Bacchus": the Greek god of wine and fertility.

4. The lost civilization of Atlantis, described in Plato's dialogues *Timaeus* and *Critias*.

5. Last Inca emperor (r. 1532–33), captured and held for ransom before being strangled by Pizarro's soldiers. "Moctezuma": Montezuma II (1466–1520), Aztec emperor in Mexico, captured and slain by Spanish invaders.

6. Words spoken to a fellow prisoner by the last Aztec emperor (d. 1525) while he was being tortured by Spanish invaders.

7. Of Germanic or British ancestry; here, North Americans.

III

Realism across the Globe

As the world grew closer together in the nineteenth century, thanks to rapidly expanding empires and new methods of transportation and communication, including the steamship and the telegraph, literary movements were able to spread fast, too. Writers could find inspiration in texts composed across the world; they could nurture new ideas at home that then spread quickly outward; and they could readily mix and fuse traditions that came from different continents. "World literature" as a globally interconnected phenomenon became a reality in this period. Symbolism, for example—the poetic movement launched by **Charles Baudelaire** in Paris—had an impact as far away as Nicaragua and Japan, and the *ghazal*, an Arabic poetic form used for many centuries in India and Persia, inspired imitators in nineteenth-century Europe, including **Johann Wolfgang von Goethe**, who made it a popular poetic form in Germany, and Thomas Hardy in Britain.

One of the most powerfully influential global artistic movements in the nineteenth century was realism. It began in Britain and France, hotbeds of industrial and political revolution, but it soon spread worldwide. And yet realism in literature did not always arise in response to European influences.

Leo Tolstoi Ploughing a Field, 1882, by Ilya Yefimovich Repin.

For example, **Higuchi Ichiyō**, a Japanese woman writer, published fiction at the end of the nineteenth century that departed from Japanese literary conventions, startling and enchanting her readers with a new style and subject matter that felt fresh and lifelike. She focused on poor and marginal characters in the city as they struggle to make choices in a forbidding economic environment. She also purposefully incorporated colloquial speech and lively dialogue that sounded more natural than the speech of traditional literary characters. And she did all this without ever having read a European novel. Similarly, it would be a mistake to see **Joaquim Maria Machado de Assis** in Brazil, **Rabindranath Tagore** in India, and Rebecca Harding Davis in the United States as mere imitators of the European model: they invented techniques, subjects, and plots, they altered conventions, and they experimented with styles to generate realisms all their own.

Despite its rich variety, realist writing around the world tended to share some crucial aims and characteristics. In the nineteenth century many artists felt a new urgency to tell the unvarnished truth about the world, to observe social life unsentimentally, and to convey it as objectively as possible. To be sure, the struggle to give a realistic representation of the world—sometimes called verisimilitude or mimesis—was nothing new. But while artists for many generations had been aiming at truth in their representations of the world, the nineteenth century ushered in a new realist philosophy, shocking new subject matter, and a specific new constellation of literary techniques.

The revolutionary overturning of old regimes and hierarchies, the rise of democracy and the middle class, and the industrial revolution—which created smoky, grimy cities teeming with an impoverished working class—had already inspired writers to throw off old literary forms and conventions. In Europe and the Americas, the Romantic poets (described in detail in this volume) had sought to liberate literature from the grip of traditional courtly manners and traditions to focus instead on nature as a model of freedom and beauty. For them, the natural environment offered an antidote to the arti-

The Stonebreakers, 1848, by Gustave Courbet. A realist masterpiece that was destroyed in the Allied bombing of Dresden during World War II, this painting now exists only in reproductions and photographs.

fices and injustices of human societies. Realist writers, by and large, lost faith in this ideal: nature no longer seemed to provide a plausible alternative. Now all that was left of reality was what you could see with your naked eyes: gritty, ugly industries; the power of money; starving, broken workers; social hierarchies; dirt, decay, and disease. The realists thus shocked their audiences by representing characters who for centuries had been considered too low and coarse for art: ragged orphans and exhausted workers, washerwomen and prostitutes, drunks and thieves. They routinely chose the city over the countryside for their settings. And they were willing to lavish their descriptive attention on squalid surroundings—sickening slums, smoggy factories, dusty barrooms. Gone was the equation of art with beauty: visual art and literature could now be deliberately, powerfully hideous.

The realists were not only concerned with the unfortunate, however. In throwing off the ideals associated with earlier art forms, realist artists often threw their energies into representing the commonplace—the mundane experience of ordinary people. They wanted to capture the world as it was, and that meant describing plausible individuals in recognizable circumstances. Realism is as closely associated with middle-class characters, then, as it is with the poor, and many of the most famous realist writers of the nineteenth century—including Honoré de Balzac, Charles Dickens, and **Fyodor Dostoyevsky**—wrote fiction that deliberately cut across different classes, showing encounters between rich and poor in an attempt to give a realistic picture of a whole society.

While some realist writers tried to capture entire nations and social classes, others focused intensively on a few individuals. Some put their emphasis on internal, psychological reality, others on the shaping force of external circumstances. Usually those who stuck to the small scale implied larger social relationships, and they used individual characters to represent whole groups, but their fictions do feel more local and intimate than the vast and sprawling novels of the period—*Bleak House* or *War and Peace*—that contain many characters and strive to represent a whole nation. These differences were in part philosophical, revolving around the question of what it is possible to know. What *is* reality? Can we rely on our senses, or do we need to turn to facts and statistics, theories about hidden causes and social structures? Can we see reality from a single, individual perspective, or do we need to take a bird's-eye view?

The realists did not always agree about what constituted reality or how best to capture it in words or paint, but in general they resisted symbols and allegories, sentimentality and sensationalism, otherworldly ideals and timeless values in favor of the literal, the specific, and observable—the social world as it appeared in the here and the now. They tended to focus on the immediate, material causes of social misery and looked to scientists and social thinkers for solutions, rather than aspiring to transcendent or beautiful ideals. Though frequently the writers themselves were religious, realism was typically a secular project that put its emphasis on empirical experience—what we can know through our senses—rather than on providential explanations. Many realist writers were influenced by currents in science, and a later offshoot of realism, called naturalism, turned to the evolutionary science of Charles Darwin for a brutal explanatory model: human beings would only survive to the extent that they could adapt to their social environments; those who proved unfit would die.

Realist writers introduced a whole

Reading by Lamplight, 1858, by James Abbott McNeill Whistler.

new range of formal techniques that transformed the literary landscape. Most wrote novels or short stories, though realist drama changed the history of theater in the late nineteenth century. The novel had the advantage of being relatively formless: it could be long or short; it could include many central characters or a single protagonist; it could be told in the first person or the third person; it could focus on domestic settings or foreign travel; and it could entwine many stories or follow a single main path. Unlike more traditional and compact forms, such as the sonnet or *ghazal*, it could swallow up other kinds of writing—letters, dialogue, description, history, biography, satire, even poetry—without being bound by the rules of any of those particular forms itself. In Europe, the novel was a new genre in the eighteenth century—hence its name "novel"—and its flexibility as a form allowed it to adapt to many different kinds of philosophies and social circumstances. Often written and read by more women than men, novels were a popular form that did not acquire a serious, highbrow status until the beginning of the twentieth century.

The novel and drama suited the aims of realism in some very specific ways. Prose is of course prosaic—suited to capturing ordinariness and even ugliness. Realist writers often opted for plain, unstylized diction and usually tried to convey the many ways of speaking that characterized the social groups they represented, including dialect speech. Prose and drama lend themselves much better to this linguistic variety than does poetry, with its strict forms and connotations of artful beauty. Fiction also lends itself well to movement between action and description: it can pause the plot to include highly detailed depictions of the characters and their environments. For writers wanting to capture the whole social world in a style that seemed objective, the omniscient third-person narrator provided the perfect, impersonal perspective. Other writers opted for first-person narrators, guided only by their own senses and experience as they try to make sense of the world. Fiction can accommodate both of these perspectives easily, and some realist novels even move back and forth between the narrator's bird's-eye view and the characters' more restricted knowledge.

The elements of both character and plot raised particular challenges and opportunities for realist writers. Some realists tried to present uniquely individual characters, conveying some of the complexity of real people in the world; others felt that the truth lay instead in types, and they used individual characters to represent whole social groups—the outraged worker, the subjugated wife, the social climber. As for plot, realist writers often tried to steer clear of sensational events and neat endings, which jeopardized the goal of unvarnished truth telling, but they also wanted to keep their readers absorbed. One solution was to put characters in believable social situations where they faced ethical dilemmas. The dramatic interest of the plot then lay in having the character make a difficult choice. Should the heroine choose respectable poverty or agree to a luxurious but disreputable life as a kept woman? Should the hero climb the social ladder at the expense of an innocent victim?

One of the advantages of dramatizing ethical predicaments is that these allowed fiction to engage the question of moral action in the new social environments of the nineteenth century. Can individuals have an impact on unjust social relationships? What responsibility does each of us have toward others in a city, a nation, or a densely interconnected world? For many realists, the purpose of describing the social world in great detail—with a particular emphasis on poverty and injustice—was to prompt readers to try to change that world.

With its emphasis on ordinary language, new social circumstances, and plausible human predicaments, realism transformed the literary landscape across the globe, inviting writers everywhere to try to capture the troubled, painful, struggling worlds of their own experience. And the mark these writers left remains palpable everywhere today, as realism continues to exert a powerful cultural force, still part of the daily fare of television, fiction, drama, and film around the world. Realism is nothing if not a capacious, roomy genre—able to move across borders and oceans, and as it moves, to take up new social relationships, new styles, new perspectives, and new resolutions.

FYODOR DOSTOYEVSKY

1821–1881

At seven o'clock on a bitter winter morning in 1849, a young man, meagerly dressed and shivering, went to meet his death. He had been convicted of circulating subversive writings that attacked both the Russian Orthodox Church and the tsar. Led to a platform surrounded by a crowd, he looked out over a cart filled with coffins. He heard his name and faced a firing squad. A priest administered his last rites and pressed him to confess. His cap was pulled over his face. Then, just as the firing squad took aim, a carriage screeched to a halt, and a messenger leapt out, shouting, "Long live the tsar! The good tsar!" Fyodor Dostoyevsky had been allowed to live. Astonished and thankful, he pledged his lifelong loyalty to the tsar. Drawing on this and other experiences from his eventful life, he would go on to write some of the most gripping fiction of the nineteenth century, works characterized by dramatic extremes of authority and subjection. Intense and unforgettable, Dostoyevsky's characters are often, like their author, wracked by violence, guilt, obsession, and addiction.

LIFE

Fyodor Dostoyevsky was born in 1821, the son of a doctor in Moscow. He was the second of six children. The family lived next to a hospital for poor people, which also housed a morgue. Their father was stern and efficient, their mother compassionate, and both were devout members of the Russian Orthodox Church. The children were encouraged to read widely, and Fyodor became an admirer of such writers as William Shakespeare, Pierre Corneille, **Johann Wolfgang von Goethe**, and Charles Dickens.

In 1837 Dostoyevsky's beloved mother died, and his father sent him to be educated at the military Academy for Engineers in St. Petersburg. On the way there, he witnessed an act of violence that later became a famous scene in *Crime and Punishment*, one of his best-known novels. A government courier, after throwing back a few shots of vodka, jumped into a carriage and started beating the peasant driver mercilessly. The driver, in turn, began to thrash his horses. Dostoyevsky retained a lifelong fascination with what he considered the basic human desire to subdue those weaker than oneself. After his mother's death, his father withdrew and became violent, drinking excessively, talking aloud to his dead wife, and beating his servants. In 1839 he was mysteriously murdered on his own estate, probably by his serfs.

Once Dostoyevsky had finished his engineering courses, he worked at a government job, which he found as "tiresome as potatoes." He lived beyond his means, gambling and eating in expensive restaurants. Soon he quit his job to write *Poor Folk*, his first novel, which turned out to be a great success, especially with political radicals. In the revolutionary year 1848, he took up with a group of subversive St. Petersburg socialists and atheists. A spy who had infiltrated the group informed on them, leading to Dostoyevsky's arrest and death sentence.

After being pardoned at the last moment by the tsar, the writer was exiled to hard labor in remote Siberia.

For four years he marched with shackles on his legs, moving snow and firing bricks. "Every minute," he wrote later, "weighed upon my soul like a stone." The only book he was allowed was the New Testament, and he was not permitted to write letters or receive them. Dostoyevsky's thinking and writing would be transformed by the experience: in Siberia, he found renewed faith in the Orthodox Christianity of his childhood and artistic inspiration in the religious and folk traditions of the poorest Russian people.

Dostoyevsky served out the next four years of his sentence as a soldier in the small town of Semipalatinsk, where he fell in love for the first time with a married woman. In 1857, after her husband died, they were married. Then began a period of restlessness. The marriage was not a success. The couple traveled to Western Europe, where they were poor and unhappy. Ill with epilepsy and subject to increasingly serious episodes of the disease, Dostoyevsky gambled compulsively, squandering all of the money he had begged relatives to give him. As Dostoyevsky and his wife grew ever more estranged and her health declined from tuberculosis, he fell in love with another woman who disappointed him and then left him.

It was in 1864, during the lowest point of his bitter wandering, that he composed *Notes from Underground*. Soon after this his wife died, and he began work on the manuscript that would become *Crime and Punishment*, a novel about a young man named Raskolnikov who believes that he is superior to the ordinary run of humanity and therefore not subject to the usual moral laws. He kills two women with an axe and is consumed both with guilt and with the terror of being caught. Dostoyevsky burned the first draft of this novel and then rewrote it from scratch. All the while, he was miserably poor, forced to plead with acquaintances for money and to sell everything he owned, including most of his clothes.

The next phase of the writer's life proved slightly more stable. He married a much younger woman with good business sense who managed his publications and their finances better than he had done on his own, though he remained in debt until the last year of his life. They had four children. The last, Alyosha, died from epilepsy at the age of three, and Dostoyevsky, heartbroken, blamed himself for having passed on the disease. His final novel, *The Brothers Karamazov*, features not only the murder of a father but also a saintly son named Alyosha. This novel proved extremely popular, hailed by fellow writer **Leo Tolstoy** as the best of the century. A life packed with dramatic incidents and great suffering came to an end soon after. At the time of his death in 1881, Dostoyevsky was acclaimed as one of the greatest Russian writers of all time. Thirty thousand people attended his funeral.

TIMES

By the middle of the nineteenth century, Russians had a long tradition of ambivalence toward Western Europe. On the one hand, Russia had been instituting Western-inspired reforms since the late seventeenth century, borrowing ideas about military organization, industry, law, and culture from France, Britain, and Germany. Most highborn Russians spoke French almost as a native language. On the other hand, the Russians had proudly fought off the invasion of Napoleon's French troops in 1812, and some saw European influences as weakening and corrupting Russian traditions. Tsar Nicholas I, who ruled the Russian empire from 1825 to 1855, instituted a policy he called Official Nationalism. He believed in exerting absolute power himself, and he imposed a regime of strict suppression, punishing dissenters, censoring subversive publications, and demanding allegiance to the Russian nation. He also insisted that everyone at court speak Russian. Nicholas I was followed by a very different kind of leader, Tsar Alexander II, who looked to the West for reformist ideas. His most sweeping reform was the abolition of serfdom—the possession of peasants by landowners, a system very much like slavery. He also introduced trial by jury and modest forms of representative government. His relatively liberal administration came to an end when he was assassinated in 1881.

Russian thinkers in this period tended to divide themselves into two broad camps. The first, called the Westernizers, favored European-style modernizations. Many of these were moderate liberals who defended gradual progress toward rights and freedoms, welcoming Alexander II's reforms, but others were more radical and utopian, imagining that only a thoroughgoing revolution would bring about the change Russia needed. Both liberals and radicals believed that the Western European Enlightenment, with its emphasis on reason and on universal rights, offered the best model for Russia's future.

Other Russians resisted this wholehearted embrace of Western Enlightenment values. Most of these, known as Slavophiles, envisioned all of the Slavic peoples uniting around a unique set of spiritual and cultural traditions, including a shared loyalty to the Orthodox Church. Dostoyevsky, after his brief flirtation with European radicalism, helped to bring into being a movement called "Native Soil" conservatism. He imagined all of Russia, rich and poor, joined in a new national union that would be spiritually superior to all of Western Europe. Somewhat ambivalent about the Orthodox Church, he was always drawn to the image of Christ as a loving figure of universal reconciliation and self-sacrifice who could regenerate the nation. He saw the Russian peasantry as a repository of great spiritual wealth, and he felt that intellectuals must now return to their native soil to create a new bond with the vast mass of the people through *sobornost*, or spiritual oneness.

These "native soil" views sometimes come as a surprise to readers of Dostoyevsky's fiction, since he delves so compellingly into the minds of dogmatic atheists and violent killers that it seems he must in some way have shared their perspective. But part of what makes Dostoyevsky remarkable is his capacity to see from multiple, often conflicting viewpoints, and perhaps this is not surprising, given the extraordinary range of his experiences: his pious childhood, his fraternizing with socialists and atheists, his incarceration in a Siberian prison with murderous convicts and devout peasants, his humiliating poverty, his addiction to gambling, and his misery in love.

WORK

From the outset, *Notes from Underground* poses questions about what kind of human one should be. The narrator begins, "I am a sick man. . . . I am a spiteful man. I am a most unpleasant man." But if this character is sick, then what does it mean to be healthy? If he is spiteful and unpleasant, are others good and generous? Or, as the underground man suggests at times, are we all actually versions of him, and is humanity therefore sick, spiteful, and unpleasant? In the first few pages, the narrator compares himself to an insect, a mouse, a monkey, a slave, a peasant, and a civilized European. Later he mocks those who see humans as musical instruments—mechanical devices. But if we are not bugs, animals, machines, slaves, or civilized people, then what is the proper model for thinking about what it means to be human?

Dostoyevsky does not give us a character who can answer any of these questions to our satisfaction. Constantly contradicting himself, he calls himself a "paradoxicalist," taking pleasure in spitefulness and pride in pain. One of the most tortuous aspects of the narrator's experience is his acute self-awareness. He is horrified at being seen by others and then more troubled still by the idea that he may not be seen. And he cannot escape his obsessive self-consciousness even when alone, since he is always watching and judging himself and imagining himself through the eyes of others. Indeed, although he is painfully lonely, he is never truly free of the social world. We see him always in dialogue, constantly responding to another's views, anticipating someone else's response, even when that someone else is himself.

The "underground man" moves back and forth between casting his intense self-awareness as unique and seeing it as representative of all humanity. But Dostoyevsky also hints at a third possibility: that his antihero is a particular social type, a representative of a specifically *modern* condition. The "underground man" is a new kind of rootless urban intellectual, bombarded with fashionably progressive ideas about science, who cannot reason his way to any kind of satisfying conclusion. *Notes from Underground* is packed with references to contemporary ideas. For example, the socialist utopian novel *What Is to Be Done?*, published in 1863 (just a year prior to *Notes from Underground*), with its vision of an intrinsically good human nature governed by scientific laws, is one of the central targets of Dostoyevsky's biting critique, as is Charles Darwin's theory of evolution, first translated into Russian in 1864. The narrator also mocks an 1863 controversy over N. N. Ge's painting *The Last Supper*, which offered a startling realism, showing Jesus recumbent and thoughtful instead of upright and authoritative, and presenting his disciples as scared and puzzled. This attention to up-to-date ideas was no accident: Dostoyevsky saw his own time as a "thunderous epoch permeated with so many colossal, astounding, and rapidly shifting actual events" that he could not imagine writing historical fiction, such as Leo Tolstoy's hugely popular *War and Peace*, which was set in 1812. *Notes from Underground*, then, may be less about the human condition in general than about the specific dilemma of being an educated man in modern, urban Russia.

Dostoyevsky captures this troubled mindset through a carefully crafted and complex work of literature. It is split into two quite distinct parts: in the first section we hear about the narrator from his own perspective in the present, and in the second we move backwards in time to see him through his encounters with others. The genre of *Notes from Underground* has long puzzled readers. It certainly draws on the tradition of the confession, as the narrator makes a declaration of guilt to an implied audience. And yet religious confessions require feelings of repentance, whereas Dostoyevsky's narrator defends himself and resists expressions of contrition. Is this novel, as some readers have believed, a parody of a confession? In many ways, the narrator is most like **Jean-Jacques Rousseau**, whose secular ***Confessions*** was the first text to explore the intimate psychological life of the author, including petty experiences of guilt and shame. And yet *Notes from Underground* is hardly a straightforward autobiography. The text's split structure does not follow a chronological arc. Instead, it gives us a picture of the narrator in two different pieces, first present and then past.

On first reading, this text may seem to meander with the narrator's tortured perceptions, but in fact it is tightly organized. After the long first section, in which he is entirely alone, we see him engaging with a sequence of other people, each of whom is lower on the social ladder than the one before. First, he becomes obsessed with a stranger—a military officer who is socially superior to him and snubs him by failing to recognize his existence. Next he meets with a group of his peers, schoolmates who refuse to take him seriously as an equal. In the final section we see him try to assert his superiority over two others: his dignified servant Apollon and the compassionate, self-sacrificing prostitute Liza.

However extreme and contradictory his characters, Dostoyevsky laid claim to a specific version of realism in his fiction. "They call me a psychologist," he said, but "it's not true. I'm merely a realist in a higher sense, that is to say I describe all the depths of the human soul." Reaching low, into the depths of the soul, as a way of achieving a "higher realism," his literature is nothing if not paradoxical. But Dostoyevsky's brilliance lies precisely in its capacity to fold together extremes—it is in the poorest prostitute that one finds the greatest spiritual wealth, and in the cruelest spite that a man can experience pleasure. Not surprisingly, then, Dostoyevsky's realism did not involve attention to the humdrum, as did the work of other realists, but offered up extremes of emotion and violence. "What most people regard as fantastic and exceptional is sometimes for me the very essence of reality," he wrote. "Everyday trivialities and a conventional view of them, in my opinion, not only fall short of realism but are even contrary to it."

Dostoyevsky influenced an astonishing array of writers and thinkers. From **Franz Kafka** and **William Faulkner** to **Gabriel García Márquez** and Ralph Ellison, some of the most imaginative minds of the following century acknowledged him as an inspiration. Perhaps the most unexpected of these was Albert Einstein. "Dostoevsky," he wrote, "gives me more than any scientist."

Notes from Underground[1]

I

Underground[2]

I

I am a sick man. . . .[3] I am a spiteful man. I am a most unpleasant man. I think my liver is diseased. Then again, I don't know a thing about my illness; I'm not even sure what hurts. I'm not being treated and never have been, though I respect both medicine and doctors. Besides, I'm extremely superstitious—

1. Translated by Michael Katz.
2. Both the author of these notes and the *Notes* themselves are fictitious, of course. Nevertheless, people like the author of these notes not only may, but actually must exist in our society, considering the general circumstances under which our society was formed. I wanted to bring before the public with more prominence than usual one of the characters of the recent past. He's a representative of the current generation. In the excerpt entitled "Underground" this person introduces himself and his views, and, as it were, wants to explain the reasons why he appeared and why he had to appear in our midst. The following excerpt [*Apropos of Wet Snow*] contains the actual "notes" of this person about several events in his life [Dostoyevsky's note].
3. The ellipses are Dostoyevsky's and do not indicate omissions from the text.

well at least enough to respect medicine. (I'm sufficiently educated not to be superstitious; but I am, anyway.) No, gentlemen, it's out of spite that I don't wish to be treated. Now then, that's something you probably won't understand. Well, I do. Of course, I won't really be able to explain to you precisely who will be hurt by my spite in this case; I know perfectly well that I can't possibly "get even" with doctors by refusing their treatment; I know better than anyone that all this is going to hurt me alone, and no one else. Even so, if I refuse to be treated, it's out of spite. My liver hurts? Good, let it hurt even more!

I've been living this way for some time—about twenty years. I'm forty now. I used to be in the civil service. But no more. I was a nasty official. I was rude and took pleasure in it. After all, since I didn't accept bribes, at least I had to reward myself in some way. (That's a poor joke, but I won't cross it out. I wrote it thinking that it would be very witty; but now, having realized that I merely wanted to show off disgracefully, I'll make a point of not crossing it out!) When petitioners used to approach my desk for information, I'd gnash my teeth and feel unending pleasure if I succeeded in causing someone distress. I almost always succeeded. For the most part they were all timid people: naturally, since they were petitioners. But among the dandies there was a certain officer whom I particularly couldn't bear. He simply refused to be humble, and he clanged his saber in a loathsome manner. I waged war with him over that saber for about a year and a half. At last I prevailed. He stopped clanging. All this, however, happened a long time ago, during my youth. But do you know, gentlemen, what the main component of my spite really was? Why, the whole point, the most disgusting thing, was the fact that I was shamefully aware at every moment, even at the moment of my greatest bitterness, that not only was I not a spiteful man, I was not even an embittered one, and that I was merely scaring sparrows to no effect and consoling myself by doing so. I was foaming at the mouth—but just bring me some trinket to play with, just serve me a nice cup of tea with sugar, and I'd probably have calmed down. My heart might even have been touched, although I'd probably have gnashed my teeth out of shame and then suffered from insomnia for several months afterward. That's just my usual way.

I was lying about myself just now when I said that I was a nasty official. I lied out of spite. I was merely having some fun at the expense of both the petitioners and that officer, but I could never really become spiteful. At all times I was aware of a great many elements in me that were just the opposite of that. I felt how they swarmed inside me, these contradictory elements. I knew that they had been swarming inside me my whole life and were begging to be let out; but I wouldn't let them out, I wouldn't, I deliberately wouldn't let them out. They tormented me to the point of shame; they drove me to convulsions and—and finally I got fed up with them, oh how fed up! Perhaps it seems to you, gentlemen, that I'm repenting about something, that I'm asking your forgiveness for something? I'm sure that's how it seems to you. . . . But really, I can assure you, I don't care if that's how it seems. . . .

Not only couldn't I become spiteful, I couldn't become anything at all: neither spiteful nor good, neither a scoundrel nor an honest man, neither a hero nor an insect. Now I live out my days in my corner, taunting myself with the spiteful and entirely useless consolation that an intelligent man cannot seriously become anything and that only a fool can become something. Yes, sir, an intelligent man in the nineteenth century must be, is morally obliged to be, principally a characterless creature; a man possessing character, a man of action, is fundamentally a limited creature. That's my conviction at the age of forty. I'm forty now; and, after all, forty is an entire lifetime; why it's extreme old age. It's rude to live past forty, it's indecent, immoral! Who lives more than forty years? Answer sincerely, honestly. I'll tell you who: only fools and rascals. I'll tell those old men that right to their faces, all those venerable old men, all those silver-haired and sweet-smelling old men! I'll say it to the whole world right to its face! I have a right to say it because I myself will live to sixty. I'll make it to seventy! Even to eighty! . . . Wait! Let me catch my breath. . . .

You probably think, gentlemen, that I want to amuse you. You're wrong about that, too. I'm not at all the cheerful fellow I seem to be, or that I may seem to be; however, if you're irritated by all this talk (and I can already sense that you are irritated), and if you decide to ask me just who I really am, then I'll tell you: I'm a collegiate assessor. I worked in order to have something to eat (but only for that reason); and last year, when a distant relative of mine left me six thousand rubles in his will, I retired immediately and settled down in this corner. I used to live in this corner before, but now I've settled down in it. My room is nasty, squalid, on the outskirts of town. My servant is an old peasant woman, spiteful out of stupidity; besides, she has a foul smell. I'm told that the Petersburg climate is becoming bad for my health, and that it's very expensive to live in Petersburg with my meager resources. I know all that; I know it better than all those wise and experienced advisers and admonishers. But I shall remain in Petersburg; I shall not leave Petersburg! I shall not leave here because . . . Oh, what difference does it really make whether I leave Petersburg or not?

Now, then, what can a decent man talk about with the greatest pleasure?

Answer: about himself.

Well, then, I too will talk about myself.

II

Now I would like to tell you, gentlemen, whether or not you want to hear it, why it is that I couldn't even become an insect. I'll tell you solemnly that I wished to become an insect many times. But not even that wish was granted. I swear to you, gentlemen, that being overly conscious is a disease, a genuine, full-fledged disease. Ordinary human consciousness would be more than sufficient for everyday human needs—that is, even half or a quarter of the amount of consciousness that's available to a cultured man in our unfortunate nineteenth century, especially to one who has the particular misfortune of living in St. Petersburg, the most abstract and premeditated city in the whole world.[4] (Cities can be either premeditated or unpremeditated.) It would have been entirely sufficient, for example, to have the consciousness with which all so-called spontaneous people and men of action are endowed. I'll bet that you think I'm writing all this to show off, to make fun of these men of action, that I'm clanging my saber just like that officer did to show off in bad taste. But, gentlemen, who could possibly be proud of his illnesses and want to show them off?

4. St. Petersburg was conceived of as an imposing city; plans called for regular streets, broad avenues, and spacious squares.

But what am I saying? Everyone does that; people do take pride in their illnesses, and I, perhaps, more than anyone else. Let's not argue; my objection is absurd. Nevertheless, I remain firmly convinced that not only is being overly conscious a disease, but so is being conscious at all. I insist on it. But let's leave that alone for a moment. Tell me this: why was it, as if on purpose, at the very moment, indeed, at the precise moment that I was most capable of becoming conscious of the subtleties of everything that was "beautiful and sublime,"[5] as we used to say at one time, that I didn't become conscious, and instead did such unseemly things, things that . . . well, in short, probably everyone does, but it seemed as if they occurred to me deliberately at the precise moment when I was most conscious that they shouldn't be done at all? The more conscious I was of what was good, of everything "beautiful and sublime," the more deeply I sank into the morass and the more capable I was of becoming entirely bogged down in it. But the main thing is that all this didn't seem to be occurring accidentally; rather, it was as if it all had to be so. It was as if this were my most normal condition, not an illness or an affliction at all, so that finally I even lost the desire to struggle against it. It ended when I almost came to believe (perhaps I really did believe) that this might really have been my normal condition. But at first, in the beginning, what agonies I suffered during that struggle! I didn't believe that others were experiencing the same thing; therefore, I kept it a secret about myself all my life. I was ashamed (perhaps I still am even now); I reached the point where I felt some secret, abnormal, despicable little pleasure in returning home to my little corner on some disgusting Petersburg night, acutely aware that once again I'd committed some revolting act that day, that what had been done could not be undone, and I used to gnaw and gnaw at myself inwardly, secretly, nagging away, consuming myself until finally the bitterness turned into some kind of shameful, accursed sweetness and at last into genuine, earnest pleasure! Yes, into pleasure, real pleasure! I absolutely mean that. . . . That's why I first began to speak out, because I want to know for certain whether other people share this same pleasure. Let me explain: the pleasure resulted precisely from the overly acute consciousness of one's own humiliation; from the feeling that one had reached the limit; that it was disgusting, but couldn't be otherwise; you had no other choice—you could never become a different person; and that even if there were still time and faith enough for you to change into something else, most likely you wouldn't even want to change, and if you did, you wouldn't have done anything, perhaps because there really was nothing for you to change into. But the main thing and the final point is that all of this was taking place according to normal and fundamental laws of overly acute consciousness and of the inertia which results directly from these laws; consequently, not only couldn't one change, one simply couldn't do anything at all. Hence it follows, for example, as a result of this overly acute consciousness, that one is absolutely right in being a scoundrel, as if this were some consolation to the scoundrel. But enough of this. . . . Oh, my,

5. This phrase originated in Edmund Burke's *Philosophical Inquiry into the Origin of Our Ideas of the Sublime and Beautiful* (1756) and was repeated in Immanuel Kant's *Observations on the Feeling of the Beautiful and the Sublime* (1756). It became a cliché in the writings of Russian critics during the 1830s.

I've gone on rather a long time, but have I really explained anything? How can I explain this pleasure? But I will explain it! I shall see it through to the end! That's why I've taken up my pen. . . .

For example, I'm terribly proud. I'm as mistrustful and as sensitive as a hunchback or a dwarf; but, in truth, I've experienced some moments when, if someone had slapped my face, I might even have been grateful for it. I'm being serious. I probably would have been able to derive a peculiar sort of pleasure from it—the pleasure of despair, naturally, but the most intense pleasures occur in despair, especially when you're very acutely aware of the hopelessness of your own predicament. As for a slap in the face—why, here the consciousness of being beaten to a pulp would overwhelm you. The main thing is, no matter how I try, it still turns out that I'm always the first to be blamed for everything and, what's even worse, I'm always the innocent victim, so to speak, according to the laws of nature. Therefore, in the first place, I'm guilty inasmuch as I'm smarter than everyone around me. (I've always considered myself smarter than everyone around me, and sometimes, believe me, I've been ashamed of it. At the least, all my life I've looked away and never could look people straight in the eye.) Finally, I'm to blame because even if there were any magnanimity in me, it would only have caused more suffering as a result of my being aware of its utter uselessness. After all, I probably wouldn't have been able to make use of that magnanimity: neither to forgive, as the offender, perhaps, had slapped me in accordance with the laws of nature, and there's no way to forgive the laws of nature; nor to forget, because even if there were any laws of nature, it's offensive nonetheless. Finally, even if I wanted to be entirely unmagnanimous, and had wanted to take revenge on the offender, I couldn't be revenged on anyone for anything because, most likely, I would never have decided to do anything, even if I could have. Why not? I'd like to say a few words about that separately.

III

Let's consider people who know how to take revenge and how to stand up for themselves in general. How, for example, do they do it? Let's suppose that they're seized by an impulse to take revenge—then for a while nothing else remains in their entire being except for that impulse. Such an individual simply rushes toward his goal like an enraged bull with lowered horns; only a wall can stop him. (By the way, when actually faced with a wall such individuals, that is, spontaneous people and men of action, genuinely give up. For them a wall doesn't constitute the evasion that it does for those of us who think and consequently do nothing; it's not an excuse to turn aside from the path, a pretext in which a person like me usually doesn't believe, but one for which he's always extremely grateful. No, they give up in all sincerity. For them the wall possesses some kind of soothing, morally decisive and definitive meaning, perhaps even something mystical . . . But more about the wall later.) Well, then, I consider such a spontaneous individual to be a genuine, normal person, just as tender mother nature wished to see him when she lovingly gave birth to him on earth. I'm green with envy at such a man. He's stupid, I won't argue with you about that; but perhaps a normal man is supposed to be stupid—how do we know? Perhaps it's even very beautiful. And I'm all the more convinced of the suspicion, so to speak, that if, for example, one were to take the antithesis of a normal man—that is, a man of overly acute consciousness, who emerged, of course, not from the bosom of nature, but from a laboratory test tube (this is almost mysticism, gentlemen, but I suspect that it's the case), then this test tube man sometimes gives up so completely in the face of his antithesis that he himself, with his overly acute consciousness, honestly considers himself not as a person, but a mouse. It may be an acutely conscious mouse, but a mouse nonetheless, while the other one is a person and consequently, . . . and so on and so forth. But the main thing is that he, he himself, considers himself to be a mouse; nobody asks him to do so, and that's the important point. Now let's take a look at this mouse in action. Let's assume, for instance, that it feels offended (it almost always feels offended), and that it also wishes to be revenged. It may even contain more accumulated malice than *l'homme de la nature et de la vérité*.[6] The mean, nasty, little desire to pay the offender back with evil may indeed rankle in it even more despicably than in *l'homme de la nature et de la vérité*, because *l'homme de la nature et de la vérité*, with his innate stupidity, considers his revenge nothing more than justice, pure and simple; but the mouse, as a result of its overly acute consciousness, rejects the idea of justice. Finally, we come to the act itself, to the very act of revenge. In addition to its original nastiness, the mouse has already managed to pile up all sorts of other nastiness around itself in the form of hesitations and doubts; so many unresolved questions have emerged from that one single question, that some kind of fatal blow is concocted unwillingly, some kind of stinking mess consisting of doubts, anxieties and, finally, spittle showered upon it by the spontaneous men of action who stand by solemnly as judges and arbiters, roaring with laughter until their sides split. Of course, the only thing left to do is dismiss it with a wave of its paw and a smile of assumed contempt which it doesn't even believe in, and creep ignominiously back into its mousehole. There, in its disgusting, stinking underground, our offended, crushed, and ridiculed mouse immediately plunges into cold, malicious, and, above all, everlasting spitefulness. For forty years on end it will recall its insult down to the last, most shameful detail; and each time it will add more shameful details of its own, spitefully teasing and irritating itself with its own fantasy. It will become ashamed of that fantasy, but it will still remember it, rehearse it again and again, fabricating all sorts of incredible stories about itself under the pretext that they too could have happened; it won't forgive a thing. Perhaps it will even begin to take revenge, but only in little bits and pieces, in trivial ways, from behind the stove, incognito, not believing in its right to be revenged, nor in the success of its own revenge, and knowing in advance that from all its attempts to take revenge, it will suffer a hundred times more than the object of its vengeance, who might not even feel a thing. On its deathbed it will recall everything all over again, with interest compounded over all those years and. . . . But it's precisely in that cold, abominable state of half-despair and half-belief, in that conscious burial of itself alive in the underground for forty years because of

6. "The man of nature and truth" (French). The basic idea is borrowed from Jean-Jacques Rousseau's *Confessions* (1782–89), namely, that human beings in a state of nature are honest and direct and that they are corrupted only by civilization.

its pain, in that powerfully created, yet partly dubious hopelessness of its own predicament, in all that venom of unfulfilled desire turned inward, in all that fever of vacillation, of resolutions adopted once and for all and followed a moment later by repentance—herein precisely lies the essence of that strange enjoyment I was talking about earlier. It's so subtle, sometimes so difficult to analyze, that even slightly limited people, or those who simply have strong nerves, won't understand anything about it. "Perhaps," you'll add with a smirk, "even those who've never received a slap in the face won't understand," and by so doing you'll be hinting to me ever so politely that perhaps during my life I too have received such a slap in the face and that therefore I'm speaking as an expert. I'll bet that's what you're thinking. Well, rest assured, gentlemen, I've never received such a slap, although it's really all the same to me what you think about it. Perhaps I may even regret the fact that I've given so few slaps during my lifetime. But that's enough, not another word about this subject which you find so extremely interesting.

I'll proceed calmly about people with strong nerves who don't understand certain refinements of pleasure. For example, although under particular circumstances these gentlemen may bellow like bulls as loudly as possible, and although, let's suppose, this behavior bestows on them the greatest honor, yet, as I've already said, when confronted with impossibility, they submit immediately. Impossibility—does that mean a stone wall? What kind of stone wall? Why, of course, the laws of nature, the conclusions of natural science and mathematics. As soon as they prove to you, for example, that it's from a monkey you're descended,[7] there's no reason to make faces; just accept it as it is. As soon as they prove to you that in truth one drop of your own fat is dearer to you than the lives of one hundred thousand of your fellow creatures and that this will finally put an end to all the so-called virtues, obligations, and other such similar ravings and prejudices, just accept that too; there's nothing more to do, since two times two is a fact of mathematics. Just you try to object.

"For goodness sake," they'll shout at you, "it's impossible to protest: it's two times two makes four! Nature doesn't ask for your opinion; it doesn't care about your desires or whether you like or dislike its laws. You're obliged to accept it as it is, and consequently, all its conclusions. A wall, you see, is a wall . . . etc. etc." Good Lord, what do I care about the laws of nature and arithmetic when for some reason I dislike all these laws and I dislike the fact that two times two makes four? Of course, I won't break through that wall with my head if I really don't have the strength to do so, nor will I reconcile myself to it just because I'm faced with such a stone wall and lack the strength.

As though such a stone wall actually offered some consolation and contained some real word of conciliation, for the sole reason that it means two times two makes four. Oh, absurdity of absurdities! How much better it is to understand it all, to be aware of everything, all the impossibilities and stone walls; not to be reconciled with any of those impossibilities or stone walls if it so disgusts you; to reach, by using the most inevitable logical combinations, the most revolting conclusions on the eternal theme that you are somehow or other to blame even for that stone wall, even though it's absolutely clear once

7. A reference to the theory of evolution by natural selection developed by Charles Darwin (1809–1882). A book on the subject was translated into Russian in 1864.

again that you're in no way to blame, and, as a result of all this, while silently and impotently gnashing your teeth, you sink voluptuously into inertia, musing on the fact that, as it turns out, there's no one to be angry with; that an object cannot be found, and perhaps never will be; that there's been a substitution, some sleight of hand, a bit of cheating, and that it's all a mess—you can't tell who's who or what's what; but in spite of all these uncertainties and sleights-of-hand, it hurts you just the same, and the more you don't know, the more it hurts!

IV

"Ha, ha, ha! Why, you'll be finding enjoyment in a toothache next!" you cry out with a laugh.

"Well, what of it? There is some enjoyment even in a toothache," I reply. I've had a toothache for a whole month; I know what's what. In this instance, of course, people don't rage in silence; they moan. But these moans are insincere; they're malicious, and malice is the whole point. These moans express the sufferer's enjoyment; if he didn't enjoy it, he would never have begun to moan. This is a good example, gentlemen, and I'll develop it. In the first place, these moans express all the aimlessness of the pain which consciousness finds so humiliating, the whole system of natural laws about which you really don't give a damn, but as a result of which you're suffering nonetheless, while nature isn't. They express the consciousness that while there's no real enemy to be identified, the pain exists nonetheless; the awareness that, in spite of all possible Wagenheims,[8] you're still a complete slave to your teeth; that if someone so wishes, your teeth will stop aching, but that if he doesn't so wish, they'll go on aching for three more months; and finally, that if you still disagree and protest, all there's left to do for consolation is flagellate yourself or beat your fist against the wall as hard as you can, and absolutely nothing else. Well, then, it's these bloody insults, these jeers coming from nowhere, that finally generate enjoyment that can sometimes reach the highest degree of voluptuousness. I beseech you, gentlemen, to listen to the moans of an educated man of the nineteenth century who's suffering from a toothache, especially on the second or third day of his distress, when he begins to moan in a very different way than he did on the first day, that is, not simply because his tooth aches; not the way some coarse peasant moans, but as a man affected by progress and European civilization, a man "who's renounced both the soil and the common people," as they say nowadays. His moans become somehow nasty, despicably spiteful, and they go on for days and nights. Yet he himself knows that his moans do him no good; he knows better than anyone else that he's merely irritating himself and others in vain; he knows that the audience for whom he's trying so hard, and his whole family, have now begun to listen to him with loathing; they don't believe him for a second, and they realize full well that he could moan in a different, much simpler way, without all the flourishes and affectation, and that he's only indulging himself out of spite and malice. Well, it's precisely in this

8. The *General Address Book of St. Petersburg* listed eight dentists named Wagenheim; contemporary readers would have recognized the name from signs throughout the city.

awareness and shame that the voluptuousness resides. "It seems I'm disturbing you, tearing at your heart, preventing anyone in the house from getting any sleep. Well, then, you won't sleep; you too must be aware at all times that I have a toothache. I'm no longer the hero I wanted to pass for earlier, but simply a nasty little man, a rogue. So be it! I'm delighted that you've seen through me. Does it make you feel bad to hear my wretched little moans? Well, then, feel bad. Now let me add an even nastier flourish. . . ." You still don't understand, gentlemen? No, it's clear that one has to develop further and become even more conscious in order to understand all the nuances of this voluptuousness! Are you laughing? I'm delighted. Of course my jokes are in bad taste, gentlemen; they're uneven, contradictory, and lacking in self-assurance. But that's because I have no respect for myself. Can a man possessing consciousness ever really respect himself?

V

Well, and is it possible, is it really possible for a man to respect himself if he even presumes to find enjoyment in the feeling of his own humiliation? I'm not saying this out of any feigned repentance. In general I could never bear to say: "I'm sorry, Daddy, and I won't do it again," not because I was incapable of saying it, but, on the contrary, perhaps precisely because I was all too capable, and how! As if on purpose it would happen that I'd get myself into some sort of mess for which I was not to blame in any way whatsoever. That was the most repulsive part of it. What's more, I'd feel touched deep in my soul; I'd repent and shed tears, deceiving even myself of course, though not feigning in the least. It seemed that my heart was somehow playing dirty tricks on me. . . . Here one couldn't even blame the laws of nature, although it was these very laws that continually hurt me during my entire life. It's disgusting to recall all this, and it was disgusting even then. Of course, a moment or so later I would realize in anger that it was all lies, lies, revolting, made-up lies, that is, all that repentance, all that tenderness, all those vows to mend my ways. But you'll ask why I mauled and tortured myself in that way? The answer is because it was so very boring to sit idly by with my arms folded; so I'd get into trouble. That's the way it was. Observe yourselves better, gentlemen; then you'll understand that it's true. I used to think up adventures for myself, inventing a life so that at least I could live. How many times did it happen, well, let's say, for example, that I took offense, deliberately, for no reason at all? All the while I knew there was no reason for it; I put on airs nonetheless, and would take it so far that finally I really did feel offended. I've been drawn into such silly tricks all my life, so that finally I lost control over myself. Another time, even twice, I tried hard to fall in love. I even suffered, gentlemen, I can assure you. In the depths of my soul I really didn't believe that I was suffering; there was a stir of mockery, but suffer I did, and in a genuine, normal way at that; I was jealous, I was beside myself with anger. . . . And all as a result of boredom, gentlemen, sheer boredom; I was overcome by inertia. You see, the direct, legitimate, immediate result of consciousness is inertia, that is, the conscious sitting idly by with one's arms folded. I've referred to this before. I repeat, I repeat emphatically: all spontaneous men and men of action are so active precisely because they're stupid and limited. How can one explain this? Here's how: as a result of their limitations they mistake immediate and secondary causes for primary ones, and thus they're convinced more quickly and easily than other people that they've located an indisputable basis for action, and this puts them at ease; that's the main point. For, in order to begin to act, one must first be absolutely at ease, with no lingering doubts whatsoever. Well, how can I, for example, ever feel at ease? Where are the primary causes I can rely upon, where's the foundation? Where shall I find it? I exercise myself in thinking, and consequently, with me every primary cause drags in another, an even more primary one, and so on to infinity. This is precisely the essence of all consciousness and thought. And here again, it must be the laws of nature. What's the final result? Why, the very same thing. Remember: I was talking about revenge before. (You probably didn't follow.) I said: a man takes revenge because he finds justice in it. That means, he's found a primary cause, a foundation: namely, justice. Therefore, he's completely at ease, and, as a result, he takes revenge peacefully and successfully, convinced that he's performing an honest and just deed. But I don't see any justice here at all, nor do I find any virtue in it whatever; consequently, if I begin to take revenge, it's only out of spite. Of course, spite could overcome everything, all my doubts, and therefore could successfully serve instead of a primary cause precisely because it's not a cause at all. But what do I do if I don't even feel spite (that's where I began before)? After all, as a result of those damned laws of consciousness, my spite is subject to chemical disintegration. You look—and the object vanishes, the arguments evaporate, a guilty party can't be identified, the offense ceases to be one and becomes a matter of fate, something like a toothache for which no one's to blame, and, as a consequence, there remains only the same recourse: that is, to bash the wall even harder. So you throw up your hands because you haven't found a primary cause. Just try to let yourself be carried away blindly by your feelings, without reflection, without a primary cause, suppressing consciousness even for a moment; hate or love, anything, just in order not to sit idly by with your arms folded. The day after tomorrow at the very latest, you'll begin to despise yourself for having deceived yourself knowingly. The result: a soap bubble and inertia. Oh, gentlemen, perhaps I consider myself to be an intelligent man simply because for my whole life I haven't been able to begin or finish anything. All right, suppose I am a babbler, a harmless, annoying babbler, like the rest of us. But then what is to be done[9] if the direct and single vocation of every intelligent man consists in babbling, that is, in deliberately talking in endless circles?

VI

Oh, if only I did nothing simply as a result of laziness. Lord, how I'd respect myself then. I'd respect myself precisely because at least I'd be capable of being lazy; at least I'd possess one more or less positive trait of which I could

9. Reference to a then-new novel by Nikolai Chernyshevsky (1828–1889) called *What Is to Be Done?* (1863). Dostoyevsky disliked the main idea of the novel, which was that Russians could be freed from the delusions of tradition and faith by scientific knowledge and could build a rational new nation; *Notes from Underground* is in part a response to Chernyshevsky.

be certain. Question: who am I? Answer: a sluggard. Why, it would have been very pleasant to hear that said about oneself. It would mean that I'd been positively identified; it would mean that there was something to be said about me. "A sluggard!" Why, that's a calling and a vocation, a whole career! Don't joke, it's true. Then, by rights I'd be a member of the very best club and would occupy myself exclusively by being able to respect myself continually. I knew a gentleman who prided himself all his life on being a connoisseur of Lafite.[1] He considered it his positive virtue and never doubted himself. He died not merely with a clean conscience, but with a triumphant one, and he was absolutely correct. I should have chosen a career for myself too: I would have been a sluggard and a glutton, not an ordinary one, but one who, for example, sympathized with everything beautiful and sublime. How do you like that? I've dreamt about it for a long time. The "beautiful and sublime" have been a real pain in the neck during my forty years, but then it's been *my* forty years, whereas then—oh, then it would have been otherwise! I would've found myself a suitable activity at once—namely, drinking to everything beautiful and sublime. I would have seized upon every opportunity first to shed a tear into my glass and then drink to everything beautiful and sublime. Then I would have turned everything into the beautiful and sublime; I would have sought out the beautiful and sublime in the nastiest, most indisputable trash. I would have become as tearful as a wet sponge. An artist, for example, has painted a portrait of Ge.[2] At once I drink to the artist who painted that portrait of Ge because I love everything beautiful and sublime. An author has written the words, "Just as you please,"[3] at once I drink to "Just as you please," because I love everything "beautiful and sublime." I'd demand respect for myself in doing this, I'd persecute anyone who didn't pay me any respect. I'd live peacefully and die triumphantly—why, it's charming, perfectly charming! And what a belly I'd have grown by then, what a triple chin I'd have acquired, what a red nose I'd have developed—so that just looking at me any passerby would have said, "Now that's a real plus! That's something really positive!" Say what you like, gentlemen, it's extremely pleasant to hear such comments in our negative age.

VII

But these are all golden dreams. Oh, tell me who was first to announce, first to proclaim that man does nasty things simply because he doesn't know his own true interest; and that if he were to be enlightened, if his eyes were to be opened to his true, normal interests, he would stop doing nasty things at once and would immediately become good and noble, because, being so enlightened and understanding his real advantage, he would realize that his own advantage really did lie in the good; and that it's well known that there's not a single man capable of acting knowingly against his own interest; conse-

1. A variety of red wine from Médoc in France.
2. N. N. Ge (1831–1894), Russian artist who rebelled against official styles in favor of a new realism in art; just before *Notes from Underground* appeared, Ge's *Last Supper* (1863) provoked considerable controversy in St. Petersburg because the painter had refused the conventional imagery of Jesus seated at a long table and instead showed him reclined and meditative, with his disciples confused and frightened.
3. An attack on the writer M. E. Saltykov-Shchedrin, who published a sympathetic review of Ge's painting titled *Just As You Please*.

quently, he would, so to speak, begin to do good out of necessity. Oh, the child! Oh, the pure, innocent babe! Well, in the first place, when was it during all these millennia, that man has ever acted only in his own self interest? What does one do with the millions of facts bearing witness to the one fact that people knowingly, that is, possessing full knowledge of their own true interests, have relegated them to the background and have rushed down a different path, that of risk and chance, compelled by no one and nothing, but merely as if they didn't want to follow the beaten track, and so they stubbornly, willfully forged another way, a difficult and absurd one, searching for it almost in the darkness? Why, then, this means that stubbornness and willfulness were really more pleasing to them than any kind of advantage. . . . Advantage! What is advantage? Will you take it upon yourself to define with absolute precision what constitutes man's advantage? And what if it turns out that man's advantage sometimes not only may, but even must in certain circumstances, consist precisely in his desiring something harmful to himself instead of something advantageous? And if this is so, if this can ever occur, then the whole theory falls to pieces. What do you think, can such a thing happen? You're laughing; laugh, gentlemen, but answer me: have man's advantages ever been calculated with absolute certainty? Aren't there some which don't fit, can't be made to fit into any classification? Why, as far as I know, you gentlemen have derived your list of human advantages from averages of statistical data and from scientific-economic formulas. But your advantages are prosperity, wealth, freedom, peace, and so on and so forth; so that a man who, for example, expressly and knowingly acts in opposition to this whole list, would be, in your opinion, and in mine, too, of course, either an obscurantist or a complete madman, wouldn't he? But now here's what's astonishing: why is it that when all these statisticians, sages, and lovers of humanity enumerate man's advantages, they invariably leave one out? They don't even take it into consideration in the form in which it should be considered, although the entire calculation depends upon it. There would be no great harm in considering it, this advantage, and adding it to the list. But the whole point is that this particular advantage doesn't fit into any classification and can't be found on any list. I have a friend, for instance. . . . But gentlemen! Why, he's your friend, too! In fact, he's everyone's friend! When he's preparing to do something, this gentleman straight away explains to you eloquently and clearly just how he must act according to the laws of nature and truth. And that's not all: with excitement and passion he'll tell you all about genuine, normal human interests; with scorn he'll reproach the shortsighted fools who understand neither their own advantage nor the real meaning of virtue; and then—exactly a quarter of an hour later, without any sudden outside cause, but precisely because of something internal that's stronger than all his interests—he does a complete about-face; that is, he does something which clearly contradicts what he's been saying: it goes against the laws of reason and his own advantage, in a word, against everything. . . . I warn you that my friend is a collective personage; therefore it's rather difficult to blame only him. That's just it, gentlemen; in fact, isn't there something dearer to every man than his own best advantage, or (so as not to violate the rules of logic) isn't there one more advantageous advantage (exactly the one omitted, the one we mentioned before), which is more important and more advantageous than all others and, on behalf of which, a man will, if necessary, go against all laws, that is, against reason, honor, peace, and prosperity—in a word, against all those splendid and useful things, merely in order to attain this fundamental, most advantageous advantage which is dearer to him than everything else?

"Well, it's advantage all the same," you say, interrupting me. Be so kind as to allow me to explain further; besides, the point is not my pun, but the fact that this advantage is remarkable precisely because it destroys all our classifications and constantly demolishes all systems devised by lovers of humanity for the happiness of mankind. In a word, it interferes with everything. But, before I name this advantage, I want to compromise myself personally; therefore I boldly declare that all these splendid systems, all these theories to explain to mankind its real, normal interests so that, by necessarily striving to achieve them, it would immediately become good and noble—are, for the time being, in my opinion, nothing more than logical exercises! Yes, sir, logical exercises! Why, even to maintain a theory of mankind's regeneration through a system of its own advantages, why, in my opinion, that's almost the same as . . . well, claiming, for instance, following Buckle,[4] that man has become kinder as a result of civilization; consequently, he's becoming less bloodthirsty and less inclined to war. Why, logically it all even seems to follow. But man is so partial to systems and abstract conclusions that he's ready to distort the truth intentionally, ready to deny everything that he himself has ever seen and heard, merely in order to justify his own logic. That's why I take this example, because it's such a glaring one. Just look around: rivers of blood are being spilt, and in the most cheerful way, as if it were champagne. Take this entire nineteenth century of ours during which even Buckle lived. Take Napoleon—both the great and the present one.[5] Take North America—that eternal union.[6] Take, finally, that ridiculous Schleswig-Holstein[7]. . . . What is it that civilization makes kinder in us? Civilization merely promotes a wider variety of sensations in man and . . . absolutely nothing else. And through the development of this variety man may even reach the point where he takes pleasure in spilling blood. Why, that's even happened to him already. Haven't you noticed that the most refined bloodshedders are almost always the most civilized gentlemen to whom all these Attila the Huns and Stenka Razins[8] are scarcely fit to hold a candle; and if they're not as conspicuous as Attila and Stenka Razin, it's precisely because they're too common and have become too familiar to us. At least if man hasn't become more bloodthirsty as a result of civilization, surely he's become bloodthirsty in a nastier, more repulsive way than before. Previously man saw justice in bloodshed and exterminated whomever he wished with a clear conscience; whereas now, though we con-

4. In his *History of Civilization in England* (1857–61), Henry Thomas Buckle (1821–1862) argued that the development of civilization necessarily leads to the cessation of war. Russia had recently been involved in fierce fighting in the Crimea (1853–56).

5. The French emperors Napoleon I (1769–1821) and his nephew Napoleon III (1808–1873), both of whom engaged in numerous wars, though on vastly different scales.

6. The United States was in the middle of its Civil War (1861–65).

7. The German duchies of Schleswig and Holstein, held by Denmark since 1773, were reunited with Prussia after a brief war in 1864.

8. Cossack leader (d. 1671) who organized a peasant rebellion in Russia. Attila (406?–453 C.E.), king of the Huns, who conducted devastating wars against the Roman emperors.

sider bloodshed to be abominable, we nevertheless engage in this abomination even more than before. Which is worse? Decide for yourselves. They say that Cleopatra (forgive an example from Roman history) loved to stick gold pins into the breasts of her slave girls and take pleasure in their screams and writhing. You'll say that this took place, relatively speaking, in barbaric times; that these are barbaric times too, because (also comparatively speaking), gold pins are used even now; that even now, although man has learned on occasion to see more clearly than in barbaric times, *he's still far from having learned* how to act in accordance with the dictates of reason and science. Nevertheless, you're still absolutely convinced that he will learn how to do so, as soon as he gets rid of some bad, old habits and as soon as common sense and science have completely re-educated human nature and have turned it in the proper direction. You're convinced that then man will voluntarily stop committing blunders, and that he will, so to speak, never willingly set his own will in opposition to his own normal interests. More than that: then, you say, science itself will teach man (though, in my opinion, that's already a luxury) that in fact he possesses neither a will nor any whim of his own, that he never did, and that he himself is nothing more than a kind of piano key or an organ stop;[9] that, moreover, there still exist laws of nature, so that everything he's done has been not in accordance with his own desire, but in and of itself, according to the laws of nature. Consequently, we need only discover these laws of nature, and man will no longer have to answer for his own actions and will find it extremely easy to live. All human actions, it goes without saying, will then be tabulated according to these laws, mathematically, like tables of logarithms up to 108,000, and will be entered on a schedule; or even better, certain edifying works will be published, like our contemporary encyclopedic dictionaries, in which everything will be accurately calculated and specified so that there'll be no more actions or adventures left on earth.

At that time, it's still you speaking, new economic relations will be established, all ready-made, also calculated with mathematical precision, so that all possible questions will disappear in a single instant, simply because all possible answers will have been provided. Then the crystal palace[1] will be built. And then . . . Well, in a word, those will be our halcyon days. Of course, there's no way to guarantee (now this is me talking) that it won't be, for instance, terribly boring then (because there won't be anything left to do, once everything has been calculated according to tables); on the other hand, everything will be extremely rational. Of course, what don't people think up out of boredom! Why, even gold pins get stuck into other people out of boredom, but that wouldn't matter. What's really bad (this is me talking again) is that for all I know, people might even be grateful for those gold pins. For man is stupid, phenomenally stupid. That is, although he's not really stupid at all, he's really so ungrateful that it's hard to find another being quite like him.

9. A reference to the last discourse of the French philosopher Denis Diderot (1713–1784) in the *Conversation of D'Alembert and Diderot* (1769).

1. An allusion to the crystal palace described in Vera Pavlovna's fourth dream in Chernyshevsky's *What Is to Be Done?* and to the actual building designed by Sir Joseph Paxton, erected for the Great Exhibition in London in 1851 and at that time admired as the newest wonder of architecture; Dostoevsky described it in *Winter Notes on Summer Impressions* (1863).

Why, I, for example, wouldn't be surprised in the least, if, suddenly, for no reason at all, in the midst of this future, universal rationalism, some gentleman with an offensive, rather, a retrograde and derisive expression on his face were to stand up, put his hands on his hips, and declare to us all: "How about it, gentlemen, what if we knock over all this rationalism with one swift kick for the sole purpose of sending all these logarithms to hell, so that once again we can live according to our own stupid will!" But that wouldn't matter either; what's so annoying is that he would undoubtedly find some followers; such is the way man is made. And all because of the most foolish reason, which, it seems, is hardly worth mentioning: namely, that man, always and everywhere, whoever he is, has preferred to act as he wished, and not at all as reason and advantage have dictated; one might even desire something opposed to one's own advantage, and sometimes (this is now my idea) one *positively must do so*. One's very own free, unfettered desire, one's own whim, no matter how wild, one's own fantasy, even though sometimes roused to the point of madness—all this constitutes precisely that previously omitted, most advantageous advantage which isn't included under any classification and because of which all systems and theories are constantly smashed to smithereens. Where did these sages ever get the idea that man needs any normal, virtuous desire? How did they ever imagine that man needs any kind of rational, advantageous desire? Man needs only one thing—his own *independent* desire, whatever that independence might cost and wherever it might lead. And as far as desire goes, the devil only knows. . . .

VIII

"Ha, ha, ha! But in reality even this desire, if I may say so, doesn't exist!" you interrupt me with a laugh. "Why science has already managed to dissect man so now we know that desire and so-called free choice are nothing more than . . ."

Wait, gentlemen, I myself wanted to begin like that. I must confess that even I got frightened. I was just about to declare that the devil only knows what desire depends on and perhaps we should be grateful for that, but then I remembered about science and I . . . stopped short. But now you've gone and brought it up. Well, after all, what if someday they really do discover the formula for all our desires and whims, that is, the thing that governs them, precise laws that produce them, how exactly they're applied, where they lead in each and every case, and so on and so forth, that is, the genuine mathematical formula—why, then all at once man might stop desiring, yes, indeed, he probably would. Who would want to desire according to some table? And that's not all: he would immediately be transformed from a person into an organ stop or something of that sort; because what is man without desire, without will, and without wishes if not a stop in an organ pipe? What do you think? Let's consider the probabilities—can this really happen or not?

"Hmmm . . . ," you decide, "our desires are mistaken for the most part because of an erroneous view of our own advantage. Consequently, we sometimes desire pure rubbish because, in our own stupidity, we consider it the easiest way to achieve some previously assumed advantage. Well, and when all this has been analyzed, calculated on paper (that's entirely possible, since it's repugnant and senseless to assume in advance that man will never come to understand the laws of nature) then, of course, all so-called desires will no longer exist. For if someday desires are completely reconciled with reason, we'll follow reason instead of desire simply because it would be impossible, for example, while retaining one's reason, to *desire* rubbish, and thus knowingly oppose one's reason, and desire something harmful to oneself. . . . And, since all desires and reasons can really be tabulated, since someday the laws of our so-called free choice are sure to be discovered, then, all joking aside, it may be possible to establish something like a table, so that we could actually desire according to it. If, for example, someday they calculate and demonstrate to me that I made a rude gesture because I couldn't possibly refrain from it, that I had to make precisely that gesture, well, in that case, what sort of *free choice* would there be, especially if I'm a learned man and have completed a course of study somewhere? Why, then I'd be able to calculate in advance my entire life for the next thirty years; in a word, if such a table were to be drawn up, there'd be nothing left for us to do; we'd simply have to accept it. In general, we should be repeating endlessly to ourselves that at such a time and in such circumstances nature certainly won't ask our opinion; that we must accept it as is, and not as we fantasize it, and that if we really aspire to prepare a table, a schedule, and, well . . . well, even a laboratory test tube, there's nothing to be done—one must even accept the test tube! If not, it'll be accepted even without you. . . ."

Yes, but that's just where I hit a snag! Gentlemen, you'll excuse me for all this philosophizing; it's a result of my forty years in the underground! Allow me to fantasize. Don't you see: reason is a fine thing, gentlemen, there's no doubt about it, but it's only reason, and it satisfies only man's rational faculty, whereas desire is a manifestation of all life, that is, of all human life, which includes both reason, as well as all of life's itches and scratches. And although in this manifestation life often turns out to be fairly worthless, it's life all the same, and not merely the extraction of square roots. Why, take me, for instance; I quite naturally want to live in order to satisfy all my faculties of life, not merely my rational faculty, that is, some one-twentieth of all my faculties. What does reason know? Reason knows only what it's managed to learn. (Some things it may never learn; while this offers no comfort, why not admit it openly?) But human nature acts as a whole, with all that it contains, consciously and unconsciously; and although it may tell lies, it's still alive. I suspect, gentlemen, that you're looking at me with compassion; you repeat that an enlightened and cultured man, in a word, man as he will be in the future, cannot knowingly desire something disadvantageous to himself, and that this is pure mathematics. I agree with you: it really is mathematics. But I repeat for the one-hundredth time, there is one case, only one, when a man may intentionally, consciously desire even something harmful to himself, something stupid, even very stupid, namely: in order *to have the right* to desire something even very stupid and not be bound by an obligation to desire only what's smart. After all, this very stupid thing, one's own whim, gentlemen, may in fact be the most advantageous thing on earth for people like me, especially in certain cases. In particular, it may be more advantageous than any other advantage, even in a case where it causes obvious harm and contradicts the most sensible conclusions of reason about advantage—because in any case it preserves for us what's most important and precious, that is, our personality and our individuality. There are some people who maintain that in fact this is more precious to man than anything else; of course, desire can, if it so chooses, coincide with reason, especially if it doesn't abuse this option, and chooses to coincide in moderation; this is useful and sometimes even commendable. But very often, even most of the time, desire absolutely and stubbornly disagrees with reason and . . . and . . . and, do you know, sometimes this is also useful and even very commendable? Let's assume, gentlemen, that man isn't stupid. (And really, this can't possibly be said about him at all, if only because if he's stupid, then who on earth is smart?) But even if he's not stupid, he is, nevertheless, monstrously ungrateful. Phenomenally ungrateful. I even believe that the best definition of man is this: a creature who walks on two legs and is ungrateful. But that's still not all; that's still not his main defect. His main defect is his perpetual misbehavior, perpetual from the time of the Great Flood to the Schleswig-Holstein period of human destiny. Misbehavior, and consequently, imprudence; for it's long been known that imprudence results from nothing else but misbehavior. Just cast a glance at the history of mankind; well, what do you see? Is it majestic? Well, perhaps it's majestic; why, the Colossus of Rhodes,[2] for example—that alone is worth something! Not without reason did Mr Anaevsky[3] report that some people consider it to be the product of human hands, while others maintain that it was created by nature itself. Is it colorful? Well, perhaps it's also colorful; just consider the dress uniforms, both military and civilian, of all nations at all times—why, that alone is worth something, and if you include everyday uniforms, it'll make your eyes bulge; not one historian will be able to sort it all out. Is it monotonous? Well, perhaps it's monotonous, too: men fight and fight; now they're fighting; they fought first and they fought last—you'll agree that it's really much too monotonous. In short, anything can be said about world history, anything that might occur to the most disordered imagination. There's only one thing that can't possibly be said about it—that it's rational. You'll choke on the word. Yet here's just the sort of thing you'll encounter all the time: why, in life you're constantly running up against people who are so well-behaved and so rational, such wise men and lovers of humanity who set themselves the lifelong goal of behaving as morally and rationally as possible, so to speak, to be a beacon for their nearest and dearest, simply in order to prove that it's really possible to live one's life in a moral and rational way. And so what? It's a well-known fact that many of these lovers of humanity, sooner or later, by the end of their lives, have betrayed themselves: they've pulled off some caper, sometimes even quite an indecent one. Now I ask you: what can one expect from man as a creature endowed with such strange qualities? Why, shower him with all sorts of earthly blessings, submerge him in happiness over his head so that only little bubbles appear on the surface of this happiness, as if on water, give him such economic prosperity that he'll have absolutely nothing left to do except sleep, eat gingerbread, and worry about the continuation of world history—even then, out of pure ingratitude, sheer perversity, he'll commit some repulsive act. He'll even risk losing his gingerbread, and will intentionally desire the most wicked rubbish, the most uneconomical absurdity, simply in order to inject his own pernicious fantastic element into all this positive rationality. He wants to hold onto those most fantastic dreams, his own indecent stupidity solely for the purpose of assur-

2. A large bronze statue of the Greek sun god, Helios, built between 292 and 280 B.C.E. in the harbor of Rhodes (an island in the Aegean Sea) and considered one of the Seven Wonders of the Ancient World.

3. A. E. Anaevsky was a critic whose articles were frequently ridiculed in literary polemics of the period.

ing himself (as if it were necessary) that men are still men and not piano keys, and that even if the laws of nature play upon them with their own hands, they're still threatened by being overplayed until they won't possibly desire anything more than a schedule. But that's not all: even if man really turned out to be a piano key, even if this could be demonstrated to him by natural science and pure mathematics, even then he still won't become reasonable; he'll intentionally do something to the contrary, simply out of ingratitude, merely to have his own way. If he lacks the means, he'll cause destruction and chaos, he'll devise all kinds of suffering and have his own way! He'll leash a curse upon the world; and, since man alone can do so (it's his privilege and the thing that most distinguishes him from other animals), perhaps only through this curse will he achieve his goal, that is, become really convinced that he's a man and not a piano key! If you say that one can also calculate all this according to a table, this chaos and darkness, these curses, so that the mere possibility of calculating it all in advance would stop everything and that reason alone would prevail—in that case man would go insane deliberately in order not to have reason, but to have his own way! I believe this, I vouch for it, because, after all, the whole of man's work seems to consist only in proving to himself constantly that he's a man and not an organ stop! Even if he has to lose his own skin, he'll prove it; even if he has to become a troglodyte, he'll prove it. And after that, how can one not sin, how can one not praise the fact that all this hasn't yet come to pass and that desire still depends on the devil knows what . . . ?

You'll shout at me (if you still choose to favor me with your shouts) that no one's really depriving me of my will; that they're merely attempting to arrange things so that my will, by its own free choice, will coincide with my normal interests, with the laws of nature, and with arithmetic.

But gentlemen, what sort of free choice will there be when it comes down to tables and arithmetic, when all that's left is two times two makes four? Two times two makes four even without my will. Is that what you call free choice?

IX

Gentlemen, I'm joking of course, and I myself know that it's not a very good joke; but, after all, you can't take everything as a joke. Perhaps I'm gnashing my teeth while I joke. I'm tormented by questions, gentlemen; answer them for me. Now, for example, you want to cure man of his old habits and improve his will according to the demands of science and common sense. But how do you know not only whether it's possible, but even if it's *necessary* to remake him in this way? Why do you conclude that human desire *must* undoubtedly be improved? In short, how do you know that such improvement will really be to man's advantage? And, to be perfectly frank, why are you so *absolutely* convinced that not to oppose man's real, normal advantage guaranteed by the conclusions of reason and arithmetic is really always to man's advantage and constitutes a law for all humanity? After all, this is still only an assumption of yours. Let's suppose that it's a law of logic, but perhaps not a law of humanity. Perhaps, gentlemen, you're wondering if I'm insane? Allow me to explain. I agree that man is primarily a creative animal, destined to strive consciously toward a goal and to engage in the art of engineering, that, is, externally and incessantly building new roads for himself *wherever they lead*. But sometimes he may want to swerve aside precisely because he's *compelled* to build these roads, and perhaps also because, no matter how stupid the spontaneous man of action may generally be, nevertheless it sometimes occurs to him that the road, as it turns out, almost always leads *somewhere or other*, and that the main thing isn't so much where it goes, but the fact that it does, and that the well-behaved child, disregarding the art of engineering, shouldn't yield to pernicious idleness which, as is well known, constitutes the mother of all vices. Man loves to create and build roads; that's indisputable. But why is he also so passionately fond of destruction and chaos? Now, then, tell me. But I myself want to say a few words about this separately. Perhaps the reason that he's so fond of destruction and chaos (after all, it's indisputable that he sometimes really loves it, and that's a fact) is that he himself has an instinctive fear of achieving his goal and completing the project under construction? How do you know if perhaps he loves his building only from afar, but not from close up; perhaps he only likes building it, but not living in it, leaving it afterward *aux animaux domestiques*,[4] such as ants or sheep, or so on and so forth. Now ants have altogether different tastes. They have one astonishing structure of a similar type, forever indestructible—the anthill.

The worthy ants began with the anthill, and most likely, they will end with the anthill, which does great credit to their perseverance and steadfastness. But man is a frivolous and unseemly creature and perhaps, like a chess player, he loves only the process of achieving his goal, and not the goal itself. And, who knows (one can't vouch for it), perhaps the only goal on earth toward which mankind is striving consists merely in this incessant process of achieving or to put it another way, in life itself, and not particularly in the goal which, of course, must always be none other than two times two makes four, that is, a formula; after all, two times two makes four is no longer life, gentlemen, but the beginning of death. At least man has always been somewhat afraid of this two times two makes four, and I'm afraid of it now, too. Let's suppose that the only thing man does is search for this two times two makes four; he sails across oceans, sacrifices his own life in the quest; but to seek it out and find it—really and truly, he's very frightened. After all, he feels that as soon as he finds it, there'll be nothing left to search for. Workers, after finishing work, at least receive their wages, go off to a tavern, and then wind up at a police station—now that's a full week's occupation. But where will man go? At any rate a certain awkwardness can be observed each time he approaches the achievement of similar goals. He loves the process, but he's not so fond of the achievement, and that, of course is terribly amusing. In short, man is made in a comical way; obviously there's some sort of catch in all this. But two times two makes four is an insufferable thing, nevertheless. Two times two makes four—why, in my opinion, it's mere insolence. Two times two makes four stands there brazenly with its hands on its hips, blocking your path and spitting at you. I agree that two times two makes four is a splendid thing; but if we're going to lavish praise, then two times two makes five is sometimes also a very charming little thing.

And why are you so firmly, so triumphantly convinced that only the normal and positive—in short, only well-being is advantageous to man? Doesn't reason ever make mistakes about advantage? After all, perhaps man likes some-

4. "To domestic animals" (French).

thing other than well-being? Perhaps he loves suffering just as much? Perhaps suffering is just as advantageous to him as well-being? Man sometimes loves suffering terribly, to the point of passion, and that's a fact. There's no reason to study world history on this point; if indeed you're a man and have lived at all, just ask yourself. As far as my own personal opinion is concerned, to love only well-being is somehow even indecent. Whether good or bad, it's sometimes also very pleasant to demolish something. After all, I'm not standing up for suffering here, nor for well-being, either. I'm standing up for . . . my own whim and for its being guaranteed to me whenever necessary. For instance, suffering is not permitted in vaudevilles,[5] that I know. It's also inconceivable in the crystal palace; suffering is doubt and negation. What sort of crystal palace would it be if any doubt were allowed? Yet, I'm convinced that man will never renounce real suffering, that is, destruction and chaos. After all, suffering is the sole cause of consciousness. Although I stated earlier that in my opinion consciousness is man's greatest misfortune, still I know that man loves it and would not exchange it for any other sort of satisfaction. Consciousness, for example, is infinitely higher than two times two. Of course, after two times two, there's nothing left, not merely nothing to do, but nothing to learn. Then the only thing possible will be to plug up your five senses and plunge into contemplation. Well, even if you reach the same result with consciousness, that is, having nothing left to do, at least you'll be able to flog yourself from time to time, and that will liven things up a bit. Although it may be reactionary, it's still better than nothing.

X[6]

You believe in the crystal palace, eternally indestructible, that is, one at which you can never stick out your tongue furtively nor make a rude gesture, even with your fist hidden away. Well, perhaps I'm so afraid of this building precisely because it's made of crystal and it's eternally indestructible, and because it won't be possible to stick one's tongue out even furtively.

Don't you see: if it were a chicken coop instead of a palace, and if it should rain, then perhaps I could crawl into it so as not to get drenched; but I would still not mistake a chicken coop for a palace out of gratitude, just because it sheltered me from the rain. You're laughing, you're even saying that in this case there's no difference between a chicken coop and a mansion. Yes, I reply, if the only reason for living is to keep from getting drenched.

But what if I've taken it into my head that this is not the only reason for living, and, that if one is to live at all, one might as well live in a mansion? Such is my wish, my desire. You'll expunge it from me only when you've changed my desires. Well, then, change them, tempt me with something else, give me some other ideal. In the meantime, I still won't mistake a chicken coop for a palace. But let's say that the crystal palace is a hoax, that according to the laws of nature it shouldn't exist, and that I've invented it only out of my own stupidity, as a result of certain antiquated, irrational habits of my generation. But what do I care if it doesn't exist? What difference does it make if

5. A dramatic genre, popular on the Russian stage, consisting of scenes from contemporary life acted with a satirical twist, often in racy dialogue.

6. This chapter was badly mutilated by the censor, as Dostoyevsky makes clear in the letter to his brother Mikhail, dated March 26, 1864.

it exists only in my own desires, or, to be more precise, if it exists as long as my desires exist? Perhaps you're laughing again? Laugh, if you wish; I'll resist all your laughter and I still won't say I'm satiated if I'm really hungry; I know all the same that I won't accept a compromise, an infinitely recurring zero, just because it exists according to the laws of nature and it *really* does exist. I won't accept as the crown of my desires a large building with tenements for poor tenants to be rented for a thousand years and, just in case, with the name of the dentist Wagenheim on the sign. Destroy my desires, eradicate my ideals, show me something better and I'll follow you. You may say, perhaps, that it's not worth getting involved; but, in that case, I'll say the same thing in reply. We're having a serious discussion; if you don't grant me your attention, I won't grovel for it. I still have my underground.

And, as long as I'm still alive and feel desire—may my arm wither away before it contributes even one little brick to that building! Never mind that I myself have just rejected the crystal palace for the sole reason that it won't be possible to tease it by sticking out one's tongue at it. I didn't say that because I'm so fond of sticking out my tongue. Perhaps the only reason I got angry is that among all your buildings there's still not a single one where you don't feel compelled to stick out your tongue. On the contrary, I'd let my tongue be cut off out of sheer gratitude, if only things could be so arranged that I'd no longer want to stick it out. What do I care if things can't be so arranged and if I must settle for some tenements? Why was I made with such desires? Can it be that I was made this way only in order to reach the conclusion that my entire way of being is merely a fraud? Can this be the whole purpose? I don't believe it.

By the way, do you know what? I'm convinced that we underground men should be kept in check. Although capable of sitting around quietly in the underground for some forty years, once he emerges into the light of day and bursts into speech, he talks on and on and on. . . .

XI

The final result, gentlemen, is that it's better to do nothing! Conscious inertia is better! And so, long live the underground! Even though I said that I envy the normal man to the point of exasperation, I still wouldn't want to be him under the circumstances in which I see him (although I still won't keep from envying him. No, no, in any case the underground is more advantageous!) At least there one can . . . Hey, but I'm lying once again! I'm lying because I know myself as surely as two times two, that it isn't really the underground that's better, but something different, altogether different, something that I long for, but I'll never be able to find! To hell with the underground! Why, here's what would be better: if I myself were to believe even a fraction of everything I've written. I swear to you, gentlemen, that I don't believe one word, not one little word of all that I've scribbled. That is, I do believe it, perhaps, but at the very same time, I don't know why, I feel and suspect that I'm lying like a trooper.

"Then why did you write all this?" you ask me.

"What if I'd shut you up in the underground for forty years with nothing to do and then came back forty years later to see what had become of you? Can a man really be left alone for forty years with nothing to do?"

"Isn't it disgraceful, isn't it humiliating!" you might say, shaking your head in contempt. "You long for life, but you try to solve life's problems by means of a logical tangle. How importunate, how insolent your outbursts, and how frightened you are at the same time! You talk rubbish, but you're constantly afraid of them and make apologies. You maintain that you fear nothing, but at the same time you try to ingratiate yourself with us. You assure us that you're gnashing your teeth, yet at the same time you try to be witty and amuse us. You know that your witticisms are not very clever, but apparently you're pleased by their literary merit. Perhaps you really have suffered, but you don't even respect your own suffering. There's some truth in you, too, but no chastity; out of the pettiest vanity you bring your truth out into the open, into the market-place, and you shame it. . . . You really want to say something, but you conceal your final word out of fear because you lack the resolve to utter it; you have only cowardly impudence. You boast about your consciousness, but you merely vacillate, because even though your mind is working, your heart has been blackened by depravity, and without a pure heart, there can be no full, genuine consciousness. And how importunate you are; how you force yourself upon others; you behave in such an affected manner. Lies, lies, lies!"

Of course, it was I who just invented all these words for you. That, too, comes from the underground. For forty years in a row I've been listening to all your words through a crack. I've invented them myself, since that's all that's occurred to me. It's no wonder that I've learned it all by heart and that it's taken on such a literary form. . . .

But can you really be so gullible as to imagine that I'll print all this and give it to you to read? And here's another problem I have: why do I keep calling you "gentlemen"? Why do I address you as if you really were my readers? Confessions such as the one I plan to set forth here aren't published and given to other people to read. Anyway, I don't possess sufficient fortitude, nor do I consider it necessary to do so. But don't you see, a certain notion has come into my mind, and I wish to realize it at any cost. Here's the point.

Every man has within his own reminiscences certain things he doesn't reveal to anyone, except, perhaps, to his friends. There are also some that he won't reveal even to his friends, only to himself perhaps, and even then, in secret. Finally, there are some which a man is afraid to reveal even to himself; every decent man has accumulated a fair number of such things. In fact, it can even be said that the more decent the man, the more of these things he's accumulated. Anyway, only recently I myself decided to recall some of my earlier adventures; up to now I've always avoided them, even with a certain anxiety. But having decided not only to recall them, but even to write them down, now is when I wish to try an experiment: is it possible to be absolutely honest even with one's own self and not to fear the whole truth? Incidentally, I'll mention that Heine maintains that faithful autobiographies are almost impossible, and that a man is sure to lie about himself.[7] In Heine's opinion, Rousseau, for example, undoubtedly told untruths about himself in his confession and even lied intentionally, out of vanity. I'm convinced that Heine is correct; I understand perfectly well that sometimes it's possible out

7. A reference to the work *On Germany* (1853–54) by the German poet Heinrich Heine (1797–1856), in which on the very first page Heine speaks of Rousseau as lying and inventing disgraceful incidents about himself for his *Confessions*.

of vanity alone to impute all sorts of crimes to oneself, and I can even understand what sort of vanity that might be. But Heine was making judgments about a person who confessed to the public. I, however, am writing for myself alone and declare once and for all that if I write as if I were addressing readers, that's only for show, because it's easier for me to write that way. It's a form, simply a form; I shall never have any readers. I've already stated that. . . . I don't want to be restricted in any way by editing my notes. I won't attempt to introduce any order or system. I'll write down whatever comes to mind.

Well, now, for example, someone might seize upon my words and ask me, if you really aren't counting on any readers, why do you make such compacts with yourself, and on paper no less; that is, if you're not going to introduce any order or system, if you're going to write down whatever comes to mind, etc., etc.? Why do you go on explaining? Why do you keep apologizing?

"Well, imagine that," I reply.

This, by the way, contains an entire psychology. Perhaps it's just that I'm a coward. Or perhaps it's that I imagine an audience before me on purpose, so that I behave more decently when I'm writing things down. There may be a thousand reasons.

But here's something else: why is it that I want to write? If it's not for the public, then why can't I simply recall it all in my own mind and not commit it to paper?

Quite so; but somehow it appears more dignified on paper. There's something more impressive about it; I'll be a better judge of myself; the style will be improved. Besides, perhaps I'll actually experience some relief from the process of writing it all down. Today, for example, I'm particularly oppressed by one very old memory from my distant past. It came to me vividly several days ago and since then it's stayed with me, like an annoying musical motif that doesn't want to leave you alone. And yet you must get rid of it. I have hundreds of such memories; but at times a single one emerges from those hundreds and oppresses me. For some reason I believe that if I write it down I can get rid of it. Why not try?

Lastly, I'm bored, and I never do anything. Writing things down actually seems like work. They say that work makes a man become good and honest. Well, at least there's chance.

It's snowing today, an almost wet, yellow, dull snow. It was snowing yesterday too, a few days ago as well. I think it was apropos of the wet snow that I recalled this episode and now it doesn't want to leave me alone. And so, let it be a tale apropos of wet snow.

II

Apropos of Wet Snow

When from the darkness of delusion
I saved your fallen soul
With ardent words of conviction,
And, full of profound torment,
Wringing your hands, you cursed
The vice that had ensnared you;

When, punishing by recollection
Your forgetful conscience,
You told me the tale
Of all that had happened before,
And, suddenly, covering your face,
Full of shame and horror,
You tearfully resolved,
Indignant, shaken . . .
Etc., etc., etc.
From the poetry of N. A. Nekrasov[8]

I

At that time I was only twenty-four years old. Even then my life was gloomy, disordered, and solitary to the point of savagery. I didn't associate with anyone; I even avoided talking, and I retreated further and further into my corner. At work in the office I even tried not to look at anyone; I was aware not only that my colleagues considered me eccentric, but that they always seemed to regard me with a kind of loathing. Sometimes I wondered why it was that no one else thinks that others regard him with loathing. One of our office-workers had a repulsive pock-marked face which even appeared somewhat villainous. It seemed to me that with such a disreputable face I'd never have dared look at anyone. Another man had a uniform so worn that there was a foul smell emanating from him. Yet, neither of these two gentlemen was embarrassed—neither because of his clothes, nor his face, nor in any moral way. Neither one imagined that other people regarded him with loathing; and if either had so imagined, it wouldn't have mattered at all, as long as their supervisor chose not to view him that way. It's perfectly clear to me now, because of my unlimited vanity and the great demands I accordingly made on myself, that I frequently regarded myself with a furious dissatisfaction verging on loathing; as a result, I intentionally ascribed my own view to everyone else. For example, I despised my own face; I considered it hideous, and I even suspected that there was something repulsive in its expression. Therefore, every time I arrived at work, I took pains to behave as independently as possible, so that I couldn't be suspected of any malice, and I tried to assume as noble an expression as possible. "It may not be a handsome face," I thought, "but let it be noble, expressive, and above all, extremely *intelligent*." But I was agonizingly certain that my face couldn't possibly express all these virtues. Worst of all, I considered it positively stupid. I'd have been reconciled if it had looked intelligent. In fact, I'd even have agreed to have it appear repulsive, on the condition that at the same time people would find my face terribly intelligent.

Of course, I hated all my fellow office-workers from the first to the last and despised every one of them; yet, at the same time it was as if I were afraid of them. Sometimes it happened that I would even regard them as superior to me. At this time these changes would suddenly occur: first I would despise them, then I would regard them as superior to me. A cultured and decent

8. A Russian poet and editor of radical sympathies (1821–1878). The poem quoted dates from 1845 and is untitled. It ends with the lines "And enter my house bold and free / To become its full mistress!"

man cannot be vain without making unlimited demands on himself and without hating himself, at times to the point of contempt. But, whether hating them or regarding them as superior, I almost always lowered my eyes when meeting anyone. I even conducted experiments: could I endure someone's gaze? I'd always be the first to lower my eyes. This infuriated me to the point of madness. I slavishly worshipped the conventional in everything external. I embraced the common practice and feared any eccentricity with all my soul. But how could I sustain it? I was morbidly refined, as befits any cultured man of our time. All others resembled one another as sheep in a flock. Perhaps I was the only one in the whole office who constantly thought of himself as a coward and a slave; and I thought so precisely because I was so cultured. But not only did I think so, it actually was so: I was a coward and a slave. I say this without any embarrassment. Every decent man of our time is and must be a coward and a slave. This is his normal condition. I'm deeply convinced of it. This is how he's made and what he's meant to be. And not only at the present time, as the result of some accidental circumstance, but in general at all times, a decent man must be a coward and a slave. This is a law of nature for all decent men on earth. If one of them should happen to be brave about something or other, we shouldn't be comforted or distracted: he'll still lose his nerve about something else. That's the single and eternal way out. Only asses and their mongrels are brave, and even then, only until they come up against a wall. It's not worthwhile paying them any attention because they really don't mean anything at all.

There was one more circumstance tormenting me at that time: no one was like me, and I wasn't like anyone else. "I'm alone," I mused, "and they are *everyone*"; and I sank deep into thought.

From all this it's clear that I was still just a boy.

The exact opposite would also occur. Sometimes I would find it repulsive to go to the office: it reached the point where I would often return home from work ill. Then suddenly, for no good reason at all, a flash of skepticism and indifference would set in (everything came to me in flashes); I would laugh at my own intolerance and fastidiousness, and reproach myself for my *romanticism*. Sometimes I didn't even want to talk to anyone; at other times it reached a point where I not only started talking, but I even thought about striking up a friendship with others. All my fastidiousness would suddenly disappear for no good reason at all. Who knows? Perhaps I never really had any, and it was all affected, borrowed from books. I still haven't answered this question, even up to now. And once I really did become friends with others; I began to visit their houses, play préférence,[9] drink vodka, talk about promotions. . . . But allow me to digress.

We Russians, generally speaking, have never had any of those stupid, transcendent German romantics, or even worse, French romantics, on whom nothing produces any effect whatever: the earth might tremble beneath them, all of France might perish on the barricades, but they remain the same, not even changing for decency's sake; they go on singing their transcendent songs, so to speak, to their dying day, because they're such fools. We here on Russian soil have no fools. It's a well-known fact; that's precisely what distin-

9. A card game for three players.

guishes us from foreigners. Consequently, transcendent natures cannot be found among us in their pure form. That's the result of our "positive" publicists and critics of that period, who hunted for the Kostanzhouglo and the Uncle Pyotr Ivanoviches,[1] foolishly mistaking them for our ideal and slandering our own romantics, considering them to be the same kind of transcendents as one finds in Germany or France. On the contrary, the characteristics of our romantics are absolutely and directly opposed to the transcendent Europeans; not one of those European standards can apply here. (Allow me to use the word "romantic"—it's an old-fashioned little word, well-respected and deserving, familiar to everyone.) The characteristics of our romantics are to understand everything, *to see everything, often to see it much more clearly than our most positive minds*; not to be reconciled with anyone or anything, but, at the same time, not to balk at anything; to circumvent everything, to yield on every point, to treat everyone diplomatically; never to lose sight of some useful, practical goal (an apartment at government expense, a nice pension, a decoration)—to keep an eye on that goal through all his excesses and his volumes of lyrical verse, and, at the same time, to preserve intact the "beautiful and sublime" to the end of their lives; and, incidentally, to preserve themselves as well, wrapped up in cotton like precious jewelry, if only, for example, for the sake of that same "beautiful and sublime." Our romantic has a very broad nature and is the biggest rogue of all, I can assure you of that . . . even by my own experience. Of course, all this is true if the romantic is smart. But what am I saying? A romantic is always smart; I merely wanted to observe that although we've had some romantic fools, they really don't count at all, simply because while still in their prime they would degenerate completely into Germans, and, in order to preserve their precious jewels more comfortably, they'd settle over there, either in Weimar or in the Black Forest. For instance, I genuinely despised my official position and refrained from throwing it over merely out of necessity, because I myself sat there working and received good money for doing it. And, as a result, please note, I still refrained from throwing it over. Our romantic would sooner lose his mind (which, by the way, very rarely occurs) than give it up, if he didn't have another job in mind; nor is he ever kicked out, unless he's hauled off to the insane asylum as the "King of Spain,"[2] and only if he's gone completely mad. Then again, it's really only the weaklings and towheads who go mad in our country. An enormous number of romantics later rise to significant rank. What extraordinary versatility! And what a capacity for the most contradictory sensations! I used to be consoled by these thoughts back then, and still am even nowadays. That's why there are so many "broad natures" among us, people who never lose their ideals, no matter how low they fall; even though they never lift a finger for the sake of their ideals, even though they're outrageous villains and thieves, nevertheless they respect their original ideals to

1. A character in Ivan Goncharov's novel *A Common Story* (1847); a high bureaucrat, a factory owner who teaches lessons of sobriety and good sense to the romantic hero, Alexander Aduyev. Konstanzhouglo is the ideal efficient landowner in the second part of Nikolai Gogol's novel *Dead Souls* (1852).

2. An allusion to the hero of Gogol's short story "Diary of a Madman" (1835). Poprishchin, a low-ranking civil servant, sees his aspirations crushed by the enormous bureaucracy. He ends by going insane and imagining himself to be king of Spain.

the point of tears and are extremely honest men at heart. Yes, only among us Russians can the most outrageous scoundrel be absolutely, even sublimely honest at heart, while at the same time never ceasing to be a scoundrel. I repeat, nearly always do our romantics turn out to be very efficient rascals (I use the word "rascal" affectionately); they suddenly manifest such a sense of reality and positive knowledge that their astonished superiors and the general public can only click their tongues at them in amazement.

Their versatility is really astounding; God only knows what it will turn into, how it will develop under subsequent conditions, and what it holds for us in the future. The material is not all that bad! I'm not saying this out of some ridiculous patriotism or jingoism. However, I'm sure that once again you think I'm joking. But who knows? Perhaps it's quite the contrary, that is, you're convinced that this is what I really think. In any case, gentlemen, I'll consider that both of these opinions constitute an honor and a particular pleasure. And do forgive me for this digression.

Naturally, I didn't sustain any friendships with my colleagues, and soon I severed all relations after quarreling with them; and, because of my youthful inexperience at the same time, I even stopped greeting them, as if I'd cut them off entirely. That, however, happened to me only once. On the whole, I was always alone.

At home I spent most of my time reading. I tried to stifle all that was constantly seething within me with external sensations. And of all external sensations available, only reading was possible for me. Of course, reading helped a great deal—it agitated, delighted, and tormented me. But at times it was terribly boring. I still longed to be active; and suddenly I sank into dark, subterranean, loathsome depravity—more precisely, petty vice. My nasty little passions were sharp and painful as a result of my constant, morbid irritability. I experienced hysterical fits accompanied by tears and convulsions. Besides reading, I had nowhere else to go—that is, there was nothing to respect in my surroundings, nothing to attract me. In addition, I was overwhelmed by depression; I possessed a hysterical craving for contradictions and contrasts; and, as a result, I plunged into depravity. I haven't said all this to justify myself. . . . But, no, I'm lying. I did want to justify myself. It's for myself, gentlemen, that I include this little observation. I don't want to lie. I've given my word.

I indulged in depravity all alone, at night, furtively, timidly, sordidly, with a feeling of shame that never left me even in my most loathsome moments and drove me at such times to the point of profanity. Even then I was carrying around the underground in my soul. I was terribly afraid of being seen, met, recognized. I visited all sorts of dismal places.

Once, passing by some wretched little tavern late at night, I saw through a lighted window some gentlemen fighting with billiard cues; one of them was thrown out the window. At some other time I would have been disgusted; but just then I was overcome by such a mood that I envied the gentleman who'd been tossed out; I envied him so much that I even walked into the tavern and entered the billiard room. "Perhaps," I thought, "I'll get into a fight, and they'll throw me out the window, too."

I wasn't drunk, but what could I do—after all, depression can drive a man to this kind of hysteria. But nothing came of it. It turned out that I was incapable of being tossed out the window; I left without getting into a fight.

As soon as I set foot inside, some officer put me in my place.

I was standing next to the billiard table inadvertently blocking his way as he wanted to get by; he took hold of me by the shoulders and without a word of warning or explanation, moved me from where I was standing to another place, and he went past as if he hadn't even noticed me. I could have forgiven even a beating, but I could never forgive his moving me out of the way and entirely failing to notice me.

The devil knows what I would have given for a genuine, ordinary quarrel, a decent one, a more *literary* one, so to speak. But I'd been treated as if I were a fly. The officer was about six feet tall, while I'm small and scrawny. The quarrel, however, was in my hands; all I had to do was protest, and of course they would've thrown me out the window. But I reconsidered and preferred . . . to withdraw resentfully.

I left the tavern confused and upset and went straight home; the next night I continued my petty vice more timidly, more furtively, more gloomily than before, as if I had tears in my eyes—but I continued nonetheless. Don't conclude, however, that I retreated from that officer as a result of any cowardice; I've never been a coward at heart, although I've constantly acted like one in deed, but—wait before you laugh—I can explain this. I can explain anything, you may rest assured.

Oh, if only this officer had been the kind who'd have agreed to fight a duel! But no, he was precisely one of those types (alas, long gone) who preferred to act with their billiard cues or, like Gogol's Lieutenant Pirogov,[3] by appealing to the authorities. They didn't fight duels; in any case, they'd have considered fighting a duel with someone like me, a lowly civilian, to be indecent. In general, they considered duels to be somehow inconceivable, free-thinking, French, while they themselves, especially if they happened to be six feet tall, offended other people rather frequently.

In this case I retreated not out of any cowardice, but because of my unlimited vanity. I wasn't afraid of his height, nor did I think I'd receive a painful beating and get thrown out the window. In fact, I'd have had sufficient physical courage; it was moral fortitude I lacked. I was afraid that everyone present—from the insolent billiard marker to the foul-smelling, pimply little clerks with greasy collars who used to hang about—wouldn't understand and would laugh when I started to protest and speak to them in literary Russian. Because, to this very day, it's still impossible for us to speak about a point of honor, that is, not about honor itself, but a point of honor (*point d'honneur*), except in literary language. One can't even refer to a "point of honor" in everyday language. I was fully convinced (a sense of reality, in spite of all my romanticism!) that they would all simply split their sides laughing, and that the officer, instead of giving me a simple beating, that is, an inoffensive one, would certainly apply his knee to my back and drive me around the billiard table; only then perhaps would he have the mercy to throw me out the window. Naturally, this wretched story of mine couldn't possibly end with this alone. Afterward I used to meet this officer frequently on the street and I observed him very carefully. I don't know whether he ever recognized me. Probably not; I reached that conclusion

3. One of two main characters in Gogol's short story "Nevsky Prospect" (1835). A shallow and self-satisfied officer, he mistakes the wife of a German artisan for a woman of easy virtue and receives a sound thrashing. He decides to lodge an official complaint but, after consuming a cream-filled pastry, thinks better of it.

from various observations. As for me, I stared at him with malice and hatred, and continued to do so for several years! My malice increased and became stronger over time. At first I began to make discreet inquiries about him. This was difficult for me to do, since I had so few acquaintances. But once, as I was following him at a distance as though tied to him, someone called to him on the street: that's how I learned his name. Another time I followed him back to his own apartment and for a ten-kopeck piece learned from the doorman where and how he lived, on what floor, with whom, etc.—in a word, all that could be learned from a doorman. One morning, although I never engaged in literary activities, it suddenly occurred to me to draft a description of this officer as a kind of exposé, a caricature, in the form of a tale. I wrote it with great pleasure. I exposed him; I even slandered him. At first I altered his name only slightly, so that it could be easily recognized; but then, upon careful reflection, I changed it. Then I sent the tale off to *Notes of the Fatherland*.[4] But such exposés were no longer in fashion, and they didn't publish my tale. I was very annoyed by that. At times I simply choked on my spite. Finally, I resolved to challenge my opponent to a duel. I composed a beautiful, charming letter to him, imploring him to apologize to me; in case he refused, I hinted rather strongly at a duel. The letter was composed in such a way that if that officer had possessed even the smallest understanding of the "beautiful and sublime," he would have come running, thrown his arms around me, and offered his friendship. That would have been splendid! We would have led such a wonderful life! Such a life! He would have shielded me with his rank; I would have ennobled him with my culture, and, well, with my ideas. Who knows what might have come of it! Imagine it, two years had already passed since he'd insulted me; my challenge was the most ridiculous anachronism, in spite of all the cleverness of my letter in explaining and disguising that fact. But, thank God (to this day I thank the Almighty with tears in my eyes), I didn't send that letter. A shiver runs up and down my spine when I think what might have happened if I had. Then suddenly . . . suddenly, I got my revenge in the simplest manner, a stroke of genius! A brilliant idea suddenly occurred to me. Sometimes on holidays I used to stroll along Nevsky Prospect at about four o'clock in the afternoon, usually on the sunny side. That is, I didn't really stroll; rather, I experienced innumerable torments, humiliations, and bilious attacks. But that's undoubtedly just what I needed. I darted in and out like a fish among the strollers, constantly stepping aside before generals, cavalry officers, hussars, and young ladies. At those moments I used to experience painful spasms in my heart and a burning sensation in my back merely at the thought of my dismal apparel as well as the wretchedness and vulgarity of my darting little figure. This was sheer torture, uninterrupted and unbearable humiliation at the thought, which soon became an incessant and immediate sensation, that I was a fly in the eyes of society, a disgusting, obscene fly—smarter than the rest, more cultured, even nobler—all that goes without saying, but a fly, nonetheless, who incessantly steps aside, insulted and injured by everyone. For what reason did I inflict this torment on myself? Why did I stroll along Nevsky Prospect? I don't know. But something simply *drew* me there at every opportunity.

Then I began to experience surges of that pleasure about which I've already spoken in the first chapter. After the incident with the officer I was drawn

4. A radical literary and political journal published in St. Petersburg from 1839 to 1867.

there even more strongly; I used to encounter him along Nevsky most often, and it was there that I could admire him. He would also go there, mostly on holidays. He, too, would give way before generals and individuals of superior rank; he, too, would spin like a top among them. But he would simply trample people like me, or even those slightly superior; he would walk directly toward them, as if there were empty space ahead of him; and under no circumstance would he ever step aside. I revelled in my malice as I observed him, and . . . bitterly stepped aside before him every time. I was tortured by the fact that even on the street I found it impossible to stand on an equal footing with him. "Why is it you're always first to step aside?" I badgered myself in insane hysteria, at times waking up at three in the morning. "Why always you and not he? After all, there's no law about it; it isn't written down anywhere. Let it be equal, as it usually is when people of breeding meet: he steps aside halfway and you halfway, and you pass by showing each other mutual respect." But that was never the case, and I continued to step aside, while he didn't even notice that I was yielding to him. Then a most astounding idea suddenly dawned on me. "What if," I thought, "what if I were to meet him and . . . not step aside? Deliberately not step aside, even if it meant bumping into him: how would that be?" This bold idea gradually took such a hold that it afforded me no peace. I dreamt about it incessantly, horribly, and even went to Nevsky more frequently so that I could imagine more clearly how I would do it. I was in ecstasy. The scheme was becoming more and more possible and even probable to me. "Of course, I wouldn't really collide with him," I thought, already feeling more generous toward him in my joy, "but I simply won't turn aside. I'll bump into him, not very painfully, but just so, shoulder to shoulder, as much as decency allows. I'll bump into him the same amount as he bumps into me." At last I made up my mind completely. But the preparations took a very long time. First, in order to look as presentable as possible during the execution of my scheme, I had to worry about my clothes. "In any case, what if, for example, it should occasion a public scandal? (And the public there was *superflu*:[5] a countess, Princess D., and the entire literary world.) It was essential to be well-dressed; that inspires respect and in a certain sense will place us immediately on an equal footing in the eyes of high society." With that goal in mind I requested my salary in advance, and I purchased a pair of black gloves and a decent hat at Churkin's store. Black gloves seemed to me more dignified, more *bon ton*[6] than the lemon-colored ones I'd considered at first. "That would be too glaring, as if the person wanted to be noticed"; so I didn't buy the lemon-colored ones. I'd already procured a fine shirt with white bone cufflinks; but my overcoat constituted a major obstacle. In and of itself it was not too bad at all; it kept me warm; but it was quilted and had a raccoon collar, the epitome of bad taste. At all costs I had to replace the collar with a beaver one, just like on an officer's coat. For this purpose I began to frequent the Shopping Arcade; and, after several attempts, I turned up some cheap German beaver. Although these German beavers wear out very quickly and soon begin to look shabby, at first, when they're brand new, they look very fine indeed; after all, I only needed it for a single occasion. I asked the price: it was still expensive. After considerable reflection I resolved to sell my raccoon collar. I decided to request

5. "Excessively refined" (French).

6. "In good taste" (French).

a loan for the remaining amount—a rather significant sum for me—from Anton Antonych Setochkin, my office chief, a modest man, but a serious and solid one, who never lent money to anyone, but to whom, upon entering the civil service, I'd once been specially recommended by an important person who'd secured the position for me. I suffered terribly. It seemed monstrous and shameful to ask Anton Antonych for money. I didn't sleep for two or three nights in a row; in general I wasn't getting much sleep those days, and I always had a fever. I would have either a vague sinking feeling in my heart, or else my heart would suddenly begin to thump, thump, thump! . . . At first Anton Antonych was surprised, then he frowned, thought it over, and finally gave me the loan, after securing from me a note authorizing him to deduct the sum from my salary two weeks later. In this way everything was finally ready; the splendid beaver reigned in place of the mangy raccoon, and I gradually began to get down to business. It was impossible to set about it all at once, in a foolhardy way; one had to proceed in this matter very carefully, step by step. But I confess that after many attempts I was ready to despair: we didn't bump into each other, no matter what! No matter how I prepared, no matter how determined I was—it seems that we're just about to bump, when I look up—and once again I've stepped aside while he's gone by without even noticing me. I even used to pray as I approached him that God would grant me determination. One time I'd fully resolved to do it, but the result was that I merely stumbled and fell at his feet because, at the very last moment, only a few inches away from him, I lost my nerve. He stepped over me very calmly, and I bounced to one side like a rubber ball. That night I lay ill with a fever once again and was delirious. Then, everything suddenly ended in the best possible way. The night before I decided once and for all not to go through with my pernicious scheme and to give it all up without success; with that in mind I went to Nevsky Prospect for one last time simply in order to see how I'd abandon the whole thing. Suddenly, three paces away from my enemy, I made up my mind unexpectedly; I closed my eyes and—we bumped into each other forcefully, shoulder to shoulder! I didn't yield an inch and walked by him on a completely equal footing! He didn't even turn around to look at me and pretended that he hadn't even noticed; but he was merely pretending, I'm convinced of that. To this very day I'm convinced of that! Naturally, I got the worst of it; he was stronger, but that wasn't the point. The point was that I'd achieved my goal, I'd maintained my dignity, I hadn't yielded one step, and I'd publicly placed myself on an equal social footing with him. I returned home feeling completely avenged for everything. I was ecstatic. I rejoiced and sang Italian arias. Of course, I won't describe what happened to me three days later; if you've read the first part entitled "Underground," you can guess for yourself. The officer was later transferred somewhere else; I haven't seen him for some fourteen years. I wonder what he's doing nowadays, that dear friend of mine! Whom is he trampling underfoot?

II

But when this phase of my nice, little dissipation ended I felt terribly nauseated. Remorse set in; I tried to drive it away because it was too disgusting. Little by little, however, I got used to that, too. I got used to it all; that is, it wasn't that I got used to it, rather, I somehow voluntarily consented to endure it. But I had a way out that reconciled everything—to escape into "all that was beautiful and sublime," in my dreams, of course. I was a terrible dreamer; I dreamt for three months in a row, tucked away in my little corner. And well you may believe that in those moments I was not at all like the gentleman who, in his faint-hearted anxiety, had sewn a German beaver onto the collar of his old overcoat. I suddenly became a hero. If my six-foot-tall lieutenant had come to see me then, I'd never have admitted him. I couldn't even conceive of him at that time. It's hard to describe now what my dreams consisted of then, and how I could've been so satisfied with them, but I was. Besides, even now I can take pride in them at certain times. My dreams were particularly sweet and vivid after my little debauchery; they were filled with remorse and tears, curses and ecstasy. There were moments of such positive intoxication, such happiness, that I felt not even the slightest trace of mockery within me, really and truly. It was all faith, hope and love. That's just it: at the time I believed blindly that by some kind of miracle, some external circumstance, everything would suddenly open up and expand; a vista of appropriate activity would suddenly appear—beneficent, beautiful, and most of all, *ready-made* (what precisely, I never knew, but, most of all, it had to be ready-made), and that I would suddenly step forth into God's world, almost riding on a white horse and wearing a laurel wreath. I couldn't conceive of a secondary role; and that's precisely why in reality I very quietly took on the lowest one. Either a hero or dirt—there was no middle ground. That was my ruin because in the dirt I consoled myself knowing that at other times I was a hero, and that the hero covered himself with dirt; that is to say, an ordinary man would be ashamed to wallow in filth, but a hero is too noble to become defiled; consequently, he can wallow. It's remarkable that these surges of everything "beautiful and sublime" occurred even during my petty depravity, and precisely when I'd sunk to the lowest depths. They occurred in separate spurts, as if to remind me of themselves; however, they failed to banish my depravity by their appearance. On the contrary, they seemed to add spice to it by means of contrast; they came in just the right amount to serve as a tasty sauce. This sauce consisted of contradictions, suffering, and agonizing internal analysis; all of these torments and trifles lent a certain piquancy, even some meaning to my depravity—in a word, they completely fulfilled the function of a tasty sauce. Nor was all this even lacking in a measure of profundity. Besides, I would never have consented to the simple, tasteless, spontaneous little debauchery of an ordinary clerk and have endured all that filth! How could it have attracted me then and lured me into the street late at night? No, sir, I had a noble loophole for everything. . . .

But how much love, oh Lord, how much love I experienced at times in those dreams of mine, in those "escapes into everything beautiful and sublime." Even though it was fantastic love, even though it was never directed at anything human, there was still so much love that afterward, in reality, I no longer felt any impulse to direct it: that would have been an unnecessary luxury. However, everything always ended in a most satisfactory way by a lazy and intoxicating transition into art, that is, into beautiful forms of being, ready-made, largely borrowed from poets and novelists, and adapted to serve every possible need. For instance, I would triumph over everyone; naturally, everyone else grovelled in the dust and was voluntarily impelled to acknowledge my superiority, while I would forgive them all for everything. Or else, being a famous poet and chamberlain, I would fall in love; I'd receive an enormous fortune and would immediately sacrifice it all for the benefit of humanity, at the same time confessing before all peoples my own infamies, which, needless to say, were not simple infamies, but contained a great amount of "the beautiful and sublime," something in the style of Manfred.[7] Everyone would weep and kiss me (otherwise what idiots they would have been), while I went about barefoot and hungry preaching new ideas and defeating all the reactionaries of Austerlitz.[8] Then a march would be played, a general amnesty declared, and the Pope would agree to leave Rome and go to Brazil;[9] a ball would be hosted for all of Italy at the Villa Borghese on the shores of Lake Como,[1] since Lake Como would have been moved to Rome for this very occasion; then there would be a scene in the bushes, etc., etc.—as if you didn't know. You'll say that it's tasteless and repugnant to drag all this out into the open after all the raptures and tears to which I've confessed. But why is it so repugnant? Do you really think I'm ashamed of all this or that it's any more stupid than anything in your own lives, gentlemen? Besides, you can rest assured that some of it was not at all badly composed. . . . Not everything occurred on the shores of Lake Como. But you're right; in fact, it is tasteless and repugnant. And the most repugnant thing of all is that now I've begun to justify myself before you. And even more repugnant is that now I've made that observation. But enough, otherwise there'll be no end to it: each thing will be more repugnant than the last. . . .

I was never able to dream for more than three months in a row, and I began to feel an irresistible urge to plunge into society. To me plunging into society meant paying a visit to my office chief, Anton Antonych Setochkin. He's the only lasting acquaintance I've made during my lifetime; I too now marvel at this circumstance. But even then I would visit him only when my dreams had reached such a degree of happiness that it was absolutely essential for me to embrace people and all humanity at once; for that reason I needed to have at least one person on hand who actually existed. However, one could only call upon Anton Antonych on Tuesdays (his receiving day); consequently, I always had to adjust the urge to embrace all humanity so that it occurred on Tuesday. This Anton Antonych lived near Five Corners,[2] on the fourth floor, in four small, low-ceilinged rooms, each smaller than the last, all very frugal and yellowish in appearance. He lived with his two daughters and an aunt who used to serve tea. The daughters, one thirteen, the other fourteen, had little snub noses. I was very embarrassed by them because they used to whisper all the time and giggle to each other. The host usually sat in his study on a leather couch in front of a table together with some gray-haired guest, a civil servant either from our office or another one. I never saw more than two or three guests there, and

7. The romantic hero of Byron's poetic tragedy *Manfred* (1817), a lonely, defiant figure whose past conceals some mysterious crime.

8. The site of Napoleon's great victory in December 1805 over the combined armies of the Russian tsar Alexander I and the Austrian emperor Francis II.

9. Napoleon announced his annexation of the Papal States to France in 1809 and was promptly excommunicated by Pope Pius VII. The pope was imprisoned and forced to sign a new concordat, but in 1814 he returned to Rome in triumph.

1. Located in the foothills of the Italian Alps in Lombardy. Villa Borghese was the elegant summer palace built by Scipione Cardinal Borghese outside the Porta del Popolo in Rome.

2. A well-known landmark in St. Petersburg.

they were always the same ones. They talked about excise taxes, debates in the Senate, salaries, promotions, His Excellency and how to please him, and so on and so forth. I had the patience to sit there like a fool next to these people for four hours or so; I listened without daring to say a word to them or even knowing what to talk about. I sat there in a stupor; several times I broke into a sweat; I felt numbed by paralysis; but it was good and useful. Upon returning home I would postpone for some time my desire to embrace all humanity.

I had one other sort of acquaintance, however, named Simonov, a former schoolmate of mine. In fact, I had a number of schoolmates in Petersburg, but I didn't associate with them, and I'd even stopped greeting them along the street. I might even have transferred into a different department at the office so as not to be with them and to cut myself off from my hated childhood once and for all. Curses on that school and those horrible years of penal servitude. In short, I broke with my schoolmates as soon as I was released. There remained only two or three people whom I would greet upon encountering them. One was Simonov, who hadn't distinguished himself in school in any way; he was even-tempered and quiet, but I detected in him a certain independence of character, even honesty. I don't even think that he was all that limited. At one time he and I experienced some rather bright moments, but they didn't last very long and somehow were suddenly clouded over. Evidently he was burdened by these recollections, and seemed in constant fear that I would lapse into that former mode. I suspect that he found me repulsive, but not being absolutely sure, I used to visit him nonetheless.

So once, on a Thursday, unable to endure my solitude, and knowing that on that day Anton Antonych's door was locked, I remembered Simonov. As I climbed the stairs to his apartment on the fourth floor, I was thinking how burdensome this man found my presence and that my going to see him was rather useless. But since it always turned out, as if on purpose, that such reflections would impel me to put myself even further into an ambiguous situation, I went right in. It had been almost a year since I'd last seen Simonov.

III

I found two more of my former schoolmates there with him. Apparently they were discussing some important matter. None of them paid any attention to me when I entered, which was strange since I hadn't seen them for several years. Evidently they considered me some sort of ordinary house fly. They hadn't even treated me like that when we were in school together, although they'd all hated me. Of course, I understood that they must despise me now for my failure in the service and for the fact that I'd sunk so low, was badly dressed, and so on, which, in their eyes, constituted proof of my ineptitude and insignificance. But I still hadn't expected such a degree of contempt. Simonov was even surprised by my visit. All this disconcerted me; I sat down in some distress and began to listen to what they were saying.

The discussion was serious, even heated, and concerned a farewell dinner which these gentlemen wanted to organize jointly as early as the following day for their friend Zverkov, an army officer who was heading for a distant province. Monsieur Zverkov had also been my schoolmate all along. I'd begun to hate him especially in the upper grades. In the lower grades he was merely an attractive, lively lad whom everyone liked. However, I'd hated him in the lower grades, too, precisely because he was such an attractive, lively lad. He was perpetually a poor student and had gotten worse as time went on; he managed to graduate, however, because he had influential connections. During his last year at school he'd come into an inheritance of some two hundred serfs, and, since almost all the rest of us were poor, he'd even begun to brag. He was an extremely uncouth fellow, but a nice lad nonetheless, even when he was bragging. In spite of our superficial, fantastic, and high-flown notions of honor and pride, all of us, except for a very few, would fawn upon Zverkov, the more so the more he bragged. They didn't fawn for any advantage; they fawned simply because he was a man endowed by nature with gifts. Moreover, we'd somehow come to regard Zverkov as a cunning fellow and an expert on good manners. This latter point particularly infuriated me. I hated the shrill, self-confident tone of his voice, his adoration for his own witticisms, which were terribly stupid in spite of his bold tongue; I hated his handsome, stupid face (for which, however, I'd gladly have exchanged my own intelligent one), and the impudent bearing typical of officers during the 1840s. I hated the way he talked about his future successes with women. (He'd decided not to get involved with them yet, since he still hadn't received his officer's epaulettes; he awaited those epaulettes impatiently.) And he talked about all the duels he'd have to fight. I remember how once, although I was usually very taciturn, I suddenly clashed with Zverkov when, during our free time, he was discussing future exploits with his friends; getting a bit carried away with the game like a little puppy playing in the sun, he suddenly declared that not a single girl in his village would escape his attention—that it was his *droit de seigneur*,[3] and that if the peasants even dared protest, he'd have them all flogged, those bearded rascals; and he'd double their quit-rent.[4] Our louts applauded, but I attacked him—not out of any pity for the poor girls or their fathers, but simply because everyone else was applauding such a little insect. I got the better of him that time, but Zverkov, although stupid, was also cheerful and impudent. Therefore he laughed it off to such an extent that, in fact, I really didn't get the better of him. The laugh remained on his side. Later he got the better of me several times, but without malice, just so, in jest, in passing, in fun. I was filled with spite and hatred, but I didn't respond. After graduation he took a few steps toward me; I didn't object strongly because I found it flattering; but soon we came to a natural parting of the ways. Afterward I heard about his barrack-room successes as a lieutenant and about his *binges*. Then there were other rumors—about his *successes* in the service. He no longer bowed to me on the street; I suspected that he was afraid to compromise himself by acknowledging such an insignificant person as myself. I also saw him in the theater once, in the third tier, already sporting an officer's gold braids. He was fawning and grovelling before the daughters of some aged general. In those three years he'd let himself go, although he was still as handsome and agile as before; he sagged somehow and had begun to put on weight; it was clear that by the age of thirty he'd be totally

3. "Lord's privilege" (French); the feudal lord's right to spend the first night with the bride of a newly married serf.

4. The annual sum paid in cash or produce by serfs to landowners for the right to farm their land in feudal Russia, as opposed to the *corvée*, a certain amount of labor owed.

flabby. So it was for this Zverkov, who was finally ready to depart, that our schoolmates were organizing a farewell dinner. They'd kept up during these three years, although I'm sure that inwardly they didn't consider themselves on an equal footing with him.

One of Simonov's two guests was Ferfichkin, a Russified German, a short man with a face like a monkey, a fool who made fun of everybody, my bitterest enemy from the lower grades—a despicable, impudent show-off who affected the most ticklish sense of ambition, although, of course, he was a coward at heart. He was one of Zverkov's admirers and played up to him for his own reasons, frequently borrowing money from him. Simonov's other guest, Trudolyubov, was insignificant, a military man, tall, with a cold demeanor, rather honest, who worshipped success of any kind and was capable of talking only about promotions. He was a distant relative of Zverkov's, and that, silly to say, lent him some importance among us. He'd always regarded me as a nonentity; he treated me not altogether politely, but tolerably.

"Well, if each of us contributes seven rubles," said Trudolyubov, "with three of us that makes twenty-one altogether—we can have a good dinner. Of course, Zverkov won't have to pay."

"Naturally," Simonov agreed, "since we're inviting him."

"Do you really think," Ferfichkin broke in arrogantly and excitedly, just like an insolent lackey bragging about his master-the-general's medals, "do you really think Zverkov will let us pay for everything? He'll accept out of decency, but then he'll order *half a dozen bottles* on his own."

"What will the four of us do with half a dozen bottles?" asked Trudolyubov, only taking note of the number.

"So then, three of us plus Zverkov makes four, twenty-one rubles, in the Hôtel de Paris, tomorrow at five o'clock," concluded Simonov definitively, since he'd been chosen to make the arrangements.

"Why only twenty-one?" I asked in trepidation, even, apparently, somewhat offended. "If you count me in, you'll have twenty-eight rubles instead of twenty-one."

It seemed to me that to include myself so suddenly and unexpectedly would appear as quite a splendid gesture and that they'd all be smitten at once and regard me with respect.

"Do you really want to come, too?" Simonov inquired with displeasure, managing somehow to avoid looking at me. He knew me inside out.

It was infuriating that he knew me inside out.

"And why not? After all, I was his schoolmate, too, and I must admit that I even feel a bit offended that you've left me out," I continued, just about to boil over again.

"And how were we supposed to find you?" Ferfichkin interjected rudely.

"You never got along very well with Zverkov," added Trudolyubov frowning. But I'd already latched on and wouldn't let go.

"I think no one has a right to judge that," I objected in a trembling voice, as if God knows what had happened. "Perhaps that's precisely why I want to take part now, since we didn't get along so well before."

"Well, who can figure you out . . . such lofty sentiments . . . ," Trudolyubov said with an ironic smile.

"We'll put your name down," Simonov decided, turning to me. "Tomorrow at five o'clock at the Hôtel de Paris. Don't make any mistakes."

"What about the money?" Ferfichkin started to say in an undertone to Simonov while nodding at me, but he broke off because Simonov looked embarrassed.

"That'll do," Trudolyubov said getting up. "If he really wants to come so much, let him."

"But this is our own circle of friends," Ferfichkin grumbled, also picking up his hat. "It's not an official gathering. Perhaps we really don't want you at all. . . ."

They left. Ferfichkin didn't even say goodbye to me as he went out; Trudolyubov barely nodded without looking at me. Simonov, with whom I was left alone, was irritated and perplexed, and he regarded me in a strange way. He neither sat down nor invited me to.

"Hmmm . . . yes . . . , so, tomorrow. Will you contribute your share of the money now? I'm asking just to know for sure," he muttered in embarrassment.

I flared up; but in doing so, I remembered that I'd owed Simonov fifteen rubles for a very long time, which debt, moreover, I'd forgotten, but had also never repaid.

"You must agree, Simonov, that I couldn't have known when I came here . . . oh, what a nuisance, but I've forgotten. . . ."

He broke off and began to pace around the room in even greater irritation. As he paced, he began to walk on his heels and stomp more loudly.

"I'm not detaining you, am I?" I asked after a few moments of silence.

"Oh, no!" he replied with a start. "That is, in fact, yes. You see, I still have to stop by at . . . It's not very far from here . . . ," he added in an apologetic way with some embarrassment.

"Oh, good heavens! Why didn't you say so?" I exclaimed, seizing my cap; moreover I did so with a surprisingly familiar air, coming from God knows where.

"But it's really not far . . . only a few steps away . . . ," Simonov repeated, accompanying me into the hallway with a bustling air which didn't suit him well at all. "So, then, tomorrow at five o'clock sharp!" he shouted to me on the stairs. He was very pleased that I was leaving. However, I was furious.

"What possessed me, what on earth possessed me to interfere?" I gnashed my teeth as I walked along the street. "And for such a scoundrel, a pig like Zverkov! Naturally, I shouldn't go. Of course, to hell with them. Am I bound to go, or what? Tomorrow I'll inform Simonov by post. . . ."

But the real reason I was so furious was that I was sure I'd go. I'd go on purpose. The more tactless, the more indecent it was for me to go, the more certain I'd be to do it.

There was even a definite impediment to my going: I didn't have any money. All I had was nine rubles. But of those, I had to hand over seven the next day to my servant Apollon for his monthly wages; he lived in and received seven rubles for his meals.

Considering Apollon's character it was impossible not to pay him. But more about that rascal, that plague of mine, later.

In any case, I knew that I wouldn't pay him his wages and that I'd definitely go.

That night I had the most hideous dreams. No wonder: all evening I was burdened with recollections of my years of penal servitude at school and I couldn't get rid of them. I'd been sent off to that school by distant relatives on whom I was dependent and about whom I've heard nothing since. They dispatched me, a lonely boy, crushed by their reproaches, already introspective, taciturn, and regarding everything around him savagely. My schoolmates received me with spiteful and pitiless jibes because I wasn't like any of them. But I couldn't tolerate their jibes; I couldn't possibly get along with them as easily as they got along with each other. I hated them all at once and took refuge from everyone in fearful, wounded and excessive pride. Their crudeness irritated me. Cynically they mocked my face and my awkward build; yet, what stupid faces they all had! Facial expressions at our school somehow degenerated and became particularly stupid. Many attractive lads had come to us, but in a few years they too were repulsive to look at. When I was only sixteen I wondered about them gloomily; even then I was astounded by the pettiness of their thoughts and the stupidity of their studies, games and conversations. They failed to understand essential things and took no interest in important, weighty subjects, so that I couldn't help considering them beneath me. It wasn't my wounded vanity that drove me to it; and, for God's sake, don't repeat any of those nauseating and hackneyed clichés, such as, "I was merely a dreamer, whereas they already understood life." They didn't understand a thing, not one thing about life, and I swear, that's what annoyed me most about them. On the contrary, they accepted the most obvious, glaring reality in a fantastically stupid way, and even then they'd begun to worship nothing but success. Everything that was just, but oppressed and humiliated, they ridiculed hard-heartedly and shamelessly. They mistook rank for intelligence; at the age of sixteen they were already talking about occupying comfortable little niches. Of course, much of this was due to their stupidity and the poor examples that had constantly surrounded them in their childhood and youth. They were monstrously depraved. Naturally, even this was more superficial, more affected cynicism; of course, their youth and a certain freshness shone through their depravity; but even this freshness was unattractive and manifested itself in a kind of rakishness. I hated them terribly, although, perhaps, I was even worse than they were. They returned the feeling and didn't conceal their loathing for me. But I no longer wanted their affection; on the contrary, I constantly longed for their humiliation. In order to avoid their jibes, I began to study as hard as I could on purpose and made my way to the top of the class. That impressed them. In addition, they all began to realize that I'd read certain books which they could never read and that I understood certain things (not included in our special course) about which they'd never even heard. They regarded this with savagery and sarcasm, but they submitted morally, all the more since even the teachers paid me some attention on this account. Their jibes ceased, but their hostility remained, and relations between us became cold and strained. In the end I myself couldn't stand it: as the years went by, my need for people, for friends, increased. I made several attempts to get closer to some of them; but these attempts always turned out to be unnatural and ended of their own accord. Once I even had a friend of sorts. But I was already a despot at heart; I wanted to exercise unlimited power over his soul; I wanted to instill in him contempt for his surroundings; and I demanded from him a disdainful and definitive break with those surroundings. I frightened him with my passionate friendship, and I reduced him to tears and convulsions. He was a naive and giving soul, but as soon as he'd surrendered himself to me totally, I began to despise him and reject him immediately—as if I only needed to achieve a victory over him, merely to subjugate him. But I was unable to conquer them all; my one friend was not at all like them, but rather a rare exception. The first thing I did upon leaving school was abandon the special job in the civil service for which I'd been trained, in order to sever all ties, break with my past, cover it over with dust. . . . The devil only knows why, after all that, I'd dragged myself over to see this Simonov! . . .

Early the next morning I roused myself from bed, jumped up in anxiety, just as if everything was about to start happening all at once. But I believed that some radical change in my life was imminent and was sure to occur that very day. Perhaps because I wasn't used to it, but all my life, at any external event, albeit a trivial one, it always seemed that some sort of radical change would occur. I went off to work as usual, but returned home two hours earlier in order to prepare. The most important thing, I thought, was not to arrive there first, or else they'd all think I was too eager. But there were thousands of most important things, and they all reduced me to the point of impotence. I polished my boots once again with my own hands. Apollon wouldn't polish them twice in one day for anything in the world; he considered it indecent. So I polished them myself, after stealing the brushes from the hallway so that he wouldn't notice and then despise me for it afterward. Next I carefully examined my clothes and found that everything was old, shabby, and worn out. I'd become too slovenly. My uniform was in better shape, but I couldn't go to dinner in a uniform. Worst of all, there was an enormous yellow stain on the knee of my trousers. I had an inkling that the spot alone would rob me of nine-tenths of my dignity. I also knew that it was unseemly for me to think that. "But this isn't the time for thinking. Reality is now looming," I thought, and my heart sank. I also knew perfectly well at that time, that I was monstrously exaggerating all these facts. But what could be done? I was no longer able to control myself, and was shaking with fever. In despair I imagined how haughtily and coldly that "scoundrel" Zverkov would greet me; with what dull and totally relentless contempt that dullard Trudolyubov would regard me; how nastily and impudently that insect Ferfichkin would giggle at me in order to win Zverkov's approval; how well Simonov would understand all this and how he'd despise me for my wretched vanity and cowardice; and worst of all, how petty all this would be, not *literary*, but commonplace. Of course, it would have been better not to go at all. But that was no longer possible; once I began to feel drawn to something, I plunged right in, head first. I'd have reproached myself for the rest of my life: "So, you retreated, you retreated before reality, you retreated!" On the contrary, I desperately wanted to prove to all this "rabble" that I really wasn't the coward I imagined myself to be. But that's not all: in the strongest paroxysm of cowardly fever I dreamt of gaining the upper hand, of conquering them, of carrying them away, compelling them to love me—if only "for the nobility of my thought and my indisputable wit." They would abandon Zverkov; he'd sit by in silence and embarassment, and I'd crush him. Afterward, perhaps, I'd be reconciled with Zverkov and drink to our *friendship*, but what was most spiteful and insulting for me was that I knew even then, I knew completely and for sure, that I didn't need any of this at all; that in fact I really didn't want to crush them, conquer them, or attract them, and that if I could have ever achieved all that, I'd be the first to say that it wasn't worth a damn. Oh, how I prayed to God that this day would pass quickly! With inexpressible anxiety I approached the window, opened the transom,[5] and peered out into the murky mist of the thickly falling wet snow. . . .

At last my worthless old wall clock sputtered out five o'clock. I grabbed my hat, and, trying not to look at Apollon—who'd been waiting since early morning to receive his wages, but didn't want to be the first one to mention it out of pride—I slipped out the door past him and intentionally hired a smart cab with my last half-ruble in order to arrive at the Hôtel de Paris in style.

IV

I knew since the day before that I'd be the first one to arrive. But it was no longer a question of who was first.

Not only was no one else there, but I even had difficulty finding our room. The table hadn't even been set. What did it all mean? After many inquiries I finally learned from the waiters that dinner had been ordered for closer to six o'clock, instead of five. This was also confirmed in the buffet. It was too embarrassing to ask any more questions. It was still only twenty-five minutes past five. If they'd changed the time, they should have let me know; that's what the city mail was for. They shouldn't have subjected me to such "shame" in my own eyes and . . . and, at least not in front of the waiters. I sat down. A waiter began to set the table. I felt even more ashamed in his presence. Toward six o'clock candles were brought into the room in addition to the lighted lamps already there, yet it hadn't occurred to the waiters to bring them in as soon as I'd arrived. In the next room two gloomy customers, angry-looking and silent, were dining at separate tables. In one of the distant rooms there was a great deal of noise, even shouting. One could hear the laughter of a whole crowd of people, including nasty little squeals in French—there were ladies present at that dinner. In short, it was disgusting. Rarely had I passed a more unpleasant hour, so that when they all arrived together precisely at six o'clock, I was initially overjoyed to see them, as if they were my liberators, and I almost forgot that I was supposed to appear offended.

Zverkov, obviously the leader, entered ahead of the rest. Both he and they were laughing; but, upon seeing me, Zverkov drew himself up, approached me unhurriedly, bowed slightly from the waist almost coquettishly, and extended his hand politely, but not too, with a kind of careful civility, almost as if he were a general both offering his hand, but also guarding against something. I'd imagined, on the contrary, that as soon as he entered he'd burst into his former, shrill laughter with occasional squeals, and that he'd immediately launch into his stale jokes and witticisms. I'd been preparing for them since the previous evening; but in no way did I expect such condescension, such courtesy characteristic of a general. Could it be that he now considered himself so immeasurably superior to me in all respects? If he'd merely wanted to offend me by this superior attitude, it wouldn't have been so bad, I thought; I'd manage to pay him back somehow. But what if, without any desire to offend, the notion had crept into his dumb sheep's brain that he

5. A small hinged pane in the window of a Russian house, used for ventilation especially during the winter when the main part of the window is sealed.

really was immeasurably superior to me and that he could only treat me in a patronizing way? From this possibility alone I began to gasp for air.

"Have you been waiting long?" Trudolyubov asked.

"I arrived at five o'clock sharp, just as I was told yesterday," I answered loudly and with irritation presaging an imminent explosion.

"Didn't you let him know that we changed the time?" Trudolyubov asked, turning to Simonov.

"No, I didn't. I forgot," he replied, but without any regret; then, not even apologizing to me, he went off to order the hors d'oeuvres.

"So you've been here for a whole hour, you poor fellow!" Zverkov cried sarcastically, because according to his notions, this must really have been terribly amusing. That scoundrel Ferfichkin chimed in after him with nasty, ringing laughter that sounded like a dog's yapping. My situation seemed very amusing and awkward to him, too.

"It's not the least bit funny!" I shouted at Ferfichkin, getting more and more irritated. "The others are to blame, not me. They neglected to inform me. It's, it's, it's . . . simply preposterous."

"It's not only preposterous, it's more than that," muttered Trudolyubov, naively interceding on my behalf. "You're being too kind. It's pure rudeness. Of course, it wasn't intentional. And how could Simonov have . . . hmm!"

"If a trick like that had been played on me," said Ferfichkin, "I'd . . ."

"Oh, you'd have ordered yourself something to eat," interrupted Zverkov, "or simply asked to have dinner served without waiting for the rest of us."

"You'll agree that I could've done that without asking anyone's permission," I snapped. "If I did wait, it was only because . . ."

"Let's be seated, gentlemen," cried Simonov upon entering. "Everything's ready. I can vouch for the champagne; it's excellently chilled. . . . Moreover, I didn't know where your apartment was, so how could I find you?" he said turning to me suddenly, but once again not looking directly at me. Obviously he was holding something against me. I suspect he got to thinking after what had happened yesterday.

Everyone sat down; I did, too. The table was round. Trudolyubov sat on my left, Simonov, on my right. Zverkov sat across; Ferfichkin, next to him, between Trudolyubov and him.

"Tell-l-l me now, are you . . . in a government department?" Zverkov continued to attend to me. Seeing that I was embarrassed, he imagined in earnest that he had to be nice to me, encouraging me to speak. "Does he want me to throw a bottle at his head, or what?" I thought in a rage. Unaccustomed as I was to all this, I was unnaturally quick to take offense.

"In such and such an office," I replied abruptly, looking at my plate.

"And . . . is it p-p-profitable? Tell-l-l me, what ma-a-de you decide to leave your previous position?"

"What ma-a-a-a-de me leave my previous position was simply that I wanted to," I dragged my words out three times longer than he did, hardly able to control myself. Ferfichkin snorted. Simonov looked at me ironically; Trudolyubov stopped eating and began to stare at me with curiosity.

Zverkov was jarred, but didn't want to show it.

"Well-l, and how is the support?"

"What support?"

"I mean, the s-salary?"

"Why are you cross-examining me?"

However, I told him right away what my salary was. I blushed terribly.

"That's not very much," Zverkov observed pompously.

"No, sir, it's not enough to dine in café-restaurants!" added Ferfichkin insolently.

"In my opinion, it's really very little," Trudolyubov observed in earnest.

"And how thin you've grown, how you've changed . . . since . . . ," Zverkov added, with a touch of venom now, and with a kind of impudent sympathy, examining me and my apparel.

"Stop embarrassing him," Ferfichkin cried with a giggle.

"My dear sir, I'll have you know that I'm not embarrassed," I broke in at last. "Listen! I'm dining in this 'café-restaurant' at my own expense, my own, not anyone else's; note that, Monsieur Ferfichkin."

"Wha-at? And who isn't dining at his own expense? You seem to be . . ." Ferfichkin seized hold of my words, turned as red as a lobster, and looked me straight in the eye with fury.

"Just so-o," I replied, feeling that I'd gone a bit too far, "and I suggest that it would be much better if we engaged in more intelligent conversation."

"It seems that you're determined to display your intelligence."

"Don't worry, that would be quite unnecessary here."

"What's all this cackling, my dear sir? Huh? Have you taken leave of your senses in that *duh*-partment of yours?"

"Enough, gentlemen, enough," cried Zverkov authoritatively.

"How stupid this is!" muttered Simonov.

"Really, it is stupid. We're gathered here in a congenial group to have a farewell dinner for our good friend, while you're still settling old scores," Trudolyubov said, rudely addressing only me. "You forced yourself upon us yesterday; don't disturb the general harmony now. . . ."

"Enough, enough," cried Zverkov. "Stop it, gentlemen, this'll never do. Let me tell you instead how I very nearly got married a few days ago . . ."

There followed some scandalous, libelous anecdote about how this gentleman very nearly got married a few days ago. There wasn't one word about marriage, however; instead, generals, colonels, and even gentlemen of the bed chamber figured prominently in the story, while Zverkov played the leading role among them all. Approving laughter followed; Ferfichkin even squealed.

Everyone had abandoned me by now, and I sat there completely crushed and humiliated.

"Good Lord, what kind of company is this for me?" I wondered. "And what a fool I've made of myself in front of them all! But I let Ferfichkin go too far. These numbskulls think they're doing me an honor by allowing me to sit with them at their table, when they don't understand that it's I who's done them the honor, and not the reverse. 'How thin I've grown! What clothes!' Oh, these damned trousers! Zverkov's already noticed the yellow spot on my knee. . . . What's the use? Right now, this very moment, I should stand up, take my hat, and simply leave without saying a single word. . . . Out of contempt! And tomorrow—I'll even be ready for a duel. Scoundrels! It's not the seven rubles I care about. But they may think that . . . To hell with it! I don't care about the seven rubles. I'm leaving at once! . . ."

Of course, I stayed.

In my misery I drank Lafite and sherry by the glassful. Being unaccustomed to it, I got drunk very quickly; the more intoxicated I became, the greater my annoyance. Suddenly I felt like offending them all in the most impudent manner—and then I'd leave. To seize the moment and show them all who I really was—let them say: even though he's ridiculous, he's clever . . . and . . . and . . . in short, to hell with them!

I surveyed them all arrogantly with my dazed eyes. But they seemed to have forgotten all about me. *They* were noisy, boisterous and merry. Zverkov kept on talking. I began to listen. He was talking about some magnificent lady whom he'd finally driven to make a declaration of love. (Of course, he was lying like a trooper.) He said that he'd been assisted in this matter particularly by a certain princeling, the hussar Kolya, who possessed some three thousand serfs.

"And yet, this same Kolya who has three thousand serfs hasn't even come to see you off," I said, breaking into the conversation suddenly. For a moment silence fell.

"You're drunk already," Trudolyubov said, finally deigning to notice me, and glancing contemptuously in my direction. Zverkov examined me in silence as if I were an insect. I lowered my eyes. Simonov quickly began to pour champagne.

Trudolyubov raised his glass, followed by everyone but me.

"To your health and to a good journey!" he cried to Zverkov. "To old times, gentlemen, and to our future, hurrah!"

Everyone drank up and pressed around to exchange kisses with Zverkov. I didn't budge; my full glass stood before me untouched.

"Aren't you going to drink?" Trudolyubov roared at me, having lost his patience and turning to me menacingly.

"I wish to make my own speech, all by myself . . . and then I'll drink, Mr. Trudolyubov."

"Nasty shrew!" Simonov muttered.

I sat up in my chair, feverishly seized hold of my glass, and prepared for something extraordinary, although I didn't know quite what I'd say.

"*Silence!*" cried Ferfichkin. "And now for some real intelligence!" Zverkov waited very gravely, aware of what was coming.

"Mr. Lieutenant Zverkov," I began, "you must know that I detest phrases, phrasemongers, and corsetted waists. . . . That's the first point; the second will follow."

Everyone stirred uncomfortably.

"The second point: I hate obscene stories and the men who tell them.[6] I especially hate the men who tell them!"

"The third point: I love truth, sincerity and honesty," I continued almost automatically, because I was beginning to become numb with horror, not knowing how I could be speaking this way. . . . "I love thought, Monsieur Zverkov. I love genuine comradery, on an equal footing, but not . . . hmmm . . . I

6. A phrase borrowed from the inveterate liar Nozdryov, one of the provincial landowners in the first volume of Gogol's *Dead Souls* (1842).

love . . . But, after all, why not? I too will drink to your health, Monsieur Zverkov. Seduce those Circassian[7] maidens, shoot the enemies of the fatherland, and . . . and . . . To your health, Monsieur Zverkov!"

Zverkov rose from his chair, bowed, and said: "I'm most grateful."

He was terribly offended and had even turned pale.

"To hell with him," Trudolyubov roared, banging his fist down on the table.

"No, sir, people should be whacked in the face for saying such things!" squealed Ferfichkin.

"We ought to throw him out!" muttered Simonov.

"Not a word, gentlemen, not a move!" Zverkov cried triumphantly, putting a stop to this universal indignation. "I'm grateful to you all, but I can show him myself how much I value his words."

"Mr. Ferfichkin, tomorrow you'll give me satisfaction for the words you've just uttered!" I said loudly, turning to Ferfichkin with dignity.

"Do you mean a duel? Very well," he replied, but I must have looked so ridiculous as I issued my challenge, it must have seemed so out of keeping with my entire appearance, that everyone, including Ferfichkin, collapsed into laughter.

"Yes, of course, throw him out! Why, he's quite drunk already," Trudolyubov declared in disgust.

"I shall never forgive myself for letting him join us," Simonov muttered again.

"Now's the time to throw a bottle at the lot of them," I thought. So I grabbed a bottle and . . . poured myself another full glass.

". . . No, it's better to sit it out to the very end!" I went on thinking. "You'd be glad, gentlemen, if I left. But nothing doing! I'll stay here deliberately and keep on drinking to the very end, as a sign that I accord you no importance whatsoever. I'll sit here and drink because this is a tavern, and I've paid good money to get in. I'll sit here and drink because I consider you to be so many pawns, nonexistent pawns. I'll sit here and drink . . . and sing too, if I want to, yes, sir, I'll sing because I have the right to . . . sing . . . hmm."

But I didn't sing. I just tried not to look at any of them; I assumed the most carefree poses and waited impatiently until they would be the first to speak to me. But, alas, they did not. How much, how very much I longed to be reconciled with them at that moment! The clock struck eight, then nine. They moved from the table to the sofa. Zverkov sprawled on the couch, placing one foot on the round table. They brought the wine over, too. He really had ordered three bottles at his own expense. Naturally, he didn't invite me to join them. Everyone surrounded him on the sofa. They listened to him almost with reverence. It was obvious they liked him. "What for? What for?" I wondered to myself. From time to time they were moved to drunken ecstasy and exchanged kisses. They talked about the Caucasus,[8] the nature of true passion, card games, profitable positions in the service; they talked about the income of a certain hussar Podkharzhevsky, whom none of them knew personally, and

7. Women from the region between the Black Sea and the Caspian Sea, famous for their beauty and much in demand as concubines in the Ottoman Empire.

8. Region in which various peoples opposed Russian rule, and thus a constant source of trouble for the Russian Empire.

they rejoiced that his income was so large; they talked about the unusual beauty and charm of Princess D., whom none of them had ever seen; finally, they arrived at the question of Shakespeare's immortality.

I smiled contemptuously and paced up and down the other side of the room, directly behind the sofa, along the wall from the table to the stove and back again. I wanted to show them with all my might that I could get along without them; meanwhile, I deliberately stomped my boots, thumping my heels. But all this was in vain. *They* paid me no attention. I had the forbearance to pace like that, right in front of them, from eight o'clock until eleven, in the very same place, from the table to the stove and from the stove back to the table. "I'm pacing just as I please, and no one can stop me." A waiter who came into the room paused several times to look at me; my head was spinning from all those turns; there were moments when it seemed that I was delirious. During those three hours I broke out in a sweat three times and then dried out. At times I was pierced to the heart with a most profound, venomous thought: ten years would pass, twenty, forty; and still, even after forty years, I'd remember with loathing and humiliation these filthiest, most absurd, and horrendous moments of my entire life. It was impossible to humiliate myself more shamelessly or more willingly, and I fully understood that, fully; nevertheless, I continued to pace from the table to the stove and back again. "Oh, if you only knew what thoughts and feelings I'm capable of, and how cultured I really am!" I thought at moments, mentally addressing the sofa where my enemies were seated. But my enemies behaved as if I weren't even in the room. Once, and only once, they turned to me, precisely when Zverkov started in about Shakespeare, and I suddenly burst into contemptuous laughter. I snorted so affectedly and repulsively that they broke off their conversation immediately and stared at me in silence for about two minutes, in earnest, without laughing, as I paced up and down, from the table to the stove, while *I paid not the slightest bit of attention to them.* But nothing came of it; they didn't speak to me. A few moments later they abandoned me again. The clock struck eleven.

"Gentlemen," exclaimed Zverkov, getting up from the sofa, "Now let's all go *to that place*."[9]

"Of course, of course!" the others replied.

I turned abruptly to Zverkov. I was so exhausted, so broken, that I'd have slit my own throat to be done with all this! I was feverish; my hair, which had been soaked through with sweat, had dried and now stuck to my forehead and temples.

"Zverkov, I ask your forgiveness," I said harshly and decisively. "Ferfichkin, yours too, and everyone's, everyone's. I've insulted you all!"

"Aha! So a duel isn't really your sort of thing!" hissed Ferfichkin venomously.

His remark was like a painful stab to my heart.

"No, I'm not afraid of a duel, Ferfichkin! I'm ready to fight with you tomorrow, even after we're reconciled. I even insist upon it, and you can't refuse me. I want to prove that I'm not afraid of a duel. You'll shoot first, and I'll fire into the air."

"He's amusing himself," Simonov observed.

9. I.e., a brothel.

"He's simply taken leave of his senses!" Trudolyubov added.

"Allow us to pass; why are you blocking our way? . . . Well, what is it you want?" Zverkov asked contemptuously. They were all flushed, their eyes glazed. They'd drunk a great deal.

"I ask for your friendship, Zverkov, I've insulted you, but . . ."

"Insulted me? You? In-sul-ted me? My dear sir, I want you to know that never, under any circumstances, could you possibly insult *me*!"

"And that's enough from you. Out of the way!" Trudolyubov added. "Let's go."

"Olympia is mine, gentlemen, that's agreed!" cried Zverkov.

"We won't argue, we won't," they replied, laughing.

I stood there as if spat on. The party left the room noisily, and Trudolyubov struck up a stupid song. Simonov remained behind for a brief moment to tip the waiters. All of a sudden I went up to him.

"Simonov! Give me six rubles," I said decisively and desperately.

He looked at me in extreme amazement with his dulled eyes. He was drunk, too.

"Are you really going *to that place* with us?"

"Yes!"

"I have no money!" he snapped; then he laughed contemptuously and headed out of the room.

I grabbed hold of his overcoat. It was a nightmare.

"Simonov! I know that you have some money. Why do you refuse me? Am I really such a scoundrel? Beware of refusing me: if you only knew, if you only knew why I'm asking. Everything depends on it, my entire future, all my plans. . . ."

Simonov took out the money and almost threw it at me.

"Take it, if you have no shame!" he said mercilessly, then ran out to catch up with the others.

I remained behind for a minute. The disorder, the leftovers, a broken glass on the floor, spilled wine, cigarette butts, drunkenness and delirium in my head, agonizing torment in my heart; and finally, a waiter who'd seen and heard everything and who was now looking at me with curiosity.

"To that place!" I cried. "Either they'll all fall on their knees, embracing me, begging for my friendship, or . . . or else, I'll give Zverkov a slap in the face."

V

"So here it is, here it is at last, a confrontation with reality," I muttered, rushing headlong down the stairs. "This is no longer the Pope leaving Rome and going to Brazil; this is no ball on the shores of Lake Como!"

"You're a scoundrel," the thought flashed through my mind, "if you laugh at that now."

"So what!" I cried in reply. "Everything is lost now, anyway!"

There was no sign of them, but it didn't matter. I knew where they were going.

At the entrance stood a solitary, late-night cabby in a coarse peasant coat powdered with wet, seemingly warm snow that was still falling. It was steamy and stuffy outside. The little shaggy piebald nag was also dusted with snow and was coughing; I remember that very well. I headed for the rough-hewn sledge; but as soon as I raised one foot to get in, the recollection of how Simonov had just given me six rubles hit me with such force that I tumbled into the sledge like a sack.

"No! There's a lot I have to do to make up for that!" I cried. "But make up for it I will or else I'll perish on the spot this very night. Let's go!" We set off. There was an entire whirlwind spinning around inside my head.

"They won't fall on their knees to beg for my friendship. That's a mirage, an indecent mirage, disgusting, romantic, and fantastic; it's just like the ball on the shores of Lake Como. Consequently, I *must* give Zverkov a slap in the face! I am obligated to do it. And so, it's all decided; I'm rushing there to give him a slap in the face."

"Hurry up!"

The cabby tugged at the reins.

"As soon as I go in, I'll slap him. Should I say a few words first before I slap him in the face? No! I'll simply go in and slap him. They'll all be sitting there in the drawing room; he'll be on the sofa with Olympia. That damned Olympia! She once ridiculed my face and refused me. I'll drag Olympia around by the hair and Zverkov by the ears. No, better grab one ear and lead him around the room like that. Perhaps they'll begin to beat me, and then they'll throw me out. That's even likely. So what? I'll still have slapped him first; the initiative will be mine. According to the laws of honor, that's all that matters. He'll be branded, and nothing can wipe away that slap except a duel.[1] He'll have to fight. So just let them beat me now! Let them, the ingrates! Trudolyubov will hit me hardest, he's so strong. Ferfichkin will sneak up alongside and will undoubtedly grab my hair, I'm sure he will. But let them, let them. That's why I've come. At last these blockheads will be forced to grasp the tragedy in all this! As they drag me to the door, I'll tell them that they really aren't even worth the tip of my little finger!"

"Hurry up, driver, hurry up!" I shouted to the cabby.

He was rather startled and cracked his whip. I'd shouted very savagely.

"We'll fight at daybreak, and that's settled. I'm through with the department. Ferfichkin recently said duh-partment, instead of department. But where will I get pistols? What nonsense! I'll take my salary in advance and buy them. And powder? Bullets? That's what the second will attend to. And how will I manage to do all this by daybreak? And where will I find a second? I have no acquaintances. . . ."

"Nonsense!" I shouted, whipping myself up into even more of a frenzy, "Nonsense!"

"The first person I meet on the street will have to act as my second, just as he would pull a drowning man from the water. The most extraordinary possibilities have to be allowed for. Even if tomorrow I were to ask the director himself to act as my second, he too would have to agree merely out of a sense of chivalry, and he would keep it a secret! Anton Antonych . . ."

The fact of the matter was that at that very moment I was more clearly and vividly aware than anyone else on earth of the disgusting absurdity of my intentions and the whole opposite side of the coin, but . . .

"Hurry up, driver, hurry, you rascal, hurry up!"

1. Duels as a means of resolving points of honor were officially discouraged but still fairly common.

"Hey, sir!" that son of the earth replied.

A sudden chill came over me.

"Wouldn't it be better . . . wouldn't it be better . . . to go straight home right now? Oh, my God! Why, why did I invite myself to that dinner yesterday? But no, it's impossible. And my pacing for three hours from the table to the stove? No, they, and no one else will have to pay me back for that pacing! They must wipe out that disgrace!"

"Hurry up!"

"What if they turn me over to the police? They wouldn't dare! They'd be afraid of a scandal. And what if Zverkov refuses the duel out of contempt? That's even likely; but I'll show them. . . . I'll rush to the posting station when he's supposed to leave tomorrow; I'll grab hold of his leg, tear off his overcoat just as he's about to climb into the carriage. I'll fasten my teeth on his arm and bite him. 'Look, everyone, see what a desperate man can be driven to!' Let him hit me on the head while others hit me from behind. I'll shout to the whole crowd, 'Behold, here's a young puppy who's going off to charm Circassian maidens with my spit on his face!'"

"Naturally, it'll all be over after that. The department will banish me from the face of the earth. They'll arrest me, try me, drive me out of the service, send me to prison; ship me off to Siberia for resettlement. Never mind! Fifteen years later when they let me out of jail, a beggar in rags, I'll drag myself off to see him. I'll find him in some provincial town. He'll be married and happy. He'll have a grown daughter. . . . I'll say, 'Look, you monster, look at my sunken cheeks and my rags. I've lost everything—career, happiness, art, science, a *beloved woman*—all because of you. Here are the pistols. I came here to load my pistol, and . . . and I forgive you.' Then I'll fire into the air, and he'll never hear another word from me again. . . ."

I was actually about to cry, even though I knew for a fact at that very moment that all this was straight out of Silvio and Lermontov's *Masquerade*.[2] Suddenly I felt terribly ashamed, so ashamed that I stopped the horse, climbed out of the sledge, and stood there amidst the snow in the middle of the street. The driver looked at me in amazement and sighed.

What was I to do? I couldn't go there—that was absurd; and I couldn't drop the whole thing, because then it would seem like . . . Oh, Lord! How could I drop it? After such insults!

"No!" I cried, throwing myself back into the sledge. "It's predestined; it's fate! Drive on, hurry up, *to that place*!"

In my impatience, I struck the driver on the neck with my fist.

"What's the matter with you? Why are you hitting me?" cried the poor little peasant, whipping his nag so that she began to kick up her hind legs.

Wet snow was falling in big flakes; I unbuttoned my coat, not caring about the snow. I forgot about everything else because now, having finally resolved on the slap, *I felt with horror that it was imminent* and that *nothing on earth could possibly stop it*. Lonely street lamps shone gloomily in the snowy mist like torches at a funeral. Snow got in under my overcoat, my jacket, and my necktie, and melted there. I didn't button up; after all, everything was lost,

2. A drama by Mikhail Lermontov (1835) about romantic conventions of love and honor. Silvio is the protagonist of Alexander Pushkin's short story "The Shot" (1830), about a man dedicated to revenge. Both works conclude with bizarre twists.

anyway. At last we arrived. I jumped out, almost beside myself, ran up the stairs, and began to pound at the door with my hands and feet. My legs, especially my knees, felt terribly weak. The door opened rather quickly; it was as if they knew I was coming. (In fact, Simonov had warned them that there might be someone else, since at this place one had to give notice and in general take precautions. It was one of those "fashionable shops" of the period that have now been eliminated by the police. During the day it really was a shop; but in the evening men with recommendations were able to visit as guests.) I walked rapidly through the darkened shop into a familiar drawing-room where there was only one small lit candle, and I stopped in dismay: there was no one there.

"Where are they?" I asked.

Naturally, by now they'd all dispersed. . . .

Before me stood a person with a stupid smile, the madam herself, who knew me slightly. In a moment a door opened, and another person came in.

Without paying much attention to anything, I walked around the room, and, apparently, was talking to myself. It was as if I'd been delivered from death, and I felt it joyously in my whole being. I'd have given him the slap, certainly, I'd certainly have given him the slap. But now they weren't here and . . . everything had vanished, everything had changed! . . . I looked around. I still couldn't take it all in. I glanced up mechanically at the girl who'd come in: before me there flashed a fresh, young, slightly pale face with straight dark brows and a serious, seemingly astonished look. I liked that immediately; I would have hated her if she'd been smiling. I began to look at her more carefully, as though with some effort: I'd still not managed to collect my thoughts. There was something simple and kind in her face, but somehow it was strangely serious. I was sure that she was at a disadvantage as a result, and that none of those fools had even noticed her. She couldn't be called a beauty, however, even though she was tall, strong, and well built. She was dressed very simply. Something despicable took hold of me; I went up to her. . . .

I happened to glance into a mirror. My overwrought face appeared extremely repulsive: it was pale, spiteful and mean; and my hair was dishevelled. "It doesn't matter. I'm glad," I thought. "In fact, I'm even delighted that I'll seem so repulsive to her; that pleases me. . . ."

VI

Somewhere behind a partition a clock was wheezing as if under some strong pressure, as though someone were strangling it. After this unnaturally prolonged wheezing there followed a thin, nasty, somehow unexpectedly hurried chime, as if someone had suddenly leapt forward. It struck two. I recovered, although I really hadn't been asleep, only lying there half-conscious.

It was almost totally dark in the narrow, cramped, low-ceilinged room, which was crammed with an enormous wardrobe and cluttered with cartons, rags, and all sorts of old clothes. The candle burning on the table at one end of the room flickered faintly from time to time, and almost went out completely. In a few moments total darkness would set in.

It didn't take long for me to come to my senses; all at once, without any effort, everything returned to me, as though it had been lying in ambush ready to pounce on me again. Even in my unconscious state some point had constantly remained in my memory, never to be forgotten, around which my sleepy visions had gloomily revolved. But it was a strange thing: everything that had happened to me that day now seemed, upon awakening, to have occurred in the distant past, as if I'd long since left it all behind.

My mind was in a daze. It was as though something were hanging over me, provoking, agitating, and disturbing me. Misery and bile were welling inside me, seeking an outlet. Suddenly I noticed beside me two wide-open eyes, examining me curiously and persistently. The gaze was coldly detached, sullen, as if belonging to a total stranger. I found it oppressive.

A dismal thought was conceived in my brain and spread throughout my whole body like a nasty sensation, such as one feels upon entering a damp, mouldy underground cellar. It was somehow unnatural that only now these two eyes had decided to examine me. I also recalled that during the course of the last two hours I hadn't said one word to this creature, and that I had considered it quite unnecessary; that had even given me pleasure for some reason. Now I'd suddenly realized starkly how absurd, how revolting as a spider, was the idea of debauchery, which, without love, crudely and shamelessly begins precisely at the point where genuine love is consummated. We looked at each other in this way for some time, but she didn't lower her gaze before mine, nor did she alter her stare, so that finally, for some reason, I felt very uneasy.

"What's your name?" I asked abruptly, to put an end to it quickly.

"Liza," she replied, almost in a whisper, but somehow in a very unfriendly way; and she turned her eyes away.

I remained silent.

"The weather today . . . snow . . . foul!" I observed, almost to myself, drearily placing one arm behind my head and staring at the ceiling.

She didn't answer. The whole thing was obscene.

"Are you from around here?" I asked her a moment later, almost angrily, turning my head slightly toward her.

"No."

"Where are you from?"

"Riga," she answered unwillingly.

"German?"

"No, Russian."

"Have you been here long?"

"Where?"

"In this house."

"Two weeks." She spoke more and more curtly. The candle had gone out completely; I could no longer see her face.

"Are your mother and father still living?"

"Yes . . . no . . . they are."

"Where are they?"

"There . . . in Riga."

"Who are they?"

"Just . . ."

"Just what? What do they do?"

"Tradespeople."

"Have you always lived with them?"

"Yes."

"How old are you?"

"Twenty."

"Why did you leave them?"

"Just because . . ."

That "just because" meant: leave me alone, it makes me sick. We fell silent.

Only God knows why, but I didn't leave. I too started to feel sick and more depressed. Images of the previous day began to come to mind all on their own, without my willing it, in a disordered way. I suddenly recalled a scene that I'd witnessed on the street that morning as I was anxiously hurrying to work. "Today some people were carrying a coffin and nearly dropped it," I suddenly said aloud, having no desire whatever to begin a conversation, but just so, almost accidentally.

"A coffin?"

"Yes, in the Haymarket; they were carrying it up from an underground cellar."

"From a cellar?"

"Not a cellar, but from a basement . . . well, you know . . . from downstairs . . . from a house of ill repute . . . There was such filth all around. . . . Eggshells, garbage . . . it smelled foul . . . it was disgusting."

Silence.

"A nasty day to be buried!" I began again to break the silence.

"Why nasty?"

"Snow, slush . . ." (I yawned.)

"It doesn't matter," she said suddenly after a brief silence.

"No, it's foul. . . ." (I yawned again.) "The grave diggers must have been cursing because they were getting wet out there in the snow. And there must have been water in the grave."

"Why water in the grave?" she asked with some curiosity, but she spoke even more rudely and curtly than before. Something suddenly began to goad me on.

"Naturally, water on the bottom, six inches or so. You can't ever dig a dry grave at Volkovo cemetery."

"Why not?"

"What do you mean, why not? The place is waterlogged. It's all swamp. So they bury them right in the water. I've seen it myself . . . many times. . . ."

(I'd never seen it, and I'd never been to Volkovo cemetery, but I'd heard about it from other people.)

"Doesn't it matter to you if you die?"

"Why should I die?" she replied, as though defending herself.

"Well, someday you'll die; you'll die just like that woman did this morning. She was a . . . she was also a young girl . . . she died of consumption."

"The wench should have died in the hospital. . . ." (She knows all about it, I thought, and she even said "wench" instead of "girl.")

"She owed money to her madam," I retorted, more and more goaded on by the argument. "She worked right up to the end, even though she had consumption. The cabbies standing around were chatting with the soldiers, telling them all about it. Her former acquaintances, most likely. They were all laughing. They were planning to drink to her memory at the tavern." (I invented a great deal of this.)

Silence, deep silence. She didn't even stir.

"Do you think it would be better to die in a hospital?"

"Isn't it just the same? . . . Besides, why should I die?" she added irritably.

"If not now, then later?"

"Well, then later . . ."

"That's what you think! Now you're young and pretty and fresh—that's your value. But after a year of this life, you won't be like that any more; you'll fade."

"In a year?"

"In any case, after a year your price will be lower," I continued, gloating. "You'll move out of here into a worse place, into some other house. And a year later, into a third, each worse and worse, and seven years from now you'll end up in a cellar on the Haymarket. Even that won't be so bad. The real trouble will come when you get some disease, let's say a weakness in the chest . . . or you catch cold or something. In this kind of life it's no laughing matter to get sick. It takes hold of you and may never let go. And so, you die."

"Well, then, I'll die," she answered now quite angrily and stirred quickly.

"That'll be a pity."

"For what?"

"A pity to lose a life."

Silence.

"Did you have a sweetheart? Huh?"

"What's it to you?"

"Oh, I'm not interrogating you. What do I care? Why are you angry? Of course, you may have had your own troubles. What's it to me? Just the same, I'm sorry."

"For whom?"

"I'm sorry for you."

"No need . . . ," she whispered barely audibly and stirred once again.

That provoked me at once. What! I was being so gentle with her, while she . . .

"Well, and what do you think? Are you on the right path then?"

"I don't think anything."

"That's just the trouble—you don't think. Wake up, while there's still time. And there is time. You're still young and pretty; you could fall in love, get married, be happy.[3] . . ."

"Not all married women are happy," she snapped in her former, rude manner.

"Not all, of course, but it's still better than this. A lot better. You can even live without happiness as long as there's love. Even in sorrow life can be good; it's good to be alive, no matter how you live. But what's there besides . . . stench? Phew!"

I turned away in disgust; I was no longer coldly philosophizing. I began to feel what I was saying and grew excited. I'd been longing to expound these cherished *little ideas* that I'd been nurturing in my corner. Something had suddenly caught fire in me, some kind of goal had "manifested itself" before me.

"Pay no attention to the fact that I'm here. I'm no model for you. I may be even worse than you are. Moreover, I was drunk when I came here." I hastened nonetheless to justify myself. "Besides, a man is no example to a woman. It's a different thing altogether; even though I degrade and defile myself, I'm still no one's slave; if I want to leave, I just get up and go. I shake

3. A popular theme treated by Gogol, Chernyshevsky, and Nekrasov, among others. Typically, an innocent and idealistic young man attempts to rehabilitate a prostitute or "fallen" woman.

it all off and I'm a different man. But you must realize right from the start that you're a slave. Yes, a slave! You give away everything, all your freedom. Later, if you want to break this chain, you won't be able to; it'll bind you ever more tightly. That's the kind of evil chain it is. I know. I won't say anything else; you might not even understand me. But tell me this, aren't you already in debt to your madam? There, you see!" I added, even though she hadn't answered, but had merely remained silent; but she was listening with all her might. "There's your chain! You'll never buy yourself out. That's the way it's done. It's just like selling your soul to the devil. . . .

"And besides . . . I may be just as unfortunate, how do you know, and I may be wallowing in mud on purpose, also out of misery. After all, people drink out of misery. Well, I came here out of misery. Now, tell me, what's so good about this place? Here you and I were . . . intimate . . . just a little while ago, and all that time we didn't say one word to each other; afterward you began to examine me like a wild creature, and I did the same. Is that the way people love? Is that how one person is supposed to encounter another? It's a disgrace, that's what it is!"

"Yes!" she agreed with me sharply and hastily. The haste of her answer surprised even me. It meant that perhaps the very same idea was flitting through her head while she'd been examining me earlier. It meant that she too was capable of some thought. . . . "Devil take it; this is odd, this *kinship*," I thought, almost rubbing my hands together. "Surely I can handle such a young soul."

It was the sport that attracted me most of all.

She turned her face closer to mine, and in the darkness it seemed that she propped her head up on her arm. Perhaps she was examining me. I felt sorry that I couldn't see her eyes. I heard her breathing deeply.

"Why did you come here?" I began with some authority.

"Just so . . ."

"But think how nice it would be living in your father's house! There you'd be warm and free; you'd have a nest of your own."

"And what if it's worse than that?"

"I must establish the right tone," flashed through my mind. "I won't get far with sentimentality."

However, that merely flashed through my mind. I swear that she really did interest me. Besides, I was somewhat exhausted and provoked. After all, artifice goes along so easily with feeling.

"Who can say?" I hastened to reply. "All sorts of things can happen. Why, I was sure that someone had wronged you and was more to blame than you are. After all, I know nothing of your life story, but a girl like you doesn't wind up in this sort of place on her own accord. . . ."

"What kind of a girl am I?" she whispered hardly audibly; but I heard it.

"What the hell! Now I'm flattering her. That's disgusting! But, perhaps it's a good thing. . . ." She remained silent.

"You see, Liza, I'll tell you about myself. If I'd had a family when I was growing up, I wouldn't be the person I am now. I think about this often. After all, no matter how bad it is in your own family—it's still your own father and mother, and not enemies or strangers. Even if they show you their love only once a year, you still know that you're at home. I grew up without a family; that must be why I turned out the way I did—so unfeeling."

I waited again.

"She might not understand," I thought. "Besides, it's absurd—all this moralizing."

"If I were a father and had a daughter, I think that I'd have loved her more than my sons, really," I began indirectly, talking about something else in order to distract her. I confess that I was blushing.

"Why's that?"

Ah, so she's listening!

"Just because. I don't know why, Liza. You see, I knew a father who was a stern, strict man, but he would kneel before his daughter and kiss her hands and feet; he couldn't get enough of her, really. She'd go dancing at a party, and he'd stand in one spot for five hours, never taking his eyes off her. He was crazy about her; I can understand that. At night she'd be tired and fall asleep, but he'd wake up, go in to kiss her, and make the sign of the cross over her while she slept. He used to wear a dirty old jacket and was stingy with everyone else, but would spend his last kopeck on her, buying her expensive presents; it afforded him great joy if she liked his presents. A father always loves his daughters more than their mother does. Some girls have a very nice time living at home. I think that I wouldn't even have let my daughter get married."

"Why not?" she asked with a barely perceptible smile.

"I'd be jealous, so help me God. Why, how could she kiss someone else? How could she love a stranger more than her own father? It's even painful to think about it. Of course, it's all nonsense; naturally, everyone finally comes to his senses. But I think that before I'd let her marry, I'd have tortured myself with worry. I'd have found fault with all her suitors. Nevertheless, I'd have ended up by allowing her to marry whomever she loved. After all, the one she loves always seems the worst of all to the father. That's how it is. That causes a lot of trouble in many families."

"Some are glad to sell their daughters, rather than let them marry honorably," she said suddenly.

Aha, so that's it!

"That happens, Liza, in those wretched families where there's neither God nor love," I retorted heatedly. "And where there's no love, there's also no good sense. There are such families, it's true, but I'm not talking about them. Obviously, from the way you talk, you didn't see much kindness in your own family. You must be very unfortunate. Hmm . . . But all this results primarily from poverty."

"And is it any better among the gentry? Honest folk live decently even in poverty."

"Hmmm . . . Yes. Perhaps. There's something else, Liza. Man only likes to count his troubles; he doesn't calculate his happiness. If he figured as he should, he'd see that everyone gets his share. So, let's say that all goes well in a particular family; it enjoys God's blessing, the husband turns out to be a good man, he loves you, cherishes you, and never leaves you. Life is good in that family. Sometimes, even though there's a measure of sorrow, life's still good. Where isn't there sorrow? If you choose to get married, *you'll find out for yourself*. Consider even the first years of a marriage to the one you love: what happiness, what pure bliss there can be sometimes! Almost without exception. At first even quarrels with your husband turn out well. For some women, the more they love their husbands, the more they pick fights with them. It's true; I once knew a woman like that. 'That's how it is,' she'd say. 'I love you very much and I'm tormenting you out of love, so that you'll feel it.' Did you know that one can torment a person intentionally out of love? It's mostly women who do that. Then she thinks to herself, 'I'll love him so much afterward, I'll be so affectionate, it's no sin to torment him a little now.' At home everyone would rejoice over you, and it would be so pleasant, cheerful, serene, and honorable. . . . Some other women are very jealous. If her husband goes away, I knew one like that, she can't stand it; she jumps up at night and goes off on the sly to see. Is he there? Is he in that house? Is he with that one? Now that's bad. Even she herself knows that it's bad; her heart sinks and she suffers because she really loves him. It's all out of love. And how nice it is to make up after a quarrel, to admit one's guilt or forgive him! How nice it is for both of them, how good they both feel at once, just as if they'd met again, married again, and begun their love all over again. No one, no one at all has to know what goes on between a husband and wife, if they love each other. However their quarrel ends, they should never call in either one of their mothers to act as judge or to hear complaints about the other one. They must act as their own judges. Love is God's mystery and should be hidden from other people's eyes, no matter what happens. This makes it holier, much better. They respect each other more, and a great deal is based on this respect. And, if there's been love, if they got married out of love, why should love disappear? Can't it be sustained? It rarely happens that it can't be sustained. If the husband turns out to be a kind and honest man, how can the love disappear? The first phase of married love will pass, that's true, but it's followed by an even better kind of love. Souls are joined together and all their concerns are managed in common; there'll be no secrets from one another. When children arrive, each and every stage, even a very difficult one, will seem happy, as long as there's both love and courage. Even work is cheerful; even when you deny yourself bread for your children's sake, you're still happy. After all, they'll love you for it afterward; you're really saving for your own future. Your children will grow up, and you'll feel that you're a model for them, a support. Even after you die, they'll carry your thoughts and feelings all during their life. They'll take on your image and likeness, since they received it from you. Consequently, it's a great obligation. How can a mother and father keep from growing closer? They say it's difficult to raise children. Who says that? It's heavenly joy! Do you love little children, Liza? I love them dearly. You know—a rosy little boy, suckling at your breast; what husband's heart could turn against his wife seeing her sitting there holding his child? The chubby, rosy little baby sprawls and snuggles; his little hands and feet are plump; his little nails are clean and tiny, so tiny it's even funny to see them; his little eyes look as if he already understood everything. As he suckles, he tugs at your breast playfully with his little hand. When the father approaches, the child lets go of the breast, bends way back, looks at his father, and laughs—as if God only knows how funny it is—and then takes to suckling again. Afterward, when he starts cutting teeth, he'll sometimes bite his mother's breast; looking at her sideways his little eyes seem to say, 'See, I bit you!' Isn't this pure bliss—the three of them, husband, wife, and child, all together? You can forgive a great deal for such moments. No, Liza, I think you must first learn how to live by yourself, and only afterward blame others."

"It's by means of images," I thought to myself, "just such images that I can get to you," although I was speaking with considerable feeling, I swear it; and all at once I blushed. "And what if she suddenly bursts out laughing—where will I hide then?" That thought drove me into a rage. By the end of my speech I'd really become excited, and now my pride was suffering somehow. The silence lasted for a while. I even considered shaking her.

"Somehow you . . ." she began suddenly and then stopped.

But I understood everything already: something was trembling in her voice now, not shrill, rude or unyielding as before, but something soft and timid, so timid that I suddenly was rather ashamed to watch her and felt guilty.

"What?" I asked with tender curiosity.

"Well, you . . ."

"What?"

"You somehow . . . it sounds just like a book," she said, and once again something which was noticeably sarcastic was suddenly heard in her voice.

Her remark wounded me dreadfully. That's not what I'd expected.

Yet, I didn't understand that she was intentionally disguising her feelings with sarcasm; that was usually the last resort of people who are timid and chaste of heart, whose souls have been coarsely and impudently invaded; and who, until the last moment, refuse to yield out of pride and are afraid to express their own feelings to you. I should've guessed it from the timidity with which on several occasions she tried to be sarcastic, until she finally managed to express it. But I hadn't guessed, and a malicious impulse took hold of me.

"Just you wait," I thought.

VII

"That's enough, Liza. What do books have to do with it, when this disgusts me as an outsider? And not only as an outsider. All this has awakened in my heart . . . Can it be, can it really be that you don't find it repulsive here? No, clearly habit means a great deal. The devil only knows what habit can do to a person. But do you seriously think that you'll never grow old, that you'll always be pretty, and that they'll keep you on here forever and ever? I'm not even talking about the filth. . . . Besides, I want to say this about your present life: even though you're still young, good-looking, nice, with soul and feelings, do you know, that when I came to a little while ago, I was immediately disgusted to be here with you! Why, a man has to be drunk to wind up here. But if you were in a different place, living as nice people do, I might not only chase after you, I might actually fall in love with you. I'd rejoice at a look from you, let alone a word; I'd wait for you at the gate and kneel down before you; I'd think of you as my betrothed and even consider that an honor. I wouldn't dare have any impure thoughts about you. But here, I know that I need only whistle, and you, whether you want to or not, will come to me, and that I don't have to do your bidding, whereas you have to do mine. The lowliest peasant may hire himself out as a laborer, but he doesn't make a complete slave of himself; he knows that it's only for a limited term. But what's your term? Just think about it. What are you giving up here? What are you enslaving? Why, you're enslaving your soul, something you don't really own, together with your body! You're giving away your love to be defiled by any drunkard! Love! After all, that's all there is! It's a precious jewel, a maiden's treasure, that's what it is! Why, to earn that love a man might be ready to offer up his own soul, to face death. But what's your love worth now? You've been bought, all of you; and why should anyone strive for your love, when you offer everything even without it? Why, there's no greater insult for a girl, don't you understand? Now, I've heard that they console you foolish girls, they allow you to see your own lovers here. But that's merely child's play, deception, making fun of you, while you believe it. And do you really think he loves you, that lover of yours? I don't believe it. How can he, if he knows that you can be called away from him at any moment? He'd have to be depraved after all that. Does he possess even one drop of respect for you? What do you have in common with him? He's laughing at you and stealing from you at the same time—so much for his love. It's not too bad, as long as he doesn't beat you. But perhaps he does. Go on, ask him, if you have such a lover, whether he'll ever marry you. Why, he'll burst out laughing right in your face, if he doesn't spit at you or smack you. He himself may be worth no more than a few lousy kopecks. And for what, do you think, did you ruin your whole life here? For the coffee they give you to drink, or for the plentiful supply of food? Why do you think they feed you so well? Another girl, an honest one, would choke on every bite, because she'd know why she was being fed so well. You're in debt here, you'll be in debt, and will remain so until the end, until such time comes as the customers begin to spurn you. And that time will come very soon; don't count on your youth. Why, here youth flies by like a stagecoach. They'll kick you out. And they'll not merely kick you out, but for a long time before that they'll pester you, reproach you, and abuse you—as if you hadn't ruined your health for the madam, hadn't given up your youth and your soul for her in vain, but rather, as if you'd ruined her, ravaged her, and robbed her. And don't expect any support. Your friends will also attack you to curry her favor, because they're all in bondage here and have long since lost both conscience and pity. They've become despicable, and there's nothing on earth more despicable, more repulsive, or more insulting than their abuse. You'll lose everything here, everything, without exception—your health, youth, beauty, and hope—and at the age of twenty-two you'll look as if you were thirty-five, and even that won't be too awful if you're not ill. Thank God for that. Why, you probably think that you're not even working, that it's all play! But there's no harder work or more onerous task than this one in the whole world and there never has been. I'd think that one's heart alone would be worn out by crying. Yet you dare not utter one word, not one syllable; when they drive you out, you leave as if you were the guilty one. You'll move to another place, then to a third, then somewhere else, and finally you'll wind up in the Haymarket. And there they'll start beating you for no good reason at all; it's a local custom; the clients there don't know how to be nice without beating you. You don't think it's so disgusting there? Maybe you should go and have a look sometime, and see it with your own eyes. Once, at New Year's, I saw a woman in a doorway. Her own kind had pushed her outside as a joke, to freeze her for a little while because she was wailing too much; they shut the door behind her. At nine o'clock in the morning she was already dead drunk, dishevelled, half-naked, and all beaten up. Her face was powdered, but her eyes were bruised; blood was streaming from her nose and mouth; a certain cabby had just fixed her up. She was sitting on a stone step, holding a piece of salted fish in her hand; she was howling, wailing something about her 'fate,' and slapping the fish against the stone step. Cabbies and drunken soldiers had gathered around the steps and were taunting her. Don't you think you'll wind up the same way? I wouldn't want to believe it myself, but how do you know, perhaps eight or ten years ago this same girl, the one with the salted fish, arrived here from somewhere or other, all fresh like a little cherub, innocent, and pure; she knew no evil and blushed at every word. Perhaps she was just like you—proud, easily offended, unlike all the rest; she looked like a queen and knew that total happiness awaited the man who would love her and whom she would also love. Do you see how it all ended? What if at the very moment she was slapping the fish against that filthy step, dead drunk and dishevelled, what if, even at that very moment she'd recalled her earlier, chaste years in her father's house when she was still going to school, and when her neighbor's son used to wait for her along the path and assure her that he'd love her all his life and devote himself entirely to her, and when they vowed to love one another forever and get married as soon as they grew up! No, Liza, you'd be lucky, very lucky, if you died quickly from consumption somewhere in a corner, in a cellar, like that other girl. In a hospital, you say? All right—they'll take you off, but what if the madam still requires your services? Consumption is quite a disease—it's not like dying from a fever. A person continues to hope right up until the last minute and declares that he's in good health. He consoles himself. Now that's useful for your madam. Don't worry, that's the way it is. You've sold your soul; besides, you owe her money—that means you don't dare say a thing. And while you're dying, they'll all abandon you, turn away from you—because there's nothing left to get from you. They'll even reproach you for taking up space for no good reason and for taking so long to die. You won't even be able to ask for something to drink, without their hurling abuse at you: 'When will you croak, you old bitch? You keep on moaning and don't let us get any sleep—and you drive our customers away.' That's for sure; I've overheard such words myself. And as you're breathing your last, they'll shove you into the filthiest corner of the cellar—into darkness and dampness; lying there alone, what will you think about then? After you die, some stranger will lay you out hurriedly, grumbling all the while, impatiently—no one will bless you, no one will sigh over you; they'll merely want to get rid of you as quickly as possible. They'll buy you a wooden trough and carry you out as they did that poor woman I saw today; then they'll go off to a tavern and drink to your memory. There'll be slush, filth, and wet snow in your grave—why bother for the likes of you? 'Let her down, Vanyukha; after all, it's her fate to go down with her legs up, that's the sort of girl she was. Pull up on that rope, you rascall!' 'It's okay like that.' 'How's it okay? See, it's lying on its side. Was she a human being or not? Oh, never mind, cover it up.' They won't want to spend much time arguing over you. They'll cover your coffin quickly with wet, blue clay and then go off to the tavern. . . . That'll be the end of your memory on earth; for other women, children will visit their graves, fathers, husbands—but for you—no tears, no sighs; no remembrances. No one, absolutely no one in the whole world, will ever come to visit you; your name will disappear from the face of the earth, just as if you'd never been born and had never existed. Mud and filth, no matter how you pound on the lid of your coffin at night when other corpses arise: 'Let me out, kind people, let me live on earth for a little while! I lived, but I didn't really see life; my life went down the drain; they drank it away in a tavern at the Haymarket; let me out, kind people, let me live in the world once again!'"

I was so carried away by my own pathos that I began to feel a lump forming in my throat, and . . . I suddenly stopped, rose up in fright, and, leaning over apprehensively, I began to listen carefully as my own heart pounded. There was cause for dismay.

For a while I felt that I'd turned her soul inside out and had broken her heart; the more I became convinced of this, the more I strived to reach my goal as quickly and forcefully as possible. It was the sport, the sport that attracted me; but it wasn't only the sport. . . .

I knew that I was speaking clumsily, artificially, even bookishly; in short, I didn't know how to speak except "like a book." But that didn't bother me, for I knew, I had a premonition, that I would be understood and that this bookishness itself might even help things along. But now, having achieved this effect, I suddenly lost all my nerve. No, never, never before had I witnessed such despair! She was lying there, her face pressed deep into a pillow she was clutching with her hands. Her heart was bursting. Her young body was shuddering as if she were having convulsions. Suppressed sobs shook her breast, tore her apart, and suddenly burst forth in cries and moans. Then she pressed her face even deeper into the pillow: she didn't want anyone, not one living soul, to hear her anguish and her tears. She bit the pillow; she bit her hand until it bled (I noticed that afterward); or else, thrusting her fingers into her dishevelled hair, she became rigid with the strain, holding her breath and clenching her teeth. I was about to say something, to ask her to calm down; but I felt that I didn't dare. Suddenly, all in a kind of chill, almost in a panic, I groped hurriedly to get out of there as quickly as possible. It was dark: no matter how I tried, I couldn't end it quickly. Suddenly I felt a box of matches and a candlestick with a whole unused candle. As soon as the room was lit up, Liza started suddenly, sat up, and looked at me almost senselessly, with a distorted face and a half-crazy smile. I sat down next to her and took her hands; she came to and threw herself at me, wanting to embrace me, yet not daring to. Then she quietly lowered her head before me.

"Liza, my friend, I shouldn't have . . . you must forgive me," I began, but she squeezed my hands so tightly in her fingers that I realized I was saying the wrong thing and stopped.

"Here's my address, Liza. Come to see me."

"I will," she whispered resolutely, still not lifting her head.

"I'm going now, good-bye . . . until we meet again."

I stood up; she did, too, and suddenly blushed all over, shuddered, seized a shawl lying on a chair, threw it over her shoulders, and wrapped herself up to her chin. After doing this, she smiled again somewhat painfully, blushed, and looked at me strangely. I felt awful. I hastened to leave, to get away.

"Wait," she said suddenly as we were standing in the hallway near the door, and she stopped me by putting her hand on my overcoat. She quickly put the candle down and ran off; obviously she'd remembered something or wanted to show me something. As she left she was blushing all over, her eyes were gleaming, and a smile had appeared on her lips—what on earth did it all mean? I waited against my own will; she returned a moment later with a glance that seemed to beg forgiveness for something. All in all it was no longer the same face or the same glance as before—sullen, distrustful, obstinate. Now her glance was imploring, soft, and, at the same time, trusting, affectionate, and timid. That's how children look at people whom they love very much, or when they're asking for something. Her eyes were light hazel, lovely, full of life, as capable of expressing love as brooding hatred.

Without any explanation, as if I were some kind of higher being who was supposed to know everything, she held a piece of paper out toward me. At that moment her whole face was shining with a most naive, almost childlike triumph. I unfolded the paper. It was a letter to her from some medical student containing a high-flown, flowery, but very respectful declaration of love. I don't remember the exact words now, but I can well recall the genuine emotion that can't be feigned shining through that high style. When I'd finished reading the letter, I met her ardent, curious, and childishly impatient gaze. She'd fixed her eyes on my face and was waiting eagerly to see what I'd say. In a few words, hurriedly, but with some joy and pride, she explained that she'd once been at a dance somewhere, in a private house, at the home of some "very, very good people, *family people*, where they *knew nothing*, nothing at all," because she'd arrived at this place only recently and was just . . . well, she hadn't quite decided whether she'd stay here and she'd certainly leave as soon as she'd paid off her debt. . . . Well, and this student was there; he danced with her all evening and talked to her. It turned out he was from Riga; he'd known her as a child, they'd played together, but that had been a long time ago; he was acquainted with her parents—but he knew nothing, absolutely nothing *about this place* and he didn't even suspect it! And so, the very next day, after the dance, (only some three days ago), he'd sent her this letter through the friend with whom she'd gone to the party . . . and . . . well, that's the whole story."

She lowered her sparkling eyes somewhat bashfully after she finished speaking.

The poor little thing, she'd saved this student's letter as a treasure and had run to fetch this one treasure of hers, not wanting me to leave without knowing that she too was the object of sincere, honest love, and that someone exists who had spoken to her respectfully. Probably that letter was fated to lie in her box without results. But that didn't matter; I'm sure that she'll guard it as a treasure her whole life, as her pride and vindication; and now, at a moment like this, she remembered it and brought it out to exult naively before me, to raise herself in my eyes, so that I could see it for myself and could also think well of her. I didn't say a thing; I shook her hand and left. I really wanted to get away. . . . I walked all the way home in spite of the fact that wet snow was still falling in large flakes. I was exhausted, oppressed, and perplexed. But the truth was already glimmering behind that perplexity. The ugly truth!

VIII

It was some time, however, before I agreed to acknowledge that truth. I awoke the next morning after a few hours of deep, leaden sleep. Instantly recalling the events of the previous day, even I was astonished at my *sentimentality* with Liza last night, at all of yesterday's "horror and pity." "Why, it's an attack of old woman's nervous hysteria, phew!" I decided. "And why on earth did I force my address on her? What if she comes? Then again, let her come, it doesn't make any difference. . . ." But *obviously* that was not the main, most important matter: I had to make haste and rescue at all costs my reputation in the eyes of Zverkov and Simonov. That was my main task. I even forgot all about Liza in the concerns of that morning.

First of all I had to repay last night's debt to Simonov immediately. I resolved on desperate means: I would borrow the sum of fifteen rubles from Anton Antonych. As luck would have it, he was in a splendid mood that morning and gave me the money at once, at my first request. I was so delighted that I signed a promissory note with a somewhat dashing air, and told him *casually* that on the previous evening "I'd been living it up with some friends at the Hôtel de Paris. We were holding a farewell dinner for a comrade, one might even say, a childhood friend, and, you know—he's a great carouser, very spoiled—well, naturally; he comes from a good family, has considerable wealth and a brilliant career; he's witty and charming, and has affairs with certain ladies, you understand. We drank up an extra 'half-dozen bottles' and . . ." There was nothing to it; I said all this very easily, casually, and complacently.

Upon arriving home I wrote to Simonov at once.

To this very day I recall with admiration the truly gentlemanly, good-natured, candid tone of my letter. Cleverly and nobly, and, above all, without unnecessary words, I blamed myself for everything. I justified myself, "if only I could be allowed to justify myself," by saying that, being so totally unaccustomed to wine, I'd gotten drunk with the first glass, which (supposedly) I'd consumed even before their arrival, as I waited for them in the Hôtel de Paris between the hours of five and six o'clock. In particular, I begged for Simonov's pardon; I asked him to convey my apology to all the others, especially to Zverkov, whom, "I recall, as if in a dream," it seems, I'd insulted. I added that I'd have called upon each of them, but was suffering from a bad headache, and, worst of all, I was ashamed. I was particularly satisfied by the "certain lightness," almost casualness (though, still very proper), unexpectedly reflected in my style; better than all possible arguments, it conveyed to them at once that I regarded "all of last night's unpleasantness" in a rather detached way, and that I was not at all, not in the least struck down on the spot as you, gentlemen, probably suspect. On the contrary, I regard this all serenely, as any self-respecting gentleman would. The true story, as they say, is no reproach to an honest young man.

"Why, there's even a hint of aristocratic playfulness in it," I thought admiringly as I reread my note. "And it's all because I'm such a cultured and educated man! Others in my place wouldn't know how to extricate themselves, but I've gotten out of it, and I'm having a good time once again, all because I'm an 'educated and cultured man of our time.' It may even be true that the whole thing occurred as a result of that wine yesterday. Hmmm . . . well, no, it wasn't really the wine. And I didn't have anything to drink between five and six o'clock when I was waiting for them. I lied to Simonov; it was a bold-faced lie—yet I'm not ashamed of it even now. . . ."

But, to hell with it, anyway! The main thing is, I got out of it.

I put six rubles in the letter, sealed it up, and asked Apollon to take it to Simonov. When he heard that there was money in it, Apollon became more respectful and agreed to deliver it. Toward evening I went out for a stroll. My head was still aching and spinning from the events of the day before. But as evening approached and twilight deepened, my impressions changed and became more confused, as did my thoughts. Something hadn't yet died within me, deep within my heart and conscience; it didn't want to die, and it expressed itself as burning anguish. I jostled my way along the more populous, commercial streets, along Meshchanskaya, Sadovaya, near the Yusupov Garden. I particularly liked to stroll along these streets at twilight, just as they became most crowded with all sorts of pedestrians, merchants, and tradesmen, with faces preoccupied to the point of hostility, on their way home from a hard day's work. It was precisely the cheap bustle that I liked, the crass prosaic quality. But this time all that street bustle irritated me even more. I couldn't get a hold of myself or puzzle out what was wrong. Something was rising, rising up in my soul continually, painfully, and didn't want to settle down. I returned home completely distraught. It was just as if some crime were weighing on my soul.

I was constantly tormented by the thought that Liza might come to see me. It was strange, but from all of yesterday's recollections, the one of her tormented me most, somehow separately from all the others. I'd managed to forget the rest by evening, to shrug everything off, and I still remained completely satisfied with my letter to Simonov. But in regard to Liza, I was not at all satisfied. It was as though I were tormented by her alone. "What if she comes?" I thought continually. "Well, so what? It doesn't matter. Let her come. Hmm. The only unpleasant thing is that she'll see, for instance, how I live. Yesterday I appeared before her such a . . . hero . . . but now, hmm! Besides, it's revolting that I've sunk so low. The squalor of my apartment. And I dared go to dinner last night wearing such clothes! And that oilcloth sofa of mine with its stuffing hanging out! And my dressing gown that doesn't quite cover me! What rags! . . . She'll see it all—and she'll see Apollon. That swine will surely insult her. He'll pick on her, just to be rude to me. Of course, I'll be frightened, as usual. I'll begin to fawn before her, wrap myself up in my dressing gown. I'll start to smile and tell lies. Ugh, the indecency! And that's not even the worst part! There's something even more important, nastier, meaner! Yes, meaner! Once again, I'll put on that dishonest, deceitful mask! . . ."

When I reached this thought, I simply flared up.

"Why deceitful? How deceitful? Yesterday I spoke sincerely. I recall that there was genuine feeling in me, too. I was trying no less than to arouse noble feelings in her . . . and if she wept, that's a good thing; it will have a beneficial effect. . . ."

But I still couldn't calm down.

All that evening, even after I returned home, even after nine o'clock, when by my calculations Liza could no longer have come, her image continued to haunt me, and, what's most important, she always appeared in one and the same form. Of all that had occurred yesterday, it was one moment in particular which stood out most vividly: that was when I lit up the room with a match and saw her pale, distorted face with its tormented gaze. What a pitiful, unnatural, distorted smile she'd had at that moment! But little did I know then that even fifteen years later I'd still picture Liza to myself with that same pitiful, distorted, and unnecessary smile which she'd had at that moment.

The next day I was once again prepared to dismiss all this business as nonsense, as the result of overstimulated nerves; but most of all, as exaggeration. I was well aware of this weakness of mine and sometimes was even afraid of it; "I exaggerate everything, that's my problem," I kept repeating to myself hour after hour. And yet, "yet, Liza may still come, all the same"; that was the refrain which concluded my reflections. I was so distressed that I sometimes became furious. "She'll come! She'll definitely come!" If not today, then tomorrow, she'll seek me out! That's just like the damned romanticism of all these *pure hearts*! Oh, the squalor, the stupidity, the narrowness of these "filthy, sentimental souls!' How could all this not be understood, how on earth could it not be understood? . . ." But at this point I would stop myself, even in the midst of great confusion.

"And how few, how very few words were needed," I thought in passing, "how little idyllic sentiment (what's more, the sentiment was artificial, bookish, composed) was necessary to turn a whole human soul according to my wishes at once. That's innocence for you! That's virgin soil!"

At times the thought occurred that I might go to her myself "to tell her everything," and to beg her not to come to me. But at this thought such venom arose in me that it seemed I'd have crushed that "damned" Liza if she'd suddenly turned up next to me. I'd have insulted her, spat at her, struck her, and chased her away!

One day passed, however, then a second, and a third; she still hadn't come, and I began to calm down. I felt particularly reassured and relaxed after nine o'clock in the evening, and even began to daydream sweetly at times. For instance, I'd save Liza, precisely because she'd come to me, and I'd talk to her. . . . I'd develop her mind, educate her. At last I'd notice that she loved me, loved me passionately. I'd pretend I didn't understand. (For that matter, I didn't know why I'd pretend; most likely just for the effect.) At last, all embarrassed, beautiful, trembling, and sobbing, she'd throw herself at my feet and declare that I was her saviour and she loved me more than anything in the world. I'd be surprised, but . . . "Liza," I'd say, "Do you really think that I haven't noticed your love? I've seen everything. I guessed, but dared not be first to make a claim on your heart because I had such influence over you, and because I was afraid you might deliberately force yourself to respond to my love out of gratitude, that you might forcibly evoke within yourself a feeling that didn't really exist. No, I didn't want that because it would be . . . despotism. . . . It would be indelicate (well, in short, here I launched on some European, George Sandian,[4] inexplicably lofty subtleties . . .). But now, now—you're mine, you're my creation, you're pure and lovely, you're my beautiful wife."

And enter my house bold and free
To become its full mistress![5]

4. George Sand was the pseudonym of the French woman novelist Aurore Dudevant (1804–1876), famous also as a promoter of feminism.

5. The last lines of the poem by Nekrasov used as the epigraph of Part II of this story (see pp. 600–601).

"Then we'd begin to live happily together, travel abroad, etc., etc." In short, it began to seem crude even to me, and I ended it all by sticking my tongue out at myself.

"Besides, they won't let her out of there, the 'bitch,'" I thought. "After all, it seems unlikely that they'd release them for strolls, especially in the evening (for some reason I was convinced that she had to report there every evening, precisely at seven o'clock). Moreover, she said that she'd yet to become completely enslaved there, and that she still had certain rights; that means, hmm. Devil take it, she'll come, she's bound to come!"

It was a good thing I was distracted at the time by Apollon's rudeness. He made me lose all patience. He was the bane of my existence, a punishment inflicted on me by Providence. We'd been squabbling constantly for several years now and I hated him. My God, how I hated him! I think that I never hated anyone in my whole life as much as I hated him, especially at those times. He was an elderly, dignified man who worked part-time as a tailor. But for some unknown reason he despised me, even beyond all measure, and looked down upon me intolerably. However, he looked down on everyone. You need only glance at that flaxen, slicked-down hair, at that single lock brushed over his forehead and greased with vegetable oil, at his strong mouth, always drawn up in the shape of the letter V,[6] and you felt that you were standing before a creature who never doubted himself. He was a pedant of the highest order, the greatest one I'd ever met on earth; in addition he possessed a sense of self-esteem appropriate perhaps only to Alexander the Great, King of Macedonia. He was in love with every one of his buttons, every one of his fingernails—absolutely in love, and he looked it! He treated me quite despotically, spoke to me exceedingly little, and, if he happened to look at me, cast a steady, majestically self-assured, and constantly mocking glance that sometimes infuriated me. He carried out his tasks as if he were doing me the greatest of favors. Moreover, he did almost nothing at all for me; nor did he assume that he was obliged to do anything. There could be no doubt that he considered me the greatest fool on earth, and, that if he "kept me on," it was only because he could receive his wages from me every month. He agreed to "do nothing" for seven rubles a month. I'll be forgiven many of my sins because of him. Sometimes my hatred reached such a point that his gait alone would throw me into convulsions. But the most repulsive thing about him was his lisping. His tongue was a bit larger than normal or something of the sort; as a result, he constantly lisped and hissed. Apparently, he was terribly proud of it, imagining that it endowed him with enormous dignity. He spoke slowly, in measured tones, with his hands behind his back and his eyes fixed on the ground. It particularly infuriated me when he used to read the Psalter to himself behind his partition. I endured many battles on account of it. He was terribly fond of reading during the evening in a slow, even singsong voice, as if chanting over the dead. It's curious, but that's how he ended up: now he hires himself out to recite the Psalter over the dead; in addition, he exterminates rats and makes shoe polish. But at that time I couldn't get rid of him; it was as if he were chemically linked to my own existence. Besides, he'd never have agreed to leave for anything. It was impossible for me to live in a

6. The last letter of the old Russian alphabet, triangular in shape.

furnished room: my own apartment was my private residence, my shell, my case, where I hid from all humanity. Apollon, the devil only knows why, seemed to belong to this apartment, and for seven long years I couldn't get rid of him.

It was impossible, for example, to delay paying him his wages for even two or three days. He'd make such a fuss that I wouldn't know where to hide. But in those days I was so embittered by everyone that I decided, heaven knows why or for what reason, to *punish* Apollon by not paying him his wages for two whole weeks. I'd been planning to do this for some time now, about two years, simply in order to teach him that he had no right to put on such airs around me, and that if I chose to, I could always withhold his wages. I resolved to say nothing to him about it and even remain silent on purpose, to conquer his pride and force him to be the first one to mention it. Then I would pull all seven rubles out of a drawer and show him that I actually had the money and had intentionally set it aside, but that "I didn't want to, didn't want to, simply didn't want to pay him his wages, and that I didn't want to simply because *that's what I wanted*," because such was "my will as his master," because he was disrespectful and because he was rude. But, if he were to ask respectfully, then I might relent and pay him; if not, he might have to wait another two weeks, or three, or even a whole month. . . .

But, no matter how angry I was, he still won. I couldn't even hold out for four days. He began as he always did, because there had already been several such cases (and, let me add, I knew all this beforehand; I knew his vile tactics by heart), to wit: he would begin by fixing an extremely severe gaze on me. He would keep it up for several minutes in a row, especially when meeting me or accompanying me outside of the house. If, for example, I held out and pretended not to notice these stares, then he, maintaining his silence as before, would proceed to further tortures. Suddenly, for no reason at all, he'd enter my room quietly and slowly, while I was pacing or reading; he'd stop at the door, place one hand behind his back, thrust one foot forward, and fix his gaze on me, no longer merely severe, but now utterly contemptuous. If I were suddenly to ask him what he wanted, he wouldn't answer at all. He'd continue to stare at me reproachfully for several more seconds; then, compressing his lips in a particular way and assuming a very meaningful air, he'd turn slowly on the spot and slowly withdraw to his own room. Two hours later he'd emerge again and suddenly appear before me in the same way. It's happened sometimes that in my fury I hadn't even asked what he wanted, but simply raised my head sharply and imperiously, and begun to stare reproachfully back at him. We would stare at each other thus for some two minutes or more; at last he'd turn slowly and self-importantly, and withdraw for another few hours.

If all this failed to bring me back to my senses and I continued to rebel, he'd suddenly begin to sigh while staring at me. He'd sigh heavily and deeply, as if trying to measure with each sigh the depth of my moral decline. Naturally, it would end with his complete victory: I'd rage and shout, but I was always forced to do just as he wished on the main point of dispute.

This time his usual maneuvers of "severe stares" had scarcely begun when I lost my temper at once and lashed out at him in a rage. I was irritated enough even without that.

"Wait!" I shouted in a frenzy, as he was slowly and silently turning with one hand behind his back, about to withdraw to his own room. "Wait! Come back, come back, I tell you!" I must have bellowed so unnaturally that he turned around and even began to scrutinize me with a certain amazement. He continued, however, not to utter one word, and that was what infuriated me most of all.

"How dare you come in here without asking permission and stare at me? Answer me!"

But after regarding me serenely for half a minute, he started to turn around again.

"Wait!" I roared, rushing up to him. "Don't move! There! Now answer me: why do you come in here to stare?"

"If you've got any orders for me now, it's my job to do 'em," he replied after another pause, lisping softly and deliberately, raising his eyebrows, and calmly shifting his head from one side to the other—what's more, he did all this with horrifying composure.

"That's not it! That's not what I'm asking you about, you executioner!" I shouted, shaking with rage. "I'll tell you myself, you executioner, why you came in here. You know that I haven't paid you your wages, but you're so proud that you don't want to bow down and ask me for them. That's why you came in here to punish me and torment me with your stupid stares, and you don't even sus-s-pect, you torturer, how stupid it all is, how stupid, stupid, stupid, stupid!"

He would have turned around silently once again, but I grabbed hold of him.

"Listen," I shouted to him. "Here's the money, you see! Here it is! (I pulled it out of a drawer.) All seven rubles. But you won't get it, you won't until you come to me respectfully, with your head bowed, to ask my forgiveness. Do you hear?"

"That can't be!" he replied with some kind of unnatural self-confidence.

"It will be!" I shrieked. "I give you my word of honor, it will be!"

"I have nothing to ask your forgiveness for," he said as if he hadn't even noticed my shrieks, "because it was you who called me an 'executioner,' and I can always go lodge a complaint against you at the police station."

"Go! Lodge a complaint!" I roared. "Go at once, this minute, this very second! You're still an executioner! Executioner! Executioner!" But he only looked at me, then turned and, no longer heeding my shouts, calmly withdrew to his own room without looking back.

"If it hadn't been for Liza, none of this would have happened!" I thought to myself. Then, after waiting a minute, pompously and solemnly, but with my heart pounding heavily and forcefully, I went in to see him behind the screen.

"Apollon!" I said softly and deliberately, though gasping for breath, "go at once, without delay to fetch the police supervisor!"

He'd already seated himself at his table, put on his eyeglasses, and picked up something to sew. But, upon hearing my order, he suddenly snorted with laughter.

"At once! Go this very moment! Go, go, or you can't imagine what will happen to you!"

"You're really not in your right mind," he replied, not even lifting his head, lisping just as slowly, and continuing to thread his needle. "Who's ever heard of a man being sent to fetch a policeman against himself? And as for trying to frighten me, you're only wasting your time, because nothing will happen to me."

"Go," I screeched, seizing him by the shoulder. I felt that I might strike him at any moment.

I never even heard the door from the hallway suddenly open at that very moment, quietly and slowly, and that someone walked in, stopped, and began to examine us in bewilderment. I glanced up, almost died from shame, and ran back into my own room. There, clutching my hair with both hands, I leaned my head against the wall and froze in that position.

Two minutes later I heard Apollon's deliberate footsteps.

"There's *some woman* asking for you," he said, staring at me with particular severity; then he stood aside and let her in—it was Liza. He didn't want to leave, and he scrutinized us mockingly.

"Get out, get out!" I commanded him all flustered. At that moment my clock strained, wheezed, and struck seven.

IX

And enter my house bold and free,
To become its full mistress!
From the same poem.[7]

I stood before her, crushed, humiliated, abominably ashamed; I think I was smiling as I tried with all my might to wrap myself up in my tattered, quilted dressing gown—exactly as I'd imagined this scene the other day during a fit of depression. Apollon, after standing over us for a few minutes, left, but that didn't make things any easier for me. Worst of all was that she suddenly became embarrassed too, more than I'd ever expected. At the sight of me, of course.

"Sit down," I said mechanically and moved a chair up to the table for her, while I sat on the sofa. She immediately and obediently sat down, staring at me wide-eyed, and, obviously, expecting something from me at once. This naive expectation infuriated me, but I restrained myself.

She should have tried not to notice anything, as if everything were just as it should be, but she . . . And I vaguely felt that she'd have to pay dearly *for everything*.

"You've found me in an awkward situation, Liza," I began, stammering and realizing that this was precisely the wrong way to begin.

"No, no, don't imagine anything!" I cried, seeing that she'd suddenly blushed. "I'm not ashamed of my poverty. . . . On the contrary, I regard it with pride. I'm poor, but noble. . . . One can be poor and noble," I muttered. "But . . . would you like some tea?"

"No . . . ," she started to say.

"Wait!"

I jumped up and ran to Apollon. I had to get away somehow.

"Apollon," I whispered in feverish haste, tossing down the seven rubles which had been in my fist the whole time, "here are your wages. There, you see, I've given them to you. But now you must rescue me: bring us some tea and a dozen rusks from the tavern at once. If you don't go, you'll make me a very miserable

7. I.e., from the poem quoted on pp. 600–601 and 640.

man. You have no idea who this woman is. . . . This means—everything! You may think she's . . . But you've no idea at all who this woman really is!"

Apollon, who'd already sat down to work and had put his glasses on again, at first glanced sideways in silence at the money without abandoning his needle; then, paying no attention to me and making no reply, he continued to fuss with the needle he was still trying to thread. I waited there for about three minutes standing before him with my arms folded *à la Napoleon*.[8] My temples were soaked in sweat. I was pale, I felt that myself. But, thank God, he must have taken pity just looking at me. After finishing with the thread, he stood up slowly from his place, slowly pushed back his chair, slowly took off his glasses, slowly counted the money and finally, after inquiring over his shoulder whether he should get a whole pot, slowly walked out of the room. As I was returning to Liza, it occurred to me: shouldn't I run away just as I was, in my shabby dressing gown, no matter where, and let come what may.

I sat down again. She looked at me uneasily. We sat in silence for several minutes.

"I'll kill him." I shouted suddenly, striking the table so hard with my fist that ink splashed out of the inkwell.

"Oh, what are you saying?" she exclaimed, startled.

"I'll kill him, I'll kill him!" I shrieked, striking the table in an absolute frenzy, but understanding full well at the same time how stupid it was to be in such a frenzy.

"You don't understand, Liza, what this executioner is doing to me. He's my executioner. . . . He's just gone out for some rusks; he . . ."

And suddenly I burst into tears. It was a nervous attack. I felt so ashamed amidst my sobs, but I couldn't help it. She got frightened.

"What's the matter? What's wrong with you?" she cried, fussing around me.

"Water, give me some water, over there!" I muttered in a faint voice, realizing full well, however, that I could've done both without the water and without the faint voice. But I was *putting on an act*, as it's called, in order to maintain decorum, although my nervous attack was genuine.

She gave me some water while looking at me like a lost soul. At that very moment Apollon brought in the tea. It suddenly seemed that this ordinary and prosaic tea was horribly inappropriate and trivial after everything that had happened, and I blushed. Liza stared at Apollon with considerable alarm. He left without looking at us.

"Liza, do you despise me?" I asked, looking her straight in the eye, trembling with impatience to find out what she thought.

She was embarrassed and didn't know what to say.

"Have some tea," I said angrily. I was angry at myself, but she was the one who'd have to pay, naturally. A terrible anger against her suddenly welled up in my heart; I think I could've killed her. To take revenge I swore inwardly not to say one more word to her during the rest of her visit. "She's the cause of it all," I thought.

Our silence continued for about five minutes. The tea stood on the table; we didn't touch it. It reached the point of my not wanting to drink on purpose, to make it even more difficult for her; it would be awkward for her to

8. In the style of Napoleon.

begin alone. Several times she glanced at me in sad perplexity. I stubbornly remained silent. I was the main sufferer, of course, because I was fully aware of the despicable meanness of my own spiteful stupidity; yet, at the same time, I couldn't restrain myself.

"I want to . . . get away from . . . that place . . . once and for all," she began just to break the silence somehow; but, poor girl, that was just the thing she shouldn't have said at that moment, stupid enough as it was to such a person as me, stupid as I was. My own heart even ached with pity for her tactlessness and unnecessary straightforwardness. But something hideous immediately suppressed all my pity; it provoked me even further. Let the whole world go to hell. Another five minutes passed.

"Have I disturbed you?" she began timidly, barely audibly, and started to get up.

But as soon as I saw this first glimpse of injured dignity, I began to shake with rage and immediately exploded.

"Why did you come here? Tell me why, please," I began, gasping and neglecting the logical order of my words. I wanted to say it all at once, without pausing for breath; I didn't even worry about how to begin.

"Why did you come here? Answer me! Answer!" I cried, hardly aware of what I was saying. "I'll tell you, my dear woman, why you came here. You came here because I spoke some *words of pity* to you that time. Now you've softened, and want to hear more 'words of pity.' Well, you should know that I was laughing at you then. And I'm laughing at you now. Why are you trembling? Yes, I was laughing at you! I'd been insulted, just prior to that, at dinner, by those men who arrived just before me that evening. I came intending to thrash one of them, the officer; but I didn't succeed; I couldn't find him; I had to avenge my insult on someone, to get my own back; you turned up and I took my anger out at you, and I laughed at you. I'd been humiliated, and I wanted to humiliate someone else; I'd been treated like a rag, and I wanted to exert some power. . . . That's what it was; you thought that I'd come there on purpose to save you, right? Is that what you thought? Is that it?"

I knew that she might get confused and might not grasp all the details, but I also knew that she'd understand the essence of it very well. That's just what happened. She turned white as a sheet; she wanted to say something. Her lips were painfully twisted, but she collapsed onto a chair just as if she'd been struck down with an ax. Subsequently she listened to me with her mouth gaping, her eyes wide open, shaking with awful fear. It was the cynicism, the cynicism of my words that crushed her. . . .

"To save you!" I continued, jumping up from my chair and rushing up and down the room in front of her, "to save you from what? Why, I may be even worse than you are. When I recited that sermon to you, why didn't you throw it back in my face? You should have said to me, 'Why did you come here? To preach morality or what?' Power, it was the power I needed then, I craved the sport, I wanted to reduce you to tears, humiliation, hysteria—that's what I needed then! But I couldn't have endured it myself, because I'm such a wretch. I got scared. The devil only knows why I foolishly gave you my address. Afterward, even before I got home, I cursed you like nothing on earth on account of that address. I hated you already because I'd lied to you then, because it was all playing with words, dreaming in my own mind. But, do you know what I really want now? For you to get lost, that's what! I need some peace. Why, I'd sell the whole world for a kopeck if people would only stop bothering me. Should the world go to hell, or should I go without my tea? I say, let the world go to hell as long as I can always have my tea. Did you know that or not? And I know perfectly well that I'm a scoundrel, a bastard, an egotist, and a sluggard. I've been shaking from fear for the last three days wondering whether you'd ever come. Do you know what disturbed me most of all these last three days? The fact that I'd appeared to you then as such a hero, and that now you'd suddenly see me in this torn dressing gown, dilapidated and revolting. I said before that I wasn't ashamed of my poverty; well, you should know that I am ashamed, I'm ashamed of it more than anything, more afraid of it than anything, more than if I were a thief, because I'm so vain; it's as if the skin's been stripped away from my body so that even wafts of air cause pain. By now surely even you've guessed that I'll never forgive you for having come upon me in this dressing gown as I was attacking Apollon like a vicious dog. Your saviour, your former hero, behaving like a mangy, shaggy mongrel, attacking his own lackey, while that lackey stood there laughing at me! Nor will I ever forgive you for those tears which, like an embarrassed old woman, I couldn't hold back before you. And I'll never forgive *you* for all that I'm confessing now. Yes—you, you alone must pay for everything because you turned up like this, because I'm a scoundrel, because I'm the nastiest, most ridiculous, pettiest, stupidest, most envious worm of all those living on earth who're no better than me in any way, but who, the devil knows why, never get embarrassed, while all my life I have to endure insults from every louse—that's my fate. What do I care that you don't understand any of this? What do I care, what do I care about you and whether or not you perish there? Why, don't you realize how much I'll hate you now after having said all this with your being here listening to me? After all, a man can only talk like this once in his whole life, and then only in hysteria! . . . What more do you want? Why, after all this, are you still hanging around here tormenting me? Why don't you leave?"

But at this point a very strange thing suddenly occurred.

I'd become so accustomed to inventing and imagining everything according to books, and picturing everything on earth to myself just as I'd conceived of it in my dreams, that at first I couldn't even comprehend the meaning of this strange occurrence. But here's what happened: Liza, insulted and crushed by me, understood much more than I'd imagined. She understood out of all this what a woman always understands first of all, if she sincerely loves—namely, that I myself was unhappy.

The frightened and insulted expression on her face was replaced at first by grieved amazement. When I began to call myself a scoundrel and a bastard, and my tears had begun to flow (I'd pronounced this whole tirade in tears), her whole face was convulsed by a spasm. She wanted to get up and stop me; when I'd finished, she paid no attention to my shouting, "Why are you here? Why don't you leave?" She only noticed that it must have been very painful for me to utter all this. Besides, she was so defenseless, the poor girl. She considered herself immeasurably beneath me. How could she get angry or take offense? Suddenly she jumped up from the chair with a kind of uncontrollable impulse, and yearning toward me, but being too timid and not daring to stir from her place, she extended her arms in my direction. . . . At this moment my heart leapt inside me, too. Then suddenly she threw herself at me, put her arms around my neck, and burst into tears. I, too, couldn't restrain myself and sobbed as I'd never done before.

"They won't let me . . . I can't be . . . good!" I barely managed to say; then I went over to the sofa, fell upon it face down, and sobbed in genuine hysterics for a quarter of an hour. She knelt down, embraced me, and remained motionless in that position.

But the trouble was that my hysterics had to end sometime. And so (after all, I'm writing the whole loathsome truth), lying there on the sofa and pressing my face firmly into that nasty leather cushion of mine, I began to sense gradually, distantly, involuntarily, but irresistibly, that it would be awkward for me to raise my head and look Liza straight in the eye. What was I ashamed of? I don't know, but I was ashamed. It also occurred to my overwrought brain that now our roles were completely reversed; now she was the heroine, and I was the same sort of humiliated and oppressed creature she'd been in front of me that evening—only four days ago. . . . And all this came to me during those few minutes as I lay face down on the sofa!

My God! Was it possible that I envied her?

I don't know; to this very day I still can't decide. But then, of course, I was even less able to understand it. After all, I couldn't live without exercising power and tyrannizing over another person. . . . But . . . but, then, you really can't explain a thing by reason; consequently, it's useless to try.

However, I regained control of myself and raised my head; I had to sooner or later. . . . And so, I'm convinced to this day that it was precisely because I felt too ashamed to look at her, that another feeling was suddenly kindled and burst into flame in my heart—the feeling of domination and possession. My eyes gleamed with passion; I pressed her hands tightly. How I hated her and felt drawn to her simultaneously! One feeling intensified the other. It was almost like revenge! . . . At first there was a look of something resembling bewilderment, or even fear, on her face, but only for a brief moment. She embraced me warmly and rapturously.

X

A quarter of an hour later I was rushing back and forth across the room in furious impatience, constantly approaching the screen to peer at Liza through the crack. She was sitting on the floor, her head leaning against the bed, and she must have been crying. But she didn't leave, and that's what irritated me. By this time she knew absolutely everything. I'd insulted her once and for all, but . . . there's nothing more to be said. She guessed that my outburst of passion was merely revenge, a new humiliation for her, and that to my former, almost aimless, hatred there was added now a *personal*, *envious* hatred of her. . . . However, I don't think that she understood all this explicitly; on the other hand, she fully understood that I was a despicable man, and, most important, that I was incapable of loving her.

I know that I'll be told this is incredible—that it's impossible to be as spiteful and stupid as I am; you may even add that it was impossible not to return, or at least to appreciate, this love. But why is this so incredible? In the first place, I could no longer love because, I repeat, for me love meant tyrannizing and demonstrating my moral superiority. All my life I could never even conceive of any other kind of love, and I've now reached the point that I sometimes think that love consists precisely in a voluntary gift by the beloved person of the right to tyrannize over him. Even in my underground dreams I couldn't conceive of love in any way other than a struggle. It always began with hatred and ended with moral subjugation; afterward, I could never imagine what to do with the subjugated object. And what's so incredible about that, since I'd previously managed to corrupt myself morally; I'd already become unaccustomed to "real life," and only a short while ago had taken it into my head to reproach her and shame her for having come to hear "words of pity" from me. But I never could've guessed that she'd come not to hear words of pity at all, but to love me, because it's in that kind of love that a woman finds her resurrection, all her salvation from whatever kind of ruin, and her rebirth, as it can't appear in any other form. However, I didn't hate her so much as I rushed around the room and peered through the crack behind the screen. I merely found it unbearably painful that she was still there. I wanted her to disappear. I longed for "peace and quiet"; I wanted to remain alone in my underground. "Real life" oppressed me—so unfamiliar was it—that I even found it hard to breathe.

But several minutes passed, and she still didn't stir, as if she were oblivious. I was shameless enough to tap gently on the screen to remind her. . . . She started suddenly, jumped up, and hurried to find her shawl, hat, and coat, as if she wanted to escape from me. . . . Two minutes later she slowly emerged from behind the screen and looked at me sadly. I smiled spitefully; it was forced, however, for *appearance's sake only*; and I turned away from her look.

"Good-bye," she said, going toward the door.

Suddenly I ran up to her, grabbed her hand, opened it, put something in . . . and closed it again. Then I turned away at once and bolted to the other corner, so that at least I wouldn't be able to see. . . .

I was just about to lie—to write that I'd done all this accidentally, without knowing what I was doing, in complete confusion, out of foolishness. But I don't want to lie; therefore I'll say straight out, that I opened her hand and placed something in it . . . out of spite. It occurred to me to do this while I was rushing back and forth across the room and she was sitting there behind the screen. But here's what I can say for sure: although I did this cruel thing deliberately, it was not from my heart, but from my stupid head. This cruelty of mine was so artificial, cerebral, intentionally invented, *bookish*, that I couldn't stand it myself even for one minute—at first I bolted to the corner so as not to see, and then, out of shame and in despair, I rushed out after Liza. I opened the door into the hallway and listened. "Liza! Liza!" I called down the stairs, but timidly, in a soft voice.

There was no answer; I thought I could hear her footsteps at the bottom of the stairs.

"Liza!" I cried more loudly.

No answer. But at that moment I heard down below the sound of the tight outer glass door opening heavily with a creak and then closing again tightly. The sound rose up the stairs.

She'd gone. I returned to my room deep in thought. I felt horribly oppressed.

I stood by the table near the chair where she'd been sitting and stared senselessly into space. A minute or so passed, then I suddenly started: right before me on the chair I saw . . . in a word, I saw the crumpled blue five-ruble note, the very one I'd thrust into her hand a few moments before. It was the same one; it couldn't be any other; I had none other in my apartment. So she'd managed to toss it down on the table when I'd bolted to the other corner.

So what? I might have expected her to do that. Might have expected it? No. I was such an egotist, in fact, I so lacked respect for other people, that I couldn't even conceive that she'd ever do that. I couldn't stand it. A moment later, like a madman, I hurried to get dressed. I threw on whatever I happened to find, and rushed headlong after her. She couldn't have gone more than two hundred paces when I ran out on the street.

It was quiet; it was snowing heavily, and the snow was falling almost perpendicularly, blanketing the sidewalk and the deserted street. There were no passers-by; no sound could be heard. The street lights were flickering dismally and vainly. I ran about two hundred paces to the crossroads and stopped.

"Where did she go? And why am I running after her? Why? To fall down before her, sob with remorse, kiss her feet, and beg her forgiveness! That's just what I wanted. My heart was being torn apart; never, never will I recall that moment with indifference. But—why?" I wondered. "Won't I grow to hate her, perhaps as soon as tomorrow, precisely because I'm kissing her feet today? Will I ever be able to make her happy? Haven't I found out once again today, for the hundredth time, what I'm really worth? Won't I torment her?"

I stood in the snow, peering into the murky mist, and thought about all this.

"And wouldn't it be better, wouldn't it," I fantasized once I was home again, stifling the stabbing pain in my heart with such fantasies, "wouldn't it be better if she were to carry away the insult with her forever? Such an insult—after all, is purification; it's the most caustic and painful form of consciousness. Tomorrow I would have defiled her soul and wearied her heart. But now that insult will never die within her; no matter how abominable the filth that awaits her, that insult will elevate and purify her . . . by hatred . . . hmm . . . perhaps by forgiveness as well. But will that make it any easier for her?"

And now, in fact, I'll pose an idle question of my own. Which is better: cheap happiness or sublime suffering? Well, come on, which is better?

These were my thoughts as I sat home that evening, barely alive with the anguish in my soul. I'd never before endured so much suffering and remorse; but could there exist even the slightest doubt that when I went rushing out of my apartment, I'd turn back again after going only halfway? I never met Liza afterward, and I never heard anything more about her. I'll also add that for a long time I remained satisfied with my theory about the use of insults and hatred, in spite of the fact that I myself almost fell ill from anguish at the time.

Even now, after so many years, all this comes back to me as *very unpleasant*. A great deal that comes back to me now is very unpleasant, but . . . perhaps I should end these *Notes* here? I think that I made a mistake in beginning to write them. At least, I was ashamed all the time I was writing this *tale*: consequently, it's not really literature, but corrective punishment. After all, to tell you long stories about how, for example, I ruined my life through moral decay in my corner, by the lack of appropriate surroundings, by isolation from any living beings, and by futile malice in the underground—so help me God, that's not very interesting. A novel needs a hero, whereas here all the traits of an anti-hero have been assembled *deliberately*; but the most important thing is that all this produces an extremely unpleasant impression because we've all become estranged from life, we're all cripples, every one of us, more or less. We've become so estranged that at times we feel some kind of revulsion for genuine "real life," and therefore we can't bear to be reminded of it. Why, we've reached a point where we almost regard "real life" as hard work, as a job, and we've all agreed in private that it's really better in books. And why do we sometimes fuss, indulge in whims, and make demands? We don't know ourselves. It'd be even worse if all our whimsical desires were fulfilled. Go on, try it. Give us, for example, a little more independence; untie the hands of any one of us, broaden our sphere of activity, relax the controls, and . . . I can assure you, we'll immediately ask to have the controls reinstated. I know that you may get angry at me for saying this, you may shout and stamp your feet: "Speak for yourself," you'll say, "and for your own miseries in the underground, but don't you dare say *'all of us.'*" If you'll allow me, gentlemen; after all, I'm not trying to justify myself by saying *all of us*. What concerns me in particular, is that in my life I've only taken to an extreme that which you haven't even dared to take halfway; what's more, you've mistaken your cowardice for good sense; and, in so deceiving yourself, you've consoled yourself. So, in fact, I may even be "more alive" than you are. Just take a closer look! Why, we don't even know where this "real life" lives nowadays, what it really is, and what it's called. Leave us alone without books and we'll get confused and lose our way at once—we won't know what to join, what to hold on to, what to love or what to hate, what to respect or what to despise. We're even oppressed by being men—men with real bodies and blood of *our very own*. We're ashamed of it; we consider it a disgrace and we strive to become some kind of impossible "general-human-beings." We're stillborn; for some time now we haven't been conceived by living fathers; we like it more and more. We're developing a taste for it. Soon we'll conceive of a way to be born from ideas. But enough; I don't want to write any more "from Underground. . . ."

However, the "notes" of this paradoxalist don't end here. He couldn't resist and kept on writing. But it also seems to us that we might as well stop here.

GUSTAVE FLAUBERT

1821–1880

Living mostly as a hermit in a small country town, Gustave Flaubert threw himself into the making of art. He saw literature as a realm superior to the "stupidity" and "mediocrity" of lived experience. He labored over every sentence he wrote, sometimes taking as much as a week to complete a paragraph, determined to perfect the style of each phrase. He did travel, spending months at a time in Paris and taking journeys to North Africa, Syria, Turkey, and Italy. He was even in Paris to witness the revolution of 1848, as workers rose up against the monarchy and demanded the vote. But Flaubert's greatest excitement lay in the tormented process of writing: "I get drunk on ink as others do on wine," he wrote. "I love my work with a frenetic and perverted love, as the ascetic loves the hair shirt that scratches his belly."

LIFE

Gustave Flaubert was the son of a chief surgeon in the provincial French town of Rouen. When he was fourteen, he developed an unrequited passion for an older married woman. A few years later he went to Paris to study law, which he hated. Anxious and unhappy, he failed his exams and suffered a sudden nervous breakdown, which sent him back to his family home in the small town of Croisset near Rouen, where he would stay for most of his life with his mother. It was there that he began to write seriously.

In 1846, on a visit to Paris, he met the beautiful Louise Colet, a professional writer who lived and worked among bohemian artists. This was Flaubert's only serious love affair, though it would take place mostly by correspondence—for him reality never lived up to the imagination—and he treated her coldly. Otherwise, he frequented prostitutes and had some fleeting sexual relationships with men. His mother declared that his "passion for sentences" had "dried up" his heart.

Flaubert's works did not make it easily into the world. In 1849 he asked his two closest friends to read a draft of his first novel, *The Temptation of Saint Anthony*. "We think you should throw it in the fire and never speak of it again," they advised. He put it aside and labored for five years on his masterpiece, *Madame Bovary* (1857). He said he wanted to write "a book about nothing," one held together by the "internal force of its style" alone. The protagonist he developed for this was a doctor's wife who longs to lead a romantic life like that of the heroines she encounters in books. She seeks out grand love affairs but is doomed to a narrow middle-class life among mediocrities in the provinces. Though sales of *Madame Bovary* were strong, critics denounced it as repugnant, consumed with the ugly banality of everyday life and offering nothing uplifting or consoling. One critic famously charged that Flaubert wielded his pen as a surgeon wields a scalpel. The novel was so shocking in its distanced and ironic treatment of adultery that Flaubert was tried for "offending public morals and religion." Although he was acquitted, *Madame Bovary* maintained its reputation as an immoral book for decades. Now it is viewed as one of the great works of nineteenth-century realism—perhaps the greatest. In 1869 Flaubert published *Sentimental Education*, a novel about the generation that lived through the revolutions of 1848. It flopped with the public, and the reviewers at the time sneered, although it has been enormously influential and highly regarded since.

Flaubert returned to *The Temptation of Saint Anthony* late in life, burying his manuscript in the ground temporarily when the Prussians invaded Normandy in 1870. In a period of despondency, when he was struggling financially and grieving over the loss of his mother and several close friends, he wrote *Three Tales* (1877), which included *A Simple Heart*. As Flaubert's body succumbed to syphilis, he told his niece, "Sometimes I think I'm liquefying like an old Camembert cheese." He died from a brain hemorrhage in 1880.

WORK

"It's no easy business to be simple," Flaubert said, pointing us to the great paradox at the center of *A Simple*

Heart. On the one hand, this is a straightforward tale of a relatively uneventful life: there is nothing complex or convoluted about the prose, about the chronology of events, or about the protagonist's experience. On the other hand, the sophisticated Flaubert invites us to see the world from the perspective of a naïve, exploited, illiterate servant woman whose last great love is a stuffed parrot, and allows us to understand her viewpoint as serious and sad rather than absurd or contemptible. The contemporary British novelist Julian Barnes, in a novel called *Flaubert's Parrot*, puts it this way: "Imagine the technical difficulty of writing a story in which a badly stuffed bird with a ridiculous name ends up standing for one third of the Trinity, and in which the intention is neither satirical, sentimental nor blasphemous. Imagine further telling the story from the point of view of an ignorant old woman without making it sound derogatory or coy." If we remember that Flaubert labored over every single sentence, suffering the "torments of style," we can read the simplicity he represents here as the result of a complex and careful artistic process.

Three elements of the story's highly refined technique are worth noticing. First of all, its economy: Flaubert distills his protagonist's experience into brief, clipped sentences. No word is wasted, and often it is tiny details that carry rich significance. For example, when the narrator tells us that Félicité's nephew keeps her "amused by telling her stories full of nautical jargon," he suggests that she cherishes precisely what she cannot understand—a language of her nephew's that is foreign to her. Second, Flaubert is famous for the impersonality or objectivity of his narrative style: he never intrudes his own feelings or opinions, maintaining a deliberate detachment. He wrote that "the author in his work should be like God in the universe—present everywhere and visible nowhere." Finally, it is worth paying attention to the story's structure: Félicité's experience follows the same pattern again and again—she falls in love and experiences a short period of happiness; this is followed by some kind of parting or death and a long spell of grief. But each time she falls in love with a new object, and the sequence of beloved objects is itself intriguing: first it is a lover, then the little girl in her care, then her nephew, then an elderly neighbor, then a live parrot, and finally the same parrot, stuffed. If on the one hand Flaubert seems to suggest a decline from human to animal to dead thing, on the other hand he suggests an ascent, as Félicité moves from erotic love to a wider, more charitable love and finally to a kind of mystical and heavenly adoration.

The parrot's role in the text goes beyond Félicité's love for it. As an animal from overseas brought to the town by an outsider-bureaucrat, it is above all a strange and foreign thing. Yet parrots learn to repeat human phrases, and so it becomes a strange echo of the social world it inhabits. First it learns Félicité's own expressions of respect and humility: "Your servant, sir!" and "Hail Mary!" Later it imitates Madame Aubain, and when the doorbell rings, it screams out "Félicité! The door, the door!" And yet it refuses to obey the rules of class and decorum itself, mocking the corrupt Boulais with screeches of laughter and leaving its droppings everywhere. At once symbolizing the stupidity and rote clichés of human life and acting as a focus for sincere love and spiritual veneration, the parrot remains one of Flaubert's most startling and fascinating figures.

Félicité too emerges as more complex than she may at first appear. On the one hand, Flaubert uses her to explore the psychology of servitude: what makes a person willingly accept the monotony and humiliation of spending a lifetime serving the needs of callous and thoughtless others? Intellectually, she is certainly simple: she has so little power of abstract thought that she cannot understand how a map works, and her understanding of religious doctrine is limited indeed. Compared to an animal herself, she bears numerous interesting relations to animals in the text. On the other hand, Flaubert allows her simplicity to feel powerful and moving and even sometimes surprising. For example, Félicité experiences an intense identification with Virginie at the moment of her first communion, and then disappointment with her own experience of taking communion the following day. She herself cannot interpret this difference, but Flaubert implies that sincere feeling may take place by way of concrete realities—people and objects—rather than abstractions. Indeed, Félicité endows not only animals but her cherished collection of things with meaning and value. And along the way, although she is cheated, exploited, discounted, and misguided, she reaches moments of heroism and even sublimity.

Flaubert wrote the story at a moment when he himself was thinking back over his life with sadness. Félicité's life is set in the very places that had been his own haunts in childhood: all of the place names are real, and many of the farms and beach scenes evoke specific spots the writer remembered with fondness. Flaubert's early readers assumed that the detached writer must feel scorn for his simple heroine, but he declared otherwise: *A Simple Heart* is "not at all ironic, as you suppose, but on the contrary very serious and very sad. I want to arouse people's pity, to make sensitive souls weep, since I am one myself."

A Simple Heart[1]

I

For half a century the women of Pont-l'Évêque[2] envied Mme Aubain her maidservant Félicité.

In return for a hundred francs a year she did all the cooking and the housework, the sewing, the washing, and the ironing. She could bridle a horse, fatten poultry, and churn butter, and she remained faithful to her mistress, who was by no means an easy person to get on with.

Mme Aubain had married a young fellow who was good-looking but badly-off, and who died at the beginning of 1809, leaving her with two small children and a pile of debts. She then sold all her property except for the farms of Toucques and Geffosses, which together brought in five thousand francs a year at the most, and left her house at Saint-Melaine for one behind the covered market which was cheaper to run and had belonged to her family.

This house had a slate roof and stood between an alley-way and a lane leading down to the river. Inside there were differences in level which were the cause of many a stumble. A narrow entrance-hall separated the kitchen

1. Translated by Robert Baldick.

2. Town in the rural French province of Normandy.

from the parlour, where Mme Aubain sat all day long in a wicker easy-chair by the window. Eight mahogany chairs were lined up against the white-painted wainscoting, and under the barometer stood an old piano loaded with a pyramid of boxes and cartons. On either side of the chimney-piece, which was carved out of yellow marble in the Louis Quinze style, there was a tapestry-covered arm-chair, and in the middle was a clock designed to look like a temple of Vesta.[3] The whole room smelt a little musty, as the floor was on a lower level than the garden.

On the first floor was 'Madame's' bedroom—very spacious, with a patterned wallpaper of pale flowers and a portrait of 'Monsieur' dressed in what had once been the height of fashion. It opened into a smaller room in which there were two cots, without mattresses. Then came the drawing-room, which was always shut up and full of furniture covered with dustsheets. Next there was a passage leading to the study, where books and papers filled the shelves of a book-case in three sections built round a big writing-table of dark wood. The two end panels were hidden under pen-and-ink drawings, landscapes in gouache, and etchings by Audran,[4] souvenirs of better days and bygone luxury. On the second floor a dormer window gave light to Félicité's room, which looked out over the fields.

Every day Félicité got up at dawn, so as not to miss Mass, and worked until evening without stopping. Then, once dinner was over, the plates and dishes put away, and the door bolted, she piled ashes on the log fire and went to sleep in front of the hearth, with her rosary in her hands. Nobody could be more stubborn when it came to haggling over prices, and as for cleanliness, the shine on her saucepans was the despair of all the other servants. Being of a thrifty nature, she ate slowly, picking up from the table the crumbs from her loaf of bread—a twelve-pound loaf which was baked specially for her and lasted her twenty days.

All the year round she wore a kerchief of printed calico fastened behind with a pin, a bonnet which covered her hair, grey stockings, a red skirt, and over her jacket a bibbed apron such as hospital nurses wear.

Her face was thin and her voice was sharp. At twenty-five she was often taken for forty; once she reached fifty, she stopped looking any age in particular. Always silent and upright and deliberate in her movements, she looked like a wooden doll driven by clock-work.

2

Like everyone else, she had had her love-story.

Her father, a mason, had been killed when he fell off some scaffolding. Then her mother died, and when her sisters went their separate ways, a farmer took her in, sending her, small as she was, to look after the cows out in the fields. She went about in rags, shivering with cold, used to lie flat on the ground to

3. The ancient temple of Vesta, Roman goddess of the hearth, is a round building with a conical roof supported by columns. "Louis Quinze style": ornate furniture style dating from the 18th century.

4. Claude Audran III (1658–1734), French painter, sculptor, engraver, and decorator.

drink water out of the ponds, would be beaten for no reason at all, and was finally turned out of the house for stealing thirty sous,[5] a theft of which she was innocent. She found work at another farm, looking after the poultry, and as she was liked by her employers the other servants were jealous of her.

One August evening—she was eighteen at the time—they took her off to the fête[6] at Colleville. From the start she was dazed and bewildered by the noise of the fiddles, the lamps in the trees, the medley of gaily coloured dresses, the gold crosses and lace, and the throng of people jigging up and down. She was standing shyly on one side when a smart young fellow, who had been leaning on the shaft of a cart, smoking his pipe, came up and asked her to dance. He treated her to cider, coffee, girdle-cake, and a silk neckerchief, and imagining that she knew what he was after, offered to see her home. At the edge of a field of oats, he pushed her roughly to the ground. Thoroughly frightened, she started screaming for help. He took to his heels.

Another night, on the road to Beaumont, she tried to get past a big, slow-moving waggon loaded with hay, and as she was squeezing by she recognized Théodore.

He greeted her quite calmly, saying that she must forgive him for the way he had behaved to her, as 'it was the drink that did it.'

She did not know what to say in reply and felt like running off.

Straight away he began talking about the crops and the notabilities of the commune, saying that his father had left Colleville for the farm at Les Écots, so that they were now neighbours.

'Ah!' she said.

He added that his family wanted to see him settled but that he was in no hurry and was waiting to find a wife to suit his fancy. She lowered her head. Then he asked her if she was thinking of getting married. She answered with a smile that it was mean of him to make fun of her.

'But I'm not making fun of you!' he said. 'I swear I'm not!'

He put his left arm round her waist, and she walked on supported by his embrace. Soon they slowed down. There was a gentle breeze blowing, the stars were shining, the huge load of hay was swaying about in front of them, and the four horses were raising clouds of dust as they shambled along. Then, without being told, they turned off to the right. He kissed her once more and she disappeared into the darkness.

The following week Théodore got her to grant him several rendezvous.

They would meet at the bottom of a farm-yard, behind a wall, under a solitary tree. She was not ignorant of life as young ladies are, for the animals had taught her a great deal; but her reason and an instinctive sense of honour prevented her from giving way. The resistance she put up inflamed Théodore's passion to such an extent that in order to satisfy it (or perhaps out of sheer naivety) he proposed to her. At first she refused to believe him, but he swore that he was serious.

Soon afterwards he had a disturbing piece of news to tell her: the year before, his parents had paid a man to do his military service for him, but now

5. About the price of a good dinner.

6. "Festival" (French).

he might be called up again any day, and the idea of going into the army frightened him. In Félicité's eyes this cowardice of his appeared to be a proof of his affection, and she loved him all the more for it. Every night she would steal out to meet him, and every night Théodore would plague her with his worries and entreaties.

In the end he said that he was going to the Prefecture himself to make inquiries, and that he would come and tell her how matters stood the following Sunday, between eleven and midnight.

At the appointed hour she hurried to meet her sweetheart, but found one of his friends waiting for her instead.

He told her that she would not see Théodore again. To make sure of avoiding conscription, he had married a very rich old woman, Mme Lehoussais of Toucques.

Her reaction was an outburst of frenzied grief. She threw herself on the ground, screaming and calling on God, and lay moaning all alone in the open until sunrise. Then she went back to the farm and announced her intention of leaving. At the end of the month, when she had received her wages, she wrapped her small belongings up in a kerchief and made her way to Pont-l'Évêque.

In front of the inn there, she sought information from a woman in a widow's bonnet, who, as it happened, was looking for a cook. The girl did not know much about cooking, but she seemed so willing and expected so little that finally Mme Aubain ended up by saying: 'Very well, I will take you on.'

A quarter of an hour later Félicité was installed in her house.

At first she lived there in a kind of fearful awe caused by 'the style of the house' and by the memory of 'Monsieur' brooding over everything. Paul and Virginie, the boy aged seven and the girl barely four, seemed to her to be made of some precious substance. She used to carry them about pick-a-back,[7] and when Mme Aubain told her not to keep on kissing them she was cut to the quick. All the same, she was happy now, for her pleasant surroundings had dispelled her grief.

On Thursdays, a few regular visitors came in to play Boston,[8] and Félicité got the cards and the footwarmers ready beforehand. They always arrived punctually at eight, and left before the clock struck eleven.

Every Monday morning the second-hand dealer who lived down the alley put all his junk out on the pavement. Then the hum of voices began to fill the town, mingled with the neighing of horses, the bleating of lambs, the grunting of pigs, and the rattle of carts in the streets.

About midday, when the market was in full swing, a tall old peasant with a hooked nose and his cap on the back of his head would appear at the door. This was Robelin, the farmer from Geffosses. A little later, and Liébard, the farmer from Toucques, would arrive—a short, fat, red-faced fellow in a grey jacket and leather gaiters fitted with spurs.

Both men had hens or cheeses they wanted to sell to 'Madame.' But Félicité was up to all their tricks and invariably outwitted them, so that they went away full of respect for her.

7. Piggy-back.

8. A card game.

From time to time Mme Aubain had a visit from an uncle of hers, the Marquis de Grémanville, who had been ruined by loose living and was now living at Falaise on his last remaining scrap of property. He always turned up at lunch-time, accompanied by a hideous poodle which dirtied all the furniture with its paws. However hard he tried to behave like a gentleman, even going so far as to raise his hat every time he mentioned 'my late father,' the force of habit was usually too much for him, for he would start pouring himself one glass after another and telling bawdy stories. Félicité used to push him gently out of the house, saying politely: 'You've had quite enough, Monsieur de Grémanville. See you another time!' and shutting the door on him.

She used to open it with pleasure to M. Bourais, who was a retired solicitor. His white tie and his bald head, his frilled shirt-front and his ample brown frock-coat, the way he had of rounding his arm to take a pinch of snuff, and indeed everything about him made an overwhelming impression on her such as we feel when we meet some outstanding personality.

As he looked after 'Madame's' property, he used to shut himself up with her for hours in 'Monsieur's' study. He lived in dread of compromising his reputation, had a tremendous respect for the Bench, and laid claim to some knowledge of Latin.

To give the children a little painless instruction, he made them a present of a geography book with illustrations. These represented scenes in different parts of the world, such as cannibals wearing feather head-dresses, a monkey carrying off a young lady, Bedouins in the desert, a whale being harpooned, and so on.

Paul explained these pictures to Félicité, and that indeed was all the education she ever had. As for the children, they were taught by Guyot, a poor devil employed at the Town Hall, who was famous for his beautiful handwriting, and who had a habit of sharpening his penknife on his boots.

When the weather was fine the whole household used to set off early for a day at the Geffosses farm.

The farm-yard there was on a slope, with the house in the middle; and the sea, in the distance, looked like a streak of grey. Félicité would take some slices of cold meat out of her basket, and they would have their lunch in a room adjoining the dairy. It was all that remained of a country house which had fallen into ruin, and the wallpaper hung in shreds, fluttering in the draught. Mme Aubain used to sit with bowed head, absorbed in her memories, so that the children were afraid to talk. 'Why don't you run along and play?' she would say, and away they went.

Paul climbed up into the barn, caught birds, played ducks and drakes on the pond, or banged with a stick on the great casks, which sounded just like drums.

Virginie fed the rabbits, or scampered off to pick cornflowers, showing her little embroidered knickers as she ran.

One autumn evening they came home through the fields. The moon, which was in its first quarter, lit up part of the sky, and there was some mist floating like a scarf over the winding Toucques. The cattle, lying out in the middle of the pasture, looked peacefully at the four people walking by. In the third field a few got up and made a half circle in front of them.

'Don't be frightened!' said Félicité, and crooning softly, she stroked the back of the nearest animal. It turned about and the others did the same. But while they were crossing the next field they suddenly heard a dreadful bellowing. It came from a bull which had been hidden by the mist, and which now came towards the two women.

Mme Aubain started to run.

'No! No!' said Félicité. 'Not so fast!'

All the same they quickened their pace, hearing behind them a sound of heavy breathing which came nearer and nearer. The bull's hooves thudded like hammers on the turf, and they realized that it had broken into a gallop. Turning round, Félicité tore up some clods of earth and flung them at its eyes. It lowered its muzzle and thrust its horns forward, trembling with rage and bellowing horribly.

By now Mme Aubain had got to the end of the field with her two children and was frantically looking for a way over the high bank. Félicité was still backing away from the bull, hurling clods of turf which blinded it, and shouting: 'Hurry! Hurry!'

Mme Aubain got down into the ditch, pushed first Virginie and then Paul up the other side, fell once or twice trying to climb the bank, and finally managed it with a valiant effort.

The bull had driven Félicité back against a gate, and its slaver was spurting into her face. In another second it would have gored her, but she just had time to slip between two of the bars, and the great beast halted in amazement.

This adventure was talked about at Pont-l'Évêque for a good many years, but Félicité never prided herself in the least on what she had done, as it never occurred to her that she had done anything heroic.

Virginie claimed all her attention, for the fright had affected the little girl's nerves, and M. Poupart, the doctor, recommended sea-bathing at Trouville.

In those days the resort had few visitors. Mme Aubain made inquiries, consulted Bourais, and got everything ready as though for a long journey.

Her luggage went off in Liébard's cart the day before she left. The next morning he brought along two horses, one of which had a woman's saddle with a velvet back, while the other carried a cloak rolled up to make a kind of seat on its crupper. Mme Aubain sat on this, with Liébard in front. Félicité looked after Virginie on the other horse, and Paul mounted M. Lechaptois's donkey, which he had lent them on condition they took great care of it.

The road was so bad that it took two hours to travel the five miles to Toucques. The horses sank into the mud up to their pasterns and had to jerk their hind-quarters to get out; often they stumbled in the ruts, or else they had to jump. In some places, Liébard's mare came to a sudden stop, and while he waited patiently for her to move off again, he talked about the people whose properties bordered the road, adding moral reflexions to each story. For instance, in the middle of Toucques, as they were passing underneath some windows set in a mass of nasturtiums, he shrugged his shoulders and said:

'There's a Madame Lehoussais lives here. Now instead of taking a young man, she . . .'

Félicité did not hear the rest, for the horses had broken into a trot and the donkey was galloping along. All three turned down a bridle-path, a gate swung open, a couple of boys appeared, and everyone dismounted in front of a manure-heap right outside the farm-house door.

Old Mother Liébard welcomed her mistress with every appearance of pleasure. She served up a sirloin of beef for lunch, with tripe and black pudding, a fricassee of chicken, sparkling cider, a fruit tart and brandy-plums, garnishing the whole meal with compliments to Madame, who seemed to be enjoying better health, to Mademoiselle, who had turned into a 'proper little beauty,' and to Monsieur Paul, who had 'filled out a lot.' Nor did she forget their deceased grandparents, whom the Liébards had known personally, having been in the family's service for several generations.

Like its occupants, the farm had an air of antiquity. The ceiling-beams were worm-eaten, the walls black with smoke, and the window-panes grey with dust. There was an oak dresser laden with all sorts of odds and ends—jugs, plates, pewter bowls, wolf-traps, sheep-shears, and an enormous syringe which amused the children. In the three yards outside there was not a single tree without either mushrooms at its base or mistletoe in its branches. Several had been blown down and had taken root again at the middle; all of them were bent under the weight of their apples. The thatched roofs, which looked like brown velvet and varied in thickness, weathered the fiercest winds, but the cart-shed was tumbling down. Mme Aubain said that she would have it seen to, and ordered the animals to be reharnessed.

It took them another half-hour to reach Trouville. The little caravan dismounted to make their way along the Écores, a cliff jutting right out over the boats moored below; and three minutes later they got to the end of the quay and entered the courtyard of the Golden Lamb, the inn kept by Mère David.

After the first few days Virginie felt stronger, as a result of the change of air and the sea-bathing. Not having a costume, she went into the water in her chemise and her maid dressed her afterwards in a customs officer's hut which was used by the bathers.

In the afternoons they took the donkey and went off beyond the Roches-Noires,[9] in the direction of Hennequeville. To begin with, the path went uphill between gentle slopes like the lawns in a park, and then came out on a plateau where pastureland and ploughed fields alternated. On either side there were holly-bushes standing out from the tangle of brambles, and here and there a big dead tree spread its zigzag branches against the blue sky.

They almost always rested in the same field, with Deauville on their left, Le Havre on their right, and the open sea in front. The water glittered in the sunshine, smooth as a mirror, and so still that the murmur it made was scarcely audible; unseen sparrows could be heard twittering, and the sky covered the whole scene with its huge canopy. Mme Aubain sat doing her needlework, Virginie plaited rushes beside her, Félicité gathered lavender, and Paul, feeling profoundly bored, longed to get up and go.

Sometimes they crossed the Toucques in a boat and hunted for shells. When the tide went out, sea-urchins, ormers, and jelly-fish were left behind; and the children scampered around, snatching at the foam-flakes carried on the wind.

9. "Black rocks," visible on the Normandy coast at low tide.

The sleepy waves, breaking on the sand, spread themselves out along the shore. The beach stretched as far as the eye could see, bounded on the land side by the dunes which separated it from the Marais, a broad meadow in the shape of an arena. When they came back that way, Trouville, on the distant hillside, grew bigger at every step, and with its medley of oddly assorted houses seemed to blossom out in gay disorder.

On exceptionally hot days they stayed in their room. The sun shone in dazzling bars of light between the slats of the blind. There was not a sound to be heard in the village, and not a soul to be seen down in the street. Everything seemed more peaceful in the prevailing silence. In the distance caulkers were hammering away at the boats, and the smell of tar was wafted along by a sluggish breeze.

The principal amusement consisted in watching the fishing-boats come in. As soon as they had passed the buoys, they started tacking. With their canvas partly lowered and their foresails blown out like balloons they glided through the splashing waves as far as the middle of the harbour, where they suddenly dropped anchor. Then each boat came alongside the quay, and the crew threw ashore their catch of quivering fish. A line of carts stood waiting, and women in cotton bonnets rushed forward to take the baskets and kiss their men.

One day one of these women spoke to Félicité, who came back to the inn soon after in a state of great excitement. She explained that she had found one of her sisters—and Nastasie Barette, now Leroux, made her appearance, with a baby at her breast, another child holding her right hand, and on her left a little sailor-boy, his arms akimbo and his cap over one ear.

Mme Aubain sent her off after a quarter of an hour. From then on they were forever hanging round the kitchen or loitering about when the family went for a walk, though the husband kept out of sight.

Félicité became quite attached to them. She bought them a blanket, several shirts, and a stove; and it was clear that they were bent on getting all they could out of her.

This weakness of hers annoyed Mme Aubain, who in any event disliked the familiar way in which the nephew spoke to Paul. And so, as Virginie had started coughing and the good weather was over, she decided to go back to Pont-l'Évêque.

M. Bourais advised her on the choice of a school; Caen[1] was considered the best, so it was there that Paul was sent. He said good-bye bravely, feeling really rather pleased to be going to a place where he would have friends of his own.

Mme Aubain resigned herself to the loss of her son, knowing that it was unavoidable. Virginie soon got used to it. Félicité missed the din he used to make, but she was given something new to do which served as a distraction: from Christmas onwards she had to take the little girl to catechism every day.

3

After genuflecting at the door, she walked up the centre aisle under the nave, opened the door of Mme Aubain's pew, sat down, and started looking about her.

1. A cathedral school.

The choir stalls were all occupied, with the boys on the right and the girls on the left, while the curé[2] stood by the lectern. In one of the stained-glass windows in the apse the Holy Ghost looked down on the Virgin; another window showed her kneeling before the Infant Jesus; and behind the tabernacle there was a wood-carving of St. Michael slaying the dragon.[3]

The priest began with a brief outline of sacred history. Listening to him, Félicité saw in imagination the Garden of Eden, the Flood, the Tower of Babel, cities burning, peoples dying, and idols being overthrown; and this dazzling vision left her with a great respect for the Almighty and profound fear of His wrath.

Then she wept as she listened to the story of the Passion.[4] Why had they crucified Him, when He loved children, fed the multitudes, healed the blind, and had chosen out of humility to be born among the poor, on the litter of a stable? The sowing of the seed, the reaping of the harvest, the pressing of the grapes—all those familiar things of which the Gospels speak had their place in her life. God had sanctified them in passing, so that she loved the lambs more tenderly for love of the Lamb of God, and the doves for the sake of the Holy Ghost.

She found it difficult, however, to imagine what the Holy Ghost looked like, for it was not just a bird but a fire as well, and sometimes a breath.[5] She wondered whether that was its light she had seen flitting about the edge of the marshes at night, whether that was its breath she had felt driving the clouds across the sky, whether that was its voice she had heard in the sweet music of the bells. And she sat in silent adoration, delighting in the coolness of the walls and the quiet of the church.

Of dogma she neither understood nor even tried to understand anything. The curé discoursed, the children repeated their lesson, and she finally dropped off to sleep, waking up suddenly at the sound of their sabots[6] clattering across the flagstones as they left the church.

It was in this manner, simply by hearing it expounded, that she learnt her catechism, for her religious education had been neglected in her youth. From then on she copied all Virginie's observances, fasting when she did and going to confession with her. On the feast of Corpus Christi the two of them made an altar of repose together.[7]

The preparations for Virginie's first communion caused her great anxiety. She worried over her shoes, her rosary, her missal, and her gloves. And how she trembled as she helped Mme Aubain to dress the child!

All through the Mass her heart was in her mouth. One side of the choir was hidden from her by M. Bourais, but directly opposite her she could see the flock of maidens, looking like a field of snow with their white crowns perched on top of their veils; and she recognized her little darling from a distance by

2. "Priest" (French).
3. Satan, depicted as a dragon in the Book of Revelation, is cast out of heaven by St. Michael.
4. The crucifixion and death of Christ.
5. The Holy Spirit appears as both fire and breath (or wind) in the Bible.
6. Heavy wooden shoes.
7. The resting-place for the Eucharist during the Tridduum, the holiest three days of the Christian year. "Corpus Christi": "Body of Christ" (Latin), a liturgical celebration of Christ's gift of himself, in the form of bread and wine, during the mass.

her dainty neck and her rapt attitude. The bell tinkled.[8] Every head bowed low, and there was a silence. Then, to the thunderous accompaniment of the organ, choir and congregation joined in singing the *Agnus Dei*.[9] Next the boys' procession began, and after that the girls got up from their seats. Slowly, their hands joined in prayer, they went towards the brightly lit altar, knelt on the first step, received the Host one by one, and went back to their places in the same order. When it was Virginie's turn, Félicité leant forward to see her, and in one of those imaginative flights born of real affection, it seemed to her that she herself was in the child's place. Virginie's face became her own, Virginie's dress clothed her, Virginie's heart was beating in her breast; and as she closed her eyes and opened her mouth, she almost fainted away.

Early next morning she went to the sacristy and asked M. le Curé to give her communion. She received the sacrament with all due reverence, but did not feel the same rapture as she had the day before.

Mme Aubain wanted her daughter to possess every accomplishment, and since Guyot could not teach her English or music, she decided to send her as a boarder to the Ursuline[1] Convent at Honfleur.

Virginie raised no objection, but Félicité went about sighing at Madame's lack of feeling. Then she thought that perhaps her mistress was right: such matters, after all, lay outside her province.

Finally the day arrived when an old waggonette stopped at their door, and a nun got down from it who had come to fetch Mademoiselle. Félicité hoisted the luggage up on top, gave the driver some parting instructions, and put six pots of jam, a dozen pears, and a bunch of violets in the boot.

At the last moment Virginie burst into a fit of sobbing. She threw her arms round her mother, who kissed her on the forehead, saying: 'Come now, be brave, be brave.' The step was pulled up and the carriage drove away.

Then Mme Aubain broke down, and that evening all her friends, M. and Mme Lormeau, Mme Lechaptois, the Rochefeuille sisters, M. de Houppeville, and Bourais, came in to console her.

To begin with she missed her daughter badly. But she had a letter from her three times a week, wrote back on the other days, walked round her garden, did a little reading, and thus contrived to fill the empty hours.

As for Félicité, she went into Virginie's room every morning from sheer force of habit and looked round it. It upset her not having to brush the child's hair any more, tie her bootlaces, or tuck her up in bed; and she missed seeing her sweet face all the time and holding her hand when they went out together. For want of something to do, she tried making lace, but her fingers were too clumsy and broke the threads. She could not settle to anything, lost her sleep, and, to use her own words, was 'eaten up inside.'

To 'occupy her mind,' she asked if her nephew Victor might come and see her, and permission was granted.

He used to arrive after Mass on Sunday, his cheeks flushed, his chest bare, and smelling of the countryside through which he had come. She laid a place

8. The bell marks the moment of transubstantiation during the mass.
9. "Lamb of God" (Latin); a plea for God's mercy.
1. Catholic religious order concerned with the education of girls.

for him straight away, opposite hers, and they had lunch together. Eating as little as possible herself, in order to save the expense, she stuffed him so full of food that he fell asleep after the meal. When the first bell for vespers rang, she woke him up, brushed his trousers, tied his tie, and set off for church, leaning on his arm with all a mother's pride.

His parents always told him to get something out of her—a packet of brown sugar perhaps, some soap, or a little brandy, sometimes even money. He brought her his clothes to be mended, and she did the work gladly, thankful for anything that would force him to come again.

In August his father took him on a coasting trip. The children's holidays were just beginning, and it cheered her up to have them home again. But Paul was turning capricious and Virginie was getting too old to be addressed familiarly—a state of affairs which put a barrier of constraint between them.

Victor went to Morlaix, Dunkirk, and Brighton in turn, and brought her a present after each trip. The first time it was a box covered with shells, the second a coffee cup, the third a big gingerbread man. He was growing quite handsome, with his trim figure, his little moustache, his frank open eyes, and the little leather cap that he wore on the back of his head like a pilot. He kept her amused by telling her stories full of nautical jargon.

One Monday—it was the fourteenth of July 1819,[2] a date she never forgot—Victor told her that he had signed on for an ocean voyage, and that on the Wednesday night he would be taking the Honfleur packet to join his schooner, which was due to sail shortly from Le Havre. He might be away, he said, for two years.

The prospect of such a long absence made Félicité extremely unhappy, and she felt she must bid him godspeed once more. So on the Wednesday evening, when Madame's dinner was over, she put on her clogs and swiftly covered the ten miles between Pont-l'Évêque and Honfleur.

When she arrived at the Calvary[3] she turned right instead of left, got lost in the shipyards, and had to retrace her steps. Some people she spoke to advised her to hurry. She went right round the harbour, which was full of boats, constantly tripping over moorings. Then the ground fell away, rays of light crisscrossed in front of her, and for a moment she thought she was going mad, for she could see horses up in the sky.

On the quayside more horses were neighing, frightened by the sea. A derrick was hoisting them into the air and dropping them into one of the boats, which was already crowded with passengers elbowing their way between barrels of cider, baskets of cheese, and sacks of grain. Hens were cackling and the captain swearing, while a cabin-boy stood leaning on the cats-head, completely indifferent to it all. Félicité, who had not recognized him, shouted: 'Victor!' and he raised his head. She rushed forward, but at that very moment the gangway was pulled ashore.

2. The national holiday called Bastille Day, which commemorates the start of the French Revolution.

3. Public crucifix.

The packet moved out of the harbour with women singing as they hauled it along, its ribs creaking and heavy waves lashing its bows. The sail swung round, hiding everyone on board from view, and against the silvery, moonlit sea the boat appeared as a dark shape that grew ever fainter, until at last it vanished in the distance.

As Félicité was passing the Calvary, she felt a longing to commend to God's mercy all that she held most dear; and she stood there praying for a long time, her face bathed in tears, her eyes fixed upon the clouds. The town was asleep, except for the customs officers walking up and down. Water was pouring ceaselessly through the holes in the sluice-gate, making as much noise as a torrent. The clocks struck two.

The convent parlour would not be open before daybreak, and Madame would be annoyed if she were late; so, although she would have liked to give a kiss to the other child, she set off for home. The maids at the inn were just waking up as she got to Pont-l'Évêque.

So the poor lad was going to be tossed by the waves for months on end! His previous voyages had caused her no alarm. People came back from England and Brittany; but America, the Colonies, the Islands, were all so far away, somewhere at the other end of the world.

From then on Félicité thought of nothing but her nephew. On sunny days she hoped he was not too thirsty, and when there was a storm she was afraid he would be struck by lightning. Listening to the wind howling in the chimney or blowing slates off the roof, she saw him being buffeted by the very same storm, perched on the top of a broken mast, with his whole body bent backwards under a sheet of foam; or again—and these were reminiscences of the illustrated geography-book—he was being eaten by savages, captured by monkeys in a forest, or dying on a desert shore. But she never spoke of her worries.

Mme Aubain had worries of her own about her daughter. The good nuns said that she was an affectionate child, but very delicate. The slightest emotion upset her, and she had to give up playing the piano.

Her mother insisted on regular letters from the convent. One morning when the postman had not called, she lost patience and walked up and down the room, between her chair and the window. It was really extraordinary! Four days without any news!

Thinking her own example would comfort her, Félicité said:

'I've been six months, Madame, without news.'

'News of whom?'

The servant answered gently:

'Why—of my nephew.'

'Oh, your nephew!' And Mme Aubain started pacing up and down again, with a shrug of her shoulders that seemed to say: 'I wasn't thinking of him—and indeed, why should I? Who cares about a young, good-for-nothing cabin-boy? Whereas my daughter—why, just think!'

Although she had been brought up the hard way, Félicité was indignant with Madame, but she soon forgot. It struck her as perfectly natural to lose one's head where the little girl was concerned. For her, the two children were of equal importance; they were linked together in her heart by a single bond, and their destinies should be the same.

The chemist[4] told her that Victor's ship had arrived at Havana: he had seen this piece of information in a newspaper.

Because of its association with cigars, she imagined Havana as a place where nobody did anything but smoke, and pictured Victor walking about among crowds of Negroes in a cloud of tobacco-smoke. Was it possible, she wondered, 'in case of need' to come back by land? And how far was it from Pont-l'Évêque? To find out she asked M. Bourais.

He reached for his atlas, and launched forth into an explanation of latitudes and longitudes, smiling like the pedant he was at Félicité's bewilderment. Finally he pointed with his pencil at a minute black dot inside a ragged oval patch, saying:

'There it is.'

She bent over the map, but the network of coloured lines meant nothing to her and only tired her eyes. So when Bourais asked her to tell him what was puzzling her, she begged him to show her the house where Victor was living. He threw up his hands, sneezed, and roared with laughter, delighted to come across such simplicity. And Félicité—whose intelligence was so limited that she probably expected to see an actual portrait of her nephew—could not make out why he was laughing.

It was a fortnight later that Liébard came into the kitchen at market-time, as he usually did, and handed her a letter from her brother-in-law. As neither of them could read, she turned to her mistress for help.

Mme Aubain, who was counting the stitches in her knitting, put it down and unsealed the letter. She gave a start, and, looking hard at Félicité, said quietly:

'They have some bad news for you . . . Your nephew . . .'

He was dead. That was all the letter had to say.

Félicité dropped on to a chair, leaning her head against the wall and closing her eyelids, which suddenly turned pink. Then, with her head bowed, her hands dangling, and her eyes set, she kept repeating:

'Poor little lad! Poor little lad!'

Liébard looked at her and sighed. Mme Aubain was trembling slightly. She suggested that she should go and see her sister at Trouville, but Félicité shook her head to indicate that there was no need for that.

There was a silence. Old Liébard thought it advisable to go.

Then Félicité said:

'It doesn't matter a bit, not to them it doesn't.'

Her head fell forward again, and from time to time she unconsciously picked up the knitting needles lying on the worktable.

Some women went past carrying a tray full of dripping linen.

Catching sight of them through the window, she remembered her own washing; she had passed the lye through it the day before and today it needed rinsing. So she left the room.

Her board and tub were on the bank of the Toucques. She threw a pile of chemises down by the water's edge, rolled up her sleeves, and picked up her battledore. The lusty blows she gave with it could be heard in all the neighbouring gardens.

4. Pharmacist.

The fields were empty, the river rippling in the wind; at the bottom long weeds were waving to and fro, like the hair of corpses floating in the water. She held back her grief, and was very brave until the evening; but in her room she gave way to it completely, lying on her mattress with her face buried in the pillow and her fists pressed against her temples.

Long afterwards she learnt the circumstances of Victor's death from the captain of his ship. He had gone down with yellow fever, and they had bled him too much at the hospital. Four doctors had held him at once. He had died straight away, and the chief doctor had said:

'Good! There goes another!'

His parents had always treated him cruelly. She preferred not to see them again, and they made no advances, either because they had forgotten about her or out of the callousness of the poor.

Meanwhile Virginie was growing weaker. Difficulty in breathing, fits of coughing, protracted bouts of fever, and mottled patches on the cheekbones all indicated some deep-seated complaint. M. Poupart had advised a stay in Provence. Mme Aubain decided to follow this suggestion, and, if it had not been for the weather at Pont-l'Évêque, she would have brought her daughter home at once.

She arranged with a jobmaster[5] to drive her out to the convent every Tuesday. There was a terrace in the garden, overlooking the Seine, and there Virginie, leaning on her mother's arm, walked up and down over the fallen vine-leaves. Sometimes, while she was looking at the sails in the distance, or at the long stretch of horizon from the Château de Tancarville to the lighthouses of Le Havre, the sun would break through the clouds and make her blink. Afterwards they would rest in the arbour. Her mother had secured a little cask of excellent Malaga,[6] and, laughing at the idea of getting tipsy, Virginie used to drink a thimbleful, but no more.

Her strength revived. Autumn slipped by, and Félicité assured Mme Aubain that there was nothing to fear. But one evening, coming back from some errand in the neighbourhood, she found M. Poupart's gig standing at the door. He was in the hall, and Mme Aubain was tying on her bonnet.

'Give me my foot warmer, purse, gloves. Quickly now!'

Virginie had pneumonia and was perhaps past recovery.

'Not yet!' said the doctor; and the two of them got into the carriage with snow-flakes swirling around them. Night was falling and it was very cold.

Félicité rushed into the church to light a candle, and then ran after the gig. She caught up with it an hour later, jumped lightly up behind, and hung on to the fringe. But then a thought struck her: the courtyard had not been locked up, and burglars might get in. So she jumped down again.

At dawn the next day she went to the doctor's. He had come home and gone out again on his rounds. Then she waited at the inn, thinking that somebody who was a stranger to the district might call there with a letter. Finally, when it was twilight, she got into the coach for Lisieux.

5. One who loans horses and carriages.

6. A Spanish dessert wine.

The convent was at the bottom of a steep lane. When she was half-way down the hill, she heard a strange sound which she recognized as a death-bell tolling.

'It's for somebody else,' she thought, as she banged the door-knocker hard.

After a few minutes she heard the sound of shuffling feet, the door opened a little way, and a nun appeared.

The good sister said with an air of compunction that 'she had just passed away.' At that moment the bell of Saint-Léonard was tolled more vigorously than ever.

Félicité went up to the second floor. From the doorway of the room she could see Virginie lying on her back, her hands clasped together, her mouth open, her head tilted back under a black crucifix that leant over her, her face whiter than the curtains that hung motionless on either side. Mme Aubain was clinging to the foot of the bed and sobbing desperately. The Mother Superior stood on the right. Three candlesticks on the chest of drawers added touches of red to the scene, and fog was whitening the windows. Some nuns led Mme Aubain away.

For two nights Félicité never left the dead girl. She said the same prayers over and over again, sprinkled holy water on the sheets, then sat down again to watch. At the end of her first vigil, she noticed that the child's face had gone yellow, the lips were turning blue, the nose looked sharper, and the eyes were sunken. She kissed them several times, and would not have been particularly surprised if Virginie had opened them again: to minds like hers the supernatural is a simple matter. She laid her out, wrapped her in a shroud, put her in her coffin, placed a wreath on her, and spread out her hair. It was fair and amazingly long for her age. Félicité cut off a big lock, half of which she slipped into her bosom, resolving never to part with it.

The body was brought back to Pont-l'Évêque at the request of Mme Aubain, who followed the hearse in a closed carriage.

After the Requiem Mass, it took another three-quarters of an hour to reach the cemetery. Paul walked in front, sobbing. Then came M. Bourais, and after him the principal inhabitants of the town, the women all wearing long black veils, and Félicité. She was thinking about her nephew; and since she had been unable to pay him these last honours, she felt an added grief, just as if they were burying him with Virginie.

Mme Aubain's despair passed all bounds. First of all she rebelled against God, considering it unfair of Him to have taken her daughter from her—for she had never done any harm, and her conscience was quite clear. But was it? She ought to have taken Virginie to the south; other doctors would have saved her life. She blamed herself, wished she could have joined her daughter, and cried out in anguish in her dreams. One dream in particular obsessed her. Her husband, dressed like a sailor, came back from a long voyage, and told her amid tears that he had been ordered to take Virginie away—whereupon they put their heads together to discover somewhere to hide her.

One day she came in from the garden utterly distraught. A few minutes earlier—and she pointed to the spot—father and daughter had appeared to her, doing nothing, but simply looking at her.

For several months she stayed in her room in a kind of stupor. Félicité scolded her gently telling her that she must take care of herself for her son's sake, and also in remembrance of 'her.'

'Her?' repeated Mme Aubain, as if she were waking from a sleep. 'Oh, yes, of course! You don't forget her, do you!' This was an allusion to the cemetery, where she herself was strictly forbidden to go.

Félicité went there every day. She would set out on the stroke of four, going past the houses, up the hill, and through the gate, until she came to Virginie's grave. There was a little column of pink marble with a tablet at its base, and a tiny garden enclosed by chains. The beds were hidden under a carpet of flowers. She watered their leaves and changed the sand, going down on her knees to fork the ground thoroughly. The result was that when Mme Aubain was able to come here, she experienced a feeling of relief, a kind of consolation.

Then the years slipped by, each one like the last, with nothing to vary the rhythm of the great festivals: Easter, the Assumption, All Saints' Day.[7] Domestic events marked dates that later served as points of reference. Thus in 1825 a couple of glaziers whitewashed the hall; in 1827 a piece of the roof fell into the courtyard and nearly killed a man; and in the summer of 1828 it was Madame's turn to provide the bread for consecration. About this time Bourais went away in a mysterious fashion; and one by one the old acquaintances disappeared: Guyot, Liébard, Mme Lechaptois, Robelin, and Uncle Grémanville, who had been paralysed for a long time.

One night the driver of the mail-coach brought Pont-l'Évêque news of the July Revolution.[8] A few days later a new sub-prefect[9] was appointed. This was the Baron de Larsonnière, who had been a consul in America, and who brought with him, besides his wife, his sister-in-law and three young ladies who were almost grown-up. They were to be seen on their lawn, dressed in loose-fitting smocks; and they had a Negro servant and a parrot. They paid a call on Mme Aubain, who made a point of returning it. As soon as Félicité saw them coming, she would run and tell her mistress. But only one thing could really awaken her interest, and that was her son's letters.

He seemed to be incapable of following any career and spent all his time in taverns. She paid his debts, but he contracted new ones, and the sighs Mme Aubain heaved as she knitted by the window reached Félicité at her spinning-wheel in the kitchen.

The two women used to walk up and down together beside the espalier, forever talking of Virginie and debating whether such and such a thing would have appealed to her, or what she would have said on such and such an occasion.

All her little belongings were in a cupboard in the children's bedroom. Mme Aubain went through them as seldom as possible. One summer day she resigned herself to doing so, and the moths were sent fluttering out of the cupboard.

Virginie's frocks hung in a row underneath a shelf containing three dolls, a few hoops, a set of toy furniture, and the wash-basin she had used. Besides the frocks, they took out her petticoats, her stockings and her handkerchiefs, and spread them out on the two beds before folding them up again.

7. Catholic holy days that mark the arrival of souls into heaven.

8. The July Revolution of 1830 toppled the French king Charles X and established a new constitutional monarchy.

9. Government official responsible for a region.

The sunlight streamed in on these pathetic objects, bringing out the stains and showing up the creases made by the child's movements. The air was warm, the sky was blue, a blackbird was singing, and everything seemed to be utterly at peace.

They found a little chestnut-coloured hat, made of plush with a long nap; but the moths had ruined it. Félicité asked if she might have it. The two women looked at each other and their eyes filled with tears. Then the mistress opened her arms, the maid threw herself into them, and they clasped each other in a warm embrace, satisfying their grief in a kiss which made them equal.

It was the first time that such a thing had happened, for Mme Aubain was not of a demonstrative nature. Félicité was as grateful as if she had received a great favour, and henceforth loved her mistress with dog-like devotion and religious veneration.

Her heart grew softer as time went by.

When she heard the drums of a regiment coming down the street she stood at the door with a jug of cider and offered the soldiers a drink. She looked after the people who went down with cholera. She watched over the Polish refugees,[1] and one of them actually expressed a desire to marry her. But they fell out, for when she came back from the Angelus[2] one morning, she found that he had got into her kitchen and was calmly eating an oil-and-vinegar salad.

After the Poles it was Père Colmiche, an old man who was said to have committed fearful atrocities in '93.[3] He lived by the river in a ruined pig-sty. The boys of the town used to peer at him through the cracks in the walls, and threw pebbles at him which landed on the litter where he lay, constantly shaken by fits of coughing. His hair was extremely long, his eyelids inflamed, and on one arm there was a swelling bigger than his head. Félicité brought him some linen, tried to clean out his filthy hovel, and even wondered if she could install him in the wash-house without annoying Madame. When the tumour had burst, she changed his dressings every day, brought him some cake now and then, and put him out in the sun on a truss of hay. The poor old fellow would thank her in a faint whisper, slavering and trembling all the while, fearful of losing her and stretching his hands out as soon as he saw her moving away.

He died, and she had a Mass said for the repose of his soul.

That same day a great piece of good fortune came her way. Just as she was serving dinner, Mme de Larsonnière's Negro appeared carrying the parrot in its cage, complete with perch, chain, and padlock. The Baroness had written a note informing Mme Aubain that her husband had been promoted to a Prefecture and they were leaving that evening; she begged her to accept the parrot as a keepsake and a token of her regard.

This bird had engrossed Félicité's thoughts for a long time, for it came from America, and that word reminded her of Victor. So she had asked the Negro all about it, and once she had even gone so far as to say:

'How pleased Madame would be if it were hers!'

1. After the July Revolution, a spirit of revolt spread throughout Europe, prompting Poles and other Europeans to seek refuge in France.
2. A daily prayer to the Virgin Mary.
3. I.e., 1793, the height of the Reign of Terror during the French Revolution when thousands of people were guillotined.

The Negro had repeated this remark to his mistress, who, unable to take the parrot with her, was glad to get rid of it in this way.

4

His name was Loulou. His body was green, the tips of his wings were pink, his poll blue, and his breast golden.

Unfortunately he had a tiresome mania for biting his perch, and also used to pull his feathers out, scatter his droppings everywhere, and upset his bath water. He annoyed Mme Aubain, and so she gave him to Félicité for good.

Félicité started training him, and soon he could say: 'Nice boy! Your servant, sir! Hail, Mary!' He was put near the door, and several people who spoke to him said how strange it was that he did not answer to the name of Jacquot, as all parrots were called Jacquot.[4] They likened him to a turkey or a block of wood, and every sneer cut Félicité to the quick. How odd, she thought, that Loulou should be so stubborn, refusing to talk whenever anyone looked at him!

For all that, he liked having people around him, because on Sundays, while the Rochefeuille sisters, M. Houppeville and some new friends—the apothecary Onfroy, M. Varin, and Captain Mathieu—were having their game of cards, he would beat on the window-panes with his wings and make such a din that it was impossible to hear oneself speak.

Bourais's face obviously struck him as terribly funny, for as soon as he saw it he was seized with uncontrollable laughter. His shrieks rang round the courtyard, the echo repeated them, and the neighbours came to their windows and started laughing too. To avoid being seen by the bird, M. Bourais used to creep along by the wall, hiding his face behind his hat, until he got to the river, and then come into the house from the garden. The looks he gave the parrot were far from tender.

Loulou had once been cuffed by the butcher's boy for poking his head into his basket; and since then he was always trying to give him a nip through his shirt. Fabu threatened to wring his neck, although he was not a cruel fellow, in spite of his tattooed arms and bushy whiskers. On the contrary, he rather liked the parrot, so much so indeed that in a spirit of jovial camaraderie he tried to teach him a few swear-words. Félicité, alarmed at this development, put the bird in the kitchen. His little chain was removed and he was allowed to wander all over the house.

Coming downstairs, he used to rest the curved part of his beak on each step and then raise first his right foot, then his left; and Félicité was afraid that this sort of gymnastic performance would make him giddy. He fell ill and could neither talk nor eat for there was a swelling under his tongue such as hens sometimes have. She cured him by pulling this pellicule out with her finger-nails. One day M. Paul was silly enough to blow the smoke of his cigar at him; another time Mme Lormeau started teasing him with the end of her parasol, and he caught hold of the ferrule with his beak. Finally he got lost.

Félicité had put him down on the grass in the fresh air, and left him there for a minute. When she came back, the parrot had gone. First of all she looked for him in the bushes, by the river and on the rooftops, paying no attention to

4. A species of parrot native to the island of St. Lucia in the West Indies.

her mistress's shouts of: 'Be careful, now! You must be mad!' Next she went over all the gardens in Pont-l'Évêque, stopping passersby and asking them: 'You don't happen to have seen my parrot by any chance?' Those who did not know him already were given a description of the bird. Suddenly she thought she could make out something green flying about behind the mills at the foot of the hill. But up on the hill there was nothing to be seen. A pedlar told her that he had come upon the parrot a short time before in Mère Simon's shop at Saint-Melaine. She ran all the way there, but no one knew what she was talking about. Finally she came back home, worn out, her shoes falling to pieces, and death in her heart. She was sitting beside Madame on the garden-seat and telling her what she had been doing, when she felt something light drop on her shoulder. It was Loulou! What he had been up to, no one could discover: perhaps he had just gone for a little walk round the town.

Félicité was slow to recover from this fright, and indeed never really got over it.

As the result of a chill she had an attack of quinsy,[5] and soon after that her ears were affected. Three years later she was deaf, and she spoke at the top of her voice, even in church. Although her sins could have been proclaimed over the length and breadth of the diocese without dishonour to her or offence to others, M. le Curé thought it advisable to hear her confession in the sacristy.

Imaginary buzzings in the head added to her troubles. Often her mistress would say: 'Heavens, how stupid you are!' and she would reply: 'Yes, Madame,' at the same time looking all around her for something.

The little circle of her ideas grew narrower and narrower, and the pealing of bells and the lowing of cattle went out of her life. Every living thing moved about in a ghostly silence. Only one sound reached her ears now, and that was the voice of the parrot.

As if to amuse her, he would reproduce the click-clack of the turn-spit, the shrill call of a man selling fish, and the noise of the saw at the joiner's across the way; and when the bell rang he would imitate Mme Aubain's 'Félicité ! The door, the door !'

They held conversations with each other, he repeating *ad nauseam* the three phrases in his repertory, she replying with words which were just as disconnected but which came from the heart. In her isolation, Loulou was almost a son or a lover to her. He used to climb up her fingers, peck at her lips, and hang on to her shawl; and as she bent over him, wagging her head from side to side as nurses do, the great wings of her bonnet and the wings of the bird quivered in unison.

When clouds banked up in the sky and there was a rumbling of thunder, he would utter piercing cries, no doubt remembering the sudden downpours in his native forests. The sound of the rain falling roused him to frenzy. He would flap excitedly around, shoot up to the ceiling, knocking everything over, and fly out of the window to splash about in the garden. But he would soon come back to perch on one of the firedogs, hopping about to dry his feathers and showing tail and beak in turn.

5. Tonsillitis.

One morning in the terrible winter of 1837, when she had put him in front of the fire because of the cold she found him dead in the middle of his cage, hanging head down with his claws caught in the bars. He had probably died of a stroke, but she thought he had been poisoned with parsley,[6] and despite the absence of any proof, her suspicions fell on Fabu.

She wept so much that her mistress said to her: 'Why don't you have him stuffed?'

Félicité asked the chemist's advice, remembering that he had always been kind to the parrot. He wrote to Le Havre, and a man called Fellacher agreed to do the job. As parcels sometimes went astray on the mail-coach, she decided to take the parrot as far as Honfleur herself.

On either side of the road stretched an endless succession of apple-trees, all stripped of their leaves, and there was ice in the ditches. Dogs were barking around the farms; and Félicité, with her hands tucked under her mantlet, her little black sabots and her basket, walked briskly along the middle of the road.

She crossed the forest, passed Le Haut-Chêne, and got as far as Saint-Gatien.

Behind her, in a cloud of dust, and gathering speed as the horses galloped downhill, a mail-coach swept along like a whirlwind. When he saw this woman making no attempt to get out of the way, the driver poked his head out above the hood, and he and the postilion shouted at her. His four horses could not be held in and galloped faster, the two leaders touching her as they went by. With a jerk of the reins the driver threw them to one side, and then, in a fury, he raised his long whip and gave her such a lash, from head to waist, that she fell flat on her back.

The first thing she did on regaining consciousness was to open her basket. Fortunately nothing had happened to Loulou. She felt her right cheek burning, and when she touched it her hand turned red; it was bleeding.

She sat down on a heap of stones and dabbed her face with her handkerchief. Then she ate a crust of bread which she had taken the precaution of putting in her basket, and tried to forget her wound by looking at the bird.

As she reached the top of the hill at Ecquemauville, she saw the lights of Honfleur twinkling in the darkness like a host of stars, and the shadowy expanse of the sea beyond. Then a sudden feeling of faintness made her stop; and the misery of her childhood, the disappointment of her first love, the departure of her nephew, and the death of Virginie all came back to her at once like the waves of a rising tide, and, welling up in her throat, choked her.

When she got to the boat she insisted on speaking to the captain, and without telling him what was in her parcel, asked him to take good care of it.

Fellacher kept the parrot a long time. Every week he promised it for the next; after six months he announced that a box had been sent off, and nothing more was heard of it. It looked as though Loulou would never come back, and Félicité told herself: 'They've stolen him for sure!'

At last he arrived—looking quite magnificent, perched on a branch screwed into a mahogany base, one foot in the air, his head cocked to one side, and biting a nut which the taxidermist, out of a love of the grandiose, had gilded.

6. Fool's Parsley, a poisonous plant resembling parsley in appearance.

Félicité shut him up in her room.

This place, to which few people were ever admitted, contained such a quantity of religious bric-à-brac and miscellaneous oddments that it looked like a cross between a chapel and a bazaar.

A big wardrobe prevented the door from opening properly. Opposite the window that overlooked the garden was a little round one looking on to the courtyard. There was a table beside the bed, with a water-jug, a couple of combs, and a block of blue soap in a chipped plate. On the walls there were rosaries, medals, several pictures of the Virgin, and a holy-water stoup made out of a coconut. On the chest of drawers, which was draped with a cloth just like an altar, was the shell box Victor had given her, and also a watering-can and a ball, some copy-books, the illustrated geography book, and a pair of ankle-boots. And on the nail supporting the looking-glass, fastened by its ribbons, hung the little plush hat.

Félicité carried this form of veneration to such lengths that she even kept one of Monsieur's frock-coats. All the old rubbish Mme Aubain had no more use for, she carried off to her room. That was how there came to be artificial flowers along the edge of the chest of drawers, and a portrait of the Comte d'Artois[7] in the window-recess.

With the aid of a wall-bracket, Loulou was installed on a chimney-breast that jutted out into the room. Every morning when she awoke, she saw him in the light of the dawn, and then she remembered the old days, and the smallest details of insignificant actions, not in sorrow but in absolute tranquillity.

Having no intercourse with anyone, she lived in the torpid state of a sleepwalker. The Corpus Christi processions roused her from this condition, for she would go round the neighbours collecting candlesticks and mats to decorate the altar of repose which they used to set up in the street.

In church she was forever gazing at the Holy Ghost, and one day she noticed that it had something of the parrot about it. This resemblance struck her as even more obvious in a colour-print depicting the baptism of Our Lord. With its red wings and its emerald-green body, it was the very image of Loulou.

She bought the print and hung it in the place of the Comte d'Artois, so that she could include them both in a single glance. They were linked together in her mind, the parrot being sanctified by this connexion with the Holy Ghost, which itself acquired new life and meaning in her eyes. God the Father could not have chosen a dove as a means of expressing Himself, since doves cannot talk, but rather one of Loulou's ancestors. And although Félicité used to say her prayers with her eyes on the picture, from time to time she would turn slightly towards the bird.

She wanted to join the Children of Mary,[8] but Mme Aubain dissuaded her from doing so.

An important event now loomed up—Paul's wedding.

After starting as a lawyer's clerk, he had been in business, in the Customs, and in Inland Revenue, and had even begun trying to get into the Department

7. Charles Philippe, Comte d' Artois (1757–1836), reigned as King Charles X from 1824 until 1830, when he was overthrown in the July Revolution.

8. Society of laywomen who pledge to imitate the Virgin Mary.

of Woods and Forests, when, at the age of thirty-six, by some heaven-sent inspiration, he suddenly discovered his real vocation—in the Wills and Probate Department. There he proved so capable that one of the auditors had offered him his daughter in marriage and promised to use his influence on his behalf.

Paul, grown serious-minded, brought her to see his mother. She criticized the way things were done at Pont-l'Évêque, put on airs, and hurt Félicité's feelings. Mme Aubain was relieved to see her go.

The following week came news of M. Bourais's death in an inn in Lower Brittany. Rumours that he had committed suicide were confirmed, and doubts arose as to his honesty. Mme Aubain went over her accounts and was soon conversant with the full catalogue of his misdeeds—embezzlement of interest, secret sales of timber, forged receipts, etc. Besides all this, he was the father of an illegitimate child, and had had 'relations with a person at Dozulé.'

These infamies upset Mme Aubain greatly. In March 1853 she was afflicted with a pain in the chest; her tongue seemed to be covered with a film; leeches failed to make her breathing any easier; and on the ninth evening of her illness she died. She had just reached the age of seventy-two.

She was thought to be younger because of her brown hair, worn in bandeaux round her pale, pock-marked face. There were few friends to mourn her, for she had a haughty manner which put people off. Yet Félicité wept for her as servants rarely weep for their masters. That Madame should die before her upset her ideas, seemed to be contrary to the order of things, monstrous and unthinkable.

Ten days later—the time it took to travel hot-foot from Besançon—the heirs arrived. The daughter-in-law ransacked every drawer, picked out some pieces of furniture and sold the rest; and then back they went to the Wills and Probate Department.

Madame's arm-chair, her pedestal table, her foot warmer, and the eight chairs had all gone. Yellow squares in the centre of the wall-panels showed where the pictures had hung. They had carried off the two cots with their mattresses, and no trace remained in the cupboard of all Virginie's things. Félicité climbed the stairs to her room, numbed with sadness.

The next day there was a notice on the door, and the apothecary shouted in her ear that the house was up for sale.

She swayed on her feet, and was obliged to sit down.

What distressed her most of all was the idea of leaving her room, which was so suitable for poor Loulou. Fixing an anguished look on him as she appealed to the Holy Ghost, she contracted the idolatrous habit of kneeling in front of the parrot to say her prayers. Sometimes the sun, as it came through the little window, caught his glass eye, so that it shot out a great luminous ray which sent her into ecstasies.

She had a pension of three hundred and eighty francs a year which her mistress had left her. The garden kept her in vegetables. As for clothes, she had enough to last her till the end of her days, and she saved on lighting by going to bed as soon as darkness fell.

She went out as little as possible, to avoid the second-hand dealer's shop, where some of the old furniture was on display. Ever since her fit of giddiness, she had been dragging one leg; and as her strength was failing, Mère Simon, whose grocery business had come to grief, came in every morning to chop wood and pump water for her.

Her eyes grew weaker. The shutters were not opened any more. Years went by, and nobody rented the house and nobody bought it.

For fear of being evicted, Félicité never asked for any repairs to be done. The laths in the roof rotted, and all through one winter her bolster was wet. After Easter she began spitting blood.

When this happened Mère Simon called in a doctor. Félicité wanted to know what was the matter with her, but she was so deaf that only one word reached her: 'Pneumonia.' It was a word she knew, and she answered gently: 'Ah! like Madame,' thinking it natural that she should follow in her mistress's footsteps.

The time to set up the altars of repose was drawing near.

The first altar was always at the foot of the hill, the second in front of the post office, the third about half-way up the street. There was some argument as to the siting of this one, and finally the women of the parish picked on Mme Aubain's courtyard.

The fever and the tightness of the chest grew worse. Félicité fretted over not doing anything for the altar. If only she could have put something on it! Then she thought of the parrot. The neighbours protested that it would not be seemly, but the curé gave his permission, and this made her so happy that she begged him to accept Loulou, the only thing of value she possessed, when she died.

From Tuesday to Saturday, the eve of Corpus Christi, she coughed more and more frequently. In the evening her face looked pinched and drawn, her lips stuck to her gums, and she started vomiting. At dawn the next day, feeling very low, she sent for a priest.

Three good women stood by her while she was given extreme unction. Then she said that she had to speak to Fabu.

He arrived in his Sunday best, very ill at ease in this funereal atmosphere.

'Forgive me,' she said, making an effort to stretch out her arm. 'I thought it was you who had killed him.'

What could she mean by such nonsense? To think that she had suspected a man like him of murder! He got very indignant and was obviously going to make a scene.

'Can't you see,' they said, 'that she isn't in her right mind any more?'

From time to time Félicité would start talking to shadows. The women went away. Mère Simon had her lunch.

A little later she picked Loulou up and held him out to Félicité, saying:

'Come now, say good-bye to him.'

Although the parrot was not a corpse, the worms were eating him up. One of his wings was broken, and the stuffing was coming out of his stomach. But she was blind by now, and she kissed him on the forehead and pressed him against her cheek. Mère Simon took him away from her to put him on the altar.

5

The scents of summer came up from the meadows; there was a buzzing of flies; the sun was glittering in the river and warming the slates of the roof. Mère Simon had come back into the room and was gently nodding off to sleep.

The noise of church bells woke her up; the congregation was coming out from vespers. Félicité's delirium abated. Thinking of the procession, she could see it as clearly as if she had been following it.

All the school-children, the choristers, and the firemen were walking along the pavements, while advancing up the middle of the street came the church officer armed with his halberd, the beadle carrying a great cross, the schoolmaster keeping an eye on the boys, and the nun fussing over her little girls—three of the prettiest, looking like curly-headed angels, were throwing rose-petals into the air. Then came the deacon, with both arms outstretched, conducting the band, and a couple of censer-bearers who turned round at every step to face the Holy Sacrament, which the curé, wearing his splendid chasuble, was carrying under a canopy of poppy-red velvet held aloft by four churchwardens. A crowd of people surged along behind, between the white cloths covering the walls of the houses, and eventually they got to the bottom of the hill.

A cold sweat moistened Félicité's temples. Mère Simon sponged it up with a cloth, telling herself that one day she would have to go the same way.

The hum of the crowd increased in volume, was very loud for a moment, then faded away.

A fusillade shook the window-panes. It was the postilions saluting the monstrance. Félicité rolled her eyes and said as loud as she could: 'Is he all right?'—worrying about the parrot.

She entered into her death-agony. Her breath, coming ever faster, with a rattling sound, made her sides heave. Bubbles of froth appeared at the corners of her mouth, and her whole body trembled.

Soon the booming of the ophicleides,[9] the clear voices of the children, and the deep voices of the men could be heard near at hand. Now and then everything was quiet, and the tramping of feet, deadened by a carpet of flowers, sounded like a flock moving across pasture-land.

The clergy appeared in the courtyard. Mère Simon climbed on to a chair to reach the little round window, from which she had a full view of the altar below.

It was hung with green garlands and adorned with a flounce in English needle-point lace. In the middle was a little frame containing some relics, there were two orange-trees at the corners, and all the way along stood silver candlesticks and china vases holding sunflowers, lilies, peonies, foxgloves, and bunches of hydrangea. This pyramid of bright colours stretched from the first floor right down to the carpet which was spread out over the pavement. Some rare objects caught the eye: a silver-gilt sugar-basin wreathed in violets, some pendants of Alençon gems gleaming on a bed of moss, and two Chinese screens with landscape decorations. Loulou, hidden under roses, showed nothing but his blue poll, which looked like a plaque of lapis lazuli.

The churchwardens, the choristers, and the children lined up along the three sides of the courtyard. The priest went slowly up the steps and placed his great

9. Bugles.

shining gold sun[1] on the lace altar cloth. Everyone knelt down. There was a deep silence. And the censers, swinging at full tilt, slid up and down their chains.

A blue cloud of incense was wafted up into Félicité's room. She opened her nostrils wide and breathed it in with a mystical, sensuous fervour. Then she closed her eyes. Her lips smiled. Her heart-beats grew slower and slower, each a little fainter and gentler, like a fountain running dry, an echo fading away. And as she breathed her last, she thought she could see, in the opening heavens, a gigantic parrot hovering above her head.

1. Used in Catholic services, the vessel called a "monstrance" resembles a sun.

LEO TOLSTOY

1828–1910

A gambler, womanizer, and aristocrat of the highest rank, Count Leo Tolstoy was also a vegetarian, pacifist, and anarchist, and a passionate advocate for the Russian peasantry. He was world-famous for his wisdom on the subject of marriage, but suffered through a remarkably stormy marriage himself. He became widely known as a moral and religious sage, but was excommunicated from the Russian Orthodox Church. He produced some of the century's best fiction but came to believe that novels were immoral. And yet this heap of contradictions should not be seen as the mark of a hypocrite. Tolstoy was always fully conscious of the disparity between his ideals and his life. "Blame *me*," he wrote, "and not the path I tread." This painful self-division reflects his intense, lifelong struggle to find the best way to live in the world—how to respond to the pressures of guilt and pleasure, authority and money, sex and war. And it suggests the source of one of his great talents as a writer: the capacity to represent a vast, various, and conflicting array of desires and ideals.

LIFE

Born in 1828, Tolstoy was the fourth of five children. Both of his parents belonged to the highest class of Russian society—aristocrats who had access to the tsar and the tsar's court. And yet Tolstoy never took advantage of his high birth to pursue a grand career as a diplomat or courtier. Having lost his mother at the age of two and his father at nine, he spent his youth in relative isolation. Much of his long life was passed on the family estate, Yasnaya Polyana, about 130 miles from Moscow, in the company of his close family members and his serfs—Russian peasants who were the property of aristocratic landowners, much like slaves.

Despite the fact that he was an orphan and moved from one guardian to another, Tolstoy looked back on his childhood as idyllic. He was close to his siblings, and together they imagined a perfect society based on the ideal of universal love. At the age of fourteen Tolstoy started to visit brothels, which prompted terrible bouts of remorse and self-revulsion. After his first experience, he claimed to have stood next to the bed and wept. A few years later he started to write in a diary, which he then kept compulsively for the rest of his life. This daily writing often furnished material for his fiction, as well as developing his skills and habits as a writer. Here, he would explore questions about how to act and what to believe, wondering about the purpose and meaning of life. He would also repeatedly make vows to give up his dalliances with women, and just as often break his promise. Thus began a chronicle of sex and shame, played out in countless affairs with women, almost all of them members of the peasant class.

Intending to take up a diplomatic career, Tolstoy went to the provincial university at Kazan to study Arabic, Turko-Tartar, French, and German. He later switched to law, a course of study open only to the highest-ranking aristocrats. But this too he dropped in 1847 when he inherited the family estate, a large sum of money, and the ownership of over three hundred serfs. This sudden inheritance allowed him to drift aimlessly for a while, moving in aristocratic circles in the cities of St. Petersburg and Moscow, where he spent night after night at gambling tables.

Tolstoy's life changed radically in 1851 when he followed his older brother Nikolay, a soldier, to the mountains of the Caucasus, where the Russian army was protecting the hotly contested boundary between Russia and the Ottoman and Persian empires. It was here, observing military life and conflict, that Tolstoy began publishing his work. He decided to join the army and to serve in the war between Russia and Britain in Crimea. There he witnessed appalling devastation, incompetence, and confusion. He also gambled away his fortune, observed the heat of battle and the pettiness of military life, and became a literary sensation with his detailed descriptions of the war in *Sebastopol Sketches* (1854). He began to be known in literary circles as an emerging genius, and in government circles as a potentially dangerous critic.

Although he had been an indifferent student, Tolstoy was a great reader, and from adolescence he passionately admired the French Romantic **Jean-Jacques Rousseau**, who argued against the artificiality of social manners and institutions in favor of the simplicity of life in and through nature. Tolstoy read widely in European and American literature, from **Johann Wolfgang von Goethe** to Harriet Beecher Stowe. One of his greatest influences was the English novelist Charles Dickens, who was highly popular in Russia. Tolstoy would often read a Dickens novel when he needed a catalyst to begin writing himself.

At the age of thirty-four, Tolstoy, now a famous writer, married Sofya Andreyevna Bers, an eighteen-year-old, upper-class St. Petersburg girl. A day after he proposed, he offered his fiancée the chance to read his diaries, which recorded, among other things, twenty years of sexual activity with prostitutes, gypsies, and serfs. "I forgive you," she said to him after reading it, "but it's dreadful." From the beginning, both Tolstoys wrote constantly about one another in their diaries, and read each other's accounts, leading to many jealous battles—and perhaps the most documented marriage in history. Over their long and tumultuous life together, Sofya bore thirteen children, made four handwritten copies of the 1,500-page *War and Peace*, and did her best to protect her husband's literary property.

By his mid-thirties, Tolstoy had run afoul of the Russian government. As a local justice of the peace, he had made eccentric and radical decisions, taking the side of serfs against his fellow landowners, and he had founded an experimental school for peasant children at Yasnaya Polyana based on new theories of education emerging out of France, Belgium, Germany, and England. Instead of cramming children with information, Tolstoy argued, it made sense for education to draw on their own experience. This seemed dangerously foreign, and his writing seemed unsettling, too. The tsar, concerned about threats to his life and his regime, had a team of censors who excised paragraphs from a number of Tolstoy's early short stories. In 1862 the police made a raid on his house. They found little evidence of subversive writings or activity, but the search infuriated Tolstoy, whose antigovernment sentiment increased as he grew older. Arguing that governments always relied on violence, he became a vocal anarchist and pacifist, advocating civil disobedience rather than submission to the state.

Tolstoy's two greatest works, *War and Peace* (1865–69) and *Anna Karenina* (1875–77), were hugely popular and established him as the greatest novelist of the Russian experience. *War and Peace* was an epic that recounted Napoleon's invasion of Russia in 1812, a huge swarming story of a nation's resistance to a foreign power. Tolstoy unsettles the myth of Napoleon as one of the world's greatest heroes, interpreting history instead as a struggle of anonymous collective forces; events are the consequences of waves of irrational communal feeling. *Anna Karenina* is a moving story of marriage and adultery that juxtaposes characters who are searching for meaning and fulfillment. Its hero, Levin, ends a painful struggle with the promise of salvation, adopting the ideal of a simple life in which we should "remember God." So bound up with national pride were these two works that they survived successive waves of censorship. In fact, the repressive Russian government was so fearful of making a martyr out of the much-beloved novelist that they left Tolstoy almost entirely alone, even while they imprisoned and executed a vast number of his fellow writers for subversive antitsarist sentiment. As Tolstoy became an increasingly outspoken critic of the state, his own fiction protected him.

After he published *Anna Karenina* Tolstoy underwent an acute personal and spiritual crisis, thrown into such despair by the pointlessness of existence that he considered suicide (a despair shared by some of the characters in the novel). Then he had a conversion experience that set him on a new path. After exploring and rejecting the Russian Orthodox Church, he began to pursue his own search for God. It was the peasants who seemed to Tolstoy to know how to live best, and in the late 1870s he started to try to live a peasant life, dressing like them, eating peasant food, and even making his own shoes. Rereading the Gospels closely, he founded his own religion. This involved rejecting any idea of an afterlife and following the model of Jesus' life as closely as possible, giving away wealth and rejecting all forms of violence. Tolstoy's first work of fiction after his conversion was *The Death of Ivan Ilyich* in 1886.

The last decades of his life saw Tolstoy writing mostly religious and philosophical treatises. By the 1880s the writer was arguing in favor of complete sexual abstinence. He condemned literature and singled out Shakespeare as particularly bad. He became an outspoken vegetarian. At one point, an elderly relative visiting Yasnaya Polyana asked that meat be served to her; when she came to the table, she discovered a meat cleaver at her place and a live chicken tied to her chair. In his later years, many followers saw Tolstoy as a wise prophet and made long journeys to Yasnaya Polyana from distant places to meet the great man. They often reported that he seemed larger than life—saintly and heroic.

At Tolstoy's death in 1910 students rioted, anarchists were rounded up by the police, and thousands of people followed his coffin. Seven years later, when Russia erupted in political turmoil, some saw the first tide of communism as a "Tolstoyan revolution." But Tolstoy left another kind of political legacy as well. So influential was his notion of nonviolent resistance for a young Indian man named Mohandas Gandhi that he called his first political base "Tolstoy farm."

TIMES

In the century leading up to Tolstoy's birth, Russian society was divided into three major groups: the aristocracy, which was small in number but exerted all of the nation's political power; town merchants, who had fixed duties and privileges; and serfs, who made up the vast majority of the population but had no power at all. The aristocrats were the only Russians who could attend universities, hold civil service positions, and remain exempt from taxation. Meanwhile, serfs had neither freedom nor authority: one tsar after another reduced serfs' rights, and by the middle of the eighteenth century, serfs were forbidden to travel and had the legal status of personal property, exactly like slaves. When Tolstoy was young, 23 million Russians were privately owned serfs.

This drastically lopsided political and social system was clearly unstable, and anxious tsars struggled to stave off outright revolution. Alexander II emancipated the serfs in 1861 for purely pragmatic reasons: "It is better to abolish serfdom from above," he explained, "than to wait for the time when it will begin to abolish itself from below." The emancipation did not put an end to social unrest, however. By 1880 there had been six attempts to kill the tsar by anarchists and nihilists. Alexander increased his secret police force, imposed severe censorship, and promised political reforms. In 1881 an assassin succeeded in killing him, and he was succeeded by his son, Alexander III, who rejected his father's reform efforts in favor of harsh and repressive measures, including even tighter censorship and persecution of non-Orthodox minorities, especially Jews. Most writers were persecuted—thrown in jail or kept under house arrest. In this context, it is astonishing that Tolstoy managed to remain free, especially given his sharp and vocal criticism of both church and state.

In Russian intellectual circles, one urgent question constantly reemerged in the nineteenth century: should Russia follow the lead of a modernizing Western Europe in terms of culture, politics, and industry, or should the nation instead reach for models drawn from its own religious and national history, developing its own distinctive heritage? On the one side, the so-called Westernizers, based largely in St. Petersburg, argued for liberal democracy, religious freedom, and the emancipation of the serfs. They spoke French, and often felt ashamed of Russian backwardness. On the other side, the Moscow-based Slavophiles resisted rationalism and technological innovation, embraced the Russian Orthodox Church, and typically favored bringing together all Slavic peoples under the Russian tsar. Tolstoy belonged to neither camp—or to both. While he favored European models of education and rejected the Orthodox Church, he also prized the Russian peasantry as a source of national renewal and meaning.

WORK

Tolstoy's great novels, *War and Peace* and *Anna Karenina*, told vast and sweeping realist stories of life in nineteenth-century Russia, filled with vivid depictions of aristocratic pursuits, military battles, and the complexities of love and marriage. Later he turned to a different kind of writing, producing impassioned and often didactic stories and nonfiction essays in favor of spiritual principles. *The Death of Ivan Ilyich*, the story included here, falls midway between these two phases of his career. As the first piece of fiction written after the writer's conversion, it has seemed to many readers to combine Tolstoy's earlier, richly realistic representations of contemporary life with his later turn to religious ideals.

There may be a biographical source for this novella. In 1856—thirty years before he began writing it—Tolstoy's brother Dmitry had died of tuberculosis in the arms of a prostitute. Revolted by his brother's emaciated body and the smell of illness, Tolstoy felt remarkably little concern for Dmitry and selfishly rushed back to St. Petersburg to enjoy his growing literary fame. This experience—Dmitry's death, his own indifference, and his resulting guilt—seems to have provided the writer with the contrasting perspectives he explores in *The Death of Ivan Ilyich*.

This is the story of an average man of the prosperous middle class who faces the unbearable fact that he is soon going to die. Tolstoy is famous for peppering his prose with startlingly opinionated, intrusive judgments, and among the most famous of these is the narrator's assessment of his protagonist's life at the opening of chapter II: "Ivan Ilyich's life had been the most simple and most ordinary and therefore most terrible." The relationship between terror and ordinariness here appears straightforward and categorical, but the story then asks us to think about how we respond to such blunt claims of truth. Ivan Ilyich himself knows that everyone must die—"Caius is a man, men are mortal, therefore Caius is mortal"—but he rebels against applying this to himself: "he was not Caius, not an abstract man, but a creature quite, quite separate from all others." What, Tolstoy asks us, is the relationship between abstract, universal truths and our intensely felt personal experience?

Ordinary social life, it seems, allows us to avoid this question, as characters immerse themselves in card games, interior decorating, career advancement, financial dealings, and the desire to "live pleasantly." Ivan Ilyich, whose first symptoms of illness appear when he tries to hang his curtains properly, comes to see his family, friends, and doctors as false and deceitful. Gerasim, the peasant, represents the only appealing alternative described in the narrative.

Tolstoy experiments with perspective, choosing to begin the story at its chronological endpoint, as the news of Ivan Ilyich's death comes to his acquaintances. For them it appears as an interruption of ordinary life, and we see the event through their uncomfortable eyes. It is only after this introduction that the narrator switches to Ivan Ilyich's perspective. In the first draft, two characters, Peter Ivanovich and Ivan Ilyich, told the story in the first person. Later Tolstoy shifted to a third-person omniscient narrator, who filters our experience through these two characters.

Tolstoy not only multiplies perspectives, he also multiplies metaphors: dying is like being "thrust into a narrow, deep black sack"; it is also like a "stone falling downwards," like flying, and "like the sensation one sometimes experiences in a railway carriage when one thinks one is going backwards while one is really going forwards." Death emerges variously as nothingness, a black hole, a judge (like the character himself), and perhaps most memorably, as "*It.*" In Russian this pronoun is feminine and thus closer to the English "*She.*" As death slowly comes to the protagonist, language itself begins to break down. In the final chapter, he starts screaming, "I won't," but this becomes simply "Oh! Oh! Oh!"—a sound that lasts for three solid days. In his final moments of illumination, the protagonist tries to ask his son to "forgive" him but says only "forgo." As Ivan Ilyich's viewpoint develops and changes, the story narrows in time and space; the focus tightens, his range of movements contracts, the chapters get shorter, and the time of the events shrinks.

Guy de Maupassant, a French writer whom Tolstoy admired, read *The Death of Ivan Ilyich* late in his own life, and said, sadly: "I realize that everything I have done now was to no purpose, and that my ten volumes are worthless."

The Death of Ivan Ilyich[1]

I

During a break in the hearing of the Melvinsky case, the members of the court and the prosecutor met in Ivan Yegorovich Shebek's room in the big law courts building and began talking about the famous Krasovsky case. Fyodor Vasilyevich became heated, contending that it didn't come under their jurisdiction; Ivan Yegorovich held his ground; while Pyotr Ivanovich, not having joined in the argument at the beginning, took no part in it and was looking through the *Gazette*, which had just been delivered.

"Gentlemen!" he said. "Ivan Ilyich has died."

"He hasn't!"

"Look, read this," he said to Fyodor Vasilyevich, handing him a fresh copy which still smelled of ink.

Within a black border was printed: "Praskovya Fyodorovna Golovina with deep sorrow informs family and friends of the passing of her beloved spouse Ivan Ilyich Golovin, member of the Court of Justice, which took place on the 4th of February of this year 1882. The funeral will be on Friday at 1 p.m."

Ivan Ilyich was a colleague of the gentlemen meeting there and they all liked him. He had been ill for several weeks; people were saying his illness was incurable. His position had been kept for him, but there had been conjectures that, in the event of his death, Alekseyev might be appointed to his position, and either Vinnikov or Shtabel to Alekseyev's. So on hearing of Ivan Ilyich's death the first thought of each of the gentlemen meeting in the room was of the significance the death might have for the transfer or promotion of the members themselves or their friends.

Now I will probably get Shtabel's or Vinnikov's position, thought Fyodor Vasilyevich. *It was promised to me long ago and this promotion means a raise of eight hundred rubles, plus a private office.*

1. Translated by Peter Carson.

Now I must ask about the transfer of my brother-in-law from Kaluga, thought Pyotr Ivanovich. *My wife will be very pleased. Now she won't be able to say that I've never done anything for her family.*

"I thought he wouldn't leave his bed," Pyotr Ivanovich said aloud. "Such a pity."

"What was actually wrong with him?"

"The doctors couldn't make a diagnosis. That is, they did, but different ones. When I saw him the last time, I thought he would recover."

"And I didn't go and see him after the holidays. I kept meaning to."

"Did he have any money?"

"I think his wife had a very small income. But next to nothing."

"Yes, we'll have to go and see her. They lived a terribly long way off."

"That is, a long way from you. Everything's a long way from you."

"He just can't forgive me for living on the other side of the river," said Pyotr Ivanovich, smiling at Shebek. And they started talking about distances in the city, and went back into the courtroom.

Apart from the thoughts the death brought each of them about the possible moves and changes at work that might follow, the actual fact of the death of a close acquaintance evoked, as always, in all who learned of it a complacent feeling that it was "he who had died, not I."

So—he's dead; but here I am still, each thought or felt. At this point his closer acquaintances, the so-called friends of Ivan Ilyich, involuntarily thought that they now needed to carry out the very tedious requirements of etiquette and go to the requiem service and pay a visit of condolence to the widow.

Closest of all were Fyodor Vasilyevich and Pyotr Ivanovich.

Pyotr Ivanovich was a friend from law school and considered himself under an obligation to Ivan Ilyich.

Having given his wife over dinner the news of Ivan Ilyich's death and his thoughts about the possibility of his brother-in-law's transfer to their district, Pyotr Ivanovich didn't lie down to have a rest but put on a formal tailcoat and drove to Ivan Ilyich's.

At the entrance to Ivan Ilyich's apartment stood a carriage and two cabs. Downstairs in the hall by the coatrack, leaning against the wall, was the brocade-covered lid of the coffin with tassels and a gold braid that had been cleaned with powder. Two ladies in black were taking off their fur coats. One of them, Ivan Ilyich's sister, he knew; the other was an unknown lady. Pyotr Ivanovich's colleague Schwarz was coming downstairs and, seeing from the top step who had come in, he winked at him as if to say, "Ivan Ilyich has made a silly mess of things; you and I have done things differently."

Schwarz's face with his English side-whiskers and his whole thin figure in a tailcoat as usual had an elegant solemnity, and this solemnity, which was always at odds with Schwarz's playful character, was especially piquant here. So Pyotr Ivanovich thought.

Pyotr Ivanovich let the ladies go in front of him and slowly followed them up the stairs. Schwarz didn't come down but stayed at the top. Pyotr Ivanovich understood why: he obviously wanted to arrange where they should play *vint*[2] today. The ladies went up the stairs to the widow but Schwarz, with a serious

2. A Russian card game, similar to whist and bridge.

set to his strong lips and a playful look, indicated by a twitch of his eyebrows that Pyotr Ivanovich should go to the right, into the room where the corpse lay.

Pyotr Ivanovich went in, feeling, as is always the case, at a loss as to what he should do there. One thing he did know was that in these circumstances it never does any harm to cross oneself. He wasn't altogether sure whether one should also bow and so he chose a middle course: entering the room, he started to cross himself and made a kind of slight bow. Insofar as the movements of his head and hands would allow, he looked round the room at the same time. Two young men, probably nephews, one of them a gymnasium[3] pupil, were crossing themselves as they left the room. An old woman stood motionless, and a lady with oddly arched eyebrows was saying something to her in a whisper. A church lector[4] in a frock coat with a vigorous and decisive way to him was reading something out loudly with an expression that permitted no contradiction; the peasant manservant Gerasim, stepping lightly in front of Pyotr Ivanovich, scattered something on the ground. Seeing that, Pyotr Ivanovich at once sensed the faint smell of a decomposing body. On his last visit to Ivan Ilyich he had seen this peasant in the study; he carried out the duties of a sick-nurse, and Ivan Ilyich was especially fond of him. Pyotr Ivanovich kept crossing himself and bowing slightly in an intermediate direction between the coffin, the lector, and the icons on a table in the corner. Then, when he thought the movement of crossing himself with his hand had gone on for too long, he stopped and started to examine the dead man.

The dead man lay, as dead men always do, especially heavily, his stiffened limbs sunk in the padded lining of the coffin with his head bent back forever on the pillow, and, as always with dead men, his yellow waxen forehead sticking out, showing bald patches on his hollow temples, his nose protruding as if it pressed on his upper lip. He had greatly changed, had become even thinner since Pyotr Ivanovich had seen him, but like all dead men, his face was handsomer, above all more imposing than when he was alive. On his face was an expression that said what had to be done had been done, and done properly. This expression also held a reproach or reminder to the living. Pyotr Ivanovich found this reminder inappropriate—or at the least one not applying to himself. This gave Pyotr Ivanovich an unpleasant feeling, and so he hurriedly crossed himself once more and turned, too hurriedly he thought, and not in accordance with propriety, and went to the door. Schwarz was waiting for him in the next room, his legs wide apart and both hands playing behind his back with his top hat. One look at Schwarz's playful, neat, and elegant figure refreshed Pyotr Ivanovich. Pyotr Ivanovich felt that Schwarz stood above all this and didn't allow himself to give in to depressing thoughts. The very way he looked stated the following: the fact of Ivan Ilyich's requiem cannot serve as a sufficient reason to consider the order of the courts disrupted; in other words, nothing can stop us unsealing and shuffling a pack of cards this evening while the manservant puts out four fresh candles; in general there are no grounds for assuming that this fact can prevent us from spending a pleasant evening, even today. He said this in a whisper to Pyotr Ivanovich as he came in, proposing they meet for

3. School for preparing students to enter university.

4. High position in the minor orders of the Eastern Orthodox Church, responsible for reading from scripture during services.

a game at Fyodor Vasilyevich's. But apparently Pyotr Ivanovich was not fated to play *vint* this evening. Praskovya Fyodorovna, a short, plump woman who broadened from the shoulders down in spite of all her efforts to achieve the opposite, was dressed all in black with her head covered in lace and with oddly arched eyebrows like the lady standing by the coffin. She came out of her rooms with the other ladies, and taking them to the door where the dead man lay, said:

"Now there'll be the requiem; do go in."

Schwarz stopped, making a vague bow—clearly neither accepting nor rejecting this proposal. Praskovya Fyodorovna, recognizing Pyotr Ivanovich, sighed, went right up to him, took him by the hand, and said:

"I know that you were a true friend of Ivan Ilyich . . ." and looked at him, waiting for an action on his part that corresponded to these words.

Pyotr Ivanovich knew that just as in that room one had had to cross oneself, so here one must press the hand, sigh, and say, "Believe me!" And that's what he did. And having done it he felt that the desired result had been obtained: he was moved and she was moved.

"Come while they haven't started in there; I need to talk to you," said the widow. "Give me your hand."

Pyotr Ivanovich gave his hand and they went off into the inner rooms, past Schwarz who winked sadly at Pyotr Ivanovich. "There's your *vint* gone! Don't take it out on us; we'll find another partner. Maybe you can cut in once you've gotten free," said his playful look.

Pyotr Ivanovich sighed even more deeply and sadly, and Praskovya Fyodorovna gratefully pressed his hand. They went into her dimly lit drawing room hung with pink cretonne[5] and sat down by a table, she on a sofa and Pyotr Ivanovich on a low pouf built on springs that awkwardly gave way as he sat down. (Praskovya Fyodorovna was going to warn him to sit on another chair but found such a warning inappropriate for the situation and changed her mind.) As he sat down on the pouf, Pyotr Ivanovich remembered how Ivan Ilyich had arranged this drawing room and consulted him about this very pink cretonne with green leaves. On her way to sit down on the sofa, as she passed the table (the whole drawing room was full of furniture and knickknacks), the widow caught the lace of her black mantilla on the carving of the table. Pyotr Ivanovich got up to unhook her, and the sprung pouf now released below began to sway and push at him. The widow started to unhook the lace herself and Pyotr Ivanovich sat down again, quelling the rebellious pouf underneath him. But the widow hadn't unhooked it all, and Pyotr Ivanovich again got up and the pouf again rebelled and even made a noise. When all this was over she took out a clean cambric handkerchief and began to cry. Pyotr Ivanovich felt chilled by the episode of the lace and the battle with the pouf and sat frowning. This awkward situation was interrupted by Sokolov, Ivan Ilyich's butler, reporting that the place in the cemetery Praskovya Fyodorovna had selected would cost two hundred rubles. She stopped crying and, looking at Pyotr Ivanovich with the air of a victim, said in French[6] that

5. Heavy upholstery fabric, often printed with a fancy or gaudy pattern.
6. It was common for members of the upper classes in Russia in the 19th century to speak French to one another.

she was suffering greatly. Pyotr Ivanovich made a silent sign expressing a firm conviction that it couldn't be otherwise.

"Do smoke, please," she said in a gracious and, at the same time, broken voice and talked to Sokolov about the matter of the price of the place in the cemetery. Pyotr Ivanovich smoked and heard her asking very detailed questions about the different prices of plots and deciding on the one that should be bought. When that was done, she went on to give instructions about the singers. Sokolov went out.

"I do everything myself," she said to Pyotr Ivanovich, moving some albums lying on the table to one side. Noticing that his ash was posing a threat to the table, she speedily pushed an ashtray towards Pyotr Ivanovich and said, "I find it a pretence to state that because of grief I can't deal with practical matters. On the contrary, if there is something that can . . . not console . . . but distract me, then it's bothering about him." She again took out her handkerchief as if she were going to cry, and suddenly, as if pulling herself together, she shook herself and began to speak quietly:

"However, I have to talk to you about something."

Pyotr Ivanovich bowed, not letting the pouf release its springs, which had at once started to move underneath him.

"He suffered terribly in the last days."

"Did he suffer very much?" Pyotr Ivanovich asked.

"Oh. Terribly! At the end he never stopped screaming, not for minutes, for hours. For three whole days he screamed without drawing breath. It was unbearable. I can't understand how I bore it; one could hear it from three doors away. Oh, what I've been through!"

"And was he really conscious?" Pyotr Ivanovich asked.

"Yes," she whispered, "till the final moment. He said goodbye to us a quarter of an hour before he died and asked as well for Volodya to be taken out."

The thought of the sufferings of a man he had known so well, first as a cheerful lad, a schoolboy, then as an adult colleague, suddenly horrified Pyotr Ivanovich in spite of his unpleasant consciousness of his own and this woman's pretense. He saw again that forehead, the nose pressing on the lip, and he became fearful for himself.

Three days of terrible suffering and death. That can happen to me too, now, any minute, he thought, and for a moment he became frightened. But right away, he didn't know how, there came to his aid the ordinary thought that this had happened to Ivan Ilyich and not to him; and this ought not and could not happen to him; that in thinking like this he was giving in to gloomy thoughts, which one shouldn't, as had been clear from Schwarz's face. And having reached this conclusion, Pyotr Ivanovich was reassured and started to ask with interest about the details of Ivan Ilyich's end, as if death were an adventure peculiar to Ivan Ilyich but absolutely not to himself.

After some talk about the details of the truly terrible physical sufferings which Ivan Ilyich had undergone (details that Pyotr Ivanovich learned only by way of the effect that Ivan Ilyich's torment had had on Praskovya Fyodorovna's nerves), the widow apparently found it necessary to move on to business.

"Ah, Pyotr Ivanovich, it's so hard, so terribly hard." And she again started to cry.

Pyotr Ivanovich sighed and waited for her to blow her nose. When she had blown her nose, he said:

"Believe me . . ." and again she talked away and unburdened herself of what was clearly her main business with him—how on her husband's death she could get money from the treasury. She gave the appearance of asking Pyotr Ivanovich for advice about the pension, but he saw that she already knew down to the smallest details even what he didn't know—everything that one could extract from the public purse on this death—but that she wanted to learn if one couldn't somehow extract a bit more money. Pyotr Ivanovich tried to think of a way, but, having thought a little and out of politeness abusing the government for its meanness, he said that he thought one couldn't get more. Then she sighed and clearly began to think of a way to get rid of her visitor. He understood this, put out his cigarette, got up, shook her hand, and went into the hall.

In the dining room with the clock that Ivan Ilyich had been so pleased to buy in a junk shop, Pyotr Ivanovich met the priest and also a few acquaintances who had come to the requiem, and he saw a beautiful young lady he knew, Ivan Ilyich's daughter. She was all in black. That made her very slender waist seem even more so. She had a somber, decisive, almost angry expression. She bowed to Pyotr Ivanovich as if he had done something wrong. Behind the daughter, with a similarly offended expression, stood a rich young man whom Pyotr Ivanovich knew, an examining magistrate who he'd heard was her fiancé. He glumly bowed to them and was about to go on into the room where the dead man lay when from under the stairs there appeared the figure of the son, a gymnasium student, who looked terribly like Ivan Ilyich. He was a little Ivan Ilyich just as Pyotr Ivanovich remembered him at law school. His eyes were tearstained and had the look that the eyes of boys with impure thoughts have at the age of thirteen or fourteen. When he recognized Pyotr Ivanovich the boy began to scowl sullenly and shamefacedly. Pyotr Ivanovich nodded to him and went into the dead man's room. The requiem began—candles, groans, incense, tears, sobs. Pyotr Ivanovich stood frowning, looking at the feet in front of him. He didn't look once at the dead man and right until the end didn't give in to any depressing influences. He was one of the first to leave. There was no one in the hall. Gerasim, the peasant manservant, darted out of the dead man's study, rummaged with his strong hands among all the fur coats to find Pyotr Ivanovich's, and gave it to him.

"So, Gerasim my friend," said Pyotr Ivanovich in order to say something. "It's sad, isn't it?"

"It's God's will. We'll all be there," said Gerasim, showing his white, regular, peasant's teeth, and like a man in the full swing of intensive work, briskly opened the door, called the coachman, helped Pyotr Ivanovich in, and jumped back to the steps as if trying to think what else he might do.

It was particularly pleasant for Pyotr Ivanovich to breathe the fresh air after the smells of incense, the dead body, and the carbolic acid.[7]

"Where to, sir?" asked the coachman.

"It's not late. So I'll still drop in at Fyodor Vasilyevich's."

7. Phenol, used as a disinfectant.

And off Pyotr Ivanovich went. And indeed he found his friends finishing the first rubber;[8] it was easy for him to cut in as a fifth.

II

Ivan Ilyich's past life had been very simple and ordinary and very awful.

Ivan Ilyich had died at the age of forty-five, a member of the Court of Justice. He was the son of a St. Petersburg civil servant who had in various ministries and departments the kind of career that brings people to a position in which, although it is quite clear that they are incapable of performing any meaningful job, they still by reason of their long past service and seniority cannot be dismissed; so they receive invented, fictitious positions and thousands of rubles, from six to ten thousand, which are not fictitious, with which they live on to a ripe old age.

Such was Privy Councillor Ilya Yefimovich Golovin, the superfluous member of various superfluous institutions.

He had three sons, Ivan Ilyich being the second. The eldest had the same kind of career as his father, only in a different ministry, and he was already approaching the age at which salary starts increasing automatically. The third son was a failure. Wherever he had been in various positions he had made a mess of things and he was now working in the railways. Both his father and his brothers, and especially their wives, not only didn't like to see him but didn't even mention his existence unless absolutely compelled to do so. Their sister was married to Baron Gref, the same kind of St. Petersburg civil servant as his father-in-law. Ivan Ilyich was *le phénix de la famille*,[9] as they said. He wasn't as cold and precise as the eldest or as hopeless as the youngest. He was somewhere between them—a clever, lively, pleasant, and decent man. He had been educated with his younger brother in the law school. The younger one didn't finish and was expelled from the fifth class. Ivan Ilyich completed the course with good marks. In law school he was already what he would later be during his entire life: a capable, cheerful, good-natured, and sociable man, but one who strictly did what he considered his duty, and he considered his duty to be everything that it was considered to be by his superiors. Neither as a boy nor afterward as a grown man did he seek to ingratiate himself, but there was in him from a young age the characteristic of being drawn to people of high station like a fly toward the light; he adopted their habits and their views on life and established friendly relations with them. All the passions of childhood and youth went by without leaving much of a trace in him; he gave in both to sensuality and to vanity, and—toward the end, in the senior classes—to liberalism,[1] but always within the defined limits that his sense accurately indicated to him as correct.

At law school he had done things that previously had seemed to him quite vile and had filled him with self-disgust while he did them; but later, seeing these things were done by people in high positions and were not thought by

8. A round of a card game.
9. "The phoenix of the family" (French). The word *phoenix* is used here to mean "rare bird," "prodigy."
1. Here meaning libertinism, wild sexual behavior.

them to be bad, he didn't quite think of them as good but completely forgot them and wasn't at all troubled by memories of them.

Having left law school in the tenth class and received money from his father for fitting himself out, Ivan Ilyich ordered clothes at Sharmer's, hung on his watch chain a medallion with the inscription *respice finem*, took his leave of the princely patron of the school and his tutor, dined with his schoolmates at Donon's,[2] and, equipped with a new and fashionable trunk, linen, clothes, shaving and toilet things, and traveling rug ordered and bought from the very best shops, he went off to a provincial city to the post of assistant to the governor for special projects, which his father had procured for him.

In the provincial city Ivan Ilyich at once established for himself the kind of easy and pleasant position he had had at law school. He worked, made his career, and at the same time amused himself in a pleasant and seemly way; from time to time he went around the district towns on a mission from his chief. He behaved to both superiors and inferiors with dignity and he carried out the responsibilities he had been given, mainly for the affairs of religious dissenters,[3] with an exactness and incorruptible honesty of which he could not but be proud.

In his work, despite his youth and liking for frivolous amusement, he was exceptionally reserved, formal, and even severe; but in society he was often playful and witty and always good-humored, well-behaved and *bon enfant*,[4] as his chief and his chief's wife, with whom he was one of the family, used to say of him.

There was also in the provincial city an affair with one of the ladies who attached herself to the smart lawyer; there was a little dressmaker; there were drinking sessions with visiting aides-de-camp and trips to a remote street after supper; there was also some fawning deference to his chief and even to his chief's wife, but all this wore such a high tone of probity that it couldn't be described in bad words; all this could only go under the rubric of the French expression *il faut que jeunesse se passe*.[5] Everything took place with clean hands, in clean shirts, with French words, and, most importantly, in the highest society, consequently with the approval of people in high position.

Ivan Ilyich worked in this way for five years, and then there came changes in his official life. New legal bodies were founded; new men were needed.

And Ivan Ilyich was this new man.

Ivan Ilyich was offered the position of examining magistrate and he accepted it, despite the fact that this position was in another province and he had to abandon the relationships he had established and establish new ones. His friends saw Ivan Ilyich off: they took a group photograph, they presented him with a silver cigarette case, and off he went to his new position.

As an examining magistrate Ivan Ilyich was just as *comme il faut*,[6] well-behaved, capable of separating his official duties from his private life and of

2. One of St. Petersburg's better restaurants. "Sharmer's": a fashionable St. Petersburg tailor. "*Respice finem*": "regard the end" (a Latin motto).

3. The Old Believers, a large group of Russians (about 25 million in 1900), members of a sect that originated in a break with the Orthodox Church in the 17th century; they were subject to many legal restrictions.

4. A nice boy (French).

5. "Youth must have its fling" [translators' note].

6. Literally, "as one must" (French); proper.

inspiring general respect as he had been as a special projects officer. The actual work of a magistrate had much more interest and attraction for him than his previous work. In his previous position it had been pleasant to walk with a light step in his Sharmer uniform past trembling petitioners and envious officials waiting to be seen, straight into his chief's room to sit down with him over a cup of tea with a cigarette. But there were few people who depended directly on his say-so—only district police officers and religious schismatics when he was sent on missions—and he liked to treat such people dependent on him politely, almost as comrades; he liked to let them feel that here he was, someone who could crush them, treating them in a simple and friendly way. There were only a few such people then. Now, as an examining magistrate, Ivan Ilyich felt that all of them, all without exception, even the most important, self-satisfied people, were in his hands, and that he only had to write certain words on headed paper and this or that important, self-satisfied man would be brought to him as a defendant or a witness, and if he wouldn't let him sit down, would have to stand before him and answer his questions. Ivan Ilyich never abused this power of his—on the contrary he tried to use it lightly—but the consciousness of this power and the possibility of using it lightly constituted for him the chief interest and attraction of his new job. In the work itself, in the actual investigations, Ivan Ilyich very quickly mastered a way of setting aside all circumstances that didn't relate to the investigation and expressing the most complicated case in a terminology in which the case only appeared on paper in its externals and his personal view was completely excluded, and most importantly all requisite formality was observed. This work was something new. And he was one of the first people who worked out the practical application of the statutes of 1864.[7]

Moving to a new city to the post of examining magistrate, Ivan Ilyich made new acquaintances and connections, positioned himself afresh, and adopted a slightly different tone. He positioned himself at a certain respectable distance from the governing authorities, but chose the best circle of the lawyers and nobles who lived in the city and adopted a tone of slight dissatisfaction with government, moderate liberalism, and enlightened civic-mindedness. Moreover, without changing the elegance of his dress, in his new job Ivan Ilyich stopped shaving his chin and let his beard grow freely.

Ivan Ilyich's life turned out very pleasantly in the new city as well: the society that took a critical view of the governor was good and friendly; his salary was larger; and a not inconsiderable pleasure was added to his life by *vint*, which Ivan Ilyich started to play, having an ability to play cards cheerfully, quick-wittedly, and very shrewdly so that generally he won.

After two years working in the new city Ivan Ilyich met his future wife. Praskovya Fyodorovna Mikhel was the most attractive, cleverest, most brilliant girl of the group in which Ivan Ilyich moved. Among the other amusements and relaxations from the labors of a magistrate Ivan Ilyich developed a playful, easy relationship with Praskovya Fyodorovna.

While he had been a special assignments official Ivan Ilyich used to dance as a matter of course; as an examining magistrate he now danced only on

7. The emancipation of the serfs in 1861 was followed by a thorough all-round reform of judicial proceedings [translators' note].

special occasions. He danced now in the sense that although he was a part of the new institutions and in the fifth grade,[8] when it came to dancing, then he could show that in this field he could do things better than others. So from time to time at the end of an evening he used to dance with Praskovya Fyodorovna, and it was during these dances in particular that he conquered her. She fell in love with him. Ivan Ilyich didn't have a clear, defined intention of marrying, but when the girl fell in love with him, he asked himself a question. "Actually, why not get married?" he said to himself.

Miss Praskovya Fyodorovna was from a good noble family, was not bad-looking, and had a bit of money. Ivan Ilyich could aspire to a more brilliant match, but this too was a good match. Ivan Ilyich had his salary; she, he hoped, would have as much again. The family connection was good; she was a sweet, pretty, and absolutely decent woman. To say that Ivan Ilyich married because he fell in love with his bride and found in her sympathy for his views on life would have been as unjust as to say that he married because people in his social circle approved of the match. Ivan Ilyich married because of both considerations: he was doing something pleasant for himself in acquiring such a wife, and at the same time he was doing something his superiors thought a right thing to do.

And so Ivan Ilyich married.

The actual process of marriage and the first period of married life, with its conjugal caresses, new furniture, new china, and new linen, went very well until his wife's pregnancy, so that Ivan Ilyich was beginning to think that marriage not only would not destroy the character of an easy, pleasant, cheerful life, one wholly decorous and approved of by society, which Ivan Ilyich thought the true quality of life, but would enhance it further. But then from the first months of his wife's pregnancy something new appeared, something unexpected, unpleasant, oppressive, and indecorous that one couldn't expect and from which one couldn't escape.

His wife for no reason, so Ivan Ilyich thought, as he said to himself, began *de gaieté de coeur*[9] to destroy the pleasant tenor and decorum of life. She was jealous of him without any cause, demanded attentions to herself from him, found fault with everything, and made crude and unpleasant scenes.

At first Ivan Ilyich had hoped to be freed from the unpleasantness of this situation by the same easy and decorous attitude to life which had rescued him before—he tried to ignore his wife's state of mind and continued to live pleasantly and decorously as before: he invited friends home for a game of cards; he tried to go out to his club or see his friends. But on one occasion his wife started to abuse him rudely with such energy and continued to abuse him so persistently every time he didn't fulfill her demands, clearly having made a firm decision not to stop until he would submit—that is, sit at home and be miserable like her—that Ivan Ilyich was horrified. He understood that married life—at any rate with his wife—does not always make for the pleasures and decorum of life but on the contrary often destroys them, and therefore it was essential to protect himself from this destruction. And Ivan Ilyich began to seek the means for this. His official work was one thing that impressed Pras-

8. That is, the government service sector of the Table of Ranks; the fifth grade was reserved for high-ranking civil servants.

9. Literally, "from gaiety of heart" (French); that is, from sheer impulsiveness.

kovya Fyodorovna, and Ivan Ilyich through his official work and the duties that arose out of it began to fight his wife, securing his own independent world.

A child was born. There were attempts at feeding and various failures in this, along with the real and imaginary illnesses of child and mother. Sympathy for all this was demanded from Ivan Ilyich but he could understand nothing of it. So the requirement of Ivan Ilyich to fence in a world for himself outside of the family became all the more pressing.

As his wife became more irritable and demanding, so Ivan Ilyich moved the center of gravity of his life more and more into his official work. He came to like his work more and became more ambitious than he had been before.

Very soon, not more than a year after their marriage, Ivan Ilyich understood that married life, which offers certain conveniences, in reality is a very complicated and difficult business with which, in order to do one's duty—that is, to lead a decorous life that is approved of by society—one has to develop a defined relationship as one does with one's work.

And Ivan Ilyich did develop for himself such a relationship with married life. He required of family life only those conveniences it could give him, of dinner at home, a mistress of the house, a bed, and most importantly, that decorum of external appearances which were defined by public opinion. For the rest he looked for cheerfulness and pleasure, and if he found them was very grateful; if he met rejection and querulousness, he at once went off into the separate world of official work that he had fenced in for himself and found pleasure there.

Ivan Ilyich was valued as a good official and in three years he was made assistant prosecutor. His new responsibilities, their importance, the ability to bring anyone to trial and send him to prison, the public nature of his speeches, the success Ivan Ilyich had in this work—all of this tied him even more closely to his official work.

More children came. His wife became more and more querulous and angry, but the relationship Ivan Ilyich had developed with domestic life had made him almost impervious to her querulousness.

After seven years of working in one city Ivan Ilyich was promoted to the position of prosecutor in a different province. They moved; they now had little money and his wife didn't like the place to which they had moved. Though his salary was more than it had been, life cost more; also two children died, and so family life became even more unpleasant for Ivan Ilyich.

Praskovya Fyodorovna blamed her husband for all the misfortunes that befell them in their new home. Most subjects of conversation between husband and wife, particularly the education of the children, led to questions that recalled past disputes, and quarrels were ready to break out at every minute. There remained only rare periods of tenderness that came to the married couple but did not last long. These were islands on which they landed for a while but then again sailed off into the sea of hidden animosity which expressed itself in their alienation from each other. This alienation might have distressed Ivan Ilyich if he had thought that it should not be like this, but he now recognized this situation not just as normal but as the actual goal of his family life. His object was to free himself more and more from these unpleasant things and to give them a character of innocuous decorum; he achieved it by spending less and less time with his family and when he was forced to do it, he tried to protect his situation by the presence of outsiders. The important thing was that Ivan

Ilyich had his official work. For him all the interest of life was concentrated in that official world, and this interest absorbed him. The consciousness of his power, of his ability to bring down anyone he chose to, his importance, even in externals when he entered the court and at meetings with subordinates, his mastery of conducting the work—all this made him feel glad, and together with talking to his friends, with dinners and *vint*, it filled up his life. So overall Ivan Ilyich's life continued to go on as he thought that it should: pleasantly and with decorum.

So he lived for another seven years. His elder daughter was now sixteen, another child had died, and there only remained a boy at the gymnasium, a subject of dissension. Ivan Ilyich had wanted to send him to law school but to spite him Praskovya Fyodorovna had sent the boy to the gymnasium. The daughter was taught at home and had grown into a good-looking girl; the boy too wasn't bad at his studies.

III

That was Ivan Ilyich's life for seventeen years after his marriage. He was now a senior prosecutor, having refused various promotions in the expectation of a more desirable position, when something very unpleasant happened which completely destroyed the tranquility of his life. Ivan Ilyich was expecting the position of president of the tribunal in a university town, but somehow Hoppe overtook him and got the place. Ivan Ilyich was angry, started to make accusations, and quarreled with him and his closest superiors; they cooled towards him and passed him over for the next appointment.

That was in 1880. That year was the hardest in Ivan Ilyich's life. In that year his salary wasn't sufficient for living; everyone forgot him, and what appeared to him to be the greatest, the cruelest injustice toward him was found by others to be something completely ordinary. Even his father didn't see it as his duty to help him. He felt everyone had abandoned him, considering his situation on a 3,500-ruble[1] salary quite normal and even fortunate. He alone knew that with his consciousness of the injustices done to him, his wife's constant nagging, and the debts he was beginning to run, living above his means—he alone knew that his situation was far from normal.

In the summer of that year, to ease his finances he took some leave and went with his wife to spend the summer at Praskovya Fyodorovna's brother's home.

In the country, without his work, Ivan Ilyich for the first time felt not just boredom but unbearable depression, felt that he could not live like that and that he absolutely had to take some decisive action.

Having spent a sleepless night pacing the terrace, Ivan Ilyich decided to go to Petersburg to make a petition and, in order to punish *them*, those who could not appreciate him, to transfer to another ministry.

The next day, in spite of all the attempts of his wife and brother-in-law to dissuade him, he traveled to Petersburg.

He went for one thing: to obtain a five-thousand-ruble[2] salary. He was no longer holding out for any particular ministry or direction or type of work. He

1. The equivalent of nearly $100,000 in today's US currency.

2. The equivalent of over $140,000, in today's US currency.

just needed a position, a position on five thousand rubles, in government, in banking, in the railways, in the Empress Maria's Foundations,[3] even in customs, but he absolutely had to have five thousand rubles and he absolutely had to leave the ministry where they couldn't appreciate him.

And now this trip of Ivan Ilyich's was crowned with amazing, unexpected success. In Kursk he was joined in a first-class carriage by F. S. Ilyin, someone he knew, who told him about a telegram the governor of Kursk had just received that announced a reorganization to take place in the ministry: Pyotr Ivanovich's position was going to be taken by Ivan Semyonovich.

The planned upheaval, apart from its significance for Russia, had a particular significance for Ivan Ilyich: by promoting a new face, Pyotr Petrovich, and of course Zakhar Ivanovich, his classmate and friend, it was highly propitious for him.

In Moscow the news was confirmed. And when he reached Petersburg, Ivan Ilyich found Zakhar Ivanovich and got the promise of a sure place in his old ministry of justice.

After a week he telegraphed his wife: *Zakhar has Miller's place stop*[4] *I receive position at next report.*

Thanks to this change of personnel Ivan Ilyich got this position in his old ministry, which placed him two ranks above his old colleagues as well as a salary of 5,000 rubles and 3,500 for removal expenses. All his anger against his former enemies and the entire ministry was forgotten, and Ivan Ilyich was altogether happy.

Ivan Ilyich returned to the country more cheerful and content than he had ever been. Praskovya Fyodorovna cheered up too and a truce was established between them. Ivan Ilyich told her how in Petersburg everyone had feted him, how all his old enemies had been shamed and were now crawling before him, how he was envied for his position, and especially how highly he was regarded by everyone in Petersburg.

Praskovya Fyodorovna listened to all this and appeared to believe it, and she didn't contradict him in anything but just made plans for their new life in the city to which they were moving. And Ivan Ilyich joyfully saw that these plans were his plans, that the plans were tallying, and that his life which had faltered was again taking on its true and natural character of cheerful pleasantness and decorum.

Ivan Ilyich had come just for a short time. On September 10 he had to take up the new job and furthermore he needed time to settle in their new home, to move everything from the provincial city, and to buy and order many more things; in a word, to settle as had been decided in his own mind and almost exactly as had been decided in that of Praskovya Fyodorovna.

And now, when everything had worked out so well and he and his wife were agreed about their goals (and furthermore weren't living much together), they got on harmoniously as they hadn't done since the first years of married life. Ivan Ilyich thought of taking his family away with him immediately but the insistence of his brother-in-law and his wife, who had suddenly become

3. Reference to the charitable organization founded by the Empress Maria, wife of Paul I, late in the 18th century.

4. Indicating a period (full stop) in a telegram.

particularly friendly and familial towards Ivan Ilyich and his family, resulted in Ivan Ilyich going away alone.

Ivan Ilyich left, and the cheerful state of mind brought about by his success and the harmony with his wife, one reinforcing the other, stayed with him the whole time. A delightful apartment was found, the very one husband and wife had been dreaming of. High, spacious, old-fashioned reception rooms; a comfortable, imposing study; rooms for his wife and daughter; a schoolroom for his son—everything as if devised purposely for them. Ivan Ilyich set about arranging it himself: he chose wallpaper, he bought more furniture (antiques in particular whose style he found particularly *comme il faut*), he had things upholstered, and it all grew and grew and approached the ideal he had composed for himself. Even when he had half arranged things, his arrangements exceeded his expectation. He understood the *comme il faut* look, elegant without vulgarity, which everything would take on once it was ready. As he went to sleep he imagined to himself how the reception room would be. Looking at the drawing room, which wasn't yet finished, he could already see the fireplace, the screen, the whatnot and the little chairs disposed about the room, the plates and saucers on the walls, and the bronzes all standing in their places. He was pleased by the thought that he would surprise Pasha and Lizanka, his wife and daughter, who also had a taste for this. They were certainly not expecting this. He was particularly successful in finding old things and buying them cheaply; they gave everything a particularly aristocratic air. In his letters he deliberately described everything in less attractive terms than the reality to surprise them. All this absorbed him so much that even his new job absorbed him less than he had expected—though he loved his work. During sittings of the court he had moments of absent-mindedness; he started thinking about whether the curtain pelmets[5] should be straight or curved. He was so absorbed by this that he often did things himself; he even moved the furniture about and rehung the curtains himself. Once he got up on a ladder to show a slow-witted decorator how he wanted the drapes hung; he missed his footing and fell, but being a strong and agile man he held his balance and only knocked his side on the handle of the window frame. The bruise was painful but soon disappeared. During all this time Ivan Ilyich felt particularly well and cheerful. He wrote, "I feel I'm fifteen years younger." He thought the work would be finished in September but it dragged on till mid-October. But the apartment was delightful—it wasn't just he who said this but everyone who saw it said so to him.

In actual fact it was the same as the houses of all people who are not so rich but want to be like the rich and so are only like one another: brocade, ebony, flowers, carpets, and bronzes, everything dark and shiny—everything that all people of a certain type do to be like all people of a certain type. And what he had was so like that that one couldn't even notice it, but to him it all looked somehow special. When he met his family at the railway station and took them to his apartment, all finished and lit up, and a manservant in a white tie opened the door into the flower-decked hall, and they went into the drawing room and study, he was very happy, he took them everywhere, drank in their praise, and beamed with pleasure. That evening, when over tea Pras-

5. Fabric borders above windows, used to hide curtain fittings.

kovya Fyodorovna asked him among other things how he had fallen, he laughed and in front of them showed how he had gone flying and frightened the decorator.

"It's lucky I am a gymnast. Someone else might have been killed but I only knocked myself a bit here; when you touch it—it hurts, but it'll pass; it's just a bruise."

And they started to live in the new home which, as always, once they had settled in properly, turned out to have one room too few, with the new income which, as always, turned out to be too little (only not by very much—five hundred rubles). And life was very good. Especially good at first when all was not yet done and more still had to be done: things to be bought, ordered, moved, adjusted. Although there were some disagreements between husband and wife, they were both so pleased and there was so much to do that everything was finished without serious quarrels. When there was nothing left to do, it became a bit more boring and something seemed lacking, but now friendships were made and habits established and life filled up.

After spending the morning in court Ivan Ilyich returned for dinner, and at first his mood was good, although it suffered a little, specifically because of their home. (Every stain on a tablecloth or brocade or broken curtain cord irritated him; he had put so much work into the arrangement that every disruption of it was painful to him.) But in general Ivan Ilyich's life went on just as in his view life should flow: easily, pleasantly, and decorously. He rose at nine, drank his coffee, read the newspapers, then put on his uniform and drove to the court. There the harness in which he worked was already molded for him and he slipped into it right away: petitioners, chancery inquiries, the chancery itself, public and executive sittings of the court. In all of these one had to know how to exclude anything raw and vital, which always destroys the even flow of official work: one couldn't admit any human relationships except official ones; the occasion for a relationship had to be solely official and so had the relationship itself. For example, a man would come in and want to find out something. Outside his official role Ivan Ilyich could not have any relationship with him; but if this man had a relationship with him as a member of the court—one that could be expressed on headed paper—then within the bounds of this relationship Ivan Ilyich would do everything, absolutely everything he could, and in doing this would observe the semblance of friendly relations, that is, courtesy. As soon as the official relationship was ended, so was any other. This ability to separate out the official side without combining it with his real life Ivan Ilyich possessed in the highest degree, and by his talents and long practice he had developed it to such a point that he even sometimes, like a virtuoso, would allow himself as if in jest to combine personal and official relationships. He would allow himself this because he always felt in himself the power to split off the official again when necessary and to reject the personal. Ivan Ilyich handled this work of his not just easily, agreeably, and decorously but even with the mastery of a virtuoso. Between cases he would smoke, drink tea, chat a bit about politics, a bit about generalities, a bit about cards, and most of all about official appointments. And he would return home tired but with the feeling of a virtuoso who had given a lucid performance of his part, one of the first violins in the orchestra. At home mother and daughter would go out somewhere or someone came to see them;

his son was at the gymnasium, preparing his lessons with tutors and diligently studying the things they teach in a gymnasium. Everything was good. After dinner, if there were no guests, Ivan Ilyich would sometimes read a book about which people were talking a lot, and in the evenings he would sit down to his work, that is, read his papers, consult the law, examine testimony, and check it against the law. All this he found neither boring nor amusing. It was boring if he could be playing *vint*; but if there was no *vint*—then all the same this was better than sitting by himself or with his wife. Ivan Ilyich's pleasures were little dinners to which he would invite ladies and gentlemen who were important in terms of worldly position and spending his time with them: that was just like the usual way such people spend their time, just as his drawing room was like all drawing rooms.

Once they even had an evening party, with dancing. And Ivan Ilyich felt cheerful and everything was good, except he had a big quarrel with his wife over the cakes and sweets: Praskovya Fyodorovna had her own plan, but Ivan Ilyich insisted on getting everything from an expensive confectioner and the quarrel was because there were cakes left over and the confectioner's bill came to forty-five rubles.[6] The quarrel was a big and unpleasant one to such a point that Praskovya Fyodorovna called him "an idiot and a misery," and he took his head in his hands and in a fit of temper said something about divorce. But the actual party was enjoyable. The very best society was there and Ivan Ilyich danced with Princess Trufonova, sister of the famous founder of the Goodbye Sorrow Society. His official pleasures were pleasures of pride; his social pleasures were pleasures of vanity; but Ivan Ilyich's real pleasures were the pleasures of playing *vint*. He admitted that after all the various unhappy events in his life the pleasure that burnt like a candle above all others was to sit down at *vint* with good players and partners who didn't shout, definitely in a four (when you're five it's really annoying to have to stand out, although you pretend you very much like it), and to have an intelligent, serious game (when the cards are right), and then to have supper and drink a glass of wine. After *vint*, especially after a little win (a big win was unpleasant), Ivan Ilyich went to bed in an especially good mood.

That's how they lived. They formed around them a group of the best society, important people went to them and young people, too.

Husband, wife, and daughter were agreed in their views of their circle of acquaintances, and without any formal understanding they dropped and were rid of all sorts of shabby little friends and relatives who used to drop in to see them, spouting endearments into the drawing room with Japanese plates hanging on the wall. Soon these shabby little friends stopped dropping in and the Golovins were left with just the very best society. Young men paid court to Lizanka and Petrishchev, an examining magistrate, the son of Dmitry Ivanovich Petrishchev and sole heir to his property, began to pay so much attention to her that Ivan Ilyich even talked about it to Praskovya Fyodorovna. Shouldn't they bring them together in a troika ride or organize some theatricals? That's how they lived. And everything went on like that, without any change, and everything was very good.

6. The equivalent of over $1,200 in today's US currency.

IV

They were all in good health. One couldn't call poor health the fact that Ivan Ilyich sometimes said he had an odd taste in his mouth and something felt uncomfortable on the left side of his stomach.

But it happened that this discomfort started to grow and to become not quite pain but the consciousness of a constant heaviness in his side accompanied by a bad mood. This bad mood, which got worse and worse, began to spoil the pleasant course of the easy and decorous life that had been established in the Golovin house. Husband and wife began to quarrel more and more often, and soon the ease and pleasantness disappeared and only decorum was preserved, with difficulty. Again scenes became more frequent. Again there remained just some islands of calm, and only a few of those, on which husband and wife could meet without an outburst.

And Praskovya Fyodorovna now said, not without cause, that her husband had a difficult character. With her natural habit of exaggeration she said he had always had this dreadful character, and that one needed her good nature to stand it for twenty years. It was true that the quarrels now started with him. His fault-finding always began just before dinner and often when he was starting to eat, over the soup. He would remark that one of the dishes was damaged, or the food wasn't right, or his son had his elbow on the table, or it was his daughter's hairstyle. And he blamed Praskovya Fyodorovna for everything. At first Praskovya Fyodorovna answered back and was rude to him, but a couple of times at the beginning of dinner he flew into such a rage that she understood this was a morbid condition brought on by the intake of food, so she controlled herself and didn't answer back but ate her dinner quickly. Praskovya Fyodorovna regarded her self-control as greatly to her own credit. Having decided that her husband had a dreadful character and that he had created the unhappiness of her life, she started to feel sorry for herself. And the more she felt sorry for herself, the more she hated her husband. She began to wish that he would die, but she couldn't wish for that because then there would be no salary. And that irritated her even more. She considered herself terribly unhappy precisely because even his death could not rescue her and she became irritated; she concealed it and her concealed irritation increased his own irritation.

After one scene, in which Ivan Ilyich was particularly unfair, and after which in explaining himself he said he was indeed prone to irritability but that it came from his illness, she said to him that if he was ill then he must get treatment, and demanded from him that he see a famous doctor.

He went. Everything was as he had expected; everything happened as it always does. The waiting and the doctor's assumed pompousness, something familiar to him that he knew from himself in court, and the tapping and the auscultation[7] and the questions requiring predetermined and clearly unnecessary answers, and the meaningful air suggesting that you just submit to us, we'll fix everything—we know, we have no doubts about how to fix everything, in the very same way for any man you choose. Everything was precisely as in

7. Listening to internal organs, as with a stethoscope.

court. Just as he in court put on an air towards the accused, so in precisely the same way the famous doctor put on an air towards him.

The doctor said: such and such shows that you have such and such inside; but if that isn't confirmed by examining such and such, then one must assume you have such and such. If one does assume such and such, then . . . and so forth. Only one question was important to Ivan Ilyich: was his condition dangerous or not? But the doctor ignored this inappropriate question. From the doctor's point of view the question was pointless and wasn't the one under discussion; it was only a question of assessing various possibilities—a floating kidney, chronic catarrh, or an infection of the appendix. It wasn't a question of Ivan Ilyich's life but an argument between a floating kidney and the appendix. And before Ivan Ilyich's eyes the doctor resolved the argument brilliantly in favor of the floating kidney, with the reservation that an examination of his urine could provide new evidence and then the case would be looked at again. All this was very precisely what Ivan Ilyich himself had done a thousand times with defendants and as brilliantly. The doctor did his summing-up just as brilliantly, triumphantly, even cheerfully, looking at the defendant over his glasses. From the doctor's summing-up Ivan Ilyich drew the conclusion that things were bad, that it didn't matter much to the doctor or probably to anyone else, but that for him things were bad. And Ivan Ilyich was painfully struck by this conclusion that aroused in him a feeling of great self-pity and of great anger toward this doctor who was indifferent to such an important question.

But he didn't say anything and got up, put the money on the desk, and said with a sigh:

"Probably we patients often put inappropriate questions to you. In general terms, is this a dangerous illness or not?"

The doctor gave him one stern look through his glasses as if to say: Accused, if you will not stay within the boundaries of the questions that are put to you, then I will be compelled to give instructions for your removal from the courtroom.

"I have already told you what I consider necessary and proper," said the doctor. "An examination will show the rest." And the doctor bowed.

Ivan Ilyich slowly went out, despondently got into the sleigh, and went home. For the whole journey he ceaselessly went over everything the doctor had said, trying to turn those confused, unclear, scientific words into simple language and to read in them an answer to the question: Am I in a bad way, or a very bad way, or aren't things yet so bad? And he thought that the sense of everything the doctor had said was that he was in a very bad way. Everything in the streets looked sad to Ivan Ilyich. The cab drivers were sad, the houses were sad, the passersby, the shops. This pain, this dull nagging pain that didn't stop for a single second, combined with the doctor's unclear pronouncements acquired another more serious meaning. Ivan Ilyich listened to his pain with a new heavy feeling.

He arrived home and started to tell his wife. His wife listened but in the middle of his account his daughter came in wearing a hat: she and her mother were going out. She sat down for a moment to listen to this boring stuff but she couldn't stand it for long, and her mother didn't listen to the end.

"Now I'm very pleased," his wife said. "So mind you take your medicine properly. Give me the prescription, I'll send Gerasim to the chemist's." And she went to dress.

While she was in the room he was barely able to breathe and he sighed heavily when she went out.

"Well then," he said. "Perhaps it's not so bad."

He began to take the medicines and to follow the doctor's directions, which changed after the urine examination. But it was the case now that there had been some kind of confusion in the examination and in what followed from it. It was impossible to get through to the doctor himself, but it turned out that what was happening was not what the doctor had told him. Either he had forgotten or he had lied or he had concealed something from Ivan Ilyich.

But Ivan Ilyich still started to follow the directions precisely and in doing so at first found some comfort.

From the time he visited the doctor Ivan Ilyich's chief occupations became the precise following of the doctor's directions about hygiene and the monitoring of his pain and all his bodily functions. Ivan Ilyich's chief interests became human illness and human health. When others talked in front of him about people who were ill or had died or had gotten better, and in particular about any illness that resembled his own, he would listen, trying to conceal his agitation, ask questions, and apply what was said to his own illness.

The pain got no less but Ivan Ilyich made an effort to force himself to think he was better. And he could deceive himself as long as nothing disturbed him. But as soon as there was some unpleasantness with his wife or something went wrong at work or he had bad cards at *vint*, he at once felt the full force of his illness. In the past he had endured things going wrong in the expectation that *I'll soon put things right, I'll overcome, I'll be successful, I'll get a grand slam.* Now anything that went wrong brought him down and cast him into despair. He would say to himself, "I was just starting to get better and the medicine was already beginning to work, and along comes this cursed accident or unpleasantness. . . ." And he was angry with the accident or with the people who were causing him unpleasantnesses and killing him, and he felt that this anger was killing him but he couldn't restrain himself. One might have thought it would have been clear to him that this anger against circumstances and people made his illness worse, and that therefore he shouldn't pay any attention to unpleasant incidents, but his reasoning was quite the reverse: He said he needed calm; he watched out for anything that might breach that calm and at the smallest breach he got angry. His condition was made worse by the fact that he consulted medical books and doctors. His deterioration progressed so evenly that comparing one day with another he could deceive himself—there was little difference. But when he consulted doctors, he thought he was getting worse and that very quickly. And in spite of that he constantly consulted doctors.

That month he went to see another celebrity doctor; this other celebrity doctor said almost the same as the first but put the questions differently. And consulting this celebrity doctor only deepened Ivan Ilyich's doubt and terror. A friend of a friend—a very good doctor—diagnosed his illness quite differently, and in spite of promising recovery, his questions and assumptions confused Ivan Ilyich even more and increased his doubts. A homeopath diagnosed his illness again quite differently and gave him some medicine, and Ivan Ilyich took it in secret from everyone for about a week. But after a week, feeling no relief and having lost confidence both in the previous treatments and in this one, he fell into greater despair. On one occasion a lady he knew was talking about the healing powers of icons.[8] Ivan Ilyich found himself listening carefully and believing the reality of this. This incident frightened him. "Have I really become so feeble-minded?" he said to himself. "What rubbish! It's all nonsense. I mustn't give in to hypochondria, but having chosen one doctor I must firmly stick to his treatment. That's what I'll do. Now it's settled. I'm not going to think and I'm going to follow the treatment strictly till the summer. Then there'll be something to show. Let's now have an end to all this wavering!" It was easy to say that but impossible to put it into action. The pain in his side wore him down; it seemed to keep getting worse; it became constant; the taste in his mouth became stronger; he thought a disgusting smell was coming from his mouth; and his appetite and strength were going. He couldn't deceive himself: something terrible, new, and important was happening in him, something more important than anything that had happened to Ivan Ilyich in his life. And only he knew about this; all those around him either didn't understand or didn't want to understand and thought that everything in the world was going on as before. That was what tormented Ivan Ilyich most of all. He could see that his household—chiefly his wife and daughter who were in the full swing of visits and parties—understood nothing, and they were vexed that he was so gloomy and demanding, as if he were guilty in that. Although they tried to conceal it, he saw that he was a burden to them, but that his wife had evolved a particular attitude to his illness and adhered to that irrespective of what he said and did. Her attitude was like this:

"You know," she would say to friends, "Ivan Ilyich can't strictly follow a prescribed treatment, as most good people can. Today he'll take his drops and eat what he's been told to and go to bed in good time, but tomorrow if I don't look properly, he'll suddenly forget to take them and eat oysters (which are forbidden him) and sit down to *vint* till one in the morning."

"When did I do that?" Ivan Ilyich would say crossly. "Once at Pyotr Ivanovich's."

"Yesterday with Shebek."

"I just couldn't sleep from the pain . . ."

"Well, whatever it was from, like that you won't get better and you make us miserable."

Praskovya Fyodorovna's public attitude to her husband's illness, which she expressed to others and to him, was that this illness was Ivan Ilyich's own fault and that the whole illness was a new unpleasantness he was bringing down on his wife. Ivan Ilyich felt that this came out in her involuntarily, but that didn't make it any easier for him.

In court Ivan Ilyich noticed or thought he noticed the same strange attitude to him: now he would think that people were scrutinizing him like a man whose position was soon going to be vacant; now all of a sudden his friends would start to joke in an amicable way about his hypochondria, as if this thing, this awful, terrible, unheard-of thing that had grown in him and was ceaselessly gnawing at him and irrepressibly dragging him somewhere, were the most pleasant subject for a joke. He was especially irritated by Schwarz with his playfulness and energy and *comme il faut* ways, all of which reminded Ivan Ilyich of himself ten years back.

8. Paintings of religious images, commonly used for devotional purposes in the Russian Orthodox Church.

Friends came to make up a game; they sat down. They dealt, bending the new cards; he put diamonds next to diamonds, seven of them. His partner bid no trumps—and held two diamonds. What could be better? Things were cheerful and bright—they had a grand slam. And suddenly Ivan Ilyich felt that gnawing pain, that taste in the mouth, and there seemed to him to be something absurd in the fact that he could rejoice in a grand slam.

He looked at Mikhail Mikhaylovich, his partner, rapping his powerful hand on the table and politely and condescendingly refraining from scooping up the tricks but pushing the cards toward Ivan Ilyich to give him the pleasure of picking them up without straining himself and stretching out his arm. "Does he think I'm so weak I can't stretch out my arm?" Ivan Ilyich thought. He forgot about trumps and trumped his partner, losing the grand slam by three tricks—and what was really dreadful was that he saw how Mikhail Mikhaylovich was suffering, but he didn't care. And it was dreadful to think just why he didn't care.

They all saw he was feeling bad and said to him, "We can stop if you are tired. You must rest." Rest? No, he wasn't tired at all, and they finished the rubber. They were all gloomy and silent. Ivan Ilyich felt he had brought down this gloom upon them and he couldn't dispel it. They had supper and went their ways, and Ivan Ilyich was left alone with the knowledge that his life had been poisoned for him, that it was poisoning the lives of others, and that this poison wasn't losing its power but was penetrating his whole being more and more.

And with this knowledge, with the physical pain, and with the terror, he had to get into bed and often be unable to sleep from the pain the greater part of the night. And the next morning he had to get up again, dress, go to court, talk, write, or if he didn't go to court he had to stay at home with those twenty-four hours of the day, each one of which was a torment. And he had to live like that on the brink of the abyss, all alone, without a single person who could understand and take pity on him.

V

A month went by like that and then another. Before the new year his brother-in-law came to the city and stayed with them. Ivan Ilyich was in court. Praskovya Fyodorovna had gone out shopping. When Ivan Ilyich went into his study he found his brother-in-law, a healthy, full-blooded fellow, unpacking his suitcase himself. He raised his head when he heard Ivan Ilyich's footsteps and looked at him for a second in silence. That look revealed everything to Ivan Ilyich. His brother-in-law opened his mouth to say "oh" and stopped himself. That movement confirmed everything.

"So, I've changed, haven't I?"

"Yes . . . there is a change."

And however much afterwards Ivan Ilyich turned the conversation with his brother-in-law to his appearance, his brother-in-law said nothing. Praskovya Fyodorovna arrived, his brother-in-law went out to her. Ivan Ilyich locked his door and started to examine himself in the mirror—face-on, then from the side. He took up a photograph of himself with his wife and compared the image with the one he saw in the mirror. The change was huge. Then he bared his arms to the elbow, looked, rolled his sleeves down again, and sat on an ottoman, and his mood became darker than night.

"You mustn't, you mustn't," he said to himself; he jumped up, went to the desk, opened a case file, and began to read it, but he couldn't. He unlocked the door and went into the salon. The drawing-room door was shut. He tiptoed to it and began to listen.

"No, you're exaggerating," said Praskovya Fyodorovna.

"Exaggerating? You don't see—he's a dead man, look at his eyes. There's no light in them. What's the matter with him?"

"Nobody knows. Nikolayev [that was the second doctor] said something, but I don't know what. Leshchetitsky [that was the celebrated doctor] said the opposite . . ."

Ivan Ilyich moved away, went to his room, lay down, and started to think: *A kidney, a floating kidney.* He remembered everything the doctor had told him—how it had become detached and was floating. And with an effort of the imagination he tried to understand his kidney and to halt it and strengthen it; so little was needed for that, he thought. *No, I'll go again to Pyotr Ivanovich.* (That was the friend who had a friend who was a doctor.) He rang, gave orders for the horse to be harnessed, and got ready to leave.

"Where are you off to, *Jean?*"[9] his wife said, using a particularly sad and unusually kind expression.

This unusual kindness angered him. He looked at her morosely.

"I have to go to Pyotr Ivanovich."

He went to his friend who had a friend who was a doctor. He found him at home and had a long conversation with him.

When he considered both the anatomical and physiological details of what, in the doctor's opinion, had been happening inside him, he understood everything.

There was something, a little something in the appendix. All that might be put right. Stimulate the activity of one organ, weaken the activity of another; the something would be absorbed and everything would be put right. He got back a little late for dinner, talked cheerfully for a bit, but for a long time he couldn't go to his room to work. Finally he went into his study and at once sat down to work. He read his cases and worked, but the consciousness that he had set something aside—an important and intimate matter which he would take up once his work was over—did not leave him. When he had finished his cases, he remembered that this intimate matter was his thinking about his appendix. But he didn't indulge it; he went to the drawing room for tea. There were guests, including the examining magistrate, his daughter's intended; they talked and played the piano and sang. Ivan Ilyich spent the evening, as Praskovya Fyodorovna noticed, more cheerfully than he had spent others, but he didn't forget for one minute that he had set aside some important thinking about his appendix. At eleven o'clock he said goodnight and went to his room. Since he had become ill he slept in a little room next to his study. He went in, undressed, and picked up a novel of Zola's,[1] which he didn't read.

9. French for Ivan (in English, John).

1. Émile Zola (1840–1902), French novelist, author of the Rougon-Macquart novels (*Nana*, *Germinal*, etc.). Tolstoy condemned Zola for his naturalistic theories and considered his novels crude.

He began thinking instead. The desired cure of the appendix took place in his imagination. Matter was absorbed, matter was expelled, and normal activity was restored. "Yes, that's how it all is," he said to himself. "Only nature needs a little help." He remembered his medicine, sat up, took it, watching for the beneficial effects of the medicine and the removal of the pain. "Just take it regularly and avoid unhealthy influences; I already feel a bit better, much better." He started to feel his side—it wasn't painful to the touch. "Yes, I can't feel it; I'm really much better now." He put out the candle and lay on his side. "The appendix is getting better; things are being absorbed." Suddenly he felt the familiar old dull nagging pain, the persistent, quiet, serious pain. The familiar nastiness in his mouth. His heart began to pump, his head turned. "My God, my God!" he said. "It's here again, it's here again and it's never going to stop." And suddenly his case presented itself to him from a different perspective. "Appendix! Kidney!" he said to himself. "It's not a case of the appendix or of the kidney, but of life . . . and death. Yes, I had life and now it's passing, passing, and I can't hold it back. That's it. Why deceive oneself? Isn't it obvious to everyone but myself that I am dying, and it's only a question of the number of weeks, days—maybe now. There was light and now there's darkness. I was here but now I'm going there! Where?" A chill came over him, his breathing stopped. He could only hear the beating of his heart.

"I won't exist, so what will exist? Nothing will exist. So where will I be when I don't exist? Is this really death? No, I don't want it." He got up quickly, tried to light a candle, groped with shaking hands, dropped the candle and candlestick on the floor, and slumped back again onto the pillow. "Why? Nothing matters," he said to himself, looking into the darkness with open eyes. "Death. Yes, death. And none of them knows and they don't want to know and they have no pity for me. They're enjoying themselves." Outside the door he could hear the distant noise of music and singing. "They don't care but they too will die. Fools. It'll come to me first, to them later; they too will have the same. But they're having fun, the beasts!" Anger choked him. And he felt painful, unbearable misery. "It cannot be that we're all doomed to this terrible fear." He raised himself.

"Something's not right; I must calm down, I must think over everything from the outset." And he began to think. "Yes, the start of my illness. I knocked my side, and I stayed just the same that day and the next; it ached a bit, then more, then the doctors, then depression, despair, the doctors again; and I kept getting nearer and nearer to the abyss. Less strength. Nearer and nearer. And now I've wasted away, there's no light in my eyes. And death, and I think about my appendix. I think of how to mend my appendix, but this is death. Is it really death?" Again horror came over him; he bent down, tried to find the matches, and banged his elbow on the nighttable. It got in his way and hurt him; he got angry with it; in his irritation he banged his elbow harder and knocked the nighttable over. And in his despair he fell back, gasping for breath, expecting death to come now.

Now the guests were leaving. Praskovya Fyodorovna was seeing them out. She heard something fall and came in.

"What's the matter with you?"

"Nothing. I knocked it over by mistake."

She went out and brought back a candle. He lay breathing heavily and very fast, like a man who has run a mile, looking at her with motionless eyes.

"What's the matter with you, *Jean*?"

"Nothing. I . . . knocked . . . it . . . over." (*What should I say? She won't understand*, he thought.)

Indeed she didn't. She picked the table up, lit a candle for him, and quickly went out; she had to see a guest out.

When she returned, he was lying in the same position, on his back, looking up.

"How are you feeling? Is it worse?"

"Yes, it is."

She shook her head and sat down.

"You know, *Jean*, I am wondering whether we shouldn't ask Leshchetitsky to the house."

That meant asking the celebrated doctor regardless of cost. He smiled venomously and said, "No." She sat for a while, then went over to him and kissed him on the forehead.

When she kissed him he hated her with all his might and made an effort not to push her away.

"Good night. With God's help you'll go to sleep."

"Yes."

VI

Ivan Ilyich saw that he was dying and was in constant despair.

Ivan Ilyich knew in the very depths of his soul that he was dying but not only could he not get accustomed to this, he simply didn't understand it; he just couldn't understand it.

All his life the example of a syllogism he had studied in Kiesewetter's[2] logic—"Caius is a man, men are mortal, therefore Caius is mortal"—had seemed to him to be true only in relation to Caius but in no way to himself. There was Caius the man, man in general, and it was quite justified, but he wasn't Caius and he wasn't man in general, and he had always been something quite, quite special apart from all other beings; he was Vanya,[3] with Mama, with Papa, with Mitya and Volodya, with his toys and the coachman, with Nyanya, then with Katenka, with all the joys, sorrows, passions of childhood, boyhood, youth. Did Caius know the smell of the striped leather ball Vanya loved so much? Did Caius kiss his mother's hand like that and did the silken folds of Caius's mother's dress rustle like that for him? Was Caius in love like that? Could Caius chair a session like that?

And Caius is indeed mortal and it's right that he should die, but for me, Vanya, Ivan Ilyich, with all my feelings and thoughts—for me it's quite different. And it cannot be that I should die. It would be too horrible.

That's what he felt.

"If I had to die like Caius, then I would know it, an inner voice would be telling me, but nothing like that happened in me, and I and all my friends—we understood that things weren't at all like with Caius. But now there's this!" he said to himself. "It can't be. It can't be, but it is. How has this happened? How can one understand it?"

2. Karl Kiesewetter (1766–1819) was a German popularizer of Kant's philosophy. His *Outline of Logic According to Kantian Principles* (1796) was widely used in Russian adaptations as a schoolbook.

3. Diminutive, familiar form of Ivan.

And he couldn't understand it and tried to banish this thought as false, inaccurate, morbid, and to replace it with other true and healthy thoughts. But this thought, and not just the thought but reality as it were came and stopped in front of him.

And in the place of this thought he called up others in turn in the hope of finding support in them. He tried to return to his previous ways of thought, which had concealed the thought of death from him. But—strangely—everything which previously had concealed and covered up and obliterated the awareness of death now could no longer produce this result. Ivan Ilyich now spent most of his time attempting to restore his previous ways of feeling that had concealed death. Now he would say to himself, "I'll take up some work, that's what I live by." And he went to court, banishing all his doubts; he talked to friends and sat down, absentmindedly looking over the crowd of people with a pensive look as he used to and supporting both wasted hands on the arms of his oak chair; leaning over toward a friend as usual, moving the papers of a case, whispering together, and then suddenly raising his eyes and sitting up straight, he would pronounce the particular words and open the case. But suddenly in the middle of it, the pain in his side, ignoring the stages of the case's development, began its own gnawing work. Ivan Ilyich listened and tried not to think about it, but it kept on. It came and stood right in front of him and looked at him, and he became petrified; the fire in his eyes died down, and he again began to ask himself, "Is it alone the truth?" And his friends and staff saw with surprise and dismay that he, such a brilliant, subtle judge, was getting confused and making mistakes. He would give himself a shake, make an effort to recover himself, and somehow or other bring the session to an end, and he would return home with the depressing awareness that his work as a judge couldn't hide from him as it used to what he wanted it to hide; that with his work as a judge he couldn't be rid of It. And what was worst of all was that It was distracting him not to make him do anything but only for him to look at It, right in the eye, look at it and without doing anything endure inexpressible sufferings.

And to rescue himself from this condition, Ivan Ilyich looked for relief—for new screens—and new screens appeared and for a short time seemed to offer him salvation, but very soon they again not so much collapsed as let the light through, as if It penetrated everything and nothing could hide it.

Latterly he would go into the drawing room he had arranged—the drawing room where he had fallen—how venomously comic it was to think of it—for the arrangement of which he had sacrificed his life, for he knew that his illness had started with that injury; he would go in and see that something had made a scratch on a polished table. He would look for the cause and find it in the bronze ornament of an album that had become bent at the edge. He would pick up the album, an expensive one he had lovingly compiled, and be cross at the carelessness of his daughter and her friends—things were torn and the photographs bent. He would carefully set things to rights and bend the decoration back again.

He then would have the thought of moving this whole *établissement*[4] of albums over into another corner by the flowers. He would call the manservant; either his daughter or his wife would come to his help; they would disagree,

4. Arrangement (French).

contradict him; he would argue, get angry, but everything would be all right because he didn't remember It, couldn't see It.

And then his wife would say when he himself was moving something, "Let the servants do it, you'll hurt yourself again," and suddenly It would flash through the screens; he would see It flash just for a moment, and he still would hope It would disappear, but without wanting to he would pay attention to his side—the same thing would still be sitting there, still aching, and he couldn't forget it, and It would be looking at him quite openly from behind the flowers. Why?

It's true, it was here on these curtains that I lost my life as if in an assault. Did I really? How terrible and how stupid! It can't be so! It can't be, but it is.

He would go into his study, lie down, and be left alone with It. Face-to-face with It, but nothing to be done with It. Just look at It and turn cold.

VII

How it happened in the third month of Ivan Ilyich's illness is impossible to say because it happened step by step, imperceptibly, but it did happen that his wife and his daughter and his son and the servants and his friends and the doctors and, above all, he himself knew that all interest others had in him lay solely in whether he would soon, at last, vacate his place, free the living from the constraint brought about by his presence, and be liberated himself from his sufferings.

He slept less and less; they gave him opium and started to inject morphine. But that gave him no relief. The dull pangs he felt in his half-somnolent state at first gave him relief as being something new, but then they became as agonizing as outright pain or even more so.

They prepared special food to the doctors' prescriptions, but this food he found more and more tasteless, more and more disgusting.

Special contrivances had to be made for excretion, and every time this was a torment for him. A torment because of the uncleanliness, the loss of decorum, and the odor, from the consciousness that another person had to take part in this.

But some comfort for Ivan Ilyich did come out of this unpleasant business. Gerasim, the manservant, always came to take things out for him.

Gerasim was a clean, fresh young peasant who had filled out on city food. He was always cheerful and sunny. At first Ivan Ilyich was embarrassed by seeing this man, always dressed in his clean, traditional clothes, having to do this repulsive job.

Once getting up from the pan and lacking the strength to pull up his trousers, he collapsed into an easy chair and looked with horror at his feeble bare thighs with their sharply defined muscles.

Gerasim came in with firm, light steps in his heavy boots, giving off a pleasant smell of tar from the boots and of fresh winter air; he had on a clean hessian[5] apron and a clean cotton shirt, the sleeves rolled up over his strong, young, bare arms; without looking at Ivan Ilyich, he went to the vessel, obviously masking the joy in living shining out from his face so as not to hurt the sick man.

"Gerasim," Ivan Ilyich said weakly.

5. Coarse, strong fabric made from hemp.

Gerasim started, obviously scared he had made some mistake, and with a quick movement turned toward the sick man his fresh, kind, simple, young face, which was just beginning to grow a beard.

"Do you need something, sir?"

"I think this must be unpleasant for you. You must forgive me. I can't manage."

"No, sir." Gerasim's eyes were shining and he showed his young white teeth. "What's a little trouble? You've got an illness."

And with strong, dexterous hands he did his usual job and went out, treading lightly. And in five minutes, treading just as lightly, he came back.

Ivan Ilyich was still sitting there like that in the armchair.

"Gerasim," he said when Gerasim had put down the clean, rinsed vessel, "please, come here and help me." Gerasim came. "Lift me up. It's difficult by myself and I've sent Dmitry away."

Gerasim came over to him; he put his strong arms around him and, gently and deftly, the same way he walked, lifted and supported him; he pulled up his trousers with one hand and was going to sit him down. But Ivan Ilyich asked Gerasim to take him to the sofa. Effortlessly and with next to no pressure, Gerasim led him, almost carrying him, to the sofa and sat him down.

"Thank you. How easily, how well . . . you do everything."

Gerasim again smiled and was about to go out. But Ivan Ilyich felt so good with him around that he didn't want to let him go.

"Now. Please move this chair over to me. No, that one, underneath my legs. I feel better when my legs are higher."

Gerasim brought the chair, placed it without making any noise, lowering it in one movement to the floor, and lifted Ivan Ilyich's legs onto the chair; Ivan Ilyich thought he felt better the moment Gerasim raised up his legs.

"I feel better when my legs are higher," Ivan Ilyich said. "Put that cushion under me."

Gerasim did that. Again he lifted his legs up and put the cushion into position. Again Ivan Ilyich felt better when Gerasim held his legs up. When he lowered them, he thought he felt worse.

"Gerasim," he said to him, "are you busy now?"

"No sir, not at all," said Gerasim, who had learned from the townsfolk how to talk to the gentry.

"What do you still have to do?"

"What is there to do? I've done everything; I've just got to chop the wood for tomorrow."

"So hold my legs up a bit higher, can you do that?"

"Of course I can." Gerasim lifted up his legs and Ivan Ilyich thought that in this position he felt absolutely no pain.

"But what about the wood?"

"Don't worry, sir. We'll manage."

Ivan Ilyich told Gerasim to sit down and hold up his legs, and he talked to him. And—strange to say—he thought he felt better while Gerasim held up his legs.

From that day Ivan Ilyich started sometimes to call Gerasim in to him and made him hold up his legs on his shoulders, and he liked to talk to him. Gerasim did this easily, willingly, simply, and with a goodness of heart that touched Ivan

Ilyich. In all other people Ivan Ilyich was offended by health, strength, high spirits; only Gerasim's strength and high spirits didn't depress but calmed Ivan Ilyich.

Ivan Ilyich's chief torment was the lie—that lie, for some reason recognized by everyone, that he was only ill but not dying, and that he only needed rest and treatment and then there would be some very good outcome. But he knew that whatever they did, there would be no outcome except even more painful suffering and death. And he was tormented by this lie; he was tormented by their unwillingness to acknowledge what everyone knew and he knew, by their wanting to lie to him about his terrible situation, by their wanting him to and making him take part in that lie himself. The lie, this lie being perpetrated above him on the eve of his death, the lie which could only bring down this terrible solemn act of his death to the level of all their visits and curtains and sturgeon for dinner . . . was horribly painful for Ivan Ilyich. And, strangely, many times when they were performing their tricks above him, he was within a hair's breadth of crying out to them, "Stop lying; you know and I know that I am dying; so at least stop lying." But he never had the strength to do it. The terrible, horrific act of his dying, he saw, had been brought down by all those surrounding him to the level of a casual unpleasantness, some breach of decorum (as one treats a man who, entering a drawing room, emits a bad smell); brought down by that very "decorum" he had served his whole life, he saw that no one had pity for him because no one even wanted to understand his situation. Only Gerasim understood his situation and felt pity for him. And so Ivan Ilyich only felt comfortable with Gerasim. He felt comfortable when Gerasim held up his legs, sometimes for whole nights without a break, and wouldn't go off to bed, saying, "Please, sir, don't worry, Ivan Ilyich, I'll still get plenty of sleep"; or when he would suddenly add, going over to the familiar "thou," "You're sick, so why shouldn't I do something for you?" Gerasim was the only one not to lie; everything showed he was the only one who understood what the matter was and didn't think it necessary to hide it, and simply felt pity for his wasted, feeble master. He even once said directly when Ivan Ilyich was dismissing him:

"We'll all die. So why not take a little trouble?" He said this, conveying by it that he wasn't bothered by the work precisely because he was doing it for a dying man and hoped that in his time someone would do this work for him.

Apart from this lie, or as a consequence of it, what was most painful for Ivan Ilyich was that no one had pity on him as he wanted them to have pity; at some moments after prolonged sufferings Ivan Ilyich wanted most of all, however much he felt ashamed to admit it, for someone to have pity on him like a sick child. He wanted them to caress him, to kiss him, to cry over him as one caresses and comforts children. He knew he was an important legal official, that he had a graying beard and that therefore this was impossible, but he still wanted it. And in his relations with Gerasim there was something close to that, and therefore his relations with Gerasim comforted him. Ivan Ilyich would want to cry, would want them to caress him and cry over him; then in would come his friend, the lawyer Shebek, and instead of crying and caresses Ivan Ilyich would assume a serious, stern, pensive expression and out of inertia would give his opinion on the meaning of a verdict of the court of appeal and stubbornly insist on it. This lie all around him and inside him more than anything poisoned the last days of Ivan Ilyich's life.

VIII

It was morning. It was morning only because Gerasim had gone out and Pyotr the manservant came in, put out the candles, opened one curtain, and started quietly to tidy up. Whether it was morning or evening, Friday or Sunday, was immaterial, it was all one and the same: the gnawing, agonizing pain that didn't abate for a moment; the consciousness of life departing without hope but still not yet departed; the same terrible, hateful death advancing, which was the only reality, and always the same lie. What did days, weeks, and times of day matter here?

"Would you like some tea?"

He has to have order; masters should drink tea in the mornings, he thought and only said:

"No."

"Would you like to move to the sofa?"

He has to tidy the chamber, and I'm in the way; I am dirt, disorder, he thought and only said:

"No, leave me be."

The manservant did some more things. Ivan Ilyich stretched out his hand. Pyotr came up to serve.

"What do you want?"

"My watch."

Pyotr got the watch, which was lying right there, and handed it to him.

"Half past eight. Have they got up?"

"No, sir. Vasily Ivanovich"—that was his son—"has gone to the gymnasium, but Praskovya Fyodorovna gave orders to wake her if you asked for her. Shall I?"

"No, don't." *Shall I try some tea?* he thought. "Yes, tea . . . bring it."

Pyotr went to the door. Ivan Ilyich felt terrified of being left alone. *How can I detain him? Yes, my medicine*. "Pyotr, give me my medicine." *Why not, maybe the medicine will still help*. He took the spoon and drank. *No, it won't help. It's all nonsense and a sham*, he decided as soon as he sensed the familiar sickly, hopeless taste. *No, I can't believe in it anymore. But the pain, why the pain, if it would just go down even for a minute*. And he groaned. Pyotr turned round again. "No, go away. Bring me some tea."

Pyotr went out. Left alone, Ivan Ilyich groaned not so much from the pain, however frightful it was, as from anguish. "Always the same, always these endless days and nights. If only it could be soon. What could be soon? Death, darkness. No, no. Anything is better than death!"

When Pyotr came in with the tea on a tray, Ivan Ilyich looked distractedly at him for a long time, not taking in who and what he was. Pyotr was embarrassed by this stare. And when Pyotr was embarrassed, Ivan Ilyich came to himself.

"Yes," he said, "tea . . . good, put it down. Only help me wash and give me a clean shirt."

And Ivan Ilyich began to wash. Stopping to rest, he washed his hands, his face, cleaned his teeth, began to brush his hair, and looked in the mirror. He felt frightened, especially frightened by the way his hair stuck flat to his forehead.

When his shirt was being changed, he knew that he would be even more frightened if he looked at his body, and so he didn't look at himself. But now it was all done. He put on a dressing gown, covered himself with a blanket, and sat in an armchair to have his tea. For one minute he felt refreshed, but as soon as he began to drink the tea, again the same taste, the same pain. With an effort he finished the tea and lay down, stretching out his legs. He lay down and sent Pyotr away.

Always the same. There'd be a small flash of hope, then a sea of despair would surge, and always pain, always pain, always despair, and always the same. It was horribly depressing being alone; he wanted to ask for someone but he knew in advance that with others there it would be even worse. "If only I could have morphine again—and lose consciousness. I'll tell him, the doctor, to think of something else. Like this it's impossible, impossible."

An hour, a couple of hours would go by like that. But now there's a bell in the hall. Maybe it's the doctor. It is; it's the doctor, fresh, bright, plump, cheerful, his expression saying, "You've gotten frightened of something there but now we'll fix all that for you." The doctor knows that this expression isn't appropriate here, but he has assumed it once and for all and he can't take it off, like a man who has put on a tailcoat in the morning and is paying visits.

The doctor rubs his hands briskly and reassuringly.

"I'm cold. There's a cracking frost. Let me warm myself up," he says, his expression being as if one just had to wait a little for him to warm himself, and when he had, then he would set everything to rights.

"So, how are we?"

Ivan Ilyich feels the doctor wants to say, "How are things?" but feels one can't talk like that, and he says, "How did you spend the night?"

Ivan Ilyich looks at the doctor, his expression asking, "Will you really never be ashamed of telling lies?" But the doctor doesn't want to understand the question.

And Ivan Ilyich says:

"Just as dreadfully. The pain isn't going, it isn't going away. If I could just have something!"

"Yes, you patients are always like that. Well, sir, now I've warmed up, even our very particular Praskovya Fyodorovna wouldn't have anything to say against my temperature. So, sir, good morning." And the doctor shakes his hand.

And, dropping all his earlier playfulness, the doctor begins to examine the patient with a serious expression, takes pulse and temperature, and then begin the tappings and auscultations.

Ivan Ilyich knows firmly and without any doubt that all this is nonsense, an empty fraud, but when the doctor on his knees stretches over him, applying his ear first higher, then lower, and performs over him various gymnastic exercises, Ivan Ilyich succumbs to all this as he used to succumb to lawyers' speeches when he knew very well that they were lying and why they were lying.

The doctor, kneeling on the sofa, was still tapping something when there was a rustling at the door of Praskovya Fyodorovna's silk dress, and they could hear her scolding Pyotr for not informing her of the doctor's arrival.

She comes in, kisses her husband, and at once starts to make it clear that she has got up long ago and that it's because of a misunderstanding that she wasn't there when the doctor came.

Ivan Ilyich looks at her, examines her closely, and holds against her the whiteness and plumpness and cleanliness of her arms and neck, the gloss of her hair and the shine of her eyes that are so full of life. He hates her with his whole soul. And her touch makes him suffer from a surge of hatred towards her.

Her attitude to him and to his illness is always the same. Just as the doctor has developed for himself an attitude toward his patients which he hasn't been able to put aside, so has she developed a simple attitude towards him—he isn't doing something he should be doing, and it's his fault, and she lovingly scolds him for this—and she hasn't yet managed to put this attitude toward him aside.

"He just doesn't listen. He doesn't take his medicine when he should. And above all—he lies in a position that has to be bad for him—with his legs up."

She described how he makes Gerasim hold his legs.

The doctor smiled a smile of amiable scorn, as if saying, "What can one do? Sometimes these patients dream up such silly things; but one can forgive them."

When the examination was over the doctor looked at his watch, and then Praskovya Fyodorovna announced to Ivan Ilyich that whatever he might want, today she had asked in a famous doctor and he and Mikhail Danilovich (that was the usual doctor's name) would examine him together and discuss the case.

"So please don't go against this. I'm doing this for myself," she said ironically, letting him understand that she did everything for him and just by her saying this he was given no right to refuse her. He said nothing and frowned. He felt that the lies surrounding him had become so tangled that it was difficult now to see anything clearly.

Everything she did for him she did only for herself, and she told him so, as if that was something so unlikely that he had to understand it in the opposite sense.

Indeed the famous doctor did arrive at half past eleven. Again there started the auscultations and serious conversations, both in front of Ivan Ilyich and in another room, about his kidney and appendix, and questions and answers delivered with such a serious air that again, instead of the real question about life and death which now was the only one that confronted him, there came a question about his kidney and appendix, which were doing something not quite as they should be and which Mikhail Danilovich and the celebrity doctor would get to grips with right away and make them correct themselves.

The famous doctor said his goodbyes with a serious expression, but one that hadn't given up hope. And to the timid question Ivan Ilyich put to him, raising eyes that were shining with fear and hope—is there any possibility of recovery?—he answered that though one couldn't guarantee it, there was a possibility. The look of hope with which Ivan Ilyich said goodbye to the doctor was so pitiful that, when she saw it, Praskovya Fyodorovna burst into tears as she went through the study doors to give the famous doctor his fee.

The rise in his spirits brought about by the doctor's encouragement didn't last long. Again it was the same room, the same pictures, curtains, wallpaper, medicine bottles, and his same hurting, suffering body. And Ivan Ilyich started to groan; they gave him an injection and he lost consciousness.

When he came to, it was beginning to get dark; they brought in his dinner. With some effort he took some broth; and again all those same things and again night was coming on.

After dinner at seven o'clock Praskovya Fyodorovna came into his room dressed for an evening out, her breasts large and lifted and traces of powder on her face. That morning she had reminded him that they were going to the theater. Sarah Bernhardt[6] was visiting and they had a box which Ivan Ilyich had insisted they take. Now he had forgotten that, and her clothes outraged him. But he concealed his outrage when he remembered that he himself had insisted they get a box and go because it was a cultural treat for their children.

Praskovya Fyodorovna came in pleased with herself but also with a kind of guilty feeling. She sat down, asked about his health—as he could see, just for the sake of asking rather than to learn, knowing that there was nothing to learn—and began to say what she needed to: that she wouldn't have gone out for anything but the box was taken and Hélène was going and their daughter and Petrishchev (the examining magistrate, their daughter's fiancé), and it was impossible to let them go alone. But it would be so much more agreeable for her to sit with him. He must just do what the doctor had ordered without her.

"Yes, and Fyodor Petrovich—the fiancé—wanted to come in. Can he? Liza, too."

"Let them come in."

His daughter came in all dressed up with her young body bared, that body which made him suffer so. But she was flaunting it. Strong, healthy, clearly in love and angry at the illness, suffering, and death that stood in the way of her happiness.

Fyodor Petrovich came too, in a tailcoat, his hair curled à la Capoul,[7] his long sinewy neck encased in a white collar, with a huge white shirtfront and with powerful thighs squeezed into narrow black trousers, with one white glove pulled onto his hand and an opera hat.

After him the schoolboy crept in inconspicuously in a new school uniform, poor fellow, wearing white gloves and with terrible dark patches under his eyes, the meaning of which Ivan Ilyich knew.

His son always made him feel sorry for him. And the look he gave him was terrible, full of sympathy and fear. Apart from Gerasim, only Vasya understood him and felt pity for him, so Ivan Ilyich thought.

They all sat down, asked again about his health. A silence fell. Liza asked her mother about the opera glasses. There ensued an argument between mother and daughter about who had put them where. It felt unpleasant.

Fyodor Petrovich asked Ivan Ilyich if he had seen Sarah Bernhardt. At first Ivan Ilyich didn't understand what he was being asked and then said:

"No, but have you?"

"Yes, in *Adrienne Lecouvreur*."[8]

Praskovya Fyodorovna said that she was particularly good in something or other. Their daughter disagreed. There began a conversation about the elegance and realism of her acting—that conversation which is always exactly the same.

In the middle of the conversation Fyodor Petrovich looked at Ivan Ilyich and fell silent. The others looked and fell silent. Ivan Ilyich looked straight

6. Stage name of French actress Rosine Bernard (1844–1923), famed for romantic and tragic roles.

7. That is, worn in tight curls in the manner of famed French tenor Victor Capoul (1839–1924).

8. A play (1849) by the French dramatist Eugène Scribe (1791–1861), in which the heroine was a famous actress of the 18th century. Tolstoy considered Scribe, who wrote over 400 plays, a shoddy, commercial playwright.

ahead with shining eyes, clearly becoming angry with them. This had to be put right, but it was quite impossible to put right. Somehow this silence had to be broken. No one had the resolve, and they all became frightened that somehow the decorous lie would collapse and the true state of things would become obvious to all. Liza was the first to take the resolve. She broke the silence. She wanted to hide what they were all feeling, but she said it wrong.

"So, *if we are going to go*, it's time," she said, looking at her watch, a present from her father, and she gave a barely perceptible smile to the young man, which meant something known to them alone, and got up, her dress rustling.

They all got up, said goodbye, and went off.

When they had gone out, Ivan Ilyich thought he felt better: the lie wasn't there—it had gone out with them—but the pain remained. The same constant pain, the same constant fear made nothing more difficult, nothing easier. Everything was worse.

Again minute followed minute, hour followed hour; it was always the same and there was still no end and the inevitable end became more terrifying.

"Yes, send me Gerasim," he said in reply to a question Pyotr asked.

IX

His wife came back late at night. She walked on tiptoe but he heard her; he opened his eyes and quickly shut them again. She wanted to send Gerasim away and sit with him herself. He opened his eyes and said:

"No. Go away."

"Are you in a lot of pain?"

"It doesn't matter."

"Take some opium."

He agreed and drank. She went out.

Till three o'clock he was in a tormented stupor. He thought that in some way they were pushing him and his pain into a narrow, deep, black sack; they kept pushing further but they couldn't push them right in. And this terrible business for him was crowned by his suffering. And he was both struggling and wanting to drop right down, both fighting against it and assisting. And suddenly he was free and fell and came to. The same Gerasim was still sitting on the bed at his feet, dozing quietly, patiently. And Ivan Ilyich was lying there, having lifted his emaciated legs in their socks onto Gerasim's shoulders; there was the same candle with its shade and the same unceasing pain.

"Go, Gerasim," he whispered.

"It doesn't matter, sir, I'll sit a bit longer."

"No, go."

He removed his legs and lay on his side on top of his arm, and he began to feel sorry for himself. He waited for Gerasim to go out into the next room and he couldn't control himself anymore, and he burst into tears like a child. He wept for his helplessness, for his horrible loneliness, for people's cruelty, for God's cruelty, for God's absence.

"Why have you done all this? Why have you brought me here? Why, why do you torment me so horribly?"

He didn't expect an answer, but he also wept because there wasn't and couldn't be an answer. The pain increased again but he didn't move or call anyone. He said to himself, "More, go on, beat me! But why? What have I done to you, why?"

Then he calmed down; he not only stopped weeping, he stopped breathing and became all attention, as if he were listening not to a voice speaking in sounds but to the voice of his soul, to the train of thoughts rising within him.

"What do you want?" was the first clear idea capable of being expressed in words that he heard. "What do you want? What do you want?" he repeated to himself. "What? Not to suffer. To live," he answered.

And again he became absorbed with such intense attention that even the pain did not distract him.

"To live? To live how?" asked the voice of his soul.

"Yes, to live, as I lived before: well and pleasantly."

"As you lived before, well, pleasantly?" asked the voice. And he began to go over in his imagination the best moments of his pleasant life. But—strange to relate—all these best moments of a pleasant life now seemed quite different from what they had seemed then. All of them—except for his first memories of childhood. There in childhood was something so truly pleasant with which he could live, if it returned. But the person who had experienced those pleasant things no longer existed: it was like a memory of something else.

As soon as the process began which had resulted in Ivan Ilyich, the man of today, all the things which had seemed joys melted away before his eyes and were changed into something worthless and often vile.

And the further from childhood, the nearer to the present, the more worthless and dubious were the joys. That began with law school. There was still something there truly good: there was gaiety, there was friendship, there were hopes. But in the senior classes these good moments were already less frequent. After that, at the time of his first period of service with the governor, again good moments appeared: there were memories of love for a woman. After that all this became confused and there was even less of what was good. Further on there was still less good, and the further he went the less there was.

Marriage . . . so casually entered, and disillusionment, and the smell that came from his wife's mouth, and sensuality, hypocrisy! And that deadly work of his and those worries about money, and on for a year, and two, and ten, and twenty—and always the same. And the further he went, the more deadly it became. "As if I were walking downhill at a regular pace, imagining I was walking uphill. That's how it was. In the eyes of the world I was walking uphill, and to just that extent life was slipping away from under me . . . And now it's time, to die!

"So what is this? Why? It can't be. It can't be that life was so meaningless and vile. But if it was indeed so meaningless and vile, then why die and die suffering? Something is wrong.

"Maybe I have lived not as I should have"—the thought suddenly came into his head. "But how so when I did everything in the proper way?" he said to himself, and immediately rejected this solution of the whole riddle of life as something wholly impossible.

"What do you want now? To live? To live how? To live as you lived in court when the court officer pronounces, 'The court is opening!' The court is opening, opening, the court," he repeated to himself. "Here's the court! But I'm not guilty!" he shouted angrily. "For what?" And he stopped weeping and, turning his face to the wall, he began to think of just the one thing: why all this horror, for what?

But however much he thought, he found no answer. And when there came to him the thought, as it often did, that all this was happening because he had lived wrongly, he at once remembered all the correctness of his life and rejected this strange thought.

X

Two more weeks went by. Ivan Ilyich didn't get up from the sofa anymore. He didn't want to lie in bed and instead lay on the sofa. And, lying almost all the time with his face to the wall, he suffered in his loneliness all those same insoluble sufferings and in his loneliness thought the same insoluble thoughts. What is this? Is it really true that this is death? And a voice within answered: Yes, it's true. Why these torments? And the voice answered: That's the way it is; there is no why. Apart from that there was nothing more.

From the very start of his illness, when Ivan Ilyich went to the doctor for the first time, his life was divided into two diametrically opposed moods, which alternated with each other: on the one hand despair and the expectation of an incomprehensible and horrible death, on the other hope and the absorbed observation of the activity of his body. Now he had before his eyes just a kidney or appendix which for a time had deviated from the performance of its duties; now there was just incomprehensible, horrible death from which it was impossible to escape in any way.

From the very beginning of his illness these two moods alternated with each other; but the more the illness progressed, the more fantastic and questionable became thoughts about his kidney and the more real the consciousness of approaching death.

He only had to remember what he had been three months previously and what he was now—to remember how he had been walking downhill at a regular pace—for all possibility of hope to crumble.

In the recent loneliness in which he found himself, lying with his face to the back of the sofa, loneliness in the midst of a crowded city and his numerous acquaintances and family—loneliness that could not be more absolute anywhere, either at the bottom of the sea or underneath the earth—in his recent terrible loneliness Ivan Ilyich lived only by his imagination in the past. One after another pictures of his past presented themselves to him. It always began with the closest in time and went back to the most remote, to his childhood, and rested there. If Ivan Ilyich thought of the stewed prunes he was offered to eat now, he remembered the moist, wrinkled French prunes of his childhood, their particular taste and the flow of saliva when he got to the stone, and alongside this memory of taste there arose a whole row of memories of that time: his *nyanya*, his brother, his toys. "You mustn't think of that. . . . It's too painful," Ivan Ilyich said to himself, and was again transported into the present. A button on the back of the sofa and the creases in its morocco leather. "Morocco is expensive and wears badly; there was a quarrel because of it. But it was different leather and a different row when we ripped our father's briefcase and were punished, but Mama brought us some pies." And again he stopped in his childhood and again it was painful for Ivan Ilyich, and he tried to push it away and think of something else.

And here again, together with this train of memories, another train of memories went through his mind—of how his illness had intensified and grown. It was the same; the further back he went, the more life there was. There was more good in life and more of life itself. And the two merged together. *As my torments kept getting worse and worse, so the whole of life became worse and worse,* he thought. One bright spot, there, at the start of his life, and after that everything blacker and blacker, and everything quicker and quicker. *In inverse ratio to the square of the distance from death,* thought Ivan Ilyich. And an image of a stone flying downward with increasing speed became fixed in his mind. Life, a sequence of increasing sufferings, flies quicker and quicker to the end, to the most terrible suffering of all. *I am flying* . . . He shivered, moved, tried to resist, but he now knew that resistance was impossible, and again, with eyes that were tired of looking but which couldn't help looking at what was in front of him, he gazed at the back of the sofa and waited—waited for that terrible fall, the crash, and annihilation. "I can't resist," he said to himself. "But if I could just understand why. That too I can't. I might be able to explain it if I said I had lived not as I should have. But it's impossible to admit that," he said to himself, remembering all the lawfulness, the correctness, and the decorum of his life. "It's impossible to admit that now," he said to himself, grimacing with his lips, as if anyone could see this smile of his and be deceived by it. "There's no explanation! Torment, death. . . . Why?"

XI

Two weeks went by like that. In those weeks an event took place that had been desired by Ivan Ilyich and his wife: Petrishchev made a formal proposal. It happened in the evening. The next day Praskovya Fyodorovna went in to her husband, wondering how to announce Fyodor Petrovich's proposal to him, but that very night Ivan Ilyich had taken a turn for the worse. Praskovya Fyodorovna found him on the same sofa, but in a new position. He was lying on his back, groaning and looking ahead with a fixed gaze.

She started talking about medicines. He turned his eyes to her. She didn't finish what she had begun to say; there was so much anger expressed in those eyes, aimed directly at her.

"For Christ's sake, let me die in peace," he said.

She was about to go, but at that moment his daughter came in and went up to say good morning. He looked at his daughter as he had at his wife and to her questions about his health he drily said to her that he would soon liberate them all from himself. They both said nothing, sat briefly, and went out.

"What can we be blamed for?" Liza said to her mother. "As if we'd done this! I'm sorry for Papa, but why must he torment us?"

The doctor came at the usual time. Ivan Ilyich answered him "yes, no," not taking his angry eyes from him, and finally said:

"You know that you won't be of any help, so leave me."

"We can relieve the suffering," the doctor said.

"You can't do that either; leave me."

The doctor went out into the drawing room and informed Praskovya Fyodorovna that things were very bad and that there was only one resource—opium, to relieve the suffering, which must be terrible.

The doctor said that Ivan Ilyich's physical sufferings were terrible, and that was true; but even more terrible than his physical sufferings were his mental sufferings, and there was his chief torment.

His mental sufferings lay in the fact that that night, as he looked at Gerasim's sleepy, good-natured face with its high cheekbones, there suddenly had entered his head the thought: *But what if in actual fact all my life, my conscious life, has been "wrong"?*

It occurred to him that the notion that had previously seemed to him a complete impossibility—that he had not lived his life as he should have done—could be the truth. It occurred to him that his barely noticeable attempts at struggling against what was considered good by those in high positions above him, those barely noticeable attempts which he had immediately rejected, could be genuine, and everything else wrong. His work and the structure of his life and his family and his social and professional interests—all that could be wrong. He tried to defend all that to himself. And suddenly he felt the fragility of what he was defending. And there was nothing to defend.

"But if this is so," he said to himself, "and I am leaving life with the realization that I have lost everything I was given and that it's impossible to put right, then what?" He lay on his back and started to go over his whole life afresh. When in the morning he saw the manservant, then his wife, then his daughter, then the doctor—every one of their movements, every one of their words confirmed for him the terrible truth that had been disclosed to him in the night. He saw in them himself, everything by which he had lived, and saw clearly that all this was wrong, all this was a terrible, huge fraud concealing both life and death. This realization increased, increased tenfold his physical sufferings. He groaned and tossed about and pulled at the clothes on him. He felt suffocated and crushed. And he hated them for that.

They gave him a big dose of opium; he lost consciousness, but at dinnertime the same began again. He drove them all away from him and tossed about from side to side.

His wife came to him and said:

"*Jean*, my dear, do this for me. It can't do any harm, but it often helps. So, it's nothing. And people in good health often . . ."

He opened his eyes wide.

"What? Take communion? Why? There's no need to! But then . . ."

She started crying.

"Yes, my dear? I'll call for our man, he's so sweet."

"Fine, very well," he said.

When the priest came and took his confession, he was calmed; he felt a kind of relief from his doubts and, as a consequence of that, from his sufferings, and a moment of hope came to him. He again began to think of his appendix and the possibility of curing it. He received communion with tears in his eyes.

When, after communion, he was put to bed, for a moment he felt comfortable and hope for life appeared again. He began to think of the operation being suggested to him. "To live, I want to live," he said to himself. His wife came to congratulate him on taking communion; she said the usual words and added:

"You feel better, don't you?"

Without looking at her he said, "Yes."

Her clothes, her body, the expression of her face, the sound of her voice—everything said to him one thing: "Wrong. Everything by which you have lived and are living is a lie, a fraud, concealing life and death from you." And as soon as he thought that, hatred rose up in him, and together with hatred agonizing physical suffering, and with those sufferings an awareness of the end, nearby and unavoidable. Something new happened: his breath started to strain and come in spurts and be squeezed out.

His expression when he said "yes" was terrible. Having said that yes, he looked her straight in the eye and with unusual strength for his weakness turned himself facedown and cried:

"Go away, go away, leave me!"

XII

From that minute began three days of unceasing screams that were so horrible one couldn't hear them from two doors away without feeling horror. The minute he answered his wife, he understood that he was lost, that there was no return, that the end had come, the very end, but the doubt still wasn't resolved; it still remained doubt.

"Oh! Oh! Oh!" he cried out in various tones. He began to cry out, "I don't want to, no!" and went on like that crying out the letter O.

For the whole three days, during which time did not exist for him, he tossed about in the black sack into which he was being pushed by an invisible, insurmountable force. He struggled as a man condemned to death struggles in the arms of the executioner, knowing he cannot save himself; and with every minute he felt that for all his efforts at struggling he was coming nearer and nearer to what filled him with horror. He felt that his agony lay both in being pushed into that black hole and even more in being unable to get into it. He was prevented from climbing in by his declaration that his life had been good. This justification of his life caught on something and stopped him from going forward, and that distressed him most of all.

Suddenly some kind of force struck him in the chest and on the side; his breath was constricted even more; he collapsed into the hole and there at the bottom of the hole some light was showing. There happened to him what he used to experience in a railway carriage when you think you are going forward but are going backward and suddenly realize your true direction.

"Yes, everything was wrong," he said to himself, "but it doesn't matter. I can, I can do what is right. But what is right?" he asked himself, and at once fell silent.

It was the end of the third day, an hour before his death. At that very moment the gymnasium schoolboy quietly slipped into his father's room and approached his bed. The dying man was still crying out despairingly and waving his arms about. One of his hands hit the schoolboy's head. The schoolboy took it, pressed it to his lips, and wept.

At that very moment Ivan Ilyich fell through and saw a light, and it was revealed to him that his life had been wrong but that it was still possible to mend things. He asked himself, "What is right?" and fell silent, listening. Now he felt someone was kissing his hand. He opened his eyes and looked at his son. He felt sorry for him. His wife came to him. He looked at her. She looked at him, mouth open and tears on her nose and cheeks that she hadn't wiped away. He felt sorry for her.

"Yes, I make them unhappy," he thought. "They are sorry for me, but it'll be better for them when I die." He wanted to say that but didn't have the strength to utter it. "However, why say things? One must act," he thought. With a look to his wife he pointed to his son and said:

"Take him away . . . sorry for him . . . and for you . . ." He wanted to add "forgive" but said "give," and not having the strength to correct himself, waved his hand, knowing that He who needed to understand would understand.

And suddenly it became clear to him that what had been oppressing him and not coming to an end—now everything was coming to an end at once, on two sides, on ten sides, on every side. He was sorry for them, he must make it so they had no pain. Free them and free himself from these sufferings. "So good and so simple," he thought. "And the pain?" he asked himself. "Where's it gone? Well, where are you, pain?"

He began to listen.

"There it is. So—let the pain be. And death? Where is it?"

He searched for his old habitual fear of death and didn't find it. Where was death? What death? There was no fear, because there was no death.

Instead of death there was light.

"So that's it!" he suddenly said aloud. "Such joy!"

For him all this took place in a moment, and the significance of this moment didn't change. For those there his death agony lasted two hours more. Something bubbled in his chest; his emaciated body shivered. Then the gurgling and wheezing became less and less frequent.

"It is finished!" someone said above him.

He heard these words and repeated them in his heart. "Death is finished," he said to himself. "It is no more."

He breathed in, stopped halfway, stretched himself, and died.

HENRIK IBSEN

1828–1906

Writing in an era when drama had become a second-rate occupation, with most gifted writers turning instead to novels or poetry, Henrik Ibsen restored prestige and relevance to the theater. Over the course of the nineteenth century, the invention of new theatrical machinery and techniques had turned theater into spectacle. Theater producers spent their time and money on special effects, dazzling audiences with lighting, horses, or even nautical battles in addition to, of course, trying to sign the latest acting stars. One might compare nineteenth-century theater with present-day Hollywood and its focus on blockbuster action movies packed with special effects and star actors. Ibsen showed Europe that theater could be more than just spectacle, that it could be an art form addressing the most serious moral and social questions of the time. The theatergoing public was first shocked, and later thrilled, to have controversial themes presented on the stage, and to have them presented not through special effects but through carefully drawn characters and well-constructed dramatic situations. Honing his dramatic technique over half a century, Ibsen almost single-handedly brought a new seriousness to the theater, and he has been regarded as the originator of modern drama ever since.

Ibsen achieved his unparalleled success against all odds. He was born in Skien, a small town in Norway, far removed from the cultural centers of Europe, and he spoke Norwegian, a marginal language unlikely to launch a European career in literature. When Ibsen left his provincial home at the age of fifteen, he was apprenticed to a chemist. Only at the age of twenty-two was he able to free himself from his apprenticeship—and from a liaison with a maid that had resulted in an illegitimate child—and move to the capital, Christiania (now Oslo), to study for the university entrance exam. During this time his first play was performed. After a few years spent learning the craft, he assumed positions of greater responsibility—as artistic director and dramaturge—at theaters in Bergen and Christiania.

Ibsen at first learned from the standard dramatic form of the time, the so-called well-made play. Popularized by the French playwrights Victorien Sardou and Augustine-Eugène Scribe, the well-made play revolved around complicated plots and well-timed confrontations. Immensely popular with audiences, well-made plays excelled at fast-moving action, intrigues, alliances, and sudden revelations.

But Ibsen would soon turn against these sensational formulas. In two plays, *Brand* (1866) and *Peer Gynt* (1867), Ibsen startlingly rejected not only the well-made play, but the theater as such. He wrote these works as "dramatic poems," plays that were not supposed to be performed but were written exclusively to be read. All the rules that governed conventional stage action could thus be circumvented entirely. Drawing on literary models such as **Goethe**'s ***Faust*** and Byron's *Don Juan*, *Peer Gynt* freely mixes fantasy and reality, conjuring mountain trolls, mad German philosophers, and the devil himself. The play established Ibsen as a writer of European significance.

And so Europe, rather than Norway, became Ibsen's home: he would spend the next twenty-seven years on the continent, mostly in Italy and Germany, before moving back to Norway at the age of sixty-three. After *Brand* and *Peer Gynt* had secured his Europe-wide reputation, he changed course and started writing for the stage once more, but in an entirely different style. He gave up on Norway's past and chose to write, once and for all, about the world he knew best: the contemporary Norwegian middle class. His singular purpose was to lay bare the ugly reality behind the façade of middle-class respectability, to expose the lies of bourgeois characters and indeed of bourgeois society as a whole. The five plays of this period, *The Pillars of Society* (1877), *A Doll's House* (1879), *Ghosts* (1881), *Enemy of the People* (1882), and *The Wild Duck* (1884), made Ibsen notorious throughout Europe and established him as an author of shock, confrontation, and revolt.

The main reason why these plays caused such consternation and excitement is that they introduced realism to the theater. Realism had already been established in the novel, but not in drama. In these realist plays, Ibsen wrote in ordinary language and devoted his drama to undoing deceit and pretense, to unveiling hidden motives and past misdeeds so that the truth would shine forth on the stage. Realism, for Ibsen, meant creating a theater of emotional and moral truth, where audiences could understand both the subjective experience and the objective conditions of modern life.

After becoming notorious with his realist plays, Ibsen changed course once more. He had been trying to write modern versions of Greek tragedy for a long while, but it was only in the last phase of his career that he managed to give definite shape to the tragedy of modern middle-class life. Of these plays *Hedda Gabler* (1890) is the most compelling and famous. It is set in the same bourgeois milieu as his realist plays, but is no longer directed towards social deceptions and pretense. Instead it is interested in the bourgeois characters themselves, presenting them in all their complexity, with the hidden yearnings and fantasies that take them outside of the constricted worlds in which they live.

Hedda Gabler is a play about the daughter of a general who marries Tesman, an aspiring scholar waiting for his university post. As the play begins, we see almost immediately that the marriage is unequal and unsettled. Tesman is eager to start his new life and he is clearly proud of his trophy wife. Hedda, by contrast, is dismissive of his affectionate tone and also his values. She snubs him, is impatient, abruptly changes the topic of conversation, and sulks. There is a clear class difference between them. As the daughter of a general, Hedda is used to an upper-middle-class life. Tesman, by contrast, is lower middle class, with all the difference in habit and taste that entails. The collision between Hedda's and Tesman's respective classes, expectations, and attitudes centers on the bourgeois home. Gradually we learn that Hedda only married Tesman and convinced him to get the house out of boredom, feeling that no other options were available to her. But now she finds herself trapped: trapped in her marriage and trapped in the house.

Far from merely a setting for the characters, the house and its furnishings emerge as the main object of Hedda's scorn. The play revolves around furniture and what it represents: class and taste. Hedda despises those objects associated with Tesman and his class, and she admires the remnants of her former life. Tesman's scholarly study is also a set of objects: the handicrafts of the Middle Ages. For Ibsen tangible things become pawns in larger struggles between classes and wills.

Hedda Gabler, bored and without a function except to bear children—a thought she rejects with horror—manipulates every single character in the play, from Tesman and his aunt to Løvborg and his companion, her old school friend, Mrs. Elvsted. She gets them to do her bidding through force, lies, flattery, and utter ruthlessness. As the play progresses, we find her destroying careers and lives without blinking an eye. Hedda sees plotting as an end in itself and for this reason she is often seen as a modern version of Medea or Lady Macbeth.

The main victim of Hedda's plotting is Tesman's rival, Løvborg, who has written nothing less than a book about the future (after completing one about the history of civilization). Ibsen again here focuses on an object, Løvberg's sole manuscript, which becomes a central plot device, a stage prop that drives the action forward. Ibsen had learned from the well-made play how to weave objects and characters into suspenseful plots. But these props are rich in meaning too, throwing light on characters and themes, multifaceted devices that develop a life of their own.

Hedda Gabler may be a manipulator, but she is a manipulator with a vision. She is driven by her hunger for a more fulfilling, ideal, and beautiful life. She fantasizes about acts of heroism and beauty, and she tries to bring about such acts by directing the people around her the way a director assigns roles to actors. She shares her desire for a better life with many tragic characters of Ibsen's later plays, characters who cannot get rid of the chains that bind them to their houses, their objects, their habits, their class, and their past. Ibsen's attitude towards his characters' desire for beauty tends to be ambivalent. On the one hand, he sympathizes with them, even with the cold-hearted Hedda Gabler. On the other hand, his plays show that the single-minded desire to achieve an ideal life leads to destruction. Hedda Gabler's vision is an escape fantasy, the stuff of historical and idealist plays of the kind Ibsen had written in his youth. Ibsen saw both: the intense longing to live a life of ideals as well as the destructive effects of that idealism.

Since his own time, Ibsen's work has inspired important actors and directors worldwide. In England, George Bernard Shaw and the writer William Archer led what some have called the Ibsen campaign, turning the Norwegian playwright into the central figure in modern British drama, and the influential Russian director Konstantin Stanislavski, whose Moscow Art Theater promoted an acting style based on authentic emotional responses, drew on Ibsen's drama. His later plays, including *Hedda Gabler*, have attracted a different set of directors, less interested in naturalism and truth telling than in symbolism and poetry. Film directors drawn to surrealism and suggestive stage craft, such as Ingmar Bergman, continue to be attracted first and foremost to Ibsen's late plays.

Ibsen's influential career is full of enigmas and contradictions. He began with historical dramas, looking to the past, and yet he would become the herald of modern drama. He rejected the dramatic techniques of standard nineteenth-century drama, but he also managed to transform them into something that seemed new, shocking, and modern to his audience. He received the most attention for his realist plays but later turned realism itself in a more poetic and symbolist direction. In the end, he created a dramatic oeuvre of unparalleled variety and complexity, and this versatility has allowed him to become one of the most popular dramatists of all time. Today, he ranks second only to Shakespeare as the world's most-performed playwright. Shocking and novel when it was first presented to audiences, Ibsen's work has also stood the test of time.

Hedda Gabler[1]

Characters

GEORGE TESMAN, *research fellow in cultural history*
HEDDA TESMAN, *his wife*
MISS JULIANE TESMAN, *his aunt*
MRS. ELVSTED
JUDGE BRACK
EILERT LØVBORG
BERTA, *the maid to the Tesmans*

The action takes place in the fashionable west side of Christiania, Norway's capital.

1. Translated by Rick Davis and Brian Johnston.

Act 1

A large, pleasantly and tastefully furnished drawing room, decorated in somber tones. In the rear wall is a wide doorway with the curtains pulled back. This doorway leads into a smaller room decorated in the same style. In the right wall of the drawing room is a folding door leading into the hall. In the opposite wall, a glass door, also with its curtains pulled back. Outside, through the windows, part of a covered veranda can be seen, along with trees in their autumn colors. In the foreground, an oval table surrounded by chairs. Downstage, near the right wall, is a broad, dark porcelain stove, a high-backed armchair, a footstool with cushions and two stools. Up in the right-hand corner, a corner-sofa and a small round table. Downstage, on the left side, a little distance from the wall, a sofa. Beyond the glass door, a piano. On both sides of the upstage doorway stand shelves displaying terra cotta and majolica objects. By the back wall of the inner room, a sofa, a table and a couple of chairs can be seen. Above the sofa hangs the portrait of a handsome elderly man in a general's uniform. Above the table, a hanging lamp with an opalescent glass shade. There are many flowers arranged in vases and glasses all around the drawing room. More flowers lie on the tables. The floors of both rooms are covered with thick rugs.

Morning light. The sun shines in through the glass door.

[MISS JULIE TESMAN, *with hat and parasol, comes in from the hall, followed by* BERTA, *who carries a bouquet wrapped in paper.* MISS TESMAN *is a kindly, seemingly good-natured lady of about sixty-five, neatly but simply dressed in a grey visiting outfit.* BERTA *is a housemaid, getting on in years, with a homely and somewhat rustic appearance.*]

MISS TESMAN [*Stops just inside the doorway, listens, and speaks softly.*] Well—I believe they're just now getting up!

BERTA [*Also softly.*] That's what I said, Miss. Just think—the steamer got in so late last night, and then—Lord, the young mistress wanted so much unpacked before she could settle down.

MISS TESMAN Well, well. Let them have a good night's sleep at least. But—they'll have some fresh morning air when they come down. [*She crosses to the glass door and throws it wide open.*]

BERTA [*By the table, perplexed, holding the bouquet.*] Hmm. Bless me if I can find a spot for these. I think I'd better put them down here, Miss. [*Puts the bouquet down on the front of the piano.*]

MISS TESMAN So, Berta dear, now you have a new mistress. As God's my witness, giving you up was a heavy blow.

BERTA And me, Miss—what can I say? I've been in yours and Miss Rina's service for so many blessed years—

MISS TESMAN We must bear it patiently, Berta. Truly, there's no other way. You know George has to have you in the house with him—he simply has to. You've looked after him since he was a little boy.

BERTA Yes, but Miss—I keep worrying about her, lying there at home—so completely helpless, poor thing. And that new girl! She'll never learn how to take care of sick people.

MISS TESMAN Oh, I'll teach her how soon enough. And I'll be doing most of the work myself, you know. Don't you worry about my sister, Berta dear.

BERTA Yes, but there's something else, Miss. I'm so afraid I won't satisfy the new mistress—

MISS TESMAN Ffft—Good Lord—there might be a thing or two at first—

BERTA Because she's so particular about things—

MISS TESMAN Well, what do you expect? General Gabler's daughter—the way she lived in the general's day! Do you remember how she would go out riding with her father? In that long black outfit, with the feather in her hat?

BERTA Oh, yes—I remember that all right. But I never thought she'd make a match with our Mr. Tesman.

MISS TESMAN Neither did I. But—while I'm thinking about it, don't call George "Mister Tesman" any more. Now it's "Doctor Tesman."

BERTA Yes—that's what the young mistress said as soon as they came in last night. So it's true?

MISS TESMAN Yes, it's really true. Think of it, Berta—they've made him a doctor. While he was away, you understand. I didn't know a thing about it, until he told me himself, down at the pier.

BERTA Well, he's so smart he could be anything he wanted to be. But I never thought he'd take up curing people too!

MISS TESMAN No, no, no. He's not that kind of doctor. [*Nods significantly.*] As far as that goes, you might have to start calling him something even grander soon.

BERTA Oh no! What could that be?

MISS TESMAN [*Smiling.*] Hmm—wouldn't you like to know? [*Emotionally.*] Oh, dear God . . . if our sainted Joseph could look up from his grave and see what's become of his little boy. [*She looks around.*] But, Berta—what's this now? Why have you taken all the slipcovers off the furniture?

BERTA The mistress told me to. She said she can't stand covers on chairs.

MISS TESMAN But are they going to use this for their everyday living room?

BERTA Yes, they will. At least she will. He—the doctor—he didn't say anything.

[GEORGE TESMAN *enters, humming, from the right of the inner room, carrying an open, empty suitcase. He is a youthful-looking man of thirty-three, of medium height, with an open, round, and cheerful face, blond hair and beard. He wears glasses and is dressed in comfortable, somewhat disheveled clothes.*]

MISS TESMAN Good morning, good morning, George!

TESMAN Aunt Julie! Dear Aunt Julie! [*Goes over and shakes her hand.*] All the way here—so early in the day! Hm!

MISS TESMAN Yes, you know me—I just had to peek in on you a little.

TESMAN And after a short night's sleep at that!

MISS TESMAN Oh, that's nothing at all to me.

TESMAN So—you got home all right from the pier, hm?

MISS TESMAN Yes, as it turned out, thanks be to God. The Judge was kind enough to see me right to the door.

TESMAN We felt so bad that we couldn't take you in the carriage—but you saw how many trunks and boxes Hedda had to bring.

MISS TESMAN Yes, it was amazing.

BERTA [*To* TESMAN.] Perhaps I should go in and ask the mistress if there's anything I can help her with.

TESMAN No, thank you, Berta. You don't have to do that. If she needs you, she'll ring—that's what she said.

BERTA [*Going out to right.*] Very well.

TESMAN Ah—but—Berta—take this suitcase with you.

BERTA [*Takes the case.*] I'll put it in the attic.

TESMAN Just imagine, Auntie. I'd stuffed that whole suitcase with notes—just notes! The things I managed to collect in those archives—really incredible! Ancient, remarkable things that no one had any inkling of.

MISS TESMAN Ah yes—you certainly haven't wasted any time on your honeymoon.

TESMAN Yes—I can really say that's true. But, Auntie, take off your hat—Here, let's see. Let me undo that ribbon, hm?

MISS TESMAN [*While he does so.*] Ah, dear God—this is just what it was like when you were home with us.

TESMAN [*Examining the hat as he holds it.*] My, my—isn't this a fine, elegant hat you've got for yourself.

MISS TESMAN I bought it for Hedda's sake.

TESMAN For Hedda's—hm?

MISS TESMAN Yes, so Hedda won't feel ashamed of me if we go out for a walk together.

TESMAN [*Patting her cheek.*] You think of everything, Auntie Julie, don't you? [*Putting her hat on a chair by the table.*] And now—let's just settle down here on the sofa until Hedda comes. [*They sit. She puts her parasol down near the sofa.*]

MISS TESMAN [*Takes both his hands and gazes at him.*] What a blessing to have you here, bright as day, right before my eyes again, George. Sainted Joseph's own boy!

TESMAN For me too. To see you again, Aunt Julie—who've been both father and mother to me.

MISS TESMAN Yes, I know you'll always have a soft spot for your old aunts.

TESMAN But no improvement at all with Rina, hm?

MISS TESMAN Oh dear no—and none to be expected poor thing. She lies there just as she has all these years. But I pray that Our Lord lets me keep her just a little longer. Otherwise I don't know what I'd do with my life, George. Especially now, you know—when I don't have you to take care of any more.

TESMAN [*Patting her on the back.*] There. There. There.

MISS TESMAN Oh—just to think that you've become a married man, George. And that you're the one who carried off Hedda Gabler! Beautiful Hedda Gabler. Imagine—with all her suitors.

TESMAN [*Hums a little and smiles complacently.*] Yes, I believe I have quite a few friends in town who envy me, hm?

MISS TESMAN And then—you got to take such a long honeymoon—more than five—almost six months . . .

TESMAN Yes, but it was also part of my research, you know. All those archives I had to wade through—and all the books I had to read!

MISS TESMAN I suppose you're right. [*Confidentially and more quietly.*] But listen, George—isn't there something—something extra you want to tell me?

TESMAN About the trip?

MISS TESMAN Yes.

TESMAN No—I can't think of anything I didn't mention in my letters. I was given my doctorate—but I told you that yesterday.

MISS TESMAN So you did. But I mean—whether you might have any—any kind of—prospects—?

TESMAN Prospects?

MISS TESMAN Good Lord, George—I'm your old aunt.

TESMAN Well of course I have prospects.

MISS TESMAN Aha!

TESMAN I have excellent prospects of becoming a professor one of these days. But Aunt Julie dear, you already know that.

MISS TESMAN [*With a little laugh.*] You're right, I do. [*Changing the subject.*] But about your trip. It must have cost a lot.

TESMAN Well, thank God, that huge fellowship paid for a good part of it.

MISS TESMAN But how did you make it last for the both of you?

TESMAN That's the tricky part, isn't it?

MISS TESMAN And on top of that, when you're travelling with a lady! That's always going to cost you more, or so I've heard.

TESMAN You're right—it was a bit more costly. But Hedda just had to have that trip, Auntie. She really had to. There was no choice.

MISS TESMAN Well, I suppose not. These days a honeymoon trip is essential, it seems. But now tell me—have you had a good look around the house?

TESMAN Absolutely! I've been up since dawn.

MISS TESMAN And what do you think about all of it?

TESMAN It's splendid! Only I can't think of what we'll do with those two empty rooms between the back parlor and Hedda's bedroom.

MISS TESMAN [*Lightly laughing.*] My dear George—when the time comes, you'll think of what to do with them.

TESMAN Oh, of course—as I add to my library, hm?

MISS TESMAN That's right, my boy—of course I was thinking about your library.

TESMAN Most of all I'm just so happy for Hedda. Before we got engaged she'd always say how she couldn't imagine living anywhere but here—in Prime Minister Falk's house.

MISS TESMAN Yes—imagine. And then it came up for sale just after you left for your trip.

TESMAN Aunt Julie, we really had luck on our side, hm?

MISS TESMAN But the expense, George. This will all be costly for you.

TESMAN [*Looks at her disconcertedly.*] Yes. It might be. It might be, Auntie.

MISS TESMAN Ah, God only knows.

TESMAN How much, do you think? Approximately. Hm?

MISS TESMAN I can't possibly tell before all the bills are in.

TESMAN Luckily Judge Brack lined up favorable terms for me—he wrote as much to Hedda.

MISS TESMAN That's right—don't you ever worry about that, my boy. All this furniture, and the carpets? I put up the security for it.

TESMAN Security? You? Dear Auntie Julie, what kind of security could you give?

MISS TESMAN I took out a mortgage on our annuity.

TESMAN What? On your—and Aunt Rina's annuity!

MISS TESMAN I couldn't think of any other way.

TESMAN [*Standing in front of her.*] Have you gone completely out of your mind, Auntie? That annuity is all you and Aunt Rina have to live on.

MISS TESMAN Now, now, take it easy. It's just a formality, you understand. Judge Brack said so. He was good enough to arrange it all for me. Just a formality, he said.

TESMAN That could very well be, but all the same . . .

MISS TESMAN You'll be earning your own living now, after all. And, good Lord, so what if we do have to open the purse a little, spend a little bit at first? That would only make us happy.

TESMAN Auntie . . . you never get tired of sacrificing yourself for me.

MISS TESMAN [*Rises and lays her hands on his shoulders.*] What joy do I have in the world, my dearest boy, other than smoothing out the path for you? You, without a father or mother to take care of you . . . but we've reached our destination, my dear. Maybe things looked black from time to time. But, praise God, George, you've come out on top!

TESMAN Yes, it's really amazing how everything has gone according to plan.

MISS TESMAN And those who were against you—those who would have blocked your way—they're at the bottom of the pit. They've fallen, George. And the most dangerous one, he fell the farthest. Now he just lies there where he fell, the poor sinner.

TESMAN Have you heard anything about Eilert—since I went away, I mean?

MISS TESMAN Nothing, except they say he published a new book.

TESMAN What? Eilert Løvborg? Just recently, hm?

MISS TESMAN That's what they say. God only knows how there could be anything to it. But when *your* book comes out—now that will be something else again, won't it, George? What's it going to be about?

TESMAN It will deal with the Domestic Craftsmanship Practices of Medieval Brabant.[2]

MISS TESMAN Just think—you can write about that kind of thing too.

TESMAN However, it might be quite a while before that book is ready. I've got all these incredible collections that have to be put in order first.

MISS TESMAN Ordering and collecting—you're certainly good at that. You're not the son of sainted Joseph for nothing.

TESMAN And I'm so eager to get going. Especially now that I've got my own snug house and home to work in.

MISS TESMAN And most of all, now that you've got her—your heart's desire, dear, dear George!

2. In the Middle Ages, Brabant was a duchy located in parts of what are now Belgium and the Netherlands.

TESMAN [*Embracing her.*] Yes, Auntie Julie! Hedda . . . that's the most beautiful thing of all! [*Looking toward the doorway.*] I think that's her, hm?

[HEDDA *comes in from the left side of the inner room. She is a lady of twenty-nine. Her face and figure are aristocratic and elegant. Her complexion is pale. Her eyes are steel-grey, cold and clear. Her hair is an attractive medium brown but not particularly full. She is wearing a tasteful, somewhat loose-fitting morning gown.*]

MISS TESMAN [*Going to meet* HEDDA.] Good morning, Hedda, my dear. Good morning.

HEDDA [*Extending her hand.*] Good morning, Miss Tesman, my dear. You're here so early. How nice of you.

MISS TESMAN [*Looking somewhat embarrassed.*] Well now, how did the young mistress sleep in her new home?

HEDDA Fine thanks. Well enough.

TESMAN [*Laughing.*] Well enough! That's a good one, Hedda. You were sleeping like a log when I got up.

HEDDA Yes, lucky for me. But of course you have to get used to anything new, Miss Tesman. A little at a time. [*Looks toward the window.*] Uch! Look at that. The maid opened the door. I'm drowning in all this sunlight.

MISS TESMAN [*Going to the door.*] Well then, let's close it.

HEDDA No, no, don't do that. Tesman my dear, just close the curtains. That gives a gentler light.

TESMAN [*By the door.*] All right, all right. Now then, Hedda. You've got both fresh air and sunlight.

HEDDA Yes, fresh air. That's what I need with all these flowers all over the place. But Miss Tesman, won't you sit down?

MISS TESMAN No, but thank you. Now that I know everything's all right here, I've got to see about getting home again. Home to that poor dear who's lying there in pain.

TESMAN Be sure to give her my respects, won't you? And tell her I'll stop by and look in on her later today.

MISS TESMAN Yes, yes I'll certainly do that. But would you believe it, George? [*She rustles around in the pocket of her skirt.*] I almost forgot. Here, I brought something for you.

TESMAN And what might that be, Auntie, hm?

MISS TESMAN [*Brings out a flat package wrapped in newspaper and hands it to him.*] Here you are, my dear boy.

TESMAN [*Opening it.*] Oh my Lord. You kept them for me, Aunt Julie. Hedda, isn't this touching, hm?

HEDDA Well, what is it?

TESMAN My old house slippers. My slippers.

HEDDA Oh yes, I remember how often you talked about them on our trip.

TESMAN Yes, well, I really missed them. [*Goes over to her.*] Now you can see them for yourself, Hedda.

HEDDA [*Moves over to the stove.*] Oh, no thanks. I don't really care to.

TESMAN [*Following after her.*] Just think, Aunt Rina lying there embroidering for me, sick as she was. Oh, you couldn't possibly believe how many memories are tangled up in these slippers.

HEDDA [*By the table.*] Not for me.

MISS TESMAN Hedda's quite right about that, George.

TESMAN Yes, but now that she's in the family I thought—

HEDDA That maid won't last, Tesman.

MISS TESMAN Berta—?

TESMAN What makes you say that, hm?

HEDDA [*Pointing.*] Look, she's left her old hat lying there on that chair.

TESMAN [*Terrified, dropping the slippers on the floor.*] Hedda—!

HEDDA What if someone came in and saw that.

TESMAN But Hedda—that's Aunt Julie's hat.

HEDDA Really?

MISS TESMAN [*Taking the hat.*] Yes, it really is. And for that matter it's not so old either, my dear little Hedda.

HEDDA Oh, I really didn't get a good look at it, Miss Tesman.

MISS TESMAN [*Tying the hat on her head.*] Actually I've never worn it before today—and the good Lord knows that's true.

TESMAN And an elegant hat it is too. Really magnificent.

MISS TESMAN [*She looks around.*] Oh that's as may be, George. My parasol? Ah, here it is. [*She takes it.*] That's mine too. [*She mutters.*] Not Berta's.

TESMAN A new hat and a new parasol. Just think, Hedda.

HEDDA Very charming, very attractive.

TESMAN That's true, hm? But Auntie, take a good look at Hedda before you go. Look at how charming and attractive she is.

MISS TESMAN Oh my dear, that's nothing new. Hedda's been lovely all her life. [*She nods and goes across to the right.*]

TESMAN [*Following her.*] Yes, but have you noticed how she's blossomed, how well she's filled out on our trip?

HEDDA Oh, leave it alone!

MISS TESMAN [*Stops and turns.*] Filled out?

TESMAN Yes, Aunt Julie. You can't see it so well right now in that gown—but I, who have a little better opportunity to—

HEDDA [*By the glass door impatiently.*] Oh you don't have the opportunity for anything.

TESMAN It was that mountain air down in the Tyrol.

HEDDA [*Curtly interrupting.*] I'm the same as when I left.

TESMAN You keep saying that. But it's true, isn't it Auntie?

MISS TESMAN [*Folding her hands and gazing at* HEDDA.] Lovely . . . lovely . . . lovely. That's Hedda. [*She goes over to her and with both her hands takes her head, bends it down, kisses her hair.*] God bless and keep Hedda Tesman for George's sake.

HEDDA [*Gently freeing herself.*] Ah—! Let me out!

MISS TESMAN [*With quiet emotion.*] I'll come look in on you two every single day.

TESMAN Yes, Auntie, do that, won't you, hm?

MISS TESMAN Good-bye, good-bye.

[*She goes out through the hall door.* TESMAN *follows her out. The door remains half open.* TESMAN *is heard repeating his greetings to Aunt Rina and his thanks for the slippers. While this is happening,* HEDDA *walks around the room raising her arms and clenching her fists as if in a rage. Then she draws the curtains back from the door, stands there and looks out. After a short time,* TESMAN *comes in and closes the door behind him.*]

TESMAN [*Picking up the slippers from the floor.*] What are you looking at, Hedda?

HEDDA [*Calm and controlled again.*] Just the leaves. So yellow and so withered.

TESMAN [*Wrapping up the slippers and placing them on the table.*] Yes, well—we're into September now.

HEDDA [*Once more uneasy.*] Yes—It's already—already September.

TESMAN Didn't you think Aunt Julie was acting strange just now, almost formal? What do you suppose got into her?

HEDDA I really don't know her. Isn't that the way she usually is?

TESMAN No, not like today.

HEDDA [*Leaving the glass door.*] Do you think she was upset by the hat business?

TESMAN Not really. Maybe a little, for just a moment—

HEDDA But where did she get her manners, flinging her hat around any way she likes here in the drawing room. People just don't act that way.

TESMAN Well, I'm sure she won't do it again.

HEDDA Anyway, I'll smooth everything over with her soon enough.

TESMAN Yes, Hedda, if you would do that.

HEDDA When you visit them later today, invite her here for the evening.

TESMAN Yes, that's just what I'll do. And there's one more thing you can do that would really make her happy.

HEDDA Well?

TESMAN If you just bring yourself to call her Aunt Julie, for my sake, Hedda, hm?

HEDDA Tesman, for God's sake, don't ask me to do that. I've told you that before. I'll try to call her Aunt once in a while and that's enough.

TESMAN Oh well, I just thought that now that you're part of the family . . .

HEDDA Hmm. I don't know—[*She crosses upstage to the doorway.*]

TESMAN [*After a pause.*] Is something the matter, Hedda?

HEDDA I was just looking at my old piano. It really doesn't go with these other things.

TESMAN As soon as my salary starts coming in, we'll see about trading it in for a new one.

HEDDA Oh, no, don't trade it in. I could never let it go. We'll leave it in the back room instead. And then we'll get a new one to put in here. I mean, as soon as we get the chance.

TESMAN [*A little dejectedly.*] Yes, I suppose we could do that.

HEDDA [*Taking the bouquet from the piano.*] These flowers weren't here when we got in last night.

TESMAN I suppose Aunt Julie brought them.

HEDDA [*Looks into the bouquet.*] Here's a card. [*Takes it out and reads.*] "Will call again later today." Guess who it's from.

TESMAN Who is it, hm?

HEDDA It says Mrs. Elvsted.

TESMAN Really. Mrs. Elvsted. She used to be Miss Rysing.

HEDDA Yes, that's the one. She had all that irritating hair she'd always be fussing with. An old flame of yours, I've heard.

TESMAN [*Laughs.*] Oh, not for long and before I knew you, Hedda. And she's here in town. How about that.

HEDDA Strange that she should come visiting us. I hardly know her except from school.

TESMAN Yes, and of course I haven't seen her since—well God knows how long. How could she stand it holed up out there so far from everything, hm?

HEDDA [*Reflects a moment and then suddenly speaks.*] Just a minute, Tesman. Doesn't he live out that way, Eilert Løvborg, I mean?

TESMAN Yes, right up in that area.

[BERTA *comes in from the hallway.*]

BERTA Ma'am, she's back again. The lady who came by with the flowers an hour ago. [*Pointing.*] Those you've got in your hand, Ma'am.

HEDDA Is she then? Please ask her to come in.

[BERTA *opens the door for* MRS. ELVSTED *and then leaves.* MRS. ELVSTED *is slender with soft, pretty features. Her eyes are light blue, large, round and slightly protruding. Her expression is one of alarm and question. Her hair is remarkably light, almost a white gold and exceptionally rich and full. She is a couple of years younger than Hedda. Her costume is a dark visiting dress, tasteful but not of the latest fashion.*]

HEDDA [*Goes to meet her in a friendly manner.*] Hello my dear Mrs. Elvsted. So delightful to see you again.

MRS. ELVSTED [*Nervous, trying to control herself.*] Yes, it's been so long since we've seen each other.

TESMAN [*Shakes her hand.*] And we could say the same, hm?

HEDDA Thank you for the lovely flowers.

MRS. ELVSTED I would have come yesterday right away but I heard you were on a trip—

TESMAN So you've just come into town, hm?

MRS. ELVSTED Yesterday around noon. I was absolutely desperate when I heard you weren't home.

HEDDA Desperate, why?

TESMAN My dear Miss Rysing—I mean Mrs. Elvsted.

HEDDA There isn't some sort of trouble—?

MRS. ELVSTED Yes there is—and I don't know another living soul to turn to here in town.

HEDDA [*Sets the flowers down on the table.*] All right then, let's sit down here on the sofa.

MRS. ELVSTED Oh no, I'm too upset to sit down.

HEDDA No you're not. Come over here. [*She draws* MRS. ELVSTED *to the sofa and sits beside her.*]

TESMAN Well, and now Mrs.—

HEDDA Did something happen up at your place?

MRS. ELVSTED Yes—That's it—well, not exactly—Oh, I don't want you to misunderstand me—

HEDDA Well then the best thing is just to tell it straight out, Mrs. Elvsted—why?

TESMAN That's why you came here, hm?

MRS. ELVSTED Yes, of course. So I'd better tell you, if you don't already know, that Eilert Løvborg is in town.

HEDDA Løvborg?

TESMAN Eilert Løvborg's back again? Just think, Hedda.

HEDDA Good Lord, Tesman, I can hear.

MRS. ELVSTED He's been back now for about a week. The whole week alone here where he can fall in with all kinds of bad company. This town's a dangerous place for him.

HEDDA But my dear Mrs. Elvsted, how does this involve you?

MRS. ELVSTED [*With a scared expression, speaking quickly.*] He was the children's tutor.

HEDDA Your children?

MRS. ELVSTED My husband's. I don't have any.

HEDDA The stepchildren then?

MRS. ELVSTED Yes.

TESMAN [*Somewhat awkwardly.*] But was he sufficiently—I don't know how to say this—sufficiently regular in his habits to be trusted with that kind of job, hm?

MRS. ELVSTED For the past two years no one could say anything against him.

TESMAN Really, nothing. Just think, Hedda.

HEDDA I hear.

MRS. ELVSTED Nothing at all, I assure you. Not in any way. But even so, now that I know he's here in the city alone and with money in his pocket I'm deathly afraid for him.

TESMAN But why isn't he up there with you and your husband, hm?

MRS. ELVSTED When the book came out he was too excited to stay up there with us.

TESMAN Yes, that's right. Aunt Julie said he'd come out with a new book.

MRS. ELVSTED Yes, a major new book on the progress of civilization—in its entirety I mean. That was two weeks ago. And it's been selling wonderfully. Everyone's reading it. It's created a huge sensation—why?

TESMAN All that really? Must be something he had lying around from his better days.

MRS. ELVSTED From before, you mean?

TESMAN Yes.

MRS. ELVSTED No, he wrote the whole thing while he was up there living with us. Just in the last year.

TESMAN That's wonderful to hear, Hedda. Just think!

MRS. ELVSTED Yes, if only it continues.

HEDDA Have you met him here in town?

MRS. ELVSTED No, not yet. I had a terrible time hunting down his address but this morning I finally found it.

HEDDA [*Looks searchingly.*] I can't help thinking this is a little odd on your husband's part.

MRS. ELVSTED [*Starts nervously.*] My husband—What?

HEDDA That he'd send you to town on this errand. That he didn't come himself to look for his friend.

MRS. ELVSTED Oh no, no, no. My husband doesn't have time for that. And anyway I had to do some shopping too.

HEDDA [*Smiling slightly.*] Oh well, that's different then.

MRS. ELVSTED [*Gets up quickly, ill at ease.*] And now I beg you, Mr. Tesman, please be kind to Eilert Løvborg if he comes here—and I'm sure he will. You were such good friends in the old days. You have interests in common. The same area of research, as far as I can tell.

TESMAN Yes, that used to be the case anyway.

MRS. ELVSTED Yes, that's why I'm asking you—from the bottom of my heart to be sure to—that you'll—that you'll keep a watchful eye on him. Oh, Mr. Tesman, will you do that—will you promise me that?

TESMAN Yes, with all my heart, Mrs. Rysing.

HEDDA Elvsted.

TESMAN I'll do anything in my power for Eilert. You can be sure of it.

MRS. ELVSTED Oh, that is so kind of you. [*She presses his hands.*] Many, many thanks. [*Frightened.*] Because my husband thinks so highly of him.

HEDDA [*Rising.*] You should write to him, Tesman. He might not come to you on his own.

TESMAN Yes, that's the way to do it, Hedda, hm?

HEDDA And the sooner the better. Right now, I think.

MRS. ELVSTED [*Beseechingly.*] Yes, if you only could.

TESMAN I'll write to him this moment. Do you have his address, Mrs. Elvsted?

MRS. ELVSTED Yes. [*She takes a small slip of paper from her pocket and hands it to him.*] Here it is.

TESMAN Good, good. I'll go write him—[*Looks around just a minute.*]—Where are my slippers? Ah, here they are. [*Takes the packet and is about to leave.*]

HEDDA Make sure your note is very friendly—nice and long too.

TESMAN Yes, you can count on me.

MRS. ELVSTED But please don't say a word about my asking you to do it.

TESMAN Oh, that goes without saying.

[TESMAN *leaves to the right through the rear room.*]

HEDDA [*Goes over to* MRS. ELVSTED, *smiles and speaks softly.*] There, now we've killed two birds with one stone.

MRS. ELVSTED What do you mean?

HEDDA Didn't you see that I wanted him out of the way?

MRS. ELVSTED Yes, to write the letter—

HEDDA So I could talk to you alone.

MRS. ELVSTED [*Confused.*] About this thing?

HEDDA Yes, exactly, about this thing.

MRS. ELVSTED [*Apprehensively.*] But there's nothing more to it, Mrs. Tesman, really there isn't.

HEDDA Ah, but there is indeed. There's a great deal more. I can see that much. Come here, let's sit down together. Have a real heart-to-heart talk.

[*She forces* MRS. ELVSTED *into the armchair by the stove and sits down herself on one of the small stools.*]

MRS. ELVSTED [*Nervously looking at her watch.*] Mrs. Tesman, I was just thinking of leaving.

HEDDA Now you can't be in such a hurry, can you? Talk to me a little bit about how things are at home.

MRS. ELVSTED Oh, that's the last thing I want to talk about.

HEDDA But to me? Good Lord, we went to the same school.

MRS. ELVSTED Yes, but you were one class ahead of me. Oh, I was so afraid of you then.

HEDDA Afraid of me?

MRS. ELVSTED Horribly afraid. Whenever we'd meet on the stairs you always used to pull my hair.

HEDDA No, did I do that?

MRS. ELVSTED Yes, you did—and once you said you'd burn it off.

HEDDA Oh, just silly talk, you know.

MRS. ELVSTED Yes, but I was so stupid in those days and anyway since then we've gotten to be so distant from each other. Our circles have just been totally different.

HEDDA Well let's see if we can get closer again. Listen now, I know we were good friends in school. We used to call each other by our first names.

MRS. ELVSTED No, no, I think you're mistaken.

HEDDA I certainly am not. I remember it perfectly and so we have to be perfectly open with each other just like in the old days. [*Moves the stool closer.*] There now. [*Kisses her cheek.*] Now you must call me Hedda.

MRS. ELVSTED [*Pressing and patting her hands.*] Oh, you're being so friendly to me. I'm just not used to that.

HEDDA There, there, there. I'll stop being so formal with you and I'll call you my dear Thora.

MRS. ELVSTED My name is Thea.

HEDDA That's right, of course, I meant Thea. [*Looks at her compassionately.*] So you're not used to friendship, Thea, in your own home?

MRS. ELVSTED If I only had a home, but I don't. I've never had one.

HEDDA [*Glances at her.*] I suspected it might be something like that.

MRS. ELVSTED [*Staring helplessly before her.*] Yes, yes, yes.

HEDDA I can't exactly remember now, but didn't you go up to Sheriff Elvsted's as a housekeeper?

MRS. ELVSTED Actually I was supposed to be a governess but his wife—at that time—she was an invalid, mostly bedridden, so I had to take care of the house too.

HEDDA So in the end you became mistress of your own house.

MRS. ELVSTED [*Heavily.*] Yes, that's what I became.

HEDDA Let me see. How long has that been?

MRS. ELVSTED Since I was married?

HEDDA Yes.

MRS. ELVSTED Five years now.

HEDDA That's right, it must be about that.

MRS. ELVSTED Oh these five years—! Or the last two or three anyway—! Ah, Mrs. Tesman, if you could just imagine.

HEDDA [*Slaps her lightly on the hand.*] Mrs. Tesman; really, Thea.

MRS. ELVSTED No, no, of course, I'll try to remember. Anyway, Hedda, if you could only imagine.

HEDDA [*Casually.*] It seems to me that Eilert Løvborg's been living up there for about three years, hasn't he?

MRS. ELVSTED [*Looks uncertainly at her.*] Eilert Løvborg? Yes, that's about right.

HEDDA Did you know him from before—from here in town?

MRS. ELVSTED Hardly at all. I mean his name of course.

HEDDA But up there he'd come to visit you at the house?

MRS. ELVSTED Yes, every day. He'd read to the children. I couldn't manage everything myself, you see.

HEDDA No, of course not. And what about your husband? His work must take him out of the house quite a bit.

MRS. ELVSTED Yes, as you might imagine. He's the sheriff so he has to go traveling around the whole district.

HEDDA [*Leaning against the arm of the chair.*] Thea, my poor sweet Thea—You've got to tell me everything just the way it is.

MRS. ELVSTED All right, but you've got to ask the questions.

HEDDA So, Thea, what's your husband really like? I mean, you know, to be with? Is he good to you?

MRS. ELVSTED [*Evasively.*] He thinks he does everything for the best.

HEDDA I just think he's a little too old for you. He's twenty years older, isn't he?

MRS. ELVSTED [*Irritatedly.*] There's that too. There's a lot of things. I just can't stand being with him. We don't have a single thought in common, not a single thing in the world, he and I.

HEDDA But doesn't he care for you at all in his own way?

MRS. ELVSTED I can't tell what he feels. I think I'm just useful to him, and it doesn't cost very much to keep me. I'm very inexpensive.

HEDDA That's a mistake.

MRS. ELVSTED [*Shaking her head.*] Can't be any other way, not with him. He only cares about himself and maybe about the children a little.

HEDDA And also for Eilert Løvborg, Thea.

MRS. ELVSTED [*Stares at her.*] For Eilert Løvborg? Why do you think that?

HEDDA Well, my dear, he sent you all the way into town to look for him. [*Smiling almost imperceptibly.*] And besides, you said so yourself, to Tesman.

MRS. ELVSTED [*With a nervous shudder.*] Oh yes, I suppose I did. No, I'd better just tell you the whole thing. It's bound to come to light sooner or later anyway.

HEDDA But my dear Thea.

MRS. ELVSTED All right, short and sweet. My husband doesn't know that I'm gone.

HEDDA What, your husband doesn't know?

MRS. ELVSTED Of course not. Anyway he's not at home. He was out traveling. I just couldn't stand it any longer, Hedda, it was impossible. I would have been so completely alone up there.

HEDDA Well, then what?

MRS. ELVSTED Then I packed some of my things, just the necessities, all in secret, and I left the house.

HEDDA Just like that?

MRS. ELVSTED Yes, and I took the train to town.

HEDDA Oh, my good, dear Thea. You dared to do that!

MRS. ELVSTED [*Gets up and walks across the floor.*] Well, what else could I do?

HEDDA What do you think your husband will say when you go home again?

MRS. ELVSTED [*By the table looking at her.*] Up there to him?

HEDDA Of course, of course.

MRS. ELVSTED I'm never going back up there.

HEDDA [*Gets up and goes closer to her.*] So you've really done it? You've really run away from everything?

MRS. ELVSTED Yes, I couldn't think of anything else to do.

HEDDA But you did it—so openly.

MRS. ELVSTED Oh, you can't keep something like that a secret anyway.

HEDDA Well, what do you think people will say about you, Thea?

MRS. ELVSTED They'll say whatever they want, God knows. [*She sits tired and depressed on the sofa.*] But I only did what I had to do.

HEDDA [*After a brief pause.*] So what will you do with yourself now?

MRS. ELVSTED I don't know yet. All I know is that I've got to live here where Eilert Løvborg lives if I'm going to live at all.

HEDDA [*Moves a chair closer from the table, sits beside her and strokes her hands.*] Thea, my dear, how did it come about, this—bond between you and Eilert Løvborg?

MRS. ELVSTED Oh, it just happened, little by little. I started to have a kind of power over him.

HEDDA Really?

MRS. ELVSTED He gave up his old ways—and not because I begged him to. I never dared do that. But he started to notice that those kinds of things upset me, so he gave them up.

HEDDA [*Concealing an involuntary, derisive smile.*] So you rehabilitated him, as they say. You, little Thea.

MRS. ELVSTED That's what he said, anyway. And for his part he's made a real human being out of me. Taught me to think, to understand all sorts of things.

HEDDA So he read to you too, did he?

MRS. ELVSTED No, not exactly, but he talked to me. Talked without stopping about all sorts of great things. And then there was that wonderful time when I shared in his work, when I helped him.

HEDDA You got to do that?

MRS. ELVSTED Yes. Whenever he wrote anything, we had to agree on it first.

HEDDA Like two good comrades.

MRS. ELVSTED [*Eagerly.*] Yes, comrades. Imagine, Hedda, that's what he called it too. I should feel so happy, but I can't yet because I don't know how long it will last.

HEDDA Are you that unsure of him?

MRS. ELVSTED [*Dejectedly.*] There's the shadow of a woman between Eilert Løvborg and me.

HEDDA [*Stares intently at her.*] Who could that be?

MRS. ELVSTED I don't know. Someone from his past. Someone he's never really been able to forget.

HEDDA What has he told you about all this?

MRS. ELVSTED He's only talked about it once and very vaguely.

HEDDA Yes, what did he say?

MRS. ELVSTED He said that when they broke up she was going to shoot him with a pistol.

HEDDA [*Calm and controlled.*] That's nonsense, people just don't act that way here.

MRS. ELVSTED No they don't—so I think it's got to be that red-haired singer that he once—

HEDDA Yes, that could well be.

MRS. ELVSTED Because I remember they used to say about her that she went around with loaded pistols.

HEDDA Well, then it's her, of course.

MRS. ELVSTED [*Wringing her hands.*] Yes, but Hedda, just think, I hear this singer is in town again. Oh, I'm so afraid.

HEDDA [*Glancing toward the back room.*] Shh, here comes Tesman. [*She gets up and whispers.*] Now, Thea, all of this is strictly between you and me.

MRS. ELVSTED [*Jumping up.*] Oh yes, yes, for God's sake!

[GEORGE TESMAN, *a letter in his hand, comes in from the right side of the inner room.*]

TESMAN There now, the epistle is prepared.

HEDDA Well done—but Mrs. Elvsted's got to leave now, I think. Just a minute, I'll follow you as far as the garden gate.

TESMAN Hedda dear, do you think Berta could see to this?

HEDDA [*Takes the letter.*] I'll instruct her.

[BERTA *comes in from the hall.*]

BERTA Judge Brack is here. Says he'd like to pay his respects.

HEDDA Yes, ask the Judge to be so good as to come in, and then—listen here now—Put this letter in the mailbox.

BERTA [*Takes the letter.*] Yes, ma'am.

[*She opens the door for* JUDGE BRACK *and then goes out.* JUDGE BRACK *is forty-five years old, short, well built and moves easily. He has a round face and an aristocratic profile. His short hair is still almost black. His eyes are lively and ironic. He has thick eyebrows and a thick moustache, trimmed square at the ends. He is wearing outdoor clothing, elegant, but a little too young in style. He has a monocle in one eye. Now and then he lets it drop.*]

BRACK [*Bows with his hat in his hand.*] Does one dare to call so early?

HEDDA One does dare.

TESMAN [*Shakes his hand.*] You're welcome any time. Judge Brack, Mrs. Rysing. [HEDDA *sighs.*]

BRACK [*Bows.*] Aha, delighted.

HEDDA [*Looks at him laughing.*] Nice to see you by daylight for a change, Judge.

BRACK Do I look different?

HEDDA Yes, younger.

BRACK You're too kind.

TESMAN Well, how about Hedda, hm? Doesn't she look fine? Hasn't she filled out?

HEDDA Stop it now. You should be thanking Judge Brack for all of his hard work—

BRACK Nonsense. It was my pleasure.

HEDDA There's a loyal soul. But here's my friend burning to get away. Excuse me, Judge, I'll be right back.

[*Mutual good-byes.* MRS. ELVSTED *and* HEDDA *leave by the hall door.*]

BRACK Well, now, your wife's satisfied, more or less?

TESMAN Oh yes, we can't thank you enough. I gather there might be a little more rearrangement here and there and one or two things still missing. A couple of small things yet to be procured.

BRACK Is that so?

TESMAN But nothing for you to worry about. Hedda said that she'd look for everything herself. Let's sit down.

BRACK Thanks. Just for a minute. [*Sits by the table.*] Now, my dear Tesman, there's something we need to talk about.

TESMAN Oh yes, ah, I understand. [*Sits down.*] Time for a new topic. Time for the serious part of the celebration, hm?

BRACK Oh, I wouldn't worry too much about the finances just yet—although I must tell you that it would have been better if we'd managed things a little more frugally.

TESMAN But there was no way to do that. You know Hedda, Judge, you know her well. I couldn't possibly ask her to live in a middle-class house.

BRACK No, that's precisely the problem.

TESMAN And luckily it can't be too long before I get my appointment.[3]

BRACK Well, you know, these things often drag on and on.

TESMAN Have you heard anything further, hm?

BRACK Nothing certain. [*Changing the subject.*] But there is one thing. I've got a piece of news for you.

TESMAN Well?

BRACK Your old friend Eilert Løvborg's back in town.

TESMAN I already know.

BRACK Oh, how did you find out?

TESMAN She told me, that lady who just left with Hedda.

BRACK Oh, I see. I didn't quite get her name.

TESMAN Mrs. Elvsted.

BRACK Ah yes, the sheriff's wife. Yes, he's been staying up there with them.

TESMAN And I'm so glad to hear that he's become a responsible person again.

BRACK Yes, one is given to understand that.

TESMAN And he's come out with a new book, hm?

BRACK He has indeed.

TESMAN And it's caused quite a sensation.

BRACK It's caused an extraordinary sensation.

3. Tesman expects to be appointed to a professorship. These positions were much less numerous and more socially prominent than their contemporary American counterparts.

TESMAN Just think, isn't that wonderful to hear. With all his remarkable talents, I was absolutely certain he was down for good.

BRACK That was certainly the general opinion.

TESMAN But I can't imagine what he'll do with himself now. What will he live on, hm?

[*During these last words,* HEDDA *has entered from the hallway.*]

HEDDA [*To* BRACK, *laughing a little scornfully.*] Tesman is constantly going around worrying about what to live on.

TESMAN My Lord, we're talking about Eilert Løvborg, dear.

HEDDA [*Looking quickly at him.*] Oh yes? [*Sits down in the armchair by the stove and asks casually.*] What's the matter with him?

TESMAN Well, he must have spent his inheritance a long time ago, and he can't really write a new book every year, hm? So I was just asking what was going to become of him.

BRACK Perhaps I can enlighten you on that score.

TESMAN Oh?

BRACK You might remember that he has some relatives with more than a little influence.

TESMAN Unfortunately they've pretty much washed their hands of him.

BRACK In the old days they thought of him as the family's great shining hope.

TESMAN Yes, in the old days, possibly, but he took care of that himself.

HEDDA Who knows? [*Smiles slightly.*] Up at the Elvsteds' he's been the target of a reclamation project.

BRACK And there's this new book.

TESMAN Well, God willing, they'll help him out some way or another. I've just written to him, Hedda, asking him to come over this evening.

BRACK But my dear Tesman, you're coming to my stag party[4] this evening. You promised me on the pier last night.

HEDDA Had you forgotten, Tesman?

TESMAN Yes, to be perfectly honest, I had.

BRACK For that matter, you can be sure he won't come.

TESMAN Why do you say that, hm?

BRACK [*Somewhat hesitantly getting up and leaning his hands on the back of his chair.*] My dear Tesman, you too, Mrs. Tesman, in good conscience I can't let you go on living in ignorance of something like this.

TESMAN Something about Eilert, hm?

BRACK About both of you.

TESMAN My dear Judge, tell me what it is.

BRACK You ought to prepare yourself for the fact that your appointment might not come through as quickly as you expect.

TESMAN [*Jumps up in alarm.*] Has something held it up?

BRACK The appointment might just possibly be subject to a competition.

TESMAN A competition! Just think of that, Hedda!

HEDDA [*Leans further back in her chair.*] Ah yes—yes.

TESMAN But who on earth would it—surely not with—?

BRACK Yes, precisely, with Eilert Løvborg.

4. A party for men only, whether single or married.

TESMAN [*Clasping his hands together.*] No, no, this is absolutely unthinkable, absolutely unthinkable, hm?

BRACK Hmm—well, we might just have to learn to get used to it.

TESMAN No, but Judge Brack, that would be incredibly inconsiderate. [*Waving his arms.*] Because—well—just look, I'm a married man. We went and got married on this very prospect, Hedda and I. Went and got ourselves heavily into debt. Borrowed money from Aunt Julie too. I mean, good Lord, I was as much as promised the position, hm?

BRACK Now, now, you'll almost certainly get it but first there'll have to be a contest.

HEDDA [*Motionless in the armchair.*] Just think, Tesman, it will be a sort of match.

TESMAN But Hedda, my dear, how can you be so calm about this?

HEDDA Oh I'm not, not at all. I can't wait for the final score.

BRACK In any case, Mrs. Tesman, it's a good thing that you know how matters stand. I mean, before you embark on any more of these little purchases I hear you're threatening to make.

HEDDA What's that got to do with this?

BRACK Well, well, that's another matter. Good-bye. [*To* TESMAN.] I'll come by for you when I take my afternoon walk.

TESMAN Oh yes, yes, forgive me—I don't know if I'm coming or going.

HEDDA [*Reclining, stretching out her hand.*] Good-bye, Judge, and do come again.

BRACK Many thanks. Good-bye, good-bye.

TESMAN [*Following him to the door.*] Good-bye, Judge. You'll have to excuse me.

[JUDGE BRACK *goes out through the hallway door.*]

TESMAN [*Pacing about the floor.*] We should never let ourselves get lost in a wonderland, Hedda, hm?

HEDDA [*Looking at him and smiling.*] Do you do that?

TESMAN Yes, well, it can't be denied. It was like living in wonderland to go and get married and set up housekeeping on nothing more than prospects.

HEDDA You may be right about that.

TESMAN Well, at least we have our home, Hedda, our wonderful home. The home both of us dreamt about, that both of us craved, I could almost say, hm?

HEDDA [*Rises slowly and wearily.*] The agreement was that we would live in society, that we would entertain.

TESMAN Yes, good Lord, I was so looking forward to that. Just think, to see you as a hostess in our own circle. Hm. Well, well, well, for the time being at least we'll just have to make do with each other, Hedda. We'll have Aunt Julie here now and then. Oh you, you should have such a completely different—

HEDDA To begin with, I suppose I can't have the liveried footmen.[5]

TESMAN Ah no, unfortunately not. No footmen. We can't even think about that right now.

5. Uniformed servants.

HEDDA And the horse!

TESMAN [*Horrified.*] The horse.

HEDDA I suppose I mustn't think about that any more.

TESMAN No, God help us, you can see that for yourself.

HEDDA [*Walking across the floor.*] Well, at least I've got one thing to amuse myself with.

TESMAN [*Beaming with pleasure.*] Ah, thank God for that, and what is that, Hedda?

HEDDA [*In the center doorway looking at him with veiled scorn.*] My pistols, George.

TESMAN [*Alarmed.*] Pistols?

HEDDA [*With cold eyes.*] General Gabler's pistols.

[*She goes through the inner room and out to the left.*]

TESMAN [*Running to the center doorway and shouting after her.*] No, for the love of God, Hedda, dearest, don't touch those dangerous things. For my sake, Hedda, hm?

Act 2

The TESMANS' *rooms as in the first act except that the piano has been moved out and an elegant little writing table with a bookshelf has been put in its place. Next to the sofa a smaller table has been placed. Most of the bouquets have been removed.* MRS. ELVSTED'*s bouquet stands on the larger table in the foreground. It is afternoon.*

[HEDDA, *dressed to receive visitors, is alone in the room. She stands by the open glass door loading a pistol. The matching pistol lies in an open pistol case on the writing table.*]

HEDDA [*Looking down into the garden and calling.*] Hello again, Judge.

BRACK [*Is heard some distance below.*] Likewise, Mrs. Tesman.

HEDDA [*Raises the pistol and aims.*] Now, Judge Brack, I am going to shoot you.

BRACK [*Shouting from below.*] No, no, no. Don't stand there aiming at me like that.

HEDDA That's what you get for coming up the back way. [*She shoots.*]

BRACK Are you out of your mind?

HEDDA Oh, good Lord, did I hit you?

BRACK [*Still outside.*] Stop this nonsense.

HEDDA Then come on in, Judge.

[JUDGE BRACK, *dressed for a bachelor party, comes in through the glass doors. He carries a light overcoat over his arm.*]

BRACK In the devil's name, are you still playing this game? What were you shooting at?

HEDDA Oh, I just stand here and shoot at the sky.

BRACK [*Gently taking the pistol out of her hands.*] With your permission, ma'am? [*Looks at it.*] Ah, this one. I know it well. [*Looks around.*] And where do we keep the case? I see, here it is. [*Puts the pistol inside and shuts the case.*] All right, we're through with these little games for today.

HEDDA Then what in God's name am I to do with myself?

BRACK No visitors?

HEDDA [*Closes the glass door.*] Not a single one. Our circle is still in the country.

BRACK Tesman's not home either, I suppose.

HEDDA [*At the writing table, locks the pistol case in the drawer.*] No, as soon as he finished eating he was off to the aunts. He wasn't expecting you so early.

BRACK Hmm, I never thought of that. Stupid of me.

HEDDA [*Turns her head, looks at him.*] Why stupid?

BRACK Then I would have come a little earlier.

HEDDA [*Going across the floor.*] Then you wouldn't have found anyone here at all. I've been in my dressing room since lunch.

BRACK Isn't there even one little crack in the door wide enough for a negotiation?

HEDDA Now that's something you forgot to provide for.

BRACK That was also stupid of me.

HEDDA So we'll just have to flop down here and wait. Tesman won't be home any time soon.

BRACK Well, well, Lord knows I can be patient.

[HEDDA *sits in the corner of the sofa.* BRACK *lays his overcoat over the back of the nearest chair and sits down, keeps his hat in his hand. Short silence. They look at each other.*]

HEDDA So?

BRACK [*In the same tone.*] So?

HEDDA I asked first.

BRACK [*Leaning a little forward.*] Yes, why don't we allow ourselves a cozy little chat, Mrs. Hedda.

HEDDA [*Leaning further back in the sofa.*] Doesn't it feel like an eternity since we last talked together? A few words last night and this morning, but I don't count them.

BRACK Like this, between ourselves, just the two of us?

HEDDA Well, yes, more or less.

BRACK I wished you were back home every single day.

HEDDA The whole time I was wishing the same thing.

BRACK You, really, Mrs. Hedda? Here I thought you were having a wonderful time on your trip.

HEDDA Oh yes, you can just imagine.

BRACK But that's what Tesman always wrote.

HEDDA Yes, him! He thinks it's the greatest thing in the world to go scratching around in libraries. He loves sitting and copying out old parchments or whatever they are.

BRACK [*Somewhat maliciously.*] Well, that's his calling in the world, at least in part.

HEDDA Yes, so it is, and no doubt it's—but for me, oh dear Judge, I've been so desperately bored.

BRACK [*Sympathetically.*] Do you really mean that? You're serious?

HEDDA Yes, you can imagine it for yourself. Six whole months never meeting with a soul who knew the slightest thing about our circle. No one we could talk with about our kinds of things.

BRACK Ah no, I'd agree with you there. That would be a loss.

HEDDA Then what was most unbearable of all.

BRACK Yes?

HEDDA To be together forever and always—with one and the same person.

BRACK [*Nodding agreement.*] Early and late, yes, night and day, every waking and sleeping hour.

HEDDA That's it, forever and always.

BRACK Yes, all right, but with our excellent Tesman I would have imagined that you might—

HEDDA Tesman is—a specialist, dear Judge.

BRACK Undeniably.

HEDDA And specialists aren't so much fun to travel with. Not for the long run anyway.

BRACK Not even the specialist that one loves?

HEDDA Uch, don't use that syrupy word.

BRACK [*Startled.*] Mrs. Hedda.

HEDDA [*Half laughing, half bitterly.*] Well, give it a try for yourself. Hearing about the history of civilization every hour of the day.

BRACK Forever and always.

HEDDA Yes, yes, yes. And then his particular interest, domestic crafts in the Middle Ages. Uch, the most revolting thing of all.

BRACK [*Looks at her curiously.*] But, tell me now, I don't quite understand how—hmmm.

HEDDA That we're together? George Tesman and I, you mean?

BRACK Well, yes. That's a good way of putting it.

HEDDA Good Lord, do you think it's so remarkable?

BRACK I think—yes and no, Mrs. Hedda.

HEDDA I'd danced myself out, dear Judge. My time was up. [*Shudders slightly.*] Uch, no, I'm not going to say that or even think it.

BRACK You certainly have no reason to think it.

HEDDA Ah, reasons—[*Looks watchfully at him.*] And George Tesman? Well, he'd certainly be called a most acceptable man in every way.

BRACK Acceptable and solid, God knows.

HEDDA And I can't find anything about him that's actually ridiculous, can you?

BRACK Ridiculous? No—I wouldn't quite say that.

HEDDA Hmm. Well, he's a very diligent archivist anyway. Some day he might do something interesting with all of it. Who knows.

BRACK [*Looking at her uncertainly.*] I thought you believed, like everyone else, that he'd turn out to be a great man.

HEDDA [*With a weary expression.*] Yes, I did. And then when he went around constantly begging with all his strength, begging for permission to let him take care of me, well, I didn't see why I shouldn't take him up on it.

BRACK Ah well, from that point of view . . .

HEDDA It was a great deal more than any of my other admirers were offering.

BRACK [*Laughing.*] Well, of course I can't answer for all the others, but as far as I'm concerned you know very well that I've always maintained a certain respect for the marriage bond, that is, in an abstract kind of way, Mrs. Hedda.

HEDDA [*Playfully.*] Oh, I never had any hopes for you.

BRACK All I ask is an intimate circle of good friends, friends I can be of service to in any way necessary. Places where I am allowed to come and go as a trusted friend.

HEDDA Of the man of the house, you mean.

BRACK [*Bowing.*] No, to be honest, of the lady. Of the man as well, you understand, because you know that kind of—how should I put this—that kind of triangular arrangement is really a magnificent convenience for everyone concerned.

HEDDA Yes, you can't imagine how many times I longed for a third person on that trip. Ach, huddled together alone in a railway compartment.

BRACK Fortunately, the wedding trip is over now.

HEDDA [*Shaking her head.*] Oh no, it's a very long trip. It's nowhere near over. I've only come to a little stopover on the line.

BRACK Then you should jump out, stretch your legs a little, Mrs. Hedda.

HEDDA I'd never jump out.

BRACK Really?

HEDDA No, because there's always someone at the stop who—

BRACK [*Laughing.*] Who's looking at your legs, you mean?

HEDDA Yes, exactly.

BRACK Yes, but for heaven's sake.

HEDDA [*With a disdainful gesture.*] I don't hold with that sort of thing. I'd rather remain sitting, just like I am now, a couple alone. On a train.

BRACK But what if a third man climbed into the compartment with the couple?

HEDDA Ah yes. Now that's quite different.

BRACK An understanding friend, a proven friend—

HEDDA Who can be entertaining on all kinds of topics—

BRACK And not a specialist in any way!

HEDDA [*With an audible sigh.*] Yes, that would be a relief.

BRACK [*Hears the front door open and glances toward it.*] The triangle is complete.

HEDDA [*Half audibly.*] And there goes the train.

[GEORGE TESMAN *in a gray walking suit and with a soft felt hat comes in from the hallway. He is carrying a large stack of unbound books under his arm and in his pockets.*]

TESMAN [*Goes to the table by the corner, sofa.*] Phew—hot work lugging all these here. [*Puts the books down.*] Would you believe I'm actually sweating, Hedda? And you're already here, Judge, hm. Berta didn't mention anything about that.

BRACK [*Getting up.*] I came up through the garden.

HEDDA What are all those books you've got there?

TESMAN [*Stands leafing through them.*] All the new works by my fellow specialists. I've absolutely got to have them.

HEDDA By your fellow specialists.

BRACK Ah, the specialists, Mrs. Tesman. [BRACK *and* HEDDA *exchange a knowing smile.*]

HEDDA You need even more of these specialized works?

TESMAN Oh, yes, my dear Hedda, you can never have too many of these. You have to keep up with what's being written and published.

HEDDA Yes, you certainly must do that.

TESMAN [*Searches among the books.*] And look here, I've got Eilert Løvborg's new book too. (*Holds it out.*) Maybe you'd like to look at it, Hedda, hm?

HEDDA No thanks—or maybe later.

TESMAN I skimmed it a little on the way.

HEDDA And what's your opinion as a specialist?

TESMAN I think the argument's remarkably thorough. He never wrote like this before. [*Collects the books together.*] Now I've got to get all these inside. Oh, it's going to be such fun to cut the pages.[6] Then I'll go and change. [*To* BRACK.] We don't have to leave right away, hm?

BRACK No, not at all. No hurry at all.

TESMAN Good, I'll take my time then. [*Leaves with the books but stands in the doorway and turns.*] Oh, Hedda, by the way, Aunt Julie won't be coming over this evening.

HEDDA Really? Because of that hat business?

TESMAN Not at all. How could you think that of Aunt Julie? No, it's just that Aunt Rina is very ill.

HEDDA She always is.

TESMAN Yes, but today she's gotten quite a bit worse.

HEDDA Well, then it's only right that the other one should stay at home with her. I'll just have to make the best of it.

TESMAN My dear, you just can't believe how glad Aunt Julie was, in spite of everything, at how healthy and rounded out you looked after the trip.

HEDDA [*Half audibly getting up.*] Oh, these eternal aunts.

TESMAN Hm?

HEDDA [*Goes over to the glass door.*] Nothing.

TESMAN Oh, all right. [*He goes out through the rear room and to the right.*]

BRACK What were you saying about a hat?

HEDDA Oh, just a little run-in with Miss Tesman this morning. She'd put her hat down there on that chair [*Looks at him smiling.*] and I pretended I thought it was the maid's.

BRACK [*Shaking his head.*] My dear Mrs. Hedda, how could you do such a thing to that harmless old lady.

HEDDA [*Nervously walking across the floor.*] Oh, you know—these things just come over me like that and I can't resist them. [*Flings herself into the armchair by the stove.*] I can't explain it, even to myself.

BRACK [*Behind the armchair.*] You're not really happy—that's the heart of it.

HEDDA [*Staring in front of her.*] And why should I be happy? Maybe you can tell me.

BRACK Yes. Among other things, be happy you've got the home that you've always longed for.

6. Books used to be sold with the pages folded but uncut; one had to cut the pages to read the book.

HEDDA [*Looks up at him and laughs.*] You also believe that myth?

BRACK There's nothing to it?

HEDDA Yes, heavens, there's something to it.

BRACK So?

HEDDA And here's what it is. I used George Tesman to walk me home from parties last summer.

BRACK Yes, regrettably I had to go another way.

HEDDA Oh yes, you certainly were going a different way last summer.

BRACK [*Laughs.*] Shame on you, Mrs. Hedda. So you and Tesman . . .

HEDDA So we walked past here one evening and Tesman, the poor thing, was twisting and turning in his agony because he didn't have the slightest idea what to talk about and I felt sorry that such a learned man—

BRACK [*Smiling skeptically.*] You did . . .

HEDDA Yes, if you will, I did, and so just to help him out of his torment I said, without really thinking about it, that this was the house I would love to live in.

BRACK That was all?

HEDDA For that evening.

BRACK But afterward?

HEDDA Yes, dear Judge, my thoughtlessness has had its consequences.

BRACK Unfortunately, our thoughtlessness often does, Mrs. Hedda.

HEDDA Thanks, I'm sure. But it so happens that George Tesman and I found our common ground in this passion for Prime Minister Falk's villa. And after that it all followed. The engagement, the marriage, the honeymoon and everything else. Yes, yes, Judge, I almost said: you make your bed, you have to lie in it.

BRACK That's priceless. Essentially what you're telling me is you didn't care about any of this here.

HEDDA God knows I didn't.

BRACK What about now, now that we've made it into a lovely home for you?

HEDDA Ach, I feel an air of lavender and dried roses in every room—or maybe Aunt Julie brought that in with her.

BRACK [*Laughing.*] No, I think that's probably a relic of the eminent prime minister's late wife.

HEDDA Yes, that's it, there's something deathly about it. It reminds me of a corsage the day after the ball. [*Folds her hands at the back of her neck, leans back in her chair and gazes at him.*] Oh, my dear Judge, you can't imagine how I'm going to bore myself out here.

BRACK What if life suddenly should offer you some purpose or other, something to live for? What about that, Mrs. Hedda?

HEDDA A purpose? Something really tempting for me?

BRACK Preferably something like that, of course.

HEDDA God knows what sort of purpose that would be. I often wonder if—[*Breaks off.*] No, that wouldn't work out either.

BRACK Who knows. Let me hear.

HEDDA If I could get Tesman to go into politics, I mean.

BRACK [*Laughing.*] Tesman? No, you have to see that politics, anything like that, is not for him. Not in his line at all.

HEDDA No, I can see that. But what if I could get him to try just the same?

BRACK Yes, but why should he do that if he's not up to it? Why would you want him to?

HEDDA Because I'm bored, do you hear me? [*After a pause.*] So you don't think there's any way that Tesman could become a cabinet minister?

BRACK Hmm, you see my dear Mrs. Hedda, that requires a certain amount of wealth in the first place.

HEDDA [*Rises impatiently.*] Yes, that's it, this shabby little world I've ended up in. [*Crosses the floor.*] That's what makes life so contemptible, so completely ridiculous. That's just what it is.

BRACK I think the problem's somewhere else.

HEDDA Where's that?

BRACK You've never had to live through anything that really shakes you up.

HEDDA Anything serious, you mean.

BRACK Yes, you could call it that. Perhaps now, though, it's on its way.

HEDDA [*Tosses her head.*] You mean that competition for that stupid professorship? That's Tesman's business. I'm not going to waste a single thought on it.

BRACK No, forget about that. But when you find yourself facing what one calls in elegant language a profound and solemn calling—[*Smiling.*] a new calling, my dear little Mrs. Hedda.

HEDDA [*Angry.*] Quiet. You'll never see anything like that.

BRACK [*Gently.*] We'll talk about it again in a year's time, at the very latest.

HEDDA [*Curtly.*] I don't have any talent for that, Judge. I don't want anything to do with that kind of calling.

BRACK Why shouldn't you, like most other women, have an innate talent for a vocation that—

HEDDA [*Over by the glass door.*] Oh, please be quiet. I often think I only have one talent, one talent in the world.

BRACK [*Approaching.*] And what is that may I ask?

HEDDA [*Standing, staring out.*] Boring the life right out of me. Now you know. [*Turns, glances toward the inner room and laughs.*] Perfect timing; here comes the professor.

BRACK [*Warning softly.*] Now, now, now, Mrs. Hedda.

[GEORGE TESMAN, *in evening dress, carrying his gloves and hat, comes in from the right of the rear room.*]

TESMAN Hedda, no message from Eilert Løvborg?

HEDDA No.

BRACK Do you really think he'll come?

TESMAN Yes, I'm almost certain he will. What you told us this morning was just idle gossip.

BRACK Oh?

TESMAN Yes, at least Aunt Julie said she couldn't possibly believe that he would stand in my way anymore. Just think.

BRACK So, then everything's all right.

TESMAN [*Puts his hat with his gloves inside on a chair to the right.*] Yes, but I'd like to wait for him as long as I can.

BRACK We have plenty of time. No one's coming to my place until seven or even half past.

TESMAN Meanwhile, we can keep Hedda company and see what happens, hm?

HEDDA [*Sets* BRACK's *overcoat and hat on the corner sofa.*] At the very worst, Mr. Løvborg can stay here with me.

BRACK [*Offering to take his things.*] At the worst, Mrs. Tesman, what do you mean?

HEDDA If he won't go out with you and Tesman.

TESMAN [*Looking at her uncertainly.*] But, Hedda dear, do you think that would be quite right, him staying here with you? Remember, Aunt Julie can't come.

HEDDA No, but Mrs. Elvsted will be coming and the three of us can have a cup of tea together.

TESMAN Yes, that's all right then.

BRACK [*Smiling.*] And I might add, that would be the best plan for him.

HEDDA Why so?

BRACK Good Lord, Mrs. Tesman, you've had enough to say about my little bachelor parties in the past. Don't you agree they should be open only to men of the highest principle?

HEDDA That's just what Mr. Løvborg is now, a reclaimed sinner.

[BERTA *comes in from the hall doorway.*]

BERTA Madam, there's a gentleman who wishes to—

HEDDA Yes, please, show him in.

TESMAN [*Softly.*] It's got to be him. Just think.

[EILERT LØVBORG *enters from the hallway. He is slim and lean, the same age as* TESMAN, *but he looks older and somewhat haggard. His hair and beard are dark brown. His face is longish, pale, with patches of red over the cheekbones. He is dressed in an elegant suit, black, quite new dark gloves and top hat. He stops just inside the doorway and bows hastily. He seems somewhat embarrassed.*]

TESMAN [*Goes to him and shakes his hands.*] Oh my dear Eilert, we meet again at long last.

LØVBORG [*Speaks in a low voice.*] Thanks for the letter, George. [*Approaches* HEDDA.] May I shake your hand also, Mrs. Tesman?

HEDDA [*Takes his hand.*] Welcome, Mr. Løvborg. [*With a gesture.*] I don't know if you two gentlemen—

LØVBORG [*Bowing.*] Judge Brack, I believe.

BRACK [*Similarly.*] Indeed. It's been quite a few years—

TESMAN [*To* LØVBORG, *his hands on his shoulders.*] And now Eilert, make yourself completely at home. Right, Hedda? I hear you're going to settle down here in town, hm?

LØVBORG Yes, I will.

TESMAN Well, that's only sensible. Listen, I got your new book. I haven't really had time to read it yet.

LØVBORG You can save yourself the trouble.

TESMAN What do you mean?

LØVBORG There's not much to it.

TESMAN How can you say that?

BRACK But everyone's been praising it so highly.

LØVBORG Exactly as I intended—so I wrote the sort of book that everyone can agree with.

BRACK Very clever.

TESMAN Yes, but my dear Eilert.

LØVBORG Because I want to reestablish my position, begin again.

TESMAN [*A little downcast.*] Yes, I suppose you'd want to, hm.

LØVBORG [*Smiling, putting down his hat and pulling a package wrapped in paper from his coat pocket.*] But when this comes out, George Tesman—this is what you should read. It's the real thing. I've put my whole self into it.

TESMAN Oh yes? What's it about?

LØVBORG It's the sequel.

TESMAN Sequel to what?

LØVBORG To my book.

TESMAN The new one?

LØVBORG Of course.

TESMAN But my dear Eilert, that one takes us right to the present day.

LØVBORG So it does—and this one takes us into the future.

TESMAN The future. Good Lord! We don't know anything about that.

LØVBORG No, we don't—but there are still one or two things to say about it, just the same. [*Opens the packages.*] Here, you'll see.

TESMAN That's not your handwriting, is it?

LØVBORG I dictated it. [*Turns the pages.*] It's written in two sections. The first is about the cultural forces which will shape the future, and this other section [*Turning the pages.*] is about the future course of civilization.

TESMAN Extraordinary. It would never occur to me to write about something like that.

HEDDA [*By the glass door, drumming on the pane.*] Hmm, no, no.

LØVBORG [*Puts the papers back in the packet and sets it on the table.*] I brought it along because I thought I might read some of it to you tonight.

TESMAN Ah, that was very kind of you, Eilert, but this evening [*Looks at* BRACK.] I'm not sure it can be arranged—

LØVBORG Some other time then, there's no hurry.

BRACK I should tell you, Mr. Løvborg, we're having a little party at my place this evening, mostly for Tesman, you understand—

LØVBORG [*Looking for his hat.*] Aha, well then I'll—

BRACK No, listen, why don't you join us?

LØVBORG [*Briefly but firmly.*] No, that I can't do, but many thanks just the same.

BRACK Oh come now, you certainly can do that. We'll be a small, select circle and I guarantee we'll be "lively," as Mrs. Hed—Mrs. Tesman would say.

LØVBORG No doubt, but even so—

BRACK And then you could bring your manuscript along and read it to Tesman at my place. I've got plenty of rooms.

TESMAN Think about that, Eilert. You could do that, hm?

HEDDA [*Intervening.*] Now, my dear, Mr. Løvborg simply doesn't want to. I'm quite sure Mr. Løvborg would rather settle down here and have supper with me.

LØVBORG [*Staring at her.*] With you, Mrs. Tesman?

HEDDA And with Mrs. Elvsted.

LØVBORG Ah—[*Casually.*] I saw her this morning very briefly.

HEDDA Oh did you? Well, she's coming here; so you might almost say it's essential that you stay here, Mr. Løvborg. Otherwise she'll have no one to see her home.

LØVBORG That's true. Yes, Mrs. Tesman, many thanks. I'll stay.

HEDDA I'll go and have a word with the maid.

[*She goes over to the hall door and rings.* BERTA *enters.* HEDDA *speaks quietly to her and points toward the rear room.* BERTA *nods and goes out again.*]

TESMAN [*At the same time to* LØVBORG.] Listen, Eilert, your lecture—Is it about this new subject? About the future?

LØVBORG Yes.

TESMAN Because I heard down at the bookstore that you'd be giving a lecture series here this fall.

LØVBORG I plan to. Please don't hold it against me.

TESMAN No, God forbid, but—?

LØVBORG I can easily see how this might make things awkward.

TESMAN [*Dejectedly.*] Oh, for my part, I can't expect you to—

LØVBORG But I'll wait until you get your appointment.

TESMAN You will? Yes but—yes but—you won't be competing then?

LØVBORG No. I only want to conquer you in the marketplace of ideas.

TESMAN But, good Lord, Aunt Julie was right after all. Oh yes, yes, I was quite sure of it. Hedda, imagine, my dear—Eilert Løvborg won't stand in our way.

HEDDA [*Curtly.*] Our way? Leave me out of it.

[*She goes up toward the rear room where* BERTA *is placing a tray with decanters and glasses on the table.* HEDDA *nods approvingly, comes forward again.* BERTA *goes out.*]

TESMAN [*Meanwhile.*] So, Judge Brack, what do you say about all this?

BRACK Well now, I say that honor and victory, hmm—they have a powerful appeal—

TESMAN Yes, yes, I suppose they do but all the same—

HEDDA [*Looking at* TESMAN *with a cold smile.*] You look like you've been struck by lightning.

TESMAN Yes, that's about it—or something like that, I think—

BRACK That was quite a thunderstorm that passed over us, Mrs. Tesman.

HEDDA [*Pointing toward the rear room.*] Won't you gentlemen go in there and have a glass of punch?

BRACK [*Looking at his watch.*] For the road? Yes, not a bad idea.

TESMAN Wonderful, Hedda, wonderful! And I'm in such a fantastic mood now.

HEDDA You too, Mr. Løvborg, if you please.

LØVBORG [*Dismissively.*] No, thank you, not for me.

BRACK Good Lord, cold punch isn't exactly poison, you know.

LØVBORG Maybe not for everybody.

HEDDA Then I'll keep Mr. Løvborg company in the meantime.

TESMAN Yes, yes, Hedda dear, you do that.

[TESMAN *and* BRACK *go into the rear room, sit down and drink punch, smoking cigarettes and talking animatedly during the following.* EILERT LØVBORG *remains standing by the stove and* HEDDA *goes to the writing table.*]

HEDDA [*In a slightly raised voice.*] Now, if you like, I'll show you some photographs. Tesman and I—we took a trip to the Tyrol on the way home.

[*She comes over with an album and lays it on the table by the sofa, seating herself in the farthest corner.* EILERT LØVBORG *comes closer, stooping and looking at her. Then he takes a chair and sits on her left side with his back to the rear room.*]

HEDDA [*Opening the album.*] Do you see these mountains, Mr. Løvborg? That's the Ortler group. Tesman's written a little caption. Here. "The Ortler group near Meran."[7]

LØVBORG [*Who has not taken his eyes off her from the beginning, says softly and slowly.*] Hedda Gabler.

HEDDA [*Glances quickly at him.*] Shh, now.

LØVBORG [*Repeating softly.*] Hedda Gabler.

HEDDA [*Staring at the album.*] Yes, so I was once, when we knew each other.

LØVBORG And from now—for the rest of my life—do I have to teach myself never to say Hedda Gabler?

HEDDA [*Turning the pages.*] Yes, you have to. And I think you'd better start practicing now. The sooner the better, I'd say.

LØVBORG [*In a resentful voice.*] Hedda Gabler married—and then—with George Tesman.

HEDDA That's how it goes.

LØVBORG Ah, Hedda, Hedda—how could you have thrown yourself away like that?

HEDDA [*Looks sharply at him.*] What? Now stop that.

LØVBORG Stop what, what do you mean?

HEDDA Calling me Hedda and[8]—

[TESMAN *comes in and goes toward the sofa.*]

HEDDA [*Hears him approaching and says casually.*] And this one here, Mr. Løvborg, this was taken from the Ampezzo Valley. Would you just look at these mountain peaks. [*Looks warmly up at* TESMAN.] George, dear, what were these extraordinary mountains called?

TESMAN Let me see. Ah, yes, those are the Dolomites.

HEDDA Of course. Those, Mr. Løvborg, are the Dolomites.

TESMAN Hedda, dear, I just wanted to ask you if we should bring some punch in here, for you at least.

HEDDA Yes, thank you my dear. And a few pastries perhaps.

TESMAN Any cigarettes?

HEDDA No.

TESMAN Good.

[*He goes into the rear room and off to the right.* BRACK *remains sitting, from time to time keeping his eye on* HEDDA *and* LØVBORG.]

7. I.e., Merano, a city in the Austrian Tyrol, since 1918 in Italy. The scenic features mentioned here and later are tourist attractions. The Ortler group and the Dolomites are Alpine mountain ranges. The Ampezzo Valley lies beyond the Dolomites to the east. The Brenner Pass is a major route through the Alps to Austria.

8. This line is interpolated in an attempt to suggest the difference between the informal *du* (thee or thou) and the formal *de* (you) in the Norwegian text. Løvborg has just addressed Hedda in the informal manner and she is warning him not to [translators' note].

LØVBORG [*Quietly, as before.*] Then answer me, Hedda—how could you go and do such a thing?

HEDDA [*Apparently absorbed in the album.*] If you keep talking to me that way, I just won't speak to you.

LØVBORG Not even when we're alone together?

HEDDA No. You can think whatever you want but you can't talk about it.

LØVBORG Ah, I see. It offends your love for George Tesman.

HEDDA [*Glances at him and smiles.*] Love? Don't be absurd.

LØVBORG Not love then either?

HEDDA But even so—nothing unfaithful. I will not allow it.

LØVBORG Answer me just one thing—

HEDDA Shh.

[TESMAN, *with a tray, enters from the rear room.*]

TESMAN Here we are, here come the treats. [*He places the tray on the table.*]

HEDDA Why are you serving us yourself?

TESMAN [*Filling the glasses.*] I have such a good time waiting on you, Hedda.

HEDDA But now you've gone and poured two drinks and Mr. Løvborg definitely does not want—

TESMAN No, but Mrs. Elvsted's coming soon.

HEDDA Yes, that's right, Mrs. Elvsted.

TESMAN Did you forget about her?

HEDDA We were just sitting here so completely wrapped up in these. [*Shows him a picture.*] Do you remember this little village?

TESMAN Yes, that's the one below the Brenner Pass. We spent the night there—

HEDDA —and ran into all those lively summer visitors.

TESMAN Ah yes, that was it. Imagine—if you could have been with us, Eilert, just think. [*He goes in again and sits with* BRACK.]

LØVBORG Just answer me one thing—

HEDDA Yes?

LØVBORG In our relationship—wasn't there any love there either? No trace? Not a glimmer of love in any of it?

HEDDA I wonder if there really was. For me it was like we were two good comrades, two really good, faithful friends. [*Smiling.*] I remember you were particularly frank and open.

LØVBORG That's how you wanted it.

HEDDA When I look back on it, there was something really beautiful—something fascinating, something brave about this secret comradeship, this secret intimacy that no living soul had any idea about.

LØVBORG Yes, Hedda, that's true isn't it? That was it. When I'd come to your father's in the afternoon—and the General would sit in the window reading his newspaper with his back toward the room—

HEDDA And us on the corner sofa.

LØVBORG Always with the same illustrated magazine in front of us.

HEDDA Instead of an album, yes.

LØVBORG Yes, Hedda—and when I made all those confessions to you—telling you things about myself that no one else knew in those days. Sat there and told you how I'd lost whole days and nights in drunken frenzy, frenzy that would last for days on end. Ah, Hedda—what kind of power was in you that drew these confessions out of me?

HEDDA You think it was a power in me?

LØVBORG Yes. I can't account for it in any other way. And you'd ask me all those ambiguous leading questions—

HEDDA Which you understood implicitly—

LØVBORG How did you sit there and question me so fearlessly?

HEDDA Ambiguously?

LØVBORG Yes, but fearlessly all the same. Questioning me about—About things like that.

HEDDA And how could you answer them, Mr. Løvborg?

LØVBORG Yes, yes. That's just what I don't understand anymore. But now tell me, Hedda, wasn't it love underneath it all? Wasn't that part of it? You wanted to purify me, to cleanse me—when I'd seek you out to make my confessions. Wasn't that it?

HEDDA No, no, not exactly.

LØVBORG Then what drove you?

HEDDA Do you find it so hard to explain that a young girl—when it becomes possible—in secret—

LØVBORG Yes?

HEDDA That she wants a glimpse of a world that—

LØVBORG That—

HEDDA That is not permitted to her.

LØVBORG So that was it.

HEDDA That too, that too—I almost believe it.

LØVBORG Comrades in a quest for life. So why couldn't it go on?

HEDDA That was your own fault.

LØVBORG You broke it off.

HEDDA Yes, when it looked like reality threatened to spoil the situation. Shame on you, Eilert Løvborg, how could you do violence to your comrade in arms?

LØVBORG [*Clenching his hands together.*] Well, why didn't you do it for real? Why didn't you shoot me dead right then and there like you threatened to?

HEDDA Oh, I'm much too afraid of scandal.

LØVBORG Yes, Hedda, underneath it all, you're a coward.

HEDDA A terrible coward. [*Changes her tone.*] Lucky for you. And now you've got plenty of consolation up there at the Elvsteds'.

LØVBORG I know what Thea's confided to you.

HEDDA And no doubt you've confided to her about us.

LØVBORG Not one word. She's too stupid to understand things like this.

HEDDA Stupid?

LØVBORG In things like this she's stupid.

HEDDA And I'm a coward. [*Leans closer to him without looking him in the eyes and says softly.*] Now I'll confide something to you.

LØVBORG [*In suspense.*] What?

HEDDA My not daring to shoot you—

LØVBORG Yes?!

HEDDA —that wasn't my worst cowardice that evening.

LØVBORG [*Stares at her a moment, understands and whispers passionately.*] Ah, Hedda Gabler, now I see the hidden reason why we're such comrades. This craving for life in you—

HEDDA [*Quietly, with a sharp glance at him.*] Watch out, don't believe anything of the sort.

[*It starts to get dark. The hall door is opened by* BERTA.]

HEDDA [*Clapping the album shut and crying out with a smile.*] Ah, finally. Thea, darling, do come in.

[MRS. ELVSTED *enters from the hall. She is in evening dress. The door is closed after her.*]

HEDDA [*On the sofa, stretching out her arms.*] Thea, my sweet, you can't imagine how I've been expecting you.

[MRS. ELVSTED, *in passing, exchanges a greeting with the gentlemen in the inner room, crosses to the table, shakes* HEDDA'*s hand.* EILERT LØVBORG *has risen. He and* MRS. ELVSTED *greet each other with a single nod.*]

MRS. ELVSTED Perhaps I should go in and have a word with your husband.

HEDDA Not at all. Let them sit there. They'll be on their way soon.

MRS. ELVSTED They're leaving?

HEDDA Yes, they're going out on a little binge.

MRS. ELVSTED [*Quickly to* LØVBORG.] You're not?

LØVBORG No.

HEDDA Mr. Løvborg . . . he'll stay here with us.

MRS. ELVSTED [*Takes a chair and sits down beside him.*] It's so nice to be here.

HEDDA No, you don't, little Thea, not there. Come right over here next to me. I want to be in the middle between you.

MRS. ELVSTED All right, whatever you like. [*She goes around the table and sits on the sofa to the right of* HEDDA. LØVBORG *takes his chair again.*]

LØVBORG [*After a brief pause, to* HEDDA.] Isn't she lovely to look at?

HEDDA [*Gently stroking her hair.*] Only to look at?

LØVBORG Yes. We're true comrades, the two of us. We trust each other completely and that's why we can sit here and talk so openly and boldly together.

HEDDA With no ambiguity, Mr. Løvborg.

LØVBORG Well—

MRS. ELVSTED [*Softly, clinging to* HEDDA.] Oh, Hedda, I'm so lucky. Just think, he says I've inspired him too.

HEDDA [*Regards her with a smile.*] No, dear, does he say that?

LØVBORG And she has the courage to take action, Mrs. Tesman.

MRS. ELVSTED Oh God, me, courage?

LØVBORG Tremendous courage when it comes to comradeship.

HEDDA Yes, courage—yes! That's the crucial thing.

LØVBORG Why is that, do you suppose?

HEDDA Because then—maybe—life has a chance to be lived. [*Suddenly changing her tone.*] But now, my dearest Thea. Why don't you treat yourself to a nice cold glass of punch?

MRS. ELVSTED No thank you, I never drink anything like that.

HEDDA Then for you, Mr. Løvborg.

LØVBORG No thank you, not for me either.

MRS. ELVSTED No, not for him either.

HEDDA [*Looking steadily at him.*] But if I insisted.

LØVBORG Doesn't matter.

HEDDA [*Laughing.*] Then I have absolutely no power over you? Ah, poor me.

LØVBORG Not in that area.

HEDDA But seriously now, I really think you should, for your own sake.

MRS. ELVSTED No, Hedda—

LØVBORG Why is that?

HEDDA Or to be more precise, for others' sakes.

LØVBORG Oh?

HEDDA Because otherwise people might get the idea that you don't, deep down inside, feel really bold, really sure of yourself.

LØVBORG Oh, from now on people can think whatever they like.

MRS. ELVSTED Yes, that's right, isn't it.

HEDDA I saw it so clearly with Judge Brack a few minutes ago.

LØVBORG What did you see?

HEDDA That condescending little smile when you didn't dare join them at the table.

LØVBORG Didn't dare? I'd just rather stay here and talk with you, of course.

MRS. ELVSTED That's only reasonable, Hedda.

HEDDA How was the Judge supposed to know that? I saw how he smiled and shot a glance at Tesman when you didn't dare join them in their silly little party.

LØVBORG Didn't dare. You're saying I don't dare.

HEDDA Oh, I'm not. But that's how Judge Brack sees it.

LØVBORG Well let him.

HEDDA So you won't join them?

LØVBORG I'm staying here with you and Thea.

MRS. ELVSTED Yes, Hedda, you can be sure he is.

HEDDA [*Smiling and nodding approvingly to* LØVBORG.] What a strong foundation you've got. Principles to last a lifetime. That's what a man ought to have. [*Turns to* MRS. ELVSTED.] See now, wasn't that what I told you when you came here this morning in such a panic—

LØVBORG [*Startled.*] Panic?

MRS. ELVSTED [*Terrified.*] Hedda, Hedda, no.

HEDDA Just see for yourself. No reason at all to come running here in mortal terror. [*Changing her tone.*] There, now all three of us can be quite jolly.

LØVBORG [*Shocked.*] What does this mean, Mrs. Tesman?

MRS. ELVSTED Oh God, oh God, Hedda. What are you doing? What are you saying?

HEDDA Keep calm now. That disgusting Judge is sitting there watching you.

LØVBORG In mortal terror on my account?

MRS. ELVSTED [*Quietly wailing.*] Oh, Hedda—

LØVBORG [*Looks at her steadily for a moment; his face is drawn.*] So that, then, was how my brave, bold comrade trusted me.

MRS. ELVSTED [*Pleading.*] Oh, my dearest friend, listen to me—

LØVBORG [*Takes one of the glasses of punch, raises it and says in a low, hoarse voice.*] Your health, Thea. [*Empties the glass, takes another.*]

MRS. ELVSTED [*Softly.*] Oh Hedda, Hedda—how could you want this to happen?

HEDDA Want it? I want this? Are you mad?

LØVBORG And your health too, Mrs. Tesman. Thanks for the truth. Long may it live. [*He drinks and goes to refill the glass.*]

HEDDA [*Placing her hand on his arm.*] That's enough for now. Remember, you're going to the party.

MRS. ELVSTED No, no, no.

HEDDA Shh. They're watching us.

LØVBORG [*Putting down the glass.*] Thea, be honest with me now.

MRS. ELVSTED Yes.

LØVBORG Was your husband told that you came here to look for me?

MRS. ELVSTED [*Wringing her hands.*] Oh, Hedda, listen to what he's asking me!

LØVBORG Did he arrange for you to come to town to spy on me? Maybe he put you up to it himself. Aha, that's it. He needed me back in the office again. Or did he just miss me at the card table?

MRS. ELVSTED [*Softly moaning.*] Oh, Løvborg, Løvborg—

LØVBORG [*Grabs a glass intending to fill it.*] Skøal to the old Sheriff too.

HEDDA [*Preventing him.*] No more now. Remember, you're going out to read to Tesman.

LØVBORG [*Calmly putting down his glass.*] Thea, that was stupid of me. What I did just now. Taking it like that I mean. Don't be angry with me, my dear, dear comrade. You'll see. Both of you and everyone else will see that even though I once was fallen—now I've raised myself up again, with your help, Thea.

MRS. ELVSTED [*Radiant with joy.*] Oh God be praised.

[*Meanwhile* BRACK *has been looking at his watch. He and* TESMAN *get up and come into the drawing room.*]

BRACK [*Taking his hat and overcoat.*] Well, Mrs. Tesman, our time is up.

HEDDA Yes, it must be.

LØVBORG [*Rising.*] Mine too.

MRS. ELVSTED [*Quietly pleading.*] Løvborg, don't do it.

HEDDA [*Pinching her arm.*] They can hear you.

MRS. ELVSTED [*Crying out faintly.*] Ow.

LØVBORG [*To* BRACK.] You were kind enough to ask me along.

BRACK So you're coming after all.

LØVBORG Yes, thanks.

BRACK I'm delighted.

LØVBORG [*Putting the manuscript packet in his pocket and saying to* TESMAN.] I'd really like you to look at one or two things before I send it off.

TESMAN Just think, that will be splendid. But, Hedda dear, how will you get Mrs. Elvsted home?

HEDDA Oh, there's always a way out.

LØVBORG [*Looking at the ladies.*] Mrs. Elvsted? Well, of course, I'll come back for her. [*Coming closer.*] Around ten o'clock, Mrs. Tesman, will that do?

HEDDA Yes, that will be fine.

TESMAN Well, everything's all right then; but don't expect me that early, Hedda.

HEDDA No dear, you stay just as long—as long as you like.

MRS. ELVSTED [*With suppressed anxiety.*] Mr. Løvborg—I'll stay here until you come.

LØVBORG [*His hat in his hand.*] That's understood.

BRACK All aboard then, the party train's pulling out. Gentlemen, I trust it will be a lively trip, as a certain lovely lady suggested.

HEDDA Ah yes, if only that lovely lady could be there—invisible, of course.

BRACK Why invisible?

HEDDA To hear a little of your liveliness, Judge, uncensored.

BRACK [*Laughing.*] Not recommended for the lovely lady.

TESMAN [*Also laughing.*] You really are the limit, Hedda. Think of it.

BRACK Well, well, my ladies. Good night. Good night.

LØVBORG [*Bowing as he leaves.*] Until ten o'clock, then.

[BRACK, LØVBORG *and* TESMAN *leave through the hall door. At the same time* BERTA *comes in from the rear room with a lighted lamp which she places on the drawing room table, going out the way she came in.*]

MRS. ELVSTED [*Has gotten up and wanders uneasily about the room.*] Oh, Hedda, where is all this going?

HEDDA Ten o'clock—then he'll appear. I see him before me with vine leaves in his hair,[9] burning bright and bold.

MRS. ELVSTED Yes, if only it could be like that.

HEDDA And then you'll see—then he'll have power over himself again. Then he'll be a free man for the rest of his days.

MRS. ELVSTED Oh God yes—if only he'd come back just the way you see him.

HEDDA He'll come back just that way and no other. [*Gets up and comes closer.*] You can doubt him as much as you like. I believe in him. And so we'll see—

MRS. ELVSTED There's something behind this, something else you're trying to do.

HEDDA Yes, there is. Just once in my life I want to help shape someone's destiny.

MRS. ELVSTED Don't you do that already?

HEDDA I don't and I never have.

MRS. ELVSTED Not even your husband?

HEDDA Oh yes, that was a real bargain. Oh, if you could only understand how destitute I am while you get to be so rich. [*She passionately throws her arms around her.*] I think I'll burn your hair off after all.

MRS. ELVSTED Let me go, let me go. I'm afraid of you.

BERTA [*In the doorway.*] Tea is ready in the dining room, Madam.

HEDDA Good. We're on our way.

MRS. ELVSTED No, no, no! I'd rather go home alone! Right now!

9. Like Bacchus, the Greek god of wine, and his followers.

HEDDA Nonsense! First you're going to have some tea, you little bubble-head, and then—at ten o'clock—Eilert Løvborg—with vine leaves in his hair! [*She pulls* MRS. ELVSTED *toward the doorway almost by force.*]

Act 3

The room at the TESMANS'. *The curtains are drawn across the center doorway and also across the glass door. The lamp covered with a shade burns low on the table. In the stove, with its door standing open, there has been a fire that is almost burned out.*

[MRS. ELVSTED, *wrapped in a large shawl and with her feet on a footstool, sits sunk back in an armchair.* HEDDA, *fully dressed, lies sleeping on the sofa with a rug over her.*]

MRS. ELVSTED [*After a pause suddenly straightens herself in the chair and listens intently. Then she sinks back wearily and moans softly.*] STILL NOT BACK . . . OH GOD, OH GOD . . . STILL NOT BACK.

[BERTA *enters tiptoeing carefully through the hall doorway; she has a letter in her hand.*]

MRS. ELVSTED Ah—did someone come?

BERTA Yes, a girl came by just now with this letter.

MRS. ELVSTED [*Quickly stretching out her hand.*] A letter? Let me have it.

BERTA No ma'am, it's for the doctor.

MRS. ELVSTED Oh.

BERTA It was Miss Tesman's maid who brought it. I'll put it on the table here.

MRS. ELVSTED Yes, do that.

BERTA [*Puts down the letter.*] I'd better put out the lamp; it's starting to smoke.

MRS. ELVSTED Yes, put it out. It'll be light soon anyway.

BERTA [*Putting out the light.*] Oh, ma'am, it's already light.

MRS. ELVSTED So, morning and still not back—!

BERTA Oh, dear Lord—I knew all along it would go like this.

MRS. ELVSTED You knew?

BERTA Yes, when I saw a certain person was back in town. And then when he went off with them—oh we'd heard plenty about that gentleman.

MRS. ELVSTED Don't speak so loud, you'll wake your mistress.

BERTA [*Looks over to the sofa and sighs.*] No, dear Lord—let her sleep, poor thing. Shouldn't I build the stove up a little more?

MRS. ELVSTED Not for me, thanks.

BERTA Well, well then. [*She goes out quietly through the hall doorway.*]

HEDDA [*Awakened by the closing door, looks up.*] What's that?

MRS. ELVSTED Only the maid.

HEDDA [*Looking around.*] In here—! Oh, now I remember. [*Straightens up, stretches sitting on the sofa and rubs her eyes.*] What time is it, Thea?

MRS. ELVSTED [*Looks at her watch.*] It's after seven.

HEDDA What time did Tesman get in?

MRS. ELVSTED He hasn't.

HEDDA Still?

MRS. ELVSTED [*Getting up.*] No one's come back.

HEDDA And we sat here waiting and watching until almost four.

MRS. ELVSTED [*Wringing her hands.*] Waiting for him!

HEDDA [*Yawning and speaking with her hand over her mouth.*] Oh yes—we could have saved ourselves the trouble.

MRS. ELVSTED Did you finally manage to sleep?

HEDDA Yes, I think I slept quite well. Did you?

MRS. ELVSTED Not a wink. I couldn't, Hedda. It was just impossible for me.

HEDDA [*Gets up and goes over to her.*] Now, now, now. There's nothing to worry about. I know perfectly well how it all turned out.

MRS. ELVSTED Yes, what do you think? Can you tell me?

HEDDA Well, of course they dragged it out dreadfully up at Judge Brack's.

MRS. ELVSTED Oh God yes—that must be true. But all the same—

HEDDA And then you see, Tesman didn't want to come home and create a fuss by ringing the bell in the middle of the night. [*Laughing.*] He probably didn't want to show himself either right after a wild party like that.

MRS. ELVSTED For goodness sake—where would he have gone?

HEDDA Well, naturally, he went over to his aunts' and laid himself down to sleep there. They still have his old room standing ready for him.

MRS. ELVSTED No, he's not with them. A letter just came for him from Miss Tesman. It's over there.

HEDDA Oh? [*Looks at the inscription.*] Yes, that's Aunt Julie's hand all right. So then, he's still over at Judge Brack's and Eilert Løvborg—he's sitting—reading aloud with vine leaves in his hair.

MRS. ELVSTED Oh, Hedda, you don't even believe what you're saying.

HEDDA You are such a little noodlehead, Thea.

MRS. ELVSTED Yes, unfortunately I probably am.

HEDDA And you look like you're dead on your feet.

MRS. ELVSTED Yes, I am. Dead on my feet.

HEDDA And so now you're going to do what I tell you. You'll go into my room and lie down on my bed.

MRS. ELVSTED Oh no, no—I couldn't get to sleep anyway.

HEDDA Yes, you certainly will.

MRS. ELVSTED But your husband's bound to be home any time now and I've got to find out right away—

HEDDA I'll tell you as soon as he comes.

MRS. ELVSTED Promise me that, Hedda?

HEDDA Yes, that you can count on. Now just go in and sleep for a while.

MRS. ELVSTED Thanks. At least I'll give it a try. [*She goes in through the back room.*]

[HEDDA *goes over to the glass door and draws back the curtains. Full daylight floods the room. She then takes a small hand mirror from the writing table, looks in it and arranges her hair. Then she goes to the hall door and presses the bell. Soon after* BERTA *enters the doorway.*]

BERTA Did Madam want something?

HEDDA Yes, build up the stove a little bit. I'm freezing in here.

BERTA Lord, in no time at all it'll be warm in here. [*She rakes the embers and puts a log inside. She stands and listens.*] There's the front doorbell, Madam.

HEDDA So, go answer it. I'll take care of the stove myself.

BERTA It'll be burning soon enough. [*She goes out through the hall door.*]

[HEDDA *kneels on the footstool and puts more logs into the stove. After a brief moment,* GEORGE TESMAN *comes in from the hall. He looks weary and rather serious. He creeps on tiptoes toward the doorway and is about to slip through the curtains.*]

HEDDA [*By the stove, without looking up.*] Good morning.

TESMAN [*Turning around.*] Hedda. [*Comes nearer.*] What in the world—Up so early, hm?

HEDDA Yes, up quite early today.

TESMAN And here I was so sure you'd still be in bed. Just think, Hedda.

HEDDA Not so loud. Mrs. Elvsted's lying down in my room.

TESMAN Has Mrs. Elvsted been here all night?

HEDDA Yes. No one came to pick her up.

TESMAN No, no, they couldn't have.

HEDDA [*Shuts the door of the stove and gets up.*] So, did you have a jolly time at the Judge's?

TESMAN Were you worried about me?

HEDDA No, that would never occur to me. I asked if you had a good time.

TESMAN Yes, I really did, for once, in a manner of speaking—Mostly in the beginning, I'd say. We'd arrived an hour early. How about that? And Brack had so much to get ready. But then Eilert read to me.

HEDDA [*Sits at the right of the table.*] So, tell me.

TESMAN Hedda, you can't imagine what this new work will be like. It's one of the most brilliant things ever written, no doubt about it. Think of that.

HEDDA Yes, yes, but that's not what I'm interested in.

TESMAN But I have to confess something, Hedda. After he read—something horrible came over me.

HEDDA Something horrible?

TESMAN I sat there envying Eilert for being able to write like that. Think of it, Hedda.

HEDDA Yes, yes, I'm thinking.

TESMAN And then, that whole time, knowing that he—even with all the incredible powers at his command—is still beyond redemption.

HEDDA You mean he's got more of life's courage in him than the others?

TESMAN No, for heaven sakes—he just has no control over his pleasures.

HEDDA And what happened then—at the end?

TESMAN Well, Hedda, I guess you'd have to say it was a bacchanal.

HEDDA Did he have vine leaves in his hair?

TESMAN Vine leaves? No, I didn't see anything like that. But he did make a long wild speech for the woman who had inspired him in his work. Yes—that's how he put it.

HEDDA Did he name her?

TESMAN No, he didn't, but I can only guess that it must be Mrs. Elvsted. Wouldn't you say?

HEDDA Hmm—where did you leave him?

TESMAN On the way back. Most of our group broke up at the same time and Brack came along with us to get a little fresh air. And you see, we agreed to follow Eilert home because—well—he was so far gone.

HEDDA He must have been.

TESMAN But here's the strangest part, Hedda! Or maybe I should say the saddest. I'm almost ashamed for Eilert's sake—to tell you—

HEDDA So?

TESMAN There we were walking along, you see, and I happened to drop back a bit, just for a couple of minutes, you understand.

HEDDA Yes, yes, good Lord but—

TESMAN And then when I was hurrying to catch up—can you guess what I found in the gutter, hm?

HEDDA How can I possibly guess?

TESMAN Don't ever tell a soul, Hedda. Do you hear? Promise me that for Eilert's sake. [*Pulls a package out of his coat pocket.*] Just think—this is what I found.

HEDDA That's the package he had with him here yesterday, isn't it?

TESMAN That's it. His precious, irreplaceable manuscript—all of it. And he's lost it—without even noticing it. Oh just think, Hedda—the pity of it—

HEDDA Well, why didn't you give it back to him right away?

TESMAN Oh, I didn't dare do that—The condition he was in—

HEDDA You didn't tell any of the others that you found it either?

TESMAN Absolutely not. I couldn't, you see, for Eilert's sake.

HEDDA So nobody knows you have Eilert's manuscript? Nobody at all?

TESMAN No. And they mustn't find out either.

HEDDA What did you talk to him about later?

TESMAN I didn't get a chance to talk to him any more. We got to the city limits, and he and a couple of the others went a different direction. Just think—

HEDDA Aha, they must have followed him home then.

TESMAN Yes, I suppose so. Brack also went his way.

HEDDA And, in the meantime, what became of the bacchanal?

TESMAN Well, I and some of the others followed one of the revelers up to his place and had morning coffee with him—or maybe we should call it morning-after coffee, hm? Now, I'll rest a bit—and as soon as I think Eilert has managed to sleep it off, poor man, then I've got to go over to him with this.

HEDDA [*Reaching out for the envelope.*] No, don't give it back. Not yet, I mean. Let me read it first.

TESMAN Oh no.

HEDDA Oh, for God's sake.

TESMAN I don't dare do that.

HEDDA You don't dare?

TESMAN No, you can imagine how completely desperate he'll be when he wakes up and realizes he can't find the manuscript. He's got no copy of it. He said so himself.

HEDDA [*Looks searchingly at him.*] Couldn't it be written again?

TESMAN No, I don't believe that could ever be done because the inspiration—you see—

HEDDA Yes, yes—That's the thing, isn't it? [*Casually.*] But, oh yes—there's a letter here for you.

TESMAN No, think of that.

HEDDA [*Hands it to him.*] It came early this morning.

TESMAN From Aunt Julie, Hedda. What can it be? [*Puts the manuscript on the other stool, opens the letter and jumps up.*] Oh Hedda—poor Aunt Rina's almost breathing her last.

HEDDA It's only what's expected.

TESMAN And if I want to see her one more time, I've got to hurry. I'll charge over there right away.

HEDDA [*Suppressing a smile.*] You'll charge?

TESMAN Oh, Hedda dearest—if you could just bring yourself to follow me. Just think.

HEDDA [*Rises and says wearily and dismissively.*] No, no. Don't ask me to do anything like that. I won't look at sickness and death. Let me stay free from everything ugly.

TESMAN Oh, good Lord, then—[*Darting around.*] My hat—? My overcoat—? Ah, in the hall—Oh, I hope I'm not too late, Hedda, hm?

HEDDA Then charge right over—

[BERTA *appears in the hallway.*]

BERTA Judge Brack is outside.

HEDDA Ask him to come in.

TESMAN At a time like this! No, I can't possibly deal with him now.

HEDDA But I can. [*To* BERTA.] Ask the Judge in.

[BERTA *goes out.*]

HEDDA [*In a whisper.*] The package, Tesman. [*She snatches it off the stool.*]

TESMAN Yes, give it to me.

HEDDA No, I'll hide it until you get back.

[*She goes over to the writing table and sticks the package in the bookcase.* TESMAN *stands flustered, and can't get his gloves on.* BRACK *enters through the hall doorway.*]

HEDDA [*Nodding to him.*] Well, you're an early bird.

BRACK Yes, wouldn't you say. [*To* TESMAN.] You're going out?

TESMAN Yes, I've got to go over to my aunt's. Just think, the poor dear is dying.

BRACK Good Lord, is she really? Then don't let me hold you up for even a moment, at a time like this—

TESMAN Yes, I really must run—Good-bye. Good-bye. [*He hurries through the hall doorway.*]

HEDDA [*Approaches.*] So, things were livelier than usual at your place last night, Judge.

BRACK Oh yes, so much so that I haven't even been able to change clothes, Mrs. Hedda.

HEDDA You too.

BRACK As you see. But, what has Tesman been telling you about last night's adventures?

HEDDA Oh, just some boring things. He went someplace to drink coffee.

BRACK I've already looked into the coffee party. Eilert Løvborg wasn't part of that group, I presume.

HEDDA No, they followed him home before that.

BRACK Tesman too?

HEDDA No, but a couple of others, he said.

BRACK [*Smiles.*] George Tesman is a very naïve soul, Mrs. Hedda.

HEDDA God knows, he is. But is there something more behind this?

BRACK I'd have to say so.

HEDDA Well then, Judge, let's be seated. Then you can speak freely. [*She sits to the left side of the table,* BRACK *at the long side near her.*] Well, then—

BRACK I had certain reasons for keeping track of my guests—or, more precisely, some of my guests' movements last night.

HEDDA For example, Eilert Løvborg?

BRACK Yes, indeed.

HEDDA Now I'm hungry for more.

BRACK Do you know where he and a couple of the others spent the rest of the night, Mrs. Hedda?

HEDDA Why don't you tell me, if it can be told.

BRACK Oh, it's certainly worth the telling. It appears that they found their way into a particularly animated soirée.[1]

HEDDA A lively one?

BRACK The liveliest.

HEDDA Tell me more, Judge.

BRACK Løvborg had received an invitation earlier—I knew all about that. But he declined because, as you know, he's made himself into a new man.

HEDDA Up at the Elvsteds', yes. But he went just the same?

BRACK Well, you see, Mrs. Hedda—unfortunately, the spirit really seized him at my place last evening.

HEDDA Yes, I hear he was quite inspired.

BRACK Inspired to a rather powerful degree. And so, he started to reconsider, I assume, because we men, alas, are not always so true to our principles as we ought to be.

HEDDA Present company excepted, Judge Brack. So, Løvborg—?

BRACK Short and sweet—He ended up at the salon of a certain Miss Diana.

HEDDA Miss Diana?

BRACK Yes, it was Miss Diana's soirée for a select circle of ladies and their admirers.

HEDDA Is she a redhead?

BRACK Exactly.

HEDDA A sort of a—singer?

BRACK Oh, yes—She's also that. And a mighty huntress—of men, Mrs. Hedda. You must have heard of her. Eilert Løvborg was one of her most strenuous admirers—in his better days.

HEDDA And how did all this end?

1. "Evening party" (French).

BRACK Apparently less amicably than it began. Miss Diana, after giving him the warmest of welcomes, soon turned to assault and battery.

HEDDA Against Løvborg?

BRACK Oh, yes. He accused her, or one of her ladies, of robbing him. He insisted that his pocketbook was missing, along with some other things. In short, he seems to have created a dreadful spectacle.

HEDDA And what did that lead to?

BRACK A regular brawl between both the men and the women. Luckily the police finally got there.

HEDDA The police too?

BRACK Yes. It's going to be quite a costly little romp for Eilert Løvborg. What a madman.

HEDDA Well!

BRACK Apparently, he resisted arrest. It seems he struck one of the officers on the ear, and ripped his uniform to shreds, so he had to go to the police station.

HEDDA How do you know all this?

BRACK From the police themselves.

HEDDA [*Gazing before her.*] So, that's how it ended? He had no vine leaves in his hair.

BRACK Vine leaves, Mrs. Hedda?

HEDDA [*Changing her tone.*] Tell me now, Judge, why do you go around snooping and spying on Eilert Løvborg?

BRACK For starters, I'm not a completely disinterested party—especially if the hearing uncovers the fact that he came straight from my place.

HEDDA There's going to be a hearing?

BRACK You can count on it. Be that as it may, however—My real concern was my duty as a friend of the house to inform you and Tesman of Løvborg's nocturnal adventures.

HEDDA Why, Judge Brack?

BRACK Well, I have an active suspicion that he'll try to use you as a kind of screen.

HEDDA Oh! What makes you think that?

BRACK Good God—we're not that blind, Mrs. Hedda. Wait and see. This Mrs. Elvsted—she won't be in such a hurry to leave town again.

HEDDA If there's anything going on between those two, there's plenty of places they can meet.

BRACK Not one single home. Every respectable house will be closed to Eilert Løvborg from now on.

HEDDA And mine should be too—Is that what you're saying?

BRACK Yes. I have to admit it would be more than painful for me if this man secured a foothold here. If this—utterly superfluous—and intrusive individual—were to force himself into—

HEDDA Into the triangle?

BRACK Precisely! It would leave me without a home.

HEDDA [*Looks smilingly at him.*] I see—The one cock of the walk—That's your goal.

BRACK [*Slowly nodding and dropping his voice.*] Yes, that's my goal. And it's a goal that I'll fight for—with every means at my disposal.

HEDDA [*Her smile fading.*] You're really a dangerous man, aren't you—when push comes to shove.

BRACK You think so?

HEDDA Yes, I'm starting to. And that's all right—just as long as you don't have any kind of hold on me.

BRACK [*Laughing ambiguously.*] Yes, Mrs. Hedda—you might be right about that. Of course, then, who knows whether I might not find some way or other—

HEDDA Now listen, Judge Brack! That sounds like you're threatening me.

BRACK [*Gets up.*] Oh, far from it. A triangle, you see—is best fortified by free defenders.

HEDDA I think so too.

BRACK Well, I've had my say so I should be getting back. Good-bye, Mrs. Hedda. [*He goes toward the glass doors.*]

HEDDA Out through the garden?

BRACK Yes, it's shorter for me.

HEDDA And then, it's also the back way.

BRACK That's true. I have nothing against back ways. Sometimes they can be very piquant.

HEDDA When there's sharpshooting.

BRACK [*In the doorway, laughing at her.*] Oh, no—you never shoot your tame cocks.

HEDDA [*Also laughing.*] Oh, no, especially when there's only one—

[*Laughing and nodding they take their farewells. He leaves. She closes the door after him.* HEDDA *stands for a while, serious, looking out. Then she goes and peers through the curtains in the back wall. She goes to the writing table, takes Løvborg's package from the bookcase, and is about to leaf through it.* BERTA*'s voice, raised in indignation, is heard out in the hall.* HEDDA *turns and listens. She quickly locks the package in the drawer and sets the key on the writing table.* EILERT LØVBORG, *wearing his overcoat and carrying his hat, bursts through the hall doorway. He looks somewhat confused and excited.*]

LØVBORG [*Turned toward the hallway.*] And I'm telling you, I've got to go in! And that's that! [*He closes the door, sees* HEDDA, *controls himself immediately, and bows.*]

HEDDA [*By the writing table.*] Well, Mr. Løvborg, it's pretty late to be calling for Thea.

LØVBORG Or a little early to be calling on you. I apologize.

HEDDA How do you know that she's still here?

LØVBORG I went to where she was staying. They told me she'd been out all night.

HEDDA [*Goes to the table.*] Did you notice anything special when they told you that?

LØVBORG [*Looks inquiringly at her.*] Notice anything?

HEDDA I mean—did they seem to have any thought on the subject—one way or the other?

LØVBORG [*Suddenly understanding.*] Oh, of course, it's true. I'm dragging her down with me. Still, I didn't notice anything. Tesman isn't up yet, I suppose?

HEDDA No, I don't think so.
LØVBORG When did he get home?
HEDDA Very late.
LØVBORG Did he tell you anything?
HEDDA Yes. I heard Judge Brack's was very lively.
LØVBORG Nothing else?
HEDDA No, I don't think so. I was terribly tired, though—

[MRS. ELVSTED *comes in through the curtains at the back.*]

MRS. ELVSTED [*Runs toward him.*] Oh, Løvborg—at last!
LØVBORG Yes, at last, and too late.
MRS. ELVSTED [*Looking anxiously at him.*] What's too late?
LØVBORG Everything's too late. I'm finished.
MRS. ELVSTED Oh no, no—Don't say that!
LØVBORG You'll say it too, when you've heard—
MRS. ELVSTED I won't listen—
HEDDA Shall I leave you two alone?
LØVBORG No, stay—You too, I beg you.
MRS. ELVSTED But I won't listen to anything you tell me.
LØVBORG I don't want to talk about last night.
MRS. ELVSTED What is it, then?
LØVBORG We've got to go our separate ways.
MRS. ELVSTED Separate!
HEDDA [*Involuntarily.*] I knew it!
LØVBORG Because I have no more use for you, Thea.
MRS. ELVSTED You can stand there and say that! No more use for me! Can't I help you now, like I did before? Won't we go on working together?
LØVBORG I don't plan to work any more.
MRS. ELVSTED [*Desperately.*] Then what do I have to live for?
LØVBORG Just try to live your life as if you'd never known me.
MRS. ELVSTED I can't do that.
LØVBORG Try, Thea. Try, if you can. Go back home.
MRS. ELVSTED [*Defiantly.*] Where you are, that's where I want to be. I won't let myself be just driven off like this. I want to stay at your side—be with you when the book comes out.
HEDDA [*Half aloud, tensely.*] Ah, the book—Yes.
LØVBORG [*Looking at her.*] Mine and Thea's, because that's what it is.
MRS. ELVSTED Yes, that's what I feel it is. That's why I have a right to be with you when it comes out. I want to see you covered in honor and glory again, and the joy. I want to share that with you too.
LØVBORG Thea—our book's never coming out.
HEDDA Ah!
MRS. ELVSTED Never coming out?
LØVBORG It can't ever come out.
MRS. ELVSTED [*In anxious foreboding.*] Løvborg, what have you done with the manuscript?
HEDDA [*Looking intently at him.*] Yes, the manuscript—?
MRS. ELVSTED What have you—?
LØVBORG Oh, Thea, don't ask me that.
MRS. ELVSTED Yes, yes, I've got to know. I have the right to know.

LØVBORG The manuscript—all right then, the manuscript—I've ripped it up into a thousand pieces.

MRS. ELVSTED [*Screams.*] Oh no, no!

HEDDA [*Involuntarily.*] But that's just not—!

LØVBORG [*Looking at her.*] Not true, you think?

HEDDA [*Controls herself.*] All right then. Of course it is, if you say so. It sounds so ridiculous.

LØVBORG But it's true, just the same.

MRS. ELVSTED [*Wringing her hands.*] Oh God—oh God, Hedda. Torn his own work to pieces.

LØVBORG I've torn my own life to pieces. I might as well tear up my life's work too—

MRS. ELVSTED And you did that last night!

LØVBORG Yes. Do you hear me? A thousand pieces. Scattered them all over the fjord.[2] Way out where there's pure salt water. Let them drift in it. Drift with the current in the wind. Then, after a while, they'll sink. Deeper and deeper. Like me, Thea.

MRS. ELVSTED You know, Løvborg, all this with the book—? For the rest of my life, it will be just like you'd killed a little child.

LØVBORG You're right. Like murdering a child.

MRS. ELVSTED But then, how could you—! That child was partly mine, too.

HEDDA [*Almost inaudibly.*] Ah, the child—

MRS. ELVSTED [*Sighs heavily.*] So it's finished? All right, Hedda, now I'm going.

HEDDA You're not going back?

MRS. ELVSTED Oh, I don't know what I'm going to do. I can't see anything out in front of me. [*She goes out through the hall doorway.*]

HEDDA [*Standing a while, waiting.*] Don't you want to see her home, Mr. Løvborg?

LØVBORG Through the streets? So that people can get a good look at us together?

HEDDA I don't know what else happened to you last night but if it's so completely beyond redemption—

LØVBORG It won't stop there. I know that much. And I can't bring myself to live that kind of life again either. Not again. Once I had the courage to live life to the fullest, to break every rule. But she's taken that out of me.

HEDDA [*Staring straight ahead.*] That sweet little fool has gotten hold of a human destiny. [*Looks at him.*] And you're so heartless to her.

LØVBORG Don't call it heartless.

HEDDA To go and destroy the thing that has filled her soul for this whole long, long time. You don't call that heartless?

LØVBORG I can tell you the truth, Hedda.

HEDDA The truth?

LØVBORG First, promise me—Give me your word that Thea will never find out what I'm about to confide to you.

2. "Inlet of the sea" (Norwegian).

HEDDA You have my word.

LØVBORG Good. Then I'll tell you—What I stood here and described—It wasn't true.

HEDDA About the manuscript?

LØVBORG Yes. I haven't ripped it up. I didn't throw it in the fjord, either.

HEDDA No, well—so—Where is it?

LØVBORG I've destroyed it just the same. Utterly and completely, Hedda!

HEDDA I don't understand any of this.

LØVBORG Thea said that what I'd done seemed to her like murdering a child.

HEDDA Yes, she did.

LØVBORG But killing his child—that's not the worst thing a father can do to it.

HEDDA Not the worst?

LØVBORG No. And the worst—that is what I wanted to spare Thea from hearing.

HEDDA And what is the worst?

LØVBORG Imagine, Hedda, a man—in the very early hours of the morning—after a wild night of debauchery, came home to the mother of his child and said, "Listen—I've been here and there to this place and that place, and I had our child with me in this place and that place. And the child got away from me. Just got away. The devil knows whose hands it's fallen into, who's got a hold of it."

HEDDA Well—when you get right down to it—it's only a book—

LØVBORG All of Thea's soul was in that book.

HEDDA Yes, I can see that.

LØVBORG And so, you must also see that there's no future for her and me.

HEDDA So, what will your road be now?

LØVBORG None. Only to see to it that I put an end to it all. The sooner the better.

HEDDA [*Comes a step closer.*] Eilert Løvborg—Listen to me now—Can you see to it that—that when you do it, you bathe it in beauty?

LØVBORG In beauty? [*Smiles.*] With vine leaves in my hair, as you used to imagine?

HEDDA Ah, no. No vine leaves—I don't believe in them any longer. But in beauty, yes! For once! Good-bye. You've got to go now. And don't come here any more.

LØVBORG Good-bye, Mrs. Tesman. And give my regards to George Tesman. [*He is about to leave.*]

HEDDA No, wait! Take a souvenir to remember me by.

[*She goes over to the writing table, opens the drawer and the pistol case. She returns to* LØVBORG *with one of the pistols.*]

LØVBORG [*Looks at her.*] That's the souvenir?

HEDDA [*Nodding slowly.*] Do you recognize it? It was aimed at you once.

LØVBORG You should have used it then.

HEDDA Here, you use it now.

LØVBORG [*Puts the pistol in his breast pocket.*] Thanks.

HEDDA In beauty, Eilert Løvborg. Promise me that.

LØVBORG Good-bye, Hedda Gabler. [*He goes out the hall doorway.*]

[HEDDA *listens a moment at the door. Afterward, she goes to the writing table and takes out the package with the manuscript, looks inside the wrapper, pulls some of the pages half out and looks at them. She then takes it all over to the armchair by the stove and sits down. She has the package in her lap. Soon after she opens the stove door and then opens the package.*]

HEDDA [*Throws one of the sheets into the fire and whispers to herself.*] Now, I'm burning your child, Thea—You with your curly hair. [*Throws a few more sheets into the fire.*] Your child and Eilert Løvborg's. [*Throws in the rest.*] Now I'm burning—burning the child.

Act 4

The same room at the TESMANS'. *It is evening. The drawing room is in darkness. The rear room is lit with a hanging lamp over the table. The curtains are drawn across the glass door.*

[HEDDA, *dressed in black, wanders up and down in the darkened room. Then she goes into the rear room, and over to the left side. Some chords are heard from the piano. Then she emerges again, and goes into the drawing room.* BERTA *comes in from the right of the rear room, with a lighted lamp, which she places on the table in front of the sofa, in the salon. Her eyes show signs of crying, and she has black ribbons on her cap. She goes quietly and carefully to the right.* HEDDA *goes over to the glass door, draws the curtains aside a little, and stares out into the darkness. Soon after,* MISS TESMAN *enters from the hallway dressed in black with a hat and a veil.* HEDDA *goes over to her and shakes her hand.*]

MISS TESMAN Yes, here I am, Hedda—in mourning black. My poor sister's struggle is over at last.

HEDDA As you can see, I've already heard. Tesman sent me a note.

MISS TESMAN Yes, he promised he would but I thought I should bring the news myself. This news of death into this house of life.

HEDDA That was very kind of you.

MISS TESMAN Ah, Rina shouldn't have left us right now. Hedda's house is no place for sorrow at a time like this.

HEDDA [*Changing the subject.*] She died peacefully, Miss Tesman?

MISS TESMAN Yes, so gently—Such a peaceful release. And she was happy beyond words that she got to see George once more and could say a proper good-bye to him. Is it possible he's not home yet?

HEDDA No. He wrote saying I shouldn't expect him too early. But, please sit down.

MISS TESMAN No, thank you, my dear—blessed Hedda. I'd like to, but I have so little time. She'll be dressed and arranged the best that I can. She'll look really splendid when she goes to her grave.

HEDDA Can I help you with anything?

MISS TESMAN Oh, don't even think about it. These kinds of things aren't for Hedda Tesman's hands or her thoughts either. Not at this time. No, no.

HEDDA Ah—thoughts—Now they're not so easy to master—

MISS TESMAN [*Continuing.*] Yes, dear God, that's how this world goes. Over at my house we'll be sewing a linen shroud for Aunt Rina, and here there will be sewing too, but of a whole different kind, praise God.

[GEORGE TESMAN *enters through a hall door.*]

HEDDA Well, it's good you're finally here.

TESMAN You here, Aunt Julie, with Hedda. Just think.

MISS TESMAN I was just about to go, my dear boy. Well. Did you manage to finish everything you promised to?

TESMAN No, I'm afraid I've forgotten half of it. I have to run over there tomorrow again. Today my brain is just so confused. I can't keep hold of two thoughts in a row.

MISS TESMAN George, my dear, you mustn't take it like that.

TESMAN Oh? How should I take it, do you think?

MISS TESMAN You must be joyful in your sorrow. You must be glad for what has happened, just as I am.

TESMAN Ah, yes. You're thinking of Aunt Rina.

HEDDA You'll be lonely now, Miss Tesman.

MISS TESMAN For the first few days, yes. But that won't last long, I hope. Our sainted Rina's little room won't stand empty. That much I know.

TESMAN Really? Who'll be moving in there, hm?

MISS TESMAN Oh, there's always some poor invalid or other who needs care and attention, unfortunately.

HEDDA You'd really take on a cross like that again?

MISS TESMAN Cross? God forgive you child. It's not a cross for me.

HEDDA But a complete stranger—

MISS TESMAN It's easy to make friends with sick people. And I so badly need someone to live for. Well, God be praised and thanked—there'll be a thing or two to keep an old aunt busy here in this house soon enough.

HEDDA Oh, please don't think about us.

TESMAN Yes. The three of us could be quite cozy here if only—

HEDDA If only—?

TESMAN [*Uneasily.*] Oh, it's nothing. Everything'll be fine. Let's hope, hm?

MISS TESMAN Well, well, you two have plenty to talk about, I'm sure. [*Smiling.*] And Hedda may have something to tell you, George. Now it's home to Rina. [*Turning in the doorway.*] Dear Lord, isn't it strange to think about. Now Rina's both with me and our sainted Joseph.

TESMAN Yes, just think, Aunt Julie, hm?

[MISS TESMAN *leaves through the hall door.*]

HEDDA [*Follows* TESMAN *with cold, searching eyes.*] I think all this has hit you harder than your aunt.

TESMAN Oh, it's not just this death. It's Eilert I'm worried about.

HEDDA [*Quickly.*] Any news?

TESMAN I wanted to run to him this afternoon and tell him that his manuscript was safe—in good hands.

HEDDA Oh? Did you find him?

TESMAN No, he wasn't home. But later I met Mrs. Elvsted, and she told me he'd been here early this morning.

HEDDA Yes, just after you left.

TESMAN And apparently he said that he'd ripped the manuscript up into a thousand pieces, hm?

HEDDA That's what he said.

TESMAN But, good God, he must have been absolutely crazy. So you didn't dare give it back to him, Hedda?

HEDDA No, he didn't get it back.

TESMAN But, you told him we had it?

HEDDA No. [*Quickly.*] Did you tell Mrs. Elvsted?

TESMAN No, I didn't want to. But you should have told him. What would happen if in his desperation he went and did something to himself? Let me have the manuscript, Hedda. I'll run it over to him right away. Where did you put it?

HEDDA [*Cold and impassively leaning on the armchair.*] I don't have it any more.

TESMAN Don't have it! What in the world do you mean?

HEDDA I burned it up—every page.

TESMAN [*Leaps up in terror.*] Burned? Burned? Eilert's manuscript!

HEDDA Don't shout like that. The maid will hear you.

TESMAN Burned! But good God—! No, no, no—That's absolutely impossible.

HEDDA Yes, but all the same it's true.

TESMAN Do you have any idea what you've done, Hedda? That's—that's criminal appropriation of lost property. Think about that. Yes, just ask Judge Brack, then you'll see.

HEDDA Then it's probably wise for you not to talk about it, isn't it? To the Judge or anyone else.

TESMAN How could you have gone and done something so appalling? What came over you? Answer me that, Hedda, hm?

HEDDA [*Suppressing an almost imperceptible smile.*] I did it for your sake, George.

TESMAN My sake?

HEDDA Remember you came home this morning and talked about how he had read to you?

TESMAN Yes, yes.

HEDDA You confessed that you envied him.

TESMAN Good God, I didn't mean it literally.

HEDDA Nevertheless, I couldn't stand the idea that someone would over shadow you.

TESMAN [*Exclaiming between doubt and joy.*] Hedda—Oh, is this true?—What you're saying?—Yes, but. Yes, but. I never noticed that you loved me this way before. Think of that!

HEDDA Well, you need to know—that at a time like this—[*Violently breaking off.*] No, no—go and ask your Aunt Julie. She'll provide all the details.

TESMAN Oh, I almost think I understand you, Hedda. [*Clasps his hands together.*] No, good God—Can it be, hm?

HEDDA Don't shout like that. The maid can hear you.

TESMAN [*Laughing in extraordinary joy.*] The maid! Oh, Hedda, you are priceless. The maid—why it's—why it's Berta. I'll go tell Berta myself.

HEDDA [*Clenching her hands as if frantic.*] Oh, I'm dying—Dying of all this.

TESMAN All what, Hedda, what?

HEDDA [*Coldly controlled again.*] All this—absurdity—George.

TESMAN Absurdity? I'm so incredibly happy. Even so, maybe I shouldn't say anything to Berta.

HEDDA Oh yes, go ahead. Why not?

TESMAN No, no. Not right now. But Aunt Julie, yes, absolutely. And then, you're calling me George. Just think. Oh, Aunt Julie will be so happy—so happy.

HEDDA When she hears I've burned Eilert Løvborg's manuscript for your sake?

TESMAN No, no, you're right. All this with the manuscript. No. Of course, nobody can find out about that. But, Hedda—you're burning for me—Aunt Julie really must share in that. But I wonder—all this—I wonder if it's typical with young wives, hm?

HEDDA You'd better ask Aunt Julie about that too.

TESMAN Oh yes, I certainly will when I get the chance. [*Looking uneasy and thoughtful again.*] No, but, oh no, the manuscript. Good Lord, it's awful to think about poor Eilert, just the same.

[MRS. ELVSTED, *dressed as for her first visit with hat and coat, enters through the hall door.*]

MRS. ELVSTED [*Greets them hurriedly and speaks in agitation.*] Oh, Hedda, don't be offended that I've come back again.

HEDDA What happened to you, Thea?

TESMAN Something about Eilert Løvborg?

MRS. ELVSTED Oh yes, I'm terrified that he's had an accident.

HEDDA [*Grips her arm.*] Ah, do you think so?

TESMAN Good Lord, where did you get that idea, Mrs. Elvsted?

MRS. ELVSTED I heard them talking at the boarding house—just as I came in. There are the most incredible rumors about him going around town today.

TESMAN Oh yes, imagine, I heard them too. And still I can swear he went straight home to sleep. Just think.

HEDDA So—What were they saying at the boarding house?

MRS. ELVSTED Oh, I couldn't get any details, either because they didn't know or—or they saw me and stopped talking. And I didn't dare ask.

TESMAN [*Uneasily pacing the floor.*] Let's just hope—you misunderstood.

MRS. ELVSTED No, I'm sure they were talking about him. Then I heard them say something about the hospital—

TESMAN Hospital?

HEDDA No—That's impossible.

MRS. ELVSTED I'm deathly afraid for him, so I went up to his lodgings and asked about him there.

HEDDA You dared to do that?

MRS. ELVSTED What else should I have done? I couldn't stand the uncertainty any longer.

TESMAN You didn't find him there either, hm?

MRS. ELVSTED No. And the people there didn't know anything at all. They said he hadn't been home since yesterday afternoon.

TESMAN Yesterday? How could they say that?

MRS. ELVSTED It could only mean one thing—Something terrible's happened to him.

TESMAN You know, Hedda—What if I were to go into town and ask around at different places—?

HEDDA No! You stay out of this.

[JUDGE BRACK, *carrying his hat, enters through the hall door, which* BERTA *opens and closes after him. He looks serious and bows in silence.*]

TESMAN Oh, here you are, Judge, hm?

BRACK Yes, it was essential for me to see you this evening.

TESMAN I see you got the message from Aunt Julie.

BRACK Yes, that too.

TESMAN Isn't it sad, hm?

BRACK Well, my dear Tesman, that depends on how you look at it.

TESMAN [*Looks at him uneasily.*] Has anything else happened?

BRACK Yes, it has.

HEDDA [*Tensely.*] Something sad, Judge Brack?

BRACK Once again, it depends on how you look at it, Mrs. Tesman.

MRS. ELVSTED [*In an uncontrollable outburst.*] It's Eilert Løvborg.

BRACK [*Looks briefly at her.*] How did you guess, Mrs. Elvsted? Do you already know something—?

MRS. ELVSTED [*Confused.*] No, no, I don't know anything but—

TESMAN Well, for God's sake, tell us what it is.

BRACK [*Shrugging his shoulders.*] Well then—I'm sorry to tell you—that Eilert Løvborg has been taken to the hospital. He is dying.

MRS. ELVSTED [*Crying out.*] Oh God, oh God.

TESMAN Dying?

HEDDA [*Involuntarily.*] So quickly—?

MRS. ELVSTED [*Wailing.*] And we were quarrelling when we parted, Hedda.

HEDDA [*Whispers.*] Now, Thea—Thea.

MRS. ELVSTED [*Not noticing her.*] I'm going to him. I've got to see him alive.

BRACK It would do you no good, Mrs. Elvsted. No visitors are allowed.

MRS. ELVSTED At least tell me what happened. What—?

TESMAN Yes, because he certainly wouldn't have tried to—hm?

HEDDA Yes, I'm sure that's what he did.

TESMAN Hedda. How can you—

BRACK [*Who is watching her all the time.*] Unfortunately, Mrs. Tesman, you've guessed right.

MRS. ELVSTED Oh, how awful.

TESMAN To himself, too. Think of it.

HEDDA Shot himself!

BRACK Right again, Mrs. Tesman.

MRS. ELVSTED [*Tries to compose herself.*] When did this happen, Mr. Brack?

BRACK Just this afternoon, between three and four.

TESMAN Oh, my God—Where did he do it, hm?

BRACK [*Slightly uncertain.*] Where? Oh, I suppose at his lodgings.

MRS. ELVSTED No, that can't be. I was there between six and seven.

BRACK Well then, some other place. I don't know precisely. All I know is that he was found—he'd shot himself—in the chest.

MRS. ELVSTED Oh, how awful to think that he should die like that.

HEDDA [*To* BRACK.] In the chest?

BRACK Yes, like I said.

HEDDA Not through the temple?

BRACK The chest, Mrs. Tesman.

HEDDA Well, well. The chest is also good.

BRACK What was that, Mrs. Tesman?

HEDDA [*Evasively.*] Oh, nothing—nothing.

TESMAN And the wound is fatal, hm?

BRACK The wound is absolutely fatal. In fact, it's probably already over.

MRS. ELVSTED Yes, yes, I can feel it. It's over. It's all over. Oh, Hedda—!

TESMAN Tell me, how did you find out about all this?

BRACK [*Curtly.*] From a police officer. One I spoke with.

HEDDA [*Raising her voice.*] Finally—an action.

TESMAN God help us, Hedda, what are you saying?

HEDDA I'm saying that here, in this—there is beauty.

BRACK Uhm, Mrs. Tesman.

TESMAN Beauty! No, don't even think it.

MRS. ELVSTED Oh, Hedda. How can you talk about beauty?

HEDDA Eilert Løvborg has come to terms with himself. He's had the courage to do what had to be done.

MRS. ELVSTED No, don't ever believe it was anything like that. What he did, he did in a moment of madness.

TESMAN It was desperation.

MRS. ELVSTED Yes, madness. Just like when he tore his book in pieces.

BRACK [*Startled.*] The book. You mean his manuscript? Did he tear it up?

MRS. ELVSTED Yes, last night.

TESMAN [*Whispering softly.*] Oh, Hedda, we'll never get out from under all this.

BRACK Hmm, that's very odd.

TESMAN [*Pacing the floor.*] To think that Eilert Løvborg should leave the world this way. And then not to leave behind the work that would have made his name immortal.

MRS. ELVSTED Oh, what if it could be put together again.

TESMAN Yes—just think—what if it could? I don't know what I wouldn't give—

MRS. ELVSTED Maybe it can, Mr. Tesman.

TESMAN What do you mean?

MRS. ELVSTED [*Searching in the pocket of her skirt.*] See this? I saved all the notes he dictated from.

HEDDA [*A step closer.*] Ah.

TESMAN You saved them, Mrs. Elvsted, hm?

MRS. ELVSTED Yes, they're all here. I brought them with me when I came to town, and here they've been. Tucked away in my pocket—

TESMAN Oh, let me see them.

MRS. ELVSTED [*Gives him a bundle of small papers.*] But they're all mixed up, completely out of order.

TESMAN Just think. What if we could sort them out. Perhaps if the two of us helped each other.

MRS. ELVSTED Oh yes. Let's at least give it a try—

TESMAN It will happen. It must happen. I'll give my whole life to this.

HEDDA You, George, your life?

TESMAN Yes, or, anyway, all the time I have. Every spare minute. My own research will just have to be put aside. Hedda—you understand, don't you, hm? I owe this to Eilert's memory.

HEDDA Maybe so.

TESMAN Now, my dear Mrs. Elvsted, let's pull ourselves together. God knows there's no point brooding about what's happened. We've got to try to find some peace of mind so that—

MRS. ELVSTED Yes, yes, Mr. Tesman. I'll do my best.

TESMAN Well. So, come along then. We've got to get started on these notes right away. Where should we sit? Here? No. In the back room. Excuse us, Judge. Come with me, Mrs. Elvsted.

MRS. ELVSTED Oh God—if only it can be done.

[TESMAN *and* MRS. ELVSTED *go into the rear room. She takes her hat and coat off. Both sit at the table under the hanging lamp and immerse themselves in eager examination of the papers. Hedda goes across to the stove and sits in the armchair. Soon after,* BRACK *goes over to her.*]

HEDDA [*Softly.*] Ah, Judge—This act of Eilert Løvborg's—there's a sense of liberation in it.

BRACK Liberation, Mrs. Hedda? Yes, I guess it's a liberation for him, all right.

HEDDA I mean, for me. It's a liberation for me to know that in this world an act of such courage, done in full, free will, is possible. Something bathed in a bright shaft of sudden beauty.

BRACK [*Smiles.*] Hmm—Dear Mrs. Hedda—

HEDDA Oh, I know what you're going to say, because you're a kind of specialist too, after all, just like—Ah well.

BRACK [*Looking steadily at her.*] Eilert Løvborg meant more to you than you might admit—even to yourself. Or am I wrong?

HEDDA I don't answer questions like that. All I know is that Eilert Løvborg had the courage to live life his own way, and now—his last great act—bathed in beauty. He—had the will to break away from the banquet of life—so soon.

BRACK It pains me, Mrs. Hedda—but I'm forced to shatter this pretty illusion of yours.

HEDDA Illusion?

BRACK Which would have been taken away from you soon enough.

HEDDA And what's that?

BRACK He didn't shoot himself—so freely.

HEDDA Not freely?

BRACK No. This whole Eilert Løvborg business didn't come off exactly the way I described it.

HEDDA [*In suspense.*] Are you hiding something? What is it?

BRACK I employed a few euphemisms for poor Mrs. Elvsted's sake.
HEDDA Such as—?
BRACK First, of course, he's already dead.
HEDDA At the hospital?
BRACK Yes. And without regaining consciousness.
HEDDA What else?
BRACK The incident took place somewhere other than his room.
HEDDA That's insignificant.
BRACK Not completely. I have to tell you—Eilert Løvborg was found shot in—Miss Diana's boudoir.
HEDDA [*About to jump up but sinks back again.*] That's impossible, Judge. He can't have gone there again today.
BRACK He was there this afternoon. He came to demand the return of something that he said they'd taken from him. He talked crazily about a lost child.
HEDDA Ah, so that's why—
BRACK I thought maybe he was referring to his manuscript but I hear he'd already destroyed that himself so I guess it was his pocketbook.
HEDDA Possibly. So—that's where he was found.
BRACK Right there, with a discharged pistol in his coat pocket, and a fatal bullet wound.
HEDDA In the chest, yes?
BRACK No—lower down.
HEDDA [*Looks up at him with an expression of revulsion.*] That too! Oh absurdity—! It hangs like a curse over everything I so much as touch.
BRACK There's still one more thing, Mrs. Hedda. Also in the ugly category.
HEDDA And what is that?
BRACK The pistol he had with him—
HEDDA [*Breathless.*] Well, what about it?
BRACK He must have stolen it.
HEDDA [*Jumping up.*] Stolen? That's not true. He didn't.
BRACK There's no other explanation possible. He must have stolen it—Shh.

[TESMAN *and* MRS. ELVSTED *have gotten up from the table in the rear room and come into the living room.*]

TESMAN [*With papers in both hands.*] Hedda, my dear—I can hardly see anything in there under that lamp. Just think—
HEDDA I'm thinking.
TESMAN Do you think you might let us sit a while at your desk, hm?
HEDDA Oh, gladly. [*Quickly.*] No, wait. Let me just clean it up a bit first.
TESMAN Oh, not necessary, Hedda. There's plenty of room.
HEDDA No, no, I'll just straighten it up, I'm telling you. I'll just move these things here under the piano for a while.

[*She has pulled an object covered with sheet music out of the bookcase. She adds a few more sheets and carries the whole pile out to the left of the rear room.* TESMAN *puts the papers on the desk and brings over the lamp from the corner table. He and* MRS. ELVSTED *sit and continue their work.*]

HEDDA Well, Thea, my sweet. Are things moving along with the memorial?
MRS. ELVSTED [*Looks up at her dejectedly.*] Oh, God—It's going to be so difficult to find the order in all of this.

TESMAN But it must be done. There's simply no other choice. And finding the order in other people's papers—that's precisely what I'm meant for.

[HEDDA *goes over to the stove and sits on one of the stools.* BRACK *stands over her, leaning over the armchair.*]

HEDDA [*Whispers.*] What were you saying about the pistol?

BRACK [*Softly.*] That he must have stolen it.

HEDDA Why stolen exactly?

BRACK Because there shouldn't be any other way to explain it, Mrs. Hedda.

HEDDA I see.

BRACK [*Looks briefly at her.*] Eilert Løvborg was here this morning, am I correct?

HEDDA Yes.

BRACK Were you alone with him?

HEDDA Yes, for a while.

BRACK You didn't leave the room at all while he was here?

HEDDA No.

BRACK Think again. Weren't you out of the room, even for one moment?

HEDDA Yes. Perhaps. Just for a moment—out in the hallway.

BRACK And where was your pistol case at that time?

HEDDA I put it under the—

BRACK Well, Mrs. Hedda—

HEDDA It was over there on the writing table.

BRACK Have you looked since then to see if both pistols are there?

HEDDA No.

BRACK It's not necessary. I saw the pistol Løvborg had, and I recognized it immediately from yesterday, and from before as well.

HEDDA Have you got it?

BRACK No, the police have it.

HEDDA What will the police do with that pistol?

BRACK Try to track down its owner.

HEDDA Do you think they can do that?

BRACK [*Bends over her and whispers.*] No, Hedda Gabler, not as long as I keep quiet.

HEDDA [*Looking fearfully at him.*] And what if you don't keep quiet—then what?

BRACK Then the way out is to claim that the pistol was stolen.

HEDDA I'd rather die.

BRACK [*Smiling.*] People make those threats but they don't act on them.

HEDDA [*Without answering.*] So—let's say the pistol is not stolen and the owner is found out? What happens then?

BRACK Well, Hedda—then there'll be a scandal.

HEDDA A scandal?

BRACK Oh, yes, a scandal. Just what you're so desperately afraid of. You'd have to appear in court, naturally. You and Miss Diana. She'd have to detail how it all occurred. Whether it was an accident or a homicide. Was he trying to draw the pistol to threaten her? Is that when the gun went off? Did she snatch it out of his hands to shoot him, and then put the pistol back in his pocket? That would be thoroughly in character for her. She's a feisty little thing, that Miss Diana.

HEDDA But all this ugliness has got nothing to do with me.

BRACK No. But you would have to answer one question. Why did you give the pistol to Eilert Løvborg? And what conclusions would people draw from the fact that you gave it to him?

HEDDA [*Lowers her head.*] That's true. I didn't think of that.

BRACK Well. Fortunately you have nothing to worry about as long as I keep quiet.

HEDDA [*Looking up at him.*] So I'm in your power now, Judge. You have a hold over me from now on.

BRACK [*Whispering more softly.*] Dearest Hedda—Believe me—I won't abuse my position.

HEDDA But in your power. Totally subject to your demands—And your will. Not free. Not free at all. [*She gets up silently.*] No, that's one thought I just can't stand. Never!

BRACK [*Looks mockingly at her.*] One can usually learn to live with the inevitable.

HEDDA [*Returning his look.*] Maybe so. [*She goes over to the writing table, suppressing an involuntary smile and imitating* TESMAN's *intonation.*] Well, George, this is going to work out, hm?

TESMAN Oh, Lord knows, dear. Anyway, at this rate, it's going to be months of work.

HEDDA [*As before.*] No, just think. [*Runs her fingers lightly through* MRS. ELVSTED's *hair.*] Doesn't it seem strange, Thea. Here you are, sitting together with Tesman—just like you used to sit with Eilert Løvborg.

MRS. ELVSTED Oh, God, if only I could inspire your husband too.

HEDDA Oh, that will come—in time.

TESMAN Yes, you know what, Hedda—I really think I'm beginning to feel something like that. But why don't you go over and sit with Judge Brack some more.

HEDDA Can't you two find any use for me here?

TESMAN No, nothing in the world. [*Turning his head.*] From now on, my dear Judge, you'll have to be kind enough to keep Hedda company.

BRACK [*With a glance at* HEDDA.] That will be an infinite pleasure for me.

HEDDA Thanks, but I'm tired tonight. I'll go in there and lie down on the sofa for a while.

TESMAN Yes, do that, Hedda, hm?

[HEDDA *goes into the rear room and draws the curtains after her. Short pause. Suddenly she is heard to play a wild dance melody on the piano.*]

MRS. ELVSTED [*Jumping up from her chair.*] Oh—what's that?

TESMAN [*Running to the doorway.*] Oh, Hedda, my dear—Don't play dance music tonight. Just think of poor Aunt Rina and of Eilert Løvborg too.

HEDDA [*Putting her head out from between the curtains.*] And Aunt Julie and all the rest of them too. From now on I shall be quiet. [*She closes the curtains again.*]

TESMAN [*At the writing table.*] This can't be making her very happy—See ing us at this melancholy work. You know what, Mrs. Elvsted—You're going to move in with Aunt Julie. Then I can come over in the evening, and we can sit and work there, hm?

MRS. ELVSTED Yes, maybe that would be the best—

HEDDA [*From the rear room.*] I can hear you perfectly well, Tesman. So, how am I supposed to get through the evenings out here?

TESMAN [*Leafing through the papers.*] Oh, I'm sure Judge Brack will be good enough to call on you.

BRACK [*In the armchair, shouts merrily.*] I'd be delighted, Mrs. Tesman. Every evening. Oh, we're going to have some good times together, the two of us.

HEDDA [*Loudly and clearly.*] Yes, that's what you're hoping for, isn't it, Judge? You, the one and only cock of the walk—

[*A shot is heard within.* TESMAN, MRS. ELVSTED *and* BRACK *all jump to their feet.*]

TESMAN Oh, she's playing around with those pistols again.

[*He pulls the curtains aside and runs in.* MRS. ELVSTED *follows.* HEDDA *is stretched out lifeless on the sofa. Confusion and cries.* BERTA *comes running in from the right.*]

[*Shrieking to* BRACK.] Shot herself! Shot herself in the temple! Just think!

BRACK [*Half prostrate in the armchair.*] But God have mercy—People just don't act that way!

END OF PLAY

JOAQUIM MARIA MACHADO DE ASSIS

1839–1908

No one could have predicted that Joaquim Maria Machado de Assis would become Brazil's greatest writer. Born the grandson of freed slaves in a dilapidated corner of Rio de Janeiro, subject to fits of epilepsy, afflicted with a pronounced stutter, and having no more than an elementary school education, this man of color became the first president of Brazil's Academy of Letters and one of the most innovative, playful, and technically adventurous writers of the whole nineteenth century. Particularly skilled at revealing gaps between high-flown rhetoric and bleak reality, Machado—as he is called—used his fiction to expose hypocrisy and pretension at the heart of Brazilian society.

Machado's father was a housepainter of mixed race, his mother a white Portuguese woman who died when he was a small child. He taught himself largely by listening in on lessons at a girls' school where his stepmother worked in the kitchen. In his early teens he took a job as an apprentice printer and began to write for publication. By the age of twenty-five he was a literary star, having established himself as an editor, translator, poet, and writer of criticism and drama. Elegant, reserved, and courteous, he was happily married to the sister of a close poet friend. Despite his literary success, he took bureaucratic posts in the Brazilian government to ensure a steady income.

Machado eventually became best known for his novels and short stories, which in the 1880s broke with all established schools and styles. Drawing on a huge range of influences that included Shakespeare and **Jonathan Swift**, Machado often anticipated twentieth-century Modernist fiction by experimenting with unreliable narrators and mischievous addresses to the reader. But he also expanded the possibilities of realism, exploring the complex psychology and social structures of modern urban life.

The city of Rio de Janeiro was an especially strange and frustrating place to live in the late nineteenth century. Brazil abolished slavery only in 1888, when Machado was forty-nine years old—the last country in the Americas to do so. Over the previous three centuries Brazil had brought in four and a half million Africans, more slaves than any other nation in the New World. Even very poor people—some of them free blacks—often owned a slave or two. The social life of Rio de Janeiro looked quite peculiar to nineteenth-century observers: its elite class turned to Europe for fashion and ideas, imitating especially the upper classes in France and Britain; its "middle class" was typically quite poor, composed of white immigrants from Europe and free black workers; and the whole city was propped up by slave labor.

Machado, more than any of his contemporaries, set out to expose the attitudes and the lies that sustained this lopsided society. Slavery often remains on the margins of Machado's work, but he had a longstanding fascination with questions of authority and control. How do people wield power? Why do others submit? "The Cane" (1891), our selection below, follows a subtle chain of influence, as a young seminary student tries to figure out how to escape a career in the priesthood. He locates his best chance of help in his godfather's mistress, who herself is eager to show her power over both her lover and her slaves. As the main character is torn between ideals of justice and compassion on the one hand and a desire to realize his own freedom on the other, Machado reveals the subtle and conflicting sources of power at work organizing Brazilian society.

The Cane[1]

Damião ran away from the seminary at eleven o'clock on a Friday morning in August. I don't know which year it was exactly, but certainly before 1850.[2] After only a few minutes, he stopped running, suddenly filled with embarrassment. He had not considered how people might react to the sight of a fleeing, frightened seminarian. Being unfamiliar with the streets, he walked aimlessly up and down, and finally stopped. Where could he go? He could not go home, because, his father, after giving him a sound beating, would send him straight back to the seminary. He had not planned where exactly he might take refuge, because he had intended making his escape at some later date; however, a chance incident had precipitated his departure. Where could

1. Translated by Margaret Jull Costa.
2. The end of the international slave trade in Brazil.

he go? There was his godfather, João Carneiro, but he was a spineless creature, incapable of doing anything on his own initiative. He had been the one to take him to the seminary in the first place, presenting him to the rector with these words:

"I bring you a great man of the future."

"We welcome great men," the rector said, "as long as they are humble and good. True greatness lies in simplicity. Come in, boy."

That had been his introduction to the seminary. Shortly afterwards, he had run away. We see him now standing in the street, frightened, uncertain, not knowing where to turn for shelter or advice; in his mind, he reviewed his various relatives and friends, but none seemed quite right. Then a thought occurred to him:

"I'll appeal to Sinhá[3] Rita! She'll send for my godfather and tell him she wants me to leave the seminary. Perhaps that way . . ."

Sinhá Rita was a widow and João Carneiro's mistress. Damião had a vague understanding of what this meant, and it occurred to him that he might be able to take advantage of the situation. But where did she live? He was so disoriented that it took him a few minutes to find the house, which was in Largo do Capim.[4]

"Good heavens! Whatever's the matter?" cried Sinhá Rita, sitting bolt upright on the sofa on which she was reclining.

Damião had burst in unannounced, looking utterly terrified, for when he reached Sinhá Rita's house, he saw a priest coming down the street, and, in sheer panic, he violently pushed open the Sinhá Rita's front door, which, fortunately for him, was neither locked nor bolted. Once inside, he peered through the shutters to watch the priest, who had clearly failed to notice him and walked on by.

"Whatever's the matter, Senhor Damião?" she said again, for she had recognized him now. "What are *you* doing here?"

Damião, who was trembling so much he could barely speak, told her not to be afraid, it was nothing very important and he would explain everything.

"All right, sit down and explain yourself then."

"First, I swear that I haven't committed a crime of any kind . . ."

Sinhá Rita stared at him in alarm, and all the young girls in the room—boarders and day pupils—froze over their lace-making pillows, their bobbins and hands suddenly motionless. Sinhá Rita earned her living largely from teaching lace-making, cut-work, and embroidery. While the boy was catching his breath, she ordered the girls to go back to their tasks, while she waited for Damião to speak. Finally, he told her everything, about how much he hated the seminary and how he was certain he would not make a good priest. He spoke with great passion and begged her to save him.

"But how? I can't do anything."

"You could if you wanted to."

"No," she said, shaking her head, "I'm not getting involved in family matters, besides, I hardly know your family, and they say your father has a very nasty temper on him!"

3. Variant of Portuguese word *senhora*, or "mistress"; used by slaves as a form of address.

4. Street in Rio de Janeiro where there was a hangman's scaffold and a slave cemetery.

Damião saw that he was lost. In desperation, he knelt at her feet and kissed her hands.

"Please help me, Sinhá Rita. Please, for the love of God, by everything you hold most sacred, by the soul of your late husband, save me from death, because I will kill myself if I have to go back."

Flattered by the boy's pleas, Sinhá Rita tried to reason with him. The life of a priest was a very holy and pleasant one, she said; in time, he would see that it was best to overcome his dislike of the seminary and then, one day . . .

"No, never!" insisted Damião, shaking his head and again kissing her hands and saying it would be the death of him.

Sinhá Rita hesitated for a while longer. Then she asked why he could not speak to his godfather.

"My godfather? He's even worse than Papa. He never listens to me. I shouldn't think he listens to anyone . . ."

"Doesn't listen, eh?" Sinhá Rita responded, her pride wounded. "I'll show you if he listens or not."

She summoned a slave-boy and ordered him to go straight to Senhor João Carneiro's house, and if the gentleman wasn't at home, then he should ask where he could be found and run and tell him that she needed to speak to him urgently.

"Off you go."

Damião sighed loudly and sadly. To justify the authority with which she had issued these orders, she explained to him that Senhor João Carneiro had been a friend of her late husband and had brought her several new pupils. Then, when he remained leaning in the doorway, looking glum, she tweaked his nose and said, smiling:

"Don't you worry, my little priest, it'll all be fine."

According to her birth certificate, Sinhá Rita was forty years old, but her eyes were only twenty-seven. She was a handsome, lively woman, who enjoyed both her food and a joke; however, when she had a mind to, she could be extremely fierce. She tried to cheer the boy up and, despite the situation, this did not prove difficult. Soon they were both laughing; she was telling him stories and asking him to reciprocate, which he did with considerable humour. One particularly extravagant tale, which required him to pull funny faces, made one of Sinhá Rita's pupils laugh so much that she neglected her work. Sinhá Rita picked up a cane lying next to the sofa and threatened her:

"Remember the cane, Lucrécia!"

The girl bowed her head, waiting for the blow, but the blow did not come. It had only been a warning. If, by the evening, she had not finished her work, then Lucrécia would receive the usual punishment. Damião looked at her; she was a scrawny little black girl, all skin and bone, with a scar on her forehead and a burn mark on her left hand. She was about eleven years old. Damião noticed, too, that she kept coughing, quietly, as if not wanting to disturb their conversation. He felt sorry for her and decided to take her side if she did not finish her work. Sinhá Rita would be sure to forgive her . . . Besides, she had been laughing at *him*, so it was his fault, if being funny can be a fault.

At this point, João Carneiro arrived. He blanched when he saw his godson there and looked at Sinhá Rita, who came straight to the point. She told him he had to remove the boy from the seminary, that the child had no vocation for the ecclesiastical life, and it was far better to have no priest at all than a bad priest. One could just as easily love and serve Our Lord in the outside world. For the first few minutes, João Carneiro was too taken aback to reply; in the end, however, he did open his mouth to scold his godson for coming and bothering "complete strangers" and threatened him with punishment.

"What do you mean 'punishment'!" Sinhá Rita broke in. "Punish him for what? Go on, talk to his father."

"I can't promise anything, in fact, I think it's highly unlikely, if not impossible . . ."

"Well, I'm telling you that it has to be possible. If you really try," she went on in a rather insinuating tone, "I'm sure you can sort something out. You just have to ask nicely and he'll give in. Because, Senhor João Carneiro, your godson is not going back to the seminary."

"But, Senhora . . ."

"Go on, off you go."

João Carneiro did not want to go, but neither could he stay. He was caught between two opposing forces. He really didn't care if the boy ended up being a cleric, a lawyer or a doctor, or something else entirely, however useless, but he was being asked to do battle with the father's deepest feelings and could not guarantee the result. If he failed, that would mean another battle with Sinhá Rita, whose final words had a threatening note to them: "your godson is not going back to the seminary." Either way, there was sure to be a ruckus. João Carneiro stood there, wide-eyed, his eyelids twitching, his chest heaving. He kept shooting pleading glances at Sinhá Rita, glances in which there was just a hint of censure. Why couldn't she ask him for something else, anything? Why couldn't she ask him to walk in the rain all the way to Tijuca or Jacarepaguá?[5] But to persuade a father to change his mind about his son's career . . . He knew the boy's father well, and knew that he was perfectly capable of smashing a glass in his face. Ah, if only the boy would just drop down dead of an apoplectic fit! That would be a solution—cruel, yes, but final.

"What do you say?" demanded Sinhá Rita.

He made a gesture as if asking for more time. He stroked his beard, looking for some way out. A papal decree dissolving the Church or, at the very least, abolishing all seminaries, that would do the trick. João Carneiro could then go home and enjoy a quiet game of cards. It was like asking Napoleon's barber to lead the battle of Austerlitz . . . [6] Alas, the Church was still there, so were the seminaries, and his godson was still standing waiting by the wall, eyes downcast, with no convenient apoplectic fit in sight.

"Go on, off you go," said Sinhá Rita, handing him his hat and cane.

There was nothing for it. The barber put away his razor, buckled on his sword, and went off to battle. Damião breathed more easily, although, outwardly, he remained grave-faced, eyes fixed on the floor. This time, Sinhá Rita pinched his chin.

"Come on, don't be so glum, let's have something to eat."

"Do you really think he'll succeed?"

5. Neighborhoods in Rio de Janeiro.
6. In 1805, the defining victory in Napoleon's military career, often considered the height of his tactical genius; Austerlitz is the present-day Slavkov, a town in the Czech Republic.

"He has to," retorted Sinhá Rita proudly. "Come along, the soup's getting cold."

Despite Sinhá Rita's natural joviality and his own naturally playful self, Damião felt less happy over supper than he had earlier on. He had no confidence in his spineless godfather. Nevertheless, he ate well and, towards the end, was once again telling jokes as he had in the morning. Over dessert, he heard the sound of people in the next room, and asked if they had come for him.

"No, it'll be the ladies."

They got up and went into the drawing-room. The "ladies" were five neighbours who came every evening after supper to have coffee with Sinhá Rita and stayed until nightfall.

Once the pupils had finished their supper, they returned to their lace-making pillows. Sinhá Rita presided over this gaggle of women, some of whom were resident and others not. The whisper of bobbins and the chatter of the ladies were such worldly sounds, so far removed from theology and Latin, that the boy let himself be carried along by them and forgot about everything else. At first, the ladies were a little shy, but soon recovered. One of them sang a popular ballad accompanied on the guitar by Sinhá Rita, and the evening passed quickly. Before the soirée ended, Sinhá Rita asked Damião to tell them the story she had particularly liked. The same one that had made Lucrécia laugh.

"Come on, Senhor Damião, don't play hard to get. Our guests are just about to leave. You'll really love this one, ladies."

Damião had no option but to obey. Despite the expectation created by Sinhá Rita's words—which rather diminished the joke and its effect—the story did nevertheless make the ladies laugh. Pleased with himself, Damião glanced over at Lucrécia to see if she had laughed as well, but she had her head bent over her work, intent now on finishing her task. She certainly wasn't laughing, or perhaps only to herself, in the same way as she kept her cough to herself.

The ladies left, and darkness fell. Damião's heart also grew blacker with the onset of night. What would be happening at his father's house? Every few minutes, he went over to peer out of the window, but returned each time feeling more discouraged. No sign of his godfather. His father had doubtless sent him packing, then summoned a couple of slaves and gone to the police station to demand that a constable come with him to arrest his son and take him back to the seminary. Damião asked Sinhá Rita if there was a back entrance to the house and ran out into the garden to see if he could climb over the wall. He also asked if there was an escape route down Rua da Vala or if she could perhaps speak to one of her neighbours, who might be kind enough to take him in. The problem was his cassock: could Sinhá Rita lend him a jacket or an old overcoat? Sinhá Rita did indeed have a jacket, left behind by João Carneiro, either as a souvenir or out of sheer absentmindedness.

"I have an old jacket of my husband's," she said, laughing, "but why are you so frightened? It will all work out, don't you worry."

At last, when night had fallen, a slave arrived bearing a letter for Sinhá Rita from his godfather. No agreement had yet been reached; the father had reacted furiously and tried to smash everything in the room; he had roared out his disapproval, saying that if his lazy rapscallion of a son refused to go back to the seminary, he would have him thrown in jail or sent to the prison ship. João Carneiro had battled very hard to persuade Damião's father not to rush into a decision, but to sleep on it and ponder deeply whether it was right to give the Church such a rebellious, immoral child. He explained in the letter that he had only used such language as a way of winning the argument. Not that he considered the argument won, by any means, but tomorrow he would go and see the man again and try to win him round. He concluded by saying that, meanwhile, the boy could stay at his house.

Damião finished reading the letter and looked at Sinhá Rita. She's my last hope, he thought. Sinhá Rita ordered a bottle of ink to be brought, and she wrote this response on the bottom half of João Carneiro's letter: "My dear Joãozinho,[7] either you save the boy or you'll never see me again." She sealed the letter with glue and gave it to the slave for him to deliver with all speed. She again tried to cheer up the reluctant seminarian, who had again donned the monkish hood of humility and consternation. She told him not to worry, that she would sort things out.

"They'll see what I'm made of! No one's going to get the better of me!"

It was time to collect in the lace work. Sinhá Rita examined each piece, and all the girls had completed their daily task. Only Lucrécia was still at her lace-making pillow, furiously working the bobbins, even though it was too dark to see. Sinhá Rita went over to her, saw that the work was unfinished and flew into a rage, seizing her by one ear.

"You lazy girl!"

"Please, Senhora, please, for the love of God and Our Lady in Heaven."

"You idler! Our Lady doesn't protect good-for-nothings like you!"

Lucrécia broke away and fled the room. Sinhá Rita went after her and caught her by the arm.

"Come here!"

"Please, Senhora, please forgive me!"

"No, I won't forgive you!"

And they came back into the room: Lucrécia dragged along by her ear, struggling and crying and pleading; and Sinhá Rita declaring that she must be punished.

"Where's that cane?"

The cane was next to the sofa. From the other side of the room, Sinhá Rita, not wanting to let the girl go, shouted to Damião.

"Senhor Damião, give me that cane, will you?"

Damião froze. Oh, cruel moment! A kind of cloud passed before his eyes. Had he not sworn to help the young girl, who had, after all, only got behind with her work because of him?

"Give me the cane, Senhor Damião!"

Damião began to walk over to the sofa. The young black girl begged him by all that he held most sacred, his mother, his father, Our Lord . . .

"Help me, sir!"

Sinhá Rita, face aflame, eyes bulging, was demanding the cane, still not letting go of the girl, who was now convulsed by a coughing fit. Damião was terribly touched by her plight, but . . . he had to get out of that seminary. He went over to the sofa, picked up the cane and handed it to Sinhá Rita.

7. Diminutive nickname for João, an endearment.

JOSÉ LÓPEZ PORTILLO Y ROJAS

1850–1923

José López Portillo y Rojas was a Mexican fiction writer, poet, journalist, editor, and law professor. He was also a career politician. Born to a wealthy and prominent family in Guadalajara, Mexico, he studied law and traveled widely as a young man in the United States, Europe and the Middle East. His first book was a travel memoir called *Egypt and Palestine.* He would go on to hold many positions in the Mexican government, including governor of the State of Jalisco and secretary of foreign affairs.

For much of his political career, López Portillo worked in the so-called Porfiriato, the administration of Porfirio Díaz, a military general turned dictator who opened Mexico to foreign investors and imposed a repressive order at home. From 1876 to 1909, Díaz's corrupt regime rewarded his friends and punished his enemies, all the while conserving traditional hierarchies of class and race. One of his mottoes was "*pan o palo*" ("bread or beating"), a choice between accepting the benevolence of the regime and taking violent consequences for refusing. The Díaz administration did encourage the growth of a new urban middle class, but the vast majority of the nation continued to work on rural farms, tilling the fields for a handful of landowners who grew increasingly wealthy under Díaz, even as wages for the workers stagnated.

The Porfiriato came to an end in 1911. Díaz had announced that Mexico was ready for a democratic election. Instead of abiding by the will of the voters, however, he imprisoned his opponent and declared himself the winner. Revolutionary violence broke out across the country, as farm workers, miners, labor unions, discontented elites, and indigenous people rejected the Porfiriato. The Mexican Revolution would last for nearly a decade. It ended in a profound political and economic restructuring of the country, including the passage of a democratic constitution that is still in force today.

The writer's role, according to López Portillo, was to try to convey society as realistically as possible—to hold up a "faithful mirror" to the social world. He praised novelists such as Harriet Beecher Stowe and Charles Dickens for helping to change their societies by revealing their faults. But López Portillo was certainly no revolutionary himself. He thought of his own fiction as improving conditions within the Porfiriato, rather than overturning the whole regime. For him, stability and order were cherished values. He worried that corrupt moral behavior, more than political repression or economic inequality, was preventing the nation from developing.

López Portillo emerged as one of the most important Latin American realists. He and other realists in the region typically focused on the grinding poverty of rural life. In "Unclaimed Watch," however, López Portillo turns to a different social landscape—the self-satisfied world of the urban middle class. Like many other realist fictions around the world, the story is set in the recognizably modern space of the contemporary city; the narrator gives us names of real streets in Mexico City, including 16th of September Street and Plaza de la Constitución, both of which commemorate Mexican independence from Spain. Throughout the story, the author reminds us of an up-to-date urban setting crisscrossed by trolley cars, journalists, and pickpockets.

"Unclaimed Watch" is realist in yet another way as well. López Portillo refuses to give us a heroic central character and instead focuses on the ordinariness of his protagonist—with his bad digestion, his colorful language, and his annoyance toward his wife. The narrator draws attention to the distance between his characters' grand images of themselves—as the brave fighter and the grieving widow—and their much more commonplace reality. And yet he mocks them gently: there remains a loving connection between the husband and wife, and López Portillo shows some sympathy for his characters, despite their shortcomings, rather than demonizing or vilifying them.

The author left not only a powerful literary legacy but also a political legacy. His grandson, José López Portillo y Pacheco, served as president of Mexico from 1976 to 1982.

Unclaimed Watch[1]

I

"The insolence of these reporters is positively unbearable!" exclaimed Judge Felix Zendejas, as he angrily struck the table with the newspaper he had just finished reading.

Don Felix was a middle-aged man, in his thirties or forties; he was overweight, had a round face with a ruddy complexion, a full beard, sparkling eyes, a long nose, bushy eyebrows, and a character that was as vigorous as his facial features. He always spoke at the top of his lungs, and when he discussed something he never discussed it, he preached it dogmatically. He would not tolerate objections; he was always right, or pretended to be so, and if somebody disagreed with him, he'd fly off the handle, the discussion would degenerate into an argument, and soon the argument would wind up in a quarrel. It could be said that the material he was made of was melinite or roburite,[2] since with the slightest amount of friction or jarring he'd become inflamed, would roar like thunder, and then burst into a terrifying conflagration; a dangerous blasting cap disguised as a man.

During the meal, he exchanged few words with his wife Otilia because he had been so absorbed in reading the newspaper, which he had found quite interesting, all the more so because it had hurt his gall bladder; he had such an excitable temper that he was purposely and constantly looking for excuses to blow up.

From his reading, Zendejas came to the conclusion that "these scribbling dogs," as he irreverently called reporters, were continuing every day to denounce robberies, and more robberies, committed in various ways in different parts of the city—all of them alarming in nature because they revealed so precarious a state of affairs in the metropolis which seemed to have been converted into the crossroads of the *camino real*.[3] Assaults on homes were becoming daily

1. Translated by Roberta H. Kimble.
2. Explosive materials.
3. Spanish for "royal road," referring to main roads connecting towns or cities.

occurrences; in plain daylight, in the middle of the street, the bandits performed their escapades, and their audacity had reached such heights that even the center of the city had turned into a stage for their scandalous acts. The paper said they had snatched purses from two or three women and taken bracelets right off other women's arms, and rings right off their fingers; and had ripped a pair of diamond earrings from the blushing lobes of one distinguished woman's precious ears, leaving them split in two, or rather, in four. The repeated perpetrations of these atrocities indicated the existence in Mexico City of a band of ruffians, or rather a tribe of Apaches, and this tribe was thriving in comfort, as though it were operating in the open and unprotected countryside.

After reading through what the paper had to say, Zendejas flew into such a rage that you could have roasted beans on his skin, and with a little more fuel he would have been pawing and snorting like an untamed bull bedecked with *banderillas*.[4]

"We absolutely *must* find some way to put an end to this outrage!" he repeated, pounding the paper with his fist.

His wife, who was used to his perpetual raging, as a salamander is used to living in fire (no doubt by virtue of the law of adaptation to one's surroundings), did not in any way become discouraged when she felt the air around her filled with rumbling and bellowing. She even dared to observe, with perfect calm:

"But, Felix, don't you think that the bandits' insolence is worse than that of the reporters?"

She was about twenty-eight years old, had a dark complexion, graceful movements, dark eyes, and straight hair, with the distinguishing characteristic that she would comb it in a Greek or Roman style, or whatever style occurred to her, but always over her ears in soft waves.

At this remark, her husband cast a look at her that any painter would have represented as flames darting from his pupils; but she didn't worry or get upset over that hot shower with which Zendejas enveloped her, and she calmly continued to sip a cup of tea.

"You, too, Otilia?" shouted the judge in his deep bass voice. "As if these mercenary pens weren't enough to make me rage! The same old tune, every day! Robbery everywhere, all the time. At that rate, there wouldn't be a single person living in the capital who hadn't been held up. . . . Why, not even if there were a hundred thousand thieves packed into this city! If you ask me, it's all a pack of lies that these sensationalist reporters dream up just to boost sales."

"Excuse me, dear, but I don't think it's such a bad idea for reporters to deal with such matters; I find it appropriate and even necessary."

"The fact is, it's a lot of fuss about nothing."

"You don't know that for certain."

"I do know it, and you don't. If things were as bad as these papers claim, there'd be many more arrests of thieves and pickpockets. . . . In my district there have been very few."

"But the number will go up once the police become more active, don't you think so?"

4. Sharp decorative sticks planted in the shoulders of the bull in a bullfight.

"No, I don't think so."

"Time will tell."

Otilia's calm disposition had the virtue of neutralizing the hurricanes and earthquakes raging within Zendejas; which should come as no surprise, since it is a well-known fact that passivity is the best antidote for violence, just as woolen mattresses are for cannon-balls.

"Besides," debated her husband, "do you think it's right for those dogs (the reporters) to make the judges responsible for everything that goes on? Let them skin the policemen alive and eat the police chiefs! But the judges! What have we got to do with all this nonsense? And yet, they won't leave us alone."

"Delayed or twisted justice gives very bad results, Felix."

"I never delay or twist it. Was that comment directed at me?"

"Heaven forbid! I'd never say, or even think, such a thing. I know you are honest and hard-working; but your colleagues. . . . What about your colleagues?"

"My colleagues are . . . the way they are. Some good, some bad."

"So you see, they could use a little prodding."

"Well then, let them prod the others; but why me? Tell me, wife, why is it my fault that in front of the Cathedral after the twelve o'clock Mass they snatched a gaudy pearl necklace from that silly hick mentioned here (pointing to the paper) who had the bad taste to walk around half-choking herself?"

"It's obviously not your fault; but they weren't talking about you in the paper."

"Not me personally, but I feel they're alluding to me when they talk about the corps to which I belong."

"What corps is that? You don't belong to the militia."

"The honorable judicial corps."

"Only in that sense; but that's another matter."

"No, my dear lady, it is not, because when they say such things, when they keep shouting, 'It's the judges' fault. Things are the way they are because they're pardoning dozens of bandits each day!' Or when they shout. 'They're a bunch of good-for-nothings! Criminal cases are sleeping as soundly as the just.' When they start saying things like that, everyone who's a judge must take up the cudgel. Furthermore, all you need is a little common sense to realize that these attacks are absurd. We're pardoning dozens of bandits each day, are we? Let's just suppose it's the truth. Well then, how can you say criminal cases are sleeping soundly? If there are daily pardons, obviously the criminal cases are not sleeping soundly. On the other hand, if the criminal cases are sleeping soundly, that's unjust, so how can you say they are sleeping soundly as the just? These reporters are a bunch of idiots who don't know what they're talking about."

Don Felix reached the depths of resorting to the minutiae of dialectic in order to give vent to his anger; he moved from one point to another; he complicated and confused matters; but that didn't bother him at all; what was important for him was to cut, to split, to chop, and to smash, just like a stampeding buffalo in the jungle.

"You are right about that," answered his wife. "The paragraph is very badly written."

"You admit I'm right?"

"Indirectly; but don't get upset over such a small matter. Do your duty; don't pardon the guilty, work diligently, and just let the world go on spinning."

"I already do all that, woman, without your telling me. I don't need anyone to prod me. But what I'll never do will be to let the world just go on spinning."

It occurred to Otilia to reply, "Well then, stop it!" But fearing that Zendejas wouldn't know how to take her little joke, she just smiled and said aloud:

"What are you planning to do then?"

"Send the editor of this paper a very harsh letter telling those awful reporters what's what."

"I wouldn't do that if I were you, Felix."

"Why not, wife?"

"Because I think it would be like stirring up a hornets' nest."

"Well, I could handle it. I'd beat the nest and the hornets too!"

"I'm sure you would, but you couldn't get away without being stung."

"A few stings wouldn't bother me."

"In that case, then, don't worry about what the papers say or how they exaggerate."

Her observation precluded any reply; Zendejas felt trapped and he couldn't come up with a good response. Therefore, changing his tactics, he shouted:

"What makes me most indignant is knowing that not just women but also full-grown men are claiming to be victims of the criminals. How can that be! Don't they have any guts? Why don't they defend themselves? It's understandable that timid females get things snatched from them and end up complaining; but men, big strong men! . . . That's really grotesque."

"But what can you do to stop some quick hand from pulling your watch or your wallet out of your pocket!"

"For strong hands, there is no such thing as quick hands. Nobody has stuck his hands in my pocket, and I pity the man who dares to try it! He'd pay dearly for it. My clothing is as sensitive as my skin, and if anything so much as brushes against me, I throw out my hand, and it's caught, held, then crushed to smithereens."

"But what if you were surprised in a deserted street by armed thieves?"

"Nobody surprises me. I'm always on my guard, keeping an eye out for anything and everything. I'm fully aware of who's in front of me, who's at my side, and who's behind me; where he's got his hands and what moves he's making. . . ."

"But what if you're coming around a corner?"

"I never do that haphazardly the way most people do. Instead, before I turn the corner, I step down off the sidewalk so I've got a good view of both sides of the street corner. . . . Plus I never forget my revolver, and if necessary, I keep my hand on the handle in plain view, or inside my pocket."

"I pray you won't find yourself put to the test."

"Oh, quite the contrary. I wish I had the chance to teach those troublemakers a good lesson. I'm sure they'd never want to try anything again! If every man would defend himself and fight back against these criminals, this 'plague,' which the press says is devastating the city today, would already be over and done with."

Otilia said nothing, but she did say a few prayers to herself, in hopes that her husband would never be attacked, because she didn't want him to get hurt, and she didn't want him to hurt anyone else either.

That's how the after-dinner conversation ended.

Next on the agenda: Zendejas got up and went to his room to take his usual little afternoon nap, because he couldn't do without it if he wanted to keep a clear head on his shoulders. You see, he had the unfortunate habit of eating well and digesting badly. Actually it is quite common in the human species for appetite and indigestion to rule on equal terms.

Meanwhile Otilia got busy putting the food away in the icebox and giving some orders to the servants.

II

As soon as Zendejas found himself in his bedroom, he closed the door and the window, to keep the light and noise from bothering him; next he took off his jacket and vest; then he put his watch on the nightstand, where he could consult it from time to time, so as not to oversleep; he unbuttoned his pants to give his ample stomach plenty of room to expand, for it grew abruptly after the intake of food. After that, he stretched himself out lazily, half dizzy from the pleasant feeling of drowsiness creeping over his encephalic mass.

The animal mechanism of that respectable official was well disciplined. Of course, since the person who controlled it was endowed with extraordinary *energy!* Don Felix always did exactly what he demanded of himself, and no more, and he expected the same from everyone else, by golly! Even his sleep was subject to his will, and when he said he would *sleep for twelve hours*, he snored away for half the day; but when he decided to rest for five minutes, he'd open his eyes after a twelfth of an hour, or at the most, one or two seconds later. Naturally! Everything is subject to a man's will; it's just that men lack *energy*. He was one of the few *energetic* men around. He never let himself be led by the tide nor did he let himself be caught with his guard down and everyone who had to deal with him soon realized that, because as far as he was concerned there were no valid excuses, compromises, or halfway measures: everything was strictly business, straightforward and to the point. By golly!

As proof of all this, he leaped out of bed half an hour later than he had intended; which nobody suspected, and which will be consigned to the archives of history until the end of time. Nevertheless, knowing within himself that he had slept beyond what he had planned put him in such a dreadful mood that he got up as though possessed, threw on the clothes he had taken off, and quickly (but carefully) buttoned up the ones he had left undone so as to facilitate the expansion of his abdominal organs. Then he grabbed his revolver and hat and left the room, with the angry face typical of a man of strong character who wouldn't put up with anyone's looking askance at him or even slightly touching his coat.

Otilia, who had gone up to the adjoining room to make sure the children didn't make any noise and was waiting there so she could say good-bye when her husband left, couldn't help remarking:

"You've slept a little more than usual today."

"Exactly what I intended," answered Zendejas. "No more, no less."

"I am glad that you were able to rest, you were tired."

"Who told you I was tired? I could work twenty-four hours a day without feeling the least bit tired."

"Yes, you're a very strong man."

"Whenever I see those spoiled brats of the new generation, they just make me laugh: they're all so feeble and depraved. Not like me. There's real muscle here. . . ."

And flexing his right arm, he used his left hand to point to the sinuous mountain of his well-developed biceps. After that he pinched his thighs, which he thought were like bronze, and he ended up by striking a few strong blows on his chest, which protruded like that of a wet nurse. That tangible display of his physique filled him with vanity and helped calm his bad mood; so by the time he and his young wife had walked slowly to the front hallway, he had already forgotten the delay incurred thanks to the god Morpheus.[5]

"Well, see you later, Otilia," he said to his wife, as he lovingly squeezed her hand.

"See you later, Felix," she answered lovingly. "Don't come home late . . . you know we live on the outskirts and times are bad."

"Don't worry about me," replied the judge confidently.

"Try not to walk by yourself."

The judge responded to her advice with a kind of snort, because it wounded him that his wife didn't think he was brave enough to handle even the giant enemies of Don Quijote.[6] Aloud, all he said was:

"Take care of the children."

He set out down the street immediately, while Otilia stayed by the door, watching him with loving eyes until he turned the corner. Then the young woman went in and continued with the usual daily chores which took up most of her time; for she was an extremely meticulous housekeeper. Her only worry was what time Zendejas would be coming home because the street where they lived was so isolated, and there had been so many assaults that she just couldn't relax.

Meanwhile, propelled by his contrary nature which continually buoyed his spirits; and also by the belligerent pride that filled his conceited person, Don Felix went along saying to himself: "That was some advice Otilia gave me! Don't come home late, and make sure not to walk by myself. . . . As if I were a timid, scared little boy! It looks like she doesn't know me very well. . . . I'm not afraid of either shadows or ghosts, and as for men, I'm as much a man as any of them. . . . Well now, so my wife won't offend me like that again, I'm going to teach her a lesson by returning home late, alone, and by the most deserted streets . . . and if anyone dares to get in my way, I swear I'll strangle him, or slap his face, or kick him in the pants, or I'll kill him. . . ."

He was so engrossed in visualizing a possible attack and the different degrees of effectiveness of his own various defense tactics, that, without realizing it, he was acting out with energetic and unconscious gestures the exploits he planned to perform; he'd cup his right hand, stretch it out in front of him, and then shake it vigorously, as though he'd caught the culprit by the scruff of his neck; or he'd throw punches in the air, as though there were faces all around him just asking for it; or, raising his legs up high, one after the other, he'd kick furiously at parts (which may not and should not be men-

5. The Greek god of dreams and sleep.

6. Don Quijote is the protagonist of a famous 17-century Spanish novel by Miguel de Cervantes, who imagines that he is living in a world of heroic chivalric adventure when in fact his life is quite ordinary; he rushes into battle against windmills, which he sees as ferocious giants.

tioned) of the human anatomy belonging to the figures who paraded through the limbo of his feverish imagination.

Anyone who saw him acting in that wild fashion without any bugles announcing the imminent arrival of the enemy would have declared him a raving lunatic and not what he really was: a fairly sane, though high-strung, judge. Fortunately, however, the street was deserted, and there was nobody to witness his unbridled mime; so he was able to arrive at the courthouse with his usual dignity and be greeted by the employees as respectfully as ever.

Seated at his desk, he set to work with great determination and gave his attention to studying several cases that were at the sentencing stage, in order to polish them off by means of brilliant decisions through which both his incomparable acumen and his never sufficiently appreciated *energy* would shine. And he became so absorbed in his task that time passed without his noticing it; the sun went down and night fell, but even then he went on, showing no signs of fatigue or boredom; rather, he continued to work with the same persistence, in spite of the dim, red light which the supreme government had put at his disposal since there were only two incandescent light bulbs in the main office, and they were so old that they had lost their brightness and looked like dying cigarette butts inserted in glass globes hanging from the ceiling. Fortunately, the judge had eyes like a cat.

Another judge, equally industrious, who had also stayed late reading tedious briefs and scribbling notes, came to distract the judge from his work at about eight o'clock:

"You sure are hard at it, partner!" he said.

"That's what you have to do to keep up with the work," answered Zendejas.

"I'm the same way, partner."

"We have to silence those who slander us. They say we're lazy, and we've got to prove we're not by our actions."

"I agree. . . . But listen, old pal, don't you think we've worked enough for now and that we're entitled to a little amusement, as a reward for all our hard work?"

"You're right, partner," answered Don Felix, stretching and yawning. "It's time to put this aside."

"And go to The Principal[7] to see the first show."

"Excellent idea," agreed Zendejas.

The invitation struck him just right. With his mind made up to go home late, alone, and by the most deserted streets (to prove to his better half that he wasn't afraid, that he didn't even know what *that* was, and that he was hardly aware of *such a thing* from hearsay), he took advantage of this opportunity to kill time and show up at home sometime after midnight. Therefore, within a few minutes he had put away the cases and the lawbooks in their respective places, washed his face, put on his hat, gone outside with his colleague, and headed for the old theater.

Both judges argued at the box office over who should pay; but Zendejas, who wouldn't tolerate anyone's disagreeing with him or placing obstacles in his way, got to buy the tickets. And so the two dignified magistrates pompously entered the temple of happiness and took seats down front, where they

7. One of the major theaters in Mexico City through the nineteenth century.

could have a better view of the actresses. They also provided themselves with good pairs of opera glasses, which throughout the show never left their eyes, so that they were able to enjoy looking at the vaudeville stars and chorus girls at such close range, it almost seemed they could reach out and pinch them.

The show consisted of clever repartee, laughter and cavorting, lively singing and dancing, off-color jokes, and clapping and shouting as if there were no tomorrow. Those two good gentlemen, who were not really as good as they seemed, enjoyed the suggestive pranks on stage until they could barely stand it. They roared at the most risqué scenes of the zarzuelas[8] with such uncontrollable laughter that it sounded like the crashing of two heavily flowing waterfalls side by side; totally uninhibited, they communicated to each other their delight in all they saw; they applauded gleefully, stamped on the wooden floor with their feet, and called for encores of the raciest songs and the most alluring dances like a couple of schoolboys on vacation who find everything new and fun and full of excitement.

It was after nine-thirty when they left the theater, and they went straight to the Bach Restaurant where they dined slowly and sumptuously until well after eleven when they left to go to their respective homes. After walking together for a few blocks, they cordially took leave of each other:

"See you tomorrow, partner. Sleep well!"

"Good night, partner. I hope the meal won't upset your stomach!"

Zendejas stationed himself on the corner of 16th of September Street[9] to wait for the trolley that would take him to his destination, which was the Colonia Roma;[1] but his luck was so bad that, one after another, he watched all the trolleys from the Plaza de la Constitución[2] go by—all, that is, except the one he needed. We said he had bad luck, but we ought to correct ourselves, because the truth is, he felt just the opposite, that things were turning out just the way he wanted because now he would get home even later, which was exactly what he had intended all along, owing to his own pride and petty sense of honor as a brave and daring man.

It was shortly before midnight when he got aboard a Tacubaya[3] trolley, having finally decided that, according to his plans and intentions, it was time to go home. When he got off at the Insurgentes stop, it had already struck twelve; he crossed Chapultepec Avenue[4] and turned down one of the wide streets into the new neighborhood; on purpose he walked along choosing the newest and most deserted streets, where there were few houses and absolutely no pedestrians. He had a vehement desire to meet up with some nocturnal thief so he could teach him a lesson, but not a living soul appeared in

8. Musical comedies, with popular songs, dances, and solos.
9. Mexico City street that commemorates a revolt against the Spaniards in 1810 and is celebrated each year as Mexican Independence Day.
1. A neighborhood in Mexico City.
2. The Plaza de la Constitución is the main square in Mexico City, named for a Spanish Constitution of 1812, which guaranteed freedom of the press, universal male suffrage, and other liberal reforms.
3. Then a wealthy neighborhood on the outskirts of Mexico City.
4. Street in Mexico City that follows an Aztec aqueduct, a portion of which remains visible. *Insurgentes*: a long street in Mexico City; its name means "rebels" in Spanish.

that deserted place. Nevertheless, true to his habits, and so as not to be taken by surprise by whoever might come along, he continued to take all the precautions that prudence advised; and in addition to never letting his hand leave his pistol, not for even a second, he would step down off the sidewalk before reaching each corner, look in all directions, and listen intently to every noise.

He'd been walking quite a distance when, as he crossed one of the most isolated avenues, he caught the sound of heavy, uneven footsteps coming from the opposite direction, and soon he saw the dark silhouette of a suspicious-looking man appear at the next intersection. When the man moved into the circle of light projected by the street lamp, Zendejas noticed that he was elegantly dressed and, furthermore, that he was lit to the gills. So drunk was he that he wasn't only staggering, he was reeling; but when Don Felix saw him approaching, he said to himself: "I don't like the looks of this ostentatious display of drunkenness. Not at all! Who knows . . . he might be pretending so he can catch me off guard. Keep an eye on him, Zendejas!"

And he didn't take his eyes off him, as the saying goes, even though, it seemed that, broad as the street was, it wasn't broad enough for the wild gyrations executed by that off-balance body. Plus the fact that in his mad joy, he was singing in a mournful, off-key voice:

Grace! Grace!
My, what a face!

or else:

Sal! Sal!
My, what a gal!

or else:

Fay! Fay!
Oh, how gay!

It almost made you think that the priest of Bacchus had just come from celebrating some of the mysteries of the cult—in the company of one or more priestesses—and for this and other reasons, as he went on his way, he seemed to be recalling some of their names, the charm of the flames ("the sparks of the dames"). Surely that was another reason why he was taking so many steps in the wrong direction now, in addition to all the others that he must have taken previously!

Don Felix formulated his plan as soon as he analyzed that fellow's irregular pattern. . . . Not so irregular! . . . Taking into account geometry as well as morals and public safety! If he really *was* drunk, he had to avoid being surprised. He watched, and each time the man strayed from a straight path, he'd say to himself:

"Now he's going to the right? Well then, I have to go right! . . . Now he's going in a straight line? Well, I guess I have to be ready to go either way! . . . Oh, hell! He sure does change direction quickly! . . . No, the important thing is not to let him run into me! . . . He's going to run into me! . . . No, he's not going to run into me! Great Scott!"

As Don Felix spouted out this last exclamation, the drunk, or whatever he was, had already run into him, like an erratic asteroid colliding with a well-behaved planet in a fixed orbit. How could the accident have occurred, in spite of Zendejas's precautions? Neither the judge nor the drunkard ever managed to find out.

The fact was that at the least expected moment. Don Felix found himself face to face, or rather, stomach to stomach, with the living pendulum who had seemed to be everywhere at once in his stubborn efforts to escape the perpendicular line.

"Idiot!" screamed Zendejas, full of anger.

"What? What?" muttered the fellow slurring his words. "Why don't people watch where they're going? . . . They're always getting in the way! . . . They won't let a man pass! . . .

"Go to hell!" shouted Don Felix again, trying to disentangle himself from that inert body that prevented him from moving.

With some effort, by pulling his foot back and poking with his elbow at the mass on top of him, Zendejas finally freed himself of the weight and left the drunkard a short distance away, half standing and half falling. Then the judge grabbed him by the lapels of his jacket, and as punishment shook him furiously several times, finally letting him go so he could follow the laws of his dangerous instability. The poor man spun around on the heel of one shoe, threw one foot into the air, almost fell, then raised his other foot, went through a few more strange contortions like a doll bending over and straightening up, and then finally managed to recover some semblance of balance. As he continued on his way, it seemed his slow, laborious, zigzagging walk had never been interrupted.

No sooner did he find himself free of Zendejas's grasp than he recovered his good humor, and he continued droning in his off-key voice, which was occasionally interrupted by a hiccup:

Don't kill me, don't kill me
With pistol or dagger!

Don Felix also continued on his way, enraged like a wild bull, as much from the bumping as from that miserable wretch's making fun of his terrible, unleashed anger. But suddenly a strange thought occurred to him. What if that drunk was really a thief? And what if that stumble had been planned, just a strategy used to rob him without his noticing it? No sooner had he thought this than he found himself checking his watch pocket. . . . And, in fact, he found . . . that he did not find his silver pocket watch or the gold-plated watch chain from which it hung.

Having discovered this, he turned around quick as a flash and, let's not say he ran, but rather he flew, after the enigmatic person, who was moving away as best he could with his stumbling feet and noisy steps punishing the asphalt of the public streets.

As soon as he was within reach, the judge grabbed him fiercely by the scruff of his neck with his left hand, just as he had gone over it in his mind as he was leaving his house, while, with his right hand, he took out and started to flaunt his relucent, redoubtable revolver.

"Halt, villain!" he shouted.

"Again? . . . Don't yank so hard!" mumbled the man.

"You're no drunk, you're faking it!" shouted Zendejas.

"Oh! Oh! Police! Police!" roared the drunk.

"If only they *would* come," yelled Don Felix, "so they could lock you up down at headquarters, assign a judge, and put you on trial."

"Put me on what?"

"Trial."

"Well then, in that case, my friend, I'll try. What can I do for you?"

"Hand over the watch."

"What watch do I owe you?"

"The one you took from me, you thief."

"This watch is mine, all mine . . . with an automatic winder and it chimes the hours."

"Chimes? What kind of humbug is that! You're a member of the band."[5]

"I'm not a musician. . . . I'm a property owner."

"Sure, someone else's property."

As this conversation took place, the drunk was trying to defend himself, but he didn't have enough strength; at the same time, Don Felix didn't know what to do with him, because with each step the drunk would fall on top of him or slip out of his hands, to one side or the other, on the verge of collapsing. Exasperated, the judge dropped him violently and without mercy, and when he had him on the ground, he pointed his weapon at the drunk's chest, and again demanded:

"The watch and the chain, or I'll blow your brains out!"

All the drunk could exclaim was:

"Holy smoke! . . . Holy smoke! . . . Holy smoke!"

He wouldn't, or couldn't, move either hand or foot. Zendejas took the only option left to him: with his own hand he transferred the watch and chain he found on the drunkard's person into his own coat pocket. After that, he stood up and gave the man on the ground a few more kicks, and he was about to set out for home again when he heard the man muttering through his clenched teeth:

"Holy smoke! . . . This guy must be one of the members of the band!"

"So you still haven't had enough? . . . Well, take that! . . . And that! . . . Thief! . . . Villain! . . . Scoundrel!"

Each one of these exclamations was punctuated with furious kicks, which the judge showered on the stranger, who did nothing but mutter at each blow:

"Holy smoke! . . . Holy smoke! . . . Holy smoke! . . . "

Tired at last of administering a beating without glory, Zendejas left the drunk (fake or real, he couldn't figure out which) and resolutely resumed his walk home, while the stranger staggered to his feet, after several unsuccessful attempts, and gradually moved away with a mixture of long and short steps, forward and backward, and leaning alarmingly like the Tower of Pisa, now toward the right, now toward the left.

5. That is, the band of thieves.

III

Otilia didn't know how to interpret her husband's not arriving on time, and she was extremely upset. Rarely did ten o'clock find Zendejas away from home, so that when the young woman realized it was past midnight and her husband had not yet returned, she imagined the worst, as always occurs in cases like this.

"Surely something has happened to him," she was saying to herself. "There's no other way to explain why he's out so late. . . . Could it have been the robbers? . . . And if they recognized him and he defended himself, as he most certainly would, they might have wounded him, or maybe even killed him. . . . Heaven forbid! . . . May the Mother of God be with him!"

With thoughts like these in her head, she went on crocheting the never-ending quilt which she meant to use as a bedspread in the master bedroom, but every now and then she'd stop moving her agile, feverish fingers, either to wipe away a tear as it slipped down from her eyelashes, or else to make the sign of the cross in the direction of the street from which the absent man was supposed to come. . . . What would she do if she were left a widow? There was no other man in the whole world like Felix. . . . And her poor children? There were three of them, and they were still so young. Savings? They had none; his salary was small, and they struggled to make ends meet. They lacked many of the necessities of life and they had learned to do without them. There's no use; they'd be forced out into the street; she'd have to give up the house, which, though it was on the outskirts, was comfortable and gave them privacy; she'd end up renting a flat in some apartment house. How dark and dingy those flats are! The children would all get sick there.

Her imagination continued working ceaselessly. She'd have to take in sewing jobs to support herself and the children. What a miserable life! The children would be running around dirty and barefoot; they wouldn't be able to attend a private school; they'd have to go to the public ones, with all the riffraff; and they'd learn bad habits; they'd get mixed up with the wrong kind of people; it would be their undoing. . . .

She went so far along that road of speculative adversities that she saw herself in total poverty, a widow, and all alone in the world. Black clothing covered her attractive body, and the black veil of widowhood draped over her shoulders. How well the outfit looked on her! It gave her an exceptionally intriguing appearance. Would she have suitors again? . . . If her charm and youth were taken into account, perhaps she would, but then again, considering her poverty, perhaps not. . . . Many men might be attracted to her, but only ones with bad intentions. . . . And would she give in? Or wouldn't she? . . . Human nature is so frail! Women are so sentimental! And men are so evil! Let nobody say, "Never shall I taste of this water." Oh, Lord!

And Otilia burst into tears without really knowing whether she was crying so hard because of the tenderness she felt over Don Felix's unfortunate and premature death, or whether it was because she'd been left a widow or because of her orphaned children and their wretched clothing or because they were being ruined in the public schools; or maybe it was seeing herself, so young and attractive dressed in black, or because she had no admirers, or because she saw herself being seduced by perverted men who would take advantage of her inexperience, her sensitivity, and her helplessness . . . but especially her sensitivity! . . . Because she knew herself well: she was extremely sensitive. That was her weakness; that was the slit in the plate of armor that was her virtue. . . . If anyone were sharp enough to notice it, that's where he'd plunge his dagger, and she would be a lost woman. . . . Oh, how horrible! How wretched is the fate of a young, beautiful, unprotected woman with a sensitive heart. . . . Why couldn't she have been born with a piece of stone for a heart? . . . That organ would be her downfall; she knew it, but there was nothing she could do about it.

Fortunately the doorbell rang several times just as the young woman's wild imagination pushed her over this precipice and engulfed her in the depths of those calamities, passions, and adventures from which it was not possible, no, to emerge with dry eyes. . . . Fortunately, the ringing of that little electric bell came just in time to save her, pulling her out of that abyss of gloom and tragic events into which she had thrown herself headlong. The young woman's dangerously sensitive heart jumped for joy repeatedly when it discovered it was free from all those risks: widowhood, black clothing, the death of her children, the feeling of being stalked, slipping, and falling into disgrace. In contrast, the doorbell sounded joyous and triumphant. It chimed in that special way, which said Zendejas was returning victorious and happy, for having put the morning star in its place, or for having taken a swipe at some insolent bum, or for having given some busybody a good kick in the pants. Otilia sensed all that as she ran to open the door, rejoicing that she was free from all the misfortunes, snares, and traps that the terrifying future seemed to hold in store for her.

Don Felix, in fact, did come in beaming over the results of the battle he had just won against the clever thief who had accosted him on a public street, and over the recovery of his watch and chain.

"Felix!" exclaimed Otilia in a faint voice, as she threw herself into his arms. "What have you been doing? Why are you so late? You've had me terribly worried."

"Don't be upset, wife," answered Zendejas. "Nothing happened to me, and nothing ever could. I could go for a walk alone anywhere in the Republic, and no one would dare touch me."

"Where have you been?"

"At work, at the theater, at the restaurant. . . ."

"It never dawned on me that that's where you'd be. Meanwhile I've been sitting here alone, unable to sleep, and imagining the most horrible things. . . . I've been so upset thinking about you. . . ."

The young woman was careful not to tell Don Felix about the mourning clothes, the sensitivity of her heart, and the seduction which she had seen looming on the horizon.

Holding hands, they went into the living room.

"Wait a minute! You've been crying!" exclaimed Don Felix, drying the tears running down her face with his handkerchief.

"Of course, because I love you so much and I was so afraid for you!" she answered, leaning her head on the judge's shoulder.

"You silly little girl," Zendejas went on lovingly. "There's no reason to be alarmed."

"Felix, can I ask you a favor?"

"Whatever you want."

"Don't come home late anymore."

"I promise, dear. There's no reason to now, since I've accomplished what I set out to do."

"What do you mean, Felix?"

"I had a good scuffle with a robber . . . one of those guys the press talks about so much."

"Really? How did that happen? . . . Tell me, Felix," asked the young woman, extremely interested.

Zendejas, complying with his wife's request, told her about his recent adventure, not exactly the way it happened, but embellished with minor incidents and details which, though not really factual, helped a great deal to bring out the fierceness of the battle, the strength of the champion, and the brilliance of the victory. The young woman, fascinated, listened to his story and felt proud that her husband was such a strong, brave man; but, like all loving and delicately sentimental wives, she couldn't help worrying about the injuries that her husband's robust body might have suffered in such a terrible encounter, so she asked the judge in her sweetest voice:

"Let me see your hand: it's not swollen, is it? . . . You didn't twist your ankle, did you?"

"Both are still firm and strong," replied Don Felix with obvious satisfaction, waving his clenched fist and shaking his right foot in the air.

"Thank Goodness!" exclaimed his wife, heaving a sigh of relief.

"It just goes to prove what I've been trying to tell you all along," Don Felix went on. "If all the men around here with hair on their chests would do what I did when attacked by those thieves, if they'd beat them up and get back the stolen goods, this plague of robberies would soon be over. . . ."

"Maybe you're right. . . . So . . . that thief took your watch and chain away from you?"

"Yes, by pretending to be drunk. He fell on top of me like a dead man, and while I was trying to get him off me, he swiped them without my feeling a thing."

"Those pickpockets certainly are quick. . . ."

"Yes, they are, but fortunately I soon realized what must have happened. . . . If it weren't for that, I'd have lost a couple of my most prized possessions."

As he said this, Zendejas took them out of his pocket to look at them gloatingly. Otilia stared at them too, curious and interested, as is always the case when one looks at things that have been lost and are now found; but upon seeing them, instead of rejoicing, both husband and wife found themselves confused. Why?

"But, Felix. . . . What have you done?" asked the frightened Otilia.

"Why do you ask, woman?" replied the judge, hardly knowing what he was saying.

"Because this watch and chain are not yours."

"How can that be?" responded Zendejas in a feeble voice when he realized that his wife was right.

"You can see for yourself," she went on, taking both objects in her hands to examine them closely. "This is a gold watch, and yours is made of silver. . . . It looks like a repeating one."

The young woman pushed a spring on the side, and a clear, silvery little bell gave the time in quarter-hours and even minutes.

"And look, it has initials on the lid: A.B.C.; they must stand for the owner's name. . . . It's a very good watch, quite valuable."

Zendejas was left in a daze, and he felt drops of sweat covering his forehead.

"And the chain," his wife went on, continuing her analysis, "is wide and expensive looking, made out of fourteen-carat gold mesh, and look at this charm at the end of it: made of the same metal and shaped like a little elephant, with ruby eyes and fine enameled feet and ears."

With that painful evidence in front of him, Zendejas lost almost all the cold as well as the hot blood in his veins, turned white as a sheet, and murmured with supreme anxiety:

"That makes me a thief, one of the band!"

"That's crazy! . . . Don't say such things."

"Yes, I am a half-wit, a stupid ass," repeated Don Felix, feeling desperate.

And, in keeping with his impetuous nature, he started to beat himself soundly on the head with his fists, until his wife stopped the savage attack by grabbing his wrists.

"Let me go," he said indignantly. "I deserve this, and more. Let them throw me in jail. I'm a criminal . . . an impostor of a judge."

"No, Felix, it's just that you made a mistake. It was night time, the man was drunk, and he fell on top of you. Anybody would have thought the same thing."

"Plus, I've lost my watch," added Zendejas.

"That's right," said his wife. "How do you explain that?"

The judge perceived a ray of hope. In the course of passing judgments and handing down sentences, he had grown accustomed to deducing, inferring, or subtilizing.

"I've got it!" he exclaimed, cheerful and calm once again. "The drunk was a fake, and he'd robbed that watch and chain from somebody else, before he ever ran into me. . . . Then he robbed me of mine, and in trying to get back the one that belonged to me, I hit on the pocket where he'd put the other's possessions; but he got away with mine."

The explanation seemed unlikely; Otilia stood and thought a moment.

"Could be," she murmured at last. "Are you sure you were wearing your watch?"

"I never forget it," replied the judge firmly.

"Well, even so, let's go check your room."

"There's no point in it."

"But there's nothing to lose. . . ."

"As you wish."

And the couple adjourned to Zendejas's bedroom, where they found the judge's silver watch, with his inexpensive plated watch chain, lying peacefully on the nightstand, exactly where their owner had left them when he climbed into bed to take his nap.

Felix felt terrified, as if he had seen Medusa's head.

"It's here," he murmured painfully. "So that gentleman (he no longer called him a drunk or a thief) has been robbed by this hand. Not the slightest doubt remains."

Otilia, grieved, made no reply, and her husband went on:

"What happened can be easily explained now: that man, who must be rich and carefree, was out on a binge in that neighborhood. . . . He had more than a few too many, and he was really drunk. I mistook him for a thief and carried off his property. . . . I stole at night, on a public street, and while armed. . . . I'm ruined. . . . First thing tomorrow I'm turning myself in to the authorities: a good judge begins his work at home."

"There's no way," objected Otilia, horrified at the thought. "It would make you look ridiculous, a regular Don Quixote."

"Why would it be ridiculous?" asked Zendejas, angrily.

"Because we'd never hear the end of it: how you had it out with some old man in a drunken stupor who couldn't even defend himself, and what a great hero you are!"

"No, that's not fair because on numerous occasions I have demonstrated that the weak and the strong are all alike to me, and that I fear no one, no, not even Lucifer himself."

"But people are mean, especially the envious ones."

"You're right about that: the envious ones, the envious ones!" repeated Zendejas. "All my brave friends envy me," he went on, thinking to himself. "And how they'd love to take advantage of the quid pro quo,[6] to make me the laughingstock of the city!" Then he continued aloud: "But what should I do then? I certainly can't keep someone else's property!"

"Let me think a minute," replied Otilia, concerned. ". . . Let me see those initials again. . . . A.B.C. What was the man like? Describe him to me, Felix."

"Let me see. . . . Kind of on the old side, heavy, almost as heavy as I am, clean-shaven."

"With glasses?"

"I think so, but he lost them in the scuffle."

"Listen," the young woman continued thoughtfully. "Couldn't it be Antonio Bravo Caicedo? . . . A.B.C.: the initials fit."

"You mean the rich and famous one? Why, his name is known all over this city!"

"That's the one."

"There's no way, dear."

"Why not?"

"Because he's such a serious person; his conduct is beyond reproach; wherever he goes, he's always accompanied by his daughters, who are very beautiful; and, wait a minute, if I'm not mistaken, he's. . . ."

"He's what, Felix?"

"An active member of the Temperance Society."[7]

6. Literally, "something for something" (Latin); here meaning advantage or opportunity.

7. A group that advocated restrictions on the consumption of alcohol.

"That doesn't matter," answered his wife. "Men are so contradictory, and so evil. . . ." (She was thinking, at that point, about the dangers of her widowhood.)

"You're right about that; they certainly are evil." Out of instinct the judge refrained from saying *we* certainly are evil, no doubt because he remembered the mental and visual excesses he had just committed at The Principal.

Anyway, there followed a long discussion between husband and wife, in which they examined the situation in detail and analyzed all suppositions from every possible angle; and the more they dug into the matter, the more they suspected that the watch and chain belonged to that elderly, rich, and hypocritical Antonio Bravo Caicedo; a thousand indications proved it, a thousand small details made it undeniable. Who would have thought it! . . . That such a respectable man would really be so unrespectable! How true is the saying "The flesh is weak. . . ." But Bravo Caicedo was fat. . . . What a complicated affair! . . . From the looks of things one might conclude that the fatter the flesh, the weaker it is. . . .

Having solved for the unknown quantity, or rather, for the unknown man, they still needed to find a way to return the stolen goods. Should they send the objects to the owner's house? No, that would mean compromising him, exposing him, embarrassing him. . . . And then, even though the most likely explanation was that that august person was the clumsy drunkard of the encounter, nevertheless, there was still the possibility that some other individual was the true owner of the jewelry. Antonio Bravo Caicedo (A.B.C.), it's true, had a monopoly on the production of pulque,[8] but not on the first three letters of the alphabet.

IV

In short, after looking at it, considering it, and wracking their brains over it, the honorable couple resolved that the property in question should be deposited at the courthouse with Zendejas, and that he should place an announcement about it in the newspapers, one written so cleverly that it would neither denounce the judge himself, nor bring the rich old man's disgraceful behavior into public view.

Having decided upon this course of action, Don Felix, being an honorable man, refused to lay his head on his pillow before relieving his conscience of its heavy burden. The document had to be sketched out and written in its final form so that the next day it would be ready to send to two or three of the evening papers when their doors opened. The judge worked feverishly, made several rough drafts, consulted Otilia, crossed out, made changes, added, erased, and scribbled away on several sheets of paper, until, finally, when it was almost dawn, he finished the arduous task of giving shape to the little paragraph, whose definitive version was conceived in the following words:

8. A Mexican alcoholic drink.

NOTICE

This morning shortly after the office opened, a gold watch was left at this courthouse. Self-winding, with a chain, also of gold, and topped by a small elephant charm with ruby eyes and black enameled ears and feet. The watch contains the initials A.B.C. inside its cover. The serial number is 40180, and it is a Longines.[9] All this is being made known to the public so that the objects can be claimed by their owner. They were placed in the hands of the undersigned judge, along with a paper containing an exact and specific description of the person from whom the jewelry was removed by mistake. There is mention of the street, the hour, and other pertinent details.

But the repeated publication of those lines proved useless. To this very day, as this story is being written, nobody has shown up to claim the watch and chain; perhaps because Antonio Bravo Caicedo is not the owner of the jewelry, or, maybe because he is, but wishes to remain anonymous at all costs. So that, if any reader's initials are A.B.C., if he was walking through the Colonia Roma that night and had had a bit too much to drink, if he had something to do with Grace, Fay, or Sal, and, finally, if he lost these objects in a street scuffle, he knows that he can go to claim them at the courthouse where they are on deposit.

9. An expensive Swiss watch.

ANTON CHEKHOV
1860–1904

Anton Chekhov visited the literary giant **Leo Tolstoy** late in the great novelist's life. Tolstoy embraced him warmly, and said: "I can't stand your plays. Shakespeare's are terrible, but yours are worse!" Tolstoy particularly objected that the dramas lacked purpose. "Where does one get to with your heroes?" he asked the young dramatist. "From the sofa to the privy and from the privy back to the sofa?" The ever-modest Chekhov was apparently amused, finding it hard to take offense at a judgment that likened him to Shakespeare. And perhaps he was pleased, too, that Tolstoy's perplexity got at the very heart of Chekhov's innovative writing, which both puzzled and startled his early audiences by refusing grand actions and melodramatic plots: no deaths, no great love affairs, no shocking revelations. Tolstoy was looking for heroes, and Chekhov refuses to give us any, typically offering a constellation of characters, each of whom—even the most minor—can lay claim to a separate life and perspective. Aged servants and bumbling tutors have as much to say as aristocrats and beauties. His plays are like life, Chekhov said, "just as complex and just as simple."

LIFE

Anton Chekhov was born in the thriving Russian seaport town of Taganrog in 1860. His grandfather had been a serf who eventually saved enough money to purchase his freedom. Chekhov himself never forgot how narrowly he had escaped being born into serfdom, and he struggled his whole life against feelings of subservience and inferiority. Chekhov's father owned a grimy and decrepit grocery store and forced his children to work there. A tyrannical man, he had outbursts of temper, beat his children, insulted his wife, and held fervent religious beliefs. When Chekhov was sixteen, his father went bankrupt and slunk off to Moscow to escape his debtors, where his family soon joined him. They left only Anton behind in Taganrog to fend for himself. Survival was difficult. His parents insisted that he send them money, so he sold the family furniture and lived with relatives, begging them for small sums.

In 1879, Chekhov won a scholarship to study medicine at Moscow University. In Moscow he found his family poverty-stricken and gloomy, his two older brothers spending what money they earned on drinking and women. Anton took financial responsibility for all of them, writing humorous stories for magazines to make money while studying medicine. He was so prolific that by the age of 26, he had published over 400 short pieces in popular magazines, as well as two books of stories.

During this period, Chekhov developed two techniques as a writer that would serve him for the rest of his life. First, his medical training taught him to pay close attention to details; readers have long praised his skill as an objective observer of subtle signs and gestures. Second, his work as a humor writer demanded brevity; he wrote frequently for a magazine called *Splinters*, which had a strict limit of 100 words, and so forced the young writer to express his ideas within tight constraints. Once when friend found him condensing a story by Tolstoy, he explained that he frequently did this kind of exercise to practice conciseness.

In his third year of medical school, Chekhov began writing for more serious literary magazines. He was launched on two careers, managing to work as both a physician and a writer until he died. "Medicine is my lawful wife," he once said; "Writing is my mistress." His medical practice was draining, since he often treated poor patients for nothing and was called out to visit the sick in the middle of the night. Alarmingly, he started showing symptoms of tuberculosis in 1884.

Chekhov's first full-length play, *Ivanov*, went on stage in 1887. The production was a disaster: none of the actors had learned their lines, and one was clearly drunk on stage. Chekhov later dismissed his early plays as conventional and frivolous. It would be another decade before his drama would be treated as seriously as his short fiction, which was making him famous. He won the prestigious Pushkin Prize for his short stories in 1888.

Surprising everyone who knew him, Chekhov decided to write a report about Sakhalin, a penal colony off the coast of Siberia that was notorious for its appalling conditions. What he found was worse even than he had imagined: a "perfect hell," as he described it. Chained to wheelbarrows, flogged, starved, sometimes even raped and murdered, the prisoners endured a life of daily horror. The women survived mostly by prostitution. Since the Russian government had never collected much information about the prisoners and their families, Chekhov decided to perform a full census of the island himself. This was a massive task, and the writer took notes on the brutal conditions as he moved, offering his medical services to sick prisoners. When he returned, he lobbied for reform of Sakhalin, especially for the island's children, and in 1894 published a long and detailed book on the colony, filled with statistics and shocking truths. The press praised the book, the public was scandalized by the conditions in Sakhalin, and the government began to undertake reforms.

In the 1890s Chekhov finally turned his hand to writing drama again, and this time the plays he wrote were radically experimental, casting off the conventions of sensational melodrama that had dominated Russian theater and ushering in a new style that stressed ensembles rather than heroes and moods rather than actions. The first of these dramas, *The Seagull*, had such a disastrous opening that Chekhov vowed never to write another play. But this failure marked the beginning of a new era in Russian drama. In 1897, a theater opened in Moscow insisting on naturalistic, modern styles, and its great director, Konstantin Stanislavsky, saw *The Seagull* as the ideal play to mark this innovation. His new production astonished its first audiences. When the curtain fell on the first act, there was total silence. The hush went on for so long that one actress began to sob. But then the audience burst into wild applause. The actors were too stunned to take their bow. What followed were rave reviews and packed houses. Stanislavky's production of *The Seagull* was hailed as "one of the greatest events in the history of Russian theater and one of the greatest new developments in the history of world drama." The Moscow Art Theatre took the seagull as its emblem, and it staged all of Chekhov's late dramatic works, including his very last, *The Cherry Orchard*, our selection here.

The Moscow Art Theatre launched a new phase in Chekhov's personal life as well. He fell in love with one of the actresses in *The Seagull*, Olga Knipper, and married her in 1901, at the age of 41. They moved to Yalta, where they hoped that his health would improve. It did not. Chekhov died of tuberculosis in 1904.

TIMES

Huge social inequalities, fast-paced economic change, and rising political instability produced the pervasive anxiety that characterized Russia at the end of the nineteenth century. The country had begun a phase of rapid industrialization—about a century later than most of Western Europe—and saw a dramatic rise in the production of coal, steel, iron, oil, textiles, and beet sugar after 1850. Its population exploded from 50 million in 1860 to about 100 million in 1900. Russian cities grew quickly, and the railroad expanded dramatically. Tsar Alexander II officially abolished serfdom in 1860, diminishing the traditional influence of landowners, while business and bureaucratic sectors grew and employed ever larger numbers. Newly rich merchants and professionals began to buy property from the old aristocracy.

This profound shift in wealth and power brought a sense of impending crisis. Social groups that had new access to wealth and education frequently expressed anger at the autocratic tsarist regime, and voices across the class spectrum criticized the government for allowing the poor to suffer. Anarchists and other revolutionary groups assassinated numerous high-ranking officials, including Tsar Alexander II himself in 1881. The government tried to crack down on social turmoil with widespread arrests. Writers and intellectuals lived in constant fear that they would be thrown into prison, and their work was subject to frequent censorship. Chekhov was among the writers who signed a petition for freedom of the press, which brought him under the surveillance of the tsar's secret police. The end of the century witnessed massive demonstrations against tsarist authority, with students often acting as the leading agitators. In 1901, the Russian minister of education tried to draft 200 student leaders into the army. In *The Cherry Orchard*, the perpetual student Trofimov would have evoked these dissidents for contemporary audiences, and in fact the censors forced Chekhov to revise his character's most inflammatory speeches.

In the final years of Chekhov's life, Russian society was turning ever more volatile. Tsar Nicholas II was a weak-willed leader, inclined to bow to the dictates of reactionary ministers. Russian liberals clamored for constitutional reforms, while increasingly visible socialists responded to widespread crop failures, cholera epidemics, and grinding rural poverty by demanding outright revolution. In 1904, mounting tensions between Japan and Russia exploded into war. The very day that Chekhov died, July 15, 1904, a homemade bomb thrown by a socialist revolutionary killed the minister of the interior in his carriage. A year later, the Imperial Guard killed a thousand peaceful demonstrators, who had been singing patriotic songs and hymns. "Bloody Sunday," as this event came to be called, inflamed antimonarchical sentiment, launched the Russian Revolution of 1905, and heralded the ultimate end of tsarism. In 1917 the Bolshevik-led revolution would bring about a wholly new kind of social organization—the communist state.

Writers and artists working in this atmosphere of violence and instability hotly debated the proper role of the arts. Should art act as provocative political opposition, offering criticism of the status quo and images of a better future? Should it instead glorify the nation, prompting patriotism and loyalty? Or should art retain a fierce independence from politics, dedicated to purely aesthetic aims and aspirations? Chekhov had friends who propounded all of these positions, but he managed to elude them all. Throughout his career, for example, Chekhov stood up for oppressed and marginalized groups, but his stories and plays often steered clear of strong political and moral messages. From the 1930s onward, Chekhov became a favorite among Soviet leaders, who saw him as a proponent of communist ideals and insisted that his plays be produced across the USSR. Meanwhile, in the West, his work was taken to stand for individualism—and against Soviet collectivism. Throughout the twentieth century, Chekhov remained widely popular around the world—and exceptionally difficult to categorize.

WORK

Chekhov made a lasting mark on two major genres, short fiction and drama. When twenty-five famous short-story writers in our own time were asked to name the authors who had had the greatest influence on their art, ten of them—including Eudora Welty, Nadine Gordimer, and Raymond Carver—named Chekhov, more than any other writer. (Tied for second place, with five votes each, were Henry James and James Joyce.) Chekhov's special aptitude—and what makes him seem especially modern—is his reliance on small, delicate details in place of sensational actions or sudden plot twists. The driving force of his narratives is often not external events at all but mental processes that are subtle and unsettling: unexpected emotions, ambivalent desires, and gradually dawning recognitions.

Vladimir Nabokov called "The Lady with the Dog" (our second selection below) "one of the greatest stories ever written." Contradictory impulses propel the two main characters from the beginning: the jaded philanderer Gurov scorns women and yet craves their company, while the bored young woman he casually seduces at a seaside resort deceives a husband she condemns as a "flunky" but is then rocked by waves of remorse. Gurov thinks of the affair as a passing thrill, but later, in the woman's absence, he is surprised to discover that he has actually fallen in love with her. Chekhov invites us to recognize this as a major crisis in Gurov's life—his old life becomes unbearable—but it does not interrupt the narrative as a sudden turning point. Instead, the crisis unfolds as a series of fleeting, quiet moments of painful perception. Chekhov does not judge his characters' adultery, as most of his contemporaries would have done, but hints at the value of their transformation, as both are slowly estranged from their earlier selves. And in characteristically Chekhovian fashion, he does not end with a clear or comforting resolution but with a fragile, fleeting, inconclusive moment of genuine intimacy.

Chekhov's drama, like his short fiction, is so subtle and subdued that audiences have often had trouble fitting his work into conventional categories. From the very beginning, for example, there has been a dispute over whether *The Cherry Orchard* is a comedy or a tragedy. The original director Stanislavsky saw the play as a tear-jerker. He wept when he read the text for the first time, and many directors since have foregrounded the pain and loss at the center of the play. Chekhov himself, however, insisted that it was a comic farce, to be played at an almost breakneck speed. (He imagined the fourth act taking a quick twelve minutes, while Stanislavsky stretched it to last forty.) Conventional comedies end in marriage, tragedies in death, and this play does end with the death of the ancient servant Firs, whom the family has forgotten to send to a nursing home. On the other hand, slapstick moments occur throughout the play, as when Varya smacks her beloved Lopakhin over the head by mistake. Carlotta's magic tricks and Yepikhidov's comically grandiose language compete for attention with passages of poetic beauty. Chekhov wrote that directors like Stanislavsky were misreading him: "First they turn me into a weeper and then into a boring writer." In the century since, directors and actors have continued to wrestle with the question of the proper mood and pace for *The Cherry Orchard*, which can change significantly from production to production.

Productions of *The Cherry Orchard* also have to grapple with the political implications of the play. Since 1917, it has been difficult to avoid reading the play as a warning of the coming Russian Revolution. The single event in the drama—the sale of a beautiful but unprofitable aristocratic estate—suggests the passing of the old regime and the coming of a new order. Like the vast expanse of Russia, the orchard is huge—bigger, in fact, than any real orchard—and like all Russian land it is owned by the few rather than the many. Toward the end of Act II Trofimov says explicitly, "This whole country is our orchard." But Chekhov does not agitate for revolution here: instead he captures a feeling of stagnation, the quiet before the storm.

Soviet directors tended to cast the workers as heroic characters—serious and grand—while the aristocrats appeared decadent and foolish. But it is equally plausible to represent the socialist student as a naïve idealist with his head so high in the clouds that he cannot even make it down a flight of stairs. Many Western productions have played *The Cherry Orchard* in this way. A third perspective—probably closest to Chekhov's own—is to see the cast as an ensemble, with no characters claiming the heroic center. In such productions,

Chekhov offers us representatives from many social groups, all comically misguided but all sympathetic as well.

At the same time that Chekhov gives us a surprisingly wide cross-section of Russian society, he diminishes the usual scale of the dramatic action. The only major event in the play, the sale of the orchard, takes place offstage, and what happens onstage is largely banter, offhand remarks, distracted conversation, foundering intentions, and other markers of sheer ordinariness. Notably, Chekhov paid considerable attention to writing meticulous stage directions, which some readers have found poetic in themselves, and which suggest that he cared a great deal about the smallest details of clothing, setting, and blocking—the arrangement of characters onstage.

Chekhov is perhaps at his most innovative when it comes to the play's extraordinarily complex structure. His drama is more like a musical composition than a traditional dramatic plot: certain words, themes, and images appear, then reappear later, somewhat changed, like symphonic leitmotifs. The play organizes itself around multiple, overlapping patterns: it follows the cycle of the cherry trees, from their first blossoming in an unseasonably cold early spring to the axe that chops them down at the end, but it also follows the fates of three young women, Anya, Varya, and Dunyasha, all of whom consider the possibility of marriage, just as it tracks the intensity of loss, from the mother's loss of her child to the aristocrats' loss of their land. Echoes and resonances among the characters reverberate in visible groupings onstage: clusters of characters converge and then disperse; and their collective moods shift, like a network of emotions that has its own life. Chekhov's play also follows the model of music in quite a literal way: it organizes itself around specific, nonverbal *sounds*: the sad, mysterious noise that sounds like a harp string breaking or an echo in a mine shaft, the noise of the axes chopping down the cherry trees, and more comically, Yepikhidov's squeaking boots (which resonate with Pishchik's name, meaning "squeaker"). Throughout, too, music plays a prominent role: among Chekhov's many specific stage directions are details about the music played by the Jewish orchestra, Yepikhidov's guitar, and Ranevskaya's humming. As one director wrote to Chekhov: "Your play is abstract, like a Tchaikovsky symphony."

Although Chekhov's admirers have disagreed about the nature of *The Cherry Orchard*, from those who compared it to a musical abstraction to those who praised it as a politically charged historical chronicle, there has been no disputing its radical originality and its contribution to the history of drama. As Chekhov himself said, in characteristically self-effacing fashion: "I think that, however boring it may be, there's something new about my play."

The Cherry Orchard

A Comedy in Four Acts[1]

CHARACTERS

LIUBÓV RANYÉVSKAYA [Lyúba, Liúba Andréyevna], *who owns the estate*
ÁNYA, *her daughter, seventeen years old*
VÁRYA, *her adopted daughter, twenty-four years old*
LEONÍD GÁYEV [Lonya, Lyónya Andréyich], *Liubóv's brother*
YERMOLÁI LOPÁKHIN [Yermolái Alexéyich], *a businessman*
PÉTYA TROFÍMOV, *a graduate student*
BORÍS SEMYÓNOV-PÍSHCHIK, *who owns land in the neighborhood*
CARLOTTA, *the governess*
SEMYÓN YEPIKHÓDOV, *an accountant*
DUNYÁSHA [Avdótya Fyódorovna, Dunyáhsa Kozoyédov], *the maid*
FIRS, *the butler, eighty-seven years old*
YÁSHA, *the valet*
A HOMELESS MAN
THE STATIONMASTER
THE POSTMASTER
GUESTS, SERVANTS

The action takes place on Ranyévskaya's estate.

Act 1

[*A room they still call the nursery. A side door leads to* ÁNYA*'s room. Almost dawn; the sun is about to rise. It's May; the cherry orchard is already in bloom, but there's a chill in the air. The windows are shut. Enter* DUNYÁSHA *with a lamp, and* LOPÁKHIN *with a book in his hand.*]

LOPÁKHIN The train's finally in, thank God. What time is it?
DUNYÁSHA Almost two. [*She blows out the lamp.*] It's getting light.
LOPÁKHIN How late is the train this time? Must be at least two hours. [*He yawns and stretches.*] That was dumb. I came over on purpose just to meet them at the station, and then I fell asleep. Sat right here and fell asleep. Too bad. You should have woke me up.
DUNYÁSHA I thought you already left. [*She listens.*] Listen, that must be them.
LOPÁKHIN [*he listens*] No, they still have the luggage to get, and all that. [*Pause*] She's been away five years now; no telling how she's changed. She was always a good person. Very gentle, never caused a fuss. I remember one time when I was a kid, fifteen or so, they had my old man working in the store down by the village, and he hit me, hard, right in the face; my nose started to bleed. And we had to come up here to make a delivery or something; he was still drunk. And Liubóv Andréyevna—she wasn't much older than I was, kind of thin—she brought me inside the house, right into the nursery here, and washed the blood off my face for me. "Don't cry," she told me. "Don't cry, poor boy; you'll live long enough to get married." [*Pause*] Poor boy . . . Well, my father was poor, but take a look at me now, all dressed up, brand-new suit and tan shoes. Silk purse out of a sow's ear, I guess . . . I'm rich now, got lots of money, but when you think about it, I

1. Translated by Paul Schmidt.

guess I'm still a poor boy from the country. [*He flips the pages of the book.*] I tried reading this book, couldn't figure out a word it said. Put me to sleep.

[*Pause.*]

DUNYÁSHA The dogs were barking all night long; they know their mistress is coming home.

LOPÁKHIN Don't be silly.

DUNYÁSHA I'm so excited I'm shaking. I may faint.

LOPÁKHIN You're getting too full of yourself, Dunyásha. Look at you, all dressed up like that, and that hairdo. You watch out for that. You got to remember who you are.

[*Enter* YEPIKHÓDOV *with a bunch of flowers; he wears a jacket and tie and brightly polished boots, which squeak loudly. As he comes in, he drops the flowers.*]

YEPIKHÓDOV [*picking up the flowers*] Here. The gardener sent these over; he said put them on the dining room table. [*He gives the flowers to* DUNYÁSHA.]

LOPÁKHIN And bring me a beer.

DUNYÁSHA Right away.

[*She goes out.*]

YEPIKHÓDOV It's freezing this morning—it must be in the thirties—and the cherry blossoms are out already. I cannot abide the climate here. [*He sighs.*] I never have abided it, ever. [*Beat*][2] Yermolái Alexéyich, would you examinate something for me, please? Day before yesterday I bought myself a new pair of boots, and listen to them squeak, will you? I just cannot endear it. Do you know anything I can put on them?

LOPÁKHIN Will you shut up? You drive me crazy.

YEPIKHÓDOV Every day something awful happens to me. It's like a habit. But I don't complain. I just try to keep smiling.

[*Enter* DUNYÁSHA; *she brings* LOPÁKHIN *a beer.*]

YEPIKHÓDOV I'm going. [*He bumps into a chair, which falls over.*] You see? [*He seems proud of it.*] You see what I was referring about? Excuse my expressivity, but what a concurrence. It's almost uncanny, isn't it?

[*He leaves.*]

DUNYÁSHA You know what? That Yepikhódov proposed to me!

LOPÁKHIN Oh?

DUNYÁSHA I just don't know what to think. He's kind of nice. . . . He's a real quiet boy, but then he opens his mouth, and you can't ever understand what he's talking about. I mean, it sounds nice, but it just doesn't make any sense. I do like him, though. Kind of. And he's crazy about me. It's funny, you know, every day something awful happens to him. People around here call him Double Trouble.

LOPÁKHIN [*he listens*] That must be them.

DUNYÁSHA It's them! Oh, I don't know what's the matter with me! I feel so funny; I'm cold all over.

LOPÁKHIN It really is them this time. Let's go; we should be there at the door. You think she'll recognize me? It's been five years.

2. Pause.

DUNYÁSHA [*excited*] Oh, my God! I'm going to faint! I think I'm going to faint!

[*The sound of two carriages outside the house.* LOPÁKHIN *and* DUNYÁSHA *hurry out. The stage is empty. The sound outside gets louder.* FIRS, *leaning heavily on his cane, crosses the room, heading for the door; he wears an old-fashioned butler's livery and a top hat; he says something to himself, but you can't make out the words. The offstage noise and bustle increases. A voice: "Here we are . . . this way." Enter* LIUBÓV ANDRÉYEVNA, ÁNYA, *and* CARLOTTA, *dressed in traveling clothes.* VÁRYA *wears an overcoat, and a kerchief on her head.* GÁYEV, SEMYÓNOV-PÍSHCHIK, LOPÁKHIN, DUNYÁSHA *with a bundle and an umbrella, Servants with the luggage—all pass across the stage.*]

ÁNYA Here we are. Oh, Mama, do you remember this room?

LIUBÓV ANDRÉYEVNA The nursery!

VÁRYA It's freezing; my hands are like ice. We kept your room exactly as you left it, Mama. The white and lavender one.

LIUBÓV ANDRÉYEVNA The nursery! Oh, this house, this beautiful house! I slept in this room when I was a child. . . . [*She weeps.*] And I feel like a child again! [*She hugs* GÁYEV, VÁRYA, *then* GÁYEV *again.*] And Várya hasn't changed at all—still looks like a nun! And Dunyásha dear! Of course I remember you! [*She hugs* DUNYÁSHA.]

GÁYEV The train was two hours late. What kind of efficiency is that? Eh?

CARLOTTA And my dog loves nuts.

SEMYÓNOV-PÍSHCHIK Really! I don't believe it!

[*Everyone leaves, except* ÁNYA *and* DUNYÁSHA.]

DUNYÁSHA We've been up all night, waiting. . . . [*She takes* ÁNYA*'s coat and hat.*]

ÁNYA I've been up for four nights now. . . . I didn't sleep the whole trip. And now I'm freezing.

DUNYÁSHA When you went away it was still winter, it was snowing, and now look! Oh, sweetie, you're back! [*She laughs and hugs Ánya.*] I've been up all night, waiting to see you. Sweetheart, I just can't wait—I've got to tell you what happened. I can't wait another minute!

ÁNYA [*wearily*] Now what?

DUNYÁSHA Yepikhódov proposed the day after Easter! He wants to marry me!

ÁNYA That's all you ever think about. . . . [*She fixes her hair.*] I lost all my hairpins. . . .

DUNYÁSHA I just don't know what to do about him. He really, really loves me!

ÁNYA [*looking through the door to her room*] My own room, just as if I'd never left. I'm back home! Tomorrow I'll get up and go for a walk in the orchard. I just wish I could get some sleep. I didn't sleep the whole trip, I was so worried.

DUNYÁSHA Pétya's here. He got here day before yesterday.

ÁNYA [*joyfully*] Pétya!

DUNYÁSHA He's staying out in the barn. Said he didn't want to bother anybody. [*She looks at her watch.*] He told me to get him up, but Várya said not to. You let him sleep, she said.

[*Enter* VÁRYA. *She has a big bunch of keys attached to her belt.*]

VÁRYA Dunyásha, go get the coffee. Mama wants her coffee.

DUNYÁSHA Oh, I forgot!

[*She goes out.*]

VÁRYA You're back. Thank God! You're home again! [*She embraces Ánya.*] My angel is home again! My beautiful darling!

ÁNYA You won't believe what I've been through!

VÁRYA I can imagine.

ÁNYA I left just before Easter; it was cold. Carlotta never shut up the whole trip; she kept doing those silly tricks of hers. I don't know why you had to stick me with her.

VÁRYA Darling, you couldn't go all that way by yourself! You're only seventeen!

ÁNYA We got to Paris, it was cold and snowy, and my French is just awful! Mama was living in this fifth-floor apartment, we had to walk up, we get there and there's all these French people, some old priest reading some book, and it was crowded, and everybody was smoking these awful cigarettes—and I felt so sorry for Mama, I just threw my arms around her and couldn't let go. And she was so glad to see me, she cried—

VÁRYA [*almost crying*] I know, I know . . .

ÁNYA And she sold the villa in Mentón,[3] and the money was already gone, all of it! And I spent everything you gave me for the trip; I haven't got a thing left. And Mama still doesn't understand! We have dinner at the train station, and she orders the most expensive things on the menu, and then she tips the waiters a ruble[4] each! And Carlotta does the same! And Yásha expects the same treatment—he's just awful. You know, Yásha, that flunky of Mama's—he came back with us.

VÁRYA I saw him, the lazy good-for-nothing.

ÁNYA So what happened? Did you get the interest paid?

VÁRYA With what?

ÁNYA Oh, my God, my God . . .

VÁRYA The place goes up for sale in August.

ÁNYA Oh, my God.

[LOPÁKHIN *sticks his head in the doorway and makes a mooing sound, then goes away.*]

VÁRYA Oh, that man! I'd like to— [*She shakes her fist.*]

ÁNYA [*she hugs her*] Várya, did he propose yet? [VÁRYA *shakes her head no.*] But you know he loves you! Why don't the two of you just sit down and be honest with each other? What are you waiting for?

VÁRYA I don't think anything will ever come of it. He's always so busy, he never has time for me. He just isn't interested! It's hard for me when I see him, but I don't care anymore. Everybody talks about us getting married, people even congratulate me, but there's nothing. . . . I mean, it's all just a dream. [*A change of tone*] Oh, you've got a new pin, a little bee. . . .

ÁNYA [*with a sigh*] I know. Mama bought it for me. [*She goes into her room and starts to giggle, like a little girl.*] You know what? In Paris I went for a ride in a balloon!

VÁRYA Oh, darling, you're back! My angel is home again!

3. Resort town on the French Riviera.

4. Basic unit of Russian currency, worth about $20; one ruble is equal to one hundred kopecks.

[DUNYÁSHA *comes in, carrying a tray with coffee things, and begins setting them out on the table.* VÁRYA *stands at the doorway and talks to* ÁNYA *in the other room.*]

You know, dear, I spend the livelong day trying to keep this house going, and all I do is dream. I want to see you married off to somebody rich, then I can rest easy. And I think then I'll go away by myself, maybe live in a convent, or just go traveling: Kiev, Moscow . . . spend all my time making visits to churches. I'd start walking and just go and go and go. That would be heaven!

ÁNYA Listen to the birds in the orchard! What time is it?

VÁRYA It must be almost three. You should get some sleep, darling. [*She goes into* ÁNYA'*s room.*] Yes, that would be heaven!

[*Enter* YÁSHA *with a suitcase and a lap robe. He walks with an affected manner.*]

YÁSHA I beg pardon! May I intrude?

DUNYÁSHA I didn't even recognize you, Yásha. You got so different there in France.

YÁSHA *I'm* sorry—who are you exactly?

DUNYÁSHA When you left, I wasn't any higher than this. [*She holds her hand a distance from the floor.*] I'm Dunyásha. You know, Dunyásha Kozoyédov. Don't you remember me?

YÁSHA Well! You sure turned out cute, didn't you? [*He looks around carefully, then grabs and kisses her; she screams and drops a saucer;* YÁSHA *leaves in a hurry.*]

VÁRYA [*at the door, annoyed*] Now what happened?

DUNYÁSHA [*almost in tears*] I broke a saucer.

VÁRYA [*ironically*] Well, isn't that lucky!

ÁNYA [*entering*] Somebody should let Mama know Pétya's here.

VÁRYA I told them to let him sleep.

ÁNYA [*lost in thought*] Father died six years ago, and a month later our little brother, Grísha, drowned. Sweet boy, he was only seven. And Mama couldn't face it, that's why she went away, just went away and never looked back. [*Shivers.*] And I understand exactly how she felt. I wish she knew that.

[*Pause.*]

And Pétya Trofímov was Grísha's tutor. He might remind her . . .

[*Enter* FIRS *in his old-fashioned butler's livery. He crosses to the table and begins looking over the coffee things.*]

FIRS The missus will have her breakfast here. [*He puts on a pair of white gloves.*] Is the coffee ready? [*To* DUNYÁSHA, *crossly*] Where's the cream? Go get the cream!

DUNYÁSHA Oh, my God, I'm sorry. . . .

[*Hurries off.*]

FIRS [*he starts fussing with the coffee things*] Young flibbertigibbet . . . [*He mumbles to himself.*] They're all back from Paris. . . . In the old days they went to Paris too . . . had to go the whole way in a horse and buggy. [*He laughs.*]

VÁRYA Firs, what are you talking about?

FIRS Beg pardon? [*Joyfully*] The missus is home! Going to see her at last! Now I can die happy. . . . [*He starts to cry with joy.*]

[*Enter* LIUBÓV, GÁYEV, LOPÁKHIN, *and* SEMYÓNOV-PÍSHCHIK, *who wears a crumpled linen suit. As* GÁYEV *enters, he gestures as if he were making a billiard shot.*]

LIUBÓV ANDRÉYEVNA How did it go? I'm trying to remember. . . . Yellow ball in the side pocket! Bank shot off the corner!

GÁYEV And right down the middle! Oh, sister, sister, just think . . . when you and I were little we used to sleep in this room, and now I'm almost fifty-one! Strange, isn't it?

LOPÁKHIN Time sure passes. . . .

GÁYEV [*beat*] Say again?

LOPÁKHIN I said, time sure passes.

GÁYEV [*looking at* LOPÁKHIN] Who's wearing that cheap cologne?

ÁNYA I'm going to bed. Good night, Mama. [*She kisses her mother.*]

LIUBÓV ANDRÉYEVNA Oh, my darling little girl, my baby! Are you glad you're home? I still can't quite believe I'm here.

ÁNYA Good night, Uncle.

GÁYEV [*he kisses her*] God bless you, dear. You're getting to look so much like your mother! Liúba, she looks just like you when you were her age. She really does.

[ÁNYA *says good night to* LOPÁKHIN *and* PÍSHCHIK, *goes into her room, and closes the door behind her.*]

LIUBÓV ANDRÉYEVNA She's tired to death.

PÍSHCHIK Well, that's such a long trip!

VÁRYA Gentlemen, please. It's almost three; time you were going.

LIUBÓV ANDRÉYEVNA [*laughs*] You're the same as ever, Várya. [*Hugs and kisses her.*] Just let me have my coffee, then we'll all be going.

[FIRS *puts a pillow beneath her feet.*]

Thank you, dear. I've really gotten addicted to coffee; I drink it day and night. You old darling, you! Thank you.

VÁRYA I'll just go make sure they've got everything unloaded.

[*Goes out.*]

LIUBÓV ANDRÉYEVNA I can't believe I'm really here! [*Laughs.*] I feel like jumping up and waving my arms in the air! [*Covers her face with her hands.*] It's still like a dream. I love this country, really I do, I adore it. I started to cry every time I looked out the train windows. [*Almost in tears*] But I do need my coffee! Thank you, Firs, thank you, darling. I'm so glad you're still alive.

FIRS Day before yesterday.

GÁYEV He doesn't hear too well anymore.

LOPÁKHIN Time for me to go. I have to leave for Hárkow[5] at five. I'm really disappointed; I was looking forward to seeing you, have a chance to talk. . . . You look wonderful, just the way you always did.

PÍSHCHIK [*breathes hard*] Better than she always did. That Paris outfit. . . . She makes me feel young again!

LOPÁKHIN Your brother here thinks I'm crude, calls me a money grubber. That doesn't bother me; he can call me whatever he wants. I just hope you'll trust me the way you used to, look at me the way you used to. . . . My God, my father slaved for your father and grandfather, my whole family worked for yours; but you, you treated me different. You did so much for me I forgot about all that. Fact is, I . . . I love you like you were family . . . more, even.

5. Kharkov, city in present-day Ukraine.

LIUBÓV ANDRÉYEVNA I can't sit still; I'm just not in the mood! [*Gets up excitedly, moves about the room.*] I'm so happy I could die! I know I sound stupid—go ahead, laugh. . . . Dear old bookcase. . . . [*Kisses the bookcase.*] My little desk . . .

GÁYEV Did I tell you Nanny died while you were away?

LIUBÓV ANDRÉYEVNA [*sits back down and drinks her coffee*] Yes, you wrote me. God rest her.

GÁYEV Stásy died too. And Petrúsha Kosói quit and moved into town; he works at the police station. [*Takes out a little box of hard candies and puts one in his mouth.*]

PÍSHCHIK Dáshenka—you remember Dáshenka? My daughter? Anyway, she sends her regards. . . .

LOPÁKHIN Well, I'd like to give you some very good news. [*Looks at his watch.*] Afraid there's no time to talk now, though; I've got to go. Well, just to make it short, you know you haven't kept up the mortgage payments on your place here. So now they foreclosed and your estate is up for sale. At auction. They set a date already, August twenty-second, but don't you worry, you can rest easy. We can take care of this—I've got a great idea. Now listen, here's how it works: your place here is fifteen miles from town, and it's only a short drive from the train station. All you've got to do is clear out the old cherry orchard, plus that land down by the river, and subdivide! You lease the plots, build vacation homes, and I swear that'll bring you in twenty-five thousand[6] a year, maybe more.

GÁYEV What an outrageous thing to say!

LIUBÓV ANDRÉYEVNA Excuse me . . . Excuse me, I don't think I quite understand. . . .

LOPÁKHIN You'll get at least twenty-five hundred an acre! And if you start advertising right away, I swear to God come this fall you won't have a single plot left. You see what I'm saying? Your troubles are over! Congratulations! The location is terrific; the river's a real selling point. Only thing is, you've got to start clearing right away. Get rid of all the old buildings. This house, for instance, will have to go. You can't get people to live in a barn like this anymore. And you'll have to cut down that old cherry orchard.

LIUBÓV ANDRÉYEVNA Cut down the cherry orchard? My dear man, you don't understand! Our cherry orchard is a landmark! It's famous for miles around!

LOPÁKHIN The only thing famous about it is how big it is. You only get cherries every two years, and even then you can't get rid of them. Nobody buys them. It's just not a commercial crop.

GÁYEV Our cherry orchard is mentioned in the encyclopedia![7]

LOPÁKHIN [*looks at his watch*] We have to think of something to do and then do it. Otherwise the cherry orchard will be sold at auction on August twenty-second, this house and all the land with it. Make up your minds! Believe me, I've thought this through; there isn't any other way to do it. There just isn't.

FIRS Back in the old days, forty, fifty years ago, they used to make dried cherries, pickled cherries, preserved cherries, cherry jam, and sometimes—

6. Roughly equivalent to $500,000 today (all references to money are in rubles).

7. Probably a reference to the *Great Russian Encyclopedic Dictionary* (1890–1906), an authoritative 86-volume reference work published by F. A. Brockhaus and I. A. Efron.

GÁYEV Oh, Firs, just shut up.

FIRS —sometimes they sent them off to Moscow by the wagonload. People paid a lot for them! Back then the dried cherries were soft and juicy and sweet, and they smelled just lovely; back then they knew how to fix them. . . .

LIUBÓV ANDRÉYEVNA Does anybody know how to fix them nowadays?

FIRS Nope. They all forgot.

PÍSHCHIK Tell us about Paris. What was it like? Did you eat frogs?

LIUBÓV ANDRÉYEVNA I ate crocodiles.

PÍSHCHIK Crocodiles? Really! I don't believe it!

LOPÁKHIN You see, it used to be out here in the country there were only landlords and poor farmers, but now all of a sudden there are summer people moving in; they want vacation homes. Every town you can name is surrounded by them—it's the coming thing. In twenty years they'll expand and multiply! Right now maybe they're only places to relax on the weekend, but I bet you eventually people will put down roots out here, they'll create neighborhoods, and then your cherry orchard will blossom and bear fruit once again—and even bring in a profit!

GÁYEV [*indignantly*] That's outrageous!

[*Enter* VÁRYA *and* YÁSHA.]

VÁRYA Mama, a couple of telegrams came for you. [*Takes a key and opens the old bookcase; the lock creaks.*] Here they are.

LIUBÓV ANDRÉYEVNA They're from Paris. [*She tears them up without opening them.*] I'm through with Paris.

GÁYEV Liúba, have you any idea how old this bookcase is? Last week I pulled out the bottom drawer, and there was the date on the back, burned right into the wood. A hundred years! This bookcase is exactly a hundred years old! What do you say to that, eh? We should have a birthday celebration. Of course, it's an inanimate object, any way you look at it, but still, it's a . . . well, it's a . . . a bookcase.

PÍSHCHIK A hundred years old! Really! I don't believe it!

GÁYEV Yes, yes, it is. [*He caresses the bookcase.*] Dear old bookcase! Wonderful old bookcase! I rejoice in your existence. For a hundred years now you have borne the shining ideals of goodness and justice, a hundred years have not dimmed your silent summons to useful labor. To generations of our family [*Almost in tears*] you have offered courage, a belief in a better future, you have instructed us in ideals of goodness and social awareness. . . .

[*Pause.*]

LOPÁKHIN Right. Well . . .

LIUBÓV ANDRÉYEVNA Oh, Lonya, you're still the same as ever!

GÁYEV [*somewhat embarrassed*] Yellow ball in the side pocket! Bank shot off the center!

LOPÁKHIN Well, I've got to be off.

YÁSHA [*gives* LIUBÓV *a pillbox*] Isn't it perhaps time for your pills?

PÍSHCHIK No, no, no, dear lady! Never take medicine! Won't do any good! Won't do any harm either, though. Watch! [*Takes the pillbox, dumps the contents into his hand, puts them in his mouth, and swallows them with a swig of beer.*] There! All gone!

LIUBÓV ANDRÉYEVNA [*alarmed*] Are you out of your mind?

PÍSHCHIK I have just taken all your pills for you.

LOPÁKHIN What a glutton.

[*Everybody laughs.*]

FIRS He was here over the holidays, ate half a crock of pickles. . . . [*Mumbles.*]

LIUBÓV ANDRÉYEVNA What's he mumbling about?

VÁRYA He's been going on like that for the last three years. We're used to it by now.

YÁSHA He's getting senile.

[*Enter* CARLOTTA, *in a white dress with a lorgnette on a chain. She starts to cross the room.*]

LOPÁKHIN Oh, excuse me, Carlotta, I didn't get a chance to say hello yet. [*Tries to kiss her hand.*]

CARLOTTA [*takes her hand away*] I let you kiss my hand, first thing I know, you'll want to kiss my elbow, then my shoulder . . .

LOPÁKHIN This isn't my lucky day.

[*Everybody laughs.*]

Carlotta, show us a trick!

LIUBÓV ANDRÉYEVNA Yes, do, Carlotta—show us a trick!

CARLOTTA Not now. I'm off to bed.

[*Leaves.*]

LOPÁKHIN Well, I'll see you in three weeks. [*Kisses* LIUBÓV*'s hand.*] Goodbye now. I've got to be off. [*To* GÁYEV] Goodbye. [*Hugs* PÍSHCHIK.] So long. [*Shakes hands with* VÁRYA, *then with* FIRS *and* YÁSHA.] I sort of hate to leave. [*To* LIUBÓV] Think over what I said about subdividing the place. You decide to do it, let me know, and I'll take care of everything. I'll get you a loan of fifty thousand. Think it over now, seriously.

VÁRYA [*angry*] Will you please just go?

LOPÁKHIN I'm going, I'm going.

[*Leaves.*]

GÁYEV What a bore. Oh, excuse me, *pardon*,[8] I forgot—that's Várya's boyfriend. He's going to marry our Várya.

VÁRYA Uncle, will you please not talk nonsense?

LIUBÓV ANDRÉYEVNA Oh, but Várya, that's wonderful! He's a fine man!

PÍSHCHIK One of the finest, in fact . . . the very, very finest . . . My Dáshenka always says . . . she says . . . she says a lot of things. [*Snores, but immediately wakes up.*] Dear lady, yes, always respected you, hmm. . . . You think you could lend me, say, two hundred and forty rubles? Mortgage payment, you know, due tomorrow . . .

VÁRYA [*terrified*] We can't; we don't have any!

LIUBÓV ANDRÉYEVNA I'm afraid that's the truth. We haven't any money.

PÍSHCHIK I'll get it somewhere. [*Laughs.*] I never give up hope. There was that time I thought I was finished, it was all over, and all of a sudden—boom! The railroad cut across some of my land and paid me for it. You'll see, something will turn up tomorrow or the next day. Dáshenka will win two hundred thousand in the lottery; she just bought a ticket.

LIUBÓV ANDRÉYEVNA Well, the coffee's gone. We might as well go to bed.

8. Gáyev uses the French word *pardon* (excuse me); it was typical for upper-class Russians in the 19th century to speak French to one another.

FIRS [*takes out a clothes brush and brushes* GÁYEV*'s clothes; scolds him*] You've got on the wrong trousers again. What am I supposed to do with you?

VÁRYA [*softly*] Ánya's asleep. [*Quietly opens the window.*] The sun's coming up; it's not as cold as it was. Look, Mama, what wonderful trees! Smell the perfume! Oh, Lord! And the orioles are singing!

GÁYEV [*opens another window*] The whole orchard is white. You remember, Liúba? That long path, stretched out like a ribbon, on and on, the way it used to shine in the moonlight? You remember? You haven't forgotten?

LIUBÓV ANDRÉYEVNA Oh, my childhood! My innocence! I slept in this room, I could look out over the orchard, when I woke up in the morning I was happy, and it all looked exactly the same as this! Nothing has changed! [*Laughs delightedly.*] White, white, all white! My whole orchard is white! Autumn was dark and drizzly, and winter was cold, but now you're young again, flowering with happiness—the angels of heaven have never abandoned you. If only I could shake off this weight I've been carrying so long. If only I could forget my past!

GÁYEV Yes, and now they're selling the orchard to pay our debts. Strange, isn't it?

LIUBÓV ANDRÉYEVNA Look! There . . . in the orchard . . . it's Mother! In her white dress! [*Laughs delightedly.*] It's Mother!

GÁYEV Where?

VÁRYA Oh, Mama, for God's sake . . .

LIUBÓV ANDRÉYEVNA It's all right; I was just imagining things. There to the right, by the path to the summerhouse, that little white tree all bent over . . . it looked just like a woman.

[*Enter* TROFÍMOV. *He is dressed like a student and wears wire-rimmed glasses.*]

What a glorious orchard! All those white blossoms, and the blue sky—

TROFÍMOV Liubóv Andréyevna!

[*She turns to look at him.*]

I don't mean to disturb you; I just wanted to say hello. [*Shakes her hand warmly.*] They told me to wait until later, but I couldn't. . . .

[LIUBÓV *stares at him, bewildered.*]

VÁRYA It's Pétya Trofímov. . . .

TROFÍMOV Pétya Trofímov—I was your little boy Grísha's tutor. . . . Have I really changed all that much?

[LIUBÓV *embraces him and begins to weep softly.*]

GÁYEV [*embarrassed*] Liúba, that'll do, that'll do. . . .

VÁRYA [*weeps*] Oh, Pétya, I told you to wait till tomorrow.

LIUBÓV ANDRÉYEVNA Grísha . . . my little boy. Grísha . . . my son . . .

VÁRYA Oh, Mama, don't; it was God's will.

TROFÍMOV [*gently, almost in tears*] There, there . . .

LIUBÓV ANDRÉYEVNA [*weeps softly*] My little boy drowned, lost forever . . . Why? What for? My dear boy, why? [*Quiets down.*] Ánya's asleep, and here I am carrying on like this. . . . Pétya, what's happened to you? You used to be such a nice-looking boy. What happened? You look dreadful. You've gotten so old!

TROFÍMOV Some lady on the train called me a high-class tramp.

LIUBÓV ANDRÉYEVNA You were only a boy then, just out of high school, you were adorable, and now you've got glasses and you're losing your hair. And haven't you graduated yet? [*Goes to the door.*]

TROFÍMOV I suppose I'm what you'd call a permanent graduate student.

LIUBÓV ANDRÉYEVNA [*kisses* GÁYEV, *then* VÁRYA] Time for bed. You've gotten old too, Leoníd.

PÍSHCHIK [*follows* LIUBÓV] Time for bed, time to go . . . Ooh, my gout! I'd better stay the night. Now, dear, look, look . . . Liubóv Andréyevna, tomorrow morning I need . . . two hundred and forty rubles. . . .

GÁYEV He never gives up, does he?

PÍSHCHIK Two hundred and forty rubles; my mortgage payment due. . . .

LIUBÓV ANDRÉYEVNA Darling, I simply have no money.

PÍSHCHIK But, dear, I'll give it right back. . . . It's such a *trivial* amount. . . .

LIUBÓV ANDRÉYEVNA Oh, all right. Leoníd will get it for you. Leoníd, you give him the money.

GÁYEV I should give him money? That'll be the day.

LIUBÓV ANDRÉYEVNA We have to give it to him; he needs it. He'll give it back.

[*Exit* LIUBÓV, TROFÍMOV, PÍSHCHIK, *and* FIRS. GÁYEV, VÁRYA, *and* YÁSHA *remain.*]

GÁYEV She still thinks money grows on trees. [*To* YÁSHA] My good man, will you leave us, please? Go back to the barn, where you belong.

YÁSHA [*smiles*] Leoníd Andréyich, you're the same as you always were.

GÁYEV What say? [*To* VÁRYA] What did he just say?

VÁRYA [*to* YÁSHA] Your mother came in from the country to see you. She's been sitting in the kitchen for two days now, waiting.

YÁSHA Oh, for God's sake, can't she leave me alone?

VÁRYA You are really disgraceful!

YÁSHA That's all I need right now. Why couldn't she wait till tomorrow? [*Goes out.*]

VÁRYA Mama hasn't changed; she's the same as she always was. If it were up to her, she'd give away everything.

GÁYEV Yes. . . . [*Pause*] Someone gets sick, you know, and the doctor tries one thing after another, that means there's no cure. I've been thinking and thinking, racking my brains, I come up with one thing, then another, but the truth is, none of them will work. It would be wonderful if somebody left us a lot of money, it would be wonderful if we could marry off Ánya to somebody with a lot of money, it would be wonderful if we could go see Ánya's godmother in Yároslavl,[9] try to borrow the money from her. She's very, very rich.

VÁRYA [*weeps*] If only God would help us!

GÁYEV Oh, stop crying. She's very, very rich, but she doesn't like us. Because in the first place, my sister married a mere lawyer instead of a man with a title. . . .

[ÁNYA *appears in the doorway.*]

She married a lawyer, and then her behavior has not been—how shall I put it?—particularly exemplary. She's a lovely woman, goodhearted, charming, and of course she's my sister and I love her very much, and there are extenuating circumstances and such, but the fact is, she's what you'd have to call a . . . a loose woman. And she doesn't care who knows it; you can feel it in every move she makes.

9. Russian city northeast of Moscow.

VÁRYA [*whispers*] Ánya's here.

GÁYEV What say? [*Pause*] Funny, I must have gotten something in my eye: I can't see too well. . . . Did I tell you what happened Thursday, when I was at the county courthouse?

[ÁNYA *comes into the room.*]

VÁRYA Why aren't you asleep?

ÁNYA I tried. I couldn't sleep.

GÁYEV Kitten . . . [*Kisses* ÁNYA*'s cheek, then her hands.*] My dear child . . . [*Almost in tears*] You're more than just my niece, you're my angel, you know that? You're my whole world, believe me, believe me. . . .

ÁNYA I believe you, Uncle. And I love you; we all love you. . . . But, Uncle dear, you should learn not to talk so much. The things you were saying just now about Mama, about your own sister . . . What were you saying all that for?

GÁYEV I know, I know. . . . [*Covers his face with her hand.*] It's awful, I know. My God, a few minutes ago I made a speech to a piece of furniture. . . . It was so stupid! The thing is, I never realize how stupid I sound until I'm done.

VÁRYA She's right, Uncle. You just have to learn to keep still, that's all.

ÁNYA If you do, you'll feel much better about yourself, you know you will. . . .

GÁYEV I will, I will, I promise. [*Kisses* ÁNYA*'s and* VÁRYA*'s hands.*] I'll keep still. Only right now I have to talk a little more. Business! On Thursday I was at the county courthouse; there was a group of us talking—just this and that—and it turns out I might be able to arrange a promissory note for enough money to pay off the mortgage.

VÁRYA If only God would help us!

GÁYEV I'm going in on Tuesday, I'll talk to them again. [*To* VÁRYA] Don't whine! [*To* ÁNYA] Your mother will talk to Lopákhin; he can't refuse to help her. And you, as soon as you're rested, you go to Yároslavl, go talk to your godmother. There. We'll be operating on three fronts at once; we're sure to succeed. We *will* pay off this mortgage, I know we will. . . . [*He pops a hard candy into his mouth.*] I swear by my honor, I swear by anything you want, the estate will not be sold! [*Excitedly*] I swear by my own happiness! Here, you have my hand on it. You may call me . . . dishonorable, call me anything you will, if I ever let this estate go on the auction block! I swear by my entire existence!

ÁNYA [*her calm mood has returned; she is happy*] You're so smart, Uncle! You're such a wonderful man! [*Hugs* GÁYEV.] Now I feel better! So much better! I'm happy again!

[*Enter* FIRS.]

FIRS [*reproachfully*] Leoníd Andréyich, why aren't you in bed, like decent God-fearing people?

GÁYEV I'm coming, I'm coming. You go to bed, Firs. I can get undressed by myself. All right, children, nighty-night. We can talk about the details tomorrow, now it's time for bed. [*Kisses* ÁNYA *and* VÁRYA.] I am a man of the eighties, you know. People don't think much of that era now, but I can tell you frankly that I have had the courage of my convictions and often had to pay the price.[1]

1. When Alexander III (1845–1894) became tsar in 1881, he initiated repressive measures to combat liberal and revolutionary elements in Russian society.

But these local peasants all love me. You have to get to know them, that's all. You have to get to know them, and—

ÁNYA Uncle. You're at it again.

VÁRYA Just be quiet, Uncle.

FIRS [*angrily*] Leoníd Andréyich!

GÁYEV I'm coming, I'm coming. . . . Go to bed now. Yellow ball in the side pocket! Clean shot!

[*Goes out;* FIRS *follows him, limping.*]

ÁNYA I feel much better. I don't much want to go to Yároslavl, I don't like my godmother, but I feel better now. Thanks to Uncle [*Sits down.*]

VÁRYA We've got to get some sleep. I'm going to bed. Oh, there's something came up since you left. You know we've got all those old retired servants living out back—Paulina, old Karp, and the rest of them. And what happened, they started inviting people in to spend the night. Well, it's annoying, but I never said a thing. Then what happened was, they started telling everybody all they were getting to eat was beans. Because I was so cheap, you see. It was that old Karp was doing it. So I said to myself, All right, that's the way you want it, all right, just wait, and I sent for him [*Yawns*], and in he comes, so I say, Karp, you're such an idiot—[*Looks at* ÁNYA.] Ánya!

[*Pause.*]

She's asleep. [*Lifts* ÁNYA *by the arms.*] Come on, time for bed. . . . Come on, let's go. . . . [*Leads her off.*] My angel fell asleep! Come on. . . . [*They start out.*]

[*In the distance, beyond the orchard, a shepherd plays a pipe.* TROFÍMOV *enters, sees* ÁNYA *and* VÁRYA, *stops.*]

VÁRYA Shh! She's asleep. . . . Come on, darling, let's go. . . .

ÁNYA [*softly, half asleep*] I was so tired. . . . All those bells . . . Uncle dear . . . and Mama. Uncle and Mama.

VÁRYA Come on, darling, come on. . . .

[*They go off into* ÁNYA*'s room.*]

TROFÍMOV [*deeply moved*] My sunshine! My springtime!

Curtain.

Act 2

[*An open space. The overgrown rain of an abandoned chapel. There is a well beside it and some large stones that must once have been grave markers. An old bench. Beyond, the road to the Gáyev estate. On one side a shadowy row of poplar trees; they mark the limits of the cherry orchard. A row of telegraph poles, and on the far distant horizon, on a clear day, you can just make out the city. It's late afternoon, almost sunset.* CARLOTTA, YÁSHA, *and* DUNYÁSHA *are sitting on the bench;* YEPIKHÓDOV *stands nearby, strumming his guitar; each seems lost in his own thoughts.* CARLOTTA *wears an old military cap and is adjusting the strap on a hunting rifle.*]

CARLOTTA [*meditatively*] I haven't got a birth certificate, so I don't know how old I really am. I just think of myself as young. When I was a little girl, Mama and my father used to travel around to fairs and put on shows, good ones. I did back flips, things like that. And after they died this German woman brought me up, taught me a few things. And that was it. Then I grew up and had to go to work. As a governess. Where I'm from . . . who I am . . . no idea. Who my parents were—maybe they weren't even married—no idea. [*Takes a large cucumber pickle out of her pocket and takes a bite.*] No idea at all.

[*Pause.*]

And I feel like talking all the time, but there's no one to talk to. No one.

YEPIKHÓDOV [*plays the guitar and sings*]

"What do I care for the rest of the world,
or care what it cares for me . . . "[2]

Very agreeable, playing a mandolin.

DUNYÁSHA That's not a mandolin, it's a guitar. [*Takes out a compact with a mirror and powders herself.*]

YEPIKHÓDOV When a man is madly in love, a guitar is a mandolin. [*Sings.*]

"As long as my heart is on fire with love,
and the one I love loves me."

[YÁSHA *sings harmony.*]

CARLOTTA Oof! You people sound like hyenas.

DUNYÁSHA But it must have been just lovely, being in Europe.

YÁSHA Oh, it was. Quite, quite lovely. I have to agree with you there. [*Yawns, then lights a cigar.*]

YEPIKHÓDOV That's understandable. In Europe, things have already come to a complex.

YÁSHA [*beat*] I suppose you could say that.

YEPIKHÓDOV I'm a true product of the educational system; I read all the time. All the right books too, but I have no chosen directive in life. For me, strictly speaking, it's live or shoot myself. That's why I always carry a loaded pistol. See? [*Takes out a revolver.*]

CARLOTTA All done. Time to go. [*Slings the rifle over her shoulder.*] You're a very smart man, Yepikhódov, and a very scary one. Ooh! The women must adore you. [*Starts off.*] They're all so dumb, these smart boys. Never anyone to talk to . . . Always alone, all by myself, no one to talk to . . . and I still don't know who I am. Or why. No idea.

[*Walks slowly off.*]

YEPIKHÓDOV I should explain, by the way, for the sake of expressivity, that fate has been, ah, *rigorous* to me. I am, strictly speaking, tempest-tossed. Always have been. Now, you may say to me, Oh, you're imagining things, but then why, when I wake up this morning—here's an example—and I look down, why is there this spider on my stomach? Detrimentally large too. [*Makes a circle with his two hands.*] Big as that. Or take a beer, let's say. I go to drink it, what do I see floating around in it? Something highly unappreciative, like a cockroach.

[*Pause.*]

Have you ever read Henry Thomas Buckle?[3]

[*Pause.*]

2. Words from a popular turn-of-the-century ballad.

3. English historian (1821–1862) who wrote *A History of Civilization in England* (1857–61), considered daringly freethinking and materialistic.

May I design to disturb you, Avdótya Fyódorovna, with something I have to say?

DUNYÁSHA So say it.

YEPIKHÓDOV Preferentially alone. [*Sighs.*]

DUNYÁSHA [*embarrassed*] All right. . . . Only first get me my wrap; it's by the kitchen door. It's getting kind of damp.

YEPIKHÓDOV Ah, I see. Yes, get the wrap, of course. Now I know what to do with my gun.

[*Takes his guitar and goes off, strumming.*]

YÁSHA Double Trouble. He's an idiot, if you ask me. [*Yawns.*]

DUNYÁSHA I hope to God he doesn't shoot himself.

[*Pause.*]

I get upset over every little thing anymore. Ever since I started working for them here, I've gotten used to their *lifestyle*. Just look at my hands. Look at how white they are, just like I was rich. I'm different now from like I was. I'm more delicate, I'm more sensitive; everything upsets me. . . . It's just awful how things upset me. So if you cheat on me, Yásha, I may just have a nervous breakdown.

YÁSHA [*kisses her*] Oh, you little cutie! Just remember, though: a girl has to watch her step. What I'm after is a *nice* girl.

DUNYÁSHA I really love you, Yásha, I really do. You're so smart, you know so many things. . . .

[*Pause.*]

YÁSHA [*yawns*] Yeah. . . . But my theory is, a girl says she loves you, she's not a nice girl.

[*Pause.*]

Nothing like smoking a cigar out here in the fresh air. . . . [*Listens.*] Somebody's coming. . . . It's them. . . .

[DUNYÁSHA *hugs him impulsively.*]

YÁSHA Go on back to the house. Go back the other way, make believe you've been swimming down by the river, so they don't think we've been . . . we've been getting together out here like this. I don't want them to think that.

DUNYÁSHA [*a little cough*] That cigar smoke is giving me a headache. . . .

[*Goes out.*]

[YÁSHA *sits beside the chapel wall. Enter* LIUBÓV, GÁYEV, *and* LOPÁKHIN.]

LOPÁKHIN You have to make up your mind one way or the other; time's running out. There's no argument left. You want to subdivide or don't you? Just give me an answer, one word, yes or no.

LIUBÓV ANDRÉYEVNA Who's been smoking those cheap cigars? [*Sits down.*]

GÁYEV Everything's so convenient, now that there's the railroad. We went into town just to have lunch. Yellow ball in the side pocket! What do you say—why don't we go back to the house, eh? Have ourselves a little game . . .

LIUBÓV ANDRÉYEVNA Let's wait till later.

LOPÁKHIN Just one word! [*Imploringly*] Why don't you give me an answer?

GÁYEV [*yawns*] To what?

LIUBÓV ANDRÉYEVNA [*rummages in her purse*] Yesterday I had a lot of money, today it's all gone. My poor Várya feeds us all on soup to economize, the poor old people get nothing but beans, and I just spend and spend. . . . [*Drops her purse; gold coins spill out.*] Oh, I've spilled everything. . . .

YÁSHA Here, allow me. [*Picks up the money.*]

LIUBÓV ANDRÉYEVNA Oh, please do, Yásha: thank you. And why I had to go into that town for lunch—that stupid restaurant of yours, those stupid musicians, those stupid tablecloths; they smelled of soap. . . . Why do we drink so much, Lyónya? And eat so much? Why do we talk so much? The whole time we were in the restaurant, you kept talking, and none of it made any sense. Talking about the seventies, about Symbolism.[4] And to who? The waiters! Talking about Symbolism to waiters!

LOPÁKHIN Yes.

GÁYEV [*makes a deprecating gesture*] I'm incorrigible, I suppose. . . . [*To* YÁSHA, *irritably*] What are *you* doing here? Why are you always underfoot every time I turn around?

YÁSHA [*laughs*] Because every time I hear your voice it makes me laugh.

GÁYEV Either he goes or I do!

LIUBÓV ANDRÉYEVNA Yásha, please . . . just go 'way, will you?

YÁSHA [*gives* LIUBÓV *her purse*] I'm going. Right now. [*Barely containing his laughter*] Right this very minute . . .

[*Goes out.*]

LOPÁKHIN You know who Derigánov is? You know how much money he has? You know he's planning to buy your property? They say he's coming to the auction himself.

LIUBÓV ANDRÉYEVNA Who told you that?

LOPÁKHIN Everybody in town knows about it.

GÁYEV The old lady in Yároslavl promised to send money. . . . But when, and how much, she didn't say.

LOPÁKHIN How much will she send? A hundred thousand? Two hundred?

LIUBÓV ANDRÉYEVNA Ten or fifteen thousand. And we're lucky to get that much.

LOPÁKHIN Excuse me, but you people . . . I have never met anyone so unbusinesslike, so impractical, so . . . so *crazy* as the pair of you! Somebody tells you flat out your land is about to be sold, you don't even seem to understand!

LIUBÓV ANDRÉYEVNA But what should we do? Just tell us what we should do!

LOPÁKHIN I tell you every day what you should do! Every day I come out here and say the same thing. The cherry orchard and the rest of the land has to be subdivided and developed for leisure homes, and it has to be done right away. The auction date is getting closer! Can't you understand? All you have to do is make up your mind to subdivide, you'll have more money than even you can spend! Your troubles will be over!

LIUBÓV ANDRÉYEVNA Subdivide, leisure homes . . . excuse me, but it's all so hopelessly vulgar.

GÁYEV I couldn't agree more.

4. Symbolism was an unsettling artistic movement, launched by French poets Stéphane Mallarmé and Paul Verlaine in the late 19th century; they emphasized evocative images and sounds rather than logic or facts. "The seventies": a time of peasant unrest in Russia.

LOPÁKHIN You people drive me crazy! Another minute, I'll be shouting my head off! Oh, I give up, I give up! Why do I even bother? [*To* GÁYEV] You're worse than an old lady!

GÁYEV What say?

LOPÁKHIN I said you're an old lady! [*Starts to leave.*]

LIUBÓV ANDRÉYEVNA [*fearfully*] No, no, no, please, my dear, don't go. Please. I'm sure we'll think of something.

LOPÁKHIN What's there to think of?

LIUBÓV ANDRÉYEVNA Please. Don't go. Things are easier when you're around. . . .

[*Pause.*]

I keep waiting for something to happen. It's as if the house were about to fall down around our ears or something. . . .

GÁYEV [*meditatively*] Yellow ball in the side pocket . . . Clean shot down the middle . . .

LIUBÓV ANDRÉYEVNA We're guilty of so many sins, I know—

LOPÁKHIN Sins? What are you talking about?

GÁYEV [*pops a hard candy into his mouth*] People say I've eaten up my entire inheritance in candy. [*Laughs.*]

LIUBÓV ANDRÉYEVNA All my sins . . . I've always wasted money, just thrown it away like a madwoman, and I married a man who never paid a bill in his life. He was an alcoholic; he drank himself to death—on champagne. And I was so unhappy I fell in love with another man, *unfortunately*, and had an affair with him, and that was when—that was the first thing, my first punishment, right down there, in the river, my little boy drowned, and I left, I went to France, I left and never wanted to come back, I never wanted to see that river again, I just closed my eyes and *ran*, forgot about everything, and that man followed me. He just wouldn't let up. And he was so mean to me, so cruel! I bought a villa in Mentón because he got sick while we were there, and for the next three years I never had a moment's peace, day or night. He tormented me from his sickbed. I could feel my soul dry up. And last year I couldn't afford the villa anymore, so I sold it and we moved to Paris, and once we were in Paris he took everything I had left and ran off with another woman, and I tried to kill myself. It was so stupid, and so shameful! Finally all I wanted was to come back home, to where I was born, to my daughter. [*Wipes away her tears.*] Oh, dear God, dear God, forgive me! Forgive me my sins! Don't punish me again! [*Takes a telegram from her purse.*] This came today, from Paris. . . . He says he's sorry, he wants me back. . . . [*Tears up the telegram.*] Where's [*Listens.*] . . . where's that music coming from?

GÁYEV That's our famous local orchestra. Those Jewish musicians, you remember? Four fiddles, a clarinet, and a double bass.

LIUBÓV ANDRÉYEVNA Are they still around? We should have them over some evening and throw a party.

LOPÁKHIN [*listens*] I don't hear anything. [*Sings to himself.*]

"Ooh-la-la . . .
Just a little bit of money
makes a lady very French . . ."[5]

5. Satirical reference to Russian efforts to imitate Parisian culture since the time of Tsar Peter the Great (1672–1725).

[*Laughs.*] I went to the theater last night, saw this musical. Very funny.

LIUBÓV ANDRÉYEVNA I doubt there was anything funny about it. You ought to stop going to see playacting and take a good look at your own reality. What a boring life you lead! And what uninteresting things you talk about.

LOPÁKHIN Well . . . yeah, there's some truth to that. It is a pretty dumb life we lead. . . .

[*Pause.*]

My father was a . . . he was a dirt farmer, an idiot, never understood me, never taught me anything, just got drunk and beat me up. With a stick. Fact is, I'm not much better myself. Never did well in school, my writing's terrible, I'm ashamed if anybody sees it. I write like a pig.

LIUBÓV ANDRÉYEVNA My dear man, you should get married.

LOPÁKHIN Yes. . . . Yes, I should.

LIUBÓV ANDRÉYEVNA And you should marry our Várya. She's a wonderful girl.

LOPÁKHIN She is.

LIUBÓV ANDRÉYEVNA Her people were quite ordinary, but she works like a dog, and the main thing is, she loves you. And you like her, I know you do. You always have.

LOPÁKHIN Look, I've got nothing against it. I . . . She's wonderful girl.

[*Pause.*]

GÁYEV They offered me a position at the bank. Six thousand a year. Did I tell you?

LIUBÓV ANDRÉYEVNA Don't be silly! You stay right here where you belong.

[*Enter* FIRS, *carrying an overcoat.*]

FIRS Sir, sir, please put this on. It's getting damp.

GÁYEV [*puts it on*] Firs, you're getting to be a bore.

FIRS That so? Went out this morning, didn't even tell me. [*Tries to adjust* GÁYEV*'s clothes.*]

LIUBÓV ANDRÉYEVNA Poor Firs! You've gotten so old!

FIRS Beg pardon?

LOPÁKHIN She said you got very old!

FIRS I've lived a long time. They were trying to marry me off way back before your daddy was born. [*Laughs.*] By the time we got our freedom back,[6] I was already head butler. I had all the freedom I needed, so I stayed right here with the masters.

[*Pause.*]

I remember everybody got all excited about it, but they never even knew what they were getting excited about.

LOPÁKHIN Oh, sure, things were wonderful back in the good old days! They had the right to beat you if they wanted, remember?

FIRS [*doesn't hear*] That's right. Masters stood by the servants, servants stood by the masters. Nowadays it's all mixed up; you can't tell who's who.

GÁYEV Shut up, Firs. . . . I have to go into town tomorrow. A friend promised to introduce me to someone who might be able to arrange a loan. Some general.

6. Tsar Alexander II emancipated the serfs in 1861.

LOPÁKHIN That's never going to work. Trust me, you won't get enough even for the interest payments.

LIUBÓV ANDRÉYEVNA He's imagining things. There's no general.

[*Enter* ÁNYA, VÁRYA, *and* TROFÍMOV.]

GÁYEV Here come our young people.

ÁNYA Mama's resting.

LIUBÓV ANDRÉYEVNA [*tenderly*] Here we are, dears, over here. [*Kisses* ÁNYA *and* VÁRYA.] If you only knew how much I love you both. Come sit here by me . . . that's right.

[*They all sit down.*]

LOPÁKHIN Our permanent graduate student seems to spend all his time studying the ladies.

TROFÍMOV Mind your own business.

LOPÁKHIN Almost in his fifties, he's still in school.

TROFÍMOV Just stop the silly jokes, will you?

LOPÁKHIN Oh, the *scholar* is losing his temper!

TROFÍMOV Will you please just leave me alone?

LOPÁKHIN [*laughs*] Let me ask you a question: You look at me, what do you see?

TROFÍMOV When I look at you, Yermolái Alexéyich, what I see is a rich man. One who will soon be a millionaire. You are as necessary a part of the evolution of the species as the wild animal that eats up anything in its path.

[*Everybody laughs.*]

VÁRYA Forget biology, Pétya. You should stick to counting stars.

LIUBÓV ANDRÉYEVNA I want to hear more about what we were talking about last night.

TROFÍMOV What were we talking about?

GÁYEV About human dignity.

TROFÍMOV We talked about a lot last night, but we never got anywhere. You people talk about human dignity as if it were something mystical. I suppose it is, in a way, for you anyway, but when you really get down to it, what have humans got to be proud of? Biologically we're pretty minor specimens—besides which, the great majority of human beings are vulgar and unhappy and totally *un*dignified. We should stop patting ourselves on the back and get to work.

GÁYEV You still have to die.

TROFÍMOV Who says? Anyway, what does that mean, to die? Maybe we have a hundred senses, and all we lose when we die are the five we're familiar with, and the other ninety-five go on living.

LIUBÓV ANDRÉYEVNA Oh, Pétya, you're so smart!

LOPÍKHIN [*with irony*] Oh, yes, very.

TROFÍMOV Remember, human beings are constantly progressing, and their power keeps growing. Things that seem impossible to us nowadays, the day will come when they're not a problem at all, only we have to work toward that day. We have to seek out the truth. We don't do that, you know. Most of the people in this country aren't working toward anything. People I come in contact with—at the university, for instance—they're supposed to be educated, but they're not interested in the truth. They're not interested in much of anything, actually. They certainly don't *do* much. They call themselves intellectuals and think that gives them the right to look down on the rest of the world. They never read anything worthwhile, they're completely ignorant where science is concerned, they talk about art and they don't even know what it is they're talking about. They take themselves so seriously, they're full of theories and ideas, but just go look at the cities they live in. Miles and miles of slums, where people go hungry and where they live packed into unheated tenements full of cockroaches and garbage, and their lives are full of violence and immorality. So what are all the theories for? To keep people like us from seeing all that. Where are the day-care centers they talk so much about, and the literacy programs? It's all just talk. You go out to the parts of town where the poor people live, you can't find them. All you find is dirt and ignorance and crime. That's why I don't like all this talk, all these theories. Bothers me, makes me afraid. If that's all our talk is good for, we'd better just shut up.

LOPÁKHIN I get up at five and work from morning to night, and you know, my business involves a lot of money, my own and other people's, so I see lots of people, see what they're like. And you just try to get anything accomplished: you'll see how few decent, honest people there really are. Sometimes at night I can't sleep, and I think: Dear God, you gave us this beautiful earth to live on, these great forests, these wide fields, the broad horizons . . . by rights we should be giants.

LIUBÓV ANDRÉYEVNA What do you want giants for? The only good giants are in fairy tales. Real ones would scare you to death.

[*Upstage,* YEPIKHÓDOV *strolls by, playing his guitar.*]

[*Dreamily*] There goes Yepikhódov. . . .

ÁNYA [*dreamily*] There goes Yepikhódov. . . .

GÁYEV The sun, ladies and gentlemen, has just set.

TROFÍMOV Yes.

GÁYEV [*as if reciting a poem, but not too loud*] O wondrous nature, cast upon us your eternal rays, forever beautiful, forever indifferent. . . . Mother, we call you; life and death reside within you; you bring forth and lay waste—

VÁRYA [*pleading*] Uncle, please!

ÁNYA Uncle, you're doing it again.

TROFÍMOV We'd rather have the yellow ball in the side pocket.

GÁYEV Sorry, sorry. I'll keep still.

[*They all sit in silence. The only sound we hear is old* FIRS *mumbling. Suddenly a distant sound seems to fall from the sky, a sad sound, like a harp string breaking. It dies away.*]

LIUBÓV ANDRÉYEVNA What was that?

LOPÁKHIN Can't tell. Sounds like it could be an echo from a mine shaft. But it must be far away.

GÁYEV Or some kind of bird . . . like a heron.

TROFÍMOV Or an owl.

LIUBÓV ANDRÉYEVNA [*shivers*] Makes me nervous.

[*Pause.*]

FIRS It's like just before the trouble started. They heard an owl screech, and the kettle wouldn't stop whistling. . . .

GÁYEV Before what trouble?

FIRS The day we got our freedom back.

[*Pause.*]

LIUBÓV ANDRÉYEVNA My dears, it's getting dark; we should be going in. [*To* ÁNYA] You've got tears in your eyes, darling. What's the matter? [*Hugs* ÁNYA.]

ÁNYA Nothing, Mama. It's all right.

TROFÍMOV Someone's coming.

[*Enter a* HOMELESS MAN *in a white cap and an overcoat; he's slightly drunk.*]

HOMELESS MAN Can anyone please tell me, can I get to the train station this way?

GÁYEV Of course you can. Just follow this road.

HOMELESS MAN Much obliged. [*Bows.*] Wonderful weather we're having . . . [*Recites.*] "Behold one of the poor in spirit, just trying to inherit a little of the earth. . . ."[7] [*To* VÁRYA] Listen, you think you could spare some money for a hungry man?

[VÁRYA *is terrified; she screams.*]

LOPÁKHIN [*angrily*] Now hold on just a minute!

LIUBÓV ANDRÉYEVNA [*panicked*] Here . . . here . . . take this. [*Fumbles in her purse.*] Oh, I don't seem to have anything smaller. Here, take this. [*Gives him a gold piece.*]

HOMELESS MAN Very much obliged!

[*Goes out.*]

[*Everybody laughs.*]

VÁRYA Get me out of here! Oh, please get me out! Mama, how could you! We can't even feed the servants, and you go and give him a gold piece!

LIUBÓV ANDRÉYEVNA I know, darling, I'm just stupid about money. When we get home I'll give you whatever I've got left; you can take care of it. Yermolái Alexéyich, can you lend me some money?

LOPÁKHIN Of course.

LIUBÓV ANDRÉYEVNA My darlings, it really is time to go in. Várya dear, we've just gotten you engaged. Congratulations.

VÁRYA [*almost in tears*] Mama, that's nothing to joke about!

LOPÁKHIN Amelia, get thee to a nunnery![8]

GÁYEV Look how my hands shake. I don't know if I could play billiards anymore. . . .

LOPÁKHIN Nymph, in thy horizons be all my sins remembered![9]

LIUBÓV ANDRÉYEVNA Please, let's go. It's almost suppertime.

VÁRYA He scared me half to death. I can feel my heart pounding.

LOPÁKHIN But keep in mind, the cherry orchard is going to be sold. On August twenty-second! You hear what I'm saying? You've got to think about this! You've got to!

[*They all go off except* ÁNYA *and* TROFÍMOV.]

ÁNYA [*laughs*] I'm so glad that tramp scared Várya off. Now we can be alone.

TROFÍMOV Várya's afraid we're going to fall in love; that's why she never leaves us alone. She's so narrow-minded; she simply can't understand that we are

7. Reference to Jesus's Sermon on the Mount: "Blessed are the poor in spirit, for theirs is the kingdom of heaven. . . . Blessed are the meek, for they shall inherit the earth" (Matthew 5.3, 5).

8. Hamlet, in Shakespeare's play, suspects Ophelia of spying for her father and sends her off with "Get thee to a nunnery!" (3.1.22).

9. Lopákhin transforms a line from *Hamlet*: "Nymph, in thy orisons, / Be all my sins remembered" (3.1.91–92).

above love. Our goal is to get rid of the silly illusions that keep us from being free and happy. We are moving forward, toward the future! Toward one bright star that burns ahead of us! Forward, friends! Come join us in our journey!

ÁNYA [*claps her hands*] Oh, you talk so beautifully!

[*Pause.*]

It's just heavenly out here today!

TROFÍMOV Yes, the weather's been really good lately.

ÁNYA I don't know what it is you've done to me, Pétya, but I don't love the cherry orchard anymore, not the way I used to. I used to think there was no place on earth like our orchard.

TROFÍMOV This whole country is our orchard. It's a big country and a beautiful one; it has lots of wonderful places in it.

[*Pause.*]

Just think, Ánya: your grandfather, and his father, and his father's fathers, they *owned* the people who slaved away for them all over this estate, and now the voices and faces of human beings hide behind every cherry in the orchard, every leaf, every tree trunk. Can't you see them? And hear them? And owning human beings has left its mark on all of you. Look at your mother and your uncle! They live off the labor of others, they always have, and they've never even noticed! They owe their entire lives to those other people, people they wouldn't even let walk through the front gate of their beloved cherry orchard! This whole country has fallen behind; it'll take us at least two hundred years to catch up. The thing is, we don't have any real sense of our own history; all we do is sit around and talk, talk, talk, then we feel depressed, so we go out and get drunk. If there's one thing that's clear to me, it's this: if we want to have any real life in the present, we have to do something to make up for our past, we have to get over it, and the only way to do that is to make sacrifices, get down to work, and work harder than we've ever worked before. Do you understand what I mean, Ánya?

ÁNYA The house we live in isn't our house anymore. It hasn't ever been, really. And I'll leave it all behind, I promise you I will.

TROFÍMOV Yes, you will! Throw away your house keys and go as far away as you can! You'll be free as the wind.

ÁNYA [*radiant*] I love the way you say things!

TROFÍMOV You have to understand me, Ánya. I'm not thirty yet, I'm still young; I may still be in school, but I've learned a lot. Winter comes, sometimes I get cold and hungry, or sick and upset, I don't have a cent to my name; things work out or they don't. . . . But no matter what, my heart and soul are always full of feelings, all kinds . . . I can't even explain them. And I feel happiness coming, Ánya, I can feel it. I can almost see it—

ÁNYA [*dreamily*] Look, the moon's rising.

[*The sound of* YEPIKHÓDOV's *guitar, still playing the same mournful song. The moon rises. Somewhere beyond the poplar trees,* VÁRYA *can be heard calling.*]

VÁRYA [*off*] Ánya! Ánya, where are you?

TROFÍMOV Yes, the moon is rising.

[*Pause.*]

It's happiness, that's what it is: it's rising, it's coming closer and closer, I can hear it. And even if we miss it, if we never find it, that's all right! Someone will!

VÁRYA [*off*] Ánya! Ánya, where are you?

TROFÍMOV [*angrily*] That Várya! Why won't she let us alone!

ÁNYA Don't let her bother you. Let's take a walk by the river. It's so nice there.

TROFÍMOV All right, let's go.

[*They leave. The stage is empty.*]

VÁRYA [*off*] Ánya! Ánya!

Curtain.

Act 3

[*A sitting room, separated from the ballroom in back by an archway. The chandeliers are lit. From the entrance hall comes the sounds of an orchestra, the Jewish musicians* GÁYEV *mentioned in Act 2. Evening. In the ballroom, everyone is dancing a grande ronde.* SEMYÓNOV-PÍSHCHIK*'s voice is heard calling the figures of the dance: "Promenade à une paire!"*[1] *The dancers dance through the sitting room in pairs in the following order:* PÍSHCHIK *and* CARLOTTA, TROFÍMOV *and* LIUBÓV ANDREYÉVNA, ÁNYA *and the* POSTMASTER, VÁRYA *and the* STATIONMASTER, *etc.* VÁRYA *is in tears, which she tries to wipe away as she dances. The final pair includes* DUNYÁSHA. *As the dancers return to the ballroom,* PÍSHCHIK *calls out: "Grande roude, balancez!" and "Les cavaliers à genoux et remercier vos dames."*[2] FIRS *in his butler's uniform crosses the stage, carrying a seltzer bottle on a tray.* PÍSHCHIK *and* TROFÍMOV *come into the sitting room.*]

PÍSHCHIK I'm prone to strokes, already had two of 'em, I really shouldn't be dancing, but you know what they say: When in Rome. Besides, I'm really strong as a horse. Speaking of Romans, my father—what a joker he was—he used to claim our family was descended from the emperor Caligula's horse—you know, the one he made a senator?[3] [*Sits down.*] The only problem is we have no money. [*His head nods, he snores, then immediately wakes up.*] So the only thing I ever think about is money.

TROFÍMOV Your father was right. You do look a little like a horse.

PÍSHCHIK Nothing wrong with horses. Wonderful animals. If I had one, I could sell it. . . .

[*From the adjacent billiard room come the sounds of a game.* VÁRYA *appears in the archway.*]

TROFÍMOV [*teases her*] Mrs. Lopákhin! Mrs. Lopákhin!

VÁRYA [*angrily*] High-class tramp!

TROFÍMOV Yes, I'm a high-class tramp, and I'm proud of it!

VÁRYA [*bitterly*] We've hired an orchestra! And what are we supposed to pay them with?

[*Goes out.*]

1. "Promenade with your partner!" (French).
2. "Make a large circle, swing with your arms! Gentlemen, kneel and thank your ladies!" (French).
3. The mad emperor Caligula (12–41 C.E.) brought his favorite horse into the Roman senate to make it a senator.

TROFÍMOV [*to* PÍSHCHIK] All the energy you've used trying to find money to pay your mortgage, if you'd spent that energy on something else, you could have moved the world.

PÍSHCHIK Nietzsche,[4] you know, the philosopher—a great thinker, Nietzsche, a man of genius, one of the great minds of the century—now Nietzsche, you know, says, in his memoirs, that counterfeit money's just as good as real. . . .

TROFÍMOV I didn't know you'd read Nietzsche.

PÍSHCHIK Well . . . actually, Dáshenka told me. And I'm desperate enough. I'm ready to start counterfeiting. I need three hundred and ten rubles, day after tomorrow. All I've got so far is a hundred and thirty. . . . [*He feels in his pockets anxiously.*] It's gone! My money's gone! [*Almost in tears*] I've lost my money! [*Joyfully*] Oh, here it is! It slipped down into the lining of my coat! God, I'm all in a sweat!

[*Enter* LIUBÓV *and* CARLOTTA.]

LIUBÓV ANDREYÉVNA [*she hums a dance tune*] Why is it taking so long? What's Leoníd doing all this time in town? He should be back by now. [*Calls to* DUNYÁSHA *in the ballroom.*] Dunyásha, tell the musicians they can take a break.

TROFÍMOV They probably postponed the auction.

LIUBÓV ANDREYÉVNA I suppose it was a mistake to hire an orchestra. Or to have a party in the first place. Oh, well . . . what difference does it make? [*Sits down and hums quietly.*]

CARLOTTA [*hands* PÍSHCHIK *a deck of cards*] Here's the deck. Pick a card, any card. . . . No, no, just think of one.

PÍSHCHIK All right, I'm thinking of one.

CARLOTTA Good. Now shuffle the deck. Very good. Now give it to me. Observe, my dear Píshchik! *Eins, zwei, drei!*[5] Now look in your jacket pocket, and you will find your card.

PÍSHCHIK [*takes a card from his jacket pocket*] That's it, the eight of spades! [*Amazed*] Really! I don't believe it!

CARLOTTA [*holds out the deck to* TROFÍMOV] Quick, what's the top card?

TROFÍMOV The top card? Oh . . . uh . . . the queen of spades.

CARLOTTA Correct! [*To* PÍSHCHIK] Now which card's on top?

PÍSHCHIK Ace of hearts!

CARLOTTA Correct! [*Claps her hands, and the deck disappears.*] Well, isn't this a lovely day we're having?

[*A mysterious woman's voice answers; it seems to come from the floorboards: "A lovely day indeed. I couldn't agree more."*]

Whoever you are, I adore you!

[*The voice: "I adore you too!"*]

MASTER [*applauds*] Bravo! A lady ventriloquist!

PÍSHCHIK [*amazed*] Really! I don't believe it! Carlotta, you are amazing! I'm completely in love with you!

4. Friedrich Nietzsche (1844–1900), influential German philosopher.

5. "One, two, three!" (German).

CARLOTTA In love? [*Shrugs her shoulders.*] What do you know about love? *Guter Mensch aber schlechter Musikant.*[6]

TROFÍMOV [*slaps* PÍSHCHIK *on the shoulder*] You're just an old horse!

CARLOTTA All right, everybody, watch closely! One more trick! [*Takes a lap robe from a chair.*] See, what a lovely blanket! I'm thinking of selling it. [*Shakes out the lap robe and holds it up.*] Who wants to buy?

PÍSHCHIK [*amazed*] Really! I don't believe it!

CARLOTTA *Eins, zwei, drei!* [*Quickly raises the lap robe.*]

[ÁNYA *appears behind the lap robe; she curtsies, runs to her mother and kisses her, then runs back into the ballroom. General applause and cries of delight.*]

LIUBÓV ANDREYÉVNA [*applauding*] Bravo! Bravo!

CARLOTTA Now one more! *Eins, zwei, drei!*

[*She raises the lap robe;* VÁRYA *appears; she takes a bow.*]

PÍSHCHIK Really! I don't believe it!

CARLOTTA That's all. The show is over.

[*Throws the lap robe to* PÍSHCHIK, *takes a bow, goes through the ballroom and out.*]

PÍSHCHIK [*goes after her*] Enchanting! What a woman! What a woman! [*Goes out.*]

LIUBÓV ANDRÉYEVNA Leoníd still isn't back from town yet. I don't understand what could be taking him so long! It's got to be all over by now: either the estate has been sold or they've postponed the auction. Why does he have to keep us in suspense like this?

VÁRYA [*tries to comfort her*] Uncle bought the estate, I'm sure he has.

TROFÍMOV [*ironically*] Oh, I'm sure.

VÁRYA Ánya's godmother sent him a power of attorney to buy the estate in her name; she agreed to take over the mortgage. She did it for Ánya. So God *has* helped us. Uncle has saved the estate.

LIUBÓV ANDREYÉVNA The old lady in Yároslavl sent us fifteen thousand to buy the place in her name—she doesn't trust us—but that's not even enough to pay the interest. [*Covers her face with her hands.*] My fate . . . my entire life . . . It's all being decided today.

TROFÍMOV [*teases* VÁRYA] Mrs. Lopákhin! Mrs. Lopákhin!

VÁRYA [*angrily*] And you're a permanent graduate student! Who's been suspended twice!

LIUBÓV ANDRÉYEVNA Don't get so angry, Várya; he's only teasing you. What's wrong with that? And what's wrong with Lopákhin? If you want to marry him, do; he's a nice man. Interesting, even. If you don't want to marry him, don't; nobody's forcing you.

VÁRYA It's not a joking matter, Mama, believe me. I'm serious about him. He is a nice man, and I like him.

LIUBÓV ANDRÉYEVNA Then go ahead and marry him! I don't understand what you're waiting for!

VÁRYA Mama, I can't propose to him myself! For two years now everybody's been telling me to marry him, everybody, but he never mentions it. Or he

6. "A good man but a bad musician" (German); that is, an incompetent (from the poet Heinrich Heine).

jokes about it! Look, I understand, he's busy getting rich, he doesn't have time for me. Oh, if I had just a little money—I don't care how much, even a couple of hundred—I'd get out of here and go someplace far away. I'd go join a convent.

TROFÍMOV Now, there's an exalted idea!

VÁRYA [*to* TROFÍMOV] I thought students were supposed to be smart! [*Her tone softens; almost crying.*] Oh, Pétya, you used to be so nice-looking, and now you're getting old! [*To* LIUBÓV, *in a normal tone*] It's just that I need something to do all the time, Mama; it's the way I am. I can't sit around and do nothing.

[*Enter* YÁSHA.]

YÁSHA [*barely controlling his laughter*] Yepikhódov broke a billiard cue!

[*Goes out.*]

VÁRYA What is Yepikhódov doing here? Who asked him to come? And what's he doing playing billiards? I just don't understand these people. . . .

[*Goes out.*]

LIUBÓV ANDRÉYEVNA Pétya, don't tease her like that; you can see she's upset already.

TROFÍMOV Oh, she's such a busybody, always poking her nose into other people's business. She hasn't left Ánya and me alone the whole summer; she's afraid we're having a . . . an *affair*. What business is it of hers? Besides, it's not true. I'd never do anything so sordid. We're above love!

LIUBÓV ANDRÉYEVNA And I, I suppose, am beneath love. [*Upset*] Why isn't Leoníd back yet? I just want to know: has the estate been sold or not? The whole disaster seems so impossible to me, I don't know what to think, or do. . . . Oh, God, I'm losing my mind! I want to scream, or do something completely stupid . . . Help me, Pétya! Save me! Say something, say something!

TROFÍMOV Whether they sell it or not, does it make any difference really? You can't go back to the past. Everything here came to an end a long time ago. Try to calm down. You can't go on deceiving yourself; at least once in your life you have to look the truth straight in the eye.

LIUBÓV ANDRÉYEVNA What truth? You seem so sure what's truth and what isn't, but I'm not. I've lost any sense of it. I've lost sight of the truth. You're so sure of yourself, aren't you, so sure you have all the answers to everything, but darling, have you ever really had to live with one of your answers? You're too young. Of course *you* look into the future and see a brave new world, you don't expect any difficulties, but that's because you know nothing about life! Yes, you have more courage than my generation has, and better morals, and you're better educated, but for God's sake have a little sense of what it's like for me, and be easier on me. Pétya, I was born here! My parents lived here all their lives; so did my grandfather. I love this house! Without the cherry orchard my life makes no sense, and if you have to sell it, you might as well sell me with it. [*She embraces* TROFÍMOV *and kisses his forehead.*] And it was here my son drowned, you know that. . . . [*Weeps.*] Have some feeling for me, Pétya, you're such a good, sweet boy.

TROFÍMOV I pity you. [*Beat*] I do, from the bottom of my heart.

LIUBÓV ANDRÉYEVNA You should have said that differently, just a little differently. . . . [*Takes out her handkerchief; a telegram falls to the floor.*] You can't imagine how miserable I am today. All this noise, and every new sound makes me shake. I can't get away from it, but then when I'm alone in my room I can't stand the silence. Don't judge me, Pétya! I love you like one of my own family; I'd be very happy to see you and Ánya married, you know I would, only, darling, you must finish school first! You have *got* to graduate! You don't do anything except drift around from place to place—what kind of life is that? It's true, isn't it? Isn't that the truth? And we have to do something about that beard of yours; it's so scraggly. . . . [*Laughs.*] You've gotten so funny-looking!

TROFÍMOV [*picks up the telegram*] I have no desire to be good-looking.

LIUBÓV ANDRÉYEVNA The telegram's from Paris. I get a new one every day. One yesterday, now again today. That madman is sick again and in trouble. . . . He wants me to forgive him, he wants me back . . . and I suppose I should go back to Paris to be with him. Now see, Pétya, you're giving me that superior look, but darling, what am I supposed to do? He's sick, he's alone, he's unhappy, and who has he got to look after him? To give him his medicine and keep him out of trouble? And I love him—why do I have to pretend I don't, or not talk about it? I love him. That's just the way it is: I love him. I love him! He's a millstone around my neck, and he'll drown me with him, but he's *my* millstone! I love him and I can't live without him! [*Grabs* TROFÍMOV'*s hand.*] Don't judge me, Pétya, don't think badly of me, just don't say anything, please just don't say anything. . . .

TROFÍMOV [*almost in tears*] But for God's sake, you have to face the facts! He robbed you blind!

LIUBÓV ANDRÉYEVNA No, no, please, you mustn't say that, you mustn't—

TROFÍMOV He doesn't care a thing for you—you're the only person who doesn't seem to understand that! He's rotten!

LIUBÓV ANDRÉYEVNA [*gets angry but tries to control it*] And you, you're what? Twenty-six, twenty-seven? Listen to you: you sound like you'd never even graduated to long pants!

TROFÍMOV That's fine with me!

LIUBÓV ANDRÉYEVNA You're supposed to be a man; at your age you ought to know something about love. You ought to be in love yourself! [*Angrily*] Really! You think you're so smart, you're just a kid who doesn't know the first thing about it, you're probably a virgin, you're ridiculous, you're grotesque—

TROFÍMOV [*horrified*] What are you saying!

LIUBÓV ANDREYÉVNA "I'm above love!" You're not above love; you've just never gotten down to it! You're all wet, like Firs says. At your age, you ought to be sleeping with someone!

TROFÍMOV [*horrified*] What a terrible thing to say! That's terrible! [*He runs toward the ballroom, covering his ears.*] That's just horrible. . . . I can't listen to that; I'm leaving. [*Goes out, but reappears immediately.*] All is over between us!

[*Goes out into the entrance hall.*]

LIUBÓV ANDRÉYEVNA [*calls after him*] Pétya, wait a minute! Come back! I was just joking, Pétya, don't be so silly! Pétya!

[*A great clatter from the entrance hall; someone has fallen downstairs.* ÁNYA *and* VÁRYA *scream.*]

What happened?

[ÁNYA *and* VÁRYA *suddenly howl with laughter.*]

ÁNYA [*runs in, laughing*] Pétya just fell headfirst down the stairs!

[*Runs out.*]

LIUBÓV ANDRÉYEVNA Oh, what a silly boy!

[*The* STATIONMASTER *in the ballroom gets on a chair and begins declaiming the opening lines of "The Magdalen" by Alexei Tolstoy.*[7]]

STATIONMASTER "The splendid ballroom gleams with gold and candles,
a crowd of dancers whirls around the room;
and there apart, an empty glass beside her,
behold the fallen beauty, the lost, the doomed.

Her lavish gown and jewels make all eyes wonder,
her shameless glance bespeaks a life of sin;
young men and old cast longing glances at her—
see, how her fatal beauty draws them in!"

[*Everyone gathers to listen, but soon the orchestra returns and the strains of a waltz are heard from the entrance hall. The reading breaks off, and everybody begins to dance.* TROFÍMOV, ÁNYA, *and* VÁRYA *come in from the entrance hall.*]

LIUBÓV ANDRÉYEVNA Pétya . . . oh, darling, I'm *so* sorry. . . . You sweet thing, please forgive me. . . . Come on, let's dance. [*Dances with* TROFÍMOV.]

[ÁNYA *and* VÁRYA *dance together.* FIRS *enters, leans his walking stick against the side door.* YÁSHA *appears and stands watching the dancers.*]

YÁSHA What's the matter, pops?

FIRS I don't feel so good. The old days, we had a dance, we had generals and barons and admirals; nowadays we have to send out for the postmaster and the stationmaster. And they're none too eager to come, either. Oh, I'm getting old and feeble. The old master, their grandfather, anybody got sick, he used to dose 'em all with sealing wax. Didn't matter what they had, they all got sealing wax. I've been taking sealing wax myself now for nigh onto twenty years. Take some every day. That's probably why I'm still alive.

YÁSHA You're getting boring, pops. [*Yawns.*] Time for you to crawl off and die.

FIRS Oh, you . . . you young flibbertigibbet. [*Mumbles.*]

[TROFÍMOV *and* LIUBÓV *dance through the ballroom, into the sitting room.*]

LIUBÓV ANDRÉYEVNA *Merci.*[8] I need to sit down and rest a bit. . . . [*Sits.*] I'm so tired.

[*Enter* ÁNYA.]

ÁNYA [*upset*] There was a man in the kitchen just now, he said the cherry orchard's already been sold!

LIUBÓV ANDRÉYEVNA Who bought it?

ÁNYA He didn't say. And he's gone now. [*Dances with* TROFÍMOV; *they dance off across the ballroom.*]

YÁSHA That was just some old guy talking crazy. It wasn't anybody from around here.

FIRS And Leoníd Andréyich still isn't back. All he had on was his topcoat; you watch, he'll catch cold. He's all wet, that one.

LIUBÓV ANDRÉYEVNA I'll never live through this. Yásha, go out and see if anybody knows who bought it.

7. Russian writer (1817–1875), a distant relative of Leo Tolstoy, and author of *The Magdalen*, a play about a prostitute.

8. "Thank you" (French).

YÁSHA It was just some old guy. He left long ago. [*Laughs.*]

LIUBÓV ANDRÉYEVNA [*somewhat annoyed*] What are you laughing at? What's so funny?

YÁSHA That Yepikhódov. What a dope. Old Double Trouble.

LIUBÓV ANDRÉYEVNA Firs, suppose the estate is sold—where are you going to go?

FIRS I'll go wherever you tell me to.

LIUBÓV ANDRÉYEVNA What's the matter? Your face looks so funny. . . . Are you sick? You should go to bed.

FIRS Yes . . . [*Smirks.*] Yes, sure, go to bed, and then who'll take care of things? I'm the only one you've got.

YÁSHA Liubóv Andréyevna, there's a favor I have *got* to ask you; it's very important. If you go back to Paris, please take me with you. Please! You've got to! I positively cannot stay around here. [*Looks around, lowers his voice.*] You can see for yourself this place is hopeless. The whole country's a mess, nobody has any culture, it's boring, the food is lousy, and there's that old Firs drooling all over the place and talking like an idiot. Please, take me with you—you've just got to!

[*Enter* PÍSHCHIK.]

PÍSHCHIK Beautiful lady, what about a waltz? Just one little waltz! [LIUBÓV *crosses to him.*] You dazzler, you! And what about a loan, just one little loan, just a hundred and eighty, that's all I need. [*They begin to dance.*] Just a hundred and eighty . . .

[*They dance off into the ballroom.*]

YÁSHA [*sings to himself*] "Can't you see my heart is breaking . . ."

[*In the ballroom, a figure appears dressed in checkered trousers and a gray top hat, jumping and waving its arms. We hear shouts of "Bravo, Carlotta!"*]

DUNYÁSHA [*stops to powder her nose*] The missus told me to dance—there's too many gentlemen and not enough ladies—so I did, I've been dancing all night and my heart won't stop beating, and you know what, Firs? Just now, the postmaster, you know? He said something almost made me faint.

[*The orchestra stops playing.*]

FIRS What did he say?

DUNYÁSHA That I was like a flower. That's what he said.

YÁSHA [*yawns*] What does he know about it?

[*Goes out.*]

DUNYÁSHA Just like a flower. I'm a very romantic girl, really. I just adore that kind of talk.

FIRS You're out of your mind.

[*Enter* YEPIKHÓDOV.]

YEPIKHÓDOV [*to* DUNYÁSHA] Why are you deliberating not to notice me? You act as if I wasn't here, like I was a bug or something. [*Sighs.*] Ah, life!

DUNYÁSHA Excuse me?

YEPIKHÓDOV Of course, you may be right. [*Sighs.*] But if you look at it, let's say, from a . . . a point of view, then you're the faulty one—excuse my expressivity—because you led me on. Into this predictament. Look at me! Every day something awful happens to me. It's like a habit. But I can look disaster in the face and keep smiling. You gave me your word, you know, and you even—

DUNYÁSHA Do you mind? Let's talk about it later. Right now I'd rather be left alone. With my dreams. [*Plays with a fan.*]

YEPIKHÓDOV Every day. Something awful. But all I do—excuse my expressivity—is try to keep smiling. Sometimes I even laugh.

[*Enter* VÁRYA *from the ballroom.*]

VÁRYA [*to* YEPIKHÓDOV] Are you still here? I thought I told you to go home. Really, you have no consideration. [*To* DUNYÁSHA] Dunyásha, go back to the kitchen! [*To* YEPIKHÓDOV] You come in here and start playing billiards, you break one of our cues, now you hang around in here as if we'd invited you.

YEPIKHÓDOV Excuse my expressivity, but you have no right to penalize me.

VÁRYA I'm not penalizing you, I'm telling you! All you do here is wander around and bump into the furniture. You're supposed to be working for us, and you don't do a thing. I don't know why we hired you in the first place.

YEPIKHÓDOV [*offended*] Whether I work or not or wander around or not or play billiards or not is none of your business! You do not have the know-it-all to make my estimation!

VÁRYA How dare you talk to me like that! [*In a rage*] How dare you! What do you mean, I don't have the know-it-all? You get yourself out of here right this minute! Right this minute!

YEPIKHÓDOV [*apprehensively*] I wish you wouldn't use language like that—

VÁRYA [*beside herself*] Get out of here right this minute! Out! [*He goes to the door; she follows him.*] Double Trouble! I don't want to see hide or hair of you, I don't want to lay eyes on you ever again! [YEPIKHÓDOV *goes out; from behind the door we hear him screech: "I'll call the police on you!"*] Oh, you coming back for more? [*Grabs the stick that* FIRS *has left by the door.*] Come on . . . Come on . . . Come on, I'll show you! All right, all right, you asked for it—[*Swings the stick; the door opens, and she hits* LOPÁKHIN *over the head as he enters.*]

LOPÁKHIN Thanks a lot.

VÁRYA [*still angry, sarcastic*] Oh, I'm so sorry!

LOPÁKHIN S'all right. Always appreciate a warm welcome.

VÁRYA I don't need appreciation. [*Walks off, then turns and asks gently.*] I didn't hurt you, did I?

LOPÁKHIN No, I'm fine. Just a whopping big lump, that's all.

[*Voices from the ballroom: "Lopákhin! Lopákhin's here! He's back! Lopákhin's back!" People crowd into the sitting room.*]

PÍSHCHIK The great man in person! [*Hugs* LOPÁKHIN.] Is that cognac I smell? It is! You've been celebrating! Well, so have we. Join the party!

LIUBÓV ANDRÉYEVNA It's you, Yermolái Alexéyich. Where have you been all this time? Where's Leoníd?

LOPÁKHIN He's coming; we took the same train.

LIUBÓV ANDRÉYEVNA What happened? Did they have the auction? Tell me!

LOPÁKHIN [*embarrassed, afraid to show his joy*] The auction was all over by four this afternoon, but we missed the train. We had to wait for the nine-thirty. [*Exhales heavily.*] Oof! My head is really spinning. . . .

[*Enter* GÁYEV; *he holds a wrapped package in one hand, wipes his eyes with the other.*]

LIUBÓV ANDRÉYEVNA Lyónya, what's the matter? Lyónya! [*Impatiently, beginning to cry*] For God's sake, what happened!

GÁYEV [*weeps and can't answer her; makes a despairing gesture with his free hand and turns to* FIRS] Here, take these . . . some anchovies . . . imported. I haven't eaten a thing all day. You have no idea what I've been through! [*The door to the billiard room is open; we hear the click of billiard balls and*

YÁSHA's *voice: "Seven ball in the left pocket!"* GÁYEV's *expression changes; he stops crying.*] I'm all worn out. Firs, come help me get ready for bed.

[*Goes through the ballroom and out;* FIRS *follows him.*]

PÍSHCHIK What about the auction? Tell us what happened!

LIUBÓV ANDRÉYEVNA Is the cherry orchard sold?

LOPÁKHIN It's sold.

LIUBÓV ANDRÉYEVNA Who bought it?

LOPÁKHIN I did.

[*Pause.* LIUBÓV *is overcome; she would fall, if she weren't standing beside a table and the armchair.* VÁRYA *takes the keys from her belt, throws them on the floor, crosses the room, and goes out.*]

I did! I bought it! No, wait, don't go, please. I'm still a little mixed up about it, I can't talk yet. . . . [*Laughs.*] We get to the auction, and there's Derigánov, all ready and waiting. Leoníd Andréyich only had fifteen thousand, so right away Derigánov raises the bid to thirty, that's on top of the balance on the mortgage. So I see what he's up to, and I bid against him. Raise it to forty. He bids forty-five. I bid fifty-five. See, he was raising by five, and I double him, I raise him ten each time. Anyway, finally it's all over, and I got it! Ninety thousand plus the balance on the mortgage.[9] And now the cherry orchard is mine! Mine! [*A loud laugh*] My God, the cherry orchard belongs to me! Tell me I'm drunk, tell me it's all a dream, I'm making this up—[*Stomps on the floor.*] And don't anybody laugh! My God, if my father and my grandfather could be here now and see this, see *me*, their Yermolái, the boy they beat, who went barefoot in winter and never went to school, see how that poor boy just bought the most beautiful estate in the whole world! I bought the estate where my father and my grandfather slaved away their lives, where they wouldn't even let them in the kitchen! My God, I must be dreaming—I can't believe all this is happening! [*Picks up* VÁRYA's *keys; smiles gently.*] See, she threw away her keys; she knows she isn't running the place anymore. . . . [*Jingles the keys.*] Well, that's all right.

[*The orchestra starts tuning up again.*]

That's it, let's have some music—come on, I want to hear it! Everybody come watch! Come on and watch what I do! I'm going to chop down every tree in that cherry orchard, every goddamn one of them, and then I'm going to develop that land! Watch me! I'm going to do something our children and grandchildren can be proud of! Come on, you musicians, play!

[*The orchestra begins to play,* LIUBÓV *curls up in the armchair and weeps bitterly.*]

LOPÁKHIN [*reproachfully*] Oh, why didn't you listen to me? You dear woman, you dear good woman, you can't ever go back to the past. [*With tears in his eyes*] Oh, if only we could change things, if only life were different, this unhappy, messy life . . .

PÍSHCHIK [*takes his arm; quietly*] She's crying. Come on, we'll go in the other room, leave her alone for a while. Come on. . . . [*Leads him into the ballroom.*]

LOPÁKHIN What's the matter? Tell the band to keep playing! Louder! [*Ironic*] It's my house now! The cherry orchard belongs to me! I can do what I want

9. The winning bid for the estate was equivalent to nearly $2 million today—about twice what Lopákhin had offered to lend Liubóv and her family to save the estate (act 1).

to! [*Bumps into a small table, almost knocking over a candlestick.*] Don't worry about that: I can pay for it! I can pay for everything!

[*Goes out with* PÍSHCHIK.]

[*The sitting room is empty except for* LIUBÓV, *who sits lightly clenched and weeping bitterly. The orchestra plays softly. Suddenly* ÁNYA *and* TROFÍMOV *enter.* ÁNYA *goes and kneels before her mother.* TROFÍMOV *remains by the archway.*]

ÁNYA Mama! Mama, you're crying. Mama dear, I love you, I'll take care of you. The cherry orchard is sold, it's gone now, that's the truth, Mama, that's the truth, but don't cry. You still have your life to lead, you're still a good person. . . . Come with me, Mama, we'll go away, someplace far away from here. We'll plant a new orchard, even better than this one, you'll see, Mama, you'll understand, and you'll feel a new kind of joy, like a light in your soul. . . . Let's go, Mama. Let's go!

Curtain.

Act 4

[*The same room as Act 1. The curtains have been taken down, the pictures are gone from the walls, and there are only a few pieces of furniture shoved into a corner, as if for sale. The place feels empty. By the doorway, a pile of trunks, suitcases, etc. The door on the right is open; we hear* ÁNYA *and* VÁRYA *talking in the room beyond.* LOPÁKHIN *stands waiting. Beside him,* YÁSHA *holds a tray of glasses filled with champagne. Through the door we see* YEPIKHÓDOV *in the front hall, fastening the straps on a trunk. The sound of murmured voices offstage; some of the local people have come to say goodbye.* GÁYEV*'s voice: "Thank you all, good people, thanks, thanks very much for coming."*]

YÁSHA It's some of these poor yokels, come to say goodbye. I'm of the opinion, you know, these people around here . . . ? They're okay, but they're . . . they're just a bunch of know-nothings.

[*The murmur of voices dies away.* LIUBÓV *and* GÁYEV *come in from the entrance hall; she has stopped crying, but she is shaking slightly, and her face is pale. She cannot speak.*]

GÁYEV You gave them all the money you had, Liúba. You can't do that! You can't do that anymore!

LIUBÓV ANDREYÉVNA I couldn't help it! I just couldn't help it!

[*They both go out.* LOPÁKHIN *follows them to the door.*]

LOPÁKHIN Wait, please. How about a little glass of champagne, just to celebrate? I forgot to bring some from town, but I got this one bottle at the station. It was all they had.

[*Pause.*]

No? What's the matter, don't you want any? [*Comes back from the door.*] If I'd known that, I wouldn't have bought it. I don't feel like any myself.

[YÁSHA *carefully puts the tray down on a chair.*]

Go on, Yásha, you might as well have one.

YASHA *Bon voyage!* And here's to the girls we leave behind! [*Drinks.*] This is not your real French champagne, I can tell.

LOPÁKHIN Cost me enough.

[*Pause.*]

It's cold as hell in here.

YÁSHA They figured they were going away today anyway—they decided not to heat the place. [*Laughs.*]

LOPÁKHIN What's with you?

YÁSHA I'm laughing because everything worked out just the way I wanted.

LOPÁKHIN It's October already, but the sun's out; it feels like summer. Good weather for home builders. [*Looks at his watch, then at the door.*] Listen, everybody, you got forty-six minutes till train time! And it's twenty minutes from here to the station, so you better get a move on.

[*Enter* TROFÍMOV *from outside; he's wearing an overcoat.*]

TROFÍMOV It must be time to go. The carts are here. Where the hell are my galoshes? I've lost them somewhere. [*At the door*] Ánya, where are my galoshes? I can't find them anyplace!

LOPÁKHIN I'm off to Hárkov. I'll be taking the same train as you. Off to Hárkov, spend the winter there. I've been hanging around here too long, doing nothing; I can't stand that. I got to keep working, otherwise I don't know what to do with my hands; if they're not doing something, they feel like they don't belong to me.

TROFÍMOV So. We're leaving, and you're going back to your useful labors in the real world.

LOPÁKHIN Have a glass of champagne.

TROFÍMOV No, thanks.

LOPÁKHIN So you're off to Moscow?

TROFÍMOV Yes. I'll go into town with them today, and then leave tomorrow for Moscow.

LOPAKHIN Sure. I'll bet all those professors are waiting for you to show up, wouldn't want to start their lectures without you!

TROFÍMOV Mind your own business.

LOPÁKHIN How long you say you've been at that university?

TROFÍMOV Come on! Think up something new, will you? You're getting boring. [*Pokes around, looking for his galoshes.*] You know, we probably won't ever see each other again, so you mind my giving you a little advice? As a farewell present? Don't wave your arms around so much. Bad habit. And this development you're putting in out here—you think that's going to improve the world? You think your leisure home buyers are going to turn into yeoman farmers? That's a lot of arm waving too. Well, what the hell. I like you anyway. You've got nice hands. Gentle and sensitive. You could have been an artist. And you're like that inside too—gentle and sensitive.

LOPÁKHIN [*hugs him*] Goodbye, boy. Thanks for everything. Here, let me give you a little money. You may need it for the trip.

TROFÍMOV What for? I don't need money!

LOPÁKHIN What *for*? You don't have any!

TROFÍMOV I do too. Thanks all the same. I got paid for a translation I did. I have money right here in my pocket. [*Worried*] I just wish I could find my galoshes!

VÁRYA [*from the next room*] Here they are! The smelly things . . . [*Throws a pair of galoshes into the room.*]

TROFÍMOV What are you always getting mad for? Hmm . . . These aren't my galoshes.

LOPÁKHIN This past spring I planted a big crop of poppies. Three hundred acres. Sold the poppy seed, made forty thousand clear. And when those poppies were all in flower, what a picture that was! So look, I just made forty thousand, I can afford to loan you some money. Why turn up your nose at it? Because you think I'm just a dirt farmer?

TROFÍMOV So your father was a dirt farmer. Mine worked in a drugstore. What does that prove?

[LOPÁKHIN *takes out his wallet.*]

Forget it, forget it. Look, you could give me a couple of hundred thousand, I still wouldn't take it. I'm a free man. And you people, everything you think is so valuable, it doesn't mean a thing to me. I don't care whether you're rich or poor; you've got no power over me. I can do without you, I can go right on past you, because I am proud and I am strong. Humanity is moving onward, toward a higher truth and a higher happiness, higher than anyone can imagine. And I'm ahead of the rest!

LOPÁKHIN You think you'll ever get there?

TROFÍMOV I'll get there.

[*Pause.*]

I'll get there. Or I'll make sure the rest of them get there.

[*From the orchard comes the sound of axes; they've started chopping down the cherry trees.*]

LOPÁKHIN Well, boy, goodbye. Time to go. You and I don't see eye to eye, but life goes on anyway. Whenever I work real hard, round the clock practically, that clears my mind somehow, and for a minute I think maybe I know what we're all here for. But God, boy, think of the thousands of people in this country who don't know what they're doing or why they're doing it. But . . . I guess that doesn't have much to do with the price of eggs. They told me Leoníd Andréyich got a job at the bank, six thousand a year. He won't last; he's too lazy.

ÁNYA [*at the door*] Mama asks you to please wait until she's gone before you start cutting down the orchard.

TROFÍMOV I agree. That isn't very tactful, you know.

[*Goes out into the front hall.*]

LOPÁKHIN All right, all right, I'll take care of it. God, these people . . .

[*Goes out after him.*]

ÁNYA Have they taken Firs to the nursing home?

YÁSHA I told them about it this morning. So I imagine they have.

ÁNYA [*to* YEPIKHÓDOV, *who crosses the room*] Yepikhódov, could you please go and make sure they've taken Firs to the nursing home?

YÁSHA [*offended*] I already told them this morning! Why keep asking?

YEPIKHÓDOV The aged Firs, in my ultimate opinion, is beyond nursing. They ought to take him to the cemetery. And I can only envy him. [*Sets a suitcase down on a cardboard hatbox and crushes it.*] There. Finally. Wouldn't you know.

[*Goes out.*]

YÁSHA [*snickers*] Old Double Trouble.

VÁRYA [*from the next room*] Have they taken Firs to the nursing home?

ÁNYA They took him this morning.

VÁRYA Then why didn't they take the letter for the doctor?

ÁNYA They must have forgotten. We'll have to send someone after them with it.

VÁRYA Where's Yásha? Tell him his mother is here; she wants to say goodbye.

YÁSHA [*with a dismissive gesture*] What a bore! Why can't she just leave me alone?

[DUNYÁSHA *has been drifting in and out, fussing with the baggage; now that she sees* YÁSHA *alone, she goes to him.*]

DUNYÁSHA Oh . . . oh, Yásha, why won't you even look at me? You're going away . . . you're leaving me behind. . . . [*Starts to cry and throws her arms around his neck.*]

YÁSHA What are you crying about? [*Drinks some champagne.*] Six days from now, I'll be back in Paris. Tomorrow we get on the express train, and we're off! And that's the last you'll ever see of me! I can't hardly believe it myself. *Vive la France!*[1] I can't live around here anymore; it's just not my kind of place. They're all so ignorant, and I can't stand that. [*Drinks more champagne.*] What are you crying about? If you'd been a nice girl, you wouldn't have anything to cry about.

DUNYÁSHA [*powders her nose in a mirror*] Don't forget to send me a letter from Paris. Because I loved you, Yásha, I really did. I'm a very sensitive person, Yásha, I really am—

YÁSHA Watch it, someone's coming. [*He starts fussing with the luggage, whistling quietly.*]

[*Enter* LIUBÓV, GÁYEV, ÁNYA, *and* CARLOTTA.]

GÁYEV We should be going. We're already a little late. [*Looks at* YÁSHA.] Who smells like herring?

LIUBÓV ANDRÉYEVNA We've only got ten minutes; then we absolutely must start out. [*Glances around the room.*] Goodbye, house! Wonderful old house! Winter's almost here, and come spring you'll be gone. They'll tear you down. Think of everything these walls have seen! [*Kisses* ÁNYA *with great feeling.*] My treasure, look at you! You're radiant today! Your eyes are shining like diamonds! Are you happy? Really happy?

ÁNYA Oh, yes, Mama, really! We're starting a new life!

GÁYEV She's right—everything worked out extremely well. Before the cherry orchard was sold we were at our wit's end—remember how painful it was?—and now everything's finally settled, once and for all, no turning back, and see? We've all calmed down. We're even rather happy. I'm going to work at the bank, I'm about to become a financier! Yellow ball in the side pocket . . . And you look better than you have in a long time, Lyúba; you do, you know.

LIUBÓV ANDRÉYEVNA I know. My nerves have quieted down. You're quite right.

[*Someone holds out her hat and coat.*]

And I sleep much better now. Take my things, Yásha, will you? It's time to go. [*To* ÁNYA] Darling, we'll see each other soon enough. I'm off to Paris—I kept the money your godmother in Yároslavl sent to buy the estate. [*A hard laugh*] Thank God for the old lady! That ought to get me through the winter at least. . . .

ÁNYA And you'll come back soon, won't you? You promise? I'll study hard and get my diploma, and then I'll get a job and help you out. We can read

1. "Long live France!" (French).

together the way we used to, can't we? [*Kisses her mother's hands.*] We'll spend long autumn evenings together; we'll read lots of books and learn all about the wonderful new world of the future. . . . [*Dreamily*] Don't forget, Mama, you promised. . . .

LIUBÓV ANDRÉYEVNA I will, my angel, I promise. [*Embraces her.*]

[*Enter* LOPÁKHIN. CARLOTTA *hums a tune under her breath.*]

GÁYEV Carlotta must be happy; she's singing!

CARLOTTA [*picks up a bundle that looks like a baby in swaddling clothes*] Here's my little baby. Bye, bye, baby . . .

[*We hear a baby's voice: "Wah! Wah!"*]

Shh, baby, shh, shh . . . good little children don't cry. . . .

[*Again: "Wah! Wah!"*]

I feel so sorry for the poor thing. [*Hurls the bundle to the floor.*] You will find me a job, won't you? I can't go on like this anymore.

LOPÁKHIN Don't worry, Carlotta; we'll take care of you.

GÁYEV Everybody's just thrown us away. Várya's leaving. . . . All of a sudden we're useless.

CARLOTTA How can I live in that town of yours? There must be someplace I can go. . . . [*Hums.*] What difference does it make . . . ?

[*Enter* PÍSHCHIK.]

LOPÁKHIN Here comes the wonder boy.

PÍSHCHIK [*panting*] Ooh, give me a minute . . . I'm all worn out. Good morning, good morning, good morning. Could I get a drink of water?

GÁYEV [*sarcastic*] You're sure it isn't money you want? You'll all have to excuse me if I remove myself from the approaching negotiations.

[*Goes out.*]

PÍSHCHIK I'm so glad to see you all. . . . Dear lady . . . I've been a stranger, I know. [*To* LOPÁKHIN] And you're here too. Delighted, delighted, a man I admire, always have. . . . Here. Here. This is for you. [*Gives* LOPÁKHIN *money.*] Four hundred. And I still owe you eight hundred and forty.

LOPÁKHIN [*a bewildered shrug*] I must be dreaming. Where did you get money?

PÍSHCHIK Wait a minute; let me cool off. Well, it was an absolutely extraordinary thing. These Englishmen showed up, they poked around on my land, found some kind of white clay. . . . [*To* LIUBÓV] Here . . . Here's the four hundred. You've been so kind . . . so sweet . . . [*Gives her money.*] And you'll have the rest before you know it. [*Takes a drink of water.*] You know, there was a young man on the train just now, he was saying . . . there was this philosopher, he said, who wanted us all to jump off the roof. "Jump!" he said. "Jump!" That was his whole philosophy. [*Amazed*] Really! I don't believe it! Give me some more water. . . .

LOPÁKHIN What Englishmen are you talking about?

PÍSHCHIK I gave them a lease on the land, the place where the clay is, a twenty-four-year lease. And now excuse me, but I'm off. Lots of people to see, pay back what I owe. I owe money all over the place. [*Takes a drink of water.*] Well, I just wanted to say hello. I'll come by again on Thursday.

LIUBÓV ANDRÉYEVNA But we're leaving for town today. And tomorrow I'm going back to Paris.

PÍSHCHIK What? [*Astonished*] Leaving for town? Oh, my . . . Oh, of course; the furniture's gone. And all these trunks. I didn't realize. [*Almost in tears*] I didn't realize. Great thinkers, these English . . . God bless you all. And be happy. I didn't realize. Well, all things must come to an end. [*Kisses* LIUBÓV's *hand.*] I'll come to an end myself one of these days. And when I do, I want you all to say: "Semyónov-Píshchik . . . he was a good old horse. God bless him." Wonderful weather we're having. Yes. . . . [*Starts out, overcome with emotion, stops in the doorway and turns.*] Oh, by the way, Dáshenka says hello.

[*Goes out.*]

LIUBÓV ANDRÉYEVNA Now we can go. There are just two things still on my mind. The first is old Firs. [*Looks at her watch.*] We've still got five minutes. . . .

ÁNYA Mama, they took Firs to the nursing home this morning. Yásha took care of it.

LIUBÓV ANDRÉYEVNA . . . And then there's our Várya. She's used to getting up early and working around here all day long, and now she's . . . out of a job. Like a fish out of water. Poor thing—she's so nervous, she cries, she's losing weight . . .

[*Pause.*]

You know, Yermolái Alexéyich—well, of course you know—I'd always dreamed . . . always dreamed she'd marry you; you know we all think it's a wonderful idea. . . . [*Whispers to* ÁNYA, *who nods to* CARLOTTA; *they both leave.*] She loves you, you like her. . . . I don't know why, I just don't know why the two of you keep avoiding the issue. Really!

LOPÁKHIN I don't know why either. It's all a little funny. Well, I don't mind. If there's still time, I'll do it. . . . All right, *basta*,[2] let's just get it over with. But I don't know, I don't think I can propose without you—

LIUBÓV ANDRÉYEVNA Of course you can. All it takes is a minute. I'll send her right in. . . .

LOPÁKHIN We've even got some champagne all ready. [*Looks at the tray of empty glasses.*] Or at least we did. Somebody must have drunk it all up.

[YÁSHA *coughs.*]

Guzzled it down, I should say.

LIUBÓV ANDRÉYEVNA Wonderful! We'll leave you alone. Yásha, *allez!*[3] I'll go call her. [*At the door*] Várya, leave that alone; come here a minute, will you? Come on, dear!

[*Goes out with* YÁSHA.]

LOPÁKHIN [*looks at his watch*] Well . . .

[*Pause. A few stifled laughs and whispers behind the door. Finally* VÁRYA *enters.*]

VÁRYA [*examines the luggage; takes her time*] That's funny, I can't find them. . . .

LOPÁKHIN What are you looking for?

VÁRYA I packed them myself, and now I don't remember where.

[*Pause.*]

LOPÁKHIN What . . . ah . . . where are you off to, Várya?

VÁRYA Me? I'm going to work for the Ragúlins. I talked to them about it already; they need a housekeeper. And look after things, you know. . . .

2. "That's enough" (Italian).

3. "Go on!" (French).

LOPÁKHIN All the way over there? That's fifty miles away.

[*Pause.*]

Well, looks like this is the end of things around here. . . .

VÁRYA [*still examining the luggage*] Where are they . . . ? Or maybe I put them in the trunk. You're right: this is the end of things here. The end of one life—

LOPÁKHIN I'm going too. To Hárkov. Taking the same train, actually. I've got a million things waiting for me. I'm leaving Yepikhódov, though. Hired him to take charge here.

VÁRYA You hired *who*?

LOPÁKHIN Last year this time it was snowing already, remember? Today it's still sunny. Nice day. A little chilly, though . . . It was freezing this morning; must have been in the thirties.

VÁRYA I didn't notice.

[*Pause.*]

Anyway, the thermometer's broken.

[*Pause. A voice from outside calls: "Lopákhin!"*]

LOPÁKHIN [*as if he'd been waiting for the call*] I'm coming!

[*Goes out.*]

[VÁRYA *sits down on the floor, leans her head on a bundle of dresses, and cries. The door opens;* LIUBÓV *enters carefully.*]

LIUBÓV ANDRÉYEVNA Well?

[*Pause.*]

We have to go.

VÁRYA [*already stopped crying, wipes her eyes*] Right, Mama, we have to go. I can get to the Ragúlins' today, if I don't miss the train.

LIUBÓV ANDRÉYEVNA Ánya, get your coat on.

[*Enter* ÁNYA, GÁYEV, CARLOTTA. GÁYEV *wears a winter overcoat. Servants and drivers come in to pick up the luggage.* YEPIKHÓDOV *directs the operation.*]

Well, we're ready to start.

ÁNYA [*joyfully*] Ready to start!

GÁYEV My dear friends, my very dear friends! On this occasion, this farewell to our beloved house, I cannot keep still. I feel I must say a few words to express the emotion that overwhelms me, overwhelms us all—

ÁNYA [*pleads*] Uncle, please!

VÁRYA That's enough, Uncle.

GÁYEV [*crushed*] All right . . . Yellow ball in the side pocket . . . I'll keep still.

[*Enter* TROFÍMOV, *then* LOPÁKHIN.]

TROFÍMOV Ladies and gentlemen, time to go! You'll be late!

LOPÁKHIN Yepikhódov, get my coat.

LIUBÓV ANDRÉYEVNA Let me stay a little minute longer. I never really noticed these walls before, or the ceilings. I want a last look, one last long look. . . .

GÁYEV I remember when I was six, I was watching out that window, right over there. It was a holy day, Trinity Sunday,[4] I think, and I saw Father on his way to church. . . .

LIUBÓV ANDRÉYEVNA Have we got everything?

LOPÁKHIN I guess so. [*To* YEPIKHÓDOV, *who helps him on with his coat*] You keep an eye on things, Yepikhódov.

4. Also known as Pentecost, a Christian holy day occurring on the seventh Sunday after Easter.

YEPIKHÓDOV [*loud, businesslike tone*] You can count on me, Yermolái Alexéyich!

LOPÁKHIN Why are you talking like that all of a sudden?

YEPIKHÓDOV I just had a drink—water. . . . It went down the wrong way.

YÁSHA [*with contempt*] Dumb hick!

LIUBÓV ANDRÉYEVNA We're all going away. There won't be a soul left on the place. . . .

LOPÁKHIN But wait till you see what happens here come spring!

[VÁRYA *grabs an umbrella from the luggage, as if she were going to hit him.* LOPÁKHIN *pretends to be terrified.*]

VÁRYA Don't get excited. It was just a joke.

TROFÍMOV You've all got to get moving! It's time to go! You'll miss your train!

VÁRYA Here's your galoshes, Pétya, behind this suitcase. [*With tears in her eyes*] Smelly old things . . .

TROFÍMOV [*puts them on*] It's time to go!

GÁYEV [*deeply moved, afraid he'll start crying*] Yes, the train . . . mustn't miss the train . . . Yellow ball in the side pocket, white in the corner . . .

LIUBÓV ANDRÉYEVNA Let's go!

LOPÁKHIN Everybody here? Nobody left? [*Closes and locks the door, left.*] Got to lock up; I've got a few things stored here. All right, let's go!

ÁNYA Goodbye, house! Goodbye, old life!

TROFÍMOV No, hello, new life!

[*Goes out with* ÁNYA.]

[VÁRYA *looks around the room again; she's not eager to go.* YÁSHA *goes out with* CARLOTTA *and her little dog.*]

LOPÁKHIN So. Until next spring. Come on, let's go, everybody. Goodbye!

[LIUBÓV *and* GÁYEV *are left alone. It's as if they'd been waiting for this moment. They throw their arms around each other and burst out crying, but try to keep the others outside from hearing.*]

GÁYEV [*in despair*] Oh, sister, sister . . .

LIUBÓV ANDRÉYEVNA Oh, my orchard, my beautiful orchard! My life, my youth, my happiness, goodbye! Goodbye! Goodbye!

[ÁNYA'*s voice, joyful: "Mama!"* TROFÍMOV'*s voice, joyful, excited: "Yoo-hoo!"*]

These walls, these windows, for the last time . . . And Mama loved this room . . .

GÁYEV Oh, sister, sister . . .

[ÁNYA: *"Mama!"* TROFÍMOV: *"Yoo-hoo!"*]

LIUBÓV ANDRÉYEVNA We're coming!

[*They leave.*]

[*The stage is empty. We hear the sound of the door being locked, then the carriages as they drive away. It grows very quiet. In the silence, we hear the occasional sound of an ax chopping down the cherry trees, a mournful, lonely sound. Then we hear steps. Enter* FIRS *from the door, right. He wears his usual butler's livery, but with bedroom slippers. He's very ill.*]

FIRS [*goes to the door, tries the handle*] Locked. They're gone. [*Sits on the sofa.*] They forgot about me. That's all right; I'll just sit here for a bit. . . . And Leoníd Andréyich probably forgot his winter coat. [*A worried sigh*] I should have looked. . . . He's still all wet, that one. . . . [*Mumbles something we can't make out.*] Well, it's all over now, and I never even had a life to live. . . . [*Lies back.*] I'll just lie here for a bit. . . . No strength left, nothing left, not a thing . . . Oh, you. You young flibbertigibbet. [*Lies there, no longer moving.*]

[*In the distance we hear a sound that seems to come from the sky, a sad sound, like a string snapping. It dies away. Everything grows quiet. We can hear the occasional sound of an ax on a tree.*]

Curtain.

The Lady with the Dog[1]

I

People were telling one another that a newcomer had been seen on the promenade—a lady with a dog. Dmitri Dmitrich Gurov had been a fortnight in Yalta,[2] and was accustomed to its ways, and he, too, had begun to take an interest in fresh arrivals. From his seat in Vernet's outdoor café, he caught sight of a young woman in a toque, passing along the promenade; she was fair and not very tall; after her trotted a white Pomeranian.

Later he encountered her in the municipal park and in the square several times a day. She was always alone, wearing the same toque, and the Pomeranian always trotted at her side. Nobody knew who she was, and people referred to her simply as "the lady with the dog."

"If she's here without her husband, and without any friends," thought Gurov, "it wouldn't be a bad idea to make her acquaintance."

He was not yet forty but had a twelve-year-old daughter and two sons in high school. He had been talked into marrying in his second year at college, and his wife now looked nearly twice as old as he did. She was a tall woman with dark eyebrows, erect, dignified, imposing, and, as she said of herself, a "thinker." She was a great reader, omitted the "hard sign"[3] at the end of words in her letters, and called her husband "Dimitry" instead of Dmitry; and though he secretly considered her shallow, narrow-minded, and dowdy, he stood in awe of her, and disliked being at home. He had first begun deceiving her long ago and he was now constantly unfaithful to her, and this was no doubt why he spoke slightingly of women, to whom he referred as *the lower race*.

He considered that the ample lessons he had received from bitter experience entitled him to call them whatever he liked, but without this "lower race" he could not have existed a single day. He was bored and ill-at-ease in the company of men, with whom he was always cold and reserved, but felt quite at home among women, and knew exactly what to say to them, and how to behave; he could even be silent in their company without feeling the slightest awkwardness. There was an elusive charm in his appearance and disposition which attracted women and caught their sympathies. He knew this and was himself attracted to them by some invisible force.

Repeated and bitter experience had taught him that every fresh intimacy, while at first introducing such pleasant variety into everyday life, and offer-

1. Translated by Ivy Litvinov.
2. A fashionable seaside resort in the Crimea.
3. Certain progressive intellectuals, anticipating the reform of the Russian alphabet, omitted the hard sign after consonants in writing; here, however, it is an affectation.

ing itself as a charming, light adventure, inevitably developed, among decent people (especially in Moscow, where they are so irresolute and slow to move), into a problem of excessive complication leading to an intolerably irksome situation. But every time he encountered an attractive woman he forgot all about this experience, the desire for life surged up in him, and everything suddenly seemed simple and amusing.

One evening, then, while he was dining at the restaurant in the park, the lady in the toque came strolling up and took a seat at a neighboring table. Her expression, gait, dress, coiffure, all told him that she was from the upper classes, that she was married, that she was in Yalta for the first time, alone and bored. . . . The accounts of the laxity of morals among visitors to Yalta are greatly exaggerated, and he paid no heed to them, knowing that for the most part they were invented by people who would gladly have transgressed themselves, had they known how to set about it. But when the lady sat down at a neighboring table a few yards away from him, these stories of easy conquests, of excursions to the mountains, came back to him, and the seductive idea of a brisk transitory liaison, an affair with a woman whose very name he did not know, suddenly took possession of his mind.

He snapped his fingers at the Pomeranian and, when it trotted up to him, shook his forefinger at it. The Pomeranian growled. Gurov shook his finger again.

The lady glanced at him and instantly lowered her eyes.

"He doesn't bite," she said, and blushed.

"May I give him a bone?" he asked, and on her nod of consent added in friendly tones: "Have you been long in Yalta?"

"About five days."

"And I am dragging out my second week here."

Neither spoke for a few minutes.

"The days pass quickly, and yet one is so bored here," she said, not looking at him.

"It's the thing to say it's boring here. People never complain of boredom in godforsaken holes like Belyev or Zhizdra, but when they get here it's: 'Oh, the dullness! Oh, the dust!' You'd think they'd come from Granada[4] to say the least."

She laughed. Then they both went on eating in silence, like complete strangers. But after dinner they left the restaurant together, and embarked upon the light, jesting talk of people free and contented, for whom it is all the same where they go, or what they talk about. They strolled along, remarking on the strange light over the sea. The water was a warm, tender purple, the moonlight lay on its surface in a golden strip. They said how close it was, after the hot day. Gurov told her he was from Moscow, that he was really a philologist, but worked in a bank; that he had at one time trained himself to sing in a private opera company, but had given up the idea; that he owned two houses in Moscow. . . . And from her he learned that she had grown up in Petersburg,[5] but had gotten married in the town of S., where she had been living two years, that she would stay another month in Yalta, and that perhaps her husband,

4. A famous medieval city in Spain, once capital of the Moorish kingdom of Granada and now a tourist center known for its art and architecture. Belyev and Zhizdra are small provincial towns.

5. St. Petersburg, the former capital of Russia: an important port and cultural center.

who also needed a rest, would join her. She was quite unable to explain whether her husband was a member of the province council, or on the board of the *zemstvo*,[6] and was greatly amused at herself for this. Further, Gurov learned that her name was Anna Sergeyevna.

Back in his own room he thought about her, and felt sure he would meet her the next day. It was inevitable. As he went to bed he reminded himself that only a very short time ago she had been a schoolgirl, like his own daughter, learning her lessons, he remembered how much there was of shyness and constraint in her laughter, in her way of conversing with a stranger—it was probably the first time in her life that she found herself alone, and in a situation in which men could follow her and watch her, and speak to her, all the time with a secret aim she could not fail to divine. He recalled her slender, delicate neck, her fine gray eyes.

"And yet there's something pathetic about her," he thought to himself as he fell asleep.

II

A week had passed since the beginning of their acquaintance. It was a holiday. Indoors it was stuffy, but the dust rose in clouds out of doors, and people's hats blew off. It was a parching day and Gurov kept going to the outdoor café for fruit drinks and ices to offer Anna Sergeyevna. The heat was overpowering.

In the evening, when the wind had dropped, they walked to the pier to see the steamer come in. There were a great many people strolling about the landing-place; some, bunches of flowers in their hands, were meeting friends. Two peculiarities of the smart Yalta crowd stood out distinctly—the elderly ladies all tried to dress very youthfully, and there seemed to be an inordinate number of generals about.

Owing to the roughness of the sea the steamer arrived late, after the sun had gone down, and it had to maneuver for some time before it could get alongside the pier. Anna Sergeyevna scanned the steamer and passengers through her lorgnette,[7] as if looking for someone she knew, and when she turned to Gurov her eyes were glistening. She talked a great deal, firing off abrupt questions and forgetting immediately what it was she had wanted to know. Then she lost her lorgnette in the crush.

The smart crowd began dispersing, features could no longer be made out, the wind had quite dropped, and Gurov and Anna Sergeyevna stood there as if waiting for someone else to come off the steamer. Anna Sergeyevna had fallen silent, every now and then smelling her flowers, but not looking at Gurov.

"It's turned out a fine evening," he said. "What shall we do? We might go for a drive."

She made no reply.

He looked steadily at her and suddenly took her in his arms and kissed her lips, and the fragrance and dampness of the flowers closed round him, but the next moment he looked behind him in alarm—had anyone seen them?

"Let's go to your room," he murmured.

And they walked off together, very quickly.

6. District administration.

7. Small eyeglasses on a short handle.

Her room was stuffy and smelt of some scent she had bought in the Japanese shop.[8] Gurov looked at her, thinking to himself: "How full of strange encounters life is!" He could remember carefree, good-natured women who were exhilarated by love-making and grateful to him for the happiness he gave them, however short-lived; and there had been others—his wife among them—whose caresses were insincere, affected, hysterical, mixed up with a great deal of quite unnecessary talk, and whose expression seemed to say that all this was not just lovemaking or passion, but something much more significant; then there had been two or three beautiful, cold women, over whose features flitted a predatory expression, betraying a determination to wring from life more than it could give, women no longer in their first youth, capricious, irrational, despotic, brainless, and when Gurov had cooled to these, their beauty aroused in him nothing but repulsion, and the lace trimming on their underclothes reminded him of fish-scales.

But here the timidity and awkwardness of youth and inexperience were still apparent; and there was a feeling of embarrassment in the atmosphere, as if someone had just knocked at the door. Anna Sergeyevna, "the lady with the dog," seemed to regard the affair as something very special, very serious, as if she had become a fallen woman, an attitude he found odd and disconcerting. Her features lengthened and drooped, and her long hair hung mournfully on either side of her face. She assumed a pose of dismal meditation, like a repentant sinner in some classical painting.[9]

"It isn't right," she said. "You will never respect me anymore."

On the table was a watermelon. Gurov cut himself a slice from it and began slowly eating it. At least half an hour passed in silence.

Anna Sergeyevna was very touching, revealing the purity of a decent, naïve woman who had seen very little of life. The solitary candle burning on the table scarcely lit up her face, but it was obvious that her heart was heavy.

"Why should I stop respecting you?" asked Gurov. "You don't know what you're saying."

"May God forgive me!" she exclaimed, and her eyes filled with tears. "It's terrible."

"No need to seek to justify yourself."

"How can I justify myself? I'm a wicked, fallen woman, I despise myself and have not the least thought of self-justification. It isn't my husband I have deceived, it's myself. And not only now, I have been deceiving myself for ever so long. My husband is no doubt an honest, worthy man, but he's a flunky. I don't know what it is he does at his office, but I know he's a flunky. I was only twenty when I married him, and I was devoured by curiosity, I wanted something higher. I told myself that there must be a different kind of life I wanted to live, to live. . . . I was burning with curiosity . . . you'll never understand that, but I swear to God I could no longer control myself, nothing could hold me back, I told my husband I was ill, and I came here. . . . And I started going about

8. Probably a tourist shop with imported goods.

9. A famous painting of Mary Magdalen (see Luke 7.36–50) by the French classical artist Georges de la Tour (1593–1652) shows her seated at a table meditating, her face and long hair illuminated by a candle.

like one possessed, like a madwoman . . . and now I have become an ordinary, worthless woman, and everyone has the right to despise me."

Gurov listened to her, bored to death. The naïve accents, the remorse, all was so unexpected, so out of place. But for the tears in her eyes, she might have been jesting or play-acting.

"I don't understand," he said gently. "What is it you want?"

She hid her face against his breast and pressed closer to him.

"Do believe me, I implore you to believe me," she said. "I love all that is honest and pure in life, vice is revolting to me, I don't know what I'm doing. The common people say they are snared by the Devil. And now I can say that I have been snared by the Devil, too."

"Come, come," he murmured.

He gazed into her fixed, terrified eyes, kissed her, and soothed her with gentle affectionate words, and gradually she calmed down and regained her cheerfulness. Soon they were laughing together again.

When, a little later, they went out, there was not a soul on the promenade, the town and its cypresses looked dead, but the sea was still roaring as it dashed against the beach. A solitary fishing-boat tossed on the waves, its lamp blinking sleepily.

They found a carriage and drove to Oreanda.[1]

"I discovered your name in the hall, just now," said Gurov, "written up on the board. Von Diederitz. Is your husband a German?"

"No. His grandfather was, I think, but he belongs to the Orthodox Church himself."

When they got out of the carriage at Oreanda they sat down on a bench not far from the church, and looked down at the sea, without talking. Yalta could be dimly discerned through the morning mist, and white clouds rested motionless on the summits of the mountains. Not a leaf stirred, the grasshoppers chirruped, and the monotonous hollow roar of the sea came up to them, speaking of peace, of the eternal sleep lying in wait for us all. The sea had roared like this long before there was any Yalta or Oreanda, it was roaring now, and it would go on roaring, just as indifferently and hollowly, when we had passed away. And it may be that in this continuity, this utter indifference of life and death, lies the secret of our ultimate salvation, of the stream of life on our planet, and of its never-ceasing movement towards perfection.

Side by side with a young woman, who looked so exquisite in the early light, soothed and enchanted by the sight of all this magical beauty—sea, mountains, clouds and the vast expanse of the sky—Gurov told himself that, when you came to think of it, everything in the world is beautiful really, everything but our own thoughts and actions, when we lose sight of the higher aims of life, and of our dignity as human beings.

Someone approached them—a watchman, probably—looked at them and went away. And there was something mysterious and beautiful even in this. The steamer from Feodosia[2] could be seen coming towards the pier, lit up by the dawn, its lamps out.

1. A hotel and beach compound near Yalta; the whole area is known as the Ukrainian Riviera.

2. A coastal town seventy miles northeast of Yalta.

"There's dew on the grass," said Anna Sergeyevna, breaking the silence.

"Yes. Time to go home."

They went back to the town.

After this they met every day at noon on the promenade, lunching and dining together, going for walks, and admiring the sea. She complained of sleeplessness, of palpitations, asked the same questions over and over again, alternately surrendering to jealousy and the fear that he did not really respect her. And often, when there was nobody in sight in the square or the park, he would draw her to him and kiss her passionately. The utter idleness, these kisses in broad daylight, accompanied by furtive glances and the fear of discovery, the heat, the smell of the sea, and the idle, smart, well-fed people continually crossing their field of vision, seemed to have given him a new lease of life. He told Anna Sergeyevna she was beautiful and seductive, made love to her with impetuous passion, and never left her side, while she was always pensive, always trying to force from him the admission that he did not respect her, that he did not love her a bit, and considered her just an ordinary woman. Almost every night they drove out of town, to Oreanda, the waterfall, or some other beauty-spot. And these excursions were invariably a success, each contributing fresh impressions of majestic beauty.

All this time they kept expecting her husband to arrive. But a letter came in which he told his wife that he was having trouble with his eyes, and implored her to come home as soon as possible. Anna Sergeyevna made hasty preparations for leaving.

"It's a good thing I'm going," she said to Gurov. "It's the intervention of fate."

She left Yalta in a carriage, and he went with her as far as the railway station. The drive took nearly a whole day. When she got into the express train, after the second bell had been rung, she said:

"Let me have one more look at you. . . . One last look. That's right."

She did not weep, but was mournful, and seemed ill, the muscles of her cheeks twitching.

"I shall think of you . . . I shall think of you all the time," she said. "God bless you! Think kindly of me. We are parting forever, it must be so, because we ought never to have met. Good-bye—God bless you."

The train steamed rapidly out of the station, its lights soon disappearing, and a minute later even the sound it made was silenced, as if everything were conspiring to bring this sweet oblivion, this madness, to an end as quickly as possible. And Gurov, standing alone on the platform and gazing into the dark distance, listened to the shrilling of the grasshoppers and the humming of the telegraph wires, with a feeling that he had only just awakened. And he told himself that this had been just one more of the many adventures in his life, and that it, too, was over, leaving nothing but a memory. . . . He was moved and sad, and felt a slight remorse. After all, this young woman whom he would never again see had not been really happy with him. He had been friendly and affectionate with her, but in his whole behaviour, in the tones of his voice, in his very caresses, there had been a shade of irony, the insulting indulgence of the fortunate male, who was, moreover, almost twice her age. She had insisted in calling him good, remarkable, high-minded. Evidently he had appeared to her different from his real self, in a word he had involuntarily deceived her. . . .

There was an autumnal feeling in the air, and the evening was chilly.

"It's time for me to be going north, too," thought Gurov, as he walked away from the platform. "High time!"

III

When he got back to Moscow it was beginning to look like winter; the stoves were heated every day, and it was still dark when the children got up to go to school and drank their tea, so that the nurse had to light the lamp for a short time. Frost had set in. When the first snow falls, and one goes for one's first sleigh-ride, it is pleasant to see the white ground, the white roofs; one breathes freely and lightly, and remembers the days of one's youth. The ancient lime-trees and birches, white with hoarfrost, have a good-natured look, they are closer to the heart than cypresses and palms, and beneath their branches one is no longer haunted by the memory of mountains and the sea.

Gurov had always lived in Moscow, and he returned to Moscow on a fine frosty day, and when he put on his fur-lined overcoat and thick gloves, and sauntered down Petrovka Street, and when, on Saturday evening, he heard the church bells ringing, his recent journey and the places he had visited lost their charm for him. He became gradually immersed in Moscow life, reading with avidity three newspapers a day, while declaring he never read Moscow newspapers on principle. Once more he was caught up in a whirl of restaurants, clubs, banquets, and celebrations, once more he glowed with the flattering consciousness that well-known lawyers and actors came to his house, that he played cards in the Medical Club opposite a professor. He could once again eat a whole serving of Moscow Fish Stew served in a pan.

He had believed that in a month's time Anna Sergeyevna would be nothing but a vague memory, and that hereafter, with her wistful smile, she would only occasionally appear to him in dreams, like others before her. But the month was now well over and winter was in full swing, and all was as clear in his memory as if he had parted with Anna Sergeyevna only the day before. And his recollections grew ever more insistent. When the voices of his children at their lessons reached him in his study through the evening stillness, when he heard a song, or the sounds of a music-box in a restaurant, when the wind howled in the chimney, it all came back to him: early morning on the pier, the misty mountains, the steamer from Feodosia, the kisses. He would pace up and down his room for a long time, smiling at his memories, and then memory turned into dreaming, and what had happened mingled in his imagination with what was going to happen. Anna Sergeyevna did not come to him in his dreams, she accompanied him everywhere, like his shadow, following him everywhere he went. When he closed his eyes, she seemed to stand before him in the flesh, still lovelier, younger, tenderer than she had really been, and looking back, he saw himself, too, as better than he had been in Yalta. In the evenings she looked out at him from the bookshelves, the fireplace, the corner, he could hear her breathing, the sweet rustle of her skirts. In the streets he followed women with his eyes, to see if there were any like her. . . .

He began to feel an overwhelming desire to share his memories with someone. But he could not speak of his love at home, and outside his home who was there for him to confide in? Not the tenants living in his house, and certainly not his colleagues at the bank. And what was there to tell? Was it love that he had felt? Had there been anything exquisite, poetic, anything instructive or even amusing about his relations with Anna Sergeyevna? He had to content himself with uttering vague generalizations about love and women, and nobody guessed what he meant, though his wife's dark eyebrows twitched as she said:

"The role of a coxcomb doesn't suit you a bit, Dimitry."

One evening, leaving the Medical Club with one of his card-partners, a government official, he could not refrain from remarking:

"If you only knew what a charming woman I met in Yalta!"

The official got into his sleigh, and just before driving off, turned and called out:

"Dmitry Dmitrich!"

"Yes?"

"You were quite right, you know—the sturgeon was just a *leetle* off."

These words, in themselves so commonplace, for some reason infuriated Gurov, seemed to him humiliating, gross. What savage manners, what people! What wasted evenings, what tedious, empty days! Frantic card-playing, gluttony, drunkenness, perpetual talk always about the same thing. The greater part of one's time and energy went on business that was no use to anyone, and on discussing the same thing over and over again, and there was nothing to show for it all but a stunted, earth-bound existence and a round of trivialities, and there was nowhere to escape to, you might as well be in a madhouse or a convict settlement.

Gurov lay awake all night, raging, and went about the whole of the next day with a headache. He slept badly on the succeeding nights, too, sitting up in bed, thinking, or pacing the floor of his room. He was sick of his children, sick of the bank, felt not the slightest desire to go anywhere or talk about anything.

When the Christmas holidays came, he packed his things, telling his wife he had to go to Petersburg in the interests of a certain young man, and set off for the town of S. To what end? He hardly knew himself. He only knew that he must see Anna Sergeyevna, must speak to her, arrange a meeting, if possible.

He arrived at S. in the morning and engaged the best suite in the hotel, which had a carpet of gray military frieze, and a dusty ink-pot on the table, surmounted by a headless rider, holding his hat in his raised hand. The hall porter told him what he wanted to know: von Diederitz had a house of his own in Staro-Goncharnaya Street. It wasn't far from the hotel, he lived on a grand scale, luxuriously, kept carriage-horses, the whole town knew him. The hall porter pronounced the name "Drideritz."

Gurov strolled over to Staro-Goncharnaya Street and discovered the house. In front of it was a long gray fence with inverted nails hammered into the tops of the palings.

"A fence like that is enough to make anyone want to run away," thought Gurov, looking at the windows of the house and the fence.

He reasoned that since it was a holiday, Anna's husband would probably be at home. In any case it would be tactless to embarrass her by calling at the house. And a note might fall into the hands of the husband, and bring about catastrophe. The best thing would be to wait about on the chance of seeing her. And he walked up and down the street, hovering in the vicinity of the fence, watching for his chance. A beggar entered the gate, only to be attacked by dogs, then, an hour later, the faint, vague sounds of a piano reached his ears. That would be Anna Sergeyevna playing. Suddenly the front door opened and an old woman came out, followed by a familiar white Pomeranian. Gurov tried to call to it, but his heart beat violently, and in his agitation he could not remember its name.

He walked on, hating the gray fence more and more, and now ready to tell himself irately that Anna Sergeyevna had forgotten him, had already, perhaps, found distraction in another—what could be more natural in a young woman who had to look at this accursed fence from morning to night? He went back to his hotel and sat on the sofa in his suite for some time, not knowing what to do, then he ordered dinner, and after dinner, had a long sleep.

"What a foolish, restless business," he thought, waking up and looking towards the dark windowpanes. It was evening by now. "Well, I've had my sleep out. And what am I to do in the night?"

He sat up in bed, covered by the cheap gray quilt, which reminded him of a hospital blanket, and in his vexation he fell to taunting himself.

"You and your lady with a dog . . . there's adventure for you! See what you get for your pains."

On his arrival at the station that morning he had noticed a poster announcing in enormous letters the first performance at the local theatre of *The Geisha*.[3] Remembering this; he got up and made for the theatre.

"It's highly probable that she goes to first nights," he told himself.

The theatre was full. It was a typical provincial theatre, with a mist collecting over the chandeliers, and the crowd in the gallery fidgeting noisily. In the first row of the stalls the local dandies stood waiting for the curtain to go up, their hands clasped behind them. There, in the front seat of the governor's box, sat the governor's daughter, wearing a boa, the governor himself hiding modestly behind the drapes, so that only his hands were visible. The curtain stirred, the orchestra took a long time tuning up their instruments. Gurov's eyes roamed eagerly over the audience as they filed in and occupied their seats.

Anna Sergeyevna came in, too. She seated herself in the third row of the stalls, and when Gurov's glance fell on her, his heart seemed to stop, and he knew in a flash that the whole world contained no one nearer or dearer to him, no one more important to his happiness. This little woman, lost in the provincial crowd, in no way remarkable, holding a silly lorgnette in her hand, now filled his whole life, was his grief, his joy, all that he desired. Lulled by the sounds coming from the wretched orchestra, with its feeble, amateurish violinists, he thought how beautiful she was . . . thought and dreamed. . . .

Anna Sergeyevna was accompanied by a tall, round-shouldered young man with small whiskers, who nodded at every step before taking the seat beside her and seemed to be continually bowing to someone. This must be her husband, whom, in a fit of bitterness, at Yalta, she had called a "flunky." And there really was something of a lackey's servility in his lanky figure, his side-

3. An operetta (1896) by the English composer Sidney Jones.

whiskers, and the little bald spot on the top of his head. And he smiled sweetly, and the badge of some scientific society gleaming in his buttonhole was like the number on a footman's livery.

The husband went out to smoke in the first interval, and she was left alone in her seat. Gurov, who had taken a seat in the stalls, went up to her and said in a trembling voice, with a forced smile: "How d'you do?"

She glanced up at him and turned pale, then looked at him again in alarm, unable to believe her eyes, squeezing her fan and lorgnette in one hand, evidently struggling to overcome a feeling of faintness. Neither of them said a word. She sat there, and he stood beside her, disconcerted by her embarrassment, and not daring to sit down. The violins and flutes sang out as they were tuned, and there was a tense sensation in the atmosphere, as if they were being watched from all the boxes. At last she got up and moved rapidly towards one of the exits. He followed her and they wandered aimlessly along corridors, up and down stairs; figures flashed by in the uniforms of legal officials, high-school teachers and civil servants, all wearing badges; ladies, coats hanging from pegs flashed by; there was a sharp draft, bringing with it an odor of cigarette butts. And Gurov, whose heart was beating violently, thought:

"What on earth are all these people, this orchestra for? . . ."

The next minute he suddenly remembered how, after seeing Anna Sergeyevna off that evening at the station, he had told himself that all was over, and they would never meet again. And how far away the end seemed to be now!

She stopped on a dark narrow staircase over which was a notice bearing the inscription "To the upper circle."[4]

"How you frightened me!" she said, breathing heavily, still pale and half-stunned. "Oh, how you frightened me! I'm almost dead! Why did you come? Oh, why?"

"But, Anna," he said, in low, hasty tones. "But, Anna. . . . Try to understand . . . do try. . . ."

She cast him a glance of fear, entreaty, love, and then gazed at him steadily, as if to fix his features firmly in her memory.

"I've been so unhappy," she continued, taking no notice of his words. "I could think of nothing but you the whole time, I lived on the thoughts of you. I tried to forget—why, oh, why did you come?"

On the landing above them were two schoolboys, smoking and looking down, but Gurov did not care, and, drawing Anna Sergeyevna towards him, began kissing her face, her lips, her hands.

"What are you doing, oh, what are you doing?" she said in horror, drawing back. "We have both gone mad. Go away this very night, this moment. . . . By all that is sacred, I implore you. . . . Somebody is coming."

Someone was ascending the stairs.

"You must go away," went on Anna Sergeyevna in a whisper. "D'you hear me, Dmitry Dmitrich? I'll come to you in Moscow. I have never been happy, I am unhappy now, and I shall never be happy—never! Do not make me suffer still more! I will come to you in Moscow, I swear it! And now we must part! My dear one, my kind one, my darling, we must part."

4. The stalls or back rows; a medium-priced area behind the orchestra seats on the main floor.

She pressed his hand and hurried down the stairs, looking back at him continually, and her eyes showed that she was in truth unhappy. Gurov stood where he was for a short time, listening, and when all was quiet, went to look for his coat, and left the theatre.

IV

And Anna Sergeyevna began going to Moscow to see him. Every two or three months she left the town of S., telling her husband that she was going to consult a specialist on female diseases, and her husband believed her and did not believe her. In Moscow she always stayed at the Slavyanski Bazaar,[5] sending a man in a red cap to Gurov the moment she arrived. Gurov went to her, and no one in Moscow knew anything about it.

One winter morning he went to see her as usual (the messenger had been to him the evening before, but had not found him at home). His daughter was with him, for her school was on the way and he thought he might as well see her to it.

"It is forty degrees," said Gurov to his daughter, "and yet it is snowing. You see it is only above freezing close to the ground, the temperature in the upper layers of the atmosphere is quite different."

"Why doesn't it ever thunder in winter, Papa?"

He explained this, too. As he was speaking, he kept reminding himself that he was going to a rendezvous and that not a living soul knew about it, or, probably, ever would. He led a double life—one in public, in the sight of all whom it concerned, full of conventional truth and conventional deception, exactly like the lives of his friends and acquaintances, and another which flowed in secret. And, owing to some strange, possibly quite accidental chain of circumstances, everything that was important, interesting, essential, everything about which he was sincere and never deceived himself, everything that composed the kernel of his life, went on in secret, while everything that was false in him, everything that composed the husk in which he hid himself and the truth which was in him—his work at the bank, discussions at the club, his "lower race," his attendance at anniversary celebrations with his wife—was on the surface. He began to judge others by himself, no longer believing what he saw, and always assuming that the real, the only interesting life of every individual goes on as under cover of night, secretly. Every individual existence revolves around mystery, and perhaps that is the chief reason that all cultivated individuals insisted so strongly on the respect due to personal secrets.

After leaving his daughter at the door of her school Gurov set off for the Slavyanski Bazaar. Taking off his overcoat in the lobby, he went upstairs and knocked softly on the door. Anna Sergeyevna, wearing the gray dress he liked most, exhausted by her journey and by suspense, had been expecting him since the evening before. She was pale and looked at him without smiling, but was in his arms almost before he was fairly in the room. Their kiss was lingering, prolonged, as if they had not met for years.

5. A luxurious hotel in Moscow.

"Well, how are you?" he asked. "Anything new?"

"Wait, I'll tell you in a minute. . . . I can't. . . ."

She could not speak, because she was crying. Turning away, she held her handkerchief to her eyes.

"I'll wait till she's had her cry out," he thought, and sank into a chair.

He rang for tea, and a little later, while he was drinking it, she was still standing there, her face to the window. She wept from emotion, from her bitter consciousness of the sadness of their life; they could only see one another in secret, hiding from people, as if they were thieves. Was not their life a broken one?

"Don't cry," he said.

It was quite obvious to him that this love of theirs would not soon come to an end, and that no one could say when this end would be. Anna Sergeyevna loved him ever more fondly, worshipped him, and there would have been no point in telling her that one day it must end. Indeed, she would not have believed him.

He moved over and took her by the shoulders, intending to fondle her with light words, but suddenly he caught sight of himself in the looking-glass.

His hair was already beginning to turn gray. It struck him as strange that he should have aged so much in the last few years. The shoulders on which his hands lay were warm and quivering. He felt a pity for this life, still so warm and exquisite, but probably soon to fade and droop like his own. Why did she love him so? Women had always believed him different from what he really was, had loved in him not himself but the man their imagination pictured him, a man they had sought for eagerly all their lives. And afterwards when they discovered their mistake, they went on loving him just the same. And not one of them had ever been happy with him. Time had passed, he had met one woman after another, become intimate with each, parted with each, but had never loved. There had been all sorts of things between them, but never love.

And only now, when he was gray-haired, had he fallen in love properly, thoroughly, for the first time in his life.

He and Anna Sergeyevna loved one another as people who are very close and intimate, as husband and wife, as dear friends love one another. It seemed to them that fate had intended them for one another, and they could not understand why she should have a husband, and he a wife. They were like two migrating birds, the male and the female, who had been caught and put into separate cages. They forgave one another all that they were ashamed of in the past and in the present, and felt that this love of theirs had changed them both.

Formerly, in moments of melancholy, he had consoled himself by the first argument that came into his head, but now arguments were nothing to him, he felt profound pity, desired to be sincere, tender.

"Stop crying, my dearest," he said. "You've had your cry, now stop. . . . Now let us have a talk, let us try and think what we are to do."

Then they discussed their situation for a long time, trying to think how they could get rid of the necessity for hiding, deception, living in different towns, being so long without meeting. How were they to shake off these intolerable fetters?

"How? How?" he repeated, clutching his head. "How?"

And it seemed to them that they were within an inch of arriving at a decision, and that then a new, beautiful life would begin. And they both realized that the end was still far, far away, and that the hardest, the most complicated part was only just beginning.

RABINDRANATH TAGORE

1861–1941

Rabindranath Tagore, the first Asian to receive the Nobel Prize, won the award in 1913 for literature, specifically for his contribution to poetry. But, by the end of his career in 1941, Tagore had become an international influence not only with his poetry but also with his novels, novellas, short stories, plays, and essays; and his continuing, broader impact on the modern world has been as much due to his other artistic work as a musician, painter, and performer, as to his activism as an educator, political thinker, and cosmopolitan intellectual. The challenge he poses for readers today is to understand how he interwove these roles into a remarkably productive career, and how he combined his diverse talents into coherent individual works.

LIFE AND TIMES

Tagore was born in Calcutta in 1861, into one of India's most famous families. His grandfather, Dwarkanath Tagore, amassed a great fortune in agriculture, mining, banking, and trade in British India, and helped establish such major institutions in the city as Hindu College (known as Presidency College today), Calcutta Medical College, the National Library, and the Agricultural and Horticultural Society of India. Dwarkanath also cofounded the Brahmo Sabha, an influential association dedicated to far-reaching reforms of Hindu religious and social life, which Rabindranath's father, Debendranath, expanded and renamed as the Brahmo Samaj (the Brahmo Samaj had a transformative effect on **Pandita Ramabai**). Growing up in an exceptionally talented family and a stimulating cultural environment, almost all of Debendranath's fourteen surviving children—of whom Rabindranath was the youngest—became notable writers, artists, intellectuals, and civil servants in a late-colonial India that was shaped by this legacy of reformist activism.

Tagore was educated in several schools in Calcutta but rebelled against formal education so strongly that, after the age of fourteen, he was trained by tutors at home in history, science, mathematics, literature, and art, as well as in Bengali, Sanskrit, and English. He spent 1878–80 in England, first in Brighton and then in London, but returned to India after failing to complete a law degree at University College. Back in Calcutta, he published his first book of poems in Bengali in

1880; two years later, his family arranged his marriage to Mrinalini Devi, with whom he had three daughters and two sons. What followed proved to be one of the most fertile periods in his artistic career: between 1891 and 1895 he wrote forty-two short stories, single-handedly establishing this modern genre in India, besides inventing what we now recognize as Indian realism and aesthetic modernism.

A reformist and activist in education, Tagore founded a school at Shantiniketan, about a hundred miles northwest of Calcutta, in 1901; twenty years later, he launched a college called Vishwa Bharati at the same site, which became Vishwa Bharati University in 1951 (a decade after his death), an unconventional "open-air" teaching and research institution that continues to serve as an international model for alternative education in the arts and humanities today. Tagore's two elder daughters were married in 1901, but the next few years brought several tragedies to the family: his wife died in 1902, his middle daughter the following year, his father in 1905, and his younger son two years later. Despite this emotional devastation, Tagore remained productive and innovative during the first decade of the twentieth century, publishing several important works, including the novel *Chokher Bali* (*A Speck of Sand in the Eye*, 1903), and a book of poems, *Gitanjali* (*An Offering of Songs*, 1910), which was the primary citation by the Noble Prize Committee in 1913.

After the award, Tagore's range of activities and influence became truly global, as he visited some thirty countries, including Russia, China, Japan, Vietnam, Argentina, the United States, Iran, Iraq, Bulgaria, Germany, and Sweden. He lectured on the most pressing issues of the time, speaking out in *Nationalism* (1917), a pioneering early-twentieth-century critique of this phenomenon, and he became a moral and political authority in the international arena. In 1919 he rejected the British knighthood bestowed on him a few years earlier, in protest against the British massacre of Indians at a peaceful rally in Jallianwalla Bagh, Amritsar. Even though his health deteriorated in the late 1930s, he continued to write poems and stories until the final months of his life.

Although Tagore's career as a writer was full, it was only one part of his creative life. Over several decades he also wrote more than 2,200 songs and set them to music; unique in style, they constitute an entire genre of modern South Asian music, known as *Rabindra-sangit*. India and Bangladesh would both use songs written and set to music by Tagore for their national anthems. In 1928 he also took up drawing and painting, and produced a large number of artworks in the last dozen years of his life, mostly in graphite, pen and ink, wash, and watercolor; his visual art has been exhibited in several major cities around the world. Moreover, he wrote or composed more than sixty-five works for the stage, including short and long plays as well as operatic works and dance-dramas, and Tagore himself performed in them in India as well as during his visits to Europe.

Tagore's influence on modern life and literature has been as multifarious and far-reaching as his output in many media. In his own time, he became a notable representative of universal humanism, especially of a "spiritual" version of it; seventy years after his death, he continues to be celebrated as a model of cosmopolitanism. Tagore has left a lasting impression in many unexpected places around the world. Modern education in the Czech Republic, for example, still carries the impact of his pedagogic experiments in the arts and humanities. The main waterfront in the beautiful resort town of Balatonfured, Hungary, is called the Tagore Promenade; dozens of artists gather there regularly to paint in the open air. The Abbey Theater in

Dublin staged Tagore's play *The Post Office* (1912); James Joyce watched a performance during one of his rare visits to his native city, and he modeled the twin characters Shem and Shaun in *Finnegans Wake* (1939) on the central character in the play.

WORK

Tagore was fluent in Bengali and English, but he wrote almost all his literary works originally in Bengali. In the second half of his six-decade-long career he translated and supervised the translation of most of his work into English; he also wrote numerous book reviews, articles, and public lectures directly in English, and carried on an extensive English correspondence with many associates around the world. He described himself as first and foremost a poet; his language in his verse as well as his prose was always lyrical. The hallmark of his prose style was its poetic and musical quality: it was infused with the rhythms and melodic sounds of spoken Bengali, as well as with the figures of speech and thought that we normally associate with poetry.

Tagore was not a systematic thinker, and he was rarely successful in explaining his ideas and philosophical positions at length in expository prose; but his insights and intuitions ran deep, and he was able to express them in imaginative structures of startling originality. He was equally at home in song, narrative, and drama; many of his poems, tales, and plays display an effortless organic unity, as though they "came to him" fully formed, without needing any conscious artistry or intervention on his part. One of the unusual aspects of Tagore's work is that each of the genres in which he wrote serves a different artistic function, and all the genres together complement each other imaginatively.

Our selection here consists of two short stories, and like many of Tagore's shorter pieces of fiction, they are realistic in style, organization, and effect. The first, "Punishment" (1892), is set in the Bengal countryside (probably in what is now west-central Bangladesh) in the late nineteenth century. It is told crisply from the perspective of a narrator whose omniscience and veracity play crucial roles in the story; and its theme is the administration of justice, in this case in the British colonial justice system. "Punishment," in fact, is the first modern short story in world literature about the legal phenomenon that lawyers and judges call "the Rashomon effect." Named after the famous Japanese art film *Rashomon* (1950), directed by Akira Kurosawa, this is a universal phenomenon: whenever there are two or more eyewitnesses to an event or a crime, even their most truthful accounts of what happened differ fundamentally from each other. When a judge or a jury has to decide a case solely on the basis of eyewitness accounts, without material evidence to clinch the matter, there is no purely rational way to choose between equally reliable but conflicting eyewitness testimonies given under oath. In Tagore's story, written nearly seventy years before the movie, the problem of conflicting testimony goes much deeper: for different reasons, the various eyewitnesses produce dishonest as well as truthful accounts of a spontaneous murder. When the colonial judge (an Englishman) assesses the witnesses' stories, he has no means of separating the truth from the fabrications, even though the murderer confesses fully in court. The judge then arrives at a decision that is blatantly biased (by class and gender), bringing the story to its famous surprise ending. The narrative combines social realism with psychological realism to confront the troubling questions of what constitutes justice under such circumstances and how we might solve this most intractable of problems.

The second story, "Kabuliwala" (1894), seeks to dismantle the social distinction between biological and surrogate parenthood, and it represents love—rather than biology—as the only validation of fatherhood. The central puzzle in the story appears at the beginning, where the little girl Mini asks the first-person narrator what his relationship with her mother is; what he is unable to explain to her is that her biological father, his younger brother, died in her infancy, leaving her mother a widow; and that, following Hindu custom, he as the elder brother has assumed the role of surrogate husband and father. Given the strictures in conventional Hindu society against widows, the alternative would have been to segregate the girl's mother, deprive her of the normal comforts of home and family life, and leave her to raise the child in stigmatizing conditions.

The story famously extends this validation of surrogate parenthood, paternal love, and the rehabilitation of widows within the framework of the extended family by bringing in a second, symbolic father figure: Rahmat, the "traveling salesman" from Kabul, Afghanistan, who comes to Calcutta every winter to sell dry fruit as well as luxury items such as hand-embroidered woolen shawls. A Pathan by ethnicity and a Muslim by religion, Rahmat leaves behind a young family in Kabul during his wanderings; he intensely misses his own daughters, and cultivates a deeply affectionate relationship—based predominantly on wonderful storytelling skills—with Mini. Despite the early suspicions of Mini's mother, and despite even the fact that Rahmat, in an unfortunate moment of rage, subsequently commits a serious crime in the neighborhood, the narrator of the story recognizes him as an innocent and affectionate father figure for Mini, and allows him to meet her even on her wedding day, after his release from prison. Like "Punishment," this story mixes psychological realism with social realism, but does so in order to explore the treatment of women in the Hindu society of colonial Bengal, as well as the related phenomena of fatherhood, paternal love, and surrogate parenthood.

Both these stories are drawn from Tagore's early work, and both represent his writing in the realistic mode. His poetry, novelistic fiction, and plays take us in other directions, but his short stories remain among his most memorable pieces. Tagore is not a writer who fits into the usual model of linear development in which the later writing supersedes the earlier on the grounds of maturity. Since he attempts rather different kinds of effects in different genres, his output in any one genre frequently brings together his best qualities, regardless of chronology. "Punishment" and "Kabuliwala" already display the skills for which Tagore is most celebrated: vivid and diverse characters who come alive in a few brushstrokes and invite our deeper sympathies; evolving human situations that refuse to stand still; problems and dilemmas that turn up in many different times, places, and guises; and insights into the larger rhythms and patterns of life that fully engage our emotions and reveal a great deal about ourselves.

Punishment[1]

I

When the brothers Dukhiram Rui and Chidam Rui went out in the morning with their heavy farm-knives, to work in the fields, their wives would quarrel and shout. But the people nearby were as used to the uproar as they were to other customary, natural sounds. When they heard the shrill screams of the women, they would say, "They're at it again"—that is, what was happening was only to be expected: it was not a violation of Nature's rules. When the sun rises at dawn, no one asks why; and whenever the two wives in this *kuri*-caste[2] household let fly at each other, no one was at all curious to investigate the cause.

Of course this wrangling and disturbance affected the husbands more than the neighbours, but they did not count it a major nuisance. It was as if they were riding together along life's road in a cart whose rattling, clattering, unsprung wheels were inseparable from the journey. Indeed, days when there was no noise, when everything was uncannily silent, carried a greater threat of unpredictable doom.

The day on which our story begins was like this. When the brothers returned home at dusk, exhausted by their work, they found the house eerily quiet. Outside, too, it was extremely sultry. There had been a sharp shower in the afternoon, and clouds were still massing. There was not a breath of wind. Weeds and scrub round the house had shot up after the rain: the heavy scent of damp vegetation, from these and from the waterlogged jute-fields, formed a solid wall all around. Frogs croaked from the milkman's pond behind the house, and the buzz of crickets filled the leaden sky.

Not far off the swollen Padma[3] looked flat and sinister under the mounting clouds. It had flooded most of the grain-fields, and had come close to the houses. Here and there, roots of mango and jackfruit trees on the slipping bank stuck up out of the water, like helpless hands clawing at the air for a last fingerhold.

That day, Dukhiram and Chidam had been working near the zamindar's office. On a sandbank opposite, paddy[4] had ripened. The paddy needed to be cut before the sandbank was washed away, but the village people were busy either in their own fields or in cutting jute: so a messenger came from the office and forcibly engaged the two brothers. As the office roof was leaking in places, they also had to mend that and make some new wickerwork panels: it had taken them all day. They couldn't come home for lunch; they just had a snack from the office. At times they were soaked by the rain; they were not paid normal labourers' wages; indeed, they were paid mainly in insults and sneers.

When the two brothers returned at dusk, wading through mud and water, they found the younger wife, Chandara, stretched on the ground with her sari[5] spread out. Like the sky, she had wept buckets in the afternoon, but had now given way to sultry exhaustion. The elder wife, Radha, sat on the verandah sullenly: her eighteen-month son had been crying, but when the brothers came in they saw him lying naked in a corner of the yard, asleep.

1. Translated by William Radice.
2. In Bengal, a low caste originally of bird catchers, but by the 19th century, general laborers.
3. A major river in what is now Bangladesh.
4. The rice crop. "Zamindar": landlord.
5. A long strip of cloth draped around the body; Indian women's traditional clothing.

Dukhiram, famished, said gruffly, "Give me my food."

Like a spark on a sack of gunpowder, the elder wife exploded, shrieking out, "Where is there food? Did you give me anything to cook? Must I earn money myself to buy it?"

After a whole day of toil and humiliation, to return—raging with hunger—to a dark, joyless, foodless house, to be met by Radha's sarcasm, especially her final jibe, was suddenly unendurable. "What?" he roared, like a furious tiger, and then, without thinking, plunged his knife into her head. Radha collapsed into her sister-in-law's lap, and in minutes she was dead.

"What have you done?" screamed Chandara, her clothes soaked with blood. Chidam pressed his hand over her mouth. Dukhiram, throwing aside the knife, fell to his knees with his head in his hands, stunned. The little boy woke up and started to wail in terror.

Outside there was complete quiet. The herd-boys were returning with the cattle. Those who had been cutting paddy on the far sandbanks were crossing back in groups in a small boat—with a couple of bundles of paddy on their heads as payment. Everyone was heading for home.

Ramlochan Chakravarti, pillar of the village, had been to the post office with a letter, and was now back in his house, placidly smoking. Suddenly he remembered that his sub-tenant Dukhiram was very behind with his rent: he had promised to pay some today. Deciding that the brothers must be home by now, he threw his chadar[6] over his shoulders, took his umbrella, and stepped out.

As he entered the Ruis' house, he felt uneasy. There was no lamp alight. On the dark verandah, the dim shapes of three or four people could be seen. In a corner of the verandah there were fitful, muffled sobs: the little boy was trying to cry for his mother, but was stopped each time by Chidam.

"Dukhi," said Ramlochan nervously, "are you there?"

Dukhiram had been sitting like a statue for a long time; now, on hearing his name, he burst into tears like a helpless child.

Chidam quickly came down from the verandah into the yard, to meet Ramlochan. "Have the women been quarelling again?" Ramlochan asked. "I heard them yelling all day."

Chidam, all this time, had been unable to think what to do. Various impossible stories occurred to him. All he had decided was that later that night he would move the body somewhere. He had never expected Ramlochan to come. He could think of no swift reply. "Yes," he stumbled, "today they were quarrelling terribly."

"But why is Dukhi crying so?" asked Ramlochan, stepping towards the verandah.

Seeing no way out now, Chidam blurted, "In their quarrel, *Choṭobau* struck at *Baṛobau*'s[7] head with a farm-knife."

When immediate danger threatens, it is hard to think of other dangers. Chidam's only thought was to escape from the terrible truth—he forgot that a lie can be even more terrible. A reply to Ramlochan's question had come instantly to mind, and he had blurted it out.

"Good grief," said Ramlochan in horror. "What are you saying? Is she dead?"

"She's dead," said Chidam, clasping Ramlochan's feet.

6. In Bengal, a sheet of cloth draped around the shoulders, usually worn by men but sometimes by women.

7. "Elder Daughter-in-Law"; members of a family address each other by kinship terms. *Choṭobau*: "Younger Daughter-in-Law."

Ramlochan was trapped. "*Rām, Rām,*"[8] he thought, "what a mess I've got into this evening. What if I have to be a witness in court?" Chidam was still clinging to his feet, saying, "*Thākur,*[9] how can I save my wife?"

Ramlochan was the village's chief source of advice on legal matters. Reflecting further he said, "I think I know a way. Run to the police station: say that your brother Dukhi returned in the evening wanting his food, and because it wasn't ready he struck his wife on the head with his knife. I'm sure that if you say that, she'll get off."

Chidam felt a sickening dryness in his throat. He stood up and said, "*Thākur,* if I lose my wife I can get another, but if my brother is hanged, how can I replace him?" In laying the blame on his wife, he had not seen it that way. He had spoken without thought; now, imperceptibly, logic and awareness were returning to his mind.

Ramlochan appreciated his logic. "Then say what actually happened," he said. "You can't protect yourself on all sides."

He had soon, after leaving, spread it round the village that Chandara Rui had, in a quarrel with her sister-in-law, split her head open with a farm-knife. Police charged into the village like a river in flood. Both the guilty and the innocent were equally afraid.

II

Chidam decided he would have to stick to the path he had chalked out for himself. The story he had given to Ramlochan Chakravarti had gone all round the village; who knew what would happen if another story was circulated? But he realized that if he kept to the story he would have to wrap it in five more stories if his wife was to be saved.

Chidam asked Chandara to take the blame on to herself. She was dumbfounded. He reassured her: "Don't worry—if you do what I tell you, you'll be quite safe." But whatever his words, his throat was dry and his face was pale.

Chandara was not more than seventeen or eighteen. She was buxom, well-rounded, compact and sturdy—so trim in her movements that in walking, turning, bending or climbing there was no awkwardness at all. She was like a brand-new boat: neat and shapely, gliding with ease, not a loose joint anywhere. Everything amused and intrigued her; she loved to gossip; her bright, restless, deep black eyes missed nothing as she walked to the *ghāt,*[1] pitcher on her hip, parting her veil slightly with her finger.

The elder wife had been her exact opposite: unkempt, sloppy and slovenly. She was utterly disorganized in her dress, housework, and the care of her child. She never had any proper work in hand, yet never seemed to have time for anything. The younger wife usually refrained from comment, for at the mildest barb Radha would rage and stamp and let fly at her, disturbing everyone around.

Each wife was matched by her husband to an extraordinary degree. Dukhiram was a huge man—his bones were immense, his nose was squat, in his eyes and expression he seemed not to understand the world very well, yet he never questioned it either. He was innocent yet fearsome: a rare combination

8. God's name, repeated to express great emotion.

9. "Master" or "lord," term of address for gods and upper-class (*brāhmaṇa*) men. *Tagore* is an anglicized form of *Thākur*.

1. Steps leading down to a pond or river; meeting place, especially for women, who go there to get water or to wash clothes.

of power and helplessness. Chidam, however, seemed to have been carefully carved from shiny black rock. There was not an inch of excess fat on him, not a wrinkle or dimple anywhere. Each limb was a perfect blend of strength and finesse. Whether jumping from a riverbank, or punting[2] a boat, or climbing up bamboo-shoots for sticks, he showed complete dexterity, effortless grace. His long black hair was combed with oil back from his brow and down to his shoulders—he took great care over his dress and appearance. Although he was not unresponsive to the beauty of other women in the village, and was keen to make himself charming in their eyes, his real love was for his young wife. They quarrelled sometimes, but there was mutual respect too: neither could defeat the other. There was a further reason why the bond between them was firm: Chidam felt that a wife as nimble and sharp as Chandara could not be wholly trusted, and Chandara felt that all eyes were on her husband—that if she didn't bind him tightly to her she might one day lose him.

A little before the events in this story, however, they had a major row. Chandara had noticed that when her husband's work took him away for two days or more, he brought no extra earnings. Finding this ominous, she also began to overstep the mark. She would hang around by the *ghāt*, or wander about talking rather too much about Kashi Majumdar's middle son.

Something now seemed to poison Chidam's life. He could not settle his attention on his work. One day his sister-in-law rounded on him: she shook her finger and said in the name of her dead father, "That girl runs before the storm. How can I restrain her? Who knows what ruin she will bring?"

Chandara came out of the next room and said sweetly, "What's the matter, *Didi*?"[3] and a fierce quarrel broke out between them.

Chidam glared at his wife and said, "If I ever hear that you've been to the *ghāt* on your own, I'll break every bone in your body."

"The bones will mend again," said Chandara, starting to leave. Chidam sprang at her, grabbed her by the hair, dragged her back to the room and locked her in.

When he returned from work that evening he found that the room was empty. Chandara had fled three villages away, to her maternal uncle's house. With great difficulty Chidam persuaded her to return, but he had to surrender to her. It was as hard to restrain his wife as to hold a handful of mercury; she always slipped through his fingers. He did not have to use force any more, but there was no peace in the house. Ever-fearful love for his elusive young wife wracked him with intense pain. He even once or twice wondered if it would be better if she were dead: at least he would get some peace then. Human beings can hate each other more than death.

It was at this time that the crisis hit the house.

When her husband asked her to admit to the murder, Chandara stared at him, stunned; her black eyes burnt him like fire. Then she shrank back, as if to escape his devilish clutches. She turned her heart and soul away from him. "You've nothing to fear," said Chidam. He taught her repeatedly what she should say to the police and the magistrate. Chandara paid no attention—sat like a wooden statue whenever he spoke.

2. Propelling a boat with a long pole.
3. "Elder Sister," respectful form of address for Bengali women.

Dukhiram relied on Chidam for everything. When he told him to lay the blame on Chandara, Dukhiram said, "But what will happen to her?" "I'll save her," said Chidam. His burly brother was content with that.

III

This was what he instructed his wife to say: "The elder wife was about to attack me with the vegetable-slicer. I picked up a farm-knife to stop her, and it somehow cut into her." This was all Ramlochan's invention. He had generously supplied Chidam with the proofs and embroidery that the story would require.

The police came to investigate. The villagers were sure now that Chandara had murdered her sister-in-law, and all the witnesses confirmed this. When the police questioned Chandara, she said, "Yes, I killed her."

"Why did you kill her?"

"I couldn't stand her anymore."

"Was there a brawl between you?"

"No."

"Did she attack you first?"

"No."

"Did she ill-treat you?"

"No."

Everyone was amazed at these replies, and Chidam was completely thrown off balance. "She's not telling the truth," he said. "The elder wife first—"

The inspector silenced him sharply. He continued according to the rules of cross-examination and repeatedly received the same reply: Chandara would not accept that she had been attacked in any way by her sister-in-law. Such an obstinate girl was never seen! She seemed absolutely bent on going to the gallows; nothing would stop her. Such fierce, passionate pride! In her thoughts, Chandara was saying to her husband, "I shall give my youth to the gallows instead of to you. My final ties in this life will be with them."

Chandara was arrested, and left her home for ever, by the paths she knew so well, past the festival carriage, the market-place, the *ghāt*, the Majumdars' house, the post office, the school—an ordinary, harmless, flirtatious, fun-loving village wife; leaving a shameful impression on all the people she knew. A bevy of boys followed her, and the women of the village, her friends and companions—some of them peering through their veils, some from their doorsteps, some from behind trees—watched the police leading her away and shuddered with embarrassment, fear and contempt.

To the Deputy Magistrate, Chandara again confessed her guilt, claiming no ill-treatment from her sister-in-law at the time of the murder. But when Chidam was called to the witness-box he broke down completely, weeping, clasping his hands and saying, "I swear to you, sir, my wife is innocent." The magistrate sternly told him to control himself, and began to question him. Bit by bit the true story came out.

The magistrate did not believe him, because the chief, most trustworthy, most educated witness—Ramlochan Chakravarti—said: "I appeared on the scene a little after the murder. Chidam confessed everything to me and clung to my feet saying, 'Tell me how I can save my wife.' I did not say anything one way or the other. Then Chidam said, 'If I say that my elder brother killed his wife in a fit of fury because his food wasn't ready, then she'll get off.' I said, 'Be careful, you rogue:

don't say a single false word in court—there's no worse offence than that.'" Ramlochan had previously prepared lots of stories that would save Chandara, but when he found that she herself was bending her neck to receive the noose, he decided, "Why take the risk of giving false evidence now? I'd better say what little I know." So Ramlochan said what he knew—or rather said a little more than he knew.

The Deputy Magistrate committed the case to a sessions trial.[4] Meanwhile in fields, houses, markets and bazaars, the sad or happy affairs of the world carried on; and just as in previous years, torrential monsoon rains fell on to the new rice-crop.

Police, defendant and witnesses were all in court. In the civil court opposite hordes of people were waiting for their cases. A Calcutta lawyer had come on a suit about the sharing of a pond behind a kitchen; the plaintiff had thirty-nine witnesses. Hundreds of people were anxiously waiting for hair-splitting judgements, certain that nothing, at present, was more important. Chidam stared out of the window at the constant throng, and it seemed like a dream. A *koel*-bird[5] was hooting from a huge banyan tree in the compound: no courts or cases in *his* world!

Chandara said to the judge, "Sir, how many times must I go on saying the same thing?"

The judge explained, "Do you know the penalty for the crime you have confessed?"

"No," said Chandara.

"It is death by the hanging."

"Then please give it to me, sir," said Chandara. "Do what you like—I can't take any more."

When her husband was called to the court, she turned away. "Look at the witness," said the judge, "and say who he is."

"He is my husband," said Chandara, covering her face with her hands.

"Does he not love you?"

"He loves me greatly."

"Do you not love him?"

"I love him greatly."

When Chidam was questioned, he said, "I killed her."

"Why?"

"I wanted my food and my sister-in-law didn't give it to me."

When Dukhiram came to give evidence, he fainted. When he had come round again, he answered, "Sir, I killed her."

"Why?"

"I wanted a meal and she didn't give it to me."

After extensive cross-examination of various other witnesses, the judge concluded that the brothers had confessed to the crime in order to save the younger wife from the shame of the noose. But Chandara had, from the police investigation right through to the sessions trial, said the same thing repeatedly—she had not budged an inch from her story. Two barristers did their utmost to save her from the death-sentence, but in the end were defeated by her.

Who, on that auspicious night when, at a very young age, a dusky, diminutive, round-faced girl had left her childhood dolls in her father's house and come to her in-laws' house, could have imagined these events? Her father, on

4. A trial that is settled through a special *sessions* court in one continuous sitting.

5. Common Indian songbird.

his deathbed, had happily reflected that at least he had made proper arrangements for his daughter's future.

In gaol,[6] just before the hanging, a kindly Civil Surgeon asked Chandara, "Do you want to see anyone?"

"I'd like to see my mother," she replied.

"Your husband wants to see you," said the doctor. "Shall I call him?"

"To hell with him,"[7] said Chandara.

Kabuliwala[1]

My five-year-old daughter Mini cannot stop chattering for even a moment. From the time she came into this world, it took her hardly a year to acquire the gift of language, and thereafter she has not wasted a single moment of her waking hours in silence. Her mother scolds her sometimes to stop her from talking, but I cannot do that. Mini holding her peace is such an unnatural sight that I cannot bear it for long; so her conversations with me proceed with a great deal of vigour.

One morning, I had just started on the seventeenth chapter of my novel when Mini came in and started off. 'Baba, Ramdayal the doorman calls a crow a *kauwa* instead of a *kak*.[2] He doesn't know a thing, does he?'

Before I could explain to her about the diversity of languages in this world, she was off on another tack. 'You know, Baba,[3] Bhola was saying that an elephant pours water from the sky with his trunk and that's how we get rain.[4] What rubbish he talks day and night!'

She didn't wait for my opinion on the matter, but came up suddenly with, 'Baba, who's Ma to you?'

My sister-in-law, I said to myself;[5] but aloud I said, 'Mini, go and play with Bhola. I have work to do.'

Whereupon she flopped down close to my feet and, tapping her knees and clapping her hands, started a game of knick-knack, chanting *Agdumbagdum*.[6] Meanwhile, in my seventeenth chapter, Pratapsingh was leaping with Kanchanmala on a dark night from his high prison window down to the river below.

My room faces the street. Mini suddenly stopped her game, sped across to the window and started yelling, 'Kabuliwala, Kabuliwala!'

A tall, turbanned[7] Afghan pedlar in a dirty costume, with a sack over his shoulder and a few boxes of grapes in his hands, was making his way down the

6. Jail.
7. "Death to him" (literal trans.); an expression usually uttered in jest.
1. Translated by Madhuchhanda Karlekar.
2. *Kauwa* is the Hindi word for "crow," whereas *kak* is the word for it in Bengali. Mini, whose mother tongue is Bengali, is too young at this moment in the story to know that the doorman, Ramdayal, is a Hindi speaker, not a Bengali.
3. "Baba" is Mini's word for her father, equivalent to the English "Dad."
4. Bhola, a servant in the household, has told Mini a simplified version of an ancient Indian myth, according to which Airavat, the divine elephant of Lord Indra (the principal god of the Vedic pantheon), is responsible for rain on earth.
5. Here the narrator reveals to the reader (but not to Mini) that he is, most likely, the elder brother of the deceased husband of Mini's mother. In orthodox Hinduism, a widow loses all her privileges with respect to "normal family life"; to prevent that from happening, a brother-in-law may assume the role of surrogate husband or guardian, and that of surrogate father to the widow's children.
6. A nonsense-rhyme that playfully mimics the meaningless sounds of a magic spell.
7. Traditional headgear for Indian men, a turban is a long scarf wrapped around the head, worn (instead of a hat) for protection from the elements, to designate social status, and for ceremonial purposes.

street. What came over my dear daughter I do not know, but she started calling out to him frantically. Now we'll have another nuisance walking in, sack and all, thought I. There goes my seventeenth chapter.

But as soon as the Kabuliwala looked up smilingly and started towards us, Mini turned tail and ran off into the house: not a sign of her could be seen. She was somehow possessed of a blind belief that if one searched the Kabuli's sack, one would find a couple of humanlings like her concealed in it.

In the meantime, the Kabuliwala had walked in with a smile and a big salaam. Although Pratapsingh and Kanchanmala's fate was in jeopardy, I could not very well have called this man in and then turned him away without buying anything.

So I bought some of his stuff, and then we got talking of this and that. We chatted about Abdur Rahman and the Frontier Policy[8] of the Russians and the English.

Finally, as he got up to leave, he asked, 'Babu, where did your little girl go?'

I thought I ought to break Mini's irrational fear, so I called for her to come and meet him. She came and hung close to me, keeping a wary eye on the Kabuliwala and his sack. He brought out some raisins and dried apricots from his sack and held them out to her. She would not touch them, but clung to my knee and looked at him with redoubled suspicion. That's how the first meeting went.

A few days later, I was going out one morning on some work when I saw my girl perched on a bench beside the front door, chattering away without a stop, while the Kabuliwala sat at her feet, listening with a smile and expressing his own opinion now and then in broken Bengali. Mini in her five years of existence had never found such a patient audience, except for her father. I noticed that the train of her little sari[9] had been tucked into her waist and filled with raisins and nuts. 'Why have you given her all that?' I asked the man. 'You mustn't any more.' I took out an eight-anna bit and handed it to him. He accepted it without demur and put it into his sack.

When I came back, I found that half-rupee had set off a full-scale row.

Mini's mother was holding out a shiny coin and questioning her sternly, 'Where did you get this?'

'The Kabuliwala gave it to me,' said Mini.

'Why did you take it from him?' asked her mother.

'I didn't ask for it, he gave it to me of his own,' said Mini, close to tears.

I stepped in at this point and rescued her from impending danger.

What I gathered was that this was not the second time she had met the Kabuliwala. He had been coming almost every day, bribing her with his goodies, and had already won quite a large space in her greedy little heart.

I noticed that these two friends shared a few stock jokes between them. For instance, the minute she saw Rahamat[1] my girl would laugh and ask

8. Abdur Rahman Khan was the Amir (ruler) of Afghanistan from 1880 to 1901, immediately after the Second Anglo-Afghan War. Under Abdur Rahman, Afghanistan was a separate state, geographically sandwiched between the northwestern end of the British-Indian empire and Tsarist Russia. "Frontier Policy" refers to the triangular politics of the region around the close of the nineteenth century, characterized as "the Great Game" in Rudyard Kipling's novel *Kim* (1901).

9. A long strip of cloth draped around the body; Indian women's traditional clothing.

1. His name indicates that Rahamat, the Kabuliwala ("the man from Kabul"), is a Muslim; the narrator and his family are Hindus.

him, 'Kabuliwala, Kabuliwala, what have you got in your sack?' And Rahamat would answer with a big smile and an unnecessary nasal in the first syllable, 'Hanti!'[2]

In other words, the subtle point of his joke was that his sack contained a Nellyphant. It was not very subtle really, but it seemed to amuse them both immensely. And I too enjoyed the simple laughter of that elderly man and the little girl filling the autumn morning.

There was another routine exchange the two of them went through. Rahamat would tell Mini in his halting Bengali, 'Khonkhi,[3] you must never go to your in-laws' house.'

Bengali girls are usually taught from childhood about the in-laws' house they must go to. But we, being a little more modern, had not filled our daughter's head with that sort of talk. Mini did not quite catch the significance of Rahamat's words; but as not to reply would go against her nature, she asked him back, 'Will you go to your in-laws?'

Rahamat would shake his big fist and say, 'I'll beat up my father-in-law!'

And Mini, imagining the plight of that unknown creature called a father-in-law, would go into gales of laughter.

It was early autumn: the season when, in olden times, kings would march out on conquest. I myself have never been anywhere outside Calcutta; probably that is why my mind constantly travels across the world. Within my own home, I feel like an eternal outsider, longing continually for the big world. The minute I hear the name of some foreign country, off I go on my imaginary travels; and so too when I meet someone from a foreign land. I imagine some little cottage far across the rivers, seas and forests, where one can live a joyous life of freedom.

Yet am I so much a vegetable, anchored by my root, that the thought of actually venturing out of my little corner unnerves me. For this reason, sitting at my table every morning and talking to the Kabuliwala served me in lieu of travel. The Kabuli talked of his homeland in broken Bengali, and I pictured it all in my mind's eye: tall, impassable mountains on either side, burnt red with heat, and a caravan moving along the narrow desert track between them; turbanned traders and other travellers, some on camel-back, others on foot, some with spears in hand, others holding old-fashioned flintlock rifles.

Mini's mother is a very timid sort of person. If she hears a sound outside, she imagines that every drunken man in the world is charging towards our house. After all these years (not very many really), she is still not convinced that the world is not crawling with all kinds of horrors—thieves, robbers, drunks, snakes, tigers, malaria, caterpillars, cockroaches and British soldiers.

Hence she could not trust Rahamat the Kabuliwala either. She told me over and over again to keep a close watch on him. When I tried to laugh off her doubts, she asked me a series of pertinent questions. Are children never kidnapped? Is there or is there not a slave trade in Afghanistan? Is it quite impossible for a hulking big Kabuli to steal a little child?

I had to admit it was not impossible, but unbelievable. Not everyone has the same strength of conviction, however, so my wife remained as suspicious as

2. "Hanti" is Rahamat's mispronunciation of the Hindi word *hathi*, "elephant."

3. Rahamat's mispronunciation of *khuki*, a common term of endearment for a young girl in Bengali.

ever. Still, I could not very well stop Rahamat, for no fault of his own, from visiting our home.

Rahamat would visit his native land every year in the middle of Magh.[4] Being a money-lender, he had a very busy time collecting all his dues from various people before he left. He trudged from house to house all day, but he still found time to look Mini up. It really seemed as if they were hatching a conspiracy. If he could not come in the morning, he certainly would in the evening. Seeing that big man sitting in a dark corner in his baggy clothes, with all his various bags and sacks, made one apprehensive. But when Mini came running up so happily to meet him with her usual 'Kabuliwala, Kabuliwala,' and the two friends of unmatched years shared their simple old jokes together, it gladdened one's heart.

One morning, I was busy correcting proofs in my little room. The winter on its way out had thrown a sudden chill over the past few days, making everyone shiver. A little strip of sunlight had forced itself through the window and fallen under my table; I was enjoying its warmth upon my feet. It must have been around eight o'clock. The early risers with muffled heads had finished their morning walks and returned home. Just then I heard a deep voice coming from the street outside.

I looked out and saw two policemen approaching with our Rahamat bound in ropes between them. Behind them walked a long line of curious street urchins. There was blood on Rahamat's clothes, and one of the policemen was holding a blood-stained knife. I rushed out, stopped the policemen and asked what it was all about.

Partly from the policemen and partly from Rahamat, I learnt that one of our neighbours owed Rahamat money for a Rampuri shawl[5] he had bought. The man had told lies, denied the debt, and started an argument, in the midst of which Rahamat had pulled out a knife and stabbed him.

Rahamat was still hurling filthy abuse at the liar when Mini came skipping out of the house with her 'Kabuliwala, Kabuliwala!'

Rahamat's face instantly relaxed into a happy smile. As he had no sack on his shoulder that day, the usual exchange regarding its contents could not take place. So Mini asked him straight off, 'Will you go to your in-laws' house?'

'That's just where I'm going,' Rahamat answered with a laugh.

He saw that Mini did not find this answer funny, so he held out his hands and added, 'I would have beaten up my father-in-law, but what can I do? My hands are tied.'

Charged with causing grievous harm, Rahamat was sentenced to several years in prison.

We almost forgot about him. Year after year, as we went about our daily business in the safety of our home, never once did we think of how that freedom-loving man from the mountains was spending his time in prison.

4. Late winter month in the Bengali calendar.

5. An expensive, hand-embroidered woolen wrap made in Rampur, now in Uttar Pradesh, India, near the Nepal border. Between the late 18th and mid-20th century, Rampur was a Shi'a Muslim kingdom ruled by descendants of Afghan Rohilla ethnicity, and it became a center for handicrafts such as the Rampuri cap and the Rampuri knife.

As for Mini's flighty little heart, her own father cannot deny its shameful conduct. She forgot her old friend quite easily, and found a new one in Nabi the groom. Gradually, as she grew older, girlfriends took the place of men: so much so that she was hardly ever seen in her father's study. We were practically not on talking terms anymore.

Years went by. It was autumn again. Mini was going to be married. A match had been arranged, and the wedding day fixed during the Puja vacation. Along with Durga of Mount Kailas, my Mini too would leave her father's house in darkness and set off for her husband's home.[6]

It was a beautiful day. The rain-washed autumn sunshine was like pure gold. Even the mouldy brickwork of the houses huddled along our old Calcutta lane looked lovely as they basked in the golden haze.

The wedding shehnai had been playing since dawn. Each note of the music seemed to be playing tearfully in my own rib-cage. The piercing Bhairavi raga[7] intensified the pain of the impending farewell, spilling it across the world outside like the autumn sunlight. My Mini was to be married that day.

The house was in commotion from the early morning, with people milling around. Down in the courtyard, bamboo poles had been fixed and an awning set up. From every room in the house, one heard the tinkle of chandeliers being fitted up, with endless yelling and shouting of orders.

I was sitting in my study looking through the bills, when all of a sudden Rahamat appeared.

I did not recognise him at first. He did not have his sack, nor his long hair, nor that robust look of old. I finally placed him by his smile.

'Ah, Rahamat, how long have you been back?' I said.

'I came out of prison last evening,' he replied.

His words jarred on my ears. I had never seen a murderer in flesh and blood, but my heart shrank at the sight of this man. I wanted him to go away that very minute and not spoil the auspicious day.

'There's a ceremony in the house today, and I'm very busy. You had better go now,' I told him.

He got up when he heard this and prepared to leave right away; but he stopped half-way and asked, 'Can't I see Khonkhi for just a short while?'

He must have thought that Mini would remain exactly as before: that she would come running up with her usual 'Kabuliwala, Kabuliwala!' and share their familiar jokes. He had even brought a box of grapes, and some nuts and raisins in a paper packet—no doubt begged from a fellow Kabuli, since he no longer had his own sack of wares.

'I told you there's a ceremony in the house,' I said again. 'You can't meet anyone else today.'

6. Durga is the fearsome form of the goddess Pārvatī, Lord Śiva's consort; she is worshipped widely in Bengal as a "mother goddess," in preference to the male gods in the Hindu pantheon. The annual festival called Durga Puja ("Worship of Durga") is celebrated over six days in September or October on the lunar calendar; Durga is associated with Mount Kailash (in the Himalayas) which, in Hindu mythology, is her and Śiva's "heavenly abode" on earth.

7. The *shehnai*, a double-reed conical oboe, is played at Hindu weddings; its music is associated with purity and sanctity. In Indian classical music, a *rāga* ("musical mode") is a tonal structure with a framework of progressions and melodic and rhythmic patterns; any particular composition is set to a specific *rāga*. Compositions in the Bhairavi *rāga* are prized for their emotion-charged melodies, sung or played at dawn or early in the morning.

He seemed a little upset. He stood up without a word, looked steadily at me for a while, said 'Salaam,[8] Babu,' and left.

I felt sorry for him. I was thinking of calling him back when I saw him returning on his own.

'I'd brought these grapes, raisins and nuts for Khonkhi. Will you give them to her, please?' he said.

I was about to pay him for them when he suddenly caught hold of my hand and said, 'You're a very kind man. I'll always remember you, but please don't pay me for these. Babu, just as you have a daughter, I too have a daughter at home. I remember her face when I bring these things for Khonkhi. I don't come here to trade.'

With that he plunged a hand into his big loose shirt and brought out a soiled piece of paper from near his breast. He unfolded it very carefully with both hands and laid it on my table.

I saw the black imprint of a little hand on that paper: not a photograph, nor a painting, just a rough print of a little hand made from burnt charcoal smeared on the palm. He brought back this little memento of his daughter with him every year, held it close to his big lonely heart as he roamed the streets of Calcutta, as if the touch of her little soft hand brought some comfort to his great pining heart.

My eyes were moist as I examined that scrap of paper. I forgot that he was just a dry-fruit vendor from Kabul, and I a well-born Bengali gentleman. I knew then that he and I were really just the same. He was a father, and so was I. The rough print of his little mountain-dwelling Parvati's[9] hand reminded me of my own Mini. I sent for her that very minute. The women were very reluctant to let her out, but I paid no heed. She came out, dressed in her red silk sari and bridal make-up, and stood shyly at the door.

Rahamat was quite taken aback when he saw her. He did not know how to pick up the thread of their old friendship. Finally he laughed and said, 'Are you going to your in-laws, Khonkhi?'

Mini now knew what 'in-laws' meant. She could not answer him back as before, but blushed and turned her face away. I recalled the day she had met the Kabuliwala for the first time, and my heart ached.

After Mini had left, Rahamat gave a deep sigh and sat down on the floor. It struck him suddenly that his daughter too would have grown as old. He would have to make friends with her again: she would not be the same girl he had left behind. Who knows how she had fared in these eight years? The shehnai played on in the mellow morning sunshine, and Rahamat, sitting in a narrow city lane, saw visions of the barren Afghan mountains.

I took out a banknote from my purse and handed it to him. 'Go home to your daughter, Rahamat,' I said. 'Have a happy reunion, and may your joy bring good fortune to my Mini.'

By gifting him that money, I had to cut down on a few frills for the wedding. The electric lights were not as dazzling as we had planned, and the big band had to be cancelled. The women were most upset; but to me the ceremony was the brighter for being bathed in a great beneficent light.

8. *Salaam*, from the Arabic and corresponding to the Hebrew *shalom*, is a common greeting and expression at parting in northern India. *Babu* is a masculine honorific term, used to address social superiors.

9. In Hinduism, the goddess Pārvatī is Lord Śiva's consort; she is the daughter of the Himalayas (mythologized as an old man), and dwells with her husband in the mountains. Here the narrator sympathetically imagines Rahamat's daughter as a little "goddess" in the Kabul Valley, among the Hindu Kush mountains, just west of the Himalayas.

HIGUCHI ICHIYŌ

1872–1896

The first major Japanese woman writer in six centuries, the poverty-stricken, barely educated Higuchi Ichiyō seemed to emerge out of nowhere. She crafted brief, sensitive stories that borrowed from the luxuriant language of classical Japanese literature while representing a stark and sordid modern world: bedraggled orphans in the streets, mistreated prostitutes, and the urban working class—potters, rickshaw drivers, seamstresses. Knowing nothing about European literary movements, she developed a realism all her own, focusing on the lives of poor and insignificant city dwellers. She was quickly hailed as one of the great writers of her time—praised as inventive, highly skillful, and deeply moving. She died suddenly at the age of twenty-four, leaving a mark on Japanese literature in a writing career that lasted just four years.

LIFE

Higuchi Natsu was born at a time when Japanese women were not expected to receive much in the way of education, but she read as widely as she could, immersing herself in classical literature. She especially loved *The Tale of Genji* and from an early age wrote poetry in a classical style. Her father was determined to leave his peasant roots behind, and he managed to become a bureaucrat in Tokyo. Intrigued by the fast money he saw entrepreneurs earning around him, he then sunk all of his money into a business that failed miserably. He died, destitute, when Ichiyō was seventeen. She packed up her mother and sister and moved to the fringes of Tokyo's red-light district, where she took in sewing and laundry while struggling to make literary connections. The family had barely enough money to put food on the table.

The young woman met her literary mentor, Nakarai Tōsui, while working as his washerwoman. He was a journalist and hack novelist, writing in an increasingly outmoded style that was deliberately playful, even frivolous. He appeared handsome, elegant, and sophisticated. She fell in love with him immediately, as she records in her lively diary, but he did not reciprocate her feeling; eventually she had to break with him when gossip about them began to compromise her reputation. In the meanwhile, however, he did launch her career as a writer, helping her to get her first stories published under the pen name Higuchi Ichiyō (the second name meaning "single leaf").

Ichiyō's novella *Child's Play*, which appeared in 1895 and 1896, made her suddenly famous. It follows a number of children living on the margins of Tokyo's red-light district as they come of age. Leaders of Japan's literary establishment were astonished by the fresh talent of a writer unschooled in Western fiction, and the general public was equally enthusiastic. She began to publish one brilliant story after another for a miraculous fourteen months. Fan clubs arose; students begged her to teach them about *The Tale of Genji*; and one besotted enthusiast stole the handwritten nameplate from her door so that he could have a piece of her writing. But by this time, having lived on a meager diet in grim poverty for years, Ichiyō was suffering from an advanced case of tuberculosis. No doctor could save her.

TIMES

In 1868 a new Japanese emperor took the name Meiji ("enlightened rule"). At the time, the Japanese economy was mostly agricultural, and the nation did not have a strong military. Europe and the United States had been putting pressure on Japan to sign unbalanced trade treaties, and the Japanese realized that they had little power to resist. But this situation was about to change dramatically. By 1912, the end of the Meiji period, the government of the military dictator, or *shogun*, and his *samurai*, in power since the seventeenth century, had fallen in favor of a constitutional monarchy, with a representative system of local government and a bicameral legislature. The new regime had established a new legal system and a ministry of education to oversee the training of future generations, while newspapers sprang up to circulate information and debate about the modern state. The country had built up its military, winning wars against China and Russia, and established itself as an international power. Perhaps most important, Japan had invested in industry—importing new technologies from the West, installing telegraph and telephone lines, and laying railways. Suddenly whole new industries opened up, and with the collapse of old feudal structures, people found themselves free to move around in search of work. "Advances" could be seen everywhere, from new brick buildings several stories high to streetlights and telegraph poles, and fashionable people wore bowler hats and petticoats, following the styles from London and Paris. As Tokyo grew into a modern metropolis, the number of rats was alleged to have topped eight million.

Writers, too, got caught up in the enthusiasm for modernization and looked in the direction of Europe for ideas. Japanese audiences eagerly read new translations: Defoe's *Robinson Crusoe*, Aesop's *Fables*, *Hamlet*, **Dostoyevsky**'s *Crime and Punishment*. Many male writers were now educated at the new Japanese universities, fully exposed to the latest intellectual currents from around the world. Encouraged to think of themselves as potential leaders of the new Japan, they became purposefully worldly. The new novelists found European realism especially intriguing, and they began to write fiction that examined the subtlest feelings of ordinary, middle-class people and explored the contemporary social world.

WORK

Isolated from the male writers who were at the time inspired by European literature to reinvent the Japanese novel as serious social and psychological fiction, Ichiyō belonged to no established or emerging school of writing. Her mentor, Nakarai, with his frivolous, unfashionable style, was clearly not the right guide to bring her into the modern age. And so she accomplished this feat almost entirely alone. Drawing on the materials of her lived experience—her own marginal social status, her struggles with money, and her squalid surroundings—she began to paint a rich picture of the alleyways and brothels in Tokyo's poorest neighborhoods, where threadbare merchants and day-laborers, fortune-tellers and hangers-on, jugglers and minstrels catered to the rough and colorful "pleasure quarter." She had a particular predilection for adolescent characters, and some of her readers saw these figures as metaphors for the new Japan, on the brink of full maturity and feeling all of the excitement, the pain—and the disappointment—of growing up. Indeed, unlike many writers in the West, Ichiyō tended to cast the experience of coming of age as a loss and a threat rather than a fulfilling promise.

"Separate Ways," Ichiyō's final short story, captures the world of Tokyo's struggling poor almost entirely in a compact dialogue between its two main characters. Here she shows a woman at a crossroads, able to choose between two kinds of life—one of respectable independence and poverty, the other of sexual dependence and luxury—but she gives us the woman's choice mostly through the eyes of a feisty street urchin who is her friend. Throughout, in fact, the narrator remains very much in the background, offering very little explicit description and no judgment of her characters or their feelings; we learn almost everything we know about them through what they say and what is said about them. Although it is an unsentimental, restrained narrator who takes us into Tokyo's urban underclass, the dialogue itself is full of feeling—colloquial, spirited, disapproving, even aggressive. Thus we are immersed in a contentious social world, and like the story's characters, must find our way to our own judgments about how best to live in that world.

While focusing on the modern urban poor, Ichiyō throughout her career preserved an attachment to the style of classical Japanese literature, filling her elegantly brief stories with skillful plays on words, literary allusions, and passages of lyrical beauty that were quite different from the new literary realism of male writers borrowing from Western models. Poised perfectly between old and new, Higuchi Ichiyō has been called both the last woman writer of old Japan and the first woman writer of Japanese modernity.

Separate Ways[1]

There was someone outside, tapping at her window.

"Okyō? Are you home?"

"Who is it? I'm already in bed," she lied. "Come back in the morning."

"I don't care if you are in bed. Open up! It's me—Kichizō, from the umbrella shop."

"What a bothersome boy you are. Why do you come so late at night? I suppose you want some rice cakes again," she chuckled. "Just a minute. I'm coming."

Okyō, a stylish woman in her early twenties, put her sewing down and hurried into the front hall. Her abundant hair was tied back simply—she was too busy to fuss with it—and over her kimono she wore a long apron and a jacket. She opened the lattice, then the storm door.

"Sorry," Kichizō said as he barged in.

Dwarf, they called him. He was a pugnacious little one. He was sixteen, and he worked as an apprentice at the umbrella shop, but to look at him one would think he was eleven or twelve. He had spindly shoulders and a small face. He was a bright-looking boy, but so short that people teased him and dubbed him "Dwarf."

"Pardon me." He went right for the brazier.

"You won't find enough fire in there to toast any of your rice cakes. Go get some charcoal from the cinder box in the kitchen. You can heat the cakes

1. Translated by Robert Lyons Danly.

yourself. I've got to get this done tonight." She took up her sewing again. "The owner of the pawnshop on the corner ordered it to wear on New Year's."[2]

"Hmm. What a waste, on that old baldie. Why don't I wear it first?"

"Don't be ridiculous. Don't you know what they say? 'He who wears another's clothes will never get anywhere in life.' You're a hopeless one, you are. You shouldn't say such things."

"I never did expect to be successful. I'll wear anybody's clothes—it's all the same to me. Remember what you promised once? When your luck changes, you said you'd make me a good kimono. Will you really?" He wasn't joking now.

"If only I could sew you a nice kimono, it would be a happy day. I'd gladly do it. But look at me. I don't have enough money to dress myself properly. I'm sewing to support myself. These aren't gifts I'm making." She smiled at him. "It's a dream, that promise."

"That's all right. I'm not asking for it now. Wait until some good luck comes. At least say you will. Don't you want to make me happy? That would be a sight, though, wouldn't it?" The boy had a wistful smile on his face. "Me dressed up in a fancy kimono!"

"And if you succeed first, Kichizō, promise me you'll do the same. That's a pledge I'd like to see come true."

"Don't count on it. I'm not going to succeed."

"How do you know?"

"I know, that's all. Even if someone came along and insisted on helping me, I'd still rather stay where I am. Oiling umbrellas suits me fine. I was born to wear a plain kimono with workman's sleeves[3] and a short band around my waist. To me, all 'good luck' means is squeezing a little money from the change when I'm sent to buy persimmon juice.[4] If I hit the target someday, shooting arrows through a bamboo pole,[5] that's about all the good luck I can hope for. But someone like you, from a good family—why, fortune will come to greet you in a carriage. I don't mean a man's going to come and take you for his mistress, or something. Don't get the wrong idea." He toyed with the fire in the brazier and sighed over his fate.

"It won't be a fine carriage that comes for me. I'll be going to hell in a handcart." Okyō leaned against her yardstick and turned to Kichizō. "I've had so many troubles on my mind, sometimes it feels as if my heart's on fire."

Kichizō went to fetch the charcoal from the kitchen, as he always did.

"Aren't you going to have any rice cakes?"

Okyō shook her head. "No thank you."

"Then I'll go ahead. That old tightwad at the umbrella shop is always complaining. He doesn't know how to treat people properly. I was sorry when the old woman died. *She* was never like that. These new people! I don't talk to any of them. Okyō, what do you think of Hanji at the shop? He's a mean one, isn't he? He's so stuck-up. He's the owner's son, but, you know, I still can't think of him as a future boss. Whenever I have the chance, I like to pick a

2. New Year's Day is the most significant holiday of the year in Japan.

3. The kimono is a traditional Japanese robe; workman's sleeves are short.

4. Persimmons are a common fruit in Japan, sometimes used for fermented drinks.

5. A game played at carnivals that involved trying to hit a target.

fight and cut him down to size." Kichizō set the rice cakes on the wire net above the brazier. "Oh, it's hot!" he shouted, blowing on his fingers. "I wonder why it is—you seem almost like a sister to me, Okyō. Are you sure you never had a younger brother?"

"I was an only child. I never had any brothers or sisters."

"So there really is no connection between us. Boy, I'd sure be glad if someone like you would come and tell me she was my sister. I'd hug her so tight . . . After that, I wouldn't care if I died. What was I, born from a piece of wood? I've never run into anyone who was a relative of mine. You don't know how many times I've thought about it: if I'm never, ever going to meet anyone from my own family, I'd be better off dying right now. Wouldn't I? But it's odd. I still want to go on living. I have this funny dream. The few people who've been the least bit kind to me all of a sudden turn out to be my mother and father and my brother and sister. And then I think, I want to live a little longer. Maybe if I wait another year, someone will tell me the truth. So I go on oiling umbrellas, even if it doesn't interest me a bit. Do you suppose there's anyone in the world as strange as I am? I don't have a mother or a father, Okyō. How could a child be born without either parent? It makes me pretty odd." He tapped at the rice cakes and decided they were done.

"Don't you have some kind of proof of your identity? A charm with your name on it, for instance?[6] There must be something you have, some clue to your family's whereabouts."

"Nothing. My friends used to tease me. They said I was left underneath a bridge when I was born, so I'd be taken for a beggar's baby. It may be true. Who knows? I may be the child of a tramp. One of those men who pass by in rags every day could be a kinsman. That old crippled lady with one eye who comes begging every morning—for all I know, she could be my mother. I used to wear a lion's mask and do acrobatics in the street," he said dejectedly, "before I worked at the umbrella shop. Okyō, if I were a beggar's boy, you wouldn't have been so nice to me, would you? You wouldn't have given me a second look."

"You shouldn't joke like that, Kichizō. I don't know what kind of people your parents were, but it makes no difference to me. These silly things you're saying—you're not yourself tonight. If I were you, I wouldn't let it bother me. Even if I were the child of an outcast, I'd make something of myself, whether I had any parents or not, no matter who my brothers were. Why are you whining around so?"

"I don't know," he said, staring at the floor. "There's something wrong with me. I don't seem to have any get-up-and-go."

She was dead now, but in the last generation the old woman Omatsu, fat as a *sumō* wrestler, had made a tidy fortune at the umbrella shop. It was a winter's night six years before that she had picked up Kichizō, performing his tumbler's act along the road, as she was returning from a pilgrimage.

"It's all right," she had assured him. "If the master gives us any trouble, we'll worry about it when the time comes. I'll tell him what a poor boy you are, how your companions abandoned you when your feet were too sore to go on walking. Don't worry about it. No one will raise an eyebrow. There's always room

6. Children were given paper charms with their names on them to carry for safety and good luck.

for a child or two. Who's going to care if we spread out a few boards for you to sleep on in the kitchen, and give you a little bit to eat? There's no risk in that. Why, even with a formal apprenticeship boys have been known to disappear. It doesn't prevent them from running off with things that don't belong to them. There are all kinds of people in this world. You know what they say: 'You don't know a horse till you ride it.' How can we tell whether we can use you in the shop if we don't give you a try? But listen, if you don't want to go back to that slum of yours, you're going to have to work hard. And learn how things are done. You'll have to make up your mind: this is where your home is. You're going to have to work, you know."

And work he did. Today, by himself, Kichizō could treat as many umbrellas as three adults, humming a tune as he went about his business. Seeing this, people would praise the dead lady's foresight: "Granny knew what she was doing."

The old woman, to whom he owed so much, had been dead two years now, and the present owners of the shop and their son Hanji were hard for Kichizō to take. But what was he to do? Even if he didn't like them, he had nowhere else to go. Had not his anger and resentment at them caused his very bones and muscles to contract? "Dwarf! Dwarf!" everybody taunted him. "Eating fish on the anniversary of your parents' death! It serves you right that you're so short. Round and round we go—look at him! The tiny monk who'll never grow!"[7]

In his work, he could take revenge on the sniveling bullies, and he was perfectly ready to answer them with a clenched fist. But his valor sometimes left him. He didn't even know the date of his parents' death, he had no way to observe the yearly abstinences. It made him miserable, and he would throw himself down underneath the umbrellas drying in the yard and push his face against the ground to stifle his tears.

The boy was a little fireball. He had a violence about him that frightened the entire neighborhood. The sleeves of his plain kimono would swing as he flailed his arms, and the smell of oil from the umbrellas followed him through every season. There was no one to calm his temper, and he suffered all the more. If anyone were to show Kichizō a moment's kindness, he knew that he would cling to him and find it hard ever to let go.

In the spring Okyō the seamstress had moved into the neighborhood. With her quick wit, she was soon friendly with everyone. Her landlord was the owner of the umbrella shop, and so she was especially cordial to the members of the shop. "Bring over your mending anytime, boys. I don't care what condition it's in. There are so many people at your house, the mistress won't have time to tend to it. I'm always sewing anyway, one more stitch is nothing. Come and visit when you have time. I get lonely living by myself. I like people who speak their minds, and that rambunctious Kichizō—he's one of my favorites. Listen, the next time you lose your temper," she would tell him, "instead of hitting the little white dog at the rice shop, come over to my place. I'll give you my mallet, and you can take out your anger on the fulling block. That way, people won't be so upset with you. And you'll be helping me—it'll do us both good."

In no time Kichizō began to make himself at home. It was "Okyō, this" and "Okyō, that" until he had given the other workmen at the shop something new

7. Song from a children's game.

to tease him about. "Why, he's the mirror image of the great Chōemon!" they would laugh. "At the River Katsura, Ohan will have to carry *him*! Can't you see the little runt perched on top of her sash for the ride across the river? What a farce!"[8]

Kichizō was not without retort. "If you're so manly, why don't you ever visit Okyō? Which one of you can tell me each day what sweets she's put in the cookie jar? Take the pawnbroker with the bald spot. He's head over heels in love with her, always ordering sewing from her and coming round on one pretext or another, sending her aprons and neckpieces and sashes—trying to win her over. But she's never given him the time of day. Let alone treat him the way she does me! Kichizō from the umbrella shop—*I'm* the one who can go there any hour of the night, and when she hears it's me, she'll open the door in her nightgown. 'You haven't come to see me all day. Did something happen? I've been worried about you.' That's how she greets me. Who else gets treated that way? 'Hulking men are like big trees: not always good supports.' Size has nothing to do with it. Look at how the tiny peppercorn is prized."

"Listen to him!" they would yell, pelting Kichizō across the back.

But all he did was smile nonchalantly. "Thank you very much." If only he had a little height, no one would dare to tease him. As it was, the disdain he showed them was dismissed as nothing more than the impertinence of a little fool. He was the butt of all their jokes and the gossip they exchanged over tobacco.

On the night of the thirtieth of December, Kichizō was returning home. He had been up the hill to call on a customer with apologies for the late filling of an order. On his way back now he kept his arms folded across his chest and walked briskly, kicking a stone with the tip of his sandal. It rolled to the left and then to the right, and finally Kichizō kicked it into a ditch, chuckling aloud to himself. There was no one around to hear him. The moon above shone brightly on the white winter roads, but the boy was oblivious to the cold. He felt invigorated. He thought he would stop by Okyō's on the way home. As he crossed over to the back street, he was suddenly startled: someone appeared from behind him and covered his eyes. Whoever it was, the person could not keep from laughing.

"Who is it? Come on, who is it?" When he touched the hands held over his eyes, he knew who it was. "Ah, Okyō! I can tell by your snaky fingers. You shouldn't scare people."

Kichizō freed himself and Okyō laughed. "Oh, too bad! I've been discovered."

Over her usual jacket she was wearing a hood that came down almost to her eyes. She looked smart tonight, Kichizō thought as he surveyed her appearance. "Where've you been? I thought you told me you were too busy even to eat the next few days." The boy did not hide his suspicion. "Were you taking something to a customer?"

"I went to make some of my New Year's calls early," she said innocently.

"You're lying. No one receives greetings on the thirtieth. Where did you go? To your relatives?"

8. Reference to a puppet play by the late-18th-century playwright Suga Sensuke, *The River Katsura and the Floodgate of Eternal Love* (1776), a story of two lovers, a middle-aged man named Chōemon and a teenaged girl named Ohan. In one scene Chōemon carries Ohan across the Katsura River.

"As a matter of fact, I *am* going to a relative's—to live with a relative I hardly know. Tomorrow I'll be moving. It's so sudden, it probably surprises you. It *is* unexpected, even I feel a little startled. Anyway, you should be happy for me. It's not a bad thing that's happened."

"Really? You're not teasing, are you? You shouldn't scare me like this. If you went away, what would I do for fun? Don't ever joke about such things. You and your nonsense!" He shook his head at her.

"I'm not joking. It's just as you said once—good luck has come riding in a fancy carriage. So I can't very well stay on in a back tenement, can I? Now I'll be able to sew you that kimono, Kichizō."

"I don't want it. When you say 'Good luck has come,' you mean you're going off someplace worthless. That's what Hanji said the other day. 'You know Okyō the seamstress?' he said. 'Her uncle—the one who gives rub-downs over by the vegetable market—he's helped her find a new position. She's going into service with some rich family. Or so they say. But it sounds fishy to me—she's too old to learn sewing from some housewife. Somebody's going to set her up. I'm sure of it. She'll be wearing tasseled coats the next time we see her, la-de-da, and her hair all done up in ringlets, like a kept woman. You wait. With a face like hers, you don't think she's about to spend her whole life sewing, do you?' That's what he said. I told him he was full of it, and we had a big fight. But you *are* going to do it, aren't you? You're going off to be someone's mistress!"

"It's not that I want to. I don't have much choice. I suppose I won't be able to see you anymore, Kichizō, will I?"

With these few words, Kichizō withered. "I don't know, maybe it's a step up for you, but don't do it. It's not as if you can't make a living with your sewing. The only one you have to feed is yourself. When you're good at your work, why give it up for something so stupid? It's disgusting of you. Don't go through with it. It's not too late to change your mind." The boy was unyielding in his notion of integrity.

"Oh, dear," Okyō sighed. She stopped walking. "Kichizō, I'm sick of all the washing and sewing. Anything would be better. I'm tired of these drab clothes. I'd like to wear a crepe kimono, too, for a change—even if it is tainted."

They were bold words, and yet it didn't sound as if she herself fully comprehended them. "Anyway," she laughed, "come home with me. Hurry up now."

"What! I'm too disgusted. You go ahead," he said, but his long, sad shadow followed after her.

Soon they came to their street. Okyō stopped beneath the window where Kichizō always tapped for her. "Every night you come and knock at this window. After tomorrow night," she sighed, "I won't be able to hear your voice calling anymore. How terrible the world is."

"It's not the world. It's you."

Okyō went in first and lit a lamp. "Kichizō, come get warm," she called when she had the fire in the brazier going.

He stood by the pillar. "No, thanks."

"Aren't you chilly? It won't do to catch a cold."

"I don't care." He looked down at the floor as he spoke. "Leave me alone."

"What's the matter with you? You're acting funny. Is it something I said? If it is, please tell me. When you stand around with a long face like that and won't talk to me, it makes me worry."

"You don't have to worry about anything. This is Kichizō from the umbrella shop you're talking to. I don't need any woman to take care of me." He rubbed his back against the pillar. "How pointless everything turns out. What a life! People are friendly, and then they disappear. It's always the ones I like. Granny at the umbrella shop, and Kinu, the one with short hair, at the dyer's shop. First Granny dies of palsy. Then Kinu goes and throws herself into the well behind the dyer's—she didn't want to marry. Now you're going off. I'm always disappointed in the end. Why should I be surprised, I suppose? What am I but a boy who oils umbrellas? So what if I do the work of a hundred men? I'm not going to win any prizes for it. Morning and night, the only title I ever hear is 'Dwarf' . . . 'Dwarf'! I wonder if I'll ever get any taller. 'All things come to him who waits,' they say, but I wait and wait, and all I get is more unhappiness. Just the day before yesterday I had a fight with Hanji over you. Ha! I was so sure he was wrong. I told him you were the last person rotten enough to go off and do that kind of thing. Not five days have passed, and I have to eat crow. How could I have thought of you as a sister? You, with all your lies and tricks, and your selfishness. This is the last you'll ever see of me. Ever. Thanks for your kindness. Go on and do what you want. From now on, I won't have anything to do with anyone. It's not worth it. Good-by, Okyō."

He went to the front door and began to put his sandals on.

"Kichizō! You're wrong. I'm leaving here, but I'm not abandoning *you*. You're like my little brother. How can you turn on me?" From behind, she hugged him with all her might. "You're too impatient. You jump to conclusions."

"You mean you're not going to be someone's mistress?" Kichizō turned around.

"It's not the sort of thing anybody wants to do. But it's been decided. You can't change things."

He stared at her with tears in his eyes.

"Take your hands off me, Okyō."

ORATURE

The written word reached only a tiny sliver of the world's population before the twentieth century. The United Nations estimates that around 10 percent of the world was literate in 1850. By the 1920s the number was up to 28 percent. But low levels of literacy worldwide did not mean that people lacked stories and poetry, philosophy and religious wisdom. For most of human history, people used the spoken word to pass on laws, skills, common values, founding legends, and thrilling tales. In fact, world literature as we know it today would not exist without the nourishment of oral traditions. Homer's great ancient Greek epics, the *Iliad* and the *Odyssey*, began as oral tales, becoming "literature" only after generations had passed them down from memory. From Walt Disney's *Snow White* to **Toni Morrison**'s Nobel Prize–winning fiction, from experimental poetry to African jazz, long and complex histories of oral performance continue to circulate as a living part of world culture, whether we recognize them or not.

The Ugandan linguist Pio Zirimu coined the term *orature* to convey the serious artistic value of oral expression. In most predominantly oral cultures, performance is a highly refined skill. Those who recite stories and poems aloud adopt individual performance styles and alter details for dramatic effect. A talented few come to be renowned as great artists. Unlike the fixed written word, an oral tradition is not a single, knowable object: live performances involve vocal modulations and cadences, dramatic silences and bodily movements that change with each telling; and performers often introduce creative transformations, adapting old stories to suit new circumstances. Live audiences respond to the teller in ways that can shape the telling, and they sometimes participate in the performance.

The relationship between oral literature and the written word took on a new importance in the nineteenth century. When it comes to reading and writing, this was a time of great unevenness and rapid change. In traditional agrarian societies such as Russia, where most people worked the land, only 5 percent of the population could read. But in the United States and Protestant Europe, where churches formed schools to teach people how to read the Bible, and industrialization and urbanization demanded new skills and new mobility, literacy rates reached almost universal levels. Around mid-century, about 60 percent of French and British people could read, 30 percent of Japanese people, and 5 percent across the Ottoman Empire. In some regions literacy rates varied by gender: in Brazil 12 percent of women were literate compared to 20 percent of men, and India's female literacy was at 8 percent across the country, while in the Kerala region almost a third of adult women could read. In the United States, the most important differentiating factor was race: while the United States boasted an 80 percent overall literacy rate in 1870, four-fifths of African Americans were illiterate because under slavery they had been denied education.

Zovave storyteller (North Africa, 1857). Photograph by Gustave le Gray.

Literacy rates rose dramatically in many places over the course of the century: in Argentina, adult literacy stood at less than one-third in 1869, but thanks to education reforms launched by Domingo Faustino Sarmiento, it rose to two-thirds by 1914. Toward the end of the nineteenth century, British colonial administrators in South Africa actually worried that too many black people were literate and so were beginning to rebel against the expectation that they would perform only the most menial kinds of work. Literacy, as the American slave **Frederick Douglass** had discovered, could be a powerful tool of resistance and political freedom. But so too could orature, which often eluded official scrutiny and could bring a sense of cohesion and solidarity to social groups under threat.

Interest in oral traditions rose sharply in the nineteenth century, as many nations made the shift to widespread literacy. When people learn how to read, they usually stop developing the skills and methods of memorization, and this means that oral traditions fade as literacy rates rise. Thanks to the huge upsurge in literacy, the nineteenth century saw the end of many vibrant oral traditions around the world. This threat of disappearing cultural riches prompted some, like **Jacob and Wilhelm Grimm**, to try to preserve spoken stories in print before they vanished. The Grimms' fairy tales, first published in 1812, included "Snow White" and "Hansel and Gretel," stories that had been passed down orally for generations. For the Grimms, fairy tales were important because they were thought to reveal a deep, longstanding cultural life that bound the German people together. And the Grimms were not the only ones to turn to folktales and fairy tales to build nationalist sentiment: around the world, traditional oral stories were often thought to be the authentic expressions of a unified people.

The nineteenth century was also a time when European powers were conquering peoples around the world, and some Europeans became fascinated by similarities between their own oral traditions and those they found thriving elsewhere. Did folktales provide a key to understanding a universal human nature? Did all cultures tell the same basic stories? The examples collected below suggest intriguing similarities between African stories and those told by slaves in the Americas and peasants in Europe: all of these groups return again and again to tales of oppressive labor. Many Europeans assumed that cultures in Africa and Asia represented "immature" stages in a single story of human development, and that one could see Europe as it had once been by studying Iroquois or Zulu culture in the present. In the 1870s, for example, a German scholar by the name of Willem Bleek took advantage of the imprisonment of a number of nomadic Kung people by the British in southern Africa. These prisoners were the perfect subjects to teach him about oral traditions, he realized, since they could not wander off, as nomadic people were inclined to do. Acknowledging that the Kung were in danger of extinction because their traditional hunting and gathering lands had been seized by European settlers, Bleek said that he had made an urgent journey to collect their stories so that Europeans could come to know a disappearing race "that had made little, if any, advance since the far-distant days when members of it shot their flint-headed arrows at reindeer in France." Bleek assumed that oral stories from Africa needed to be transcribed as a way for Europeans to understand their own past—the prehistory of civilization—before they themselves eradicated that prehistory through colonization.

Although orature might have seemed fragile in the context of rapid industrialization and modernization, sometimes it survived, forceful and vigorous. The twelve million African slaves who crossed the ocean between the seventeenth and the nineteenth centuries carried stories, styles, and cadences to the United States, Latin America, and the Caribbean, which pervaded their new home cultures. The roots of jazz and hip-hop rhythms, for example, can be traced to African musical traditions. Collected below are two stories of **Anansi** the spider-trickster, a character who originates with the Ashanti people in West Africa and then travels on the slave ships, appearing in lots of different retellings in the Americas.

As vibrant oral cultures continued to coexist with rising literacy in the nineteenth century, many people tried their hands at translating oral stories and poems into written form. Among these were colonial administrators, missionaries, curious travelers, and scholars of language, folklore, and anthropology, as well as representatives of cultures under threat. The selections here reveal a range of motives: the British in West Africa, for example, wanted to study local lore so that they could control the Ashanti people, while the Hawaiian folklorist **Mary Pukui** feared that her own traditions were disappearing. Whether intending to oppress or to conserve, all of these writers had to make difficult choices in the translation from oral to written forms: should they try to express the particular style of one performer, or should they listen to multiple versions of the same story to try to distill the common features of a tradition? Should the written version convey the idiosyncratic features of spoken language—interjections, cadences, repetitions, and colloquialisms—or should it follow a tidier, more conventionally literary style? The transcriber of "**A Donegal Fairy**," an Irish tale, opts for the former, trying to keep the texture of the particular oral performance intact, down to the details of local pronunciation and conversational interruptions.

However they were preserved and transcribed, a vast range of oral traditions have survived into our time, nourishing the richness of modern world cultures, sometimes unseen or overlooked but nonetheless still vital. Many of the most prominent twentieth- and twenty-first-century writers around the world have drawn inspiration from orature. **William Butler Yeats**, the Irish poet, collected and published traditional tales from his own country and drew from them for his groundbreaking Modernist poetry, while the Nigerian novelist **Chinua Achebe** has made complex use of Igbo orature. American Indian writers, such as **Leslie Marmon Silko**, frequently ground their fiction in folktales passed down orally through the generations, while Indian-born **Salman Rushdie** deliberately stylizes traditional oral storytelling in his novels. Surprisingly, perhaps, even the most modern, technologically driven cultures have been built on oral foundations.

GERMAN FOLKTALE: THE THREE SPINNERS

The folktales and fairy tales collected by the brothers Grimm—Jacob (1785–1863) and Wilhelm (1786–1859)—have become some of the most famous stories in the world: "Little Red Riding Hood," "Rapunzel," "Hansel and Gretel," "Rumpelstiltskin," "Snow White," "Cinderella," and "Sleeping Beauty." The Grimm versions can be surprising or even shocking today. They include scenes of sexual and physical violence that seem like strange material for children. But in fact these stories were originally entertainment for a whole village.

The Grimms were the editors of these stories rather than their authors. They were serious German scholars who came of age just as Napoleon's French armies invaded and imposed new laws and customs, threatening to wipe out generations of traditional German lore. Eager to preserve a national heritage, the brothers set about collecting the stories told by peasants. Ironically, however, they did not hear actual peasants tell the tales. Instead, most of their sources were educated women who had absorbed traditional stories from household servants and nursemaids in their childhoods. The Grimms then heavily edited the stories. They were keen to preserve a rustic feel, sometimes inserting old proverbs for effect. But they also added new material that explored the psychological motives of the characters. In this way, they joined traditional folk elements with rounded characters who appealed to a growing middle-class audience. This combination would prove enormously popular, influencing many other collectors of folktales around the world and making these tales classics well beyond Germany within a generation.

"The Three Spinners" is not one of the most famous Grimm fairy tales, but it reveals the ways that traditional folktales could appeal to poor peasants. It is primarily about the burden of physical work, which is so oppressive that it deforms the very body of the worker. The story shows how the different social classes have strikingly different relationships to work, and it is interesting to speculate what its happy ending would have meant to those facing a life of hard and unrelenting labor.

The Three Spinners[1]

There was once a girl who was idle and would not spin, and her mother, say what she would, could not bring her to it. At last the mother lost her temper and beat her, at which the girl began to weep loudly. Now at this very moment the Queen drove by, and when she heard the weeping she stopped her carriage, went into the house, and asked the mother why she was beating her daughter so that the cries could be heard out in the road?

The woman was ashamed to tell how lazy her daughter was, and said,—

"I cannot get her to leave off spinning. She insists on spinning for ever and ever, and I am poor, and cannot get the flax for her." Then the Queen answered,—

1. Translated by Jack Zipes.

"There is nothing I like better to hear than spinning, and I am never happier than when the wheels are humming. Let me have your daughter with me in the palace; I have flax enough, and there she shall spin as much as she likes."

The mother was well pleased with this, and the Queen took the girl with her. When they had arrived at the palace, the Queen led the girl up into three rooms which were filled from the bottom to the top with the finest flax.

"Now spin me this flax," said she, "and when you have done it, you shall have my eldest son for a husband, even if you are poor. I care not for that; you are a hard-working girl, and that is enough."

The girl was scared out of her wits, for she could not have spun the flax, no, not if she had lived till she was three hundred years old, and had sat at it every day from morning till night. So when she was alone, she began to weep, and sat thus for three days without moving a finger. On the third day the Queen came, and wondered when she saw nothing had been spun yet; but the girl said she had not been able to begin because she felt so badly at leaving her mother's house. The Queen was sorry for her, but said when she was going away,—

"To-morrow you must begin to work."

When the girl was alone again, she did not know what to do, and in her distress went to the window. There she saw three women coming toward her; the first had a broad flat foot, the second had such a great under lip that it hung down over her chin, and the third had a broad thumb. They stood before the window, and looked up, and asked the girl what was the matter with her? She told her trouble, and they said they would help her, but added,—

"If you will invite us to the wedding, not be ashamed of us, and will call us your aunts; and if you will place us at your table, we will spin the flax for you, and that in a very short time."

"With all my heart," she replied; "do but come in and begin the work at once." Then she let in the three strange women, and cleared a place in the first room, where they sat down and began their spinning. One drew the thread and trod the wheel, the second wetted the thread, the third twisted it, and struck the table with her finger; and as often as she struck it, a skein of thread, that was spun in the finest manner possible, fell to the ground. The girl hid the three spinners from the Queen, and showed her, whenever she came, the great heap of spun thread, until the Queen could not praise her enough. When the first room was empty she went to the second, and at last to the third, and that too was quickly cleared. Then the three women took leave, and said to the girl,—

"Do not forget what you have promised us,—it will make your fortune."

When the maiden showed the Queen the empty rooms, and the great heap of yarn, she gave orders for the wedding. Her son was glad that he was to have such a clever and hard-working wife, and praised her well.

"I have three aunts," said the girl, "and as they have been very kind to me, I should not like to forget them in my good fortune; let me ask them to the wedding, and let them sit with us at table." The Queen and the bridegroom said,—

"Why not?" So when the feast began, the three women entered in strange dress, and the bride said,—

"Welcome, dear aunts."

"Ah," said the bridegroom, "how do you come by these odious friends?" He went to the one with the broad flat foot, and said,—

"How do you come by such a broad foot?"

"By treading," she answered, "by treading." Then the bridegroom went to the second and said,—

"How do you come by your falling lip?"

"By licking," she answered, "by licking." Then he asked the third,—

"How do you come by your broad thumb?"

"By twisting the thread," she answered, "by twisting the thread." On this the King's son took fright and said,—

"Neither now nor ever shall my beautiful bride touch a spinning-wheel." And thus she got rid of the hateful flax-spinning.

ENGLISH FOLKTALE: TOM TIT TOT

An Australian-born Jew who settled in the United States, Joseph Jacobs (1854–1916) might seem a surprising person to have collected folklore for the sake of preserving a traditional English culture. He complained that the Grimms had had too much of an effect on England, wiping out local traditions, and he set about gathering authentically English stories and editing them for children so that they could grow up absorbing their national heritage, hearing each story "as a good old nurse" would have told it. He worried that the middle and upper classes had lost access to the lore that continued to thrive among working people, and argued, like the Grimms, for folktales as a key to national unity: it is "no unpatriotic task," he wrote, "to help to bridge over this gulf, by giving a common fund of nursery literature to all classes of the English people."

Jacobs took most of the stories from published sources. He then actively created his own versions of these tales, reducing the frequency of dialect speech but adding local words here and there for effect. Jacobs felt that "Tom Tit Tot," the first story in his volume, was "one of the best folktales that have ever been collected," better than any French or German version of the same story, including "Rumpelstiltskin" and "The Three Spinners." He praised it particularly for its humor and claimed that the tale reveals the staying power of the ancient superstition that to know someone's name gives you power over that person.

Tom Tit Tot

Once upon a time there was a woman, and she baked five pies. And when they came out of the oven, they were that overbaked the crusts were too hard to eat. So she says to her daughter:

"Darter," says she, "put you them there pies on the shelf, and leave 'em there a little, and they'll come again."—She meant, you know, the crust would get soft.

But the girl, she says to herself: "Well, if they'll come again, I'll eat 'em now." And she set to work and ate 'em all, first and last.

Well, come supper-time the woman said: "Go you, and get one o' them there pies. I dare say they've come again now."

The girl went and she looked, and there was nothing but the dishes. So back she came and says she: "Noo, they ain't come again."

"Not one of 'em?" says the mother.

"Not one of 'em," says she.

"Well, come again, or not come again," said the woman, "I'll have one for supper."

"But you can't, if they ain't come," said the girl.

"But I can," says she. "Go you, and bring the best of 'em."

"Best or worst," says the girl, "I've ate 'em all, and you can't have one till that's come again."

Well, the woman she was done, and she took her spinning to the door to spin, and as she span she sang:

"My darter ha' ate five, five pies to-day.
My darter ha' ate five, five pies to-day."

The king was coming down the street, and he heard her sing, but what she sang he couldn't hear, so he stopped and said:

"What was that you were singing, my good woman?"

The woman was ashamed to let him hear what her daughter had been doing, so she sang, instead of that:

"My darter ha' spun five, five skeins to-day.
My darter ha' spun five, five skeins to-day."

"Stars o' mine!" said the king, "I never heard tell of any one that could do that."

Then he said: "Look you here, I want a wife, and I'll marry your daughter. But look you here," says he, "eleven months out of the year she shall have all she likes to eat, and all the gowns she likes to get, and all the company she likes to keep; but the last month of the year she'll have to spin five skeins every day, and if she don't I shall kill her."

"All right," says the woman; for she thought what a grand marriage that was. And as for the five skeins, when the time came, there'd be plenty of ways of getting out of it, and likeliest, he'd have forgotten all about it.

Well, so they were married. And for eleven months the girl had all she liked to eat, and all the gowns she liked to get, and all the company she liked to keep.

But when the time was getting over, she began to think about the skeins and to wonder if he had 'em in mind. But not one word did he say about 'em, and she thought he'd wholly forgotten 'em.

However, the last day of the last month he takes her to a room she'd never set eyes on before. There was nothing in it but a spinning-wheel and a stool. And says he: "Now, my dear, here you'll be shut in to-morrow with some victuals and some flax, and if you haven't spun five skeins by the night, your head 'll go off."

And away he went about his business.

Well, she was that frightened, she'd always been such a gatless[1] girl, that she didn't so much as know how to spin, and what was she to do to-morrow with

1. Careless.

no one to come nigh her to help her? She sat down on a stool in the kitchen, and law! how she did cry!

However, all of a sudden she heard a sort of a knocking low down on the door. She upped and oped it, and what should she see but a small little black thing with a long tail. That looked up at her right curious, and that said:

"What are you a-crying for?"

"What's that to you?" says she.

"Never you mind," that said, "but tell me what you're a-crying for."

"That won't do me no good if I do," says she.

"You don't know that," that said, and twirled that's tail round.

"Well," says she, "that won't do no harm, if that don't do no good," and she upped and told about the pies, and the skeins, and everything.

"This is what I'll do," says the little black thing, "I'll come to your window every morning and take the flax and bring it spun at night."

"What's your pay?" says she.

That looked out of the corner of that's eyes, and that said: "I'll give you three guesses every night to guess my name, and if you haven't guessed it before the month's up you shall be mine."

Well, she thought she'd be sure to guess that's name before the month was up. "All right," says she, "I agree."

"All right," that says, and law! how that twirled that's tail.

Well, the next day, her husband took her into the room, and there was the flax and the day's food.

"Now there's the flax," says he, "and if that ain't spun up this night, off goes your head." And then he went out and locked the door.

He'd hardly gone, when there was a knocking against the window.

She upped and she oped it, and there sure enough was the little old thing sitting on the ledge.

"Where's the flax?" says he.

"Here it be," says she. And she gave it to him.

Well, come the evening a knocking came again to the window. She upped and she oped it, and there was the little old thing with five skeins of flax on his arm.

"Here it be," says he, and he gave it to her.

"Now, what's my name?" says he.

"What, is that Bill?" says she.

"Noo, that ain't," says he, and he twirled his tail.

"Is that Ned?" says she.

"Noo, that ain't," says he, and he twirled his tail.

"Well, is that Mark?" says she.

"Noo, that ain't," says he, and he twirled his tail harder, and away he flew.

Well, when her husband came in, there were the five skeins ready for him. "I see I shan't have to kill you to-night, my dear," says he; "you'll have your food and your flax in the morning," says he, and away he goes.

Well, every day the flax and the food were brought, and every day that there little black impet used to come mornings and evenings. And all the day the girl sate trying to think of names to say to it when it came at night. But she never hit on the right one. And as it got towards the end of the month, the impet began to look so maliceful, and that twirled that's tail faster and faster each time she gave a guess.

At last it came to the last day but one. The impet came at night along with the five skeins, and that said:

"What, ain't you got my name yet?"

"Is that Nicodemus?" says she.

"Noo, t'ain't," that says.

"Is that Sammle?" says she.

"Noo, t'ain't," that says.

"A-well, is that Methusalem?" says she.

"Noo, t'ain't that neither," that says.

Then that looks at her with that's eyes like a coal o' fire, and that says: "Woman, there's only to-morrow night, and then you'll be mine!" And away it flew.

Well, she felt that horrid. However, she heard the king coming along the passage. In he came, and when he sees the five skeins, he says, says he:

"Well, my dear," says he. "I don't see but what you'll have your skeins ready to-morrow night as well, and as I reckon I shan't have to kill you, I'll have supper in here to-night." So they brought supper, and another stool for him, and down the two sate.

Well, he hadn't eaten but a mouthful or so, when he stops and begins to laugh.

"What is it?" says she

"A-why," says he, "I was out a-hunting to-day, and I got away to a place in the wood I'd never seen before. And there was an old chalk pit. And I heard a kind of a sort of a humming. So I got off my hobby,[2] and I went right quiet to the pit, and I looked down. Well, what should there be but the funniest little black thing you ever set eyes on. And what was that doing, but that had a little spinning-wheel, and that was spinning wonderful fast, and twirling that's tail. And as that span that sang:

"Nimmy nimmy not
My name's Tom Tit Tot."

Well, when the girl heard this, she felt as if she could have jumped out of her skin for joy, but she didn't say a word.

Next day that there little thing looked so maliceful when he came for the flax. And when night came, she heard that knocking against the window panes. She oped the window, and that come right in on the ledge. That was grinning from ear to ear, and Oo! that's tail was twirling round so fast.

"What's my name?" that says, as that gave her the skeins.

"Is that Solomon?" she says, pretending to be afeard.

"Noo, t'ain't," that says, and that came further into the room.

"Well, is that Zebedee?" says she again.

"Noo, 'tain't," says the impet. And then that laughed and twirled that's tail till you couldn't hardly see it.

"Take time, woman," that says; "next guess, and you're mine." And that stretched out that's black hands at her.

2. Small horse.

Well, she backed a step or two, and she looked at it, and then she laughed out, and says she, pointing her finger at it:

"Nimmy nimmy *not*
Your name's Tom Tit Tot."

Well, when that heard her, that gave an awful shriek and away that flew into the dark, and she never saw it anymore.

IRISH FOLKTALES: A DONEGAL FAIRY *AND* THE BREWERY OF EGG-SHELLS

"Poetry in Ireland," wrote the great poet **William Butler Yeats**, "has always been mysteriously connected with magic." Frustrated by the schooling of Irish children by the British government, who saw fairy tales and local superstitions as primitive and backward, Yeats collected and published *Fairy and Folk Tales of Ireland* in 1889, aiming to celebrate the poetic value of Irish orature as the most inspiring source of art in a rapidly modernizing age: for Yeats it had a "simplicity sought for so much in these days by all the poets, and not to be had at any price."

Yeats drew his stories from previous collections. "The Brewery of Egg-Shells" came from a compilation put together by Thomas Crofton Croker (1798–1854), who had traveled around Ireland transcribing local stories and describing customs. His book *The Fairy Legends and Traditions of the South of Ireland* (1825) was popular throughout the nineteenth century. Letitia Maclintock, who transcribed "A Donegal Fairy," was a novelist in her own right. Little is known about her, but Yeats praised her for capturing the distinctive dialect speech of Northern Ireland. Her story appears without a narrator to frame it, as though being told directly by "old Matt Craig," the man she claimed was her source.

A Donegal Fairy

Ay, it's a bad thing to displeasure the gentry,[1] sure enough—they can be unfriendly if they're angered, an' they can be the very best o' gude neighbours if they're treated kindly.

My mother's sister was her lone in the house one day, wi' a big pot o' water boiling on the fire, and ane o' the wee folk fell down the chimney, and slipped wi' his leg in the hot water.

1. Respectful term for fairies in order not to offend them.

He let a terrible squeal out o' him, an' in a minute the house was full o' wee crathurs[2] pulling him out o' the pot, an' carrying him across the floor.

"Did she scald you?" my aunt heard them saying to him.

"Na, na, it was mysel' scalded my ainsel'," [3] quoth the wee fellow.

"A weel, a weel," says they. "If it was your ainsel scalded yoursel', we'll say nothing, but if she had scalded you, we'd ha' made her pay."

The Brewery of Egg-Shells

Mrs. Sullivan fancied that her youngest child had been exchanged by "fairies theft,"[1] and certainly appearances warranted such a conclusion; for in one night her healthy, blue-eyed boy had become shrivelled up into almost nothing, and never ceased squalling and crying. This naturally made poor Mrs. Sullivan very unhappy; and all the neighbours, by way of comforting her, said that her own child was, beyond any kind of doubt, with the good people,[2] and that one of themselves was put in his place.

Mrs. Sullivan of course could not disbelieve what every one told her, but she did not wish to hurt the thing; for although its face was so withered, and its body wasted away to a mere skeleton, it had still a strong resemblance to her own boy. She, therefore, could not find it in her heart to roast it alive on the griddle, or to burn its nose off with the red-hot tongs, or to throw it out in the snow on the road-side, notwithstanding these, and several like proceedings, were strongly recommended to her for the recovery of her child.

One day who should Mrs. Sullivan meet but a cunning woman, well known about the country by the name of Ellen Leah (or Grey Ellen). She had the gift, however she got it, of telling where the dead were, and what was good for the rest of their souls; and could charm away warts and wens, and do a great many wonderful things of the same nature.

"You're in grief this morning, Mrs. Sullivan," were the first words of Ellen Leah to her.

"You may say that, Ellen," said Mrs. Sullivan, "and good cause I have to be in grief, for there was my own fine child whipped off from me out of his cradle, without as much as 'by your leave' or 'ask your pardon,' and an ugly dony[3] bit of a shrivelled-up fairy put in his place; no wonder, then, that you see me in grief, Ellen."

"Small blame to you, Mrs. Sullivan," said Ellen Leah, "but are you sure 'tis a fairy?"

"Sure!" echoed Mrs. Sullivan, "sure enough I am to my sorrow, and can I doubt my own two eyes? Every mother's soul must feel for me!"

"Will you take an old woman's advice?" said Ellen Leah, fixing her wild and mysterious gaze upon the unhappy mother; and, after a pause, she added, "but maybe you'll call it foolish?"

2. Creatures.
3. My own self.

1. Fairies were said to steal human infants and replace them with supernatural creatures.
2. Fairies.
3. A fairy trick intended to fool humans.

"Can you get me back my child, my own child, Ellen?" said Mrs. Sullivan with great energy.

"If you do as I bid you," returned Ellen Leah, "you'll know." Mrs. Sullivan was silent in expectation, and Ellen continued, "Put down the big pot, full of water, on the fire, and make it boil like mad; then get a dozen new-laid eggs, break them, and keep the shells, but throw away the rest; when that is done, put the shells in the pot of boiling water, and you will soon know whether it is your own boy or a fairy. If you find that it is a fairy in the cradle, take the red-hot poker and cram it down his ugly throat, and you will not have much trouble with him after that I promise you."

Home went Mrs. Sullivan, and did as Ellen Leah desired. She put the pot on the fire, and plenty of turf[4] under it, and set the water boiling at such a rate, that if ever water was red-hot, it surely was.

The child was lying, for a wonder, quite easy and quiet in the cradle, every now and then cocking his eye, that would twinkle as keen as a star in a frosty night, over at the great fire, and the big pot upon it; and he looked on with great attention at Mrs. Sullivan breaking the eggs and putting down the egg-shells to boil. At last he asked, with the voice of a very old man, "What are you doing, mammy?"

Mrs. Sullivan's heart, as she said herself, was up in her mouth ready to choke her, at hearing the child speak. But she contrived to put the poker in the fire, and to answer, without making any wonder at the words, "I'm brewing, *a vick*" (my son).

"And what are you brewing, mammy?" said the little imp, whose supernatural gift of speech now proved beyond question that he was a fairy substitute.

"I wish the poker was red," thought Mrs. Sullivan; but it was a large one, and took a long time heating; so she determined to keep him in talk until the poker was in a proper state to thrust down his throat, and therefore repeated the question.

"Is it what I'm brewing, *a vick*," said she, "you want to know?"

"Yes, mammy: what are you brewing?" returned the fairy.

"Egg-shells, *a vick*," said Mrs. Sullivan.

"Oh!" shrieked the imp, starting up in the cradle, and clapping his hands together, "I'm fifteen hundred years in the world, and I never saw a brewery of egg-shells before!" The poker was by this time quite red, and Mrs. Sullivan, seizing it, ran furiously towards the cradle; but somehow or other her foot slipped, and she fell flat on the floor, and the poker flew out of her hand to the other end of the house. However, she got up without much loss of time and went to the cradle, intending to pitch the wicked thing that was in it into the pot of boiling water, when there she saw her own child in a sweet sleep, one of his soft round arms rested upon the pillow—his features were as placid as if their repose had never been disturbed, save the rosy mouth, which moved with a gentle and regular breathing.

4. Peat, a low-burning fuel cut from bogs in Ireland.

TWO ANANSI STORIES: GHANA, JAMAICA

Tricky, mischievous, mostly clever but sometimes very foolish, the spider Anansi manages to outsmart most other animals and sometimes even the gods. He is a trickster—a character who compensates for his physical weakness by using his cunning to play tricks on powerful characters. He can be a shape-shifter, and sometimes takes the form of a human, or a human-spider hybrid. Spiders spin webs that connect spaces: they are therefore border-crossers, and belong to no one place. They also hide in corners, and disappear easily. Anansi usually breaks taboos and upsets expectations. And he is almost always selfish, aiming to survive in hard conditions, stealing food and money or bamboozling other creatures into working to get food for him. Anansi's maneuvers do not always succeed: sometimes they backfire and he is temporarily set back, but he is nothing if not resilient, and he simply returns to his old tricks again in the next story.

For the Ashanti people of West Africa, where he originates, Anansi is almost always the underdog, though he sometimes takes on qualities of the gods. Ashanti village elders typically tell Anansi stories after dark, with an audience sitting in a circle to listen. Sometimes in the middle of a telling, an actor will enter the circle and start impersonating one of the characters, to the great amusement of those watching. The stories typically reinforce a shared sense of moral norms and appropriate behavior precisely by having Anansi break taboos in a humorous way. One characteristic of the African versions of the Anansi stories is that they often explain how the world has come to be the way it is. In Ghana, stories of all kinds are called *Anansesem*, and the first tale included here explains why all stories belong to Anansi.

The first English-language transcriber of the Anansi stories was R. S. Rattray, an anthropologist for the British government, which had established a colony called the Gold Coast (now Ghana). The more the British knew, they thought, the more successfully they would be able to assert and maintain power over the Ashanti. The collection of oral traditions was thus considered "of incalculable importance from an administrative point of view." The version included here comes out of a later collaboration between American anthropologist Harold Courlander and a student from Ghana, Albert Kofi Prempeh.

Trickster figures are found in many cultures, but what is most remarkable about the Anansi stories is their global reach. They can be found not only in West Africa but also in the Bahamas, Jamaica, Haiti, Trinidad, Barbados, Curaçao, Grenada, Costa Rica, Belize, Colombia, Nicaragua, Suriname, and the United States. The stories vary, and the character's name changes from place to place—Ananse, Annancy, Nansi, Aunt Nancy, Bre Nancy, Anansi Tori, and Ti Malice—but this oral tradition has remained remarkably resilient despite its transmission through centuries and across oceans.

The geographical scope of the Anansi tradition has everything to do with the slave trade. Enforced illiteracy meant that slaves who were taken from West Africa to the New World had severely restricted educations, but it also meant that they kept alive oral traditions that might have faded under different conditions. Oppressed by a system that was based on a hypocritical morality, and surrounded by an abundance that was denied to them, slaves might well find Anansi appealing: his egocentrism, his willingness to use cunning to survive, his undermining of authority, and his resistance to moral constraints all suggested ways of coping with cruel and hypocritical slaveholders.

As Anansi traveled to the Caribbean, Latin America, and the United States, he tended to lose the divine qualities which he sometimes had in West Africa. In the American versions, he also faces harsher realities; moreover, he is more inclined to trick characters who are weaker than he is, and more frequently his tricks go wrong and he loses. Sometimes his arrogance or his greed brings about a downfall. He also adapts to new social conditions, sometimes getting involved in gambling and bootlegging. The stories are frequently entangled with tales and characters from other traditions, including European and American Indian orature.

Walter Jekyll, a British folklorist, collected the Jamaican version of the Anansi story included here, published in 1906. The "men and boys" who told the stories he collected were his own paid workers. (The British government had abolished slavery in Jamaica in 1834.) Around the same time that he was transcribing these stories, Jekyll met and encouraged a young Jamaican poet, Claude McKay, urging him to write in his native dialect. With money and advice, Jekyll helped McKay to move to the United States, where he became a leading writer in New York's Harlem Renaissance. With Anansi, then, we see how far-flung oral traditions can cross the world, meet, enrich, and transform one another, all without the need of writing.

All Stories Are Anansi's[1]

In the beginning, all tales and stories belonged to Nyame, the Sky God. But Kwaku Anansi, the spider, yearned to be the owner of all the stories known in the world, and he went to Nyame and offered to buy them.

The Sky God said: "I am willing to sell the stories, but the price is high. Many people have come to me offering to buy, but the price was too high for them. Rich and powerful families have not been able to pay. Do you think you can do it?"

Anansi replied to the Sky God: "I can do it. What is the price?"

"My price is three things," the Sky God said. "I must first have Mmoboro, the hornets. I must then have Onini, the great python. I must then have Osebo, the leopard. For these things I will sell you the right to tell all stories."

Anansi said: "I will bring them."

He went home and made his plans. He first cut a gourd from a vine and made a small hole in it. He took a large calabash and filled it with water. He went to the tree where the hornets lived. He poured some of the water over himself, so that he was dripping. He threw some water over the hornets, so that they too were dripping. Then he put the calabash on his head, as though to protect himself from a storm, and called out to the hornets: "Are you foolish people? Why do you stay in the rain that is falling?"

1. Translated by Harold Courlander and Albert Kofi Prempeh.

The hornets answered: "Where shall we go?"

"Go here, in this dry gourd," Anansi told them.

The hornets thanked him and flew into the gourd through the small hole. When the last of them had entered, Anansi plugged the hole with a ball of grass, saying: "Oh, yes, but you are really foolish people!"

He took his gourd full of hornets to Nyame, the Sky God. The Sky God accepted them. He said: "There are two more things."

Anansi returned to the forest and cut a long bamboo pole and some strong vines. Then he walked toward the house of Onini, the python, talking to himself. He said: "My wife is stupid. I say he is longer and stronger. My wife says he is shorter and weaker. I give him more respect. She gives him less respect. Is she right or am I right? I am right, he is longer. I am right, he is stronger."

When Onini, the python, heard Anansi talking to himself, he said: "Why are you arguing this way with yourself?"

The spider replied: "Ah, I have had a dispute with my wife. She says you are shorter and weaker than this bamboo pole. I say you are longer and stronger."

Onini said: "It's useless and silly to argue when you can find out the truth. Bring the pole and we will measure."

So Anansi laid the pole on the ground, and the python came and stretched himself out beside it.

"You seem a little short," Anansi said.

The python stretched further.

"A little more," Anansi said.

"I can stretch no more," Onini said.

"When you stretch at one end, you get shorter at the other end," Anansi said. "Let me tie you at the front so you don't slip."

He tied Onini's head to the pole. Then he went to the other end and tied the tail to the pole. He wrapped the vine all around Onini, until the python couldn't move.

"Onini," Anansi said, "it turns out that my wife was right and I was wrong. You are shorter than the pole and weaker. My opinion wasn't as good as my wife's. But you were even more foolish than I, and you are now my prisoner."

Anansi carried the python to Nyame, the Sky God, who said: "There is one thing more."

Osebo, the leopard, was next. Anansi went into the forest and dug a deep pit where the leopard was accustomed to walk. He covered it with small branches and leaves and put dust on it, so that it was impossible to tell where the pit was. Anansi went away and hid. When Osebo came prowling in the black of night, he stepped into the trap Anansi had prepared and fell to the bottom. Anansi heard the sound of the leopard falling, and he said: "Ah, Osebo, you are half-foolish!"

When morning came, Anansi went to the pit and saw the leopard there.

"Osebo," he asked, "what are you doing in this hole?"

"I have fallen into a trap," Osebo said. "Help me out."

"I would gladly help you," Anansi said. "But I'm sure that if I bring you out, I will have no thanks for it. You will get hungry, and later on you will be wanting to eat me and my children."

"I swear it won't happen!" Osebo said.

"Very well. Since you swear it, I will take you out," Anansi said.

He bent a tall green tree toward the ground, so that its top was over the pit, and he tied it that way. Then he tied a rope to the top of the tree and dropped the other end of it into the pit.

"Tie this to your tail," he said.

Osebo tied the rope to his tail.

"Is it well tied?" Anansi asked.

"Yes, it is well tied," the leopard said.

"In that case," Anansi said, "you are not merely half-foolish, you are all-foolish."

And he took his knife and cut the other rope, the one that held the tree bowed to the ground. The tree straightened up with a snap, pulling Osebo out of the hole. He hung in the air head downward, twisting and turning. And while he hung this way, Anansi killed him with his weapons.

Then he took the body of the leopard and carried it to Nyame, the Sky God, saying: "Here is the third thing. Now I have paid the price."

Nyame said to him: "Kwaku Anansi, great warriors and chiefs have tried, but they have been unable to do it. You have done it. Therefore, I will give you the stories. From this day onward, all stories belong to you. Whenever a man tells a story, he must acknowledge that it is Anansi's tale."

In this way Anansi, the spider, became the owner of all stories that are told. To Anansi all these tales belong.

Annancy, Monkey and Tiger

One day Annancy an' Tiger get in a rum-shop, drink an' drink, an' then Monkey commence to boast. Monkey was a great boaster.

Annancy say:—"You boast well; I wonder if you have sense as how you boast."

Monkey say:—"Get 'way you foolish fellah you, can come an' ask me if me have sense. You go t'rough de whole world you never see a man again have the sense I have."

Annancy say:—"Bro'er Monkey, how many sense you have, tell me?"

Monkey say:—"I have dem so till I can't count dem to you, for dem dé[1] all over me body."

Annancy say:—"Me no have much, only two, one fe[2] me an' one fe me friend."

One day Monkey was travelling an' was going to pass where Tiger live. Annancy was working on that same road.

As Monkey passing, Tiger was into a stone-hole an' jump out on the fellah an' catch him. All his sense was gone, no sense to let him get 'way. Tiger was so glad, have him before him well ready to kill.

1. There.

2. For.

Here come the clever man Mr. Annancy.

When he saw his friend Monkey in the hand of such a wicked man he was frighten, but he is going to use his sense.

He said:—"Marnin', Bro'er Tiger, I see you catch dat fellah; I was so glad to see you hold him so close in hand. You must eat him now. But before you eat him take you two hand an' cover you face an' kneel down with you face up to Massa God an' say, 'T'ank God fe what I goin' to receive.'"

An' so Tiger do.

An' by the time Tiger open his eyes Monkey an' Annancy was gone.

When they get to a distant Annancy said to Monkey:—"T'ink you say you have sense all over you 'kin, why you no been get 'way when Bro'er Tiger catch you?"

Monkey don't have nothing to say.

Annancy say:—"Me no tell you say me have two sense, one fe me an' one fe me friend? Well! a him me use to-day."

From that day Tiger hate Annancy up to now.

Jack Mantora me no choose any.[3]

3. Jamaican storytellers typically end Annancy stories with these words, indicating that the moral is not intended for any particular listener.

US SLAVE STORY: ALL GOD'S CHILLEN HAD WINGS

Geographically and culturally isolated from the mainland, the islands off the coast of Georgia and South Carolina are home to a group of African Americans called "Gullah," who retained African stories, rituals, intonations, common words, and even grammatical constructions well into the twentieth century. Many of their linguistic practices can be traced to Bantu, a family of languages found across central and southern Africa. In the early part of the twentieth century, Caesar Grant, a Gullah worker on John's Island off the coast of South Carolina, told a story of slaves making plans in a language not understood by their masters and escaping from a cruel slave driver by intoning an African word that allows them to fly away. Like "**The Three Spinners**" and "**Tom Tit Tot**," it offered the fantasy of an escape from a life of painful labor. A white novelist named John Bennett wrote Grant's story down, though he felt free to translate many of the teller's Gullah phrases into standard English. Bennett published the story in 1943, concerned that the grim and ghostly Gullah stories common in Charleston would vanish with the older generations who had lived under slavery.

Across the American South there were many versions of this legend of slaves who could fly. The great African American poet Langston Hughes (1902–1967) claimed that this story was important because it showed that there was more to slave folklore than humorous trickster tales. Later, the US novelist **Toni Morrison** (b. 1931) shaped her novel *Song of Solomon* around this oral tradition. The image of flying slaves, she has said, "is everywhere—people used to talk about it, it's in the spirituals and gospels. Perhaps it was wishful thinking: escape, death, and all that. But suppose it wasn't. What might that mean?"

All God's Chillen Had Wings[1]

Once all Africans could fly like birds; but owing to their many transgressions, their wings were taken away. There remained, here and there, in the sea islands and out-of-the-way places in the low country, some who had been overlooked, and had retained the power of flight, though they looked like other men.

There was a cruel master on one of the sea islands who worked his people till they died. When they died he bought others to take their places. These also he killed with overwork in the burning summer sun, through the middle hours of the day, although this was against the law.

One day, when all the worn-out Negroes were dead of overwork, he bought, of a broker in the town, a company of native Africans just brought into the country, and put them at once to work in the cottonfield.

He drove them hard. They went to work at sunrise and did not stop until dark. They were driven with unsparing harshness all day long, men, women and children. There was no pause for rest during the unendurable heat of the midsummer noon, though trees were plenty and near. But through the hardest hours, when fair plantations gave their Negroes rest, this man's driver pushed the work along without a moment's stop for breath, until all grew weak with heat and thirst.

There was among them one young woman who had lately borne a child. It was her first; she had not fully recovered from bearing, and should not have been sent to the field until her strength had come back. She had her child with her, as the other women had, astraddle on her hip, or piggyback.

The baby cried. She spoke to quiet it. The driver could not understand her words. She took her breast with her hand and threw it over her shoulder that the child might suck and be content. Then she went back to chopping knot-grass; but being very weak, and sick with the great heat, she stumbled, slipped and fell.

The driver struck her with his lash until she rose and staggered on.

She spoke to an old man near her, the oldest man of them all, tall and strong, with a forked beard. He replied; but the driver could not understand what they said; their talk was strange to him.

She returned to work; but in a little while she fell again. Again the driver lashed her until she got to her feet. Again she spoke to the old man. But he said: "Not yet, daughter; not yet." So she went on working, though she was very ill.

1. Translated by John Bennett.

Soon she stumbled and fell again. But when the driver came running with his lash to drive her on with her work, she turned to the old man and asked: "Is it time yet, daddy?" He answered: "Yes, daughter; the time has come. Go; and peace be with you!". . . and stretched out his arms toward her . . . so.

With that she leaped straight up into the air and was gone like a bird, flying over field and wood.

The driver and overseer ran after her as far as the edge of the field; but she was gone, high over their heads, over the fence, and over the top of the woods, gone, with her baby astraddle of her hip, sucking at her breast.

Then the driver hurried the rest to make up for her loss; and the sun was very hot indeed. So hot that soon a man fell down. The overseer himself lashed him to his feet. As he got up from where he had fallen the old man called to him in an unknown tongue. My grandfather told me the words that he said; but it was a long time ago, and I have forgotten them. But when he had spoken, the man turned and laughed at the overseer, and leaped up into the air, and was gone, like a gull, flying over field and wood.

Soon another man fell. The driver lashed him. He turned to the old man. The old man cried out to him, and stretched out his arms as he had done for the other two; and he, like them, leaped up, and was gone through the air, flying like a bird over field and wood.

Then the overseer cried to the driver, and the master cried to them both: "Beat the old devil! He is the doer!"

The overseer and the driver ran at the old man with lashes ready; and the master ran too, with a picket pulled from the fence, to beat the life out of the old man who had made those Negroes fly.

But the old man laughed in their faces, and said something loudly to all the Negroes in the field, the new Negroes and the old Negroes.

And as he spoke to them they all remembered what they had forgotten, and recalled the power which once had been theirs. Then all the Negroes, old and new, stood up together; the old man raised his hands; and they all leaped up into the air with a great shout; and in a moment were gone, flying, like a flock of crows, over the field, over the fence, and over the top of the wood; and behind them flew the old man.

The men went clapping their hands; and the women went singing; and those who had children gave them their breasts; and the children laughed and sucked as their mothers flew, and were not afraid.

The master, the overseer, and the driver looked after them as they flew, beyond the wood, beyond the river, miles on miles, until they passed beyond the last rim of the world and disappeared in the sky like a handful of leaves. They were never seen again.

Where they went I do not know; I never was told. Nor what it was that the old man said . . . that I have forgotten. But as he went over the last fence he made a sign in the master's face, and cried "Kuli-ba! Kuli-ba!" I don't know what that means.

But if I could only find the old wood sawyer, he could tell you more; for he was there at the time, and saw the Africans fly away with their women and children. He is an old, old man, over ninety years of age, and remembers a great many strange things.

US SLAVE SPIRITUALS AND SECULAR SONGS

In 1801 a Methodist preacher named Richard Allen (1760–1831), who had been born into slavery, published the first hymnal intended specifically for African American congregations. He collected and wrote songs of religious faith in the face of persecution which would come to be known as *spirituals*. Sung not only in churches but also during times of work and leisure, African American spirituals played many roles: often they were outlets for fervent belief and strong emotion, but they might also help to synchronize work rhythms, and they could even be used to pass on coded information about secret meetings or plans to escape. Typically these songs have a double meaning: on the one hand, they express a desire to flee an oppressive earthly world into the arms of a loving Christian God who understands suffering; on the other hand, they suggest dreams of escape from slavery in this world, using the underground railroad system of safe houses, for example, to reach Canada. Some incorporated specific instructions, such as constellations of stars that would lead the way for slaves on the run. "Steal Away to Jesus" is famous for having functioned as a signal for escaped slaves.

Combining European Protestant church music with African musical rhythms and patterns of call-and-response, slave songs created a new hybrid tradition. This music laid the groundwork for jazz and the blues, and has influenced rock, reggae, and hip-hop artists. In the twentieth century, musicians in apartheid South Africa adopted some of the styles and patterns of American jazz, completing a global circuit in which oral traditions that had moved west with the slave trade returned to Africa in a new form. Certainly music around the world as we know it today would not have been the same without the songs of American slaves.

No More Auction Block

No more auction block for me,
No more, no more,
No more auction block for me,
Many thousand gone.

No more peck of corn for me,
No more, no more,
No more peck of corn for me,
Many thousand gone.

No more pint of salt for me,
No more, no more,
No more pint of salt for me,
Many thousand gone.

No more driver's lash for me,
No more, no more,
No more driver's lash for me,
Many thousand gone.

Swing Low, Sweet Chariot

Swing low, sweet chariot,
Coming for to carry me home,
Swing low, sweet chariot,
Coming for to carry me home.

I looked over Jordan[1] and what did I see
Coming for to carry me home,
A band of angels, coming after me,
Coming for to carry me home.

If you get there before I do,
Coming for to carry me home,
Tell all my friends I'm coming too,
Coming for to carry me home.

Swing low, sweet chariot,
Coming for to carry me home,
Swing low, sweet chariot,
Coming for to carry me home.

Steal Away to Jesus

Steal away, steal away, steal away to Jesus,
Steal away, steal away home,
I ain't got long to stay here.

My Lord, He calls me,
He calls me by the thunder,
The trumpet sounds within-a my soul,
I ain't got long to stay here.

Steal away, steal away, steal away to Jesus,
Steal away, steal away home,
I ain't got long to stay here.

Green trees a-bending,
Po' sinner stands a-trembling,
The trumpet sounds within-a my soul,
I ain't got long to stay here.

1. A river that appears in the Bible; for slaves, crossing Jordan symbolized going to heaven and escaping from slavery.

Steal away, steal away, steal away to Jesus,
Steal away, steal away home,
I ain't got long to stay here.

Promises of Freedom

My ole Mistiss promise me,
W'en she died, she'd set me free.
She lived so long dat 'er head got bal',
An' she give out'n de notion a dyin' at all.

My ole Mistiss say to me:
"Sambo, I'se gwine ter set you free."
But w'en dat head git slick an' bal',
De Lawd couldn' a' killed 'er wid a big green maul.

My ole Mistiss never die,
Wid 'er nose all hooked an' skin all dry.
But my ole Miss, she's somehow gone,
An' she lef' "Uncle Sambo" a-hillin' up co'n.

Ole Mosser lakwise promise me,
W'en he died, he'd set me free.
But ole Mosser go an' make his Will
Fer to leave me a-plowin' ole Beck still.

Yes, my ole Mosser promise me;
But "his papers" didn't leave me free.
A dose of pizen he'ped 'im along.
May de Devil preach 'is funer'l song.

MALAGASY WISDOM POETRY

While many songs and stories that flourished in the nineteenth century focused on the realities of backbreaking labor, scarce resources, and the desire for freedom, not all oral traditions offered such grim fare. On the island of Madagascar, off the east coast of Africa, oral poetry conveyed traditional knowledge and explored the delights and torments of love. *Ohabolana*, the Malagasy word for wise proverbs, expresses cultural values and guides for living. There are *ohabolana* for a huge range of different emotions and circumstances. Widely respected as ancient and authoritative, these are typically brief and rhythmic, which means that they can be easily remembered and transmitted. *Hainteny*, or Malagasy wisdom poetry, deals mostly with love, including initial attraction, the joy of union, jealousy, feelings of abandonment, and bitter blame. Despite the patriarchal social structure, Malagasy women are comparatively free, and love poetry can be spoken by a man or a woman. Some are dialogues, spoken by two sparring parties as in a contest. Much of the complexity of *hainteny* does not translate: poems about thunder may include words that sound thunderous, for example, and double meanings are common in the original. But the selection included here gives a sense of the wit, profundity, and compact poetic structure characteristic of the Malagasy oral tradition.

Both *ohabolana* and *hainteny* are traditions that belonged originally to the Merina people, a group who arrived on Madagascar from the Malay-Indonesian archipelago in the fifteenth century. Despite many waves of migration from East Africa, Indonesia, and India, this large island shares the Malagasy language and many Malagasy cultural institutions and traditions. The culture remained predominantly oral until 1850. Much of the traditional poetry and prose has been recorded, but some is irretrievably lost, in part thanks to Protestant missionaries in the nineteenth century who excised and distorted a great deal as they transcribed. "I have . . . thought it necessary to cut out anything that might be considered 'dirty,'" wrote a Norwegian missionary in 1877, "which has thus reduced the collection very considerably." (Since Malagasy people accept sex before marriage, their own cultural expectations and those of Christian missionaries often came into conflict.) The selections included here were transcribed by the French writer Jean Paulhan (1884–1968), who worked as a teacher in Madagascar between 1908 and 1910. His translations of Malagasy oral poetry inspired the surrealist French poets Guillaume Apollinaire (1880–1918) and Paul Éluard (1895–1952).

Ohabolana[1]

Life is like the aroma of a cooking-pot:
when it is uncovered, it escapes [i.e., departs].

God is not the property of one person alone.

Death is not a condemnation,
but part of a tax.

I hate the passage of time,
for it causes beauty to pass.

Man falls no lower than his knees.

Sometimes she is like spilled coral
and sometimes like a startled swarm of beetles.

1. Both stories translated by Leonard Fox.

Justice is like a fire:
if it is covered, it burns [you].

Justice resembles a dream:
it cannot be acquired except in bed;
and it is like a straight tree:
it cannot be found except in the forest.

Hainteny

I love you.
- And how do you love me?
- I love you as I love money.
- Then you do not love me,
for if you are hungry, you will exchange me for food.
- I love you as I love the door.
- Then you do not love me:
it is surely loved, but it is pushed continually.
- I love you as I love the *lambamena*.[1]
- Then you do not love me,
for we will be united only in death.
- I love you as I love the *voatavo*:[2]
fresh, I eat you;
dry, I make you into a cup;
broken, I fashion you into a *valiha*[3] bridge:
I will play there along the edge of the road.

How, then, do you love me?
- I love you as I love rice.
- Then you do not love me,
for you will make a meal of me when you are hungry.
How, then, do you love me?
- I love you as I love water.
- Then you do not love me,
for you will make your love follow your sweat.
How, then, do you love me?
- I love you as I love my *lamba*.[4]
- Then you do not love me,
for if you are in debt, you will exchange me
and no longer remember me.
How, then, do you love me?
- I love you as I love honey.
- Then you do not love me,
for there are still dregs that you remove.
How, then, do you love me?
- I love you as I love the ruling prince.

1. Shroud.
2. Gourd or pumpkin.
3. A zither made of bamboo.
4. Traditional shawl.

- Then you truly love me.
- His passage inspires awe,
his glance causes me shame.
- You truly love me, then;
my desires are fulfilled,
my searching is complete.
- I love you as I love my father and mother:
alive in the same house,
dead in the same wood.

I am a friendless child
who plays alone with the dust,
a chick that has fallen into a ditch:
if it calls out, its voice is small;
if it flies, its wings are weak;
if it waits, it fears the savage cat.
Do not make our love a love of stones:
broken, they cannot be joined.
But make it a love of lips:
although angry, they approach each other.

What does blame resemble?
It resembles the wind:
I have heard its name, but I have not seen its face.
But what does blame resemble?
It is not heaped up like the clouds;
it does not lie on its back like the hills;
it is not the passing man, to whom is said, "Enter the house;"
it is not the visitor, to whom is said, "Return;"
it is not the seated man, to whom is said, "May I pass?"
But it resembles the slippery path:
he who is not careful falls.
A rock at the side of the road:
he who does not see it trips.
A deep abyss:
he who looks at it becomes dizzy
and it kills him when he falls.
Like the freezing cold:
unseen, it numbs.
May it be removed!
Removed in the morning, may it have no meal!
Removed in the evening, may it have no bed!
Removed in the summer, may the floods take it!
Removed in the winter, may it be burned with the grass!
Above, let it not press down;
below, let it not be revived;
on two sides, let it not crush;
in front, let it not be able to stop;
behind, let it not be able to pursue!

HAWAIIAN FOLKTALE: THE DESPOTIC CHIEFS OF KAU

By the early nineteenth century, foreign traders and missionaries had begun to disrupt the traditions that had organized the social life of the Hawaiian islands for over a thousand years. Descended mostly from Polynesian settlers, Hawaiians had long been ruled by a number of independent royal chiefs who governed separate regions, presiding over an intricate system of sacred laws. But merchants, missionaries, whale traders, and sugar growers from overseas brought new technologies and new social and cultural values with them, reorganizing the Hawaiian economy and eroding traditional laws and structures of authority. In 1810 Western powers helped a single Hawaiian chief to take advantage of a crumbling social system to establish leadership over all of the islands. King Kamehemaha I ruled over a new constitutional monarchy. The United States annexed Hawaii in 1898; it remained a territory until 1959, when it became the fiftieth state.

Born in Honolulu in 1895, Mary Wiggen Pukui was descended from New England settlers on her father's side and Hawaiian high chiefs and priestesses on her mother's. She was raised by her grandmother, a sacred high priestess, and charged with the responsibility of studying Hawaiian genealogies, language, and customs. As she matured, she worried that, given the huge upheavals in Hawaii, ancient oral traditions would be forgotten unless she recorded them, and she spent a lifetime editing and translating books, including the first Hawaiian dictionary. As a young woman, she advised an American anthropologist, Martha Warren Beckwith, who was interested in the similarities between Hawaiian folklore and legends told by the Maori people in New Zealand. Pukui told Warren traditional stories, including "The Despotic Chiefs of Kau." Here an oral tradition transmits political theory, exploring weak and wrong forms of government. This trio of brief stories makes it clear that chiefs must fear and respect the people they govern and cannot impose a merely arbitrary rule. In the 1970s, Pukui became a hero for Hawaiians who were beginning to reclaim local history, language, music, and stories in what is often called the "Hawaiian Renaissance."

The Despotic Chiefs of Kau[1]

That district lying between Ko-na and Pu-na, namely, Ka-u,[2] was called in old days a land of oppression because of three despotic chiefs who lived there. These are the tales told about them.

1. Translated by Mary Kawne Pukui and Laura C.S. Green.
2. Southern region of the island of Hawai'i, containing many volcanoes.

1. *Halaea*

A greedy chief was Ha-la-e-a. Every day he visited the fleet of fishing canoes and took all the fish he could find for himself and his retainers. Then he would hold a feast, carousing and often wantonly wasting the food that remained. As for the fishermen, they were obliged to catch the fish without ever having any to take home to their families. Day after day they ate herbs for food.

This conduct of the chief greatly vexed the common people and they sought means to rid themselves of Ha-la-e-a's oppression. Never did they go out upon the ocean without hearing on their return the voice of their chief crying, "The fish is mine! give me the fish!"

At last came the season of the *ahi*[3] fish, and proclamation was made summoning the head fishermen to accompany their chief to the fishing-grounds. So they gathered together and prepared their canoes, looking after the nets, the bait, and whatever else was required for the expedition. Also they held a council at which it was agreed to deposit all their fish in the chief's canoe and themselves return to the shore without even a backward glance. At the day appointed everything was in readiness from Wai-ahu-kini to Ke-au-hou.

When the first canoe-load was conveyed to the chief's canoe even then could the voice of the chief be heard protesting, "Bring me the fish! bring me the fish!" But when the second, third, fourth, fifth, and the succeeding canoes had deposited their loads into the chief's canoe and he saw there was danger of swamping the canoe with their weight he called out, "The chief has fish enough!"—"Not so!" cried the men. "Here is all the fish that the chief desires!" They piled in the last load and the canoe began to sink rapidly. The chief looked about for help, but there was no canoe at hand and no man to show compassion; all had gone back to land.

So perished Ha-la-e-a in the sea surrounded by the objects of his greed.

2. *Koihala*

An irresolute chief was Ko-i-ha-la. When the chief was visiting in Ko-na, he despatched a messenger to Ka-u with the order for food to be prepared and taken to Wai-ahu-kini, there to meet him. When all was in readiness, the servants bore it to Wai-ahu-kini. As they sat awaiting his appearance, they saw the chief's canoe heading for Kai-li-kii, so they took up the food again and went on to the place where they expected him to land. Not so! when they got to Kai-li-kii he was heading for Ka-pu-a.

Again the men shouldered the food and followed toward the mountain, but as they reached Ka-pu-a they perceived the chief heading for Ka-alu-alu and they immediately proceeded thither.

By this time they were hungry and tired and they therefore agreed to watch and, if the chief did not arrive shortly, to eat the food themselves. The chief delayed landing, simply sitting idly in the canoe and gazing at the men. So the servants ate the food that had been prepared and then they filled with stones the *ti*-leaf[4] packets in which the fish had been wrapped and the empty

3. A kind of tuna.
4. A plant with glossy leaves that are used to wrap meat and fish for cooking.

calabashes of vegetable food. The chief, seeing these things, paddled furiously until he reached Ka-alu-alu. Hence has arisen the proverb, *"Kau ino auwaa o Kaalualu,"* that is, "The canoes arrive hurriedly at Ka-alu-alu." Hastening up the beach to the spot where the men sat he cried, "Say! let us eat! let the chief eat!"—"Yes, indeed!" answered the servants. "Here is vegetable food and fish!" Whereupon they stoned the despotic chief to death.

3. *Kohaikalani*

An evil man was the chief, causing heavy burdens to be laid upon his people whenever opportunity offered. When he built a temple for himself on the hill Ka-u-la-ka-lani, he commanded the men of the place to bring large smooth pebbles from Ka-wa many miles distant. Patiently they bore the heavy loads slung on a pole over their shoulders from the sea-shore to the hill where the foundation of the temple was to be laid. When much stone had been collected, two priests (*kahuna*) arrived to superintend the erection of the structure and upon seeing the quantity of stone brought from Ka-wa they turned to the men and exclaimed, "Look you! there was stone enough already without your exerting yourselves to bring more from Ka-wa! It is clear that your chief intends when this temple is completed to offer your bodies as sacrifice. Hence when he commands you to bring hither an *ohia* tree to be used in the building you must tell him to select one for himself and that you will then help him pull it up here. In this way you may save your lives."[5]

The people heeded the priests' warning and when they were commanded to descend the cliff after a tree they replied, "O heavenly one! listen! It is better for you to choose the tree to your liking and uproot it, and we will haul it up hither." The chief consented. He was so strong that with one pull he uprooted a great tree. He lopped the branches and then proposed to ascend the cliff and pull the tree up from the top while the men pushed from below. This however they refused to do,—they would pull while the chief pushed from below; and to this the chief acquiesced. The men pulled at the tree until half the distance up the cliff was covered, then they released the rope. The great tree rolled over on top of the chief and death came to the oppressor.

Since the rule of these despotic chiefs, Ka-u has become noted as a land where everyone looks out for himself and his own family. The rulers fear to say "We are great chiefs" lest a reckoning come from the people. In old days Ka-u was a despotic district—one chief would command and be instantly obeyed, one would give orders which were at once fulfilled. Thus did they live. But these days of civilization have overturned all those customs.

5. When a new temple was built, chiefs would use their enemies as sacrifices. "*Ohia*": tall hardwood trees often used for building temples.

NAVAJO CEREMONY: THE NIGHT CHANT

Navajo ceremonialism ranks among the glories of native American achievement. Directed primarily toward restoring a harmony between individuals and the environment, the ceremonies called Nightway, Mountainway, Beautyway, Enemyway, and Blessingway—to name only a few of the best known—create a spiritual universe of song, prayer, drama, and graphic art. These are healing ceremonies that have proven their therapeutic power and earned the respect of Western medicine. In fact, they cross the boundaries of art, religion, and science. Their shared quest for *beauty*—a broad term that includes perfection, normality, success, and well-being—reflects a central value of Navajo culture, located mostly in the southwestern United States, in Arizona and New Mexico.

With its induction of new initiates, its unique all-night sing, and its lofty portrayal of deities, the famous Nightway chant occupies a place of honor among these "ways." Its nineteenth-century translator, Washington Matthews, a US army surgeon posted to New Mexico, called it by the name "Night Chant." Although a large audience of relatives, friends, and visitors usually attend the Nightway ceremony, a single person is its focus. Each of the Navajo ceremonials is said to be effective against a particular group of illnesses, and the Night Chant heals strokes and other disorders of the brain. It remains in huge demand every year. But the value of the ceremony also goes beyond the task of healing one person: the host who sponsors it gains prestige, and it provides opportunities for broader cultural reaffirmation, socializing, and spiritual renewal.

Performed in only fall or winter, the Night Chant falls into two four-day parts, followed by a climactic ninth-night reprise, the night of nights, in which the ceremonial leader, or chanter, summons the long-awaited spirit of thunder. At this point the ceremony breaks free in a torrent of song that continues unabated until dawn. In the first part the emphasis is on rites that exorcise evil influences and invoke the distant gods. The second part is distinguished by spacious and intricate sand paintings made of dry pigments sprinkled on the earth. The paintings depict the gods and allow the sick to take on some divine invulnerability. Through it all, the ceremonial leader directs the song recitals and intones the prescribed prayers. The two selections included here are the prayer to thunder that begins the final night and the last of the Finishing Songs that bring it to a close.

From The Night Chant[1]

Prayer to Thunder[2]

* * *

In Tsegíhi,[3]
In the house made of the dawn,

1. Translated by Washington Matthews.
2. In performance each line is first recited by the chanter, then repeated by the patient.
3. Pronounced *tsay-gee'-hee*, a distant canyon and site of the *house made of the dawn* (line 2), a prehistoric ruin, regarded as the home of deities.

In the house made of the evening twilight,
In the house made of the dark cloud,
In the house made of the he-rain,
In the house made of the dark mist,
In the house made of the she-rain,[4]
In the house made of pollen,[5]
In the house made of grasshoppers,
Where the dark mist curtains the doorway,
The path to which is on the rainbow,
Where the zigzag lightning stands high on top,
Where the he-rain stands high on top,
Oh, male divinity![6]
With your moccasins of dark cloud, come to us.
With your leggings of dark cloud, come to us.
With your shirt of dark cloud, come to us.
With your headdress of dark cloud, come to us.
With your mind enveloped in dark cloud, come to us.
With the dark thunder above you, come to us soaring.
With the shapen cloud at your feet, come to us soaring.
With the far darkness made of the dark cloud
over your head, come to us soaring.
With the far darkness made of the he-rain
over your head, come to us soaring.
With the far darkness made of the dark mist
over your head, come to us soaring.
With the far darkness made of the she-rain
over your head, come to us soaring.
With the zigzag lightning flung out on high
over your head, come to us soaring.
With the rainbow hanging high over your head,
come to us soaring.
With the far darkness made of the dark cloud on
the ends of your wings, come to us soaring.
With the far darkness made of the he-rain on
the ends of your wings, come to us soaring.
With the far darkness made of the dark mist
on the ends of your wings, come to us soaring.
With the far darkness made of the she-rain
on the ends of your wings, come to us soaring.
With the zigzag lightning flung out on high
on the ends of your wings, come to us soaring.
With the rainbow hanging high on the ends of
your wings, come to us soaring.
With the near darkness made of the dark cloud, of
the he-rain, of the dark mist, and of the
she-rain, come to us.
With the darkness on the earth, come to us.

4. Rain without thunder. "He-rain": rain with thunder.
5. Emblem of peace, of happiness, of prosperity [translator's note].
6. Thunder, regarded as a bird.

With these I wish the foam floating on the flowing
water over the roots of the great corn.
I have made your sacrifice.
I have prepared a smoke[7] for you.
My feet restore for me.
My limbs restore for me.
My body restore for me.
My mind restore for me.
My voice restore for me.
Today, take out your spell for me.
Today, take away your spell for me.
Away from me you have taken it.
Far off from me it is taken.
Far off you have done it.
Happily I recover.
Happily my interior becomes cool.
Happily my eyes regain their power.
Happily my head becomes cool.
Happily my limbs regain their power.
Happily I hear again.
Happily for me *the spell*[8] is taken off.
Happily may I walk.
Impervious to pain, may I walk.
Feeling light within, may I walk.
With lively feelings, may I walk.
Happily abundant dark clouds I desire.
Happily abundant dark mists I desire.
Happily abundant passing showers I desire.
Happily an abundance of vegetation I desire.
Happily an abundance of pollen I desire.
Happily abundant dew I desire.
Happily may fair white corn, to the ends of the
earth, come with you.
Happily may fair yellow corn, to the ends of the
earth, come with you.
Happily may fair blue corn, to the ends of the
earth, come with you.
Happily may fair corn of all kinds, to the ends
of the earth, come with you.
Happily may fair plants of all kinds, to the ends
of the earth, come with you.
Happily may fair goods of all kinds, to the ends
of the earth, come with you.
Happily may fair jewels of all kinds, to the ends
of the earth, come with you.
With these before you, happily may they come with you.
With these behind you, happily may they come with you.
With these below you, happily may they come with you.

7. Painted reed filled with native tobacco, offered as a sacrifice.

8. Words added by the translator.

With these above you, happily may they come with you.
With these all around you, happily may they come with you.
Thus happily you accomplish your tasks.
Happily the old men will regard you.
Happily the old women will regard you.
Happily the young men will regard you.
Happily the young women will regard you.
Happily the boys will regard you.
Happily the girls will regard you.
Happily the children will regard you.
Happily the chiefs will regard you.
Happily, as they scatter in different directions,
  they will regard you.
Happily, as they approach their homes, they will
  regard you.
Happily may their roads home be on the trail of pollen.
Happily may they all get back.
In beauty I walk.
With beauty before me, I walk.
With beauty behind me, I walk.
With beauty below me, I walk.
With beauty above me, I walk.
With beauty all around me, I walk.
It is finished in beauty,
It is finished in beauty,
It is finished in beauty,
It is finished in beauty.

Finishing Song

From the pond in the white valley—
  The young man doubts it—
  He takes up his sacrifice,
  With that he now heals.
With that your kindred thank you now.

From the pools in the green meadow[9]—
  The young woman doubts it—
  He takes up his sacrifice,[1]
  With that he now heals.
With that your kindred thank you now.

9. A contrast of landscapes, of the beginning and end of a stream. It rises in a green valley in the mountains and flows down to the lower plains, where it spreads into a single sheet of water. As the dry season approaches, it shrinks, leaving a white saline efflorescence called alkali. The male is associated with the sterile, unattractive alkali flat in the first stanza, while the female is named with the pleasant mountain meadow in the second stanza [adapted from translator's note].

1. The deity accepts the sacrificial offering (see p. 919, n. 7) and effects the healing that benefits the patient and his kindred—though young men and young women, with the irreverence of youth, may doubt the truth of the ceremony.

Selected Bibliographies

I. An Age of Revolutions in Europe and the Americas

The excellent, classic resource for the industrial and political revolutions of the period is E. J. Hobsbawm, *The Age of Revolution, 1789–1848* (1962). Another fine introduction to the upheavals of the period is Charles Breunig, *Age of Revolution and Reaction, 1789–1850* (1977). For the global implications of the industrial revolution, see E. J. Hobsbawm, *Industry and Empire* (1990) and Peter N. Stearns, *The Industrial Revolution in World History* (3rd ed. 2007). Gavin Weightman tells absorbing stories about particular inventors, entrepreneurs, and industrial breakthroughs in *The Industrial Revolutionaries* (2010). Good scholarly works on the French Revolution include William Doyle, *The Oxford History of the French Revolution* (2003) and Simon Schama, *Citizens* (1990). Alan Schom's *Napoleon Bonaparte: A Life* (1998) is a lively biography; see also J. Christopher Herold, *The Age of Napoleon* (2002). *Latin American Independence: An Anthology of Sources*, ed. John Chasteen and Sarah C. Chambers (2010), contains fascinating source materials; for a historical overview, see Michael Eakin, *The History of Latin America* (2007). A detailed account of the upheavals of 1848 can be found in Mike Rapport, *1848: Year of Revolution* (2009).

Anna Laetitia Barbauld
William McCarthy has written a long and exceptionally detailed scholarly biography: *Anna Letitia Barbauld: Voice of the Enlightenment* (2008). For a scholarly introduction to Barbauld's life and work, see Anne Janowitz, *Women Romantic Poets: Anna Barbauld and Mary Robinson* (2004). Janowitz also offers a specific account of Barbauld's entry into polemical debates in "Amiable and Radical Sociability: Anna Barbauld's 'Free Familiar Conversation,'" in *Romantic Sociability: Social Networks and Literary Culture in Britain, 1770–1840*, ed. Gillian Russell and Clara Tuite (2002), 62–81.

Charles Baudelaire
There have been many English translations of Baudelaire's poetry, including those by the well-known poets included here. The most comprehensive collection is Walter Martin's *Charles Baudelaire: Complete Poems* (2002), which includes juvenilia and poems that have been ascribed to Baudelaire; Keith Waldrop's prose translation of *Flowers of Evil*, with French and English on facing pages, is widely respected (2006). Baudelaire's essays on painting and the other arts, including his studies of Delacroix, Poe, and Wagner, have been considered the beginning of modern criticism: see *The Painter of Modern Life and Other Essays*, trans. Jonathan Mayne (1964). The definitive biography is Claude Pichois and Jean Ziegler, *Charles Baudelaire*, trans. G. Robb (1991). The most famous essays on Baudelaire as a modern writer are Walter Benjamin's *Charles Baudelaire*, trans. Harry Zohn (1973). For useful introductions, see Lois Boe Hyslop, *Charles Baudelaire Revisited* (1992); Laurence Porter, ed., *Approaches to Teaching Baudelaire's* Flowers of Evil (2000); and Rosemary Lloyd, *Baudelaire's World* (2002). Strong readings of individual works include Barbara Johnson's classic deconstructive approach, "Poetry and Its Double: Two *Invitations au voyage*," in *The Critical Difference* (1980), 23–51; Jonathan Culler's introduction to *Charles Baudelaire: The Flowers of Evil* (1993); and the collection

of readings in William J. Thompson, ed., *Understanding* Les Fleurs du Mal (1997). For more on the city, see Ross Chambers, "Baudelaire's Paris," in *The Cambridge Companion to Baudelaire*, ed. Rosemary Lloyd (2005), 101–16.

Andrés Bello
The best work on Andrés Bello is Julio Ramos, *Divergent Modernities*, trans. John D. Blance (1999). See also Iván Jaksić's thoughtful introduction to *The Selected Writings of Andrés Bello*, trans. Frances M. López-Morillas (1997); and Iván Jaksić, *Andrés Bello: Scholarship and Nation-Building in Nineteenth-Century Latin America* (2001). For an excellent reading of this poem as a response to Virgil, see *Bello and Bolívar: Poetry and Politics in the Spanish American Revolution* (1992).

William Blake
The standard edition of the works is David V. Erdman's *The Complete Poetry and Prose of William Blake* (rev. 1988). Peter Ackroyd's marvelously well-written biography *William Blake: A Life* (1996) is to be recommended, as is the more scholarly, detailed life by G. E. Bentley Jr., *The Stranger from Paradise* (2003). Martin K. Nurmi's *William Blake* (1976) is a helpful introduction to the man and his work. For excellent critical and contextual readings, see *The Cambridge Companion to William Blake*, ed. Morris Eaves (2003), which suggests a range of approaches to reading and teaching Blake, including serious attention to Blake's images and processes of image-making. Also helpful are Jacob Brunowski, *William Blake and the Age of Revolution* (1965); W. J. T. Mitchell, *Blake's Composite Art: A Study of the Illuminated Poetry* (1978); and Saree Makdisi, *William Blake and the Impossible History of the 1790s* (2003).

Rosalía de Castro
There is an excellent collection of Rosalía de Castro's poetry in English, with a helpful introduction, by Michael Smith, called *Selected Poems* (2007); see also *Poems*, eds. Anna-Marie Aldaz, Barbara N. Gantt, and Anne C. Bromley (1991). Kathleen Kulp-Hill has also written a good introduction to the poet's life and work: *Rosalía de Castro* (1977).

Samuel Taylor Coleridge
Princeton University Press has published a fine multivolume *Complete Works of Coleridge*, ed. J. C. C. Mays and Joyce Crick (1971–2001). For a life of Coleridge, see Richard Holmes's prize-winning two-volume biography, *Coleridge: Early Visions, 1772–1804* (1989) and *Coleridge: Darker Reflections, 1804–1834* (1998). Kelvin Everest provides an excellent reading of "Frost at Midnight" in *Coleridge's Secret Ministry* (1979), 258–70. For a reading of this poem as a response to the French Revolution, see Paul Magnuson, "The Politics of 'Frost at Midnight,'" *The Wordsworth Circle* 22 (1991): 3–11. An analysis of global contexts for the two other poems appears in Tim Fulford's essay "Slavery and Superstition in the Supernatural Poems," in *The Cambridge Companion to Coleridge* (2002), 45–58. See also John Drew, "'Kubla Khan' and Orientalism," in *Coleridge's Visionary Languages*, ed. Tim Fulford and Morton D. Paley (1993), 41–49; and Patrick J. Keane, *Coleridge's Submerged Politics* (1994).

Rubén Darío
Rubén Darío's work has been translated into English more than once, but the best version remains Lysander Kemp's *Selected Poems* (1965). Also from 1965 is Charles Watland's *Poet-Errant: A Biography of Rubén Darío*, the only book-length biography in English. It is carefully documented and reliable. Keith Ellis offers five different ways of reading Darío—biographical, socio-political, literary historical, formal, and structural—in *Critical Approaches to Rubén Darío* (1974), and Octavio Paz discusses Darío's work in the title essay of *The Siren and the Seashell* (1970). Cathy Login Jrade in *Rubén Darío and the Romantic Search for Unity* (1983) and Dolores Ackel Fiore in *Rubén Darío in Search of Inspiration* (1963) explore influences on Darío from ancient to contemporary times. A brief review essay by the influential scholar Roberto González Echevarría, called "Master of Modernismo," does a beautiful job of capturing Darío's importance to Spanish American literary history (*The Nation*, January 25, 2006).

Emily Dickinson
R. W. Franklin's three-volume edition of Emily Dickinson's work is carefully comprehensive and preserves as much as possible her spelling and punctuation: *The Poems of Emily Dickinson: The Variorum Edition* (1998). Franklin has also put together a more accessible, one-volume version: *The Poems of Emily Dickinson: Reading Edition* (2005) and a facsimile edition, which allows readers to see her

handwritten pages (1981). The classic biography is the award-winning *Life of Emily Dickinson* by Richard B. Sewall (1974). Alfred Habegger has added fresh material and perspectives in *My Wars Are Laid Away in Books: The Life of Emily Dickinson* (2001). The poet Adrienne Rich has a wonderful essay on Dickinson's sense of her own genius in *Critical Essays on Emily Dickinson*, ed. Paul J. Ferlazzo (1984), 175–95. For critical readings, see Sharon Cameron, *Lyric Time: Dickinson and the Limits of Genre* (1979); J. Dobson, *Dickinson and the Strategies of Reticence* (1989); E. Phillips, *Emily Dickinson: Personae and Performance* (1996); Elizabeth A. Petrino, *Emily Dickinson and Her Contemporaries: Women's Verse in America, 1820–85* (1998); and Virginia Jackson, *Dickinson's Misery: A Theory of Lyric Reading* (2005). For Dickinson in context, see *The Emily Dickinson Handbook*, ed. Gudrun Grabher, Roland Hagenbüchle, and Cristanne Miller (1998); Paula Bernat Bennett, "Emily Dickinson and her American Women Poet Peers," in *The Cambridge Companion to Emily Dickinson* (2002), 215–35; and *A Historical Guide to Emily Dickinson*, ed. Vivian R. Pollak (2004).

Frederick Douglass

Douglass himself wrote three autobiographies: not only the *Narrative*, but also *My Bondage and My Freedom* (1855) and *The Life and Times of Frederick Douglass, Written by Himself* (1892). For a more recent scholarly account, see William S. McFeely's *Frederick Douglass* (1991). Excellent critical and historical studies include *The Cambridge Companion to Frederick Douglass*, ed. Maurice S. Lee (2009); William L. Andrews, *To Tell a Free Story* (1986); Houston A. Baker, *Blues, Ideology, and Afro-American Literature* (1991); Audrey A. Fisch, *American Slaves in Victorian England* (2000); Dwight A. McBride, *Impossible Witnesses: Truth, Abolitionism, and Slave Testimony* (2001); and John Stauffer, *Giants: The Parallel Lives of Frederick Douglass and Abraham Lincoln* (2008). On the question of gender in the narrative, see Deborah E. McDowell, "In the First Place: Making Frederick Douglass and the Afro-American Narrative Tradition," in *Critical Essays on Frederick Douglass*, ed. William L. Andrews (1991), 192–211.

Olaudah Equiano

Henry Louis Gates Jr.'s famous analysis of the "trope of the talking book" is found in his book *The Signifying Monkey: A Theory of Afro-American Literary Criticism* (1988), 127–69. Angelo Costanzo's *Surprizing Narrative: Olaudah Equiano and the Beginnings of Black Autobiography* (1987) has been influential. For a consideration of Equiano's career as a public figure, see John Bugg, "The Other Interesting Narrative: Olaudah Equiano's Public Book Tour," *PMLA: Publications of the Modern Language Association of America* 121:5 (October 2006): 1424–42. Vincent Carretta's biography, *Equiano the African: Biography of a Self-Made Man* (2005) makes the highly controversial case that Equiano was born not in Africa but in South Carolina; there is a lively debate between Carretta and Paul Lovejoy in the pages of the journal *Slavery and Abolition*, vol. 27 (December 2006): 317–47, and vol. 28 (April 2007): 115–19 and 121–25.

Johann Wolfgang von Goethe

Nicholas Boyle's two-volume biography, *Goethe: The Poet and the Age* (1991), is the most recent and one of the most extensive, informative biographies of Goethe and his work. More compact is John R. Williams's *The Life of Goethe: A Critical Biography* (1998), which is divided by genre and thus allows for a good, concise overview of Goethe's dramatic work. A classic study of *Faust* in English is Stuart Atkins's *Goethe's* Faust: *A Literary Analysis* (1964), a close textual analysis of the play in the tradition of the New Critics. John R. Williams's *Goethe's* Faust (1987) is more varied in its method and includes a useful discussion of the different sources, versions, and revisions that led to the final text. Most attuned to literary form is Benjamin Bennett's *Goethe's Theory of Poetry* (1986), which discusses Goethe's use and interruption of the traditional tragic plot as well as other stylistic devices. Focusing on Goethe's theater practice is Marvin Carlson's *Goethe and the Weimar Theatre* (1978). Goethe's *Faust* has also attracted the attention of philosophers and cultural critics. An early example was the Marxist critic Georg Lukács, whose *Goethe and His Age* (1940, 1969) places Goethe within the history of political and social upheaval. This line of interpretation was later taken up by Marshall Berman, whose powerful *All That Is Sold Melts into Air* (1982) reads *Faust* alongside Marx and Engels's *Communist Manifesto*, written some fifteen years after Goethe's death, as an expression of modernist upheaval and productivity.

John Keats

Andrew Motion's *Keats* (1999) is a fine biography. William Walsh's *Introduction to Keats* (1981) is a critical biography with strong readings of the poetry. Jack Stillinger's edition of Keats's *Complete Poems* (1978) remains the standard. For a brilliant and sustained reading of the odes, see Helen Vendler, *The Odes of John Keats* (1983); see also Geoffrey Hartman's *The Fate of Reading* (1975), 57–73. William Keach writes about the reception of Keats as a political member of the Cockney School in "Cockney Couplets: Keats and the Politics of Style," *Studies in Romanticism* 25 (summer 1986): 182–96; see also Jeffrey Cox, *Poetry and Politics in the Cockney School* (1998).

Giacomo Leopardi

Ottavio Casale has put together a wonderful collection of selections from Leopardi's poetry and prose, including his diary, woven together to make a critical biography: *A Leopardi Reader* (1981). The only full-length English biography of Leopardi dates from 1935 (revised in 1953): Iris Origo's *Leopardi: A Study in Solitude*. For insightful readings of the poetry, see J. H. Whitfield, *Giacomo Leopardi* (1954) and Daniela Bini, *A Fragrance from the Desert* (1983).

Stéphane Mallarmé

The fullest English edition of Mallarmé's work can be found in *Stéphane Mallarmé: Collected Poems*, trans. Henry Weinfield (1995). Rosemary Lloyd has written a strong biography, *Mallarmé: The Poet and His Circle* (1999). Roger Pearson's briefer *Stéphane Mallarmé* (2010) weaves together biography with readings of the work and thought. Malcolm Bowie's *Mallarmé and the Art of Being Difficult* (1978; repr. 2008) offers a wonderful starting point for tackling Mallarmé's poetry, inviting us to ask not "What does this poem mean?" but rather "How can this poem be read fully and with enjoyment?" Harold Bloom's *Stéphane Mallarmé: Modern Critical Views* (1987) brings together some of the finest, and also most sophisticated and difficult, readings of Mallarmé, including Jacques Derrida's famous philosophical reading of Mallarmé, which can also be found in *Dissemination*, trans. Barbara Johnson (1981).

Herman Melville

Andrew Delbanco's *Melville: His World and Work* (2005) is a well-written and comprehensive biography. Leo Marx's suggestive essay, "Parable of the Walls," is collected in *Herman Melville's* Billy Budd, *"Benito Cereno," Bartleby the Scrivener, and Other Tales*, ed. Harold Bloom (1987). For a wonderful reading of Bartleby as a response to Thoreau, see Michael Paul Rogin, *Subversive Genealogy: The Politics and Art of Herman Melville* (1983). Barbara Foley links the story to the worker uprisings of the 1840s in "From Wall Street to Astor Place: Historicizing Melville's 'Bartleby,'" *American Literature* (March 2000), 87–116. Other excellent essays on the texts are collected in *Melville's Short Novels: Authoritative Texts, Contexts, Criticism*, ed. Dan McCall (2002).

Arthur Rimbaud

Graham Robb's *Rimbaud* (2000) recounts Rimbaud's tempestuous life in vivid and persuasive terms. Frederic St. Aubyn's *Arthur Rimbaud* (1988) weaves together a brief biography with readings of the poems. Other useful introductions include Cecil Arthur Hackett, *Rimbaud, a Critical Introduction* (1981) and Harold Bloom, ed., *Arthur Rimbaud* (1988). For a focus on the self in Rimbaud, see James Lawler, *Rimbaud's Theatre of the Self* (1992) and Susan Harrow, *The Material, the Real, and the Fractured Self* (2004). David Evans thinks in intriguing ways about the use of rhythm in Baudelaire, Mallarmé, and Rimbaud in *Rhythm, Illusion, and the Poetic Idea* (2004).

Romantic Poets and Their Successors

Hugh Honour's *Romanticism* (1974) offers an extremely useful brief introduction to the arts in their intellectual and political context. Michael Ferber, *A Companion to European Romanticism* (2005) provides a rich set of introductory essays to Romantic movements across genres and nations, but of course it is limited to Europe. *From Romanticism to Modernismo in Latin America* (1997), a collection of essays edited by David Foster Williams and Daniel Altamiranda, adds to the global story of the movement, though a number of the articles are in Spanish. Classic studies of British Romanticism are by M. H. Abrams, *The Mirror and the Lamp* (1971) and *Natural Supernaturalism* (1973); see also Robin Jarvis, *The Romantic Period: The Intellectual and Cultural Context of English Literature* (2004). *The Literature of German Romanticism* (2004), by Dennis F. Mahoney, provides a detailed account. An introduction to American Romanticism geared to students is Jennifer Hurley, ed., *Literary Movements and Genres: American Romanticism* (1999). For the relationship between Romantic artists and those of the avant-garde, see Renato Poggioli, *The Theory of the Avant-Garde* (1968).

Christina Rossetti
The most comprehensive edition is *The Complete Poems of Christina Rossetti*, ed. R. W. Crump (1979–1990). Jan Marsh's biography is excellent and detailed: *Christina Rossetti: A Writer's Life* (1994). Fine book-length studies include Antony Harrison, *Christina Rossetti in Context* (1988); Diane D'Amico, *Christina Rossetti: Faith, Gender, and Time* (1999); and Constance W. Hassett, *Christina Rossetti: The Patience of Style* (2006). There are rich close readings of individual Rossetti poems in Isobel Armstrong, *Victorian Poetry: Poetry, Poetics, and Politics* (1993).

Jean-Jacques Rousseau
Leo Damrosch has written an excellent, lively biography, *Jean-Jacques Rousseau: Restless Genius* (2005). For a study of Rousseau's impact, see Thomas McFarland, *Romanticism and the Heritage of Rousseau* (1995). An appealing and readable account of the relationship between Hume and Rousseau, including a meditation on the ideas of both, can be found in David Edmonds and John Eidinow, *Rousseau's Dog: Two Great Thinkers at War in the Age of Enlightenment* (2006). For classic readings of *The Confessions*, see Jean Starobinski, *Jean-Jacques Rousseau: Transparency and Obstruction*, trans. Arthur Goldhammer (1988); Huntington Williams, *Rousseau and Romantic Autobiography* (1983); and Christopher Kelly, *Rousseau's Exemplary Life: The Confessions as Political Philosophy* (1987). One of the most important works of contemporary French philosophy is Jacques Derrida's reading of *The Confessions* in *Of Grammatology*, trans. Gayatri Chakravorty Spivak (1976). James Olney reads Rousseau as part of the history of autobiography in *Memory and Narrative: The Weave of Life-Writing* (1999). For a look at gender in Rousseau, see Linda Zerilli, *Signifying Women: Culture and Chaos in Rousseau, Burke, and Mill* (1994), and Lynda Lange, ed., *Feminist Interpretations of Jean-Jacques Rousseau* (2002). The distinguished historian Robert Darnton writes about Rousseau's reception in "Readers Respond to Rousseau" in *Jean-Jacques Rousseau: Politics, Art, and Autobiography*, ed. John T. Scott (2006), 303–40.

Alfred, Lord Tennyson
Christopher Ricks has edited *The Poems of Tennyson* (1987). Leonee Ormond's *Alfred Tennyson: A Literary Life* (1993) is a fine biography. For excellent contextual and critical readings, see Alan Sinfield, *Alfred Tennyson* (1986), Herbert F. Tucker, *Tennyson and the Doom of Romanticism* (1988), and Isobel Armstrong, *Victorian Poetry: Poetry, Poetics, and Politics* (1993).

William Wordsworth
The best editions of Wordsworth's poetry are the volumes in "The Cornell Wordsworth" series, ed. Stephen Parrish (1974–2008). A good serious biography of the poet is Stephen Gill's *William Wordsworth: A Life* (1989); for a stunningly sensitive and intelligent reading of Wordsworth's poetry with his politics, see David Bromwich's *Disowned by Memory: Wordsworth's Poetry of the 1790s* (1998). Other fine studies include Geoffrey Hartman's *Wordsworth's Poetry* (1964), Alan Liu's *Wordsworth: A Sense of History* (1989), and Theresa M. Kelley's *Wordsworth's Revisionary Aesthetics* (1988). For a study of Wordsworth's ecological consciousness, see Jonathan Bate, *Romantic Ecology* (1991) and *The Song of the Earth* (2000); for a general look at audiences of Wordsworth's historical moment, see Richard Altick's classic study, *The English Common Reader* (1957), and William St. Clair, *The Reading Nation in the Romantic Period* (2004).

II. At the Crossroads of Empire

Oscar Chapuis has written a two-part historical account of Vietnam in English: *A History of Vietnam: From Hong Bang to Tu Duc* (1995) and *The Last Emperors of Vietnam: From Tu Duc to Bao Dai* (2000). D. R. SarDesai's *India: The Definitive History* (2007) is a well-written overview. *The Cambridge Illustrated History of China* (2010) by Patricia Buckley Ebrey offers a useful and clear introduction. For a look at European imperial power in East Asia in the period, see H. L. Wesseling, *The European Colonial Empires: 1815–1919* (2004) and Andrew Porter, *The Oxford History of the British Empire: The Nineteenth Century* (1999). For a fascinating study of the role of British and U.S. culture in China, see James L. Hevia, *English Lessons: The Pedagogy of Imperialism in Nineteenth-Century China* (2003).

Elizabeth Barrett Browning

The Complete Works of Elizabeth Barrett Browning, ed. Sandra Donaldson et al. (2010), is the only scholarly edition of her works. The standard biography is Margaret Foster's *Elizabeth Barrett Browning* (1989). The story of the Brownings' romance has been retold many times in fiction and film. A particularly appealing version is Virginia Woolf's novel *Flush*, which relates the Brownings' courtship from the perspective of her dog. Helpful critical and contextual commentary can be found in Simon Avery and Rebecca Stott, *Elizabeth Barrett Browning* (2003). For a close reading of "The Cry of the Children," see Caroline Levine, "Strategic Formalism: Toward a New Method in Cultural Studies," in *Victorian Studies* (2006).

Anna Bunina

Wendy Rosslyn's *Anna Bunina (1774–1829) and the Origins of Women's Poetry in Russia* (1997) is a fine critical biography that includes a rich context for thinking about nineteenth century Russian writers and audiences. Catriona Kelly's *A History of Russian Women's Writing, 1820–1992* (1998) gives a broad history of women's writing in Russia and includes a brief discussion of Bunina.

Ghalib

Ghalib's poetry and prose have been translated and discussed widely in English. New poetic translations, with a comprehensive introduction and notes, are found in Vinay Dharwadker, *Ghalib: Ghazals* (2011); Aijaz Ahmad, *Ghazals of Ghalib* (1971) includes translations by American poets, with commentary on individual poems. For historical context, biographical interpretation, and analysis of the Urdu and Persian writings, see Ralph Russell and Khurshidul Islam, *Ghalib: Life and Letters* (1994); and Ralph Russell, *Ghalib: The Poet and His Age* (1997). Daud Rahbar, *Urdu Letters of Mirza Asadu'llah Khan Ghalib* (1987) is a large translated selection; Pavan K. Verma, *Ghalib: The Man, the Times* (1988) is an informative popular biography. Agha Shahid Ali's *Ravishing Disunities: Real Ghazals in English* (2000) collects recent experiments in the form by a large number of British, American, South Asian, and diasporic poets.

Heinrich Heine

Heine has been translated into English many times. The most comprehensive edition is Hal Draper's *The Complete Poems of Heinrich Heine* (1982). The best English-language biography is Jeffrey L. Sammons's *Heinrich Heine* (1979). Hanna Spencer provides a useful introduction to the work in *Heinrich Heine* (1982). For a series of contextualizing essays by leading Heine scholars, see Roger F. Cook, *A Companion to the Works of Heinrich Heine* (2002).

Liu E

Harold Shadick's 1952 translation remains the standard: *The Travels of Lao Ts'an* (1952). Shadick provides some helpful introductory material, though he also adopts a strongly pro-Western stance. C. T. Hsia has an excellent brief essay on the novel called "Liu E's *The Travels of Lao Can*," in *Masterworks of Asian Literature in Comparative Perspective*, ed. Barbara Stoler Miller (1994). For an intriguing reading of *The Travels of Lao Can* as a "court case novel," see David Der-Wei Wang, *Fin-de-siècle Splendor: Repressed Modernities of Late Qing Fiction, 1849–1911* (1997).

José Martí

Esther Allen's *José Martí: Selected Writings* (2002) features Martí's fine prose as well as his poetry and includes a valuable essay about the poet's life, work, and reception, by renowned Latin American scholar Roberto González Echevarría. *José Martí: Major Poems*, trans. Elinor Randall, ed. Philip S. Foner (1982), provides good translations and a helpful biographical and critical introduction.

Adam Mickiewicz

David J. Welsh's *Adam Mickiewicz* (1966), R. R. Koropeckyj's *Adam Mickiewicz: The Life of a Romantic* (2008), and R. R. Koropeckyj's

"Adam Mickiewicz as a Polish National Icon" in *History of the Literary Cultures of East-Central Europe*, ed. Marcel Cornis-Pope and John Neubauer (2010), 19–39, are excellent resources.

Nguyễn Du
There have been a number of recent translations of *The Tale of Kiều*, the best of which is Huỳnh Sanh Thông's revised bilingual edition (1983). This includes an excellent introduction by Alexander B. Woodside, which offers both historical and literary contexts for the poem. Nathalie Huynh Chau Nguyen's *Vietnamese Voices* (2003) explores the femininity of the central character and tracks the powerful influence of *Kiều* on modern Vietnamese literature. The 2007 film *Saigon Eclipse*, directed by Othello Khanh, is a contemporary retelling of the story.

Pandita Ramabai
The best recent source is *Pandita Ramabai Through Her Own Words: Selected Works* (2000), ed. Meera Kosambi, which contains reliable new translations of several Marathi texts alongside the works written originally in English. Kosambi's introduction to the book, and her various essays mentioned in its bibliography, offer a balanced and comprehensive account of Ramabai's life and writing. For the wider historical and literary contexts of Ramabai's career, see the two volumes by Susie Tharu and K. Lalitha, *Women Writing in India* (1992) and Antoinette Burton, *At the Heart of the Empire: Indians and the Colonial Encounter in Late-Victorian Britain* (1998).

Percy Bysshe Shelley
A comprehensive, three-volume edition of the poetry has been put together by Kelvin Everest, *The Poems of Shelley* (1989–2010); for Shelley's other influential writings, see *Shelley's Poetry and Prose*, ed. Neil Fraistat and Donald Reiman (2002). James Bieri has written a lengthy and well-researched biography, *Percy Bysshe Shelley* (2008). For readings of the poetry in the context of Shelley's politics, see Stuart Curran, "Shelley and the End(s) of Ideology," from *The Most Unfailing Herald*, ed. Alan M. Weinberg and Romaine Hill (1996), 21–30; see also James Chandler, *England in 1819* (1998). Shelley's style and form have been richly treated by William Keach, *Shelley's Style* (1984), and Susan J. Wolfson, *Formal Charges: The Shaping of Poetry in British Romanticism* (1997), 193–206.

Lola Rodríguez de Tió
Frances R. Aparicio, *Listening to Salsa: Gender, Latin Popular Music, and Puerto Rican Cultures* (1998); Vicki L Ruiz and Virginia Sanchez Korrol, *Latina Legacies: Identity, Biography, and Community* (2005).

Speranza, Lady Jane Wilde
Horace Wyndham, *Speranza: A Biography of Lady Wilde* (1953); Emer O'Sullivan, *The Fall of the House of Wilde: Oscar Wilde and His Family* (2016).

Walt Whitman
The standard scholarly edition of Whitman's works took many years and a number of volumes: *The Collected Writings of Walt Whitman*, ed. Gay Wilson Allen and Sculley Bradley (1961–2004). Whitman's additions and revisions are so extensive that they are difficult to capture in print. An excellent new online edition called *The Walt Whitman Archive*, ed. Kenneth M. Price and Ed Folsom, has the advantage of incorporating multiple texts, including facsimiles of original editions, poems published in periodicals, and editions of *Leaves of Grass* printed outside of the United States. The best-known scholarly biography is Gay Allen Wilson, *The Solitary Singer* (rev. 1985). Another fine biography is Jerome Loving, *Walt Whitman: The Song of Himself* (1998). David S. Reynolds has brought together a series of essays that contextualize the poet in *A Historical Guide to Walt Whitman* (2000). Ezra Greenspan's Walt Whitman's *Song of Myself: A Sourcebook and Critical Edition* (2005) brings together a rich collection of reviews and critical responses starting in the nineteenth century, and offers a good overview of the historical context for Whitman's work. For critical studies, see Mark Bauerlein, *Whitman and the American Idiom* (1991); Jimmie M. Killingsworth, *Whitman's Poetry of the Body: Sexuality, Politics, and the Text* (1989); Michael Moon, *Disseminating Whitman: Revision and Corporeality in Leaves of Grass* (1991); *Whitman East and West: New Contexts for Reading Walt Whitman*, ed. Ed Folsom (2002); and Susan Belasco, Ed Folsom, and Kenneth M. Price, eds., *Leaves of Grass: The Sesquicentennial Essays* (2007). For a valuable approach to teaching "Out of the Cradle Endlessly Rocking," see Dennis K. Renner, "Reconciling Varied Approaches to 'Out of the Cradle Endlessly Rocking,'" in *Approaches to Teaching Whitman's "Leaves of Grass,"* ed. Donald D. Kummings (1990), 67–73.

III. Realism across the World

Erich Auerbach's beautiful classic work of criticism, *Mimesis* (1946), explores a number of different attempts to capture reality in the Western tradition, including nineteenth-century realism. Pam Morris's *Realism* (2003) is a fine introduction to the concept, focusing exclusively on French and British literary examples. For a historical understanding of the rise of realism, with a special focus on the visual arts, see Linda Nochlin, *Realism* (1972). György Lukács has been one of the most influential theorists of the realist novel: see his *Theory of the Novel* (1920) and *Studies in European Realism* (1948). For the roots of British realism in eighteenth-century thought and social experience, Ian Watt's *Rise of the Novel* (1957) is a landmark study. An overview of Russian realism can be found in Dmitrij Cizevskij and Dmitrij Tschižewskij, *The History of Nineteenth-Century Russian Literature: The Age of Realism* (1974).

Anton Chekhov
Donald Rayfield's detailed biography *Anton Chekhov: A Life* (2000) is the most substantial in English. Rayfield's *Understanding Chekhov: A Critical Study of Chekhov's Prose and Drama* (1999) brings together biography and criticism. A more popular book on Chekhov is Janet Malcolm's *Reading Chekhov: A Critical Journey* (2001), which combines travel writing, biography, and criticism in a lively and intelligent—though not scholarly—combination. Dana Gioia's short essay on "Anton Chekhov's 'The Lady with the Pet Dog,'" in *Eclectic Literary Review* (Fall/Winter 1998) is concise and illuminating. See also Vladimir Nabokov's wonderful essay on Chekhov in his *Lectures on Russian Literature* (1981). Three fine collections of essays offer an array of good historical and critical responses to Chekhov's drama: *A Chekhov Companion*, ed. Toby W. Clyman (1985); the second *Critical Essays on Anton Chekhov*, ed. Thomas A. Eekman (1989); and *The Cambridge Companion to Chekhov*, ed. Vera Gottlieb and Paul Allain (2000). Jean-Louis Barrault's poetic essay "Why *The Cherry Orchard*?" explores the musical structure of the play (included in *Anton Chekhov's Selected Plays*, ed. Laurence Senelick [2005], pp. 620–28).

Fyodor Dostoyevsky
Written over the course of three decades, Joseph Frank's magisterial five-volume biography of Dostoyevsky is widely hailed as a great achievement (1976–2002). There is a helpfully condensed one-volume version of this, called *Dostoevsky: A Writer in His Time*, ed. Mary Petrusewicz (2009), that focuses mostly on the impact of events on the author's ideas. Mikhail Bakhtin makes his influential argument that Dostoyevsky's work is always multi-voiced—"polyphonic"—in *Problems of Dostoyevsky's Poetics*, trans. Caryl Emerson (1984). The Norton Critical Edition of the text contains many useful critical commentaries, including Joseph Frank's, which considers the two parts of the text as responding to two different historical contexts, the first part concerned with the mid-1860s, the second part looking back to the idealist moment of the 1840s. This edition also includes parodies and imitations of the text by Woody Allen, Ralph Ellison, and Jean-Paul Sartre. See Fyodor Dostoevsky, *Notes from Underground*, ed. Michael Katz (2000).

Gustave Flaubert
Frederick Brown's *Flaubert: A Biography* (2006) is rich in historical detail; Geoffrey Wall's *Flaubert: A Life* (2002) is more psychological in focus. Flaubert's *Selected Letters*, ed. Geoffrey Wall (1998), give access to the writer's feelings and opinions in a way that his literary texts deliberately do not. Victor Brombert offers a classic reading of *A Simple Heart* in *The Novels of Flaubert* (1966). Winifred Woodhull investigates the relationship between private experience and public, historical events in "Configurations of the Family in *Un Coeur Simple*," *Comparative Literature* 39 (1987): 139–61.

Henrik Ibsen
Overall, the best book on Ibsen is Toril Moi's *Henrik Ibsen and the Birth of Modernism* (2006). Among the early reactions to Ibsen was George Bernard Shaw's *The Quintessence of Ibsenism* (1891), which emphasizes Ibsen's

concern with pressing social and political issues, while William Archer's essays, collected by Thomas Postlewait in *William Archer on Ibsen: The Major Essays, 1889–1919* (1984), foreground Ibsen's poetic choices and techniques. Charles Lyons's compilation, *Critical Essays on Henrik Ibsen* (1987), includes landmark essays by Ibsen's modernist admirers, including James Joyce, E. M. Forster, and Georg Lukàcs. The wider cultural context of Ibsen's European success, as well as a wealth of personal detail, is captured in Michael Meyer's *Ibsen: A Biography* (1971). Michael Goldman's *Ibsen: The Dramaturgy of Fear* (1999) focuses on subtexts and psychologies. In *Ibsen and Early Modernist Theatre, 1890–1900,* Kirsten Shepherd-Barr situates Ibsen in the context of theater history, and Joan Templeton's *Ibsen's Women* is the first in-depth analysis of Ibsen's construction of female characters, including Hedda Gabler. *The Cambridge Companion to Ibsen*, ed. James McFarlane (1994), provides a good introduction into recent scholarship and contemporary approaches.

Higuchi Ichiyō

The only full-length biography of Ichiyō in English is Robert Lyons Danly's *In the Shade of Spring Leaves* (1981). Donald Keene's *Dawn to the West: Japanese Literature in the Modern Era* (1998) traces Ichiyō's life and career in some detail, locating her in a literary context. For a reading of Ichiyō in the context of other women writers, see Yukiko Tanaka, *Women Writers of Meiji and Taishō Japan: Their Lives, Works, and Critical Reception* (2000); and Rebecca Copeland and Melek Ortabasi, eds., *The Modern Murasaki: Writing by Women of Meiji Japan* (2006).

Machado de Assis

There is no full-length biography of Machado in English, but Helen Caldwell's *Machado de Assis: The Brazilian Master and his Novels* (1970) interweaves details about his life with readings of the novels, and Earl E. Fitz gives an overview of both life and work in *Machado de Assis* (1989). The most famous reading of Machado's literary innovations in their social context is Roberto Schwartz, *A Master on the Periphery of Capitalism*, trans. John Gledson (2001). Helpful and informative essays on Machado can be found in *Machado de Assis: Reflections on a Brazilian Master Writer* (1999).

Orature

For excellent introductions to thinking about oral traditions, see Eric Havelock's classic *Preface to Plato* (1963); Walter J. Ong, *Orality and Literacy* (1982); Isidore Opkewho, *African Oral Literature* (1992); and Ruth Finnegan, *The Oral and Beyond* (2007). Ngugi Wa Thiong'o makes a powerful case for studying orature in order to understand African cultures in *Decolonizing the Mind* (1986). On the Grimms, see Jack David Zipes, *The Brothers Grimm* (2002) and James M. McGlathery, ed., *The Brothers Grimm and Folktale* (1988). For an intriguing study of African American folk heroes, see *From Trickster to Badman* by John W. Roberts (1989). Leonard Fox's *Hainteny* (1990) is the best English-language introduction to Malagasy wisdom poetry. James C. Faris gives a detailed description of the Navajo Night Chant in an essay called "Context and Text" in Philip G. Cohen, ed., *Texts and Textuality* (1997).

José López Portillo Y Rojas

Roland Grass, *José López Portillo y Rojas: A Novelist of Social Reform in Mexico before the Revolution of 1910* (1970); Seymour Menton, *The Spanish American Short Story: A Critical Anthology* (1980); David William Foster, ed. *Mexican Literature: A History* (1994).

Rabindranath Tagore

Amiya Chakravarty, ed., *A Tagore Reader* (1961) and Krishna Dutta and Andrew Robinson, *Rabindranath Tagore: An Anthology* (1997) provide the best overviews of Tagore's career and work in many genres. Dutta and Robinson's *Rabindranath Tagore: The Myriad-Minded Man* (1995) and Krishna Kripalani's *Rabindranath Tagore: A Biography* (1962) offer informative accounts in English of the artist's life. Older translations, prepared under Tagore's own supervision, are still available in *Collected Poems and Plays* (1936). Among important recent translations and accounts of Tagore's work are William Radice's *Rabindranath Tagore: Selected Poems* (1985) and *Rabindranath Tagore: Selected Short Stories* (1991); Ketaki Kushari Dyson's *I Won't Let You Go* (1993), a selection of poetry; and Anand Lal's *Rabindranath Tagore: Three Plays* (2001). Some of the best new translations and critical introductions are contained in the Oxford Tagore Translations series edited by Shukanta Chaudhuri and others, which includes *Selected Short Stories* (2000) and *Selected Writings on Literature and Language* (2001).

Leo Tolstoy
A. N. Wilson's *Tolstoy* (1988) is an entertaining and readable biography. Gary R. Jahn's *Tolstoy's The Death of Ivan Il'ich* (1999) contains a number of fine interpretive essays and an excellent introduction. It also includes a set of notes on connotations of phrases in the original Russian text. For other good critical essays, see R. F. Christian, *Tolstoy: A Critical Introduction* (1969); Edward Wasiolek, ed., *Critical Essays on Tolstoy* (1986); Harold Bloom, ed., *Leo Tolstoy* (1986); *Tolstoy* by John Bayley (1997); and David Holbrook's *Tolstoy, Woman and Death* (1997). The fascinating correspondence between Tolstoy and Gandhi can be found in B. Srinivasa Murthy, ed., *Mahatma Gandhi and Leo Tolstoy: Letters* (1987).

Timeline

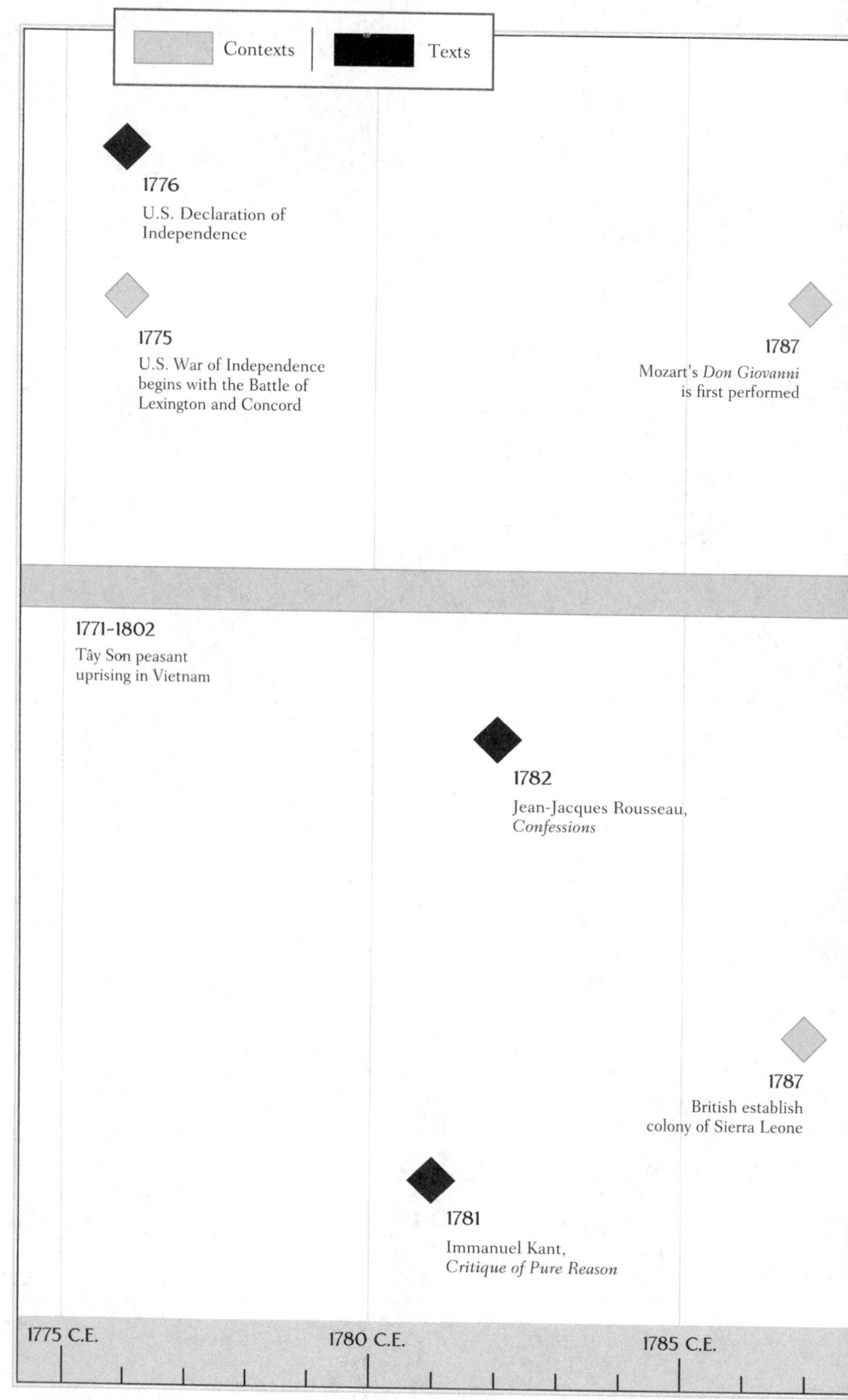
Contexts
Texts
1776
U.S. Declaration of Independence
1775
U.S. War of Independence begins with the Battle of Lexington and Concord
1787
Mozart's *Don Giovanni* is first performed
1771–1802
Tây Son peasant uprising in Vietnam
1782
Jean-Jacques Rousseau, *Confessions*
1787
British establish colony of Sierra Leone
1781
Immanuel Kant, *Critique of Pure Reason*
1775 C.E.
1780 C.E.
1785 C.E.

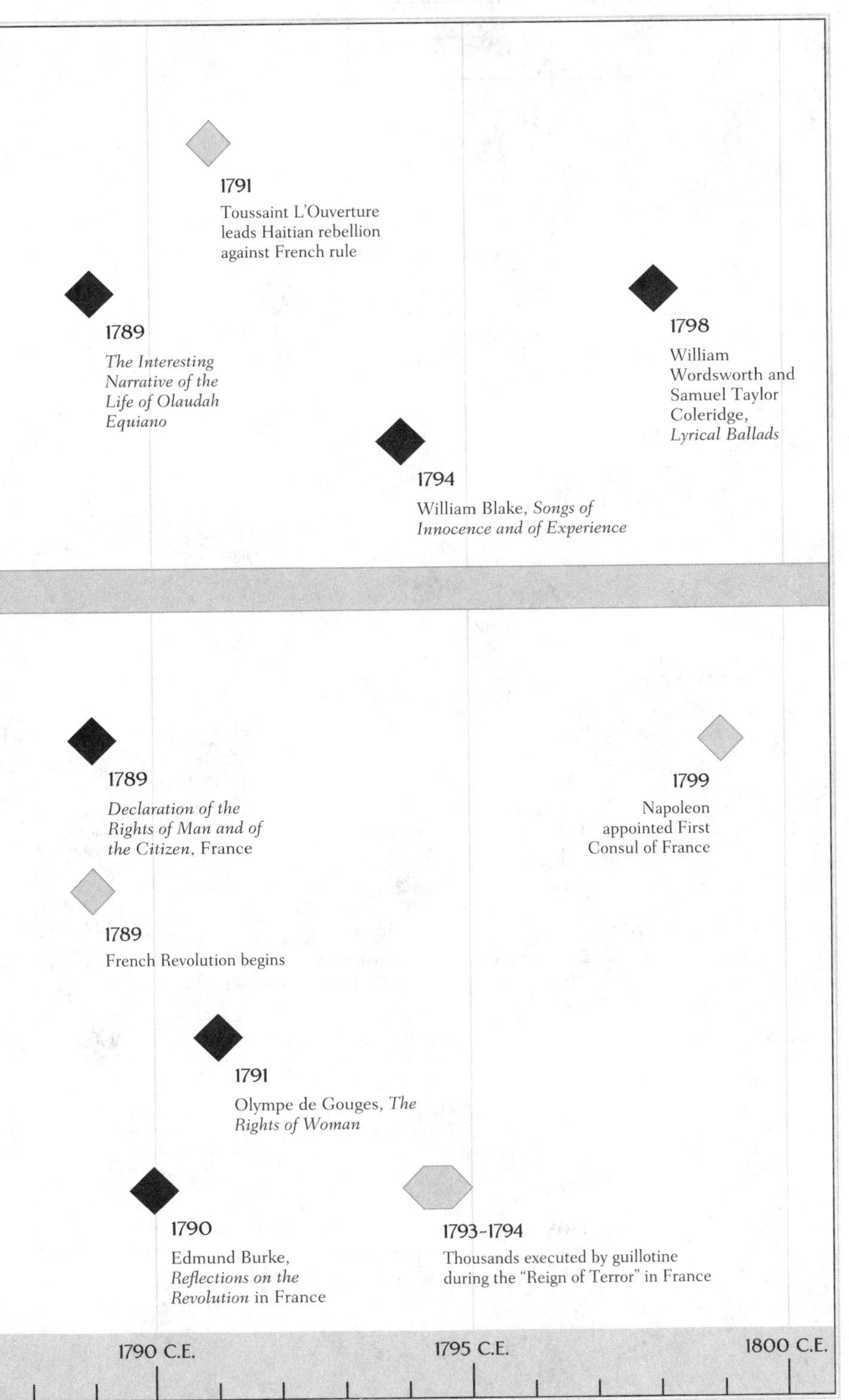
1791
Toussaint L'Ouverture leads Haitian rebellion against French rule
1789
The Interesting Narrative of the Life of Olaudah Equiano
1798
William Wordsworth and Samuel Taylor Coleridge, *Lyrical Ballads*
1794
William Blake, *Songs of Innocence and of Experience*
1789
Declaration of the Rights of Man and of the Citizen, France
1799
Napoleon appointed First Consul of France
1789
French Revolution begins
1791
Olympe de Gouges, *The Rights of Woman*
1790
Edmund Burke, *Reflections on the Revolution* in France
1793–1794
Thousands executed by guillotine during the "Reign of Terror" in France
1790 C.E.
1795 C.E.
1800 C.E.

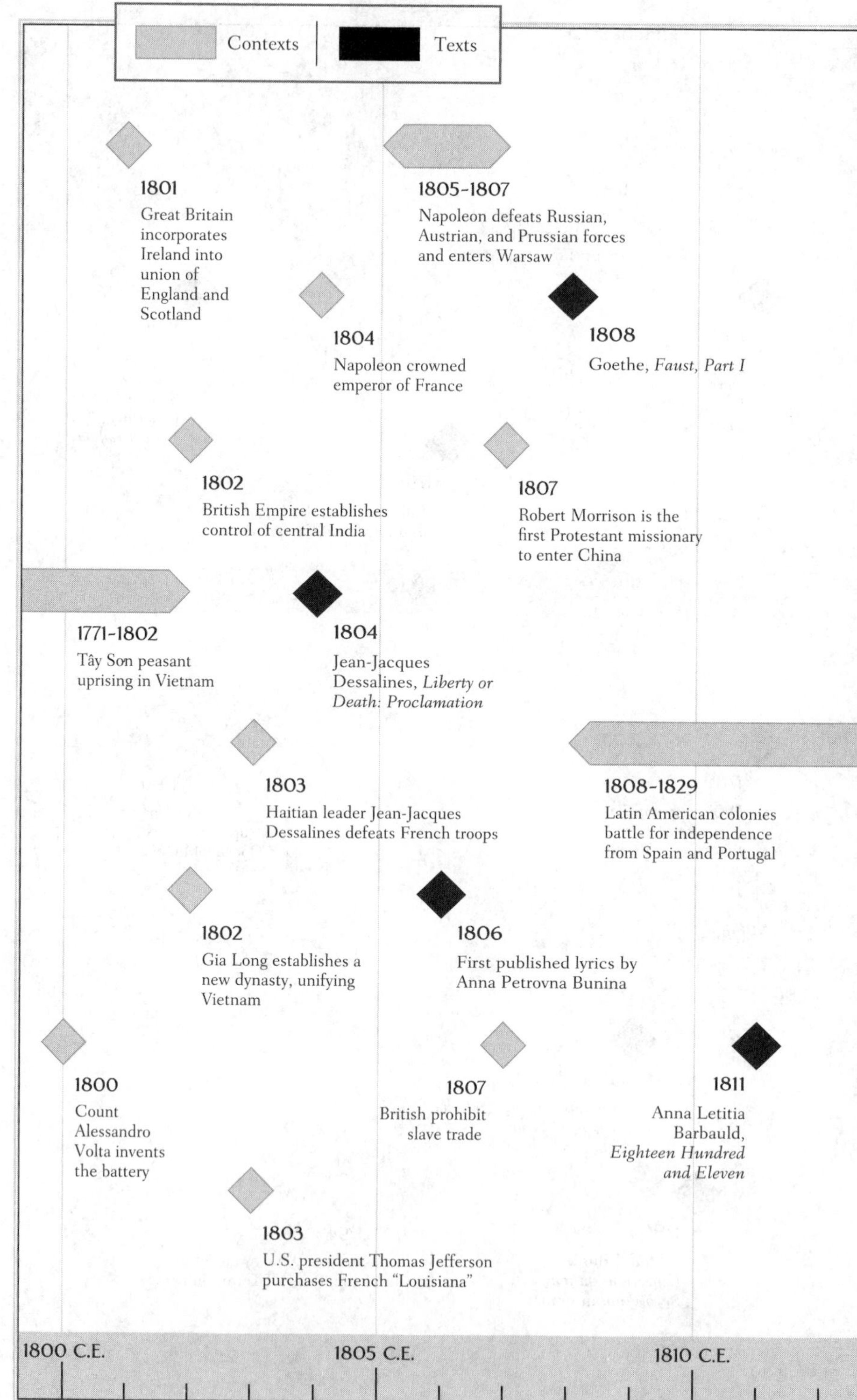
Contexts
Texts
1801
Great Britain incorporates Ireland into union of England and Scotland
1805–1807
Napoleon defeats Russian, Austrian, and Prussian forces and enters Warsaw
1804
Napoleon crowned emperor of France
1808
Goethe, *Faust, Part I*
1802
British Empire establishes control of central India
1807
Robert Morrison is the first Protestant missionary to enter China
1771–1802
Tây Sơn peasant uprising in Vietnam
1804
Jean-Jacques Dessalines, *Liberty or Death: Proclamation*
1803
Haitian leader Jean-Jacques Dessalines defeats French troops
1808–1829
Latin American colonies battle for independence from Spain and Portugal
1802
Gia Long establishes a new dynasty, unifying Vietnam
1806
First published lyrics by Anna Petrovna Bunina
1800
Count Alessandro Volta invents the battery
1807
British prohibit slave trade
1811
Anna Letitia Barbauld, *Eighteen Hundred and Eleven*
1803
U.S. president Thomas Jefferson purchases French "Louisiana"
1800 C.E.
1805 C.E.
1810 C.E.

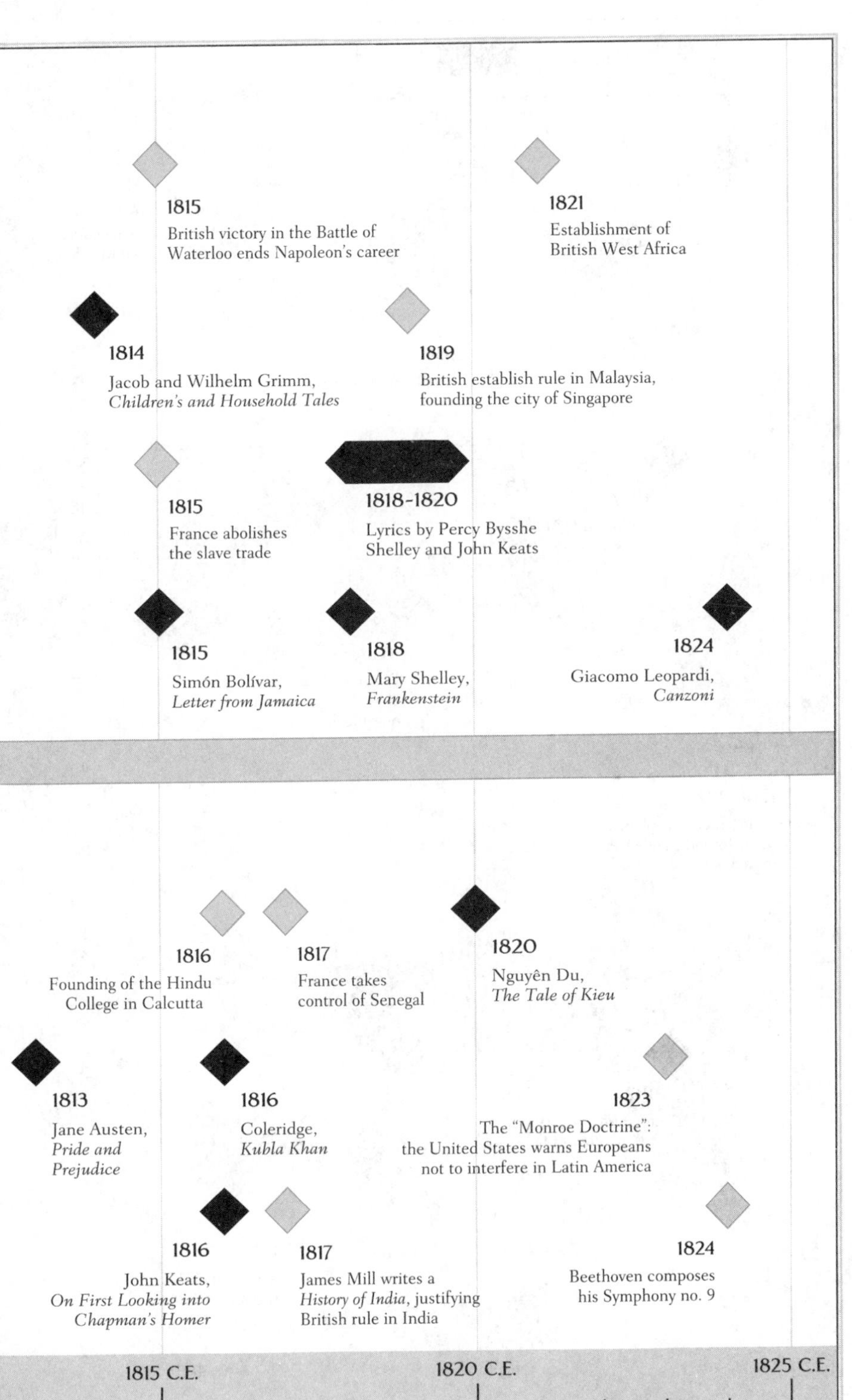
1815
British victory in the Battle of Waterloo ends Napoleon's career
1821
Establishment of British West Africa
1814
Jacob and Wilhelm Grimm, *Children's and Household Tales*
1819
British establish rule in Malaysia, founding the city of Singapore
1815
France abolishes the slave trade
1818–1820
Lyrics by Percy Bysshe Shelley and John Keats
1815
Simón Bolívar, *Letter from Jamaica*
1818
Mary Shelley, *Frankenstein*
1824
Giacomo Leopardi, *Canzoni*
1816
Founding of the Hindu College in Calcutta
1817
France takes control of Senegal
1820
Nguyên Du, *The Tale of Kieu*
1813
Jane Austen, *Pride and Prejudice*
1816
Coleridge, *Kubla Khan*
1823
The "Monroe Doctrine": the United States warns Europeans not to interfere in Latin America
1816
John Keats, *On First Looking into Chapman's Homer*
1817
James Mill writes a *History of India*, justifying British rule in India
1824
Beethoven composes his Symphony no. 9
1815 C.E.
1820 C.E.
1825 C.E.

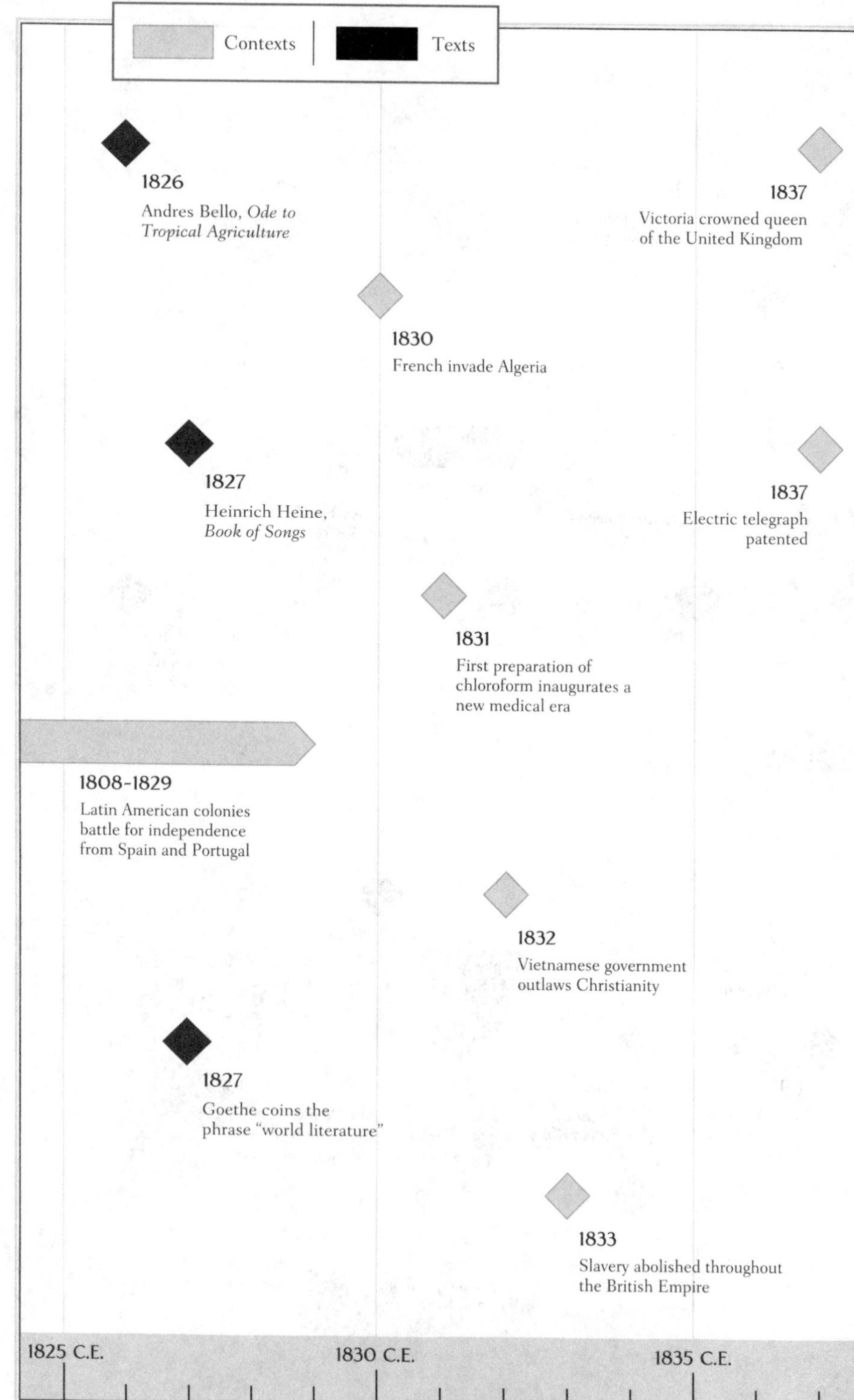
Contexts
Texts
1826
Andres Bello, *Ode to Tropical Agriculture*
1837
Victoria crowned queen of the United Kingdom
1830
French invade Algeria
1827
Heinrich Heine, *Book of Songs*
1837
Electric telegraph patented
1831
First preparation of chloroform inaugurates a new medical era
1808–1829
Latin American colonies battle for independence from Spain and Portugal
1832
Vietnamese government outlaws Christianity
1827
Goethe coins the phrase "world literature"
1833
Slavery abolished throughout the British Empire
1825 C.E.
1830 C.E.
1835 C.E.

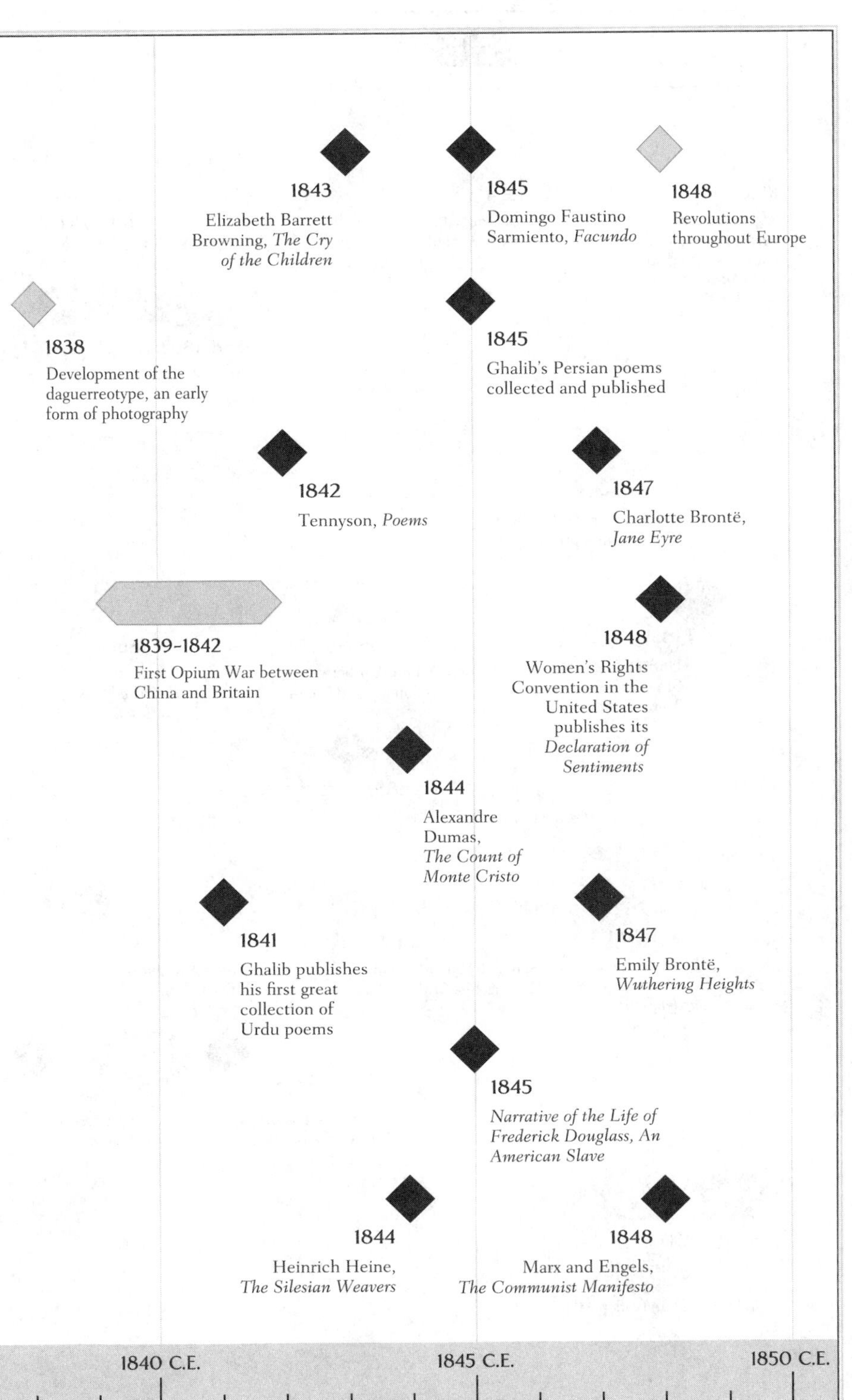
1843
Elizabeth Barrett Browning, *The Cry of the Children*
1845
Domingo Faustino Sarmiento, *Facundo*
1848
Revolutions throughout Europe
1838
Development of the daguerreotype, an early form of photography
1845
Ghalib's Persian poems collected and published
1842
Tennyson, *Poems*
1847
Charlotte Brontë, *Jane Eyre*
1839–1842
First Opium War between China and Britain
1848
Women's Rights Convention in the United States publishes its *Declaration of Sentiments*
1844
Alexandre Dumas, *The Count of Monte Cristo*
1841
Ghalib publishes his first great collection of Urdu poems
1847
Emily Brontë, *Wuthering Heights*
1845
Narrative of the Life of Frederick Douglass, An American Slave
1844
Heinrich Heine, *The Silesian Weavers*
1848
Marx and Engels, *The Communist Manifesto*
1840 C.E.
1845 C.E.
1850 C.E.

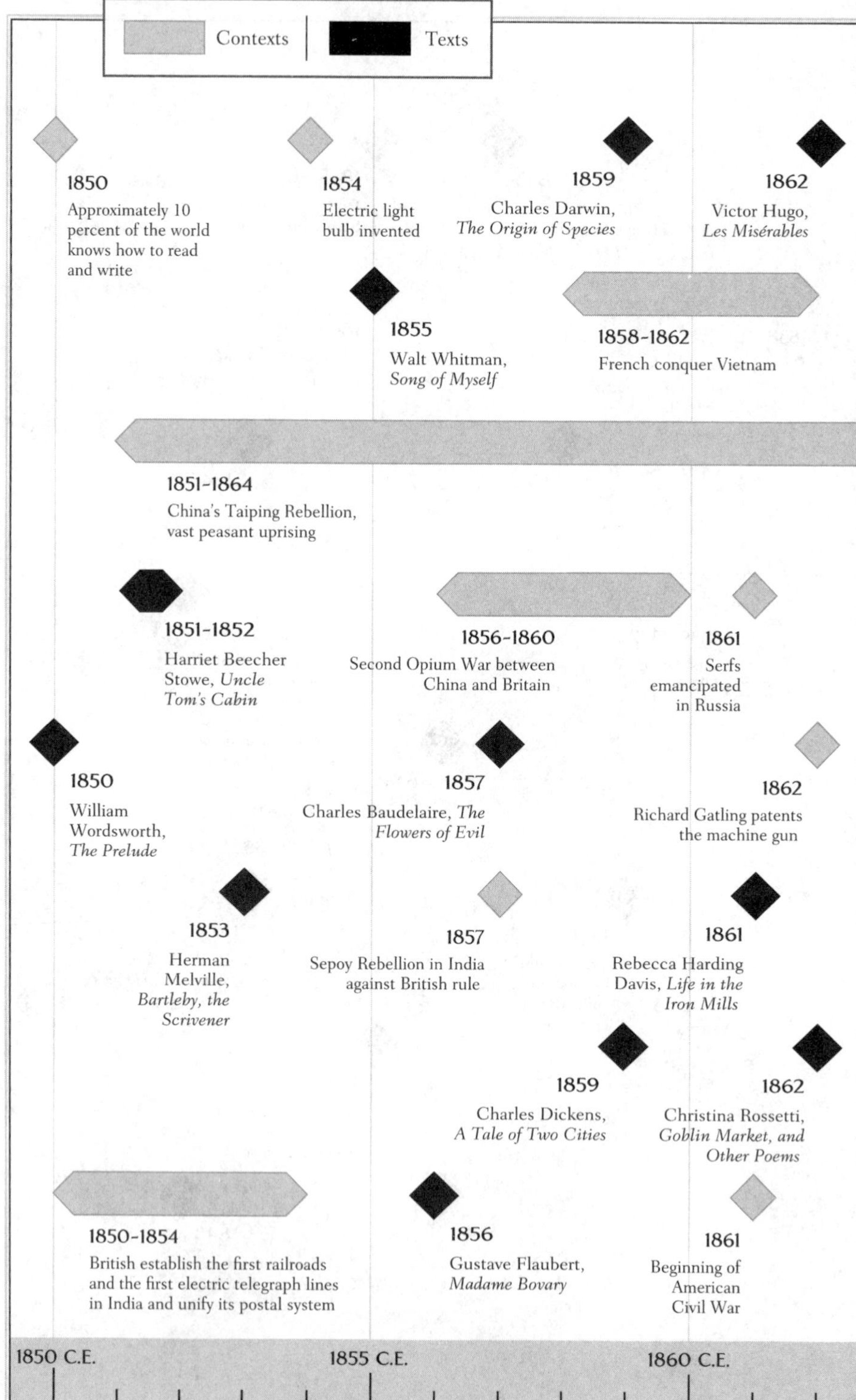
Contexts
Texts
1850
Approximately 10 percent of the world knows how to read and write
1854
Electric light bulb invented
1859
Charles Darwin, *The Origin of Species*
1862
Victor Hugo, *Les Misérables*
1855
Walt Whitman, *Song of Myself*
1858–1862
French conquer Vietnam
1851–1864
China's Taiping Rebellion, vast peasant uprising
1851–1852
Harriet Beecher Stowe, *Uncle Tom's Cabin*
1856–1860
Second Opium War between China and Britain
1861
Serfs emancipated in Russia
1850
William Wordsworth, *The Prelude*
1857
Charles Baudelaire, *The Flowers of Evil*
1862
Richard Gatling patents the machine gun
1853
Herman Melville, *Bartleby, the Scrivener*
1857
Sepoy Rebellion in India against British rule
1861
Rebecca Harding Davis, *Life in the Iron Mills*
1859
Charles Dickens, *A Tale of Two Cities*
1862
Christina Rossetti, *Goblin Market, and Other Poems*
1850–1854
British establish the first railroads and the first electric telegraph lines in India and unify its postal system
1856
Gustave Flaubert, *Madame Bovary*
1861
Beginning of American Civil War
1850 C.E.
1855 C.E.
1860 C.E.

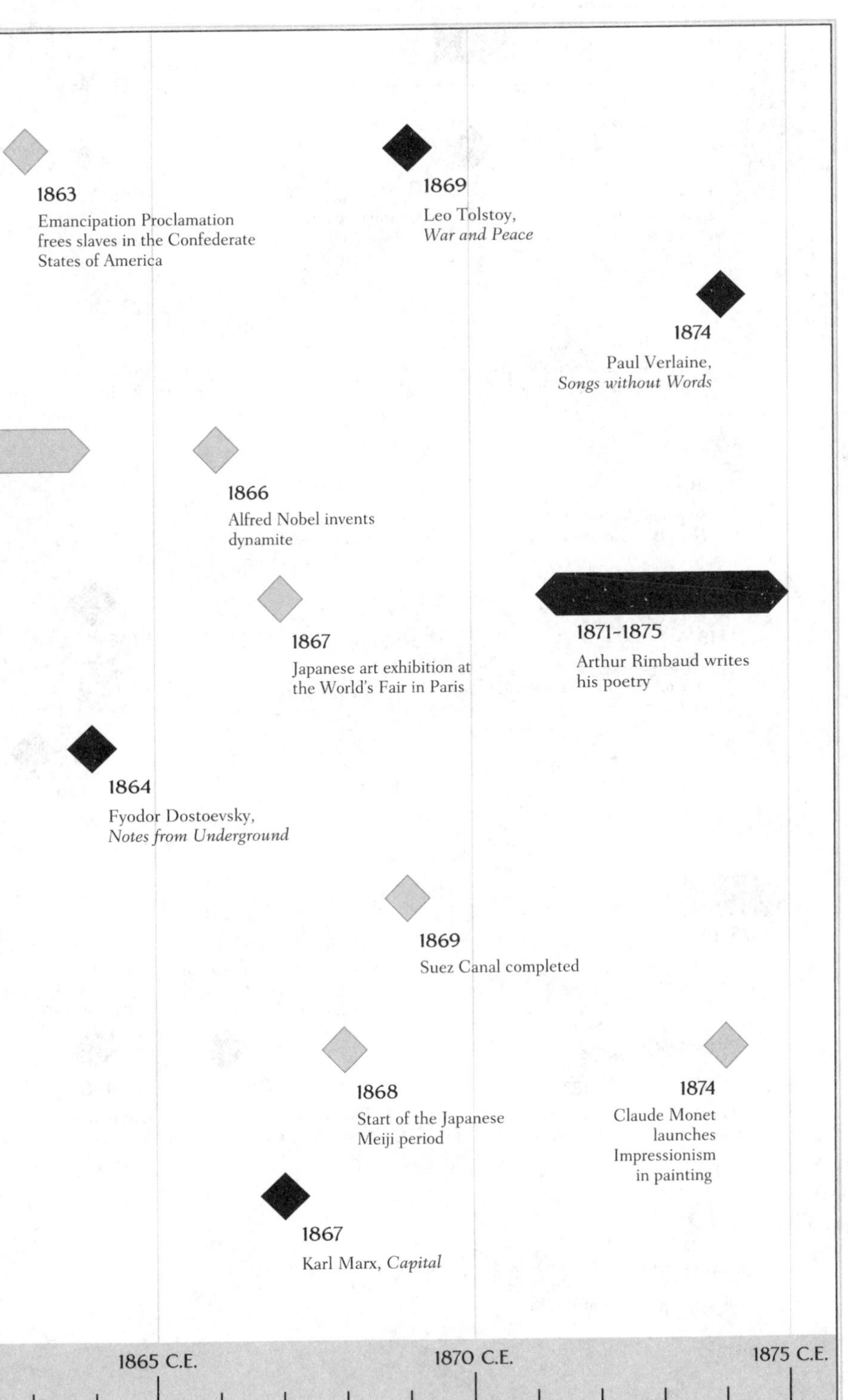
1863
Emancipation Proclamation frees slaves in the Confederate States of America
1869
Leo Tolstoy, *War and Peace*
1874
Paul Verlaine, *Songs without Words*
1866
Alfred Nobel invents dynamite
1867
Japanese art exhibition at the World's Fair in Paris
1871–1875
Arthur Rimbaud writes his poetry
1864
Fyodor Dostoevsky, *Notes from Underground*
1869
Suez Canal completed
1868
Start of the Japanese Meiji period
1874
Claude Monet launches Impressionism in painting
1867
Karl Marx, *Capital*
1865 C.E.
1870 C.E.
1875 C.E.

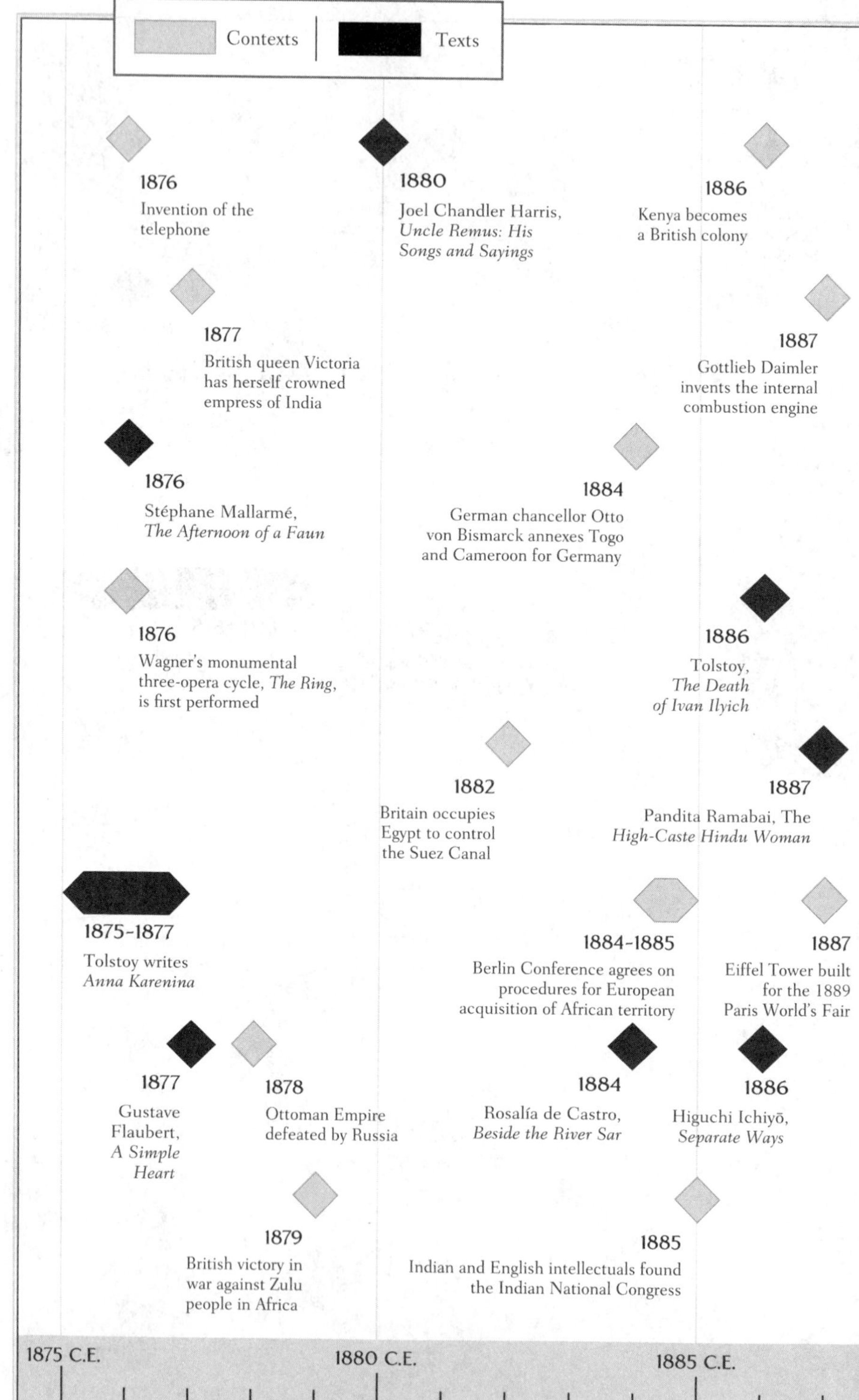

Contexts
Texts
1876
Invention of the telephone
1880
Joel Chandler Harris, *Uncle Remus: His Songs and Sayings*
1886
Kenya becomes a British colony
1877
British queen Victoria has herself crowned empress of India
1887
Gottlieb Daimler invents the internal combustion engine
1876
Stéphane Mallarmé, *The Afternoon of a Faun*
1884
German chancellor Otto von Bismarck annexes Togo and Cameroon for Germany
1876
Wagner's monumental three-opera cycle, *The Ring*, is first performed
1886
Tolstoy, *The Death of Ivan Ilyich*
1882
Britain occupies Egypt to control the Suez Canal
1887
Pandita Ramabai, The *High-Caste Hindu Woman*
1875–1877
Tolstoy writes *Anna Karenina*
1884–1885
Berlin Conference agrees on procedures for European acquisition of African territory
1887
Eiffel Tower built for the 1889 Paris World's Fair
1877
Gustave Flaubert, *A Simple Heart*
1878
Ottoman Empire defeated by Russia
1884
Rosalía de Castro, *Beside the River Sar*
1886
Higuchi Ichiyō, *Separate Ways*
1879
British victory in war against Zulu people in Africa
1885
Indian and English intellectuals found the Indian National Congress
1875 C.E.
1880 C.E.
1885 C.E.

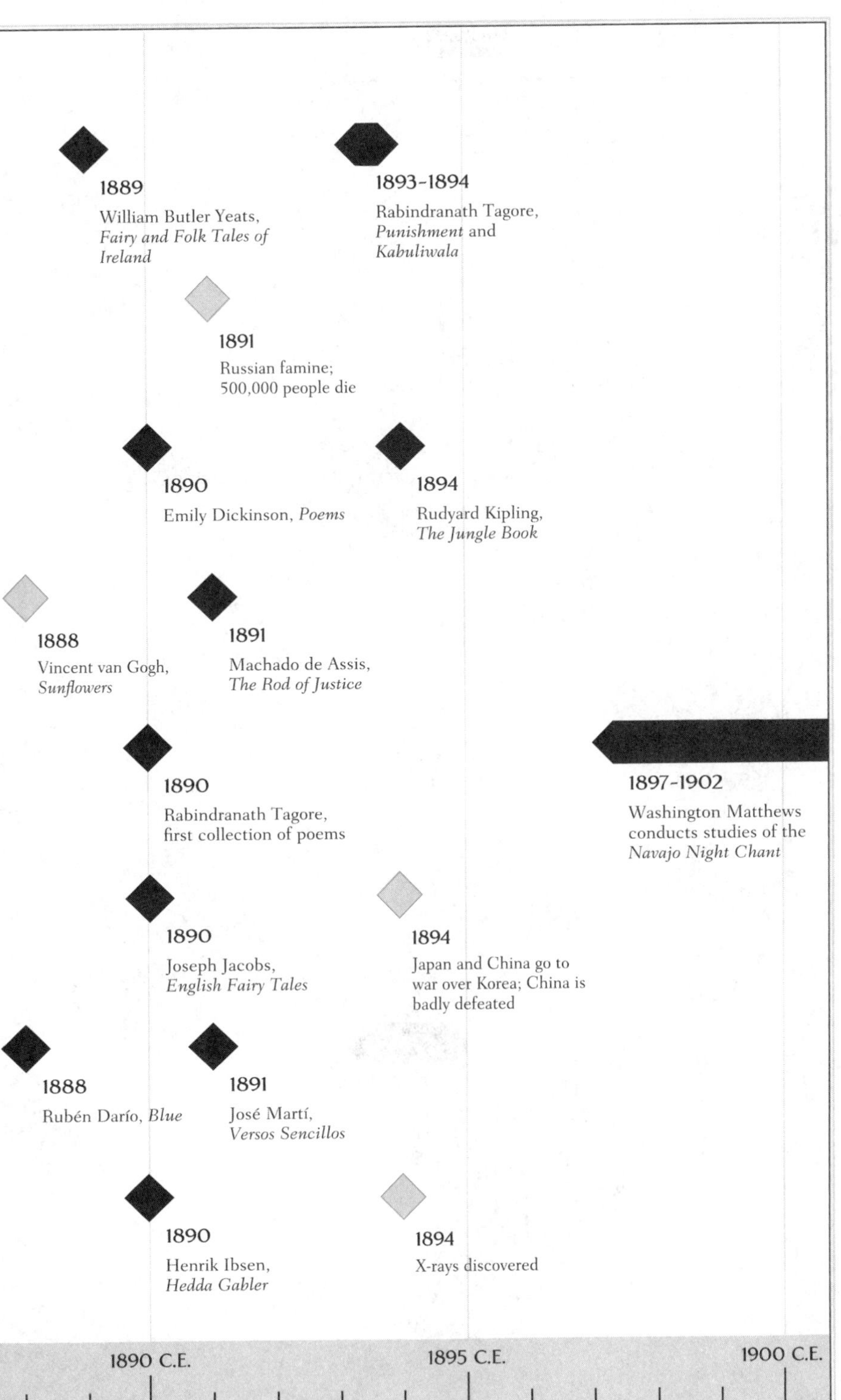

1889
William Butler Yeats, *Fairy and Folk Tales of Ireland*
1893–1894
Rabindranath Tagore, *Punishment* and *Kabuliwala*
1891
Russian famine; 500,000 people die
1890
Emily Dickinson, *Poems*
1894
Rudyard Kipling, *The Jungle Book*
1888
Vincent van Gogh, *Sunflowers*
1891
Machado de Assis, *The Rod of Justice*
1890
Rabindranath Tagore, first collection of poems
1897–1902
Washington Matthews conducts studies of the *Navajo Night Chant*
1890
Joseph Jacobs, *English Fairy Tales*
1894
Japan and China go to war over Korea; China is badly defeated
1888
Rubén Darío, *Blue*
1891
José Martí, *Versos Sencillos*
1890
Henrik Ibsen, *Hedda Gabler*
1894
X-rays discovered
1890 C.E.
1895 C.E.
1900 C.E.

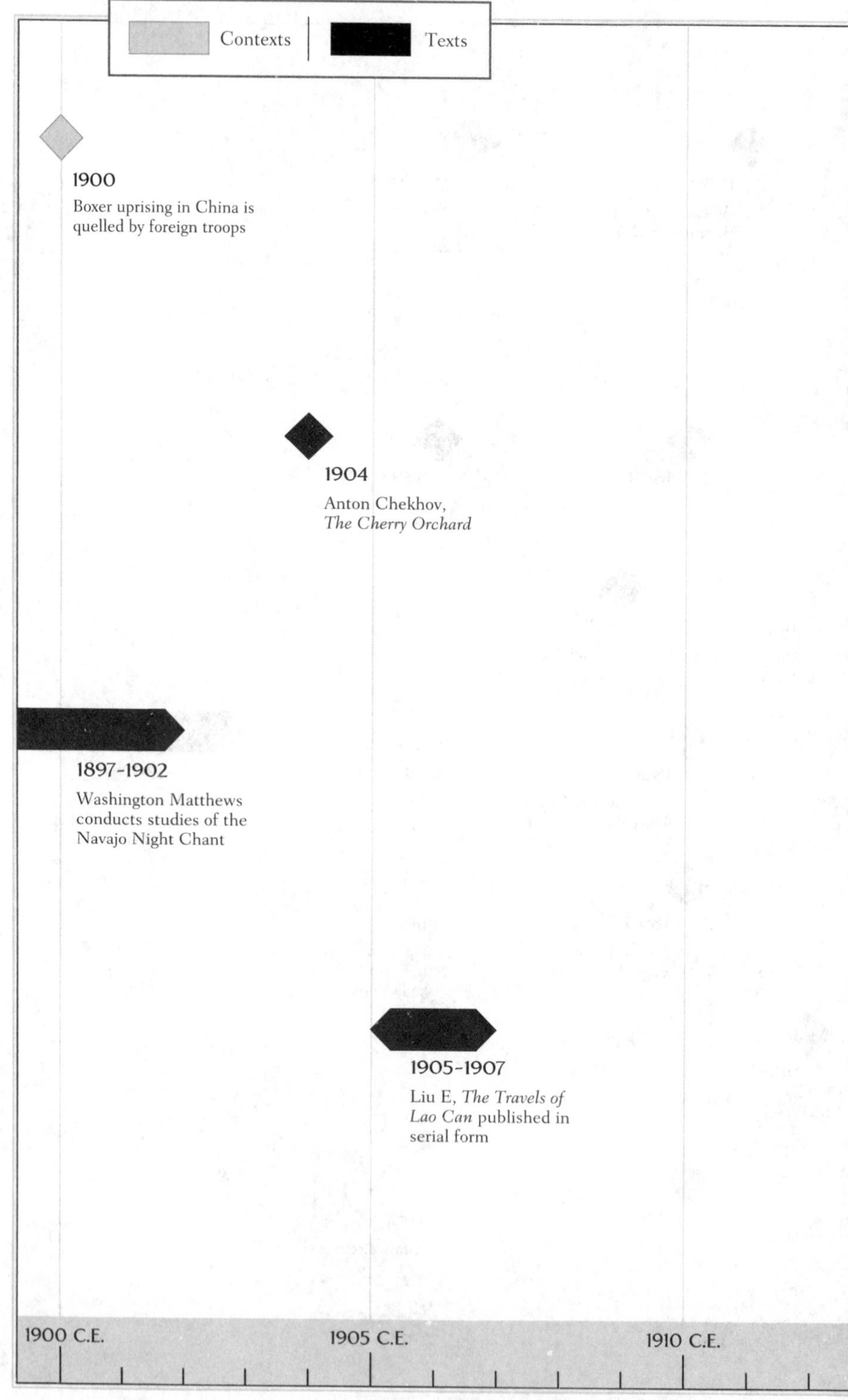
Contexts
Texts
1900
Boxer uprising in China is quelled by foreign troops
1904
Anton Chekhov, *The Cherry Orchard*
1897–1902
Washington Matthews conducts studies of the Navajo Night Chant
1905–1907
Liu E, *The Travels of Lao Can* published in serial form
1900 C.E.
1905 C.E.
1910 C.E.

1915 C.E.

1920 C.E.

1925 C.E.

Permissions Acknowledgments

All God's Chillen Had Wings: From THE DOCTOR TO THE DEAD: GROTESQUE LEGENDS AND FOLK TALES OF OLD CHARLESTON by John Bennett. Reprinted by permission of The University of South Carolina Press.

Charles Baudelaire: "To the Reader," trans. by Robert Lowell from COLLECTED POEMS by Robert Lowell. Copyright © 2003 by Harriet Lowell and Sheridan Lowell. Reprinted by permission of Farrar, Straus and Giroux. "Song of Autumn I" from ONE HUNDRED POEMS FROM LES FLEURS DU MAL, trans. by C. F. MacIntyre. Copyright © 1947 by C.F. MacIntyre. Reprinted by permission of the University of California Press. "L'Invitation au Voyage" from THINGS OF THIS WORLD by Richard Wilbur, copyright © 1956 and renewed 1984 by Richard Wilbur. Reprinted by permission of Houghton Mifflin Harcourt Publishing Company. All rights reserved. "Spleen LXXIX" trans. by Anthony Hecht, "Her Hair" trans. by Doreen Bell, "Spleen LXXVIII" trans. by Kenneth O. Hanson, "Spleen LXXXI, trans. by Sir John Squire and "Correspondences" trans. by Richard Wilbur from THE FLOWERS OF EVIL, copyright © 1965 by New Directions Publishing Corp. Reprinted by permission of New Directions Publishing Corp. "A Carcass" from FLOWERS OF EVIL, trans. by James McGowan (1993). By permission of Oxford University Press. "The Voyage" from THE MIRROR OF BAUDELAIRE, ed. and trans. by Charles Henri Ford. Reprinted by permission of the translator.

Simón Bolívar: from "Letter from Jamaica" from SELECTED WRITINGS OF BOLIVAR, comp. by Vicente Lecuna, ed. Harold A. Bierck, Jr. and trans. Lewis Bertrand, vol. 1 (Banco de Venezulea 1951).

Anna Bunina: "Conversation Between Me and the Women," trans. by Sibelan Forrester from AN ANTHOLOGY OF RUSSIAN WOMEN'S WRITING, 1777–1992, ed. by Catriona Kelly (1994). By permission of Oxford University Press.

Anton Chekhov: "The Cherry Orchard" from THE PLAYS OF ANTON CHEKHOV, A NEW TRANSLATION by Paul Schmidt. Copyright © 1997 by Paul Schmidt. Reprinted by permission of HarperCollins Publishers.

Harold Courlander: "All Stories are Anansi's" from THE HAT-SHAKING DANCE AND OTHER ASHANTI TALES FROM THE GOLD COAST by Harold Courlander with Albert Kofi Prempeh. Copyright © 1957, 1985 by Harold Courlander. Reprinted by permission of The Emma Courlander Trust.

Rubén Darío: From SELECTED POEMS OF RUBEN DARIO, trans. by Lysander Kemp. Copyright © 1965, renewed 1993. Reprinted by permission of the University of Texas Press.

Machado de Assis: "The Cane" from THE SELECTED STORIES OF MACHADO DE ASSIS. Trans. by Margaret Jull Costa and Robin Patterson. Copyright © 2018 by Margaret Jull Costa and Robin Patterson. Used by permission of Liveright Publishing Corp.

Rosalía de Castro: Poems from SELECTED POEMS, trans. by Michael Smith. Translation copyright © 2007 by Michael Smith. Reprinted by permission of Shearsman Books Ltd.

Olympe de Gouges: "The Rights of Women" from FRENCH FEMINISM: AN INDIAN ANTHOLOGY, ed. by Danielle Haase-Dubosc et al. and trans. under the direction of Nirupama Rastogi. Reprinted by permission of Sage Publications India Private Limited.

Emily Dickinson: Reprinted by permission of the publishers and the Trustees of Amherst College from THE POEMS OF EMILY DICKINSON, Thomas H. Johnson, ed. Cambridge, Mass.: The Belknap Press of Harvard University Press. Copyright © 1951, 1955 by the President and Fellows of Harvard College. Copyright © renewed 1979, 1983 by the President and Fellows of Harvard College. Copyright © 1914, 1918, 1919, 1924, 1929, 1930, 1932, 1935, 1937, 1942 by Martha Dickinson Bianchi. Copyright © 1952, 1957, 1958, 1963, 1965 by Mary L. Hampson.

Fyodor Dostoyevsky: NOTES FROM THE UNDERGROUND: A NORTON CRITICAL EDITION, trans. by Michael R. Katz. Copyright © 1989 by W. W. Norton & Company, Inc. Used by permission of W. W. Norton & Company, Inc.

Gustave Flaubert: "A Simple Heart" from THREE TALES, trans. with an introduction by Robert Baldick (Penguin Classics 1961). Copyright © 1961 by Robert Baldick. Reproduced by permission of Penguin Books Ltd.

Ghalib: Poems are translated by Vinay Dharwadker. Reprinted by permission of the translator.

Johann Wolfgang von Goethe: From FAUST: A TRAGEDY, Part One, trans. by Martin Greenberg. Revised English translation copyright © 2014 by Martin Greenberg. Used by permission of Yale University Press and revised by the translator.

Jacob and Wilhelm Grimm: "The Three Spinners" from THE COMPLETE FAIRY TALES OF THE BROTHERS GRIMM, trans. by Jack Zipes, translation copyright © 1987 by Jack Zipes. Used by permission of Bantam Books, an imprint of Random House, a division of Penguin Random House LLC. All rights reserved. Any third party use of this material, outside of this publication, is prohibited. Interested parties must apply directly to Penguin Random House LLC for permission.

Hawaiian Folktale: "The Despotic Chiefs of Kau," collected & trans. by Mary Kawne Pukui with Laura C.S. Green from FOLKTALES OF HAWAII (Bishop Museum Press 1995), p. 74–76. Reprinted by permission of the publisher.

Heinrich Heine: "The Silesian Weavers" from THE COMPLETE POEMS trans. by Hal Draper. Reprinted by permission of the translator.

Higuchi Ichiyō: "Separate Ways," from IN THE SHADE OF SPRING LEAVES: THE LIFE OF HIGUCHI ICHIYŌ WITH NINE OF HER BEST SHORT STORIES, trans. by Robert Lyons Danly. Copyright © 1981 by Robert Lyons Danly. Used by permission of W. W. Norton & Company, Inc.

Henrik Ibsen: "Hedda Gabler" from FOUR MAJOR PLAYS, Vol. 1, by Henrik Ibsen, trans. by Rick Davis and Brian Johnston. Copyright © 1995 by Rick Davis and Brian Johnston. Reprinted by permission of Smith and Kraus Publishers, Inc.

Giacomo Leopardi: Poems from A LEOPARDI READER, trans. and ed. by Ottavio M. Casale. Copyright © 1981 by the Board of Trustees of the University of Illinois. Used by permission of the Estate of Giacomo Leopardi.

Liu E: From THE TRAVELS OF LAO TS'AN by Liu T'ieh-Yun, trans. by Harold Shadick (1952). Reprinted by permission of the Estate of Harold Shadick.

José López Portillo y Rojas: "Unclaimed Watch," trans. by Roberta H. Kimble from THE SPANISH AMERICAN SHORT STORY: A CRITICAL ANTHOLOGY, ed. by Seymour Menton (1982). Reprinted by permission of UCLA Latin American Center Publications.

Machemba: Letter to Major von Wissmann, trans. from the German by Sarah Lawall and Robert Sullivan. Reprinted by permission of Sarah Lawall.

Malagasy Wisdom Poetry: "Ohabolana" and "Hainteny" from HAINTENY: THE TRADITIONAL POETRY OF MADAGASCAR, trans. by Leonard Fox (1990). Reprinted by permission of the publisher, Associated University Presses.

Stéphane Mallarmé: From COLLECTED POEMS: A BILINGUAL EDITION, ed. and trans. by Henry Michael Weinfield. Copyright © 1994 by The Regents of the University of California. Reprinted by permission of the University of California Press.

José Martí: "Guantanamera" from MAJOR POEMS: A BILINGUAL EDITION, ed. by Philip S. Foner and trans. by Elinor Randall. Copyright © 1982 by Holmes and Meier Publishers, Inc. Used with permission.

Adam Mickiewicz: "The Prisoner's Return" from FIVE CENTURIES OF POLISH POETRY, 1450–1950, trans. by Jerzy Peterkiewicz and Burns Singer in collaboration with Jon Stallworthy. Reproduced with permission of Greenwood Press via the Copyright Clearance Center.

Nguyễn Du: From THE TALE OF KIỀU, trans. by Huynh Sanh Thông. Copyright © 1983 by Yale University. Reprinted by permission of Yale University Press.

Pandita Ramabai: "Married Life" and "Legal Rights" from PANDITA RAMABAI THROUGH HER OWN WORDS: SELECTED LETTERS, ed. and trans. by Meera Kosambi. Reprinted by permission of Oxford University Press India, New Delhi.

Arthur Rimbaud: "The Drunken Boat," trans. by Stephen Stepanchev is reprinted by permission of the translator.

Lola Rodríguez de Tió: "The Puerto Rican National Anthem" (The Song of Borinquen), trans. by José Nieto, is reprinted from BORINQUEN: AN ANTHOLOGY OF PUERTO RICAN LITERATURE, ed. by María Teresa Babín and Stan Steiner (Alfred A. Knopf, 1974). Reprinted by permission of Vera John Steiner for the Estate of Stan Steiner.

Jean-Jacques Rousseau: From CONFESSIONS, trans. by Angela Scholar, ed. by Patrick Coleman (Oxford World's Classics, 2000). By permission of Oxford University Press.

Rabindranath Tagore: "Kabuliwala," trans. by Madhuchchhanda Karlekar, from RABINDRANATH TAGORE: SELECTED SHORT STORIES, ed. by Sukanta Chaudhuri. Reproduced by permission of Oxford University Press India, New Delhi. "Punishment" from RABINDRANATH TAGORE: SELECTED SHORT STORIES (Penguin Books Ltd. 1991), trans. by William Radice. Copyright © 1991 by William Radice. Reprinted with permission of John Johnson, Author's Agent, Ltd.

IMAGES

2–3 © RMN-Grand Palais/Art Resource, NY; **4** HIP/Art Resource, NY; **7** © RMN-Grand Palais/Art Resource, NY; **10** Napoleon (1769–1821) at the Battle of Waterloo, 1815 (mezzotint), Steuben, Charles Auguste (1788–1856) (after)/National Army Museum, London/Bridgeman Images; **14** © The Trustees of the British Museum/Art Resource, NY; **16–17** Niday Picture Library/Alamy Stock Photo; **304–305** Art Collection 2/Alamy Stock Photo; **432–433** SSPL/Getty Images; **435** Adoc-photos/Art Resource, NY; **438** © Hulton-Deutsch Collection/CORBIS/Corbis via Getty Images; **528–529** The Print Collector/Print Collector/Getty Images; **568–569** Bpk, Berlin/Tretyakov Gallery/Roman Beniaminson/Art Resource, NY; **570** Bpk, Berlin/Galerie Neue Meister, Staatliche Kunstsammlungen/Art Resource, NY; **572** The New York Public Library/Art Resource, NY; **888–889** The J. Paul Getty Museum

COLOR INSERT

C1 © RMN-Grand Palais/Art Resource, NY; **C2** Bpk Bildagentur/Art Resource, NY; **C3 (top)** SSPL/National Media Museum/Art Resource, NY; **C3 (bottom)** SSPL/National Media Museum/Art Resource, NY; **C4** © CORBIS/Corbis via Getty Images; **C5** V&A Images, London/Art Resource, NY; **C6** © CORBIS/Corbis via Getty Images; **C7** INTERFOTO/Alamy Stock Photo; **C8** Adoc-photos/Art Resource, NY

Index